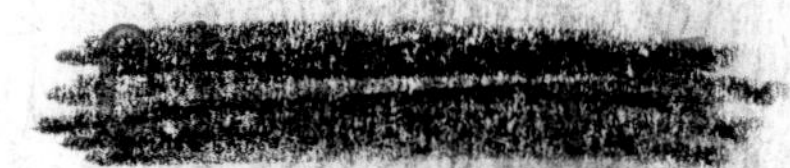

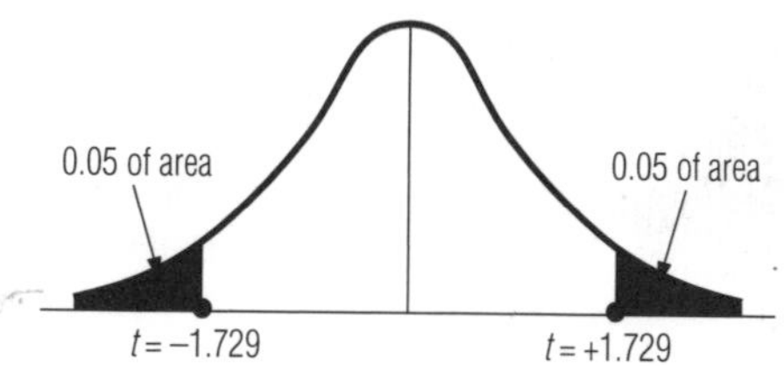

Areas in Both Tails Combined for Student's *t* Distribution

Example:
To find the value of *t* that corresponds to an area of 0.10 in both tails of the distribution combined, when there are 19 degrees of freedom, look under the 0.10 column, and proceed down to the 19 degrees of freedom row; the appropriate *t* value there is 1.729.

Degrees of Freedom	Area in Both Tails Combined			
	0.10	**0.05**	**0.02**	**0.01**
1	6.314	12.706	31.821	63.657
2	2.920	4.303	6.965	9.925
3	2.353	3.182	4.541	5.841
4	2.132	2.776	3.747	4.604
5	2.015	2.571	3.365	4.032
6	1.943	2.447	3.143	3.707
7	1.895	2.365	2.998	3.499
8	1.860	2.306	2.896	3.355
9	1.833	2.262	2.821	3.250
10	1.812	2.228	2.764	3.169
11	1.796	2.201	2.718	3.106
12	1.782	2.179	2.681	3.055
13	1.771	2.160	2.650	3.012
14	1.761	2.145	2.624	2.977
15	1.753	2.131	2.602	2.947
16	1.746	2.120	2.583	2.921
17	1.740	2.110	2.567	2.898
18	1.734	2.101	2.552	2.878
19	1.729	2.093	2.539	2.861
20	1.725	2.086	2.528	2.845
21	1.721	2.080	2.518	2.831
22	1.717	2.074	2.508	2.819
23	1.714	2.069	2.500	2.807
24	1.711	2.064	2.492	2.797
25	1.708	2.060	2.485	2.787
26	1.706	2.056	2.479	2.779
27	1.703	2.052	2.473	2.771
28	1.701	2.048	2.467	2.763
29	1.699	2.045	2.462	2.756
30	1.697	2.042	2.457	2.750
40	1.684	2.021	2.423	2.704
60	1.671	2.000	2.390	2.660
120	1.658	1.980	2.358	2.617
Normal Distribution	1.645	1.960	2.326	2.576

STATISTICS FOR MANAGEMENT

eventh Edition

STATISTICS FOR MANAGEMENT

Richard I. Levin

The University of North Carolina at Chapel Hill

David S. Rubin

The University of North Carolina at Chapel Hill

Prentice Hall, Upper Saddle River, New Jersey 07458

Library of Congress Cataloging-in-Publication Data

Levin, Richard I.
Statistics for management / Richard I. Levin, David S. Rubin. —
7th ed.
p. cm.
Includes bibliographical references and indexes.
ISBN 0-13-476292-4
1. Social sciences—Statistical methods. 2. Commercial
statistics. 3. Management—Statistical methods. I. Rubin, David
S. II. Title.
HA29.L3887 1998
519.5—dc20 96-17344
CIP

Acquisitions Editor: Tom Tucker
Assistant Editor: Audrey Regan
Associate Editor: Diane Peirano
Marketing Manager: Patrick Lynch
Editorial/Production Supervision: Kelli Rahlf, Carlisle Publishers Services
Managing Editor: Katherine Evancie
Senior Manufacturing Supervisor: Paul Smolenski
Manufacturing Manager: Vincent Scelta
Senior Designer: Suzanne Behnke
Design Director: Patricia Wosczyk
Interior Design: Lisa Jones
Cover Design: Suzanne Behnke
Composition by Carlisle Communications, Ltd.
Cover Photo: Richard Megna/Fundamental Photographs, NYC

Photo Credits

Openers

Chapter 1: *The Travelers;* **Chapter 2:** *The Image Works;* **Chapter 3:** *Photo Researchers, Inc.;* **Chapter 4:** *Monkmeyer Press;* **Chapter 5:** *Teri Stratford;* **Chapter 6:** *Tony Stone Images;* **Chapter 7:** *Stock Boston;* **Chapter 8:** *Tony Stone Images;* **Chapter 9:** *Stock Boston;* **Chapter 10:** *Stock Boston;* **Chapter 11:** *Stock Boston;* **Chapter 12:** *The Image Works;* **Chapter 13:** *Stock Boston;* **Chapter 14:** *The Image Works;* **Chapter 15:** *The Image Works;* **Chapter 16:** *The Image Works;* **Chapter 17:** *Stock Boston*

Printed in the United States of America

10 9 8 7 6 5 4 3 2

ISBN 0-13-476292-4

Prentice-Hall International (UK) Limited, *London*
Prentice-Hall of Australia Pty. Limited, *Sydney*
Prentice-Hall Canada Inc., *Toronto*
Prentice-Hall Hispanoamericana, S.A., *Mexico*
Prentice-Hall of India Private Limited, *New Delhi*
Prentice-Hall of Japan, Inc., *Tokyo*
Simon & Schuster Pte. Ltd., *Singapore*
Editora Prentice-Hall do Brasil, Ltda., *Rio de Janeiro*

Contents

Chapter 16 Index Numbers *921*

Chapter 17 Decision Theory *969*

Appendix Tables

Preface

An Opportunity for New Ideas

Writing a new edition of our textbook is an exciting time. In the two years that it takes to complete it, we get to interact with a number of adopters of our text, we benefit from the many thoughtful comments of professors who review the manuscript, our students here at the University of North Carolina at Chapel Hill always have a lot of good ideas for change, and our team at Prentice Hall organizes the whole process and provides a very high level of professional input. Even though this is the seventh edition of our book, our original goal of writing the most teacher- and student-friendly textbook in business statistics still drives our thoughts and our writing in this revision.

What Has Made This Book Different through Six Editions

Our philosophy about what a good business statistics textbook ought to be hasn't changed since the day we started writing the first edition, twenty years ago. At that time and up through this edition, we have always strived to produce a textbook that met these four goals:

- *We think a beginning business statistics textbook ought to be intuitive and easy to learn from.* In explaining statistical concepts, we begin with what students already know from their life experience and we enlarge on this knowledge by using intuitive ideas. Common sense, real-world ideas, references, patient explanations, multiple examples, and intuitive approaches all make it easier for students to learn.
- *We believe a beginning business statistics textbook ought to cover all of the topics any teacher might wish to build into a two-semester or a two-quarter course.* Not every teacher will cover every topic in our book, but we offer the most complete set of topics for the consideration of anyone who teaches this course.
- *We do not believe that using complex mathematical notation enhances the teaching of business statistics; and our own experience suggests that it may even make learning more difficult.* Complex mathematical notation belongs in advanced courses in mathematics and statistics (and we do use it there), but not here. This is a book that will make and keep you comfortable even if you didn't get an A in college algebra.
- *We believe that a beginning business statistics textbook ought to have a strong real-world focus.* Students ought to see in the book what they see in their world

every day. The approach we use, the exercises we have chosen for this edition, and the continuing focus on using statistics to solve business problems all make this book very relevant. We use a large number of real-world problems, and our explanations tend to be anecdotal, using terms and references that students read in the newspapers, see on TV, and view on their computer monitors. As our own use of statistics in our consulting practices has increased, so have the references to how and why it works in our textbook. This book is about actual managerial situations, which many of the students who use this book will face in a few years.

New Features in This Edition to Make Teaching and Learning Easier

Each of our editions and the supplements that accompanied them contained a complete set of pedagogical aids to make teaching business statistics more effective and learning it less painful. With each revision, we added new ideas, new tools, and new helpful approaches. This edition begins its own set of new features. Here is a quick preview of the twelve major changes in the seventh edition:

- End-of-section exercises have been divided into three subsets: *Basic Concepts, Applications,* and *Self-Check Exercises*. The Basic Concepts are those exercises without scenarios, Applications have scenarios, and the Self-Check Exercises have worked-out solutions right in the section.
- The set of Self-Check Exercises referenced above is found at the end of each chapter section except the introductory section. Complete *Worked-Out Answers* to each of these can be found at the end of the applications exercises in that section of the chapter.
- Minitab has been adopted throughout the book as the preferred computer software package.
- *Hints and Assumptions* are short discussions that come at the end of each section in the book, just before the end-of-section exercises. These review important assumptions and tell why we made them, they give students useful hints for working the exercises that follow, and they warn students of potential pitfalls in finding and interpreting solutions.
- The number of real-world examples in the end-of-chapter *Review and Application Exercises* has been doubled, and many of the exercises from the previous edition have been updated.
- Most of the hypothesis tests in Chapters 8 and 9 are done using the standardized scale.
- The scenarios for a quarter of the exercises in this edition have been rewritten.
- Over a hundred new exercises appear in this edition.
- All of the large, multipage data sets have been moved to the data disk, which is available with this book.
- The material on *exploratory data analysis* has been significantly expanded.
- The design of this edition has been completely changed to represent the state of the art in easy-to-follow pedagogy.

Successful Features Retained from Previous Editions

In the time between editions, we listen and learn from teachers who are using our book. The many adopters of our sixth edition reinforced our feeling that these time-tested features should also be a part of the new edition:

- Chapter *learning objectives* are prominently displayed in the chapter opening.
- The more than 1,500 *margin notes* highlight important material for students.
- A new 2-color format makes the explanations easy to follow.
- Each chapter begins with a *real-world problem,* in which a manager must make a decision. Later in the chapter, we discuss and solve this problem as part of the teaching process.
- Each chapter has a section entitled *review of Terms Introduced* in the chapter.
- An *annotated review of all Equations Introduced* is a part of every chapter.
- Each chapter has a comprehensive *Chapter Concepts Test* using multiple pedagogies.
- Chapters 2–16 have a *Computer Database Exercise* that uses data from the data disk provided with each copy of the book.
- Sections entitled *From the Textbook to the Real World* make it easier for students to see how statistical techniques are successfully applied to significant business problems.
- A *flow chart* (with numbered page citations) in Chapters 2–16 organizes the material and makes it easier for students to develop a logical, sequential approach to problem solving.
- Our *Statistics at Work* sections in each chapter allow students to think conceptually about business statistics without getting bogged down with data. This learning aid is based on the continuing story of the "Loveland Computer Company" and the experiences of its employees as they bring more and more statistical applications to the management of their business.

Teaching Supplements to the Seventh Edition

The following supplements to the text represent the most comprehensive, classroom-tested set of supplementary teaching aids available in business statistics books today. Together they provide a powerful instructor-focused package.

- A complete *Instructor's Solutions Manual* containing worked-out solutions to all of the exercises in the book.
- *Prentice-Hall's Test Manager for Windows.*
- A comprehensive *Instructor's Test Bank.*
- A complete set of *Instructor Lecture Notes,* developed in *Microsoft Powerpoint.* For each chapter of the text, these lecture notes contain learning objectives, worked-out examples, and notation and figures taken from the text.
- A *Data Disk* containing the data from the *Computer Database Exercises* and the exercises indicated by the *disk icon* within the text.

Supplements Available for Student Purchase

- A *Student Solutions Manual* containing worked-out solutions to selected even-number exercises in the text.
- *Student Lecture Notes,* which is a printed version of the *Microsoft Powerpoint* lecture notes described on page xv. Each page of the lecture notes contains printed versions of the *Microsoft Powerpoint* slides with space for students to take notes.

It Takes a Lot of People to Make a Book

Our part in the process of creating a new edition is to present ideas that we believe work in the classroom. The Prentice Hall team takes these ideas and makes them into a book. Of course, it isn't that easy.

The whole process starts with our editor, Tom Tucker, who rides herd on the process from his office in St. Paul. Tom is like a movie director; he makes sure everybody plays his or her part and that the entire process moves forward on schedule. Tom guides the project from the day we begin to discuss a seventh edition until the final book version appears on his desk. Without Tom, we'd be rudderless.

Then comes Kelli Rahlf, our production supervisor from Carlisle Publishers Services. In conjunction with Katherine Evancie, our Prentice Hall Production Manager, she manages the thousands of day-to-day activities that must all be completed before a book is produced. Together they move the rough manuscript pages through the editing and printing process, see that printed pages from the compositor reach us, keep us on schedule as we correct and return proofs, work with the bindery and the art folks, and do about a thousand other important things we never get to see but appreciate immensely.

A very helpful group of teachers reviewed the manuscript for the seventh edition and took the time to make very useful suggestions. We are happy to report that we incorporated most of them. This process gives the finished book a student–teacher focus we could not achieve without them; for their effort, we are grateful. The reviewers for this edition were Richard P. Behr, Broome Community College; Ronald L. Coccari, Cleveland State University; V. Reddy Dondeti, Norfolk State University; Mark Haggerty, Clarion University; Robert W. Hull, Western Illinois University; James R. Schmidt, University of Nebraska-Lincoln; and Edward J. Willies.

We use statistical tables in the book that were originally prepared by other folks, and we are grateful to the literary executor of the late Sir Ronald Fisher, F.R.S., to Dr. Frank Yates, F.R.S., and to Longman Group, Ltd., London, for permission to reprint tables from their book *Statistical Tables for Biological, Agricultural, and Medical Research,* sixth edition, 1974.

Dr. David O. Robinson of the Hass School of Business, Berkeley University, contributed a number of real-world exercises, produced many of the problem scenario changes, and as usual, persuaded us that it would be considerably less fun to revise a book without him.

Kevin Keyes provided a large number of new exercises, and Lisa Klein produced the index. To all of these very important, hard-working folks, we are grateful.

We're glad it's done and now we look forward to hearing from you with your comments about how well it works in your classroom. Thank you for all your help.

R.L.
D.R.

STATISTICS FOR MANAGEMENT

chapter 1

INTRODUCTION

Objectives

- To examine who really uses statistics and how statistics is used
- To provide a very short history of the use of statistics
- To present a quick review of the special features of this book that were designed to make learning statistics easier for you

Chapter Contents

1.1 Why Should I Take This Course and Who Uses Statistics Anyhow?

Every 4 years, Americans suffer through an affliction known as the presidential election. Months before the election, television, radio, and newspaper broadcasts inform us that "a poll conducted by XYZ Opinion Research shows that the Democratic (or Republican) candidate has the support of 54 percent of voters with a margin of error of plus or minus 3 percent." What does this statement mean? What is meant by the term *margin of error?* Who has actually done the polling? How many people did they interview and how many should they have interviewed to make this assertion? Can we rely on the truth of what they reported? Polling is a big business and many companies conduct polls for political candidates, new products, and even TV shows. If you have an ambition to become president, run a company, or even star in a TV show, you need to know something about statistics and statisticians.

It's the last play of the game and the Giants are behind by 4 points; they have the ball on the Chargers' 20-yard line. The Chargers' defensive coordinator calls time and goes over to the sidelines to speak to his coach. The coach knows that because a field goal won't even tie the game, the Giants will either pass or try a running play. His statistical assistant quickly consults his computer and points out that in the last 50 similar situations, the Giants have passed the ball 35 times. He also points out to the Chargers' coach that two-thirds of these passes have been short passes, right over center. The Chargers' coach instructs his defensive coordinator to expect the short pass over center. The ball is snapped, the Giants' quarterback does exactly what was predicted and there is a double-team Charger effort there to break up the pass. Statistics suggested the right defense.

The Food and Drug Administration is in final testing of a new drug that cures prostate cancer in 80 percent of clinical trials, with only a 2 percent incidence of undesirable side effects. Prostate cancer is the second largest medical killer of men and there is no present cure. The Director of Research must forward a finding on whether to release the drug for general use. She will do that only if she can be more than 99 percent certain that there won't be any significant difference between undesirable side effects in the clinical tests and those in the general population using the drug. There are statistical methods that can provide her a basis for making this important decision.

The Community Bank has learned from hard experience that there are four factors that go a long way in determining whether a borrower will repay his loan on time or will allow it to go into default. These factors are (1) the number of years at the present address, (2) the number of years in the present job, (3) whether the applicant owns his own home, and (4) whether the applicant has a checking or savings account with the Community Bank. Unfortunately, the bank doesn't know the individual effect of each of these four factors on the outcome of the loan experience. However, it has computer files full of information on applicants (both those who were granted a loan and those who were turned down) and knows, too, how each granted loan turned out. Sarah Smith applies for a loan. She has lived at her present address 4 years, owns her own home, has been in her current job only 3 months, and is not a Community Bank depositor. Using statistics, the bank can calculate the chance that Sarah will repay her loan on time if it is granted.

The word *statistics* means different things to different folks. To a football fan, statistics are rushing, passing, and first down numbers; to the Chargers' coach in the second example, statistics is the chance that the Giants will throw the short pass over center. To the manager of a power station, statistics are the amounts of pollution being released into the atmosphere. To the Food and Drug Administrator in our third example, statistics is the likely percentage of undesirable effects in the general population using the new prostate drug. To the Community Bank in the fourth example, statistics is the chance that Sarah will repay her loan on time. To the student taking this course, statistics are the grades on your quizzes and final exam in the course.

Each of these people is using the word correctly, yet each person uses it in a different way. All of them are using statistics to help them make decisions; you about your grade in this course, and the Chargers' coach about what defense to call for the final play of the game. Helping you learn why statistics is important and how to use it in your personal and professional life is the purpose of this book.

How to lie with statistics

Benjamin Disraeli once said, "There are three kinds of lies: lies, damned lies, and statistics." This rather severe castigation of statistics, made so many years ago, has come to be a rather apt description of many of the statistical deceptions we encounter in our everyday lives. Darrell Huff, in an enjoyable little book, *How to Lie with Statistics,* noted that "the crooks already know these tricks; honest men must learn them in self-defense." One goal of this book is to review some of the common ways statistics are used incorrectly.

1.2 History

Origin of the word

The word *statistik* comes from the Italian word *statista* (meaning "statesman"). It was first used by Gottfried Achenwall (1719–1772), a professor at Marlborough and Göttingen. Dr. E. A. W. Zimmerman introduced the word *statistics* into England. Its use was popularized by Sir John Sinclair in his work *Statistical Account of Scotland 1791–1799.* Long before the eighteenth century, however, people had been recording and using data.

Early government records

Official government statistics are as old as recorded history. The Old Testament contains several accounts of census taking. Governments of ancient Babylonia, Egypt, and Rome gathered detailed records of populations and resources. In the Middle Ages, governments began to register the ownership of land. In A.D. 762, Charlemagne asked for detailed descriptions of church-owned properties. Early in the ninth century, he completed a statistical enumeration of the serfs attached to the land. About 1086, William the Conqueror ordered the writing of the *Domesday Book,* a record of the ownership, extent, and value of the lands of England. This work was England's first statistical abstract.

Because of Henry VII's fear of the plague, England began to register its dead in 1532. About this same time, French law required the clergy to register baptisms, deaths, and marriages. During an outbreak of the plague in the late 1500s, the English government started publishing weekly death statistics. This practice continued, and by 1632, these *Bills of Mortality* listed births and deaths by sex. In 1662, Captain John Graunt used 30 years of these *Bills* to make predictions about the number of people who would die from various diseases and the proportions of male and female births that could be expected. Summarized in his work *Natural and Political Observations . . . Made upon the Bills of Mortality,* Graunt's study was a pioneer effort in statistical analysis. For his achievement in using past records to predict future events, Graunt was made a member of the original Royal Society.

An early prediction from statistics

The history of the development of statistical theory and practice is a lengthy one. We have only begun to list the people who have made significant contributions to this field. Later we will encounter others whose names are now attached to specific laws and methods. Many people have brought to the study of statistics refinements or innovations that, taken together, form the theoretical basis of what we will study in this book.

1.3 Subdivisions within Statistics

Managers apply some statistical technique to virtually every branch of public and private enterprise. These techniques are so diverse that statisticians commonly separate them into two broad categories: *descriptive statistics* and *inferential statistics.* Some examples will help us understand the difference between the two.

Descriptive statistics

Suppose a professor computes an average grade for one history class. Because statistics describe the performance of that one class but do not make a generalization about several classes, we can say that the professor is using *descriptive* statistics. Graphs, tables, and charts that display data so that they are easier to understand are all examples of descriptive statistics.

Inferential statistics

Now suppose that the history professor decides to use the average grade achieved by one history class to estimate the average grade achieved in all ten sections of the same history course. The process of estimating this average grade would be a problem in *inferential* statistics. Statisticians also refer to this category as *statistical inference.* Obviously, any conclusion the professor makes about the ten sections of the course is based on a generalization that goes far beyond the data for the original history class; the generalization may not be completely valid, so the professor must state how likely it is to be true. Similarly, statistical inference involves generalizations and statements about the *probability* of their validity.

Decision theory

The methods and techniques of statistical inference can also be used in a branch of statistics called *decision theory.* Knowledge of decision theory is very helpful for managers because it is used to make decisions under conditions of uncertainty when, for example, a manufacturer of stereo sets cannot specify precisely the demand for its products or when the chairperson of the English department at your school must schedule faculty teaching assignments without knowing precisely the student enrollment for next fall.

1.4 A Simple and Easy-to-Understand Approach

For students, not statisticians

This book is designed to help you get the feel of statistics: what it is, how and when to apply statistical techniques to decision-making situations, and how to interpret the results you get. Because we are not writing for professional statisticians, our writing is tailored to the backgrounds and needs of college students, who probably accept the fact that statistics can be of considerable help to them in their future occupations but are probably apprehensive about studying the subject.

We discard mathematical proofs in favor of intuitive ones. You will be guided through the learning process by reminders of what you already know, by examples with which you can identify, and by a step-by-step process instead of statements such as "it can be shown" or "it therefore follows."

Symbols are simple and explained

As you thumb through this book and compare it with other basic business statistics textbooks, you will notice a minimum of mathematical notation. In the past, the complexity of the notation has intimidated many students, who got lost in the symbols even though they were motivated and intellectually capable of understanding the ideas. Each symbol and formula that is used is explained in detail, not only at the point at which it is introduced, but also in a section at the end of the chapter.

No math beyond simple algebra is required

If you felt reasonably comfortable when you finished your high school algebra course, you have enough background to understand *everything* in this book. Nothing beyond basic algebra is assumed or used. Our goals are for you to be comfortable as you learn and for you to get a good intuitive grasp of statistical concepts and techniques. As a future manager, you will need to know when statistics can help your decision process and which tools to use. If you do need statistical help, you can find a statistical expert to handle the details.

Text problems cover a wide variety of situations

The problems used to introduce material in the chapters, the exercises at the end of each section in the chapter, and the chapter review exercises are drawn from a wide variety of situations you are already familiar with or are likely to confront quite soon. You will see problems involving all facets of the private sector of our economy: accounting, finance, individual and group behavior, marketing, and production. In addition, you will encounter managers in the public sphere coping with problems in public education, social services, the environment, consumer advocacy, and health systems.

Goals

In each problem situation, a manager is trying to use statistics creatively and productively. Helping you become comfortable doing exactly that is our goal.

1.5 Features That Make Learning Easier

In our preface, we mentioned briefly a number of learning aids that are a part of this book. Each has a particular role in helping you study and understand statistics, and if we spend a few minutes here discussing the most effective way to use some of these aids, you will not only learn more effectively, but will gain a greater understanding of how statistics is used to make managerial decisions.

Margin Notes Each of the more than 1,500 margin notes highlights the material in a paragraph or group of paragraphs. Because the notes briefly indicate the focus of the textual material, you can avoid having to read through pages of information to find what you need. Learn to read down the margin as you work through the textbook; in that way, you will get a good sense of the flow of topics and the meaning of what the text is explaining.

Application Exercises The Chapter Review Exercises include Application Exercises that come directly from real business/economic situations. Many of these are from the business press; others come from government publications. This feature will give you practice in setting up and solving problems that are faced every day by business professionals. In this edition, the number of Application Exercises has been doubled.

Review of Terms Each chapter ends with a glossary of every new term introduced in that chapter. Having all of these new terms defined again in one convenient place can be a big help. As you work through a chapter, use the glossary to reinforce your understanding of what the terms mean. Doing this is easier than going back in the chapter trying to find the definition of a particular term. When you finish studying a chapter, use the glossary to make sure you understand what each term introduced in the chapter means.

Equation Review Every equation introduced in a chapter is found in this section. All of them are explained again, and the page on which they were first introduced is given. Using this feature of the book is a very effective way to make sure you understand what each equation means and how it is used.

Chapter Concepts Test Using these tests is a good way to see how well you understand the chapter material. As a part of your study, be sure to take these tests and then compare your answers with those in the back of the book. Doing this will point out areas in which you need more work, especially before quiz time.

Statistics at Work In this set of cases, an employee of Loveland Computers applies statistics to managerial problems. The emphasis here is not on numbers; in fact, it's hard to find any numbers in these cases. As you read each of these cases, focus on what the problem is and what statistical approach might help find a solution; forget the numbers temporarily. In this way, you will develop a good appreciation for identifying problems and matching solution methods with problems, without being bogged down by numbers.

Flow Chart The flow charts at the end of the chapters will enable you to develop a systematic approach to applying statistical methods to problems. Using them helps you understand where you begin, how you proceed, and where you wind up; if you get good at using them, you will not get lost in some of the more complex word problems instructors are fond of putting on tests.

From the Textbook to the Real World Each of these will take you no more than 2 or 3 minutes to read, but doing so will show you how the concepts developed in this book are used to solve real-world problems. As you study each chapter, be sure to review the "From the Textbook to the Real World" example; see what the problem is, how statistics solves it, and what the solution adds in value. These situations also generate good classroom discussion questions.

Computer Database Exercise This running case follows a young statistical analyst as she helps HH Industries use statistics to solve important problems. In each instance, the quantity of data makes it necessary for you to use your computer as a part of the analysis. Use this feature to become comfortable with the various statistical routines available for your machine, the input formats they require, and the output formats they provide. Doing this will make it easier for you to cope with the massive amounts of data you will confront in most real problems.

Classification of Exercises This feature is new with this edition of the book. The exercises at the end of each section are divided into three categories: basic concepts to get started on, application exercises to show how statistics is used, and self-check exercises with worked-out answers to allow you to test yourself.

Self-Check Exercises with Worked-Out Answers A new feature in this edition. At the beginning of most sets of exercises, there are one or two self-check exercises for you to test yourself. The worked-out answers to these self-check exercises appear at the end of the exercise set.

Hints and Assumptions New with this edition, these provide help, direction, and things to avoid before you begin work on the exercises at the end of each section. Spending a minute reading these saves lots of time, frustration, and mistakes in working the exercises.

The authors' goals

Our own work experience has brought us into contact with thousands of situations where statistics helped decision makers. We participated personally in formulating and applying many of those solutions. It was stimulating, challenging, and, in the end, very rewarding as we saw sensible application of these ideas produce value for organizations. Although very few of you will likely end up as statistical analysts, we believe very strongly that you can learn, develop, and have fun studying statistics, and that's why we wrote this book. Good luck!

chapter 2

GROUPING AND DISPLAYING DATA TO CONVEY MEANING: Tables and Graphs

Objectives

- To show the difference between samples and populations
- To convert raw data to useful information
- To construct and use data arrays
- To construct and use frequency distributions
- To graph frequency distributions with histograms, polygons, and ogives
- To use frequency distributions to make decisions

Chapter Contents

The production manager of the Dalmon Carpet Company is responsible for the output of over 500 carpet looms. So that he does not have to measure the daily output (in yards) of each loom, he samples the output from 30 looms each day and draws a conclusion as to the average carpet production of the entire 500 looms. The table below shows the yards produced by each of the 30 looms in yesterday's sample. These production amounts are the raw data from which the production manager can draw conclusions about the entire population of looms yesterday.

Yards Produced Yesterday by Each of 30 Carpet Looms

16.2	15.4	16.0	16.6	15.9	15.8	16.0	16.8	16.9	16.8
15.7	16.4	15.2	15.8	15.9	16.1	15.6	15.9	15.6	16.0
16.4	15.8	15.7	16.2	15.6	15.9	16.3	16.3	16.0	16.3

Using the methods introduced in this chapter, we can help the production manager draw the right conclusion. ■

Some definitions

Data are collections of any number of related observations. We can collect the number of telephones that several workers install on a given day or that one worker installs per day over a period of several days, and we can call the results our data. A collection of data is called a *data set,* and a single observation a *data point.*

2.1 How Can We Arrange Data?

For data to be useful, our observations must be organized so that we can pick out patterns and come to logical conclusions. This chapter introduces the techniques of arranging data in tabular and graphical forms. Chapter 3 shows how to use numbers to describe data.

Collecting Data

Represent all groups

Statisticians select their observations so that all relevant groups are represented in the data. To determine the potential market for a new product, for example, analysts might study 100 consumers in a certain geographical area. Analysts must be certain that this group contains people representing variables such as income level, race, education, and neighborhood.

Find data by observation or from records

Data can come from actual observations or from records that are kept for normal purposes. For billing purposes and doctors' reports, a hospital, for example, will record the number of patients using the X-ray facilities. But this information can also be organized to produce data that statisticians can describe and interpret.

Use data about the past to make decisions about the future

Data can assist decision makers in educated guesses about the causes and therefore the probable effects of certain characteristics in given situations. Also, knowledge of trends from past experience can enable concerned citizens to be aware of potential outcomes and to plan in advance. Our marketing survey may reveal that the product is preferred by African-American homemakers of suburban communities, average incomes, and average education.

This product's advertising copy should address this target audience. If hospital records show that more patients used the X-ray facilities in June than in January, the hospital personnel division should determine whether this was accidental to this year or an indication of a trend, and perhaps it should adjust its hiring and vacation practices accordingly.

When data are arranged in compact, usable forms, decision makers can take reliable information from the environment and use it to make intelligent decisions. Today, computers allow statisticians to collect enormous volumes of observations and compress them instantly into tables, graphs, and numbers. These are all compact, usable forms, but are they reliable? Remember that the data that come out of a computer are only as accurate as the data that go in. As computer programmers say, "GIGO," or "Garbage In, Garbage Out." Managers must be very careful to be sure that the data they are using are based on correct assumptions and interpretations. Before relying on any interpreted data, from a computer or not, test the data by asking these questions:

Tests for data

1. Where did the data come from? Is the source biased—that is, is it likely to have an interest in supplying data points that will lead to one conclusion rather than another?
2. Do the data support or contradict other evidence we have?
3. Is evidence missing that might cause us to come to a different conclusion?
4. How many observations do we have? Do they represent all the groups we wish to study?
5. Is the conclusion logical? Have we made conclusions that the data do not support?

Study your answers to these questions. Are the data worth using? Or should we wait and collect more information before acting? If the hospital was caught short-handed because it hired too few nurses to staff the X-ray room, its administration relied on insufficient data. If the advertising agency targeted its copy only toward African-American suburban homemakers when it could have tripled its sales by appealing to white suburban homemakers, too, it also relied on insufficient data. In both cases, testing available data would have helped managers make better decisions.

Double-counting example

The effect of incomplete or biased data can be illustrated with this example. A national association of truck lines claimed in an advertisement that "75 percent of everything you use travels by truck." This might lead us to believe that cars, railroads, airplanes, ships, and other forms of transportation carry only 25 percent of what we use. Reaching such a conclusion is easy but not enlightening. Missing from the trucking assertion is the question of double counting. What did they do when something was carried to your city by rail and delivered to your house by truck? How were packages treated if they went by airmail and then by truck? When the double-counting issue (a very complex one to treat) is resolved, it turns out that trucks carry a much lower proportion of the goods you use than truckers claimed. Although trucks are involved in *delivering* a relatively high proportion of what you use, railroads and ships still carry more goods for more total miles.

Difference between Samples and Populations

Sample and *population* defined

Statisticians gather data from a sample. They use this information to make inferences about the population that the sample represents. Thus, a population is a whole, and a sample is a fraction or segment of that whole.

Function of samples

We will study samples in order to be able to describe populations. Our hospital may study a small, representative group of X-ray records rather than examining each record for

Advantages of samples

Reason why samples are used.

the last 50 years. The Gallup Poll may interview a sample of only 2,500 adult Americans in order to predict the opinion of all adults living in the United States.

Studying samples is easier than studying the whole population; it costs less and takes less time. Often, testing an airplane part for strength destroys the part; thus, testing fewer parts is desirable. Sometimes testing involves human risk; thus, use of sampling reduces that risk to an acceptable level. Finally, it has been proven that examining an entire population still allows defective items to be accepted; thus, sampling, in some instances, can *raise* the quality level. If you're wondering how that can be so, think of how tired and inattentive you might get if you had to look at thousands and thousands of items passing before you.

Function of populations

A *population* is a collection of all the elements we are studying and about which we are trying to draw conclusions. We must define this population so that it is clear whether an element is a member of the population. The population for our marketing study may be all women within a 15-mile radius of center-city Cincinnati who have annual family incomes between \$20,000 and \$45,000 and have completed at least 11 years of school. A woman living in downtown Cincinnati with a family income of \$25,000 and a college degree would be a part of this population. A woman living in San Francisco, or with a family income of \$7,000, or with 5 years of schooling would not qualify as a member of this population.

Need for a representative sample

A *sample* is a collection of some, but not all, of the elements of the population. The population of our marketing survey is *all* women who meet the qualifications listed above. Any group of women who meet these qualifications can be a sample, as long as the group is only a fraction of the whole population. A large helping of cherry filling with only a few crumbs of crust is a sample of pie, but it is not a representative sample because the proportions of the ingredients are not the same in the sample as they are in the whole.

A *representative sample* contains the relevant characteristics of the population *in the same proportions* as they are included in that population. If our population of women is one-third African-American, then a sample of the population that is representative in terms of race will also be one-third African-American. Specific methods for sampling are covered in detail in Chapter 6.

Finding a Meaningful Pattern in the Data

Data come in a variety of forms

There are many ways to sort data. We can simply collect them and keep them in order. Or if the observations are measured in numbers, we can list the data points from lowest to highest in numerical value. But if the data are skilled workers (such as carpenters, masons, and ironworkers) at construction sites, or the different types of automobiles manufactured by all automakers, or the various colors of sweaters manufactured by a given firm, we must organize them differently. We must present the data points in alphabetical order or by some other organizing principle. One useful way to organize data is to divide them into similar categories or classes and then count the number of observations that fall into each category. This method produces a *frequency distribution* and is discussed later in this chapter.

Why should we arrange data?

The purpose of organizing data is to enable us to see quickly some of the characteristics of the data we have collected. We look for things such as the range (the largest and smallest values), apparent patterns, what values the data may tend to group around, what values appear most often, and so on. The more information of this kind that we can learn from our sample, the better we can understand the population from which it came, and the better we can make decisions.

Exercises 2.1

Applications

- **2-1** When asked what they would use if they were marooned on an island with only one choice for a pain reliever, more doctors chose Bayer than Tylenol, Bufferin, or Advil. Is this conclusion drawn from a sample or a population?
- **2-2** Twenty-five percent of the cars sold in the United States in 1996 were manufactured in Japan. Is this conclusion drawn from a sample or a population?
- **2-3** An electronics firm recently introduced a new amplifier, and warranty cards indicate that 10,000 of these have been sold so far. The president of the firm, very upset after reading three letters of complaint about the new amplifiers, informed the production manager that costly control measures would be implemented immediately to ensure that the defects would not appear again. Comment on the president's reaction from the standpoint of the five tests for data given on page 9.
- **2-4** "Germany will remain ever divided" stated Walter Ulbricht after construction of the Berlin Wall in 1961. However, toward the end of 1969, the communists of East Germany began allowing free travel between the east and west, and twenty years after that, the wall was completely destroyed. Give some reasons for Ulbricht's incorrect prediction.
- **2-5** Discuss the data given in the chapter-opening problem in terms of the five tests for data given on page 9.

2.2 Examples of Raw Data

Information before it is arranged and analyzed is called *raw data.* It is "raw" because it is unprocessed by statistical methods.

Problem facing admissions staff

The carpet-loom data in the chapter-opening problem was one example of raw data. Consider a second. Suppose that the admissions staff of a university, concerned with the success of the students it selects for admission, wishes to compare the students' college performances with other achievements, such as high school grades, test scores, and extracurricular activities. Rather than study every student from every year, the staff can draw a sample of the population of all the students in a given time period and study only that group to conclude what characteristics appear to predict success. For example, the staff can compare high school grades with college grade-point averages (GPAs) for students in the sample. The staff can assign each grade a numerical value. Then it can add the grades and divide by the total number of grades to get an average for each student. Table 2-1 shows a sample of these raw data in tabular form: 20 pairs of average grades in high school and college.

Bridge-building problem

When designing a bridge, engineers are concerned with the stress that a given material, such as concrete, will withstand. Rather than test every cubic inch of concrete to determine its stress capacity, engineers take a sample of the concrete, test it, and conclude how much stress, on the average, that kind of concrete can withstand. Table 2-2 summarizes the raw data gathered from a sample of 40 batches of concrete to be used in constructing a bridge.

Table 2-1

High School and College Grade-Point Averages of 20 College Seniors

H.S.	College	H.S.	College	H.S.	College	H.S.	College
3.6	2.5	3.5	3.6	3.4	3.6	2.2	2.8
2.6	2.7	3.5	3.8	2.9	3.0	3.4	3.4
2.7	2.2	2.2	3.5	3.9	4.0	3.6	3.0
3.7	3.2	3.9	3.7	3.2	3.5	2.6	1.9
4.0	3.8	4.0	3.9	2.1	2.5	2.4	3.2

Table 2-2

Pounds of Pressure per Square Inch That Concrete Can Withstand

2500.2	2497.8	2496.9	2500.8	2491.6	2503.7	2501.3	2500.0
2500.8	2502.5	2503.2	2496.9	2495.3	2497.1	2499.7	2505.0
2490.5	2504.1	2508.2	2500.8	2502.2	2508.1	2493.8	2497.8
2499.2	2498.3	2496.7	2490.4	2493.4	2500.7	2502.0	2502.5
2506.4	2499.9	2508.4	2502.3	2491.3	2509.5	2498.4	2498.1

HINTS & ASSUMPTIONS

Data are *not* necessarily information, and having more data doesn't necessarily produce better decisions. The goal is to summarize and present data in useful ways to support prompt and effective decisions. The reason we have to organize data is to see whether there are patterns in them, patterns such as the largest and smallest values, and what value the data seem to cluster around. If the data are from a sample, we assume that they fairly represent the population from which they were drawn. All good statisticians (and users of data) recognize that using biased or incomplete data leads to poor decisions.

Exercises 2.2

Applications

■ **2-6** Look at the data in Table 2-1. Why do these data need further arranging? Can you form any conclusions from the data as they exist now?

■ **2-7** The marketing manager of a large company receives a report each month on the sales activity of one of the company's products. The report is a listing of the sales of the product by state during the previous month. Is this an example of raw data?

■ **2-8** The production manager in a large company receives a report each month from the quality control section. The report gives the reject rate for the production line (the number of rejects per 100 units produced), the machine causing the greatest number of rejects, and the average cost of repairing the rejected units. Is this an example of raw data?

Table 2-3						
Sample of Daily Production in Yards of 30 Carpet Looms	16.2	15.8	15.8	15.8	16.3	15.6
	15.7	16.0	16.2	16.1	16.8	16.0
	16.4	15.2	15.9	15.9	15.9	16.8
	15.4	15.7	15.9	16.0	16.3	16.0
	16.4	16.6	15.6	15.6	16.9	16.3

Table 2-4						
Data Array of Daily Production in Yards of 30 Carpet Looms	15.2	15.7	15.9	16.0	16.2	16.4
	15.4	15.7	15.9	16.0	16.3	16.6
	15.6	15.8	15.9	16.0	16.3	16.8
	15.6	15.8	15.9	16.1	16.3	16.8
	15.6	15.8	16.0	16.2	16.4	16.9

2.3 Arranging Data Using the Data Array and the Frequency Distribution

Data array defined

The *data array* is one of the simplest ways to present data. It arranges values in ascending or descending order. Table 2-3 repeats the carpet data from our chapter-opening problem, and Table 2-4 rearranges these numbers in a data array in ascending order.

Advantages of data arrays

Data arrays offer several advantages over raw data:

1. **We can quickly notice the lowest and highest values in the data.** In our carpet example, the range is from 15.2 to 16.9 yards.
2. **We can easily divide the data into sections.** In Table 2-4, the first 15 values (the lower half of the data) are between 15.2 and 16.0 yards, and the last 15 values (the upper half) are between 16.0 and 16.9 yards. Similarly, the lowest third of the values range from 15.2 to 15.8 yards, the middle third from 15.9 to 16.2 yards, and the upper third from 16.2 to 16.9 yards.
3. **We can see whether any values appear more than once in the array.** Equal values appear together. Table 2-4 shows that nine levels occurred more than once when the sample of 30 looms was taken.
4. **We can observe the distance between succeeding values in the data.** In Table 2-4, 16.6 and 16.8 are succeeding values. The distance between them is 0.2 yards (16.8 − 16.6).

Disadvantages of data arrays

In spite of these advantages, sometimes a data array isn't helpful. Because it lists every observation, it is a cumbersome form for displaying large quantities of data. We need to compress the information and still be able to use it for interpretation and decision making. How can we do this?

A Better Way to Arrange Data: The Frequency Distribution

Frequency distributions handle more data

One way we can compress data is to use a *frequency table* or a *frequency distribution.* To understand the difference between this and an array, take as an example the average inventory (in days) for 20 convenience stores:

Table 2-5					
Data Array of Average Inventory (in Days) for 20 Convenience Stores	2.0	3.8	4.1	4.7	5.5
	3.4	4.0	4.2	4.8	5.5
	3.4	4.1	4.3	4.9	5.5
	3.8	4.1	4.7	4.9	5.5

In Tables 2-5 and 2-6, we have taken identical data concerning the average inventory and displayed them first as an array in ascending order and then as a frequency distribution. To obtain Table 2-6, we had to divide the data in groups of similar values. Then we recorded the number of data points that fell into each group. Notice that we lose some information in constructing the frequency distribution. We no longer know, for example, that the value 5.5 appears four times or that the value 5.1 does not appear at all. Yet we gain information concerning the *pattern* of average inventories. We can see from Table 2-6 that average inventory falls most often in the range from 3.8 to 4.3 days. It is unusual to find an average inventory in the range from 2.0 to 2.5 days or from 2.6 to 3.1 days. Inventories in the ranges of 4.4 to 4.9 days and 5.0 to 5.5 days are not prevalent but occur more frequently than some others. Thus, frequency distributions sacrifice some detail but offer us new insights into patterns of data.

They lose some information

But they gain other information

Function of classes in a frequency distribution

A frequency distribution is a table that organizes data into classes, that is, into groups of values describing one characteristic of the data. The average inventory is one characteristic of the 20 convenience stores. In Table 2-5, this characteristic has 11 different values. But these same data could be divided into any number of classes. Table 2-6, for example, uses 6. We could compress the data even further and use only 2 classes: less than 3.8 and greater than or equal to 3.8. Or we could increase the number of classes by using smaller intervals, as we have done in Table 2-7.

Table 2-6	Class (Group of Similar Values of Data Points)	Frequency (Number of Observations in Each Class)
Frequency Distribution of Average Inventory (in Days) for 20 Convenience Stores (6 Classes)	2.0 to 2.5	1
	2.6 to 3.1	0
	3.2 to 3.7	2
	3.8 to 4.3	8
	4.4 to 4.9	5
	5.0 to 5.5	4

Table 2-7	Class	Frequency	Class	Frequency
Frequency Distribution of Average Inventory (in Days) for 20 Convenience Stores (12 Classes)	2.0 to 2.2	1	3.8 to 4.0	3
	2.3 to 2.5	0	4.1 to 4.3	5
	2.6 to 2.8	0	4.4 to 4.6	0
	2.9 to 3.1	0	4.7 to 4.9	5
	3.2 to 3.4	2	5.0 to 5.2	0
	3.5 to 3.7	0	5.3 to 5.5	4

Why is it called a frequency distribution?

A frequency distribution shows **the number of observations from the data set that fall into each of the classes.** If you can determine the frequency with which values occur in each class of a data set, you can construct a frequency distribution.

Characteristics of Relative Frequency Distributions

Relative frequency distribution defined

So far, we have expressed the frequency with which values occur in each class as the total number of data points that fall within that class. We can also express the frequency of each value as a *fraction* or a *percentage* of the total number of observations. The frequency of an average inventory of 4.4 to 4.9 days, for example, is 5 in Table 2-6 but 0.25 in Table 2-8. To get this value of 0.25, we divided the frequency for that class (5) by the total number of observations in the data set (20). The answer can be expressed as a fraction ($^5/_{20}$), a decimal (0.25), or a percentage (25 percent). A *relative frequency distribution* presents frequencies in terms of fractions or percentages.

Classes are all-inclusive

They are mutually exclusive

Notice in Table 2-8 that the sum of all the relative frequencies equals 1.00, or 100 percent. This is true because a relative frequency distribution pairs each class with its appropriate fraction or percentage of the total data. Therefore, the classes in any relative or simple frequency distribution are *all-inclusive.* All the data fit into one category or another. Also notice that the classes in Table 2-8 are *mutually exclusive;* that is, no data point falls into more than one category. Table 2-9 illustrates this concept by comparing mutually exclusive classes with ones that overlap. In frequency distributions, there are no overlapping classes.

Classes of qualitative data

Up to this point, our classes have consisted of numbers and have described some quantitative attribute of the items sampled. We can also classify information according to qualitative characteristics, such as race, religion, and gender, which do not fall naturally into numerical categories. Like classes of quantitative attributes, these classes must be all-inclusive and mutually exclusive. Table 2-10 shows how to construct both simple and relative frequency distributions using the qualitative attribute of occupations.

Table 2-8

Relative Frequency Distribution of Average Inventory (in Days) for 20 Convenience Stores

Class	Frequency	Relative Frequency: Fraction of Observations in Each Class
2.0 to 2.5	1	0.05
2.6 to 3.1	0	0.00
3.2 to 3.7	2	0.10
3.8 to 4.3	8	0.40
4.4 to 4.9	5	0.25
5.0 to 5.5	4	0.20
	20	**1.00 (sum of the relative frequencies of all classes)**

Table 2-9

Mutually Exclusive and Overlapping Classes

Mutually exclusive	1 to 4	5 to 8	9 to 12	13 to 16
Not mutually exclusive	1 to 4	3 to 6	5 to 8	7 to 10

Table 2-10

Occupations of Sample of 100 Graduates of Central College

Occupational Class	Frequency Distribution (1)	Relative Frequency Distribution (1) ÷ 100
Actor	5	0.05
Banker	8	0.08
Businessperson	22	0.22
Chemist	7	0.07
Doctor	10	0.10
Insurance representative	6	0.06
Journalist	2	0.02
Lawyer	14	0.14
Teacher	9	0.09
Other	17	0.17
	100	**1.00**

Table 2-11

Ages of Bunder County Residents

Class: Age (1)	Frequency (2)	Relative Frequency (2) ÷ 89,592
Birth to 7	8,873	0.0990
8 to 15	9,246	0.1032
16 to 23	12,060	0.1346
24 to 31	11,949	0.1334
32 to 39	9,853	0.1100
40 to 47	8,439	0.0942
48 to 55	8,267	0.0923
56 to 63	7,430	0.0829
64 to 71	7,283	0.0813
72 and older	6,192	0.0691
	89,592	**1.0000**

Open-ended classes for lists that are not exhaustive

Although Table 2-10 does not list every occupation held by the graduates of Central College, it is still all-inclusive. Why? The class "other" covers all the observations that fail to fit one of the enumerated categories. We will use a word like this whenever our list does not specifically list all the possibilities. For example, if our characteristic can occur in any month of the year, a complete list would include 12 categories. But if we wish to list only the 8 months from January through August, we can use the term *other* to account for our observations during the 4 months of September, October, November, and December. Although our list does not specifically list all the possibilities, it is all-inclusive. This "other" is called an *open-ended class* when it allows either the upper or the lower end of a quantitative classification scheme to be limitless. The last class in Table 2-11 ("72 and older") is open-ended.

Discrete classes

Classification schemes can be either quantitative or qualitative *and* either discrete or continuous. *Discrete classes* are separate entities that do not progress from one class to the next without a break. Such classes as the number of children in each family, the number of trucks owned by moving companies, and the occupations of Central College graduates are discrete. Discrete data are data that can take on only a limited number of values. Central College graduates can be classified as either doctors or chemists but not something in between. The closing price of AT&T stock can be $39\frac{1}{2}$ or $39\frac{7}{8}$ (but not 39.43), or your basketball team can win by 5 or 27 points (but not by 17.6 points).

Continuous classes

Continuous data do progress from one class to the next without a break. They involve numerical measurement such as the weights of cans of tomatoes, the pounds of pressure on concrete, or the high school GPAs of college seniors. Continuous data can be expressed in either fractions or whole numbers.

HINTS & ASSUMPTIONS

There are many ways to present data. Constructing a data array in either descending or ascending order is a good place to start. Showing how many times a value appears by using a frequency distribution is even more effective, and converting these frequencies to decimals (which we call relative frequencies) can help even more. Hint: We should remember that discrete variables are things that can be counted but continuous variables are things that appear at some point on a scale.

Exercises 2.3

Self-Check Exercises

SC 2-1 Here are the ages of 50 members of a county social service program:

83	51	66	61	82	65	54	56	92	60
65	87	68	64	51	70	75	66	74	68
44	55	78	69	98	67	82	77	79	62
38	88	76	99	84	47	60	42	66	74
91	71	83	80	68	65	51	56	73	55

Use these data to construct relative frequency distributions using 7 equal intervals and 13 equal intervals. State policies on social service programs require that approximately 50 percent of the program participants be older than 50.

(a) Is the program in compliance with the policy?

(b) Does your 13-interval relative frequency distribution help you answer part (a) better than your 7-interval distribution?

(c) Suppose the Director of Social Services wanted to know the proportion of program participants between 45 and 50 years old. Could you estimate the answer for her better with a 7- or a 13-interval relative frequency distribution?

SC 2-2 Using the data in Table 2-1 on page 12, arrange the data in an array from highest to lowest high school GPA. Now arrange the data in an array from highest to lowest college GPA. What can you conclude from the two arrays that you could not from the original data?

Applications

■ **2-9** Transmission Fix-It stores recorded the number of service tickets submitted by each of its 20 stores last month as follows:

823	648	321	634	752
669	427	555	904	586
722	360	468	847	641
217	588	349	308	766

The company believes that a store cannot really hope to break even financially with fewer than 475 service actions a month. It is also company policy to give a financial bonus to any store manager who generates more than 725 service actions a month. Arrange these data in a data array and indicate how many stores are not breaking even and how many are to get bonuses.

■ **2-10** Use the data from Transmission Fix-It in Exercise 2-9. The company financial VP has set up what she calls a "store watch list," that is, a list of the stores whose service activity is low enough to warrant additional attention from the home office. This category includes stores whose service activity is between 550 and 650 service actions a month. How many stores should be on that list based on last month's activity?

■ **2-11** The number of hours taken by transmission mechanics to remove, repair, and replace transmissions in one of the Transmission Fix-It stores one day last week is recorded as follows:

4.3	2.7	3.8	2.2	3.4
3.1	4.5	2.6	5.5	3.2
6.6	2.0	4.4	2.1	3.3
6.3	6.7	5.9	4.1	3.7

Construct a frequency distribution with intervals of 1.0 hour from these data. What conclusions can you reach about the productivity of mechanics from this distribution? If Transmission Fix-It management believes that more than 6.0 hours is evidence of unsatisfactory performance, does it have a major or minor problem with performance in this particular store?

■ **2-12** The Orange County Transportation Commission is concerned about the speed motorists are driving on a section of the main highway. Here are the speeds of 45 motorists:

15	32	45	46	42	39	68	47	18
31	48	49	56	52	39	48	69	61
44	42	38	52	55	58	62	58	48
56	58	48	47	52	37	64	29	55
38	29	62	49	69	18	61	55	49

Use these data to construct relative frequency distributions using 5 equal intervals and 11 equal intervals. The U.S. Department of Transportation reports that, nationally, no more than 10 percent of the motorists exceed 55 mph.

(a) Do Orange County motorists follow the U.S. DOT's report about national driving patterns?

(b) Which distribution did you use to answer part (a)?

(c) The U.S. DOT has determined that the safest speed for this highway is more than 36 but less than 59 mph. What proportion of the motorists drive within this range? Which distribution helped you answer this question?

■ **2-13** Arrange the data in Table 2-2 on page 12 in an array from highest to lowest.

(a) Suppose that state law requires bridge concrete to withstand at least 2,500 lb/sq in. How many samples would fail this test?

(b) How many samples could withstand a pressure of at least 2,497 lb/sq in. but could not withstand a pressure greater than 2,504 lb/sq in.?

(c) As you examine the array, you should notice that some samples can withstand identical amounts of pressure. List these pressures and the number of samples that can withstand each amount.

■ **2-14** A recent study concerning the habits of U.S. cable television consumers produced the following data:

Number of Channels Purchased	Number of Hours Spent Watching Television per Week
25	14
18	16
42	12
96	6
28	13
43	16
39	9
29	7
17	19
84	4
76	8
22	13
104	6

Arrange the data in an array. What conclusion(s) can you draw from these data?

■ **2-15** The Environmental Protection Agency took water samples from 12 different rivers and streams that feed into Lake Erie. These samples were tested in the EPA laboratory and rated as to the amount of solid pollution suspended in each sample. The results of the testing are given in the following table:

Sample	1	2	3	4	5	6
Pollution Rating (ppm)	37.2	51.7	68.4	54.2	49.9	33.4
Sample	7	8	9	10	11	12
Pollution Rating (ppm)	39.8	52.7	60.0	46.1	38.5	49.1

(a) Arrange the data into an array from highest to lowest.

(b) Determine the number of samples having a pollution content between 30.0 and 39.9, 40.0 and 49.9, 50.0 and 59.9, and 60.0 and 69.9.

(c) If 45.0 is the number used by the EPA to indicate excessive pollution, how many samples would be rated as having excessive pollution?

(d) What is the largest distance between any two consecutive samples?

■ **2-16** Suppose that the admissions staff mentioned in the discussion of Table 2-1 on page 12 wishes to examine the relationship between a student's differential on the college SAT examination (the difference between actual and expected score based on the student's high school GPA) and the spread between the student's high school and college GPA (the difference between the college and high school GPA). The admissions staff will use the following data:

H.S. GPA	College GPA	SAT Score	H.S. GPA	College GPA	SAT Score
3.6	2.5	1,100	3.4	3.6	1,180
2.6	2.7	940	2.9	3.0	1,010
2.7	2.2	950	3.9	4.0	1,330
3.7	3.2	1,160	3.2	3.5	1,150
4.0	3.8	1,340	2.1	2.5	940
3.5	3.6	1,180	2.2	2.8	960
3.5	3.8	1,250	3.4	3.4	1,170
2.2	3.5	1,040	3.6	3.0	1,100
3.9	3.7	1,310	2.6	1.9	860
4.0	3.9	1,330	2.4	3.2	1,070

In addition, the admissions staff has received the following information from the Educational Testing Service:

H.S. GPA	Avg. SAT Score	H.S. GPA	Avg. SAT Score
4.0	1,340	2.9	1,020
3.9	1,310	2.8	1,000
3.8	1,280	2.7	980
3.7	1,250	2.6	960
3.6	1,220	2.5	940
3.5	1,190	2.4	920
3.4	1,160	2.3	910
3.3	1,130	2.2	900
3.2	1,100	2.1	880
3.1	1,070	2.0	860
3.0	1,040		

(a) Arrange these data into an array of spreads from highest to lowest. (Consider an increase in college GPA over high school GPA as positive and a decrease in college GPA below high school GPA as negative.) Include with each spread the appropriate SAT differential. (Consider an SAT score below expected as negative and above expected as positive.)

(b What is the most common spread?

(c) For this spread in part (b), what is the most common SAT differential?

(d) From the analysis you have done, what do you conclude?

Worked-Out Answers to Self-Check Exercises

SC 2-1

7 Intervals

Class	Relative Frequency
30–39	0.02
40–49	0.06
50–59	0.16
60–69	0.32
70–79	0.20
80–89	0.16
90–99	0.08
	1.00

13 Intervals

Class	Relative Frequency	Class	Relative Frequency
35–39	0.02	70–74	0.10
40–44	0.04	75–79	0.10
45–49	0.02	80–84	0.12
50–54	0.08	85–89	0.04
55–59	0.08	90–94	0.04
60–64	0.10	95–99	0.04
65–69	0.22		1.00

(a) As can be seen from either distribution, about 90 percent of the participants are older than 50, so the program is not in compliance.
(b) In this case, both are equally easy to use.
(c) The 13-interval distribution gives a better estimate because it has a class for 45–49, whereas the 7-interval distribution lumps together all observations between 40 and 49.

SC 2-2 Data array by high school GPA:

High School GPA	College GPA	High School GPA	College GPA
4.0	3.9	3.4	3.4
4.0	3.8	3.2	3.5
3.9	4.0	2.9	3.0
3.9	3.7	2.7	2.2
3.7	3.2	2.6	2.7
3.6	3.0	2.6	1.9
3.6	2.5	2.4	3.2
3.5	3.8	2.2	3.5
3.5	3.6	2.2	2.8
3.4	3.6	2.1	2.5

Data array by college GPA:

College GPA	High School GPA	College GPA	High School GPA
4.0	3.9	3.2	3.7
3.9	4.0	3.2	2.4
3.8	4.0	3.0	3.6
3.8	3.5	3.0	2.9
3.7	3.9	2.8	2.2
3.6	3.5	2.7	2.6
3.6	3.4	2.5	3.6
3.5	3.2	2.5	2.1
3.5	2.2	2.2	2.7
3.4	3.4	1.9	2.6

From these arrays we can see that high GPAs at one level tend to go with high GPAs at the other, although there are some exceptions.

2.4 Constructing a Frequency Distribution

Classify the data

Now that we have learned how to divide a sample into classes, we can take raw data and actually construct a frequency distribution. To solve the carpet-loom problem on the first page of the chapter, follow these three steps:

Divide the range by equal classes

1. **Decide on the type and number of classes for dividing the data.** In this case, we have already chosen to classify the data by the quantitative measure of the number of yards produced rather than by a qualitative attribute such as color or pattern. Next, we need to decide how many different classes to use and the range each class should cover. The range must be divided by *equal* classes; that is, the width of the interval from the beginning of one class to the beginning of the next class must be the same for every class. If we choose a width of 0.5 yard for each class in our distribution, the classes will be those shown in Table 2-12.

Table 2-12	Class in Yards	Frequency
Daily Production in a Sample of 30 Carpet Looms with 0.5-yard Class Intervals	15.1–15.5	2
	15.6–16.0	16
	16.1–16.5	8
	16.6–17.0	4
		30

Table 2-13	Class	Width of Class Intervals	Frequency
Daily Production in a Sample of 30 Carpet Looms Using Unequal Class Intervals	15.1–15.5	15.6 − 15.1 = 0.5	2
	15.6–15.8	15.9 − 15.6 = 0.3	8
	15.9–16.1	16.2 − 15.9 = 0.3	9
	16.2–16.5	16.6 − 16.2 = 0.4	7
	16.6–16.9	17.0 − 16.6 = 0.4	4
			30

Problems with unequal classes

If the classes were unequal and the width of the intervals differed among the classes, then we would have a distribution that is much more difficult to interpret than one with equal intervals. Imagine how hard it would be to interpret the data presented in Table 2-13!

Use 6 to 15 classes

The number of classes depends on the number of data points and the range of the data collected. The more data points or the wider the range of the data, the more classes it takes to divide the data. Of course, if we have only 10 data points, it is senseless to have as many as 10 classes. As a rule, statisticians rarely use fewer than 6 or more than 15 classes.

Determine the width of the class intervals

Because we need to make the class intervals of equal size, the number of classes determines the width of each class. To find the intervals, we can use this equation:

Width of a Class Interval

$$\text{Width of class intervals} = \frac{\text{Next unit value after largest value in data} - \text{Smallest value in data}}{\text{Total number of class intervals}} \quad [2\text{-}1]$$

We must use the *next value of the same units* because we are measuring the *interval* between the first value of one class and the first value of the next class. In our carpet-loom study, the last value is 16.9, so 17.0 is the next value. We shall use six classes in this example, so the width of each class will be

$$\frac{\text{Next unit value after largest value in data} - \text{Smallest value in data}}{\text{Total number of class intervals}} \quad [2\text{-}1]$$

$$= \frac{17.0 - 15.2}{6}$$

Table 2-14 Daily Production in a Sample of 30 Carpet Looms with 0.3-yard Class Intervals	Class	Frequency
	15.2–15.4	2
	15.5–15.7	5
	15.8–16.0	11
	16.1–16.3	6
	16.4–16.6	3
	16.7–16.9	3
		30

$$= \frac{1.8}{6}$$

$$= 0.3 \text{ yd} \leftarrow \text{width of class intervals}$$

Examine the results

Step 1 is now complete. We have decided to classify the data by the quantitative measure of how many yards of carpet were produced. We have chosen 6 classes to cover the range of 15.2 to 16.9 and, as a result, will use 0.3 yard as the width of our class intervals.

Create the classes and count the frequencies

2. **Sort the data points into classes and count the number of points in each class.** This we have done in Table 2-14. Every data point fits into at least one class, and no data point fits into more than one class. Therefore, our classes are all-inclusive and mutually exclusive. Notice that the lower boundary of the first class corresponds with the smallest data point in our sample, and the upper boundary of the last class corresponds with the largest data point.
3. **Illustrate the data in a chart.** (See Figure 2-1.)

These three steps enable us to arrange the data in both tabular and graphic form. In this case, our information is displayed in Table 2-14 and in Figure 2-1. These two frequency distributions omit some of the detail contained in the raw data of Table 2-3, but they make it easier for us to notice patterns in the data. One obvious characteristic, for example, is that the class 15.8–16.0 contains the most elements; class 15.2–15.4, the fewest.

Notice any trends

Notice in Figure 2-1 that the frequencies in the classes of 0.3-yard widths follow a regular progression: The number of data points begins with 2 for the first class, builds to 5, reaches 11 in the third class, falls to 6, and tumbles to 3 in the fifth and sixth classes. We will find that the larger the width of the class intervals, the smoother this progression will

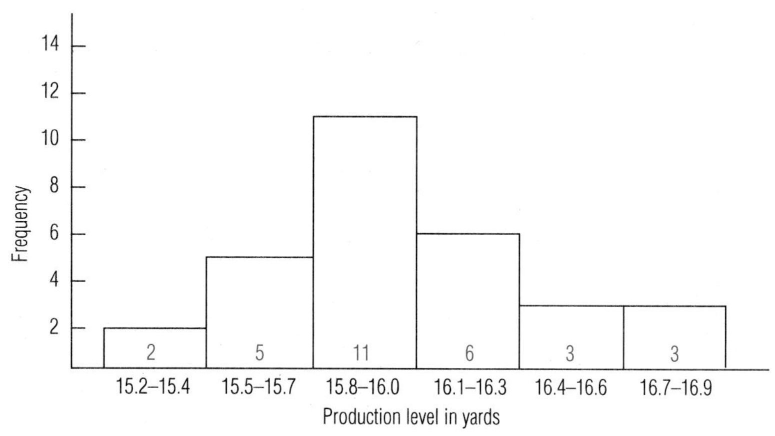

FIGURE 2-1

Frequency distribution of production levels in a sample of 30 carpet looms using 0.3-yard class intervals

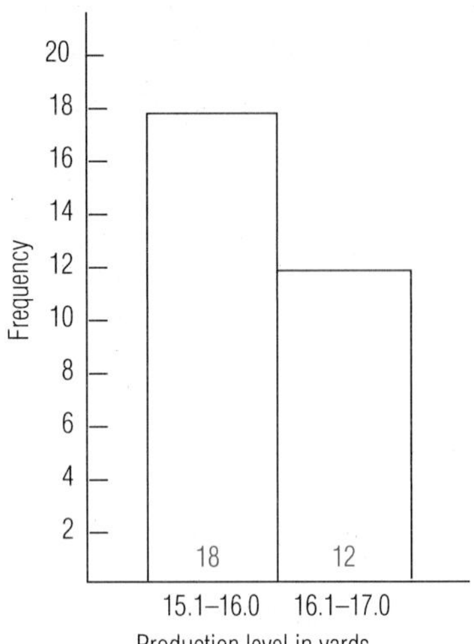

FIGURE 2-2

Frequency distribution of production levels in a sample of 30 carpet looms using 1-yard class intervals

be. However, if the classes are too wide, we lose so much information that the chart is almost meaningless. For example, if we collapse Figure 2-1 into only two categories, we obscure the pattern. This is evident in Figure 2-2.

Using the Computer to Construct Frequency Distributions

Hand calculations are cumbersome

Throughout this text, we will be using simple examples to illustrate how to do many different kinds of statistical analyses. With such examples, you can learn what sort of calculations have to be done. We hope you will also be able to understand the concepts behind the calculations, so you will appreciate why these particular calculations are appropriate. However, the fact of the matter remains that hand calculations are cumbersome, tiresome, and error-prone. Many real problems have so much data that doing the calculations by hand is not really feasible.

Software packages for statistical analysis

For this reason, most real-world statistical analysis is done on computers. You prepare the input data and interpret the results of the analysis and take appropriate actions, but the machine does all the "number crunching." There are many widely used software packages for statistical analyses, including Minitab, SAS, SPSS, and SYSTAT.* It is not our intention to teach you the details of how to use any of these to do your analyses, but we will be using primarily Minitab and occasionally the SAS System to illustrate typical sorts of outputs these packages produce.

Using the grade data

Appendix 10 contains grade data for the 199 students who used this text in our course. In Figure 2-3, we have used Minitab to create a frequency distribution of the students' raw total scores in the course. The TOTBY10 column values are the midpoints of the classes. Often, you will also be interested in *bivariate frequency distributions,* in which the data are classified with respect to two different attributes. In Figure 2-4, we have such a distribution showing the letter grades in each of the six sections of the class. The variable NUMGRADE has values 0 to 9, which correspond to letter grades F, D, C−, C, C+, B−, B, B+, A−, and A.

Appendix 11 contains earnings data for 224 companies whose 1989 last-quarter earnings were published in *The Wall Street Journal* during the week of February 12, 1990. In Figure 2-5, we have used Minitab to create a frequency distribution of those last-quarter earnings. The variable Q489 is the 1989 last-quarter earnings, rounded to the nearest dollar.

*Minitab is a registered trademark of Minitab, Inc., University Park, Pa. SAS is a registered trademark of SAS Institute, Inc., Cary, N.C. SPSS is a registered trademark of SPSS, Inc., Chicago, Ill. SYSTAT is a registered trademark of SYSTAT, Inc., Evanston, Ill.

Summary Statistics for Discrete Variables

TOTBY10	Count	Percent	Cumcnt	Cumpct
25	1	0.50	1	0.50
35	1	0.50	2	1.01
45	9	4.52	11	5.53
55	27	13.57	38	19.10
65	68	34.17	106	53.27
75	65	32.66	171	85.93
85	26	13.07	197	98.99
95	2	1.01	199	100.00
N=	199			

FIGURE 2-3

Minitab frequency distribution of raw total scores

FIGURE 2-4 Minitab bivariate frequency distribution showing grades in each section

Tabulated Statistics

ROWS: NUMGRADE COLUMNS: SECTION

	1	2	3	4	5	6	ALL
0	2	3	0	1	3	2	11
	1.01	1.51	--	0.50	1.51	1.01	5.53
1	3	6	5	2	4	6	26
	1.51	3.02	2.51	1.01	2.01	3.02	13.07
2	2	2	1	2	7	4	18
	1.01	1.01	0.50	1.01	3.52	2.01	9.05
3	9	11	3	9	6	6	44
	4.52	5.53	1.51	4.52	3.02	3.02	22.11
4	3	6	10	6	7	2	34
	1.51	3.02	5.03	3.02	3.52	1.01	17.09
5	1	5	5	1	0	3	15
	0.50	2.51	2.51	0.50	--	1.51	7.54
6	2	5	3	2	2	3	17
	1.01	2.51	1.51	1.01	1.01	1.51	8.54
7	1	1	1	2	1	1	7
	0.50	0.50	0.50	1.01	0.50	0.50	3.52
8	2	2	8	1	3	0	16
	1.01	1.01	4.02	0.50	1.51	--	8.04
9	2	5	1	0	3	0	11
	1.01	2.51	0.50	--	1.51	--	5.53
ALL	27	46	37	26	36	27	199
	13.57	23.12	18.59	13.07	18.09	13.57	100.00

CELL CONTENTS --
COUNT
% OF TBL

Summary Statistics for Discrete Variables

Q489	Count	Percent	Cumcnt	Cumpct
-5	1	0.45	1	0.45
-4	2	0.89	3	1.34
-2	1	0.45	4	1.79
-1	9	4.02	13	5.80
0	164	73.21	177	79.02
1	43	19.20	220	98.21
2	2	0.89	222	99.11
5	2	0.89	224	100.00
N=	224			

FIGURE 2-5

Minitab frequency distribution of 1989 last-quarter earnings

Because companies listed on the New York Stock Exchange (3) tend to have different financial characteristics from those listed on the American Stock Exchange (2), and because those, in turn, are different from companies listed "over-the-counter" (1), we also used Minitab to produce the bivariate distribution of the same earnings data in Figure 2-6.

HINTS & ASSUMPTIONS

When we construct a frequency distribution we need to carefully choose the classes into which we divide data. This is true even when we use a computer program to set up the classes. For example, a computer program might divide the ages of respondents to a marketing research survey into the consistent classes: 15–19, 20–24, 25–29, and so on. But if the product being researched is intended for college students, it may make more sense to set up the classes as 18, 19–22, and 23 and above. Be aware that using a computer in statistics doesn't substitute for common sense.

Exercises 2.4

Self-Check Exercises

SC 2-3 High Performance Bicycle Products Company in Chapel Hill, North Carolina, sampled its shipping records for a certain day with these results:

Time from Receipt of Order to Delivery (in Days)

4	12	8	14	11	6	7	13	13	11
11	20	5	19	10	15	24	7	29	6

Construct a frequency distribution for these data and a relative frequency distribution. Use intervals of 6 days.

(a) What statement can you make about the effectiveness of order processing from the frequency distribution?

(b) If the company wants to ensure that half of its deliveries are made in 10 or fewer days, can you determine from the frequency distribution whether they have reached this goal?

(c) What does having a relative frequency distribution permit you to do with the data that is difficult to do with only a frequency distribution?

Tabulated Statistics

ROWS: Q489 COLUMNS: EXCHANGE

	1	2	3	ALL
-5	0	0	1	1
	--	--	100.00	100.00
	--	--	1.33	0.45
	--	--	0.45	0.45
-4	1	0	1	2
	50.00	--	50.00	100.00
	0.90	--	1.33	0.89
	0.45	--	0.45	0.89
-2	1	0	0	1
	100.00	--	--	100.00
	0.90	--	--	0.45
	0.45	--	--	0.45
-1	5	2	2	9
	55.56	22.22	22.22	100.00
	4.50	5.26	2.67	4.02
	2.23	0.89	0.89	4.02
0	97	31	36	164
	59.15	18.90	21.95	100.00
	87.39	81.58	48.00	73.21
	43.30	13.84	16.07	73.21
1	7	4	32	43
	16.28	9.30	74.42	100.00
	6.31	10.53	42.67	19.20
	3.12	1.79	14.29	19.20
2	0	0	2	2
	--	--	100.00	100.00
	--	--	2.67	0.89
	--	--	0.89	0.89
5	0	1	1	2
	--	50.00	50.00	100.00
	--	2.63	1.33	0.89
	--	0.45	0.45	0.89
ALL	111	38	75	224
	49.55	16.96	33.48	100.00
	100.00	100.00	100.00	100.00
	49.55	16.96	33.48	100.00

CELL CONTENTS --
COUNT
% OF ROW
% OF COL
% OF TBL

FIGURE 2-6

Minitab bivariate frequency distribution showing earnings on each exchange

Self-Check Exercises

(continued)

SC 2-4 Mr. Franks, a safety engineer for the Mars Point Nuclear Power Generating Station, has charted the peak reactor temperature each day for the past year and has prepared the following frequency distribution:

Temperatures in °C	Frequency
Below 500	4
501–510	7
511–520	32
521–530	59
530–540	82
550–560	65
561–570	33
571–580	28
580–590	27
591–600	23
Total	**360**

List and explain any errors you can find in Mr. Franks's distribution.

Applications

■ **2-17** Universal Burger is concerned about product waste, so they sampled their burger waste record from the past year with the following results:

Number of Burgers Discarded During a Shift								
2	16	4	12	19	29	24	7	19
22	14	8	24	31	18	20	16	6

Construct a frequency distribution for these data and a relative frequency distribution. Use intervals of 5 burgers.

(a) One of Universal Burger's goals is for at least 75 percent of shifts to have no more than 16 burgers wasted. Can you determine from the frequency distribution whether this goal has been achieved?

(b) What percentage of shifts have waste of 21 or fewer burgers? Which distribution did you use to determine your answer?

■ **2-18** Refer to Table 2-2 on page 12 and construct a relative frequency distribution using intervals of 4.0 lb/sq in. What do you conclude from this distribution?

■ **2-19** The Bureau of Labor Statistics has sampled 30 communities nationwide and compiled prices in each community at the beginning and end of August in order to find out approximately how the Consumer Price Index (CPI) has changed during August. The percentage changes in prices for the 30 communities are as follows:

0.7	0.4	−0.3	0.2	−0.1	0.1	0.3	0.7	0.0	−0.4
0.1	0.5	0.2	0.3	1.0	−0.3	0.0	0.2	0.5	0.1
−0.5	−0.3	0.1	0.5	0.4	0.0	0.2	0.3	0.5	0.4

(a) Arrange the data in an array from lowest to highest.

(b) Using the following four equal-sized classes, create a frequency distribution: −0.5 to −0.2, −0.1 to 0.2, 0.3 to 0.6, and 0.7 to 1.0.

(c) How many communities had prices that either did not change or that increased less than 1.0 percent?

(d) Are these data discrete or continuous?

■ **2-20** Sarah Anne Rapp, the president of Baggit, Inc., has just obtained some raw data from a marketing survey that her company recently conducted. The survey was taken to determine the effectiveness of the new company slogan, "When you've given up on the rest, Baggit!" To determine the effect of the slogan on the sales of Luncheon Baggits, 20 people were asked how many boxes of Luncheon Baggits per month they bought before and after the slogan was used in the advertising campaign. The results were as follows:

Before/After		Before/After		Before/After		Before/After	
4	3	2	1	5	6	8	10
4	6	6	9	2	7	1	3
1	5	6	7	6	8	4	3
3	7	5	8	8	4	5	7
5	5	3	6	3	5	2	2

(a) Create both frequency and relative frequency distributions for the "Before" responses, using as classes 1–2, 3–4, 5–6, 7–8, and 9–10.

(b) Work part (a) for the "After" responses.

(c) Give the most basic reason why it makes sense to use the same classes for both the "Before" and "After" responses.

(d) For each pair of "Before/After" responses, subtract the "Before" response from the "After" response to get the number that we will call "Change" (example: $3 - 4 = -1$), and create frequency and relative frequency distributions for "Change" using classes -5 to -4, -3 to -2, -1 to 0, 1 to 2, 3 to 4, and 5 to 6.

(e) Based on your analysis, state whether the new slogan has helped sales, and give one or two reasons to support your conclusion.

■ **2-21** Here are the ages of 30 people who bought video recorders at Symphony Music Shop last week:

26	37	40	18	14	45	32	68	31	37
20	32	15	27	46	44	62	58	30	42
22	26	44	41	34	55	50	63	29	22

(a) From looking at the data just as they are, what conclusions can you come to quickly about Symphony's market?

(b) Construct a 6-category closed classification. Does having this enable you to conclude anything more about Symphony's market?

■ **2-22** Use the data from Exercise 2-21.

(a) Construct a 5-category open-ended classification. Does having this enable you to conclude anything more about Symphony's market?

(b) Now construct a relative frequency distribution to go with the 5-category open-ended classification. Does having this provide Symphony with additional information useful in its marketing? Why?

■ **2-23** John Lyon, owner of Fowler's Food Store in Chapel Hill, North Carolina, has arranged his customers' purchase amounts last week into this frequency distribution:

$ Spent	Frequency	$ Spent	Frequency	$ Spent	Frequency
0.00– 0.99	50	16.00–18.99	1,150	34.00–36.99	610
1.00– 3.99	240	19.00–21.99	980	37.00–39.99	420
4.00– 6.99	300	22.00–24.99	830	40.00–42.99	280
7.00– 9.99	460	25.00–27.99	780	43.00–45.99	100
10.00–12.99	900	28.00–30.99	760	46.00–48.99	90
13.00–15.99	1,050	31.00–33.99	720		

John says that having 17 intervals each defined by 2 numbers is cumbersome. Can you help him simplify the data he has without losing too much of their value?

■ **2-24** Here are the midpoints of the intervals for a distribution representing minutes it took the members of a university track team to complete a 5-mile cross-country run.

25 35 45

(a) Would you say that the team coach can get enough information from these midpoints to help the team?

(b) If your answer to part (a) is "no," how many intervals do seem appropriate?

■ **2-25** Barney Mason has been examining the amount of daily french fry waste (in pounds) for the past 6 months at Universal Burger and has created the following frequency distribution:

French Fry Waste in Pounds	Frequency
0.0– 3.9	37
4.0– 7.9	46
8.0–11.9	23
12.0–16.9	27
17.0–25.9	7
26.0–40.9	0
	180

List and explain any errors you can find in Barney's distribution.

■ **2-26** Construct a discrete, closed classification for the possible responses to the "marital status" portion of an employment application. Also, construct a 3-category, discrete, open-ended classification for the same responses.

■ **2-27** Stock exchange listings usually contain the company name, the high and low bids, the closing price, and the change from the previous day's closing price. Here's an example:

Name	High Bid	Low Bid	Closing	Change
Systems Associates	$11\frac{1}{2}$	$10\frac{7}{8}$	$11\frac{1}{4}$	$+\frac{1}{2}$

Is a distribution of all (a) stocks on the New York Stock Exchange by industry, (b) closing prices on a given day, and (c) changes in prices from the previous day

(1) Quantitative or qualitative?

(2) Continuous or discrete?

(3) Open-ended or closed?

Would your answer to part (c) be different if the change were expressed simply as "higher," "lower," or "unchanged"?

■ **2-28** The noise level in decibels of aircraft departing Westchester County Airport was rounded to the nearest decibel and grouped in a frequency distribution having intervals with midpoints at 100 and 130. Under 100 decibels is not considered loud at all, and anything over 140 decibels is almost deafening. If Residents for a Quieter Neighborhood is gathering data for its lawsuit against the airport, is this distribution adequate for its purpose?

■ **2-29** Use the data from Exercise 2-28. If the lawyer defending the airport is collecting data preparatory to going to trial, would she approve of the midpoints of the intervals in Exercise 2-28 for her purposes?

■ **2-30** The president of Ocean Airlines is trying to estimate when the Federal Aviation Administration (FAA) is most likely to rule on the company's application for a new route between Charlotte and Nashville. Assistants to the president have assembled the following waiting times for applications filed during the past year. The data are given in days from the date of application until an FAA ruling.

34	40	23	28	31	40	25	33	47	32
44	34	38	31	33	42	26	35	27	31
29	40	31	30	34	31	38	35	37	33
24	44	37	39	32	36	34	36	41	39
29	22	28	44	51	31	44	28	47	31

(a) Construct a frequency distribution using 10 closed intervals, equally spaced. Which interval contains the most data points?

(b) Construct a frequency distribution using 5 closed intervals, equally spaced. Which interval contains the most data points?

(c) If the president of Ocean Airlines had a relative frequency distribution for either (a) or (b), would that help him estimate the answer he needs?

■ **2-31** For the purpose of performance evaluation and quota adjustment, Ralph Williams monitored the auto sales of his 40 salespeople. Over a 1-month period, they sold the following number of cars:

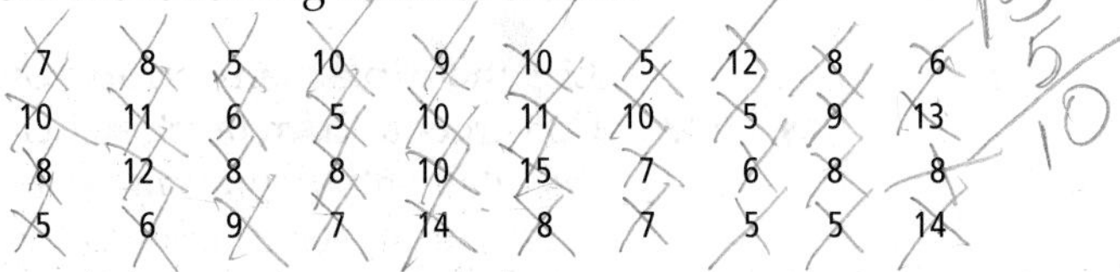

7	8	5	10	9	10	5	12	8	6
10	11	6	5	10	11	10	5	9	13
8	12	8	8	10	15	7	6	8	8
5	6	9	7	14	8	7	5	5	14

(a) Based on frequency, what would be the desired class marks (midpoints of the intervals)?

(b) Construct a frequency and relative frequency distribution having as many of these marks as possible. Make your intervals evenly spaced and at least two cars wide.

(c) If sales fewer than seven cars a month is considered unacceptable performance, which of the two answers, (a) or (b), helps you more in identifying the unsatisfactory group of salespeople?

■ **2-32** Kessler's Ice Cream Delight attempts to keep all of its 55 flavors of ice cream in stock at each of its stores. Their marketing-research director suggests that keeping better records for each store is the key to preventing stockouts. Don Martin, director of store operations, collects data to the nearest half gallon on the daily amount of each flavor of ice cream that is sold. No more than 20 gallons of any flavor are ever used on one day.

(a) Is the flavor classification discrete or continuous? Open or closed?

(b) Is the "amount of ice cream" classification discrete or continuous? Open or closed?

(c) Are the data qualitative or quantitative?

(d) What would you suggest Martin do to generate better data for market-research purposes?

■ **2-33** Doug Atkinson is the owner and ticket collector for a ferry that transports people and cars from Long Island to Connecticut. Doug has data indicating the number of people, as well as the number of cars, that have ridden the ferry during the past 2 months. For example,

JULY 3 NUMBER OF PEOPLE, 173 NUMBER OF CARS, 32

might be a typical daily entry for Doug. Doug has set up six equally spaced classes to record the daily number of people, and the class marks are 84.5, 104.5, 124.5, 144.5, 164.5, and 184.5. Doug's six equally spaced classes for the daily number of cars have class marks of 26.5, 34.5, 42.5, 50.5, 58.5, and 66.5. (The class marks are the midpoints of the intervals.)

(a) What are the upper and lower boundaries of the classes for the number of people?

(b) What are the upper and lower boundaries of the classes for the number of cars?

Worked-Out Answers to Self-Check Exercises

SC 2-3

Class	1–6	7–12	13–18	19–24	25–30
Frequency	4	8	4	3	1
Relative Frequency	0.20	0.40	0.20	0.15	0.05

(a) Assuming that the shop is open 6 days a week, we see that fully 80 percent of the orders are filled in 3 weeks or less.

(b) We can tell only that between 20 percent and 60 percent of the deliveries are made in 10 or fewer days, so the distribution does not generate enough information to determine whether the goal has been met.

(c) A relative frequency distribution lets us present frequencies as fractions or percentages.

SC 2-4 The distribution is not all-inclusive. The data point 500°C is left out, along with the points between 541°C and 549°C, inclusive. In addition, the distribution is closed on the high end, which eliminates all data points above 600°C. These omissions might explain the fact that the total number of observations is only 360, rather than 365 as might be expected for a data set compiled over one year. (Note: It is not absolutely necessary that the distribution be open-ended on the high end, especially if no data points were recorded above 600°C. However, for completeness, the distribution should be continuous over the range selected, even though no data points may fall in some of the intervals.) Finally, the classifications are not mutually exclusive. Two points, 530°C and 580°C, are contained in more than one interval. When creating a set of continuous classifications, care must be taken to avoid this error.

2.5 Graphing Frequency Distributions

Identifying the horizontal and vertical axes

Figures 2-1 and 2-2 (on pages 23 & 24) are previews of what we are going to discuss now: how to present frequency distributions graphically. Graphs give data in a two-dimensional picture. On the *horizontal* axis, we can show the values of the variable (the characteristic we are measuring), such as the carpet output in yards. On the *vertical* axis, we mark the frequencies of the classes shown on the horizontal axis. Thus, the height of the boxes in Figure 2-1 measures the number of observations in each of the classes marked on the horizontal axis. Graphs of frequency distributions and relative frequency distributions are useful because they emphasize and clarify patterns that are not so readily discernible in tables. They attract a reader's attention to patterns in the data. Graphs can also help us do problems concerning frequency distributions. They will enable us to estimate some values at a glance and will provide us with a pictorial check on the accuracy of our solutions.

Function of graphs

Histograms

Histograms described

Figures 2-1 and 2-2 (pages 23 & 24) are two examples of histograms. A *histogram* is a series of rectangles, each proportional in width to the range of values within a class and proportional in height to the number of items falling in the class. If the classes we use in the frequency distribution are of equal width, then the vertical bars in the histogram are also of equal width. The height of the bar for each class corresponds to the number of items in the class. As a result, the area contained in each rectangle (width times height) is the same percentage of the area of all the rectangles as the frequency of that class is to all the observations made.

Function of a relative frequency histogram

A histogram that uses the relative frequency of data points in each of the classes rather than the actual number of points is called a *relative frequency histogram.* The relative frequency histogram has the same shape as an absolute frequency histogram made from the same data set. This is true because in both, the relative size of each rectangle is the frequency of that class compared to the total number of observations.

Recall that the relative frequency of any class is the number of observations in that class divided by the total number of observations made. The sum of all the relative frequencies for any data set is equal to 1.0. With this in mind, we can convert the histogram of Figure 2-1 into a relative frequency histogram, such as we find in Figure 2-7. Notice that the only difference between these two is the left-hand vertical scale. Whereas the scale in Figure 2-1 is the *absolute* number of observations in each class, the scale in Figure 2-7 is the number of observations in each class as a *fraction* of the total number of observations.

FIGURE 2-7

Relative frequency distribution of production levels in a sample of 30 carpet looms using 0.3-yard class intervals

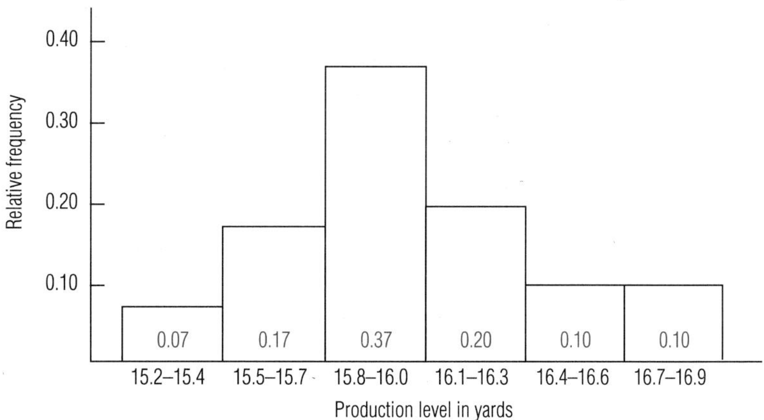

Advantage of the relative frequency histogram

Being able to present data in terms of the relative rather than the absolute frequency of observations in each class is useful because, while the absolute numbers may change (as we test more looms, for example), the relationship among the classes may remain stable. Twenty percent of all the looms may fall in the class "16.1–16.3 yards" whether we test 30 or 300 looms. It is easy to compare the data from different sizes of samples when we use relative frequency histograms.

Frequency Polygons

Use midpoints on the horizontal axis

Although less widely used, *frequency polygons* are another way to portray graphically both simple and relative frequency distributions. To construct a frequency polygon, we mark the frequencies on the vertical axis and the values of the variable we are measuring on the horizontal axis, as we did with histograms. Next, we plot each class frequency by drawing a dot above its midpoint, and connect the successive dots with straight lines to form a polygon (a many-sided figure).

Add two classes

Figure 2-8 is a frequency polygon constructed from the data in Table 2-14 on page 23. If you compare this figure with Figure 2-1, you will notice that classes have been added at *each end* of the scale of observed values. These two new classes contain zero observations but allow the polygon to reach the horizontal axis at both ends of the distribution.

Converting a frequency polygon to a histogram

How can we turn a frequency polygon into a histogram? A frequency polygon is simply a line graph that connects the midpoints of all the bars in a histogram. Therefore, we can reproduce the histogram by drawing vertical lines from the bounds of the classes (as marked on the horizontal axis) and connecting them with horizontal lines at the heights of the polygon at each midpoint. We have done this with dotted lines in Figure 2-9.

FIGURE 2-8

Frequency polygon of production levels in a sample of 30 carpet looms using 0.3-yard class intervals

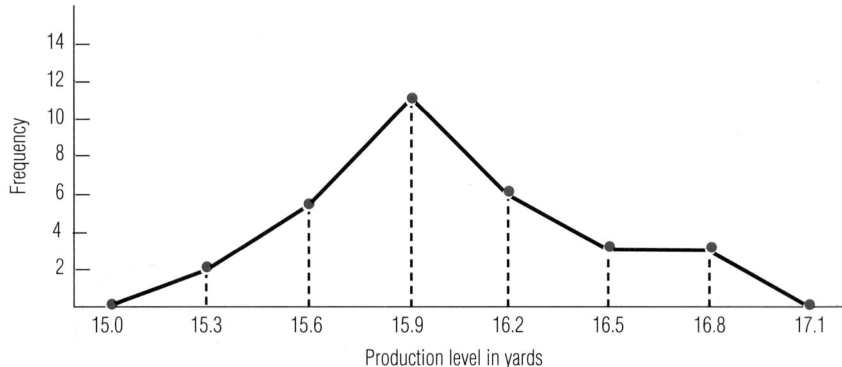

FIGURE 2-9

Histogram drawn from the points of the frequency polygon in Figure 2-8

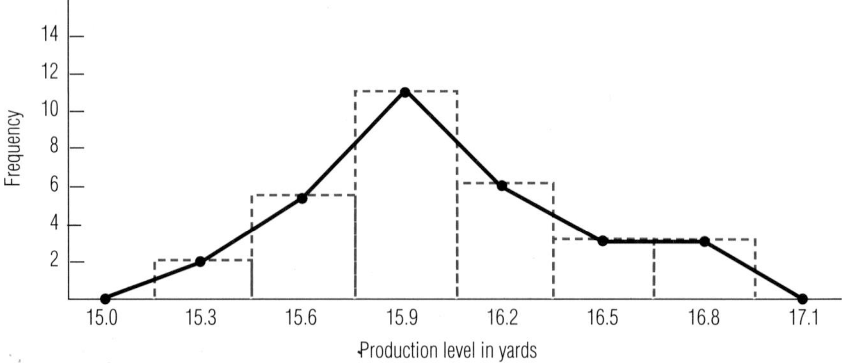

Constructing a relative frequency polygon

A frequency polygon that uses the relative frequency of data points in each of the classes rather than the actual number of points is called a *relative frequency polygon.* The relative frequency polygon has the same shape as the frequency polygon made from the same data set but a different scale of values on the vertical axis. Rather than the absolute number of observations, the scale is the number of observations in each class as a fraction of the total number of observations.

Advantages of histograms

Histograms and frequency polygons are similar. Why do we need both? The advantages of histograms are

1. The rectangle clearly shows each separate class in the distribution.
2. The area of each rectangle, relative to all the other rectangles, shows the proportion of the total number of observations that occur in that class.

Advantages of polygons

Frequency polygons, however, have certain advantages, too.

1. The frequency polygon is simpler than its histogram counterpart.
2. It sketches an outline of the data pattern more clearly.
3. The polygon becomes increasingly smooth and curvelike as we increase the number of classes and the number of observations.

Creating a frequency curve

A polygon such as the one we have just described, smoothed by added classes and data points, is called a *frequency curve.* In Figure 2-10, we have used our carpet-loom example, but we have increased the number of observations to 300 and the number of classes to 10. Notice that we have connected the points with curved lines to approximate the way the polygon would look if we had a very large number of data points and very small class intervals.

Ogives

Cumulative frequency distribution defined

A *cumulative frequency distribution* enables us to see how many observations lie above or below certain values, rather than merely recording the number of items within intervals. For

FIGURE 2-10

Frequency curve of production levels in a sample of 300 carpet looms using 0.2-yard intervals

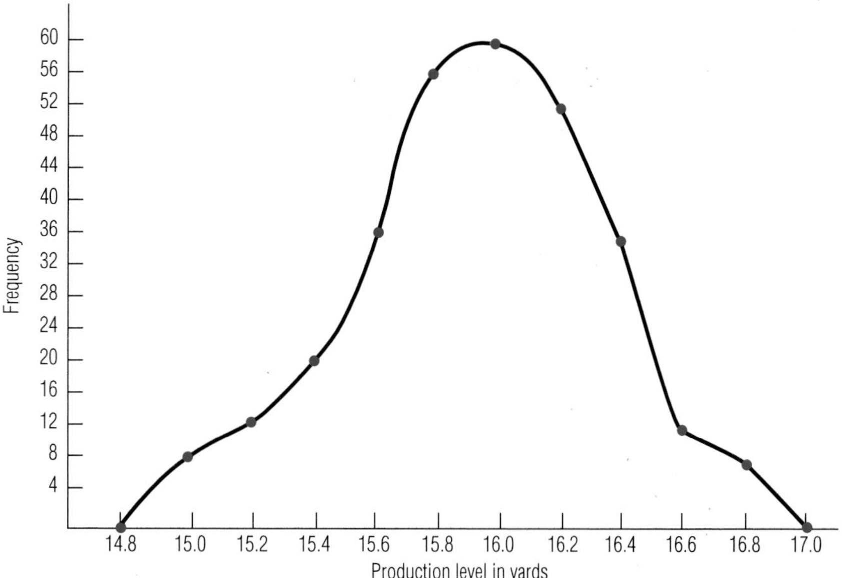

Table 2-15 Cumulative "Less-Than" Frequency Distribution of Production Levels in a Sample of 30 Carpet Looms	Class	Cumulative Frequency
	Less than 15.2	0
	Less than 15.5	2
	Less than 15.8	7
	Less than 16.1	18
	Less than 16.4	24
	Less than 16.7	27
	Less than 17.0	30

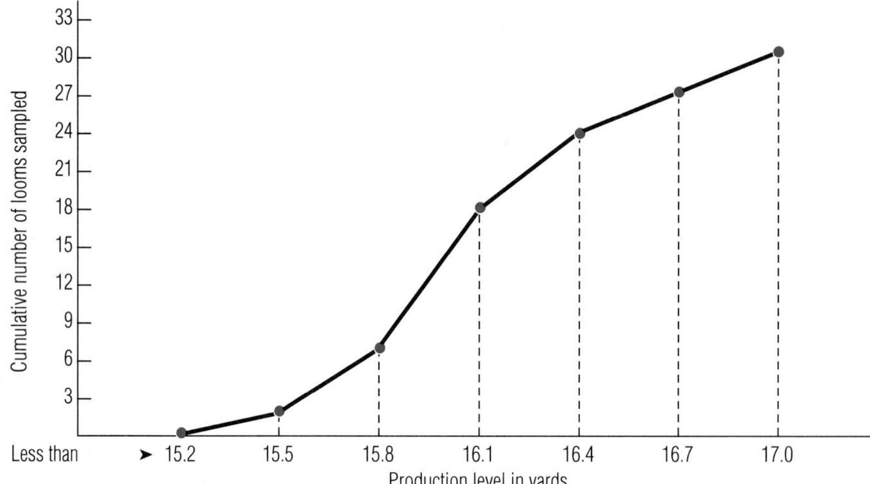

FIGURE 2-11

"Less-than" ogive of the distribution of production levels in a sample of 30 carpet looms

example, if we wish to know how many looms made less than 17.0 yards we can use a table recording the cumulative "less-than" frequencies in our sample, such as Table 2-15.

A "less-than" ogive

A graph of a cumulative frequency distribution is called an *ogive* (pronounced "**oh**-jive"). The ogive for the cumulative distribution in Table 2-15 is shown in Figure 2-11. The plotted points represent the number of looms having less production than the number of yards shown on the horizontal axis. Notice that the lower bound of the classes in the table becomes the upper bound of the cumulative distribution of the ogive.

Occasionally, the information we are using is presented in terms of "more-than" frequencies. The appropriate ogive for such information would slope down and to the right, instead of up and to the right as it did in Figure 2-11.

Ogives of relative frequencies

We can construct an ogive of a relative frequency distribution in the same manner in which we drew the ogive of an absolute frequency distribution in Figure 2-11. There will be one change—the vertical scale. As in Figure 2-7, on page 33, this scale must mark the *fraction* of the total number of observations that falls into each class.

To construct a cumulative "less-than" ogive in terms of relative frequencies, we can refer to a relative frequency distribution (such as Figure 2-7) and set up a table using the data (such as Table 2-16). Then we can convert the figures there to an ogive (as in Figure 2-12). Notice that Figures 2-11 and 2-12 are equivalent except for the left-hand vertical axis.

Approximating the data array

Suppose we now draw a line perpendicular to the vertical axis at the 0.50 mark to intersect our ogive. (We have done this in Figure 2-13.) In this way, we can read an approximate value of 16.0 for the production level in the fifteenth loom of an array of the 30.

Table 2-16 Cumulative Relative Frequency Distribution of Production Levels in a Sample of 30 Carpet Looms	Class	Cumulative Frequency	Cumulative Relative Frequency
	Less than 15.2	0	0.00
	Less than 15.5	2	0.07
	Less than 15.8	7	0.23
	Less than 16.1	18	0.60
	Less than 16.4	24	0.80
	Less than 16.7	27	0.90
	Less than 17.0	30	1.00

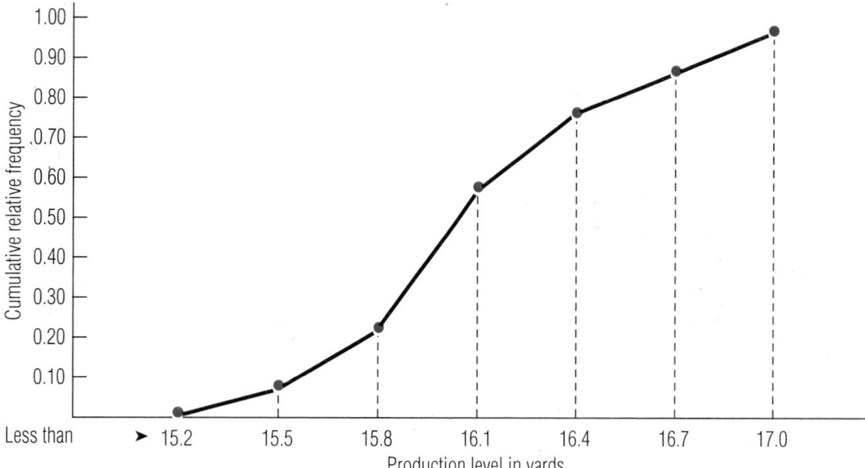

FIGURE 2-12

"Less-than" ogive of the distribution of production levels in a sample of 30 carpet looms using relative frequencies

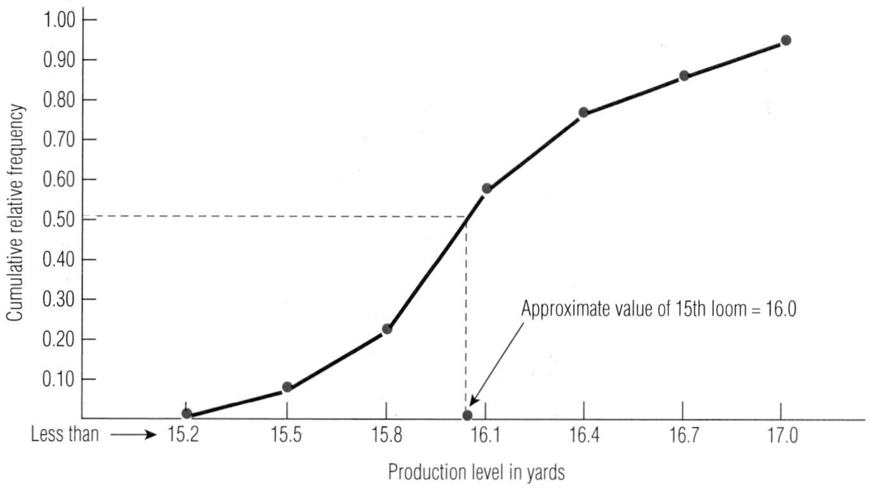

FIGURE 2-13

"Less-than" ogive of the distribution of the production levels in a sample of 30 carpet looms, indicating the approximate middle value in the original data array

Thus, we are back to the first data arrangement discussed in this chapter. From the data array, we can construct frequency distributions. From frequency distributions, we can construct cumulative frequency distributions. From these, we can graph an ogive. And from this ogive, we can approximate the values we had in the data array. However, we cannot normally recover the *exact* original data from any of the graphic representations we have discussed.

Using the Computer to Graph Frequency Distributions

Using SAS to produce histograms

Let's produce some histograms of our grade data in Appendix 10. Figure 2-14 gives a histogram of the students' raw total scores. Notice that this histogram has horizontal bars instead of the vertical bars that we have drawn so far. In addition, to the right of the bars, SAS gives the absolute frequencies, relative frequencies, and cumulative less-than frequencies (both absolute and relative). The Minitab version is in Figure 2-15.

In Figure 2-4, we looked at a bivariate frequency distribution. We can also create histograms that contain information about two variables. Figure 2-16 is a SAS vertical his-

FIGURE 2-14

SAS histogram and frequency distributions of raw total scores

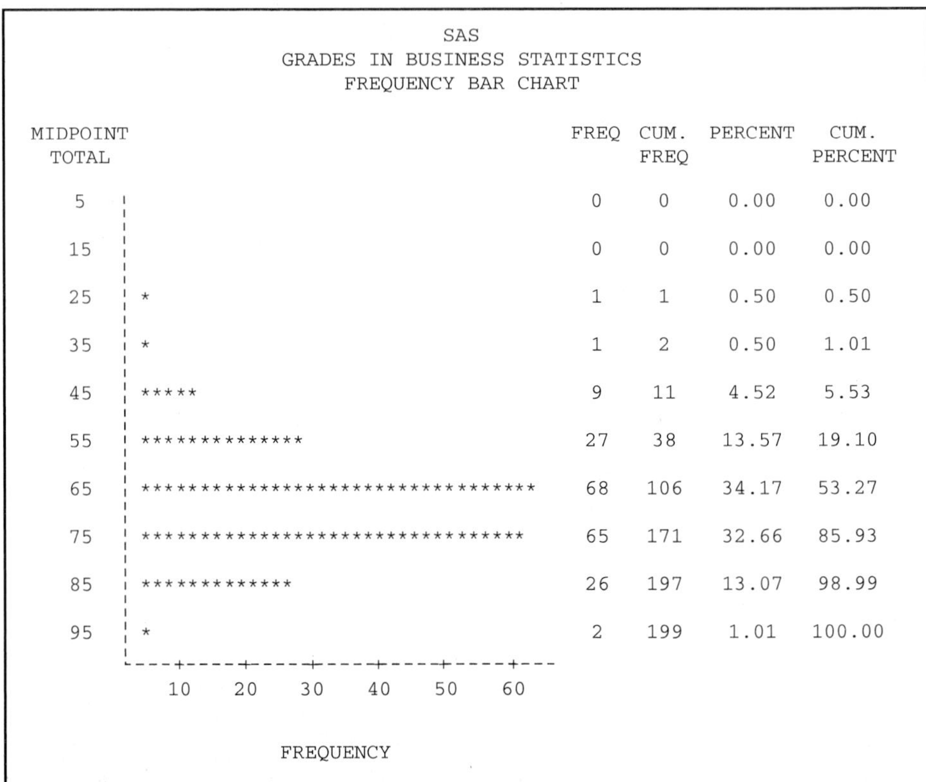

```
                                SAS
                    GRADES IN BUSINESS STATISTICS
                         FREQUENCY BAR CHART

MIDPOINT                                       FREQ  CUM.  PERCENT   CUM.
 TOTAL                                               FREQ           PERCENT

   5   |                                          0     0     0.00     0.00
  15   |                                          0     0     0.00     0.00
  25   | *                                        1     1     0.50     0.50
  35   | *                                        1     2     0.50     1.01
  45   | *****                                    9    11     4.52     5.53
  55   | **************                          27    38    13.57    19.10
  65   | **********************************      68   106    34.17    53.27
  75   | *********************************       65   171    32.66    85.93
  85   | *************                           26   197    13.07    98.99
  95   | *                                        2   199     1.01   100.00
       ----+----+----+----+----+----+---
          10   20   30   40   50   60

                  FREQUENCY
```

FIGURE 2-15

Minitab histogram and frequency distribution of grades in business statistics

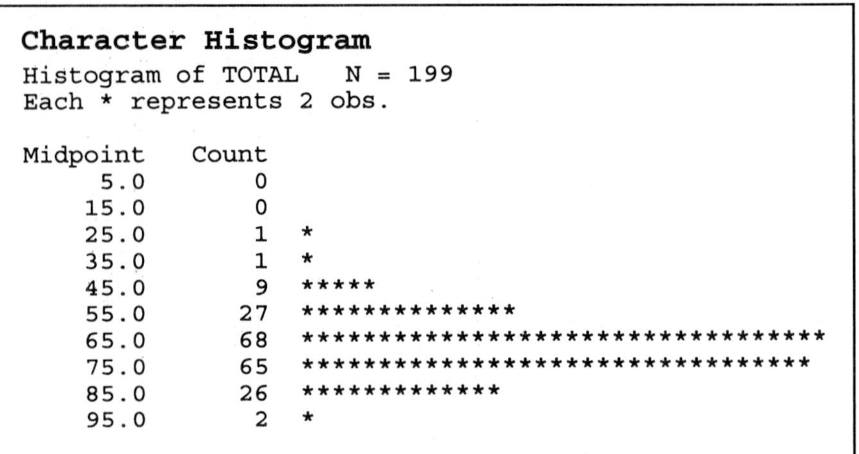

```
Character Histogram
Histogram of TOTAL    N = 199
Each * represents 2 obs.

Midpoint   Count
     5.0       0
    15.0       0
    25.0       1  *
    35.0       1  *
    45.0       9  *****
    55.0      27  **************
    65.0      68  **********************************
    75.0      65  *********************************
    85.0      26  *************
    95.0       2  *
```

togram of the students' letter grades in which each of the bars is divided into two segments showing the fractions of the students getting that grade who were in sections taught by professors and graduate teaching assistants (denoted by constructing the bars with P's and T's). Figure 2-17 is a Minitab version of the grades using two histograms of NUMGRADE (see Figure 2-4) split by INSTRNUM (1 = teaching assistant and 2 = professor).

In Figure 2-18, we have used Minitab to produce a histogram of the 1989 last-quarter earnings of the 224 companies listed in Appendix 11. Figure 2-19 gives separate Minitab histograms for the 111 OTC, 38 ASE, and 75 NYSE companies in the data set.

FIGURE 2-16 SAS histogram of grades showing type of instructor

```
                                        SAS
                           GRADES IN BUSINESS STATISTICS
                                FREQUENCY BAR CHART

FREQUENCY                      TTTTT
     |                         TTTTT
     |                         TTTTT
     |                         TTTTT
  40 +                         TTTTT
     |                         TTTTT
     |                         TTTTT
     |                         TTTTT
     |                         TTTTT
  35 +                         TTTTT
     |                         TTTTT   TTTTT
     |                         TTTTT   TTTTT
     |                         TTTTT   TTTTT
     |                         TTTTT   TTTTT
  30 +                         TTTTT   TTTTT
     |                         TTTTT   TTTTT
     |                         TTTTT   TTTTT
     |                         TTTTT   TTTTT
     |         TTTTT           TTTTT   TTTTT
  25 +         TTTTT           TTTTT   TTTTT
     |         TTTTT           TTTTT   TTTTT
     |         TTTTT           TTTTT   TTTTT
     |         TTTTT           TTTTT   TTTTT
     |         TTTTT           TTTTT   TTTTT
  20 +         TTTTT           PPPPP   TTTTT
     |         TTTTT           PPPPP   TTTTT
     |         TTTTT   TTTTT   PPPPP   PPPPP
     |         PPPPP   TTTTT   PPPPP   PPPPP           TTTTT
     |         PPPPP   TTTTT   PPPPP   PPPPP           TTTTT           TTTTT
  15 +         PPPPP   TTTTT   PPPPP   PPPPP   TTTTT   TTTTT           TTTTT
     |         PPPPP   TTTTT   PPPPP   PPPPP   TTTTT   TTTTT           TTTTT
     |         PPPPP   TTTTT   PPPPP   PPPPP   PPPPP   TTTTT           TTTTT
     |         PPPPP   TTTTT   PPPPP   PPPPP   PPPPP   TTTTT           TTTTT
     | TTTTT   PPPPP   TTTTT   PPPPP   PPPPP   PPPPP   PPPPP           TTTTT   TTTTT
  10 + TTTTT   PPPPP   TTTTT   PPPPP   PPPPP   PPPPP   PPPPP           PPPPP   TTTTT
     | TTTTT   PPPPP   TTTTT   PPPPP   PPPPP   PPPPP   PPPPP           PPPPP   TTTTT
     | TTTTT   PPPPP   TTTTT   PPPPP   PPPPP   PPPPP   PPPPP           PPPPP   TTTTT
     | TTTTT   PPPPP   PPPPP   PPPPP   PPPPP   PPPPP   PPPPP   TTTTT   PPPPP   TTTTT
     | TTTTT   PPPPP   PPPPP   PPPPP   PPPPP   PPPPP   PPPPP   TTTTT   PPPPP   PPPPP
   5 + PPPPP   PPPPP   PPPPP   PPPPP   PPPPP   PPPPP   PPPPP   TTTTT   PPPPP   PPPPP
     | PPPPP   PPPPP   PPPPP   PPPPP   PPPPP   PPPPP   PPPPP   TTTTT   PPPPP   PPPPP
     | PPPPP   PPPPP   PPPPP   PPPPP   PPPPP   PPPPP   PPPPP   PPPPP   PPPPP   PPPPP
     | PPPPP   PPPPP   PPPPP   PPPPP   PPPPP   PPPPP   PPPPP   PPPPP   PPPPP   PPPPP
     | PPPPP   PPPPP   PPPPP   PPPPP   PPPPP   PPPPP   PPPPP   PPPPP   PPPPP   PPPPP
     ---------------------------------------------------------------------------------
         F       D       C-      C       C+      B-      B       B+      A-      A

                                       GRADE

                    SYMBOL    INSTRUCT    SYMBOL    INSTRUCT
```

```
Character Histogram
Histogram of NUMGRADE   INSTRNUM = 1   N = 89

Midpoint    Count
    0.00        6   ******
    1.00        9   *********
    2.00       11   ***********
    3.00       24   ************************
    4.00       16   ****************
    5.00        2   **
    6.00        6   ******
    7.00        4   ****
    8.00        6   ******
    9.00        5   *****

Histogram of NUMGRADE   INSTRNUM = 2   N = 110

Midpoint    Count
    0.00        5   *****
    1.00       17   *****************
    2.00        7   *******
    3.00       20   ********************
    4.00       18   ******************
    5.00       13   *************
    6.00       11   ***********
    7.00        3   ***
    8.00       10   **********
    9.00        6   ******
```

FIGURE 2-17

Minitab version of grade histograms

```
Character Histogram
Histogram of LQ89   N = 224
Each * represents 5 obs.

Midpoint    Count
  -5.500        1   *
  -5.000        0
  -4.500        0
  -4.000        0
  -3.500        2   *
  -3.000        0
  -2.500        0
  -2.000        0
  -1.500        1   *
  -1.000        2   *
  -0.500       15   ***
   0.000      115   ***********************
   0.500       60   ************
   1.000       21   *****
   1.500        3   *
   2.000        1   *
   2.500        1   *
   3.000        0
   3.500        0
   4.000        0
   4.500        1   *
   5.000        1   *
```

FIGURE 2-18

Minitab histogram of 1989 last-quarter earnings

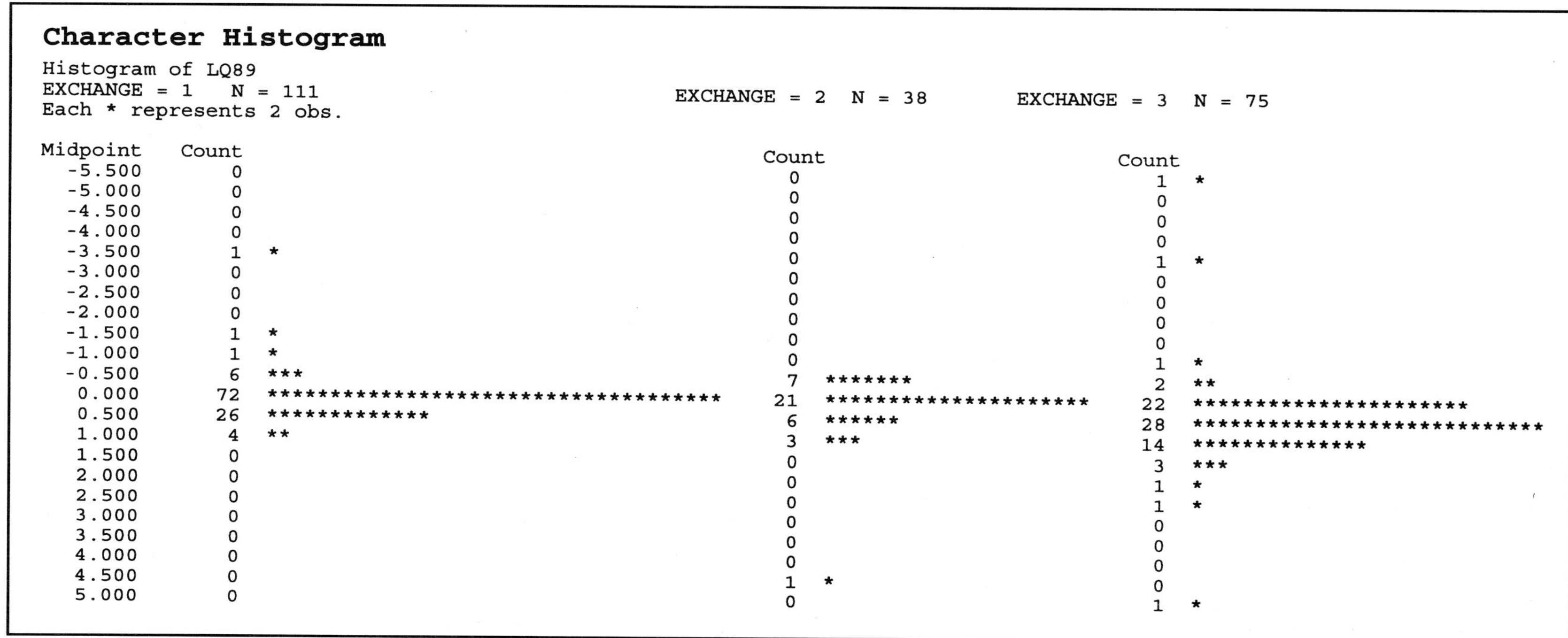

```
Character Histogram
Histogram of LQ89
EXCHANGE = 1    N = 111                                  EXCHANGE = 2  N = 38          EXCHANGE = 3  N = 75
Each * represents 2 obs.

Midpoint    Count                                        Count                         Count
  -5.500        0                                           0                              1  *
  -5.000        0                                           0                              0
  -4.500        0                                           0                              0
  -4.000        0                                           0                              0
  -3.500        1  *                                        0                              1  *
  -3.000        0                                           0                              0
  -2.500        0                                           0                              0
  -2.000        0                                           0                              0
  -1.500        1  *                                        0                              0
  -1.000        1  *                                        0                              1  *
  -0.500        6  ***                                      7  *******                     2  **
   0.000       72  ************************************    21  *********************      22  **********************
   0.500       26  *************                            6  ******                     28  ****************************
   1.000        4  **                                       3  ***                        14  **************
   1.500        0                                           0                              3  ***
   2.000        0                                           0                              1  *
   2.500        0                                           0                              1  *
   3.000        0                                           0                              0
   3.500        0                                           0                              0
   4.000        0                                           0                              0
   4.500        0                                           1  *                           0
   5.000        0                                           0                              1  *
```

FIGURE 2-19 Separate Minitab histograms by stock exchange of 1989 last-quarter earnings

HINTS & ASSUMPTIONS

Whoever said "a picture is worth a thousand words" understood intuitively what we have been covering in this section. Using graphic methods to display data gives us a quick sense of patterns and trends and what portion of our data is above or below a certain value. Warning: Some publications print graphic displays of data (histograms) in a way that is confusing by using a vertical axis that doesn't go all the way to zero. Be aware when you see one of these that small differences have been made to look too large, and that the pattern you are seeing is misleading.

Exercises 2.5

Self-Check Exercises

SC 2-5 Here is a frequency distribution of the weight of 150 people who used a ski lift a certain day. Construct a histogram for these data.

Class	Frequency	Class	Frequency
75– 89	10	150–164	23
90–104	11	165–179	9
105–119	23	180–194	9
120–134	26	195–209	6
135–149	31	210–224	2

(a) What can you see from the histogram about the data that was not immediately apparent from the frequency distribution?

(b) If each ski lift chair holds two people but is limited in total safe weight capacity to 400 pounds, what can the operator do to maximize the people capacity of the ski lift without exceeding the safe weight capacity of a chair? Do the data support your proposal?

SC 2-6 Central Carolina Hospital has the following data representing weight in pounds at birth of 200 premature babies.

Class	Frequency	Class	Frequency
0.5–0.9	10	2.5–2.9	29
1.0–1.4	19	3.0–3.4	34
1.5–1.9	24	3.5–3.9	40
2.0–2.4	27	4.0–4.4	17

Construct an ogive that will help you answer these questions:

(a) What was the approximate middle value in the original data set?

(b) If premature babies under 3.0 pounds are normally kept in an incubator for several days as a precaution, about what percentage of Central's premature babies will need an incubator?

Applications

■ **2-34** Here is a frequency distribution of the length of phone calls made by 175 people during a Labor Day weekend. Construct a histogram for these data.

Length in Minutes	Frequency
1– 7	45
8–14	32
15–21	34
22–28	22
29–35	16
36–42	12
43–49	9
50–56	5

(a) Describe the general shape of the histogram. Does there appear to be a pattern?

(b) Suppose all the people were making their calls from a room that had 10 different phones, and each person knew which time class the call would belong to. Suggest an ordering so that all calls can be completed as fast as possible.

(c) Does the order affect the length of time to complete all calls?

■ **2-35** Golden Acres is a homeowners' association that operates a trailer park outside Orlando, Florida, where retirees keep their winter homes. In addition to lot rents, a monthly facility fee of $12 is charged for social activities at the clubhouse. One board member has noted that many of the older residents never attend the clubhouse functions, and has proposed waiving the fee for association members over age 60. A survey of 25 residents reported the following ages:

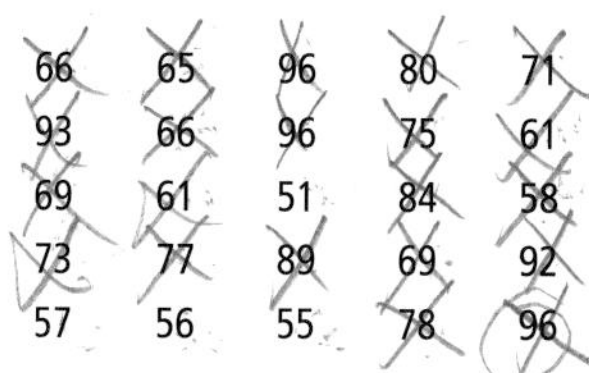

66	65	96	80	71
93	66	96	75	61
69	61	51	84	58
73	77	89	69	92
57	56	55	78	96

Construct an ogive that will help you answer these questions:

(a) Roughly what proportion of residents would be eligible for no fee?

(b) Approximately what fee would the board have to charge to the remaining (fee-paying) residents to cover the same total cost of running the clubhouse?

■ **2-36** Homer Willis, a fishing boat captain from Salter Path, North Carolina, believes that the break-even catch on his boats is 5,000 pounds per trip. Here are data on a sample of catches on 20 fishing trips Homer's boats have made recently:

6,500	6,700	3,400	3,600	2,000
7,000	5,600	4,500	8,000	5,000
4,600	8,100	6,500	9,000	4,200
4,800	7,000	7,500	6,000	5,400

Construct an ogive that will help you answer these questions:

(a) Roughly what proportion of the trips breaks even for Homer?

(b) What is the approximate middle value in the data array for Homer's boats?

(c) What catch do Homer's boats exceed 80 percent of the time?

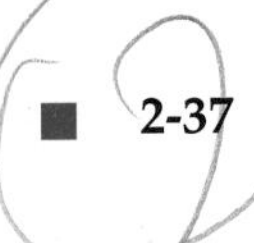

■ **2-37** The Massachusetts Friends of Fish has the following data representing pollutants (in parts per million) at 150 sites in the state:

Pollutants (in ppm)	Frequency	Pollutants (in ppm)	Frequency
5.0– 8.9	14	25.0–28.9	16
9.0–12.9	16	29.0–32.9	9
13.0–16.9	28	33.0–36.9	7
17.0–20.9	36	37.0–40.9	4
21.0–24.9	20		

Construct an ogive that will help you answer the following questions:

(a) Below what value (approximately) do the lowest one-fourth of these observations fall?

(b) If the Friends of Fish heavily monitor all sites with more than 30 ppm of pollutants, what percentage of sites will be heavily monitored?

■ **2-38** Before constructing a dam on the Colorado River, the U.S. Army Corps of Engineers performed a series of tests to measure the water flow past the proposed location of the dam. The results of the testing were used to construct the following frequency distribution:

River Flow (Thousands of Gallons per Minute)	Frequency
1,001–1,050	7
1,051–1,100	21
1,101–1,150	32
1,151–1,200	49
1,201–1,250	58
1,251–1,300	41
1,301–1,350	27
1,351–1,400	11
Total	**246**

(a) Use the data given in the table to construct a "more-than" cumulative frequency distribution and ogive.

(b) Use the data given in the table to construct a "less-than" cumulative frequency distribution and ogive.

(c) Use your ogive to estimate what proportion of the flow occurs at less than 1,300 thousands of gallons per minute.

■ **2-39** Pamela Mason, a consultant for a small local brokerage firm, was attempting to design investment programs attractive to senior citizens. She knew that if potential customers could obtain a certain level of return, they would be willing to risk an investment, but below a certain level, they would be reluctant. From a group of 50 subjects, she obtained the following data regarding the various levels of return required for each subject to invest $1,000:

Indifference Point	Frequency	Indifference Point	Frequency
$70–74	2	$90– 94	11
75–79	5	95– 99	3
80–84	10	100–104	3
85–89	14	105–109	2

(a) Construct both "more-than" and "less-than" cumulative relative frequency distributions.

(b) Graph the 2 distributions in part (a) into relative frequency ogives.

■ **2-40** At a newspaper office, the time required to set the entire front page in type was recorded for 50 days. The data, to the nearest tenth of a minute, are given below.

20.8	22.8	21.9	22.0	20.7	20.9	25.0	22.2	22.8	20.1
25.3	20.7	22.5	21.2	23.8	23.3	20.9	22.9	23.5	19.5
23.7	20.3	23.6	19.0	25.1	25.0	19.5	24.1	24.2	21.8
21.3	21.5	23.1	19.9	24.2	24.1	19.8	23.9	22.8	23.9
19.7	24.2	23.8	20.7	23.8	24.3	21.1	20.9	21.6	22.7

(a) Arrange the data in an array from lowest to highest.

(b) Construct a frequency distribution and a "less-than" cumulative frequency distribution from the data, using intervals of 0.8 minute.

(c) Construct a frequency polygon from the data.

(d) Construct a "less-than" ogive from the data.

(e) From your ogive, estimate what percentage of the time the front page can be set in less than 24 minutes.

■ **2-41** Chien-Ling Lee owns a CD store specializing in spoken-word recordings. Lee has 35 months of gross sales data, arranged as a frequency distribution.

Monthly Sales	Frequency	Monthly Sales	Frequency
$10,000–12,499	2	$20,000–22,499	6
12,500–14,999	4	22,500–24,999	8
15,000–17,499	7	25,000–27,499	2
17,500–19,999	5	27,500–29,999	1

(a) Construct a relative frequency distribution.

(b) Construct, on the same graph, a relative frequency histogram and a relative frequency polygon.

■ **2-42** The National Association of Real Estate Sellers has collected these data on a sample of 130 salespeople representing their total commission earnings annually:

Earnings	Frequency
$ 5,000 or less	5
$ 5,001–$10,000	9
$10,001–$15,000	11
$15,001–$20,000	33
$20,001–$30,000	37
$30,001–$40,000	19
$40,001–$50,000	9
Over $50,000	7

Construct an ogive that will help you answer these questions.

(a) About what proportion of the salespeople earns more than $25,000?

(b) About what does the "middle" salesperson in the sample earn?

(c) Approximately how much could a real estate salesperson whose performance was about 25 percent from the top expect to earn annually?

■ **2-43** Springfield is a college town with the usual parking problems. The city allows people who have received tickets for illegally parked cars to come in and make their case to an administrative officer and have the ticket voided. The town's administrative officer collected the following frequency distribution for the time spent on each appeal:

Minutes Spent on Appeal	Frequency	Minutes Spent on Appeal	Frequency
Less than 2	30	8– 9	70
2–3	40	10–11	50
4–5	40	12–13	50
6–7	90	14–15	30
			400

(a) Construct a "less-than" cumulative frequency distribution.

(b) Construct an ogive based on part (a).

(c) The town administrator will consider streamlining the paperwork for the appeal process if more than 50 percent of appeals take longer than 4 minutes. What is the percentage taking more than 4 minutes? What is the approximate time for the 200th (midpoint) appeal?

Worked-Out Answers to Self-Check Exercises

SC 2-5

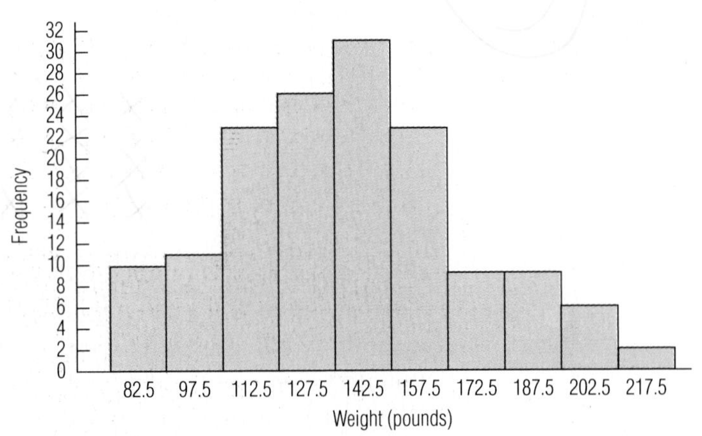

(a) The lower tail of the distribution is fatter (has more observations in it) than the upper tail.

(b) Because there are so few people who weigh 180 pounds or more, the operator can afford to pair each person who appears to be heavy with a lighter person. This can be done without greatly delaying any individual's turn at the lift.

SC 2-6

Class	Cumulative Relative Frequency	Class	Cumulative Relative Frequency
0.5–0.9	0.050	2.5–2.9	0.545
1.0–1.4	0.145	3.0–3.4	0.715
1.5–1.9	0.265	3.5–3.9	0.915
2.0–2.4	0.400	4.0–4.4	1.000

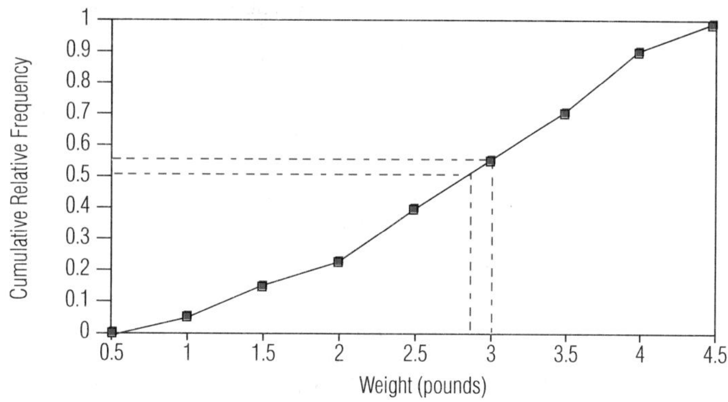

(a) The middle value was about 2.8 pounds.
(b) About 55 percent will need incubators.

Statistics at Work

Loveland Computers

Case 2: Arranging Data New Year's Day 1995, found Lee Azko staring out the window, watching a light dusting of snow fall on the Denver suburbs. Lee had graduated early from the University of Colorado, one semester short of the usual 4 years, thanks to a handful of advanced placement credits from high school. Lee was both excited and apprehensive that the next day would be the start of a serious job search for a well-trained business major, with little experience in the real world.

Contemplation of the future was interrupted by a phone call from Lee's uncle. "I was going to call you anyway to congratulate you on finishing school early. But I have another reason for calling—some things have come up in the business, and it looks as if I need someone to crunch some numbers in a hurry. Why don't you drive up tomorrow and I'll tell you what I have in mind."

Lee knew that Uncle Walter's company, Loveland Computers, had been growing by leaps and bounds. Walter Azko had developed the computer company from a strange background. Unlike Lee, Walter never finished college. "I was making too much money to stay in school," he used to explain. Walter had traveled extensively in the Far East with his parents, so it was only natural that he would begin an importing business while still a student at Boulder. He imported just about anything that could be sold cheaply and that would appeal to students: furniture, gifts, household utensils, and some clothing.

On one buying trip to Taiwan in the early 1980s, Walter was offered some personal computers. Looking back, they were awful. Not much memory and no hard drive, but they were dirt cheap and Walter soon sold them to "tekkies" at the university. The computer business grew, and within 2 years, Walter sold his retail importing business and concentrated solely on importing and selling computers.

Walter's first move was to lease a commercial building in Loveland, Colorado, where rents were much cheaper than in Boulder. From this location, he could market directly to students at the Universities at Boulder, Fort Collins, and Greeley. About an hour north of Denver's Stapleton International Airport, Loveland was a convenient site for imports coming by airfreight and a good place to recruit part-time workers. The name Loveland Computers seemed a natural.

At first, Walter Azko acted as his own sales staff, personally delivering computers from the back of his car. Walter made every sale on price alone and word-of-mouth referrals supplemented a few ads placed in the college newspapers. Because he sold directly to students and enthusiasts, it seemed that he was the only game in town. Walter's niche seemed to be an altogether different market from the one being reached by the industry giants. At the top end of the market for PCs, IBM was using expensive retail distribution, targeting the business market. And Apple was defending its high-price strategy with easy "point-and-click" graphical computing that couldn't be matched by IBM-compatible machines.

Azko began reading computer magazines and found he wasn't the only box shop (the industry name for a company that shipped boxes of computers to users with little or no additional service). One or two other companies had found cheap overseas suppliers and they were pursuing a mail-order strategy. Walter thought customers would be reluctant to buy such an expensive—and novel—piece of equipment sight unseen, but the arrival of a new shipment of computers with preinstalled hard disk drives gave him the motivation to run a few ads of his own.

So Loveland Computers joined the ranks of the national mail-order box shops, and by 1988, the company was one of the two dozen companies in this market. The mail-order companies together shared about the same percentage of the market as "Big Blue" (IBM) was maintaining: about 20 percent. But the market for PCs was huge and growing rapidly. By 1993, Loveland Computers regularly booked sales of $10 million a quarter, and even at discount prices, profits regularly amounted to 6 percent of sales. Uncle Walter had become a rich man.

Along the way, Walter Azko realized that to give customers exactly what they wanted, there were advantages in assembling computers at his ever-expanding Loveland facility. He never saw himself as a manufacturer—just an assembler of premade parts such as drive controllers and power supplies. With his contacts with overseas manufacturers, Walter was able to hunt around for the best prices, so Loveland Computers' costs remained low.

To configure new machines and to help with specifications, Walter hired a bright young engineer, Gratia Delaguardia. Gratia knew hardware: She had completed several development projects for Storage Technology. In only a few years at Loveland Computers, she built a development staff of more than two dozen and was rewarded with a partnership in the business.

Loveland Computers had a few setbacks due to misjudging demand. Walter Azko was always optimistic about sales so inventory of components was often much greater than needed. Once or twice there were embarrassing "write-downs," such as when a shipment of power supplies turned out to be useless because they produced too little current for Loveland's latest model. Gratia Delaguardia had concluded that Loveland ought to be able to manage the supplies better, but it seemed difficult to predict what the market would be like from one month to the next.

After a sleepless night, Lee Azko met with Loveland Computers' founder and president. "Come and sit over here by the window—you can see my new Mercedes 500 SL sports car," Walter Azko said, welcoming his young visitor. "Let me tell you my problem. You know that things move pretty fast around here. Seems like each model lasts about 6 months and then we replace it with something fancier. Up to this point, I've pretty much relied on the local bank for financing. But this is a hot business and we're getting some attention from folks on Wall Street. We may be doing a 'private placement'—that's where we'd raise money for expansion from one or two well-heeled investors or banks—and then, later on, we might want to take the company public. Thing is, they want to know a whole lot about our sales growth: how much is coming from which products and so on. They want to know how long each model lasts, what we should project for next year. Now, of course, I have monthly sales reports going back almost to the beginning. The good news is, it's all on disk. The bad news is, we kept changing our formats so it's very difficult to compare numbers. And, of course, no one wants to flip through, say, 48 months of reports. Your job is to organize it all so it makes sense when these city slickers come to town in their corporate jet."

"When would I start, Uncle?" asked Lee Azko, quite taken aback by the task ahead.

"You've already started," snapped Walter. "It's when you finish that's important. These folks are due in next Monday."

Lee made a mental note to cancel a ski trip planned for the weekend and pulled out a notepad and started to sketch out a plan.

Study Questions: What information should Lee gather, other than financial information relating to sales and income? What format will present the company's rapid growth most clearly in a 45-minute business presentation?

Computer Database Exercise

HH Industries

"Everybody, this is Laurel. Laurel McRae," Hal Rodgers, president of HH Industries, announced at the weekly staff meeting. "Laurel, this is Stan Hutchings, vice president in charge of sales; Peggy Noble, manager of accounting and data processing; Bob Ritchie, manager of purchasing and inventory control; and Gary Russell, operations manager.

"You all know HH Industries is doing well," Hal continued. "The last 3 years have reflected market stability and promising growth in a number of areas. However, much of what we currently base our decisions on is our collective years of experience and gut feel. Laurel is an experienced data analyst and strategic planner and is joining our team to help us analyze, in a more quantitative, statistical fashion, where we are now and where we hope to be in a few years. We may be good, but sophisticated marketing and analysis strategies show we'll have a great future. Besides, maybe we can finally find a productive use for some of this paper we generate!"

The staff chuckled. If the company didn't prosper, it wasn't due to a lack of data. Since the introduction of a tailored data-processing program in the previous fiscal year, a plethora of data, some useful and some merely confusing, had been available. Daily sales and margin (profit) figures were kept religiously, along with detailed inventory data and manifest (shipping) data. No one had quite figured out what to do with it yet, but the president and his staff kept track of simple figures of merit.

Back in her office, Laurel contemplated her recent move to the Florida Suncoast headquarters of HH Industries from the Rocky Mountain home of her first position with Cold River Toy Company. She wasn't too sure about the president's use of the word *experienced*, but she'd do her best. Her decision to leave the successful sled and toy manufacturer had been difficult, but she was confident that warehousing and distribution firms such as HH Industries were a solid bet for the future. And Laurel had been impressed during the interview process with both Hal Rodgers and the company's positive, efficient atmosphere. Soon enough she'd know whether she liked the hydraulics industry as much as she had liked toys.

"Get to know us," Hal had said. "My staff is completely available to you. Ask questions; get a look at the data we collect. I'm a little new at exactly where statistics will help us, but I have full confidence in you. You come very highly recommended, both as an analyst and as an innovative thinker."

"Well," Laurel thought, "here goes nothing." First stop, an afternoon with Stan Hutchings for some company background. Stan, she knew, had been with HH Industries longer than any other staff member and had an excellent intuitive feel for the hydraulics industry.

Days later, and after several such familiarization meetings, data began to clutter her once empty desk. Laurel reflected on what she had learned. HH Industries was a typical family-owned business. Established more than 20 years before by the Douglas family, Handy Hydraulics (as it was then known) sprang up to fill a need perceived by its founders: a source of spare and repair parts to the rapidly growing mobile hydraulics industry. The booming population of the 1960s required the support of an increasing number of construction vehicles, garbage trucks, and other large pieces of equipment, which in turn required spare and repair parts for a huge variety of hydraulic seals, pumps, cylinders, and gauges. As a distributor, Handy Hydraulics tracked down part sources and either resold directly, under the manufacturer's name, or packaged individual parts into repair kits for resale under its own name.

The first 5 years of business saw steady growth, though little actual marketing was done. Word-of-mouth and an important market niche provided a healthy atmosphere for the company. Early sales were almost all in Florida and it wasn't until after the first catalog was produced in 1974 that business began to spread northward to Alabama and Georgia.

"Brute-force" marketing was the next step, and Laurel grimaced as she thought of the poor secretary who had had to distribute mailers to prospective customers gleaned from the yellow pages of all the communities, nationwide, of over 25,000 people. The philosophy was simple: Where there are large groups of people, there are garbage trucks and construction equipment that support these communities. And it worked. The late 1970s and the early 1980s saw burgeoning growth, as new customers appeared daily. Unfortunately, and yet typical of family-run companies, management just couldn't quite keep up.

By this time, numerous competitors had sprung up throughout the United States, some of whom had originally been customers of Handy Hydraulics. It became apparent that the company's goals of maintaining nationwide prominence could be served only by opening satellite warehouses elsewhere, from which the company's emphasis on next-day service could be continued, cost-effectively, to all areas of the country. To achieve this end, the Douglas family sold Handy Hydraulics to its present parent company, BMP Enterprises, and Mr. Douglas was given a 3-year contract to remain as president. With additional capital provided by the investment firm, warehouses were opened in Arizona (1985) and Ohio (1986). However, the company was kept on tight reins by the original founder, with little thought given toward how best to manage the satellite warehouses. Similarly, no recognition was given to the importance of the changing business environment (including increased competition, new technologies and management strategies available). The result was a business out of control, suffocating itself by once-proven, but now too inflexible, policies and procedures. Something had to give.

That something occurred when Mr. Douglas retired in 1988 and BMP Enterprises brought in Hal Rodgers to try to save Handy Hydraulics. A solid business executive with good intuition and even better "people skills," Hal inherited a company that was operating by the proverbial seat of its pants. Even with over $900,000 in sales per quarter, outrageously high payroll and operating expenses were causing net losses.

Over the next 3 years, significant changes were introduced that succeeded in increasing sales while holding expenditures down. The payroll was trimmed to a bare minimum and a walk-in parts counter, once useful for public relations but now merely a costly burden, was closed. Toll-free customer order numbers were installed. The Ohio warehouse was closed down and, nearly 2 years later, a streamlined version was reopened in Pennsylvania. The company's catalog, previously consisting of two bulky three-ring binders, which had to be kept updated by continual mailings, was downsized to a "throwaway" version that more clearly and concisely represented the company's products. Finally, to publicize and celebrate the company's new image, the name was changed to HH Industries.

This was the organization that Laurel found herself contemplating. She summarized the current structure: three profit centers (Florida, Arizona, and Pennsylvania) and three product lines (seals and seal kits, finished hardware—cylinders, pumps, valves, etc.—and spare/repair parts). The company had 42 full-time and 9 part-time employees, over 3,000 active customer accounts, and approximately 15,000 line items of inventory. The corporate fiscal year ran from December to November, and quarterly sales figures now averaged close to $1.4 million. "Whew," Laurel muttered to herself. "Slightly different from toy manufacturing! But I'm getting paid to be a statistician and analyst, so let's see if I can sink my teeth into this monster."

Laurel extracted the most current year's worth of sales data (the third and fourth quarters of 1991, and the first and second quarters of 1992), both the number of orders per day and the dollar value of those orders (referred to as "sales"), by profit center. These are given in the CH02.xxx files on the data disk. From what she had seen, the entire company's mood seemed to revolve around what was called the "daily figure": total corporate sales each day. Laurel's experience, however, told her to look a little deeper. She knew, for instance, that total sales dollars were the direct result of two factors: the number of orders per day and the average dollar value per order.

1. Construct histograms and relative frequency distributions of the company's daily *average order size* (total sales divided by total orders) for the last four quarters. For each chart, use interval widths of 20 and let the first interval run from 0 to 20.
2. Construct similar quarterly charts for the company's total *number of orders per day*. Use interval widths of 10, with the first interval running from 100 to 110.
3. What changing patterns are evident in the data from quarter to quarter? What are some possible explanations?

Chapter Review

Terms Introduced in Chapter 2

Continuous Data Data that may progress from one class to the next without a break and may be expressed by either whole numbers or fractions.

Cumulative Frequency Distribution A tabular display of data showing how many observations lie above, or below, certain values.

Data A collection of any number of related observations on one or more variables.

Data Array The arrangement of raw data by observations in either ascending or descending order.

Data Point A single observation from a data set.

Data Set A collection of data.

Discrete Classes Data that do not progress from one class to the next without a break; that is, where classes represent distinct categories or counts and may be represented by whole numbers.

Frequency Curve A frequency polygon smoothed by adding classes and data points to a data set.

Frequency Distribution An organized display of data that shows the number of observations from the data set that falls into each of a set of mutually exclusive and collectively exhaustive classes.

Frequency Polygon A line graph connecting the midpoints of each class in a data set, plotted at a height corresponding to the frequency of the class.

Histogram A graph of a data set, composed of a series of rectangles, each proportional in width to the range of values in a class and proportional in height to the number of items falling in the class, or the fraction of items in the class.

Ogive A graph of a cumulative frequency distribution.

Open-Ended Class A class that allows either the upper or lower end of a quantitative classification scheme to be limitless.

Population A collection of all the elements we are studying and about which we are trying to draw conclusions.

Raw Data Information before it is arranged or analyzed by statistical methods.

Relative Frequency Distribution The display of a data set that shows the fraction or percentage of the total data set that falls into each of a set of mutually exclusive and collectively exhaustive classes.

Representative Sample A sample that contains the relevant characteristics of the population in the same proportions as they are included in that population.

Sample A collection of some, but not all, of the elements of the population under study, used to describe the population.

Equations Introduced in Chapter 2

■ **2-1**

$$\text{Width of class intervals} = \frac{\text{Next unit value after largest value in data} - \text{Smallest value in data}}{\text{Total number of class intervals}}$$

p. 22

To arrange raw data, decide the number of classes into which you will divide the data (normally between 6 and 15), and then use Equation 2-1 to determine the *width of class intervals of equal size.* This formula uses the next value of the same units because it measures the interval between the first value of one class and the first value of the next class.

● Review and Application Exercises

■ **2-44** The following set of raw data gives income and education level for a sample of individuals. Would rearranging the data help us to draw some conclusions? Rearrange the data in a way that makes them more meaningful.

Income	Education	Income	Education	Income	Education
$17,000	High school	$ 21,200	B.S.	$17,200	2 years college
20,800	B.S.	28,000	B.S.	19,600	B.A.
27,000	M.A.	30,200	High school	36,200	M.S.
70,000	M.D.	22,400	2 years college	14,400	1 year college
29,000	Ph.D.	100,000	M.D.	18,400	2 years college
14,400	10th grade	76,000	Law degree	34,400	B.A.
19,000	High school	44,000	Ph.D.	26,000	High school
23,200	M.A.	17,600	11th grade	52,000	Law degree
30,400	High school	25,800	High school	64,000	Ph.D.
25,600	B.A.	20,200	1 year college	32,800	B.S.

■ **2-45** All 50 states send the following information to the Department of Labor: the average number of workers absent daily during the 13 weeks of a financial quarter, and the percentage of absentees for each state. Is this an example of raw data? Explain.

■ **2-46** The Nebraska Department of Agriculture has these data representing weekly growth (in inches) on samples of newly planted spring corn:

0.4	1.9	1.5	0.9	0.3	1.6	0.4	1.5	1.2	0.8
0.9	0.7	0.9	0.7	0.9	1.5	0.5	1.5	1.7	1.8

(a) Arrange the data in an array from highest to lowest.
(b) Construct a relative frequency distribution using intervals of 0.25.
(c) From what you have done so far, what conclusions can you come to about growth in this sample?
(d) Construct an ogive that will help you determine what proportion of the corn grew at more than 1.0 inch a week.
(e) What was the approximate weekly growth rate of the middle item in the data array?

■ **2-47** The National Safety Council randomly sampled the tread depth of 60 right front tires on passenger vehicles stopped at a rest area on an interstate highway. From its data, it constructed the following frequency distribution:

Tread Depth (Inches)	Frequency	Tread Depth (Inches)	Frequency
$^{16}/_{32}$ (new tire)	5	$^{4}/_{32}$–$^{6}/_{32}$	7
$^{13}/_{32}$–$^{15}/_{32}$	10	$^{1}/_{32}$–$^{3}/_{32}$	4
$^{10}/_{32}$–$^{12}/_{32}$	20	$^{0}/_{32}$ bald	2
$^{7}/_{32}$–$^{9}/_{32}$	12		

(a) Approximately what was the tread depth of the thirtieth tire in the data array?
(b) If a tread depth less than $^{7}/_{32}$ inch is considered dangerous, approximately what proportion of the tires on the road are unsafe?

■ **2-48** The High Point Fastener Company produces 15 basic items. The company keeps records on the number of each item produced per month in order to examine the relative production levels. Records show the following numbers of each item were produced by the company for the last month of 20 operating days:

9,897	10,052	10,028	9,722	9,908
10,098	10,587	9,872	9,956	9,928
10,123	10,507	9,910	9,992	10,237

Construct an ogive that will help you answer these questions.

(a) On how many of its items did production exceed the break-even point of 10,000 units?

(b) What production level did 75 percent of its items exceed that month?

(c) What production level did 90 percent of its items exceed that month?

■ **2-49** The administrator of a hospital has ordered a study of the amount of time a patient must wait before being treated by emergency room personnel. The following data were collected during a typical day:

Waiting Time (Minutes)

12	16	21	20	24	3	11	17	29	18
26	4	7	14	25	1	27	15	16	5

(a) Arrange the data in an array from lowest to highest. What comment can you make about patient waiting time from your data array?

(b) Now construct a frequency distribution using 6 classes. What additional interpretation can you give to the data from the frequency distribution?

(c) From an ogive, state how long 75 percent of the patients should expect to wait based on these data.

■ **2-50** Of what additional value is a relative frequency distribution once you have already constructed a frequency distribution?

■ **2-51** Below are the weights of an entire population of 100 NFL football players.

226	198	210	233	222	175	215	191	201	175
264	204	193	244	180	185	190	216	178	190
174	183	201	238	232	257	236	222	213	207
233	205	180	267	236	186	192	245	218	193
189	180	175	184	234	234	180	252	201	187
155	175	196	172	248	198	226	185	180	175
217	190	212	198	212	228	184	219	196	212
220	213	191	170	258	192	194	180	243	230
180	135	243	180	209	202	242	259	238	227
207	218	230	224	228	188	210	205	197	169

(a) Select two samples: one sample of the first 10 elements, and another sample of the largest 10 elements.

(b) Are the two samples equally representative of the population? If not, which sample is more representative, and why?

(c) Under what conditions would the sample of the largest 10 elements be as representative as the sample of the first 10 elements?

■ **2-52** In the population under study, there are 2,000 women and 8,000 men. If we are to select a sample of 250 individuals from this population, how many should be women to make our sample considered strictly representative?

■ **2-53** The U.S. Department of Labor publishes several classifications of the unemployment rate, as well as the rate itself. Recently, the unemployment rate was 6.8 percent. The department reported the following educational categories:

Level of Education	Relative Frequency (% of Those Unemployed)
Did not complete high school	35%
Received high school diploma	31
Attended college but did not receive a degree	16
Received a college degree	9
Attended graduate school but did not receive a degree	6
Received a graduate degree	3
Total	**100%**

Using these data, construct a relative frequency histogram.

■ **2-54** Using the relative frequency distribution given in Exercise 2-63, construct a relative frequency histogram and polygon. For the purposes of the present exercise, assume that the upper limit of the last class is $51.00.

■ **2-55** Consider the following information about March 1992 nonfarm employment (in thousands of workers) in the United States, including Puerto Rico and the Virgin Islands:

12,324.3
42.4

Alabama	1,639.0	Montana	299.3
Alaska	235.5	Nebraska	730.6
Arizona	1,510.0	Nevada	638.4
Arkansas	951.1	New Hampshire	466.5
California	12,324.3	New Jersey	3,390.7
Colorado	1,552.7	New Mexico	583.3
Connecticut	1,510.6	New York	7,666.4
Delaware	335.2	North Carolina	3,068.3
District of Columbia	667.0	North Dakota	271.0
Florida	5,322.8	Ohio	4,709.9
Georgia	2,927.1	Oklahoma	1,196.9
Hawaii	546.3	Oregon	1,245.6
Idaho	400.4	Pennsylvania	4,992.1
Illinois	5,146.2	Rhode Island	413.2
Indiana	2,496.3	South Carolina	1,494.6
Iowa	1,229.2	South Dakota	295.6
Kansas	1,108.3	Tennessee	2,178.6
Kentucky	1,474.8	Texas	7,209.7
Louisiana	1,617.5	Utah	752.2
Maine	500.0	Vermont	244.8
Maryland	2,037.3	Virginia	2,792.4
Massachusetts	2,751.6	Washington	2,165.8
Michigan	3,828.9	West Virginia	622.1
Minnesota	2,117.1	Wisconsin	2,272.1
Mississippi	940.9	Wyoming	198.0
Missouri	2,275.9	Puerto Rico	842.4
		Virgin Islands	42.4

Source: Sharon R. Cohany, "Employment Data," Monthly Labor Review *115(6), (June 1992): 80–82.*

(a) Arrange the data into 10 equal-width, mutually exclusive classes.

(b) Determine the frequency and relative frequency within each class.

(c) Are these data discrete or continuous?

(d) Construct a "less-than" cumulative frequency distribution and ogive for the relative frequency distribution in part (b).

(e) Based on the ogive constructed in part (d), what proportion of states have nonfarm employment greater than 3 million?

■ **2-56** Using the frequency distribution given in Exercise 2-57 for miles per day of jogging, construct an ogive that will help you estimate what proportion of the joggers are averaging 4.0 miles or fewer daily.

■ **2-57** A sports psychologist studying the effect of jogging on college students' grades collected data from a group of college joggers. Along with some other variables, he recorded the average number of miles run per day. He compiled his results into the following distribution:

Miles per Day	Frequency
1.00–1.39	32
1.40–1.79	43
1.80–2.19	81
2.20–2.59	122
2.60–2.99	131
3.00–3.39	130
3.40–3.79	111
3.80–4.19	95
4.20–4.59	82
4.60–4.99	47
5.00 and up	53
	927

(a) Construct an ogive that will tell you approximately how many miles a day the middle jogger runs.

(b) From the ogive you constructed in part (a), approximately what proportion of college joggers run at least 3.0 miles a day?

■ **2-58** A behavioral researcher studying the success of college students in their careers conducts interviews with 100 Ivy League undergraduates, half men and half women, as the basis for the study. Comment on the adequacy of this survey.

■ **2-59** If the following age groups are included in the proportions indicated, how many of each age group should be included in a sample of 3,000 people to make the sample representative?

Age Group	Relative Proportion in Population
12–17	0.17
18–23	0.31
24–29	0.27
30–35	0.21
36+	0.04

■ **2-60** State University has three campuses, each with its own business school. Last year, State's business professors published numerous articles in prestigious professional journals, and the board of regents counted these articles as a measure of the productivity of each department.

Journal Number	Number of Publications	Campus	Journal Number	Number of Publications	Campus
9	3	North	14	20	South
12	6	North	10	18	South
3	12	South	3	12	West
15	8	West	5	6	North
2	9	West	7	5	North
5	15	South	7	15	West
1	2	North	6	2	North
15	5	West	2	3	West
12	3	North	9	1	North
11	4	North	11	8	North
7	9	North	14	10	West
6	10	West	8	17	South

(a) Construct a frequency distribution and a relative frequency distribution by journal.

(b) Construct a frequency distribution and a relative frequency distribution by university branch.

(c) Construct a frequency distribution and a relative frequency distribution by number of publications (using intervals of 3).

(d) Briefly interpret your results.

■ **2-61** A reporter wants to know how the cost of compliance with the Americans with Disabilities Act (ADA) has affected national hiring practices and sends out a form letter to 2,000 businesses in the same ZIP code as the magazine's editorial offices. A total of 880 responses are received. Comment on the data available in these responses in terms of the five tests for data.

■ **2-62** With each appliance that Central Electric produces, the company includes a warranty card for the purchaser. In addition to validating the warranty and furnishing the company with the purchaser's name and address, the card also asks for certain other information that is used for marketing studies. For each of the numbered blanks on the card, determine the most likely characteristics of the categories that would be used by the company to record the information. In particular, would they be (1) quantitative or qualitative, (2) continuous or discrete, (3) open-ended or closed? Briefly state the reasoning behind your answers.

Name ______________	Marital Status ③ ______________
Address ______________	Where was appliance purchased?
City ______________ State ______	④ ______________
Zip Code ______________	Why was appliance purchased?
Age ① ______ Yearly Income ② ______	⑤ ______________

■ **2-63** The following relative frequency distribution resulted from a study of the dollar amounts spent per visit by customers at a supermarket:

Amount Spent	Relative Frequency
$ 0–$ 5.99	1%
6.00–$10.99	3
11.00–$15.99	4
16.00–$20.99	6
21.00–$25.99	7
26.00–$30.99	9
31.00–$35.99	11
36.00–$40.99	19
41.00–$45.99	32
46.00 and above	8
Total	**100%**

Determine the class marks (midpoints) for each of the intervals.

■ **2-64** The following responses were given by two groups of hospital patients, one receiving a new treatment, the other receiving a standard treatment for an illness. The question asked was, "What degree of discomfort are you experiencing?"

Group 1			Group 2		
Mild	Moderate	Severe	Moderate	Mild	Severe
None	Severe	Mild	Severe	None	Moderate
Moderate	Mild	Mild	Mild	Moderate	Moderate
Mild	Moderate	None	Moderate	Mild	Severe
Moderate	Mild	Mild	Severe	Moderate	Moderate
None	Moderate	Severe	Severe	Mild	Moderate

Suggest a better way to display these data. Explain why it is better.

■ **2-65** The production manager of the Browner Bearing Company posted final worker performance ratings based on total units produced, percentages of rejects, and total hours worked. Is this an example of raw data? Why or why not? If not, what would the raw data be in this situation?

■ **2-66** The head of a large business department wanted to classify the specialties of its 67 members. He asked Peter Wilson, a Ph.D. candidate, to get the information from the faculty members' publications. Peter compiled the following:

Specialty	Faculty Members Publishing
Accounting only	1
Marketing only	5
Statistics only	4
Finance only	2
Accounting and marketing	7
Accounting and statistics	6
Accounting and finance	3
Marketing and finance	8
Statistics and finance	9
Statistics and marketing	21
No publications	1
	67

Construct a relative frequency distribution for the *types* of specialties. (*Hint:* The categories of your distribution will be mutually exclusive, but any individual may fall into several categories.)

■ **2-67** Lesley Niles, a summer intern at the Internet Financial Services Corporation, has been asked to investigate the low participation rates in the company's 401(k) investment program. Niles read an article in *The Wall Street Journal* commenting on families' second wage-earner income as a determinant of plan participation. Niles went from office to office and interviewed executives eligible to participate. None of the executives reported a spouse with second income over $35,000 and many families had no second income. To examine the situation, Niles decides to construct both frequency and relative frequency distributions.

(a) Develop a continuous, closed distribution with $5,000 intervals.

(b) Develop a continuous distribution open at both ends, with 6 categories. You may relax the requirement for $5,000 intervals for the open-ended categories.

■ **2-68** On December 14, 1992, the National Football League standings were as follows:

National Conference

	W	L	T	Percent
Central Division				
Minnesota	9	5	0	0.643
Green Bay	8	6	0	0.571
Chicago	5	9	0	0.357
Tampa Bay	4	10	0	0.286
Detroit	4	10	0	0.286
East Division				
Dallas	11	3	0	0.786
Washington	9	5	0	0.643
Philadelphia	9	5	0	0.643
N.Y. Giants	5	9	0	0.357
Phoenix	4	10	0	0.286
West Division				
San Francisco	12	2	0	0.857
New Orleans	11	3	0	0.786
Atlanta	6	8	0	0.429
L.A. Rams	5	9	0	0.357

American Conference

	W	L	T	Percent
Central Division				
Pittsburgh	10	4	0	0.714
Houston	8	6	0	0.571
Cleveland	7	7	0	0.500
Cincinnati	4	10	0	0.286
East Division				
Buffalo	10	4	0	0.714
Miami	8	5	0	0.615
Indianapolis	7	7	0	0.500
N.Y. Jets	4	10	0	0.286
New England	2	12	0	0.143
West Division				
Kansas City	9	5	0	0.643
San Diego	9	5	0	0.643
Denver	7	7	0	0.500
L.A. Raiders	6	7	0	0.462
Seattle	2	12	0	0.143

Source: "Pro-Football," Chicago Tribune *(December 14, 1992): sec. 3, p. 4.*

(a) Combine the "percentage won" statistics for all six divisions and arrange the data into 5 equal-width, mutually exclusive classes.

(b) Determine the frequency and relative frequency within each class.

(c) Construct a frequency polygon for the distribution in part (b).

(d) Construct a "greater-than" cumulative frequency distribution and ogive for the frequency distribution in part (b).

(e) Based on the frequency distribution in part (b), which class has teams most likely to clinch playoff berths? Each conference (National and

American) places five teams in the playoffs: the winners in each of the three geographical divisions (Central, East, and West) and the two teams in the conference with the next highest winning percentages.

■ **2-69** The Kawahondi Computer Company compiled data regarding the number of interviews required for each of its 40 salespeople to make a sale. Following are a frequency distribution and a relative frequency distribution of the number of interviews required per salesperson per sale. Fill in the missing data.

Number of Interviews (Classes)	Frequency	Relative Frequency
0– 10	?	0.075
11– 20	1	?
21– 30	4	?
31– 40	?	?
41– 50	2	?
51– 60	?	0.175
61– 70	?	0.225
71– 80	5	?
81– 90	?	0.000
91–100	?	0.025
	?	?

■ **2-70** A. T. Cline, the mine superintendent of the Grover Coal Co., has recorded the amount of time per workshift that Section Crew #3 shuts down its machinery for on-the-spot adjustments, repairs, and moving. Here are the records for the crew's last 35 shifts:

60	72	126	110	91	115	112
80	66	101	75	93	129	105
113	121	93	87	119	111	97
102	116	114	107	113	119	100
110	99	139	108	128	84	99

(a) Arrange the data in an array from highest to lowest.

(b) If Cline believes that a typical amount of downtime per shift is 108 minutes, how many of Crew #3's last 35 shifts exceeded this limit? How many were under the limit?

(c) Construct a relative frequency distribution with 10-minute intervals.

(d) Does your frequency distribution indicate that Cline should be concerned?

■ **2-71** Cline has obtained information on Section Crew #3's coal production per shift for the same 35-shift period discussed in Exercise 2-70. The values are in tons of coal mined per shift:

356	331	299	391	364	317	386
360	281	360	402	411	390	362
311	357	300	375	427	370	383
322	380	353	371	400	379	380
369	393	377	389	430	340	368

(a) Construct a relative frequency distribution with six equal intervals.

(b) If Cline considers 330 to 380 tons per shift to be an expected range of output, how many of the crew's shifts produced less than expected? How many did better than expected?

(c) Does this information affect the conclusions you reached from the preceding problem on equipment downtime?

■ **2-72** Virginia Suboleski is an aircraft maintenance supervisor. A recent delivery of bolts from a new supplier caught the eye of a clerk. Suboleski sent 25 of the bolts to a testing lab to determine the force necessary to break each of the bolts. In thousands of pounds of force, the results are as follows:

147.8	137.4	125.2	141.1	145.7
119.9	133.3	142.3	138.7	125.7
142.0	130.8	129.8	141.2	134.9
125.0	128.9	142.0	118.6	133.0
151.1	125.7	126.3	140.9	138.2

(a) Arrange the data into an array from highest to lowest.

(b) What proportion of the bolts withstood at least 120,000 pounds of force? What proportion withstood at least 150,000 pounds?

(c) If Suboleski knows that these bolts when installed on aircraft are subjected to up to 140,000 pounds of force, what proportion of the sample bolts would have failed in use? What should Suboleski recommend the company do about continuing to order from the new supplier?

■ **2-73** The telephone system used by PHM, a mail-order company, keeps track of how many customers tried to call the toll-free ordering line but could not get through because all the firm's lines were busy. This number, called the phone overflow rate, is expressed as a percentage of the total number of calls taken in a given week. Mrs. Loy has used the overflow data for the last year to prepare the following frequency distribution:

Overflow Rate	Frequency	Overflow Rate	Frequency
0.00– 2.50%	3	12.51–15.00%	4
2.51– 5.00%	7	17.51–20.00%	3
5.00– 7.50%	13	20.01–22.51%	2
7.51–10.00%	10	22.51–25.50%	2
10.00–12.50%	6	25.51 or greater	2
			52 Total number of weeks

List and explain errors you can find in Mrs. Loy's distribution.

■ **2-74** Hanna Equipment Co. sells process equipment to agricultural companies in developing countries. A recent office fire burned two staff members and destroyed most of Hanna's business records. Karl Slayden has just been hired to help rebuild the company. He has found sales records for the last 2 months:

Country	# of Sales	Country	# of Sales	Country	# of Sales
1	3	7	4	13	1
2	1	8	9	14	1
3	1	9	5	15	5
4	8	10	1	16	6
5	3	11	3	17	6
6	5	12	7	18	2

(Continued)

Country	# of Sales	Country	# of Sales	Country	# of Sales
19	2	23	1	27	1
20	1	24	7	28	5
21	1	25	3		
22	2	26	1		

(a) Arrange the sales data in an array from highest to lowest.

(b) Construct two relative frequency distributions of number of sales, one with 3 classes and one with 9 classes. Compare the two. If Slayden knows nothing about Hanna's sales patterns, think about the conclusions he might draw from each about country-to-country sales variability.

■ **2-75** Jeanne Moreno is analyzing the waiting times for cars passing through a large expressway toll plaza that is severely clogged and accident-prone in the morning. Information was collected on the number of minutes that 3,000 consecutive drivers waited in line at the toll gates:

Minutes of Waiting	Frequency	Minutes of Waiting	Frequency
less than 1	75	9–10.99	709
1–2.99	183	11–12.99	539
3–4.99	294	13–14.99	164
5–6.99	350	15–16.99	106
7–8.99	580		

(a) Construct a "less-than" cumulative frequency and cumulative relative frequency distribution.

(b) Construct an ogive based on part (a). What percentage of the drivers had to wait more than 4 minutes in line? 8 minutes?

■ **2-76** Maribor Cement Company of Montevideo, Uruguay, hired Delbert Olsen, an American manufacturing consultant, to help design and install various production reporting systems for its concrete roof tile factory. For example, today Maribor made 7,000 tiles and had a breakage rate during production of 2 percent. To measure daily tile output and breakage rate, Olsen has set up equally spaced classes for each. The class marks (midpoints of the class intervals) for daily tile output are 4,900, 5,500, 6,100, 6,700, 7,300, and 7,900. The class marks for breakage rates are 0.70, 2.10, 3.50, 4.90, 6.30, and 7.70.

(a) What are the upper and lower boundaries of the classes for the daily tile output?

(b) What are the upper and lower boundaries of the classes for the breakage rate?

■ **2-77** BMT, Inc., manufactures performance equipment for cars used in various types of racing. It has gathered the following information on the number of models of engines in different size categories used in the racing market it serves:

Class (Engine Size in Cubic Inches)	Frequency (# of Models)
101–150	1
151–200	7
201–250	7
251–300	8
301–350	17

(Continued)

Class (Engine Size in Cubic Inches)	Frequency (# of Models)
351–400	16
401–450	15
451–500	7

Construct a cumulative relative frequency distribution that will help you answer these questions:

(a) Seventy percent of the engine models available are larger than about what size?

(b) What was the approximate middle value in the original data set?

(c) If BMT has designed a fuel-injection system that can be used on racing engines up to 400 cubic inches, about what percentage of the engine models available will not be able to use BMT's system?

■ **2-78** A business group is supporting the addition of a light-rail shuttle in the central business district and has two competing bids with different numbers of seats in each car. They arrange a fact-finding trip to Denver, and in a meeting they are given the following frequency distribution of number of passengers per car:

Number of Passengers	Frequency
1–10	20
11–20	18
21–30	11
31–40	8
41–50	3
51–60	1

(a) One bid proposes light-rail cars with 30 seats and 10 standees. What percentage of the total observations are more than 30 and less than 41 passengers?

(b) The business group members have been told that street cars with fewer than 11 passengers are uneconomical to operate and more than 30 passengers lead to poor customer satisfaction. What proportion of trips would be economical and satisfying?

■ **2-79** Refer to the toll plaza problem in Exercise 2-75. Jeanne Moreno's employer, the state Department of Transportation, recently worked with a nearby complex of steel mills, with 5,000 employees, to modify the complex's shift changeover schedule so that shift changes do not coincide with the morning rush hour. Moreno wants an initial comparison to see whether waiting times at the toll plaza appear to have dropped. Here are the waiting times observed for 3,000 consecutive drivers after the mill schedule change:

Minutes of Waiting	Frequency
less than 1	177
1– 2.99	238
3– 4.99	578
5– 6.99	800
7– 8.99	713
9–10.99	326

(Continued)

Minutes of Waiting	Frequency
11–12.99	159
13–14.99	9
15–16.99	0
	3,000

(a) Construct a "less-than" cumulative frequency and cumulative relative frequency distribution.

(b) Construct an ogive based on part (a). What percentage of the drivers had to wait more than 4 minutes in line? 8 minutes?

(c) Compare your results with your answers to Exercise 2-75. Is there an obvious difference in waiting times?

■ **2-80** The manager of Fresh Foods, a grocery store in Utah, is considering expanding store hours from the present 7 A.M. to 11 P.M. schedule to 24-hour shopping. Based on information from Information Resources, Inc., a national market research firm, the estimated number of customers per hour would be as shown in the following table. Display the data in a way that would help the Board of Directors make a decision about the proposal. Are there any limitations on the use of these data for this business decision?

Hour Beginning	Number of Shoppers
Midnight	3
1 A.M.	3
2 A.M.	3
3 A.M.	3
4 A.M.	3
5 A.M.	3
6 A.M.	3
7 A.M.	35
8 A.M.	70
9 A.M.	140
10 A.M.	210
11 A.M.	280
Noon	252
1 P.M.	224
2 P.M.	168
3 P.M.	224
4 P.M.	196
5 P.M.	224
6 P.M.	168
7 P.M.	112
8 P.M.	56
9 P.M.	28
10 P.M.	14
11 P.M.	3

Source: Extrapolated from Information Resources, Inc., Grocery Shopping Times, *as reported in* The News and Observer, *Raleigh, NC (Jan. 4, 1995): F1.*

■ **2-81** Investing is increasingly a global industry, but there is market dominance in the competition for capital. The following table of data suggests that a few large exchanges in New York, Tokyo, and London dominate the field.

How would you present these data to show (a) the importance of the three major markets and (b) the qualitative difference between the U.S. and U.K. stock exchanges?

Market	Domestic Equities (in billions)	Foreign Equities (in billions)
Amsterdam	$ 225.69	n.a.
Germany	479.89	n.a.
London	1,221.86	3,127.93
Paris	455.05	n.a.
Switzerland	287.03	n.a.
Nasdaq	741.56	49.8
NYSE	4,279.63	218.56
Tokyo	3,619.02	n.a.

Source: Nicholas Bray, "London Stock Exchange Is under Siege," The Wall Street Journal *(September 29, 1995): A6.*

● Chapter Concepts Test

Circle the correct answer or fill in the blank. *Answers are in the back of the book.*

T F 1. In comparison to a data array, the frequency distribution has the advantage of representing data in compressed form.

T F 2. A "more-than" ogive is S-shaped and slopes down and to the right.

T F 3. A histogram is a series of rectangles, each proportional in width to the number of items falling within a specific class of data.

T F 4. A single observation is called a data point, whereas a collection of data is known as a tabular.

T F 5. The classes in any relative frequency distribution are both all-inclusive and mutually exclusive.

T F 6. When a sample contains the relevant characteristics of a certain population in the same proportions as they are included in that population, the sample is said to be a representative sample.

T F 7. A population is a collection of all the elements we are studying.

T F 8. If we were to connect the midpoints of the consecutive bars of a frequency histogram with a series of lines, we would be graphing a frequency polygon.

T F 9. Before information is arranged and analyzed, using statistical methods, it is known as preprocessed data.

T F 10. One disadvantage of the data array is that it does not allow us to easily find the highest and lowest values in the data set.

T F 11. Discrete data can be expressed only in whole numbers.

T F 12. As a general rule, statisticians regard a frequency distribution as incomplete if it has fewer than 20 classes.

T F 13. It is always possible to construct a histogram from a frequency polygon.

T F 14. The vertical scale of an ogive for a relative frequency distribution marks the fraction of the total number of observations that falls into each class.

T F 15. A data array is formed by arranging raw data in order of time of observation.

T F 16. A "less-than" ogive is S-shaped and slopes down and to the right.

T F 17. One advantage of a histogram in comparison with a frequency polygon is that it more clearly shows each separate class in the distribution.

T F 18. A baseball player's batting average is computed using a sample.

T F 19. A frequency distribution organizes data into groups of values describing one or more characteristics of the data.

T F 20. A series of rectangles, each proportional in width to the range of values within a class and proportional in height to the number of items falling in the class, is called a frequency polygon.

T F 21. The class widths of a frequency distribution are of equal size.

A B C D 22. Which of the following represents the most accurate scheme of classifying data?

(a) Quantitative methods.
(b) Qualitative methods.
(c) A combination of quantitative and qualitative methods.
(d) A scheme can be determined only with specific information about the situation.

A B C D 23. Which of the following is NOT an example of compressed data?

(a) Frequency distribution.
(b) Data array.
(c) Histogram.
(d) Ogive.

A B C D E 24. Which of the following statements about histogram rectangles is correct?

(a) The rectangles are proportional in height to the number of items falling in the classes.
(b) There are generally five rectangles in every histogram.
(c) The area in a rectangle depends only on the number of items in the class as compared to the number of items in all other classes.
(d) All of these.
(e) (a) and (c) but not (b).

A B C D E 25. Why is it true that classes in frequency distributions are all-inclusive?

(a) No data point falls into more than one class.
(b) There are always more classes than data points.
(c) All data fit into one class or another.
(d) All of these.
(e) (a) and (c) but not (b).

A B C D 26. When constructing a frequency distribution, the first step is

(a) Divide the data into at least five classes.
(b) Sort the data points into classes and count the number of points in each class.
(c) Decide on the type and number of classes for dividing the data.
(d) None of these.

A B C D 27. As the numbers of observations and classes increase, the shape of a frequency polygon

(a) Tends to become increasingly smooth.
(b) Tends to become jagged.
(c) Stays the same.
(d) Varies only if data become more reliable.

A B C D 28. Which of the following statements is true of cumulative frequency ogives for a particular set of data?

(a) Both "more-than" and "less-than" curves have the same slope.
(b) "More-than" curves slope up and to the right.
(c) "Less-than" curves slope down and to the right.
(d) "Less-than" curves slope up and to the right.

A B C D E 29. From an ogive constructed for a particular set of data

(a) The original data can always be reconstructed exactly.
(b) The original data can always be approximated.
(c) The original data can never be approximated or reconstructed, but valid conclusions regarding the data can be drawn.
(d) None of these.
(e) (a) and (b) but not (c).

A B C D E 30. In constructing a frequency distribution for a sample, the number of classes depends on

(a) The number of data points.
(b) The range of the data collected.
(c) The size of the population.
(d) All of these.
(e) (a) and (b) but not (c).

A B C D E 31. Which of the following statements is true?

(a) The size of a sample can never be as large as the size of the population from which it is taken.
(b) Classes describe only one characteristic of the data being organized.
(c) As a rule statisticians generally use between 6 and 15 classes.
(d) All of these.
(e) (b) and (c) but not (a).

A B C D E 32. As a general rule, statisticians tend to use which of the following number of classes when arranging data?

(a) Fewer than five.
(b) Between one and five.
(c) More than 30.
(d) Between 20 and 25.
(e) None of these.

A B C D E 33. Which of these is NOT a test for usability of data?

(a) Source.
(b) Contradiction of other evidence.
(c) Missing evidence.
(d) Number of observations.
(e) None of these.

A B C D E 34. A relative frequency distribution presents frequencies in terms of

(a) Fractions.
(b) Whole numbers.
(c) Percentages.
(d) All of the above.
(e) Both (a) and (c).

A B C D E 35. Graphs of frequency distributions are used because
(a) They have a long history in practical applications.
(b) They attract attention to data patterns.
(c) They account for biased or incomplete data.
(d) They allow for easy estimates of values.
(e) Both (b) and (d).

A B C D 36. Continuous data are differentiated from discrete data in that
(a) Discrete data classes are represented by fractions.
(b) Continuous data classes may be represented by fractions.
(c) Continuous data take on only whole numbers.
(d) Discrete data can take on any real number.

37. Double counting is a result of ______________ or ______________ data.

38. It is found that 50 of 1,000 customers in a survey contain the relevant characteristics of all customers in the survey. The 50 customers are a ______________ sample.

39. The ______________ and the ______________ are two methods of data arrangement.

40. A ______________ is a collection of all the elements in a group. A collection of some, but not all, of these elements is a ______________.

41. Dividing data points into similar classes and counting the number of observations in each class will give a ______________ distribution.

42. If data can take on only a limited number of values, the classes of these data are called ______________. Otherwise, the classes are called ______________.

43. A relative frequency distribution presents frequencies in terms of ______________ or ______________.

44. A graph of a cumulative frequency distribution is called a ______________.

45. If a collection of data is called a data set, a single observation would be called a ______________.

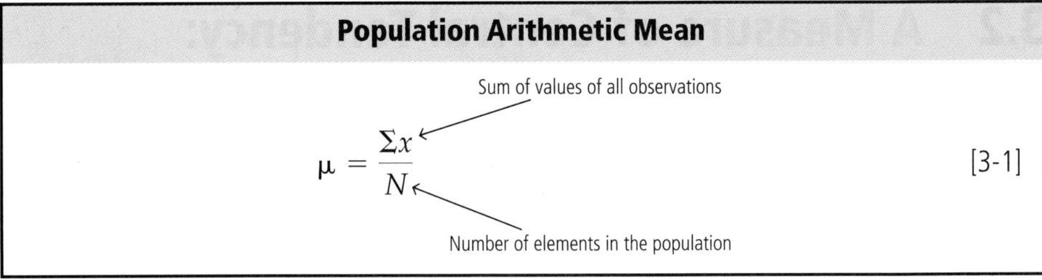

Population Arithmetic Mean

$$\mu = \frac{\Sigma x}{N} \qquad [3\text{-}1]$$

and

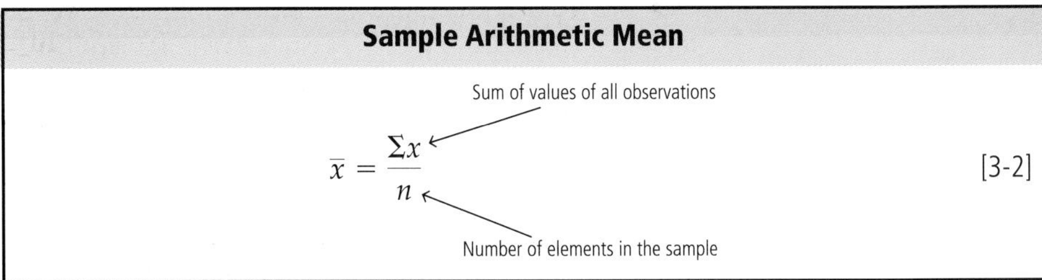

Sample Arithmetic Mean

$$\bar{x} = \frac{\Sigma x}{n} \qquad [3\text{-}2]$$

Because μ is the *population arithmetic mean,* we use N to indicate that we divide by the number of observations or elements in the population. Similarly, $\bar{x}$ is the *sample arithmetic mean* and n is the number of observations in the sample. The Greek letter sigma, Σ, indicates that all the values of x are summed together.

Another example: Table 3-2 lists the percentile increase in SAT verbal scores shown by seven different students taking an SAT preparatory course.

We compute the mean of this sample of seven students as follows:

$$\bar{x} = \frac{\Sigma x}{n} \qquad [3\text{-}2]$$

$$= \frac{9 + 7 + 7 + 6 + 4 + 4 + 2}{7}$$

$$= \frac{39}{7}$$

$$= 5.6 \text{ points per student} \longleftarrow \text{Sample mean}$$

Dealing with ungrouped data

Notice that to calculate this mean, we added every observation. Statisticians call this kind of data *ungrouped* data. The computations were not difficult because our sample size was small. But suppose we are dealing with the weights of 5,000 head of cattle and prefer not to add each of our data points separately. Or suppose we have access to only the frequency distribution of the data, not to every individual observation. In these cases, we will need a different way to calculate the arithmetic mean.

Table 3-2
SAT Verbal Scores

STUDENT	1	2	3	4	5	6	7
INCREASE	9	7	7	6	4	4	2

Calculating the Mean from Grouped Data

Dealing with grouped data

A frequency distribution consists of data that are grouped by classes. Each value of an observation falls somewhere in one of the classes. Unlike the SAT example, we do not know the separate values of every observation. Suppose we have a frequency distribution (illustrated in Table 3-3) of average monthly checking-account balances of 600 customers at a branch bank. From the information in this table, we can easily compute an *estimate* of the value of the mean of these grouped data. It is an estimate because we do not use all 600 data points in the sample. Had we used the original, ungrouped data, we could have calculated the actual value of the mean, but only by averaging the 600 separate values. For ease of calculation, we must give up accuracy.

Estimating the mean

Calculating the mean

To find the arithmetic mean of grouped data, we first calculate the midpoint of each class. To make midpoints come out in whole cents, we round up. Thus, for example, the midpoint for the first class becomes 25.00, rather than 24.995. Then we multiply each midpoint by the frequency of observations in that class, sum all these results, and divide the sum by the total number of observations in the sample. The formula looks like this:

Sample Arithmetic Mean of Grouped Data

$$\bar{x} = \frac{\Sigma(f \times x)}{n} \qquad [3\text{-}3]$$

where

- $\bar{x}$ = sample mean
- Σ = symbol meaning "the sum of"
- f = frequency (number of observations) in each class
- x = midpoint for each class in the sample
- n = number of observations in the sample

Table 3-4 illustrates how to calculate the arithmetic mean from our grouped data, using Equation 3-3.

Table 3-3 Average Monthly Balances of 600 Customers

Class (Dollars)	Frequency
0– 49.99	78
50.00– 99.99	123
100.00–149.99	187
150.00–199.99	82
200.00–249.99	51
250.00–299.99	47
300.00–349.99	13
350.00–399.99	9
400.00–449.99	6
450.00–499.99	4
	600

Table 3-4

Calculation of Arithmetic Sample Mean from Grouped Data in Table 3-3

Class (Dollars) (1)	Midpoint (x) (2)		Frequency (f) (3)		$f \times x$ (3) × (2)
0– 49.99	25.00	×	78	=	1,950
50.00– 99.99	75.00	×	123	=	9,225
100.00–149.99	125.00	×	187	=	23,375
150.00–199.99	175.00	×	82	=	14,350
200.00–249.99	225.00	×	51	=	11,475
250.00–299.99	275.00	×	47	=	12,925
300.00–349.00	325.00	×	13	=	4,225
350.00–399.99	375.00	×	9	=	3,375
400.00–449.99	425.00	×	6	=	2,550
450.00–499.99	475.00	×	4	=	1,900
			$\Sigma f = n =$ **600**		**85,350**$\leftarrow \Sigma(f \times x)$

$$\bar{x} = \frac{\Sigma(f \times x)}{n} \qquad [3\text{-}3]$$

$$= \frac{85{,}350}{600}$$

$$= 142.25 \longleftarrow \text{Sample mean (dollars)}$$

We make an assumption

In our sample of 600 customers, the average monthly checking-account balance is \$142.25. This is our approximation from the frequency distribution. Notice that because we did not know every data point in the sample, we assumed that every value in a class was equal to its midpoint. Our results, then, can only approximate the actual average monthly balance.

Coding

Assigning codes to the midpoints

In situations where a computer is not available and we have to do the arithmetic by hand, we can further simplify our calculation of the mean from grouped data. Using a technique called *coding,* we eliminate the problem of large or inconvenient midpoints. Instead of using the actual midpoints to perform our calculations, we can assign small-value consecutive integers (whole numbers) called *codes* to each of the midpoints. The integer zero can be assigned anywhere, but to keep the integers small, we will assign zero to the midpoint in the *middle* (or the one nearest to the middle) of the frequency distribution. Then we can assign negative integers to values smaller than that midpoint and positive integers to those larger, as follows:

Class	1–5	6–10	11–15	16–20	21–25	26–30	31–35	36–40	41–45
Code (u)	−4	−3	−2	−1	0	1	2	3	4
					↑ x_0				

Calculating the mean from grouped data using codes

Symbolically, statisticians use x_0 to represent the midpoint that is assigned the code 0, and u for the coded midpoint. The following formula is used to determine the sample mean using codes:

Sample Arithmetic Mean of Grouped Data Using Codes

$$\bar{x} = x_0 + w\frac{\Sigma(u \times f)}{n} \quad [3\text{-}4]$$

where

- $\bar{x}$ = mean of sample
- x_0 = value of the midpoint assigned the code 0
- w = numerical width of the class interval
- u = code assigned to each class
- f = frequency or number of observations in each class
- n = total number of observations in the sample

Keep in mind that $\Sigma(u \times f)$ simply means that we (1) multiply u by f for every class in the frequency distribution and (2) sum all of these products. Table 3-5 illustrates how to code the midpoints and find the sample mean of the annual snowfall (in inches) over 20 years in Harlan, Kentucky.

Advantages and Disadvantages of the Arithmetic Mean

Advantages of the mean

The arithmetic mean, as a single number representing a whole data set, has important advantages. First, its concept is familiar to most people and intuitively clear. Second, every data set has a mean. It is a measure that can be calculated, and it is unique because every data set has one and only one mean. Finally, the mean is useful for performing statistical procedures such as comparing the means from several data sets (a procedure we will carry out in Chapter 9).

Three disadvantages of the mean

Yet, like any statistical measure, the arithmetic mean has disadvantages of which we must be aware. **First,** although the mean is reliable in that it reflects all the values in the data set, it may also be affected by extreme values that are not representative of the rest of

Table 3-5

Annual Snowfall in Harlan, Kentucky

Class (1)	Midpoint (x) (2)	Code (u) (3)		Frequency (f) (4)		$u \times f$ (3) × (4)
0– 7	3.5	−2	×	2	=	−4
8–15	11.5	−1	×	6	=	−6
16–23	19.5←x_0	0	×	3	=	0
24–31	27.5	1	×	5	=	5
32–39	35.5	2	×	2	=	4
40–47	43.5	3	×	2	=	6
				$\Sigma f = n =$ **20**		5←$\Sigma(u \times f)$

$$\bar{x} = x_0 + w\frac{\Sigma(u \times f)}{n} \quad [3\text{-}4]$$

$$= 19.5 + 8\left(\frac{5}{20}\right)$$

$$= 19.5 + 2$$

$$= 21.5 \longleftarrow \text{Average annual snowfall}$$

the data. Notice that if the seven members of a track team have times in a mile race shown in Table 3-6, the mean time is

$$\mu = \frac{\Sigma x}{N} \tag{3-1}$$

$$= \frac{4.2 + 4.3 + 4.7 + 4.8 + 5.0 + 5.1 + 9.0}{7}$$

$$= \frac{37.1}{7}$$

$$= 5.3 \text{ minutes} \longleftarrow \text{Population mean}$$

If we compute a mean time for the first six members, however, and exclude the 9.0 value, the answer is about 4.7 minutes. The one *extreme value* of 9.0 distorts the value we get for the mean. It would be more representative to calculate the mean *without* including such an extreme value.

A **second** problem with the mean is the same one we encountered with our 600 checking-account balances: It is tedious to compute the mean because we *do* use every data point in our calculation (unless, of course, we take the short-cut method of using grouped data to approximate the mean).

The **third** disadvantage is that we are unable to compute the mean for a data set that has open-ended classes at either the high or low end of the scale. Suppose the data in Table 3-6 had been arranged in the frequency distribution shown in Table 3-7. We could not compute a mean value for these data because of the open-ended class of "5.4 and above." We have no way of knowing whether the value is 5.4, near 5.4, or far above 5.4.

Table 3-6

Times for Track-Team Members in a 1-Mile Race

MEMBER	1	2	3	4	5	6	7
TIME IN MINUTES	4.2	4.3	4.7	4.8	5.0	5.1	9.0

Table 3-7

Times for Track-Team Members in a 1-Mile Race

CLASS IN MINUTES	4.2–4.5	4.6–4.9	5.0–5.3	5.4 and above
FREQUENCY	2	2	2	1

HINTS & ASSUMPTIONS

The mean (or average) *can* be an excellent measure of central tendency (how data group around the middle point of a distribution). But unless the mean is truly representative of the data from which it was computed, we are violating an important assumption. Warning: If there are very high or very low values in the data that don't look like most of the data, the mean is *not* representative. Fortunately there are measures that can be calculated that don't suffer from this shortcoming. A helpful hint in choosing which one of these to compute is to look at the data points.

Exercises 3.2

Self-Check Exercises

SC 3-1 The frequency distribution below represents the weights in pounds of a sample of packages carried last month by a small airfreight company.

Class	Frequency	Class	Frequency
10.0–10.9	1	15.0–15.9	11
11.0–11.9	4	16.0–16.9	8
12.0–12.9	6	17.0–17.9	7
13.0–13.9	8	18.0–18.9	6
14.0–14.9	12	19.0–19.9	2

(a) Compute the sample mean using Equation 3-3.

(b) Compute the sample mean using the coding method (Equation 3-4) with 0 assigned to the fourth class.

(c) Repeat part (b) with 0 assigned to the sixth class.

(d) Explain why your answers in parts (b) and (c) are the same.

SC 3-2 Davis Furniture Company has a revolving credit agreement with the First National Bank. The loan showed the following ending monthly balances last year:

Jan.	$121,300	Apr.	$72,800	July	$58,700	Oct.	$52,800
Feb.	$112,300	May	$72,800	Aug.	$61,100	Nov.	$49,200
Mar.	$ 72,800	June	$57,300	Sept.	$50,400	Dec.	$46,100

The company is eligible for a reduced rate of interest if its average monthly balance is over $65,000. Does it qualify?

Applications

■ **3-6** Child-Care Community Nursery is eligible for a county social services grant as long as the average age of its children stays below 9. If these data represent the ages of all the children currently attending Child-Care, do they qualify for the grant?

8 5 9 10 9 12 7 12 13 7 8

■ **3-7** Child-Care Community Nursery can continue to be supported by the county social services office as long as the average annual income of the families whose children attend the nursery is below $12,500. The family incomes of the attending children are

$14,500	$15,600	$12,500	$8,600	$ 7,800	
$ 6,500	$ 5,900	$10,200	$8,800	$14,300	$13,900

(a) Does Child-Care qualify now for county support?

(b) If the answer to part (a) is no, by how much must the average family income fall for it to qualify?

(c) If the answer to part (a) is yes, by how much can average family income rise and Child-Care still stay eligible?

■ **3-8** These data represent the ages of patients admitted to a small hospital on February 28, 1996:

85	75	66	43	40
88	80	56	56	67
89	83	65	53	75
87	83	52	44	48

(a) Construct a frequency distribution with classes 40–49, 50–59, etc.
(b) Compute the sample mean from the frequency distribution.
(c) Compute the sample mean from the raw data.
(d) Compare parts (b) and (c) and comment on your answer.

■ **3-9** The frequency distribution below represents the time in seconds needed to serve a sample of customers by cashiers at BullsEye Discount Store in December 1996.

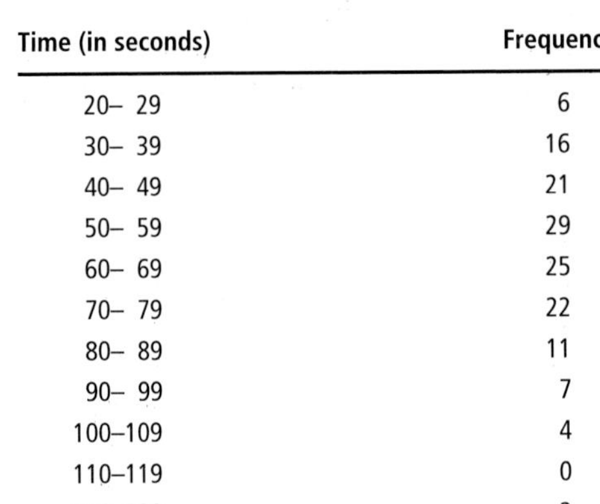

Time (in seconds)	Frequency
20– 29	6
30– 39	16
40– 49	21
50– 59	29
60– 69	25
70– 79	22
80– 89	11
90– 99	7
100–109	4
110–119	0
120–129	2

(a) Compute the sample mean using Equation 3-3.
(b) Compute the sample mean using the coding method (Equation 3-4) with 0 assigned to the 70–79 class.

■ **3-10** The owner of Pets 'R Us is interested in building a new store. The owner will build if the average number of animals sold during the first 6 months of 1995 is at least 300 and the overall monthly average for the year is at least 285. The data for 1995 are as follows:

Jan.	Feb.	Mar.	Apr.	May	June	July	Aug.	Sept.	Oct.	Nov.	Dec.
234	216	195	400	315	274	302	291	275	300	375	450

What is the owner's decision and why?

■ **3-11** A cosmetics manufacturer recently purchased a machine to fill 3-ounce cologne bottles. To test the accuracy of the machine's volume setting, 18 trial bottles were run. The resulting volumes (in ounces) for the trials were as follows:

3.02	2.89	2.92	2.84	2.90	2.97	2.95	2.94	2.93
3.01	2.97	2.95	2.90	2.94	2.96	2.99	2.99	2.97

The company does not normally recalibrate the filling machine for this cologne if the average volume is within 0.04 of 3.00 ounces. Should it recalibrate?

■ **3-12** The production manager of Hinton Press is determining the average time needed to photograph one printing plate. Using a stopwatch and observing the platemakers, he collects the following times (in seconds):

20.4	20.0	22.2	23.8	21.3	25.1	21.2	22.9	28.2	24.3
22.0	24.7	25.7	24.9	22.7	24.4	24.3	23.6	23.2	21.0

An average per-plate time of less than 23.0 seconds indicates satisfactory productivity. Should the production manager be concerned?

■ **3-13** National Tire Company holds reserve funds in short-term marketable securities. The ending daily balance (in millions) of the marketable securities account for 2 weeks is shown below:

Week 1	$1.973	$1.970	$1.972	$1.975	$1.976
Week 2	1.969	1.892	1.893	1.887	1.895

What was the average (mean) amount invested in marketable securities during

(a) The first week?

(b) The second week?

(c) The 2-week period?

(d) An average balance over the 2 weeks of more than $1.970 million would qualify National for higher interest rates. Does it qualify?

(e) If the answer to part (c) is less than $1.970 million, by how much would the last day's invested amount have to rise to qualify the company for the higher interest rates?

(f) If the answer to part (c) is more than $1.970 million, how much could the company treasurer withdraw from reserve funds on the last day and still qualify for the higher interest rates?

■ **3-14** M. T. Smith travels the eastern United States as a sales representative for a textbook publisher. She is paid on a commission basis related to volume. Her quarterly earnings over the last 3 years are given below.

	1st Quarter	2nd Quarter	3rd Quarter	4th Quarter
Year 1	$10,000	$ 5,000	$25,000	$15,000
Year 2	20,000	10,000	20,000	10,000
Year 3	30,000	15,000	45,000	50,000

(a) Calculate separately M. T.'s average earnings in each of the four quarters.

(b) Calculate separately M. T.'s average quarterly earnings in each of the 3 years.

(c) Show that the mean of the four numbers you found in part (a) is equal to the mean of the three numbers you found in part (b). Furthermore, show that both these numbers equal the mean of all 12 numbers in the data table. (This is M. T.'s average quarterly income over 3 years.)

■ **3-15** Lillian Tyson has been the chairperson of the county library committee for 10 years. She contends that during her tenure she has managed the bookmobile repair budget better than her predecessor did. Here are data for bookmobile repair for 15 years:

Student	Homework	Quizzes	Paper	Midterm	Final
1	85	89	94	87	90
2	78	84	88	91	92
3	94	88	93	86	89
4	82	79	88	84	93
5	95	90	92	82	88

■ **3-17** Jim's Videotaping Service recently placed an order for VHS videotape. Jim ordered 6 cases of High-Grade, 4 cases of Performance High-Grade, 8 cases of Standard, 3 cases of High Standard, and 1 case of Low Grade. Each case contains 24 tapes. Suppose a case of High-Grade costs $28, Performance High-Grade costs $36, Standard costs $16, High Standard costs $18, and Low costs $6.

(a) What is the average cost per case to Jim?

(b) What is the average cost per tape to Jim?

(c) Suppose Jim will sell any tape for $1.25. Is this a good business practice for Jim?

(d) How would your answer to parts (a)–(c) change if there were 48 tapes per case?

■ **3-18** Keyes Home Furnishings ran six local newspaper advertisements during December. The following frequency distribution resulted:

NUMBER OF TIMES SUBSCRIBER SAW AD DURING DECEMBER	0	1	2	3	4	5	6
FREQUENCY	897	1,082	1,325	814	307	253	198

What is the average number of times a subscriber saw a Keyes advertisement during December?

■ **3-19** The Nelson Window Company has manufacturing plants in five U.S. cities: Orlando, Minneapolis, Dallas, Pittsburgh, and Seattle. The production forecast for the next year has been completed. The Orlando division, with yearly production of 72 million windows, is predicting an 11.5 percent increase. The Pittsburgh division, with yearly production of 62 million, should grow by 6.4 percent. The Seattle division, with yearly production of 48 million, should also grow by 6.4 percent. The Minneapolis and Dallas divisions, with yearly productions of 89 and 94 million windows, respectively, are expecting to decrease production in the coming year by 9.7 and 18.2 percent, respectively. What is the average rate of change in production for the Nelson Window Company for the next year?

■ **3-20** The U.S. Postal Service handles seven basic types of letters and cards: third class, second class, first class, air mail, special delivery, registered, and certified. The mail volume during 1977 is given in the following table:

Type of Mailing	Ounces Delivered (in millions)	Price per Ounce
Third class	16,400	$0.05
Second class	24,100	0.08
First class	77,600	0.13
Air mail	1,900	0.17
Special delivery	1,300	0.35
Registered	750	0.40
Certified	800	0.45

What was the average revenue per ounce for these services during the year?

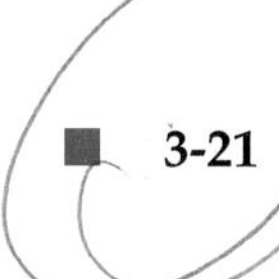

■ **3-21** Matthews, Young and Associates, a management consulting firm, has four types of professionals on its staff: managing consultants, senior associates, field staff, and office staff. Average rates charged to consulting clients for the work of each of these professional categories are \$75/hour, \$40/hour, \$30/hour, and \$15/hour. Office records indicate the following number of hours billed last year in each category: 8,000, 14,000, 24,000, and 35,000. If Matthews, Young is trying to come up with an average billing rate for estimating client charges for next year, what would you suggest they do and what do you think is an appropriate rate?

Worked-Out Answers to Self-Check Exercises

SC 3-3 With unweighted averages, we get

$$\bar{x}_c = \frac{\Sigma x}{n} = \frac{31.20}{6} = \$5.20 \text{ at the competition}$$

$$\bar{x}_D = \frac{31.50}{6} = \$5.25 \text{ at Dave's}$$

With weighted averages, we get

$$\bar{x}_c = \frac{\Sigma(w \times x)}{\Sigma w}$$

$$= \frac{7(1.29) + 9(2.97) + 12(3.49) + 8(5.00) + 6(7.50) + 3(10.95)}{7 + 9 + 12 + 8 + 6 + 3}$$

$$= \frac{195.49}{45} = \$4.344 \text{ at the competition}$$

$$\bar{x}_D = \frac{7(1.35) + 9(2.89) + 12(3.19) + 8(4.98) + 6(7.59) + 3(11.50)}{7 + 9 + 12 + 8 + 6 + 3}$$

$$= \frac{193.62}{45} = \$4.303 \text{ at Dave's}$$

Although Dave is technically correct, the word *average* in popular usage is equivalent to *unweighted average* in technical usage, and the typical customer will surely be angry with Dave's assertion (whether he or she understands the technical point or not).

SC 3-4 $$\bar{x}_w = \frac{\Sigma(w \times x)}{\Sigma w} = \frac{193.8(7.25) + 79.3(8.20) + 57.5(7.15)}{193.8 + 79.3 + 57.5}$$

$$= \frac{2466.435}{330.6} = 7.46\%$$

3.4 A Third Measure of Central Tendency: The Geometric Mean

Finding the growth rate: the geometric mean

Sometimes when we are dealing with quantities that change over a period of time, we need to know an average rate of change, such as an average growth rate over a period of several years. In such cases, the simple arithmetic mean is inappropriate, because it gives the wrong answers. What we need to find is the *geometric mean,* simply called the G.M.

Table 3-9 Growth of $100 Deposit in a Savings Account	Year	Interest Rate	Growth Factor	Savings at End of Year
	1	7%	1.07	$107.00
	2	8	1.08	115.56
	3	10	1.10	127.12
	4	12	1.12	142.37
	5	18	1.18	168.00

Consider, for example, the growth of a savings account. Suppose we deposit $100 initially and let it accrue interest at varying rates for 5 years. The growth is summarized in Table 3-9.

The entry labeled "growth factor" is equal to

$$1 + \frac{\text{interest rate}}{100}$$

The growth factor is the amount by which we multiply the savings at the beginning of the year to get the savings at the end of the year. The simple arithmetic mean growth factor would be $(1.07 + 1.08 + 1.10 + 1.12 + 1.18)/5 = 1.11$, which corresponds to an average interest rate of 11 percent per year. If the bank gives interest at a constant rate of 11 percent per year, however, a $100 deposit would grow in five years to

In this case, the arithmetic mean growth rate is incorrect

$$\$100 \times 1.11 \times 1.11 \times 1.11 \times 1.11 \times 1.11 = \$168.51$$

Table 3-9 shows that the actual figure is only $168.00. Thus, the correct average growth factor must be slightly less than 1.11.

Calculating the geometric mean

To find the correct average growth factor, we can multiply together the 5 years' growth factors and then take the fifth root of the product—the number that, when multiplied by itself four times, is equal to the product we started with. The result is the *geometric mean growth rate,* which is the appropriate average to use here. The formula for finding the geometric mean of a series of numbers is

Geometric Mean

Number of x values → n

$$\text{G.M.} = \sqrt[n]{\text{product of all } x \text{ values}} \quad [3\text{-}6]$$

If we apply this equation to our savings-account problem, we can determine that 1.1093 is the correct average growth factor.

$$\begin{aligned} \text{G.M.} &= \sqrt[n]{\text{product of all } x \text{ values}} \quad [3\text{-}6] \\ &= \sqrt[5]{1.07 \times 1.08 \times 1.10 \times 1.12 \times 1.18} \\ &= \sqrt[5]{1.679965} \\ &= 1.1093 \leftarrow \text{Average growth factor (the geometric mean of the 5 growth factors)} \end{aligned}$$

Warning: use the appropriate mean

Notice that the correct average interest rate of 10.93 percent per year obtained with the geometric mean is very close to the incorrect average rate of 11 percent obtained with the arithmetic mean. This happens because the interest rates are relatively small. Be careful, however, not to be tempted to use the arithmetic mean instead of the more complicated geometric mean. The following example demonstrates why.

In highly inflationary economies, banks must pay high interest rates to attract savings. Suppose that over 5 years in an unbelievably inflationary economy, banks pay interest at annual rates of 100, 200, 250, 300, and 400 percent, which correspond to growth factors of 2, 3, 3.5, 4, and 5. (We've calculated these growth factors just as we did in Table 3-9.)

In 5 years, an initial deposit of \$100 would grow to $\$100 \times 2 \times 3 \times 3.5 \times 4 \times 5 =$ \$42,000. The arithmetic mean growth factor is $(2 + 3 + 3.5 + 4 + 5)/5$, or 3.5. This corresponds to an average interest rate of 250 percent. Yet if the banks actually gave interest at a constant rate of 250 percent per year, then \$100 would grow to \$52,521.88 in 5 years:

$$\$100 \times 3.5 \times 3.5 \times 3.5 \times 3.5 \times 3.5 = \$52{,}521.88$$

This answer exceeds the actual \$42,000 by more than \$10,500, a sizable error.

Let's use the formula for finding the geometric mean of a series of numbers to determine the correct growth factor:

$$\begin{aligned} \text{G.M.} &= \sqrt[n]{\text{product of all } x \text{ values}} \qquad [3\text{-}6] \\ &= \sqrt[5]{2 \times 3 \times 3.5 \times 4 \times 5} \\ &= \sqrt[5]{420} \\ &= 3.347 \longleftarrow \text{Average growth factor} \end{aligned}$$

This growth factor corresponds to an average interest rate of 235 percent per year. In this case, the use of the appropriate mean *does* make a significant difference.

HINTS & ASSUMPTIONS

We use the geometric mean to show multiplicative effects over time in compound interest and inflation calculations. In certain situations, answers using the arithmetic mean and the geometric mean will not be too far apart, but even a small difference can generate a poor decision. A good working hint is to use the geometric mean whenever you are calculating the average percentage change in some variable over time. When you see a value for the average increase in inflation, for example, ask whether it's a geometric mean and be warned that if it's not, you are dealing with an incorrect value.

Exercises 3.4

Self-Check Exercises

SC 3-5 The growth in bad-debt expense for Johnston Office Supply Company over the last few years follows. Calculate the average percentage increase in bad-debt expense over this time period. If this rate continues, estimate the percentage increase in bad debts for 1997, relative to 1995.

1989	1990	1991	1992	1993	1994	1995
0.11	0.09	0.075	0.08	0.095	0.108	0.120

SC 3-6 Realistic Stereo Shops marks up its merchandise 35 percent above the cost of its latest additions to stock. Until 4 months ago, the Dynamic 400-S VHS recorder had been \$300. During the last 4 months Realistic has received 4

monthly shipments of this recorder at these unit costs: $275, $250, $240, and $225. At what average rate per month has Realistic's retail price for this unit been decreasing during these 4 months?

Applications

■ **3-22** Hayes Textiles has shown the following percentage increase in net worth over the last 5 years:

1992	1993	1994	1995	1996
5%	10.5%	9.0%	6.0%	7.5%

What is the average percentage increase in net worth over the 5-year period?

■ **3-23** MacroSwift, the U.S.-based computer software giant, has posted an increase in net worth during 7 of the last 9 years. Calculate the average percentage change in net worth over this time period. Assuming similar conditions in the years to come, estimate the percentage change for 1998, relative to 1996.

1988	1989	1990	1991	1992	1993	1994	1995	1996
0.11	0.09	0.07	0.08	−0.04	0.14	0.11	−0.03	0.06

■ **3-24** The Birch Company, a manufacturer of electrical circuit boards, has manufactured the following number of units over the past 5 years:

1992	1993	1994	1995	1996
12,500	13,250	14,310	15,741	17,630

Calculate the average percentage increase in units produced over this time period, and use this to estimate production for 1999.

■ **3-25** Bob Headen is calculating the average growth factor for his stereo store over the last 6 years. Using a geometric mean, he comes up with an answer of 1.24. Individual growth factors for the first 5 years were 1.19, 1.35, 1.23, 1.19, and 1.30, but Bob lost the records for the sixth year, after he calculated the mean. What was it?

■ **3-26** Over a 3-week period, a store owner purchased $120 worth of acrylic sheeting for new display cases in three equal purchases of $40 each. The first purchase was at $1.00 per square foot; the second, $1.10; and the third, $1.15. What was the average weekly rate of increase in the price per square foot paid for the sheeting?

■ **3-27** Lisa's Quick Stop has been attracting customers by selling milk at a price 2 percent below that of the main grocery store in town. Given below are Lisa's prices for a gallon of milk for a 2-month period. What was the average rate of change in price at Lisa's Quick Stop?

Week 1	Week 2	Week 3	Week 4	Week 5	Week 6	Week 7	Week 8
$2.30	$2.42	$2.36	$2.49	$2.24	$2.36	$2.42	$2.49

■ **3-28** Industrial Suppliers, Inc., keeps records on the cost of processing a purchase order. Over the last 5 years, this cost has been $55.00, $58.00, $61.00, $65.00, and $66.00. What has Industrial's average percentage increase been over this period? If this average rate stays the same for 3 more years, what will it cost Industrial to process a purchase order at that time?

■ **3-29** A sociologist has been studying the yearly changes in the number of convicts assigned to the largest correctional facility in the state. His data are expressed in terms of the percentage increase in the number of prisoners (a negative number indicates a percentage decrease). The sociologist's most recent data are as follows:

1991	1992	1993	1994	1995	1996
−4%	5%	10%	3%	6%	−5%

(a) Calculate the average percentage increase using only the 1992–1995 data.
(b) Rework part (a) using the data from all 6 years.
(c) A new penal code was passed in 1990. Previously, the prison population grew at a rate of about 2 percent per year. What seems to be the effect of the new code?

Worked-Out Answers to Self-Check Exercises

SC 3-5

$$\text{G.M.} = \sqrt[7]{1.11(1.09)(1.075)(1.08)(1.095)(1.108)(1.12)} = \sqrt[7]{1.908769992} = 1.09675$$

The average increase is 9.675 percent per year. The estimate for bad debt expenses in 1997 is $(1.09675)^2 - 1 = .2029$, i.e., 20.29 percent higher than in 1995.

SC 3-6 The monthly growth factors are 275/300 = 0.9167, 250/275 = 0.9091, 240/250 = 0.9600, and 225/240 = 0.9375, so

$$\text{G.M.} = \sqrt[4]{0.9167(0.9091)(0.9600)(0.9375)} = \sqrt[4]{0.7500} = 0.9306 = 1 - 0.0694$$

The price has been decreasing at an average rate of 6.94 percent per month.

3.5 A Fourth Measure of Central Tendency: The Median

Median defined

The *median* is a measure of central tendency different from any of the means we have discussed so far. The median is a single value from the data set that measures the central item in the data. This single item is the *middlemost* or *most central* item in the set of numbers. Half of the items lie above this point, and the other half lie below it.

Calculating the Median from Ungrouped Data

Finding the median of ungrouped data

To find the median of a data set, first array the data in ascending or descending order. If the data set contains an *odd* number of items, the middle item of the array is the median. If there is an *even* number of items, the median is the average of the two middle items. In formal language, the median is

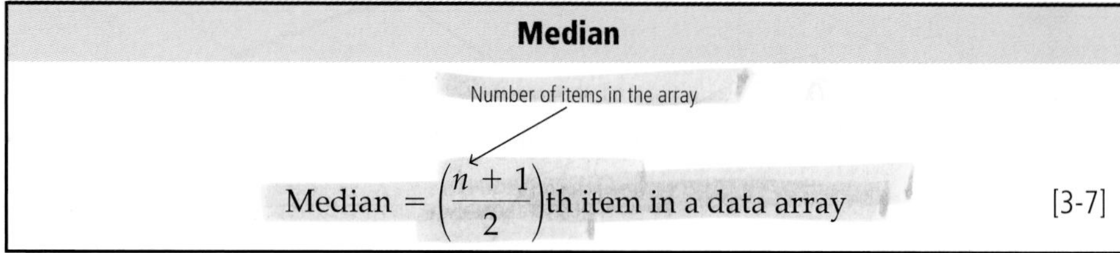

$$\text{Median} = \left(\frac{n+1}{2}\right)\text{th item in a data array} \qquad [3\text{-}7]$$

An odd number of items

Suppose we wish to find the median of seven items in a data array. According to Equation 3-7, the median is the $(7 + 1)/2 = 4$th item in the array. If we apply this to our previous example of the times for seven members of a track team, we discover that the fourth element in the array is 4.8 minutes. This is the median time for the track team. Notice that unlike the arithmetic mean we calculated earlier, the median we calculated in Table 3-10 was *not* distorted by the presence of the last value (9.0). This value could have been 15.0 or even 45.0 minutes, and the median would have been the same!

The median is not distorted by extreme values

An even number of items

Now let's calculate the median for an array with an even number of items. Consider the data shown in Table 3-11 concerning the number of patients treated daily in the emergency room of a hospital. The data are arrayed in descending order. The median of this data set would be

$$\text{Median} = \left(\frac{n+1}{2}\right)\text{th item in a data array} \tag{3-7}$$

$$= \frac{8+1}{2}$$

$$= 4.5\text{th item}$$

Because the median is the 4.5th element in the array, we need to average the fourth and fifth elements. The fourth element in Table 3-11 is 43 and the fifth is 35. The average of these two elements is equal to $(43 + 35)/2$, or 39. Therefore, 39 is the median number of patients treated in the emergency room per day during the 8-day period.

Calculating the Median from Grouped Data

Finding the median of grouped data

Often, we have access to data only after they have been grouped in a frequency distribution. For example, we do not know every observation that led to the construction of Table 3-12, the data on 600 bank customers originally introduced earlier. Instead, we have 10 class intervals and a record of the frequencies with which the observations appear in each of the intervals.

Locate the median class

Nevertheless, we can compute the median checking-account balance of these 600 customers by determining which of the 10 class intervals *contains* the median. To do this, we must add the frequencies in the frequency column in Table 3-12 until we reach the $(n + 1)/2$th item. Because there are 600 accounts, the value for $(n + 1)/2$ is 300.5 (the average of the 300th and 301st items). The problem is to find the class intervals containing the 300th and 301st

Table 3-10

Times for Track-Team Members

ITEM IN DATA ARRAY	1	2	3	4	5	6	7
TIME IN MINUTES	4.2	4.3	4.7	4.8	5.0	5.1	9.0
				↑ Median			

Table 3-11

Patients Treated in Emergency Room on 8 Consecutive Days

ITEM IN DATA ARRAY	1	2	3	4	5	6	7	8
NUMBER OF PATIENTS	86	52	49	43	35	31	30	11
				↑ Median of 39				

Table 3-12

Average Monthly Balances for 600 Customers

Class in Dollars	Frequency	
0– 49.99	78	
50.00– 99.99	123	
100.00– 149.99	187	Median class
150.00–199.99	82	
200.00–249.99	51	
250.00–299.99	47	
300.00–349.99	13	
350.00–399.99	9	
400.00–449.99	6	
450.00–499.99	4	
	600	

elements. The cumulative frequency for the first two classes is only 78 + 123 = 201. But when we moved to the third class interval, 187 elements are added to 201, for a total of 388. Therefore, the 300th and 301st observations must be located in this third class (the interval from \$100.00 to \$149.99).

The *median class* for this data set contains 187 items. If we assume that these 187 items begin at \$100.00 and are *evenly spaced over the entire class interval* from \$100.00 to \$149.99, then we can interpolate and find values for the 300th and 301st items. First, we determine that the 300th item is the 99th element in the median class:

$$300 - 201 \text{ [items in the first two classes]} = 99$$

and that the 301st item is the 100th element in the median class:

$$301 - 201 = 100$$

Then we can calculate the *width* of the 187 equal steps from \$100.00 to \$149.99, as follows:

First item of next class → \$150.00 ; First item of median class → \$100.00

$$\frac{\$150.00 - \$100.00}{187} = \$0.267 \text{ in width}$$

Now, if there are 187 steps of \$0.267 each and if 98 steps will take us to the 99th item, then the 99th item is

$$(\$0.267 \times 98) + \$100 = \$126.17$$

and the 100th item is one additional step:

$$\$126.17 + \$0.267 = \$126.44$$

Therefore, we can use \$126.17 and \$126.44 as the values of the 300th and 301st items, respectively.

The actual median for this data set is the value of the 300.5th item, that is, the average of the 300th and 301st items. This average is

$$\frac{\$126.17 + \$126.44}{2} = \$126.30$$

This figure ($126.30) is the median monthly checking account balance, as estimated from the grouped data in Table 3-12.

In summary, we can calculate the median of grouped data as follows:

Steps for finding the median of grouped data

1. Use Equation 3-7 to determine which element in the distribution is centermost (in this case, the average of the 300th and 301st items).
2. Add the frequencies in each class to find the class that contains that centermost element (the third class, or $100.00–$149.99).
3. Determine the number of elements in the class (187) and the location in the class of the median element (item 300 was the 99th element; item 301, the 100th element).
4. Learn the width of each step in the median class by dividing the class interval by the number of elements in the class (width = $0.267).
5. Determine the number of steps from the lower bound of the median class to the appropriate item for the median (98 steps for the 99th element; 99 steps for the 100th element).
6. Calculate the estimated value of the median element by multiplying the number of steps to the median element times the width of each step and by adding the result to the lower bound of the median class ($100 + 98 × $0.267 = $126.17; $126.17 + $0.267 = $126.44).
7. If, as in our example, there is an even number of elements in the distribution, average the values of the median element calculated in step 6 ($126.30).

An easier method

To shorten this procedure, statisticians use an equation to determine the median of grouped data. For a sample, this equation would be

Sample Median of Grouped Data

$$\tilde{m} = \left(\frac{(n + 1)/2 - (F + 1)}{f_m}\right)w + L_m \qquad [3\text{-}8]$$

where

- $\tilde{m}$ = sample median
- n = total number of items in the distribution
- F = sum of all the class frequencies *up to,* but *not including,* the median class
- f_m = frequency of the median class
- w = class-interval width
- L_m = lower limit of the median-class interval

If we use Equation 3-8 to compute the median of our sample of checking-account balances, then $n = 600$, $F = 201$, $f_m = 187$, $w = \$50$, and $L_m = \$100$.

$$\tilde{m} = \left(\frac{(n + 1)/2 - (F + 1)}{f_m}\right)w + L_m \qquad [3\text{-}8]$$

$$= \left(\frac{601/2 - 202}{187}\right)\$50 + \$100$$

$$= \left(\frac{98.5}{187}\right)\$50 + \$100$$

$$= (0.527)(\$50) + \$100$$

$$= \$126.35 \leftarrow \text{Estimated sample median}$$

The slight difference between this answer and our answer calculated the long way is due to rounding.

Advantages and Disadvantages of the Median

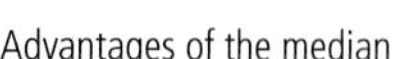

Advantages of the median

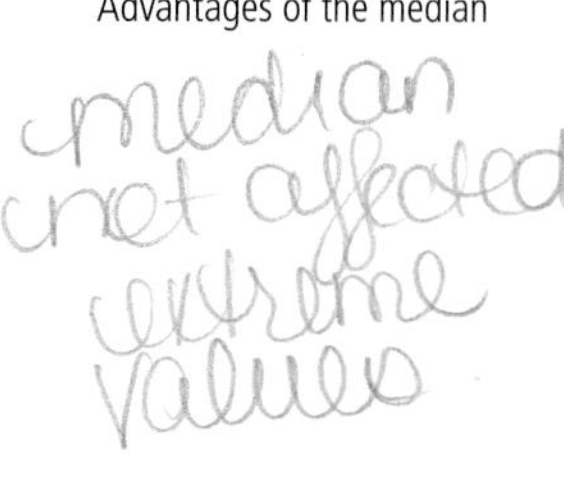

The median has several advantages over the mean. The most important, demonstrated in our track-team example in Table 3-10, is that extreme values do not affect the median as strongly as they do the mean. The median is easy to understand and can be calculated from any kind of data—even for grouped data with open-ended classes such as the frequency distribution in Table 3-7—*unless* the median falls in an open-ended class.

We can find the median even when our data are qualitative descriptions such as color or sharpness, rather than numbers. Suppose, for example, we have five runs of a printing press, the results from which must be rated according to sharpness of the image. We can array the results from best to worst: extremely sharp, very sharp, sharp, slightly blurred, and very blurred. The median of the five ratings is the $(5 + 1)/2$, or the third rating (sharp).

Disadvantages of the median

The median has some disadvantages as well. Certain statistical procedures that use the median are more complex than those that use the mean. Also, because the median is the value at the average position, we must array the data before we can perform any calculations. This is time consuming for any data set with a large number of elements. Therefore, if we want to use a sample statistic as an estimate of a population parameter, the mean is easier to use than the median. Chapter 7 will discuss estimation in detail.

HINTS & ASSUMPTIONS

In using the median, there is good news and bad news. The good news is that it is fairly quick to calculate and it avoids the effect of very large and very small values. The bad news is that you do give up some accuracy by choosing a single value to represent a distribution. With the values 2, 4, 5, 40, 100, 213, and 347, the median is 40, which has no apparent relationship to any of the other values in the distribution. Warning: Before you do any calculating, take a commonsense look at the data themselves. If the distribution looks unusual, just about anything you calculate from it will have shortcomings.

Exercises 3.5

Self-Check Exercises

SC 3-7 Swifty Markets compares prices charged for identical items in all of its food stores. Here are the prices charged by each store for a pound of bacon last week:

$1.08	0.98	1.09	1.24	1.33	1.14	1.55	1.08	1.22	1.05

(a) Calculate the median price per pound.
(b) Calculate the mean price per pound.
(c) Which value is the better measure of the central tendency of these data?

SC 3-8 For the following frequency distribution, determine
(a) The median class.
(b) The number of the item that represents the median.
(c) The width of the equal steps in the median class.
(d) The estimated value of the median for these data.

Class	Frequency	Class	Frequency
100–149.5	12	300–349.5	72
150–199.5	14	350–399.5	63
200–249.5	27	400–449.5	36
250–299.5	58	450–499.5	18

Applications

■ **3-30** Meridian Trucking maintains mileage records on all of its rolling equipment. Here are weekly mileage records for its trucks.

810	450	756	789	210	657	589	488	876	689
1,450	560	469	890	987	559	788	943	447	775

(a) Calculate the median miles a truck traveled.
(b) Calculate the mean for the 20 trucks.
(c) Compare parts (a) and (b) and explain which one is a better measure of the central tendency of the data.

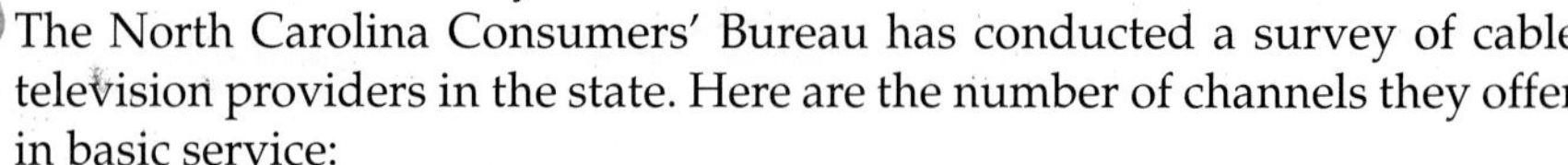

■ **3-31** The North Carolina Consumers' Bureau has conducted a survey of cable television providers in the state. Here are the number of channels they offer in basic service:

32	28	31	15	25	14	12	29	22	28	29	32	33	24	26	8	35

(a) Calculate the median number of channels provided.
(b) Calculate the mean number of channels provided.
(c) Which value is the better measure of the central tendency of these data?

■ **3-32** For the following frequency distribution,
(a) Which number item represents the median?
(b) Which class contains the median?
(c) What is the width of the equal steps in the median class?

(d) What is the estimated value of the median for these data?

(e) Use Equation 3-8 to estimate the median for the data. Are your two estimates close to one another?

Class	Frequency	Class	Frequency
10–19.5	8	60–69.5	52
20–29.5	15	70–79.5	84
30–39.5	23	80–89.5	97
40–49.5	37	90–99.5	16
50–59.5	46	100 or over	5

■ **3-33** The following data represent weights of gamefish caught on the charter boat *Slickdrifter:*

Class	Frequency
0– 24.9	5
25– 49.9	13
50– 74.9	16
75– 99.9	8
100–124.9	6

(a) Use Equation 3-8 to estimate the median weight of the fish caught.

(b) Use Equation 3-3 to compute the mean for these data.

(c) Compare parts (a) and (b) and comment on which is the better measure of the central tendency of these data.

■ **3-34** The Chicago Transit Authority thinks that excessive speed on its buses increases maintenance cost. It believes that a reasonable median time from O'Hare Airport to John Hancock Center is about 30 minutes. From the following sample data (in minutes) can you help them determine whether the buses have been driven at excessive speeds? If you conclude from these data that they have, what explanation might you get from the bus drivers?

17	32	21	22
29	19	29	34
33	22	28	33
52	29	43	39
44	34	30	41

■ **3-35** Mark Merritt, manager of Quality Upholstery Company, is researching the amount of material used in the firm's upholstery jobs. The amount varies between jobs, owing to different furniture styles and sizes. Merritt gathers the following data (in yards) from the jobs completed last week. Calculate the median yardage used on a job last week.

$5\frac{1}{4}$	$6\frac{1}{4}$	6	$7\frac{7}{8}$	$9\frac{1}{4}$	$9\frac{1}{2}$	$10\frac{1}{2}$
$5\frac{3}{8}$	6	$6\frac{1}{4}$	8	$9\frac{1}{2}$	$9\frac{7}{8}$	$10\frac{1}{4}$
$5\frac{1}{2}$	$5\frac{7}{8}$	$6\frac{1}{2}$	$8\frac{1}{4}$	$9\frac{3}{8}$	$10\frac{1}{4}$	$10\frac{1}{8}$
$5\frac{7}{8}$	$5\frac{3}{4}$	7	$8\frac{1}{2}$	$9\frac{1}{8}$	$10\frac{1}{2}$	$10\frac{1}{8}$
6	$5\frac{7}{8}$	$7\frac{1}{2}$	9	$9\frac{1}{4}$	$9\frac{7}{8}$	10

If there are 150 jobs scheduled in the next 3 weeks, use the median to predict how many yards of material will be required.

■ **3-36** If insurance claims for automobile accidents follow the distribution given, determine the median using the method outlined on page 94. Verify that you get the same answer using Equation 3-8.

Amount of Claim ($)	Frequency	Amount of Claim ($)	Frequency
less than 250	52	750–999.99	1,776
250–499.99	337	1,000 and above	1,492
500–749.99	1,066		

■ **3-37** A researcher obtained the following answers to a statement on an evaluation survey: strongly disagree, disagree, mildly disagree, agree somewhat, agree, strongly agree. Of the six answers, which is the median?

Worked-Out Answers to Self-Check Exercises

SC 3-7 We first arrange the prices in ascending order:

0.98 1.05 1.08 1.08 1.09 1.14 1.22 1.24 1.33 1.55

(a) $\text{Median} = \dfrac{1.09 + 1.14}{2} = \$1.115$, the average of items 5 and 6

(b) $\bar{x} = \dfrac{\Sigma x}{n} = \dfrac{11.76}{10} = \$1.176$

(c) Because the data are skewed slightly, the median might be a bit better than the mean, but there really isn't very much difference.

SC 3-8

Class	Frequency	Cumulative Frequency
100–149.5	12	12
150–199.5	14	26
200–249.5	27	53
250–299.5	58	111
300–349.5	72	183
350–399.5	63	246
400–449.5	36	282
450–499.5	18	300

(a) Median class = 300–349.5

(b) Average of 150th and 151st

(c) Step width = 50/72 = .6944

(d) 300 + 38(0.6944) = 326.3872 (150th)
300 + 39(0.6944) = 327.0816 (151st)
653.4688

$$\text{Median} = \frac{653.4688}{2} = 326.7344$$

3.6 A Final Measure of Central Tendency: The Mode

Mode defined

The mode is a measure of central tendency that is different from the mean but somewhat like the median because it is not actually calculated by the ordinary processes of arithmetic. The mode is *the value that is repeated most often in the data set.*

Risks in using the mode of ungrouped data

As in every other aspect of life, chance can play a role in the arrangement of data. Sometimes chance causes a single unrepresentative item to be repeated often enough to be the most frequent value in the data set. For this reason, we rarely use the mode of ungrouped data as a measure of central tendency. Table 3-13, for example, shows the number of delivery trips per day made by a Redi-mix concrete plant. The modal value is 15 because it occurs more often than any other value (three times). A mode of 15 implies that the plant activity is higher than 6.7 (6.7 is the answer we'd get if we calculated the mean). The mode tells us that 15 is the most frequent number of trips, but it fails to let us know that most of the values are under 10.

Finding the modal class of grouped data

Now let's group these data into a frequency distribution, as we have done in Table 3-14. If we select the class with the most observations, which we can call the *modal class,* we would choose 4–7 trips. This class is more representative of the activity of the plant than is the mode of 15 trips per day. For this reason, whenever we use the mode as a measure of the central tendency of a data set, we should calculate the mode from grouped data.

Calculating the Mode from Grouped Data

When data are already grouped in a frequency distribution, we must assume that the mode is located in the class with the most items, that is, the class with the highest frequency. To determine a single value for the mode from this modal class, we use Equation 3-9:

Mode

$$Mo = L_{Mo} + \left(\frac{d_1}{d_1 + d_2}\right)w \qquad [3\text{-}9]$$

Table 3-13

Delivery Trips per Day in One 20-Day Period

Trips Arrayed in Ascending Order					
0	2	5	7	15	
0	2	5	7	15	← Mode
1	4	6	8	15	
1	4	6	12	19	

Table 3-14

Frequency Distribution of Delivery Trips

CLASS IN NUMBER OF TRIPS	0–3	4–7	8–11	12 and more
FREQUENCY	6	8	1	5
		↑ Modal class		

where

- L_{Mo} = lower limit of the modal class
- d_1 = frequency of the modal class minus the frequency of the class *directly below it*
- d_2 = frequency of the modal class minus the frequency of the class *directly above it*
- w = width of the modal class interval

If we use Equation 3-9 to compute the mode of our checking-account balances (see Table 3-12), then $L_{Mo} = \$100$, $d_1 = 187 - 123 = 64$, $d_2 = 187 - 82 = 105$, and $w = \$50$.

$$Mo = L_{Mo} + \left(\frac{d_1}{d_1 + d_2}\right)w \qquad [3\text{-}9]$$

$$= \$100 + \frac{64}{64 + 105}\$50$$

$$= \$100 + (0.38)(\$50)$$

$$= \$100 + \$19$$

$$= \$119.00 \leftarrow \text{Mode}$$

Our answer of \$119 is the estimate of the mode.

Multimodal Distributions

Bimodal distributions

What happens when we have two different values that *each* appear the greatest number of times of any values in the data set? Table 3-15 shows the billing errors for one 20-day period in a hospital office. Notice that both 1 and 4 appear the greatest number of times in the data set. They each appear three times. This distribution, then, has two modes and is called a *bimodal distribution.*

In Figure 3-6, we have graphed the data in Table 3-15. Notice that there are *two* highest points on the graph. They occur at the values of 1 and 4 billing errors. The distribution in Figure 3-7 is also called bimodal, even though the two highest points are not equal. Clearly, these points are higher than the neighboring values in the frequency with which they are observed.

Table 3-15	Errors Arrayed in Ascending Order					
Billing Errors per Day in 20-Day Period	0		2		6	9
	0		4		6	9
	1		4	← Mode	7	10
	1	← Mode	4		8	12
	1		5		8	12

FIGURE 3-6

Data in Table 3-15 showing the bimodal distribution

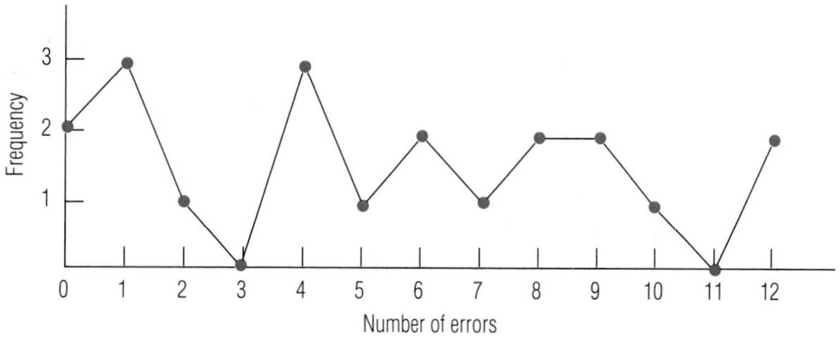

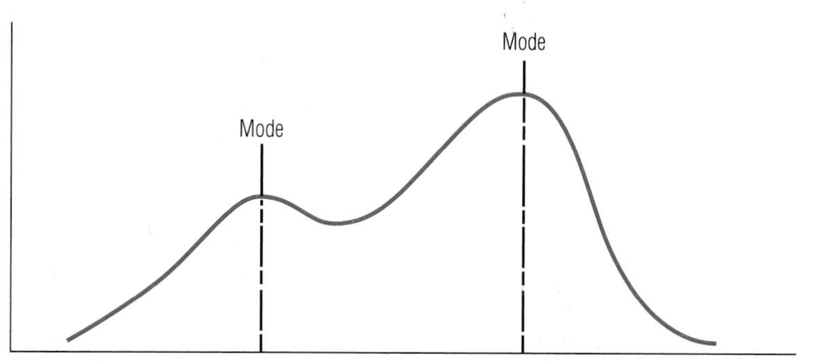

FIGURE 3-7

Bimodal distribution with two unequal modes

Advantages and Disadvantages of the Mode

Advantages of the mode

The mode, like the median, can be used as a central location for qualitative as well as quantitative data. If a printing press turns out five impressions, which we rate "very sharp," "sharp," "sharp," "sharp," and "blurred," then the modal value is "sharp." Similarly, we can talk about modal styles when, for example, furniture customers prefer Early American furniture to other styles.

Also like the median, **the mode is not unduly affected by extreme values.** Even if the high values are very high and the low values very low, we choose the most frequent value of the data set to be the modal value. We can use the mode no matter how large, how small, or how spread out the values in the data set happen to be.

A third advantage of the mode is that we can use it even when one or more of the classes are open ended. Notice, for example, that Table 3-14 contains the open-ended class "12 trips and more."

Disadvantages of the mode

Despite these advantages, the mode is not used as often to measure central tendency as are the mean and median. Too often, there is no modal value because the data set contains no values that occur more than once. Other times, every value is the mode, because every value occurs the same number of times. Clearly, the mode is a useless measure in these cases. Another disadvantage is that when data sets contain two, three, or many modes, they are difficult to interpret and compare.

Comparing the Mean, Median, and Mode

Mean, median, and mode are identical in a symmetrical distribution

When we work statistical problems, we must decide whether to use the mean, the median, or the mode as the measure of central tendency. Symmetrical distributions that contain only one mode always have the same value for the mean, the median, and the mode. In these

FIGURE 3-8

Positively (a) and negatively (b) skewed distributions, illustrating relative positions of mean, median, and mode.

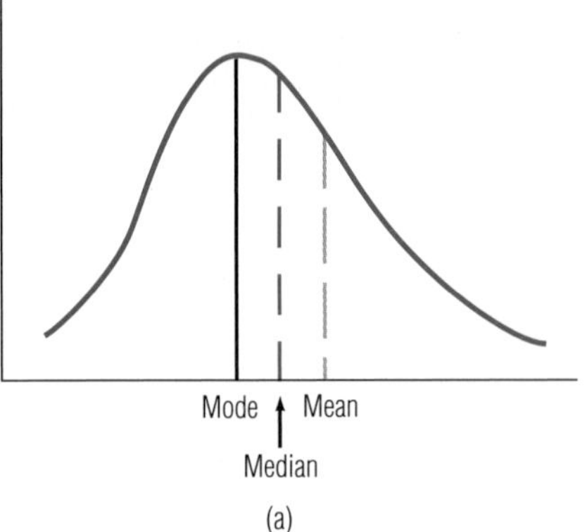

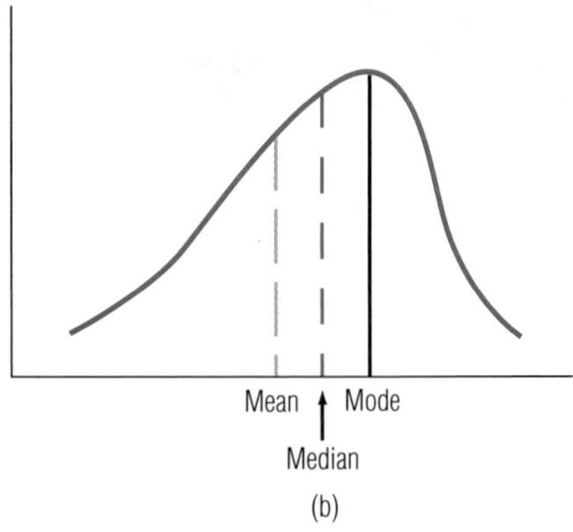

cases, we need not choose the measure of central tendency because the choice has been made for us.

In a positively skewed distribution (one skewed to the right), as illustrated in Figure 3-8(a), the mode is at the highest point of the distribution, the median is to the right of that, and the mean is to the right of both the median and mode.

In a negatively skewed distribution (one skewed to the left), as illustrated in Figure 3-8(b), the mode is still at the highest point of the distribution, the median is to the left of that, and the mean is to the left of both the median and mode.

The median may be the best location measure in skewed distributions

When the population is skewed negatively or positively, the median is often the best measure of location because it is always between the mean and the mode. The median is not as highly influenced by the frequency of occurrence of a single value as is the mode, nor is it pulled by extreme values as is the mean.

Otherwise, there are no universal guidelines for applying the mean, median, or mode as the measure of central tendency for different populations. Each case must be judged independently, according to the guidelines we have discussed.

HINTS & ASSUMPTIONS

Hint: In trying to decide on the uses of the various means, the median, and the mode, think about practical situations in which each of them would make more sense. If you are averaging a small group of factory wages fairly near each other, the arithmetic mean is very accurate and fast. If there are 500 new houses in a development all within $10,000 of each other in value, then the median is much quicker and quite accurate too. Dealing with the cumulative effects of inflation or interest requires the geometric mean if you want accuracy. A common-sense example: Although it's true that the average family has 1.65 children, automobile designers will make better decisions by using the modal value of 2.0 kids.

Exercises 3.6

Self-Check Exercises

SC 3-9 Here are the ages in years of the cars worked on by the Village Autohaus last week:

5	6	3	6	11	7	9	10	2	4	10	6	2	1	5

(a) Compute the mode for this data set.

(b) Compute the mean of the data set.

(c) Compare parts (a) and (b) and comment on which is the better measure of the central tendency of the data.

SC 3-10 The ages of a sample of the students attending Sandhills Community College this semester are:

19	17	15	20	23	41	33	21	18	20
18	33	32	29	24	19	18	20	17	22
55	19	22	25	28	30	44	19	20	39

(a) Construct a frequency distribution with intervals 15–19, 20–24, 25–29, 30–34, and 35 and older.

(b) Estimate the modal value using Equation 3-9.

(c) Now compute the mean of the raw data.

(d) Compare your answers in parts (b) and (c) and comment on which of the two is the better measure of the central tendency of these data and why.

Applications

■ **3-38** A librarian polled 20 different people as they left the library and asked them how many books they checked out. Here are the responses:

1	0	2	2	3	4	2	1	2	0	2	2	3	1	0	7	3	5	4	2

(a) Compute the mode for this data set.

(b) Compute the mean for this data set.

(c) Graph the data by plotting frequency versus number checked out. Is the mean or the mode a better measure of the central tendency of the data?

■ **3-39** The ages of residents of Twin Lakes Retirement Village have this frequency distribution:

Class	Frequency
47–51.9	4
52–56.9	9
57–61.9	13
62–66.9	42
67–71.9	39
72–76.9	20
77–81.9	9

Estimate the modal value of the distribution using Equation 3-9.

■ **3-40** What are the modal values for the following distributions?

(a) Hair Color	Black	Brunette	Redhead	Blonde			
Frequency	11	24	6	18			
(b) Blood Type	AB	0	A	B			
Frequency	4	12	35	16			
(c) Day of Birth	Mon.	Tues.	Wed.	Thurs.	Fri.	Sat.	Sun.
Frequency	22	10	32	17	13	32	14

■ **3-41** The numbers of apartments in 27 apartment complexes in Cary, North Carolina, are given below.

91	79	66	98	127	139	154	147	192
88	97	92	87	142	127	184	145	162
95	89	86	98	145	129	149	158	241

(a) Construct a frequency distribution using intervals 66–87, 88–109, . . . , 220–241.

(b) Estimate the modal value using Equation 3-9.

(c) Compute the mean of the raw data.

(d) Compare your answers in parts (b) and (c) and comment on which of the two is the better measure of central tendency of these data and why.

■ **3-42** Estimate the mode for the distribution given in Exercise 3-36.

■ **3-43** The number of solar heating systems available to the public is quite large, and their heat-storage capacities are quite varied. Here is a distribution of heat-storage capacity (in days) of 28 systems that were tested recently by University Laboratories, Inc.:

Days	Frequency
0–0.99	2
1–1.99	4
2–2.99	6
3–3.99	7
4–4.99	5
5–5.99	3
6–6.99	1

University Laboratories, Inc., knows that its report on the tests will be widely circulated and used as the basis for tax legislation on solar-heat allowances. It therefore wants the measures it uses to be as reflective of the data as possible.

(a) Compute the mean for these data.

(b) Compute the mode for these data.

(c) Compute the median for these data.

(d) Select the answer among parts (a), (b), and (c) that best reflects the central tendency of the test data and justify your choice.

■ **3-44** Ed Grant is the director of the Student Financial Aid Office at Wilderness College. He has used available data on the summer earnings of all students who have applied to his office for financial aid to develop the following frequency distribution:

Summer Earnings	Number of Students
\$ 0– 499	231
500– 999	304
1,000–1,499	400
1,500–1,999	296
2,000–2,499	123
2,500–2,999	68
3,000 or more	23

(a) Find the modal class for Ed's data.
(b) Use Equation 3-9 to find the mode for Ed's data.
(c) If student aid is restricted to those whose summer earnings were at least 10 percent lower than the modal summer earnings, how many of the applicants qualify?

Worked-Out Answers to Self-Check Exercises

SC 3-9 (a) Mode = 6

(b) $\bar{x} = \frac{\Sigma x}{n} = \frac{87}{15} = 5.8$

(c) Because the modal frequency is only 3 and because the data are reasonably symmetric, the mean is the better measure of central tendency.

SC 3-10 (a)

Class	15–19	20–24	25–29	30–34	≥ 35
Frequency	10	9	3	4	4

(b) $Mo = L_{Mo} + \frac{d_1}{d_1 + d_2}w = 15 + \left(\frac{10}{10 + 1}\right)5 = 19.55$

(c) $\bar{x} = \frac{\Sigma x}{n} = \frac{760}{30} = 25.33$

(d) Because this distribution is very skewed, the mode is a better measure of central tendency.

3.7 Dispersion: Why It Is Important

Need to measure dispersion or variability

Early in this chapter, in Figure 3-2, we illustrated two sets of data with the same central location but with one more spread out than the other. This is true of the three distributions in Figure 3-9. The mean of all three curves is the same, but curve A has less spread (or *variability*) than curve B, and curve B has less variability than curve C. If we measure only the mean of these three distributions, we will miss an important difference among the three curves. Likewise for any data, the mean, the median, and the mode tell us only part of what we need to know about the characteristics of the data. To increase our understanding of the pattern of the data, we must also measure its *dispersion*—its spread, or variability.

Uses of dispersion measures

Why is the dispersion of the distribution such an important characteristic to understand and measure? **First,** it gives us additional information that enables us to judge the reliability of our measure of the central tendency. If data are widely dispersed, such as those in

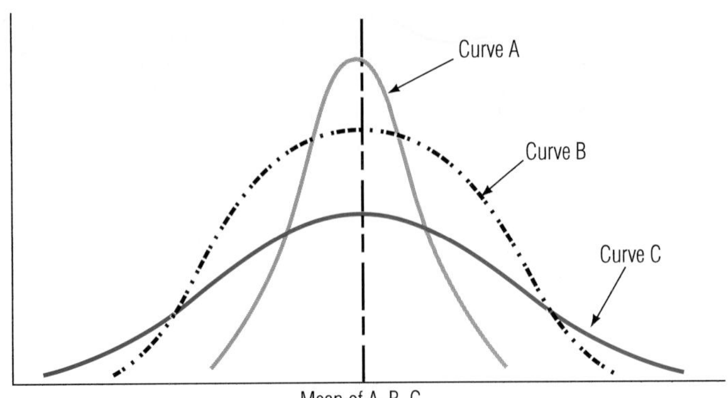

FIGURE 3-9

Three curves with the same mean but different variabilities

curve C in Figure 3-9, the central location is less representative of the data as a whole than it would be for data more closely centered around the mean, as in curve A. **Second,** because there are problems peculiar to widely dispersed data, we must be able to recognize that data are widely dispersed before we can tackle those problems. **Third,** we may wish to compare dispersions of various samples. If a wide spread of values away from the center is undesirable or presents an unacceptable risk, we need to be able to recognize and avoid choosing the distributions with the greatest dispersion.

Financial use and quality-control use

Financial analysts are concerned about the dispersion of a firm's earnings. Widely dispersed earnings—those varying from extremely high to low or even negative levels—indicate a higher risk to stockholders and creditors than do earnings remaining relatively stable. Similarly, quality control experts analyze the dispersion of a product's quality levels. A drug that is average in purity but ranges from very pure to highly impure may endanger lives.

HINTS & ASSUMPTIONS

Airline seat manufacturers make an assumption about the shape of the average flyer. In some coach sections, it's common to find seat widths of only 19″. If you weigh 250 pounds and wear a size 22 dress, sitting in a 19″ seat is like putting on a tight shoe. It's O.K. to make this assumption for an airliner, but ignoring the dispersion (or spread) of the data gets you in trouble in football. A team that averages 3.6 yards per play should theoretically win every game because 3.6 × 4 plays is more than the 10 yards necessary to retain possession. Alas, bad luck comes to us all, and the theoretically unbeatable average of 3.6 yards is affected by the occasional 20-yard loss. Warning: Don't put too much stock in averages unless you know that the dispersion is small. A recruiter for the U.S. Air Force looking for pilot trainees who average 6′ tall would get fired if he showed up with one who was 4′ and another who was 8′. Under "reason for termination" on his personnel file, it should say "disregarded dispersion."

Exercises 3.7

Basic Concepts

■ **3-45** For which of the following distributions is the mean more representative of the data as a whole? Why?

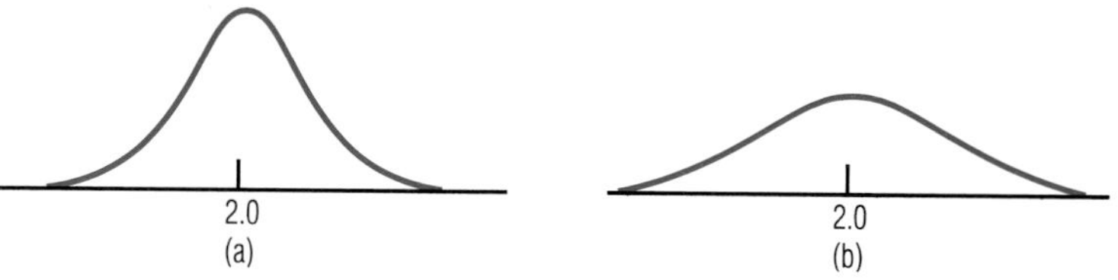

■ **3-46** Which of the following is not a valid reason for measuring the dispersion of a distribution?

(a) It provides an indication of the reliability of the statistic used to measure central tendency.

(b) It enables us to compare several samples with similar averages.

(c) It uses more data in describing a distribution.

(d) It draws attention to problems associated with very small or very large variability in distributions.

Applications

■ **3-47** To measure scholastic achievement, educators need to test students' levels of knowledge and ability. Taking students' individual differences into account, teachers can plan their curricula better. The curves that follow represent distributions based on previous scores of two different tests. Which would you select as the better for the teachers' purpose?

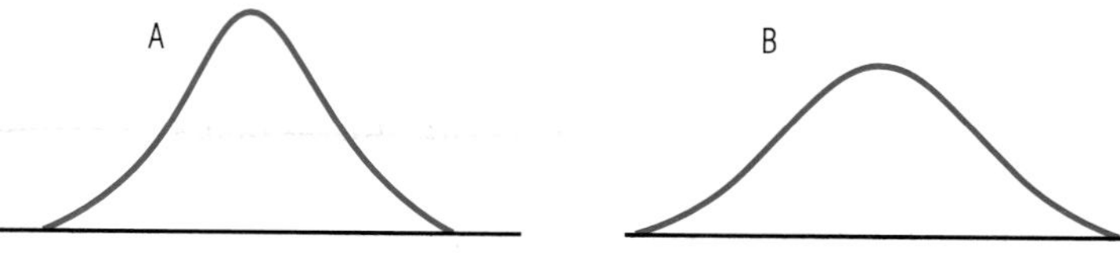

■ **3-48** A firm using two different methods to ship orders to its customers found the following distributions of delivery time for the two methods, based on past records. From available evidence, which shipment method would you recommend?

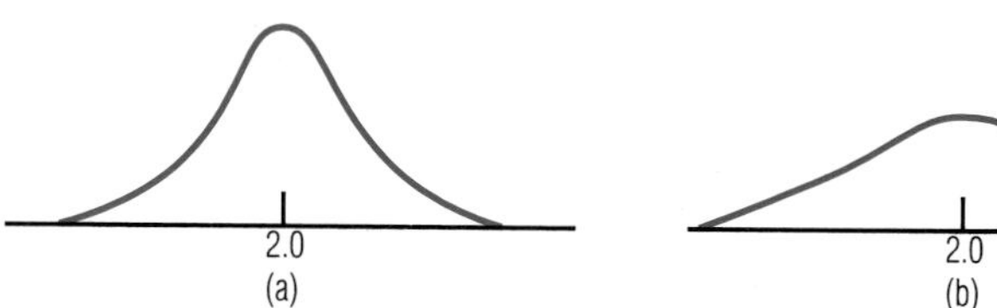

■ **3-49** Of the 3 curves shown in Figure 3-9, choose one that would best describe the distribution of values for the ages of the following groups: members of Congress, newly elected members of the House of Representatives, and the chairpersons of major congressional committees. In making your choices, disregard the common mean of the curves in Figure 3-9 and consider only the variability of the distributions. Briefly state your reasons for your choices.

■ **3-50** How do you think the concept of variability might apply to an investigation that the Federal Trade Commission (FTC) is conducting into possible price fixing by a group of manufacturers?

■ **3-51** Choose which of the three curves shown in Figure 3-9 best describes the distribution of the following characteristics of various groups. Make your choices only on the basis of the variability of the distributions. Briefly state a reason for each choice.

(a) The number of points scored by each player in a professional basketball league during an 80-game season.

(b) The salary of each of 100 people working at roughly equivalent jobs in the federal government.

(c) The grade-point average of each of the 15,000 students at a major state university.

(d) The salary of each of 100 people working at roughly equivalent jobs in a private corporation.

(e) The grade-point average of each student at a major state university who has been accepted for graduate school.

(f) The percentage of shots made by each player in a professional basketball league during an 80-game season.

3.8 Ranges: Useful Measures of Dispersion

Three distance measures

Dispersion may be measured in terms of the difference between two values selected from the data set. In this section, we shall study three of these so-called *distance measures:* the range, the interfractile range, and the interquartile range.

Range

Defining and computing the range

The *range* is the difference between the highest and lowest observed values. In equation form, we can say

Range

$$\text{Range} = \begin{matrix}\text{value of highest}\\ \text{observation}\end{matrix} - \begin{matrix}\text{value of lowest}\\ \text{observation}\end{matrix} \qquad [3\text{-}10]$$

Using this equation, we compare the ranges of annual payments from Blue Cross–Blue Shield received by the two hospitals illustrated in Table 3-16.

The range of annual payments to Cumberland is \$1,883,000 − \$863,000 = \$1,020,000. For Valley Falls, the range is \$690,000 − \$490,000 = \$200,000.

Table 3-16 Annual Payments from Blue Cross–Blue Shield (000s Omitted)						
CUMBERLAND	863	903	957	1,041	1,138	1,204
	1,354	1,624	1,698	1,745	1,802	1,883
VALLEY FALLS	490	540	560	570	590	600
	610	620	630	660	670	690

Characteristics of the range

The range is easy to understand and to find, but its usefulness as a measure of dispersion is limited. The range considers only the highest and lowest values of a distribution and fails to take account of any other observation in the data set. As a result, it ignores the nature of the variation among all the other observations, and it is heavily influenced by extreme values. Because it measures only two values, the range is likely to change drastically from one sample to the next in a given population, even though the values that fall between the highest and lowest values may be quite similar. Keep in mind, too, that open-ended distributions have no range because no "highest" or "lowest" value exists in the open-ended class.

Interfractile Range

Fractiles

In a frequency distribution, a given fraction or proportion of the data lie at or below a *fractile.* The median, for example, is the 0.5 fractile, because half the data set is less than or equal to this value. You will notice that fractiles are similar to percentages. In any distribution, 25 percent of the data lie at or below the 0.25 fractile; likewise, 25 percent of the data lie at or below the 25th percentile. The *interfractile range* is a measure of the spread between two fractiles in a frequency distribution, that is, the difference between the values of the two fractiles.

Meaning of the interfractile range

Calculating the interfractile range

Suppose we wish to find the interfractile range between the first and second *thirds* of Cumberland's receipts from Blue Cross–Blue Shield. We begin by dividing the observations into thirds, as we have done in Table 3-17. Each third contains four items ($^1/_3$ of the total of 12 items). Therefore, 33 $^1/_3$ percent of the items lie at $1,041,000 or below it, and 66 $^2/_3$ percent are less than or equal to $1,624,000. Now we can calculate the interfractile range between the $^1/_3$ and $^2/_3$ fractiles by subtracting the value $1,041,000 from the value $1,624,000. This difference of $583,000 is the spread between the top of the first third of the payments and the top of the second third.

Special fractiles: deciles, quartiles, and percentiles

Fractiles have special names, depending on the number of equal parts into which they divide the data. Fractiles that divide the data into 10 equal parts are called *deciles. Quartiles* divide the data into four equal parts. *Percentiles* divide the data into 100 equal parts.

Table 3-17 Blue Cross–Blue Shield Annual Payments to Cumberland Hospital (000s Omitted)	First Third	Second Third	Last Third
	863	1,138	1,698
	903	1,204	1,745
	957	1,354	1,802
	1,041 ← $^1/_3$ fractile	1,624 ← $^2/_3$ fractile	1,883

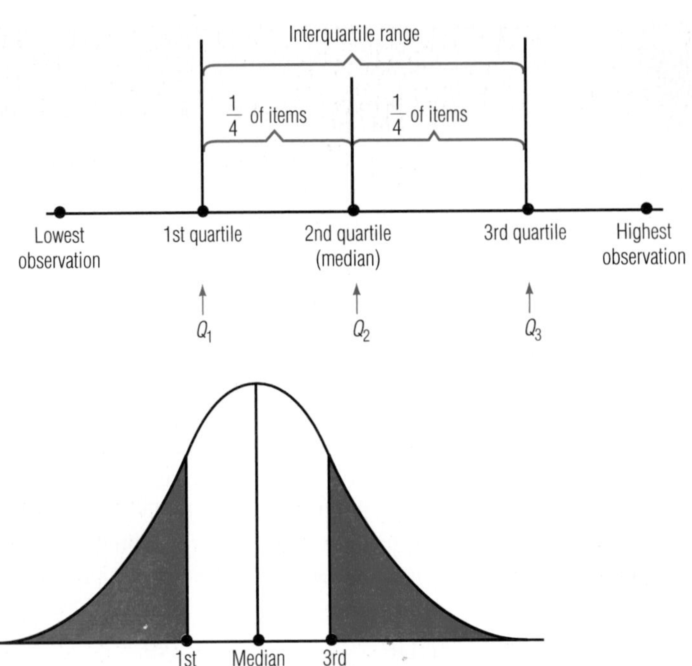

FIGURE 3-10
Interquartile range

FIGURE 3-11
Quartiles

Interquartile Range

Computing the interquartile range

The interquartile range measures approximately how far from the median we must go on either side before we can include one-half the values of the data set. To compute this range, we divide our data into four parts, each of which contains 25 percent of the items in the distribution. The *quartiles* are then the highest values in each of these four parts, and the *interquartile range* is the difference between the values of the first and third quartiles:

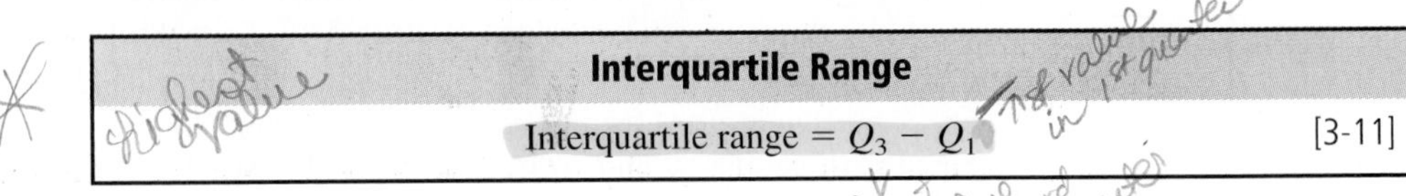

Interquartile Range

$$\text{Interquartile range} = Q_3 - Q_1 \qquad [3\text{-}11]$$

Figure 3-10 shows the concept of the interquartile range graphically. Notice in that figure that the widths of the four quartiles need *not* be the same.

In Figure 3-11, another illustration of quartiles, the quartiles divide the area under the distribution into four equal parts, each containing 25 percent of the area.

HINTS & ASSUMPTIONS

Fractile is a term used more by statisticians than by the rest of us, who are more familiar with 100 fractiles, or percentiles, especially when our percentile score on the SAT, the GMAT, or the LSAT is involved. When we get that letter indicating that our percentile score was 35, we know that 35 percent of those taking the test did worse than we did. The meaning of the range is easier to understand especially when the professor publishes the highest and lowest scores on the next statistics test. Hint: All of these terms help us deal with dispersion in data. If all the values look pretty much alike, then spending time computing dispersion values may not add much. If the data really spread out, betting your job on the average without considering dispersion is risky!

Exercises 3.8

Self-Check Exercises

SC 3-11 Here are student scores on a history quiz. Find the 80th percentile.

95	81	59	68	100	92	75	67	85	79
71	88	100	94	87	65	93	72	83	91

SC 3-12 The Casual Life Insurance Company is considering purchasing a new fleet of company cars. The financial department's director, Tom Dawkins, sampled 40 employees to determine the number of miles each drove over a 1-year period. The results of the study follow. Calculate the range and interquartile range.

3,600	4,200	4,700	4,900	5,300	5,700	6,700	7,300
7,700	8,100	8,300	8,400	8,700	8,700	8,900	9,300
9,500	9,500	9,700	10,000	10,300	10,500	10,700	10,800
11,000	11,300	11,300	11,800	12,100	12,700	12,900	13,100
13,500	13,800	14,600	14,900	16,300	17,200	18,500	20,300

Basic Concepts

■ **3-52** For the following data, compute the interquartile range.

99	75	84	61	33	45	66	97	69	55
72	91	74	93	54	76	52	91	77	68

■ **3-53** For the sample that follows, compute the

(a) Range.

(b) Interfractile range between the 20th and 80th percentiles.

(c) Interquartile range.

2,549	3,897	3,661	2,697	2,200	3,812	2,228	3,891	2,668	2,268
3,692	2,145	2,653	3,249	2,841	3,469	3,268	2,598	3,842	3,362

Applications

■ **3-54** Here are the high temperature readings during June 1995 in Phoenix, Arizona. Find the 70th percentile.

84	86	78	69	94	95	94	98	89	87	88	89	92	99	102
94	92	96	89	88	87	88	84	82	88	94	97	99	102	105

■ **3-55** These are the total fares (in dollars) collected Tuesday by the 20 taxis belonging to City Transit, Ltd.

147	95	93	127	143	101	123	83	135	129
185	92	115	126	157	93	133	51	125	132

Compute the range of these data and comment on whether you think it is a useful measure of dispersion.

■ **3-56** Redi-Mix Incorporated kept the following record of time (to the nearest 100th of a minute) its truck waited at the job to unload. Calculate the range and the interquartile range.

0.10	0.45	0.50	0.32	0.89	1.20	0.53	0.67	0.58	0.48
0.23	0.77	0.12	0.66	0.59	0.95	1.10	0.83	0.69	0.51

■ **3-57** Warlington Appliances has developed a new combination blender-crock-pot. In a marketing demonstration, a price survey determined that most of those sampled would be willing to pay around $60, with a surprisingly small interquartile range of $14.00. In an attempt to replicate the results, the demonstration and accompanying survey were repeated. The marketing department hoped to find an even smaller interquartile range. The data follow. Was its hope realized?

52	35	48	46	43	40	61	49	57	58	65	46
72	69	38	37	55	52	50	31	41	60	45	41
55	38	51	49	46	43	64	52	60	61	68	49
69	66	35	34	52	49	47	28	38	57	42	38

■ **3-58** MacroSwift has decided to develop a new software program designed for CEOs and other high-level executives. MacroSwift did not want to develop a program that required too much hard-drive space, so they polled 36 executives to determine the amount of available space on their PCs. The results are given below in megabytes.

6.3	6.7	7.9	8.4	9.7	10.6	12.4	19.4	29.1	42.6
59.8	97.6	100.4	120.6	135.5	148.6	178.6	200.1	229.6	284.6
305.6	315.6	325.9	347.5	358.6	397.8	405.6	415.9	427.8	428.6
439.5	440.9	472.3	475.9	477.2	502.6				

Calculate the range and interquartile range.

■ **3-59** The New Mexico State Highway Department is charged with maintaining all state roads in good condition. One measure of condition is the number of cracks present in each 100 feet of roadway. From the department's yearly sample, the following data were obtained:

4	7	8	9	9	10	11	12	12	13
13	13	13	14	14	14	15	15	16	16
16	16	16	17	17	17	18	18	19	19

Calculate the interfractile ranges between the 20th, 40th, 60th, and 80th percentiles.

■ **3-60** Ted Nichol is a statistical analyst who reports directly to the highest levels of management at Research Incorporated. He helped design the company slogan: "If you can't find the answer, then RESEARCH!" Ted has just received some disturbing data: the monthly dollar volume of research contracts that the company has won for the past year. Ideally, these monthly numbers should be fairly stable because too much fluctuation in the amount of work to be done can result in an inordinate amount of hiring and firing of employees. Ted's data (in thousands of dollars) follow:

253	104	633	57	500	201
43	380	467	162	220	302

Calculate the following:

(a) The interfractile range between the second and eighth deciles.

(b) The median, Q_1, and Q_3.

(c) The interquartile range.

Worked-Out Answers to Self-Check Exercises

SC 3-11 First we arrange the data in increasing order:

59	65	67	68	71	72	75	79	81	83
85	87	88	91	92	93	94	95	100	100

The 16th of these (or 93) is the 80th percentile.

SC 3-12 Range = 20,300 − 3,600 = 16,700 miles
Interquartile range = $Q_3 - Q_1$ = 12,700 − 8,100 = 4,600 miles

3.9 Dispersion: Average Deviation Measures

Two measures of average deviation

The most comprehensive descriptions of dispersion are those that deal with the average deviation from some measure of central tendency. Two of these measures are important to our study of statistics: the *variance* and the *standard deviation.* Both of these tell us an average distance of any observation in the data set from the mean of the distribution.

Population Variance

Variance

Every population has a variance, which is symbolized by σ^2 (sigma squared). To calculate the population variance, we divide the sum of the squared distances between the mean and each item in the population by the total number of items in the population. By squaring each distance, we make each number positive and, at the same time, assign more weight to the larger deviations (deviation is the distance between the mean and a value).

Formula for the variance of a population

The formula for calculating the variance is

Population Variance

$$\sigma^2 = \frac{\Sigma(x - \mu)^2}{N} = \frac{\Sigma x^2}{N} - \mu^2 \quad [3\text{-}12]$$

where

- σ^2 = population variance
- x = item or observation
- μ = population mean
- N = total number of items in the population
- Σ = sum of all the values $(x - \mu)^2$, or all the values x^2

In Equation 3-12, the middle expression, $\frac{\Sigma(x-\mu)^2}{N}$, is the definition of σ^2. The last expression, $\frac{\Sigma x^2}{N} - \mu^2$, is *mathematically* equivalent to the definition but is often much more convenient to use if we must actually compute the value of σ^2, since it frees us from calculating the deviations from the mean. However, when the x values are large and the $x - \mu$ values are small, it may be more convenient to use the middle expression, $\frac{\Sigma(x-\mu)^2}{N}$, to compute σ^2. Before we can use this formula in an example, we need to discuss an important problem concerning the variance. In solving that problem, we will learn what the standard deviation is and how to calculate it. Then we can return to the variance itself.

Units in which the variance is expressed cause a problem

Earlier, when we calculated the range, the answers were expressed in the same units as the data. (In our examples, the units were "thousands of dollars of payments.") For the variance, however, the units are the *squares of the units* of the data—for example, "squared dollars" or "dollars squared." Squared dollars or dollars squared are not intuitively clear or easily interpreted. For this reason, we have to make a significant change in the variance to compute a useful measure of deviation, one that does not give us a problem with units of measure and thus is less confusing. **This measure is called the standard deviation, and it is the square root of the variance.** The square root of 100 dollars squared is 10 dollars because we take the square root of both the value and the units in which it is measured. The standard deviation, then, is in units that are the same as the original data.

Population Standard Deviation

Relationship of standard deviation to the variance

The population standard deviation, or σ, is simply the square root of the population variance. Because the variance is the average of the squared distances of the observations from the mean, **the standard deviation is the square root of the average of the squared distances of the observations from the mean.** While the variance is expressed in the square of the units used in the data, the standard deviation is in the same units as those used in the data. The formula for the standard deviation is

Population Standard Deviation

$$\sigma = \sqrt{\sigma^2} = \sqrt{\frac{\Sigma(x-\mu)^2}{N}} = \sqrt{\frac{\Sigma x^2}{N} - \mu^2} \qquad [3\text{-}13]$$

- x = observation
- μ = population mean
- N = total number of elements in the population
- Σ = sum of all the values $(x-\mu)^2$, or all the values x^2
- σ = population standard deviation
- σ^2 = population variance

Use the positive square root

The square root of a positive number may be either positive or negative because $a^2 = (-a)^2$. When taking the square root of the variance to calculate the standard deviation, however, statisticians consider only the positive square root.

Computing the standard deviation

To calculate either the variance or the standard deviation, we construct a table, using every element of the population. If we have a population of fifteen vials of compound produced in one day and we test each vial to determine its purity, our data might look like Table 3-18. In Table 3-19, we show how to use these data to compute the mean (0.166 = 2.49/15, the column (1) sum divided by N), the deviation of each value from the mean (column 3), the square of the deviation of each value from the mean (column 4), and the sum of the squared deviations. From this, we can compute the variance, which is 0.0034 percent squared. (Table 3-19 also computes σ^2 using the second half of Equation 3-12, $\frac{\Sigma x^2}{N} - \mu^2$. Note that we get the same result but do a bit less work, since we do not have to compute the deviations from the mean.) Taking the square root of σ^2, we can compute the standard deviation, 0.058 percent.

Table 3-18 Results of Purity Test on Compounds

Observed Percentage Impurity				
0.04	0.14	0.17	0.19	0.22
0.06	0.14	0.17	0.21	0.24
0.12	0.15	0.18	0.21	0.25

Table 3-19 Determination of the Variance and Standard Deviation of Percent Impurity of Compounds

Observation (x) (1)		Mean $\mu = 2.49/15$ (2)		Deviation $(x - \mu)$ (3) = (1) − (2)	Deviation Squared $(x - \mu)^2$ (4) = [(1) − (2)]^2	Observation Squared (x^2) (5) = (1)^2
0.04	−	0.166	=	−0.126	0.016	0.0016
0.06	−	0.166	=	−0.106	0.011	0.0036
0.12	−	0.166	=	−0.046	0.002	0.0144
0.14	−	0.166	=	−0.026	0.001	0.0196
0.14	−	0.166	=	−0.026	0.001	0.0196
0.15	−	0.166	=	−0.016	0.000	0.0225
0.17	−	0.166	=	0.004	0.000	0.0289
0.17	−	0.166	=	0.004	0.000	0.0289
0.18	−	0.166	=	0.014	0.000	0.0324
0.19	−	0.166	=	0.024	0.001	0.0361
0.21	−	0.166	=	0.044	0.002	0.0441
0.21	−	0.166	=	0.044	0.002	0.0441
0.22	−	0.166	=	0.054	0.003	0.0484
0.24	−	0.166	=	0.074	0.005	0.0576
0.25	−	0.166	=	0.084	0.007	0.0625
2.49 ← Σx					**0.051** ← $\Sigma(x - \mu)^2$	**0.4643** ← Σx^2

$$\sigma^2 = \frac{\Sigma(x - \mu)^2}{N} \quad [3\text{-}12] \qquad \leftarrow \text{OR} \rightarrow \qquad \sigma^2 = \frac{\Sigma x^2}{N} - \mu^2 \quad [3\text{-}12]$$

$$= \frac{0.051}{15} \qquad\qquad = \frac{0.4643}{15} - (0.166)^2$$

$$= 0.0034 \text{ percent squared} \qquad\qquad = 0.0034 \text{ percent squared}$$

$$\sigma = \sqrt{\sigma^2} \quad [3\text{-}13]$$

$$= \sqrt{.0034}$$

$$= 0.058 \text{ percent}$$

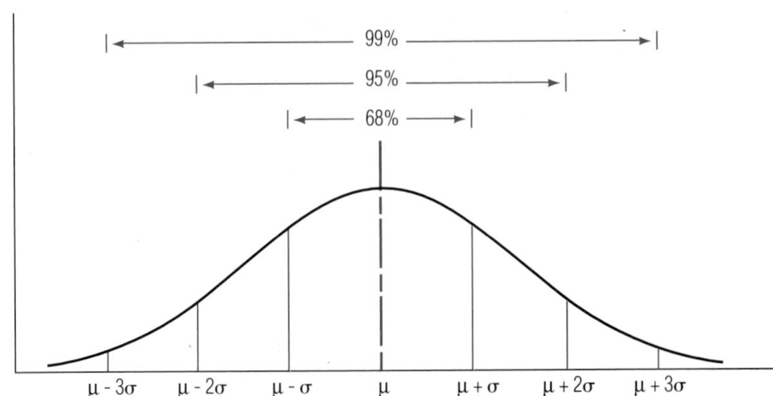

FIGURE 3-12

Location of observations around the mean of a bell-shaped frequency distribution

Uses of the Standard Deviation

Chebyshev's theorem

The standard deviation enables us to determine, with a great deal of accuracy, where the values of a frequency distribution are located in relation to the mean. We can do this according to a theorem devised by the Russian mathematician P. L. Chebyshev (1821–1894). Chebyshev's theorem says that no matter what the shape of the distribution, at least 75 percent of the values will fall within ± 2 standard deviations from the mean of the distribution, and at least 89 percent of the values will lie within ± 3 standard deviations from the mean.

We can measure with even more precision the percentage of items that fall within specific ranges under a symmetrical, bell-shaped curve such as the one in Figure 3-12. In these cases, we can say that:

1. About 68 percent of the values in the population will fall within ± 1 standard deviation from the mean.
2. About 95 percent of the values will lie within ± 2 standard deviations from the mean.
3. About 99 percent of the values will be in an interval ranging from 3 standard deviations below the mean to 3 standard deviations above the mean.

Using Chebyshev's theorem

In the light of Chebyshev's theorem, let's analyze the data in Table 3-19. There, the mean impurity of the 15 vials of compound is 0.166 percent, and the standard deviation is 0.058 percent. Chebyshev's theorem tells us that at least 75 percent of the values (at least 11 of our 15 items) are between $0.166 - 2(0.058) = 0.050$ and $0.166 + 2(0.058) = 0.282$. In fact, 93 percent of the values (14 of the 15 values) are actually in that interval. Notice that the distribution is reasonably symmetrical and that 93 percent is close to the theoretical 95 percent for an interval of plus and minus 2 standard deviations from the mean of a bell-shaped curve.

Concept of the standard score

The standard deviation is also useful in describing how far individual items in a distribution depart from the mean of the distribution. A measure called the *standard score* gives us the number of standard deviations a particular observation lies below or above the mean. If we let x symbolize the observation, the standard score computed from population data is

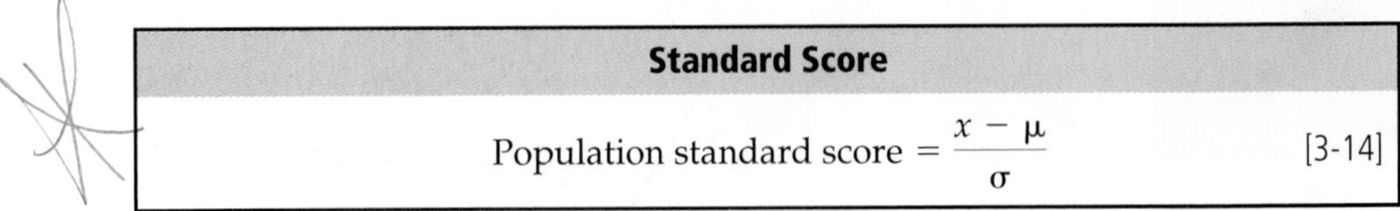

Standard Score

$$\text{Population standard score} = \frac{x - \mu}{\sigma} \qquad [3\text{-}14]$$

where

- x = observation from the population
- μ = population mean
- σ = population standard deviation

Suppose we observe a vial of compound that is 0.108 percent impure. Because our population has a mean of 0.166 and a standard deviation of 0.058, an observation of 0.108 would have a standard score of −1:

Calculating the standard score

$$\text{Standard score} = \frac{x - \mu}{\sigma} \quad [3\text{-}14]$$

$$= \frac{0.108 - 0.166}{0.058}$$

$$= -\frac{0.058}{0.058}$$

$$= -1$$

An observed impurity of 0.282 percent would have a standard score of +2:

$$\text{Standard score} = \frac{x - \mu}{\sigma} \quad [3\text{-}14]$$

$$= \frac{0.282 - 0.166}{0.058}$$

$$= \frac{0.116}{0.058}$$

$$= 2$$

Interpreting the standard score

The standard score indicates that an impurity of 0.282 percent deviates from the mean by 2(0.058) = 0.116 unit, which is equal to +2 in terms of the number of standard deviations away from the mean.

Calculation of Variance and Standard Deviation Using Grouped Data

Calculating the variance and standard deviation for grouped data

In our chapter-opening example, data on sales of 100 fast-food restaurants were already grouped in a frequency distribution. With such data, we can use the following formulas to calculate the variance and the standard deviation:

Variance of Grouped Data

$$\sigma^2 = \frac{\Sigma f(x - \mu)^2}{N} = \frac{\Sigma fx^2}{N} - \mu^2 \quad [3\text{-}15]$$

Standard Deviation of Grouped Data

$$\sigma = \sqrt{\sigma^2} = \sqrt{\frac{\Sigma f(x - \mu)^2}{N}} = \sqrt{\frac{\Sigma fx^2}{N} - \mu^2} \quad [3\text{-}16]$$

where

- σ^2 = population variance
- σ = population standard deviation
- f = frequency of each of the classes
- x = midpoint for each class
- μ = population mean
- N = size of the population

Table 3-20 shows how to apply these equations to find the variance and standard deviation of the sales of 100 fast-food restaurants.

We leave it as an exercise for the curious reader to verify that the second half of Equation 3-15, $\frac{\Sigma f x^2}{N} - \mu^2$, will yield the same value of σ^2.

Switching to sample variance and sample standard deviation

Now we are ready to compute the sample statistics that are analogous to the population variance σ^2 and the population standard deviation σ. These are the sample variance s^2 and the sample standard deviation s. In the next section, you'll notice we are changing from Greek letters (which denote population parameters) to the Roman letters of sample statistics.

Sample Standard Deviation

Computing the sample standard deviation

To compute the sample variance and the sample standard deviation, we use the same formulas as Equations 3-12 and 3-13, replacing μ with $\bar{x}$ and N with $n - 1$. The formulas look like this:

Sample Variance

$$s^2 = \frac{\Sigma(x - \bar{x})^2}{n - 1} = \frac{\Sigma x^2}{n - 1} - \frac{n\bar{x}^2}{n - 1} \quad [3\text{-}17]$$

Sample Standard Deviation

$$s = \sqrt{s^2} = \sqrt{\frac{\Sigma(x - \bar{x})^2}{n - 1}} = \sqrt{\frac{\Sigma x^2}{n - 1} - \frac{n\bar{x}^2}{n - 1}} \quad [3\text{-}18]$$

where

- s^2 = sample variance
- s = sample standard deviation
- x = value of each of the n observations
- $\bar{x}$ = mean of the sample
- $n - 1$ = number of observations in the sample minus 1

Use of $n - 1$ as the denominator

Why do we use $n - 1$ as the denominator instead of n? Statisticians can prove that if we take many samples from a given population, find the sample variance (s^2) for each sample, and average each of these together, then this average tends not to equal the population variance, σ^2, unless we use $n - 1$ as the denominator. In Chapter 7, we shall learn the statistical explanation of why this is true.

Table 3-20

Determination of the Variance and Standard Deviation of Sales of 100 Fast-Food Restaurants in the Eastern District (000s Omitted)

Class	Midpoint x (1)	Frequency f (2)	$f \times x$ (3) = (2) × (1)	Mean μ (4)	$x - \mu$ (1) − (4)	$(x-\mu)^2$ [(1) − (4)]²	$f(x-\mu)^2$ (2) × [(1) − (4)]²
700– 799	750	4	3,000	1,250	−500	250,000	1,000,000
800– 899	850	7	5,950	1,250	−400	160,000	1,120,000
900– 999	950	8	7,600	1,250	−300	90,000	720,000
1,000–1,099	1,050	10	10,500	1,250	−200	40,000	400,000
1,100–1,199	1,150	12	13,800	1,250	−100	10,000	120,000
1,200–1,299	1,250	17	21,250	1,250	0	0	0
1,300–1,399	1,350	13	17,550	1,250	100	10,000	130,000
1,400–1,499	1,450	10	14,500	1,250	200	40,000	400,000
1,500–1,599	1,550	9	13,950	1,250	300	90,000	810,000
1,600–1,699	1,650	7	11,550	1,250	400	160,000	1,120,000
1,700–1,799	1,750	2	3,500	1,250	500	250,000	500,000
1,800–1,899	1,850	1	1,850	1,250	600	360,000	360,000
		100	**125,000**				**6,680,000**

$$\bar{x} = \frac{\Sigma(f \times x)}{n} \qquad [3\text{-}3]$$

$$= \frac{125{,}000}{100}$$

$$= 1{,}250 \text{ (thousands of dollars)} \leftarrow \text{Mean}$$

$$\sigma^2 = \frac{\Sigma f(x-\mu)^2}{N} \qquad [3\text{-}15]$$

$$= \frac{6{,}680{,}000}{100}$$

$$= 66{,}800 \text{ (or 66,800 [thousands of dollars]}^2\text{)} \leftarrow \text{Variance}$$

$$\sigma = \sqrt{\sigma^2} \qquad [3\text{-}16]$$

$$= \sqrt{66{,}800}$$

$$= 258.5 \leftarrow \text{Standard deviation} = \$258{,}500$$

Table 3-21 Determination of the Sample Variance and Standard Deviation of Annual Blue Cross–Blue Shield Payments to Cumberland Hospital (000s Omitted)

Observation (x) (1)	Mean $(\bar{x})$ (2)	$x - \bar{x}$ (1) − (2)	$(x - \bar{x})^2$ [(1) − (2)]^2	x^2 (1)^2
863	1,351	−488	238,144	744,769
903	1,351	−448	200,704	815,409
957	1,351	−394	155,236	915,849
1,041	1,351	−310	96,100	1,083,681
1,138	1,351	−213	45,369	1,295,044
1,204	1,351	−147	21,609	1,449,616
1,354	1,351	3	9	1,833,316
1,624	1,351	273	74,529	2,637,376
1,698	1,351	347	120,409	2,883,204
1,745	1,351	394	155,236	3,045,025
1,802	1,351	451	203,401	3,247,204
1,883	1,351	532	283,024	3,545,689
			$\Sigma(x - \bar{x})^2 \rightarrow$ **1,593,770**	**23,496,182** $\leftarrow \Sigma x^2$

$$s^2 = \frac{\Sigma(x - \bar{x})^2}{n - 1} \qquad [3\text{-}17]$$

$$= \frac{1{,}593{,}770}{11}$$

$$= 144{,}888 \text{ (or 144,888 [thousands of dollars]}^2\text{)} \leftarrow \text{Sample variance}$$

$$s = \sqrt{s^2} \qquad [3\text{-}18]$$

$$= \sqrt{144{,}888}$$

$$= 380.64 \text{ (that is, \$380,640)} \leftarrow \text{Sample standard deviation}$$

OR

$$s^2 = \frac{\Sigma x^2}{n - 1} - \frac{n\bar{x}^2}{n - 1} \qquad [3\text{-}17]$$

$$= \frac{23{,}496{,}182}{11} - \frac{12(1{,}351)^2}{11}$$

$$= \frac{1{,}593{,}770}{11}$$

$$= 144{,}888$$

Calculating sample variance and standard deviation for hospital data

Equations 3-17 and 3-18 enable us to find the sample variance and the sample standard deviation of the annual Blue Cross–Blue Shield payments to Cumberland Hospital in Table 3-21; note that both halves of Equation 3-17 yield the same result.

Computing sample standard scores

Just as we used the population standard deviation to derive population standard scores, we may also use the sample deviation to compute sample standard scores. These sample standard scores tell us how many standard deviations a particular sample observation lies below or above the sample mean. The appropriate formula is

Standard Score of an Item in a Sample

$$\text{Sample standard score} = \frac{x - \bar{x}}{s} \qquad [3\text{-}19]$$

where

- x = observation from the sample
- $\bar{x}$ = sample mean
- s = sample standard deviation

In the example we just did, we see that the observation 863 corresponds to a standard score of −1.28:

$$\text{Sample standard score} = \frac{x - \bar{x}}{s} \tag{3-19}$$

$$= \frac{863 - 1{,}351}{380.64}$$

$$= \frac{-488}{380.64}$$

$$= -1.28$$

This section has demonstrated why the standard deviation is the measure of dispersion used most often. We can use it to compare distributions and to compute standard scores, an important element of statistical inference to be discussed later. Like the variance, the standard deviation takes into account every observation in the data set. But the standard deviation has some disadvantages, too. It is not as easy to calculate as the range, and it cannot be computed from open-ended distributions. In addition, extreme values in the data set distort the value of the standard deviation, although to a lesser extent than they do the range.

HINTS & ASSUMPTIONS

We assume when we calculate and use the standard deviation that there are not too many very large or very small values in the data set because we know that the standard deviation uses every value, and such extreme values will distort the answer. Hint: Forgetting whether to use N or $n - 1$ as the denominator for samples and populations can be avoided by associating the *smaller* value ($n - 1$) with the *smaller* set (the sample).

Exercises 3.9

Self-Check Exercises

SC 3-13 Talent, Ltd., a Hollywood casting company, is selecting a group of extras for a movie. The ages of the first 20 men to be interviewed are

50	56	55	49	52	57	56	57	56	59
54	55	61	60	51	59	62	52	54	49

The director of the movie wants men whose ages are fairly tightly grouped around 55 years. Being a statistics buff of sorts, the director suggests that a standard deviation of 3 years would be acceptable. Does this group of extras qualify?

SC 3-14 In an attempt to estimate potential future demand, the National Motor Company did a study asking married couples how many cars the average energy-minded family should own in 1998. For each couple, National averaged the husband's and wife's responses to get the overall couple response. The answers were then tabulated:

Number of cars	0	0.5	1.0	1.5	2.0	2.5
Frequency	2	14	23	7	4	2

(a) Calculate the variance and the standard deviation.

(b) Since the distribution is roughly bell-shaped, how many of the observations should theoretically fall between 0.5 and 1.5? Between 0 and 2? How many actually do fall in those intervals?

Applications

■ **3-61** The head chef of The Flying Taco has just received two dozen tomatoes from her supplier, but she isn't ready to accept them. She knows from the invoice that the average weight of a tomato is 7.5 ounces, but she insists that all be of uniform weight. She will accept them only if the average weight is 7.5 ounces and the standard deviation is less than 0.5 ounce. Here are the weights of the tomatoes:

6.3	7.2	7.3	8.1	7.8	6.8	7.5	7.8	7.2	7.5	8.1	8.2
8.0	7.4	7.6	7.7	7.6	7.4	7.5	8.4	7.4	7.6	6.2	7.4

What is the chef's decision and why?

■ **3-62** These data are a sample of the daily production rate of fiberglass boats from Hydrosport, Ltd., a Miami manufacturer:

17	21	18	27	17	21	20	22	18	23

The company production manager feels that a standard deviation of more than three boats a day indicates unacceptable production-rate variations. Should she be concerned about plant-production rates?

■ **3-63** A set of 60 observations has a mean of 66.8, a variance of 12.60, and an unknown distribution shape.

(a) Between what values should at least 75 percent of the observations fall, according to Chebyshev's theorem?

(b) If the distribution is symmetrical and bell-shaped, approximately how many observations should be found in the interval 59.7 to 73.9?

(c) Find the standard scores for the following observations from the distribution: 61.45, 75.37, 84.65, and 51.50.

■ **3-64** The number of checks cashed each day at the five branches of The Bank of Orange County during the past month had the following frequency distribution:

Class	Frequency
0–199	10
200–399	13
400–599	17
600–799	42
800–999	18

Hank Spivey, director of operations for the bank, knows that a standard deviation in check cashing of more than 200 checks per day creates staffing and organizational problems at the branches because of the uneven workload. Should Hank worry about staffing next month?

■ **3-65** The Federal Reserve Board has given permission to all member banks to raise interest rates $^1/_2$ percent for all depositors. Old rates for passbook savings were $5^1/_4$ percent; for certificates of deposit (CDs): 1-year CD, $7^1/_2$ percent; 18-month CD, $8^3/_4$ percent; 2-year CD, $9^1/_2$ percent; 3-year CD, $10^1/_2$ percent; and 5-year CD, 11 percent. The president of the First State Bank wants to know what the characteristics of the new distribution of rates will be if a full $^1/_2$ percent is added to all rates. How are the new characteristics related to the old ones?

■ **3-66** The administrator of a Georgia hospital surveyed the number of days 200 randomly chosen patients stayed in the hospital following an operation. The data are:

Hospital stay in days	1–3	4–6	7–9	10–12	13–15	16–18	19–21	22–24
Frequency	18	90	44	21	9	9	4	5

(a) Calculate the standard deviation and mean.

(b) According to Chebyshev's theorem, how many stays should be between 0 and 17 days? How many are actually in that interval?

(c) Because the distribution is roughly bell-shaped, how many stays can we expect between 0 and 17 days?

■ **3-67** FundInfo provides information to its subscribers to enable them to evaluate the performance of mutual funds they are considering as potential investment vehicles. A recent survey of funds whose stated investment goal was growth and income produced the following data on total annual rate of return over the past five years:

Annual return (%)	11.0–11.9	12.0–12.9	13.0–13.9	14.0–14.9	15.0–15.9	16.0–16.9	17.0–17.9	18.0–18.9
Frequency	2	2	8	10	11	8	3	1

(a) Calculate the mean, variance, and standard deviation of the annual rate of return for this sample of 45 funds.

(b) According to Chebyshev's theorem, between what values should at least 75 percent of the sample observations fall? What percentage of the observations actually do fall in that interval?

(c) Because the distribution is roughly bell-shaped, between what values would you expect to find 68 percent of the observations? What percentage of the observations actually do fall in that interval?

■ **3-68** Nell Berman, owner of the Earthbred Bakery, said that the average weekly production level of her company was 11,398 loaves, and the variance was 49,729. If the data used to compute the results were collected for 32 weeks, during how many weeks was the production level below 11,175? Above 11,844?

■ **3-69** The Creative Illusion Advertising Company has three offices in three cities. Wage rates differ from state to state. In the Washington, D.C. office, the average wage increase for the past year was \$1,500, and the standard deviation was \$400. In the New York office, the average raise was \$3,760, and the standard deviation was \$622. In Durham, N.C., the average increase was \$850, and the standard deviation was \$95. Three employees were interviewed. The Washington employee received a raise of \$1,100; the New York employee, a raise of \$3,200; and the Durham employee, a raise of \$500.

Which of the three had the smallest raise in relation to the mean and standard deviation of his office?

■ **3-70** American Foods heavily markets three different products nationally. One of the underlying objectives of each of the product's advertisements is to make consumers recognize that American Foods makes the product. To measure how well each ad implants recognition, a group of consumers was asked to identify as quickly as possible the company responsible for a long list of products. The first American Foods product had an average latency of 2.5 seconds, and a standard deviation of 0.004 second. The second had an average latency of 2.8 seconds, and a standard deviation of 0.006 second. The third had an average latency of 3.7 seconds, and a standard deviation of 0.09 second. One particular subject had the following latencies: 2.495 for the first, 2.79 for the second, and 3.90 for the third. For which product was this subject farthest from average performance, in standard deviation units?

■ **3-71** Sid Levinson is a doctor who specializes in the knowledge and effective use of pain-killing drugs for the seriously ill. In order to know approximately how many nurses and office personnel to employ, he has begun to keep track of the number of patients he sees each week. Each week his office manager records the number of seriously ill patients and the number of routine patients. Sid has reason to believe that the number of routine patients per week would look like a bell-shaped curve if he had enough data. (This is not true of seriously ill patients.) However, he has been collecting data for only the past five weeks.

Seriously ill patients	33	50	22	27	48
Routine patients	34	31	37	36	27

(a) Calculate the mean and variance for the number of seriously ill patients per week. Use Chebyshev's theorem to find boundaries within which the "middle 75 percent" of numbers of seriously ill patients per week should fall.

(b) Calculate the mean, variance, and standard deviation for the number of routine patients per week. Within what boundaries should the "middle 68 percent" of these weekly numbers fall?

■ **3-72** The superintendent of any local school district has two major problems: A tough job dealing with the elected school board is the first, and the second is the need to be always prepared to look for a new job because of the first problem. Tom Langley, superintendent of School District 18, is no exception. He has learned the value of understanding all numbers in any budget and being able to use them to his advantage. This year, the school board has proposed a media research budget of \$350,000. From past experience, Tom knows that actual spending always exceeds the budget proposal, and the amount by which it exceeds the proposal has a mean of \$40,000 and variance of 100,000,000 dollars squared. Tom learned about Chebyshev's theorem in college, and he thinks that this might be useful in finding a range of values within which the actual expenditure would fall 75 percent of the time in years when the budget proposal is the same as this year. Do Tom a favor and find this range.

■ **3-73** Bea Reele, a well-known clinical psychologist, keeps very accurate data on all her patients. From these data, she has developed four categories within which to place all her patients: child, young adult, adult, and elderly. For each category, she has computed the mean IQ and the variance of IQs within that category. These numbers are given in the following table. If on a certain day Bea saw four patients (one from each category), and the IQs of those patients were as follows: child, 90; young adult, 92; adult, 100; elderly, 98; then which of the patients had the IQ farthest above the mean, in standard deviation units, for that particular category?

Category	Mean IQ	IQ Variance
Child	110	81
Young adult	90	64
Adult	95	49
Elderly	90	121

Worked-Out Answers to Self-Check Exercises

SC 3-13

x	$x - \bar{x}$	$(x - \bar{x})^2$	x	$x - \bar{x}$	$(x - \bar{x})^2$
50	−5.2	27.04	54	−1.2	1.44
56	0.8	0.64	55	−0.2	0.04
55	−0.2	0.04	61	5.8	33.64
49	−6.2	38.44	60	4.8	23.04
52	−3.2	10.24	51	−4.2	17.64
57	1.8	3.24	59	3.8	14.44
56	0.8	0.64	62	6.8	46.24
57	1.8	3.24	52	−3.2	10.24
56	0.8	0.64	54	−1.2	1.44
59	3.8	14.44	49	−6.2	38.44
			1,104		**285.20**

$$\bar{x} = \frac{\Sigma x}{n} = \frac{1{,}104}{20} = 55.2 \text{ years, which is close to the desired 55 years}$$

$$s = \sqrt{\frac{\Sigma(x - \bar{x})^2}{n - 1}} = \sqrt{\frac{285.20}{19}} = 3.874 \text{ years, which shows more variability than desired}$$

SC 3-14 (a)

# of cars x	Frequency f	$f \times x$	$x - \bar{x}$	$(x - \bar{x})^2$	$f(x - \bar{x})^2$
0	2	0	−1.0288	1.0585	2.1170
0.5	14	7	−0.5288	0.2797	3.9155
1	23	23	−0.0288	0.0008	0.0191
1.5	7	10.5	0.4712	0.2220	1.5539
2	4	8	0.9712	0.9431	3.7726
2.5	2	5	1.4712	2.1643	4.3286
	52	**53.5**			**15.7067**

$$\bar{x} = \frac{\Sigma x}{n} = \frac{53.5}{52} = 1.0288 \text{ cars}$$

$$s^2 = \frac{\Sigma f(x - \bar{x})^2}{n - 1} = \frac{15.707}{51} = 0.3080 \quad \text{so} \quad s = \sqrt{0.3080} = 0.55 \text{ car}$$

(b) (0.5, 1.5) is approximately $\bar{x} \pm s$, so about 68 percent of the data, or 0.68(52) = 35.36 observations should fall in this range. In fact, 44 observations fall into this interval.

(0, 2) is approximately $\bar{x} \pm 2s$, so about 95 percent of the data, or 0.95(52) = 49.4 observations should fall in this range. In fact, 50 observations fall into this interval.

3.10 Relative Dispersion: The Coefficient of Variation

The standard deviation is an *absolute* measure of dispersion that expresses variation in the same units as the original data. The annual Blue Cross–Blue Shield payments to Cumberland Hospital (Table 3-21) have a standard deviation of $380,640. The annual Blue Cross–Blue Shield payments to Valley Falls Hospital (Table 3-16) have a standard deviation (which you can compute) of $57,390. Can we compare the values of these two standard deviations? Unfortunately, no.

Shortcomings of the standard deviation

The standard deviation cannot be the sole basis for comparing two distributions. If we have a standard deviation of 10 and a mean of 5, the values vary by an amount twice as large as the mean itself. On the other hand, if we have a standard deviation of 10 and a mean of 5,000, the variation relative to the mean is insignificant. Therefore, we cannot know the dispersion of a set of data until we know the standard deviation, the mean, *and* how the standard deviation compares with the mean.

The coefficient of variation, a relative measure

What we need is a *relative* measure that will give us a feel for the magnitude of the deviation relative to the magnitude of the mean. The *coefficient of variation* is one such relative measure of dispersion. It relates the standard deviation and the mean by expressing the standard deviation as a percentage of the mean. The unit of measure, then, is "percent" rather than the same units as the original data. For a population, the formula for the coefficient of variation is

Coefficient of Variation

Standard deviation of the population

$$\text{Population coefficient of variation} = \frac{\sigma}{\mu}(100) \qquad [3\text{-}20]$$

Mean of the population

Using this formula in an example, we may suppose that each day, laboratory technician A completes on average 40 analyses with a standard deviation of 5. Technician B completes on average 160 analyses per day with a standard deviation of 15. Which employee shows less variability?

At first glance, it appears that technician B has three times more variation in the output rate than technician A. But B completes analyses at a rate four times faster than A. Taking all this information into account, we can compute the coefficient of variation for both technicians:

Computing the coefficient of variation

$$\text{Coefficient of variation} = \frac{\sigma}{\mu}(100) \qquad [3\text{-}20]$$

$$= \frac{5}{40}(100)$$

$$= 12.5\% \leftarrow \text{For technician A}$$

and

$$\text{Coefficient of variation} = \frac{15}{160}(100)$$

$$= 9.4\% \leftarrow \text{For technician B}$$

So we find that technician B, who has more *absolute* variation in output than technician A, has less *relative* variation because the mean output for B is much greater than for A.

Using the computer to compute measures of central tendency and variability

For large data sets, we use the computer to calculate our measures of central tendency and variability. In Figure 3-13, we have used Minitab to compute some of these summary statistics for the grade data in Appendix 10. The statistics are shown for each section as well as for the course as a whole. In Figure 3-14, we have used Minitab to calculate several measures of central tendency and variability for the earnings data in Appendix 11. The statistics are given for all 224 companies together, and they are also broken down by stock exchange (1 = OTC, 2 = ASE, 3 = NYSE). The statistic TRMEAN is a "trimmed mean," a mean calculated with the top 5 percent and bottom 5 percent of the data omitted. This helps to alleviate the distortion caused by the extreme values from which the ordinary arithmetic mean suffers.

HINTS & ASSUMPTIONS

The concept and usefulness of the coefficient of variation are quickly evident if you try to compare overweight men with overweight women. Suppose a group of men and women are all 20 pounds overweight. The 20 pounds is not a good measure of the excessive weight. Average weight for men is about 160 pounds, and average weight for women is about 120 pounds. Using a simple ratio, we can see that the women are 20/120, or about 16.7 percent overweight but the men are 20/160, or about 12.5 percent overweight. Although the coefficient of variation is a bit more complex than our simple ratio example, the concept is the same: We use it to compare the amount of variation in data groups that have different means. Warning: Don't compare the dispersion in data sets by using their standard deviations unless their means are close to each other.

Exercises 3.10

Self-Check Exercises

SC 3-15 Bassart Electronics is considering employing one of two training programs. Two groups were trained for the same task. Group 1 was trained by program A; group 2, by program B. For the first group, the times required to train the employees had an average of 32.11 hours and a variance of 68.09. In the second group, the average was 19.75 hours and the variance was 71.14. Which training program has less relative variability in its performance?

SC 3-16 Southeastern Stereos, a wholesaler, was contemplating becoming the supplier to three retailers, but inventory shortages have forced Southeastern to select only one. Southeastern's credit manager is evaluating the credit record of these three retailers. Over the past 5 years, these retailers' accounts receivable have been outstanding for the following average number of days (see page 130). The credit manager feels that consistency, in addition to lowest average, is important. Based on relative dispersion, which retailer would make the best customer?

Descriptive Statistics

Variable	SECTION	N	Mean	Median	TrMean	StDev	SEMean	Min	Max	Q1	Q3
EXAM1		199	50.22	50.00	50.26	9.49	0.67	21.00	73.00	44.00	57.00
	1	27	47.15	47.00	47.32	10.86	2.09	21.00	69.00	40.00	55.00
	2	46	50.83	50.50	50.83	10.61	1.56	30.00	73.00	43.00	58.25
	3	37	53.19	55.00	53.39	8.98	1.48	35.00	68.00	47.50	60.00
	4	26	50.77	51.50	50.87	8.75	1.72	31.00	68.00	44.75	57.00
	5	36	49.47	48.50	49.16	8.16	1.36	35.00	72.00	44.00	54.75
	6	27	48.67	50.00	48.56	8.44	1.62	34.00	66.00	41.00	54.00
EXAM2		199	56.89	59.00	57.71	10.71	0.76	16.00	73.00	51.00	65.00
	1	27	53.30	56.00	54.20	13.59	2.61	16.00	68.00	49.00	63.00
	2	46	58.26	59.00	59.00	10.84	1.60	24.00	73.00	53.75	67.50
	3	37	60.51	62.00	60.76	7.60	1.25	44.00	72.00	55.00	66.00
	4	26	59.38	59.00	59.46	6.44	1.26	45.00	72.00	55.50	64.25
	5	36	55.94	57.00	56.69	11.44	1.91	25.00	72.00	48.50	65.00
	6	27	52.07	54.00	52.44	11.09	2.13	30.00	65.00	41.00	62.00
HOMEWORK		199	108.60	113.00	110.28	19.01	1.35	13.00	135.00	101.00	121.00
	1	27	109.07	112.00	111.16	20.51	3.95	32.00	134.00	106.00	121.00
	2	46	112.52	116.50	113.90	17.64	2.60	56.00	135.00	107.00	124.00
	3	37	111.78	114.00	113.73	16.80	2.76	35.00	131.00	106.50	122.00
	4	26	104.58	108.00	105.42	15.04	2.95	62.00	127.00	99.00	115.00
	5	36	107.36	114.00	110.19	24.34	4.06	13.00	133.00	98.25	124.00
	6	27	102.59	105.00	102.76	17.03	3.28	74.00	127.00	85.00	120.00
FINAL		199	45.28	45.00	45.53	10.01	0.71	13.00	74.00	39.00	52.00
	1	27	45.74	45.00	46.28	10.68	2.06	14.00	64.00	41.00	53.00
	2	46	44.76	44.00	44.98	11.90	1.75	13.00	74.00	37.75	52.25
	3	37	49.08	49.00	49.27	7.37	1.21	34.00	63.00	43.00	55.00
	4	26	44.92	45.00	44.96	8.06	1.58	29.00	60.00	37.75	51.25
	5	36	44.33	44.00	44.22	10.37	1.73	25.00	65.00	36.00	50.75
	6	27	42.11	44.00	42.60	9.44	1.82	17.00	55.00	38.00	50.00
TOTAL		199	68.57	69.51	68.95	11.24	0.80	22.01	98.11	62.69	75.97
	1	27	67.10	67.00	68.11	13.62	2.62	22.00	87.05	62.87	76.08
	2	46	69.39	71.30	69.62	12.50	1.84	37.79	98.11	63.91	76.41
	3	37	72.82	73.18	73.08	8.86	1.46	53.38	88.21	68.96	80.44
	4	26	68.60	69.38	68.90	8.08	1.59	49.05	81.06	65.50	73.59
	5	36	67.43	65.51	67.67	11.82	1.97	40.91	92.34	60.19	76.23
	6	27	64.30	64.90	64.49	9.85	1.90	43.89	79.85	58.59	75.12

FIGURE 3-13 Output from Minitab showing summary statistics for course grade data

Descriptive Statistics

Variable	MARKET	N	Mean	Median	TrMean	StDev	SEMean	Min	Max	Q1	Q3
LQ89		224	0.2105	0.1300	0.2139	0.8316	0.0556	-5.4500	5.2300	-0.0075	0.4400
	1	111	0.0766	0.1100	0.1070	0.5110	0.0485	-3.7500	1.2200	-0.0200	0.2600
	2	38	0.199	0.045	0.083	0.837	0.136	-0.560	4.740	-0.085	0.292
	3	75	0.415	0.440	0.459	1.130	0.130	-5.450	5.230	0.070	0.810

FIGURE 3-14 Output from Minitab showing summary statistics for earnings data

Lee	62.2	61.8	63.4	63.0	61.7
Forrest	62.5	61.9	62.8	63.0	60.7
Davis	62.0	61.9	63.0	63.9	61.5

Applications

■ **3-74** The weights of the Baltimore Bullets professional football team have a mean of 224 pounds with a standard deviation of 18 pounds, while the mean weight and standard deviation of their Sunday opponent, the Chicago Trailblazers, are 195 and 12, respectively. Which team exhibits the greater relative dispersion in weights?

■ **3-75** The university has decided to test three new kinds of lightbulbs. They have three identical rooms to use in the experiment. Bulb 1 has an average lifetime of 1,470 hours and a variance of 156. Bulb 2 has an average lifetime of 1,400 hours and a variance of 81. Bulb 3 has an average lifetime of 1,350 hours and a standard deviation of 6 hours. Rank the bulbs in terms of relative variability. Which was the best bulb?

■ **3-76** Students' ages in the regular daytime M.B.A. program and the evening program of Central University are described by these two samples:

Regular M.B.A.	23	29	27	22	24	21	25	26	27	24
Evening M.B.A.	27	34	30	29	28	30	34	35	28	29

If homogeneity of the class is a positive factor in learning, use a measure of relative variability to suggest which of the two groups will be easier to teach.

■ **3-77** There are a number of possible measures of sales performance, including how consistent a salesperson is in meeting established sales goals. The data that follow represent the percentage of goal met by each of three salespeople over the last 5 years.

Patricia	88	68	89	92	103
John	76	88	90	86	79
Frank	104	88	118	88	123

(a) Which salesperson is the most consistent?

(b) Comment on the adequacy of using a measure of consistency along with percentage of sales goal met to evaluate sales performance.

(c) Can you suggest a more appropriate alternative measure of consistency?

■ **3-78** The board of directors of Gothic Products is considering acquiring one of two companies and is closely examining the management of each company in regard to their inclinations toward risk. During the past five years, the first company's returns on investments had an average of 28.0 percent and a standard deviation of 5.3 percent. The second company's returns on investments had an average of 37.8 percent and a standard deviation of 4.8 percent. If we consider risk to be associated with greater relative dispersion, which of these two companies has pursued a riskier strategy?

■ **3-79** A drug company that supplies hospitals with premeasured doses of certain medications uses different machines for medications requiring different dosage amounts. One machine, designed to produce doses of 100 cc, has as its mean dose 100 cc, and a standard deviation of 5.2 cc. Another machine produces premeasured amounts of 180 cc of medication and has a standard deviation of 8.6 cc. Which machine has the lower accuracy from the standpoint of relative dispersion?

■ **3-80** HumanPower, the temporary employment agency, has tested many people's data entry skills. Infotech needs a data entry person, and the person needs to be not only quick but also consistent. HumanPower pulls the speed records for 4 employees with the data given below in terms of number of correct entries per minute. Which employee is best for Infotech based on relative dispersion?

John	63	66	68	62	69	72
Jeff	68	67	66	67	69	
Mary	62	79	75	59	72	84
Tammy	64	68	58	57	59	

■ **3-81** Wyatt Seed Company sells three grades of Early White Sugar corn seed, distinguished according to the consistency of germination of the seeds. The state seed testing laboratory has a sample of each grade of seed and its test results on the number of seeds that germinated out of packages of 100 are as follows:

Grade I (Regular)	88	91	92	89	79
Grade II (Extra)	87	92	88	90	92
Grade III (Super)	90	89	79	93	88

Does Wyatt's grading of its seeds make sense?

■ **3-82** Sunray Appliance Company has just completed a study of three possible assembly-line configurations for producing its best-selling two-slice toaster. Configuration I has yielded a mean time to construct a toaster of 34.8 minutes, and a standard deviation of 4.8 minutes. Configuration II has yielded a mean of 25.5 minutes, and a standard deviation of 7.5 minutes. Configuration III has yielded a mean of 37.5 minutes, and a standard deviation of 3.8 minutes. Which assembly-line configuration has the least relative variation in the time it takes to construct a toaster?

Worked-Out Answers to Self-Check Exercises

SC 3-15 Program A: $\text{CV} = \dfrac{\sigma}{\mu}(100) = \dfrac{\sqrt{68.09}(100)}{32.11} = 25.7$ percent

Program B: $\text{CV} = \dfrac{\sigma}{\mu}(100) = \dfrac{\sqrt{71.14}(100)}{19.75} = 42.7$ percent

Program A has less relative variability.

SC 3-16 Lee: $\bar{x} = 62.42$ $s = 0.7497$ $\text{CV} = (s/\bar{x})(100) = \dfrac{0.7497(100)}{62.42} = 1.20$ percent

Forrest: $\bar{x} = 62.18$ $s = 0.9257$ $\text{CV} = (s/\bar{x})(100) = \dfrac{0.9257(100)}{62.18} = 1.49$ percent

Davis: $\bar{x} = 62.46$ $s = 0.9762$ $\text{CV} = (s/\bar{x})(100) = \dfrac{0.9762(100)}{62.46} = 1.56$ percent

Based on relative dispersion, Lee would be the best customer, but there really isn't much difference among the three of them.

3.11 Exploratory Data Analysis (EDA)

The techniques in this section allow us to look at a lot of data and summarize it quickly using nothing more difficult than basic arithmetic and a few simple diagrams.

In one sense, that's exactly what we've been doing in Chapters 2 and 3, but in each situation where we constructed frequency distributions and histograms, we lost some information when we did this. Look at the frequency distribution in Table 3-22 of midterm test grades. It's impossible to tell from the frequency distribution how the grades from 70–79 were distributed unless you look at the original data set.

One of the most useful techniques of exploratory data analysis, *stem and leaf displays,* gets around this problem very effectively. It gives us the *rank order* of the items in the data set *and* the shape of the distribution.

To produce a stem and leaf display for the data in Table 3-22, we make a vertical list of the *stems* (the first digits of each data item) like this:

4
5
6
7
8
9
10

Then we draw a vertical line to the right of these stems, and list the *leaves* (the next digit for all the stems) to the right of the line in the order that we encountered them in the original data set.

4	8							
5	7	1	0					
6	7	6	6	3	1			
7	9	8	8	6	3	2	2	1
8	7	5	4	4	2	9		
9	9	4	3					
10	0							

Table 3-22

Grades on Midterm Quiz with Frequency Distribution

79	78	78	67	76	87	85	73	66
99	84	72	66	57	94	84	72	63
51	48	50	61	71	82	93	100	89

	Frequency
40–49	1
50–59	3
60–69	5
70–79	8
80–89	6
90–99	3
>99	1

Finally, we arrange all of the leaves in each row in rank order.

4	8
5	0 1 7
6	1 3 6 6 7
7	1 2 2 3 6 8 8 9
8	2 4 4 5 7 9
9	3 4 9
10	0

Each row in the resulting stem and leaf display is a stem and each data value on that stem is a leaf. If we pick the row **9** | 3 4 9, it means there are three items in the data set that begin with nine (93, 94, and 99).

Finally, if we turn the page 90 degrees counterclockwise and draw rectangles around the data in each stem, we get something that resembles our histograms of Chapter 2.

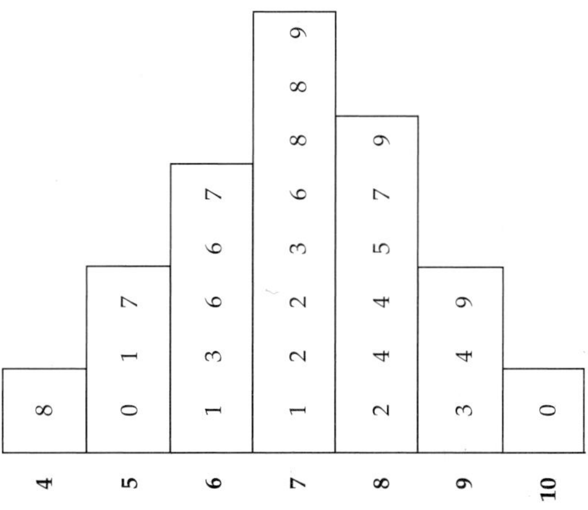

Alternatives for doing exploratory analysis

Most widely used computer packages for doing statistical analysis have the ability to do exploratory data analysis (EDA). Figure 3-15 gives the output when the SAS package is used to do an elementary exploratory analysis of the carpet-loom data from Chapter 2. We will briefly glance at this output; if you wish to learn more about EDA, the bibliography at the end of the book gives several references.

The first section of the output (headed "moments") gives the mean, standard deviation, and numerical measures of the skewness and kurtosis of the data. As we have already seen in Chapters 2 and 3, these quantities tell us about the *shape* of the data.

Quartiles, ranges, and percentiles

The next section of output (headed "quantiles") gives the quartiles and various ranges as well as several percentiles that delineate the upper (99 percent, 95 percent, 90 percent) and lower (10 percent, 5 percent, 1 percent) tails of the data. Thus, EDA not only identifies the center of the data; it also calls our attention to the noncentral, atypical values in the data. Often, closer examination of these outliers will show that they really don't belong in the data set. (Perhaps they were incorrectly recorded.) We've already seen how such outliers distort sample means.

Graphical plots of the data

SAS then gives several different plots of the data. As we have just seen, stem and leaf displays are like histograms, but they simultaneously display all the data values while grouping them. Thus, they have the histogram's advantage of summarizing the data without having its disadvantage of losing detail. Boxplots give a graphical representation of the median (the middle horizontal line in Figure 3-15), the quartiles (the top and bottom

```
ILLUSTRATING THE USE OF SAS FOR EXPLORATORY DATA ANALYSIS
                        UNIVARIATE
VARIABLE = YDS        LOOM OUTPUT IN YARDS
                          MOMENTS

          N                 30        SUM WGTS            30
          MEAN         16.0367        SUM              481.1
          STD DEV     0.411459        VARIANCE      0.169299
          SKEWNESS    0.345475        KURTOSIS      -0.10233
          USS          7720.15        CSS            4.90967
          CV           2.56574        STD MEAN     0.0751219
          T:MEAN=0     213.475        PROB>|T|        0.0001
          SGN RANK       232.5        PROB>|S|        0.0001
          NUM ~=0           30
          W:NORMAL    0.969853        PROB<W           0.571

                       QUANTILES (DEF=4)

           100% MAX       16.9            99%       16.9
            75% Q3        16.3            95%     16.845
            50% MED         16            90%      16.78
            25% Q1      15.775            10%       15.6
             0% MIN       15.2             5%      15.31
                                           1%       15.2
           RANGE           1.7
           Q3-Q1      0.524988
           MODE           15.9

                            EXTREMES

                        LOWEST         HIGHEST
                          15.2            16.4
                          15.4            16.6
                          15.6            16.8
                          15.6            16.8
                          15.6            16.9

          STEM LEAF                   #              BOXPLOT

           168 000                    3                 |
           166 0                      1                 |
           164 00                     2                 |
           162 00000                  5              +-----+
           160 00000                  5              *--+--*
           158 0000000                7              |     |
           156 00000                  5              +-----+
           154 0                      1                 |
           152 0                      1                 |
           150
               ----+----+----+----+
           MULTIPLY STEM.LEAF BY 10**-01
```

FIGURE 3-15

An exploratory analysis of the carpet-loom data from Chapter 2 using the SAS computer package

horizontal lines of the box in Figure 3-15), and the extremes (the "whiskers" extending from the box). You might want to think of a boxplot as a skeletal frequency distribution.

Figures 3-16 and 3-17 show some of the EDA that can be done with Minitab. In Figure 3-16, we have used Minitab to do a stem and leaf plot of the earnings data in Appendix 11.

Figure 3-17 shows boxplots of the earnings data as a whole and broken down by stock exchange. Once again, EDA calls our attention to the outliers, the observations far from the center of the distribution. In the boxplots, these outlying observations are denoted by O's. Closer examination of the data set shows that for the two most extreme outliers, the companies discontinued some of their operations, in one case (Airgas, Inc.) receiving a large sum for the sale of those discontinued operations, and in the other (Monarch Capital Corp.) incurring a large cost for shutting down the discontinued operations. Because of these extraordinary factors, these two data points should probably be excluded from further analyses of the data set.

```
Character Stem-and-Leaf Display

Stem-and-leaf of LQ89      N  = 224
Leaf Unit = 0.10

    1   -5 4
    1   -4
    3   -3 76
    3   -2
    4   -1 6
   57   -0 87665555543332222222221111111111110000000000000000000
(150)    0 0000000000000000000000000000000000000011111111111111111111111111+
   17    1 00111111223349
    3    2 3
    2    3
    2    4 7
    1    5 2
```

FIGURE 3-16 Minitab stem and leaf plot of 1989 last-quarter earnings

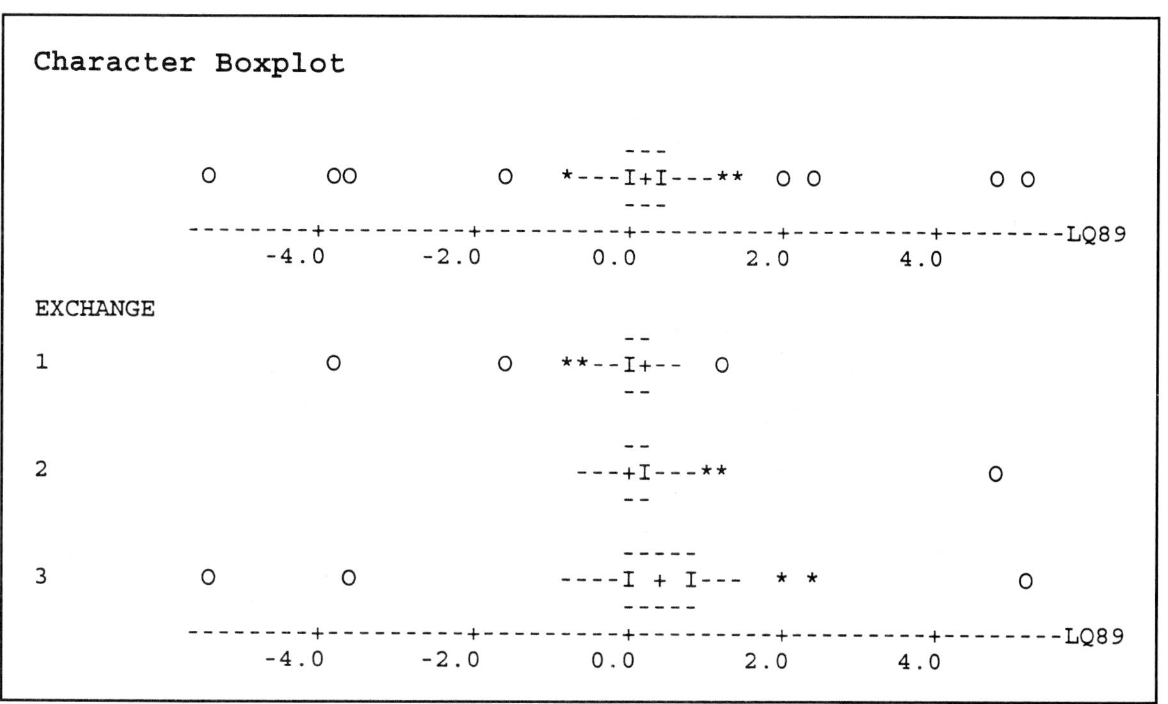

FIGURE 3-17 Minitab boxplots of the earnings data

Statistics at Work

Loveland Computers

Case 3: Central Tendency and Dispersion "Not bad for a few days' work, Lee," Uncle Walter congratulated his new assistant as he flipped through 12 pages of tables, charts, and graphs. Monday morning had come all too soon for Lee.

"Well, Nunc," replied Lee, with a familiarity possible only in a family firm, "it took a few all-nighters. But I've set things up so that we won't have to go through this kind of agony in the future. I've archived all the old data on diskettes in a common format, and I've kept the last 3 years on the hard drive. More important, I've set up some common reporting formats for each product line so the data will be collected in a consistent manner from here on out. And with the 3D spreadsheet, I can easily sum them together and give you data by month or by quarter." Warming to his audience, Lee flipped to the last page and showed a simple pie chart. "Here's the beauty of this business: You can show those New Yorkers that your average gross margin (you know, revenue minus your cost of goods sold) is 28 percent. That should impress them."

"Well maybe yes and maybe no," commented Gratia Delaguardia, Walter Azko's partner, who had just walked in. If Walter was known for his charm and his "street smarts," Gratia certainly earned the title of "the brains" of this outfit. "You're probably mixing up apples and oranges there. Some of the low-speed PCs don't have that large a gross margin any more. The profit is a little thin, but at least it's predictable. With the new technologies, we make a huge margin on our 'hit' products, but there are others where we had to cut prices to get rid of them. You'll remember our first 'portable' that weighed more than 50 pounds, Walt."

"I try to forget that one," responded the CEO tersely. "But, Lee, Gratia has a point. Don't you think you ought to break out new products—say, products within their first 6 months on sale—versus the established lines. See if the gross margins look different and whether they're all over the place like Gratia says. I'm off to the airport to pick up the investment folks. See what you can whip up by the time I get back."

***Study Questions*:** The spreadsheet program Lee is using has many built-in statistical functions. Which ones should Lee use to answer the questions about gross margins? How might the data be presented, and how will this help the new investors in their decision making? What limitations are there on assuming a bell-shaped distribution for "percentage" data?

Computer Database Exercise

HH Industries

From what Laurel could see, the trends identified in the histograms she had prepared earlier reflected several possibilities:

1. The numbers of customers buying from HH Industries are increasing, and their initial purchases are relatively small. With proper "nurturing," these customers should buy increasingly larger quantities as their confidence in the company's quality and service grows.
2. HH Industries' established customers are recognizing the expense of maintaining large inventories. Consequently, their orders will be more frequent and for smaller amounts than before.
3. Large construction or waste-management firms that have traditionally maintained their own fleets of equipment may be tending more toward contracting for repairs with smaller service shops.

In addition, there might be a seasonal trend present, which would make sense because adverse winter weather might cause construction slowdowns. (This concept will be addressed in a later chapter.)

Stan Hutchings, VP of Sales, verified that these trends were all very real possibilities. "In fact," he acknowledged, "we can probably target some promotions to take advantage of this information. But even with the decreasing dollars-per-order figures, I'm pretty sure total sales are continuing to increase; at least that's what the 'daily figure' seems to indicate. After all, that's what really matters—the total sales!"

Back in her office, Laurel contemplated Stan's "total sales" philosophy. True, the company's total sales were important, but she knew that each profit center played a key role in the overall health of the corporation. She needed to know if all three locations were pulling their own weight. In addition, Laurel was curious as to whether the trends she had identified were reflected in each profit center, or whether the majority of sales being at the Florida headquarters obscured any important information from the Arizona and Pennsylvania warehouses.

1. Calculate the mean, median, and mode for the quarterly data on the number of orders and average order size from Chapter 2. Do these numbers support Laurel's intuitive findings from the histograms? Which measure of central tendency seems most appropriate in this situation? Now calculate the company's total sales dollars for the last four quarters. Is Stan correct in his assumption that the total sales are doing well?
2. Calculate the mean number of daily orders and order size for Profit Center 3 (Pennsylvania) over the last four quarters. Does this warehouse exhibit trends similar to those of the entire company? Is Laurel's planned investigation of the performance of each profit center a good idea?

Laurel caught Hal in his office late Thursday afternoon and gave him a brief outline of her findings.

"This is all quite interesting," Hal responded. "I'd like to get opinions from the staff at Monday's meeting. Think you can have a short presentation worked up? It'd need to be heavy on the conclusions and light on the statistics for this crew!"

"Sure thing," Laurel agreed. "I still want to do some variability testing, then I'll be ready to put the whole picture together. See you back here on Monday."

3. Determine the interquartile ranges of the average order size in each quarter. Compare these to the total range in each case.
4. Using the raw data, calculate the quarterly sample variance and standard deviation values for both the number of orders and the average order size. Compute the coefficient of variation for each quarter.
5. (a) Using Chebyshev's theorem, determine the range of daily number of orders and average order size for the second quarter of 1992 that will include at least 75 percent of the data.

   (b) Examine the histograms plotted for Chapter 2 and compare them to the Chebyshev ranges calculated above. How precise is Chebyshev's theorem in establishing the range in each case?
6. Looking at each warehouse separately, calculate the coefficient of variation for both the number of orders and the average order size for the entire 12-month period. Are there significant differences between the relative dispersions experienced at each profit center?
7. How would you present your findings to the staff? What recommendations could you make about promotions, future data collection, etc.?

Chapter Review

● Terms Introduced in Chapter 3

Bimodal Distribution A distribution of data points in which two values occur more frequently than the rest of the values in the data set.

Boxplot A graphical EDA technique used to highlight the center and extremes of a data set.

Chebyshev's Theorem No matter what the shape of a distribution, at least 75 percent of the values in the population will fall within 2 standard deviations of the mean and at least 89 percent will fall within 3 standard deviations.

Coding A method of calculating the mean for grouped data by recoding values of class midpoints to more simple values.

Coefficient of Variation A relative measure of dispersion, comparable across distributions, that expresses the standard deviation as a percentage of the mean.

Deciles Fractiles that divide the data into 10 equal parts.

Dispersion The spread or variability in a set of data.

Distance Measure A measure of dispersion in terms of the difference between two values in the data set.

Exploratory Data Analysis (EDA) Methods for analyzing data that require very few prior assumptions.

Fractile In a frequency distribution, the location of a value at or above a given fraction of the data.

Geometric Mean A measure of central tendency used to measure the average rate of change or growth for some quantity, computed by taking the nth root of the product of n values representing change.

Interfractile Range A measure of the spread between two fractiles in a distribution, that is, the difference between the values of two fractiles.

Interquartile Range The difference between the values of the first and the third quartiles; this difference indicates the range of the middle half of the data set.

Kurtosis The degree of peakedness of a distribution of points.

Mean A central tendency measure representing the arithmetic average of a set of observations.

Measure of Central Tendency A measure indicating the value to be expected of a typical or middle data point.

Measure of Dispersion A measure describing how the observations in a data set are scattered or spread out.

Median The middle point of a data set, a measure of location that divides the data set into halves.

Median Class The class in a frequency distribution that contains the median value for a data set.

Mode The value most often repeated in the data set. It is represented by the highest point in the distribution curve of a data set.

Parameters Numerical values that describe the characteristics of a whole population, commonly represented by Greek letters.

Percentiles Fractiles that divide the data into 100 equal parts.

Quartiles Fractiles that divide the data into four equal parts.

Range The distance between the highest and lowest values in a data set.

Skewness The extent to which a distribution of data points is concentrated at one end or the other; the lack of symmetry.

Standard Deviation The positive square root of the variance; a measure of dispersion in the same units as the original data, rather than in the squared units of the variance.

Standard Score Expressing an observation in terms of standard deviation units above or below the mean; that is, the transformation of an observation by subtracting the mean and dividing by the standard deviation.

Statistics Numerical measures describing the characteristics of a sample. Represented by Roman letters.

Stem and Leaf Display A histogram-like display used in EDA to group data, while still displaying all the original values.

Summary Statistics Single numbers that describe certain characteristics of a data set.

Symmetrical A characteristic of a distribution in which each half is the mirror image of the other half.

Variance A measure of the average squared distance between the mean and each item in the population.

Weighted Mean An average calculated to take into account the importance of each value to the overall total, that is, an average in which each observation value is weighted by some index of its importance.

● Equations Introduced in Chapter 3

■ **3-1**

$$\mu = \frac{\Sigma x}{N}$$

p. 74

The *population arithmetic mean* is equal to the sum of the values of all the elements in the population (Σx) divided by the number of elements in the population (N).

■ 3-2
$$\bar{x} = \frac{\Sigma x}{n}$$
p. 74

To calculate the *sample arithmetic mean,* sum the values of all the elements in the sample (Σx) and divide by the number of elements in the sample (n).

■ 3-3
$$\bar{x} = \frac{\Sigma(f \times x)}{n}$$
p. 75

To find the *sample arithmetic mean of grouped data,* calculate the midpoints (x) for each class in the sample. Then multiply each midpoint by the frequency (f) of observations in the class, sum (Σ) all these results, and divide by the total number of observations in the sample (n).

■ 3-4
$$\bar{x} = x_0 + w\frac{\Sigma(u \times f)}{n}$$
p. 77

This formula enables us to calculate the *sample arithmetic mean of grouped data* using codes to eliminate dealing with large or inconvenient midpoints. Assign these codes (u) as follows: Give the value of zero to the middle midpoint (called x_0), positive consecutive integers to midpoints larger than x_0, and negative consecutive integers to smaller midpoints. Then, multiply the code assigned to each class (u) by the frequency (f) of observations in the class and sum (Σ) all these products. Divide this result by the total number of observations in the sample (n), multiply by the numerical width of the class interval (w), and add the value of the midpoint assigned the code zero (x_0).

■ 3-5
$$\bar{x}_w = \frac{\Sigma(w \times x)}{\Sigma w}$$
p. 84

The *weighted mean,* $\bar{x}_w$, is an average that takes into account how important each value is to the overall total. We can calculate this average by multiplying the weight, or proportion, of each element (w) by that element (x), summing the results (Σ), and dividing this amount by the sum of all the weights (Σw).

■ 3-6
$$\text{G.M.} = \sqrt[n]{\text{product of all } x \text{ values}}$$
p. 88

The *geometric mean,* or G.M., is appropriate to use whenever we need to measure the average rate of change (the growth rate) over a period of time. In this equation, n is equal to the number of x values dealt with in the problem.

■ 3-7
$$\text{Median} = \left(\frac{n+1}{2}\right)\text{th item in a data array}$$
where n = number of items in the data array
p. 91

The *median* is a single value that measures the central item in the data set. Half the items lie above the median, half below it. If the data set contains an odd number of items, the middle item of the array is the median. For an even number of items, the median is the average of the two middle items. Use this formula when the data are ungrouped.

■ **3-8** $$\tilde{m} = \left(\frac{(n + 1)/2 - (F + 1)}{f_m}\right)w + L_m$$ p. 94

This formula enables us to find the *sample median of grouped data.* In it, n equals the total number of items in the distribution; F equals the sum of all the class frequencies up to, but not including, the median class; f_m is the frequency of observations in the median class; w is the class-interval width; and L_m is the lower limit of the median class interval.

■ **3-9** $$Mo = L_{Mo} + \left(\frac{d_1}{d_1 + d_2}\right)w$$ p. 99

The *mode* is that value most often repeated in the data set. To find the *mode of grouped data* (symbolized *Mo*), use this formula and let L_{Mo} = lower limit of the modal class; d_1 = frequency of the modal class minus the frequency of the class directly below it; d_2 = frequency of the modal class minus the frequency of the class directly above it; and w = width of the modal class interval.

■ **3-10** $$\text{Range} = \begin{matrix}\text{value of highest} \\ \text{observation}\end{matrix} - \begin{matrix}\text{value of lowest} \\ \text{observation}\end{matrix}$$ p. 108

The *range* is the difference between the highest and lowest values in a frequency distribution.

■ **3-11** $$\text{Interquartile range} = Q_3 - Q_1$$ p. 110

The *interquartile range* measures approximately how far from the median we must go on either side before we can include one-half the values of the data set. To compute this range, divide the data into four equal parts. The *quartiles* (Q) are the highest values in each of these four parts. The *interquartile range* is the difference between the values of the first and third quartiles (Q_1 and Q_3).

■ **3-12** $$\sigma^2 = \frac{\Sigma(x - \mu)^2}{N} = \frac{\Sigma x^2}{N} - \mu^2$$ p. 113

This formula enables us to calculate the *population variance,* a measure of the average *squared* distance between the mean and each item in the population. The middle expression, $\frac{\Sigma(x - \mu)^2}{N}$, is the definition of σ^2. The last expression, $\frac{\Sigma x^2}{N} - \mu^2$, is mathematically equivalent to the definition but is often much more convenient to use because it frees us from calculating the deviations from the mean.

■ **3-13** $$\sigma = \sqrt{\sigma^2} = \sqrt{\frac{\Sigma(x - \mu)^2}{N}} = \sqrt{\frac{\Sigma x^2}{N} - \mu^2}$$ p. 114

The population standard deviation, σ, is the square root of the population variance. It is a more useful parameter than the variance because it is expressed in the same units as the data (whereas the units of the variance are the squares of the units of the data). The standard deviation is always the *positive* square root of the variance.

■ **3-14** $$\text{Population standard score} = \frac{x - \mu}{\sigma}$$ p. 116

The *standard score* of an observation is the number of standard deviations the observation lies below or above the mean of the distribution. The standard score enables us to make comparisons between distribution items that differ in order of magnitude or in the units used. Use Equation 3-14 to find the standard score of an item in a *population.*

■ **3-15** $$\sigma^2 = \frac{\Sigma f(x - \mu)^2}{N} = \frac{\Sigma fx^2}{N} - \mu^2$$ p. 117

This formula in either form enables us to calculate the *variance of data already grouped* in a frequency distribution. Here, f represents the frequency of the class and x represents the midpoint.

■ **3-16** $$\sigma = \sqrt{\sigma^2} = \sqrt{\frac{\Sigma f(x - \mu)^2}{N}} = \sqrt{\frac{\Sigma fx^2}{N} - \mu^2}$$ p. 117

Take the square root of the variance and you have the *standard deviation using grouped data.*

■ **3-17** $$s^2 = \frac{\Sigma(x - \bar{x})^2}{n - 1} = \frac{\Sigma x^2}{n - 1} - \frac{n\bar{x}^2}{n - 1}$$ p. 118

To compute the *sample variance,* use the same formula as Equation 3-12, replacing μ with $\bar{x}$ and N with $n - 1$. Chapter 7 contains an explanation of why we use $n - 1$ rather than n to calculate the sample variance.

■ **3-18** $$s = \sqrt{s^2} = \sqrt{\frac{\Sigma(x - \bar{x})^2}{n - 1}} = \sqrt{\frac{\Sigma x^2}{n - 1} - \frac{n\bar{x}^2}{n - 1}}$$ p. 118

The *sample standard deviation* is the square root of the sample variance. It is similar to Equation 3-13, except that μ is replaced by the sample mean $\bar{x}$ and N is changed to $n - 1$.

■ **3-19** $$\text{Sample standard score} = \frac{x - \bar{x}}{s}$$ p. 120

Use this equation to find the standard score of an item in a *sample.*

■ **3-20** $$\text{Population coefficient of variation} = \frac{\sigma}{\mu}(100)$$ p. 126

The *coefficient of variation* is a relative measure of dispersion that enables us to compare two distributions. It relates the standard deviation and the mean by expressing the standard deviation as a percentage of the mean.

Review and Application Exercises

■ **3-83** The weights and measures department of a state agriculture department measured the amount of granola sold in 4-ounce packets and recorded the following data:

4.01	4.00	4.02	4.02	4.03	4.00	3.98	3.99	3.99	4.01
3.99	3.98	3.97	4.00	4.02	4.01	4.02	4.00	4.01	3.99

If the sample is typical of all granola snacks marketed by this manufacturer, what is the range of weights in 95 percent of the packages?

■ **3-84** How would you react to this statement from a football fan: "The Rockland Raiders average 3.6 yards a carry in their ground game. Since they need only 10 yards for a first down, and they have four plays to get it, they can't miss if they just stick to their ground game."

■ **3-85** How would you reply to the following statement: "Variability is not an important factor because even though the outcome is more uncertain, you still have an equal chance of falling either above or below the median. Therefore, on average, the outcome will be the same."

■ **3-86** Following are three general sections of one year's defense budget, each of which was allocated the same amount of funding by Congress:

(a) Officer salaries (total).

(b) Aircraft maintenance.

(c) Food purchases (total).

Considering the distribution of possible outcomes for the funds actually spent in each of these areas, match each section to one of the curves in Figure 3-9. Support your answers.

■ **3-87** Ed's Sports Equipment Company stocks two grades of fishing line. Data on each line are

	Mean Test Strength (lb)	Standard Deviation
Master	40	Exact value unknown, but estimated to be quite large
Super	30	Exact value unknown, but estimated to be quite small

If you are going fishing for bluefish, which have been averaging 25 pounds this season, with which line would you probably land more fish?

■ **3-88** The VP of sales for Vanguard Products has been studying records regarding the performances of his sales reps. He has noticed that in the last 2 years, the average level of sales per sales rep has remained the same, while the distribution of the sales levels has widened. Salespeople's sales levels from this period have significantly larger variations from the mean than in any of the previous 2-year periods for which he has records. What conclusions might be drawn from these observations?

■ **3-89** New cars sold in December at eight Ford dealers within 50 miles of Canton, Ohio, can be described by this data set:

200	156	231	222	96	289	126	308

(a) Compute the range, interquartile range, and standard deviation of these data.

(b) Which of the three measures you have computed in part (a) best describes the variability of these data?

■ **3-90** Two economists are studying fluctuations in the price of gold. One is examining the period of 1968–1972. The other is examining the period of 1975–1979. What differences would you expect to find in the variability of their data?

■ **3-91** The Downhill Ski Boot Company runs two assembly lines in its plant. The production manager is interested in improving the consistency of the line with the greater variation. Line number 1 has a monthly average of 11,350 units, and a standard deviation of 1,050. Line number 2 has a monthly average of 9,935, and a standard deviation of 1,010. Which line has the greater relative dispersion?

■ **3-92** On June 30, 1992, the capitalizations of nine Asian/Pacific stock markets were:

Country	Capitalization (Billions of U.S. $)
Philippines	17
Indonesia	21
Thailand	44
Singapore	50
Malaysia	79
South Korea	86
Taiwan	140
Hong Kong	178
Australia	203

Source: "Asian/Pacific Stock Markets," The Chicago Tribune *(14 December 1992): sec. 4, p. 3.*

(a) Find the arithmetic mean of the data.

(b) Find the median of the data.

(c) Find the mode of the data.

(d) Which is the best measure of the central tendency of the data?

(e) Find the standard deviation of the data. (The entire population is included in the data.)

■ **3-93** The Fish and Game station on Lake Wylie keeps records of fish caught on the lake and reports its finding to the National Fish and Game Service. The catch in pounds for the last 20 days was:

101	132	145	144	130	88	156	188	169	130
90	140	130	139	99	100	208	192	165	216

Calculate the range, variance, and standard deviation for these data. In this instance, is the range a good measure of the variability? Why?

■ **3-94** The owner of Records Anonymous, a large record retailer, uses two different formulas for predicting monthly sales. The first formula has an average miss of 700 records, and a standard deviation of 35 records. The second formula has an average miss of 300 records, and a standard deviation of 16. Which formula is relatively less accurate?

■ **3-95** Using the following population data, calculate the interquartile range, variance, and standard deviation. What do your answers tell you about the cost behavior of heating fuel?

■ **3-103** Larsen (see Exercise 3-102) has just gotten the following additional information:

Equipment Group	Pieces of Machinery	Equipment Group	Pieces of Machinery
1	1	8	5
2	3	9	8
3	1	10	2
4	4	11	2
5	2	12	6
6	1	13	1
7	1	14	1

(a) What is the average downtime per piece of machinery?
(b) What is the average downtime per piece of machinery for each group when classified by group?
(c) How many groups had a higher-than-average downtime per piece of machinery?

■ **3-104** Compare and contrast the central position and skewness of the distributions of the readership volume in numbers of readers per issue for all nationally distributed
(a) Monthly magazines.
(b) Weekly news magazines.
(c) Monthly medical journals.

■ **3-105** Compare and contrast the central tendency and skewness of the distributions of the amount of taxes paid (in dollars) for all
(a) Individuals filing federal returns in the United States, where the top tax bracket is 28 percent.
(b) Individuals paying state income taxes in North Carolina, where the top tax bracket is 7 percent.
(c) Individuals paying airport taxes (contained in the price of the airplane ticket) at JFK International Airport in New York City.

■ **3-106** Allison Barrett does statistical analyses for an automobile racing team. Here are the fuel consumption figures in miles per gallon for the team's cars in recent races:

4.77	6.11	6.11	5.05	5.99	4.91	5.27	6.01
5.75	4.89	6.05	5.22	6.02	5.24	6.11	5.02

(a) Calculate the median fuel consumption.
(b) Calculate the mean fuel consumption.
(c) Group the data into five equally sized classes. What is the fuel consumption value of the modal class?
(d) Which of the three measures of central tendency is best for Allison to use when she orders fuel? Explain.

■ **3-107** Claire Chavez, an Internal Revenue Service analyst, has been asked to describe the "average" American taxpayer in terms of gross annual income. She has summary data grouping taxpayers into different income classes. Which measure of central tendency should she use?

■ **3-108** Emmot Bulb Co. sells a grab bag of flower bulbs. The bags are sold by weight; thus, the number of bulbs in each can vary depending on the varieties included. The number of bulbs in each of 20 bags sampled were:

21	33	37	56	47
36	23	26	33	37
25	33	32	47	34
26	37	37	43	45

(a) What are the mean and median number of bulbs per bag?

(b) Based on your answer, what can you conclude about the shape of the distribution of number of bulbs per bag?

■ **3-109** An engineer tested nine samples of each of three designs of a certain bearing for a new electrical winch. The following data are the number of hours it took for each bearing to fail when the winch motor was run continuously at maximum output, with a load on the winch equivalent to 1.9 times the intended capacity.

Design		
A	B	C
16	18	31
16	27	16
53	23	42
15	21	20
31	22	18
17	26	17
14	39	16
30	17	15
20	28	19

(a) Calculate the mean and median for each group.

(b) Based on your answer, which design is best and why?

■ **3-110** Table Spice Co. is installing a screener in one stage of its new processing plant to separate leaves, dirt, and insect parts from a certain expensive spice seed that it receives in bulk from growers. The firm can use a coarse 3.5-millimeter mesh screen or a finer 3-millimeter mesh. The smaller mesh will remove more debris but also will remove more seeds. The larger mesh will pass debris and remove fewer seeds. Table Spice has the following information from a sample of pieces of debris.

Debris Size (in millimeters)	Frequency
1.0 or less	12
1.01–1.5	129
1.51–2.0	186
2.01–2.5	275
2.51–3.0	341
3.01–3.5	422
3.51–4.0	6,287
4.01–4.5	8,163
4.51–5.0	6,212
5.01–5.5	2,416
more than 5.5	1,019

chapter 4

PROBABILITY I: INTRODUCTORY IDEAS

Objectives

- To examine the use of probability theory in decision making
- To explain the different ways probabilities arise
- To develop rules for calculating different kinds of probabilities
- To use probabilities to take new information into account: the definition and use of Bayes' theorem

Chapter Contents

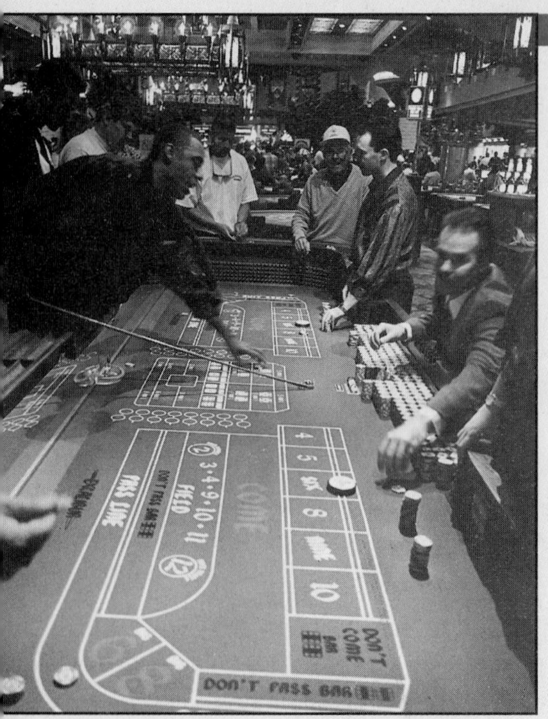

Gamblers have used odds to make bets during most of recorded history. But it wasn't until the seventeenth century that French nobleman Antoine Gombauld (1607–1684) sought a mathematical basis for success at the dice tables. He asked French mathematician Blaise Pascal (1623–1662), "What are the odds of rolling two sixes at least once in twenty-four rolls of a pair of dice?" Pascal solved the problem, having become as interested in the idea of probabilities as was Gombauld. They shared their ideas with the famous mathematician Pierre de Fermat (1601–1665), and the letters written by these three constitute the first academic journal in probability theory. We have no record of the degree of success enjoyed by these gentlemen at the dice tables, but we do know that their curiosity and research introduced many of the concepts we shall study in this chapter and the next. ■

4.1 Probability: The Study of Odds and Ends

Early probability theorists

Jacob Bernoulli (1654–1705), Abraham de Moivre (1667–1754), the Reverend Thomas Bayes (1702–1761), and Joseph Lagrange (1736–1813) developed probability formulas and techniques. In the nineteenth century, Pierre Simon, Marquis de Laplace (1749–1827), unified all these early ideas and compiled the first general theory of probability.

Need for probability theory

Probability theory was successfully applied at the gambling tables and, more relevant to our study, eventually to social and economic problems. The insurance industry, which emerged in the nineteenth century, required precise knowledge about the risk of loss in order to calculate premiums. Within 50 years, many learning centers were studying probability as a tool for understanding social phenomena. Today, the mathematical theory of probability is the basis for statistical applications in both social and decision-making research.

Examples of the use of probability theory

Probability is a part of our everyday lives. In personal and managerial decisions, we face uncertainty and use probability theory whether or not we admit the use of something so sophisticated. When we hear a weather forecast of a 70 percent chance of rain, we change our plans from a picnic to a pool game. Playing bridge, we make some probability estimate before attempting a finesse. Managers who deal with inventories of highly styled women's clothing must wonder about the chances that sales will reach or exceed a certain level, and the buyer who stocks up on skateboards considers the probability of the life of this particular fad. Before Muhammad Ali's highly publicized fight with Leon Spinks, Ali was reputed to have said, "I'll give you **odds** I'm still the greatest when it's over." And when you begin to study for the inevitable quiz attached to the use of this book, you may ask yourself, "What are the chances the professor will ask us to recall something about the history of probability theory?"

We live in a world in which we are unable to forecast the future with complete certainty. Our need to cope with uncertainty leads us to the study and use of probability theory. In many instances, we, as concerned citizens, will have some knowledge about the possible outcomes of a decision. By organizing this information and considering it systematically, we will be able to recognize our assumptions, communicate our reasoning to others, and make a sounder decision than we could by using a shot-in-the-dark approach.

Exercises 4.1

Applications

- ■ **4-1** The insurance industry uses probability theory to calculate premium rates, but life insurers know for certain that every policyholder is going to die. Does this mean that probability theory does not apply to the life insurance business? Explain.
- ■ **4-2** "Use of this product may be hazardous to your health. This product contains saccharin, which has been determined to cause cancer in laboratory animals." How might probability theory have played a part in this statement?
- ■ **4-3** Is there really any such thing as an "uncalculated risk"? Explain.
- ■ **4-4** A well-known soft drink company decides to alter the formula of its oldest and most popular product. How might probability theory be involved in such a decision?

4.2 Basic Terminology in Probability

In general, probability is the chance something will happen. Probabilities are expressed as fractions ($^1/_6$, $^1/_2$, $^8/_9$) or as decimals (0.167, 0.500, 0.889) between zero and 1. Assigning a probability of zero means that something can never happen; a probability of 1 indicates that something will always happen.

An event

In probability theory, an *event* is one or more of the possible outcomes of doing something. If we toss a coin, getting a tail would be an *event,* and getting a head would be another event. Similarly, if we are drawing from a deck of cards, selecting the ace of spades would be an event. An example of an event closer to your life, perhaps, is being picked from a class of 100 students to answer a question. When we hear the frightening predictions of highway traffic deaths, we hope not to be one of those events.

An experiment

The activity that produces such an event is referred to in probability theory as an *experiment.* Using this formal language, we could ask the question, "In a coin-toss *experiment,* what is the probability of the event *head*?" And, of course, if it is a fair coin with an equal chance of coming down on either side (and no chance of landing on its edge), we would answer "$^1/_2$" or "0.5." The set of all possible outcomes of an experiment is called the *sample space* for the experiment. In the coin-toss experiment, the sample space is

$$S = \{\text{head, tail}\}$$

In the card-drawing experiment, the sample space has 52 members: ace of hearts, deuce of hearts, and so on.

Most of us are less excited about coins or cards than we are interested in questions such as "What are the chances of making that plane connection?" or "What are my chances of getting a second job interview?" In short, we are concerned with the chances that an event will happen.

Mutually exclusive events

Events are said to be *mutually exclusive* if one and only one of them can take place at a time. Consider again our example of the coin. We have two possible outcomes, heads and tails. On any toss, either heads or tails may turn up, but not both. As a result, the events heads and tails on a single toss are said to be mutually exclusive. Similarly, you will either pass or fail this course or, before the course is over, you may drop it without a grade. Only one of those three outcomes can happen; they are said to be mutually exclusive events. The crucial question to ask in deciding whether events are really mutually exclusive is, "Can two or more of these events occur at one time?" If the answer is yes, the events are *not* mutually exclusive.

A collectively exhaustive list

When a list of the possible events that can result from an experiment includes every possible outcome, the list is said to be *collectively exhaustive.* In our coin example, the list "head and tail" is collectively exhaustive (unless, of course, the coin stands on its edge when we toss it). In a presidential campaign, the list of outcomes "Democratic candidate and Republican candidate" is *not* a collectively exhaustive list of outcomes, because an independent candidate or the candidate of another party could conceivably win.

Exercises 4.2

Self-Check Exercises

SC 4-1 Give a collectively exhaustive list of the possible outcomes of tossing two dice.

SC 4-2 Give the probability for each of the following totals in the rolling of two dice: 1, 2, 5, 6, 7, 10, and 11.

Basic Concepts

■ **4-5** Which of the following are pairs of mutually exclusive events in the drawing of one card from a standard deck of 52?

(a) A heart and a queen.
(b) A club and a red card.
(c) An even number and a spade.
(d) An ace and an even number.

Which of the following are mutually exclusive outcomes in the rolling of two dice?

(a) A total of 5 points and a 5 on one die.
(b) A total of 7 points and an even number of points on both dice.
(c) A total of 8 points and an odd number of points on both dice.
(d) A total of 9 points and a 2 on one die.
(e) A total of 10 points and a 4 on one die.

■ **4-6** A batter "takes" (does not swing at) each of the pitches he sees. Give the sample space of outcomes for the following experiments in terms of balls and strikes:

(a) Two pitches.
(b) Three pitches.

Applications

■ **4-7** Consider a stack of nine cards, all spades, numbered 2 through 10, and a die. Give a collectively exhaustive list of the possible outcomes of rolling the die and picking one card. How many elements are there in the sample space?

■ **4-8** Consider the stack of cards and the die discussed in Exercise 4-7. Give the probability for each of the following totals in the sum of the roll of the die and the value of the card drawn:

2 3 8 9 12 14 16

■ **4-9** In a recent meeting of union members supporting Joe Royal for union president, Royal's leading supporter said "chances are good" that Royal will defeat the single opponent facing him in the election.

(a) What are the "events" that could take place with regard to the election?

(b) Is your list collectively exhaustive? Are the events in your list mutually exclusive?

(c) Disregarding the supporter's comments and knowing no additional information, what probabilities would you assign to each of your events?

■ **4-10** Southern Bell is considering the distribution of funds for a campaign to increase long-distance calls within North Carolina. The following table lists the markets that the company considers worthy of focused promotions:

Market Segment	Cost of Special Campaign Aimed at Group
Minorities	$350,000
Businesspeople	$550,000
Women	$250,000
Professionals and white-collar workers	$200,000
Blue-collar workers	$250,000

There is up to $800,000 available for these special campaigns.

(a) Are the market segments listed in the table collectively exhaustive? Are they mutually exclusive?

(b) Make a collectively exhaustive and mutually exclusive list of the possible events of the spending decision.

(c) Suppose the company has decided to spend the entire $800,000 on special campaigns. Does this change your answer to part (b)? If so, what is your new answer?

Worked-Out Answers to Self-Check Exercises

SC 4-1 **(Die 1, Die 2)**

(1,1)	(1,2)	(1,3)	(1,4)	(1,5)	(1,6)
(2,1)	(2,2)	(2,3)	(2,4)	(2,5)	(2,6)
(3,1)	(3,2)	(3,3)	(3,4)	(3,5)	(3,6)
(4,1)	(4,2)	(4,3)	(4,4)	(4,5)	(4,6)
(5,1)	(5,2)	(5,3)	(5,4)	(5,5)	(5,6)
(6,1)	(6,2)	(6,3)	(6,4)	(6,5)	(6,6)

SC 4-2 $P(1) = 0/36$, $P(2) = 1/36$, $P(5) = 4/36$, $P(6) = 5/36$, $P(7) = 6/36$, $P(10) = 3/36$, $P(11) = 2/36$.

4.3 Three Types of Probability

There are three basic ways of classifying probability. These three represent rather different conceptual approaches to the study of probability theory; in fact, experts disagree about which approach is the proper one to use. Let us begin by defining the

1. Classical approach
2. Relative frequency approach
3. Subjective approach

Classical Probability

Classical probability defined

Classical probability defines the probability that an event will occur as

Probability of an Event

$$\text{Probability of an event} = \frac{\text{number of outcomes where the event occurs}}{\text{total number of possible outcomes}} \quad [4\text{-}1]$$

It must be emphasized that in order for Equation 4-1 to be valid, each of the possible outcomes must be equally likely. This is a rather complex way of defining something that may seem intuitively obvious to us, but we can use it to write our coin-toss and dice-rolling examples in symbolic form. First, we would state the question, "What is the probability of getting a head on one toss?" as

$$P(\text{Head})$$

Then, using formal terms, we get

$$P(\text{Head}) = \frac{1}{1+1}$$

Number of outcomes of one toss where the event occurs (in this case, the number that will produce a head)

Total number of possible outcomes of one toss (a head or a tail)

$$= 0.5 \text{ } or \text{ } \frac{1}{2}$$

And for the dice-rolling example:

Number of outcomes of one roll of the die that will produce a 5

$$P(5) = \frac{1}{1+1+1+1+1+1}$$

Total number of possible outcomes of one roll of the die (getting a 1, a 2, a 3, a 4, a 5, or a 6)

$$= \frac{1}{6}$$

A priori probability

Classical probability is often called *a priori* probability because if we keep using orderly examples such as fair coins, unbiased dice, and standard decks of cards, we can state the answer in advance (a priori) *without* tossing a coin, rolling a die, or drawing a card. We do not have to perform experiments to make our probability statements about fair coins, standard card decks, and unbiased dice. Instead, we can make statements based on logical reasoning before any experiments take place.

Shortcomings of the classical approach

This approach to probability is useful when we deal with card games, dice games, coin tosses, and the like, but has serious problems when we try to apply it to the less orderly decision problems we encounter in management. The classical approach to probability assumes a world that does not exist. It assumes away situations that are very unlikely but that could conceivably happen. Such occurrences as a coin landing on its edge, your classroom burning down during a discussion of probabilities, and your eating pizza while on a business trip at the North Pole are all extremely unlikely but not impossible. Nevertheless, the classical approach assumes them all away. Classical probability also assumes a kind of symmetry about the world, and that assumption can get us into trouble. Real-life situations, disorderly and unlikely as they often are, make it useful to define probabilities in other ways.

Relative Frequency of Occurrence

Suppose we begin asking ourselves complex questions such as, "What is the probability that I will live to be 85?" or "What are the chances that I will blow one of my stereo speakers if I turn my 200-watt amplifier up to wide open?" or "What is the probability that the location of a new paper plant on the river near our town will cause a substantial fish kill?" We quickly see that we may not be able to state in advance, without experimentation, what these probabilities are. Other approaches may be more useful.

Probability redefined

In the 1800s, British statisticians, interested in a theoretical foundation for calculating risk of losses in life insurance and commercial insurance, began defining probabilities from statistical data collected on births and deaths. Today, this approach is called the *relative frequency of occurrence*. It defines probability as either:

1. The observed relative frequency of an event in a very large number of trials, or
2. The proportion of times that an event occurs in the long run when conditions are stable.

Using the relative frequency of occurrence approach

This method uses the relative frequencies of past occurrences as probabilities. We determine how often something has happened in the past and use that figure to predict the probability that it will happen again in the future. Let us look at an example. Suppose an insurance company knows from past actuarial data that of all males 40 years old, about 60 out of every 100,000 will die within a 1-year period. Using this method, the company estimates the probability of death for that age group as

$$\frac{60}{100{,}000}, \text{ or } 0.0006$$

More trials, greater accuracy

A second characteristic of probabilities established by the relative frequency of occurrence method can be shown by tossing one of our fair coins 300 times. Figure 4-1 illustrates the outcomes of these 300 tosses. Here we can see that although the proportion of heads was far from 0.5 in the first 100 tosses, it seemed to stabilize and approach 0.5 as the number of tosses increased. In statistical language, we would say that the relative frequency becomes stable as the number of tosses becomes large (if we are tossing the coin under uniform conditions). Thus, when we use the relative frequency approach to establish probabilities, our probability figure will gain accuracy as we increase the number of observations. Of course, this improved accuracy is not free; although more tosses of our coin will produce a more accurate probability of heads occurring, we must bear the time and the cost of additional observations.

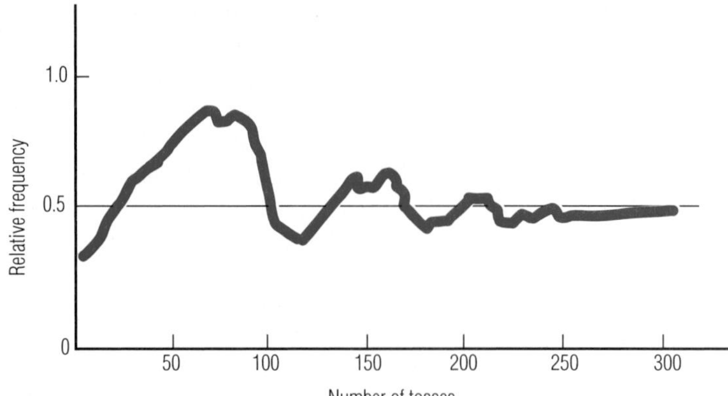

FIGURE 4-1

Relative frequency of occurrence of heads in 300 tosses of a fair coin

A limitation of relative frequency

One difficulty with the relative frequency approach is that people often use it without evaluating a sufficient number of outcomes. If you heard someone say, "My aunt and uncle got the flu this year, and they are both over 65, so everyone in that age bracket will probably get the flu," you would know that your friend did not base his assumptions on enough evidence. His observations were insufficient data for establishing a relative frequency of occurrence probability.

But what about a different kind of estimate, one that seems not to be based on statistics at all? Suppose your school's basketball team lost the first 10 games of the year. You were a loyal fan, however, and bet $100 that your team would beat Indiana's in the eleventh game. To everyone's surprise, you won your bet. We would have difficulty convincing you that you were statistically incorrect. And you would be right to be skeptical about our argument. Perhaps, without knowing that you did so, you may have based your bet on the statistical foundation described in the next approach to establishing probabilities.

Subjective Probabilities

Subjective probability defined

Subjective probabilities are based on the beliefs of the person making the probability assessment. In fact, subjective probability can be defined as the probability assigned to an event by an individual, based on whatever evidence is available. This evidence may be in the form of relative frequency of past occurrences, or it may be just an educated guess. Probably the earliest subjective probability estimate of the likelihood of rain occurred when someone's Aunt Bess said, "My corns hurt; I think we're in for a downpour." Subjective assessments of probability permit the widest flexibility of the three concepts we have discussed. The decision maker can use whatever evidence is available and temper this with personal feelings about the situation.

Subjective probability assignments are often found when events occur only once or at most a very few times. Say that it is your job to interview and select a new social services caseworker. You have narrowed your choice to three people. Each has an attractive appearance, a high level of energy, abounding self-confidence, a record of past accomplishments, and a state of mind that seems to welcome challenges. What are the chances each will relate to clients successfully? Answering this question and choosing among the three will require you to assign a subjective probability to each person's potential.

Using the subjective approach

Here is one more illustration of this kind of probability assignment. A judge is deciding whether to allow the construction of a nuclear power plant on a site where there is some evidence of a geological fault. He must ask himself, "What is the probability of a major nuclear accident at this location?" The fact that there is no relative frequency of occurrence evidence of previous accidents at this location does not excuse him from making a decision. He must use his best judgment in trying to determine the subjective probabilities of a nuclear accident.

Because most higher-level social and managerial decisions are concerned with specific, unique situations, rather than with a long series of identical situations, decision makers at this level make considerable use of subjective probabilities.

The subjective approach to assigning probabilities was introduced in 1926 by Frank Ramsey in his book *The Foundation of Mathematics and Other Logical Essays.* The concept was further developed by Bernard Koopman, Richard Good, and Leonard Savage, names that appeared regularly in advanced work in this field. Professor Savage pointed out that two reasonable people faced with the same evidence could easily come up with quite different subjective probabilities for the same event. The two people who made opposing bets on the outcome of the Indiana basketball game would understand quite well what he meant.

HINTS & ASSUMPTIONS

Warning: In classical probability problems, be sure to check whether the situation is "with replacement" after each draw or "without replacement." The chance of drawing an ace from a 52-card deck on the first draw is 4/52, or about .077. If you draw one and it is replaced, the odds of drawing an ace on the second draw are the same, 4/52. However, without replacement, the odds change to 4/51 if the first card was *not* an ace, or to 3/51 if the first card *was* an ace. In assigning subjective probabilities, it's normal for two different people to come up with different probabilities for the same event; that's the result of experience and time (we often call this combination "wisdom"). In assigning probabilities using the relative frequency of occurrence method, be sure you have observed an adequate number of outcomes. Just because red hasn't come up in 9 spins of the roulette wheel, you shouldn't bet next semester's tuition on black this spin!

Exercises 4.3

Self-Check Exercises

SC 4-3 Union shop steward B. Lou Khollar has drafted a set of wage and benefit demands to be presented to management. To get an idea of worker support for the package, he randomly polls the two largest groups of workers at his plant, the machinists (M) and the inspectors (I). He polls 30 of each group with the following results:

Opinion of Package	M	I
Strongly support	9	10
Mildly support	11	3
Undecided	2	2
Mildly oppose	4	8
Strongly oppose	4	7
	30	30

(a) What is the probability that a machinist randomly selected from the polled group mildly supports the package?

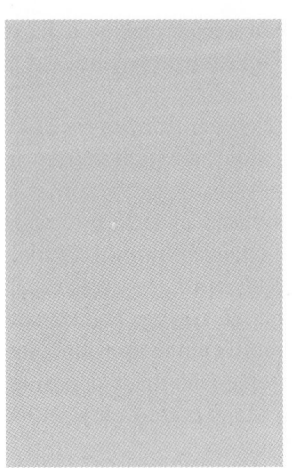

(b) What is the probability that an inspector randomly selected from the polled group is undecided about the package?

(c) What is the probability that a worker (machinist or inspector) randomly selected from the polled group strongly or mildly supports the package?

(d) What types of probability estimates are these?

SC 4-4 Classify the following probability estimates as to their type (classical, relative frequency, or subjective):

(a) The probability of scoring on a penalty shot in ice hockey is 0.47.

(b) The probability that the current mayor will resign is 0.85.

(c) The probability of rolling two sixes with two dice is 1/36.

(d) The probability that a president elected in a year ending in zero will die in office is 7/10.

(e) The probability that you will go to Europe this year is 0.14.

Basic Concepts

■ **4-11** Determine the probabilities of the following events in drawing a card from a standard deck of 52 cards:

(a) A seven.

(b) A black card.

(c) An ace or a king.

(d) A black two or a black three.

(e) A red face card (king, queen, or jack).

What type of probability estimates are these?

■ **4-12** During a recent bridge game, once the lead card had been played and the dummy's hand revealed, the declarer took a moment to count up the number of cards in each suit with the results given below:

Suit	We	They
Spades	6	7
Hearts	8	5
Diamonds	4	9
Clubs	8	5
	26	26

(a) What is the probability that a card randomly selected from the We team's hand is a spade?

(b) What is the probability that a card randomly selected from the They team's hand is a club?

(c) What is the probability that a card randomly selected from all the cards is either a spade or heart?

(d) If this type of analysis were repeated for every hand many times, what would be the long-run probability that a card drawn from the We team's hand is a spade?

Applications

■ **4-13** Below is a frequency distribution of annual sales commissions from a survey of 300 media salespeople.

Annual Commission	Frequency
$ 0– 4,999	15
5,000– 9,999	25
10,000–14,999	35
15,000–19,999	125
20,000–24,999	70
25,000+	30
	380

Based on this information, what is the probability that a media salesperson makes a commission: (a) between $5,000 and $10,000, (b) less than $15,000, (c) more than $20,000, and (d) between $15,000 and $20,000.

■ **4-14** General Buck Turgidson is preparing to make his annual budget presentation to the U.S. Senate and is speculating about his chances of getting all or part of his requested budget approved. From his 20 years of experience in making these requests, he has deduced that his chances of getting between 50 and 74 percent of his budget approved are twice as good as those of getting between 75 and 99 percent approved, and two and one-half times as good as those of getting between 25 and 49 percent approved. Further, the general believes that there is no chance of less than 25 percent of his budget being approved. Finally, the entire budget has been approved only once during the general's tenure, and the general does not expect this pattern to change. What are the probabilities of 0–24 percent, 25–49 percent, 50–74 percent, 75–99 percent, and 100 percent approval, according to the general?

■ **4-15** The office manager of an insurance company has the following data on the functioning of the copiers in the office:

Copier	Days Functioning	Days Out of Service
1	209	51
2	217	43
3	258	2
4	229	31
5	247	13

What is the probability of a copier being out of service based on these data?

■ **4-16** Classify the following probability estimates as classical, relative frequency, or subjective:

(a) The probability the Cubs will win the World Series this year is 0.175.
(b) The probability tuition will increase next year is 0.95.
(c) The probability that you will win the lottery is 0.00062.
(d) The probability a randomly selected flight will arrive on time is 0.875.
(e) The probability of tossing a coin twice and observing two heads is 0.25.
(f) The probability that your car will start on a very cold day is 0.97.

Worked-Out Answers to Self-Check Exercises

SC 4-3 (a) P(Machinist mildly supports) =

$$\frac{\text{number of machinists in "mildly support" class}}{\text{total number of machinists polled}} = 11/30$$

(b) P(Inspector undecided) $= \dfrac{\text{number of inspectors in "undecided" class}}{\text{total number of inspectors polled}}$

$= 2/30 = 1/15$

(c)

Opinion	Frequency (combined)
SS	19
MS	14
U	4
MO	12
SO	11
	60

P(Strongly or mildly support) = (19 + 14)/60 = 33/60 = 11/20

(d) Relative frequency.

SC 4-4 (a) Relative frequency. (b) Subjective.
(c) Classical. (d) Relative frequency.
(e) Subjective.

4.4 Probability Rules

Most managers who use probabilities are concerned with two conditions:

1. The case where one event *or* another will occur
2. The situation where two or more events will *both* occur

We are interested in the first case when we ask, "What is the probability that today's demand will exceed our inventory?" To illustrate the second situation, we could ask, "What is the probability that today's demand will exceed our inventory *and* that more than 10 percent of our sales force will not report for work?" In the sections to follow, we shall illustrate methods of determining answers to questions such as these under a variety of conditions.

Some Commonly Used Symbols, Definitions, and Rules

Symbol for a Marginal Probability In probability theory, we use symbols to simplify the presentation of ideas. As we discussed earlier in this chapter, the probability of the event *A* is expressed as

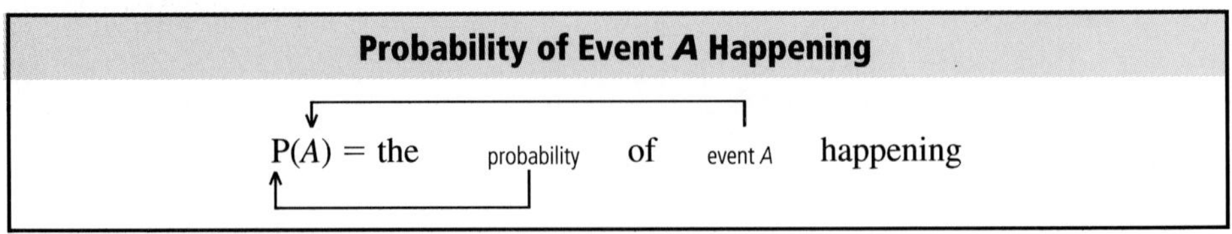

Marginal or unconditional probability

A *single* probability means that only one event can take place. It is called a *marginal* or *unconditional probability*. To illustrate, let us suppose that 50 members of a school class drew tickets to see which student would get a free trip to the National Rock Festival. Any one of the students could calculate his or her chances of winning as:

$$\text{P(Winning)} = \frac{1}{50}$$
$$= 0.02$$

Venn diagrams

In this case, a student's chance is 1 in 50 because we are certain that the possible events are mutually exclusive, that is, only one student can win at a time.

There is a nice diagrammatic way to illustrate this example and other probability concepts. We use a pictorial representation called a *Venn diagram,* after the nineteenth-century English mathematician John Venn. In these diagrams, the entire sample space is represented by a rectangle, and events are represented by parts of the rectangle. If two events *are* mutually exclusive, their parts of the rectangle will not overlap each other, as shown in Figure 4-2(a). If two events are *not* mutually exclusive, their parts of the rectangle *will* overlap, as in Figure 4-2(b).

Because probabilities behave a lot like areas, we shall let the rectangle have an area of 1 (because the probability of *something* happening is 1). Then the probability of an event is the area of *its* part of the rectangle. Figure 4-2(c) illustrates this for the National Rock Festival example. There the rectangle is divided into 50 equal, nonoverlapping parts.

Probability of one or more mutually exclusive events

Addition Rule for Mutually Exclusive Events Often, however, we are interested in the probability that one thing *or* another will occur. If these two events are mutually exclusive, we can express this probability using the addition rule for mutually exclusive events. This rule is expressed symbolically as

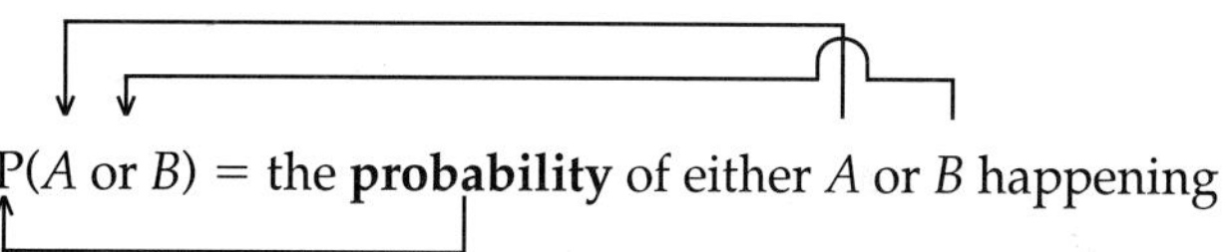

and is calculated as follows:

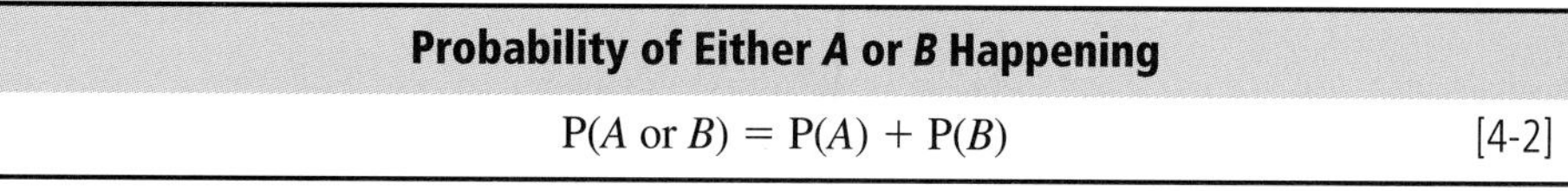

Probability of Either *A* or *B* Happening

$$P(A \text{ or } B) = P(A) + P(B) \quad [4\text{-}2]$$

FIGURE 4-2

Some Venn diagrams

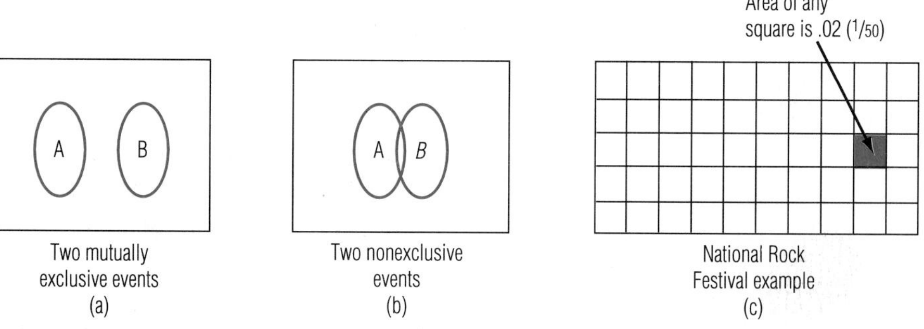

Two mutually exclusive events (a)

Two nonexclusive events (b)

National Rock Festival example (c)

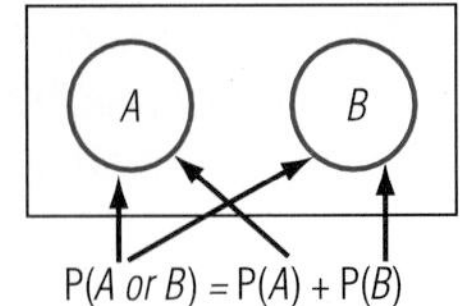

FIGURE 4-3

Venn diagram for the addition rule for mutually exclusive events

This addition rule is illustrated by the Venn diagram in Figure 4-3, where we note that the area in the two circles together (denoting the event *A* or *B*) is the sum of the areas of the circle denoting the event *A* and the circle denoting the event *B*.

Now to use this formula in an example. Five equally capable students are waiting for a summer job interview with a company that has announced that it will hire only one of the five by random drawing. The group consists of Bill, Helen, John, Sally, and Walter. If our question is, "What is the probability that John will be the candidate?" we can use Equation 4-1 and give the answer.

$$\begin{aligned} \text{P(John)} &= \frac{1}{5} \\ &= 0.2 \end{aligned}$$

However, if we ask, "What is the probability that either John *or* Sally will be the candidate?" we would use Equation 4-2:

$$\begin{aligned} \text{P(John or Sally)} &= \text{P(John)} + \text{P(Sally)} \\ &= \frac{1}{5} + \frac{1}{5} \\ &= \frac{2}{5} \\ &= 0.4 \end{aligned}$$

Let's calculate the probability of two or more events happening once more. Table 4-1 contains data on the sizes of families in a certain town. We are interested in the question, "What is the probability that a family chosen at random from this town will have four or more children (that is, four, five, six or more children)?" Using Equation 4-2, we can calculate the answer as

$$\begin{aligned} \text{P(4, 5, 6 or more)} &= \text{P(4)} + \text{P(5)} + \text{P(6 or more)} \\ &= 0.15 + 0.10 + 0.05 \\ &= 0.30 \end{aligned}$$

A special case of Equation 4-2

There is an important special case of Equation 4-2. For any event *A*, either *A* happens or it doesn't. So the events *A* and *not A* are exclusive and exhaustive. Applying Equation 4-2 yields the result

$$\text{P}(A) + \text{P}(not\ A) = 1$$

or, equivalently,

$$\text{P}(A) = 1 - \text{P}(not\ A)$$

Table 4-1

Family-Size Data

NUMBER OF CHILDREN	0	1	2	3	4	5	6 or more
PROPORTION OF FAMILIES HAVING THIS MANY CHILDREN	0.05	0.10	0.30	0.25	0.15	0.10	0.05

For example, referring back to Table 4-1, the probability of a family's having five or fewer children is most easily obtained by subtracting from 1 the probability of the family's having six or more children, and thus is seen to be 0.95.

Probability of one or more events *not* mutually exclusive

Addition Rule for Events That Are Not Mutually Exclusive If two events are not mutually exclusive, it is possible for both events to occur. In these cases, our addition rule must be modified. For example, what is the probability of drawing either an ace *or* a heart from a deck of cards? Obviously, the events ace and heart can occur together because we could draw the ace of hearts. Thus, ace and heart are not mutually exclusive events. We must adjust our Equation 4-2 to avoid double counting, that is, we have to *reduce* the probability of drawing either an ace or a heart *by the chance that we could draw both of them together.* As a result, the correct equation for the probability of one or more of two events that are not mutually exclusive is

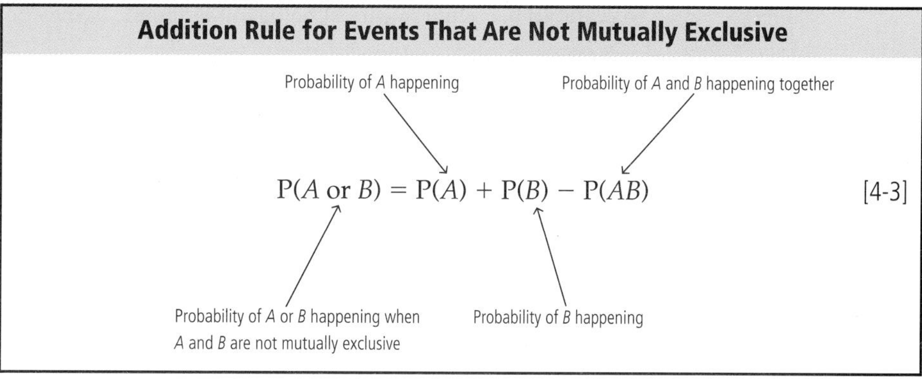
Addition Rule for Events That Are Not Mutually Exclusive

Probability of *A* happening

Probability of *A* and *B* happening together

$$P(A \text{ or } B) = P(A) + P(B) - P(AB) \quad [4\text{-}3]$$

Probability of *A* or *B* happening when *A* and *B* are not mutually exclusive

Probability of *B* happening

A Venn diagram illustrating Equation 4-3 is given in Figure 4-4. There, the event *A or B* is outlined with a heavy line. The event *A and B* is the cross-hatched wedge in the middle. If we add the areas of circles *A* and *B,* we *double count* the area of the wedge, and so we must subtract it to make sure it is counted only once.

Using Equation 4-3 to determine the probability of drawing either an ace *or* a heart, we can calculate:

$$\begin{aligned} P(\text{Ace or Heart}) &= P(\text{Ace}) + P(\text{Heart}) - P(\text{Ace and Heart}) \\ &= \frac{4}{52} + \frac{13}{52} - \frac{1}{52} \\ &= \frac{16}{52} \text{ or } \frac{4}{13} \end{aligned}$$

FIGURE 4-4

Venn diagram for the addition rule for two events not mutually exclusive

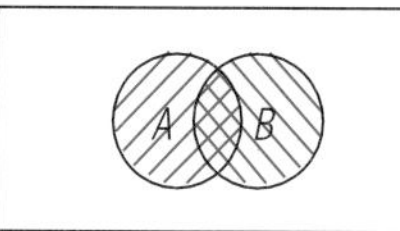

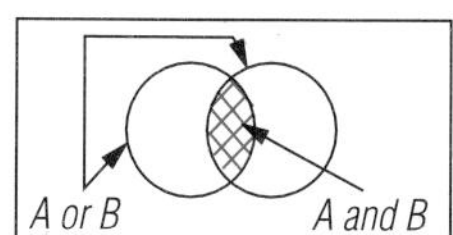

Let's do a second example. The employees of a certain company have elected five of their number to represent them on the employee–management productivity council. Profiles of the five are as follows:

1. male	age 30
2. male	32
3. female	45
4. female	20
5. male	40

This group decides to elect a spokesperson by drawing a name from a hat. Our question is, "What is the probability the spokesperson will be *either* female *or* over 35?" Using Equation 4-3, we can set up the solution to our question like this:

$$\begin{aligned}\text{P(Female or Over 35)} &= \text{P(Female)} + \text{P(Over 35)} - \text{P(Female and Over 35)} \\ &= \frac{2}{5} + \frac{2}{5} - \frac{1}{5} \\ &= \frac{3}{5}\end{aligned}$$

We can check our work by inspection and see that of the five people in the group, three would fit the requirements of being either female or over 35.

HINTS & ASSUMPTIONS

John Venn's diagrams are a useful way to avoid errors when you apply the addition rule for events that are and are not mutually exclusive. The most common error here is double counting. Hint: In applying the addition rule for mutually exclusive events, we're looking for a probability of one event or another and overlap is *not* a problem. However, with non–mutually exclusive events, both can occur together and we need to reduce our probability by the chance that they *could*. Thus, we subtract the overlap or cross-hatched area in the Venn diagram to get the correct value.

Exercises 4.4

Self-Check Exercises

SC 4-5 From the following Venn diagram, which indicates the number of outcomes of an experiment corresponding to each event and the number of outcomes that do not correspond to either event, give the probabilities indicated.

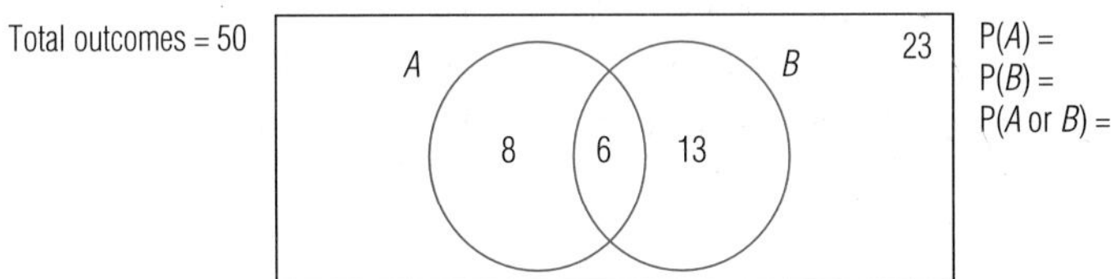

SC 4-6 An inspector of the Alaska Pipeline has the task of comparing the reliability of two pumping stations. Each station is susceptible to two kinds of failure: pump failure and leakage. When either (or both) occur, the station must be shut down. The data at hand indicate that the following probabilities prevail:

Station	P(Pump Failure)	P(Leakage)	P(Both)
1	0.07	0.10	0
2	0.09	0.12	0.06

Which station has the higher probability of being shut down?

Basic Concepts

■ **4-17** From the following Venn diagram, which indicates the number of outcomes of an experiment corresponding to each event and the number of outcomes that do not correspond to either event, give the probabilities indicated:

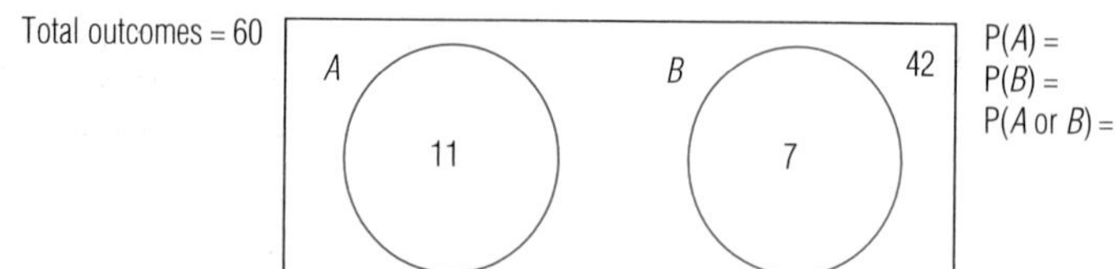

■ **4-18** Using this Venn diagram, give the probabilities indicated:

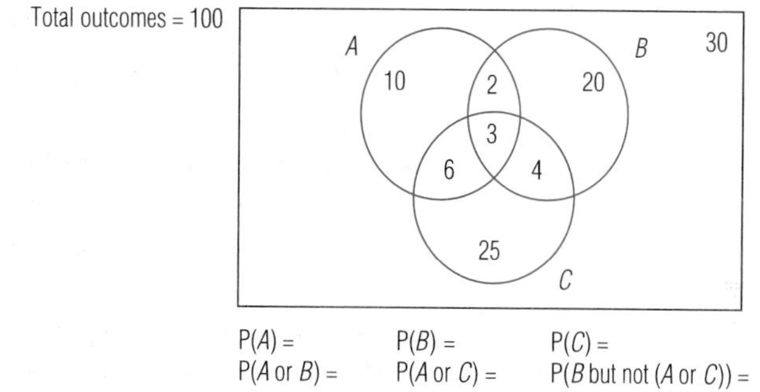

P(A) = P(B) = P(C) =
P(A or B) = P(A or C) = P(B but not (A or C)) =

■ **4-19** An urn contains 75 marbles: 35 are blue, and 25 of these blue marbles are swirled. The rest of them are red, and 30 of the red ones are swirled. The marbles that are not swirled are clear. What is the probability of drawing:

(a) A blue marble from the urn?
(b) A clear marble from the urn?
(c) A blue, swirled marble?
(d) A red, clear marble?
(e) A swirled marble?

■ **4-20** In this section, two expressions were developed for the probability of either of two events, *A* or *B*, occurring. Referring to Equations 4-2 and 4-3:

(a) What can you say about the probability of *A* and *B* occurring simultaneously when *A* and *B* are *mutually exclusive?*
(b) Develop an expression for the probability that at least one of three events, *A*, *B*, or *C*, could occur, that is, P(*A* or *B* or *C*). Do not assume that *A*, *B*, and *C* are mutually exclusive of each other.
(c) Rewrite your expression for the case in which *A* and *B* are mutually exclusive, but *A* and *C* and *B* and *C* are not mutually exclusive.
(d) Rewrite your expression for the case in which *A* and *B* and *A* and *C* are mutually exclusive, but not *B* and *C*.
(e) Rewrite your expression for the case in which *A*, *B*, and *C* are mutually exclusive of the others.

Applications

■ **4-21** An employee at Infotech must enter product information into the computer. The employee may use a light pen that transmits the information to the PC along with the keyboard to issue commands, or fill out a bubble sheet and feed it directly into the old mainframe. Historically, we know the following probabilities:

P(Light pen will fail) = 0.025
P(PC keyboard will fail) = 0.15
P(Light pen and PC keyboard will fail) = 0.005
P(Mainframe will fail) = 0.25

Data can be entered into the PC only if both the light pen and keyboard are functioning.

(a) What is the probability that the employee can use the PC to enter data?

(b) What is the probability that either the PC fails or the mainframe fails? Assume they cannot both fail at the same time.

■ **4-22** The HAL Corporation wishes to improve the resistance of its personal computer to disk-drive and keyboard failures. At present, the design of the computer is such that disk-drive failures occur only one-third as often as keyboard failures. The probability of simultaneous disk-drive and keyboard failures is 0.05.

(a) If the computer is 80 percent resistant to disk-drive and/or keyboard failure, how low must the disk-drive failure probability be?

(b) If the keyboard is improved so that it fails only twice as often as the disk-drive (and the simultaneous failure probability is still 0.05), will the disk-drive failure probability from part (a) yield a resistance to disk-drive and/or keyboard failure higher or lower than 90 percent?

■ **4-23** The Herr–McFee Company, which produces nuclear fuel rods, must X-ray and inspect each rod before shipping. Karen Wood, an inspector, has noted that for every 1,000 fuel rods she inspects, 10 have interior flaws, 8 have casing flaws, and 5 have both flaws. In her quarterly report, Karen must include the probability of flaws in fuel rods. What is this probability?

Worked-Out Answers to Self-Check Exercises

SC 4-5 $P(A) = 14/50 = 0.28 \qquad P(B) = 19/50 = 0.38$

$$P(A \text{ or } B) \, 5 \, \frac{14}{50} \, 1 \, \frac{19}{50} \, 2 \, \frac{6}{50} \, 5 \, 0.54$$

SC 4-6 P(Failure) = P(Pump failure or leakage)

Station 1: 0.07 + 0.1 − 0 = 0.17 Station 2: 0.09 + 0.12 − 0.06 = 0.15

Thus, Station 1 has the higher probability of being shut down.

4.5 Probabilities under Conditions of Statistical Independence

Independence defined

When two events happen, the outcome of the first event may or may not have an effect on the outcome of the second event. That is, the events may be either dependent or independent. In this section, we examine events that are *statistically independent:* The occurrence of one event *has no effect* on the probability of the occurrence of any other event. There are three types of probabilities under statistical independence:

1. Marginal
2. Joint
3. Conditional

Marginal Probabilities under Statistical Independence

Marginal probability of independent events

As we explained previously, a marginal or unconditional probability is the simple probability of the occurrence of an event. In a fair coin toss, P(H) = 0.5, and P(T) = 0.5; that is, the probability of heads equals 0.5 and the probability of tails equals 0.5. This is true for every toss, no matter how many tosses have been made or what their outcomes have been. Every toss stands alone and is in no way connected with any other toss. Thus, the outcome of *each* toss of a fair coin is an event that is statistically independent of the outcomes of *every other* toss of the coin.

Imagine that we have a biased or unfair coin that has been altered in such a way that heads occurs 0.90 of the time and tails 0.10 of the time. On each individual toss, P(H) = 0.90, and P(T) = 0.10. The outcome of any particular toss is completely unrelated to the outcomes of the tosses that may precede or follow it. The outcomes of several tosses of *this* coin are statistically independent events too, even though the coin is biased.

Joint Probabilities under Statistical Independence

Multiplication rule for joint, independent events

The probability of two or more independent events occurring together or in succession is the product of their marginal probabilities. Mathematically, this is stated (for two events):

Joint Probability of Two Independent Events

$$P(AB) = P(A) \times P(B) \qquad [4\text{-}4]$$

where

- P(AB) = probability of events A and B occurring together or in succession; this is known as a *joint probability*
- P(A) = marginal probability of event A occurring
- P(B) = marginal probability of event B occurring

The fair coin example

In terms of the fair coin example, the probability of heads on two successive tosses is the probability of heads on the first toss (which we shall call H_1) times the probability of heads on the second toss (H_2). That is, $P(H_1H_2) = P(H_1) \times P(H_2)$. We have shown that the events are statistically independent, because the probability of any outcome is not affected by any preceding outcome. Therefore, the probability of heads on any toss is 0.5, and $P(H_1H_2) = 0.5 \times 0.5 = 0.25$. Thus, the probability of heads on two successive tosses is 0.25.

Likewise, the probability of getting three heads on three successive tosses is $P(H_1H_2H_3) = 0.5 \times 0.5 \times 0.5 = 0.125$.

Assume next that we are going to toss an unfair coin that has P(H) = 0.8 and P(T) = 0.2. The events (outcomes) are independent, because the probabilities of all tosses are exactly the same—the individual tosses are completely separate and in no way affected by any other toss or outcome. Suppose our question is, "What is the probability of getting three heads on three successive tosses?" We use Equation 4-4 and discover that:

$$P(H_1H_2H_3) = P(H_1) \times P(H_2) \times P(H_3) = 0.8 \times 0.8 \times 0.8 = 0.512$$

(a) What is the probability that the first version of Rob's report is submitted to the FAA?

(b) What is the probability that the first version of Rob's report is approved by his group leader and department head, but is not approved by his division chief?

■ **4-31** A grocery store is reviewing its restocking policies and has analyzed the number of half-gallon containers of orange juice sold each day for the past month. The data are given below:

Number Sold	Morning	Afternoon	Evening
0–19	3	8	2
20–39	3	4	3
40–59	12	6	4
60–79	4	9	9
80–99	5	3	6
100 or more	3	0	6
	30	**30**	**30**

(a) What is the probability that on a randomly selected day the number of cartons of orange juice sold in the evening is between 80 and 99?

(b) What is the probability that 39 or fewer cartons were sold during a randomly selected afternoon?

(c) What is the probability that either 0–19 or 100 or more cartons were sold in a randomly selected morning?

■ **4-32** Bill Borde, top advertising executive for Grapevine Concepts, has just launched a publicity campaign for a new restaurant in town, The Black Angus. Bill has just installed four billboards on a highway outside of town, and he knows from experience the probabilities that each will be noticed by a randomly chosen motorist. The probability of the first billboard's being noticed by a motorist is 0.75. The probability of the second's being noticed is 0.82, the third has a probability of 0.87 of being noticed, and the probability of the fourth sign's being noticed is 0.9. Assuming that the event that a motorist notices any particular billboard is independent of whether or not he notices the others, what is the probability that

(a) All four billboards will be noticed by a randomly chosen motorist?

(b) The first and fourth, but not the second and third billboards will be noticed?

(c) Exactly one of the billboards will be noticed?

(d) None of the billboards will be noticed?

(e) The third and fourth billboards won't be noticed?

Worked-Out Answers to Self-Check Exercises

SC 4-7 (a) $P(\text{Face}_2 \mid \text{Red}_1) = 12/52 = 3/13$

(b) $P(\text{Ace}_2 \mid \text{Face}_1) = 4/52 = 1/13$

(c) $P(\text{Black jack}_2 \mid \text{Red ace}_1) = 2/52 = 1/26$

SC 4-8 (a) $3/45 = 1/15$

(b) $(7 + 6 + 5 + 4)/45 = 22/45$

(c) $(8 + 12 + 13 + 12)/180 = 45/180 = 1/4$

4.6 Probabilities under Conditions of Statistical Dependence

Dependence defined

Statistical dependence exists when the probability of some event is dependent on or affected by the occurrence of some other event. Just as with independent events, the types of probabilities under statistical dependence are

1. Conditional
2. Joint
3. Marginal

Conditional Probabilities under Statistical Dependence

Conditional and joint probabilities under statistical dependence are more involved than marginal probabilities are. We shall discuss conditional probabilities first, because the concept of joint probabilities is best illustrated by using conditional probabilities as a basis.

Examples of conditional probability of dependent events

Assume that we have one box containing 10 balls distributed as follows:

- Three are colored and dotted.
- One is colored and striped.
- Two are gray and dotted.
- Four are gray and striped.

The probability of drawing any one ball from this box is 0.1, since there are 10 balls, each with equal probability of being drawn. The discussion of the following examples will be facilitated by reference to Table 4-4 and to Figure 4-10, which shows the contents of the box in diagram form.

Example 1 Suppose someone draws a colored ball from the box. What is the probability that it is dotted? What is the probability it is striped?

Solution This question can be expressed symbolically as $P(D|C)$, or "What is the conditional probability that this ball is dotted, *given* that it is colored?"

Table 4–4

Color and Configuration of 10 Balls

Event	Probability of Event	
1	0.1	colored and dotted
2	0.1	
3	0.1	
4	0.1	colored and striped
5	0.1	gray and dotted
6	0.1	
7	0.1	gray and striped
8	0.1	
9	0.1	
10	0.1	

3/10

time be so that the probability of Litre's being awarded the contract is at least 0.65?

(c) Suppose that the probability of an investigation is 0.75 and the probability of WTR's completing its research in time is 0.85. What is the probability of Litre's being awarded the contract?

■ **4-40** A company is considering upgrading its computer system, and a major portion of the upgrade is a new operating system. The company has asked an engineer for an evaluation of the operating system. Suppose the probability of a favorable evaluation is 0.65. If the probability the company will upgrade its system given a favorable evaluation is 0.85, what is the probability that the company will upgrade and receive a favorable evaluation?

■ **4-41** The university's library has been randomly surveying patrons over the last month to see who is using the library and what services they have been using. Patrons are classified as undergraduate, graduate, or faculty. Services are classified as reference, periodicals, or books. The data for 350 people are given below. Assume a patron uses only one service per visit.

Patron	Reference	Periodicals	Books
Undergraduate	44	26	72
Graduate	24	61	20
Faculty	16	69	18
	84	**156**	**110**

Find the probability that a randomly chosen patron

(a) Is a graduate student.

(b) Visited the periodicals section, given the patron is a graduate student.

(c) Is a faculty member, given a reference section visit.

(d) Is an undergraduate who visited the book section.

■ **4-42** The southeast regional manager of General Express, a private parcel-delivery firm, is worried about the likelihood of strikes by some of his employees. He has learned that the probability of a strike by his pilots is 0.75 and the probability of a strike by his drivers is 0.65. Further, he knows that if the drivers strike, there is a 90 percent chance that the pilots will strike in sympathy.

(a) What is the probability of both groups' striking?

(b) If the pilots strike, what is the probability that the drivers will strike in sympathy?

Worked-Out Answers to Self-Check Exercises

SC 4-9 Let I = income > \$35,000 $\quad C$ = 2 cars.

$$P(C \text{ and } I) = P(C|I)P(I) = (0.75)(0.6) = 0.45$$

SC 4-10 M/W = shoplifter is male/female; F/R = shoplifter is first-time/repeat offender.

(a) $P(M) = (60 + 70)/250 = 0.520$

(b) $P(F|M) = P(F \text{ and } M)/P(M) = (60/250)/(130/250) = 0.462$

(c) $P(W|R) = P(W \text{ and } R)/P(R) = (76/250)/(146/250) = 0.521$

(d) $P(W|F) = P(W \text{ and } F)/P(F) = (44/250)/(104/250) = 0.423$

(e) $P(M \text{ and } R) = 70/250 = 0.280$

4.7 Revising Prior Estimates of Probabilities: Bayes' Theorem

At the beginning of the baseball season, the fans of last year's pennant winner thought their team had a good chance of winning again. As the season progressed, however, injuries sidelined the shortstop and the team's chief rival drafted a terrific home run hitter. The team began to lose. Late in the season, the fans realized that they must alter their prior probabilities of winning.

A similar situation often occurs in business. If a manager of a boutique finds that most of the purple and chartreuse ski jackets that she thought would sell so well are hanging on the rack, she must revise her prior probabilities and order a different color combination or have a sale.

Posterior probabilities defined

In both these cases, certain probabilities were altered after the people involved got additional information. The new probabilities are known as revised, or *posterior,* probabilities. Because probabilities can be revised as more information is gained, probability theory is of great value in managerial decision making.

Bayes' theorem

The origin of the concept of obtaining posterior probabilities with limited information is attributable to the Reverend Thomas Bayes (1702–1761), and the basic formula for conditional probability under dependence

$$P(B \mid A) = \frac{P(BA)}{P(A)} \qquad [4\text{-}6]$$

is called *Bayes' Theorem.*

Bayes, an Englishman, was a Presbyterian minister and a competent mathematician. He pondered how he might prove the existence of God by examining whatever evidence the world about him provided. Attempting to show "that the Principal End of the Divine Providence . . . is the Happiness of His Creatures," the Reverend Bayes used mathematics to study God. Unfortunately, the theological implications of his findings so alarmed the good Reverend Bayes that he refused to permit publication of his work during his lifetime. Nevertheless, his work outlived him, and modern decision theory is often called Bayesian decision theory in his honor.

Value of Bayes' theorem

Bayes' theorem offers a powerful statistical method of evaluating new information and revising our prior estimates (based upon limited information only) of the probability that things are in one state or another. **If correctly used, it makes it unnecessary to gather masses of data over long periods of time in order to make good decisions based on probabilities.**

Calculating Posterior Probabilities

Finding a new posterior estimate

Assume, as a first example of revising prior probabilities, that we have equal numbers of two types of deformed (biased or weighted) dice in a bowl. On half of them, ace (or one dot) comes up 40 percent of the time; therefore P(ace) = 0.4. On the other half, ace comes up 70 percent of the time; P(ace) = 0.7. Let us call the former type 1 and the latter type 2.

Revising probabilities based on one outcome

One die is drawn, rolled once, and comes up ace. What is the probability that it is a type 1 die? Knowing the bowl contains the same number of both types of dice, we might incorrectly answer that the probability is one-half; but we can do better than this. To answer the question correctly, we set up Table 4-6.

The sum of the probabilities of the elementary events (drawing either a type 1 or a type 2 die) is 1.0 because there are only two types of dice. The probability of each type is 0.5. The two types constitute a mutually exclusive and collectively exhaustive list.

Table 4-6 Finding the Marginal Probability of Getting an Ace

Elementary Event	Probability of Elementary Event	P(Ace|Elementary Event)	P(Ace, Elementary Event)*
Type 1	0.5	0.4	$0.4 \times 0.5 = 0.20$
Type 2	0.5	0.7	$0.7 \times 0.5 = 0.35$
	1.0		**P(ace) = 0.55**

*A comma is used to separate joint events. We can join individual letters to indicate joint events without confusion (*AB,* for example), but joining whole words in this way could produce strange looking events (aceelementaryevent) in this table, and they could be confusing.

The sum of the P(ace | elementary event) column does *not* equal 1.0. The figures 0.4 and 0.7 simply represent the conditional probabilities of getting an ace, given type 1 and type 2 dice, respectively.

The fourth column shows the joint probability of ace and type 1 occurring together ($0.4 \times 0.5 = 0.20$), and the joint probability of ace and type 2 occurring together ($0.7 \times 0.5 = 0.35$). The sum of these joint probabilities (0.55) is the marginal probability of getting an ace. Notice that in each case, the joint probability was obtained by using the formula

$$P(AB) = P(A|B) \times P(B) \tag{4-7}$$

To find the probability that the die we have drawn is type 1, we use the formula for conditional probability under statistical dependence:

$$P(B|A) = \frac{P(BA)}{P(A)} \tag{4-6}$$

Converting to our problem, we have

$$P(\text{type 1} \,|\, \text{ace}) = \frac{P(\text{type 1, ace})}{P(\text{ace})}$$

or

$$P(\text{type 1} \,|\, \text{ace}) = \frac{0.20}{0.55} = 0.364$$

Thus, the probability that we have drawn a type 1 die is 0.364.

Let us compute the probability that the die is type 2:

$$P(\text{type 2} \,|\, \text{ace}) = \frac{P(\text{type 2, ace})}{P(\text{ace})} = \frac{0.35}{0.55} = 0.636$$

Conclusion after one roll

What have we accomplished with one additional piece of information made available to us? What inferences have we been able to draw from one roll of the die? Before we rolled this die, the best we could say was that there is a 0.5 chance it is a type 1 die and a 0.5 chance it is a type 2 die. However, after rolling the die, we have been able to *alter,* or revise, *our prior probability estimate.* Our new posterior estimate is that there is a higher probability (0.636) that the die we have in our hand is a type 2 than that it is a type 1 (only 0.364).

Posterior Probabilities with More Information

Finding a new posterior estimate with more information

We may feel that one roll of the die is not sufficient to indicate its characteristics (whether it is type 1 or type 2). In this case, we can obtain additional information by rolling the die

Table 4-7 Finding the Marginal Probability of Two Aces on Two Successive Rolls

Elementary Event	Probability of Elementary Event	P(Ace| Elementary Event)	P(2 Aces| Elementary Event)	P(2 Aces, Elementary Event)
Type 1	0.5	0.4	0.16	$0.16 \times 0.5 = 0.080$
Type 2	0.5	0.7	0.49	$0.49 \times 0.5 = 0.245$
	1.0			**P(2 aces) = 0.325**

again. (Obtaining more information in most decision-making situations, of course, is more complicated and time-consuming.) Assume that the same die is rolled a second time and again comes up ace. What is the further revised probability that the die is type 1? To determine this answer, see Table 4-7.

We have one new column in this table, P(2 aces | elementary event). This column gives the *joint* probability of two aces on two successive rolls if the die is type 1 and if it is type 2: P(2 aces | type 1) = $0.4 \times 0.4 = 0.16$, and P(2 aces | type 2) = $0.7 \times 0.7 = 0.49$. In the last column, we see the joint probabilities of two aces on two successive rolls and the elementary events (type 1 and type 2). That is, P(2 aces, type 1) is equal to P(2 aces | type 1) times the probability of type 1, or $0.16 \times 0.5 = 0.080$, and P(2 aces, type 2) is equal to P(2 aces | type 2) times the probability of type 2, or $0.49 \times 0.5 = 0.245$. The sum of these (0.325) is the marginal probability of two aces on two successive rolls.

We are now ready to compute the probability that the die we have drawn is type 1, given an ace on each of two successive rolls. Using the same general formula as before, we convert to

$$P(\text{type } 1 \mid 2 \text{ aces}) = \frac{P(\text{type } 1, 2 \text{ aces})}{P(2 \text{ aces})} = \frac{0.080}{0.325} = 0.246$$

Similarly,

$$P(\text{type } 2 \mid 2 \text{ aces}) = \frac{P(\text{type } 2, 2 \text{ aces})}{P(2 \text{ aces})} = \frac{0.245}{0.325} = 0.754$$

What have we accomplished with two rolls? When we first drew the die, all we knew was that there was a probability of 0.5 that it was type 1 and a probability of 0.5 that it was type 2. In other words, there was a 50–50 chance that it was either type 1 or type 2. After rolling the die once and getting an ace, we revised these original probabilities to the following:

Probability that it is type 1, given that an ace was rolled = 0.364

Probability that it is type 2, given that an ace was rolled = 0.636

After the second roll (another ace), we revised the probabilities again:

Probability that it is type 1, given that two aces were rolled = 0.246

Probability that it is type 2, given that two aces were rolled = 0.754

Conclusion after two rolls

We have thus changed the original probabilities from 0.5 for each type to 0.246 for type 1 and 0.754 for type 2. This means that if a die turns up ace on two successive rolls, we can now assign a probability of 0.754 that it is type 2.

In both these experiments, we gained new information free of charge. We were able to roll the die twice, observe its behavior, and draw inferences from the behavior without any

Table 4-8

Posterior Probabilities with Three Trials

Event	P(Event) (1)	P(1 Strike| Event) (2)	P(3 Strikes| Event) (3)	P(Event, 3 Strikes) (4)
Correct	0.75	0.85	0.6141	0.6141 × 0.75 = 0.4606
Incorrect	0.25	0.35	0.0429	0.0429 × 0.25 = 0.0107
	1.00			**P(3 strikes) = 0.4713**

monetary cost. Obviously, there are few situations in which this is true, and managers must not only understand how to use new information to revise prior probabilities, but also be able to determine *how much that information is worth* to them before the fact. In many cases, the value of the information obtained may be considerably less than its cost.

A Problem with Three Pieces of Information

Example of posterior probability based on three trials

Consider the problem of a Little League baseball team that has been using an automatic pitching machine. If the machine is correctly set up—that is, properly adjusted—it will pitch strikes 85 percent of the time. If it is incorrectly set up, it will pitch strikes only 35 percent of the time. Past experience indicates that 75 percent of the setups of the machine are correctly done. After the machine has been set up at batting practice one day, it throws three strikes on the first three pitches. What is the revised probability that the setup has been done correctly? Table 4-8 illustrates how we can answer this question.

We can interpret the numbered table headings in Table 4-8 as follows:

1. P(event) describes the individual probabilities of correct and incorrect. P(correct) = 0.75 is given in the problem. Thus, we can compute

$$\text{P(incorrect)} = 1.00 - \text{P(correct)} = 1.00 - 0.75 = 0.25$$

2. P(1 strike | event) represents the probability of a strike given that the setup is correct or incorrect. These probabilities are given in the problem.
3. P(3 strikes | event) is the probability of getting three strikes on three successive pitches, given the event, that is, given a correct or incorrect setup. The probabilities are computed as follows:

$$\text{P(3 strikes} \mid \text{correct)} = 0.85 \times 0.85 \times 0.85 = 0.6141$$

$$\text{P(3 strikes} \mid \text{incorrect)} = 0.35 \times 0.35 \times 0.35 = 0.0429$$

4. P(event, 3 strikes) is the probability of the joint occurrence of the event (correct or incorrect) and three strikes. We can compute the probability in the problem as follows:

$$\text{P(correct, 3 strikes)} = 0.6141 \times 0.75 = 0.4606$$

$$\text{P(incorrect, 3 strikes)} = 0.0429 \times 0.25 = 0.0107$$

Notice that if A = event and S = strikes, these last two probabilities conform to the general mathematical formula for joint probabilities under conditions of dependence: $P(AS) = P(SA) = P(S \mid A) \times P(A)$, Equation 4-7.

After finishing the computation in Table 4-8, we are ready to determine the revised probability that the machine is correctly set up. We use the general formula

$$P(A|S) = \frac{P(AS)}{P(S)} \qquad [4\text{-}6]$$

and convert it to the terms and numbers in this problem:

$$P(\text{correct}|3 \text{ strikes}) = \frac{P(\text{correct, 3 strikes})}{P(3 \text{ strikes})}$$

$$= \frac{0.4606}{0.4713} = 0.9773$$

The *posterior probability* that the machine is correctly set up is 0.9773, or 97.73 percent. We have thus revised our original probability of a correct setup from 75 to 97.73 percent, based on three strikes being thrown in three pitches.

Posterior Probabilities with Inconsistent Outcomes

An example with inconsistent outcomes

In each of our problems so far, the behavior of the experiment was consistent: the die came up ace on two successive rolls, and the automatic machine three strikes on each of the first three pitches. In most situations, we would expect a less consistent distribution of outcomes. In the case of the pitching machine, for example, we might find the five pitches to be: strike, ball, strike, strike, strike. Calculating our posterior probability that the machine is correctly set up in this case is really no more difficult than it was with a set of perfectly consistent outcomes. Using the notation S = strike and B = ball, we have solved this example in Table 4-9.

Table 4-9 Posterior Probabilities with Inconsistent Outcomes

Event	P (Event)	P(*S*|Event)	P(*SBSSS*|Event)	P(Event, *SBSSS*)
Correct	0.75	0.85	0.85 × 0.15 × 0.85 × 0.85 × 0.85 = 0.07830	0.07830 × 0.75 = 0.05873
Incorrect	0.25	0.35	0.35 × 0.65 × 0.35 × 0.35 × 0.35 = 0.00975	0.00975 × 0.25 = 0.00244
	1.00			**P(*SBSSS*) = 0.06117**

$$P(\text{correct setup}|SBSSS) = \frac{P(\text{correct setup}, SBSSS)}{P(SBSSS)}$$

$$= \frac{0.05873}{0.06117}$$

$$= 0.9601$$

HINTS & ASSUMPTIONS

Bayes' theorem is a formal procedure that lets decision makers combine classical probability theory with their best intuitive sense about what is likely to happen. Warning: The real value of Bayes' theorem is not in the algebra, but rather in the ability of informed managers to make good guesses about the future. Hint: In all situations in which Bayes' theorem will be used, first use all the historical data available to you, and then (and only then) add your own intuitive judgment to the process. Intuition used to make guesses about things that are already statistically well-described is misdirected.

Exercises 4.7

Self-Check Exercises

SC 4-11 Given: The probabilities of three events, A, B, and C, occurring are $P(A) = 0.35$, $P(B) = 0.45$, and $P(C) = 0.2$. Assuming that A, B, or C has occurred, the probabilities of another event, X, occurring are $P(X|A) = 0.8$, $P(X|B) = 0.65$, and $P(X|C) = 0.3$. Find $P(A|X)$, $P(B|X)$, and $P(C|X)$.

SC 4-12 A doctor has decided to prescribe two new drugs to 200 heart patients as follows: 50 get drug A, 50 get drug B, and 100 get both. The 200 patients were chosen so that each had an 80 percent chance of having a heart attack if given neither drug. Drug A reduces the probability of a heart attack by 35 percent, drug B reduces the probability by 20 percent, and the two drugs, when taken together, work independently. If a randomly selected patient in the program has a heart attack, what is the probability that the patient was given both drugs?

Basic Concept

■ **4-43** Two related experiments are performed. The first has three possible, mutually exclusive outcomes: A, B, and C. The second has two possible, mutually exclusive outcomes: X and Y. We know $P(A) = 0.2$ and $P(B) = 0.65$. We also know the following conditional probabilities if the result of the second experiment is X: $P(X|A) = 0.75$, $P(X|B) = 0.60$, and $P(X|C) = 0.40$. Find $P(A|X)$, $P(B|X)$, and $P(C|X)$. What is the probability that the result of the second experiment is Y?

Applications

■ **4-44** Martin Coleman, credit manager for Beck's, knows that the company uses three methods to encourage collection of delinquent accounts. From past collection records, he learns that 70 percent of the accounts are called on personally, 20 percent are phoned, and 10 percent are sent a letter. The probabilities of collecting an overdue amount from an account with the three methods are 0.75, 0.60, and 0.65 respectively. Mr. Coleman has just received payment from a past-due account. What is the probability that this account

(a) Was called on personally?

(b) Received a phone call?

(c) Received a letter?

■ **4-45** A public-interest group was planning to make a court challenge to auto insurance rates in one of three cities: Atlanta, Baltimore, or Cleveland. The probability that it would choose Atlanta was 0.40; Baltimore, 0.35; and Cleveland, 0.25. The group also knew that it had a 60 percent chance of a favorable ruling if it chose Baltimore, 45 percent if it chose Atlanta, and 35 percent if it chose Cleveland. If the group did receive a favorable ruling, which city did it most likely choose?

■ **4-46** EconOcon is planning its company picnic. The only thing that will cancel the picnic is a thunderstorm. The Weather Service has predicted dry conditions with probability 0.2, moist conditions with probability 0.45, and wet conditions with probability 0.35. If the probability of a thunderstorm given dry conditions is 0.3, given moist conditions is 0.6, and given wet conditions is

0.8, what is the probability of a thunderstorm? If we know the picnic was indeed canceled, what is the probability moist conditions were in effect?

■ **4-47** An independent research group has been studying the chances that an accident at a nuclear power plant will result in radiation leakage. The group considers that the only possible types of accidents at a reactor are fire, mechanical failure, and human error, and that two or more accidents never occur together. It has performed studies that indicate that if there were a fire, a radiation leak would occur 20 percent of the time; if there were a mechanical failure, a radiation leak would occur 50 percent of the time; and if there were a human error, a radiation leak would occur 10 percent of the time. Its studies have also shown that the probability of

- A fire and a radiation leak occurring together is 0.0010.
- A mechanical failure and a radiation leak occurring together is 0.0015.
- A human error and a radiation leak occurring together is 0.0012.

(a) What are the respective probabilities of a fire, mechanical failure, and human error?

(b) What are the respective probabilities that a radiation leak was caused by a fire, mechanical failure, and human error?

(c) What is the probability of a radiation leak?

■ **4-48** A physical therapist at Enormous State University knows that the football team will play 40 percent of its games on artificial turf this season. He also knows that a football player's chances of incurring a knee injury are 50 percent higher if he is playing on artificial turf instead of grass. If a player's probability of knee injury on artificial turf is 0.42, what is the probability that

(a) A randomly selected football player incurs a knee injury?

(b) A randomly selected football player with a knee injury incurred the injury playing on grass?

■ **4-49** The physical therapist from Exercise 4-48 is also interested in studying the relationship between foot injuries and position played. His data, gathered over a 3-year period, are summarized in the following table:

	Offensive Line	Defensive Line	Offensive Backfield	Defensive Backfield
Number of players	45	56	24	20
Number injured	32	38	11	9

Given that a randomly selected player incurred a foot injury, what is the probability that he plays in the (a) offensive line, (b) defensive line, (c) offensive backfield, and (d) defensive backfield?

■ **4-50** A state Democratic official has decided that changes in the state unemployment rate will have a major effect on her party's chance of gaining or losing seats in the state senate. She has determined that if unemployment rises by 2 percent or more, the respective probabilities of losing more than 10 seats, losing 6 to 10 seats, gaining or losing 5 or fewer seats, gaining 6 to 10 seats, and gaining more than 10 seats are 0.25, 0.35, 0.15, 0.15, and 0.10, respectively. If unemployment changes by less than 2 percent, the respective probabilities are 0.10, 0.10, 0.15, 0.35, and 0.30. If unemployment falls by 2 percent or more, the respective probabilities are 0.05, 0.10, 0.10, 0.40, and 0.35. Currently this official believes that unemployment will rise by 2 percent or more with probability 0.25, change by less than 2 percent with probability 0.45, and fall by 2 percent or more with probability 0.30.

(a) If the Democrats gained seven seats, what is the probability that unemployment fell by 2 percent or more?

(b) If the Democrats lost one seat, what is the probability that unemployment changed by less than 2 percent?

■ **4-51** T. C. Fox, marketing director for Metro-Goldmine Motion Pictures, believes that the studio's upcoming release has a 60 percent chance of being a hit, a 25 percent chance of being a moderate success, and a 15 percent chance of being a flop. To test the accuracy of his opinion, T. C. has scheduled two test screenings. After each screening, the audience rates the film on a scale of 1 to 10, 10 being best. From his long experience in the industry, T. C. knows that 60 percent of the time, a hit picture will receive a rating of 7 or higher; 30 percent of the time, it will receive a rating of 4, 5, or 6; and 10 percent of the time, it will receive a rating of 3 or lower. For a moderately successful picture, the respective probabilities are 0.30, 0.45, and 0.25; for a flop, the respective probabilities are 0.15, 0.35, and 0.50.

(a) If the first test screening produces a score of 6, what is the probability that the film will be a hit?

(b) If the first test screening produces a score of 6 and the second screening yields a score of 2, what is the probability that the film will be a flop (assuming that the screening results are independent of each other)?

Worked-Out Answers to Self-Check Exercises

SC 4-11

Event	P(Event)	P(*X* | Event)	P(*X* and Event)	P(Event | *X*)
A	0.35	0.80	0.2800	0.2800/0.6325 = 0.4427
B	0.45	0.65	0.2925	0.2925/0.6325 = 0.4625
C	0.20	0.30	0.0600	0.0600/0.6325 = 0.0949
			P(*X*) = **0.6325**	

Thus, $P(A|X) = 0.4427$, $P(B|X) = 0.4625$, and $P(C|X) = 0.0949$.

SC 4-12 H = heart attack.

Event	P(Event)	P(*H* | Event)	P(*H* and Event)	P(Event | *H*)
A	0.25	(0.8)(0.65) = 0.520	0.130	0.130/0.498 = 0.2610
B	0.25	(0.8)(0.80) = 0.640	0.160	0.160/0.498 = 0.3213
A&B	0.50	(0.8)(0.65)(0.80) = 0.416	0.208	0.208/0.498 = 0.4177
			P(*H*) = **0.498**	

Thus, $P(A\&B|H) = 0.4177$.

Statistics at Work

Loveland Computers

Case 4: Probability "Aren't you going to congratulate me, Uncle Walter?" Lee Azko asked the CEO of Loveland Computers as they waved goodbye to their new-found investment bankers who were boarding their corporate jet.

"Sure, Lee, it was pretty enough stuff. But you'll find out that in business, there's more to life than gathering data. You have to make decisions, too—and often you don't have all the data you'd like because you're trying to guess what *will* happen in the future, not what *did* happen in the past. Get in the car and I'll explain.

"When we first started Loveland Computers, it was pretty much a wholesaling business. We'd bring in the computers from Taiwan, Korea, or wherever, and just ship 'em out the door with a label on them. Now that still works for some of the low-end products, but the higher-end stuff needs to be customized, so we run an assembly line here. Now I won't call it a factory, because there isn't a single thing that we 'make' here. We buy the cases from one place, the hard drives from somewhere else, and so on. Then we run the assembly line to make the machines just the way customers want them."

"Why don't you just have all the gizmos loaded on all the PCs, uncle?"

"Not a bad question, but here's the reason we can't do that. In this game, price is very important. And if you load a machine with something that a customer is never going to use—for example, going to the expense of adding a very large hard drive to a machine that's going to be used in a local area network, where most of the data will be kept on a file server—you end up pricing yourself out of the market, or selling at a loss. We can't afford to do either of those things. When we get back to the office, I want you to see Nancy Rainwater—she's the head of Production. She needs some help figuring out this month's schedule. This should give you some experience with real decision making."

Nancy Rainwater had worked for Loveland Computers for 5 years. Although Nancy was short on book learning, growing up on a farm nearby, she had learned some important practical skills about managing a workforce and getting work done on time. Her rise through the ranks to Production Supervisor had been rapid. Nancy explained her problem to Lee as follows.

"We have to decide whether to close the production line on Martin Luther King Day on the 20th of the month. Most of the workers on the line have children who will be off school that day. Your uncle, Mr. Azko, won't make it a paid vacation. But he might be open to closing the production line and letting people take the day off without pay if we can put in enough work days by the end of the month to meet our target production."

"Well, that shouldn't be too difficult to figure out—just count up the number of PCs produced on a typical day and divide that into the production target and see how many workdays you'll need," replied Lee with confidence.

"Well, I've already got that far. Not counting today, there are 19 workdays left until the end of the month, and I'll need 17 days to complete the target production."

"So let the workers take Martin Luther King Day off," Lee concluded.

"But there's more to it than that," Nancy continued. "This is 'colds and flu' season. If too many people call in sick—and believe me that happens when there's a 'bug' going around—I have to close the line for the day. I have records going back for a couple of years since I've been supervisor, and on an average winter day, there's a 1 in 30 chance that we'll have to close the line because of too many sick calls.

"And there's always a chance that we'll get a bad snowstorm—maybe even two—between now and the end of the month. Two years ago, two of the staff were in a terrible car wreck, trying to come to work on a day when the weather was real bad. So the company lawyer has told us to have a very tight 'snow day' policy. If the roads are dangerous, we close the line and lose that day's production. I'm not allowed to schedule weekend work to make up—that costs us time-and-a-half on wages and costs get out of line.

"I'd feel a lot better about closing the line for the holiday if I could be reasonably certain that we'd get in enough workdays by the end of the month. But I guess you don't have a crystal ball."

"Well, not a crystal ball, exactly. But I do have some ideas," Lee said, walking back toward the administrative offices, sketching something on a notepad. "By the way," said the younger Azko, turning back toward Nancy Rainwater, "What's *your* definition of 'reasonably certain?' "

Study Questions: What was Lee sketching on the notepad? What type of calculation will Lee make and what additional information will be needed? What difference will it make if Nancy's definition of "reasonably certain" means to meet the required production goal "75 percent of the time" or "99 percent of the time"?

Computer Database Exercise

HH Industries

Gary Russell, Operations Manager, caught Laurel on the way out of the staff meeting. "That was pretty impressive," he said. "I don't have an awful lot of experience with statistics, but it seems like a pretty powerful analysis tool. You've only been here a short while, but it looks like you're already getting some insight into our business posture that will be really useful to us."

"Thanks," answered Laurel. "That was just some basic work. But you're right—you can do some amazing things if you know where to start! Let me know if there's anything in your area I can look into for you."

"Now that you mention it," Gary grinned. "I've been meaning to ask you about something. Let me give you a little background. When HH Industries made the decision to reopen a warehouse in the Northeast after the Ohio disaster, we did a study in conjunction with UPS, the carrier we do most of our business with. Using about 6 months of shipping data, UPS ran some fancy computer program and determined the optimal location for our warehouse. It seemed like a sound methodology at the time, and there is no doubt that the warehouse is doing well, but I've got some of my own opinions about what was and what wasn't considered in the study. However, that's a story for another time. For now, I'm just interested in whether the warehouse is effectively reaching its targeted area or not. I've got some shipping data from the Pennsylvania warehouse, with packages categorized by destination zip code and weight. Think you could do anything with it?"

"I don't see why not," Laurel replied. "Aren't state zip codes arranged in some sort of consecutive order? That would help us separate out particular geographic regions."

"Sure. The first three digits indicate the area, and each state has a specific range. I'll get you that breakout when I bring back the data."

Later, entering data at her terminal, Laurel wondered about the best way to attack the problem at hand. She knew that shipping costs were based on both package weight and destination. The most critical packages, from a cost standpoint, were those designated "Next Day Air." This was where costs could add up very quickly, especially for heavier packages, as charges were 5–10 times normal UPS rates.

The following chart contains the state zip code data for use in Laurel's analysis:

State	Zip Range	State	Zip Range
MA	010–026	IA	500–528
RI	027–029	WI	530–549
NH	030–038	MN	550–567
ME	039–049	SD	570–577
VT	050–059	ND	580–588
CT	060–069	MT	590–599
NJ	070–089	IL	600–629
NY	100–149	MO	630–658
PA	150–196	KS	660–679
DE	197–199	NE	680–693
DC	200–205	LA	700–714
MD	206–219	AR	716–729
VA	220–246	OK	730–749
WV	247–268	TX	750–799
NC	270–289	CO	800–816
SC	290–299	WY	820–831
GA	300–319	ID	832–838
FL	320–346	UT	840–847
AL	350–369	AZ	850–865
TN	370–385	NM	870–884
MS	386–397	NV	889–899
KY	400–427	CA	900–961
OH	430–458	OR	970–979
IN	460–479	WA	980–994
MI	480–499		

With Gary's help, Laurel identified seven geographic regions for the purpose of the study. New England would contain MA, ME, RI, NH, VT, and CT. The Northeast would be made up of NJ, NY, PA, DE, DC, MD, VA, and WV. The Southeast would include NC, SC, GA, FL, AL, TN, and MS. KY, OH, IN and MI would be called the Midwest. North Central would indicate IA, WI, MN, SD, ND, IL, MO, KS, and NE. The South Central region would include LA, AR, OK, and TX. Finally, MT, CO, WY, ID, UT, AZ, NM, NV, CA, OR, and WA would be called the West. In addition, packages were categorized as being of normal weight (less than 10 pounds) or heavy (weighing 10 pounds or more).

1. Using the shipping data in the CH04.xxx files on the data disk, find the relative frequency of packages shipped to the seven geographic regions.
2. The target area for the Pennsylvania warehouse includes New England, the Northeast, and the Midwest. What is the probability that a package shipped from this warehouse has a destination within the target area?
3. What is the probability of a package from the Pennsylvania warehouse being shipped by Next Day Air? What is the probability of a package being classified as heavy? What is the probability of a package being heavy or being shipped by Next Day Air?
4. What is the probability of a package being heavy and being shipped within the target area? What is the probability of a package being heavy and being shipped outside of the target area?
5. Given that destination and the chance of being shipped by Next Day Air are not independent, what is the probability that, given a Next Day Air package, it is shipped within the target area?
6. If a package is sent outside of the target area, what is the chance that it is shipped by Next Day Air? What about if it is sent within the target area?
7. What can Laurel generally conclude about whether the Pennsylvania warehouse is being used effectively to reach its targeted area?

A flip side to the question, Laurel realized a couple of days later, was whether the central warehouse in Florida, which had shipped packages to the Northeast and Midwest before the Pennsylvania location came online, was now taking full advantage of this particular satellite warehouse. Though there were instances, she knew, where Pennsylvania's limited inventory prevented it from servicing *every* customer in its territory, a quick look at a random sample of Florida's shipping data would show whether things seemed to be in order. Laurel hunted Gary down, told him of her additional questions, and got some Florida shipping data from approximately the same time period as before. Then she headed back to her terminal.

Because the most expensive packages were those shipped by Next Day Air, she extracted those from the manifests and divided them into the seven geographic regions she had previously defined. Out of a total of 2,404 packages shipped, 500 fit into this category. The results are as follows:

New England	24
Northeast	42
Southeast	172
Midwest	32
North Central	63
South Central	110
West	57

8. What is the relative frequency of Next Day Air packages shipped from Florida to within the Pennsylvania warehouse's targeted area?
9. If the intended target area of the Florida warehouse is the Southeast and South Central areas, what is the probability of a Next Day Air package being shipped within that region?
10. Can Laurel give Gary any idea whether the Florida warehouse is being used efficiently, considering the location of the other two warehouses?

Chapter Review

● Terms Introduced in Chapter 4

A Priori Probability Probability estimate made prior to receiving new information.

Bayes' Theorem The formula for conditional probability under statistical dependence.

Classical Probability The number of outcomes favorable to the occurrence of an event divided by the total number of possible outcomes.

Collectively Exhaustive Events A list of events that represents all the possible outcomes of an experiment.

Conditional Probability The probability of one event occurring, given that another event has occurred.

Event One or more of the possible outcomes of doing something, or one of the possible outcomes from conducting an experiment.

Experiment The activity that results in, or produces, an event.

Joint Probability The probability of two events occurring together or in succession.

Marginal Probability The unconditional probability of one event occurring; the probability of a single event.

Mutually Exclusive Events Events that cannot happen together.

Posterior Probability A probability that has been revised after additional information was obtained.

Probability The chance that something will happen.

Probability Tree A graphical representation showing the possible outcomes of a series of experiments and their respective probabilities.

Relative Frequency of Occurrence The proportion of times that an event occurs in the long run when conditions are stable, or the observed relative frequency of an event in a very large number of trials.

Sample Space The set of all possible outcomes of an experiment.

Statistical Dependence The condition when the probability of some event is dependent on, or affected by, the occurrence of some other event.

Statistical Independence The condition when the occurrence of one event has no effect on the probability of occurrence of another event.

Subjective Probability Probabilities based on the personal beliefs of the person making the probability estimate.

Venn Diagram A pictorial representation of probability concepts in which the sample space is represented as a rectangle and the events in the sample space as portions of that rectangle.

● Equations Introduced in Chapter 4

■ **4-1** $$\text{Probability of an event} = \frac{\text{number of outcomes where the event occurs}}{\text{total number of possible outcomes}}$$ p. 164

This is the definition of the *classical* probability that an event will occur.

$$P(A) = \text{probability of event } A \text{ happening}$$ p. 170

A single probability refers to the probability of one particular event occurring, and it is called *marginal* probability.

$$P(A \text{ or } B) = \text{probability of } \textit{either } A \textit{ or } B \text{ happening}$$ p. 171

This notation represents the probability that one event *or* the other will occur.

■ **4-2** $$P(A \text{ or } B) = P(A) + P(B)$$ p. 171

The probability of either A or B happening when A and B are mutually exclusive equals the sum of the probability of event A happening and the probability of event B happening. This is the *addition rule for mutually exclusive events.*

■ **4-3** $$P(A \text{ or } B) = P(A) + P(B) - P(AB)$$ p. 173

The addition rule for events that are not mutually exclusive shows that the probability of A or B happening when A and B are not mutually exclusive is equal to the probability of event A happening plus the probability of event B happening minus the probability of A and B happening together, symbolized $P(AB)$.

■ **4-4**

$$P(AB) = P(A) \times P(B)$$

p. 177

where

- $P(AB)$ = joint probability of events A and B occurring together or in succession
- $P(A)$ = marginal probability of event A happening
- $P(B)$ = marginal probability of event B happening

The *joint* probability of two or more *independent* events occurring together or in succession is the product of their marginal probabilities.

$P(B \mid A)$ = probability of event B, *given* that event A has happened p. 181

This notation shows *conditional* probability, the probability that a second event (B) will occur if a first event (A) has already happened.

■ **4-5**

$$P(B \mid A) = P(B)$$

p. 181

For *statistically independent* events, the *conditional* probability of event B, given that event A has occurred, is simply the probability of event B. Independent events are those whose probabilities are in no way affected by the occurrence of each other.

■ **4-6**

$$P(B \mid A) = \frac{P(BA)}{P(A)}$$

and

$$P(A \mid B) = \frac{P(AB)}{P(B)}$$

p. 187

For statistically *dependent* events, the *conditional* probability of event B, given that event A has occurred, is equal to the joint probability of events A and B divided by the marginal probability of event A.

■ **4-7**

$$P(AB) = P(A \mid B) \times P(B)$$

and

$$P(BA) = P(B \mid A) \times P(A)$$

p. 188

Under conditions of statistical *dependence*, the *joint* probability of events A and B happening together or in succession is equal to the probability of event A, given that event B has already happened, multiplied by the probability that event B will happen.

● Review and Application Exercises

■ **4-52** Life insurance premiums are higher for older people, but auto insurance premiums are generally higher for younger people. What does this suggest about the risks and probabilities associated with these two areas of the insurance business?

■ **4-53** "The chance of rain today is 80 percent." Which of the following best explains this statement?

(a) It will rain 80 percent of the day today.

(b) It will rain in 80 percent of the area to which this forecast applies today.

(c) In the past, weather conditions of this sort have produced rain in this area 80 percent of the time.

■ **4-54** "There is a 0.25 probability that a restaurant in the United States will go out of business this year." When researchers make such statements, how have they arrived at their conclusions?

■ **4-55** Using probability theory, explain the success of gambling and poker establishments.

■ **4-56** Studies have shown that the chance of a new car being a "lemon" (one with multiple warranty problems) is greater for cars manufactured on Mondays and Fridays. Most consumers don't know on which day their car was manufactured. Assuming a 5-day production week, for a consumer taking a car at random from a dealer's lot,

(a) What is the chance of getting a car made on a Monday?

(b) What is the chance of getting a car made on Monday or Friday?

(c) What is the chance of getting a car made on Tuesday through Thursday?

(d) What type of probability estimates are these?

■ **4-57** Isaac T. Olduso, an engineer for Atlantic Aircraft, disagrees with his supervisor about the likelihood of landing-gear failure on the company's new airliner. Isaac contends that the probability of landing-gear failure is 0.12, while his supervisor maintains that the probability is only 0.03. The two agree that if the landing gear fails, the airplane will crash with probability 0.55. Otherwise, the probability of a crash is only 0.06. A test flight is conducted, and the airplane crashes.

(a) Using Isaac's figure, what is the probability that the airplane's landing gear failed?

(b) Repeat part (a) using the supervisor's figure.

■ **4-58** Congressman Bob Forehead has been thinking about the upcoming midterm elections and has prepared the following list of possible developments in his career during the midterm elections:

- He wins his party's nomination for reelection.
- He returns to his law practice.
- He is nominated for vice president.
- He loses his party's nomination for reelection.
- He wins reelection.

(a) Is each item on this list an "event" in the category of "Midterm Election Career Developments?"

(b) Are all of the items qualifying as "events" in part (a) mutually exclusive? If not, are any mutually exclusive?

(c) Are the events on the list collectively exhaustive?

■ **4-59** The table below is a data array of the top 25 Illinois multibank holding companies, ranked by shareholder return on equity (ROE) for the period 3/31/91 to 3/31/92. Use that information to answer the following questions. Assume that ROE is independent of total assets and dependent on equity as a percentage of assets (E/A). Assume that net income is dependent on total assets.

Rank	Holding Company	Shareholder ROE (%)	E/A (%)	Total Assets ($ 000)	Net Income ($ 000)
1	United Community Bancorp	27.20	5.61	157,492	1,784
2	Illinois Financial Services	25.16	6.72	306,048	3,846
3	FBOP Corp.	24.44	6.39	560,770	7,780
4	Alpine Bancorp, Inc.	24.12	7.18	170,382	2,248
5	River Forest Bancorp, Inc.	20.92	4.42	1,313,797	20,339
6	Pinnacle Banc Group Inc.	18.81	8.58	728,167	10,328
7	FNBC of La Grange Inc.	18.68	8.92	180,671	2,459
8	First Park Ridge Corp.	17.72	9.91	314,145	5,025
9	Palmer Bancorp Inc.	17.01	8.61	225,016	3,462
10	Northern Trust Corp.	16.66	5.83	13,154,522	132,246
11	West Suburban Bancorp	16.02	7.58	1,005,485	11,940
12	Parkway Bancorp Inc.	15.93	7.51	550,559	6,716
13	First Evergreen Corp.	15.70	7.39	1,583,884	17,187
14	LaSalle Community Bancorporation Inc.	15.30	7.08	2,814,118	27,144
15	Premier Financial Services	15.01	6.95	369,503	3,908
16	Riverdale Bancorp	14.95	5.28	221,426	2,039
17	Town & Country Bancorp Inc.	14.90	4.30	133,000	Not avail.
18	Standard Bancshares Inc.	14.83	8.87	426,025	5,267
19	Heritage Financial Services	14.35	7.57	738,726	8,200
20	National Bancorp Inc.	14.25	5.58	275,856	2,863
21	Firstbank of Illinois Co.	13.94	6.32	1,494,060	14,906
22	Banterra Corp.	13.77	6.91	393,158	3,461
23	Northern Illinois Financial Corp.	13.67	8.46	784,260	8,658
24	Heartland Bancorp Inc.	13.52	8.69	159,767	1,704
25	Sandwich Banco Inc.	13.51	6.60	308,290	2,892

Source: "Illinois' Multibank Holding Companies," Crain's Chicago Business *(19 October 1992): 22–24.*

(a) What is the probability that a randomly selected holding company will have an ROE greater than 16 percent, given that its E/A ratio is less than 7 percent?

(b) What is the probability that a randomly selected holding company will have an ROE between 14 and 16 percent (inclusive), given that its E/A ratio is greater than 7 percent?

(c) Determine the probability that a randomly selected holding company will have a net income greater than $50 million, given that its total assets are greater than $2 billion.

(d) What is the probability that a randomly selected holding company will have an ROE greater than 15 percent?

(e) Calculate the probability that a randomly selected holding company will have an ROE greater than 15 percent and have at least $2 billion in total assets.

(f) Determine the probability that a randomly selected holding company will have an ROE greater than 20 percent, given that its total assets are greater than or equal to $1 billion.

■ **4-60** Which of the following pairs of events are mutually exclusive?

(a) A defense department contractor loses a major contract, and the same contractor increases its work force by 50 percent.

(b) A man is older than his uncle, and he is younger than his cousins.

(c) A baseball team loses its last game of the year, and it wins the World Series.

(d) A bank manager discovers that a teller has been embezzling, and she promotes the same teller.

■ **4-61** The scheduling officer for a local police department is trying to decide whether to schedule additional patrol units in each of two neighborhoods. She knows that on any given day during the past year, the probabilities of major crimes and minor crimes being committed in the northern neighborhood were 0.478 and 0.602, respectively, and that the corresponding probabilities in the southern neighborhood were 0.350 and 0.523. Assume that major and minor crimes occur independently of each other and likewise that crimes in the two neighborhoods are independent of each other.

(a) What is the probability that no crime of either type is committed in the northern neighborhood on a given day?

(b) What is the probability that a crime of either type is committed in the southern neighborhood on a given day?

(c) What is the probability that no crime of either type is committed in either neighborhood on a given day?

■ **4-62** The Environmental Protection Agency is trying to assess the pollution effect of a paper mill that is to be built near Spokane, Washington. In studies of six similar plants built during the last year, the EPA determined the following pollution factors:

Plant	1	2	3	4	5	6
Sulfur dioxide emission in parts per million (ppm)	15	12	18	16	11	19

EPA defines excessive pollution as a sulfur dioxide emission of 18 ppm or greater.

(a) Calculate the probability that the new plant will be an excessive sulfur dioxide polluter.

(b) Classify this probability according to the three types discussed in the chapter: classical, relative frequency, and subjective.

(c) How would you judge the accuracy of your result?

■ **4-63** The American Cancer Society is planning to mail out questionnaires concerning breast cancer. From past experience with questionnaires, the Cancer Society knows that only 15 percent of the people receiving questionnaires will respond. It also knows that 1.3 percent of the questionnaires mailed out will have a mistake in address and never be delivered, that 2.8 percent will be lost or destroyed by the post office, that 19 percent will be mailed to people who have moved, and that only 48 percent of those who move leave a forwarding address.

(a) Do the percentages in the problem represent classical, relative frequency, or subjective probability estimates?

(b) Find the probability that the Cancer Society will get a reply from a given questionnaire.

■ **4-64** McCormick and Tryon, Inc., is a "shark watcher," hired by firms fearing takeover by larger companies. This firm has found that one of its clients, Pare and Oyd Co., is being considered for takeover by two firms. The first, Engulf and Devour, considered 20 such companies last year and took over 7. The second, R. A. Venus Corp., considered 15 such companies last year and took over 6. What is the probability of Pare and Oyd's being taken over this year, assuming that

(a) The acquisition rates of both Engulf and Devour and R. A. Venus are the same this year as they were last year?

(b) This year's acquisition rates are independent of last year's?

In each case, assume that only one firm may take over Pare and Oyd.

■ **4-65** As the administrator of a hospital, Cindy Turner wants to know what the probability is that a person checking into the hospital will require X-ray treatment and will also have hospital insurance that will cover the X-ray treatment. She knows that during the past 5 years, 23 percent of the people entering the hospital required X-rays, and that during the same period, 72 percent of the people checking into the hospital had insurance that covered X-ray treatments. What is the correct probability? Do any additional assumptions need to be made?

■ **4-66** An air traffic controller at Dulles Airport must obey regulations that require her to divert one of two airplanes if the probability of the aircraft's colliding exceeds 0.025. The controller has two inbound aircraft scheduled to arrive 10 minutes apart on the same runway. She knows that Flight 100, scheduled to arrive first, has a history of being on time, 5 minutes late, and 10 minutes late 95, 3, and 2 percent of the time, respectively. Further, she knows that Flight 200, scheduled to arrive second, has a history of being on time, 5 minutes early, and 10 minutes early 97, 2, and 1 percent of the time, respectively. The flights' timings are independent of each other.

(a) Must the controller divert one of the planes, based on this information?

(b) If she finds out that Flight 100 definitely will be 5 minutes late, must the controller divert one of the airplanes?

(c) If the controller finds out that Flight 200 definitely will be 5 minutes early, must she divert one of the airplanes?

■ **4-67** In a staff meeting called to address the problem of returned checks at the supermarket where you are interning as a financial analyst, the bank reports that 12 percent of all checks are returned for insufficient funds, and of those, in 50 percent of cases, there was cash given back to the customer. Overall, 10 percent of customers ask for cash back at the end of their transaction with the store. For 1,000 customer visits, how many transactions will involve:

(a) Insufficient funds?

(b) Cash back to the customer?

(c) Both insufficient funds and cash back?

(d) Either insufficient funds or cash back?

■ **4-68** *Working Mother* magazine got the following results when it polled some of its readers concerning the day-care arrangements they had chosen for their children between the ages of 2 and 5.

Type of Care	Number Who Chose This Type
Family day care	120
Caregiver in child's home	30
Day-care center	123
Grandmother or other relative	15
Spouse	6
On-site center at work	6
Total	**300**

Source: Vivian Cadden, "Child Care Options," Working Mother *(January 1993): 50–51.*

(a) What is the probability that a randomly selected parent chose family day care for a child in this age group?

(b) What is the probability that a randomly selected parent chose a spouse or other relative to care for a child?

■ **4-69** Which of the following pairs of events are statistically independent?

(a) The times until failure of a calculator and of a second calculator marketed by a different firm.

(b) The life-spans of the current U.S. and Russian presidents.

(c) The amounts of settlements in asbestos poisoning cases in Maryland and New York.

(d) The takeover of a company and a rise in the price of its stock.

(e) The frequency of organ donation in a community and the predominant religious orientation of that community.

■ **4-70** F. Liam Laytor, supervisor of customer relations for GLF Airlines, is studying his company's overbooking problem. He is concentrating on three late-night flights out of LaGuardia Airport in New York City. In the last year, 7, 8, and 5 percent of the passengers on the Atlanta, Kansas City, and Detroit flights, respectively, have been bumped. Further, 55, 20, and 25 percent of the late-night GLF passengers at LaGuardia take the Atlanta, Kansas City, and Detroit flights, respectively. What is the probability that a bumped passenger was scheduled to be on the

(a) Atlanta flight?

(b) Kansas City flight?

(c) Detroit flight?

■ **4-71** An electronics manufacturer is considering expansion of its plant in the next 4 years. The decision depends on the increased production that will occur if either government or consumer sales increase. Specifically, the plant will be expanded if either (1) consumer sales increase 50 percent over the present sales level or (2) a major government contract is obtained. The company also believes that both these events will not happen in the same year. The planning director has obtained the following estimates:

- The probability of consumer sales increasing by 50 percent within 1, 2, 3, and 4 years is 0.05, 0.08, 0.12, and 0.16, respectively.
- The probability of obtaining a major government contract within 1, 2, 3, and 4 years is 0.08, 0.15, 0.25, and 0.32, respectively.

What is the probability that the plant will expand

(a) Within the next year (in year 1)?

(b) Between 1 and 2 years from now (in year 2)?

(c) Between 2 and 3 years from now (in year 3)?

(d) Between 3 and 4 years from now (in year 4)?

(e) At all in the next 4 years (assume at most one expansion)?

■ **4-72** Draw Venn diagrams to represent the following situations involving three events, *A*, *B*, and *C*, which are part of a sample space of events but do not include the whole sample space.

(a) Each pair of events (*A* and *B*, *A* and *C*, and *B* and *C*) may occur together, but all three may not occur together.

(b) *A* and *B* are mutually exclusive, but not *A* and *C* nor *B* and *C*.

(c) *A*, *B*, and *C* are all mutually exclusive of one another.

(d) *A* and *B* are mutually exclusive, *B* and *C* are mutually exclusive, but *A* and *C* are not mutually exclusive.

■ **4-73** Cartoonist Barry Bludeau sends his comics to his publisher via Union Postal Delivery. UPD uses rail and truck transportation in Mr. Bludeau's part of the country. In UPD's 20 years of operation, only 2 percent of the packages carried by rail and only 3.5 percent of the packages carried by truck have been lost. Mr. Bludeau calls the claims manager to inform him that a package containing a week of comics has been lost. If UPD sends 60 percent of the packages in that area by rail, which mode of transportation was more likely used to carry the lost comics? How does the solution change if UPD loses only 2 percent of its packages, regardless of the mode of transportation?

■ **4-74** Determine the probability that

(a) Both engines on a small airplane fail, given that each engine fails with probability 0.05 and that an engine is twice as likely to fail when it is the only engine working.

(b) An automobile is recalled for brake failure and has steering problems, given that 15 percent of that model were recalled for brake failure and 2 percent had steering problems.

(c) A citizen files his or her tax return and cheats on it, given that 70 percent of all citizens file returns and 25 percent of those who file cheat.

■ **4-75** Two-fifths of clients at Show Me Realty come from an out-of-town referral network, the rest are local. The chances of selling a home on each showing are 0.075 and 0.053 for out-of-town and local clients, respectively. If a salesperson walks into Show Me's office and announces "It's a deal!" was the agent more likely to have conducted a showing for an out-of-town or local client?

■ **4-76** A senior North Carolina senator knows he will soon vote on a controversial bill. To learn his constituents' attitudes about the bill, he met with groups in three cities in his state. An aide jotted down the opinions of 15 attendees at each meeting:

Opinion	**City**		
	Chapel Hill	**Raleigh**	**Lumberton**
Strongly oppose	2	2	4
Slightly oppose	2	4	3
Neutral	3	3	5
Slightly support	2	3	2
Strongly support	6	3	1
Total	**15**	**15**	**15**

(a) What is the probability that someone from Chapel Hill is neutral about the bill? Strongly opposed?

(b) What is the probability that someone in the three city groups strongly supports the bill?

(c) What is the probability that someone from the Raleigh or Lumberton groups is neutral or slightly opposed?

■ **4-77** The breakdown by political party of the 435 members of the U.S. House of Representatives before and after the 1992 Congressional elections was

	House Seats	
	Old	**New**
Democrats	268	259
Republicans	166	175
Independents	1	1

(a) Determine the probability that a member selected at random before the 1992 election would be a Republican.

(b) Determine the probability that a member selected at random after that election would not be a Republican.

(c) Is it fair to conclude that the probability that a randomly selected Democratic incumbent was not re-elected was 9/268? Explain.

■ **4-78** A produce shipper has 10,000 boxes of bananas from Ecuador and Honduras. An inspection has determined the following information:

		# of Boxes with	
	# of Boxes	**Damaged Fruit**	**Overripe Fruit**
Ecuadoran	6,000	200	840
Honduran	4,000	365	295

(a) What is the probability that a box selected at random will contain damaged fruit? Overripe fruit?

(b) What is the probability that a randomly selected box is from Ecuador or Honduras?

(c) Given that a randomly selected box contains overripe fruit, what is the probability that it came from Honduras?

(d) If damaged fruit and overripe fruit are mutually exclusive, what is the probability that a box contains damaged or overripe fruit? What if they are not mutually exclusive?

■ **4-79** Marcia Lerner will graduate in 3 months with a master's degree in business administration. Her school's placement office indicates that the probability of receiving a job offer as the result of any given on-campus interview is about 0.07 and is statistically independent from interview to interview.

(a) What is the probability that Marcia will not get a job offer in any of her next three interviews?

(b) If she has three interviews per month, what is the probability that she will have at least one job offer by the time she finishes school?

(c) What is the probability that in her next five interviews she will get job offers on the third and fifth interviews only?

■ **4-80** A standard set of pool balls contains 15 balls numbered from 1 to 15. Pegleg Woodhull, the famous blind poolplayer, is playing a game of 8-ball, in which the 8-ball must be the last one hit into a pocket. He is allowed to touch the balls to determine their positions before taking a shot, but he does not know their numbers. Every shot Woodhull takes is successful.

(a) What is the probability that he hits the 8-ball into a pocket on his first shot, thus losing the game?

(b) What is the probability that the 8-ball is one of the first three balls he hits?

(c) What is the probability that Pegleg wins the game, that is, that the 8-ball is the last ball hit into a pocket?

■ **4-81** BMT, Inc., is trying to decide which of two oil pumps to use in its new race car engine. One pump produces 75 pounds of pressure and the other 100. BMT knows the following probabilities associated with the pumps:

	Probability of Engine Failure Due to	
	Seized Bearings	**Ruptured Head Gasket**
Pump A	0.08	0.03
Pump B	0.02	0.11

(a) If seized bearings and ruptured head gaskets are mutually exclusive, which pump should BMT use?

(b) If BMT devises a greatly improved "rupture-proof" head gasket, should it change its decision?

■ **4-82** Sandy Irick is the public relations director for a large pharmaceutical firm that has been attacked in the popular press for distributing an allegedly unsafe vaccine. The vaccine protects against a virulent contagious disease that has a 0.04 probability of killing an infected person. Twenty-five percent of the population has been vaccinated.

A researcher has told her the following: The probability of any unvaccinated individual acquiring the disease is 0.30. Once vaccinated, the probability of acquiring the disease through normal means is zero. However, 2 percent of vaccinated people will show symptoms of the disease, and 3 percent of that group will die from it. Of people who are vaccinated and show no symptoms from the vaccination, 0.05 percent will die. Irick must draw some conclusions from these data for a staff meeting in 1 hour and a news conference later in the day.

(a) If a person is vaccinated, what is the probability of dying from the vaccine? If he was not vaccinated, what is the probability of dying?

(b) What is the probability of a randomly selected person dying from either the vaccine or the normally contracted disease?

■ **4-83** The pressroom supervisor for a daily newspaper is being pressured to find ways to print the paper closer to distribution time, thus giving the editorial staff more leeway for last-minute changes. She has the option of running the presses at "normal" speed or at 110 percent of normal—"fast" speed. She estimates that they will run at the higher speed 60 percent of the time. The roll of paper (the newsprint "web") is twice as likely to tear at the higher speed, which would mean temporarily stopping the presses.

(a) If the web on a randomly selected printing run has a probability of 0.112 of tearing, what is the probability that the web will not tear at normal speed?

(b) If the probability of tearing on fast speed is 0.20, what is the probability that a randomly selected torn web occurred on normal speed?

■ **4-84** Refer to Exercise 4-83. The supervisor has noted that the web tore during each of the last four runs and that the speed of the press was not changed during these four runs. If the probabilities of tearing at fast and slow speeds were 0.14 and 0.07, respectively, what is the revised probability that the press was operating at fast speed during the last four runs?

■ **4-85** Airlines serve as "flagship carriers" in Europe, and for symbolic and strategic reasons, many have been state-owned. But governments have had to pay heavy subsidies and some airlines have been privatized. The competitive marketplace appears to reward this move. In 1994, of ten major airlines, five were privately owned and five were under state control. The five private airlines reported a profit and the five state-controlled airlines reported a loss. Consider the proposition that airline profits and losses are randomly distributed and that this result occurred by chance. If the chances of making a profit are .5, what is the chance that all five private carriers would make a profit while all state-controlled carriers were incurring losses?

Source: Brian Coleman, "Among European Airlines, the Privatized Soar to the Top," The Wall Street Journal *(19 July 1995): B4.*

■ **4-86** In the summer of 1995, Boeing successfully introduced into commercial airline service the 777, a large plane capable of carrying more than 300 passengers. They immediately sought approval from the Federal Aviation Authority for long, transoceanic flights such as the Denver to Honolulu route. The 777 is a twin-engined jet and previous FAA approvals had been given to planes with four engines (such as the 747 jumbo jet) or with extensive over-land commercial experience (such as the 767 twin jet).

In over-water flights, planes may be as far as three hours from the nearest airport. Experience with engines similar to those on the new plane suggests that the expected rate of engine failure is once every 50,000 flight hours. If failures of each of the two engines are independent events

(a) What is the probability of either engine failing during a 6-hour flight?

(b) If one engine has failed, what is the probability that the second engine will fail?

(c) What is the probability that both engines will fail?

Source: J. Cole, *"FAA to Allow Oceanic Flight by Boeing 777,"* The Wall Street Journal *(30 May 1995): A3.*

● Chapter Concepts Test

Circle the correct answer or fill in the blank. *Answers are in the back of the book.*

T F 1. In probability theory, the outcome from some experiment is known as an activity.

T F 2. The probability of two or more statistically independent events occurring together or in succession is equal to the sum of their marginal probabilities.

T F 3. Using Bayes' theorem, we may develop revised probabilities based on new information; these revised probabilities are also known as posterior probabilities.

T F 4. In classical probability, we can determine a priori probabilities based on logical reasoning before any experiments take place.

T F 5. The set of all possible outcomes of an experiment is called the sample space for the experiment.

T F 6. Under statistical dependence, a marginal probability may be computed for some simple event by taking the product of the probabilities of all joint events in which the simple event occurs.

T F 7. When a list of events resulting from some experiment includes all possible outcomes, the list is said to be collectively exclusive.

T F 8. An unconditional probability is also known as a marginal probability.

T F 9. A subjective probability may be nothing more than an educated guess.

T F 10. When the occurrence of some event has no effect on the probability of occurrence of some other event, the two events are said to be statistically independent.

T F 11. When using the relative frequency approach, probability figures become less accurate for large numbers of observations.

T F 12. Symbolically, a marginal probability is denoted $P(AB)$.

T F 13. If A and B are statistically dependent events, the probability of A and B occurring is $P(A) \times P(B)$.

T F 14. Classical probability assumes that each of the possible outcomes of an experiment is equally likely.

T F 15. One reason that decision makers at high levels often use subjective probabilities is that they are concerned with unique situations.

T F 16. In assessing the probability of some event, the relative frequency of occurrence approach gives the greatest flexibility.

T F 17. Bayes' theorem is the formula used for finding conditional probabilities under statistical dependence.

T F 18. One disadvantage of the subjective approach to probability is that it assumes away unlikely events.

T F 19. The relative frequency approach to probability will provide correct statistical probabilities after 100 trials.

T F 20. When using a subjective approach to probability, two people with the same given information can produce different but equally correct answers.

T F 21. A and B are independent events if $P(A|B) = P(B)$.

A B C D E 22. If one event is unaffected by the outcome of another event, the two events are said to be

(a) Dependent.
(b) Independent.
(c) Mutually exclusive.
(d) All of the above.
(e) Both (b) and (c).

A B C D 23. If $P(A \text{ or } B) = P(A)$, then

(a) A and B are mutually exclusive.
(b) The Venn diagram areas for A and B overlap.
(c) $P(A) + P(B)$ is the joint probability of A and B.
(d) None of the above.

A B C D 24. The simple probability of an occurrence of an event is called the

(a) Bayesian probability.
(b) Joint probability.
(c) Marginal probability.
(d) Conditional probability.

A B C D E 25. Why are the events of a coin toss mutually exclusive?

(a) The outcome of any toss is not affected by the outcomes of those preceding it.
(b) Both a head and a tail cannot turn up on any one toss.

(c) The probability of getting a head and the probability of getting a tail are the same.

(d) All of these.

(e) (a) and (b) but not (c).

26. If a Venn diagram were drawn for events *A* and *B*, which are mutually exclusive, which of the following would always be true of *A* and *B*?

(a) Their parts of the rectangle will overlap.

(b) Their parts of the rectangle will be equal in area.

(c) Their parts of the rectangle will not overlap.

(d) None of these.

(e) (b) and (c) but not (a).

27. What is the probability that a value chosen at random from a particular population is larger than the median of the population?

(a) 0.25.

(b) 0.5.

(c) 1.0.

(d) 0.67.

28. Assume that a single fair die is rolled once. Which of the following is true?

(a) The probability of rolling a number higher than 1 is 1 − P(1 is rolled).

(b) The probability of rolling a 3 is 1 − P(1, 2, 4, 5, or 6 is rolled).

(c) The probability of rolling a 5 or 6 is higher than the probability of rolling a 3 or 4.

(d) All of these.

(e) (a) and (b) but not (c).

29. If A and B are mutually exclusive events, then $P(A \text{ or } B) = P(A) + P(B)$. How does the calculation of $P(A \text{ or } B)$ change if A and B are *not* mutually exclusive?

(a) $P(AB)$ must be subtracted from $P(A) + P(B)$.

(b) $P(AB)$ must be added to $P(A) + P(B)$.

(c) $[P(A) + P(B)]$ must be multiplied by $P(AB)$.

(d) $[P(A) + P(B)]$ must be divided by $P(AB)$.

(e) None of these.

30. Leo C. Swartz, a taxi driver in Chicago, has found that the weather affects his customers' tipping. If it is raining, his customers usually tip poorly. When it is not raining, however, they usually tip well. Which of the following is true?

(a) Tips and weather are statistically independent.

(b) The weather conditions Leo cited are not mutually exclusive.

(c) P(good tip | rain) is larger than P(bad tip | rain).

(d) None of these.

(e) (a) and (c) but not (b).

31. Assume that a die is rolled twice in succession and that you are asked to draw the probability tree showing all possible outcomes of the two rolls. How many branches will your tree have?

(a) 6.

(b) 12.

(c) 36.

(d) 42.

(e) 48.

Questions 32–34 refer to the following situation: Ten numbered balls are placed in an urn. Numbers 1–4 are red and numbers 5–10 are blue.

A B C D E 32. What is the probability that a ball drawn at random from the urn is blue?
(a) 0.1.
(b) 0.4.
(c) 0.6.
(d) 1.0.
(e) Cannot be determined from the information given.

A B C D E 33. The probability of drawing the ball numbered 3, of course, is 0.1. A ball is drawn, and it is red. Which of the following is true?
(a) P(ball drawn is #3 | ball drawn is red) = 0.1.
(b) P(ball drawn is #3 | ball drawn is red) < 0.1.
(c) P(ball drawn is #3 | ball drawn is red) > 0.1.
(d) P(ball drawn is red | ball drawn is #3) = 0.25.
(e) (c) and (d) only.

A B C D E 34. In Question 33, the probability of drawing the 3 ball was reconsidered after it was found that the ball drawn was red. The new probabilities we considered are called
(a) Exhaustive.
(b) A priori.
(c) Marginal.
(d) Subjective.
(e) None of these.

A B C D E 35. Symbolically, a marginal probability is
(a) $P(AB)$.
(b) $P(BA)$.
(c) $P(B|A)$.
(d) $P(ABC)$.
(e) None of these.

A B C D 36. If we sum all the probabilities of the conditional events in which the event A occurs while under statistical dependence, the result is
(a) The marginal probability of A.
(b) The joint probability of A.
(c) The conditional probability of A.
(d) None of these.

37. One of the possible outcomes of doing something is a ____________________.
The activity that produced this outcome is a ____________________.

38. The set of all possible outcomes of an activity is the ____________________.

39. A pictorial representation of probability concepts, using symbols to represent outcomes, is a ____________________.

40. Events that cannot happen together are called ____________________.

41. The probability of one event occurring, given that another event has occurred, is called ____________________ probability.

42. In terms of its assumptions, the least restrictive approach to the study of probability is the ______________________.

43. ______________________ theorem is often used in management decisions because it provides ways to update previous probability estimates based on new information.

44. A list is ______________________ if it includes all the possible outcomes that can result from an experiment.

45. Three different approaches to probability are the ______________________ approach, the ______________________ approach, and the ______________________ approach.

● Flow Chart: Probability I: Introductory Ideas

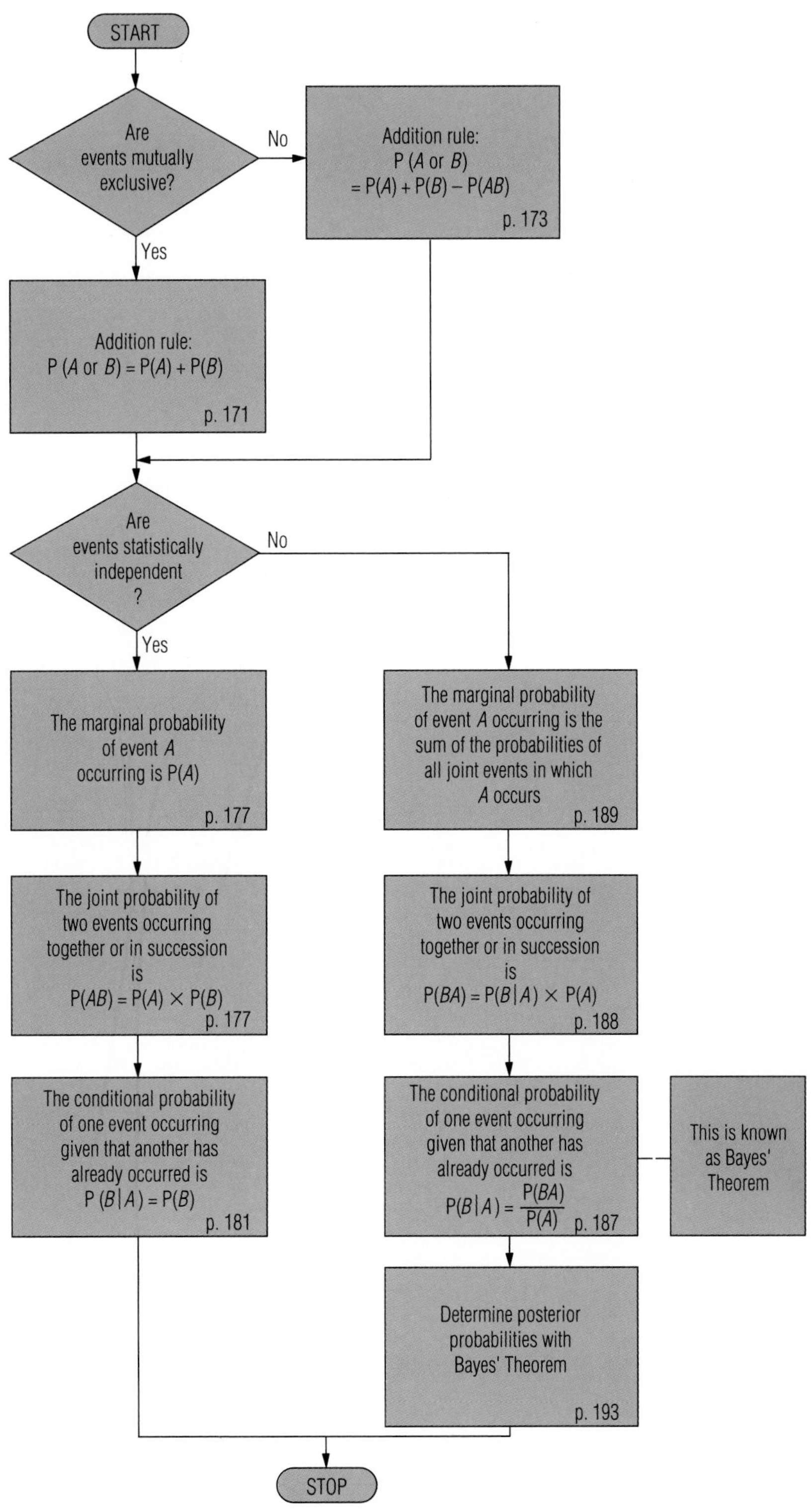
START
Are events mutually exclusive?
No
Addition rule: P (A or B) = P(A) + P(B) − P(AB)
p. 173
Yes
Addition rule: P (A or B) = P(A) + P(B)
p. 171
Are events statistically independent ?
No
Yes
The marginal probability of event A occurring is P(A)
p. 177
The marginal probability of event A occurring is the sum of the probabilities of all joint events in which A occurs
p. 189
The joint probability of two events occurring together or in succession is P(AB) = P(A) × P(B)
p. 177
The joint probability of two events occurring together or in succession is P(BA) = P(B|A) × P(A)
p. 188
The conditional probability of one event occurring given that another has already occurred is P (B|A) = P(B)
p. 181
The conditional probability of one event occurring given that another has already occurred is P(B|A) = P(BA)/P(A)
p. 187
This is known as Bayes' Theorem
Determine posterior probabilities with Bayes' Theorem
p. 193
STOP

chapter 5

PROBABILITY DISTRIBUTIONS

Objectives

- To introduce the probability distributions most commonly used in decision making
- To use the concept of expected value to make decisions
- To show which probability distribution to use and how to find its values
- To understand the limitations of each of the probability distributions you use

Chapter Contents

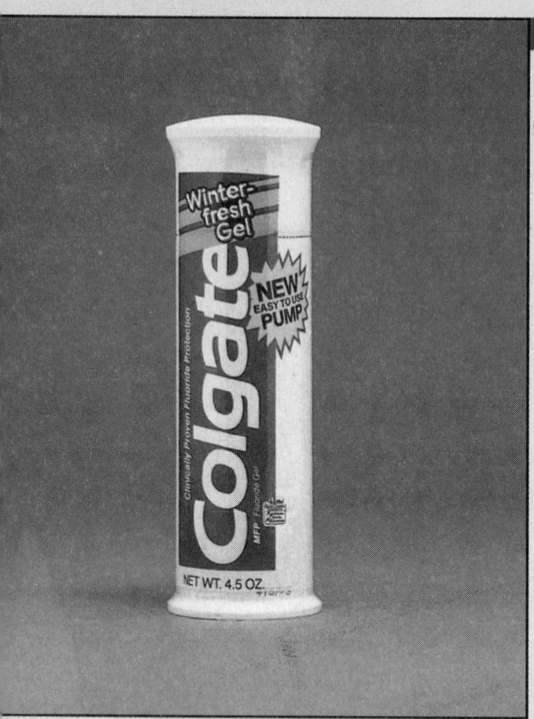

Modern filling machines are designed to work efficiently and with high reliability. Machines can fill toothpaste pumps to within 0.1 ounce of the desired level 80 percent of the time. A visitor to the plant, watching filled pumps being placed into cartons, asked, "What's the chance that exactly half the pumps in a carton selected at random will be filled to within 0.1 ounce of the desired level?" Although we cannot make an exact forecast, the ideas about probability distributions discussed in this chapter enable us to give a pretty good answer to the question. ■

5.1 What Is a Probability Distribution?

Probability distributions and frequency distributions

In Chapter 2, we described frequency distributions as a useful way of summarizing variations in observed data. We prepared frequency distributions by listing all the possible outcomes of an experiment and then indicating the observed frequency of each possible outcome. *Probability distributions* are related to frequency distributions. **In fact, we can think of a probability distribution as a theoretical frequency distribution.** Now, what does that mean? A theoretical frequency distribution is a probability distribution that describes how outcomes are *expected* to vary. Because these distributions deal with expectations, they are useful models in making inferences and decisions under conditions of uncertainty. In later chapters, we will discuss the methods we use under these conditions.

Examples of Probability Distributions

Experiment using a fair coin

To begin our study of probability distributions, let's go back to the idea of a fair coin, which we introduced in Chapter 4. Suppose we toss a fair coin twice. Table 5-1 illustrates the possible outcomes from this two-toss experiment.

Table 5-1

Possible Outcomes from Two Tosses of a Fair Coin

First Toss	Second Toss	Number of Tails on Two Tosses	Probability of the Four Possible Outcomes
T	T	2	$0.5 \times 0.5 = 0.25$
T	H	1	$0.5 \times 0.5 = 0.25$
H	H	0	$0.5 \times 0.5 = 0.25$
H	T	1	$0.5 \times 0.5 = 0.25$
			1.00

Table 5-2 Probability Distribution of the Possible Number of Tails from Two Tosses of a Fair Coin

Number of Tails, T	Tosses	Probability of This Outcome, P(*T*)
0	(*H*, *H*)	0.25
1	(*T*, *H*) + (*H*, *T*)	0.50
2	(*T*, *T*)	0.25

Now suppose that we are interested in formulating a probability distribution of the number of tails that could possibly result when we toss the coin twice. We would begin by noting any outcome that did *not* contain a tail. With a fair coin, that is only the third outcome in Table 5-1: *H, H.* Then we would note the outcomes containing only one tail (the second and fourth outcomes in Table 5-1) and, finally, we would note that the first outcome contains two tails. In Table 5-2, we rearrange the outcomes of Table 5-1 to emphasize the number of tails contained in each outcome. We must be careful to note at this point that Table 5-2 is *not* the actual outcome of tossing a fair coin twice. Rather, it is a *theoretical* outcome, that is, it represents the way in which we would *expect* our two-toss experiment to behave over time.

We can illustrate in graphic form the probability distribution in Table 5-2. To do this, we graph the number of tails we might see on two tosses against the probability that this number would happen. We show this graph in Figure 5-1.

Voting example

Consider another example. A political candidate for local office is considering the votes she can get in a coming election. Assume that votes can take on only four possible values. If the candidate's assessment is like this:

Number of votes	1,000	2,000	3,000	4,000	
Probability this will happen	0.1	0.3	0.4	0.2	**Total 1.0**

then the graph of the probability distribution representing her expectations will be like the one shown in Figure 5-2.

Difference between frequency distributions and probability distributions

Before we move on to other aspects of probability distributions, we should point out that a **frequency distribution is a listing of the observed frequencies of all the outcomes of an**

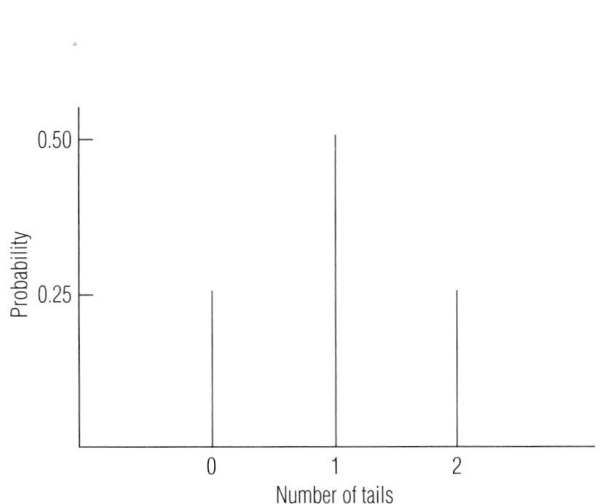

FIGURE 5-1 Probability distribution of the number of tails in two tosses of a fair coin

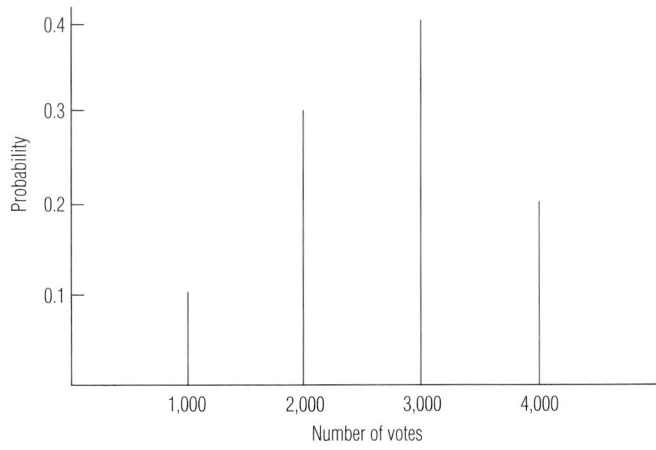

FIGURE 5-2 Probability distribution of the number of votes

Tigerhawks to replace half of its 5,000 jet fighters. Finally, there is one chance in 10 that the Air Force will replace all of its jet fighters with Tigerhawks and will buy enough Tigerhawks to expand its jet fighter fleet by 10 percent. Construct a table and draw a graph of the probability distribution of sales of Tigerhawks to the Air Force.

5.2 Random Variables

Random variable defined

A variable is random if it takes on different values as a result of the outcomes of a random experiment. A random variable can be either discrete or continuous. If a random variable is allowed to take on only a limited number of values, which can be listed, it is a *discrete random variable.* On the other hand, if it is allowed to assume any value within a given range, it is a *continuous random variable.*

Example of discrete random variables

You can think of a random variable as a value or magnitude that changes from occurrence to occurrence in no predictable sequence. A breast-cancer screening clinic, for example, has no way of knowing exactly how many women will be screened on any one day, so tomorrow's number of patients is a random variable. The values of a random variable are the numerical values corresponding to each possible outcome of the random experiment. If past daily records of the clinic indicate that the values of the random variable range from 100 to 115 patients daily, the random variable is a discrete random variable.

Creating a probability distribution

Table 5-3 illustrates the number of times each level has been reached during the last 100 days. Note that the table gives a frequency distribution. To the extent that we believe that the experience of the past 100 days has been typical, we can use this historical record to assign a probability to each possible number of patients and find a probability distribution. We have accomplished this in Table 5-4 by *normalizing* the observed frequency distribution (in this case, dividing each value in the right-hand column of Table 5-3 by 100, the total number of days for which the record has been kept). The probability distribution for the

Table 5-3

Number of Women Screened Daily During 100 Days

Number Screened	Number of Days This Level Was Observed
100	1
101	2
102	3
103	5
104	6
105	7
106	9
107	10
108	12
109	11
110	9
111	8
112	6
113	5
114	4
115	2
	100

Table 5-4 Probability Distribution for Number of Women Screened

Number Screened (Value of the Random Variable)	Probability That the Random Variable Will Take on This Value
100	0.01
101	0.02
102	0.03
103	0.05
104	0.06
105	0.07
106	0.09
107	0.10
108	0.12
109	0.11
110	0.09
111	0.08
112	0.06
113	0.05
114	0.04
115	0.02
	1.00

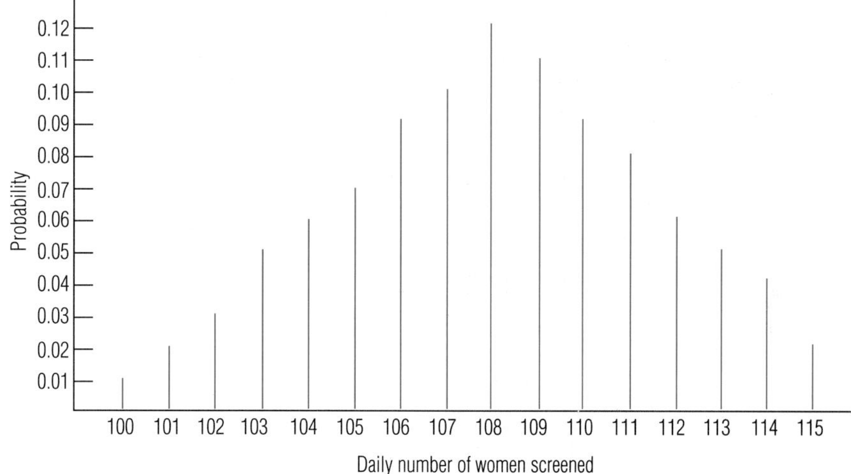

FIGURE 5-3

Probability distribution for the discrete random variable "daily number screened"

random variable "daily number screened" is illustrated graphically in Figure 5-3. Notice that the probability distribution for a random variable provides a probability for each possible value and that these probabilities must sum to 1. Table 5-4 shows that both these requirements have been met. Furthermore, both Table 5-4 and Figure 5-3 give us information about the long-run frequency of occurrence of daily patient screenings we would expect to observe if this random "experiment" were repeated.

The Expected Value of a Random Variable

Suppose you toss a coin 10 times and get 7 heads, like this:

Heads	Tails	Total
7	3	10

"Hmm, strange," you say. You then ask a friend to try tossing the coin 20 times; she gets 15 heads and 5 tails. So now you have, in all, 22 heads and 8 tails out of 30 tosses.

What did you expect? Was it something closer to 15 heads and 15 tails (half and half)? Now suppose you turn the tossing over to a machine and get 792 heads and 208 tails out of 1,000 tosses of the same coin. You might now be suspicious of the coin because it didn't live up to what you expected.

Expected value is a fundamental idea in the study of probability distributions. For many years, the concept has been put to considerable practical use by the insurance industry, and in the last 40 years, it has been widely used by many others who must make decisions under conditions of uncertainty.

Calculating expected value

To obtain the **expected value of a discrete random variable,** we multiply each value that the random variable can assume by the probability of occurrence of that value and then sum these products. Table 5-5 illustrates this procedure for our clinic problem. The total in the table tells us that the expected value of the discrete random variable "number screened" is 108.02 women. What does this mean? It means that over a long period of time, the number of daily screenings should average about 108.02. Remember that an expected value of 108.02 does *not* mean that tomorrow exactly 108.02 women will visit the clinic.

The clinic director would base her decisions on the expected value of daily screenings because the expected value is a *weighted average of the outcomes she expects in the future.* Expected value *weights* each possible outcome by the frequency with which it is expected to occur. Thus, more common occurrences are given more weight than are less common ones. As conditions change over time, the director would recompute the expected value of daily screenings and use this new figure as a basis for decision making.

Deriving expected value subjectively

In our clinic example, the director used past patients' records as the basis for calculating the expected value of daily screenings. The expected value can also be derived from the director's subjective assessments of the probability that the random variable will take on certain values. In that case, the expected value represents nothing more than her personal convictions about the possible outcome.

Table 5-5

Calculating the Expected Value of the Discrete Random Variable "Daily Number Screened"

Possible Values of the Random Variable (1)	Probability That the Random Variable Will Take on These Values (2)	(1) × (2)
100	0.01	1.00
101	0.02	2.02
102	0.03	3.06
103	0.05	5.15
104	0.06	6.24
105	0.07	7.35
106	0.09	9.54
107	0.10	10.70
108	0.12	12.96
109	0.11	11.99
110	0.09	9.90
111	0.08	8.88
112	0.06	6.72
113	0.05	5.65
114	0.04	4.56
115	0.02	2.30
Expected value of the random variable "daily number screened" →		**108.02**

In this section, we have worked with the probability distribution of a random variable in tabular form (Table 5-5) and in graphic form (Figure 5-3). In many situations, however, we will find it more convenient, in terms of the computations that must be done, to represent the probability distribution of a random variable in *algebraic* form. By doing this, we can make probability calculations by substituting numerical values directly into an algebraic formula. In the following sections, we shall illustrate some situations in which this is appropriate and methods for accomplishing it.

HINTS & ASSUMPTIONS

The expected value of a discrete random variable is nothing more than the weighted average of each possible outcome, multiplied by the probability of that outcome happening, just like we did it in Chapter 3. Warning: The use of the term *expected* can be misleading. For example, if we calculated the expected value of number of women to be screened to be 11, we *don't* think exactly this many will show up tomorrow. We are saying that, absent any other information, 11 women is the best number we can come up with as a basis for planning how many nurses we'll need to screen them. Hint: If daily patterns in the data are discernible (more women on Monday than on Friday, for example) then build this into your decision. The same holds for monthly and seasonal patterns in the data.

Exercises 5.2

Self-Check Exercises

SC 5-1 Construct a probability distribution based on the following frequency distribution.

Outcome	102	105	108	111	114	117
Frequency	10	20	45	15	20	15

(a) Draw a graph of the hypothetical probability distribution.

(b) Compute the expected value of the outcome.

SC 5-2 Bob Walters, who frequently invests in the stock market, carefully studies any potential investment. He is currently examining the possibility of investing in the Trinity Power Company. Through studying past performance, Walters has broken the potential results of the investment into five possible outcomes with accompanying probabilities. The outcomes are annual rates of return on a single share of stock that currently costs $150. Find the expected value of the return for investing in a single share of Trinity Power.

Return on investment ($)	0.00	10.00	15.00	25.00	50.00
Probability	0.20	0.25	0.30	0.15	0.10

If Walters purchases stock whenever the expected rate of return exceeds 10 percent, will he purchase the stock, according to these data?

Basic Concepts

■ **5-7** Construct a probability distribution based on the following frequency distribution:

Outcome	2	4	6	8	10	12	15
Frequency	24	22	16	12	7	3	1

(a) Draw a graph of the hypothetical probability distribution.

(b) Compute the expected value of the outcome.

■ 5-8 From the following graph of a probability distribution

(a) Construct a table of the probability distribution.

(b) Find the expected value of the random variable.

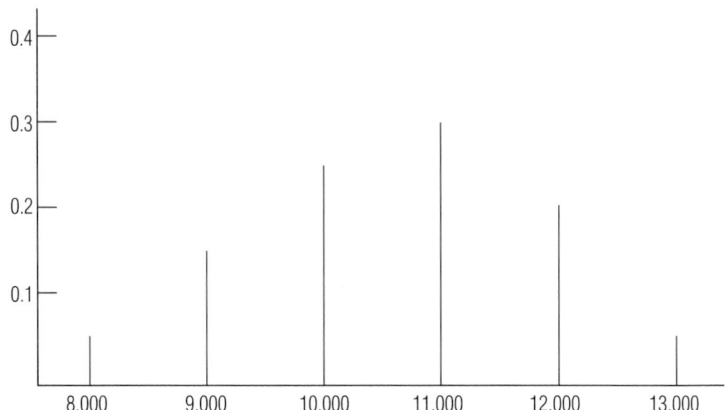

■ 5-9 The only information available to you regarding the probability distribution of a set of outcomes is the following list of frequencies:

X	0	15	30	45	60	75
Frequency	25	125	75	175	75	25

(a) Construct a probability distribution for the set of outcomes.

(b) Find the expected value of an outcome.

Applications

■ 5-10 Bill Johnson has just bought a VCR from Jim's Videotape Service at a cost of $300. He now has the option of buying an extended service warranty offering 5 years of coverage for $100. After talking to friends and reading reports, Bill believes the following maintenance expenses could be incurred during the next five years:

Expense	0	50	100	150	200	250	300
Probability	0.35	0.25	0.15	0.10	0.08	0.05	0.02

Find the expected value of the anticipated maintenance costs. Should Bill pay $100 for the warranty?

■ 5-11 Steven T. Opsine, supervisor of traffic signals for the Fairfax County division of the Virginia State Highway Administration, must decide whether to install a traffic light at the reportedly dangerous intersection of Dolley Madison Blvd. and Lewinsville Rd. Toward this end, Mr. Opsine has collected data on accidents at the intersection:

	Number of Accidents											
Year	**J**	**F**	**M**	**A**	**M**	**J**	**J**	**A**	**S**	**O**	**N**	**D**
1995	10	8	10	6	9	12	2	10	10	0	7	10
1996	12	9	7	8	4	3	7	14	8	8	8	4

S.H.A. policy is to install a traffic light at an intersection at which the monthly expected number of accidents is higher than 7. According to this criterion, should Mr. Opsine recommend that a traffic light be installed at this intersection?

■ **5-12** Alan Sarkid is the president of the Dinsdale Insurance Company and he is concerned about the high cost of claims that take a long time to settle. Consequently, he has asked his chief actuary, Dr. Ivan Acke, to analyze the distribution of time until settlement. Dr. Acke has presented him with the following graph:

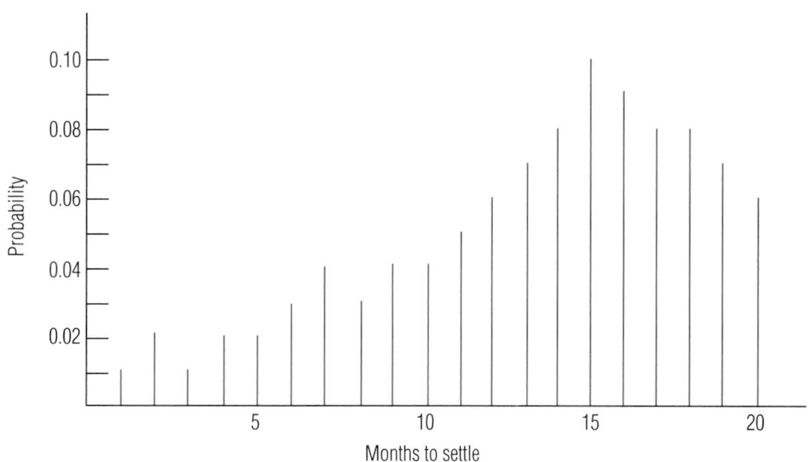

Dr. Acke also informed Mr. Sarkid of the expected amount of time to settle a claim. What is this figure?

■ **5-13** The fire marshal of Baltimore County, Maryland, is compiling a report on single-family-dwelling fires. He has the following data on the number of such fires from the last 2 years:

	Number of Fires											
Year	**J**	**F**	**M**	**A**	**M**	**J**	**J**	**A**	**S**	**O**	**N**	**D**
1995	25	30	15	10	10	5	2	2	1	4	8	10
1996	20	25	10	8	5	2	4	0	5	8	10	15

Based on these data

(a) What is the expected number of single-family-dwelling fires per month?

(b) What is the expected number of single-family-dwelling fires per winter month (January, February, March)?

■ **5-14** Ted Olson, the director of Overnight Delivery, Inc., has become concerned about the number of first-class letters lost by his firm. Because these letters are carried by both truck and airplane, Mr. Olson has broken down the lost letters for the last year into those lost from trucks and those lost from airplanes. His data are as follows:

Number Lost from	**J**	**F**	**M**	**A**	**M**	**J**	**J**	**A**	**S**	**O**	**N**	**D**
Truck	4	5	2	3	2	1	3	5	4	7	0	1
Airplane	5	6	0	2	1	3	4	2	4	7	4	0

Mr. Olson plans to investigate either the trucking or air division of the company, but not both. If he decides to investigate the division with the highest expected number of lost letters per month, which will he investigate?

Worked-Out Answers to Self-Check Exercises

SC 5-1 (a)

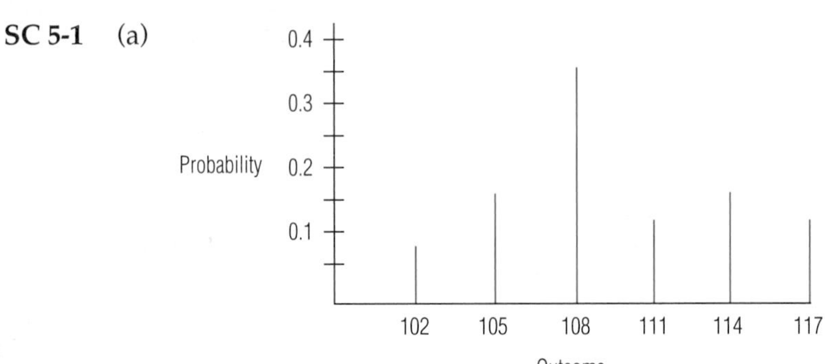

(b)

Outcome (1)	Frequency (2)	P(Outcome) (3)	(1) × (3)
102	10	0.08	8.16
105	20	0.16	16.80
108	45	0.36	38.88
111	15	0.12	13.32
114	20	0.16	18.24
117	15	0.12	14.04
	125	1.00	109.44 = Expected outcome

SC 5-2

Return (1)	P(Return) (2)	(1) × (2)
0	0.20	0.00
10	0.25	2.50
15	0.30	4.50
25	0.15	3.75
50	0.10	5.00
	1.00	15.75 = Expected return

Bob will purchase the stock because the expected return of $15.75 is greater than 10 percent of the $150 purchase price.

5.3 Use of Expected Value in Decision Making

In the preceding section, we calculated the expected value of a random variable and noted that it can have significant value to decision makers. Now we need to take a moment to illustrate how decision makers combine the probabilities that a random variable will take on certain values with the monetary gain or loss that results when it does take on those values. Doing just this enables them to make intelligent decisions under uncertain conditions.

Combining Probabilities and Monetary Values

Wholesaler problem

Let us look at the case of a fruit and vegetable wholesaler who sells strawberries. This product has a very limited useful life. If not sold on the day of delivery, it is worthless. One case of strawberries costs $20, and the wholesaler receives $50 for it. The wholesaler cannot specify the number of cases customers will call for on any one day, but her analysis of past records has produced the information in Table 5-6.

Types of Losses Defined

Obsolescence and opportunity losses

Two types of losses are incurred by the wholesaler: (1) *obsolescence losses,* caused by stocking too much fruit on any one day and having to throw it away the next day; and (2) *opportunity losses,* caused by being out of strawberries any time that customers call for them. (Customers will not wait beyond the day a case is requested.)

Table of conditional losses

Table 5-7 is a table of conditional losses. Each value in the table is conditional on a specific number of cases being stocked and a specific number being requested. The values in Table 5-7 include not only losses from decaying berries, but also those losses resulting from lost revenue when the wholesaler is unable to supply the requests she receives for the berries.

Neither of these two types of losses is incurred when the number of cases stocked on any one day is the same as the number of cases requested. When that happens, the wholesaler sells all she has stocked and incurs no losses. This situation is indicated by a colored zero in the appropriate column. Figures **above** any zero represent losses arising from spoiled berries. In each case here, the number of cases stocked is greater than the number requested. For example, if the wholesaler stocks 12 cases but receives requests for only 10 cases, she loses $40 (or $20 per case for spoiled strawberries).

Obsolescence losses

Opportunity losses

Values **below** the colored zeros represent opportunity losses resulting from requests that cannot be filled. If only 10 cases are stocked on a day that 11 requests are received, the

Table 5-6 Sales During 100 Days

Daily Sales	Number of Days Sold	Probability of Each Number Being Sold
10	15	0.15
11	20	0.20
12	40	0.40
13	25	0.25
	100	1.00

Table 5-7 Conditional Loss Table

Possible Requests for Strawberries	Possible Stock Options 10	11	12	13
10	$ 0	$20	$40	$60
11	30	0	20	40
12	60	30	0	20
13	90	60	30	0

wholesaler suffers an opportunity loss of $30 for the case she cannot sell ($50 income per case that would have been received, minus $20 cost, equals $30).

Calculating Expected Losses

Examining each possible stock action, we can compute the expected loss. We do this by weighting each of the four possible loss figures in each column of Table 5-7 by the probabilities from Table 5-6. For a stock action of 10 cases, the expected loss is computed as in Table 5-8.

Meaning of expected loss

The conditional losses in Table 5-8 are taken from the second column of Table 5-7 for a stock action of 10 cases. The fourth column total in Table 5-8 shows us that if 10 cases are stocked each day, over a long period of time, the average or expected loss will be $52.50 a day. There is no guarantee that *tomorrow's* loss will be exactly $52.50.

Optimal solution

Tables 5-9 through 5-11 show the computations of the expected loss resulting from decisions to stock 11, 12, and 13 cases, respectively. **The optimal stock action is the one that will minimize expected losses.** This action calls for the stocking of 12 cases each day, at

Table 5-8

Expected Loss from Stocking 10 Cases

Possible Requests	Conditional Loss		Probability of This Many Requests		Expected Loss
10	$ 0	×	0.15	=	$ 0.00
11	30	×	0.20	=	6.00
12	60	×	0.40	=	24.00
13	90	×	0.25	=	22.50
			1.00		$52.50

Table 5-9

Expected Loss from Stocking 11 Cases

Possible Requests	Conditional Loss		Probability of This Many Requests		Expected Loss
10	$20	×	0.15	=	$ 3.00
11	0	×	0.20	=	0.00
12	30	×	0.40	=	12.00
13	60	×	0.25	=	15.00
			1.00		$30.00

Table 5-10

Expected Loss from Stocking 12 Cases

Possible Requests	Conditional Loss		Probability of This Many Requests		Expected Loss
10	$40	×	0.15	=	$ 6.00
11	20	×	0.20	=	4.00
12	0	×	0.40	=	0.00
13	30	×	0.25	=	7.50
			1.00	Minimum expected loss →	$17.50

Table 5-11

Expected Loss from Stocking 13 Cases

Possible Requests	Conditional Loss		Probability of This Many Requests		Expected Loss
10	$60	×	0.15	=	$ 9.00
11	40	×	0.20	=	8.00
12	20	×	0.40	=	8.00
13	0	×	0.25	=	0.00
			1.00		$25.00

which point the expected loss is minimized at $17.50. We could just as easily have solved this problem by taking an alternative approach, that is, *maximizing expected gain* ($50 received per case less $20 cost per case) instead of minimizing expected loss. The answer, 12 cases, would have been the same.

In our brief treatment of expected value, we have made quite a few assumptions. To name only two, we've assumed that demand for the product can take on only four values, and that the berries are worth nothing one day later. Both these assumptions reduce the value of the answer we got. In Chapter 17, you will again encounter expected-value decision making, but there we will develop the ideas as a part of statistical decision theory (a broader use of statistical methods to make decisions), and we shall devote an entire chapter to expanding the basic ideas we have developed at this point.

HINTS & ASSUMPTIONS

Warning: In our illustrative exercise, we've allowed the random variable to take on only four values. This is unrealistic in the real world and we did it here only to make the explanation easier. Any manager facing this problem in her job would know that demand might be as low as zero on a given day (weather, holidays) and as high as perhaps 50 cases on another day. Hint: With demand ranging from zero to 50 cases, it's a computational nightmare to solve this problem by the method we just used. But don't panic, we will introduce another method in Chapter 17 that can do this easily.

Exercises 5.3

Self-Check Exercise

SC 5-3 Mario, owner of Mario's Pizza Emporium, has a difficult decision on his hands. He has found that he always sells between one and four of his famous "everything but the kitchen sink" pizzas per night. These pizzas take so long to prepare, however, that Mario prepares all of them in advance and stores them in the refrigerator. Because the ingredients go bad within one day, Mario always throws out any unsold pizzas at the end of each evening. The cost of preparing each pizza is $7, and Mario sells each one for $12. In addition to the usual costs, Mario also calculates that each "everything but" pizza that is ordered but he cannot deliver due to insufficient stock costs him $5 in future business. How many "everything but" pizzas should Mario stock each night in order to minimize expected loss if the number of pizzas ordered has the following probability distribution?

Number of pizzas demanded	1	2	3	4
Probability	0.40	0.30	0.20	0.10

Applications

■ **5-15** Harry Byrd, the director of publications for the Baltimore Orioles, is trying to decide how many programs to print for the team's upcoming three-game series with the Oakland A's. Each program costs 25¢ to print and sells for \$1.25. Any programs unsold at the end of the series must be discarded. Mr. Byrd has estimated the following probability distribution for program sales, using data from past program sales:

Programs sold	25,000	40,000	55,000	70,000
Probability	0.10	0.30	0.45	0.15

Mr. Byrd has decided to print either 25, 40, 55, or 70 thousand programs. Which number of programs will minimize the team's expected losses?

■ **5-16** Airport Rent-a-Car is a locally operated business in competition with several major firms. ARC is planning a new deal for prospective customers who want to rent a car for only one day and will return it to the airport. For \$35, the company will rent a small economy car to a customer, whose only other expense is to fill the car with gas at day's end. ARC is planning to buy a number of small cars from the manufacturer at a reduced price of \$6,300. The big question is how many to buy. Company executives have decided on the following distribution of demands per day for the service:

Number of cars rented	13	14	15	16	17	18
Probability	0.08	0.15	0.22	0.25	0.21	0.09

The company intends to offer the plan 6 days a week (312 days per year) and anticipates that its variable cost per car per day will be \$2.50. After the end of one year, the company expects to sell the cars and recapture 50 percent of the original cost. Disregarding the time value of money and any noncash expenses, use the expected-loss method to determine the optimal number of cars for ARC to buy.

■ **5-17** We Care Air needs to make a decision about Flight 105. There are currently 3 seats reserved for last-minute customers, but the airline does not know if anyone will buy them. If they release the seats now, they know they will be able to sell them for \$250 each. Last-minute customers must pay \$475 per seat. The decision must be made now, and any number of seats may be released. We Care Air has the following probability distribution to help them:

Number of last-minute customers requesting seats	0	1	2	3
Probability	0.45	0.30	0.15	0.10

The company also counts a \$150 loss of goodwill for every last-minute customer who is turned away.

(a) How much revenue will be generated by releasing all 3 seats now?

(b) What is the company's expected net revenue (revenue less loss of goodwill) if 3 seats are released now?

(c) What is the company's expected net revenue if 2 seats are released now?

(d) How many seats should be released to maximize expected revenue?

Worked-Out Answer to Self-Check Exercise

SC 5-3

Loss Table

	Pizzas Demanded				
	1	2	3	4	
Probability	0.4	0.3	0.2	0.1	
Pizzas Stocked					Expected Loss
1	0	10	20	30	10.0
2	7	0	10	20	6.8 ←
3	14	7	0	10	8.7
4	21	14	7	0	14.0

Mario should stock two "everything but" pizzas each night.

5.4 The Binomial Distribution

The binomial distribution and Bernoulli processes

One widely used probability distribution of a discrete random variable is the *binomial distribution.* It describes a variety of processes of interest to managers. The binomial distribution describes discrete, not continuous, data, resulting from an experiment known as a *Bernoulli process,* after the seventeenth-century Swiss mathematician Jacob Bernoulli. The tossing of a fair coin a fixed number of times is a Bernoulli process, and the outcomes of such tosses can be represented by the binomial probability distribution. The success or failure of interviewees on an aptitude test may also be described by a Bernoulli process. On the other hand, the frequency distribution of the lives of fluorescent lights in a factory would be measured on a continuous scale of hours and would not qualify as a binomial distribution.

Use of the Bernoulli Process

Bernoulli process described

We can use the outcomes of a fixed number of tosses of a fair coin as an example of a Bernoulli process. We can describe this process as follows:

1. Each trial (each toss, in this case) has only *two* possible outcomes: heads or tails, yes or no, success or failure.
2. The probability of the outcome of any trial (toss) remains *fixed* over time. With a fair coin, the probability of heads remains 0.5 for each toss regardless of the number of times the coin is tossed.
3. The trials are *statistically independent;* that is, the outcome of one toss does not affect the outcome of any other toss.

Characteristic probability defined

Each Bernoulli process has its own characteristic probability. Take the situation in which historically seven-tenths of all people who applied for a certain type of job passed the job test. We would say that the characteristic probability here is 0.7, but we could describe our testing results as Bernoulli only if we felt certain that the proportion of those passing the test (0.7) remained constant over time. The other characteristics of the Bernoulli process would also have to be met, of course. Each test would have only two outcomes (success or failure), and the results of each test would have to be statistically independent.

In more formal language, the symbol p represents the probability of a success (in our example, 0.7), and the symbol q ($q = 1 - p$), the probability of a failure (0.3). To represent a certain number of successes, we will use the symbol r; and to symbolize the total number of trials, we use the symbol n. In the situations we will be discussing, the number of trials is fixed before the experiment is begun.

Using this language in a simple problem, we can calculate the chances of getting exactly two heads (in any order) on three tosses of a fair coin. Symbolically, we express the values as follows:

- p = characteristic probability or probability of success = 0.5
- $q = 1 - p$ = probability of failure = 0.5
- r = number of successes desired = 2
- n = number of trials undertaken = 3

Binomial formula

We can solve the problem by using the *binomial formula:*

Binomial Formula

$$\text{Probability of } r \text{ successes in } n \text{ trials} = \frac{n!}{r!(n-r)!} p^r q^{n-r} \quad [5\text{-}1]$$

Although this formula may look somewhat complicated, it can be used quite easily. The symbol ! means *factorial,* which is computed as follows: 3! means $3 \times 2 \times 1$, or 6. To calculate 5!, we multiply $5 \times 4 \times 3 \times 2 \times 1 = 120$. Mathematicians define 0! as equal to 1. Using the binomial formula to solve our problem, we discover

$$\begin{aligned}\text{Probability of 2 successes in 3 trials} &= \frac{3!}{2!(3-2)!}(0.5)^2(0.5)^1\\ &= \frac{3 \times 2 \times 1}{(2 \times 1)(1 \times 1)}(0.5)^2(0.5)\\ &= \frac{6}{2}(0.25)(0.5)\\ &= 0.375\end{aligned}$$

Thus, there is a 0.375 probability of getting two heads on three tosses of a fair coin.

By now you've probably recognized that we can use the binomial distribution to determine the probabilities for the toothpaste pump problem we introduced at the beginning of this chapter. Recall that historically, eight-tenths of the pumps were correctly filled (successes). If we want to compute the probability of getting exactly three of six pumps (half a carton) correctly filled, we can define our symbols this way:

$$p = 0.8$$
$$q = 0.2$$
$$r = 3$$
$$n = 6$$

and then use the binomial formula as follows:

$$\text{Probability of } r \text{ successes in } n \text{ trials} = \frac{n!}{r!(n-r)!} p^r q^{n-r} \quad [5\text{-}1]$$

$$\begin{aligned} \text{Probability of 3 out of 6 pumps correctly filled} &= \frac{6 \times 5 \times 4 \times 3 \times 2 \times 1}{(3 \times 2 \times 1)(3 \times 2 \times 1)} (0.8)^3(0.2)^3 \\ &= \frac{720}{6 \times 6}(0.512)(0.008) \\ &= (20)(0.512)(0.008) \\ &= 0.08192 \end{aligned}$$

Binomial tables are available

Of course, we *could* have solved these two problems using the probability trees we developed in Chapter 4, but for larger problems, trees become quite cumbersome. In fact, using the binomial formula (Equation 5-1) is no easy task when we have to compute the value of something like 19 factorial. For this reason, binomial probability tables have been developed, and we shall use them shortly.

Some Graphic Illustrations of the Binomial Distribution

To this point, we have dealt with the binomial distribution only in terms of the binomial formula, but the binomial, like any other distribution, can be expressed graphically as well.

To illustrate several of these distributions, consider a situation at Kerr Pharmacy, where employees are often late. Five workers are in the pharmacy. The owner has studied the situation over a period of time and has determined that there is a 0.4 chance of any one employee being late and that they arrive independently of one another. How would we draw a binomial probability distribution illustrating the probabilities of 0, 1, 2, 3, 4, or 5 workers being late simultaneously? To do this, we would need to use the binomial formula, where

$$p = 0.4$$
$$q = 0.6$$
$$n = 5^*$$

and to make a separate computation for each *r*, from 0 through 5. Remember that, mathematically, any number to the zero power is defined as being equal to 1. Beginning with our binomial formula:

$$\text{Probability of } r \text{ late arrivals out of } n \text{ workers} = \frac{n!}{r!(n-r)!} p^r q^{n-r} \quad [5\text{-}1]$$

*When we define *n*, we look at the number of workers. The fact that there is a possibility that none will be late does not alter our choice of $n = 5$.

Using the Binomial Tables

Solving problems using the binomial tables

Earlier we recognized that it is tedious to calculate probabilities using the binomial formula when n is a large number. Fortunately, we can use Appendix Table 3 to determine binomial probabilities quickly.

To illustrate the use of the binomial tables, consider this problem. What is the probability that 8 of the 15 registered Democrats on Prince Street will fail to vote in the coming primary if the probability of any individual's not voting is 0.30 and if people decide independently of each other whether or not to vote? First, we represent the elements in this problem in binomial distribution notation:

$n = 15$	number of registered Democrats
$p = 0.30$	probability that any one individual won't vote
$r = 8$	number of individuals who will fail to vote

How to use the binomial tables

Then, because the problem involves 15 trials, we must find the table corresponding to $n = 15$. Because the probability of an individual's not voting is 0.30, we look through the binomial tables until we find the column headed 0.30. We then move down that column until we are opposite the $r = 8$ row, where we read the answer 0.0348. This is the probability of eight registered voters not voting.

Suppose the problem had asked us to find the probability of eight or more registered voters not voting? We would have looked under the 0.30 column and added up the probabilities there from 8 to the bottom of the column like this:

8	0.0348
9	0.0116
10	0.0030
11	0.0006
12	0.0001
13	0.0000
	0.0501

The answer is that there is a 0.0501 probability of eight or more registered voters not voting.

Suppose now that the problem asked us to find the probability of *fewer* than eight nonvoters. Again, we would have begun with the 0.30 column, but this time we would add the probabilities from 0 (the top of the $n = 15$ column) *down* to 7 (the highest value less than 8), like this:

0	0.0047
1	0.0305
2	0.0916
3	0.1700
4	0.2186
5	0.2061
6	0.1472
7	0.0811
	0.9498

The answer is that there is a 0.9498 probability of fewer than eight nonvoters.

Because r (the number of nonvoters) is *either* 8 or more, *or else* fewer than 8, it must be true that

$$P(r \geq 8) + P(r < 8) = 1$$

But according to the values we just calculated,

$$P(r \geq 8) + P(r < 8) = 0.0501 + 0.9498 = 0.9999$$

The slight difference between 1 and 0.9999 is due to rounding errors resulting from the fact that the binomial table gives the probabilities to only 4 decimal places of accuracy.

You will see that the binomial table probabilities at the tops of the columns of figures go only up to 0.50. How do you solve problems with probabilities larger than 0.5? Simply go back through the binomial tables and look this time at the probability values at the *bottoms* of the columns; these go from 0.50 through 0.99.

Measures of Central Tendency and Dispersion for the Binomial Distribution

Computing the mean and the standard deviation

Earlier in this chapter, we encountered the concept of the expected value or mean of a probability distribution. The binomial distribution has an expected value or mean (μ) and a standard deviation (σ), and we should be able to compute both these statistical measures. Intuitively, we can reason that if a certain machine produces good parts with a $p = 0.5$, then, over time, the mean of the distribution of the number of good parts in the output would be 0.5 times the total output. If there is a 0.5 chance of tossing a head with a fair coin, over a large number of tosses, the mean of the binomial distribution of the number of heads would be 0.5 times the total number of tosses.

Symbolically, we can represent the mean of a binomial distribution as

The mean

Mean of a Binomial Distribution

$$\mu = np \qquad [5\text{-}2]$$

where

- n = number of trials
- p = probability of success

And we can calculate the standard deviation of a binomial distribution by using the formula

The standard deviation

Standard Deviation of a Binomial Distribution

$$\sigma = \sqrt{npq} \qquad [5\text{-}3]$$

where

- n = number of trials
- p = probability of success
- q = probability of failure $= 1 - p$

To see how to use Equations 5-2 and 5-3, take the case of a packaging machine that produces 20 percent defective packages. If we take a random sample of 10 packages, we can compute the mean and the standard deviation of the binomial distribution of that process like this:

$$\mu = np \quad [5\text{-}2]$$
$$= (10)(0.2)$$
$$= 2 \leftarrow \text{Mean}$$

$$\sigma = \sqrt{npq} \quad [5\text{-}3]$$
$$= \sqrt{(10)(0.2)(0.8)}$$
$$= \sqrt{1.6}$$
$$= 1.265 \leftarrow \text{Standard deviation}$$

Meeting the Conditions for Using the Bernoulli Process

Problems in applying the binomial distribution to real-life situations

We need to be careful in the use of the binomial probability to make certain that the three conditions necessary for a Bernoulli process introduced earlier are met, particularly conditions 2 and 3. Condition 2 requires the probability of the outcome of any trial to remain fixed over time. In many industrial processes, however, it is extremely difficult to guarantee that this is indeed the case. Each time an industrial machine produces a part, for instance, there is some infinitesimal wear on the machine. If this wear accumulates beyond a reasonable point, the proportion of acceptable parts produced by the machine will be altered, and condition 2 for the use of the binomial distribution may be violated. This problem is not present in a coin-toss experiment, but it is an integral consideration in all real applications of the binomial probability distribution.

Condition 3 requires that the trials of a Bernoulli process be statistically independent, that is, the outcome of one trial cannot affect in any way the outcome of any other trial. Here, too, we can encounter some problems in real applications. Consider an interviewing process in which high-potential candidates are being screened for top positions. If the interviewer has talked with five unacceptable candidates in a row, he may not view the sixth with complete impartiality. The trials, therefore, might not be statistically independent.

HINTS & ASSUMPTIONS

Warning: One of the requirements for using a Bernoulli process is that the probability of the outcome must be fixed over time. This is a very difficult condition to meet in practice. Even a fully automatic machine making parts will experience some wear as the number of parts increases and this will affect the probability of producing acceptable parts. Still another condition for its use is that the trials (manufacture of parts in our machine example) be independent. This too is a condition that is hard to meet. If our machine produces a long series of bad parts, this could affect the position (or sharpness) of the metal-cutting tool in the machine. Here, as in every other situation, going from the textbook to the real world is often difficult, and smart managers use their experience and intuition to know when a Bernoulli process is appropriate.

Exercises 5.4

Self-Check Exercises

SC 5-4 For a binomial distribution with $n = 12$ and $p = 0.45$, use Appendix Table 3 to find
- (a) $P(r = 8)$.
- (b) $P(r > 4)$.
- (c) $P(r \leq 10)$.

SC 5-5 Find the mean and standard deviation of the following binomial distributions:
- (a) $n = 16, p = 0.40$.
- (b) $n = 10, p = 0.75$.
- (c) $n = 22, p = 0.15$.
- (d) $n = 350, p = 0.90$.
- (e) $n = 78, p = 0.05$.

SC 5-6 The latest nationwide political poll indicates that for Americans who are randomly selected, the probability that they are conservative is 0.55, the probability that they are liberal is 0.30, and the probability that they are middle-of-the-road is 0.15. Assuming that these probabilities are accurate, answer the following questions pertaining to a randomly chosen group of 10 Americans. (Do not use Appendix Table 3.)
- (a) What is the probability that four are liberal?
- (b) What is the probability that none are conservative?
- (c) What is the probability that two are middle-of-the-road?
- (d) What is the probability that at least eight are liberal?

Basic Concepts

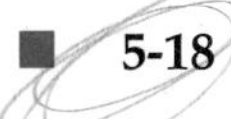

■ **5-18** For a binomial distribution with $n = 7$ and $p = 0.2$, find
- (a) $P(r = 5)$.
- (b) $P(r > 2)$.
- (c) $P(r < 8)$.
- (d) $P(r \geq 4)$.

■ **5-19** For a binomial distribution with $n = 15$ and $p = 0.2$, use Appendix Table 3 to find
- (a) $P(r = 6)$.
- (b) $P(r \geq 11)$.
- (c) $P(r \leq 4)$.

■ **5-20** Find the mean and standard deviation of the following binomial distributions:
- (a) $n = 15, p = 0.20$.
- (b) $n = 8, p = 0.42$.
- (c) $n = 72, p = 0.06$.
- (d) $n = 29, p = 0.49$.
- (e) $n = 642, p = 0.21$.

■ **5-21** For $n = 8$ trials, compute the probability that $r \geq 1$ for each of the following values of p:

(a) $p = 0.1$.
(b) $p = 0.3$.
(c) $p = 0.6$.
(d) $p = 0.4$.

Applications

■ **5-22** Harley Davidson, director of quality control for the Kyoto Motor company, is conducting his monthly spot check of automatic transmissions. In this procedure, 10 transmissions are removed from the pool of components and are checked for manufacturing defects. Historically, only 2 percent of the transmissions have such flaws. (Assume that flaws occur independently in different transmissions.)

(a) What is the probability that Harley's sample contains more than two transmissions with manufacturing flaws? (Do not use the tables.)

(b) What is the probability that none of the selected transmissions has any manufacturing flaws? (Do not use the tables.)

■ **5-23** Diane Bruns is the mayor of a large city. Lately, she has become concerned about the possibility that large numbers of people who are drawing unemployment checks are secretly employed. Her assistants estimate that 40 percent of unemployment beneficiaries fall into this category, but Ms. Bruns is not convinced. She asks one of her aides to conduct a quiet investigation of 10 randomly selected unemployment beneficiaries.

(a) If the mayor's assistants are correct, what is the probability that more than eight of the individuals investigated have jobs? (Do not use the tables.)

(b) If the mayor's assistants are correct, what is the probability that only three of the investigated individuals have jobs? (Do not use the tables.)

■ **5-24** A month later, Mayor Bruns (from Exercise 5-23) picks up the morning edition of the city's leading newspaper, the *Sun-American*, and reads an exposé of unemployment fraud. In this article, the newspaper claims that out of every 15 unemployment beneficiaries, the probability that four or more have jobs is 0.9095, and the expected number of employed beneficiaries exceeds 7. You are a special assistant to Mayor Bruns, who must respond to these claims at an afternoon press conference. She asks you to find the answers to the following two questions:

(a) Are the claims of the *Sun-American* consistent with each other?

(b) Does the first claim conflict with the opinion of the mayor's assistants?

■ **5-25** A recent study of how Americans spend their leisure time surveyed workers employed more than 5 years. They determined the probability an employee has 2 weeks of vacation time to be 0.45, 1 week of vacation time to be 0.10, and 3 or more weeks to be 0.20. Suppose 20 workers are selected at random. Answer the following questions without Appendix Table 3.

(a) What is the probability that 8 have 2 weeks of vacation time?

(b) What is the probability that only one worker has 1 week of vacation time?

(c) What is the probability that at most 2 of the workers have 3 or more weeks of vacation time?

(d) What is the probability that at least 2 workers have 1 week of vacation time?

■ **5-26** Harry Ohme is in charge of the electronics section of a large department store. He has noticed that the probability that a customer who is just browsing will buy something is 0.3. Suppose that 15 customers browse in the electronics section each hour. Use Appendix Table 3 in the back of the book to answer the following questions:

(a) What is the probability that at least one browsing customer will buy something during a specified hour?

(b) What is the probability that at least four browsing customers will buy something during a specified hour?

(c) What is the probability that no browsing customers will buy anything during a specified hour?

(d) What is the probability that no more than four browsing customers will buy something during a specified hour?

Worked-Out Answers to Self-Check Exercises

SC 5-4 Binomial ($n = 12, p = 0.45$).

(a) $P(r = 8) = 0.0762$

(b) $P(r > 4) = 1 - P(r \leq 4) = 1 - (0.0008 + 0.0075 + 0.0339 + 0.0923 + 0.1700) = 0.6955$

(c) $P(r \leq 10) = 1 - P(r \geq 11) = 1 - (0.0010 + 0.0001) = 0.9989$

SC 5-5

	n	p	$\mu = np$	$\sigma = \sqrt{npq}$
(a)	16	0.40	6.4	1.960
(b)	10	0.75	7.5	1.369
(c)	22	0.15	3.3	1.675
(d)	350	0.90	315.0	5.612
(e)	78	0.05	3.9	1.925

SC 5-6 (a) $n = 10, p = 0.30,\ P(r = 4) = \left(\frac{10!}{4!6!}\right)(0.30)^4(0.70)^6 = 0.2001$

(b) $n = 10, p = 0.55,\ P(r = 0) = \left(\frac{10!}{0!10!}\right)(0.55)^0(0.45)^{10} = 0.0003$

(c) $n = 10, p = 0.15,\ P(r = 2) = \left(\frac{10!}{2!8!}\right)(0.15)^2(0.85)^8 = 0.2759$

(d) $n = 10, p = 0.30,\ P(r \geq 8) = P(r = 8) + P(r = 9) + P(r = 10)$

$$= \left(\frac{10!}{8!2!}\right)(0.30)^8(0.70)^2 + \left(\frac{10!}{9!1!}\right)(0.30)^9(0.70)^1 + \left(\frac{10!}{10!0!}\right)(0.30)^{10}(0.70)^0$$

$$= 0.00145 + 0.00014 + 0.00001 = 0.0016$$

5.5 The Poisson Distribution

There are many discrete probability distributions, but our discussion will focus on only two: the *binomial,* which we have just concluded, and the *Poisson,* which is the subject of this section. The Poisson distribution is named for Siméon Denis Poisson (1781–1840), a French mathematician who developed the distribution from studies during the latter part of his lifetime.

Examples of Poisson distributions

The Poisson distribution is used to describe a number of processes, including the distribution of telephone calls going through a switchboard system, the demand (needs) of patients for service at a health institution, the arrivals of trucks and cars at a tollbooth, and the number of accidents at an intersection. These examples all have a common element: They can be described by a discrete random variable that takes on integer (whole) values (0, 1, 2, 3, 4, 5, and so on). The number of patients who arrive at a physician's office in a given interval of time will be 0, 1, 2, 3, 4, 5, or some other whole number. Similarly, if you count the number of cars arriving at a tollbooth on the New Jersey Turnpike during some 10-minute period, the number will be 0, 1, 2, 3, 4, 5, and so on.

Characteristics of Processes That Produce a Poisson Probability Distribution

Conditions leading to a Poisson probability distribution

The number of vehicles passing through a single turnpike tollbooth at rush hour serves as an illustration of Poisson probability distribution characteristics:

1. The average (mean) number of vehicles that arrive per rush hour can be estimated from past traffic data.
2. If we divide the rush hour into periods (intervals) of one second each, we will find these statements to be true:
   (a) The probability that exactly one vehicle will arrive at the single booth per second is a very small number and is constant for every one-second interval.
   (b) The probability that two or more vehicles will arrive within a one-second interval is so small that we can assign it a zero value.
   (c) The number of vehicles that arrive in a given one-second interval is independent of the time at which that one-second interval occurs during the rush hour.
   (d) The number of arrivals in any one-second interval is not dependent on the number of arrivals in any other one-second interval.

Now, we can generalize from these four conditions described for our tollbooth example and apply them to other processes. If these new processes meet the same four conditions, then we can use a Poisson probability distribution to describe them.

Calculating Poisson Probabilities Using Appendix Table 4a

The Poisson probability distribution, as we have explained, is concerned with certain processes that can be described by a discrete random variable. The letter X usually represents that discrete random variable, and X can take on integer values (0, 1, 2, 3, 4, 5, and so on). We use capital X to represent the random variable and lowercase x to represent a specific value that capital X can take. The probability of exactly x occurrences in a Poisson distribution is calculated with the formula

Poisson distribution formula

Poisson Formula

$$P(x) = \frac{\lambda^x \times e^{-\lambda}}{x!} \qquad [5\text{-}4]$$

Look more closely at each part of this formula:

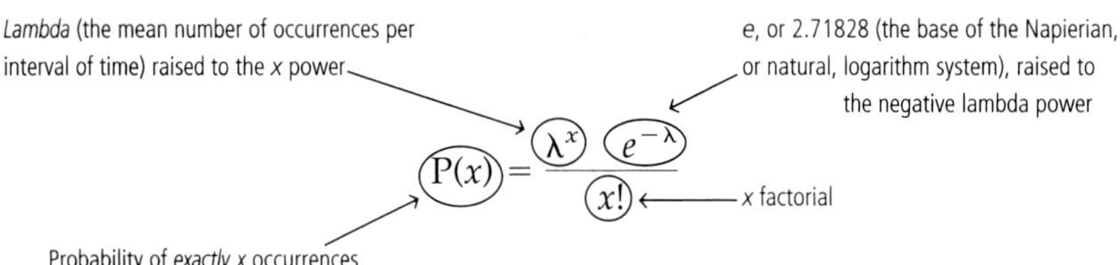

An example using the Poisson formula

Suppose that we are investigating the safety of a dangerous intersection. Past police records indicate a mean of five accidents per month at this intersection. The number of accidents is distributed according to a Poisson distribution, and the Highway Safety Division wants us to calculate the probability in any month of exactly 0, 1, 2, 3, or 4 accidents. We can use Appendix Table 4a to avoid having to calculate e's to negative powers. Applying the formula

$$P(x) = \frac{\lambda^x \times e^{-\lambda}}{x!} \qquad [5\text{-}4]$$

we can calculate the probability of no accidents:

$$\begin{aligned} P(0) &= \frac{(5)^0(e^{-5})}{0!} \\ &= \frac{(1)(0.00674)}{1} \\ &= 0.00674 \end{aligned}$$

For exactly one accident:

$$\begin{aligned} P(1) &= \frac{(5)^1(e^{-5})}{1!} \\ &= \frac{(5)(0.00674)}{1} \\ &= 0.03370 \end{aligned}$$

For exactly two accidents:

$$\begin{aligned} P(2) &= \frac{(5)^2(e^{-5})}{2!} \\ &= \frac{(25)(0.00674)}{2 \times 1} \\ &= 0.08425 \end{aligned}$$

For exactly three accidents:

$$\begin{aligned} P(3) &= \frac{(5)^3(e^{-5})}{3!} \\ &= \frac{(125)(0.00674)}{3 \times 2 \times 1} \\ &= \frac{0.8425}{6} \\ &= 0.14042 \end{aligned}$$

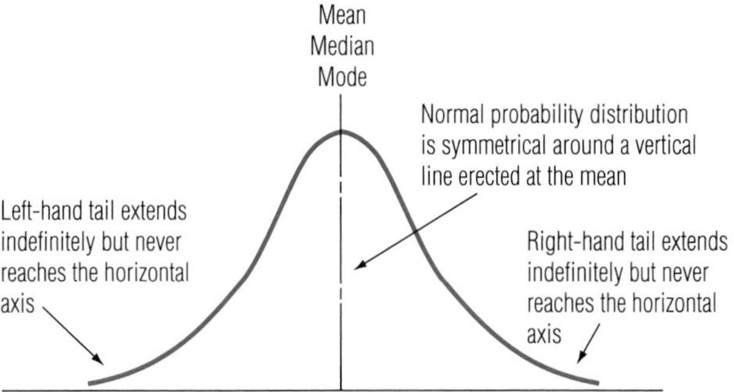

FIGURE 5-8

Frequency curve for the normal probability distribution

Table 5-14 Different Normal Probability Distributions

Nature of the Population	Its Mean	Its Standard Deviation
Annual earnings of employees at one plant	\$17,000/year	\$1,000
Length of standard 8′ building lumber	8′	0.05″
Air pollution in one community	2,500 particles per million	750 particles per million
Per capita income in a single developing country	\$1,400	\$300
Violent crimes per year in a given city	8,000	900

man characteristics (weights, heights, and IQs), outputs from physical processes (dimensions and yields), and other measures of interest to managers in both the public and private sectors.

Characteristics of the Normal Probability Distribution

Look for a moment at Figure 5-8. This diagram suggests several important features of a normal probability distribution:

1. The curve has a single peak; thus, it is unimodal. It has the bell shape that we described earlier.
2. The mean of a normally distributed population lies at the center of its normal curve.
3. Because of the symmetry of the normal probability distribution, the median and the mode of the distribution are also at the center; thus, for a normal curve, the mean, median, and mode are the same value.
4. The two tails of the normal probability distribution extend indefinitely and never touch the horizontal axis. (Graphically, of course, this is impossible to show.)

Significance of the two parameters that describe a normal distribution

Most real-life populations do not extend forever in both directions, but for such populations the normal distribution is a convenient approximation. There is no single normal curve, but rather a family of normal curves. To define a particular normal probability distribution, we need only two parameters: the mean (μ) and the standard deviation (σ). In Table 5-14, each of the populations is described only by its mean and its standard deviation, and each has a particular normal curve.

Figure 5-9 shows three normal probability distributions, each of which has the same mean but a different standard deviation. Although these curves differ in appearance, all three are "normal curves."

FIGURE 5-9

Normal probability distributions with identical means but different standard deviations

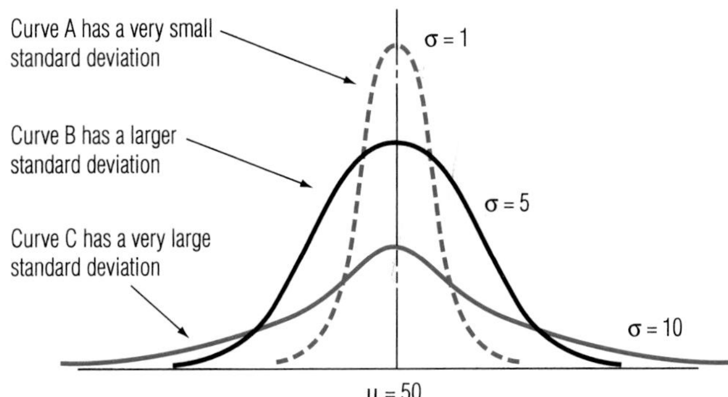

FIGURE 5-10

Normal probability distributions with different means but the same standard deviation

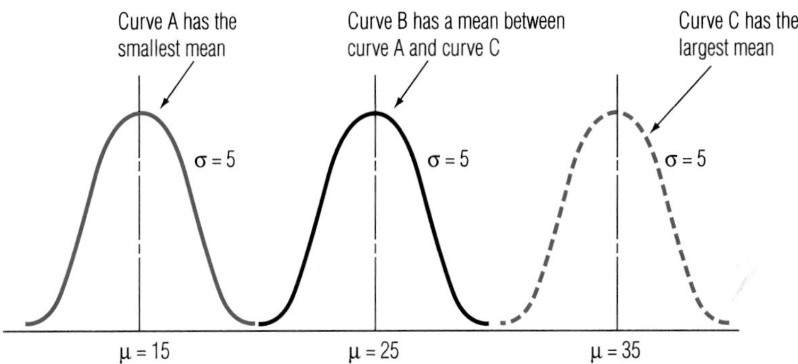

FIGURE 5-11

Three normal probability distributions, each with a different mean and a different standard deviation

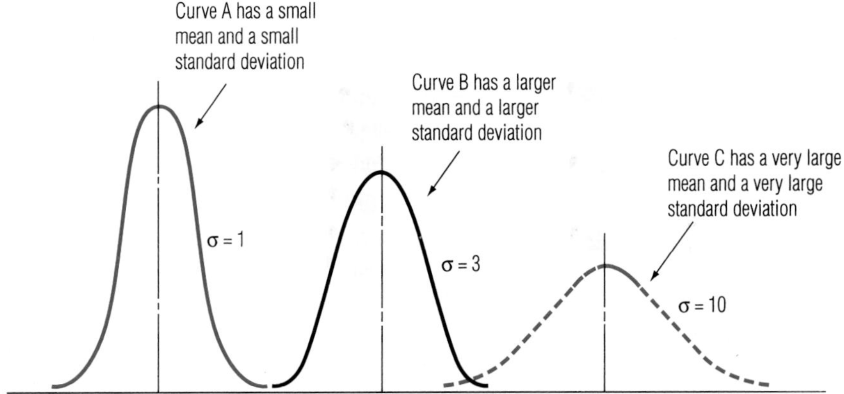

Figure 5-10 illustrates a "family" of normal curves, all with the same standard deviation, but each with a different mean.

Finally, Figure 5-11 shows three different normal probability distributions, each with a different mean *and* a different standard deviation. The normal probability distributions illustrated in Figures 5-9, 5-10, and 5-11 demonstrate that the normal curve can describe a large number of populations, differentiated only by the mean and/or the standard deviation.

Areas under the Normal Curve

Measuring the area under a normal curve

No matter what the values of μ and σ are for a normal probability distribution, the total area under the normal curve is 1.00, so that we may think of areas under the curve as probabilities. Mathematically, it is true that

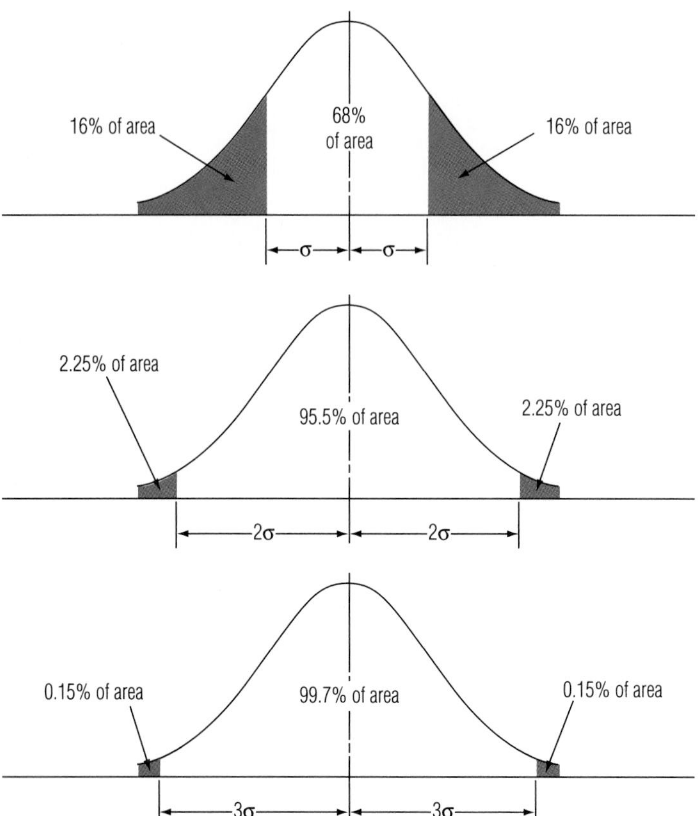

FIGURE 5-12

Relationship between the area under the curve for a normal probability distribution and the distance from the mean measured in standard deviations

1. Approximately 68 percent of all the values in a normally distributed population lie within ± 1 standard deviation from the mean.
2. Approximately 95.5 percent of all the values in a normally distributed population lie within ± 2 standard deviations from the mean.
3. Approximately 99.7 percent of all the values in a normally distributed population lie within ± 3 standard deviations from the mean.

These three statements are shown graphically in Figure 5-12.

Figure 5-12 shows three different ways of measuring the area under the normal curve. However, very few of the applications we shall make of the normal probability distribution involve intervals of *exactly* 1, 2, or 3 standard deviations (plus and minus) from the mean. What should we do about all these other cases? Fortunately, we can refer to statistical tables constructed for precisely these situations. They indicate portions of the area under the normal curve that are contained within any number of standard deviations (plus and minus) from the mean.

Standard normal probability distribution

It is not possible or necessary to have a different table for every possible normal curve. Instead, we can use a table of the *standard normal probability distribution* (a normal distribution with $\mu = 0$ and $\sigma = 1$) to find areas under any normal curve. With this table, we can determine the area, or probability, that the normally distributed random variable will lie within certain distances from the mean. These distances are defined in terms of standard deviations.

We can better understand the concept of the standard normal probability distribution by examining the special relationship of the standard deviation to the normal curve. Look at

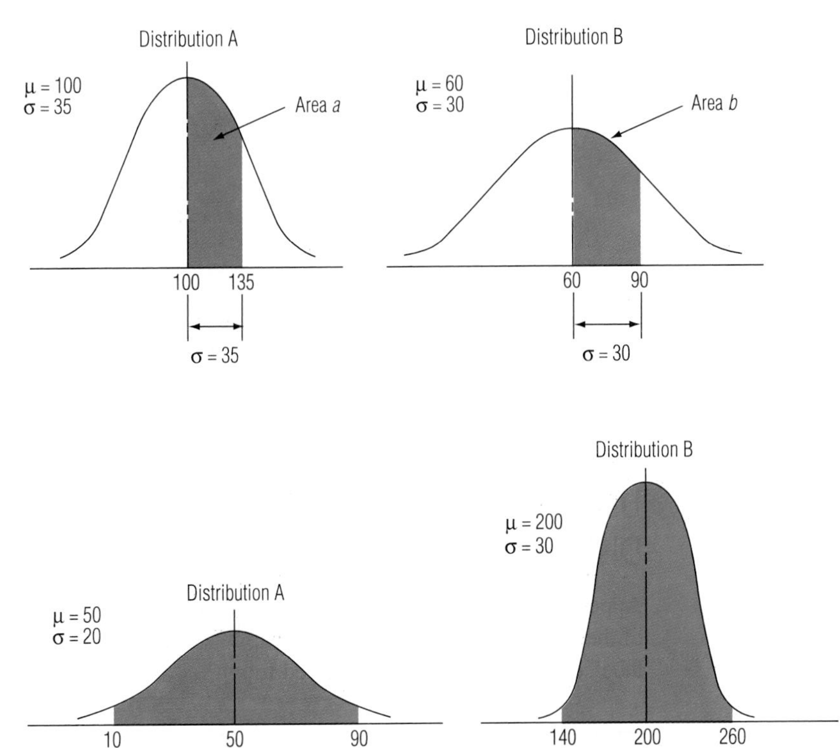

FIGURE 5-13

Two intervals, each one standard deviation to the right of the mean

FIGURE 5-14

Two intervals, each ±2 standard deviations from the mean

Figure 5-13. Here we have illustrated two normal probability distributions, each with a different mean and a different standard deviation. Both area *a* and area *b,* the shaded areas under the curves, contain the *same* proportion of the total area under the normal curve. Why? Because both these areas are defined as being the area between the mean and one standard deviation to the right of the mean. *All* intervals containing the same number of standard deviations from the mean will contain the same proportion of the total area under the curve for *any* normal probability distribution. This makes possible the use of only one standard normal probability distribution table.

Finding the percentage of the total area under the curve

Let's find out what proportion of the total area under the curve is represented by colored areas in Figure 5-13. In Figure 5-12, we saw that an interval of one standard deviation (plus *and* minus) from the mean contained about 68 percent of the total area under the curve. In Figure 5-13, however, we are interested only in the area between the mean and 1 standard deviation to the *right* of the mean (plus, *not* plus and minus). This area must be half of 68 percent, or 34 percent, for both distributions.

One more example will reinforce our point. Look at the two normal probability distributions in Figure 5-14. Each of these has a different mean and a different standard deviation. The colored area under *both* curves, however, contains the same proportion of the total area under the curve. Why? Because both colored areas fall within 2 standard deviations (plus and minus) from the mean. Two standard deviations (plus and minus) from the mean include the same proportion of the total area under *any* normal probability distribution. In this case, we can refer to Figure 5-12 again and see that the colored areas in both distributions in Figure 5-14 contain about 95.5 percent of the total area under the curve.

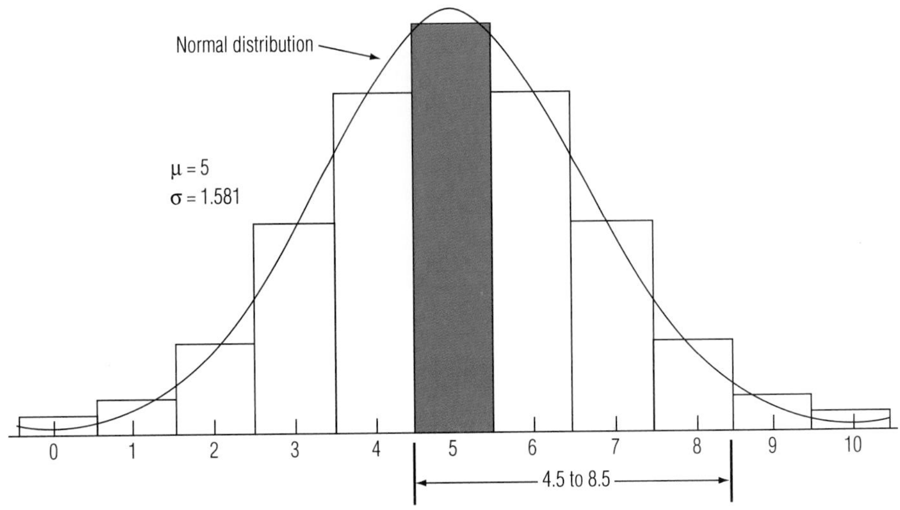

FIGURE 5-22

Binomial distribution with $n = 10$ and $p = {}^1/_2$, with a superimposed normal distribution with $\mu = 5$ and $\sigma = 1.581$

$$
\begin{aligned}
P(r = 5, 6, 7, \text{or } 8) &= P(r = 5) + P(r = 6) + P(r = 7) + P(r = 8) \\
&= 0.2461 + 0.2051 + 0.1172 + 0.0439 \\
&= 0.6123
\end{aligned}
$$

Two distributions with the same means and standard deviations

Figure 5-22 shows the binomial distribution for $n = 10$ and $p = {}^1/_2$ with a normal distribution superimposed on it with the *same* mean ($\mu = np = 10({}^1/_2) = 5$) and the *same* standard deviation ($\sigma = \sqrt{npq} = \sqrt{10({}^1/_2)({}^1/_2)} = \sqrt{2.5} = 1.581$).

Continuity correction factors

Look at the area under the normal curve between $5 - {}^1/_2$ and $5 + {}^1/_2$. We see that this area is *approximately* the same size as the area of the colored bar representing the binomial probability of getting five heads. The two ${}^1/_2$'s that we add to and subtract from 5 are called *continuity correction factors* and are used to improve the accuracy of the approximation.

Using the continuity correction factors, we see that the binomial probability of 5, 6, 7, or 8 heads can be approximated by the area under the normal curve between 4.5 and 8.5. Compute that probability by finding the z values corresponding to 4.5 and 8.5.

$$
\begin{aligned}
\text{At } x = 4.5 < z &= \frac{x - \mu}{\sigma} \qquad [5\text{-}6] \\
&= \frac{4.5 - 5}{1.581} \\
&= -0.32 \text{ standard deviation}
\end{aligned}
$$

$$
\begin{aligned}
\text{At } x = 8.5 < z &= \frac{x - \mu}{\sigma} \qquad [5\text{-}6] \\
&= \frac{8.5 - 5}{1.581} \\
&= 2.21 \text{ standard deviations}
\end{aligned}
$$

Now, from Appendix Table 1, we find

$$0.1255 \quad \text{(Probability that } z \text{ will be between } -0.32 \text{ and 0 (and, correspondingly, that } x \text{ will be between 4.5 and 5))}$$

$$+0.4864 \quad \text{(Probability that } z \text{ will be between 0 and 2.21 (and, correspondingly, that } x \text{ will be between 5 and 8.5))}$$

$$\mathbf{0.6119} \quad \text{(Probability that } x \text{ will be between 4.5 and 8.5)}$$

The error in estimating is slight

Comparing the binomial probability of 0.6123 (Appendix Table 3) with this normal approximation of 0.6119, we see that the error in the approximation is less than .1 percent.

The normal approximation to the binomial distribution is very convenient because it enables us to solve the problem without extensive tables of the binomial distribution. (You might note that Appendix Table 3, which gives binomial probabilities for values of n up to 20, is already 9 pages long.) **We should note that some care needs to be taken in using this approximation, but it is quite good whenever both *np and nq* are at least 5.**

Care must be taken

HINTS & ASSUMPTIONS

Warning: The normal distribution is the probability distribution most often used in statistics. Statisticians fear that too often, the data being analyzed are not well-described by a normal distribution. Fortunately there is a test to help you decide whether this is indeed the case, and we'll introduce it in Chapter 11 when we've laid a bit more foundation. Hint: Students who have trouble calculating probabilities using the normal distribution tend to do better when they actually sketch the distribution in question, indicate the mean and standard deviation, and then show the limits of the random variable in question (we use color but pencil shading is just as good). Visualizing the situation this way makes decisions easier (and answers more accurate).

Exercises 5.6

Self-Check Exercises

SC 5-9 Use the normal approximation to compute the binomial probabilities in parts (a)–(d) below:

(a) $n = 30, p = 0.35$, between 10 and 15 successes, inclusive.

(b) $n = 42, p = 0.62$, 30 or more successes.

(c) $n = 15, p = 0.40$, at most 7 successes.

(d) $n = 51, p = 0.42$, between 17 and 25 successes, inclusive.

SC 5-10 Dennis Hogan is the supervisor for the Conowingo Hydroelectric Dam. Mr. Hogan knows that the dam's turbines generate electricity at the peak rate only when at least 1,000,000 gallons of water pass through the dam each day. He also knows, from experience, that the daily flow is normally distributed, with the mean equal to the previous day's flow and a standard deviation of 200,000 gallons. Yesterday, 850,000 gallons flowed through the dam. What is the probability that the turbines will generate at peak rate today?

Basic Concepts

■ **5-37** Given that a random variable, X, has a normal distribution with mean 6.4 and standard deviation 2.7, find

(a) $P(4.0 < x < 5.0)$.

(b) $P(x > 2.0)$.

(c) $P(x < 7.2)$.

(d) $P((x < 3.0) \text{ or } (x > 9.0))$.

■ **5-38** Given that a random variable, X, has a binomial distribution with $n = 50$ trials and $p = 0.25$, use the normal approximation to the binomial to find

(a) $P(x > 10)$.

(b) $P(x < 18)$.

(c) $P(x > 21)$.

(d) $P(9 < x < 14)$.

■ **5-39** In a normal distribution with a standard deviation of 5.0, the probability that an observation selected at random exceeds 21 is 0.14.

(a) Find the mean of the distribution.

(b) Find the value below which 4 percent of the values in the distribution lie.

■ **5-40** Use the normal approximation to compute the binomial probabilities in parts (a.)–(e) below.

(a) $n = 35, p = 0.15$, between 7 and 10 successes inclusive.

(b) $n = 29, p = 0.25$, at least 9 successes.

(c) $n = 84, p = 0.42$, at most 40 successes.

(d) $n = 63, p = 0.11$, 10 or more successes.

(e) $n = 18, p = 0.67$, between 9 and 12 successes inclusive.

Applications

■ **5-41** The manager of a small postal substation is trying to quantify the variation in the weekly demand for mailing tubes. She has decided to assume that this demand is normally distributed. She knows that on average 100 tubes are purchased weekly and that 90 percent of the time, weekly demand is below 115.

(a) What is the standard deviation of this distribution?

(b) The manager wants to stock enough mailing tubes each week so that the probability of running out of tubes is no higher than 0.05. What is the lowest such stock level?

■ **5-42** The Gilbert Machinery Company has received a big order to produce electric motors for a manufacturing company. In order to fit in its bearing, the drive shaft of the motor must have a diameter of 5.1 ± 0.05 (inches). The company's purchasing agent realizes that there is a large stock of steel rods in inventory with a mean diameter of 5.07″, and a standard deviation of 0.07″. What is the probability of a steel rod from inventory fitting the bearing?

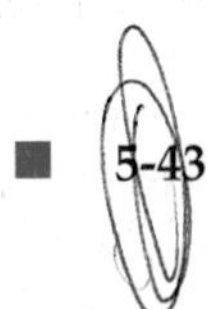

■ **5-43** The manager of a Spiffy Lube auto lubrication shop is trying to revise his policy on ordering grease gun cartridges. Currently, he orders 110 cartridges per week, but he runs out of cartridges 1 out of every 4 weeks. He knows that, on average, the shop uses 95 cartridges per week. He is also willing to assume that demand for cartridges is normally distributed.

(a) What is the standard deviation of this distribution?

(b) If the manager wants to order enough cartridges so that his probability of running out during any week is no greater than 0.2, how many cartridges should he order per week?

■ **5-44** Jarrid Medical, Inc., is developing a compact kidney dialysis machine, but its chief engineer, Mike Crowe, is having trouble controlling the variability of the rate at which fluid moves through the device. Medical standards require that the hourly flow be 4 liters, plus or minus 0.1 liter, 80 percent of the time. Mr. Crowe, in testing the prototype, has found that 68 percent of the time, the hourly flow is within 0.08 liter of 4.02 liters. Does the prototype satisfy the medical standards?

■ **5-45** Sgt. Wellborn Fitte, the U.S. Army's quartermaster at Fort Riley, Kansas, prides himself on being able to find a uniform to fit virtually any recruit. Currently, Sgt. Fitte is revising his stock requirements for fatigue caps. Based on experience, Sgt. Fitte has decided that hat size among recruits varies in such a way that it can be approximated by a normal distribution with a mean of 7″. Recently, though, he has revised his estimate of the standard deviation from 0.75 to 0.875. Present stock policy is to have on hand hats in every size (increments of $\frac{1}{8}$″) from 6 $\frac{1}{4}$″ to 7 $\frac{3}{4}$″. Assuming that a recruit is fit if his or her hat size is within this range, find the probability that a recruit is fit using

(a) The old estimate of the standard deviation.

(b) The new estimate of the standard deviation.

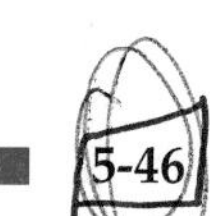

■ **5-46** Glenn Howell, VP of personnel for the Standard Insurance Company, has developed a new training program that is entirely self-paced. New employees work various stages at their own pace; completion occurs when the material is learned. Howell's program has been especially effective in speeding up the training process, as an employee's salary during training is only 67 percent of that earned upon completion of the program. In the last several years, average completion time of the program was 44 days, and the standard deviation was 12 days.

(a) Find the probability an employee will finish the program in 33 to 42 days.

(b) What is the probability of finishing the program in fewer than 30 days?

(c) Fewer than 25 or more than 60 days?

■ **5-47** On the basis of past experience, automobile inspectors in Pennsylvania have noticed that 5 percent of all cars coming in for their annual inspection fail to pass. Using the normal approximation to the binomial, find the probability that between 7 and 18 of the next 200 cars to enter the Lancaster inspection station will fail the inspection.

■ **5-48** R. V. Poppin, the concession stand manager for the local hockey rink, just had 2 cancellations on his crew. This means that if more than 72,000 people come to tonight's hockey game, the lines for hot dogs will constitute a disgrace to Mr. Poppin and will harm business at future games. Mr. Poppin knows from experience that the number of people who come to the game is normally distributed with mean 67,000 and standard deviation 4,000 people.

(a) What is the probability that there will be more than 72,000 people?

(b) Suppose Mr. Poppin can hire two temporary employees to make sure business won't be harmed in the future at an additional cost of $200. If he believes the future harm to business of having more than 72,000 fans at the game would be $5,000, should he hire the employees? Explain. (Assume there will be no harm if 72,000 or fewer fans show up, and that the harm due to too many fans doesn't depend on how many more than 72,000 show up.)

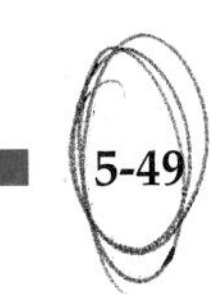

■ **5-49** Maurine Lewis, an editor for a large publishing company, calculates that it requires 11 months on average to complete the publication process from manuscript to finished book, with a standard deviation of 2.4 months. She believes that the normal distribution well describes the distribution of publication times. Out of 19 books she will handle this year, approximately how many will complete the process in less than a year?

■ **5-50** The Quickie Sales Corporation has just been given two conflicting estimates of sales for the upcoming quarter. Estimate I says that sales (in millions of dollars) will be normally distributed with $\mu = 325$ and $\sigma = 60$. Estimate II says that sales will be normally distributed with $\mu = 300$ and $\sigma = 50$. The board of directors finds that each estimate appears to be equally believable a priori. In order to determine which estimate should be used for future predictions, the board of directors has decided to meet again at the end of the quarter to use updated sales information to make a statement about the credibility of each estimate.

(a) Assuming that Estimate I is accurate, what is the probability that Quickie will have quarterly sales in excess of \$350 million?

(b) Rework part (a) assuming that Estimate II is correct.

(c) At the end of the quarter, the board of directors finds that Quickie Sales Corp. has had sales in excess of \$350 million. Given this updated information, what is the probability that Estimate I was originally the accurate one? (*Hint:* Remember Bayes' theorem.)

(d) Rework part (c) for Estimate II.

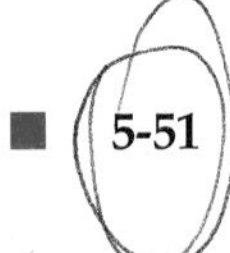

■ **5-51** The Nobb Door Company manufactures doors for recreational vehicles. It has two conflicting objectives: It wants to build doors as small as possible to save on material costs, but to preserve its good reputation with the public, it feels obligated to manufacture doors that are tall enough for 95 percent of the adult population in the United States to pass through without stooping. In order to determine the height at which to manufacture doors, Nobb is willing to assume that the height of adults in America is normally distributed with mean 73 inches and standard deviation 6 inches. How tall should Nobb's doors be?

Worked-Out Answers to Self-Check Exercises

SC 5-9 (a) $\mu = np = 30(0.35) = 10.5 \qquad \sigma = \sqrt{npq} = \sqrt{30(0.35)(0.65)} = 2.612$

$$P(10 \leq r \leq 15) = P\left(\frac{9.5 - 10.5}{2.612} \leq z \leq \frac{15.5 - 10.5}{2.612}\right)$$

$$= P(-0.38 \leq z \leq 1.91) = 0.1480 + 0.4719 = 0.6199$$

(b) $\mu = np = 42(0.62) = 26.04 \qquad \sigma = \sqrt{npq} = \sqrt{42(0.62)(0.38)} = 3.146$

$$P(r \geq 30) = P\left(z \geq \frac{29.5 - 26.04}{3.146}\right) = P(z \geq 1.10) = 0.5 - 0.3643 = 0.1357$$

(c) $\mu = np = 15(0.40) = 6 \qquad \sigma = \sqrt{npq} = \sqrt{15(0.40)(0.60)} = 1.895$

$$P(r \leq 7) = P\left(z \leq \frac{7.5 - 6}{1.897}\right) = P(z \leq 0.79) = 0.5 + 0.2852 = 0.7852$$

(d) $\mu = np = 51(0.42) = 21.42 \qquad \sigma = \sqrt{npq} = \sqrt{51(0.42)(0.58)} = 3.525$

$$P(17 \leq r \leq 25) = P\left(\frac{16.5 - 21.42}{3.525} \leq z \leq \frac{25.5 - 21.42}{3.525}\right)$$

$$P(-1.40 \leq z \leq 1.16) = 0.4192 + 0.3770 = 0.7962$$

SC 5-10 For today, $\mu = 850{,}000$, $\sigma = 200{,}000$.

$$P(x \geq 1{,}000{,}000) = P\left(z \geq \frac{1{,}000{,}000 - 850{,}000}{200{,}000}\right) = P(z \geq 0.75)$$

$$= 0.5 - 0.2734 = 0.2266$$

5.7 Choosing the Correct Probability Distribution

If we plan to use a probability to describe a situation, we must be careful to choose the right one. We need to be certain that we are not using the *Poisson* probability distribution when it is the *binomial* that more nearly describes the situation we are studying. Remember that the binomial distribution is applied when the number of trials is fixed before the experiment begins, and each trial is independent and can result in only two mutually exclusive outcomes (success/failure, either/or, yes/no). Like the binomial, the Poisson distribution applies when each trial is independent. But although the probabilities in a Poisson distribution approach zero after the first few values, the number of possible values is infinite. The results are not limited to two mutually exclusive outcomes. Under some conditions, the Poisson distribution can be used as an approximation of the binomial, but not always. All the assumptions that form the basis of a distribution must be met if our use of that distribution is to produce meaningful results.

Even though the normal probability distribution is the only continuous distribution we have discussed in this chapter, we should realize that there are other useful continuous distributions. In the chapters to come, we shall study three additional continuous distributions: Student's *t*, χ^2, and *F.* Each of these is of interest to decision makers who solve problems using statistics.

Exercises 5.7

■ **5-52** Which probability distribution is most likely the appropriate one to use for the following variables: binomial, Poisson, or normal?

(a) The life span of a female born in 1977.

(b) The number of autos passing through a tollbooth.

(d) The number of defective radios in a lot of 100.

(d) The water level in a reservoir.

■ **5-53** What characteristics of a situation help to determine which is the appropriate distribution to use?

■ **5-54** Explain in your own words the difference between discrete and continuous random variables. What difference do such classifications make in determining the probabilities of future events?

■ **5-55** In practice, managers see many different types of distributions. Often, the nature of these distributions is not as apparent as are some of the examples provided in this book. What alternatives are open to students, teachers, and researchers who want to use probability distributions in their work but who are not sure exactly which distributions are appropriate for given situations?

Statistics at Work

Loveland Computers

Case 5: Probability Distributions "So, Nancy Rainwater tells me she's 'reasonably certain' about her decision on how she's going to schedule the production line." Walter Azko was beginning to feel that hiring Lee Azko as an assistant was one of his better investments. "But don't get too comfortable, I've got another problem I want you to work on. Tomorrow, I want you to spend some time with Jeff Cohen—he's the head of purchasing here."

Jeff Cohen would be the first to say that he was surprised to find himself as the head of purchasing for a computer company. An accountant by training, he had first run into Walter Azko when he was assigned by his CPA firm to help Walter prepare the annual financial statements for his importing company. Because Walter traveled frequently and was always trying out new product lines, the financial records were a mess of invoices and check stubs for manufacturers, brokers, and shippers. Jeff's brief assignment turned into a permanent position, and when Loveland Computers was formed, he somewhat reluctantly agreed to handle purchasing, as long as Walter negotiated the deals. For Jeff, the best part of the job was that he could indulge his taste for oriental art.

Lee Azko found Jeff in a corner office that looked like a surgery room prepared for an operation: There was not so much as a paper clip on his desk, and the bookshelves contained neat rows of color-coded binders. "Let me explain my problem to you, Lee," Cohen launched in immediately. "We import our midrange line fully assembled from Singapore. Because it's a high-value product, it makes sense to pay to have it airfreighted to us. The best part of that is that we don't have to keep much inventory here in Colorado and we're not paying to have hundreds of thousands of dollars' worth of computers to sit on docks and on boats for several weeks. The computers are boxed and wrapped on pallets in a shape that just fits in the cargo hold of an MD-11 freighter. So it makes sense for us to order the midrange in lots of 200 units."

"I understand," said Lee, making a mental note that each shipment was worth about a quarter of a million dollars. "I've seen them arrive at the inbound dock."

"About half of the computers are sent on to customers without even being taken out of the box. But the rest need some assembly work on Nancy Rainwater's production line. We need to add a modem—you know, the device that lets a computer 'talk' to another machine through regular telephone lines. The modem comes on one board and just snaps into a slot. There's not much to it. I can get modems locally from several different electronics firms. But for each lot of computers, I have to decide how many modems to order. And I don't know how many customers will want a modem. If I order too many, I end up with unused inventory that just adds to my costs. The overstock eventually gets used up for customers who call in after the purchase and want a modem as an 'add on.' But if I order too few, I have to use a lot of staff time to round up a few extras, and, of course, none of the suppliers wants to give me a price break on a small lot."

"Well, you've got the records," Lee replied. "Why don't you just order the 'average' number of modems needed for each lot?"

"Because although the *average* number of modems per lot has stayed the same over the last few years, the *actual* number requested by customers on any single lot jumps around a bit. Take a look at these numbers," Jeff said as he walked across to the bookcase and pulled out a folder. "It's much worse for me to end up with too few modems in stock when a shipment of midranges comes through the production line than to have too many. So I suppose I tend to order above the average. It just seems that there ought to be a way to figure out how many to order so that we can be reasonably sure that we can operate the line without running out."

"Well, there's only one question remaining," said Lee. "You have to tell me how many times—out of 100 lots of computers—you can tolerate being wrong in your guess. Would a 95 percent success rate work for you?"

Study Questions: What calculations is Lee going to make? Why does Lee need to know Jeff Cohen's desired "success" rate for this prediction? What does Lee know about the underlying distribution of the parameter "number of modems per lot"? Finally, what additional information will Lee need?

Computer Database Exercise

HH Industries

Mary D'Angelo, Hal Rodgers' secretary, caught Laurel in the hall one Wednesday morning. "Could I stop in and see you for a few minutes? We've got a problem with our copy machines and Hal said you might be able to give me some advice."

"Sure thing," Laurel smiled. "Anytime this morning is fine." She knew the two copiers used by HH Industries were a source of frustration for the entire office staff. They had been purchased by the previous owner, Mr. Douglas, at a used-office-supply store during one of the business' leaner months. Although they were somewhat reliable for the first year or two, the repairman had recently become a familiar fixture around the office.

Mary tapped on the door and came in when Laurel beckoned. "Hal's asked me to determine our best option for dealing with the copy machine situation," she explained. "You know how aggravating it can be when the workload picks up and one of the copiers is down! What I need from you are some details about how to go about evaluating the costs of our various alternatives. I know this isn't exactly marketing analysis, but. . . ."

Laurel laughed. "This will be a welcome change. Statistics doesn't always have to be boring, boardroom stuff! Do you keep track of the daily status of the two machines?"

"I have to," Mary groaned. "It seems like one or the other is down at least once a week, and we have had to send some stuff out for reproduction recently, which is a real nuisance! I also have dated receipts for service calls during the last year or so. Will that help?"

"It sure will. Could you calculate the average service call costs for the cases when either one or both machines were down? That will help us with the evaluation. Meanwhile, I'll get started on the rest of this."

"Okay," Mary said. "I'll see you later this afternoon."

1. Using the data for copier downtime status in the CH05A.xxx files on the data disk, what is the probability that a machine will be down on any given day?
2. With 250 work days per year, how many days per year would you expect one machine to be down? Two to be down?

Mary calculated the average service call costs: $68 for one machine, $100 for two. Figuring what copier downtime cost the company was a little more difficult. Laurel and Mary decided that a reasonable measure would be 0.05 per copy (the standard fee charged by local copy shops) times the number of copies lost, which was estimated at 150 per copier per day.

3. Calculate the expected yearly cost for the company's current situation.

Next, Mary outlined for Laurel the other alternatives. "HH Industries has been presented with two proposals. First, there's a company that will lease us two copiers for $350 per month. It has data to support its claim that the probability of a machine being down on any given day is 0.05. Furthermore, service calls are included in the contract price. Second, we have the opportunity to purchase a new state-of-the-art machine that would replace both our old copiers.

The initial cost is $8,750, and it comes with a one-year guarantee under which service calls would be free. I've checked around and determined that we can expect about $175 per call after that. That sounds high, except when you consider that this machine is pretty reliable—only a 0.017 chance of it being down on any given day."

4. By using a 3-year period for comparison (and ignoring the time-value of money), which is the best alternative for HH Industries?

Hal addressed his staff at the next weekly meeting. "The last item on the agenda has to do with staffing. With phone-in orders being the lifeline of our business, it is imperative that we put as much effort as is needed toward serving our phone customers. It has been brought to my attention recently that our current staff may be inadequate to process the volume of calls we're receiving. Based on some conversations with Stan and his people, it seems unreasonable to ask someone to deal with more than eight calls per hour. Beyond that, there's just too much pressure on our people to rush folks off the line, and we haven't built our reputation for personalized service just to see it destroyed when we start to grow. Laurel, I'd like you to get together with Stan and come up with some recommendations by next week's meeting. Any questions?"

Laurel jotted down a few notes. "Peggy's staff keeps the phone bills?" she asked.

Hal nodded and stood up, signaling the end of the meeting. "Have a good one, folks."

Laurel trotted off to find Peggy, from whom she got some recent phone bills, which itemized incoming calls. She spent some time coming up with a profile of an average month, then headed toward Stan's office.

"Is Hal's figure of eight calls per hour reasonable?" she asked the VP in charge of sales.

"You've got to remember that the majority of our calls are customers ordering parts directly out of the catalog," Stan answered. "Occasionally, there will be a guy who needs to describe a part he wants matched, which takes a little legwork on the part of the sales rep, but those are definitely in the minority. Then there are the ones who just want to request a catalog. I'd say that eight is a pretty solid figure, even including short breaks. Having a phone growing out of your ear all day can get kind of uncomfortable, and we don't want to be accused of slave labor!"

"Okay," Laurel smiled. "We'll go with eight. I'll let you know soon what I come up with so we can have something for Hal next week. Catch you later."

Back in her office, Laurel set up the data. "I'll have to assume Poisson arrivals for the time being," she mused. "I can check that out a little later."

5. Using the data in the CH05B.xxx files on the data disk, calculate the average number of calls received per hour.
6. If Laurel wants to be 98 percent sure that a sales rep has to deal with only eight calls an hour, how many reps should she and Stan recommend?
7. After a little more discussion, Laurel found out from Stan that he handles an average of two calls per hour (new customers, requests for new product lines, complaints, etc.). Does this change the recommendations from question 6?

The day after the phone-line study was completed, Stan caught Laurel as she was eating lunch on the picnic table outside in the shade. "Quite a change from the Rockies, isn't it?" he asked.

"I'm afraid so," Laurel smiled, "but it does have its advantages." She crinkled her slightly sunburned nose. "The whole toy company would envy this tan! Besides, I've got a winter vacation planned to take in some cross-country skiing with an old buddy of mine from out there. To tell you the truth, I'm looking forward to a little cool weather."

"I know what you mean," said Stan. "The only thing remotely cool here is air conditioning! By the way, if you've got a minute this afternoon, stick your head in my office. I've got a study in mind, but it's not urgent or anything."

"That's the kind I like!" said Laurel. "I'll see you in a while."

Later, Stan explained to Laurel that he was interested in working up what amounted to a "typical customer profile." "That early work you did on the daily number of orders and the average order size really got me to thinking. So I had Peggy run a sales report for our active customers, giving the last year of purchases for each." He pointed to a stack of green-bar computer paper almost 2 inches thick. "It would really help me use my advertising budget efficiently," he concluded. "Like I said—no big rush on this."

"Good thing," muttered Laurel on the way back to her office. "I'm not interested in spending my weekend doing data analysis!"

8. By using the data in the CH05C.xxx files on the data disk, what distribution appears to describe the customers' purchases?
9. What are the mean, median, and standard deviation?
10. Suppose that the active customer accounts are normally distributed with μ and σ calculated in question 9. What proportion of customers would be expected to have accounts greater than \$20,000? Less than \$10,000? What proportions actually do fall in these ranges?

Chapter Review

Terms Introduced in Chapter 5

Bernoulli Process A process in which each trial has only two possible outcomes, the probability of the outcome of any trial remains fixed over time, and the trials are statistically independent.

Binomial Distribution A discrete distribution describing the results of an experiment known as a Bernoulli process.

Continuity Correction Factor Corrections used to improve the accuracy of the approximation of a binomial distribution by a normal distribution.

Continuous Probability Distribution A probability distribution in which the variable is allowed to take on any value within a given range.

Continuous Random Variable A random variable allowed to take on any value within a given range.

Discrete Probability Distribution A probability distribution in which the variable is allowed to take on only a limited number of values, which can be listed.

Discrete Random Variable A random variable that is allowed to take on only a limited number of values, which can be listed.

Expected Value A weighted average of the outcomes of an experiment.

Expected Value of a Random Variable The sum of the products of each value of the random variable with that value's probability of occurrence.

Normal Distribution A distribution of a continuous random variable with a single-peaked, bell-shaped curve. The mean lies at the center of the distribution, and the curve is symmetrical around a vertical line erected at the mean. The two tails extend indefinitely, never touching the horizontal axis.

Poisson Distribution A discrete distribution in which the probability of the occurrence of an event within a very small time period is a very small number, the probability that two or more such events will occur within the same time interval is effectively 0, and the probability of the occurrence of the event within one time period is independent of where that time period is.

Probability Distribution A list of the outcomes of an experiment with the probabilities we would expect to see associated with these outcomes.

Random Variable A variable that takes on different values as a result of the outcomes of a random experiment.

Standard Normal Probability Distribution A normal probability distribution, with mean $\mu = 0$ and standard deviation $\sigma = 1$.

Equations Introduced in Chapter 5

■ **5-1**

$$\text{Probability of } r \text{ successes in } n \text{ Bernoulli trials} = \frac{n!}{r!(n-r)!}p^r q^{n-r}$$

p. 238

where

- r = number of successes desired
- n = number of trials undertaken
- p = probability of success (characteristic probability)
- q = probability of failure ($q = 1 - p$)

This *binomial formula* enables us to calculate algebraically the probability of r successes. We can apply it to any Bernoulli process, where each trial has only two possible outcomes (a success or a failure), the probability of success remains the same trial after trial, and the trials are statistically independent.

■ 5-2 $$\mu = np$$ p. 245

The *mean of a binomial distribution* is equal to the number of trials multiplied by the probability of success.

■ 5-3 $$\sigma = \sqrt{npq}$$ p. 245

The *standard deviation of a binomial distribution* is equal to the square root of the product of the number of trials, the probability of a success, and the probability of a failure (found by taking $q = 1 - p$).

■ 5-4 $$P(x) = \frac{\lambda^x \times e^{-\lambda}}{x!}$$ p. 250

This formula enables us to calculate the probability of a discrete random variable occurring in a *Poisson distribution*. The formula states that the probability of *exactly* x occurrences is equal to λ, or lambda (the mean number of occurrences per interval of time in a Poisson distribution), raised to the xth power and multiplied by e, or 2.71828 (the base of the natural logarithm system), raised to the negative lambda power, and the product divided by x factorial. Appendix Tables 4a and 4b can be used for computing Poisson probabilities.

■ 5-5 $$P(x) = \frac{(np)^x \times e^{-np}}{x!}$$ p. 254

If we substitute in Equation 5-4 the mean of the binomial distribution (np) in place of the mean of the Poisson distribution (λ), we can use the Poisson probability distribution as a reasonable approximation of the binomial. The approximation is good when n is greater than or equal to 20 and p is less than or equal to 0.05.

■ 5-6 $$z = \frac{x - \mu}{\sigma}$$ p. 262

where

- x = value of the random variable with which we are concerned
- μ = mean of the distribution of this random variable
- σ = standard deviation of this distribution
- z = number of standard deviations from x to the mean of this distribution

Once we have derived z using this formula, we can use the Standard Normal Probability Distribution Table (which gives the values for areas under half the normal curve, beginning with 0.0 at the mean) and determine the probability that the random variable with which we are concerned is within that distance from the mean of this distribution.

Review and Application Exercises

■ **5-56** In the past 20 years, on average, only 3 percent of all checks written to the American Heart Association have bounced. This month, the A.H.A. received 200 checks. What is the probability that

(a) Exactly 10 of these checks bounced?

(b) Exactly 5 of these checks bounced?

■ **5-57** An inspector for the U.S. Department of Agriculture is about to visit a large meat-packing company. She knows that, on average, 2 percent of all sides of beef inspected by the USDA are contaminated. She also knows that if she finds that more than 5 percent of the meat-packing company's beef is contaminated, the company will be closed for at least 1 month. Out of curiosity, she wants to compute the probability that this company will be shut down as a result of her inspection. Should she assume her inspection of the company's sides of beef is a Bernoulli process? Explain.

■ **5-58** The regional office of the Environmental Protection Agency annually hires second-year law students as summer interns to help the agency prepare court cases. The agency is under a budget and wishes to keep its costs at a minimum. However, hiring student interns is less costly than hiring full-time employees. Accordingly, the agency wishes to hire the maximum number of students without overstaffing. On the average, it takes two interns all summer to research a case. The interns turn their work over to staff attorneys, who prosecute the cases in the fall when the circuit court convenes. The legal staff coordinator has to place his budget request in June of the preceding summer for the number of positions he wishes to maintain. It is therefore impossible for him to know with certainty how many cases will be researched in the following summer. The data from preceding summers are as follows:

Year	1987	1988	1989	1990	1991
Number of cases	6	4	8	7	5
Year	1992	1993	1994	1995	1996
Number of cases	6	4	5	4	5

Using these data as his probability distribution for the number of cases, the legal staff coordinator wishes to hire enough interns to research the expected number of cases that will arise. How many intern positions should be requested in the budget?

■ **5-59** Label the following probability distributions as discrete or continuous:

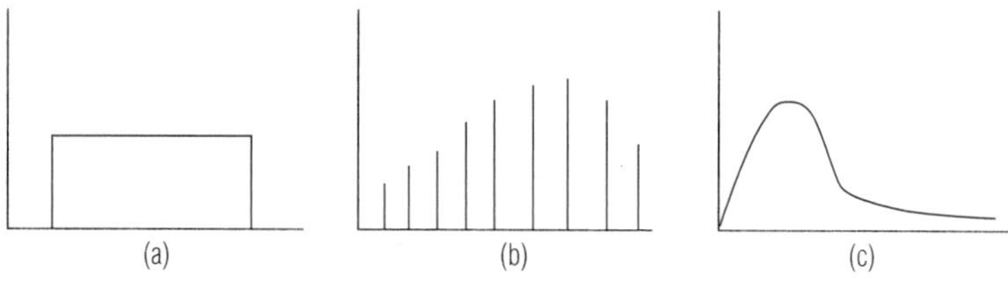

■ **5-60** Which probability distribution would you use to find binomial probabilities in the following situations: binomial, Poisson, or normal?

(a) 112 trials, probability of success 0.06.

(b) 15 trials, probability of success 0.4.

(c) 650 trials, probability of success 0.02.

(d) 59 trials, probability of success 0.1.

■ **5-61** The French bread made at La Fleur de Farine costs $8 per dozen baguettes to produce. Fresh bread sells at a premium, $16 per dozen baguettes, but it has a short shelf life. If La Fleur de Farine bakes more bread than its customers demand on any given day, the leftover day-old bread goes for croutons in local restaurants at a discounted $7 per dozen baguettes. Conversely, producing less bread than customers demand leads to lost sales. La Fleur de Farine bakes its French bread in batches of 350 dozen baguettes. The daily demand for bread is a random variable, taking the values two, three, four, or five batches, with probabilities 0.2, 0.25, 0.4, and 0.15, respectively. If La Fleur de Farine wishes to maximize expected profits, how much bread should it bake each morning?

■ **5-62** Reginald Dunfey, president of British World Airlines, is fiercely proud of his company's on-time percentage; only 2 percent of all BWA flights arrive more than 10 minutes early or late. In his upcoming speech to the BWA board of directors, Mr. Dunfey wants to include the probability that none of the 200 flights scheduled for the following week will be more than 10 minutes early or late. What is the probability? What is the probability that exactly 10 flights will be more than 10 minutes early or late?

■ **5-63** Marvin Thornbury, an attorney working for the Legal Aid Society, estimates that, on average, seven of the daily arrivals to the L.A.S. office are people who were (in their opinion) unfairly evicted. Further, he estimates that, on average, five of the daily arrivals are people whose landlords have raised their rent illegally.

(a) What is the probability that six of the daily arrivals report an unfair eviction?

(b) What is the probability that eight daily arrivals have suffered from an illegal rent increase?

■ **5-64** The City Bank of Durham has recently begun a new credit program. Customers meeting certain credit requirements can obtain a credit card accepted by participating area merchants that carries a discount. Past numbers show that 25 percent of all applicants for this card are rejected. Given that credit acceptance or rejection is a Bernoulli process, out of 15 applicants, what is the probability that

(a) Exactly four will be rejected?

(b) Exactly eight?

(c) Fewer than three?

(d) More than five?

■ **5-65** Anita Daybride is a Red Cross worker aiding earthquake victims in rural Colombia. Ms. Daybride knows that typhus is one of the most prevalent post-earthquake diseases: 44 percent of earthquake victims in rural areas contract the disease. If Anita treats 12 earthquake victims, what is the probability that

(a) Six or more have typhus?

(b) Seven or fewer?

(c) Nine or more?

■ **5-66** On average, 12 percent of those enrolled in the Federal Aviation Administration's air traffic controller training program will have to repeat the course. If the current class size at the Leesburg, Virginia, training center is 15, what is the probability that

(a) Fewer than 6 will have to repeat the course?

(b) Exactly 10 will pass the course?

(c) More than 12 will pass the course?

■ **5-67** Consider the following data about Sidley & Austin, a large law firm in Chicago:

Chicago Staff

Partners	166	Counsel	15
Associates	221	Paralegals	87

Partners' Specialties

Antitrust	10	Insurance	11
Banking	13	Intellectual property	6
Bus. reorg. & credit	6	Labor	8
Corp. & securities	28	Legislative	12
Domestic relations	0	Litigation	34
Employee benefits	4	Municipal	0
Estates & trusts	8	Real estate	8
Foreign trade	0	Taxation	7
General	0	Other	9
Health care	2		

Source: "Chicago's Largest Law Firms," Crain's Chicago Business *(12 October 1992): 20–22.*

(a) The firm is having a mandatory meeting for partners and associates. What is the probability that four of the first five employees to enter the meeting are partners?

(b) Cases coming into the firm are randomly assigned to partners for initial review and comment. Find the following probabilities:

(1) Exactly one of the next four cases to come in is assigned to a litigator.

(2) None are assigned to litigators.

(3) At least one of the next three cases to come in is assigned to a corporation and securities specialist.

■ **5-68** The Virginia Department of Health and Welfare publishes a pamphlet, *A Guide to Selecting Your Doctor.* Free copies are available to individuals, institutions, and organizations that are willing to pay the postage. Most of the copies have gone to a small number of groups who, in turn, have disseminated the literature. Mailings for 5 years have been as follows:

			Year		
	1992	**1993**	**1994**	**1995**	**1996**
Virginia Medical Association	7,000	3,000	—	2,000	4,000
Octogenarian Clubs	1,000	1,500	1,000	700	1,000
Virginia Federation of Women's Clubs	4,000	2,000	3,000	1,000	—
Medical College of Virginia	—	—	3,000	2,000	3,000
U.S. Department of Health, Education, and Welfare	1,000	—	1,000	—	1,000

In addition, an average of 2,000 copies per year were mailed or given to walk-in customers. Assistant secretary Susan Fleming, who has to estimate the number of pamphlets to print for 1997, knows that a revised edition of the pamphlet will be published in 1998. She feels that the demand in 1997 will most likely resemble that of 1994. She has constructed this assessment of the probabilities:

	Year				
	1992	1993	1994	1995	1996
Probability that 1997 will resemble this year	0.10	0.25	0.45	0.10	0.10

(a) Construct a table of the probability distribution of demand for the pamphlet, and draw a graph representing that distribution.

(b) Assuming Fleming's assessment of the probabilities was correct, how many pamphlets should she order to be certain that there will be enough for 1997?

■ **5-69** Production levels for Giles Fashion vary greatly according to consumer acceptance of the latest styles. Therefore, the company's weekly orders of wool cloth are difficult to predict in advance. On the basis of 5 years of data, the following probability distribution for the company's weekly demand for wool has been computed:

Amount of wool (lb)	2,500	3,500	4,500	5,500
Probability	0.30	0.45	0.20	0.05

From these data, the raw-materials purchaser computed the expected number of pounds required. Recently, she noticed that the company's sales were lower in the last year than in years before. Extrapolating, she observed that the company will be lucky if its weekly demand averages 2,500 this year.

(a) What was the expected weekly demand for wool based on the distribution from past data?

(b) If each pound of wool generates $5 in revenue and costs $4 to purchase, ship, and handle, how much would Giles Fashion stand to gain or lose each week if it orders wool based on the past expected value and the company's demand is only 2,500?

■ **5-70** Heidi Tanner is the manager of an exclusive shop that sells women's leather clothing and accessories. At the beginning of the fall/winter season, Ms. Tanner must decide how many full-length leather coats to order. These coats cost her $100 each and will sell for $200 each. Any coats left over at the end of the season will have to be sold at a 20 percent discount in order to make room for spring/summer inventory. From past experience, Heidi knows that demand for the coats has the following probability distribution:

Number of coats demanded	8	10	12	14	16
Probability	0.10	0.20	0.25	0.30	0.15

She also knows that any leftover coats can be sold at discount.

(a) If Heidi decides to order 14 coats, what is her expected profit?

(b) How would the answer to part (a) change if the leftover coats were sold at a 40 percent discount?

■ **5-71** The Executive Camera Company provides full expenses for its sales force. When attempting to budget automobile expenses for its employees, the financial department uses mileage figures to estimate gas, tire, and repair expenses. Distances driven average 5,650 miles a month, and have a standard deviation of 120. The financial department wants its expense estimate and subsequent budget to be adequately high and, therefore, does not want to use any of the data from drivers who drove fewer than 5,500 miles. What percentage of Executive's sales force drove 5,500 miles or more?

■ **5-72** Mission Bank is considering changing the day for scheduled maintenance for the automatic teller machine (ATM) in the lobby. The average number of people using it between 8 and 9 A.M. is 30, except on Fridays, when the average is 45. The management decision must balance the efficient use of maintenance staff while minimizing customer inconvenience.

(a) Does knowledge of the two average figures affect the manager's expected value (for inconvenienced customers)?

(b) Taking the data for all days together, the relative probability of inconveniencing 45 customers is quite small. Should the manager expect many inconvenienced customers if the maintenance day is changed to Friday?

■ **5-73** The purchasing agent in charge of procuring automobiles for the state of Minnesota's interagency motor pool was considering two different models. Both were 4-door, 4-cylinder cars with comparable service warranties. The decision was to choose the automobile that achieved the best mileage per gallon. The state had done some tests of its own, which produced the following results for the two automobiles in question:

	Average MPG	Standard Deviation
Automobile A	42	4
Automobile B	38	7

The purchasing agent was uncomfortable with the standard deviations, so she set her own decision criterion for the car that would be more likely to get more than 45 miles per gallon.

(a) Using the data provided in combination with the purchasing agent's decision criterion, which car should she choose?

(b) If the purchasing agent's criterion was to reject the automobile that more likely obtained less than 39 mpg, which car should she buy?

■ **5-74** In its third year, attendance in the Liberty Football League averaged 16,050 fans per game, and had a standard deviation of 2,500.

(a) According to these data, what is the probability that the number of fans at any given game was greater than 20,000?

(b) Fewer than 10,000?

(c) Between 14,000 and 17,500?

■ **5-75** Ted Hughes, the mayor of Chapelboro, wants to do something to reduce the number of accidents in the town involving motorists and bicyclists. Currently, the probability distribution of the number of such accidents per week is as follows:

Number of accidents	0	1	2	3	4	5
Probability	0.05	0.10	0.20	0.40	0.15	0.10

The mayor has two choices of action: He can install additional lighting on the town's streets or he can expand the number of bike lanes in the town. The respective revised probability distributions for the two options are as follows:

Number of accidents	0	1	2	3	4	5
Probability (lights)	0.10	0.20	0.30	0.25	0.10	0.05
Probability (lanes)	0.20	0.20	0.20	0.30	0.05	0.05

Which plan should the mayor approve if he wants to produce the largest possible reduction in

(a) Expected number of accidents per week?

(b) Probability of more than three accidents per week?

(c) Probability of three or more accidents per week?

■ 5-76 Copy Chums of Boulder leases office copying machines and resells returned machines at a discount. Leases are normally distributed, with a mean of 24 months and a standard deviation of 7.5 months.

(a) What is the probability that a copier will still be on lease after 28 months?

(b) What is the probability that a copier will be returned within one year?

■ 5-77 Sensurex Productions, Incorporated, has recently patented and developed an ultrasensitive smoke detector for use in both residential and commercial buildings. Whenever a detectable amount of smoke is in the air, a wailing siren is set off. In recent tests conducted in a 20′ × 15′ × 8′ room, the smoke levels that activated the smoke detector averaged 320 parts per million (ppm) of smoke in the room, and had a standard deviation of 25 ppm.

(a) If a cigarette introduces 82 ppm into the atmosphere of a 20′ × 15′ × 8′ room, what is the probability that four people smoking cigarettes simultaneously will set off the alarm?

(b) Three people?

5-78 Consider the following information about the graduates of the twenty top-ranking MBA programs in the United States:

1994 MBA Program Rank	School	Average Pay Pre-MBA	Average Pay Post-MBA	Average Number of Job Offers
1	Pennsylvania (Wharton)	$48,240	$89,930	3.02
2	Northwestern (Kellogg)	44,000	84,640	2.96
3	Chicago	42,690	83,210	2.92
4	Stanford	49,610	100,800	3.47
5	Harvard	53,910	102,630	3.60
6	Michigan	36,050	67,820	2.68
7	Indiana	34,320	58,520	2.45
8	Columbia	44,470	100,480	2.43
9	UCLA (Anderson)	44,620	74,010	2.74
10	MIT (Sloan)	41,820	80,500	3.25
11	Duke (Fuqua)	40,960	70,490	2.78
12	Virginia (Darden)	38,530	74,280	2.69
13	Dartmouth (Tuck)	45,300	95,410	2.40
14	Carnegie–Mellon	38,250	69,890	2.69
15	Cornell (Johnson)	40,740	71,970	2.40
16	NYU (Stern)	38,960	70,660	2.12
17	Texas	36,620	61,890	2.58
18	UNC (Kenan–Flagler)	38,690	69,880	3.09
19	California (Haas)	43,570	71,970	2.34
20	Purdue (Krannert)	30,600	54,720	2.19

Source: John A. Byrne and Lori Bongiorno, "The Best B-Schools," Business Week *(24 October 1994): 62–70.*

(a) Compute the mean and standard deviation for average post-MBA salaries.

(b) Assume that post-MBA salaries are normally distributed with mean and standard deviation as calculated in (a); what is the probability that a randomly selected 1994 MBA graduate

(1) Earns more than $100,000?

(2) Earns less than $60,000?

(3) Earns between $75,000 and $95,000?

(c) Compute the mean for the average number of job offers.

(d) If job offers per MBA are Poisson distributed with a mean as calculated in (c), find the probability that a randomly selected graduate received

(1) Fewer than two offers.

(2) Two or three offers.

(3) More than three job offers.

■ **5-79** Rework Exercise 5-65 using the normal approximation. Compare the approximate and exact answers.

■ **5-80** Try to use the normal approximation for Exercise 5-66. Notice that np is only 1.8. Comment on the accuracy of the approximation.

■ **5-81** Randall Finan supervises the packaging of college textbooks for Newsome-Cluett Publishers. He knows that the number of cardboard boxes he will need depends partly on the size of the books. All Newsome-Cluett books use the same size paper but may have differing numbers of pages. After pulling shipment records for the last 5 years, Finan derived the following set of probabilities:

# of pages	100	300	500	700	900	1100
Probability	0.05	0.10	0.25	0.25	0.20	0.15

(a) If Finan bases his box purchase on an expected length of 600 pages, will he have enough boxes?

(b) If all 700-page books are edited down to 500 pages, what expected number of pages should he use?

■ **5-82** D'Addario Rose Co. is planning rose production for Valentine's Day. Each rose costs $0.35 to raise and sells wholesale for $0.70. Any roses left over after Valentine's Day can be sold the next day for $0.10 wholesale. D'Addario has the following probability distribution based on previous years:

Roses sold	15,000	20,000	25,000	30,000
Probability	0.10	0.30	0.40	0.20

How many roses should D'Addario produce to minimize the firm's expected losses?

■ **5-83** A certain business school has 400 students in its MBA program. One hundred sixteen of the students are married. Without using Appendix Table 3, determine

(a) The probability that exactly 2 of 3 randomly selected students are married.

(b) The probability that exactly 4 of 13 students chosen at random are married.

■ **5-84** Kenan Football Stadium has 4 light towers with 25 high-intensity floodlights mounted on each. Sometimes an entire light tower will go dark. Smitty Moyer, head of maintenance, wonders what the distribution of light tower failures is. He knows that any individual tower has a probability of

0.11 of failing during a football game and that the towers fail independently of one another.

Construct a graph, like Figure 5-4, of a binomial probability distribution showing the probabilities of exactly 0, 1, 2, 3, or 4 towers going dark during the same game.

■ **5-85** Smitty Moyer (see Exercise 5-84) knows that the probability that any one of the 25 individual floodlights in a light tower fails during a football game is 0.05. The individual floodlights in a tower fail independently of each other.

(a) Using both the binomial and the Poisson approximation, determine the probability that seven floodlights from a given tower will fail during the same game.

(b) Using both methods, determine the probability that two will fail.

■ **5-86** Ansel Fearrington wants to borrow $75,000 from his bank for a new tractor for his farm. The loan officer doesn't have any data specifically on the bank's history of equipment loans, but he does tell Ansel that over the years, the bank has received about 1460 loan applications per year and that the probability of approval was, on average, about 0.8.

(a) Ansel is curious abo ut the average and standard deviation of the number of loans approved per year. Find these figures for him.

(b) Suppose that after careful research the loan officer tells Ansel the correct figures actually are 1,327 applications per year with an approval probability of 0.77. What are the mean and standard deviation now?

■ **5-87** Ansel Fearrington (see Exercise 5-86) learns that the loan officer has been fired for failing to follow bank lending guidelines. The bank now announces that all financially sound loan applications will be approved. Ansel guesses that three out of every five applications are unsound.

(a) If Ansel is right, what is the probability that exactly 6 of the next 10 applications will be approved?

(b) What is the probability that more than 3 will be approved?

(c) What is the probability that more than 2 but fewer than 6 will be approved?

■ **5-88** Krista Engel is campaign manager for a candidate for U.S. Senator. Staff consensus is that the candidate has the support of 40 percent of registered voters. A random sample of 300 registered voters shows that 34 percent would vote for Krista's candidate. If 40 percent of voters really are allied with her candidate, what is the probability that a sample of 300 voters would indicate 34 percent or fewer on her side? Is it likely that the 40 percent estimate is correct?

■ **5-89** Krista Engel (see Exercise 5-88) has learned that her candidate's major opponent, who has the support of 50 percent of registered voters, will likely lose the support of $^1/_4$ of those voters because of his recent support of clear-cutting of timber in national forests, a policy to which Krista's candidate is opposed.

If Krista's candidate now has the support of 34 percent of registered voters, and all the dissatisfied voters then switch to Krista's candidate, what is the probability that a new survey of 250 registered voters would show her candidate to have the support of 51 to 55 percent of the voters?

■ **5-90** *The Wall Street Journal*'s 1995 Executive Pay Survey found the following percent changes in the salaries (base plus bonus) paid to the chief executive officers (CEOs) of 39 industrial firms:

Company	Percent change	Company	Percent Change
AMP	11.2	Owens-Corning	22.7
Allied Signal	20.0	Owens-Illinois	−6.5
Armstrong	31.9	PPG Industries	5.3
Briggs & Stratton	−2.9	Paccar	17.6
Browning-Ferris	29.7	Pentair	64.1
CSX	19.1	Premark	−33.5
Caterpillar	−0.6	Raychem	5.2
Consolidated Freight	−42.3	Ryder System	−34.1
Crown Cork & Seal	−8.5	Sonoco Products	26.3
Deere	10.7	Stanley Works	−16.9
Donnelley (R.R.)	12.4	Tecumseh Products	−3.8
Dun & Bradstreet	9.7	Temple-Inland	35.6
Emerson Electric	1.3	Thomas & Betts	28.7
Engelhard	24.8	Trinova	13.1
Federal Express	8.5	Tyco	26.2
Fluor	12.5	Union Pacific	7.6
Harnischfeger	10.9	WMX Technologies	26.7
Hillenbrand	3.1	Westinghouse	47.1
Ingersoll-Rand	25.3	Yellow	−0.8
Norfolk Southern	20.3		

Source: The Wall Street Journal *(11 April 1996): R16.*

(a) What fraction of these chief executives took a pay cut in 1995? Assuming that these results are representative of the salary changes for the CEOs of all industrial firms, find the probabilities that out of six randomly chosen CEOs:

(1) Exactly five saw their pay decrease in 1995.

(2) At least five got raises in 1995.

(3) Fewer than four got raises in 1995.

(b) Compute the mean and standard deviation for these thirty-nine changes in salaries.

(c) Assume that the 1995 percent changes in salary for the CEOs of all industrial firms are normally distributed with mean and standard deviation as calculated in (b). Find the probabilities that a randomly chosen CEO had a pay change in 1995 of:

(1) At least a 25 percent increase.

(2) Less than a 5 percent increase.

(3) Between a 15 percent decrease and a 15 percent increase.

Chapter Concepts Test

Circle the correct answer or fill in the blank. *Answers are in the back of the book.*

T F 1. The expected value of an experiment is obtained by computing the arithmetic average value over all possible outcomes of the experiment.

T F 2. The value of z for some point x lying in a normal distribution is the area between x and the mean of the distribution.

T F 3. The right and left tails of the normal distribution extend indefinitely, never touching the horizontal axis.

T F 4. For a normal distribution, the mean always lies between the mode and the median.

T F 5. All but about three-tenths of 1 percent of the area in a normal distribution lies within 3 standard deviations from the mean.

T F 6. Developing a conditional loss table is cumbersome when there are many possible actions and outcomes, because the loss resulting from every action/outcome pair must be included in the table.

T F 7. The area under the curve of a normal distribution between the mean and a point 1.8 standard deviations above the mean is greater for a distribution having a mean of 100 than it is for a distribution having a mean of 0.

T F 8. The normal distribution may be used to approximate the binomial distribution when the number of trials, n, is greater than or equal to 60.

T F 9. The two types of losses we consider in solving an inventory-stocking problem are opportunity losses and activity losses.

T F 10. When the probability of success in a Bernoulli process is 50 percent ($p = 0.5$), its binomial distribution is symmetrical.

T F 11. A frequency distribution lists observed frequencies for an experiment that has already been performed; a probability distribution lists outcomes that could result *if* the experiment were performed.

T F 12. The value a random variable will take on can usually be predicted in advance of a particular occurrence.

T F 13. Once the value of p has been decided for a Bernoulli process, the value of q is calculated as $1 - p$.

T F 14. If the expected number of arrivals in an office is calculated as five per hour, one can be reasonably confident that five people will arrive within the next hour.

T F 15. The binomial distribution is not really necessary because its values can always be approximated by another distribution.

T F 16. The height of adult humans can be described by a Poisson distribution.

T F 17. Any action that minimizes expected loss will also minimize expected gain.

T F 18. After 20 trials of an experiment, a correctly shaped distribution curve is created.

T F 19. An example of an opportunity loss could be loss of sales due to the excess age of fruit on a grocery shelf.

T F 20. A distribution where the mean and median have different values can never be a normal distribution.

T F 21. The mean of a binomial distribution is given by np.

A B C D E 22. If the expected daily profit of a lemonade stand is $13.45, then:

(a) Tomorrow's profit will be $13.45.

(b) Tomorrow's profit will be less than $13.45.

(c) Tomorrow's profit will be more than $13.45.

(d) Tomorrow's loss will be $13.45.

(e) None of the above.

A B C D E 23. For a given binomial distribution with n fixed, if $p < 0.5$, then:

(a) The Poisson distribution will provide a good approximation.

(b) The Poisson distribution will provide a bad approximation.

(c) The binomial distribution will be skewed left.

(d) The binomial distribution will be skewed right.

(e) The binomial distribution will be symmetric.

A B C D 24. Suppose we have a Poisson distribution with $\lambda = 2$. Then the probability of having exactly 10 occurrences is:

(a) $\dfrac{2^{-10}e^{10}}{10!}$.

(b) $\dfrac{2^{10}e^{-2}}{2!}$.

(c) $\dfrac{10^2e^{-10}}{10!}$.

(d) $\dfrac{2^{10}e^{-2}}{10!}$.

A B C D E 25. Which of the following is a characteristic of the probability distribution for any random variable?

(a) A probability is provided for every possible value.
(b) The sum of all probabilities is 1.
(c) No given probability occurs more than once.
(d) All of these.
(e) (a) and (b) but not (c).

A B C D 26. Which of the following could never be described by a binomial distribution?

(a) The number of defective widgets produced by an assembly process.
(b) The amount of water used daily by a single household.
(c) The number of people in your class who can answer this question correctly.
(d) All of these could always be described by a binomial distribution.

A B C D E 27. If $p = 0.4$ for a particular Bernoulli process, the calculation $\left(\dfrac{7!}{3! \times 4!}\right)(0.4)^3(0.6)^4$ gives the probability of getting:

(a) Exactly three successes in seven trials.
(b) Exactly four successes in seven trials.
(c) Three or more successes in seven trials.
(d) Four or more successes in seven trials.
(e) None of these.

A B C D E 28. For binomial distributions with $p = 0.2$:

(a) A distribution for $n = 2{,}000$ would more closely approximate the normal distribution than one for $n = 50$.
(b) No matter what the value of n, the distribution is skewed to the right.
(c) The graph of this distribution with $p = 0.2$ and $n = 100$ would be the exact reverse of the graph for the binomial distribution with $n = 100$ and $p = 0.8$.
(d) All of these.
(e) (a) and (b) but not (c).

A B C D E 29. Which of the following is a necessary condition for use of a Poisson distribution?

(a) Probability of one arrival per second is constant.
(b) The number of arrivals in any 1-second interval is independent of arrivals in other intervals.
(c) The probability of two or more arrivals in the same second is zero.
(d) All of these.
(e) (b) and (c) but not (a).

A B C D E F 30. In what case would the Poisson distribution be a good approximation of the binomial?

(a) $n = 40, p = 0.32$.
(b) $n = 40, q = 0.79$.
(c) $n = 200, q = 0.98$.
(d) $n = 10, p = 0.03$.
(e) (a) and (c).
(f) All of these.

A B C D E 31. For a normal curve with $\mu = 55$ and $\sigma = 10$, how much area will be found under the curve to the right of the value 55?

(a) 1.0.
(b) 0.68.
(c) 0.5.
(d) 0.32.
(e) Cannot be determined from the information given.

A B C D E F 32. Suppose you are using a normal distribution to approximate a binomial distribution with $\mu = 5, \sigma = 2$, and wish to determine the probability of getting more than seven successes. From the normal table, you would determine the probability that z is greater than:

(a) 0.
(b) 0.5.
(c) 0.75.
(d) 1.0.
(e) 1.25.
(f) 1.5.

A B C D E F 33. For a normal curve with a mean of 120 and a standard deviation of 35, what proportion (in percent) of the area under the curve will lie between the values of 40 and 82?

(a) 12.7.
(b) 85.1.
(c) 13.8.
(d) 48.9.
(e) 12.1.
(f) 19.4.

A B C D E F 34. Which of the following normal curves looks most like the curve for $\mu = 10, \sigma = 5$?

(a) Curve for $\mu = 10, \sigma = 10$.
(b) Curve for $\mu = 20, \sigma = 10$.
(c) Curve for $\mu = 20, \sigma = 5$.
(d) Curve for $\mu = 12, \sigma = 3$.
(e) (a), (c), and (d).
(f) None of these.

A B C D E 35. A binomial distribution may be approximated by a Poisson distribution if:

(a) n is large and p is large.
(b) n is small and p is large.
(c) n is small and p is small.
(d) None of these.
(e) (a) and (b) but not (c).

A B C D E F 36. The standard deviation of a binomial distribution depends on:
(a) Probability of success.
(b) Probability of failure.
(c) Number of trials.
(d) (a) and (b) but not (c).
(e) (b) and (c) but not (a).
(f) (a), (b), and (c).

37. The weighted average of the outcomes of an experiment is referred to as the ______________________.

38. The distribution that deals only in successes and failures is referred to as the ______________________ distribution. It is usually used to describe a ______________________ process.

39. When approximating a binomial distribution by a normal distribution, a ______________________ correction factor should be used.

40. The mean of a binomial distribution, μ, can be calculated as ______________________ once n and p are known. The standard deviation, σ, is calculated as ______________________.

41. For a Poisson distribution, the symbol that represents the mean number of occurrences per interval of time is ______________________.

42. A list of the probabilities of outcomes that could result if an experiment were performed is called a ______________________.

43. The two parameters that are necessary to describe a normal distribution are the ______________________ and the ______________________.

44. A ______________________ variable is a variable that assumes different values according to the results of an experiment.

45. ______________________ distributions can take on only a limited number of values, which can be listed, while ______________________ distributions can take on any value within a range.

chapter 6

SAMPLING AND SAMPLING DISTRIBUTIONS

Objectives

- To take a sample from an entire population and use it to describe the population
- To make sure the samples you do take are an accurate representation of the population from which they came
- To introduce the concepts of sampling distributions
- To understand the trade-offs between the cost of taking larger samples and the additional accuracy this gives to decisions made from them
- To introduce experimental design: sampling procedures to gather the most information for the least cost

Chapter Contents

Although there are over 200 million TV viewers in the United States and somewhat over half that many TV sets, only about 1,000 of those sets are sampled to determine what programs Americans watch. Why select only about 1,000 sets out of 100 million? Because time and the average cost of an interview prohibit the rating companies from trying to reach millions of people. And since polls are reasonably accurate, interviewing everybody is unnecessary. In this chapter, we examine questions such as these: How many people should be interviewed? How should they be selected? How do we know when our sample accurately reflects the entire population? ■

6.1 Introduction to Sampling

Reasons for sampling

Shoppers often sample a small piece of cheese before purchasing any. They decide from one piece what the larger chunk will taste like. A chemist does the same thing when he takes a sample of alcohol from a still, determines that it is 90 proof, and infers that all the alcohol in the still is 90 proof. If the chemist tests all the alcohol or the shoppers taste all the cheese, there will be none to sell. Testing all of the product often destroys it and is unnecessary. To determine the characteristics of the whole, we have to sample only a portion.

Suppose that, as the personnel director of a large bank, you need to write a report describing all the employees who have voluntarily left the company in the last 10 years. You would have a difficult task locating all these thousands of people. They are not easily accessible as a group—many have died, moved from the community, left the country, or acquired a new name by marriage. How do you write the report? The best idea is to locate a representative sample and interview them in order to generalize about the entire group.

Time is also a factor when managers need information quickly in order to adjust an operation or change a policy. Consider an automatic machine that sorts thousands of pieces of mail daily. Why wait for an entire day's output to check whether the machine is working accurately (whether the *population characteristics* are those required by the postal service)? Instead, samples can be taken at specific intervals, and if necessary, the machine can be adjusted right away.

Census or sample

Sometimes it is possible and practical to examine every person or item in the population we wish to describe. We call this a *complete enumeration,* or *census.* We use sampling when it is not possible to count or measure every item in the population.

Examples of populations and samples

Statisticians use the word *population* to refer not only to people but to all items that have been chosen for study. In the cases we have just mentioned, the populations are all the cheese in the chunk, all the whiskey in the vat, all the employees of the large bank who voluntarily left in the last 10 years, and all mail sorted by the automatic machine since the previous sample check. **Statisticians use the word *sample* to describe a portion chosen from the population.**

Statistics and Parameters

Function of statistics and parameters

Mathematically, we can describe samples and populations by using measures such as the mean, median, mode, and standard deviation, which we introduced in Chapter 3. When these terms describe the characteristics of a sample, they are called *statistics.* When they describe the characteristics of a population, they are called *parameters.* **A statistic is a characteristic of a sample; a parameter is a characteristic of a population.**

Suppose that the mean height in inches of all tenth graders in the United States is 60 inches. In this case, 60 inches is a characteristic of the population "all tenth graders" and can be called a *population parameter.* On the other hand, if we say that the mean height in Ms. Jones's tenth-grade class in Bennetsville is 60 inches, we are using 60 inches to describe a characteristic of the sample "Ms. Jones's tenth graders." In that case, 60 inches would be a *sample statistic*. If we are convinced that the mean height of Ms. Jones's tenth graders is an accurate estimate of the mean height of all tenth graders in the United States, we could use the sample statistic "mean height of Ms. Jones's tenth graders" to estimate the population parameter "mean height of all U.S. tenth graders" without having to measure all the millions of tenth graders in the United States.

Using statistics to estimate parameters

N, μ, σ, and n, $\bar{x}$, s: standard symbols

To be consistent, statisticians use lowercase Roman letters to denote sample statistics and Greek or capital letters for population parameters. Table 6-1 lists these symbols and summarizes the definitions we have studied so far in this chapter.

Types of Sampling

Judgment and probability sampling

There are two methods of selecting samples from populations: *nonrandom* or *judgment* sampling, and *random* or *probability* sampling. In probability sampling, all the items in the population have a chance of being chosen in the sample. In judgment sampling, personal knowledge and opinion are used to identify the items from the population that are to be included in the sample. A sample selected by judgment sampling is based on someone's expertise about the population. A forest ranger, for example, would have a judgment sample if he decided ahead of time which parts of a large forested area he would walk through to estimate the total board feet of lumber that could be cut. Sometimes a judgment sample is used as a pilot or trial sample to decide how to take a random sample later. The rigorous statistical analysis that can be done with probability samples cannot be done with judgment samples. They are more convenient and can be used successfully even if we are unable to measure their validity. But if a study uses judgment sampling and loses a significant degree of representativeness, it will have purchased convenience at too high a price.

Biased Samples

The Congress is debating some gun control laws. You are asked to conduct an opinion survey. Because hunters are the ones that are most affected by the gun control laws, you went to a hunting lodge and interviewed the members there. Then you reported that in a survey done by you, about 97 percent of the respondents were in favor of repealing all gun control laws.

A couple of biased polls

A week later, the Congress took up another bill: "Should working pregnant women be given a maternity leave of one year with full pay to take care of newborn babies?" Because this issue affects women most, this time you went to all the high-rise office complexes in your city and interviewed several working women of child-bearing age. Again you reported that in a survey done by you, about 93 percent of the respondents were in favor of the one-year maternity leave with full pay.

Important

Table 6-1 **Differences between Populations and Samples**

	Population	Sample
DEFINITION	Collection of items being considered	Part or portion of the population chosen for study
CHARACTERISTICS	"Parameters"	"Statistics"
SYMBOLS	Population size = N	Sample size = n
	Population mean = μ	Sample mean = $\bar{x}$
	Population standard deviation = σ	Sample standard deviation = s

In both of these situations you picked a biased sample by choosing people who would have very strong feelings on one side of the issue. How can we be sure that pollsters we listen to and read about don't make the same mistake you did? The answer is that unless the pollsters have a strong reputation for statistically accurate polling, we can't. However, we can be alert to the risks we take when we don't ask for more information or do more research into their competence.

Exercises 6.1

Basic Concepts

- **6-1** What is the major drawback of judgment sampling?
- **6-2** Are judgment sampling and probability sampling necessarily mutually exclusive? Explain.
- **6-3** List the advantages of sampling over complete enumeration, or census.
- **6-4** What are some disadvantages of probability sampling versus judgment sampling?

Applications

- **6-5** Farlington Savings and Loan is considering a merger with Sentry Bank, but needs shareholder approval before the merger can be accomplished. At its annual meeting, to which all shareholders are invited, the president of FS&L asks the shareholders whether they approve of the deal. Eighty-five percent approve. Is this percentage a sample statistic or a population parameter?
- **6-6** Jean Mason, who was hired by Former Industries to determine employee attitudes toward the upcoming union vote, met with some difficulty after reporting her findings to management. Mason's study was based on statistical sampling, and from the beginning data, it was clear (or so Jean thought) that the employees were favoring a unionized shop. Jean's report was shrugged off with the comment, "This is no good. Nobody can make statements about employee sentiments when she talks to only a little over 15 percent of our employees. Everyone knows you have to check 50 percent to have any idea of what the outcome of the union vote will be. We didn't hire you to make guesses." Is there any defense for Jean's position?
- **6-7** A consumer protection organization is conducting a census of people who were injured by a particular brand of space heater. Each victim is asked questions about the behavior of the heater just before its malfunction; this information generally is available only from the victim, because the heater in question tends to incinerate itself upon malfunction. Early in the census, it is discovered that several of the victims were elderly and have died. Is any census of the victims now possible? Explain.

6.2 Random Sampling

In a random or probability sample, we know what the chances are that an element of the population will or will not be included in the sample. As a result, we can assess objectively the estimates of the population characteristics that result from our sample; that is, we can describe mathematically how objective our estimates are. Let us begin our explanation of this process by introducing four methods of random sampling:

1. Simple random sampling
2. Systematic sampling
3. Stratified sampling
4. Cluster sampling

Simple Random Sampling

An example of simple random sampling

Simple random sampling selects samples by methods that allow *each possible sample to have an equal probability of being picked* and *each item in the entire population to have an equal chance of being included in the sample.* We can illustrate these requirements with an example. Suppose we have a population of four students in a seminar and we want samples of two students at a time for interviewing purposes. Table 6-2 illustrates all of the possible combinations of samples of two students in a population size of four, the probability of each sample being picked, and the probability that each student will be in a sample.

Defining *finite* and *with replacement*

Our example illustrated in Table 6-2 uses a *finite* population of four students. By *finite,* we mean that the population has stated or limited size, that is to say, there is a whole number (N) that tells us how many items there are in the population. Certainly, if we sample without "replacing" the student, we shall soon exhaust our small population group. Notice, too, that if we *sample with replacement* (that is, if we replace the sampled student immediately after he or she is picked and before the second student is chosen), the same person could appear twice in the sample.

An infinite population

We have used this example only to help us think about sampling from an infinite population. An *infinite population* is a population in which it is theoretically impossible to observe all the elements. Although many populations appear to be exceedingly large, no truly infinite population of physical objects actually exists. After all, given unlimited resources and time, we could enumerate any finite population, even the grains of sand on the beaches of North America. As a practical matter, then, we will use the term *infinite population* when we are talking about a population that could not be enumerated in a reasonable period of

Table 6-2

Chances of Selecting Samples of Two Students from a Population of Four Students

Students *A*, *B*, *C*, and *D*		
Possible samples of two people: *AB, AC, AD, BC, BD, CD*		
Probability of drawing this sample of two people must be		
	$P(AB) = 1/6$	
	$P(AC) = 1/6$	
	$P(AD) = 1/6$	(There are only six possible samples
	$P(BC) = 1/6$	of two people)
	$P(BD) = 1/6$	
	$P(CD) = 1/6$	
Probability of this student in the sample must be		
	$P(A) = 1/2$	[In Chapter 4, we saw that the marginal probability is equal to the *sum* of the joint probabilities of the events within which the event is contained:
	$P(B) = 1/2$	$P(A) = P(AB) + P(AC) + P(AD) = 1/2$]
	$P(C) = 1/2$	
	$P(D) = 1/2$	

Table 6-3

1,150 Random Digits*

1581922396	2068577984	8262130892	8374856049	4637567488
0928105582	7295088579	9586111652	7055508767	6472382934
4112077556	3440672486	1882412963	0684012006	0933147914
7457477468	5435810788	9670852913	1291265730	4890031305
0099520858	3090908872	2039593181	5973470495	9776135501
7245174840	2275698645	8416549348	4676463101	2229367983
6749420382	4832630032	5670984959	5432114610	2966095680
5503161011	7413686599	1198757695	0414294470	0140121598
7164238934	7666127259	5263097712	5133648980	4011966963
3593969525	0272759769	0385998136	9999089966	7544056852
4192054466	0700014629	5169439659	8408705169	1074373131
9697426117	6488888550	4031652526	8123543276	0927534537
2007950579	9564268448	3457416988	1531027886	7016633739
4584768758	2389278610	3859431781	3643768456	4141314518
3840145867	9120831830	7228567652	1267173884	4020651657
0190453442	4800088084	1165628559	5407921254	3768932478
6766554338	5585265145	5089052204	9780623691	2195448096
6315116284	9172824179	5544814339	0016943666	3828538786
3908771938	4035554324	0840126299	4942059208	1475623997
5570024586	9324732596	1186563397	4425143189	3216653251
2999997185	0135968938	7678931194	1351031403	6002561840
7864375912	8383232768	1892857070	2323673751	3188881718
7065492027	6349104233	3382569662	4579426926	1513082455

**Based on first 834 serial numbers of selective service lottery as reported by* The New York Times, *October 30, 1940, p. 12.*

time. In this way, we will use the theoretical concept of infinite population as an approximation of a large finite population, just as we earlier used the theoretical concept of continuous random variable as an approximation of a discrete random variable that could take on many closely spaced values.

How to Do Random Sampling The easiest way to select a sample randomly is to use random numbers. These numbers can be generated either by a computer programmed to scramble numbers or by a table of random numbers, which should properly be called a *table of random digits.*

Table 6-3 illustrates a portion of such a table. Here we have 1,150 random digits in sets of 10 digits. These numbers have been generated by a completely random process. The probability that any one digit from 0 through 9 will appear is the same as that for any other digit, and the probability of one sequence of digits occurring is the same as that for any other sequence of the same length.

Using a table of random digits

To see how to use this table, suppose that we have 100 employees in a company and wish to interview a randomly chosen sample of 10. We could get such a random sample by assigning every employee a number of 00 to 99, consulting Table 6-3, and picking a systematic method of selecting two-digit numbers. In this case, let's do the following:

1. Go from the top to the bottom of the columns beginning with the left-hand column, and read only the first two digits in each row. Notice that our first number using this method would be 15, the second 09, the third 41, and so on.
2. If we reach the bottom of the last column on the right and are still short of our desired 10 two-digit numbers of 99 and under, we can go back to the beginning (the top of the left-hand column) and start reading the third and fourth digits of each number. These would begin 81, 28, and 12.

Using slips of paper

Another way to select our employees would be to write the name of each one on a slip of paper and deposit the slips in a box. After mixing them thoroughly, we could draw 10 slips at random. This method works well with a small group of people but presents problems if the people in the population number in the thousands. There is the added problem, too, of not being certain that the slips of paper are mixed well. In the draft lottery of 1970, for example, when capsules were drawn from a bowl to determine by birthdays the order for selecting draftees for the armed services, December birthdays appeared more often than the probabilities would have suggested. As it turned out, the December capsules had been placed in the bowl last, and the capsules had not been mixed properly. Thus, December capsules had the highest probability of being drawn.

Systematic Sampling

In *systematic sampling,* elements are selected from the population at a uniform interval that is measured in time, order, or space. If we wanted to interview every twentieth student on a college campus, we would choose a random starting point in the first 20 names in the student directory and then pick every twentieth name thereafter.

Characteristics of systematic sampling

Systematic sampling differs from simple random sampling in that each *element* has an equal chance of being selected but each *sample* does *not* have an equal chance of being selected. This would have been the case if, in our earlier example, we had assigned numbers between 00 and 99 to our employees and then had begun to choose a sample of 10 by picking every tenth number beginning 1, 11, 21, 31, and so forth. Employees numbered 2, 3, 4, and 5 would have had *no* chance of being selected together.

Shortcomings of systematic sampling

In systematic sampling, there is the problem of introducing an error into the sample process. Suppose we were sampling paper waste produced by households, and we decided to sample 100 households every Monday. Chances are high that our sample would not be representative, because Monday's trash would very likely include the Sunday newspaper. Thus, the amount of waste would be biased upward by our choice of this sampling procedure.

Systematic sampling has advantages, too, however. Even though systematic sampling may be inappropriate when the elements lie in a sequential pattern, this method may require less time and sometimes results in lower costs than the simple random-sample method.

Stratified Sampling

Two ways to take stratified samples

To use *stratified sampling,* we divide the population into relatively homogeneous groups, called *strata.* Then we use one of two approaches. Either we select at random from each stratum a specified number of elements corresponding to the proportion of that stratum in the population as a whole or we draw an equal number of elements from each stratum and give weight to the results according to the stratum's proportion of total population. With either approach, stratified sampling guarantees that every element in the population has a chance of being selected.

Table 6-4 Composition of Patients by Age	Age Group	Percentage of Total
	Birth–19 years	30
	20–39 years	40
	40–59 years	20
	60 years and older	10

When to use stratified sampling

Stratified sampling is appropriate when the population is already divided into groups of different sizes and we wish to acknowledge this fact. Suppose that a physician's patients are divided into four groups according to age, as shown in Table 6-4. The physician wants to find out how many hours his patients sleep. To obtain an estimate of this characteristic of the population, he could take a random sample from each of the four age groups and give weight to the samples according to the percentage of patients in that group. This would be an example of a stratified sample.

The advantage of stratified samples is that when they are properly designed, they more accurately reflect characteristics of the population from which they were chosen than do other kinds of samples.

Cluster Sampling

In *cluster sampling,* we divide the population into groups, or *clusters,* and then select a random sample of these clusters. We assume that these individual clusters are representative of the population as a whole. If a market research team is attempting to determine by sampling the average number of television sets per household in a large city, they could use a city map to divide the territory into blocks and then choose a certain number of blocks (clusters) for interviewing. Every household in each of these blocks would be interviewed. A well-designed cluster sampling procedure can produce a more precise sample at considerably less cost than that of simple random sampling.

Comparison of stratified and cluster sampling

With both stratified and cluster sampling, the population is divided into well-defined groups. We use *stratified* sampling when each group has small variation within itself but there is a wide variation between the groups. We use *cluster* sampling in the opposite case—when there is considerable variation within each group but the groups are essentially similar to each other.

Basis of Statistical Inference: Simple Random Sampling

Why we assume random sampling

Systematic sampling, stratified sampling, and cluster sampling attempt to approximate simple random sampling. All are methods that have been developed for their precision, economy, or physical ease. Even so, assume for the rest of the examples and problems in this book that we obtain our data using simple random sampling. This is necessary because the principles of simple random sampling are the foundation for *statistical inference,* the process of making inferences about populations from information contained in samples. Once these principles have been developed for simple random sampling, their extension to the other sampling methods is conceptually quite simple but somewhat involved mathematically. If you understand the basic ideas involved in simple random sampling, you will have a good grasp of what is going on in the other cases, even if you must leave the technical details to the professional statistician.

HINTS & ASSUMPTIONS

Warning: Even when precautions are taken, many so-called random samples are still not random. When you try to take a random sample of mall shoppers, you get a biased sample because many people are not willing to take the time to stop to talk to the interviewer. Nowadays, when telephone pollers try to take a random sample, often they don't get through to people with call-screening devices on their phones. There *are* ways to counter these problems in random sampling, but often the "fix" is more complicated and/or costly than the sampling organization wants to face.

Exercises 6.2

Self-Check Exercises

SC 6-1 If we have a population of 10,000 and we wish to sample 20 randomly, use the random digits table (Table 6-3) to select 20 individuals from the 10,000. List the numbers of the elements selected, based on the random digits table.

SC 6-2 A Senate study on the issue of self-rule for the District of Columbia involved surveying 2,000 people from the population of the city regarding their opinions on a number of issues related to self-rule. Washington, D.C., is a city in which many neighborhoods are poor and many neighborhoods are rich, with very few neighborhoods falling between the extremes. The researchers who were administering the survey had reasons to believe that the opinions expressed on the various questions would be highly dependent on income. Which method was more appropriate, stratified sampling or cluster sampling? Explain briefly.

Basic Concepts

■ **6-8** In the examples below, probability distributions for three natural subgroups of a larger population are shown. For which situation would you recommend stratified sampling?

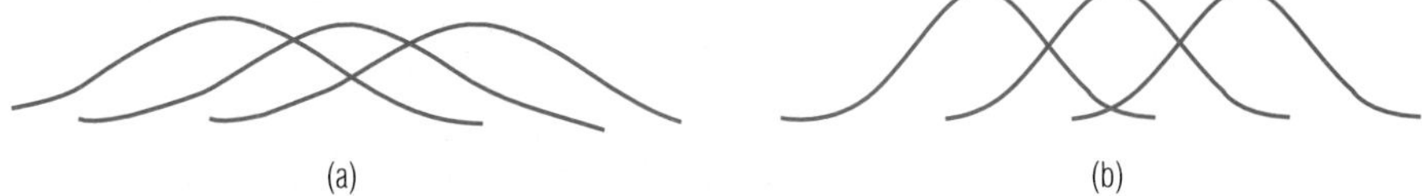

(a) (b)

■ **6-9** We wish to sample 15 pages from this textbook. Use the random digits table (Table 6-3) to select 15 pages at random and count the number of words in italics on each page. Report your results.

■ **6-10** Using a calendar, systematically sample every eighteenth day of the year, beginning with January 6.

■ **6-11** A population is made up of groups that have wide variation within each group but little variation from group to group. The appropriate type of sampling for this population is

(a) Stratified.
(b) Systematic.
(c) Cluster.
(d) Judgment.

■ **6-12** Consult Table 6-3. What is the probability that a 4 will appear as the leftmost digit in each set of 10 digits? That a 7 will appear? 2? How many times would you expect to see each of these digits in the leftmost position? How many times is each found in that position? Can you explain any differences in the number found and the number expected?

Applications

■ **6-13** The local cable television company is planning to add one channel to its basic service. There are five channels to choose from, and the company would like some input from its subscribers. There are about 20,000 subscribers, and the company knows that 35 percent of these are college students, 45 percent are white-collar workers, 15 percent are blue-collar workers, and 5 percent are other. However, the company believes there is much variation within these groups. Which of the following sampling methods is more appropriate: random, systematic, stratified, or cluster sampling?

■ **6-14** A nonprofit organization is conducting a door-to-door opinion poll on municipal day-care centers. The organization has devised a scheme for random sampling of houses, and plans to conduct the poll on weekdays from noon to 5 P.M. Will this scheme produce a random sample?

■ **6-15** Bob Peterson, public relations manager for Piedmont Power and Light, has implemented an institutional advertising campaign to promote energy consciousness among its customers. Peterson, anxious to know whether the campaign has been effective, plans to conduct a telephone survey of area residents. He plans to look in the telephone book and select random numbers with addresses that correspond to the company's service area. Will Peterson's sample be a random one?

■ **6-16** At the U.S. Mint in Philadelphia, 10 machines stamp out pennies in lots of 50. These lots are arranged sequentially on a single conveyor belt, which passes an inspection station. An inspector decides to use systematic sampling in inspecting the pennies and is trying to decide whether to inspect every fifth or every seventh lot of pennies. Which is better? Why?

■ **6-17** The state occupational safety board has decided to do a study of work-related accidents within the state, to examine some of the variables involved in the accidents, such as the type of job, the cause of the accident, the extent of the injury, the time of day, and whether the employer was negligent. It has been decided that 250 of the 2,500 work-related accidents reported last year in the state will be sampled. The accident reports are filed by date in a filing cabinet. Marsha Gulley, a department employee, has proposed that the study use a systematic sampling technique and select every tenth report in the file for the sample. Would her plan of systematic sampling be appropriate here? Explain.

■ **6-18** Bob Bennett, product manager for Clipper Mowers Company, is interested in looking at the kinds of lawn mowers used throughout the country. Assistant product manager Mary Wilson has recommended a stratified random-sampling process in which the cities and communities studied are separated into substrata, depending on the size and nature of the community. Mary Wilson proposes the following classification:

Category	Type of Community
Urban	Inner city (population 100,000+)
Suburban	Outlying areas of cities or smaller communities (pop. 20,000 to 100,000)
Rural	Small communities (fewer than 20,000 residents)

Is stratified random sampling appropriate here?

Worked-Out Answers to Self-Check Exercises

SC 6-1 Starting at the top of the third column and choosing the last 4 digits of the numbers in that column gives the following sample (reading across rows):

892	1652	2963	2913	3181	9348	4959
7695	7712	8136	9659	2526	6988	1781
7652	8559	2204	4339	6299	3397	

SC 6-2 Stratified sampling is more appropriate in this case because there appear to be two very dissimilar groups, which probably have smaller variation within each group than between groups.

6.3 Design of Experiments

Events and experiments revisited

We encountered the term *experiment* in Chapter 4, "Probability I." There we defined an *event* as one or more of the possible outcomes of doing something, and an *experiment* as an activity that would produce such events. In a coin-toss experiment, the possible events are heads and tails.

Planning Experiments

Sampling is only one part

If we are to conduct experiments that produce meaningful results in the form of usable conclusions, the way in which these experiments are designed is of the utmost importance. Sections 6.1 and 6.2 discussed ways of ensuring that random sampling was indeed being done. The way in which sampling is conducted is only a part of the total design of an experiment. In fact, the design of experiments is itself the subject of quite a number of books, some of them rather formidable in both scope and volume.

Phases of Experimental Design

A claim is made

To get a better feel for the complexity of experimental design without actually getting involved with the complex details, take an example from the many that confront us every day, and follow that example through from beginning to end.

The statement is made that a Crankmaster battery will start your car's engine better than Battery X. Crankmaster might design its experiment in the following way.

Objectives are set

Objective This is our beginning point. Crankmaster wants to test its battery against the leading competitor. Although it is possible to design an experiment that would test the two batteries on several characteristics (life, size, cranking power, weight, and cost, to name but a few), Crankmaster has decided to limit this experiment to cranking power.

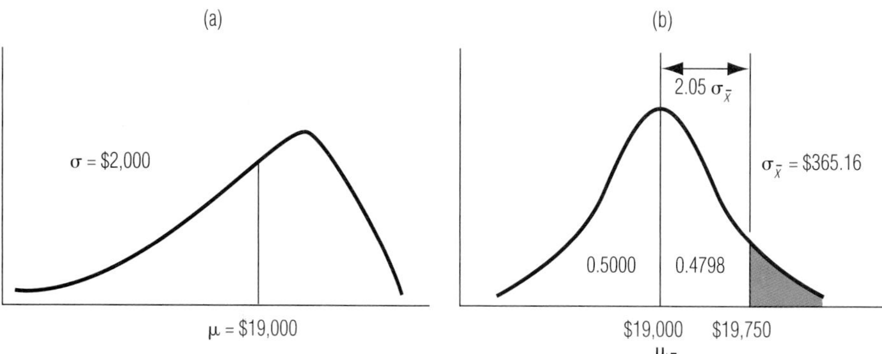

FIGURE 6-8

Population distribution and sampling distribution for bank tellers' earnings

a random sample of 30 tellers, what is the probability that their earnings will average more than \$19,750 annually? In Figure 6-8(b), we show the sampling distribution of the mean that would result, and we have colored the area representing "earnings over \$19,750."

Our first task is to calculate the standard error of the mean from the population standard deviation, as follows

$$\sigma_{\bar{x}} = \frac{\sigma}{\sqrt{n}} \quad [6\text{-}1]$$

$$= \frac{\$2{,}000}{\sqrt{30}}$$

$$= \frac{\$2{,}000}{5.477}$$

$$= \$365.16 \leftarrow \text{Standard error of the mean}$$

Because we are dealing with a sampling distribution, we must now use Equation 6-2 and the Standard Normal Probability Distribution (Appendix Table 1).

For x = \$19,750:

$$z = \frac{\bar{x} - \mu}{\sigma_{\bar{x}}} \quad [6\text{-}2]$$

$$= \frac{\$19{,}750 - \$19{,}000}{\$365.16}$$

$$= \frac{\$750.00}{\$365.16}$$

$$= 2.05 \leftarrow \text{Standard deviations from the mean of a standard normal probability distribution}$$

This gives us an area of 0.4798 for a z value of 2.05. We show this area in Figure 6-8 as the area between the mean and \$19,750. Since half, or 0.5000, of the area under the curve lies between the mean and the right-hand tail, the colored area must be

0.5000	(Area between the mean and the right-hand tail)
−0.4798	(Area between the mean and \$19,750)
0.0202	← (Area between the right-hand tail and \$19,750)

Thus, we have determined that there is slightly more than a 2 percent chance of average earnings being more than \$19,750 annually in a group of 30 tellers.

HINTS & ASSUMPTIONS

The central limit theorem is one of the most powerful concepts in statistics. What it really says is that the distribution of sample means tends to be a normal distribution. This is true *regardless* of the shape of the population distribution from which the samples were taken. Hint: Go back and look at Figures 6-6 and 6-7 on pages 318–319. Watch again how fast the distribution of sample means taken from the clearly nonnormal population in Figure 6-6 begins to look like a normal distribution in Figure 6-7 once we start to increase the sample size. And it really doesn't make any difference what the distribution of the population looks like; this will *always* happen. We could prove this to you, but first you'd have to go back and take several advanced mathematics courses to understand the proof.

Exercises 6.5

Self-Check Exercises

SC 6-5 In a sample of 25 observations from a normal distribution with mean 98.6 and standard deviation 17.2

(a) What is $P(92 < \bar{x} < 102)$?

(b) Find the corresponding probability given a sample of 36.

SC 6-6 Mary Bartel, an auditor for a large credit card company, knows that, on average, the monthly balance of any given customer is $112, and the standard deviation is $56. If Mary audits 50 randomly selected accounts, what is the probability that the sample average monthly balance is

(a) Below $100?

(b) Between $100 and $130?

Basic Concepts

■ **6-27** In a sample of 16 observations from a normal distribution with a mean of 150 and a variance of 256, what is

(a) $P(\bar{x} < 160)$?

(b) $P(\bar{x} > 142)$?

If, instead of 16 observations, 9 observations are taken, find

(c) $P(\bar{x} < 160)$.

(d) $P(\bar{x} > 142)$.

■ **6-28** In a sample of 19 observations from a normal distribution with mean 18 and standard deviation 4.8,

(a) What is $P(16 < \bar{x} < 20)$?

(b) What is $P(16 \leq \bar{x} \leq 20)$?

(c) Suppose the sample size is 48. What is the new probability in part (a)?

■ **6-29** In a normal distribution with mean 56 and standard deviation 21, how large a sample must be taken so that there will be at least a 90 percent chance that its mean is greater than 52?

■ **6-30** In a normal distribution with mean 375 and standard deviation 48, how large a sample must be taken so that the probability will be at least 0.95 that the sample mean falls between 370 and 380?

Applications

■ **6-31** An astronomer at the Mount Palomar Observatory notes that during the Geminid meteor shower, an average of 50 meteors appears each hour, with a variance of 9 meteors squared. The Geminid meteor shower will occur next week.

(a) If the astronomer watches the shower for 4 hours, what is the probability that at least 48 meteors per hour will appear?

(b) If the astronomer watches for an additional hour, will this probability rise or fall? Why?

■ **6-32** The average cost of a studio condominium in the Cedar Lakes development is $62,000 and the standard deviation is $4,200.

(a) What is the probability that a condominium in this development will cost at least $65,000?

(b) Is the probability that the average cost of a sample of two condominiums will be at least $65,000 greater or less than the probability of one condominium's costing that much? By how much?

■ **6-33** Robertson Employment Service customarily gives standard intelligence and aptitude tests to all people who seek employment through the firm. The firm has collected data for several years and has found that the distribution of scores is not normal, but is skewed to the left with a mean of 86 and a standard deviation of 16. What is the probability that in a sample of 75 applicants who take the test, the mean score will be less than 84 or greater than 90?

■ **6-34** An oil refinery has backup monitors to keep track of the refinery flows continuously and to prevent machine malfunctions from disrupting the process. One particular monitor has an average life of 4,300 hours and a standard deviation of 730 hours. In addition to the primary monitor, the refinery has set up two standby units, which are duplicates of the primary one. In the case of malfunction of one of the monitors, another will automatically take over in its place. The operating life of each monitor is independent of the others.

(a) What is the probability that a given set of monitors will last at least 13,000 hours?

(b) At most 12,630 hours?

■ **6-35** A recent study by the EPA has determined that the amount of contaminants in Minnesota lakes (in parts per million) is normally distributed with mean 64 ppm and variance 17.6. Suppose 35 lakes are randomly selected and sampled. What is the probability that the sample average amount of contaminants is

(a) Above 72 ppm?

(b) Between 64 and 72 ppm?

(c) Exactly 64 ppm?

(d) Above 94 ppm?

(e) If, in our sample, we found $\bar{x} = 100$ ppm, would you feel confident in the study conducted by the EPA? Explain briefly.

■ **6-36** Calvin Ensor, president of General Telephone Corp., is upset at the number of telephones produced by GTC that have faulty receivers. On average, 110 telephones per day are being returned because of this problem, and the standard deviation is 64. Mr. Ensor has decided that unless he can be at least 80 percent certain that, on average, no more than 120 phones per day will be returned during the next 48 days, he will order the process overhauled. Will the overhaul be ordered?

■ **6-37** Clara Voyant, whose job is predicting the future for her venture capital company, has just received the statistics describing her company's performance on 1,800 investments last year. Clara knows that, in general, investments generate profits that have a normal distribution with mean \$7,500 and standard deviation \$3,300. Even before she looked at the specific results from each of the 1,800 investments from last year, Clara was able to make some accurate predictions by using her knowledge of sampling distributions. Follow her analysis by finding the probability that the sample mean of last year's investments

(a) Exceeded \$7,700.

(b) Was less than \$7,400.

(c) Was greater than \$7,275, but less than \$7,650.

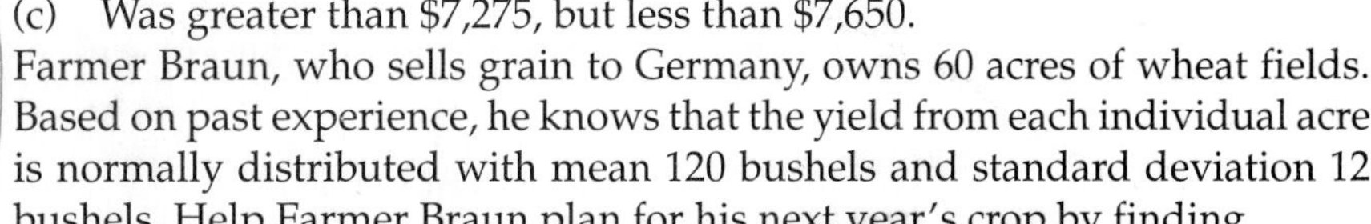

■ **6-38** Farmer Braun, who sells grain to Germany, owns 60 acres of wheat fields. Based on past experience, he knows that the yield from each individual acre is normally distributed with mean 120 bushels and standard deviation 12 bushels. Help Farmer Braun plan for his next year's crop by finding

(a) The expected mean of the yields from Farmer Braun's 60 acres of wheat.

(b) The standard deviation of the sample mean of the yields from Farmer Braun's 60 acres.

(c) The probability that the mean yield per acre will exceed 123.8 bushels.

(d) The probability that the mean yield per acre will fall between 117 and 122 bushels.

■ **6-39** A ferry carries 25 passengers. The weight of each passenger has a normal distribution with mean 168 pounds and variance 361 pounds squared. Safety regulations state that for this particular ferry, the total weight of passengers on the boat should not exceed 4,250 pounds more than 5 percent of the time. As a service to the ferry owners, find

(a) The probability that the total weight of passengers on the ferry will exceed 4,250 pounds.

(b) The 95th percentile of the distribution of the total weight of passengers on the ferry.

Is the ferry complying with safety regulations?

Worked-Out Answers to Self-Check Exercises

SC 6-5 (a) $n = 25 \quad \mu = 98.6 \quad \sigma = 17.2 \quad \sigma_{\bar{x}} = \sigma/\sqrt{n} = 17.2/\sqrt{25} = 3.44$

$$P(92 < \bar{x} < 102) = P\left(\frac{92 - 98.6}{3.44} < \frac{\bar{x} - \mu}{\sigma_{\bar{x}}} < \frac{102 - 98.6}{3.44}\right)$$

$$= P(-1.92 < z < 0.99) = 0.4726 + 0.3389 = 0.8115$$

(b) $n = 36 \quad \sigma_{\bar{x}} = \sigma/\sqrt{n} = 17.2/\sqrt{36} = 2.87$

$$P(92 < \bar{x} < 102) = P\left(\frac{92 - 98.6}{2.87} < \frac{\bar{x} - \mu}{\sigma_{\bar{x}}} < \frac{102 - 98.6}{2.87}\right)$$

$$= P(-2.30 < z < 1.18) = 0.4893 + 0.3810 = 0.8703$$

SC 6-6 The sample size of 50 is large enough to use the central limit theorem.

$$\mu = 112 \qquad \sigma = 56 \quad n = 50 \qquad \sigma_{\bar{x}} = \sigma/\sqrt{n} = 56/\sqrt{50} = 7.920$$

(a) $$P(\bar{x} < 100) = P\left(\frac{\bar{x} - \mu}{\sigma_{\bar{x}}} < \frac{100 - 112}{7.920}\right) = P(z < -1.52) = 0.5 - 0.4357 = 0.0643$$

(b) $$P(100 < \bar{x} < 130) = P\left(\frac{100 - 112}{7.920} < \frac{\bar{x} - \mu}{\sigma_{\bar{x}}} < \frac{130 - 112}{7.920}\right)$$

$$= P(-1.52 < z < 2.27) = 0.4357 + 0.4884 = 0.9241$$

6.6 An Operational Consideration in Sampling: The Relationship between Sample Size and Standard Error

Precision of the sample mean

We saw earlier in this chapter that the standard error, $\sigma_{\bar{x}}$ is a measure of dispersion of the sample means around the population mean. If the dispersion decreases (if $\sigma_{\bar{x}}$ becomes smaller), then the values taken by the sample mean tend to cluster *more* closely around μ. Conversely, if the dispersion increases (if $\sigma_{\bar{x}}$ becomes larger), the values taken by the sample mean tend to cluster *less* closely around μ. We can think of this relationship this way: **As the standard error decreases, the value of any sample mean will probably be closer to the value of the population mean.** Statisticians describe this phenomenon in another way: As the standard error decreases, the *precision* with which the sample mean can be used to estimate the population mean increases.

If we refer to Equation 6-1, we can see that as n increases, $\sigma_{\bar{x}}$ decreases. This happens because in Equation 6-1 a larger denominator on the right side would produce smaller $\sigma_{\bar{x}}$ on the left side. Two examples will show this relationship; both assume the same population standard deviation σ of 100.

$$\sigma_{\bar{x}} = \frac{\sigma}{\sqrt{n}} \qquad [6\text{-}1]$$

When $n = 10$:

$$\sigma_{\bar{x}} = \frac{100}{\sqrt{10}}$$

$$= \frac{100}{3.162}$$

$$= 31.63 \leftarrow \text{Standard error of the mean}$$

And when $n = 100$:

$$\sigma_{\bar{x}} = \frac{100}{\sqrt{100}}$$

$$= \frac{100}{10}$$

$$= 10 \leftarrow \text{Standard error of the mean}$$

Increasing the sample size: Diminishing returns

What have we shown? As we increased our sample size from 10 to 100 (a tenfold increase), the standard error dropped from 31.63 to 10, which is only about one-third of its former value. **Our examples show that, because $\sigma_{\bar{x}}$ varies inversely with the square root of n, there is diminishing return in sampling.**

It is true that sampling more items will decrease the standard error, but this benefit may not be worth the cost. A statistician would say, "The increased precision is not worth the additional sampling cost." In a statistical sense, it seldom pays to take excessively large samples. Managers should always assess *both* the worth and the cost of the additional precision they will obtain from a larger sample before they commit resources to take it.

The Finite Population Multiplier

Modifying Equation 6-1

To this point in our discussion of sampling distributions, we have used Equation 6-1 to calculate the standard error of the mean:

$$\sigma_{\bar{x}} = \frac{\sigma}{\sqrt{n}} \qquad [6\text{-}1]$$

This equation is designed for situations in which the population is infinite, or in which we sample from a finite population with replacement (that is, after each item is sampled, it is put back into the population before the next item is chosen, so that the same item can possibly be chosen more than once). If you will refer back to page 316, where we introduced Equation 6-1, you will recall our parenthesized note, which said, "Later we shall introduce an equation for finite populations." Introducing that equation is the purpose of this section.

Finding the standard error of the mean for finite populations

Many of the populations decision makers examine are finite, that is, of stated or limited size. Examples of these include the employees in a given company, the clients of a city social-services agency, the students in a specific class, and a day's production in a given manufacturing plant. Not one of these populations is infinite, so we need to modify Equation 6-1 to deal with them. The formula designed to find the standard error of the mean when the population is *finite,* and we sample *without replacement,* is

Standard Error of the Mean for Finite Populations

$$\sigma_{\bar{x}} = \frac{\sigma}{\sqrt{n}} \times \sqrt{\frac{N-n}{N-1}} \qquad [6\text{-}3]$$

where

- N = size of the population
- n = size of the sample

This new term on the right-hand side, which we multiply by our original standard error, is called the *finite population multiplier:*

Finite Population Multiplier

$$\text{Finite population multiplier} = \sqrt{\frac{N-n}{N-1}} \qquad [6\text{-}4]$$

A few examples will help us become familiar with interpreting and using Equation 6-3. Suppose we are interested in a population of 20 textile companies of the same size, all of which are experiencing excessive labor turnover. Our study indicates that the standard deviation of the distribution of annual turnover is 75 employees. If we sample five of these textile companies, without replacement, and wish to compute the standard error of the mean, we would use Equation 6-3 as follows:

$$\sigma_{\bar{x}} = \frac{\sigma}{\sqrt{n}} \times \sqrt{\frac{N-n}{N-1}} \qquad [6\text{-}3]$$

$$= \frac{75}{\sqrt{5}} \times \sqrt{\frac{20-5}{20-1}}$$

$$= (33.54)(0.888)$$

$$= 29.8 \leftarrow \text{Standard error of the mean of a finite population}$$

In this example, a finite population multiplier of 0.888 reduced the standard error from 33.54 to 29.8.

Sometimes the finite population multiplier is close to 1

In cases in which the population is very large in relation to the size of the sample, this finite population multiplier is close to 1 and has little effect on the calculation of the standard error. Say that we have a population of 1,000 items and that we have taken a sample of 20 items. If we use Equation 6-4 to calculate the finite population multiplier, the result would be

$$\text{Finite population multiplier} = \sqrt{\frac{N-n}{N-1}} \qquad [6\text{-}4]$$

$$= \sqrt{\frac{1{,}000-20}{1{,}000-1}}$$

$$= \sqrt{0.981}$$

$$= 0.99$$

Using this multiplier of 0.99 would have little effect on the calculation of the standard error of the mean.

Sampling fraction defined

This last example shows that when we sample a small fraction of the entire population (that is, when the population size N is very large relative to the sample size n), the finite population multiplier takes on a value close to 1.0. Statisticians refer to the fraction n/N as the *sampling fraction,* because it is the fraction of the population N that is contained in the sample.

When the sampling fraction is small, the standard error of the mean for finite populations is so close to the standard error of the mean for infinite populations that we might as well use the same formula for both, namely, Equation 6-1: $\sigma_{\bar{x}} = \sigma/\sqrt{n}$. The generally accepted rule is: **When the sampling fraction is less than 0.05, the finite population multiplier need not be used.**

When we use Equation 6-1, σ is constant, and so the measure of sampling precision, $\sigma_{\bar{x}}$, depends only on the sample size n and not on the proportion of the population sampled. That is, to make $\sigma_{\bar{x}}$ smaller, it is necessary only to make n larger. **Thus, it turns out that it is the absolute size of the sample that determines sampling precision, not the fraction of the population sampled.**

Sample size determines sampling precision

HINTS & ASSUMPTIONS

Although the *law of diminishing return* comes from economics, it has a definite place in statistics too. It says that there is diminishing return in sampling. Specifically, although sampling more items will decrease the standard error (the standard deviation of the distribution of sample means), the increased precision may not be worth the cost. Hint: Look again at Equation 6-1 on page 316. Because n is in the denominator, when we increase it (take larger samples) the standard error ($\sigma_{\bar{x}}$) *decreases.* Now look at page 324. When we increased the sample size from 10 to 100 (a tenfold increase) the standard error fell only from 31.63 to 10 (about a two-thirds decrease). Maybe it wasn't smart to spend so much money increasing the sample size to get this result. That's exactly why statisticians (and smart managers) focus on the concept of the "right" sample size. Another hint: In dealing with the finite population multiplier, remember that even though we can count them, some finite populations are so large that they are treated as if they were infinite. An example of this would be the number of TV households in the United States.

Exercises 6.6

Self-Check Exercises

SC 6-7 From a population of 125 items with a mean of 105 and a standard deviation of 17, 64 items were chosen.

(a) What is the standard error of the mean?

(b) What is the $P(107.5 < \bar{x} < 109)$?

SC 6-8 Jonida Martinez, researcher for the Columbian Coffee Corporation, is interested in determining the rate of coffee usage per household in the United States. She believes that yearly consumption per household is normally distributed with an unknown mean μ and a standard deviation of about 1.25 pounds.

(a) If Martinez takes a sample of 36 households and records their consumption of coffee for one year, what is the probability that the sample mean is within one-half pound of the population mean?

(b) How large a sample must she take in order to be 98 percent certain that the sample mean is within one-half pound of the population mean?

Basic Concepts

■ **6-40** From a population of 75 items with a mean of 364 and a variance of 18, 32 items were randomly selected without replacement.

(a) What is the standard error of the mean?

(b) What is the $P(363 \le \bar{x} \le 366)$?

(c) What would your answer to part (a) be if we sampled with replacement?

■ **6-41** Given a population of size $N = 80$ with a mean of 22 and a standard deviation of 3.2, what is the probability that a sample of 25 will have a mean between 21 and 23.5?

■ **6-42** For a population of size $N = 80$ with a mean of 8.2 and a standard deviation of 2.1, find the standard error of the mean for the following sample sizes:

(a) $n = 16$.

(b) $n = 25$.

(c) $n = 49$.

Applications

■ **6-43** Tread-On-Us has designed a new tire, and they don't know what the average amount of tread life is going to be. They do know that tread life is normally distributed with a standard deviation of 216.4 miles.

(a) If the company samples 800 tires and records their tread life, what is the probability the sample mean is between the true mean and 300 miles over the true mean?

(b) How large a sample must be taken to be 95 percent sure the sample mean will be within 100 miles of the true mean?

■ **6-44** An underwater salvage team is preparing to explore a site off the coast of Florida where an entire flotilla of 45 Spanish galleons sank. From historical records, the team expects these wrecks to generate an average of $225,000 in revenue when explored, and a standard deviation of $39,000. The team's financier, however, remains skeptical, and has stated that if the exploration expenses of $2.1 million are not recouped from the first nine wrecks, he will cancel the remainder of the exploration. What is the probability that the exploration continues past the first nine wrecks?

■ **6-45** An X-ray technician is taking readings from her machine to ensure that it adheres to federal safety guidelines. She knows that the standard deviation of the amount of radiation emitted by the machine is 150 millirems, but she wants to take readings until the standard error of the sampling distribution is no higher than 25 millirems. How many readings should she take?

■ **6-46** Sara Gordon is heading a fund-raising drive for Milford College. She wishes to concentrate on the current tenth-reunion class, and hopes to get contributions from 36 percent of the 250 members of that class. Past data indicate that those who contribute to the tenth-year reunion gift will donate 4 percent of their annual salaries. Sara believes that the reunion class members' annual salaries have an average of $32,000 and a standard deviation of $9,600. If her expectations are met (36 percent of the class donate 4 percent of their salaries), what is the probability that the tenth-reunion gift will be between $110,000 and $120,000?

■ **6-47** Davis Aircraft Co. is developing a new wing de-icer system, which it has installed on 30 commercial airliners. The system is designed so that the percentage of ice removed is normally distributed with mean 96 and standard deviation 7. The FAA will do a spot check of six of the airplanes with the new system, and will approve the system if at least 98 percent of the ice is removed on average. What is the probability that the system receives FAA approval?

■ **6-48** Food Place, a chain of 145 supermarkets, has been bought out by a larger nationwide supermarket chain. Before the deal is finalized, the larger chain wants to have some assurance that Food Place will be a consistent moneymaker. The larger chain has decided to look at the financial records for 36 of the Food Place stores. Food Place management claims that each store's profits have an approximately normal distribution with the same mean and a standard deviation of \$1,200. If the Food Place management is correct, what is the probability that the sample mean for the 36 stores will fall within \$200 of the actual mean?

■ **6-49** Miss Joanne Happ, chief executive officer of Southwestern Life & Surety Corp., wants to undertake a survey of the huge number of insurance policies that her company has underwritten. Miss Happ's firm makes a yearly profit on each policy that is distributed with mean \$310 and standard deviation \$150. Her personal accuracy requirements dictate that the survey must be large enough to reduce the standard error to no more than 1.5 percent of the population mean. How large should her sample be?

Worked-Out Answers to Self-Check Exercises

SC 6-7 $N = 125 \qquad \mu = 105 \qquad \sigma = 17 \qquad n = 64$

(a) $$\sigma_{\bar{x}} = \frac{\sigma}{\sqrt{n}} \times \sqrt{\frac{N-n}{N-1}} = \frac{17}{8} \times \sqrt{\frac{61}{124}} = 1.4904$$

(b) $$(107.5 < \bar{x} < 109) = P\left(\frac{107.5 - 105}{1.4904} < \frac{\bar{x} - \mu}{\sigma_{\bar{x}}} < \frac{109 - 105}{1.4904}\right)$$

$$= P(1.68 < z < 2.68) = 0.4963 - 0.4535 = 0.0428$$

SC 6-8 (a) $\sigma = 1.25 \qquad n = 36 \qquad \sigma_{\bar{x}} = \sigma/\sqrt{n} = 1.25/\sqrt{36} = 0.2083$

$$P(\mu - 0.5 \le \bar{x} \le \mu + 0.5) = P\left(\frac{-0.5}{0.2083} \le \frac{\bar{x} - \mu}{\sigma_{\bar{x}}} \le \frac{0.5}{0.2083}\right)$$

$$= P(-2.4 \le z \le 2.4) = 0.4918 + 0.4918 = 0.9836$$

(b) $$0.98 = P(\mu - 0.5 \le \bar{x} \le \mu + 0.5) = P\left(\frac{-0.5}{1.25/\sqrt{n}} \le z \le \frac{0.5}{1.25/\sqrt{n}}\right)$$

$$= P(-2.33 \le z \le 2.33)$$

Hence, $2.33 = \dfrac{0.5}{1.25/\sqrt{n}} = 0.4\sqrt{n}$ and $n = (2.33/0.4)^2 = 33.93$.

She should sample at least 34 households.

Statistics at Work

Loveland Computers

Case 6: Sampling and Sampling Distributions After less than a week on the job as an administrative assistant to Loveland Computers' CEO, Lee Azko was feeling almost overwhelmed with the range of projects that seemed to demand attention. But, there was no use denying, it sure felt good to put into practice some of the techniques that had been taught in school. And the next day on the job brought a new set of challenges.

"I guess those folks in production must like you," Walter Azko greeted Lee by the coffee machine. "I hope you're all done with purchasing because production has a quality control problem it needs help with. Go and see Nancy Rainwater again."

Lee went down to the assembly line but was greeted by an unfamiliar face. Tyronza Wilson introduced himself. "Nancy said you'd be down. I'm in charge of checking the components we use when we assemble high-end computers for customers. For most of the components, the suppliers are so reliable that we just assume they're going to work. In the very rare case there's a failure, we catch it at the end of the line, where we run the computers overnight on a test program to 'burn them in.' That means, we don't want to be surprised by a part that fails when it's been on the job for only a few hours.

"Recently, we've been having a problem with the 3-gigabyte hard drives. You know, everyone used to be happy with one or two gigabytes of storage, but new programs with fancy graphics eat up a great deal of disk space and many of the customers are specifying the large drive for their computers. To move large amounts of data, *access time* becomes very important—that's a measure of the average time that it takes to retrieve a standard amount of data from a hard drive. Because access-time performance is important to our customers, I can't just assume that every hard drive is going to work within specifications. If we wait to test access time at the end of the line and find we have a drive that's too slow, we have to completely rebuild the computer with a new drive and drive controller. That's a lot of expensive rework that we should avoid.

"But it'd be even more expensive to test every one of them at the beginning of the process—the only way I can measure the access time of each drive is to hook it up to a computer and run a diagnostic program. All told, that takes the best part of a quarter of an hour. I don't have the staff or the machines to test every one, and it's rather pointless because the vast majority of them will pass inspection.

"There's more demand than supply for the high-capacity hard drives right now, so we've been buying them all over the place. As a result, there seem to be 'good shipments' and 'bad shipments.' If the average access time of a shipment is too long, we return them to the supplier and reject their invoice. That saves us paying for something we can't use, but if I reject too many shipments, it leaves us short of disk drives to complete our orders.

"Obviously we need some kind of sampling scheme here—we need to measure the access time on a sample of each shipment and then make our decision about the lot. But I'm not sure how many we should test."

"Well, I think you have a good handle on the situation," said Lee, taking out a notepad. "Let me begin by asking you a few questions."

Study Questions: What types of sampling schemes will Lee consider and what factors will influence the choice of scheme? What questions should Lee have for Tyronza?

Computer Database Exercise

HH Industries

One of Hal Rodgers' management initiatives when he took over HH Industries was to introduce competitive procurement. He felt that many of the company's suppliers had been lulled into complacency through years of unchallenged orders. A careful study of the market revealed that a good number of HH's inventoried parts could be purchased from at least two manufacturers. Now, three years later, Hal was interested in evaluating the company's progress toward its goal.

Bob Ritchie, manager of purchasing, was in charge of the study, which brought him to Laurel's office one sunny afternoon when she was just about to escape to the beach for a few hours. "About this competitive procurement thing," he began. "I'm assuming it's a binomial distribution problem because any given purchase order was either competitively procured or not. My main question has to do with exactly how to select a truly random sample from our file cabinets full of POs. Peggy has given me the use of her part-time administrative assistant for a few days next week, and I wanted to get her started."

Laurel brightened when she realized that this particular problem could be handled quickly. Bob, she knew, had the best grasp of statistics of any of the staff, so she wouldn't have to launch into a lecture on sampling distributions, standard error, etc. She quickly summarized the advantages and disadvantages of various methods of sampling and asked Bob which ones he thought were appropriate.

"As I see it, we could do a couple of different things," he ventured. "We could randomly select a few months and examine every PO in each selected month. That sounds like what you called 'cluster sampling.' Or we could look at every twentieth PO or so, which is systematic, but sounds like almost as much work as looking at every purchase order. Finally, we could just leaf through the drawers, picking purchase orders at random until we had the sample size we wanted."

1. What method should Bob use for collecting a random sample of purchase orders? Why?

The next day, Stan caught Laurel just as she was heading out to run a few errands on her lunch hour. "Thanks for the information on our customers," he smiled. "But I have a question. I thought this statistics stuff was supposed to work with data *samples*. You used the data from all our active customers to come up with those figures. What gives?"

"Well," Laurel answered, "in this case I was merely taking advantage of the fact that we already had that data in a format that I could use, that is, on the computer. And, obviously, the larger the sample size, the more accurate the results. However, if I had had to punch in all that data, I would definitely have taken a shortcut and used a property called the central limit theorem. If you've got a few minutes this afternoon, I'll stop by and show you how it works."

"That would be terrific," said Stan. "I'll be free after a 2 P.M. meeting—about 3? Great. See you then."

2. Using the customer purchase data from Chapter 5, compute the mean and standard deviation for the purchases of the first 25 customers. Then do the same for the first 50, 100, 250, and 500.

Chapter Review

● Terms Introduced in Chapter 6

Census The measurement or examination of every element in the population.

Central Limit Theorem A result assuring that the sampling distribution of the mean approaches normality as the sample size increases, regardless of the shape of the population distribution from which the sample is selected.

Clusters Within a population, groups that are essentially similar to each other, although the groups themselves have wide internal variation.

Cluster Sampling A method of random sampling in which the population is divided into groups, or clusters of elements, and then a random sample of these clusters is selected.

Factorial Experiment An experiment in which each factor involved is used once with each other factor. In a complete factorial experiment, every level of each factor is used with each level of every other factor.

Finite Population A population having a stated or limited size.

Finite Population Multiplier A factor used to correct the standard error of the mean for studying a population of finite size that is small in relation to the size of the sample.

Infinite Population A population in which it is theoretically impossible to observe all the elements.

Judgment Sampling A method of selecting a sample from a population in which personal knowledge or expertise is used to identify the items from the population that are to be included in the sample.

Latin Square An efficient experimental design that makes it unnecessary to use a complete factorial experiment.

Parameters Values that describe the characteristics of a population.

Precision The degree of accuracy with which the sample mean can estimate the population mean, as revealed by the standard error of the mean.

Random or Probability Sampling A method of selecting a sample from a population in which all the items in the population have an equal chance of being chosen in the sample.

Sample A portion of the elements in a population chosen for direct examination or measurement.

Sampling Distribution of the Mean A probability distribution of all the possible means of samples of a given size, *n*, from a population.

Sampling Distribution of a Statistic For a given population, a probability distribution of all the possible values a statistic may take on for a given sample size.

Sampling Error Error or variation among sample statistics due to chance, that is, differences between each sample and the population, and among several samples, which are due solely to the elements we happen to choose for the sample.

Sampling Fraction The fraction or proportion of the population contained in a sample.

Sampling with Replacement A sampling procedure in which sampled items are returned to the population after being picked, so that some members of the population can appear in the sample more than once.

Sampling without Replacement A sampling procedure in which sampled items are not returned to the population after being picked, so that no member of the population can appear in the sample more than once.

Simple Random Sampling Methods of selecting samples that allow each possible sample an equal probability of being picked *and* each item in the entire population an equal chance of being included in the sample.

Standard Error The standard deviation of the sampling distribution of a statistic.

Standard Error of the Mean The standard deviation of the sampling distribution of the mean; a measure of the extent to which we expect the means from different samples to vary from the population mean, owing to the chance error in the sampling process.

Statistical Inference The process of making inferences about populations from information contained in samples.

Statistics Measures describing the characteristics of a sample.

Strata Groups within a population formed in such a way that each group is relatively homogeneous, but wider variability exists among the separate groups.

Stratified Sampling A method of random sampling in which the population is divided into homogeneous groups, or strata, and elements within each stratum are selected at random according to one of two rules: (1) A specified number of elements is drawn from each stratum corresponding to the proportion of that stratum in the population, or (2) equal numbers of elements are drawn from each stratum, and the results are weighted according to the stratum's proportion of the total population.

Systematic Sampling A method of sampling in which elements to be sampled are selected from the population at a uniform interval that is measured in time, order, or space.

• Equations Introduced in Chapter 6

■ **6-1**

$$\sigma_{\bar{x}} = \frac{\sigma}{\sqrt{n}}$$

p. 316

Use this formula to derive the standard error of the mean when the population is infinite, that is, when the elements of the population cannot be enumerated in a reasonable period of time, or when we sample with replacement. This equation states that the sampling distribution has a standard deviation, which we also call a standard error, equal to the population standard deviation divided by the square root of the sample size.

■ **6-2**

$$z = \frac{\bar{x} - \mu}{\sigma_{\bar{x}}}$$

p. 316

A modified version of Equation 5-6, this formula allows us to determine the distance of the *sample mean* $\bar{x}$ from the population mean μ when we divide the difference by the standard error of the mean $\sigma_{\bar{x}}$. Once we have derived a z value, we can use the Standard Normal Probability Distribution Table and compute the probability that the sample mean will be that distance from the population mean. Because of the central limit theorem, we can use this formula for nonnormal distributions if the sample size is at least 30.

■ 6-3

$$\sigma_{\bar{x}} = \frac{\sigma}{\sqrt{n}} \times \sqrt{\frac{N-n}{N-1}}$$

p. 325

where

- N = size of the population
- n = size of the sample

This is the formula for finding the *standard error of the mean* when the population is *finite,* that is, of stated or limited size, and the sampling is done *without* replacement.

■ 6-4

$$\text{Finite population multiplier} = \sqrt{\frac{N-n}{N-1}}$$

p. 325

In Equation 6-3, the term $\sqrt{(N-n)/(N-1)}$, which we multiply by the standard error from Equation (6-1), is called the *finite population multiplier.* When the population is small in relation to the size of the sample, the finite population multiplier reduces the size of the standard error. Any decrease in the standard error increases the precision with which the sample mean can be used to estimate the population mean.

Review and Application Exercises

■ **6-50** Crash Davis is the line supervisor for the Benicia, California, plant of a manufacturer of in-line skates. Close fit is important for in-line skating gear, so Crash tests each day's production by selecting a size 13 pair from the line and skating to get his afternoon cappuccino down the street. Crash points out that he selects each pair "at random." Is this, in fact, a random sample of the day's production, or is it judgmental?

■ **6-51** Jim Ford, advertising manager for a retail department store chain, is responsible for choosing the final advertisements from sample layouts designed by his staff. He has been in the retail advertising business for years and has been responsible for the chain's advertising for quite some time. His assistant, however, having learned the latest advertising effectiveness measurement techniques while at a New York agency, wants to do effectiveness tests for each advertisement considered, using random samples of consumers in the store's retail trading district. These tests will be quite costly. Jim is sure that his experience enables him to decide on appropriate ads, so there has been some disagreement between the two. Can you defend either position?

■ **6-52** Burt Purdue, manager of the Sea Island Development Company, wants to find out residents' feelings toward the development's recreation facilities and the improvements they would like to see implemented. The development includes residents of various ages and income levels, but a large proportion are middle-class residents between the ages of 30 and 50. As yet, Burt is unsure whether there are differences among age groups or income levels in their desire for recreation facilities. Would stratified random sampling be appropriate here?

■ **6-53** A camera manufacturer is attempting to find out what employees feel are the major problems with the company and what improvements are needed. To assess the opinions of the 37 departments, management is considering a sampling plan. It has been recommended to the personnel director that management adopt a cluster sampling plan. Management would choose six departments and interview all the employees. Upon collecting and assessing the data gathered from these employees, the company could then make changes and plan for areas of job improvement. Is a cluster sampling plan appropriate in this situation?

■ **6-54** By reviewing sales since opening 6 months ago, a restaurant owner found that the average bill for a couple was \$26, and the standard deviation was \$5.65. How large would a sample of customers have to be for the probability to be at least 95.44 percent that the mean cost per meal for the sample would fall between \$25 and \$27?

■ **6-55** The end of March in 1992 saw the following state-by-state unemployment rates in the United States.

State	Unemployment Rate (%)	State	Unemployment Rate (%)
Alabama	7.5	Montana	7.3
Alaska	10.1	Nebraska	2.8
Arizona	8.4	Nevada	6.8
Arkansas	7.0	New Hampshire	7.5
California	8.7	New Jersey	7.5
Colorado	6.3	New Mexico	7.6
Connecticut	7.4	New York	8.5
Delaware	6.4	North Carolina	6.4
District of Columbia	8.2	North Dakota	5.3
Florida	8.1	Ohio	7.8
Georgia	6.3	Oklahoma	6.8
Hawaii	3.5	Oregon	8.6
Idaho	7.8	Pennsylvania	7.6
Illinois	8.2	Rhode Island	8.9
Indiana	6.3	South Carolina	7.1
Iowa	5.3	South Dakota	4.0
Kansas	3.6	Tennessee	7.0
Kentucky	7.0	Texas	7.4
Louisiana	6.9	Utah	5.0
Maine	8.4	Vermont	7.1
Maryland	7.4	Virginia	6.8
Massachusetts	10.0	Washington	8.3
Michigan	10.0	West Virginia	12.9
Minnesota	6.3	Wisconsin	5.7
Mississippi	8.1	Wyoming	7.5
Missouri	5.6		

Source: Sharon R. Cohany, "Current Labor Statistics: Employment Data," Monthly Labor Review *115 (6), (June 1992): 80–82.*

(a) Compute the population mean and standard deviation of the unemployment rates.

(b) Using the states of Alabama, Kansas, Michigan, Nebraska, and North Carolina as a random sample (taken without replacement), determine the sample mean, $\bar{x}$.

(c) What are the mean ($\mu_{\bar{x}}$) and standard deviation ($\sigma_{\bar{x}}$) of the sampling distribution of $\bar{x}$, the sample mean of all samples of size $n = 5$, taken without replacement?

(d) Consider the sampling distribution of $\bar{x}$ for samples of size $n = 5$, taken without replacement. Is it reasonable to assume that this distribution is normal or approximately so? Explain.

(e) Notwithstanding your answer to part (d), assume that the sampling distribution of $\bar{x}$ for samples of size $n = 5$, taken without replacement, is approximately normal. What is the probability that the mean of such a random sample will lie between 5.9 and 6.5?

■ **6-56** Joan Fargo, president of Fargo-Lanna Ltd., wants to offer videotaped courses for employees during the lunch hour, and wants to get some idea of the courses that employees would like to see offered. Accordingly, she has devised a ballot that an employee can fill out in 5 minutes, listing his or her preferences among the possible courses. The ballots, which cost very little to print, will be distributed with paychecks, and the results will be tabulated by the as yet unreassigned clerical staff of a recently dissolved group within the company. Ms. Fargo plans to poll all employees. Are there any reasons to poll a sample of the employees rather than the entire population?

■ **6-57** A drug manufacturer knows that for a certain antibiotic, the average number of doses ordered for a patient is 20. Steve Simmons, a salesman for the company, after looking at one day's prescription orders for the drug in his territory, announced that the sample mean for this drug should be lower. He said, "For any sample, the mean should be lower, since the sampling mean always understates the population mean because of sample variation." Is there any truth to what Simmons said?

■ **6-58** Several weeks later at a sales meeting, Steve Simmons again demonstrated his expertise in statistics. He had drawn a graph and presented it to the group, saying, "This is a sampling distribution of means. It is a normal curve and represents a distribution of all observations in each possible sample combination." Is Simmons right? Explain.

■ **6-59** Low-Cal Foods Company uses estimates of the level of activity for various market segments to determine the nutritional composition of its diet food products. Low-Cal is considering the introduction of a liquid diet food for older women, since this segment has special weight problems not met by the competitor's diet foods. To determine the desired calorie content of this new product, Dr. Nell Watson, researcher for the company, conducted tests on a sample of women to determine calorie consumption per day. Her results showed that the average number of calories expended per day for older women is 1,328 and the standard deviation is 275. Dr. Watson estimates that the benefits she obtains with a sample size of 25 are worth \$1,720. She expects that reducing the standard error by half its current value will double the benefit. If it costs \$16 for every woman in the sample, should Watson reduce her standard error?

■ **6-60** Consider the following information about factory wages in the Chicago metropolitan area:

Job Title	Average Hourly Wage ($)	Job Title	Average Hourly Wage ($)
Assembler A	10.72	Packaging—wrapping machine operator	9.93
Assembler B	9.13	Packaging—wrapping machine packer	9.04
Assembler C	7.98	Packer—heavy	10.08
Carpenter, maintenance	13.58	Packer—light	8.82
Chemical compounder	12.64	Painter—maintenance	12.72
Chemical mixer	11.19	Painter—spray	9.78
Degreaser operator	9.11	Plastic injection molder	9.72
Drill press operator A	12.01	Polisher and buffer A	10.24
Drill press operator B	9.89	Polisher and buffer B	9.59
Drill press operator C	9.51	Punch press die setter A	12.80
Electrician	15.37	Punch press die setter B	11.31
Grinding machine operator A	12.92	Punch press heavy	9.75
Grinding machine operator B	9.89	Punch press light	8.91
Group leader A	13.55	Punch press setup and operator	11.32
Group leader B	11.28	Receiving clerk	9.98
Guard-watchman	9.86	Screw machine operator	16.01
Inspector A	11.55	Screw machine setup	12.40
Inspector B	10.11	Shear operator	10.45
Inspector C	8.57	Shipper/receiver	9.73
Janitor—heavy	9.19	Shipping clerk	10.03
Janitor—light	8.26	Solderer A	5.69
Laborer—dock hand	9.26	Solderer B	9.88
Lathe operator—turret A	12.66	Stationary engineer	16.52
Lathe operator—turret B	10.62	Stock person A	9.71
Lift truck operator	10.52	Stock person B	8.86
Machine operator	9.82	Test analyzer—junior	10.04
Maintenance machinist A	15.31	Test analyzer—senior	11.73
Maintenance machinist B	14.42	Tool and die maker A	17.66
Maintenance machinist C	12.07	Tool and die maker B	15.49
Maintenance person A	14.13	Tool and die maker C	11.72
Maintenance person B	11.19	Tool room machinist	13.55
Modelmaker	16.35	Trucker, hand	9.00
Numerical control operator A	13.99	Warehouse person	9.87
Numerical control operator B	10.69	Welder arc—acetylene prod.	12.69
Packager	7.92	Welder—spot prod.	10.01
		Wirer A	10.67
		Wirer B	8.81

Source: John J. Bohorquez, "1992 Wage and Salary Survey," Crain's Chicago Business *(28 December 1992): 28–29.*

(a) Compute the population mean and standard deviation of the wage rates.

(b) Using the job titles of Assembler C, Electrician, Electrician, Guard, Lift truck operator, Modelmaker, Punch press die setter A, Shear operator, and Wirer A as a random sample (taken *with* replacement), determine the sample mean, $\bar{x}$.

(c) What are the mean ($\mu_{\bar{x}}$) and standard deviation ($\sigma_{\bar{x}}$) of the sampling distribution of $\bar{x}$, the sample mean of all samples of size $n = 9$, taken with replacement?

(d) Consider the sampling distribution of $\bar{x}$ for samples of size $n = 9$, taken with replacement. Is it reasonable to assume that this distribution is normal or approximately so? Explain.

(e) Notwithstanding your answer to part (d), assume that the sampling distribution of $\bar{x}$ for samples of size $n = 9$, taken with replacement, is approximately normal. What is the probability that the mean of such a random sample will lie between 10.5 and 11.7?

■ **6-61** The U.S. Customs Agency routinely checks all passengers arriving from foreign countries as they enter the United States. The department reports that the number of people per day found to be carrying contraband material as they enter the United States through John F. Kennedy airport in New York averages 42 and has a standard deviation of 11. What is the probability that in five days at the airport, the average number of passengers found carrying contraband will exceed 50?

■ **6-62** HAL Corporation manufactures large computer systems and has always prided itself on the reliability of its System 666 central processing units. In fact, past experience has shown that the monthly downtime of System 666 CPUs averages 41 minutes, and has a standard deviation of 8 minutes. The computer center at a large state university maintains an installation built around six System 666 CPUs. James Kitchen, the director of the computer center, feels that a satisfactory level of service is provided to the university community if the average downtime of the six CPUs is less than 50 minutes per month. In any given month, what is the probability that Kitchen will be satisfied with the level of service?

■ **6-63** Members of the Organization for Consumer Action send more than 250 volunteers a day all over the state to increase support for a consumer protection bill that is currently before the state legislature. Usually, each volunteer will visit a household and talk briefly with the resident in the hope that the resident will sign a petition to be given to the state legislature. The number of signatures a volunteer obtains for the petition each day averages 5.8 and has a standard deviation of 0.8. What is the probability a sample of 20 volunteers will result in an average between 5.5 and 6.2 signatures per day?

■ **6-64** Jill Johnson, product manager for Southern Electric's smoke alarm, is concerned over recent complaints from consumer groups about the short life of the device. She has decided to gather evidence to counteract the complaints by testing a sample of the alarms. For the test, it costs $4 per unit in the sample. Precision is desirable for presenting persuasive statistical evidence to consumer groups, so Johnson figures the benefits she will receive for various sample sizes are determined by the formula Benefits = $\$5{,}249/\sigma_{\bar{x}}$. If Johnson wants to increase her sample until the cost equals the benefit, how many units should she sample? The population standard deviation is 265.

■ **6-65** Seventy data clerks at the Department of Motor Vehicles make an average of 18 errors per day, normally distributed with a standard deviation of 4. A field auditor can check the work of 15 clerks per day. What is the probability that the average number of errors in a group of 15 clerks checked on one day is

(a) Fewer than 15.5?

(b) Greater than 20?

■ **6-66** Mutual funds are popular with American small investors: by mid-1995, more than $2 trillion of wealth was invested in stock funds. As corporations have moved away from defined-benefit pension plans to defined-contribution plans, many employees have signed up for programs where their pension savings are automatically invested in common stocks through the purchase of mutual funds; $687 billion of all mutual funds was owned through pension plans.

The August 1995 purchase (inflows) to stock mutual funds was reported by The Investment Company Institute (a trade group) as $13.2 billion, down from $13.9 billion in July and $14.1 billion one year earlier. Stock market analysts are interested in following these inflows as an indicator of small investor sentiment. But monthly figures can vary due to irrelevant factors such as the number of paydays that fall in a given month.

Assume that a complete set of data is available for inflows to stock funds and that, over a very long period of time, you calculate a mean inflow of $13.9 billion per month and a standard deviation of $0.5 billion.

(a) Is this a sample or a complete enumeration?

(b) Is the population finite or infinite?

Source: Ellen Schultz. "Tidal Wave of Retirement Cash Anchors Mutual Funds. The Wall Street Journal *(27 September 1995): C1.*

■ **6-67** California Governor Pete Wilson ran for re-election on a promise to serve a full four-year term, and then announced a quest to seek the U.S. presidency. His absence from the state cost him approval ratings with voters, and a newspaper reported the following:

"Pete Wilson's campaign for the Republican Presidential nomination is taking its toll on his job performance rating according to a new statewide Field Poll. Four in ten Californians say he is doing a poor or very poor job."

There are about 32 million people in California, 10 to 11 million of whom cast votes in recent general elections.

(a) Is the assertion "four in ten Californians" strictly true from a statistician's point of view?

(b) What type of sampling—systematic, stratified, or cluster—would you suppose was used here?

(c) Is the population of California "infinite"?

Source: "Presidential Run Drags Governor's Rating Down." Oakland Tribune *(5 September 1995): A14.*

● Chapter Concepts Test

Circle the correct answer or fill in the blank. *Answers are in the back of the book.*

T F 1. When the items included in a sample are based on the judgment of the individual conducting the sample, the sample is said to be nonrandom.

T F 2. A statistic is a characteristic of a population.

T F 3. A sampling plan that selects members from a population at uniform intervals in time, order, or space is called stratified sampling.

T F 4. As a general rule, it is not necessary to include a finite population multiplier in a computation for standard error of the mean when the size of the sample is greater than 50.

T F 5. The probability distribution of all the possible means of samples is known as the sample distribution of the mean.

T F 6. The principles of simple random sampling are the theoretical foundation for statistical inference.

T F 7. The standard error of the mean is the standard deviation of the distribution of sample means.

T F 8. A sampling plan that divides the population into well-defined groups from which random samples are drawn is known as cluster sampling.

T F 9. With increasing sample size, the sampling distribution of the mean approaches normality, regardless of the distribution of the population.

T F 10. The standard error of the mean decreases in direct proportion to sample size.

T F 11. To perform a complete enumeration, one would need to examine every item in a population.

T F 12. In everyday life, we see many examples of infinite populations of physical objects.

T F 13. To obtain a theoretical sampling distribution, we consider all the samples of a given size.

T F 14. Large samples are always a good idea because they decrease the standard error.

T F 15. If the mean for a certain population were 15, it is likely that most of the samples we could take from that population would have means of 15.

T F 16. The precision of a sample is determined by the number of items in the sample and not the proportion of the total population that is sampled.

T F 17. The standard error of a sample statistic is the standard deviation of its sampling distribution.

T F 18. Judgment sampling has the disadvantage that it may lose some representativeness of a sample.

T F 19. The sampling fraction compares the size of a sample to the size of the population.

T F 20. Any sampling distribution can be totally described by its mean and standard deviation.

T F 21. The precision with which the sample mean can be used to estimate the population mean decreases as the standard error increases.

A B C D E 22. Which of the following is a method of selecting samples from a population?
(a) Judgment sampling.
(b) Random sampling.
(c) Probability sampling.
(d) All of these.
(e) (a) and (b) but not (c).

A B C D E 23. Choose the pair of symbols that best completes this sentence: ____________ is a parameter, whereas ____________ is a statistic.
(a) N, μ.
(b) σ, s.
(c) N, n.
(d) All of these.
(e) (b) and (c) but not (a).

A B C D E 24. In random sampling, we can describe mathematically how objective our estimates are. Why is this?
(a) We always know the chance that any population element will be included in the sample.
(b) Every sample always has an equal chance of being selected.
(c) All the samples are of exactly the same size and can be counted.
(d) None of these.
(e) (a) and (b) but not (c).

A B C D E 25. Suppose you are performing stratified sampling on a particular population and have divided it into strata of different sizes. How can you now make your sample selection?
(a) Select at random an equal number of elements from each stratum.
(b) Draw equal numbers of elements from each stratum and weigh the results.

(c) Draw numbers of elements from each stratum proportional to their weights in the population.
(d) (a) and (b) only.
(e) (b) and (c) only.

A B C D E 26. In which of the following situations would $\sigma_{\bar{x}} = \dfrac{\sigma}{\sqrt{n}}$ be the correct formula to use for computing $\sigma_{\bar{x}}$?
(a) Sampling is from an infinite population.
(b) Sampling is from a finite population with replacement.
(c) Sampling is from a finite population without replacement.
(d) (a) and (b) only.
(e) (b) and (c) only.

A B C D E 27. The dispersion among sample means is less than the dispersion among the sampled items themselves because
(a) Each sample is smaller than the population from which it is drawn.
(b) Very large values are averaged down and very small values are averaged up.
(c) The sampled items are all drawn from the same population.
(d) None of these.
(e) (b) and (c) but not (a).

A B C D 28. Suppose that a population with $N = 144$ has $\mu = 24$. What is the mean of the sampling distribution of the mean for samples of size 25?
(a) 24.
(b) 2.
(c) 4.8.
(d) Cannot be determined from the information given.

A B C D 29. The central limit theorem assures us that the sampling distribution of the mean
(a) Is always normal.
(b) Is always normal for large sample sizes.
(c) Approaches normality as sample size increases.
(d) Appears normal only when N is greater than 1,000.

A B C 30. Suppose that, for a certain population, $\sigma_{\bar{x}}$ is calculated as 20 when samples of size 25 are taken and as 10 when samples of size 100 are taken. A quadrupling of sample size, then, only halved $\sigma_{\bar{x}}$. We can conclude that increasing sample size is
(a) Always cost-effective.
(b) Sometimes cost-effective.
(c) Never cost-effective.

A B C D 31. Refer again to the data of Question 30. What must be the value of σ for this infinite population?
(a) 1,000.
(b) 500.
(c) 377.5.
(d) 100.

A B C D E 32. The finite population multiplier does not have to be used when the sampling fraction is
(a) Greater than 0.05.
(b) Greater than 0.50.
(c) Less than 0.50.
(d) Greater than 0.90.
(e) None of these.

A B C D 33. The standard error of the mean for a sample size of two or more is
(a) Always greater than the standard deviation of the population.
(b) Generally greater than the standard deviation of the population.
(c) Usually less than the standard deviation of the population.
(d) None of these.

A B C D 34. A border patrol checkpoint that stops every passenger van is using
(a) Simple random sampling.
(b) Systematic sampling.
(c) Stratified sampling.
(d) Complete enumeration.

A B C D E 35. In a normally distributed population, the sampling distribution of the mean
(a) Is normally distributed.
(b) Has a mean equal to the population mean.
(c) Has a standard deviation equal to the population standard deviation divided by the square root of the sample size.
(d) All of the above.
(e) Both (a) and (b).

A B C D 36. The central limit theorem
(a) Requires some knowledge of the frequency distribution.
(b) Permits us to use sample statistics to make inferences about population parameters.
(c) Relates the shape of a sampling distribution of the mean to the mean of the sample.
(d) Requires a sample to contain fewer than 30 observations.

37. A portion of the elements in a population chosen for direct examination or measurement is a ________________________.

38. The proportion of the population contained in a sample is the ________________________.

39. ________________________ is the process by which inferences about a population are made from information about a sample.

40. The ________________________ is the distribution obtained by finding the sampling distribution of all samples of a given size of a population.

41. ________________________ sampling should be used when each group considered has small variation within itself but there is wide variation between different groups.

42. A method of random sampling in which elements are selected from the population at uniform intervals is called ________________________ sampling.

43. ________________________ is the degree of accuracy with which the sample mean can estimate the population mean.

44. Within a population, groups that are similar to each other (although the groups themselves have wide internal variation) are called ________________________.

45. A sampling distribution of the proportion is a probability distribution of the ________________________.

Flow Chart: Sampling and Sampling Distributions

START

Use sampling and sampling distributions to make inferences about a population without counting or measuring every item in the population

Is expertise about the population used to select the sample ?

Yes

This is judgment sampling

No

This is random sampling: all items in the population have a chance of being chosen in the sample

Do you want each possible sample to have an equal probability of being picked and each item in the population to have an equal chance of being included in the sample ?

Yes

Use simple random sampling employing a table of random digits p. 300

No

Do you want each item to have an equal chance of being selected but each sample not to have an equal chance of being selected ?

Yes

Use systematic sampling p. 301

No

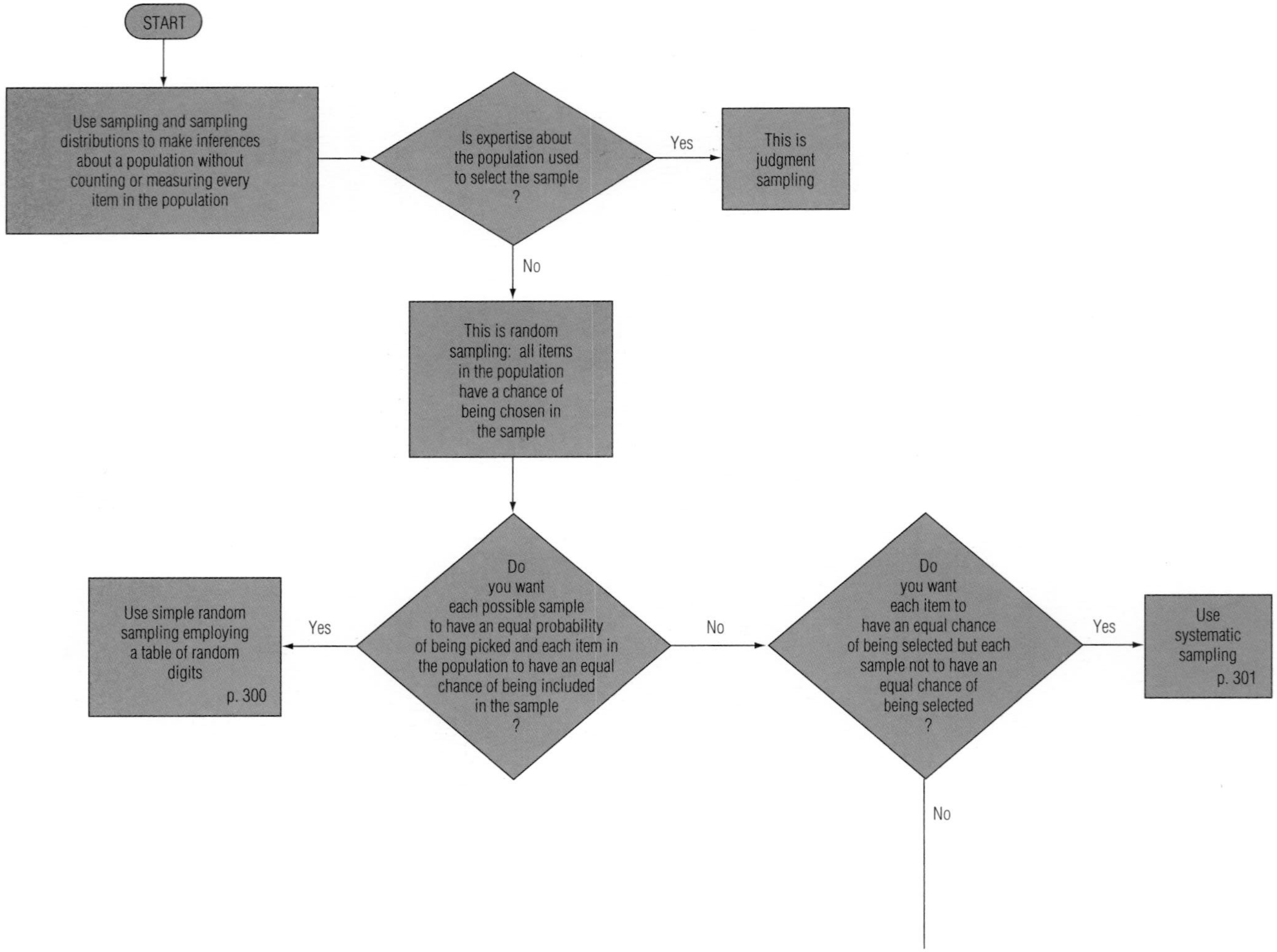

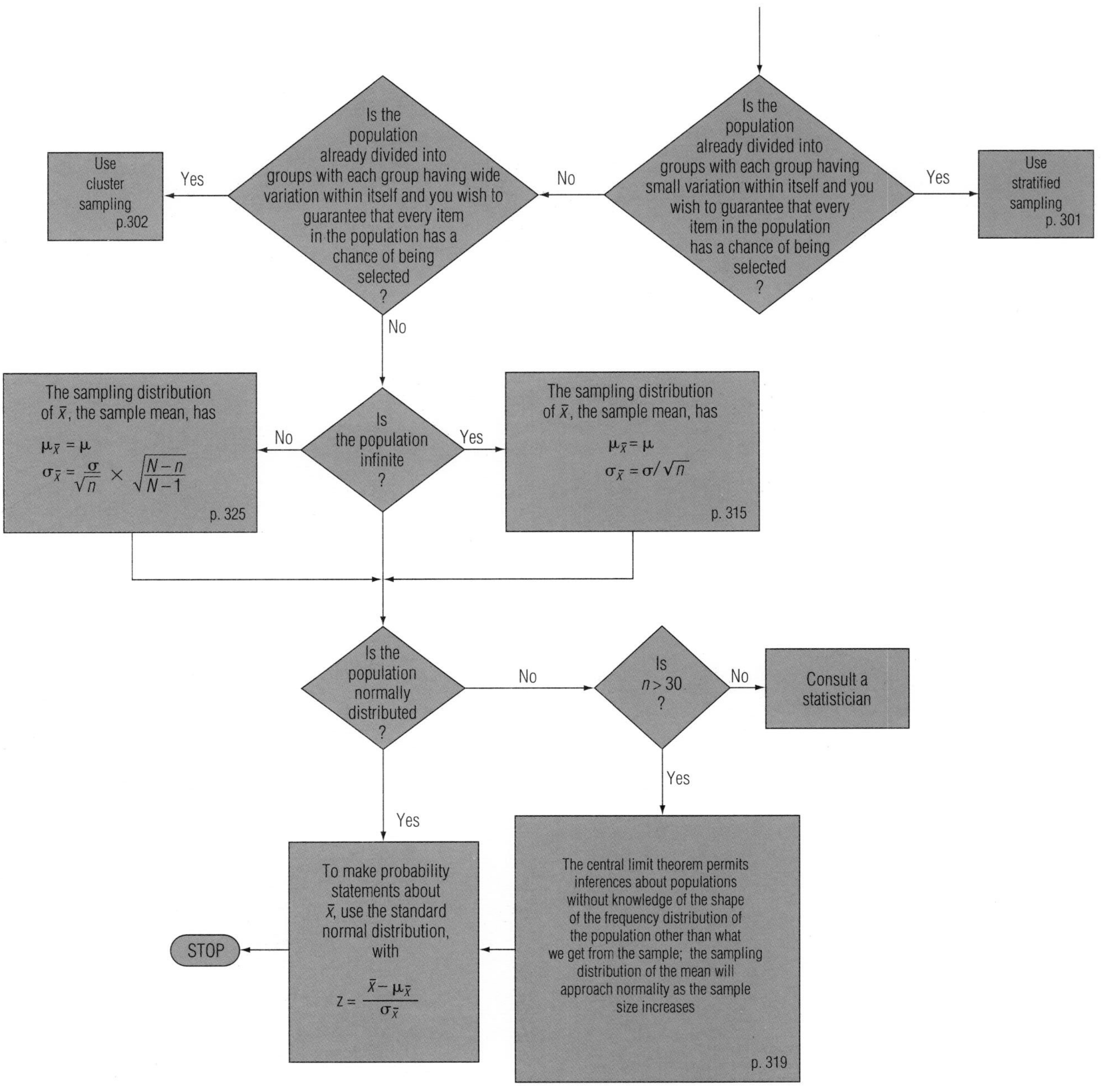

Is the population already divided into groups with each group having small variation within itself and you wish to guarantee that every item in the population has a chance of being selected ?
Yes
Use stratified sampling p. 301
No
Is the population already divided into groups with each group having wide variation within itself and you wish to guarantee that every item in the population has a chance of being selected ?
Yes
Use cluster sampling p.302
No
Is the population infinite ?
Yes
The sampling distribution of $\bar{x}$, the sample mean, has
$\mu_{\bar{x}} = \mu$
$\sigma_{\bar{x}} = \sigma/\sqrt{n}$
p. 315
No
The sampling distribution of $\bar{x}$, the sample mean, has
$\mu_{\bar{x}} = \mu$
$\sigma_{\bar{x}} = \frac{\sigma}{\sqrt{n}} \times \sqrt{\frac{N-n}{N-1}}$
p. 325
Is the population normally distributed ?
No
Is $n > 30$?
No
Consult a statistician
Yes
The central limit theorem permits inferences about populations without knowledge of the shape of the frequency distribution of the population other than what we get from the sample; the sampling distribution of the mean will approach normality as the sample size increases
p. 319
Yes
To make probability statements about $\bar{x}$, use the standard normal distribution, with
$z = \frac{\bar{x} - \mu_{\bar{x}}}{\sigma_{\bar{x}}}$
STOP

chapter 7

ESTIMATION

Objectives

- To learn how to estimate certain characteristics of a population from samples
- To learn the strengths and shortcomings of point estimates and interval estimates
- To calculate how accurate our estimates really are
- To learn how to use the t distribution to make interval estimates in some cases when the normal distribution cannot be used
- To calculate the sample size required for any desired level of precision in estimation

Chapter Contents

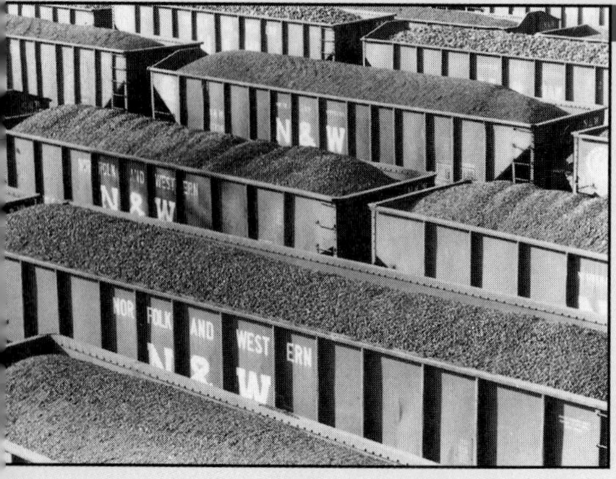

As part of the budgeting process for next year, the manager of the Far Point electric generating plant must estimate the coal he will need for this year. Last year, the plant almost ran out, so he is reluctant to budget for that same amount again. The plant manager, however, does feel that past usage data will help him *estimate* the number of tons of coal to order. A random sample of 10 plant operating weeks chosen over the last 5 years yielded a mean usage of 11,400 tons a week, and a sample standard deviation of 700 tons a week. With the data he has and the methods we shall discuss in this chapter, the plant manager can make a sensible estimate of the amount to order this year, including some idea of the accuracy of the estimate he has made. ■

7.1 Introduction

Everyone makes estimates. When you are ready to cross a street, you estimate the speed of any car that is approaching, the distance between you and that car, and your own speed. Having made these quick estimates, you decide whether to wait, walk, or run.

Reasons for estimates

All managers must make quick estimates too. The outcome of these estimates can affect their organizations as seriously as the outcome of your decision as to whether to cross the street. University department heads make estimates of next fall's enrollment in statistics. Credit managers estimate whether a purchaser will eventually pay his bills. Prospective home buyers make estimates concerning the behavior of interest rates in the mortgage market. All these people make estimates without worry about whether they are scientific but with the hope that the estimates bear a reasonable resemblance to the outcome.

Managers use estimates because in all but the most trivial decisions, they must make rational decisions without complete information and with a great deal of uncertainty about what the future will bring. As educated citizens and professionals, you will be able to make more useful estimates by applying the techniques described in this and subsequent chapters.

Making statistical inferences

The material on probability theory covered in Chapters 4, 5, and 6 forms the foundation for *statistical inference,* the branch of statistics concerned with using probability concepts to deal with uncertainty in decision making. Statistical inference is based on *estimation,* which we shall introduce in this chapter, and *hypothesis testing,* which is the subject of Chapters 8, 9, and 10. In both estimation and hypothesis testing, we shall be making inferences about characteristics of populations from information contained in samples.

Using samples

How do managers use sample statistics to estimate population parameters? The department head attempts to estimate enrollments next fall from current enrollments in the same courses. The credit manager attempts to estimate the creditworthiness of prospective customers from a sample of their past payment habits. The home buyer attempts to estimate the future course of interest rates by observing the current behavior of those rates. In each case, somebody is trying to infer something about a population from information taken from a sample.

Estimating population parameters

This chapter introduces methods that enable us to estimate with reasonable accuracy the *population proportion* (the proportion of the population that possesses a given characteristic) and the *population mean.* To calculate the exact proportion or the exact mean would be an impossible goal. Even so, we will be able to make an estimate, make a statement about the error that will probably accompany this estimate, and implement some controls to avoid as much of the error as possible. As decision makers, we will be forced at times to rely on blind hunches. Yet in other situations, in which information is available and we apply statistical concepts, we can do better than that.

Types of Estimates

Point estimate defined

We can make two types of estimates about a population: a *point estimate* and an *interval estimate.* **A point estimate is a single number that is used to estimate an unknown population parameter.** If, while watching the first members of a football team come onto the field, you say, "Why, I bet their line must average 250 pounds," you have made a point estimate. A department head would make a point estimate if she said, "Our current data indicate that this course will have 350 students in the fall."

Shortcoming of point estimates

A point estimate is often insufficient, because it is either right or wrong. If you are told only that her point estimate of enrollment is wrong, you do not know *how* wrong it is, and you cannot be certain of the estimate's reliability. If you learn that it is off by only 10 students, you would accept 350 students as a good estimate of future enrollment. But if the estimate is off by 90 students, you would reject it as an estimate of future enrollment. Therefore, a point estimate is much more useful if it is accompanied by an estimate of the error that might be involved.

Interval estimate defined

An interval estimate is a range of values used to estimate a population parameter. It indicates the error in two ways: by the extent of its range and by the probability of the true population parameter lying within that range. In this case, the department head would say something like, "I estimate that the true enrollment in this course in the fall will be between 330 and 380 and that it is very likely that the exact enrollment will fall within this interval." She has a better idea of the reliability of her estimate. If the course is taught in sections of about 100 students each, and if she had tentatively scheduled five sections, then on the basis of her estimate, she can now cancel one of those sections and offer an elective instead.

Estimator and Estimates

Estimator defined

Any sample statistic that is used to estimate a population parameter is called an *estimator*; that is, **an estimator is a sample statistic used to estimate a population parameter.** The sample mean $\bar{x}$ can be an estimator of the population mean μ, and the sample proportion can be used as an estimator of the population proportion. We can also use the sample range as an estimator of the population range.

Estimate defined

When we have observed a specific numerical value of our estimator, we call that value an *estimate.* In other words, **an estimate is a specific observed value of a statistic.** We form an estimate by taking a sample and computing the value taken by our estimator in that sample. Suppose that we calculate the mean odometer reading (mileage) from a sample of used taxis and find it to be 98,000 miles. If we use this specific value to estimate the mileage for a whole fleet of used taxis, the value 98,000 miles would be an estimate. Table 7-1 illustrates several populations, population parameters, estimators, and estimates.

Table 7-1 Populations, Population Parameters, Estimators, and Estimates

Population in Which We Are Interested	Population Parameter We Wish to Estimate	Sample Statistic We Will Use as an Estimator	Estimate We Make
Employees in a furniture factory	Mean turnover per year	Mean turnover for a period of 1 month	8.9% turnover per year
Applicants for Town Manager of Chapel Hill	Mean formal education (years)	Mean formal education of every fifth applicant	17.9 years of formal education
Teenagers in a given community	Proportion who have criminal records	Proportion of a sample of 50 teenagers who have criminal records	0.02, or 2%, have criminal records

Criteria of a Good Estimator

Qualities of a good estimator

Some statistics are better estimators than others. Fortunately, we can evaluate the quality of a statistic as an estimator by using four criteria:

1. **Unbiasedness.** This is a desirable property for a good estimator to have. The term *unbiasedness* refers to the fact that a sample mean is an *unbiased estimator* of a population mean because **the mean of the sampling distribution of sample means taken from the same population is equal to the population mean itself.** We can say that a statistic is an unbiased estimator if, on average, it tends to assume values that are above the population parameter being estimated as frequently and to the same extent as it tends to assume values that are below the population parameter being estimated.
2. **Efficiency.** Another desirable property of a good estimator is that it be efficient. *Efficiency* refers to the size of the standard error of the statistic. If we compare two statistics from a sample of the same size and try to decide which one is the more efficient estimator, we would pick the statistic that has the smaller standard error, or standard deviation of the sampling distribution. Suppose we choose a sample of a given size and must decide whether to use the sample mean or the sample median to estimate the population mean. If we calculate the standard error of the sample mean and find it to be 1.05 and then calculate the standard error of the sample median and find it to be 1.6, we would say that the sample mean is a *more efficient estimator* of the population mean *because its standard error is smaller.* It makes sense that an estimator with a smaller standard error (with less variation) will have more chance of producing an estimate nearer to the population parameter under consideration.
3. **Consistency.** A statistic is a *consistent estimator* of a population parameter if *as the sample size increases, it becomes almost certain that the value of the statistic comes very close to the value of the population parameter.* If an estimator is consistent, it becomes more reliable with large samples. Thus, if you are wondering whether to increase the sample size to get more information about a population parameter, find out first whether your statistic is a consistent estimator. If it is not, you will waste time and money by taking larger samples.
4. **Sufficiency.** An estimator is *sufficient* if it makes so much use of the information in the sample that no other estimator could extract from the sample additional information about the population parameter being estimated.

We present these criteria here to make you aware of the care that statisticians must use in picking an estimator.

Finding the best estimator

A given sample statistic is not always the best estimator of its analogous population parameter. Consider a symmetrically distributed population in which the values of the median and the mean coincide. In this instance, the sample mean would be an *unbiased* estimator of population median. Also, the sample mean would be a *consistent* estimator of the population median because, as the sample size increases, the value of the sample mean would tend to come very close to the population median. And the sample mean would be a more *efficient* estimator of the population median than the sample median itself because in large samples, the sample mean has a smaller standard error than the sample median. At the same time, the sample median in a symmetrically distributed population would be an unbiased and consistent estimator of the population mean but *not the most efficient* estimator because in large samples, its standard error is larger than that of the sample mean.

Exercises 7.1

- **7-1** What two basic tools are used in making statistical inferences?
- **7-2** Why do decision makers often measure samples rather than entire populations? What is the disadvantage?
- **7-3** Explain a shortcoming that occurs in a point estimate but not in an interval estimate. What measure is included with an interval estimate to compensate for this?
- **7-4** What is an estimator? How does an estimate differ from an estimator?
- **7-5** List and describe briefly the criteria of a good estimator.
- **7-6** What role does consistency play in determining sample size?

7.2 Point Estimates

Using the sample mean to estimate the population mean

The sample mean $\bar{x}$ is the best estimator of the population mean μ. It is unbiased, consistent, the most efficient estimator, and, as long as the sample is sufficiently large, its sampling distribution can be approximated by the normal distribution.

If we know the sampling distribution of $\bar{x}$, we can make statements about any estimate we may make from sampling information. Let's look at a medical-supplies company that produces disposable hypodermic syringes. Each syringe is wrapped in a sterile package and then jumble-packed in a large corrugated carton. Jumble packing causes the cartons to contain differing numbers of syringes. Because the syringes are sold on a per unit basis, the company needs an estimate of the number of syringes per carton for billing purposes. We have taken a sample of 35 cartons at random and recorded the number of syringes in each carton. Table 7-2 illustrates our results. Using the results of Chapter 3, we can obtain the sample mean $\bar{x}$ by finding the sum of all our results, Σx, and dividing this total by n, the number of cartons we have sampled:

Finding the sample mean

$$\bar{x} = \frac{\Sigma x}{n} \qquad [3\text{-}2]$$

Using this equation to solve our problem, we get

$$\bar{x} = \frac{3{,}570}{35}$$

$$= 102 \text{ syringes}$$

Thus, using the sample mean $\bar{x}$ as our estimator, the point estimate of the population mean μ is 102 syringes per carton. The manufactured price of a disposable hypodermic syringe

Table 7-2 Results of a Sample of 35 Cartons of Hypodermic Syringes (Syringes per Carton)

101	103	112	102	98	97	93
105	100	97	107	93	94	97
97	100	110	106	110	103	99
93	98	106	100	112	105	100
114	97	110	102	98	112	99

Table 7-3

Calculation of Sample Variance and Standard Deviation for Syringes per Carton

Values of x (Needles per Carton) (1)	x^2 (2)	Sample Mean $\bar{x}$ (3)	$(x-\bar{x})$ (4)=(1)−(3)	$(x-\bar{x})^2$ (5)=(4)^2
101	10,201	102	−1	1
105	11,025	102	3	9
97	9,409	102	−5	25
93	8,649	102	−9	81
114	12,996	102	12	144
103	10,609	102	1	1
100	10,000	102	−2	4
100	10,000	102	−2	4
98	9,604	102	−4	16
97	9,409	102	−5	25
112	12,544	102	10	100
97	9,409	102	−5	25
110	12,100	102	8	64
106	11,236	102	4	16
110	12,100	102	8	64
102	10,404	102	0	0
107	11,449	102	5	25
106	11,236	102	4	16
100	10,000	102	−2	4
102	10,404	102	0	0
98	9,604	102	−4	16
93	8,649	102	−9	81
110	12,100	102	8	64
112	12,544	102	10	100
98	9,604	102	−4	16
97	9,409	102	−5	25
94	8,836	102	−8	64
103	10,609	102	1	1
105	11,025	102	3	9
112	12,544	102	10	100
93	8,649	102	−9	81
97	9,409	102	−5	25
99	9,801	102	−3	9
100	10,000	102	−2	4
99	9,801	102	−3	9
3,570	**365,368**	Sum of all the squared differences	$\Sigma(x-\bar{x})^2$ →	**1,228**

[3-17] $$s^2 = \frac{\Sigma x^2}{n-1} - \frac{n\bar{x}^2}{n-1}$$

$$= \frac{365{,}368}{34} - \frac{35(102)^2}{34}$$

$$= \frac{1{,}228}{34}$$

$$= 36.12$$

← or →

Sum of the squared differences divided by 34, the number of items in the sample − 1 (sample variance) $\frac{\Sigma(x-\bar{x})^2}{n-1} \rightarrow 36.12$

[3-18] $$s = \sqrt{s^2}$$

$$= \sqrt{36.12}$$

$$= 6.01 \text{ syringes}$$

Sample standard deviation s $\sqrt{\frac{\Sigma(x-\bar{x})^2}{n-1}} \rightarrow 6.01$ syringes is quite small (about 25¢), so both the buyer and seller would accept the use of this point estimate as the basis for billing, and the manufacturer can save the time and expense of counting each syringe that goes into a carton.

Point Estimate of the Population Variance and Standard Deviation

Using the sample standard deviation to estimate the population standard deviation

Suppose the management of the medical-supplies company wants to estimate the variance and/or standard deviation of the distribution of the number of packaged syringes per carton. The most frequently used estimator of the population standard deviation σ is the sample standard deviation s. We can calculate the sample standard deviation as in Table 7-3 and discover that it is 6.01 syringes.

If, instead of considering

$$s^2 = \frac{\Sigma(x - \bar{x})^2}{n - 1} \tag{3-17}$$

Why is $n - 1$ the divisor?

as our sample variance, we had considered

$$s^2 = \frac{\Sigma(x - \bar{x})^2}{n}$$

the result would have some *bias* as an estimator of the population variance; specifically, it would tend to be too low. Using a divisor of $n - 1$ gives us an unbiased estimator of σ^2. Thus, we will use s^2 (as defined in Equation 3-17) and s (as defined in Equation 3-18) to estimate σ^2 and σ.

Point Estimate of the Population Proportion

Using the sample proportion to estimate the population proportion

The proportion of units that have a particular characteristic in a given population is symbolized p. If we know the proportion of units in a sample that have that same characteristic (symbolized $\bar{p}$), we can use this $\bar{p}$ as an estimator of p. It can be shown that $\bar{p}$ has all the desirable properties we discussed earlier; it is unbiased, consistent, efficient, and sufficient.

Continuing our example of the manufacturer of medical supplies, we shall try to estimate the population proportion from the sample proportion. Suppose management wishes to estimate the number of cartons that will arrive damaged, owing to poor handling in shipment after the cartons leave the factory. We can check a sample of 50 cartons from their shipping point to the arrival at their destination and then record the presence or absence of damage. If, in this case, we find that the proportion of damaged cartons in the sample is 0.08, we would say that

$$\bar{p} = 0.08 \leftarrow \text{Sample proportion damaged}$$

Because the sample proportion $\bar{p}$ is a convenient estimator of the population proportion p, we can estimate that the proportion of damaged cartons in the population will also be 0.08.

HINTS & ASSUMPTIONS

Putting all of the definitions aside, the reason we study estimators is so we can learn about populations by sampling, without counting every item in the population. Of course, there is no free lunch here either, and when we give up counting everything, we lose some accuracy. Managers would like to know the accuracy that *is* achieved when we sample, and using the ideas in this chapter, we can tell them. Hint: Determining the best sample size is not just a statistical decision. Statisticians can tell you how the standard error behaves as you increase or decrease the sample size, and market researchers can tell you what the cost of taking more or larger samples will be. But it's you who must use your judgment to combine these two inputs to make a sound *managerial* decision.

Exercises 7.2

Self-Check Exercises

SC 7-1 The Greensboro Coliseum is considering expanding its seating capacity and needs to know both the average number of people who attend events there and the variability in this number. The following are the attendances (in thousands) at nine randomly selected sporting events. Find point estimates of the mean and the variance of the population from which the sample was drawn.

8.8	14.0	21.3	7.9	12.5	20.6	16.3	14.1	13.0

SC 7-2 The Pizza Distribution Authority (PDA) has developed quite a business in Carrboro by delivering pizza orders promptly. PDA guarantees that its pizzas will be delivered in 30 minutes or less from the time the order was placed, and if the delivery is late, the pizza is free. The time that it takes to deliver each pizza order that is on time is recorded in the Official Pizza Time Book (OPTB), and the delivery time for those pizzas that are delivered late is recorded as 30 minutes in the OPTB. Twelve random entries from the OPTB are listed.

15.3	29.5	30.0	10.1	30.0	19.6
10.8	12.2	14.8	30.0	22.1	18.3

(a) Find the mean for the sample.

(b) From what population was this sample drawn?

(c) Can this sample be used to estimate the average time that it takes for PDA to deliver a pizza? Explain.

Applications

■ **7-7** Joe Jackson, a meteorologist for local television station WDUL, would like to report the average rainfall for today on this evening's newscast. The following are the rainfall measurements (in inches) for today's date for 16 randomly chosen past years. Determine the sample mean rainfall.

0.47	0.27	0.13	0.54	0.00	0.08	0.75	0.06
0.00	1.05	0.34	0.26	0.17	0.42	0.50	0.86

■ **7-8** The National Bank of Lincoln is trying to determine the number of tellers available during the lunch rush on Fridays. The bank has collected data on the number of people who entered the bank during the last 3 months on Friday from 11 A.M. to 1 P.M. Using the data below, find point estimates of the mean and standard deviation of the population from which the sample was drawn.

242	275	289	306	342	385	279	245	269	305	294	328

■ **7-9** Electric Pizza was considering national distribution of its regionally successful product and was compiling pro forma sales data. The average monthly sales figures (in thousands of dollars) from its 30 current distributors are listed. Treating them as (a) a sample and (b) a population, compute the standard deviation.

7.3	5.8	4.5	8.5	5.2	4.1
2.8	3.8	6.5	3.4	9.8	6.5
6.7	7.7	5.8	6.8	8.0	3.9
6.9	3.7	6.6	7.5	8.7	6.9
2.1	5.0	7.5	5.8	6.4	5.2

■ **7-10** In a sample of 400 textile workers, 184 expressed extreme dissatisfaction regarding a prospective plan to modify working conditions. Because this dissatisfaction was strong enough to allow management to interpret plan reaction as being highly negative, they were curious about the proportion of total workers harboring this sentiment. Give a point estimate of this proportion.

■ **7-11** The Friends of the Psychics network charges \$3 per minute to learn the secrets that can turn your life around. The network charges for whole minutes only and rounds up to benefit the company. Thus, a 2 minute 10 second call costs \$9. Below is a list of 15 randomly selected charges.

3	9	15	21	42	30	6	9	6	15	21	24	32	9	12

(a) Find the mean of the sample.
(b) Find a point estimate of the variance of the population.
(c) Can this sample be used to estimate the average length of a call? If so, what is your estimate? If not, what can we estimate using this sample?

Worked-Out Answers to Self-Check Exercises

SC 7-1 $\Sigma x^2 = 2003.65 \qquad \Sigma x = 128.5 \qquad n = 9$

$$\bar{x} = \frac{\Sigma x}{n} = \frac{128.5}{9} = 14.2778 \text{ thousands of people}$$

$$s^2 = \frac{1}{n-1}(\Sigma x^2 - n\bar{x}^2) = \frac{2003.65 - 9(14.2778)^2}{8}$$

$$= 21.119 \text{ (1,000s of people)}^2$$

SC 7-2 (a) $\bar{x} = \frac{\Sigma x}{n} = \frac{242.7}{12} = 20.225$ minutes.

(b) The population of times recorded in the OPTB.

(c) No, it cannot. Because every delivery time over 30 minutes is recorded as 30 minutes, use of these data will consistently underestimate the average of the delivery time.

7.3 Interval Estimates: Basic Concepts

The purpose of gathering samples is to learn more about a population. We can compute this information from the sample data as either *point* estimates, which we have just discussed, or as *interval* estimates, the subject of the rest of this chapter. **An interval estimate describes a range of values within which a population parameter is likely to lie.**

Start with the point estimate

Suppose the marketing research director needs an estimate of the average life in months of car batteries his company manufactures. We select a random sample of 200 batteries, record the car owners' names and addresses as listed in store records, and interview these owners about the battery life they have experienced. Our sample of 200 users has a mean battery life of 36 months. If we use the point estimate of the sample mean $\bar{x}$ as the best estimator of the population mean μ, we would report that the mean life of the company's batteries is 36 months.

Finding the likely error of this estimate

But the director also asks for a statement about the uncertainty that will be likely to accompany this estimate, that is, a statement about the range within which the unknown population mean is likely to lie. To provide such a statement, we need to find *the standard error of the mean.*

We learned from Chapter 6 that if we select and plot a large number of sample means from a population, the distribution of these means will approximate a normal curve. Furthermore, the mean of the sample means will be the same as the population mean. Our sample size of 200 is large enough that we can apply the central limit theorem, as we have done graphically in Figure 7-1. To measure the spread, or dispersion, in our distribution of sample means, we can use the following formula* and calculate the standard error of the mean:

Standard error of the mean for an infinite population → $\sigma_{\bar{x}} = \dfrac{\sigma}{\sqrt{n}}$ ← Standard deviation of the population [6-1]

Suppose we have already estimated the standard deviation of the population of the batteries and reported that it is 10 months. Using this standard deviation and the first equation from Chapter 6, we can calculate the standard error of the mean:

$$\sigma_{\bar{x}} = \frac{\sigma}{\sqrt{n}} \quad [6\text{-}1]$$

$$= \frac{10}{\sqrt{200}}$$

$$= \frac{10}{14.14}$$

$$= 0.707 \text{ month} \leftarrow \text{One standard error of the mean}$$

Making an interval estimate

We could now report to the director that our estimate of the life of the company's batteries is 36 months, and the standard error that accompanies this estimate is 0.707. In other words, the actual mean life for all the batteries *may* lie somewhere in the interval estimate of 35.293 to 36.707 months. This is helpful but insufficient information for the director. Next, we need to calculate the chance that the actual life will lie in this interval *or* in other intervals of different widths that we might choose, $\pm 2\sigma$ (2×0.707), $\pm 3\sigma$ (3×0.707), and so on.

*We have not used the finite population multiplier to calculate the standard error of the mean because the population of batteries is large enough to be considered infinite.

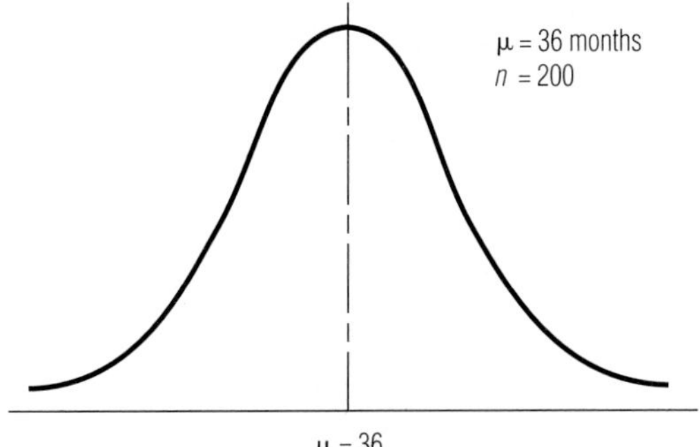

FIGURE 7-1

Sampling distribution of the mean for samples of 200 batteries

Probability of the True Population Parameter Falling within the Interval Estimate

To begin to solve this problem, we should review relevant parts of Chapter 5. There we worked with the normal probability distribution and learned that specific portions of the area under the normal curve are located between plus and minus any given number of standard deviations from the mean. In Figure 5-12, we saw how to relate these portions to specific probabilities.

Finding the chance the mean will fall in this interval estimate

Fortunately, we can apply these properties to the standard error of the mean and make the following statement about the range of values used to make an interval estimate for our battery problem.

The probability is 0.955 that the mean of a sample size of 200 will be within ± 2 standard errors of the population mean. Stated differently, 95.5 percent of all the sample means are within ± 2 standard errors from μ, and hence **μ is within ± 2 standard errors of 95.5 percent of all the sample means.** Theoretically, if we select 1,000 samples at random from a given population and then construct an interval of ± 2 standard errors around the mean of each of these samples, about 955 of these intervals will include the population mean. Similarly, the probability is 0.683 that the mean of the sample will be within ± 1 standard error of the population mean, and so forth. This theoretical concept is basic to our study of interval construction and statistical inference. In Figure 7-2, we have illustrated the concept graphically, showing five such intervals. Only the interval constructed around the sample mean $\bar{x}_4$ does not contain the population mean. In words, statisticians would describe the interval estimates represented in Figure 7-2 by saying, "The population mean μ will be located within ± 2 standard errors from the sample mean 95.5 percent of the time."

As far as any particular interval in Figure 7-2 is concerned, it either contains the population mean or it does not, because the population mean is a fixed parameter. Because we know that in 95.5 percent of all samples, the interval will contain the population mean, we say that we are 95.5 percent confident that the interval contains the population mean.

A more useful estimate of battery life

Applying this to the battery example, we can now report to the director. Our best estimate of the life of the company's batteries is 36 months, *and* we are 68.3 percent confident that the life lies in the interval from 35.293 to 36.707 months ($36 \pm 1\sigma_{\bar{x}}$). Similarly, we are 95.5 percent confident that the life falls within the interval of 34.586 to 37.414 months ($36 \pm 2\sigma_{\bar{x}}$), and we are 99.7 percent confident that battery life falls within the interval of 33.879 to 38.121 months ($36 \pm 3\sigma_{\bar{x}}$).

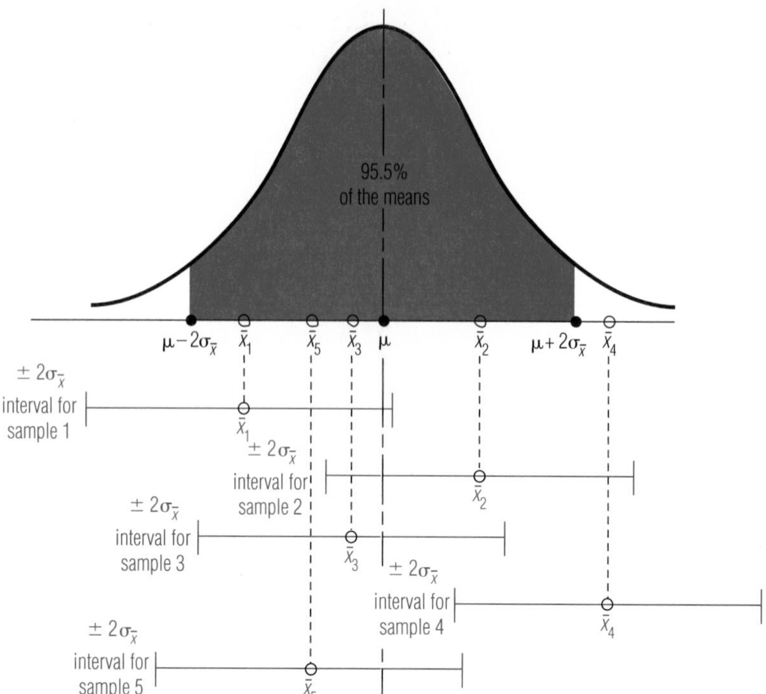

FIGURE 7-2

A number of intervals constructed around sample means; all except one include the population mean

HINTS & ASSUMPTIONS

Every time you make an estimate there is an implied error in it. For people to understand this error, it's common practice to describe it with a statement like "Our best estimate of the life of this set of tires is 40,000 miles and we are 90 percent sure that the life will be between 35,000 and 45,000 miles." But if your boss demanded to know the precise average life of a set of tires, and if she were not into sampling, you'd have to watch hundreds of thousands of sets of tires being worn out and then calculate how long they lasted on average. Warning: Even then you'd be sampling because it's impossible to watch and measure every set of tires that's being used. It's a lot less expensive and a lot faster to use sampling to find the answer. And if you understand estimates, you can tell your boss what risks she is taking in using a sample to estimate real tire life.

Exercises 7.3

Self-Check Exercises

SC 7-3 For a population with a known variance of 185, a sample of 64 individuals leads to 217 as an estimate of the mean.

(a) Find the standard error of the mean.

(b) Establish an interval estimate that should include the population mean 68.3 percent of the time.

SC 7-4 Eunice Gunterwal is a frugal undergraduate at State U. who is interested in purchasing a used car. She randomly selected 125 want ads and found

that the average price of a car in this sample was $3,250. Eunice knows that the standard deviation of used-car prices in this city is $615.

(a) Establish an interval estimate for the average price of a car so that Eunice can be 68.3 percent certain that the population mean lies within this interval.

(b) Establish an interval estimate for the average price of a car so that Miss Gunterwal can be 95.5 percent certain that the population mean lies within this interval.

Basic Concepts

■ **7-12** From a population known to have a standard deviation of 1.4, a sample of 60 individuals is taken. The mean for this sample is found to be 6.2.

(a) Find the standard error of the mean.

(b) Establish an interval estimate around the sample mean, using one standard error of the mean.

■ **7-13** From a population with known standard deviation of 1.65, a sample of 32 items resulted in 34.8 as an estimate of the mean.

(a) Find the standard error of the mean.

(b) Compute an interval estimate that should include the population mean 99.7 percent of the time.

Applications

■ **7-14** The University of North Carolina is conducting a study on the average weight of the many bricks that make up the University's walkways. Workers are sent to dig up and weigh a sample of 421 bricks and the average brick weight of this sample was 14.2 lb. It is a well-known fact that the standard deviation of brick weight is 0.8 lb.

(a) Find the standard error of the mean.

(b) What is the interval around the sample mean that will include the population mean 95.5 percent of the time?

■ **7-15** Because the owner of the Bard's Nook, a recently opened restaurant, has had difficulty estimating the quantity of food to be prepared each evening, he decided to determine the mean number of customers served each night. He selected a sample of 30 nights, which resulted in a mean of 71. The population standard deviation has been established as 3.76.

(a) Give an interval estimate that has a 68.3 percent probability of including the population mean.

(b) Give an interval estimate that has a 99.7 percent chance of including the population mean.

■ **7-16** The manager of the Neuse River Bridge is concerned about the number of cars "running" the toll gates and is considering altering the toll-collection procedure if such alteration would be cost-effective. She randomly sampled 75 hours to determine the rate of violation. The resulting average violations per hour was 7. If the population standard deviation is known to be 0.9, estimate an interval that has a 95.5 percent chance of containing the true mean.

■ **7-17** Gwen Taylor, apartment manager for WillowWood Apartments, wants to inform potential renters about how much electricity they can expect to use during August. She randomly selects 61 residents and discovers their average electricity usage in August to be 894 kilowatt hours (kwh). Gwen believes the variance in usage is about 131 $(kwh)^2$.

(a) Establish an interval estimate for the average August electricity usage so Gwen can be 68.3 percent certain the true population mean lies within this interval.

(b) Repeat part (a) with a 99.7 percent certainty.

(c) If the price per kwh is \$0.12, within what interval can Gwen be 68.3 percent certain that the average August cost for electricity will lie?

■ **7-18** The school board of Forsight County considers its most important task to be keeping the average class size in Forsight County schools less than the average class size in neighboring Hindsight County. Miss Dee Marks, the school superintendent for Forsight County, has just received reliable information indicating that the average class size in Hindsight County this year is 30.3 students. She does not yet have the figures for all 621 classes in her own school system, so Dee is forced to rely upon the 76 classes that have reported class sizes, yielding an average class size of 29.8 students. Dee knows that the class size of Forsight County classes has a distribution with an unknown mean and standard deviation equal to 8.3 students. Assuming that the sample of 76 that Miss Marks possesses is randomly chosen from the population of all Forsight County class sizes:

(a) Find an interval that Dee can be 95.5 percent certain will contain the true mean.

(b) Do you think that Dee has met her goal?

Worked-Out Answers to Self-Check Exercises

SC 7-3 $\sigma^2 = 185 \qquad \sigma = \sqrt{185} = 13.60 \qquad n = 64 \qquad \bar{x} = 217$

(a) $\sigma_{\bar{x}} = \sigma/\sqrt{n} = 13.60/\sqrt{64} = 1.70$

(b) $\bar{x} \pm \sigma_{\bar{x}} = 217 \pm 1.70 = (215.3, 218.7)$

SC 7-4 $\sigma = 615 \qquad n = 125 \qquad \bar{x} = 3{,}250 \qquad \sigma_{\bar{x}} = \sigma/\sqrt{n} = 615/\sqrt{125} = 55.01$

(a) $\bar{x} \pm \sigma_{\bar{x}} = 3{,}250 \pm 55.01 = (\$3{,}194.99, \$3{,}305.01)$

(b) $\bar{x} \pm 2\sigma_{\bar{x}} = 3{,}250 \pm 2(55.01) = 3{,}250 \pm 110.02 = (\$3{,}139.98, \$3{,}360.02)$

7.4 Interval Estimates and Confidence Intervals

In using interval estimates, we are not confined to ±1, 2, and 3 standard errors. According to Appendix Table 1, for example, ±1.64 standard errors includes about 90 percent of the area under the curve; it includes 0.4495 of the area on either side of the mean in a normal distribution. Similarly, ±2.58 standard errors includes about 99 percent of the area, or 49.51 percent on each side of the mean.

Confidence level defined

In statistics, the probability that we associate with an interval estimate is called the *confidence level.* This probability indicates how confident we are that the interval estimate will include the population parameter. A higher probability means more confidence. In estimation, the most commonly used confidence levels are 90 percent, 95 percent, and 99 percent, but we are free to apply *any* confidence level. In Figure 7-2, for example, we used a 95.5 percent confidence level.

The *confidence interval* is the range of the estimate we are making. If we report that we are 90 percent confident that the mean of the population of incomes of people in a certain community will lie between \$8,000 and \$24,000, then the range \$8,000–\$24,000 is our confidence interval. Often, however, we will express the confidence interval in standard errors rather than in numerical values. Thus, we will often express confidence intervals like this: $\bar{x} \pm 1.64\sigma_{\bar{x}}$, where

$$\bar{x} + 1.64\sigma_{\bar{x}} = \text{upper limit of the confidence interval}$$

$$\bar{x} - 1.64\sigma_{\bar{x}} = \text{lower limit of the confidence interval}$$

Thus, *confidence limits* are the upper and lower limits of the confidence interval. In this case, $\bar{x} + 1.64\sigma_{\bar{x}}$ is called the *upper confidence limit (UCL)* and $\bar{x} - 1.64\sigma_{\bar{x}}$ is the *lower confidence limit (LCL)*.

Relationship between Confidence Level and Confidence Interval

You may think that we should use a high confidence level, such as 99 percent, in all estimation problems. After all, a high confidence level seems to signify a high degree of accuracy in the estimate. In practice, however, high confidence levels will produce large confidence intervals, and such large intervals are not precise; they give very fuzzy estimates.

Consider an appliance store customer who inquires about the delivery of a new washing machine. In Table 7-4 are several of the questions the customer might ask and the likely responses. This table indicates the direct relationship that exists between the confidence level and the confidence interval for any estimate. As the customer sets a tighter and tighter confidence interval, the store manager agrees to a lower and lower confidence level. Notice, too, that when the confidence interval is too wide, as is the case with a one-year delivery, the estimate may have very little real value, even though the store manager attaches a 99 percent confidence level to that estimate. Similarly, if the confidence interval is too narrow ("Will my washing machine get home before I do?"), the estimate is associated with such a low confidence level (1 percent) that we question its value.

Table 7-4

Illustration of the Relationship between Confidence Level and Confidence Interval

Customer's Question	Store Manager's Response	Implied Confidence Level	Implied Confidence Interval
Will I get my washing machine within 1 year?	I am absolutely certain of that.	Better than 99%	1 year
Will you deliver the washing machine within 1 month?	I am almost positive it will be delivered this month.	At least 95%	1 month
Will you deliver the washing machine within 1 week?	I am pretty certain it will go out within this week.	About 80%	1 week
Will I get my washing machine tomorrow?	I am not certain we can get it to you then.	About 40%	1 day
Will my washing machine get home before I do?	There is little chance it will beat you home.	Near 1%	1 hour

Using Samplin
Interval Estima

Estimating from only one sample

In our discussion of th
described samples be
population parameter.
a population. In pract
sample from a popula
ter. We must be caref
Suppose we calcul
interval and confiden
population lies within
is 0.95 that the mear
this one sample. Inst
size and calculate a c
cent of these cases, t

HINTS & ASSUMPTIONS

Warning: There is n
intervals. When you
understand this imp
mate of the time of
rifice tightness in th
("sometime this yea
racy of the estimate
can get it to you wit

Exercises 7.4

Self-Check Exercise

SC 7-5 Given the
its of the
(a) 54 pe
(b) 75 pe
(c) 94 pe
(d) 98 pe

Basic Concepts

7-19 Define the c
7-20 Define the c
7-21 Suppose yo
limit of the
dard error,
7-22 In what wa
(a) A high
(b) A narr

Estimated Standard Error of the Mean of a Finite Population

Symbol that indicates an estimated value → $\hat{\sigma}_{\bar{x}}$; Estimate of the population standard deviation → $\hat{\sigma}$

$$\hat{\sigma}_{\bar{x}} = \frac{\hat{\sigma}}{\sqrt{n}} \times \sqrt{\frac{N-n}{N-1}} \qquad [7\text{-}2]$$

Continuing our example, we find

$$\begin{aligned}\hat{\sigma}_{\bar{x}} &= \frac{\$950.00}{\sqrt{50}} \times \sqrt{\frac{700-50}{700-1}} \\ &= \frac{\$950.00}{7.07}\sqrt{\frac{650}{699}} \\ &= (\$134.37)(0.9643) \\ &= \$129.57 \leftarrow \text{Estimate of the standard error of the mean of a finite population (derived from an } \textit{estimate} \text{ of the population standard deviation)}\end{aligned}$$

Next we consider the 90 percent confidence level, which would include 45 percent of the area on either side of the mean of the sampling distribution. Looking in the body of Appendix Table 1 for the 0.45 value, we find that about 0.45 of the area under the normal curve is located between the mean and a point 1.64 standard errors away from the mean. Therefore, 90 percent of the area is located between plus *and* minus 1.64 standard errors away from the mean, and our confidence limits are

$$\begin{aligned}\bar{x} + 1.64\hat{\sigma}_{\bar{x}} &= \$11{,}800 + 1.64(\$129.57) \\ &= \$11{,}800 + \$212.50 \\ &= \$12{,}012.50 \leftarrow \text{Upper confidence limit} \\ \bar{x} - 1.64\hat{\sigma}_{\bar{x}} &= \$11{,}800 - 1.64(\$129.57) \\ &= \$11{,}800 - \$212.50 \\ &= \$11{,}587.50 \leftarrow \text{Lower confidence limit}\end{aligned}$$

Our conclusion

Our report to the social-service agency would be: With 90 percent confidence, we estimate that the average annual income of all 700 families living in this four-square-block section falls between \$11,587.50 and \$12,012.50.

HINTS & ASSUMPTIONS

Hint: It's easy to understand how to approach these exercises if you'll go back to Figure 7-2 on page 356 for a minute. When someone states a confidence level, they are referring to the shaded area in the figure, which is defined by how many $\sigma_{\bar{x}}$ (standard errors or standard deviations of the distribution of sample means) there are on either side of the mean. Appendix Table 1 quickly converts any desired confidence level into standard errors. Because we have the information necessary to calculate *one* standard error, we can calculate the endpoints of the shaded area. These are the limits of our confidence interval. Warning: When you don't know the dispersion in the population (the population standard deviation) remember to use Equation 7-1 to estimate it.

Exercises 7.5

Self-Check Exercises

SC 7-6 From a population of 540, a sample of 60 individuals is taken. From this sample, the mean is found to be 6.2 and the standard deviation 1.368.

(a) Find the estimated standard error of the mean.

(b) Construct a 96 percent confidence interval for the mean.

SC 7-7 In an automotive safety test conducted by the North Carolina Highway Safety Research Center, the average tire pressure in a sample of 62 tires was found to be 24 pounds per square inch, and the standard deviation was 2.1 pounds per square inch.

(a) What is the estimated population standard deviation for this population? (There are about a million cars registered in North Carolina.)

(b) Calculate the estimated standard error of the mean.

(c) Construct a 95 percent confidence interval for the population mean.

Basic Concepts

■ **7-27** The manager of Cardinal Electric's lightbulb division must estimate the average number of hours that a lightbulb made by each lightbulb machine will last. A sample of 40 lightbulbs was selected from machine A and the average burning time was 1,416 hours. The standard deviation of burning time is known to be 30 hours.

(a) Compute the standard error of the mean.

(b) Construct a 90 percent confidence interval for the true population mean.

■ **7-28** Upon collecting a sample of 250 from a population with known standard deviation of 13.7, the mean is found to be 112.4.

(a) Find a 95 percent confidence interval for the mean.

(b) Find a 99 percent confidence interval for the mean.

Applications

■ **7-29** The Westview High School nurse is interested in knowing the average height of seniors at this school, but she does not have enough time to examine the records of all 430 seniors. She randomly selects 48 students. She finds the sample mean to be 64.5 inches and the standard deviation to be 2.3 inches.

(a) Find the estimated standard error of the mean.

(b) Construct a 90 percent confidence interval for the mean.

■ **7-30** Jon Jackobsen, an overzealous graduate student, has just completed a first draft of his 700-page dissertation. Jon has typed his paper himself and is interested in knowing the average number of typographical errors per page, but does not want to read the whole paper. Knowing a little bit about business statistics, Jon selected 40 pages at random to read and found that the average number of typos per page was 4.3 and the sample standard deviation was 1.2 typos per page.

(a) Calculate the estimated standard error of the mean.

(b) Construct for Jon a 90 percent confidence interval for the true average number of typos per page in his paper.

■ **7-31** The Nebraska Cable Television authority conducted a test to determine the amount of time people spend watching television per week. The NCTA surveyed 84 subscribers and found the average number of hours watched per week to be 11.6 hours and the standard deviation to be 1.8 hours.

(a) What is the estimated population standard deviation for this population? (There are about 95,000 people with cable television in Nebraska.)

(b) Calculate the estimated standard error of the mean.

(c) Construct a 98 percent confidence interval for the population mean.

■ **7-32** Joel Friedlander is a broker on the New York Stock Exchange who is curious about the amount of time between the placement and execution of a market order. Joel sampled 45 orders and found that the mean time to execution was 24.3 minutes and the standard deviation was 3.2 minutes. Help Joel by constructing a 95 percent confidence interval for the mean time to execution.

■ **7-33** Oscar T. Grady is the production manager for Citrus Groves Inc., located just north of Ocala, Florida. Oscar is concerned that the last 3 years' late freezes have damaged the 2,500 orange trees that Citrus Groves owns. In order to determine the extent of damage to the trees, Oscar has sampled the number of oranges produced per tree for 42 trees and found that the average production was 525 oranges per tree and the standard deviation was 30 oranges per tree.

(a) Estimate the population standard deviation from the sample standard deviation.

(b) Estimate the standard error of the mean for this finite population.

(c) Construct a 98 percent confidence interval for the mean per-tree output of all 2,500 trees.

(d) If the mean orange output per tree was 600 oranges 5 years ago, what can Oscar say about the possible existence of damage now?

■ **7-34** Chief of Police Kathy Ackert has recently instituted a crackdown on drug dealers in her city. Since the crackdown began, 750 of the 12,368 drug dealers in the city have been caught. The mean dollar value of drugs found on these 750 dealers is $250,000. The standard deviation of the dollar value of drugs for these 750 dealers is $41,000. Construct for Chief Ackert a 90 percent confidence interval for the mean dollar value of drugs possessed by the city's drug dealers.

Worked-Out Answers to Self-Check Exercises

SC 7-6 $\hat{\sigma} = 1.368 \qquad N = 540 \qquad n = 60 \qquad \bar{x} = 6.2$

(a) $\hat{\sigma}_{\bar{x}} = \dfrac{\hat{\sigma}}{\sqrt{n}} \times \sqrt{\dfrac{N-n}{N-1}} = \dfrac{1.368}{\sqrt{60}} \times \sqrt{\dfrac{540-60}{540-1}} = 0.167$

(b) $\bar{x} \pm 2.05\hat{\sigma}_{\bar{x}} = 6.2 \pm 2.05(0.167) = 6.2 \pm 0.342 = (5.86, 6.54)$

SC 7-7 $s = 2.1 \qquad n = 62 \qquad \bar{x} = 24$

(a) $\hat{\sigma} = s = 2.1$ psi

(b) $\hat{\sigma}_{\bar{x}} = \hat{\sigma}/\sqrt{n} = 2.1/\sqrt{62} = 0.267$ psi

(c) $\bar{x} \pm 1.96\hat{\sigma}_{\bar{x}} = 24 \pm 1.96(0.267) = 24 \pm 0.523 = (23.48, 24.52)$ psi

7.6 Calculating Interval Estimates of the Proportion from Large Samples

Review of the binomial distribution

Statisticians often use a sample to estimate a *proportion* of occurrences in a population. For example, the government estimates by a sampling procedure the unemployment rate, or the proportion of unemployed people, in the U.S. workforce.

In Chapter 5, we introduced the binomial distribution, a distribution of discrete, not continuous, data. Also, we presented the two formulas for deriving the mean and the standard deviation of the binomial distribution:

$$\mu = np \qquad [5\text{-}2]$$

$$\sigma = \sqrt{npq} \qquad [5\text{-}3]$$

where

- n = number of trials
- p = probability of success
- $q = 1 - p$ = probability of a failure

Theoretically, the binomial distribution is the correct distribution to use in constructing confidence intervals to estimate a population proportion.

Shortcomings of the binomial distribution

Because the computation of binomial probabilities is so tedious (recall that the probability of r successes in n trials is $[n!/r!(n-r)!][p^r q^{n-r}]$), using the binomial distribution to form interval estimates of a population proportion is a complex proposition. Fortunately, as the sample size increases, the binomial can be approximated by an appropriate normal distribution, which we can use to approximate the sampling distribution. Statisticians recommend that in estimation, n be large enough for both np and nq to be at least 5 when you use the normal distribution as a substitute for the binomial.

Finding the mean of the sample proportion

Symbolically, let's express the proportion of successes in a sample by $\bar{p}$ (pronounced *p bar*). Then modify Equation 5-2, so that we can use it to derive the *mean of the sampling distribution of the proportion of successes*. In words, $\mu = np$ shows that the mean of the binomial distribution is equal to the product of the number of trials, n, and the probability of success, p; that is, np equals the mean number of successes. To change this *number* of successes to the *proportion* of successes, we divide np by n and get p alone. The mean in the left-hand side of the equation becomes $\mu_{\bar{p}}$, or the mean of the sampling distribution of the proportion of successes.

Mean of the Sampling Distribution of the Proportion

$$\mu_{\bar{p}} = p \qquad [7\text{-}3]$$

Finding the standard deviation of the sample proportion

Similarly, we can modify the formula for the standard deviation of the binomial distribution, $\sqrt{npq}$, which measures the standard deviation in the number of successes. To change the number of successes to the proportion of successes, we divide $\sqrt{npq}$ by n and get $\sqrt{pq/n}$. In statistical terms, the standard deviation for the proportion of successes in a sample is symbolized

(a) Estimate the standard error of the proportion of defective chips.

(b) Construct a 98 percent confidence interval for the proportion of defective chips supplied.

■ **7-36** General Cinema sampled 55 people who viewed *GhostHunter 8* and asked them whether they planned to see it again. Only 10 of them believed the film was worthy of a second look.

(a) Estimate the standard error of the proportion of moviegoers who will view the film a second time.

(b) Construct a 90 percent confidence interval for this proportion.

■ **7-37** The product manager for the new lemon-lime Clear 'n Light dessert topping was worried about both the product's poor performance and her future with Clear 'n Light. Concerned that her marketing strategy had not properly identified the attributes of the product, she sampled 1,500 consumers and learned that 956 thought that the product was a floor wax.

(a) Estimate the standard error of the proportion of people holding this severe misconception about the dessert topping.

(b) Construct a 96 percent confidence interval for the true population proportion.

■ **7-38** Michael Gordon, a professional basketball player, shot 200 foul shots and made 174 of them.

(a) Estimate the standard error of the proportion of all foul shots Michael makes.

(b) Construct a 98 percent confidence interval for the proportion of all foul shots Michael makes.

■ **7-39** SnackMore recently surveyed 95 shoppers and found 80 percent of them purchase SnackMore fat-free brownies monthly.

(a) Estimate the standard error of the proportion.

(b) Construct a 95 percent confidence interval for the true proportion of people who purchase the brownies monthly.

■ **7-40** The owner of the Home Loan Company randomly surveyed 150 of the company's 3,000 accounts and determined that 60 percent were in excellent standing.

(a) Find a 95 percent confidence interval for the proportion in excellent standing.

(b) Based on part (a), what kind of interval estimate might you give for the absolute number of accounts that meet the requirement of excellence, keeping the same 95 percent confidence level?

■ **7-41** For a year and a half, sales have been falling consistently in all 1,500 franchises of a fast-food chain. A consulting firm has determined that 31 percent of a sample of 95 indicate clear signs of mismanagement. Construct a 98 percent confidence interval for this proportion.

■ **7-42** Student government at the local university sampled 45 textbooks at the University Student Store and determined that of these 45 textbooks, 60 percent had been marked up in price more than 50 percent over wholesale cost. Give a 96 percent confidence interval for the proportion of books marked up more than 50 percent by the University Student Store.

■ **7-43** Barry Turnbull, the noted Wall Street analyst, is interested in knowing the proportion of individual stockholders who plan to sell at least one-quarter of all their stock in the next month. Barry has conducted a random survey of 800 individuals who hold stock and has learned that 25 percent of his sample plan to sell at least one-quarter of all their stock in the next month. Barry is about to issue his much-anticipated monthly report, "The Wall Street Pulse—the Tape's Ticker," and would like to be able to report a confidence interval to his subscribers. He is more worried about being correct than he is about the width of the interval. Construct a 90 percent confidence interval for the true proportion of individual stockholders who plan to sell at least one-quarter of their stock during the next month.

Worked-Out Answers to Self-Check Exercises

SC 7-8 $n = 70 \quad \bar{p} = 0.66$

(a) $\hat{\sigma}_{\bar{p}} = \sqrt{\frac{\bar{p}\,\bar{q}}{n}} = \sqrt{\frac{0.66(0.34)}{70}} = 0.0566$

(b) $\bar{p} \pm 1.96\,\hat{\sigma}_{\bar{p}} = 0.66 \pm 1.96(0.0566) = 0.66 \pm 0.111 = (0.549, 0.771)$

SC 7-9 $n = 150 \quad \bar{p} = 0.42$

(a) $\hat{\sigma}_{\bar{p}} = \sqrt{\frac{\bar{p}\,\bar{q}}{n}} = \sqrt{\frac{0.42(0.58)}{150}} = 0.0403$

(b) $\bar{p} \pm 2.58\,\hat{\sigma}_{\bar{p}} = 0.42 \pm 2.58(0.0403) = 0.42 \pm 0.104 = (0.316, 0.524)$

7.7 Interval Estimates Using the *t* Distribution

In our three examples so far, the sample sizes were all larger than 30. We sampled 100 windshield wiper blades, 50 families living in a four-square-block section of a community, and 75 employees of a very large organization. Each time, the normal distribution was the appropriate sampling distribution to use to determine confidence intervals.

Sometimes the normal distribution is not appropriate

However, this is not always the case. How can we handle estimates where the normal distribution is *not* the appropriate sampling distribution, that is, when we are estimating the population standard deviation and the sample size is 30 or less? For example, in our chapter-opening problem of coal usage, we had data from only 10 weeks. Fortunately, another distribution exists that is appropriate in these cases. It is called the *t distribution.*

Background of the *t* distribution

Early theoretical work on *t* distributions was done by a man named W. S. Gosset in the early 1900s. Gosset was employed by the Guinness Brewery in Dublin, Ireland, which did not permit employees to publish research findings under their own names. So Gosset adopted the pen name *Student* and published under that name. Consequently, the *t* distribution is commonly called *Student's t distribution,* or simply *Student's distribution.*

Conditions for using the *t* distribution

Because it is used when the sample size is 30 or less, statisticians often associate the *t* distribution with small sample statistics. This is misleading, because the size of the sample is only *one* of the conditions that lead us to use the *t* distribution. The second condition is that the population standard deviation must be unknown. **Use of the *t* distribution for estimating is required whenever the sample size is 30 or less and the population standard deviation is not known. Furthermore, in using the *t* distribution, we assume that the population is normal or approximately normal.**

Characteristics of the *t* Distribution

t distribution compared to normal distribution

Without deriving the *t* distribution mathematically, we can gain an intuitive understanding of the relationship between the *t* distribution and the *normal* distribution. Both are symmetrical. In general, the *t* distribution is flatter than the normal distribution, and there is a

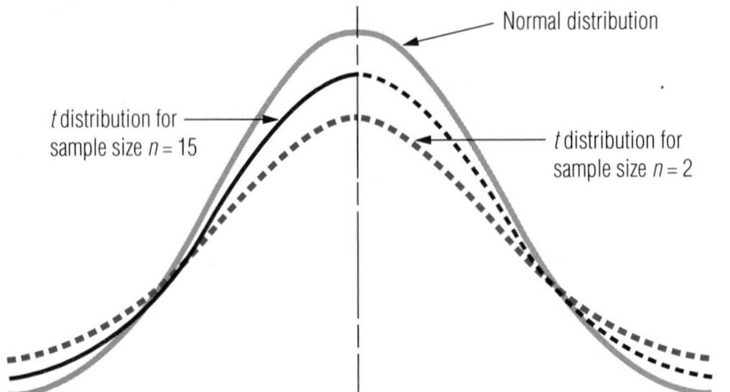

FIGURE 7-3

Normal distribution, t distribution for sample size $n = 15$, and t distribution for sample size $n = 2$

different t distribution for every possible sample size. Even so, as the sample size gets larger, the shape of the t distribution loses its flatness and becomes approximately equal to the normal distribution. In fact, for sample sizes of more than 30, the t distribution is so close to the normal distribution that we will use the normal to approximate the t.

Figure 7-3 compares one normal distribution with two t distributions of different sample sizes. This figure shows two characteristics of t distributions. **A *t* distribution is lower at the mean and higher at the tails than a normal distribution.** The figure also demonstrates how the t distribution has proportionally more of its area in its tails than the normal does. This is the reason why it will be necessary to go farther out from the mean of a t distribution to include the same area under the curve. Interval widths from t distributions are, therefore, wider than those based on the normal distribution.

Degrees of Freedom

Degrees of freedom defined

We said earlier that there is a separate t distribution for each sample size. In proper statistical language, we would say, "There is a different t distribution for each of the possible *degrees of freedom.*" **What are degrees of freedom? We can define them as the number of values we can choose freely.**

Assume that we are dealing with two sample values, a and b, and we know that they have a mean of 18. Symbolically, the situation is

$$\frac{a + b}{2} = 18$$

How can we find what values a and b can take on in this situation? The answer is that a and b can be any two values whose sum is 36, because $36 \div 2 = 18$.

Suppose we learn that a has a value of 10. Now b is no longer free to take on any value but *must* have the value of 26, because

$$\begin{array}{ll} \text{if} & a = 10 \\ \text{then} & \dfrac{10 + b}{2} = 18 \\ \text{so} & 10 + b = 36 \\ \text{therefore} & b = 26 \end{array}$$

This example shows that when there are two elements in a sample and we know the sample mean of these two elements, we are free to specify only one of the elements because the other element will be determined by the fact that the two elements sum to twice the sample mean. Statisticians say, "We have one degree of freedom."

Another example

Look at another example. There are seven elements in our sample, and we learn that the mean of these elements is 16. Symbolically, we have this situation:

$$\frac{a + b + c + d + e + f + g}{7} = 16$$

In this case, the degrees of freedom, or the number of variables we can specify freely, are $7 - 1 = 6$. We are free to give values to six variables, and then we are no longer free to specify the seventh variable. It is determined automatically.

With two sample values, we had one degree of freedom ($2 - 1 = 1$), and with seven sample values, we had six degrees of freedom ($7 - 1 = 6$). In each of these two examples, then, we had $n - 1$ degrees of freedom, assuming n is the sample size. Similarly, a sample of 23 would give us 22 degrees of freedom.

Function of degrees of freedom

We will use degrees of freedom when we select a *t* distribution to estimate a population mean, and we will use $n - 1$ degrees of freedom, where n is the sample size. For example, if we use a sample of 20 to estimate a population mean, we will use 19 degrees of freedom in order to select the appropriate *t* distribution.

Using the *t* Distribution Table

t table compared to *z* table: three differences

The table of *t* distribution values (Appendix Table 2) differs in construction from the *z* table we have used previously. **The *t* table is more compact and shows areas and *t* values for only a few percentages (10, 5, 2, and 1 percent).** Because there is a different *t* distribution for each number of degrees of freedom, a more complete table would be quite lengthy. Although we can conceive of the need for a more complete table, in fact Appendix Table 2 contains all the commonly used values of the *t* distribution.

A second difference in the *t* table is that it does *not* focus on the chance that the population parameter being estimated will fall *within* our confidence interval. Instead, it measures the chance that the population parameter we are estimating will *not* be within our confidence interval (that is, that it will lie *outside* it). If we are making an estimate at the 90 percent confidence level, we would look in the *t* table under the 0.10 column (100 percent − 90 percent = 10 percent). This 0.10 chance of error is symbolized by α, which is the Greek letter *alpha.* We would find the appropriate *t* values for confidence intervals of 95 percent, 98 percent, and 99 percent under the α columns headed 0.05, 0.02, and 0.01, respectively.

A third difference in using the *t* table is that we must specify the degrees of freedom with which we are dealing. Suppose we make an estimate at the 90 percent confidence level with a sample size of 14, which is 13 degrees of freedom. Look in Appendix Table 2 under the 0.10 column until you encounter the row labeled 13. Like a *z* value, the *t* value there of 1.771 shows that if we mark off plus and minus 1.771 $\hat{\sigma}_{\bar{x}}$'s (estimated standard errors of $\bar{x}$) on either side of the mean, the area under the curve between these two limits will be 90 percent, and the area outside these limits (the chance of error) will be 10 percent (see Figure 7-4).

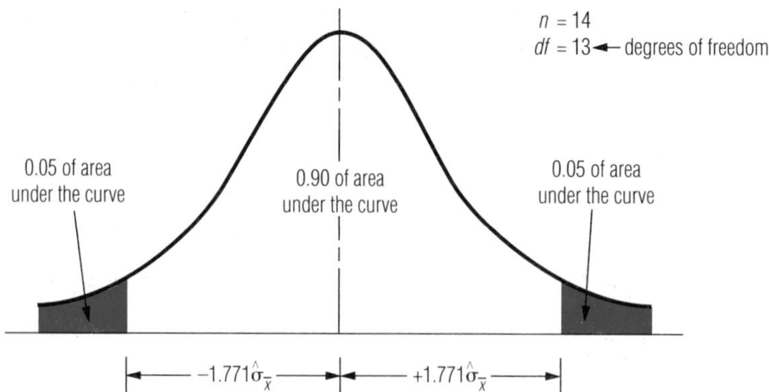

FIGURE 7-4

A t distribution for 13 degrees of freedom, showing a 90 percent confidence interval

Recall that in our chapter-opening problem, the generating plant manager wanted to estimate the coal needed for this year, and he took a sample by measuring coal usage for 10 weeks. The sample data are

$$n = 10 \text{ weeks} \leftarrow \text{Sample size}$$

$$df = 9 \leftarrow \text{Degrees of freedom}$$

$$\bar{x} = 11{,}400 \text{ tons} \leftarrow \text{Sample mean}$$

$$s = 700 \text{ tons} \leftarrow \text{Sample standard deviation}$$

Using the t table to compute confidence limits

The plant manager wants an interval estimate of the mean coal consumption, and he wants to be 95 percent confident that the mean consumption falls within that interval. **This problem requires the use of a *t* distribution because the sample size is less than 30, the population standard deviation is unknown, and the manager believes that the population is approximately normal.**

As a first step in solving this problem, recall that we *estimate* the population standard deviation with the sample standard deviation; thus

$$\hat{\sigma} = s \quad [7\text{-}1]$$

$$= 700 \text{ tons}$$

Using this estimate of the population standard deviation, we can estimate the standard error of the mean by modifying Equation 7-2 to omit the finite population multiplier (because the sample size of 10 weeks is less than 5 percent of the 5 years (260 weeks) for which data are available):

Estimated Standard Error of the Mean of an Infinite Population

$$\hat{\sigma}_{\bar{x}} = \frac{\hat{\sigma}}{\sqrt{n}} \quad [7\text{-}6]$$

Continuing our example, we find $\hat{\sigma}_{\bar{x}} = \dfrac{700}{\sqrt{10}}$

$$= \frac{700}{3.162}$$

$$= 221.38 \text{ tons} \leftarrow \text{Estimated standard error of the mean of an infinite population}$$

Now we look in Appendix Table 2 down the 0.05 column (100 percent − 95 percent = 5 percent) until we encounter the row for 9 degrees of freedom (10 − 1 = 9). There we see the t value 2.262 and can set our confidence limits accordingly:

$$\bar{x} + 2.262\hat{\sigma}_{\bar{x}} = 11{,}400 \text{ tons} + 2.262(221.38 \text{ tons})$$
$$= 11{,}400 + 500.76$$
$$= 11{,}901 \text{ tons} \leftarrow \text{Upper confidence limit}$$
$$\bar{x} - 2.262\hat{\sigma}_{\bar{x}} = 11{,}400 \text{ tons} - 2.262(221.38 \text{ tons})$$
$$= 11{,}400 - 500.76$$
$$= 10{,}899 \text{ tons} \leftarrow \text{Lower confidence limit}$$

Our conclusion

Our confidence interval is illustrated in Figure 7-5. Now we can report to the plant manager with 95 percent confidence that the mean weekly usage of coal lies between 10,899 and 11,901 tons, and he can use the 11,901-ton figure to estimate how much coal to order.

The only difference between the process we used to make this coal-usage estimate and the previous estimating problems is the use of the t distribution as the appropriate distribution. **Remember that in any estimation problem in which the sample size is 30 or less *and* the standard deviation of the population is unknown *and* the underlying population can be assumed to be normal or approximately normal, we use the t distribution.**

Summary of Confidence Limits under Various Conditions

Table 7-5 summarizes the various approaches to estimation introduced in this chapter and the confidence limits appropriate for each.

FIGURE 7-5

Coal problem: a t distribution with 9 degrees of freedom and a 95 percent confidence interval

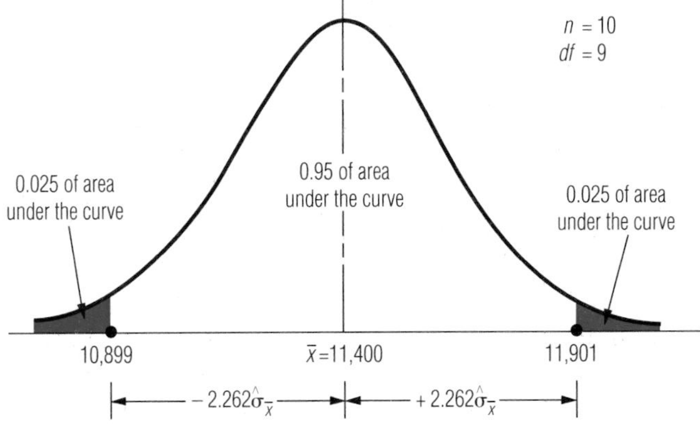

Table 7-5 Summary of Formulas for Confidence Limits Estimating Mean and Proportion

	When the Population Is Finite (and $n/N > 0.05$)	When the Population Is Infinite (or $n/N < 0.05$)
Estimating μ (the population mean): When σ (the population standard deviation) is known	Upper limit: $\bar{x} + z\frac{\sigma}{\sqrt{n}} \times \sqrt{\frac{N-n}{N-1}}$ Lower limit: $\bar{x} - z\frac{\sigma}{\sqrt{n}} \times \sqrt{\frac{N-n}{N-1}}$	$\bar{x} + z\frac{\sigma}{\sqrt{n}}$ $\bar{x} - z\frac{\sigma}{\sqrt{n}}$
When σ (the population standard deviation) is not known ($\hat{\sigma} = s$) When n (the sample size) is larger than 30	Upper limit: $\bar{x} + z\frac{\hat{\sigma}}{\sqrt{n}} \times \sqrt{\frac{N-n}{N-1}}$ Lower limit: $\bar{x} - z\frac{\hat{\sigma}}{\sqrt{n}} \times \sqrt{\frac{N-n}{N-1}}$	$\bar{x} + z\frac{\hat{\sigma}}{\sqrt{n}}$ $\bar{x} - z\frac{\hat{\sigma}}{\sqrt{n}}$
When n (the sample size) is 30 or less and the population is normal or approximately normal*	This case is beyond the scope of the text; consult a professional statistician.	$\bar{x} + t\frac{\hat{\sigma}}{\sqrt{n}}$ $\bar{x} - t\frac{\hat{\sigma}}{\sqrt{n}}$
Estimating p (the population proportion): When n (the sample size) is larger than 30 $\hat{\sigma}_{\bar{p}} = \sqrt{\frac{\bar{p}\,\bar{q}}{n}}$	This case is beyond the scope of the text; consult a professional statistician.	$\bar{p} + z\hat{\sigma}_{\bar{p}}$ $\bar{p} - z\hat{\sigma}_{\bar{p}}$

*Remember that the appropriate t distribution to use is the one with $n - 1$ degrees of freedom.

HINTS & ASSUMPTIONS

The concept of *degrees of freedom* is often difficult to grasp at first. Hint: Think of it as the number of choices you have. If you have peanut butter and cheese in your refrigerator, you can choose either a peanut butter or a cheese sandwich (unless you like peanut butter and cheese sandwiches). If you open the door and the cheese is all gone, Mr. Gosset would probably say, "You now have zero degrees of freedom." That is, if you want lunch, you have no choices left; it's peanut butter or starve. Warning: Although the t distribution is associated with small-sample statistics, remember that a sample size of less than 30 is only *one* of the conditions for its use. The others are that the population standard deviation is not known and the population is normally or approximately normally distributed.

Exercises 7.7

Self-Check Exercises

SC 7-10 For the following sample sizes and confidence levels, find the appropriate t values for constructing confidence intervals:

(a) $n = 28$; 95 percent.
(b) $n = 8$; 98 percent.
(c) $n = 13$; 90 percent.
(d) $n = 10$; 95 percent.
(e) $n = 25$; 99 percent.
(f) $n = 10$; 99 percent.

SC 7-11 Seven homemakers were randomly sampled, and it was determined that the distances they walked in their housework had an average of 39.2 miles per week and a sample standard deviation of 3.2 miles per week. Construct a 95 percent confidence interval for the population mean.

Basic Concepts

■ **7-44** For the following sample sizes and confidence levels, find the appropriate t values for constructing confidence intervals:

(a) $n = 15$; 90 percent.
(b) $n = 6$; 95 percent.
(c) $n = 19$; 99 percent.
(d) $n = 25$; 98 percent.
(e) $n = 10$; 99 percent.
(f) $n = 41$; 90 percent.

■ **7-45** Given the following sample sizes and t values used to construct confidence intervals, find the corresponding confidence levels:

(a) $n = 27$; $t = \pm 2.056$.
(b) $n = 5$; $t = \pm 2.132$.
(c) $n = 18$; $t = \pm 2.898$.

■ **7-46** A sample of 12 had a mean of 62 and a standard deviation of 10. Construct a 95 percent confidence interval for the population mean.

■ **7-47** The following sample of eight observations is from an infinite population with a normal distribution:

75.3	76.4	83.2	91.0	80.1	77.5	84.8	81.0

(a) Find the sample mean.
(b) Estimate the population standard deviation.
(c) Construct a 98 percent confidence interval for the population mean.

Applications

■ **7-48** Northern Orange County has found, much to the dismay of the county commissioners, that the population has a severe problem with dental plaque.

Every year the local dental board examines a sample of patients and rates each patient's plaque buildup on a scale from 1 to 100, with 1 representing no plaque and 100 representing a great deal of plaque. This year, the board examined 21 patients and found that they had an average Plaque Rating Score (PRS) of 72 and a standard deviation of 6.2. Construct for Orange County a 98 percent confidence interval for the mean PRS for Northern Orange County.

■ **7-49** Twelve bank tellers were randomly sampled and it was determined they made an average of 3.6 errors per day with a sample standard deviation of 0.42 error. Construct a 90 percent confidence interval for the population mean of errors per day. What assumption is implied about the number of errors bank tellers make?

■ **7-50** State Senator Hanna Rowe has ordered an investigation of the large number of boating accidents that have occurred in the state in recent summers. Acting on her instructions, her aide, Geoff Spencer, has randomly selected 9 summer months within the last few years and has compiled data on the number of boating accidents that occurred during each of these months. The mean number of boating accidents to occur in these 9 months was 31, and the standard deviation in this sample was 9 boating accidents per month. Geoff was told to construct a 90 percent confidence interval for the true mean number of boating accidents per month, but he was in such an accident himself recently, so you will have to do this for him.

Worked-Out Answers to Self-Check Exercises

SC 7-10 (a) 2.052.
(b) 2.998.
(c) 1.782.
(d) 2.262.
(e) 2.797.
(f) 3.250.

SC 7-11 $s = 3.2 \qquad n = 7 \qquad \overline{x} = 39.2 \qquad \hat{\sigma}_{\overline{x}} = s/\sqrt{n} = 3.2/\sqrt{7} = 1.2095$

$$\overline{x} \pm t\hat{\sigma}_{\overline{x}} = 39.2 \pm 2.447(1.2095) = 39.2 \pm 2.9596$$
$$= (36.240, 42.160) \text{ miles}$$

7.8 Determining the Sample Size in Estimation

In all our discussions so far, we have used for sample size the symbol n instead of a specific number. Now we need to know how to determine what number to use. How large should the sample be? If it is too small, we may fail to achieve the objective of our analysis. But if it is too large, we waste resources when we gather the sample.

What sample size is adequate?

Some sampling error will arise because we have not studied the whole population. Whenever we sample, we always miss *some* helpful information about the population. If we want a high level of precision (that is, if we want to be quite sure of our estimate), we have to sample enough of the population to provide the required information. Sampling error is controlled by selecting a sample that is adequate in size. In general, the more precision you want, the larger the sample you will need to take. Let us examine some methods that are useful in determining what sample size is necessary for any specified level of precision.

Table 7-6	Lower Confidence Limit	Upper Confidence Limit
Comparison of Two Ways of Expressing the Same Confidence Limits	a. $\bar{x} - \$500$ b. $\bar{x} - z\sigma_{\bar{x}}$	a. $\bar{x} + \$500$ b. $\bar{x} + z\sigma_{\bar{x}}$

Sample Size for Estimating a Mean

Suppose a university is performing a survey of the annual earnings of last year's graduates from its business school. It knows from past experience that the standard deviation of the annual earnings of the entire population (1,000) of these graduates is about $1,500. How large a sample size should the university take in order to estimate the mean annual earnings of last year's class within $500 and at a 95 percent confidence level?

Two ways to express a confidence limit

Exactly what is this problem asking? The university is going to take a sample of *some* size, determine the mean of the sample, $\bar{x}$, and use it as a point estimate of the population mean. It wants to be 95 percent certain that the true mean annual earnings of last year's class is not more than $500 above or below the point estimate. Row *a* in Table 7-6 summarizes in symbolic terms how the university is defining its confidence limits for us. Row *b* shows symbolically how we normally express confidence limits for an infinite population. When we compare these two sets of confidence limits, we can see that

$$z\sigma_{\bar{x}} = \$500$$

Thus, the university is actually saying that it wants $z\sigma_{\bar{x}}$ to be equal to $500. If we look in Appendix Table 1, we find that the necessary z value for a 95 percent confidence level is 1.96. Step by step:

$$\text{If} \qquad z\sigma_{\bar{x}} = \$500$$

$$\text{and} \qquad z = 1.96$$

$$\text{then} \qquad 1.96\sigma_{\bar{x}} = \$500$$

$$\text{and} \qquad \sigma_{\bar{x}} = \frac{\$500}{1.96}$$

$$= \$255 \leftarrow \text{Standard error of the mean}$$

Remember that the formula for the standard error is Equation 6-1:

$$\sigma_{\bar{x}} = \frac{\sigma}{\sqrt{n}} \leftarrow \text{Population standard deviation} \qquad [6\text{-}1]$$

Finding an adequate sample size

Using Equation 6-1, we can substitute our known population standard deviation value of $1,500 and our calculated standard error value of $255 and solve for *n:*

$$\sigma_{\bar{x}} = \frac{\sigma}{\sqrt{n}} \qquad [6\text{-}1]$$

$$\$255 = \frac{\$1{,}500}{\sqrt{n}}$$

$$(\sqrt{n})(\$255) = \$1{,}500$$

$$\sqrt{n} = \frac{\$1{,}500}{\$255}$$

$$\sqrt{n} = 5.882; \text{ now square both sides}$$

$$n = 34.6 \leftarrow \text{Sample size for precision specified}$$

Therefore, because n must be greater than or equal to 34.6, the university should take a sample of 35 business-school graduates to get the precision it wants in estimating the class's mean annual earnings.

Estimating the standard deviation from the range

In this example, we knew the standard deviation of the population, but in many cases, the standard deviation of the population is not available. Remember, too, that we have not yet taken the sample, and we are trying to decide how large to make it. We cannot estimate the population standard deviation using methods from the first part of this chapter. If we have a notion about the range of the population, we can use that to get a crude but workable estimate.

Suppose we are estimating hourly manufacturing wage rates in a city and are fairly confident that there is a \$4.00 difference between the highest and lowest wage rates. We know that plus and minus 3 standard deviations include 99.7 percent of all the area under the normal curve, that is, plus 3 standard deviations and minus 3 standard deviations include almost all of the distribution. To symbolize this relationship, we have constructed Figure 7-6, in which \$4.00 (the range) equals 6 standard deviations (plus 3 and minus 3). Thus, a rough estimate of the population standard deviation would be

$$6\hat{\sigma} = \$4.00$$

$$\hat{\sigma} = \frac{\$4.00}{6}$$

$$\text{Estimate of the population standard deviation} \rightarrow \hat{\sigma} = \$0.667$$

Our estimate of the population standard deviation using this rough method is not precise, but it may mean the difference between getting a working idea of the required sample size and knowing nothing about that sample size.

Sample Size for Estimating a Proportion

The procedures for determining sample sizes for estimating a population proportion are similar to those for estimating a population mean. Suppose we wish to poll students at a

FIGURE 7-6

Approximate relationship between the range and the population standard deviation

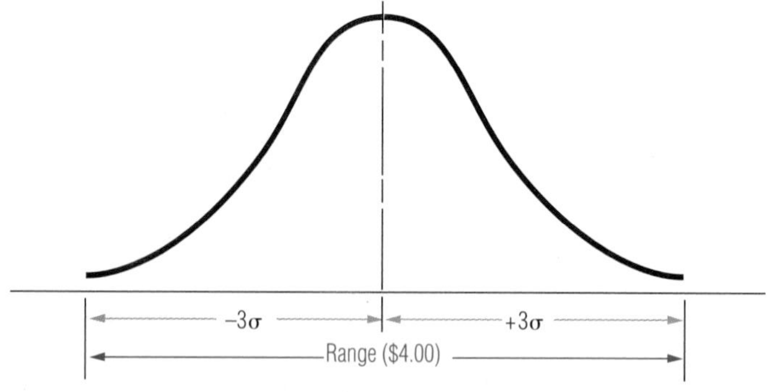

large state university. We want to determine what proportion of them is in favor of a new grading system. We would like a sample size that will enable us to be 90 percent certain of estimating the true proportion of the population of 40,000 students that is in favor of the new system within plus and minus 0.02.

We begin to solve this problem by looking in Appendix Table 1 to find the z value for a 90 percent confidence level. That value is ± 1.64 standard errors from the mean. We want our estimate to be within 0.02, so we can symbolize the step-by-step process like this:

$$\begin{aligned} &\text{If} & z\sigma_{\bar{p}} &= 0.02 \\ &\text{and} & z &= 1.64 \\ &\text{then} & 1.64\sigma_{\bar{p}} &= 0.02 \end{aligned}$$

If we now substitute the right side of Equation 7-4 for $\sigma_{\bar{p}}$, we get

$$\begin{aligned} 1.64\sqrt{\frac{pq}{n}} &= 0.02 \\ \sqrt{\frac{pq}{n}} &= 0.0122\text{; now square both sides} \\ \frac{pq}{n} &= 0.00014884\text{; now multiply both sides by } n \\ pq &= 0.00014884n \\ n &= \frac{pq}{0.00014884} \end{aligned}$$

To find n, we still need an estimate of the population parameters p and q. If we have strong feelings about the actual proportion in favor of the new system, we can use that as our best guess to calculate n. But if we have no idea what p is, then our best strategy is to guess at p in such a way that we choose n in a conservative manner (that is, so that the sample size is large enough to supply at least the precision we require no matter what p actually is). At this point in our problem, n is equal to the product of p and q divided by 0.00014884. The way to get the largest n is to generate the largest possible numerator of that expression, which happens if we pick $p = 0.5$ and $q = 0.5$. Then n becomes:

$$\begin{aligned} n &= \frac{pq}{0.00014884} \\ &= \frac{(0.5)(0.5)}{0.00014884} \\ &= \frac{0.25}{0.00014884} \\ &= 1{,}680 \leftarrow \text{Sample size for precision specified} \end{aligned}$$

As a result, to be 90 percent certain of estimating the true proportion within 0.02, we should pick a simple random sample of 1,680 students to interview.

Picking the most conservative proportion

In the problem we have just solved, we picked a value for p that represented the most conservative strategy. The value 0.5 generated the largest possible sample. We would have used another value of p if we had been able to estimate one *or* if we had a strong feeling

Table 7-7

Sample Size n Associated with Different Values of p and q

Choose This Value for p	Value of q, or $1 - p$	$\left(\frac{pq}{0.00014884}\right)$	Indicated Sample Size n
0.2	0.8	$\frac{(0.2)(0.8)}{(0.00014884)}$	= 1,075
0.3	0.7	$\frac{(0.3)(0.7)}{(0.00014884)}$	= 1,411
0.4	0.6	$\frac{(0.4)(0.6)}{(0.00014884)}$	= 1,613
0.5	0.5	$\frac{(0.5)(0.5)}{(0.00014884)}$	= 1,680 ←Most conservative
0.6	0.4	$\frac{(0.6)(0.4)}{(0.00014884)}$	= 1,613
0.7	0.3	$\frac{(0.7)(0.3)}{(0.00014884)}$	= 1,411
0.8	0.2	$\frac{(0.8)(0.2)}{(0.00014884)}$	= 1,075

about one. Whenever all these solutions are absent, assume the most conservative possible value for p, namely, $p = 0.5$.

To illustrate that 0.5 yields the largest possible sample, Table 7-7 solves the grading-system problem using several different values of p. You can see from the sample sizes associated with these different values that for the range of p's from 0.3 to 0.7, the change in the appropriate sample size is relatively small. Therefore, even if you knew that the true population proportion was 0.3 and you used a value of 0.5 for p anyway, you would have sampled only 269 more people (1,680 − 1,411) than was actually necessary for the desired degree of precision. Obviously, guessing values of p in cases like this is not so critical as it seemed at first glance.

HINTS & ASSUMPTIONS

From a commonsense perspective, if the standard deviation of the population is very small, the values cluster very tightly around their mean and just about any sample size will capture them and produce accurate information. On the other hand, if the population standard deviation is very large and the values are quite spread out, it will take a very large sample to include them and turn up accurate information. How do we get an idea about the population standard deviation before we start sampling? Companies planning to conduct market research generally conduct preliminary research on the population to estimate the standard deviation. If the product is like another that has been on the market, often it's possible to rely on previous data about the population without further estimates.

Exercises 7.8

Self-Check Exercises

SC 7-12 For a test market, find the sample size needed to estimate the true proportion of consumers satisfied with a certain new product within ±0.04 at the 90 percent confidence level. Assume you have no strong feeling about what the proportion is.

SC 7-13 A speed-reading course guarantees a certain reading rate increase within 2 days. The teacher knows a few people will not be able to achieve this increase, so before stating the guaranteed percentage of people who achieve the reading rate increase, he wants to be 98 percent confident that the percentage has been estimated to within ±5 percent of the true value. What is the most conservative sample size needed for this problem?

Basic Concepts

■ 7-51 If the population standard deviation is 78, find the sample size necessary to estimate the true mean within 50 points for a confidence level of 95 percent.

■ 7-52 We have strong indications that the proportion is around 0.7. Find the sample size needed to estimate the proportion within ±0.02 with a confidence level of 90 percent.

■ 7-53 Given a population with a standard deviation of 8.6, what size sample is needed to estimate the mean of the population within ±0.5 with 99 percent confidence?

Applications

■ 7-54 An important proposal must be voted on, and a politician wants to find the proportion of people who are in favor of the proposal. Find the sample size needed to estimate the true proportion to within ±.05 at the 95 percent confidence level. Assume you have no strong feelings about what the proportion is. How would your sample size change if you believe about 75 percent of the people favor the proposal? How would it change if only about 25 percent favor the proposal?

■ 7-55 The management of Southern Textiles has recently come under fire regarding the supposedly detrimental effects on health caused by its manufacturing process. A social scientist has advanced a theory that the employees who die from natural causes exhibit remarkable consistency in their life-span: The upper and lower limits of their life-spans differ by no more than 550 weeks (about 10 $^{1}/_{2}$ years). For a confidence level of 98 percent, how large a sample should be examined to find the average life-span of these employees within ±30 weeks?

■ 7-56 Food Tiger, a local grocery store, sells generic garbage bags and has received quite a few complaints about the strength of these bags. It seems that the generic bags are weaker than the name-brand competitor's bags and, therefore, break more often. John C. Tiger, VP in charge of purchasing, is interested in determining the average maximum weight that can be put into one of the generic bags without its breaking. If the standard deviation of garbage breaking weight is 1.2 lb, determine the number of bags that must be tested in order for Mr. Tiger to be 95 percent confident that the sample average breaking weight is within 0.5 lb of the true average.

■ 7-57 The university is considering raising tuition to improve school facilities, and they want to determine what percentage of students favor the increase. The university needs to be 90 percent confident the percentage has been estimated to within 2 percent of the true value. How large a sample is needed to guarantee this accuracy regardless of the true percentage?

■ 7-58 A local store that specializes in candles and clocks, Wicks and Ticks, is interested in obtaining an interval estimate for the mean number of customers that enter the store daily. The owners are reasonably sure that the actual standard deviation of the daily number of customers is 15 customers. Help Wicks and Ticks out of a fix by determining the sample size it should use in order to develop a 96 percent confidence interval for the true mean that will have a width of only eight customers.

Worked-Out Answers to Self-Check Exercises

SC 7-12 Assume $p = q = 0.5$.

$$0.04 = 1.64\sqrt{\frac{pq}{n}} = 1.64\sqrt{\frac{0.5(0.5)}{n}} \quad \text{so } n = \left(\frac{1.64(0.5)}{0.04}\right)^2 = 420.25 \text{ i.e., } n \geq 421.$$

SC 7-13 Assume $p = q = 0.5$.

$$0.05 = 2.33\sqrt{\frac{pq}{n}} = 2.33\sqrt{\frac{0.5(0.5)}{n}} \quad \text{so } n = \left(\frac{2.33(0.5)}{0.05}\right)^2 = 542.89 \text{ i.e., } n \geq 543.$$

So take a sample of at least 543 records of prior students.

Statistics at Work

Loveland Computers

Case 7: Estimation Although Lee Azko had felt nervous about the first job out of college, assignments in production and purchasing had already shown how "book learning" could be applied. The next assignment introduced Lee to another of Loveland Computers' departments and the no-nonsense approach of its head, Margot Derby.

"Let me tell you the situation," began Margot, the head of marketing, without bothering with introductions or small talk. "You know that we primarily consider ourselves distributors of hardware—the actual PCs that people use in their homes and businesses. When we started out, we left it up to the customers to seek out software. Sometimes, they bought directly from the companies that wrote the programs, or from national distributors with toll-free numbers. Now there are also retail outlets—almost every suburban mall has at least one store that sells computer programs.

"The reason we stayed clear of software was that there were just too many programs out there—we didn't want to guess which one would be the 'hit' product and end up with a lot of useless inventory on our hands. But the game changed. After some shakeout in software, two or three clear leaders emerged in each field—spreadsheets and word processors, for example. To match the competition we began to bundle some software with the computers for certain promotions.

"Last year, we also started loading the programs onto the hard drive for some customers. We can give them a very competitive price for the software, and preloading turns out to be an important product feature that many people are shopping for. So I'm taking another look at software, to see if we shouldn't change our strategy and do more in that line. To get some idea of the market, I had a summer intern call up 500 customers who'd owned Loveland machines for about a year. And we asked them how much they'd spent in total on software in the first year.

"I've got all the data here; it didn't take 2 minutes to come up with the mean and standard deviation from our spreadsheet program. Those investment bankers from New York took a look at a draft of my marketing plan for software; when they were down here last week, they asked me how sure I could be that the results of that telephone survey were accurate.

"Every time I pick up the newspaper, I see some opinion poll where they say: 'This is based on a survey of 1,200 adults and the margin of error is 3 percent.' How do they know that—do they keep track of all the surveys and when they're right and wrong? I only have this one set of results. I don't see how I can answer their question."

"It shouldn't be too difficult," said Lee, checking a briefcase to make sure that a calculator and a set of statistical tables were close at hand. "Why don't you show me those numbers and we can figure it out right now."

Study Questions: What distribution will Lee assume for the telephone poll results, and which statistical table will be most useful? How will Lee define *margin of error* for Margot? Is Lee likely to recommend a larger sample?

Computer Database Exercise

HH Industries

Early the following week, Bob was back in Laurel's office. "Well, we've started pulling our sample," he said. "Could you help me get a feel for exactly how many to examine? I'm interested in a 95 percent confidence level of being within plus or minus 0.05 of the actual population proportion. I think you'd agree that, for all practical purposes, we can consider our population to be infinite."

"I think you're right," Laurel agreed. "I've seen your row of filing cabinets! As far as the number to pull, it would help if we had an educated guess for the actual population parameter, but we can at least come up with a range of sample sizes for you."

1. Determine an appropriate sample size for satisfying Bob's conditions if the actual value of p (the proportion of purchase orders competitively bid) is approximately 0.2, 0.3, 0.4, or 0.5. Which should Bob choose?

About a week later, Bob knocked on Laurel's door. "Here's the raw data. Hal's goal for us at this point is to have at least 60 percent of the purchase orders competitively bid. Think this will make him happy?"

"Let's calculate our confidence interval and see," Laurel answered.

2. Estimate the proportion and standard error of the proportion for competitively bid purchase orders using the data in the CH07A.xxx files on the data disk. Construct a 95 percent confidence interval for the proportion.

Bob looked skeptically at the results. "Is there any way we can tighten those confidence interval boundaries?" he asked.

"Without any additional sampling effort, you're limited to lowering the confidence level," Laurel explained.

3. Calculate the boundaries of the confidence interval if Bob is willing to settle for a 90 percent confidence level.

"The other alternative is to try a larger sample," she continued. "Because sampling, in this case, is relatively inexpensive, why not aim for a tighter interval—say, plus or minus 0.03. We can use our initial proportion as our 'educated guess' about the population's true proportion and maintain our 95 percent confidence level."

"But how much larger a sample will that require?" asked Bob.

"I can tell you in a second," Laurel replied, pulling out her trusty calculator.

4. Under these new conditions, how many more purchase orders need to be examined?

"Good news!" Bob announced to Laurel several days later. "The new, larger sample showed a proportion of 0.58. That means I can tell the boss we're between 0.55 and 0.61 with 95 percent confidence. I'm planning on putting a short presentation together for Monday's staff meeting."

"Sounds good," said Laurel. "Just be careful how you throw around your terms. Remember we've got some statistical rookies in there and you don't want to give them the wrong impression."

5. Verify Bob's calculations. What do you think Laurel is concerned about, and how would you focus your presentation if you were Bob?

Bob's presentation went well at Monday's staff meeting. Hal asked a few questions, but was generally pleased with the results. Then he introduced the next order of business.

"As most of you know, we introduced metric parts into our inventory about a year ago. With the influx of mobile hydraulic equipment made overseas by companies like Toyota, Nissan, and Komatsu, the market for metric repair parts seemed to be ripe. And as far as I know, we were the first in our industry to carry several complete lines. At any rate, it's time to see how we're doing and estimate potential sales for the next year. Laurel, I'm afraid we're not giving you much of a break, but you can see that we definitely need you here!"

Back in her office, Laurel reviewed what she knew about HH Industries' metric product lines. Peggy was in the process of running a report that would give Laurel details on sales for the last year. Unfortunately, when metric parts were first incorporated, they weren't given a unique product code designation, which made their sales a little hard to isolate. Nevertheless, she'd do what she could.

6. Based on the data in the CH07B.xxx files on the data disk, estimate the population mean and standard deviation of weekly metric sales.
7. Estimate the standard error of the mean for this sample.
8. Construct a 95 percent confidence interval for mean weekly sales of metric parts.
9. Should HH Industries continue to carry metric parts if Hal wants to be 95 percent certain the next year's sales will be at least \$300,000? Assume there will be 50 sales weeks in the coming year.
10. Stan argued that using all 12 months of metric sales data resulted in an unreasonably low estimate, because it included the months when metric parts were first introduced. He is convinced that using the second 6 months of data will show a more accurate prediction, as sales will have leveled off. Laurel agrees. Repeat the previous calculations using just the second 25 weeks of the data.

From the Textbook to the Real World

The Berkeley Engineering Fund*

Established in 1979, the Berkeley Engineering Fund solicits contributions to support the College of Engineering at the University of California, Berkeley. Administrators use information about past numbers of donors, gifts, and dollar contributions as input to a mathematical model for predicting monthly and end-of-year contributions. Then they adjust fund-raising efforts accordingly. The model uses a binomial distribution for the numbers of donors and gifts, and a compound Poisson distribution for total dollars contributed. Since 1982, data on donor counts, timing, size of donations, and matching gifts have been recorded for parents, faculty, alumni, and friends of the college.

Parameter Estimation Forecasts are based on data from previous campaigns. Because identical mailings were used from 1982 to 1984, monthly proportions of total giving have been stable from year to year. For each mailing date, the forecasters determined distributions for the number of gifts from each of the four subgroups, as well as estimates of the mean and variance of gift size.

Evaluating the Model Parent data from 1982–1983 and 1983–1984 were used to test the Poisson assumption on which the model is based. Using both Poisson tables and a normal approximation, 95 percent confidence intervals were computed for the monthly numbers of parent donors. Figures RW7-1 and RW7-2 show these intervals for 1982–1983 and 1983–1984. Only in September of both years did the actual donor counts fall outside the 95 percent confidence intervals. This supports the assumption of a Poisson distribution.

*Source: Mark Britto and Robert M. Oliver, "Forecasting Donors and Donations," *Journal of Forcasting* 5(1986): 39–55

FIGURE RW7-1

1982–1983 fitting monthly parent donor counts

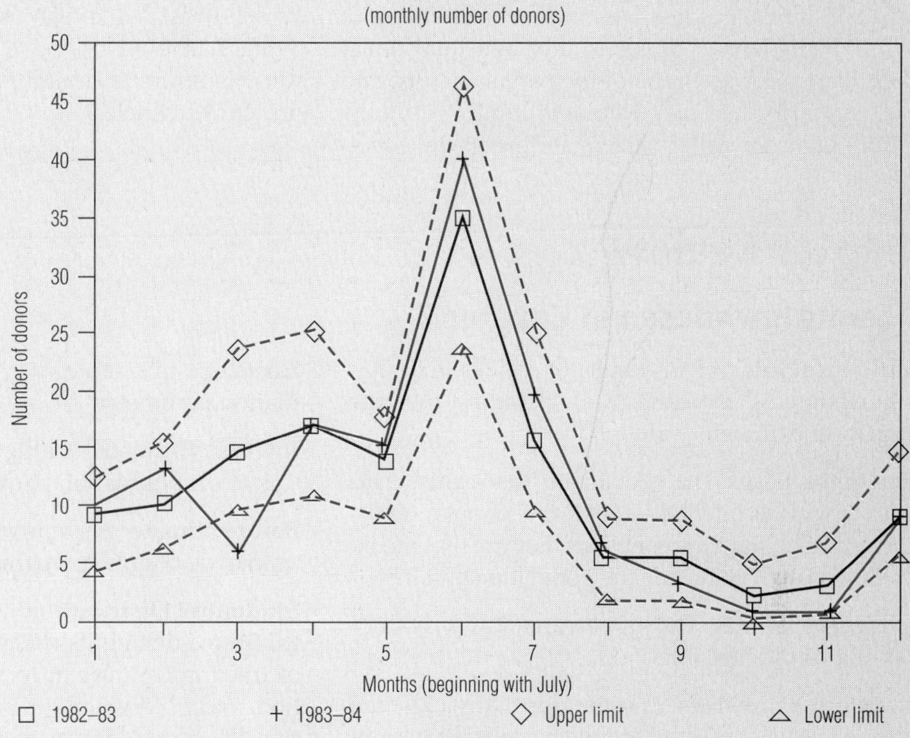

FIGURE RW7-2

1983–1984 fitting monthly parent donor counts

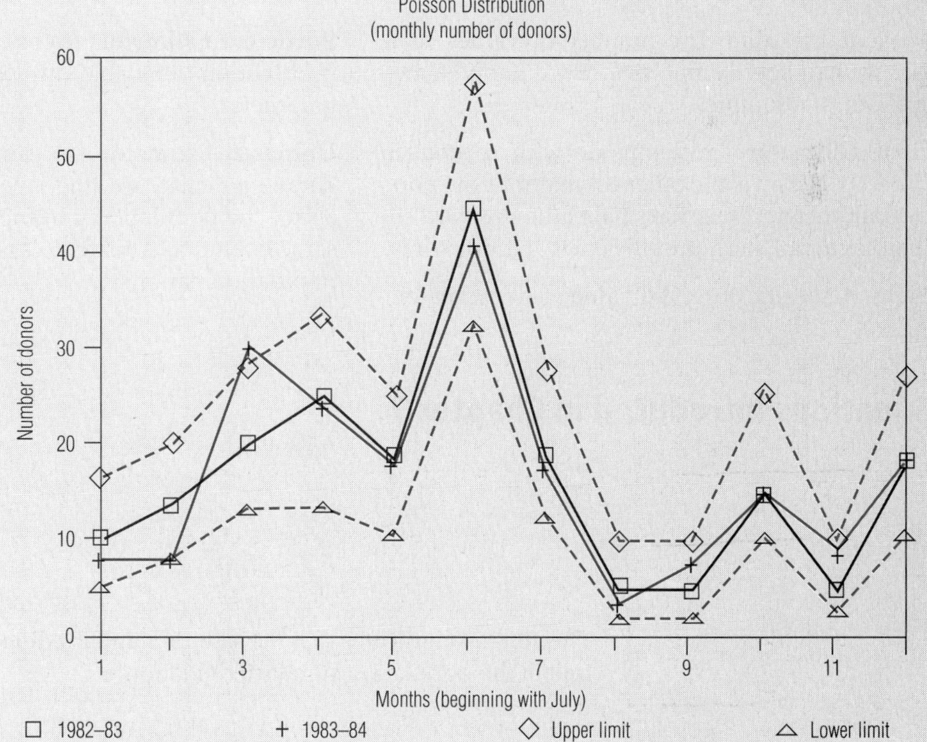

Results The model performed well in forecasting year-end totals, but less well on a month-to-month basis. Predictions of donor counts, and total donations were more accurate for the parent, faculty, and friend groups than they were for alumni. Administrators gained a better understanding of the effects of personal contacts and mailings. Because the model provided a way to predict the effects of changes in fund-raising techniques, it encouraged administrators to design strategies targeted to specific constituencies.

Chapter Review

● Terms Introduced in Chapter 7

Confidence Interval A range of values that has some designated probability of including the true population parameter value.

Confidence Level The probability that statisticians associate with an interval estimate of a population parameter, indicating how confident they are that the interval estimate will include the population parameter.

Confidence Limits The upper and lower boundaries of a confidence interval.

Consistent Estimator An estimator that yields values more closely approaching the population parameter as the sample size increases.

Degrees of Freedom The number of values in a sample we can specify freely once we know something about that sample.

Efficient Estimator An estimator with a smaller standard error than some other estimator of the population parameter; that is, the smaller the standard error of an estimator, the more efficient that estimator is.

Estimate A specific observed value of an estimator.

Estimator A sample statistic used to estimate a population parameter.

Interval Estimate A range of values to estimate an unknown population parameter.

Point Estimate A single number used to estimate an unknown population parameter.

Student's *t* Distribution A family of probability distributions distinguished by their individual degrees of freedom, similar in form to the normal distribution, and used when the population standard deviation is unknown and the sample size is relatively small ($n \leq 30$).

Sufficient Estimator An estimator that uses all the information available in the data concerning a parameter.

Unbiased Estimator An estimator of a population parameter that, on the average, assumes values above the population parameter as often, and to the same extent, as it tends to assume values below the population parameter.

● Equations Introduced in Chapter 7

■ **7-1**

Estimate of the population standard deviation

$$\hat{\sigma} = s = \sqrt{\frac{\Sigma(x - \bar{x})^2}{n - 1}}$$

p. 363

This formula indicates that the sample standard deviation can be used to estimate the population standard deviation.

■ **7-2**

$$\hat{\sigma}_{\bar{x}} = \frac{\hat{\sigma}}{\sqrt{n}} \times \sqrt{\frac{N - n}{N - 1}}$$

p. 364

This formula enables us to derive an *estimated* standard error of the mean of a *finite* population from an *estimate* of the population standard deviation. The symbol ^, called a hat, indicates that the value is estimated. Equation 7-6 is the corresponding formula for an infinite population.

■ 7-3

$$\mu_{\bar{p}} = p$$

p. 367

Use this formula to derive the *mean* of the sampling distribution of the *proportion* of successes. The right-hand side, p, is equal to $(n \times p)/n$, where the numerator is the expected number of successes in n trials and the denominator is the number of trials. Symbolically, the proportion of successes *in a sample* is written $\bar{p}$ and is pronounced *p bar.*

■ 7-4

$$\sigma_{\bar{p}} = \sqrt{\frac{pq}{n}}$$

p. 368

To get the *standard error of the proportion,* take the square root of the product of the probabilities of success and failure divided by the number of trials.

■ 7-5

$$\hat{\sigma}_{\bar{p}} = \sqrt{\frac{\bar{p}\,\bar{q}}{n}}$$

p. 368

This is the formula to use to derive an estimated standard error of the proportion when the population proportion is unknown and you are forced to use $\bar{p}$ and $\bar{q}$, the sample proportions of successes and failures.

■ 7-6

$$\hat{\sigma}_{\bar{x}} = \frac{\hat{\sigma}}{\sqrt{n}}$$

p. 374

This formula enables us to derive an *estimated* standard error of the mean of an *infinite* population from an *estimate* of the population standard deviation. It is exactly like Equation 7-2 except that it lacks the finite population multiplier.

● Review and Application Exercises

■ **7-59** From a sample of 42 gasoline stations statewide, the average price of a gallon of unleaded gas was found to be \$1.12 and the standard deviation was \$0.04 per gallon. Within what interval can we be 99.74 percent confident that the true statewide mean per-gallon price of unleaded gasoline will fall?

■ **7-60** What are the advantages of using an interval estimate over a point estimate?

■ **7-61** Why is the size of a statistic's standard error important in its use as an estimator? To which characteristic of estimator does this relate?

■ **7-62** Suzanne Jones, head registrar for the university system, needs to know what proportion of students have grade-point averages below 2.0. How many students' grades should be looked at in order to determine this proportion to within ± 0.01 with 95 percent confidence?

■ **7-63** A 95 percent confidence interval for the population mean is given by (94, 126) and a 75 percent confidence interval is given by (100.96, 119.04). What are the advantages and disadvantages of each of these interval estimates?

■ **7-64** The posted speed limit on the Cross-Bronx Expressway is 55 mph. Congestion results in much slower actual speeds. A random sample of 57 vehicles clocked speeds with an average of 23.2 mph and a standard deviation of 0.3 mph.

(a) Estimate the standard deviation of the population.

(b) Estimate the standard error of the mean for this population.

(c) What are the upper and lower limits of the confidence interval for the mean speed given a desired confidence level of 0.95?

■ **7-65** Given a sample mean of 8, a population standard deviation of 2.6, and a sample size of 32, find the confidence level associated with each of the following intervals:

(a) (7.6136, 8.3864).

(b) (6.85, 9.15).

(c) (7.195, 8.805).

■ **7-66** Based on knowledge about the desirable qualities of estimators, for what reasons might $\bar{x}$ be considered the "best" estimator of the true population mean?

■ **7-67** The president of Offshore Oil has been concerned about the number of fights on his rigs and has been considering various courses of action. In an effort to understand the catalysts of offshore fighting, he randomly sampled 41 days on which a crew had returned from mainland leave. For this sample, the average proportion of workers involved in fisticuffs each day is 0.032 and the associated standard deviation is 0.0130.

(a) Give a point estimate for the average proportion of workers involved in fights on any given day that a crew has returned from the mainland.

(b) Estimate the population standard deviation associated with this fighting rate.

(c) Find a 90 percent confidence interval for the average proportion of returning workers who get involved in fights.

■ **7-68** Given the following expressions for the limits of a confidence interval, find the confidence level associated with the interval:

(a) $\bar{x} - 1.25\sigma_{\bar{x}}$ to $\bar{x} + 1.25\sigma_{\bar{x}}$.

(b) $\bar{x} - 2.4\sigma_{\bar{x}}$ to $\bar{x} + 2.4\sigma_{\bar{x}}$.

(c) $x - 1.68\sigma_{\bar{x}}$ to $\bar{x} + 1.68\sigma_{\bar{x}}$.

■ **7-69** Harris Polls, Inc., is in the business of surveying households. From previous surveys, it is known that the standard deviation of the number of hours of television watched in a week by a household is 1.1 hours. Harris Polls would like to determine the average number of hours of television watched per week per household in the United States. Accuracy is important, so Harris Polls would like to be 98 percent certain that the sample average number of hours falls within ± 0.3 hour of the national average. Conservatively, what sample size should Harris Polls use?

■ **7-70** John Bull has just purchased a computer program that claims to pick stocks that will increase in price in the next week with an 85 percent accuracy rate. On how many stocks should John test this program in order to be 98 percent certain that the percentage of stocks that do in fact go up in the next week will be within ± 0.05 of the sample proportion?

■ **7-71** Gotchya runs a laser-tag entertainment center where adults and teenagers rent equipment and engage in mock combat. The facility is always used to capacity on weekends. The three owners want to assess the effectiveness of a new advertising campaign aimed at increasing weeknight usage. The number of paying patrons on twenty-seven randomly selected weeknights is given in the following table. Find a 95 percent confidence interval for the mean number of patrons on a weeknight.

61	57	53	60	64	57	54	58	63
59	50	60	60	57	58	62	63	60
61	54	50	54	61	51	53	62	57

7-72 Their accountants have told the owners of Gotchya, the laser-tag entertainment center discussed in Exercise 7-71, that they need to have at least fifty-five patrons in order to break even on a weeknight. The partners are willing to continue to operate on weeknights if they can be at least 95 percent certain that they will break even at least half the time. Using the data in Exercise 7-71, find a 95 percent confidence interval for the proportion of weeknights on which Gotchya will break even. Should Gotchya continue to stay open on weeknights? Explain.

The Wall Street Journal provides financial information daily for more than 3,000 mutual funds. Table RW7-1 gives information on a random sample of 35 of those funds, as of the close of trade on Friday, May 14, 1993. Use this information to answer Exercises 7-73 to 7-76.

7-73 (a) Estimate the average change in net asset value (ΔNAV) on May 14, 1993, for all of the funds listed in *The Wall Street Journal*.

(b) Estimate the standard deviation of the change in net asset value for all of those funds.

(c) Find a 95 percent confidence interval for the average change in net asset value. What assumptions do you need to make about the distribution of the individual changes in net asset value in order to derive your confidence interval?

7-74 (a) Estimate the standard deviation of the year-to-date percentage change (%YTD) in value of all of the listed funds.

(b) Assuming that the standard deviation you estimated in part (a) is close to the true population standard deviation, how large a sample would be needed to estimate the average year-to-date percentage change in value to within 0.5 percent with 99 percent confidence?

7-75 Funds for which the offering price (OP) is the same as the net asset value (NAV) are called no-load funds. Use the sample of 35 funds to estimate what fraction of all of the funds listed in *The Wall Street Journal* are no-load funds. Give a 98 percent confidence interval for this fraction.

7-76 Suppose you believe that the no-load funds should not be lumped together with the others. Assuming that the individual year-to-date percentage changes in value for the no-load funds have a distribution that is approximately normal, find a 95 confidence interval for their average year-to-date percentage change in value. Is the normality assumption necessary? Explain.

■ **7-77** In evaluating the effectiveness of a federal rehabilitation program, a survey of 52 of a prison's 900 inmates found that 35 percent were repeat offenders.

(a) Estimate the standard error of the proportion of repeat offenders.

(b) Construct a 90 percent confidence interval for the proportion of repeat offenders among the inmates of this prison.

■ **7-78** During the apple harvest, 105 separate bushels of apples were checked for bad apples (because, as you know, one bad apple can spoil the whole bunch) and it was found that there were an average of 3.2 bad apples per bushel. It is known that the standard deviation of bad apples per bushel is 0.2 for this type of apple.

(a) Calculate the standard error of the mean.

(b) Establish an interval estimate around the mean using one $\hat{\sigma}_{\bar{x}}$.

Table RW7-1

Financial Data for a Sample of 35 Mutual Funds

Fund Name	NAV	OP	ΔNAV	%YTD
AHA Balanced	12.54	12.54	−0.01	3.9%
Ambassador Index Stock	11.36	11.36	0.01	1.9
American Capital Global Equity (A)	10.44	11.08	0.01	8.2
American Capital Municipal Bond	10.33	10.85	−0.01	5.1
Atlas Growth & Income	13.69	14.04	−0.05	2.2
Babson Enterprise	16.13	16.13	0.08	6.0
Blanchard Flexible Income	5.11	5.11	0.00	5.9
Colonial Growth	14.08	14.94	−0.05	0.1
Columbia Common Stock	14.54	14.54	−0.02	3.8
Evergreen Total Return	19.96	19.96	−0.07	5.9
Fidelity Equity-Income	31.24	31.88	−0.14	8.6
Fidelity Spartan Municipal Income	11.02	11.02	0.00	5.9
First Union Value (B)	17.30	18.02	−0.04	1.8
Flag Investors Value	10.89	11.40	−0.05	2.9
Fortis Capital	17.48	18.35	0.03	−5.3
GT Global Europe	9.11	9.56	0.03	7.1
Helmsman Equity Index	11.68	11.68	0.02	1.8
Homestead Value	13.48	13.48	−0.01	7.9
IAI Emerging Growth	13.64	13.64	0.09	−2.8
John Hancock Tax Exempt	11.32	11.85	0.00	5.1
Kemper Blue Chip	13.30	14.11	0.02	−0.2
Keystone International	6.50	6.50	0.01	8.0
Marshall Stock	9.90	9.90	0.03	−1.9
MAS Equity	54.37	54.37	−0.11	−1.9
MFS Research	12.86	13.64	0.01	4.6
MIM Bond Income	9.24	9.24	0.02	−0.5
PFAMCo MidCap Growth	12.51	12.51	−0.03	2.8
Pilgrim GNMA	14.02	14.45	−0.01	3.2
PIMCO Short Term	10.03	10.03	0.01	1.8
Prudential Municipal Maryland	11.35	11.35	0.00	4.8
Putnam Global Growth	8.18	8.68	−0.01	10.1
Rightime Blue Chip	31.07	32.62	0.02	1.2
Schwab 1000	12.11	12.11	−0.01	1.3
Shearson Appreciation (A)	10.72	11.28	−0.03	0.6
Weiss Peck Greer Tudor	24.90	24.90	0.19	0.2

NAV net asset value, the price (in $) at which an investor can redeem shares of the fund
OP offering price, the price (in $) which an investor pays to purchase shares of the fund
ΔNAV the change in NAV from the previous day
%YTD the year-to-date percentage change in the value of an investment in the fund, assuming all dividends are reinvested

Source: The Wall Street Journal *(17 May 1993): C16–C19.*

■ **7-79** From a random sample of 60 buses, Montreal's mass-transit office has calculated the mean number of passengers per kilometer to be 4.1. From previous studies, the population standard deviation is known to be 1.2 passengers per kilometer.

(a) Find the standard error of the mean. (Assume that the bus fleet is very large.)

(b) Construct a 95 percent confidence interval for the mean number of passengers per kilometer for the population.

■ **7-80** The Internal Revenue Service sampled 200 tax returns recently and found that the sample average income tax refund amounted to $425.39 and the sample standard deviation was $107.10.

(a) Estimate the population mean tax refund and standard deviation.

(b) Using the estimates of part (a), construct an interval in which the population mean is 95 percent certain to fall.

■ **7-81** The Physicians Care Group operates a number of walk-in clinics. Patient charts indicate the time that a patient arrived at the clinic and the time that the patient was actually seen by a physician. Administrator Val Likmer has just received a stinging phone call from a patient complaining of an excessive wait at the Rockridge clinic. Val pulls 49 charts at random from last week's workload and calculates an average wait time of 15.2 minutes. A previous large-scale study of waiting time over several clinics had a standard deviation of 2.5 minutes. Construct a confidence interval for the average wait time with confidence level

(a) 90 percent.

(b) 99 percent.

■ **7-82** Bill Wenslaff, an engineer on the staff of a water purification plant, measures the chlorine content in 200 different samples daily. Over a period of years, he has established the population standard deviation to be 1.4 milligrams of chlorine per liter. The latest samples averaged 4.6 milligrams of chlorine per liter.

(a) Find the standard error of the mean.

(b) Establish the interval around 5.2, the population mean, that will include the sample mean with a probability of 68.3 percent.

■ **7-83** Ellen Harris, an industrial engineer, was accumulating normal times for various tasks on a labor-intensive assembly process. This process included 300 separate job stations, each performing the same assembly tasks. She sampled seven stations and obtained the following assembly times for each station: 1.9, 2.5, 2.9, 1.3, 2.6, 2.8, and 3.0 minutes.

(a) Calculate the mean assembly time and the corresponding standard deviation for the sample.

(b) Estimate the population standard deviation.

(c) Construct a 98 percent confidence interval for the mean assembly time.

■ **7-84** Larry Culler, the federal grain inspector at a seaport, found spoilage in 40 of 120 randomly selected lots of wheat shipped from the port. Construct a 95 percent confidence interval for him for the actual proportion of lots with spoilage in shipments from that port.

■ **7-85** High Fashion Marketing is considering reintroducing paisley ties. In order to avoid a fashion flop, High Fashion interviewed 90 young executives (their primary market) and found that of the 90 interviewed, 79 believed that paisley ties were fashionable and were interested in purchasing one.

Using a confidence level of 98 percent, construct a confidence interval for the proportion of all young executives who find paisley ties fashionable.

■ **7-86** The Department of Transportation has mandated that the average speed of cars on interstate highways must be no more than 67 miles per hour in order for state highway departments to retain their federal funding. North Carolina troopers, in unmarked cars, clocked a sample of 186 cars and found that the average speed was 66.3 miles per hour and the standard deviation was 0.6 mph.

(a) Find the standard error of the mean.

(b) What is the interval around the sample mean that would contain the population mean 95.5 percent of the time?

(c) Can North Carolina truthfully report that the true mean speed on its highways is 67 mph or less with 95.5 percent confidence?

■ **7-87** Mark Semmes, owner of the Aurora Restaurant, is considering purchasing new furniture. To help him decide on the amount he can afford to invest in tables and chairs, he wishes to determine the average revenue per customer. The checks for 9 randomly sampled customers had an average of \$18.30 and a standard deviation of \$3.60. Construct a 95 percent confidence interval for the size of the average check per customer.

■ **7-88** John Deer, a horticulturist at Northern Carrboro State University, knows that a certain strain of corn will always produce between 80 and 140 bushels per acre. For a confidence level of 90 percent, how many 1-acre samples must be taken in order to estimate the average production per acre to within ± 5 bushels per acre?

● Chapter Concepts Test

Circle the correct answer or fill in the blank. *Answers are in the back of the book.*

T F 1. A statistic is said to be an efficient estimator of a population parameter if, with increasing sample size, it becomes almost certain that the value of the statistic comes very close to that of the population parameter.

T F 2. An interval estimate is a range of values used to estimate the shape of a population's distribution.

T F 3. If a statistic tends to assume values higher than the population parameter as frequently as it tends to assume values that are lower, we say that the statistic is an unbiased estimate of the parameter.

T F 4. The probability that a population parameter will lie within a given interval estimate is known as the confidence level.

T F 5. With increasing sample size, the *t* distribution tends to become flatter in shape.

T F 6. We must always use the *t* distribution, rather than the normal, whenever the standard deviation of the population is not known.

T F 7. We may obtain a crude estimate of the standard deviation of some population if we have some information about its range.

T F 8. When using the *t* distribution in estimation, we must assume that the population is approximately normal.

T F 9. Using high confidence levels is not always desirable because high confidence levels produce large confidence intervals.

T F 10. There is a different *t* distribution for each possible sample size.

T F 11. A point estimate is often insufficient because it is either right or wrong.

T F 12. A sample mean is said to be an unbiased estimator of a population mean because no other estimator could extract from the sample additional information about the population mean.

T F 13. The most frequently used estimator of σ is s.

T F 14. The standard error of the proportion is calculated as $\sqrt{p(1 - p)/n}$.

T F 15. The degrees of freedom used in a t-distribution estimation are equal to the sample size.

T F 16. The t distribution is less able to be approximated by a normal distribution as the sample size increases.

T F 17. The t distribution need not be used in estimating if you know the standard deviation of the population.

T F 18. The sample median is always the best estimator of the population median.

T F 19. As the width of a confidence interval increases, the confidence level associated with the interval also increases.

T F 20. Estimating the standard error of the mean of a finite population using an estimate of the population standard deviation requires the use of the t distribution for calculating subsequent confidence intervals.

T F 21. The percentages in the t distribution table correspond to the chance that the true population parameter will fall outside our confidence interval.

T F 22. In a normal distribution, 100 percent of the population lies within ± 3 standard deviations of the mean.

A B C D E 23. When choosing an estimator of a population parameter, one should consider:

(a) Sufficiency.
(b) Clarity.
(c) Efficiency.
(d) All of these.
(e) (a) and (c) but not (b).

A B C D E 24. Suppose that 200 members of a group were asked whether they like a particular product. Fifty said yes; 150 said no. Assuming "yes" means a success, which of the following is correct?

(a) $\bar{p} = 0.33$.
(b) $\bar{p} = 0.25$.
(c) $p = 0.33$.
(d) $p = 0.25$.
(e) (b) and (d) only.

A B C D 25. Assume that you take a sample and calculate $\bar{x}$ as 100. You then calculate the upper limit of a 90 percent confidence interval for μ; its value is 112. What is the lower limit of this confidence interval?

(a) 88.
(b) 92.
(c) 100.
(d) It cannot be determined from the information given.

A B C D E 26. After taking a sample and computing $\bar{x}$, a statistician says, "I am 88 percent confident that the population mean is between 106 and 122." What does she really mean?

(a) The probability is 0.88 that μ is between 106 and 122.
(b) The probability is 0.88 that $\mu = 114$, the midpoint of the interval.
(c) Eighty-eight percent of the intervals calculated from samples of this size will contain the population mean.
(d) All of these.
(e) (a) and (c) but not (b).

A B C D E 27. Which of the following is a necessary condition for using a t distribution table?
(a) n is small.
(b) s is known but σ is not.
(c) The population is infinite.
(d) All of these.
(e) (a) and (b) but not (c).

A B C D 28. Which of the following t distributions would be expected to have the most area in its tails?
(a) $\bar{x} = 0.83$, degrees of freedom $= 12$.
(b) $\bar{x} = 15$, degrees of freedom $= 19$.
(c) $\bar{x} = 15$, $n = 19$.
(d) $\bar{x} = 8.3$, $n = 12$.

A B C D E 29. Which of the following is a difference between z tables and t tables?
(a) The t table has values for only a few percentages.
(b) The t table measures the chance that the population parameter we are estimating will be in our confidence interval.
(c) We must specify the degrees of freedom with which we are dealing when using a z table.
(d) All of these.
(e) (a) and (b) but not (c).

A B C D 30. Suppose we are attempting to estimate a population variance by using s^2. It is incorrect to calculate s^2 as $\Sigma(x - \bar{x})^2/n$ because the value would be:
(a) Biased.
(b) Inefficient.
(c) Inconsistent.
(d) Insufficient.

A B C D E 31. When considering samples with size greater than 30, we use the normal table even if the population standard deviation is unknown. Why is this?
(a) The calculation of the degrees of freedom becomes difficult for large sample sizes.
(b) The number of percentages we need for the calculation of confidence intervals exceeds the number contained in the t tables.
(c) It is difficult to calculate $\bar{x}$ (and hence s^2) for large samples.
(d) None of these.
(e) (a) and (c) but not (b).

A B C D E 32. Assume that, from a population with $N = 50$, a sample of size 15 is drawn; σ^2 is known to be 36, and s^2 for the sample is 49; $\bar{x}$ for the sample is calculated as 104. Which of the following should be used for calculating a 95 percent confidence interval for μ?
(a) Student's t distribution.
(b) Normal distribution.
(c) Finite population multiplier.
(d) (a) and (c) but not (b).
(e) (b) and (c) but not (a).

A B C D 33. We can use the normal distribution to represent the sampling distribution of the population when:
(a) The sample size is more than 10.
(b) The sample size is less than 50.
(c) The sample size is more than 5.
(d) None of these.

34. If a statistic underestimates a population parameter as much as it overestimates it, we would call it:
    (a) Consistent.
    (b) Sufficient.
    (c) Efficient.
    (d) All of these.
    (e) None of these.
35. If population proportion information is unknown, the standard error of the proportion can be estimated by the formula:
    (a) $\sqrt{npq}$.
    (b) $\sqrt{n\bar{p}\bar{q}}$.
    (c) $\sqrt{pq/n}$.
    (d) $\sqrt{\bar{p}\bar{q}/n}$.
36. The average height of the 25 students in Mr. Stanton's tenth grade math class is known to be 66″. In constructing a 95 percent confidence interval for the average height of all tenth graders, we would use:
    (a) The normal distribution with 24 degrees of freedom.
    (b) The t distribution with 24 degrees of freedom.
    (c) The t distribution with 65 degrees of freedom.
    (d) The t distribution with 25 degrees of freedom.
37. A certain normally distributed population has a known standard deviation of 1.0. What is the total width of a 95 percent confidence interval for the population mean?
    (a) 1.96.
    (b) 0.98.
    (c) 3.92.
    (d) It cannot be determined from the information given.
38. A single number used to estimate an unknown population parameter is a(n) ______________________ estimate.
39. A range of values used to estimate an unknown population parameter is a(n) ______________________ estimate.
40. Once we know something about a sample, the number of values in the sample we can specify freely is called ______________________.
41. The family of probability distributions used when the population standard deviation is unknown, the sample size is small, and the values approximate the normal is the ______________________.
42. When we give an interval estimate of a population parameter, we show how sure we are that the interval contains the actual population parameter by setting a ______________________ level.
43. The upper confidence limit and the lower confidence limit are the same ______________________ from the ______________________.
44. Theoretically, the ______________________ distribution is the correct distribution to use in constructing confidence intervals to estimate a population proportion.
45. In the absence of additional information, a value of ______________________ should be used for p when determining a sample size for estimating a population proportion.

Flow Chart: Estimation

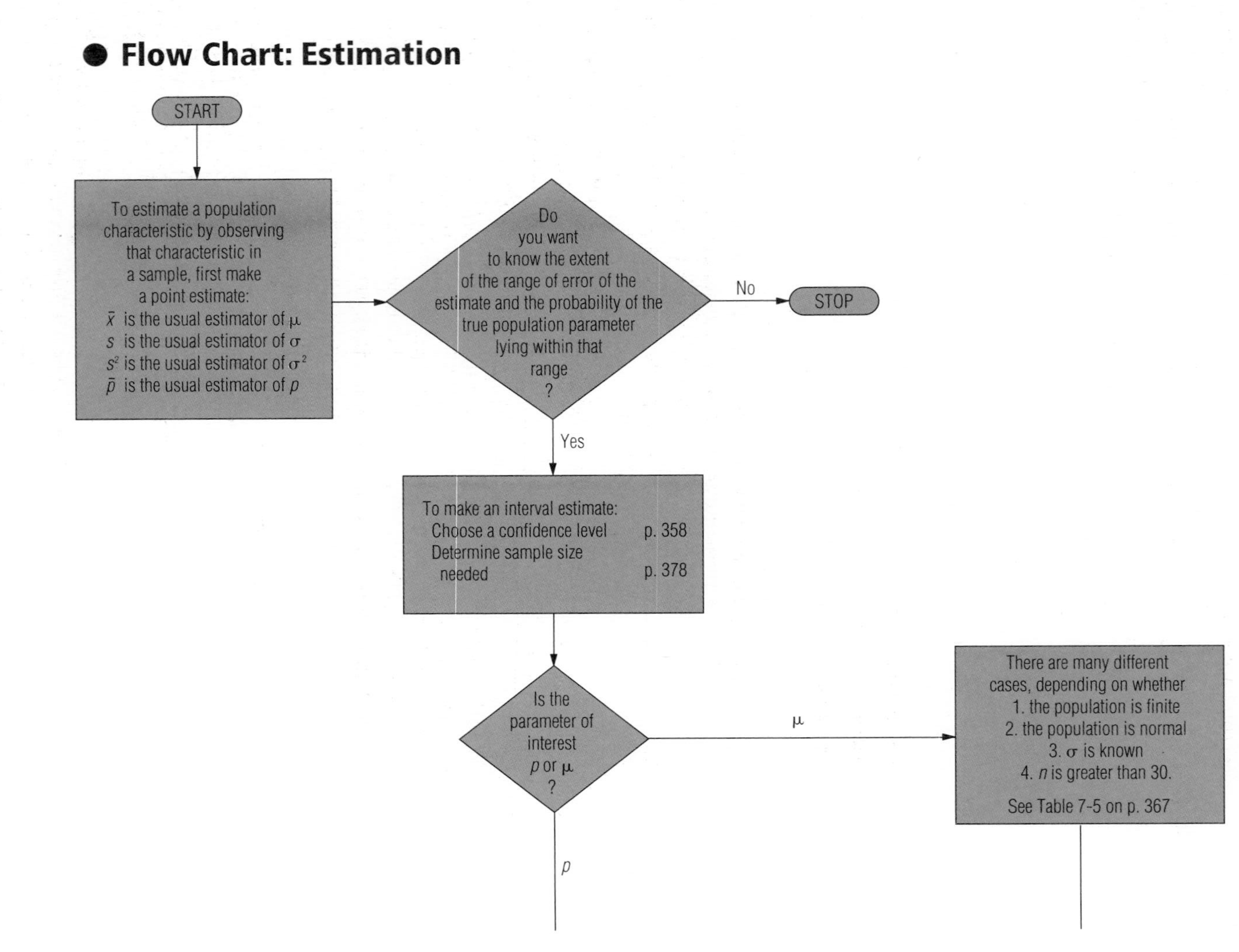

START
To estimate a population characteristic by observing that characteristic in a sample, first make a point estimate:
$\bar{x}$ is the usual estimator of μ
s is the usual estimator of σ
s^2 is the usual estimator of σ^2
$\bar{p}$ is the usual estimator of p
Do you want to know the extent of the range of error of the estimate and the probability of the true population parameter lying within that range ?
No
STOP
Yes
To make an interval estimate:
Choose a confidence level p. 358
Determine sample size needed p. 378
Is the parameter of interest p or μ ?
μ
There are many different cases, depending on whether
1. the population is finite
2. the population is normal
3. σ is known
4. n is greater than 30.
See Table 7-5 on p. 367
p

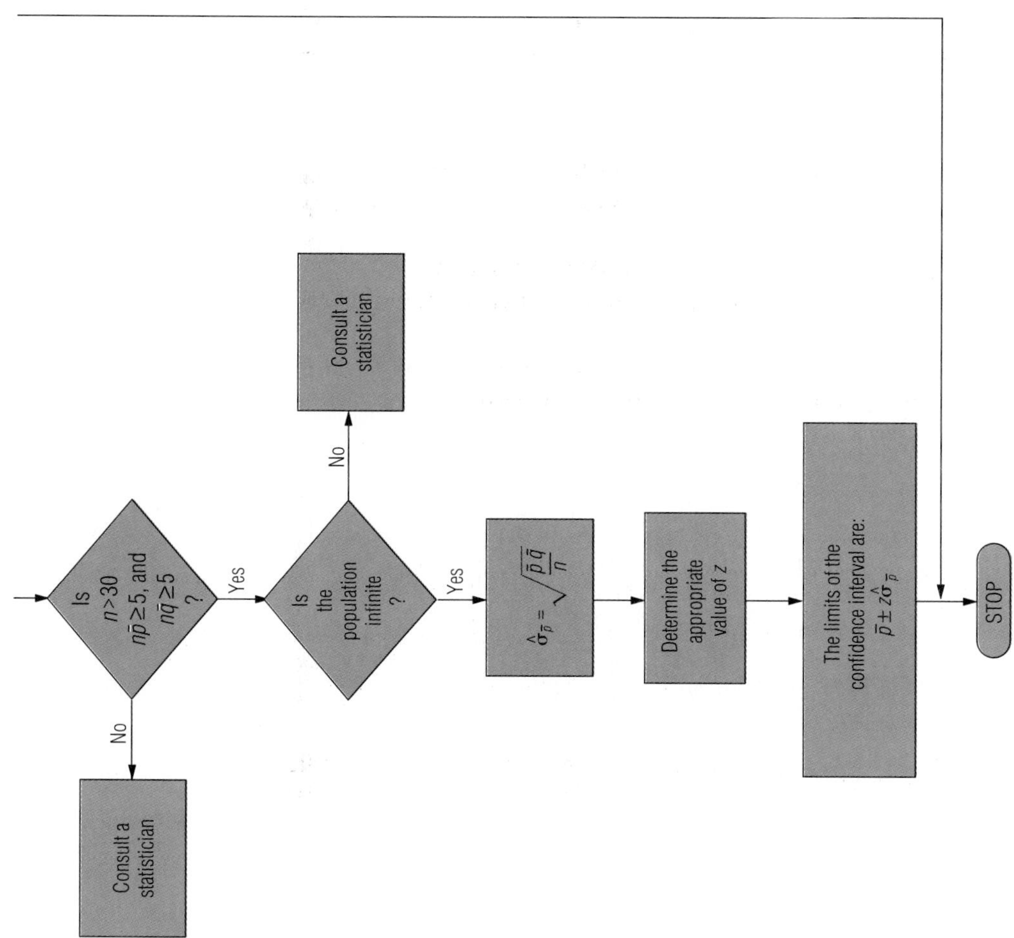

Is $n>30$ $n\bar{p}\geq 5$, and $n\bar{q}\geq 5$?
No
Consult a statistician
Yes
Is the population infinite ?
No
Consult a statistician
Yes
$\hat{\sigma}_{\bar{p}} = \sqrt{\frac{\bar{p}\,\bar{q}}{n}}$
Determine the appropriate value of z
The limits of the confidence interval are: $\bar{p} \pm z\hat{\sigma}_{\bar{p}}$
STOP

chapter 8

TESTING HYPOTHESES: ONE-SAMPLE TESTS

Objectives

- To learn how to use samples to decide whether a population possesses a particular characteristic
- To determine how unlikely it is that an observed sample could have come from a hypothesized population
- To understand the two types of errors possible when testing hypotheses
- To learn when to use one-tailed tests and when to use two-tailed tests
- To learn the five-step process for testing hypotheses
- To understand how and when to use the normal and *t* distributions for testing hypotheses about population means and proportions

Chapter Contents

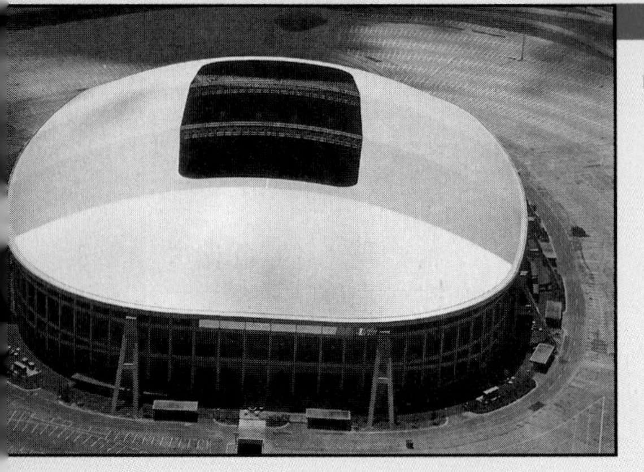

The roofing contract for a new sports complex in San Francisco has been awarded to Parkhill Associates, a large building contractor. Building specifications call for a movable roof covered by approximately 10,000 sheets of 0.04-inch-thick aluminum. The aluminum sheets cannot be appreciably thicker than 0.04 inch because the structure could not support the additional weight. Nor can the sheets be appreciably thinner than 0.04 inch because the strength of the roof would be inadequate. Because of this restriction on thickness, Parkhill carefully checks the aluminum sheets from its supplier. Of course, Parkhill does not want to measure each sheet, so it randomly samples 100. The sheets in the sample have a mean thickness of 0.0408 inch. From past experience with this supplier, Parkhill believes that these sheets come from a thickness population with a standard deviation of 0.004 inch. On the basis of these data, Parkhill must decide whether the 10,000 sheets meet specifications. In Chapter 7, we used sample statistics to estimate population parameters. Now, to solve problems like Parkhill's, we shall learn how to use characteristics of samples to test an assumption we have about the population from which that sample came. Our test for Parkhill, later in the chapter, may lead Parkhill to accept the shipment or it may indicate that Parkhill should reject the aluminum sheets sent by the supplier because they do not meet the architectural specifications. ■

8.1 Introduction

Function of hypothesis testing

Hypothesis testing begins with an assumption, called a *hypothesis,* that we make about a population parameter. Then we collect sample data, produce sample statistics, and use this information to decide how likely it is that our hypothesized population parameter is correct. Say that we assume a certain value for a population mean. To test the validity of our assumption, we gather sample data and determine the difference between the hypothesized value and the actual value of the sample mean. Then we judge whether the difference is significant. The smaller the difference, the greater the likelihood that our hypothesized value for the mean is correct. The larger the difference, the smaller the likelihood.

Unfortunately, the difference between the hypothesized population parameter and the actual statistic is more often neither so large that we automatically reject our hypothesis nor so small that we just as quickly accept it. So in hypothesis testing, as in most significant real-life decisions, clear-cut solutions are the exception, not the rule.

When to accept or reject the hypothesis

Suppose a manager of a large shopping mall tells us that the average work efficiency of her employees is at least 90 percent. How can we test the validity of her hypothesis? Using the sampling methods we learned in Chapter 6, we could calculate the efficiency of a *sample* of her employees. If we did this and the sample statistic came out to be 95 percent, we would readily accept the manager's statement. However, if the sample statistic were 46 percent, we would reject her assumption as untrue. We can interpret both these outcomes, 95 percent and 46 percent, using our common sense.

The basic problem is dealing with uncertainty

Now suppose that our sample statistic reveals an efficiency of 88 percent. This value is relatively close to 90 percent, but is it close enough for us to accept the manager's hypothesis? Whether we accept or reject the manager's hypothesis, we cannot be absolutely certain that our decision is correct; therefore, we will have to learn to deal with uncertainty in our decision making. **We cannot accept or reject a hypothesis about a population pa-**

rameter simply by intuition. Instead, we need to learn how to decide objectively, on the basis of sample information, whether to accept or reject a hunch.

Making Big Jumps

Projecting too far

College students often see ads for learning aids. One very popular such aid is a combination outline, study guide, and question set for various courses. Advertisements about such items often claim better examination scores with less studying time. Suppose a study guide for a basic statistics course is available through an organization that produces such guides for 50 different courses. If this study guide for basic statistics has been tested (and let us assume properly), the firm may advertise that "our study guides have been statistically proven to raise grades and lower study time." Of course, this assertion is quite true, but only as it applies to the basic statistics experience. There may be no evidence of statistical significance that establishes the same kind of results for the other 49 guides.

Different test conditions

Another product may be advertised as being beneficial in removing crabgrass from your lawn and may assert that the product has been "thoroughly tested" on real lawns. Even if we assume that the proper statistical procedures were, in fact, used during the tests, such claims still involve big jumps. Suppose that the test plot was in Florida and your lawn problems are in Utah. Differences in rainfall, soil fertility, airborne pollutants, temperature, dormancy hours and germination conditions may vary widely between these two locations. Claiming results for a statistically valid test under a completely different set of test conditions is invalid. One such test cannot measure effectiveness under a wide variety of environmental conditions.

Exercises 8.1

- **8-1** Why must we be required to deal with uncertainty in our decisions, even when using statistical techniques?
- **8-2** Theoretically speaking, how might one go about testing the hypothesis that a coin is fair? That a die is fair?
- **8-3** Is it possible that a false hypothesis will be accepted? How would you explain this?
- **8-4** Describe the hypothesis-testing process.
- **8-5** How would you explain a large difference between a hypothesized population parameter and a sample statistic if, in fact, the hypothesis is true?

8.2 Concepts Basic to the Hypothesis-Testing Procedure

Sports-complex problem

Before we introduce the formal statistical terms and procedures, we'll work our chapter-opening sports-complex problem all the way through. Recall that the aluminum roofing sheets have a claimed average thickness of 0.04 inch and that they will be unsatisfactory if they are too thick *or* too thin. The contractor takes a sample of 100 sheets and determines that the sample mean thickness is 0.0408 inch. On the basis of past experience, he knows that the population standard deviation is 0.004 inch. Does this sample evidence indicate that the batch of 10,000 sheets of aluminum is suitable for constructing the roof of the new sports complex?

Formulating the hypothesis

If we assume that the true mean thickness is 0.04 inch, and we know that the population standard deviation is 0.004 inch, how likely is it that we would get a sample mean of 0.0408 or more from that population? In other words, **if the true mean is 0.04 inch and the standard deviation is 0.004 inch, what are the chances of getting a sample mean that differs from 0.04 inch by 0.0008 (= 0.0408 − 0.04) inch or more?**

These questions show that **to determine whether the population mean is actually 0.04 inch, we must calculate the probability that a random sample with a mean of 0.0408 inch will be selected from a population with a μ of 0.04 inch and a σ of 0.004 inch. This probability will indicate whether it is *reasonable* to observe a sample like this if the population mean is actually 0.04 inch.** If this probability is far too low, we must conclude that the aluminum company's statement is false and that the mean thickness of the aluminum sheets is not 0.04 inch.

Let's answer the question illustrated in Figure 8-1: If the hypothesized population mean is 0.04 inch and the population standard deviation is 0.004 inch, what are the chances of getting a sample mean (0.0408 inch) that differs from 0.04 inch by 0.0008 inch? First, we calculate the standard error of the mean from the population standard deviation:

Calculating the standard error of the mean

$$\sigma_{\bar{x}} = \frac{\sigma}{\sqrt{n}} \qquad [6\text{-}1]$$

$$= \frac{0.004 \text{ in.}}{\sqrt{100}}$$

$$= \frac{0.004 \text{ in.}}{10}$$

$$= 0.0004 \text{ in.}$$

Next we use Equation 6-2 to discover that the mean of our sample (0.0408 inch) lies 2 standard errors to the right of the hypothesized population mean:

$$z = \frac{\bar{x} - \mu}{\sigma_{\bar{x}}} \qquad [6\text{-}2]$$

$$= \frac{0.0408 - 0.04}{0.0004}$$

$$= 2 \leftarrow \text{Standard errors of the mean}$$

Interpreting the probability associated with this difference

Using Appendix Table 1, we learn that 4.5 percent is the total chance of our sample mean differing from the population mean by 2 or more standard errors; that is, the chance that the sample mean would be 0.0408 inch or larger or 0.0392 inch or smaller is only 4.5 percent ($P(z \geq 2 \text{ or } z \leq -2) = 2(0.5 - 0.4772) = 0.0456$, or about 4.5 percent). **With this low a chance, Parkhill could conclude that a population with a true mean of 0.04 inch would not be likely to produce a sample like this.** The project supervisor would reject the aluminum company's statement about the mean thickness of the sheets.

The decision maker's role in formulating hypotheses

In this case, the difference between the sample mean and the hypothesized population mean is too large, and the chance that the population would produce such a random sample is far too low. Why this probability of 4.5 percent is too low, or wrong, is a

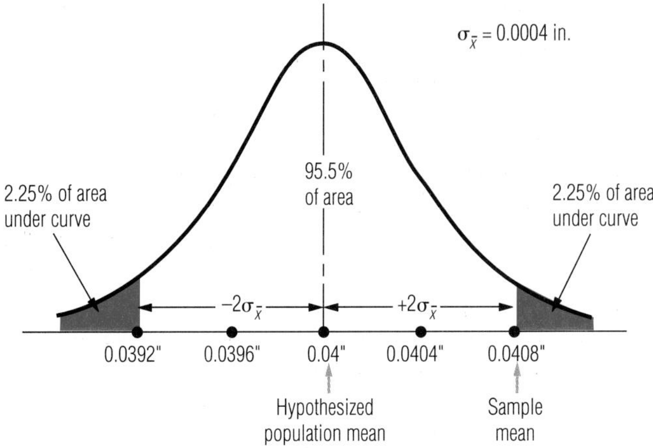

FIGURE 8-1 Probability that $\bar{x}$ will differ from hypothesized μ by 2

judgment for decision makers to make. Certain situations demand that decision makers be very sure about the characteristics of the items being tested, and then even 2 percent is too high to be attributable to chance. Other processes allow for a wider latitude or variation, and a decision maker might accept a hypothesis with a 4.5 percent probability of chance variation. In each situation, we must try to determine the costs resulting from an incorrect decision and the precise level of risk we are willing to assume.

Risk of rejection

In our example, we rejected the aluminum company's contention that the population mean is 0.04 inch. But suppose for a moment that the population mean is *actually* 0.04 inch. If we then stuck to our rejection rule of 2 standard errors or more (the 4.5 percent probability or less in the tails of Figure 8-1), we would reject a perfectly good lot of aluminum sheets 4.5 percent of the time. Therefore, **our minimum standard for an acceptable probability, 4.5 percent, is *also* the *risk* we take of *rejecting* a *hypothesis that is true*. In this or any decision making, there can be no risk-free trade-off.**

HINTS & ASSUMPTIONS

Although *hypothesis testing* sounds like some formal statistical term completely unrelated to business decision making, in fact managers propose and test hypotheses all the time. "If we drop the price of this car model by $1,500, we'll sell 50,000 cars this year" is a hypothesis. To test this hypothesis, we have to wait until the end of the year and count sales. Managerial hypotheses are based on intuition; the marketplace decides whether the manager's intuitions were correct. Hint: Hypothesis testing is about making inferences about a population from only a small sample. The bottom line in hypothesis testing is when we ask ourselves (and then decide) whether a population like we *think* this one is would be likely to produce a sample like the one we are looking at.

Exercises 8.2

Self-Check Exercises

SC 8-1 How many standard errors around the hypothesized value should we use to be 99.44 percent certain that we accept the hypothesis when it is true?

SC 8-2 An automobile manufacturer claims that a particular model gets 28 miles to the gallon. The Environmental Protection Agency, using a sample of 49 automobiles of this model, finds the sample mean to be 26.8 miles per gallon. From previous studies, the population standard deviation is known to be 5 miles per gallon. Could we reasonably expect (within 2 standard errors) that we could select such a sample if indeed the population mean is actually 28 miles per gallon?

Basic Concepts

- ■ **8-6** What do we mean when we reject a hypothesis on the basis of a sample?
- ■ **8-7** Explain why there is no single standard level of probability used to reject or accept in hypothesis testing.
- ■ **8-8** If we reject a hypothesized value because it differs from a sample statistic by more than 1.75 standard errors, what is the probability that we have rejected a hypothesis that is in fact true?
- ■ **8-9** How many standard errors around the hypothesized value should we use to be 98 percent certain that we accept the hypothesis when it is true?

Applications

- ■ **8-10** Sports and media magnate Ned Sterner is interested in purchasing the Atlanta Stalwarts if he can be reasonably certain that operating the team will not be too costly. He figures that average attendance would have to be about 28,500 fans per game to make the purchase attractive to him. Ned randomly chooses 64 home games over the past 4 years and finds from figures reported in *Sporting Reviews* that average attendance at these games was 26,100. A study he commissioned the last time he purchased a team showed that the population standard deviation for attendance at similar events had been quite stable for the past 10 years at about 6,000 fans. Using 2 standard errors as the decision criterion, should Ned purchase the Stalwarts? Can you think of any reason(s) why your conclusion might not be valid?
- ■ **8-11** *Computing World* has asserted that the amount of time owners of personal computers spend on their machines averages 23.9 hours per week and has a standard deviation of 12.6 hours per week. A random sampling of 81 of its subscribers revealed a sample mean usage of 27.2 hours per week. On the basis of this sample, is it reasonable to conclude (using 2 standard errors as the decision criterion) that *Computing World's* subscribers are different from average personal computer owners?
- ■ **8-12** A grocery store has specially packaged oranges and has claimed a bag of oranges will yield 2.5 quarts of juice. After randomly selecting 42 bags, a stocker found the average juice production per bag to be 2.2 quarts. Historically, we know the population standard deviation is 0.2 quart. Using

this sample and a decision criterion of 2.5 standard errors, could we conclude the store's claims are correct?

Worked-Out Answers to Self-Check Exercises

SC 8-1 To leave a probability of $1 - 0.9944 = 0.0056$ in the tails, the absolute value of z must be greater than or equal to 2.77, so the interval should be ± 2.77 standard errors about the hypothesized value.

SC 8-2 $\sigma = 5 \quad n = 49 \quad \bar{x} = 26.8 \quad \mu = 28$

$$\mu \pm 2\sigma_{\bar{x}} = \mu \pm 2\sigma/\sqrt{n} = 28 \pm 2(5)/\sqrt{49} = 28 \pm 1.429 = (26.571, 29.429)$$

Because $\bar{x} = 26.8 > 26.57$, it is not unreasonable to see such sample results if μ really is 28 mpg.

8.3 Testing Hypotheses

Making a formal statement of the *null hypothesis*

In hypothesis testing, we must state the assumed or hypothesized value of the population parameter *before* we begin sampling. The assumption we wish to test is called the *null hypothesis* and is symbolized H_0 or "H sub-zero."

Suppose we want to test the hypothesis that the population mean is equal to 500. We would symbolize it as follows and read it, "The null hypothesis is that the population mean is equal to 500":

$$H_0\text{: } \mu = 500$$

Why is it called the null hypothesis?

The term *null hypothesis* arises from earlier agricultural and medical applications of statistics. In order to test the effectiveness of a new fertilizer or drug, the tested hypothesis (the null hypothesis) was that it had *no effect,* that is, there was no difference between treated and untreated samples.

If we use a hypothesized value of a population mean in a problem, we would represent it symbolically as

$$\mu_{H_0}$$

This is read, "The hypothesized value of the population mean."

If our sample results fail to support the null hypothesis, we must conclude that something else is true. **Whenever we reject the hypothesis, the conclusion we do accept is called the *alternative hypothesis* and is symbolized H_1 ("H sub-one").** For the null hypothesis

$H_0\text{: } \mu = 200$ (Read: "The null hypothesis is that the population mean is equal to 200.")

we will consider three possible alternative hypotheses:

Making a formal statement of the *alternate hypothesis*

- $H_1\text{: } \mu \neq 200$ ← "The alternative hypothesis is that the population mean is *not equal* to 200"
- $H_1\text{: } \mu > 200$ ← "The alternative hypothesis is that the population mean is *greater than* 200"
- $H_1\text{: } \mu < 200$ ← "The alternative hypothesis is that the population mean is *less than* 200"

Interpreting the Significance Level

Goal of hypothesis testing

The purpose of hypothesis testing is not to question the computed value of the sample statistic but to make a judgment about the *difference* between that sample statistic and a hypothesized population parameter. The next step after stating the null and alternative hypotheses, then, is to decide what criterion to use for deciding whether to accept or reject the null hypothesis.

In our sports-complex example, we decided that a difference observed between the sample mean $\bar{x}$ and the hypothesized population mean μ_{H_0} had only a 4.5 percent, or 0.045, chance of occurring. Therefore, we rejected the null hypothesis that the population mean was 0.04 inch (H_0: $\mu = 0.04$ inch). In statistical terms, the value 0.045 is called the *significance level.*

Function of the *significance level*

What if we test a hypothesis at the 5 percent level of significance? This means that we will reject the null hypothesis if the difference between the sample statistic and the hypothesized population parameter is so large that it or a larger difference would occur, on the average, only five or fewer times in every 100 samples when the hypothesized population parameter is correct. **If we assume the hypothesis is correct, then the significance level will indicate the percentage of sample means that is outside certain limits.** (In estimation, you remember, the confidence level indicated the percentage of sample means that fell *within* the defined confidence limits.)

Area where no significant difference exists

Figure 8-2 illustrates how to interpret a 5 percent level of significance. Notice that 2.5 percent of the area under the curve is located in each tail. From Appendix Table 1, we can determine that 95 percent of all the area under the curve is included in an interval extending $1.96\sigma_{\bar{x}}$ on either side of the hypothesized mean. In 95 percent of the area, then, there is no significant difference between the observed value of the sample statistic and the hypothesized value of the population parameter. In the remaining 5 percent (the colored regions in Figure 8-2), a significant difference does exist.

Also called the area where we accept the null hypothesis

Figure 8-3 examines this same example in a different way. Here, the 0.95 of the area under the curve is where we would accept the null hypothesis. The two colored parts under the curve, representing a total of 5 percent of the area, are the regions where we would reject the null hypothesis.

FIGURE 8-2

Regions of significant difference and of no significant difference at a 5 percent level of significance

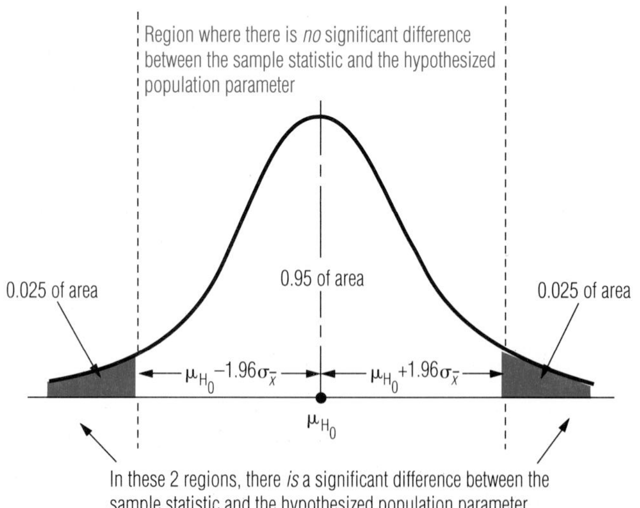
Region where there is *no* significant difference between the sample statistic and the hypothesized population parameter
0.025 of area
0.95 of area
0.025 of area
$\mu_{H_0} - 1.96\sigma_{\bar{x}}$
$\mu_{H_0} + 1.96\sigma_{\bar{x}}$
μ_{H_0}
In these 2 regions, there *is* a significant difference between the sample statistic and the hypothesized population parameter

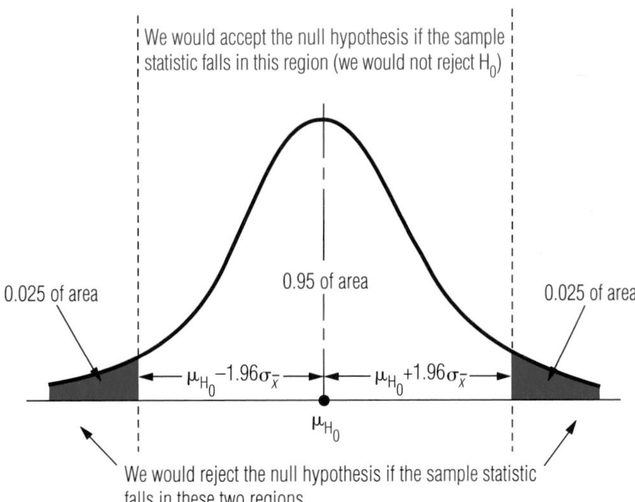

We would accept the null hypothesis if the sample statistic falls in this region (we would not reject H_0)
0.025 of area
0.95 of area
0.025 of area
$\mu_{H_0} - 1.96\sigma_{\bar{x}}$
$\mu_{H_0} + 1.96\sigma_{\bar{x}}$
μ_{H_0}
We would reject the null hypothesis if the sample statistic falls in these two regions

FIGURE 8-3

A 5 percent level of significance, with acceptance and rejection regions designated

Hypotheses are *accepted,* not *proved*

A word of caution is appropriate here. Even if our sample statistic in Figure 8-3 does fall in the nonshaded region (the region that makes up 95 percent of the area under the curve), **this *does not prove* that our null hypothesis (H_0) is true; it simply does not provide statistical evidence to reject it.** Why? Because the only way in which the hypothesis can be accepted with certainty is for us to know the population parameter; unfortunately, this is not possible. Therefore, whenever we say that we accept the null hypothesis, we actually mean that there is not sufficient statistical evidence to reject it. **Use of the term *accept,* instead of *do not reject,* has become standard. It means simply that when sample data do not cause us to reject a null hypothesis, we behave as if that hypothesis is true.**

Selecting a Significance Level

Trade-offs when choosing a significance level

There is no single standard or universal level of significance for testing hypotheses. In some instances, a 5 percent level of significance is used. Published research results often test hypotheses at the 1 percent level of significance. It is possible to test a hypothesis at *any* level of significance. But remember that our choice of the minimum standard for an acceptable probability, or the significance level, is also the risk we assume of rejecting a null hypothesis when it is true. **The higher the significance level we use for testing a hypothesis, the higher the probability of rejecting a null hypothesis when it is true.**

Examining this concept, we refer to Figure 8-4. Here we have illustrated a hypothesis test at three different significance levels: 0.01, 0.10, and 0.50. Also, we have indicated the location of the same sample mean $\bar{x}$ on each distribution. In parts *a* and *b,* we would accept the null hypothesis that the population mean is equal to the hypothesized value. But notice that in part *c,* we would reject this same null hypothesis. Why? Our significance level there of 0.50 is so high that we would rarely accept the null hypothesis when it is *not* true but, at the same time, often reject it when it *is* true.

Type I and Type II Errors

Type I and *Type II errors* defined

Statisticians use specific definitions and symbols for the concept illustrated in Figure 8-4. Rejecting a null hypothesis when it is true is called a *Type I error,* and its probability (which, as we have seen, is also the significance level of the test) is symbolized α (*alpha*). Alternatively, accepting a null hypothesis when it is false is called a *Type II error,* and its

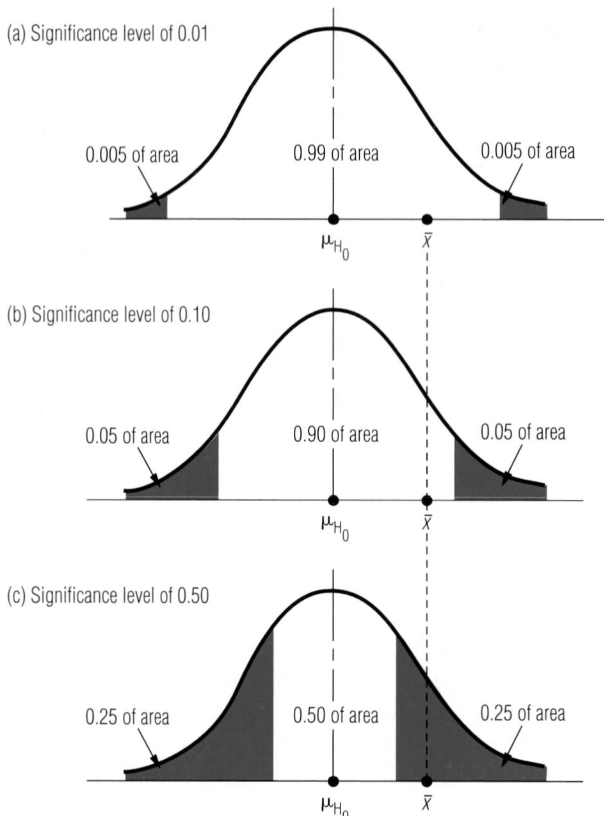

FIGURE 8-4

Three different levels of significance

probability is symbolized β (*beta*). There is a trade-off between these two errors: The probability of making one type of error can be reduced only if we are willing to increase the probability of making the other type of error. Notice in part *c*, Figure 8-4, that our acceptance region is quite small (0.50 of the area under the curve). With an acceptance region this small, we will rarely accept a null hypothesis when it is not true, but as a cost of being this sure, we will often reject a null hypothesis when it is true. Put another way, in order to get a low β, we will have to put up with a high α. To deal with this trade-off in personal and professional situations, decision makers decide the appropriate level of significance by examining the costs or penalties attached to both types of errors.

Preference for a Type I error

Suppose that making a Type I error (rejecting a null hypothesis when it is true) involves the time and trouble of reworking a batch of chemicals that should have been accepted. At the same time, making a Type II error (accepting a null hypothesis when it is false) means taking a chance that an entire group of users of this chemical compound will be poisoned. Obviously, the management of this company will prefer a Type I error to a Type II error and, as a result, will set very high levels of significance in its testing to get low βs.

Preference for a Type II error

Suppose, on the other hand, that making a Type I error involves disassembling an entire engine at the factory, but making a Type II error involves relatively inexpensive warranty repairs by the dealers. Then the manufacturer is more likely to prefer a Type II error and will set lower significance levels in its testing.

Deciding Which Distribution to Use in Hypothesis Testing

Selecting the correct distribution before the test

After deciding what level of significance to use, our next task in hypothesis testing is to determine the appropriate probability distribution. We have a choice between the normal distribution, Appendix Table 1, and the *t* distribution, Appendix Table 2. The rules for choosing the appropriate distribution are similar to those we encountered in Chapter 7 on estimation. Table 8-1 summarizes when to use the normal and *t* distributions in making tests of means. Later in this chapter, we shall examine the distributions appropriate for testing hypotheses about proportions.

Use of the finite population multiplier

Remember one more rule when testing the hypothesized value of a mean. As in estimation, use the *finite population multiplier* whenever the population is finite in size, sampling is done without replacement, and the sample is more than 5 percent of the population.

Two-Tailed and One-Tailed Tests of Hypotheses

Description of a two-tailed hypothesis test

In the tests of hypothesized population means that follow, we shall illustrate two-tailed tests and one-tailed tests. These new terms need a word of explanation. A *two-tailed test* of a hypothesis will reject the null hypothesis if the sample mean is significantly higher than *or* lower than the hypothesized population mean. Thus, in a two-tailed test, there are *two* rejection regions. This is illustrated in Figure 8-5.

A two-tailed test is appropriate when the null hypothesis is $\mu = \mu_{H_0}$ (μ_{H_0} being some specified value) and the alternative hypothesis is $\mu \neq \mu_{H_0}$. Assume that a manufacturer of lightbulbs wants to produce bulbs with a mean life of $\mu = \mu_{H_0} = 1{,}000$ hours. If the lifetime is shorter, he will lose customers to his competition; if the lifetime is longer, he will have a very high production cost because the filaments will be excessively thick. In order to see whether his production process is working properly, he takes a sample of the output to test the hypothesis H_0: $\mu = 1{,}000$. Because he does not want to deviate significantly from 1,000 hours *in either direction,* the appropriate alternative hypothesis is H_1: $\mu \neq 1{,}000$, and he uses a two-tailed test. That is, he rejects the null hypothesis if the mean life of bulbs in the sample is *either too far above* 1,000 hours *or too far below* 1,000 hours.

Sometimes a one-tailed test is appropriate

However, there are situations in which a two-tailed test is not appropriate, and we must use a one-tailed test. Consider the case of a wholesaler that buys lightbulbs from the manufacturer discussed earlier. The wholesaler buys bulbs in large lots and does not want to accept a lot of bulbs unless their mean life is at least 1,000 hours. As each shipment arrives, the wholesaler tests a sample to decide whether it should accept the shipment. The company will reject the shipment only if it feels that the mean life is below 1,000 hours. If it

Table 8-1 Conditions for Using the Normal and *t* Distributions in Testing Hypotheses About Means

	When the Population Standard Deviation Is Known	When the Population Standard Deviation Is Not Known
Sample size *n* is larger than 30	Normal distribution, *z* table	Normal distribution, *z* table
Sample size *n* is 30 or less and we assume the population is normal or approximately so	Normal distribution, *z* table	*t* distribution, *t* table

Exercises 8.3

Self-Check Exercises

SC 8-3 For the following cases, specify which probability distribution to use in a hypothesis test:

(a) H_0: $\mu = 27$, H_1: $\mu \neq 27$, $\bar{x} = 33$, $\hat{\sigma} = 4$, $n = 25$.

(b) H_0: $\mu = 98.6$, H_1: $\mu > 98.6$, $\bar{x} = 99.1$, $\sigma = 1.5$, $n = 50$.

(c) H_0: $\mu = 3.5$, H_1: $\mu < 3.5$, $\bar{x} = 2.8$, $\hat{\sigma} = 0.6$, $n = 18$.

(d) H_0: $\mu = 382$, H_1: $\mu \neq 382$, $\bar{x} = 363$, $\sigma = 68$, $n = 12$.

(e) H_0: $\mu = 57$, H_1: $\mu > 57$, $\bar{x} = 65$, $\hat{\sigma} = 12$, $n = 42$.

SC 8-4 Martha Inman, a highway safety engineer, decides to test the load-bearing capacity of a bridge that is 20 years old. Considerable data are available from similar tests on the same type of bridge. Which is appropriate, a one-tailed or a two-tailed test? If the minimum load-bearing capacity of this bridge must be 10 tons, what are the null and alternative hypotheses?

Basic Concepts

■ **8-13** Formulate null and alternative hypotheses to test whether the mean annual snowfall in Buffalo, New York, exceeds 45 inches.

■ **8-14** Describe what the null and alternative hypotheses typically represent in the hypothesis-testing process.

■ **8-15** Define the term *significance level.*

■ **8-16** Define Type I and Type II errors.

■ **8-17** In a trial, the null hypothesis is that an individual is innocent of a certain crime. Would the legal system prefer to commit a Type I or a Type II error with this hypothesis?

■ **8-18** What is the relationship between the significance level of a test and Type I error?

■ **8-19** If our goal is to accept a null hypothesis that $\mu = 36.5$ with 96 percent certainty when it's true, and our sample size is 50, diagram the acceptance and rejection regions for the following alternative hypotheses:

(a) $\mu \neq 36.5$.

(b) $\mu > 36.5$.

(c) $\mu < 36.5$.

■ **8-20** For the following cases, specify which probability distribution to use in a hypothesis test:

(a) H_0: $\mu = 15$, H_1: $\mu \neq 15$, $\bar{x} = 14.8$, $\hat{\sigma} = 3.0$, $n = 35$.

(b) H_0: $\mu = 9.9$, H_1: $\mu \neq 9.9$, $\bar{x} = 10.6$, $\sigma = 2.3$, $n = 16$.

(c) H_0: $\mu = 42$, H_1: $\mu > 42$, $\bar{x} = 44$, $\sigma = 4.0$, $n = 10$.

(d) H_0: $\mu = 148$, H_1: $\mu > 148$, $\bar{x} = 152$, $\hat{\sigma} = 16.4$, $n = 29$.

(e) H_0: $\mu = 8.6$, H_1: $\mu < 8.6$, $\bar{x} = 8.5$, $\hat{\sigma} = 0.15$, $n = 24$.

■ **8-21** Your null hypothesis is that the battery for a heart pacemaker has an average life of 300 days, with the alternative hypothesis being that the battery life is more than 300 days. You are the quality control engineer for the battery manufacturer.

(a) Would you rather make a Type I or a Type II error?

(b) Based on your answer to part (a), should you use a high or a low significance level?

■ **8-22** Under what conditions is it appropriate to use a one-tailed test? A two-tailed test?

■ **8-23** If you have decided that a one-tailed test is the appropriate test to use, how do you decide whether it should be a lower-tailed test or an upper-tailed test?

Applications

■ **8-24** The statistics department installed energy-efficient lights, heaters, and air conditioners last year. Now they want to determine whether the average monthly energy usage has decreased. Should they perform a one- or two-tailed test? If their previous average monthly energy usage was 3,124 kilowatt hours, what are the null and alternative hypotheses?

■ **8-25** Dr. Ross Darrow believes that nicotine in cigarettes causes cigarette smokers to have higher daytime heart rates on average than do nonsmokers. He also believes that smokers crave the nicotine in cigarettes rather than just smoking for the physical satisfaction of the act and, accordingly, that the average smoker will smoke more cigarettes per day if he or she switches from a brand with a high nicotine content to one with a low level of nicotine.

(a) Suppose Ross knows that nonsmokers have an average daytime heart rate of 78 beats per minute. What are the appropriate null and alternative hypotheses for testing his first belief?

(b) For the past 3 months, he has been observing a sample of 48 individuals who smoke an average of 15 high-nicotine cigarettes per day. He has just switched them to a brand with a low nicotine content. State null and alternative hypotheses for testing his second belief.

Worked-Out Answers to Self-Check Exercises

SC 8-3 (a) *t* with 24 df. (b) Normal. (c) *t* with 17 df.
(d) Normal. (e) *t* with 41 df (so we use the normal table).

SC 8-4 The engineer would be interested in whether a bridge of this age could withstand minimum load-bearing capacities necessary for safety purposes. She therefore wants its capacity to be *above* a certain minimum level, so a one-tailed test (specifically an upper-tailed or right-tailed test) would be used. The hypotheses are

$$H_0: \mu = 10 \text{ tons} \qquad H_1: \mu > 10 \text{ tons}$$

8.4 Hypothesis Testing of Means When the Population Standard Deviation Is Known

Two-Tailed Tests of Means: Testing in the Scale of the Original Variable

A manufacturer supplies the rear axles for U.S. Postal Service mail trucks. These axles must be able to withstand 80,000 pounds per square inch in stress tests, but an excessively strong axle raises production costs significantly. Long experience indicates that the standard deviation of the strength of its axles is 4,000 pounds per square inch. The manufacturer selects a sample of 100 axles from production, tests them, and finds that the mean stress capacity of the sample is 79,600 pounds per square inch. Written symbolically, the data in this case are

Setting up the problem symbolically

$$\mu_{H_0} = 80{,}000 \leftarrow \text{Hypothesized value of the population mean}$$

$$\sigma = 4{,}000 \leftarrow \text{Population standard deviation}$$

$$n = 100 \leftarrow \text{Sample size}$$

$$\bar{x} = 79{,}600 \leftarrow \text{Sample mean}$$

If the axle manufacturer uses a significance level (α) of 0.05 in testing, will the axles meet his stress requirements? Symbolically, we can state the problem:

$$H_0\text{: } \mu = 80{,}000 \leftarrow \text{Null hypothesis: The true mean is 80,000 pounds per square inch.}$$

$$H_1\text{: } \mu \neq 80{,}000 \leftarrow \text{Alternative hypothesis: The true mean is not 80,000 pounds per square inch.}$$

$$\alpha = 0.05 \leftarrow \text{Level of significance for testing this hypothesis}$$

Calculating the standard error of the mean

Because we know the population standard deviation, and because the size of the population is large enough to be treated as infinite, we can use the normal distribution in our testing. First, we calculate the standard error of the mean using Equation 6-1:

$$\sigma_{\bar{x}} = \frac{\sigma}{\sqrt{n}} \quad [6\text{-}1]$$

$$= \frac{4{,}000}{\sqrt{100}}$$

$$= \frac{4{,}000}{10}$$

$$= 400 \text{ pounds per square inch} \leftarrow \text{Standard error of the mean}$$

Illustrating the problem

Determining the limits of the acceptance region

Figure 8-8 illustrates this problem, showing the significance level of 0.05 as the two shaded regions that each contain 0.025 of the area. The 0.95 acceptance region contains two equal areas of 0.475 each. From the normal distribution table (Appendix Table 1), we can see that the appropriate z value for 0.475 of the area under the curve is 1.96. Now we can determine the limits of the acceptance region:

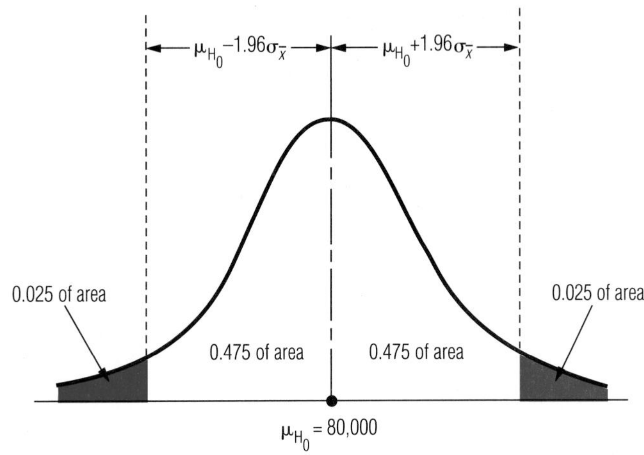

FIGURE 8-8

Two-tailed hypothesis test at the 0.05 significance level

$$\mu_{H_0} + 1.96\sigma_{\bar{x}} = 80{,}000 + 1.96(400)$$
$$= 80{,}000 + 784$$
$$= 80{,}784 \text{ pounds per square inch} \leftarrow \text{Upper limit}$$

and

$$\mu_{H_0} - 1.96\sigma_{\bar{x}} = 80{,}000 - 1.96(400)$$
$$= 80{,}000 - 784$$
$$= 79{,}216 \text{ pounds per square inch} \leftarrow \text{Lower limit}$$

Interpreting the results

Note that we have defined the limits of the acceptance region (80,784 and 79,216) and the sample mean (79,600), and illustrated them in Figure 8-9 in the scale of the original variable (pounds per square inch). In a moment, we'll show you another way to define the limits of the acceptance region and the value of the sample mean. Obviously, the sample mean lies within the acceptance region; the manufacturer should accept the null hypothesis because there is no significant difference between the hypothesized mean of 80,000 and the

FIGURE 8-9

Two-tailed hypothesis test at the 0.05 significance level, showing the acceptance region and the sample mean

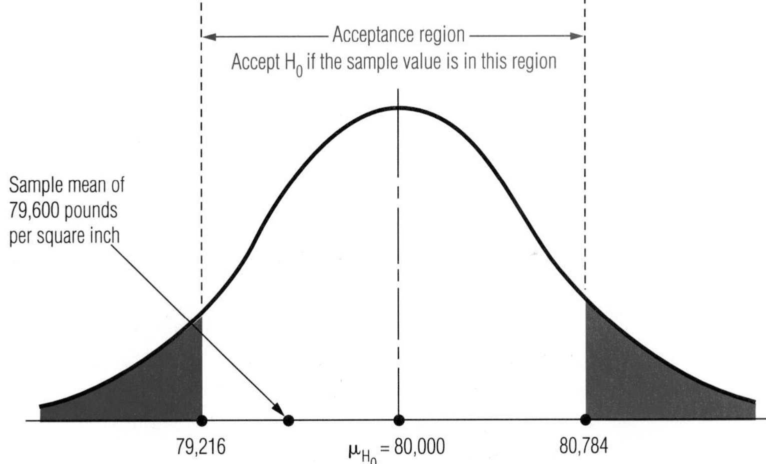

observed mean of the sample axles. On the basis of this sample, the manufacturer should accept the production run as meeting the stress requirements.

Hypothesis Testing Using the Standardized Scale

In the hypothesis test we just completed, two numbers were needed to make our decision: an *observed value* computed from the sample, and a *critical value* defining the boundary between the acceptance and rejection regions. Let's look carefully at how we obtained that critical value: After establishing our significance level of $\alpha = 0.05$, we looked in Appendix Table 1—the standard normal probability distribution—to find that ± 1.96 were the z values that left 0.025 of probability in each tail of the distribution.

Recall our discussion of standardizing normal variables in Chapter 5 (pp. 262–267): Instead of measuring the variable in its original units, the standardized variable z tells how many standard deviations above ($z > 0$) or below ($z < 0$) the mean our observation falls. So there are two different scales of measurement we are using, the original scale, or *raw scale,* and the *standardized scale.* Figure 8-10 repeats Figure 8-9, but includes both scales. Notice that our sample mean of 79,600 pounds is given on the raw scale, but that the critical z values of ± 1.96 are given on the standardized scale. **Because these two numbers are given on two different scales, we cannot compare them directly when we test our hypotheses.** ***We must convert one of them to the scale of the other.***

Converting the observed value to the standardized scale

We did our hypothesis testing on the original scale by converting the critical z values of ± 1.96 to critical values of $\bar{x}$ on the original scale. Then because the observed value of $\bar{x}$ (79,600) fell between the lower and upper limits of the acceptance region (79,216 and 80,784), we accepted the null hypothesis. **Instead of converting the critical z values to the original scale to get numbers directly comparable to the observed value of $\bar{x}$, we could have converted our observed value of $\bar{x}$ to the standardized scale, using Equation 6-2, to get an observed z value, a number directly comparable to the critical z values:**

FIGURE 8-10 Two-tailed hypothesis test at the 0.05 significance level, showing the acceptance region and the sample mean on both raw and standardized scales

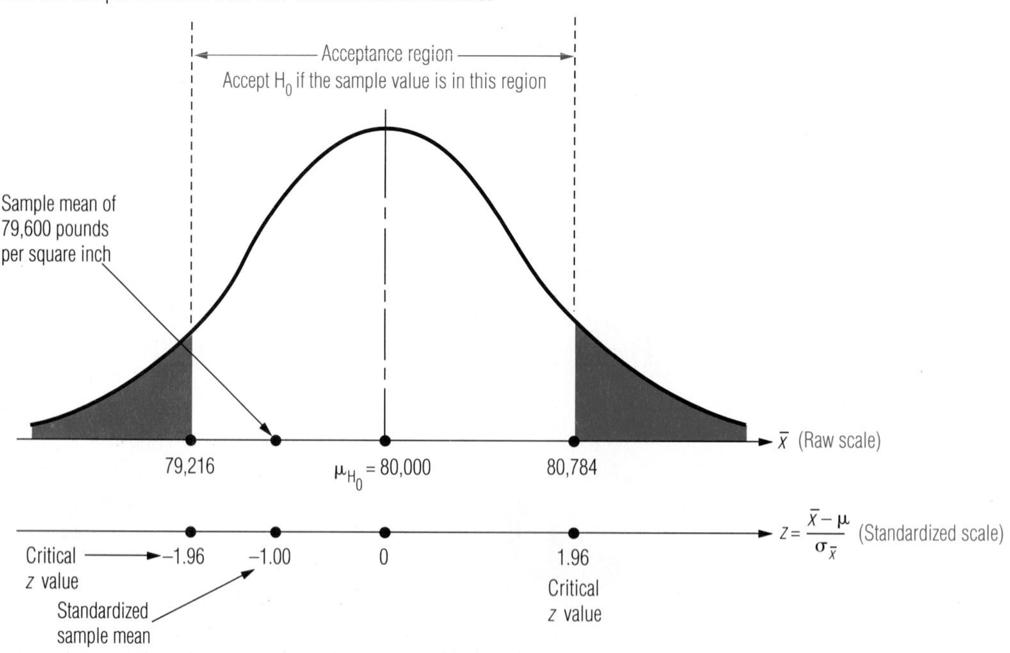

$$z = \frac{\bar{x} - \mu_{H_0}}{\sigma_{\bar{x}}} \quad [6\text{-}2]$$

$$= \frac{79{,}600 - 80{,}000}{400}$$

$$= -1.00$$

The standard error of the mean from Equation 6-1 → 400

The sample mean is one standard error below the population mean → −1.00

In Figure 8-10, we have also illustrated this observed value on the standardized scale. Notice that it falls between the ±1.96 lower and upper limits of the acceptance region on this scale. Once again, we conclude that H_0 should be accepted: The manufacturer should accept the production run as meeting the stress requirements.

How do the two methods differ?

What is the difference between the two methods we have just used to test our hypothesis? Only that we define the units (or scale of measurement) differently in each method. **However, the two methods will always lead to the same conclusions.** Some people are more comfortable using the scale of the original variable; others prefer to use the standardized scale we just explained. The output from most computer statistical packages uses the standardized scale. For the remainder of this chapter and in Chapter 9, we'll test hypotheses using the standardized scale. Our suggestion: Use the method that's more comfortable for you.

The Five-Step Process for Hypothesis Testing Using the Standardized Scale

Table 8-2 summarizes the five-step process that we will use in the remainder of this chapter and throughout Chapter 9 to test hypotheses.

One-Tailed Test of Means

For a one-tailed test of a mean, suppose a hospital uses large quantities of packaged doses of a particular drug. The individual dose of this drug is 100 cubic centimeters (100 cc). The action of the drug is such that the body will harmlessly pass off excessive doses. On the other hand, insufficient doses do not produce the desired medical effect, and they interfere with patient treatment. The hospital has purchased this drug from the same manufacturer for a number of years and knows that the population standard deviation is 2 cc. The hospital inspects 50 doses of this drug at random from a very large shipment and finds the mean of these doses to be 99.75 cc.

Table 8-2 Summary of the Five-Step Process

Step	Action
1.	Decide whether this is a two-tailed or a one-tailed test. State your hypotheses. Select a level of significance appropriate for this decision.
2.	Decide which distribution (t or z) is appropriate (see Table 8-1) and find the *critical value(s)* for the chosen level of significance from the appropriate table.
3.	Calculate the *standard error of the sample statistic.* Use the standard error to convert the observed value of the sample statistic to a standardized value.
4.	Sketch the distribution and mark the position of the standardized sample value and the critical value(s) for the test.
5.	Compare the value of the standardized sample statistic with the critical value(s) for this test and interpret the result.

$$\mu_{H_0} = 100 \leftarrow \text{Hypothesized value of the population mean}$$

$$\sigma = 2 \leftarrow \text{Population standard deviation}$$

$$n = 50 \leftarrow \text{Sample size}$$

$$\bar{x} = 99.75 \leftarrow \text{Sample mean}$$

If the hospital sets a 0.10 significance level and asks us whether the dosages in this shipment are too small, how can we find the answer?

Step 1: State your hypotheses, type of test, and significance level

To begin, we can state the problem symbolically:

$$H_0\text{: } \mu = 100 \leftarrow \text{Null hypothesis: The mean of the shipment's dosages is 100 cc}$$

$$H_1\text{: } \mu < 100 \leftarrow \text{Alternative hypothesis: The mean is less than 100 cc}$$

$$\alpha = 0.10 \leftarrow \text{Level of significance for testing this hypothesis}$$

Step 2: Choose the appropriate distribution and find the critical value

Because we know the population standard deviation, and n is larger than 30, we can use the normal distribution. From Appendix Table 1, we can determine that the value of z for 40 percent of the area under the curve is 1.28, so the critical value for our *lower-tailed* test is -1.28.

The hospital wishes to know whether the actual dosages are 100 cc or whether, in fact, the dosages are too small. The hospital must determine that the dosages are *more* than a certain amount, or it must reject the shipment. This is a *left-tailed* test, which we have shown graphically in Figure 8-11. Notice that the colored region corresponds to the 0.10 significance level. Also notice that the acceptance region consists of 40 percent on the left side of the distribution *plus* the entire right side (50 percent), for a total area of 90 percent.

Step 3: Compute the standard error and standardize the sample statistic

Now we can calculate the standard error of the mean, using the known population standard deviation and Equation 6-1 (because the population size is large enough to be considered infinite):

$$\sigma_{\bar{x}} = \frac{\sigma}{\sqrt{n}} \tag{6-1}$$

$$= \frac{2}{\sqrt{50}}$$

$$= \frac{2}{7.07}$$

$$= 0.2829 \text{ cc} \leftarrow \text{Standard error of the mean}$$

Next we use Equation 6-2 to *standardize* the sample mean, $\bar{x}$, by subtracting μ_{H_0}, the hypothesized mean, and dividing by $\sigma_{\bar{x}}$, the standard error of the mean.

$$z = \frac{\bar{x} - \mu_{H_0}}{\sigma_{\bar{x}}} \tag{6-2}$$

$$= \frac{99.75 - 100}{0.2829}$$

$$= -0.88$$

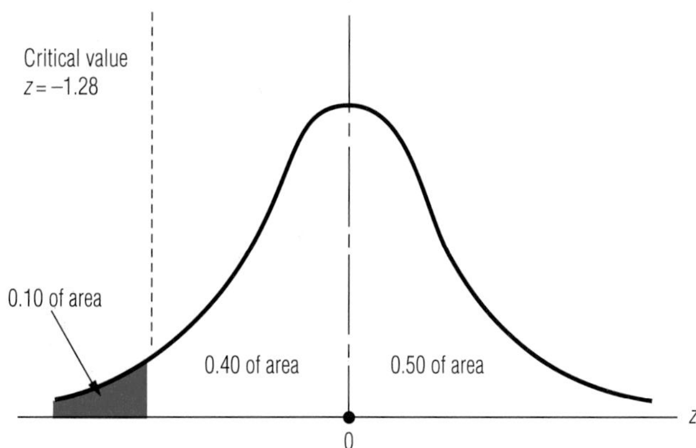

FIGURE 8-11

Left-tailed hypothesis test at the 0.10 significance level

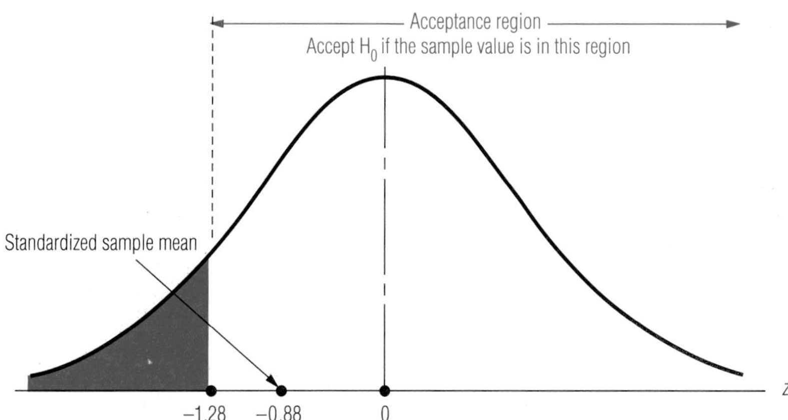

FIGURE 8-12

Left-tailed hypothesis test at the 0.10 significance level, showing the acceptance region and the standardized sample mean

Step 4: Sketch the distribution and mark the sample value and the critical value

Placing the standardized value on the z scale shows that this sample mean falls well within the acceptance region, as shown in Figure 8-12.

Step 5: Interpret the result

Therefore, the hospital should accept the null hypothesis because the observed mean of the sample is not significantly lower than our hypothesized mean of 100 cc. On the basis of this sample of 50 doses, the hospital should conclude that the doses in the shipment are sufficient.

HINTS & ASSUMPTIONS

There are a lot of managerial situations that call for a one-tailed test. For example, a concert promoter is interested in attracting enough fans to *break even or more.* If he fills up the coliseum and has to turn away customers, that adds to the prestige of the event but costs him nothing. But failing to attract enough customers can lead to financial problems. He would set up a one-tailed test worded as "greater than or equal to 10,000 fans" (if 10,000 is his break-even point). A water district that is designing pressure limits in its supply system has quite another perspective. If the pressure is too low, customers are inconvenienced and some cannot get an adequate water supply. If the pressure is too high, pipes and hoses can burst. The water engineer is interested in keeping the water pressure *close to a* certain value and would use a two-tailed test. Hint: If the question to be answered is worded as *less than, more than, less than or equal to,* or *more than or equal to,* a one-tailed test is appropriate. If the question concerns *different from* or *changed from,* use a two-tailed test.

Exercises 8.4

Self-Check Exercises

SC 8-5 Hinton Press hypothesizes that the average life of its largest web press is 14,500 hours. They know that the standard deviation of press life is 2,100 hours. From a sample of 25 presses, the company finds a sample mean of 13,000 hours. At a 0.01 significance level, should the company conclude that the average life of the presses is less than the hypothesized 14,500 hours?

SC 8-6 American Theaters knows that a certain hit movie ran an average of 84 days in each city, and the corresponding standard deviation was 10 days. The manager of the southeastern district was interested in comparing the movie's popularity in his region with that in all of American's other theaters. He randomly chose 75 theaters in his region and found that they ran the movie an average of 81.5 days.

(a) State appropriate hypotheses for testing whether there was a significant difference in the length of the picture's run between theaters in the southeastern district and all of American's other theaters.

(b) At a 1 percent significance level, test these hypotheses.

Applications

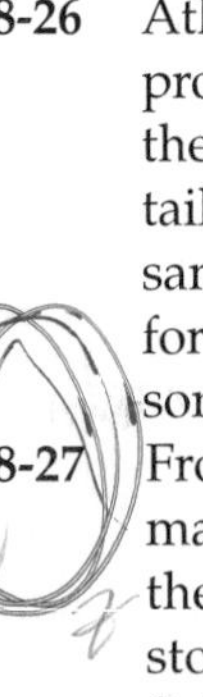

■ **8-26** Atlas Sporting Goods has implemented a special trade promotion for its propane stove and feels that the promotion should result in a price change for the consumer. Atlas knows that before the promotion began, the average retail price of the stove was $44.95, and the standard deviation was $5.75. Atlas samples 25 of its retailers after the promotion begins and finds the mean price for the stoves is now $42.95. At a 0.02 significance level, does Atlas have reason to believe that the average retail price to the consumer has decreased?

■ **8-27** From 1980 until 1985, the mean price/earnings (P/E) ratio of the approximately 1,800 stocks listed on the New York Stock Exchange was 14.35 and the standard deviation was 9.73. In a sample of 30 randomly chosen NYSE stocks, the mean P/E ratio in 1986 was 11.77. Does this sample present sufficient evidence to conclude (at the 0.05 level of significance) that in 1986 the mean P/E ratio for NYSE stocks had changed from its earlier value?

■ **8-28** Generally Electric has developed a new bulb whose design specifications call for a light output of 960 lumens compared to an earlier model that produced only 750 lumens. The company's data indicate that the standard deviation of light output for this type of bulb is 18.4 lumens. From a sample of 20 new bulbs, the testing committee found an average light output of 954 lumens per bulb. At a 0.05 significance level, can Generally Electric conclude that its new bulb is producing the specified 960 lumen output?

■ **8-29** Maxwell's Hot Chocolate is concerned about the effect of the recent year-long coffee advertising campaign on hot chocolate sales. The average weekly hot chocolate sales two years ago was 984.7 pounds and the standard deviation was 72.6 pounds. Maxwell's has randomly selected 30 weeks from the past year and found average sales of 912.1 pounds.

(a) State appropriate hypotheses for testing whether hot chocolate sales have decreased.

(b) At the 2 percent significance level, test these hypotheses.

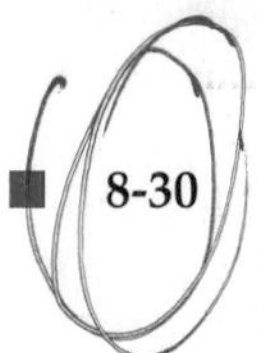

■ **8-30** The average commission charged by full-service brokerage firms on a sale of common stock is \$144, and the standard deviation is \$52. Joel Freelander has taken a random sample of 121 trades by his clients and determined that they paid an average commission of \$151. At a 0.10 significance level, can Joel conclude that his clients' commissions are higher than the industry average?

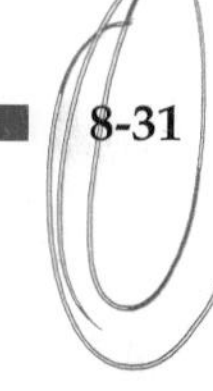

■ **8-31** Each day, the United States Customs Service has historically intercepted about \$28 million in contraband goods being smuggled into the country, with a standard deviation of \$16 million per day. On 64 randomly chosen days in 1992, the U.S. Customs Service intercepted an average of \$30.3 million in contraband goods. Does this sample indicate (at a 5 percent level of significance) that the Customs Commissioner should be concerned that smuggling has increased above its historic level?

■ **8-32** Before the 1973 oil embargo and subsequent increases in the price of crude oil, gasoline usage in the United States had grown at a seasonally adjusted rate of 0.57 percent per month, with a standard deviation of 0.10 percent per month. In 15 randomly chosen months between 1975 and 1985, gasoline usage grew at an average rate of only 0.33 percent per month. At a 0.01 level of significance, can you conclude that the growth in the use of gasoline had decreased as a result of the embargo and its consequences?

■ **8-33** The Bay City Bigleaguers, a semiprofessional baseball team, have the player who led the league in batting average for many years. For the past several years, Joe Carver's batting average has had a mean of .343, and a standard deviation of .018. This year, however, Joe's average was only .306. Joe is renegotiating his contract for next year, and the salary he will be able to obtain is highly dependent on his ability to convince the team's owner that his batting average this year was not significantly worse than in previous years. If the owner is willing to use a 0.02 significance level, will Joe's salary be cut next year?

Worked-Out Answers to Self-Check Exercises

■ **SC 8-5** $\sigma = 2{,}100 \qquad n = 25 \qquad \bar{x} = 13{,}000$

$H_0\colon \mu = 14{,}500 \qquad H_1\colon \mu < 14{,}500 \qquad \alpha = 0.01$

The lower limit of the acceptance region is $z = -2.33$, or

$$\bar{x} = \mu_{H_0} - z\sigma/\sqrt{n} = 14{,}500 - \frac{2.33(2{,}100)}{\sqrt{25}} = 13{,}521.4 \text{ hours}$$

$$\text{Because the observed } z \text{ value } = \frac{\bar{x} - \mu_{H_0}}{\sigma/\sqrt{n}} = \frac{13{,}000 - 14{,}500}{2{,}100/\sqrt{25}} = -3.57 < -2.33$$

(or $\bar{x} < 13{,}521.4$), we should reject H_0. The average life is significantly less than the hypothesized value.

■ **SC 8-6** $\sigma = 10 \qquad n = 75 \qquad \bar{x} = 81.5$

$H_0\colon \mu = 84 \qquad H_1\colon \mu \neq 84 \qquad \alpha = 0.01$

The limits of the acceptance region are $z = \pm 2.58$, or

$$\bar{x} = \mu_{H_0} \pm z\sigma/\sqrt{n} = 84 \pm \frac{2.58(10)}{\sqrt{75}} = (81.02, 86.98) \text{ days}$$

Because the observed z value $= \dfrac{\bar{x} - \mu_{H_0}}{\sigma/\sqrt{n}} = \dfrac{81.5 - 84}{10/\sqrt{75}} = -2.17$, it and $\bar{x}$ are in the acceptance region, so we do not reject H_0. The length of run in the southeast is not significantly different from the length of run in other regions.

8.5 Measuring the Power of a Hypothesis Test

What should a good hypothesis test do?

Now that we have considered two examples of hypothesis testing, a step back is appropriate to discuss what a good hypothesis test *should do*. Ideally, α and β (the probabilities of Type I and Type II errors) should both be small. Recall that a Type I error occurs when we reject a null hypothesis that is true, and that α (the significance level of the test) is the probability of making a Type I error. In other words, once we decide on the significance level, there is nothing else we can do about α. A Type II error occurs when we accept a null hypothesis that is false; the probability of a Type II error is β. What can we say about β?

Meaning of β and $1 - \beta$

Suppose the null hypothesis *is* false. Then managers would like the hypothesis test to reject it all the time. Unfortunately, hypothesis tests cannot be foolproof; sometimes when the null hypothesis is false, a test does not reject it, and thus a Type II error is made. When the null hypothesis is false, μ (the *true* population mean) does not equal μ_{H_0} (the *hypothesized* population mean); instead, μ equals some other value. For each possible value of μ for which the alternative hypothesis is true, there is a different probability (β) of incorrectly accepting the null hypothesis. Of course, we would like this β (the probability of accepting a null hypothesis when it is false) to be as small as possible, or, equivalently, we would like $1 - \beta$ (the probability of rejecting a null hypothesis when it is false) to be as large as possible.

Interpreting the values of $1 - \beta$

Because rejecting a null hypothesis when it is false is exactly what a good test should do, a high value of $1 - \beta$ (something near 1.0) means the test is working quite well (it is rejecting the null hypothesis when it is false); a low value of $1 - \beta$ (something near 0.0) means that the test is working very poorly (it's not rejecting the null hypothesis when it is false). Because the value of $1 - \beta$ is the measure of how well the test is working, it is known as the power of the test. If we plot the values of $1 - \beta$ for each value of μ for which the alternative hypothesis is true, the resulting curve is known as a *power curve*.

Computing the values of $1 - \beta$

In part *a* of Figure 8-13, we reproduce the left-tailed test from Figure 8-11, but now we are looking at the raw scale. In Figure 8-13(b), we show the power curve associated with this test. Computing the values of $1 - \beta$ to plot the power curve is not difficult; three such points are shown in Figure 8-13(b). Recall that with this test we were deciding whether to accept a drug shipment. Our test dictated that we should reject the null hypothesis if the standardized sample mean is less than -1.28, that is, if sample mean dosage is less than $100.00 - 1.28\ (0.2829)$, or 99.64 cc.

Consider point *C* on the power curve in Figure 8-13(b). The population mean dosage is 99.42 cc. Given that the population mean is 99.42 cc, we must compute the probability that the mean of a random sample of 50 doses from this population will be less than 99.64 cc (the point below which we decided to reject the null hypothesis). Now look at Figure 8-13(c). Earlier we computed the standard error of the mean to be 0.2829 cc, so 99.64 cc is $(99.64 - 99.42)/0.2829$, or 0.78 standard error above 99.42 cc. Using Appendix Table 1, we can see that the probability of observing a sample mean less than 99.64 cc and thus rejecting the null hypothesis is 0.7823, the colored area in Figure 8-13(c). Thus, the power of the test $(1 - \beta)$ at $\mu = 99.42$ is 0.7823. This simply means that if $\mu = 99.42$, the probability that this test will reject the null hypothesis when it is false is 0.7823.

Interpreting a point on the power curve

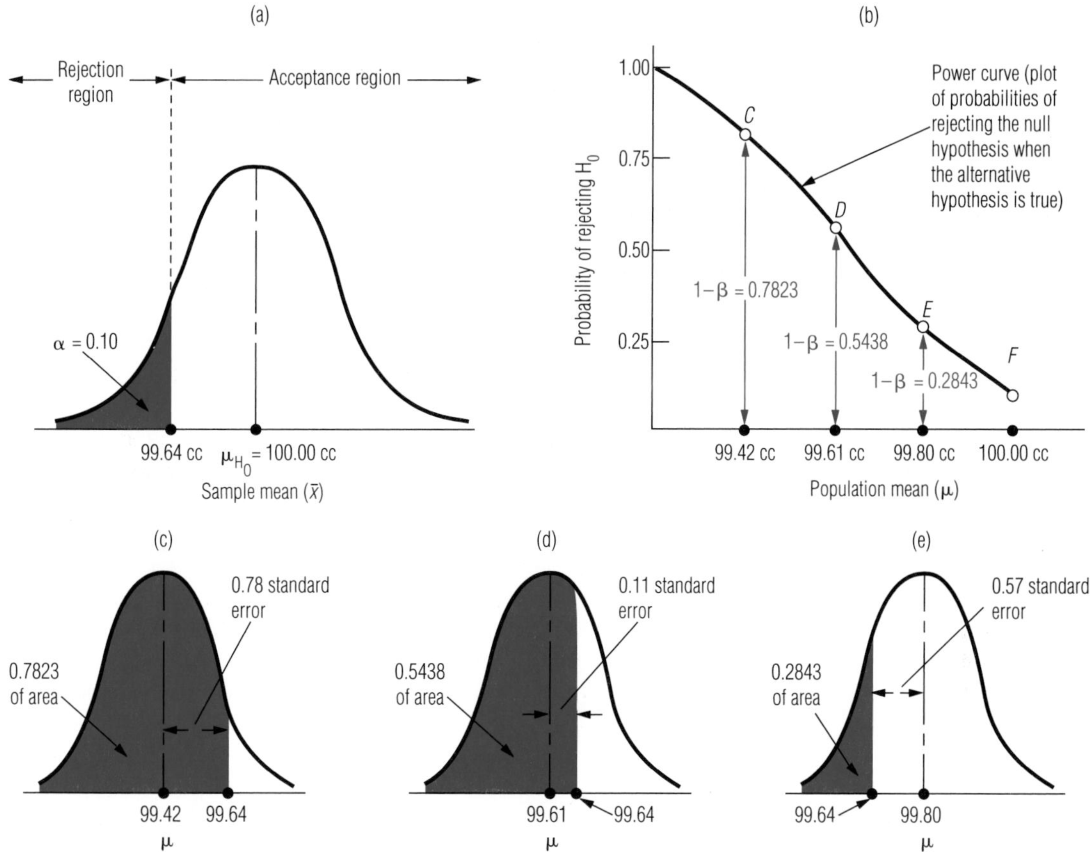

FIGURE 8-13 Left-tailed hypothesis test, associated power curve, and three values of μ.

Now look at point *D* in Figure 8-13(b). For this population mean dosage of 99.61 cc, what is the probability that the mean of a random sample of 50 doses from this population will be less than 99.64 cc and thus cause the test to reject the null hypothesis? Look at Figure 8-13(d). Here we see that 99.64 is (99.64 − 99.61)/0.2829, or 0.11 standard error above 99.61 cc. Using Appendix Table 1 again, we can see that the probability of observing a sample mean less than 99.64 cc and thus rejecting the null hypothesis is 0.5438, the colored area in Figure 8-13(d). Thus, the power of the test (1 − β) at μ = 99.61 cc is 0.5438.

Termination point of the power curve

Using the same procedure at point *E*, we find the power of the test at μ = 99.80 cc is 0.2843; this is illustrated as the colored area in Figure 8-13(e). The values of 1 − β continue to decrease to the right of point *E*. How low do they get? As the population mean gets closer and closer to 100.00 cc, the power of the test (1 − β) must get closer and closer to the probability of rejecting the null hypothesis when the population mean is exactly 100.00 cc. And we know *that* probability is nothing but the significance level of the test—in this case, 0.10. Thus, the curve terminates at point *F*, which lies at a height of 0.10 directly over the population mean.

Interpreting the power curve

What does our power curve in Figure 8-13(b) tell us? Just that as the shipment becomes less satisfactory (as the doses in the shipment become smaller), our test is more powerful (it has a greater probability of recognizing that the shipment is unsatisfactory). It also shows us, however, that because of sampling error, when the dosage is only slightly less than 100.00 cc, the power of the test to recognize this situation is quite low. Thus, if having *any* dosage below 100.00 cc is completely unsatisfactory, the test we have been discussing would not be appropriate.

HINTS & ASSUMPTIONS

Of course, we'd always like to use the hypothesis test with the greatest power. But we also know that a certain proportion of the time, all hypothesis tests will fail to reject the null hypothesis when it is false or accept it when it's true (that's statistical language that really means that when the test does fail, it will persuade us that things haven't changed when in fact they have, or persuade us that things have changed when they really haven't). That's just the price we pay for using sampling in hypothesis testing. The failure of a test to perform perfectly is due to sampling error. The only way to avoid such error is to examine everything in the population and that is either physically impossible or too expensive.

Exercises 8.5

Self-Check Exercises

SC 8-7 See Exercise 8-32. Compute the power of the test for $\mu = 0.50$, 0.45, and 0.40 percent per month.

SC 8-8 In Exercise 8-32, what happens to the power of the test for $\mu = 0.50$, 0.45, and 0.40 percent per month if the significance level is changed to 0.04?

Applications

■ **8-34** See Exercise 8-31. Compute the power of the test for μ = \$28, \$29, and \$30 million.

■ **8-35** See Exercise 8-30. Compute the power of the test for μ = \$140, \$160, and \$175.

■ **8-36** In Exercise 8-31, what happens to the power of the test for μ = \$28, \$29, and \$30 million if the significance level is changed to 0.02?

■ **8-37** In Exercise 8-30, what happens to the power of the test for μ = \$140, \$160, and \$175 if the significance level is changed to 0.05?

Worked-Out Answers to Self-Check Exercises

■ **SC 8-7** From Exercise 8-32, we have $\sigma = 0.10$, $n = 15$, H_0: $\mu = 0.57$, H_1: $\mu < 0.57$. At $\alpha = 0.01$, the lower limit of the acceptance region is

$$\mu_{H_0} - 2.33\,\sigma/\sqrt{n} = 0.57 - 2.33(0.10)/\sqrt{15} = 0.510$$

(a) At $\mu = 0.50$, the power of the test is

$$P(\bar{x} < 0.510) = P(z < \frac{0.510 - 0.50)}{0.10/\sqrt{15}} = P(z < 0.39) = 0.5 + 0.1517 = 0.6517$$

(b) At $\mu = 0.45$, the power of the test is

$$P(\bar{x} < 0.510) = P(z < \frac{0.510 - 0.45)}{0.10/\sqrt{15}} = P(z < 2.32) = 0.5 + 0.4898 = 0.9898$$

(c) At $\mu = 0.40$, the power of the test is

$$P(\bar{x} < 0.510) = P(z < \frac{0.510 - 0.40)}{0.10/\sqrt{15}} = P(z < 4.26) = 1.0000$$

■ **SC 8-8** At $\alpha = 0.04$, the lower limit of the acceptance region is

$$\mu_{H_0} - 1.75\sigma/\sqrt{n} = 0.57 - 1.75(0.10)/\sqrt{15} = 0.525$$

(a) At $\mu = 0.50$, the power of the test is

$$P(\bar{x} < 0.525) = P\left(z < \frac{0.525 - 0.50}{0.10/\sqrt{15}}\right) = P(z < 0.97) = 0.5 + 0.3340 = 0.8340$$

(b) At $\mu = 0.45$, the power of the test is

$$P(\bar{x} < 0.525) = P\left(z < \frac{0.525 - 0.45}{0.10/\sqrt{15}}\right) = P(z < 2.90) = 0.5 + 0.4981 = 0.9981$$

(c) At $\mu = 0.40$, the power of the test is

$$P(\bar{x} < 0.525) = P\left(z < \frac{0.525 - 0.40}{0.10/\sqrt{15}}\right) = P(z < 4.84) = 1.0000$$

8.6 Hypothesis Testing of Proportions: Large Samples

Two-Tailed Tests of Proportions

Dealing with proportions

In this section, we'll apply what we have learned about tests concerning means to tests for *proportions* (that is, the proportion of occurrences in a population). But before we apply it, we'll review the important conclusions we made about proportions in Chapter 7. First, remember that the binomial is the theoretically correct distribution to use in dealing with proportions. As the sample size increases, the binomial distribution approaches the normal in its characteristics, and we can use the normal distribution to approximate the sampling distribution. Specifically, *np and nq each need to be at least 5* before we can use the normal distribution as a substitute for the binomial.

Consider, as an example, a company that is evaluating the promotability of its employees, that is, determining the proportion whose ability, training, and supervisory experience qualify them for promotion to the next higher level of management. The human resources director tells the president that roughly 80 percent, or 0.8, of the employees in the company are "promotable." The president assembles a special committee to assess the promotability of all employees. This committee conducts in-depth interviews with 150 employees and finds that in its judgment only 70 percent of the sample are qualified for promotion.

$p_{H_0} = 0.8$ ← Hypothesized value of the population proportion of successes (judged promotable, in this case)

$q_{H_0} = 0.2$ ← Hypothesized value of the population proportion of failures (judged not promotable)

$n = 150$ ← Sample size

$\bar{p} = 0.7$ ← Sample proportion of promotables

$\bar{q} = 0.3$ ← Sample proportion judged not promotable

Step 1: State your hypotheses, type of test, and significance level

The president wants to test at the 0.05 significance level the hypothesis that 0.8 of the employees are promotable:

H_0: $p = 0.8$ ← Null hypothesis: 80 percent of the employees are promotable

H_1: $p \neq 0.8$ ← Alternative hypothesis: The proportion of promotable employees is not 80 percent

$\alpha = 0.05$ ← Level of significance for testing the hypothesis

Step 2: Choose the appropriate distribution and find the critical value

In this instance, the company wants to know whether the true proportion is larger or smaller than the hypothesized proportion. Thus, a two-tailed test of a proportion is appropriate, and we have shown it graphically in Figure 8-14. The significance level corresponds to the two colored regions, each containing 0.025 of the area. The acceptance region of 0.95 is illustrated as two areas of 0.475 each. Because np and nq are each larger than 5, we can use the normal approximation of the binomial distribution. From Appendix Table 1, we can determine that the critical value of z for 0.475 of the area under the curve is 1.96.

Step 3: Compute the standard error and standardize the sample statistic

We can calculate the standard error of the proportion, using the hypothesized values of p_{H_0} and q_{H_0} in Equation 7-4:

$$\sigma_{\bar{p}} = \sqrt{\frac{p_{H_0}q_{H_0}}{n}} \qquad [7\text{-}4]$$

$$= \sqrt{\frac{(0.8)(0.2)}{150}}$$

$$= \sqrt{0.0010666}$$

$$= 0.0327 \leftarrow \text{Standard error of the proportion}$$

Next we standardize the sample proportion by dividing the difference between the observed sample proportion, $\bar{p}$, and the hypothesized proportion, p_{H_0}, by the standard error of the proportion.

$$z = \frac{\bar{p} - p_{H_0}}{\sigma_{\bar{p}}}$$

$$= \frac{0.7 - 0.8}{0.0327}$$

$$= -3.06$$

Step 4: Sketch the distribution and mark the sample value and the critical values

By marking the calculated standardized sample proportion, -3.06, on a sketch of the sampling distribution, it is clear that this sample falls outside the region of acceptance, as shown in Figure 8-15.

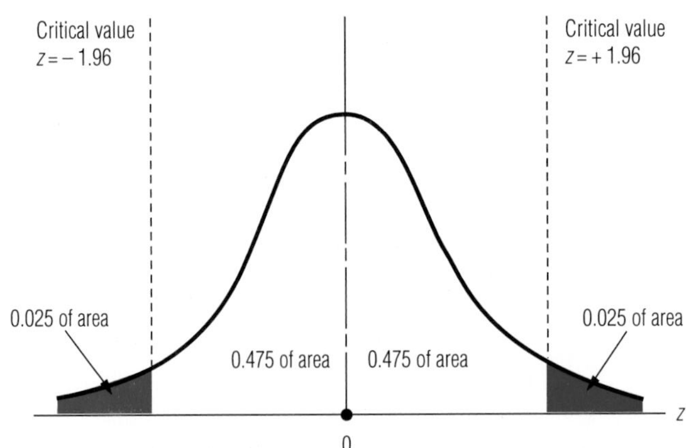

FIGURE 8-14

Two-tailed hypothesis test of a proportion at the 0.05 level of significance

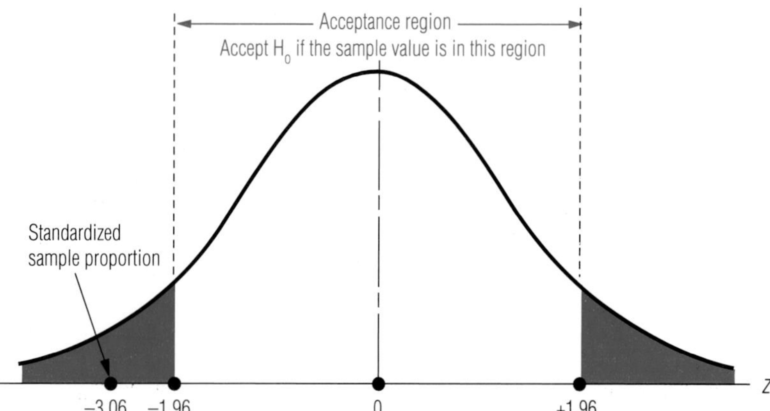

FIGURE 8-15

Two-tailed hypothesis test of a proportion at the 0.05 significance level, showing the acceptance region and the standardized sample proportion

Step 5: Interpret the result

Therefore, in this case, the president should reject the null hypothesis and conclude that there *is* a significant difference between the director of human resources' hypothesized proportion of promotable employees (0.8) and the observed proportion of promotable employees in the sample. From this, he should infer that the true proportion of promotable employees in the entire company is not 80 percent.

One-Tailed Tests of Proportions

A one-tailed test of a proportion is conceptually equivalent to a one-tailed test of a mean, as can be illustrated with this example. A member of a public interest group concerned with environmental pollution asserts at a public hearing that "fewer than 60 percent of the industrial plants in this area are complying with air-pollution standards." Attending this meeting is an official of the Environmental Protection Agency who believes that 60 percent of the plants *are* complying with the standards; she decides to test that hypothesis at the 0.02 significance level.

Step 1: State your hypotheses, type of test, and significance level

$$H_0\colon p = 0.6 \leftarrow \text{Null hypothesis: The proportion of plants complying with the air-pollution standards is 0.6}$$

$$H_1\colon p < 0.6 \leftarrow \text{Alternative hypothesis: The proportion complying with the standards is less than 0.6}$$

$$\alpha = 0.02 \leftarrow \text{Level of significance for testing the hypothesis}$$

The official makes a thorough search of the records in her office. She samples 60 plants from a population of over 10,000 plants and finds that 33 are complying with air-pollution standards. Is the assertion by the member of the public interest group a valid one?

We begin by summarizing the case symbolically:

$$p_{H_0} = 0.6 \leftarrow \text{Hypothesized value of the population proportion that is complying with air-pollution standards}$$

$$q_{H_0} = 0.4 \leftarrow \text{Hypothesized value of the population proportion that is not complying and thus polluting}$$

$$n = 60 \leftarrow \text{Sample size}$$

$$\bar{p} = 33/60, \text{ or } 0.55 \leftarrow \text{Sample proportion complying}$$

$$\bar{q} = 27/60, \text{ or } 0.45 \leftarrow \text{Sample proportion polluting}$$

This is a one-tailed test: The EPA official wonders only whether the actual proportion is less than 0.6. Specifically, this is a left-tailed test. In order to reject the null hypothesis that

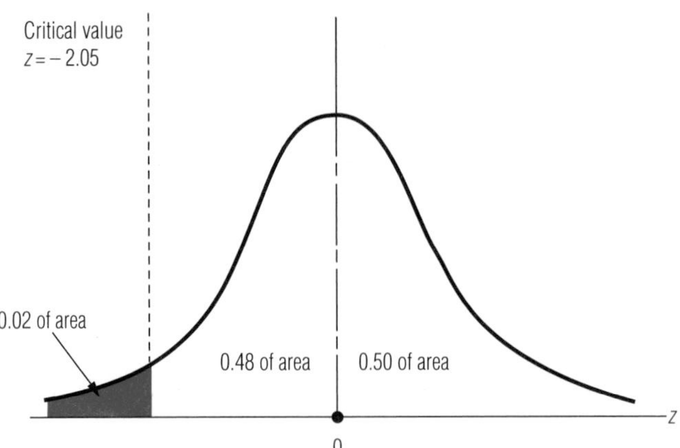

FIGURE 8-16

One-tailed hypothesis test at the 0.02 level of significance

the true proportion of plants in compliance is 60 percent, the EPA representative must accept the alternative hypothesis that fewer than 0.6 have complied. In Figure 8-16, we have shown this hypothesis test graphically.

Step 2: Choose the appropriate distribution and find the critical value

Because *np* and *nq* are each over 5, we can use the normal approximation of the binomial distribution. The critical value of *z* from Appendix Table 1 for 0.48 of the area under the curve is 2.05.

Step 3: Compute the standard error and standardize the sample statistic

Next, we can calculate the standard error of the proportion using the hypothesized population proportion as follows:

$$\sigma_{\bar{p}} = \sqrt{\frac{p_{H_0}q_{H_0}}{n}} \qquad [7\text{-}4]$$

$$= \sqrt{\frac{(0.6)(0.4)}{60}}$$

$$= \sqrt{0.004}$$

$$= 0.0632 \leftarrow \text{Standard error of the proportion}$$

And we standardize the sample proportion by dividing the difference between the observed sample proportion, $\bar{p}$, and the hypothesized proportion, p_{H_0}, by the standard error of the proportion.

$$z = \frac{\bar{p} - p_{H_0}}{\sigma_{\bar{p}}}$$

$$= \frac{0.55 - 0.6}{0.0632}$$

$$= -0.79$$

Step 4: Sketch the distribution and mark the sample value and the critical value

Figure 8-17 illustrates where the sample proportion lies in relation to the critical value, −2.05. Looking at this figure, we can see that the sample proportion lies within the acceptance region. Therefore, the EPA official should accept the null hypothesis that the true proportion of complying plants is 0.6. **Although the observed sample proportion is below 0.6, *it is not significantly below* 0.6; that is, it is not far enough below 0.6 to make us accept the assertion by the member of the public interest group.**

Step 5: Interpret the result

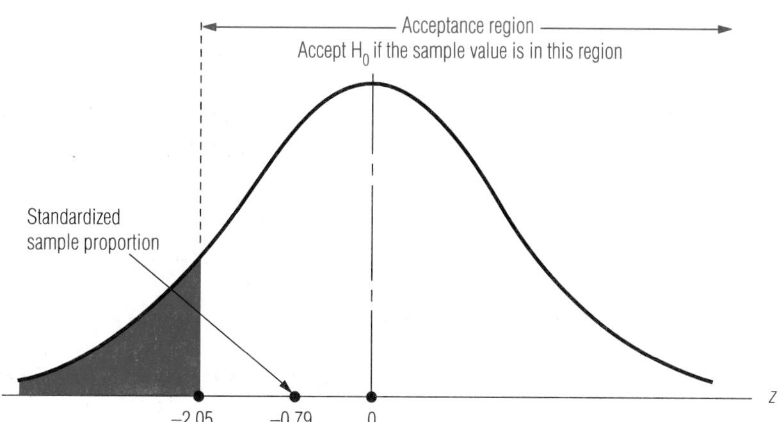

FIGURE 8-17

One-tailed (left-tailed) hypothesis test at the 0.02 significance level, showing the acceptance region and the standardized sample proportion

HINTS & ASSUMPTIONS

Warning: When we're doing hypothesis tests involving proportions, we use the binomial distribution as the sampling distribution, unless np and nq are *both* at least 5. In that case, we can use the normal distribution as an approximation of the binomial without worry. Fortunately, in practice, hypothesis tests about proportions almost always involve sufficiently large samples so that this condition is met. Even when they aren't, the arithmetic of the binomial distribution and the binomial table is not that difficult to use.

Exercises 8.6

Self-Check Exercises

SC 8-9 A ketchup manufacturer is in the process of deciding whether to produce a new extra-spicy brand. The company's marketing-research department used a national telephone survey of 6,000 households and found that the extra-spicy ketchup would be purchased by 335 of them. A much more extensive study made 2 years ago showed that 5 percent of the households would purchase the brand then. At a 2 percent significance level, should the company conclude that there is an increased interest in the extra-spicy flavor?

SC 8-10 Steve Cutter sells Big Blade lawn mowers in his hardware store, and he is interested in comparing the reliability of the mowers he sells with the reliability of Big Blade mowers sold nationwide. Steve knows that only 15 percent of all Big Blade mowers sold nationwide require repairs during the first year of ownership. A sample of 120 of Steve's customers revealed that exactly 22 of them required mower repairs in the first year of ownership. At the 0.02 level of significance, is there evidence that Steve's Big Blade mowers differ in reliability from those sold nationwide?

Applications

■ **8-38** Grant, Inc., a manufacturer of women's dress blouses, knows that its brand is carried in 19 percent of the women's clothing stores east of the Mississippi River. Grant recently sampled 85 women's clothing stores on the West Coast and found that 14.12 percent of the stores carried the brand. At the 0.04 level of significance, is there evidence that Grant has poorer distribution on the West Coast than it does east of the Mississippi?

■ **8-39** From a total of 10,200 loans made by a state employees' credit union in the most recent 5-year period, 350 were sampled to determine what proportion was made to women. This sample showed that 39 percent of the loans were made to women employees. A complete census of loans 5 years ago showed that 41 percent of the borrowers then were women. At a significance level of 0.02, can you conclude that the proportion of loans made to women has changed significantly in the past 5 years?

■ **8-40** Feronetics specializes in the use of gene-splicing techniques to produce new pharmaceutical compounds. It has recently developed a nasal spray containing interferon, which it believes will limit the transmission of the common cold within families. In the general population, 15.1 percent of all individuals will catch a rhinovirus-caused cold once another family member contracts such a cold. The interferon spray was tested on 180 people, one of whose family members subsequently contracted a rhinovirus-caused cold. Only 17 of the test subjects developed similar colds.

(a) At a significance level of 0.05, should Feronetics conclude that the new spray effectively reduces transmission of colds?

(b) What should it conclude at $\alpha = 0.02$?

(c) On the basis of these results, do you think Feronetics should be allowed to market the new spray? Explain.

■ **8-41** Some financial theoreticians believe that the stock market's daily prices constitute a "random walk with positive drift." If this is accurate, then the Dow Jones Industrial Average should show a gain on more than 50 percent of all trading days. If the average increased on 101 of 175 randomly chosen days, what do you think about the suggested theory? Use a 0.01 level of significance.

■ **8-42** MacroSwift estimated last year that 35 percent of potential software buyers were planning to wait to purchase the new operating system, Window Panes, until an upgrade had been released. After an advertising campaign to reassure the public, MacroSwift surveyed 3,000 people and found 950 who were still skeptical. At the 5 percent significance level, can the company conclude the proportion of skeptical people has decreased?

■ **8-43** Rick Douglas, the new manager of Food Barn, is interested in the percentage of customers who are totally satisfied with the store. The previous manager had 86 percent of the customers totally satisfied, and Rick claims the same is true today. Rick sampled 187 customers and found 157 were totally satisfied. At the 1 percent significance level, is there evidence that Rick's claim is valid?

Worked-Out Answers to Self-Check Exercises

■ **SC 8- 9** $n = 6{,}000 \qquad \bar{p} = 335/6{,}000 = 0.05583$

$H_0: p = 0.05 \qquad H_1: p > 0.05 \qquad \alpha = 0.02$

The upper limit of the acceptance region is $z = 2.05$, or

$$\bar{p} = p_{H_0} + z\sqrt{\frac{p_{H_0}q_{H_0}}{n}} = 0.05 + 2.05\sqrt{\frac{0.05(0.95)}{6{,}000}} = 0.05577$$

Because the observed z value $= \dfrac{\bar{p} - p_{H_0}}{\sqrt{p_{H_0}q_{H_0}/n}} = \dfrac{0.05583 - 0.05}{\sqrt{0.05(0.95)/6{,}000}} = 2.07$ > 2.05 (or $\bar{p} > 0.05577$), we should reject H_0 (but just barely). The current interest is significantly greater than the interest of 2 years ago.

■ **SC 8-10** $n = 120 \qquad \bar{p} = 22/120 = 0.1833$

$H_0: p = 0.15 \qquad H_1: p \neq 0.15 \qquad \alpha = 0.02$

The limits of the acceptance region are $z = \pm 2.33$, or

$$\bar{p} = p_{H_0} \pm z\sqrt{\frac{p_{H_0}q_{H_0}}{n}} = 0.15 \pm 2.33\sqrt{\frac{0.15(0.85)}{120}} = (0.0741, 0.2259)$$

Because the observed z value $= \dfrac{\bar{p} - p_{H_0}}{\sqrt{p_{H_0}q_{H_0}/n}} = \dfrac{0.1833 - 0.15}{\sqrt{0.15(0.85)/120}} = 1.02$ < 2.33 (or $\bar{p} = 0.1833$, which is between 0.0741 and 0.2259), we do not reject H_0. Steve's mowers are not significantly different in reliability from those sold nationwide.

8.7 Hypothesis Testing of Means When the Population Standard Deviation Is Not Known

When to use the *t* distribution

When we estimated confidence intervals in Chapter 7, we learned that the difference in size between large and small samples is important when the population standard deviation σ is unknown and must be estimated from the sample standard deviation. If the sample size n is 30 or less and σ is not known, we should use the t distribution. The appropriate t distribution has $n - 1$ degrees of freedom. These rules apply to hypothesis testing, too.

Two-Tailed Tests of Means Using the *t* Distribution

A personnel specialist of a major corporation is recruiting a large number of employees for an overseas assignment. During the testing process, management asks how things are going, and she replies, "Fine. I think the average score on the aptitude test will be around 90." When management reviews 20 of the test results compiled, it finds that the mean score is 84, and the standard deviation of this score is 11.

$$\mu_{H_0} = 90 \leftarrow \text{Hypothesized value of the population mean}$$
$$n = 20 \leftarrow \text{Sample size}$$
$$\bar{x} = 84 \leftarrow \text{Sample mean}$$
$$s = 11 \leftarrow \text{Sample standard deviation}$$

If management wants to test her hypothesis at the 0.10 level of significance, what is the procedure?

Step 1: State your hypotheses, type of test, and significance level

$$H_0\colon \mu = 90 \quad \leftarrow \text{Null hypothesis: the true population mean score is 90}$$
$$H_1\colon \mu \neq 90 \quad \leftarrow \text{Alternative hypothesis: the mean score is not 90}$$
$$\alpha = 0.10 \leftarrow \text{Level of significance for testing this hypothesis}$$

Step 2: Choose the appropriate distribution and find the critical value

Figure 8-18 illustrates this problem graphically. Because management is interested in knowing whether the true mean score is *larger* or *smaller* than the hypothesized score, a *two-tailed test* is the appropriate one to use. The significance level of 0.10 is shown in Figure 8-18 as the two colored areas, each containing 0.05 of the area under the *t* distribution. Because the sample size is 20, the appropriate number of degrees of freedom is 19, that is, 20 − 1. Therefore, we look in the *t* distribution table, Appendix Table 2, under the 0.10 column until we reach the 19 degrees of freedom row. There we find the critical value of *t*, 1.729.

Because the population standard deviation is not known, we must estimate it using the sample standard deviation and Equation 7-1:

$$\hat{\sigma} = s \tag{7-1}$$
$$= 11$$

Step 3: Compute the standard error and standardize the sample statistic

Now we can compute the standard error of the mean. Because we are using $\hat{\sigma}$, an estimate of the population standard deviation, the standard error of the mean will also be an estimate. We can use Equation 7-6, as follows:

$$\hat{\sigma}_{\bar{x}} = \frac{\hat{\sigma}}{\sqrt{n}} \tag{7-6}$$
$$= \frac{11}{\sqrt{20}}$$
$$= \frac{11}{4.47}$$
$$= 2.46 \leftarrow \text{Estimated standard error of the mean}$$

Next we standardize the sample mean, $\bar{x}$, by subtracting μ_{H_0}, the hypothesized mean, and dividing by $\hat{\sigma}_{\bar{x}}$, the estimated standard error of the mean. Because our test of hypotheses is based on the *t* distribution, we use *t* to denote the standardized statistic.

$$t = \frac{\bar{x} - \mu_{H_0}}{\hat{\sigma}_{\bar{x}}}$$
$$= \frac{84 - 90}{2.46}$$
$$= -2.44$$

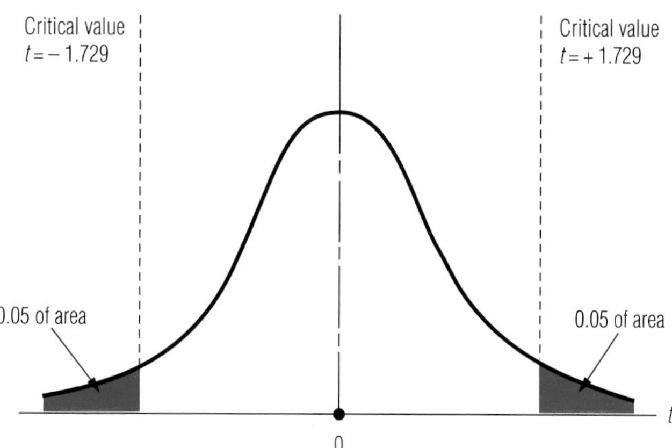

FIGURE 8-18

Two-tailed test of hypothesis at the 0.10 level of significance using the t distribution

Step 4: Sketch the distribution and mark the sample value and the critical values

Drawing this result on a sketch of the sampling distribution, we see that the sample mean falls outside the acceptance region, as shown in Figure 8-19.

Step 5: Interpret the result

Therefore, management should reject the null hypothesis (the personnel specialist's assertion that the true mean score of the employees being tested is 90).

One-Tailed Tests of Means Using the *t* Distribution

One difference from the z tables

The procedure for a one-tailed hypothesis test using the t distribution is the same conceptually as for a one-tailed test using the normal distribution and the z table. Performing such one-tailed tests may cause some difficulty, however. Notice that the column headings in Appendix Table 2 represent the *area in both tails combined.* Thus, they are appropriate to use in a two-tailed test with *two* rejection regions.

Using the t table for one-tailed tests

If we use the t distribution for a one-tailed test, we need to determine the area located in only one tail. So to find the appropriate t value for a one-tailed test at a significance level of 0.05 with 12 degrees of freedom, we would look in Appendix Table 2 under the 0.10 column opposite the 12 degrees of freedom row. The answer in this case is 1.782. **This is true because the 0.10 column represents 0.10 of the area under the curve contained in *both***

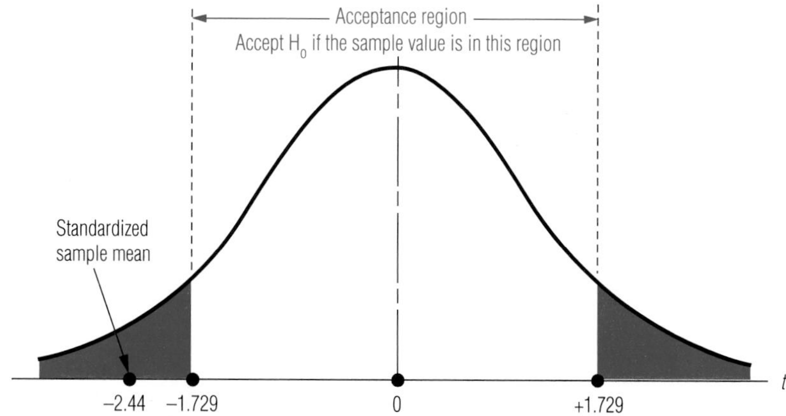

FIGURE 8-19

Two-tailed hypothesis test at the 0.10 level of significance, showing the acceptance region and the standardized sample mean

***tails combined,* so it also represents 0.05 of the area under the curve contained in each of the tails separately.**

Looking ahead

In the next chapter, we continue our work on hypothesis testing by looking at situations where decisions must be made on the basis of two samples that may or may not come from the same underlying population.

HINTS & ASSUMPTIONS

Doing hypothesis tests with the t distribution is no different from doing them with the normal distribution except that we use a different table and we have to supply the number of degrees of freedom. Hint: The number of degrees of freedom in a single-sample test is always one fewer than the sample size. Warning: Use the t distribution whenever the sample size is less than 30, the population standard deviation is not known, and the population is normal or approximately normal.

Exercises 8.7

Self-Check Exercises

SC 8-11 Given a sample mean of 83, a sample standard deviation of 12.5, and a sample size of 22, test the hypothesis that the value of the population mean is 70 against the alternative that it is more than 70. Use the 0.025 significance level.

SC 8-12 Picosoft, Ltd., a supplier of operating system software for personal computers, was planning the initial public offering of its stock in order to raise sufficient working capital to finance the development of a radically new, seventh-generation integrated system. With current earnings of \$1.61 a share, Picosoft and its underwriters were contemplating an offering price of \$21, or about 13 times earnings. In order to check the appropriateness of this price, they randomly chose seven publicly traded software firms and found that their average price/earnings ratio was 11.6, and the sample standard deviation was 1.3. At $\alpha = 0.02$, can Picosoft conclude that the stocks of publicly traded software firms have an average P/E ratio that is significantly different from 13?

Basic Concepts

■ **8-44** Given a sample mean of 94.3, a sample standard deviation of 8.4, and a sample size of 6, test the hypothesis that the value of the population mean is 100 against the alternative hypothesis that it is less than 100. Use the 0.05 significance level.

■ **8-45** If a sample of 25 observations reveals a sample mean of 52 and a sample variance of 4.2, test the hypothesis that the population mean is 65 against the alternative hypothesis that it is some other value. Use the 0.01 significance level.

reject t

calc. t = -31.7   2 tail

crit. t = 2.797

Applications

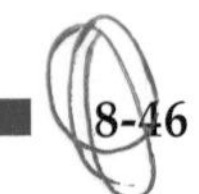

■ **8-46** Realtor Elaine Snyderman took a random sample of 12 homes in a prestigious suburb of Chicago and found the average appraised market value to be \$780,000, and the standard deviation was \$49,000. Test the hypothesis that for all homes in the area, the mean appraised value is \$825,000 against the alternative that it is less than \$825,000. Use the 0.05 level of significance.

■ **8-47** For a sample of 60 women taken from a population of over 5,000 enrolled in a weight-reducing program at a nationwide chain of health spas, the sample mean diastolic blood pressure is 101 and the sample standard deviation is 42. At a significance level of 0.02, on average, did the women enrolled in the program have diastolic blood pressure that exceeds the value of 75?

■ **8-48** The data-processing department at a large life insurance company has installed new color video display terminals to replace the monochrome units it previously used. The 95 operators trained to use the new machines averaged 7.2 hours before achieving a satisfactory level of performance. Their sample variance was 16.2 squared hours. Long experience with operators on the old monochrome terminals showed that they averaged 8.1 hours on the machines before their performances were satisfactory. At the 0.01 significance level, should the supervisor of the department conclude that the new terminals are easier to learn to operate?

■ **8-49** As the bottom fell out of the oil market in early 1986, educators in Texas worried about how the resulting loss of state revenues (estimated to be about \$100 million for each \$1 decrease in the price of a barrel of oil) would affect their budgets. The state board of education felt the situation would not be critical as long as they could be reasonably certain that the price would stay above \$18 per barrel. They surveyed 13 randomly chosen oil economists and asked them to predict how low the price would go before it bottomed out. The 13 predictions average \$21.60, and the sample standard deviation was \$4.65. At $\alpha = 0.01$, is the average prediction significantly higher than \$18.00? Should the board conclude that a budget crisis is unlikely? Explain.

■ **8-50** A television documentary on overeating claimed that Americans are about 10 pounds overweight on average. To test this claim, eighteen randomly selected individuals were examined; their average excess weight was found to be 12.4 pounds, and the sample standard deviation was 2.7 pounds. At a significance level of 0.01, is there any reason to doubt the validity of the claimed 10-pound value?

■ **8-51** XCO, a multinational manufacturer, uses a batch process to produce widgets. Each batch of widgets takes 8 hours to produce and has material and labor costs of \$8,476. Because of variations in machine efficiency and raw material purity, the number of widgets per batch is random. All widgets made can be sold for \$2.50 each, and widget production is profitable so long as the batches sell for more than \$12,500 on average. XCO sampled 16 batches and found 5,040 widgets per batch on average, with a standard deviation of 41.3 widgets. At $\alpha = 0.025$, can XCO conclude that its widget operation is profitable?

Worked-Out Answers to Self-Check Exercises

■ **SC 8-11** $s = 12.5 \qquad n = 22 \qquad \bar{x} = 83$

$H_0\colon \mu = 70 \qquad H_1\colon \mu > 70 \qquad \alpha = 0.025$

The upper limit of the acceptance region is $t = 2.080$, or

$$\bar{x} = \mu_{H_0} + t\,s/\sqrt{n} = 70 + 2.080(12.5)/\sqrt{22} = 75.54$$

Because the observed t value $= \dfrac{\bar{x} - \mu_{H_0}}{s/\sqrt{n}} = \dfrac{83 - 70}{12.5/\sqrt{22}} = 4.878 > 2.080$

(or $\bar{x} > 75.54$), we reject H_0.

■ **SC 8-12** $s = 1.3 \qquad n = 7 \qquad \bar{x} = 11.6$

$H_0\colon \mu = 13 \qquad H_1\colon \mu \neq 13 \qquad \alpha = 0.02$

The limits of the acceptance region are $t = \pm 3.143$, or

$$\bar{x} = \mu_{H_0} \pm t\,s/\sqrt{n} = 13 \pm 3.143(1.3)/\sqrt{7} = (11.46, 14.54)$$

Because the observed t value $= \dfrac{\bar{x} - \mu_{H_0}}{s/\sqrt{n}} = \dfrac{11.6 - 13}{1.3/\sqrt{7}} = -2.849 > -3.143$

(or $\bar{x} = 11.6$, which is between 11.46 and 14.54), we do not reject H_0. The average P/E ratio of publicly traded software firms is not significantly different from 13.

Statistics at Work

Loveland Computers

Case 8: One-Sample Tests of Hypotheses "Here's the other thing that has me thinking more about adding a software division," said Margot Derby, the head of Marketing at Loveland Computers, as she pulled a *Wall Street Journal* column from her desk drawer. "As you know, prices on PCs have been dropping. But, to everyone's surprise, PC buyers seem to be spending the same in total—they are making up for the discount price by buying more bells and whistles—and more software.

"The article quotes a figure for the average amount spent on software by people in the first year they own the machine. That's the same figure that we asked when we did our telephone survey, but our number came in much lower than the amount they quoted in the article. The trouble is I'm not sure which figure to use to make our business plan for a software division."

"Well, why would your number be different?" asked Lee Azko.

"We don't intend to appeal to everyone," Margot replied. "We probably have more of a 'techie' image, so our customers may be different from the 'average' customer they talk about in that article. Maybe they use custom programs they write themselves."

"Or maybe the difference doesn't mean anything at all and it's just the result of sampling error," Lee suggested.

"But I don't know how we could decide for sure. We've calculated the mean and standard deviation for our telephone sample, but the *Journal* article only gives us the mean. And I remember enough from my one stat course in college to know that we can't run a test if we don't know the population standard deviation."

Study Questions: Assume that the mean software expenditure figure quoted in the newspaper is a reliable *population mean.* Is Margot right that Lee also needs to know the population standard deviation in order to perform a test? What idea is Margot exploring here? How would the idea be stated in hypothesis-testing terms?

Computer Database Exercise

HH Industries

Hal dropped in to see Laurel the day after the staff meeting. "I've got a question," he began, "about the study you and Bob did on the competitive bidding of purchase orders. I know I'm a statistical rookie, and I'm trying hard to understand confidence intervals and such things, but isn't there any way just to get a yes-or-no answer to a question like we asked?" He paused, then went on. "I didn't want to ask dumb questions in the meeting yesterday, because I really feel as if it's my lack of knowledge that is making me question the results. Try to see it from my perspective: The figure I want, 60 percent, is *in* the confidence interval, but let's face it—most of the interval is *below* 0.6. Do you see what I'm getting at?"

Laurel nodded and smiled. "I see exactly what you mean," she said. "You're not as much of a rookie as you think, and it's not a dumb question. Confidence intervals are, by nature, somewhat confusing. I've got a textbook that you may want to borrow that will give you a little more background. And as for the yes-or-no answer, let me introduce you to hypothesis testing." Laurel went on to explain one- and two-tailed tests, illustrating with the situation at hand.

1. Perform a one-tailed hypothesis test to determine whether the proportion of competitively bid purchase orders is actually below 0.6, using $\bar{p} = 0.58$ and $n = 1{,}052$. Test at the 0.01 significance level.

Gary held the door for Laurel one morning. "I haven't seen you in a while except at our weekly staff meetings," he said, smiling. "In fact, I think it's been since you helped me with that zip code study shortly after you got here. I hear they're keeping you busy!"

"It has been rather hectic." Laurel agreed. "But I'm having a good time. Being busy is better than being bored! Recently, though, it's let up a little, which is nice. And my skiing vacation in the Rockies is coming up soon, which will be a nice break."

"Sounds like fun! Think you'd have enough time before you go to help me with a little problem?" When Laurel nodded, Gary continued. "We've been seeing some poor quality control indications from one of our O-ring suppliers. The fit of this particular type of seal is crucial, as you may know. Consequently, when Stan tells me that one or two of our customers have complained, we need to do some careful checking."

"Do you have any incoming inspection procedures?" asked Laurel, turning in to her office.

"Good question," grimaced Gary. "We do what we can, and on larger items shipped in small quantities we'll inspect each and every one. But on something like seals, we get thousands in at a time and inspecting a handful is often all we can manage. I'd really like to set up more rigorous procedures as a long-term goal."

"Sounds like this O-ring problem is a good place to start. I'll walk you through the data we need and the analysis steps, and maybe you can take it from there to evaluate other items." Laurel knew she was slowly gaining the staff's confidence, not only concerning her capabilities, but especially about the validity and usefulness of statistical analysis. "I'll swing by later this morning to get more details."

Later, Laurel found Gary in the warehouse. "Good timing," he said. "This is the latest batch coming in right now. See this dimension?" Gary scooped an O-ring from the box and indicated the innermost gap. "The required average is 0.140 inch. Historically, we've had a standard deviation of 0.003 inch. We've got a calibration instrument to measure these. What if I have my guys record the data from this batch and deliver it to your office tomorrow?"

"That's fine," answered Laurel. "Just for my own information, is too tight as bad as too loose?"

"Yep. Either way can be disastrous for the user," explained Gary.

2. At a significance level of 0.05, should Laurel conclude that the O-rings are out of tolerance? Use the data given in the CH08.xxx files on the data disk.

EPS by an average of 13.8 percent, with a standard deviation of 18.9 percent. A random sample of 35 producers of consumer goods showed that the proposal would reduce EPS by 9.1 percent on average, with a standard deviation of 8.7 percent. On the basis of these samples, is it reasonable to conclude (at $\alpha = 0.10$) that the FASB proposal will cause a greater reduction in EPS for high-technology firms than for producers of consumer goods?

Basic Concepts

■ **9-1** Two independent samples were collected. For the first sample of 42 items, the mean was 32.3 and the variance 9. The second sample of 57 items had a mean of 34 and a variance of 16.

(a) Compute the estimated standard error of the difference between the two means.

(b) Using $\alpha = 0.05$, test whether there is sufficient evidence to show the second population has a larger mean.

Applications

■ **9-2** Block Enterprises, a manufacturer of chips for computers, is in the process of deciding whether to replace its current semiautomated assembly line with a fully automated assembly line. Block has gathered some preliminary test data about hourly chip production, which is summarized in the following table, and it would like to know whether it should upgrade its assembly line. State (and test at $\alpha = 0.02$) appropriate hypotheses to help Block decide.

	$\bar{x}$	s	n
Semiautomatic line	198	32	150
Automatic line	206	29	200

■ **9-3** Two research laboratories have independently produced drugs that provide relief to arthritis sufferers. The first drug was tested on a group of 90 arthritis sufferers and produced an average of 8.5 hours of relief, and a sample standard deviation of 1.8 hours. The second drug was tested on 80 arthritis sufferers, producing an average of 7.9 hours of relief, and a sample standard deviation of 2.1 hours. At the 0.05 level of significance, does the second drug provide a significantly shorter period of relief?

■ **9-4** A sample of 32 money-market mutual funds was chosen on January 1, 1996, and the average annual rate of return over the past 30 days was found to be 3.23 percent, and the sample standard deviation was 0.51 percent. A year earlier, a sample of 38 money-market funds showed an average rate of return of 4.36 percent, and the sample standard deviation was 0.84 percent. Is it reasonable to conclude (at $\alpha = 0.05$) that money-market interest rates declined during 1995?

■ **9-5** In September 1995, the Automobile Confederation of the Carolinas surveyed 75 randomly chosen service stations in North and South Carolina and determined that the average price for regular unleaded gasoline at self-service pumps was \$1.059, and the sample standard deviation was 3.9¢. Three months later, another survey of 50 service stations found an average price of \$1.089, and the sample standard deviation was 6.8¢. At $\alpha = 0.02$, had the

Carolinas' average price of self-service regular unleaded gasoline changed significantly in this 3-month period?

■ **9-6** Notwithstanding the Equal Pay Act of 1963, in 1993 it still appeared that men earned more than women in similar jobs. A random sample of 38 male machine-tool operators found a mean hourly wage of \$11.38, and the sample standard deviation was \$1.84. A random sample of 45 female machine-tool operators found their mean wage to be \$8.42, and the sample standard deviation was \$1.31. On the basis of these samples, is it reasonable to conclude (at $\alpha = 0.01$) that the male operators are earning over \$2.00 more per hour than the female operators?

■ **9-7** BullsEye Discount store has always prided itself on customer service. The store hopes that all BullsEye stores are providing the same level of service from coast to coast, so they have surveyed some customers. In the Southeast region, a random sample of 97 customers yielded an average overall satisfaction rating of 8.8 out of 10 and the sample standard deviation was 0.7. In the Northeast region, a random sample of 84 customers resulted in an average rating of 9.0 and the sample standard deviation was 0.6. Can BullsEye conclude, at $\alpha = 0.05$, that the levels of customer satisfaction in the two markets are significantly different?

Worked-Out Answers to Self-Check Exercises

SC 9-1 $s_1 = 6 \quad n_1 = 60 \quad \bar{x}_1 = 86 \quad s_2 = 9 \quad n_2 = 75 \quad \bar{x}_2 = 82$

(a) $$\hat{\sigma}_{\bar{x}_1 - \bar{x}_2} = \sqrt{\frac{s_1^2}{n_1} + \frac{s_2^2}{n_2}} = \sqrt{\frac{36}{60} + \frac{81}{75}} = 1.296$$

(b) $H_0\colon \mu_1 = \mu_2 \quad H_1\colon \mu_1 \neq \mu_2 \quad \alpha = 0.01$

The limits of the acceptance region are $z = \pm 2.58$, or

$$\bar{x}_1 - \bar{x}_2 = 0 \pm z\hat{\sigma}_{\bar{x}_1 - \bar{x}_2} = \pm 2.58(1.296) = \pm 3.344$$

Because the observed z value $= \dfrac{(\bar{x}_1 - \bar{x}_2) - (\mu_1 - \mu_2)_{H_0}}{\hat{\sigma}_{\bar{x}_1 - \bar{x}_2}}$

$$= \frac{(86 - 82) - 0}{1.296}$$

$= 3.09 > 2.58$ (or $\bar{x}_1 - \bar{x}_2 = 86 - 82 = 4 > 3.344$), we reject H_0. It is reasonable to conclude that the two samples come from different populations.

SC 9-2 Sample 1 (HT firms): $s_1 = 18.9 \quad n_1 = 41 \quad \bar{x}_1 = 13.8$

Sample 2 (CG producers): $s_2 = 8.7 \quad n_2 = 35 \quad \bar{x}_2 = 9.1$

$H_0\colon \mu_1 = \mu_2 \quad H_1\colon \mu_1 > \mu_2 \quad \alpha = 0.10$

$$\hat{\sigma}_{\bar{x}_1 - \bar{x}_2} = \sqrt{\frac{s_1^2}{n_1} + \frac{s_2^2}{n_2}} = \sqrt{\frac{(18.9)^2}{41} + \frac{(8.7)^2}{35}} = 3.298 \text{ percent}$$

The upper limit of the acceptance region is $z = 1.28$, or

$$\bar{x}_1 - \bar{x}_2 = 0 + z\hat{\sigma}_{\bar{x}_1 - \bar{x}_2} = 1.28(3.298) = 4.221 \text{ percent}$$

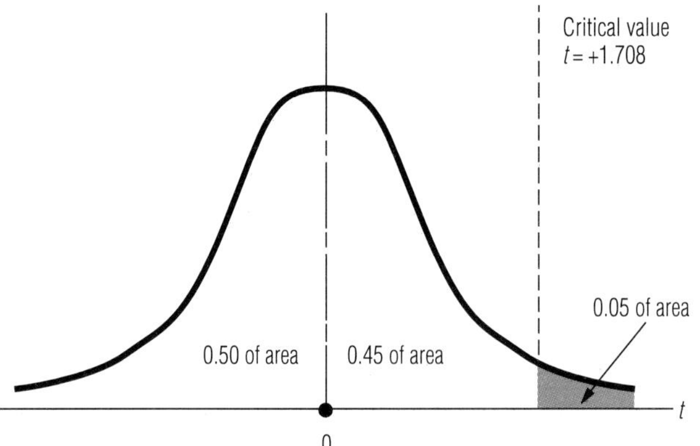

FIGURE 9-4

Right-tailed hypothesis test of the difference between two means at the 0.05 level of significance

Applying these results to our sensitivity example:

$$s_p^2 = \frac{(n_1 - 1)s_1^2 + (n_2 - 1)s_2^2}{n_1 + n_2 - 2} \quad [9\text{-}3]$$

$$= \frac{(12 - 1)(15)^2 + (15 - 1)(19)^2}{12 + 15 - 2}$$

$$= \frac{11(225) + 14(361)}{25}$$

$$= 301.160$$

Taking square roots on both sides, we get $s_p = \sqrt{301.160}$, or 17.354, so:

$$\hat{\sigma}_{\bar{x}_1 - \bar{x}_2} = s_p\sqrt{\frac{1}{n_1} + \frac{1}{n_2}} \quad [9\text{-}4]$$

$$= 17.354\sqrt{\frac{1}{12} + \frac{1}{15}}$$

$$= 17.354(0.387)$$

$$= 6.721 \leftarrow \text{Estimated standard error of the difference}$$

Concluding Step 3: Standardize the sample statistic

Next we standardize the difference of sample means, $\bar{x}_1 - \bar{x}_2$. First, we subtract $(\mu_1 - \mu_2)_{H_0}$, the hypothesized difference of the population means. Then we divide by $\hat{\sigma}_{\bar{x}_1 - \bar{x}_2}$, the estimated standard error of the difference between the sample means.

$$t = \frac{(\bar{x}_1 - \bar{x}_2) - (\mu_1 - \mu_2)_{H_0}}{\hat{\sigma}_{\bar{x}_1 - \bar{x}_2}}$$

$$= \frac{(92 - 84) - 0}{6.721}$$

$$= 1.19$$

Because our test of hypotheses is based on the t distribution, we use t to denote the standardized statistic.

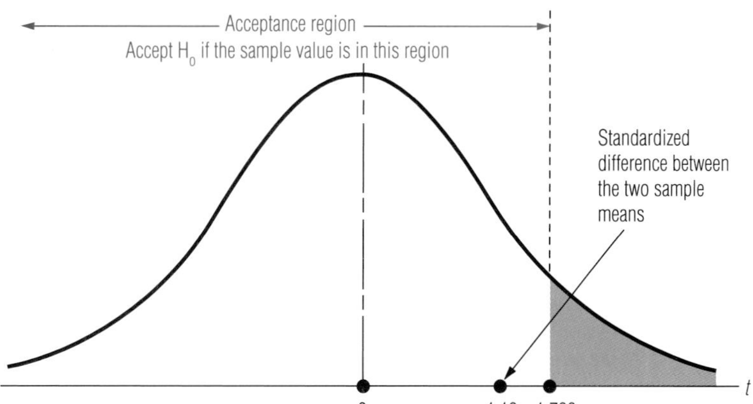

FIGURE 9-5

One-tailed test of the difference between two means at the 0.05 level of significance, showing the acceptance region and the standardized difference between the sample means

Step 4: Sketch the distribution and mark the sample value and critical value

Then we mark the standardized difference on a sketch of the sampling distribution and compare it with the critical value of $t = 1.708$, as shown in Figure 9-5. We can see in Figure 9-5 that the standardized difference between the two sample means lies within the acceptance region. Thus, we accept the null hypothesis that there is no difference between the sensitivities achieved by the two programs. The company's expenditures on the formal instructional program have not produced significantly higher sensitivities among its managers.

Step 5: Interpret the result

HINTS & ASSUMPTIONS

Hint: Because our sample sizes here are small (less than 30) and we don't know the standard deviations of the populations, the t distribution is appropriate. Like the one-sample t test we've already studied, here too we need to determine the appropriate degrees of freedom. In a one-sample test, degrees of freedom were the sample size minus one. Here, because we are using two samples, the correct degrees of freedom are the first sample size minus one plus the second sample size less one, or symbolically, $n_1 + n_2 - 2$. Assumption: We're assuming that the variances of the two populations are equal. If this is not the case, we can't do this test using the methods we've covered. Warning: To use the method explained in this section, the two samples (one from each population) must have been chosen independently of each other.

Exercises 9.3

Self-Check Exercises

SC 9-3 A consumer-research organization routinely selects several car models each year and evaluates their fuel efficiency. In this year's study of two similar subcompact models from two different automakers, the average gas mileage for 12 cars of brand A was 27.2 miles per gallon, and the standard deviation was 3.8 mpg. The nine brand B cars that were tested averaged 32.1 mpg, and the standard deviation was 4.3 mpg. At $\alpha = 0.01$, should it conclude that brand A cars have lower average gas mileage than do brand B cars?

SC 9-4 Connie Rodrigues, the Dean of Students at Midstate College, is wondering about grade distributions at the school. She has heard grumblings that the GPAs in the Business School are about 0.25 lower than those in the College of Arts and Sciences. A quick random sampling produced the following GPAs.

Business:	2.86	2.77	3.18	2.80	3.14	2.87	3.19	3.24	2.91	3.00	2.83		
Arts & Sciences:	3.35	3.32	3.36	3.63	3.41	3.37	3.45	3.43	3.44	3.17	3.26	3.18	3.41

Do these data indicate that there is a factual basis for the grumblings? State and test appropriate hypotheses at $\alpha = 0.02$.

Applications

■ **9-8** A credit-insurance organization has developed a new high-tech method of training new sales personnel. The company sampled 16 employees who were trained the original way and found average daily sales to be \$688 and the sample standard deviation was \$32.63. They also sampled 11 employees who were trained using the new method and found average daily sales to be \$706 and the sample standard deviation was \$24.84. At $\alpha = 0.05$, can the company conclude that average daily sales have increased under the new plan?

■ **9-9** A large stock-brokerage firm wants to determine how successful its new account executives have been at recruiting clients. After completing their training, new account execs spend several weeks calling prospective clients, trying to get the prospects to open accounts with the firm. The following data give the numbers of new accounts opened in their first 2 weeks by 10 randomly chosen female account execs and by 8 randomly chosen male account execs. At $\alpha = 0.05$, does it appear that the women are more effective at generating new accounts than the men are?

	Number of New Accounts									
Female account execs	12	11	14	13	13	14	13	12	14	12
Male account execs	13	10	11	12	13	12	10	12		

■ **9-10** To celebrate their first anniversary, Randy Nelson decided to buy a pair of diamond earrings for his wife Debbie. He was shown nine pairs with marquise gems weighing approximately 2 carats per pair. Because of differences in the colors and qualities of the stones, the prices varied from set to set. The average price was \$2,990, and the sample standard deviation was \$370. He also looked at six pairs with pear-shaped stones of the same 2-carat approximate weight. These earrings had an average price of \$3,065, and the standard deviation was \$805. On the basis of this evidence, can Randy conclude (at a significance level of 0.05) that pear-shaped diamonds cost more, on average, than marquise diamonds?

■ **9-11** A sample of 30-year conventional mortgage rates at 11 randomly chosen banks in California yielded a mean rate of 7.61 percent and a standard deviation of 0.39 percent. A similar sample taken at 8 randomly chosen banks in Pennsylvania had a mean rate of 7.43 percent, and a standard deviation of 0.56 percent. Do these samples provide evidence to conclude (at $\alpha = 0.10$) that conventional mortgage rates in California and Pennsylvania come from populations with different means?

■ **9-12** Because refunds are paid more quickly on tax returns that are filed electronically, the Commissioner of the Internal Revenue Service was wondering whether refunds due on returns filed by mail were smaller than those due on returns filed electronically. Looking only at returns claiming refunds, a sample of 17 filed by mail had an average refund of $563, and a standard deviation of $378. The average refund on a sample of 13 electronically filed returns was $958, and the sample standard deviation was $619. At $\alpha = 0.01$, do these data support the commissioner's speculation?

■ **9-13** Greatyear tires currently produces tires at their Wilmington, North Carolina plant during two 12-hour shifts. The night-shift employees are planning to ask for a raise because they believe they are producing more tires per shift than the day shift. "Because Greatyear is making more money during the night shift, those employees should also make more money" according to the night-shift spokesman. I.M. Checking, the Greatyear production supervisor, randomly selected some daily production runs from each shift with the results given below (in 1,000s of tires produced).

Shift				**Production (in 1,000s)**					
Day	107.5	118.6	124.6	101.6	113.6	119.6	120.6	109.6	105.9
Night	115.6	109.4	121.6	128.7	136.6	125.4	121.3	108.6	117.5

Do these data indicate, at $\alpha = 0.01$, that the night shift is producing more tires per shift?

Worked-Out Answers to Self-Check Exercises

SC 9-3 $s_A = 3.8 \quad n_A = 12 \quad \bar{x}_A = 27.2 \quad s_B = 4.3 \quad n_B = 9 \quad \bar{x}_B = 32.1$

$H_0: \mu_A = \mu_B \quad H_1: \mu_A < \mu_B \quad \alpha = 0.01$

$$s_p = \sqrt{\frac{(n_A - 1)s_A^2 + (n_B - 1)s_B^2}{n_A + n_B - 2}} = \sqrt{\frac{11(3.8)^2 + 8(4.3)^2}{19}} = 4.0181 \text{ mpg}$$

The lower limit of the acceptance region is $t = -2.539$, or

$$\bar{x}_A - \bar{x}_B = 0 - ts_p\sqrt{\frac{1}{n_A} + \frac{1}{n_B}} = -2.539(4.0181)\sqrt{\frac{1}{12} + \frac{1}{9}}$$

$$= -4.499 \text{ mpg}$$

Because the observed t value $= \dfrac{(\bar{x}_A - \bar{x}_B) - (\mu_A - \mu_B)_{H_0}}{s_p\sqrt{\dfrac{1}{n_A} + \dfrac{1}{n_B}}} = \dfrac{(27.2 - 32.1) - 0}{4.0181\sqrt{\dfrac{1}{12} + \dfrac{1}{9}}}$

$= -2.766 < -2.539$ (or $\bar{x}_A - \bar{x}_B = -4.9 < -4.499$), we reject H_0. Brand B delivers significantly higher mileage than does brand A.

SC 9-4 Sample 1 (Business): $s_B = 0.176 \quad n_B = 11 \quad \bar{x}_B = 2.98$

Sample 2 (Arts & Sciences): $s_A = 0.121 \quad n_A = 13 \quad \bar{x}_A = 3.368$

$H_0: \mu_B - \mu_A = -0.25 \quad H_1: \mu_B - \mu_A \neq -0.25 \quad \alpha = 0.02$

$$s_p = \sqrt{\frac{(n_B - 1)s_B^2 + (n_A - 1)s_A^2}{n_B + n_A - 2}} = \sqrt{\frac{10(.176)^2 + 12(.121)^2}{22}} = 0.1485$$

The limits of the acceptance region are $t = \pm 2.508$, or

$$\bar{x}_B - \bar{x}_A = (\mu_B - \mu_A)_{H_0} \pm ts_p\sqrt{\frac{1}{n_B} + \frac{1}{n_A}} = -0.25$$

$$\pm\ 2.508(0.1485)\sqrt{\frac{1}{11} + \frac{1}{13}} = (-0.4026, -0.0974)$$

Because the observed t value $= \dfrac{(\bar{x}_B - \bar{x}_A) - (\mu_B - \mu_A)_{H_0}}{s_p\sqrt{\dfrac{1}{n_B} + \dfrac{1}{n_A}}}$

$$= \frac{(2.980 - 3.368) - 0.25}{0.1485\sqrt{\dfrac{1}{11} + \dfrac{1}{13}}}$$

$= -2.268 > -2.508$ (or $\bar{x}_B - \bar{x}_A = -0.388 > -0.403$), we do not reject H_0. The Business School GPAs are about .25 below those in the College of Arts & Sciences.

9.4 Testing Differences between Means with Dependent Samples

Conditions under which paired samples aid analysis

In the examples in Sections 9.2 and 9.3, our samples were chosen *independently* of each other. In the wage example, the samples were taken in two different cities. In the sensitivity example, samples were taken of managers who had gone through two different training programs. Sometimes, however, it makes sense to take samples that are not independent of each other. Often the use of such *dependent* (or *paired*) *samples* enables us to perform a more precise analysis, because they will allow us to control for extraneous factors. With dependent samples, we still follow the same basic procedure we have followed in all our hypothesis testing. The only differences are that we will use a different formula for the estimated standard error of the sample differences and that we will require that both samples be of the same size.

A health spa has advertised a weight-reducing program and has claimed that the average participant in the program loses more than 17 pounds. A somewhat overweight executive is interested in the program but is skeptical about the claims and asks for some hard evidence. The spa allows him to select randomly the records of 10 participants and record their weights before and after the program. These data are recorded in Table 9-3. Here we have two samples (a *before* sample and an *after* sample) that are clearly dependent on each other, because the same 10 people have been observed twice.

Table 9-3

Weights Before and After a Reducing Program

Before	189	202	220	207	194	177	193	202	208	233
After	170	179	203	192	172	161	174	187	186	204

Step 1: State your hypotheses, type of test, and significance level

The overweight executive wants to test at the 5 percent significance level the claimed average weight loss of more than 17 pounds. Formally, we may state this problem:

$$H_0: \mu_1 - \mu_2 = 17 \quad \leftarrow \text{Null hypothesis: average weight loss is only 17 pounds}$$

$$H_1: \mu_1 - \mu_2 > 17 \quad \leftarrow \text{Alternative hypothesis: average weight loss exceeds 17 pounds}$$

$$\alpha = 0.05 \quad \leftarrow \text{Level of significance}$$

Conceptual understanding of differences

What we are really interested in is not the weights before and after, but their *differences*. **Conceptually, what we have *is not two samples* of before and after weights, but rather *one sample* of weight losses.** If the population of weight losses has a mean μ_l, we can restate our hypotheses as

$$H_0: \mu_l = 17$$

$$H_1: \mu_l > 17$$

Step 2: Choose the appropriate distribution and find the critical value

Figure 9-6 illustrates this problem graphically. Because we want to know whether the mean weight loss *exceeds* 17 pounds, an upper-tailed test is appropriate. The 0.05 significance level is shown in Figure 9-6 as the colored area under the t distribution. We use the t distribution because the sample size is only 10; the appropriate number of degrees of freedom is 9, $(10 - 1)$. Appendix Table 2 gives the critical value of t, 1.833.

Computing the paired differences

We begin by computing the individual losses, their mean, and standard deviation, and proceed exactly as we did when testing hypotheses about a single mean. The computations are done in Table 9-4.

Next, we use Equation 7-1 to estimate the unknown population standard deviation:

$$\hat{\sigma} = s \qquad [7\text{-}1]$$

$$= 4.40$$

FIGURE 9-6

One-tailed hypothesis test at the 0.05 level of significance

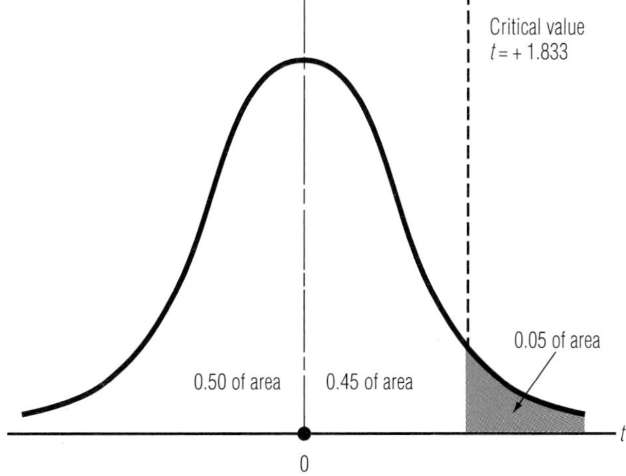

Table 9-4 Finding the Mean Weight Loss and Its Standard Deviation

Before	After	Loss x	Loss Squared x^2
189	170	19	361
202	179	23	529
220	203	17	289
207	192	15	225
194	172	22	484
177	161	16	256
193	174	19	361
202	187	15	225
208	186	22	484
233	204	29	841
		$\Sigma x =$ **197**	$\Sigma x^2 =$ **4,055**

$$\bar{x} = \frac{\Sigma x}{n} \quad [3\text{-}2]$$

$$= \frac{197}{10}$$

$$= 19.7$$

$$s = \sqrt{\frac{\Sigma x^2}{n-1} - \frac{n\bar{x}^2}{n-1}} \quad [3\text{-}18]$$

$$= \sqrt{\frac{4{,}055}{9} - \frac{10(19.7)^2}{9}}$$

$$= \sqrt{19.34}$$

$$= 4.40$$

Step 3: Compute the standard error and standardize the sample statistic

and now we can estimate the standard error of the mean:

$$\hat{\sigma}_{\bar{x}} = \frac{\hat{\sigma}}{\sqrt{n}} \quad [7\text{-}6]$$

$$= \frac{4.40}{\sqrt{10}}$$

$$= \frac{4.40}{3.16}$$

$$= 1.39 \leftarrow \text{Estimated standard error of the mean}$$

Next we standardize the observed average weight loss, $\bar{x} = 19.7$ pounds, by subtracting μ_{H_0}, the hypothesized average loss, and dividing by $\hat{\sigma}_{\bar{x}}$, the estimated standard error of the mean.

$$t = \frac{\bar{x} - \mu_{H_0}}{\hat{\sigma}_{\bar{x}}}$$

$$= \frac{19.7 - 17}{1.39}$$

$$= 1.94$$

Because our test of hypotheses is based on the t distribution, we use t to denote the standardized statistic.

Step 4: Sketch the distribution and mark the sample value and critical value

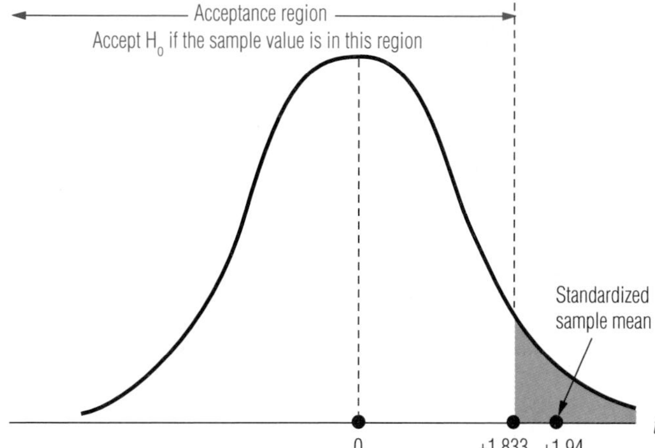

FIGURE 9-7

One-tailed hypothesis test at the 0.05 level of significance, showing the acceptance region and the standardized sample mean

Step 5: Interpret the result

Figure 9-7 illustrates the location of the sample mean weight loss on the standardized scale. We see that the sample mean lies outside the acceptance region, so the executive can reject the null hypothesis and conclude that the claimed weight loss in the program is legitimate.

How does the paired difference test differ?

Let's see how this *paired difference test* differs from a test of the difference of means of *two independent* samples. Suppose that the data in Table 9-4 represent two independent samples of 10 individuals *entering* the program and *another* 10 randomly selected individuals *leaving* the program. The means and variances of the two samples are given in Table 9-5.

A pooled estimate of σ^2

Because the sample sizes are small, we use Equation 9-3 to get a pooled estimate of σ^2 and Equation 9-4 to estimate $\sigma_{\bar{x}_1 - \bar{x}_2}$:

$$s_p^2 = \frac{(n_1 - 1)s_1^2 + (n_2 - 1)s_2^2}{n_1 + n_2 - 2} \quad [9\text{-}3]$$

$$= \frac{(10 - 1)(253.61) + (10 - 1)(201.96)}{10 + 10 - 2}$$

$$= \frac{2282.49 + 1817.64}{18}$$

$$= 227.79 \leftarrow \text{Estimate of common population variance}$$

$$\hat{\sigma}_{\bar{x}_1 - \bar{x}_2} = s_p\sqrt{\frac{1}{n_1} + \frac{1}{n_2}} \quad [9\text{-}4]$$

$$= \sqrt{227.79}\sqrt{\frac{1}{10} + \frac{1}{10}}$$

$$= 15.09(0.45)$$

$$= 6.79 \leftarrow \text{Estimate of } \sigma_{\bar{x}_1 - \bar{x}_2}$$

Table 9-5 Before and After Means and Variances	Sample	Size	Mean	Variance
	Before	10	202.5	253.61
	After	10	182.8	201.96

The appropriate test is now based on the t distribution with 18 degrees of freedom (10 + 10 − 2). With a significance level of 0.05, the critical value of t from Appendix Table 2 is 1.734. The observed difference of the sample means is

$$\bar{x}_1 - \bar{x}_2 = 202.5 - 182.8$$
$$= 19.7 \text{ pounds}$$

Now when we standardize the difference of the sample means for this independent-samples test, we get

$$t = \frac{(\bar{x}_1 - \bar{x}_2) - (\mu_1 - \mu_2)_{H_0}}{\hat{\sigma}_{\bar{x}_1 - \bar{x}_2}}$$
$$= \frac{(202.5 - 182.8) - 17}{6.79}$$
$$= 0.40$$

With independent samples, H_0 cannot be rejected

Once again, because our test of hypotheses is based on the t distribution, we use t to denote the standardized statistic. Comparing the standardized difference of the sample means (0.40) with the critical value of t, (1.734), we see that the standardized sample statistic no longer falls outside the acceptance region, so this test will *not* reject H_0.

Explaining differing results

Why did these two tests give such different results? In the paired sample test, the sample standard deviation of the individual differences was relatively small, so 19.7 pounds was significantly larger than the hypothesized weight loss of 17 pounds. With independent samples, however, the estimated standard deviation of the difference between the means depended on the standard deviations of the before weights and the after weights. Because both of these were relatively large, $\hat{\sigma}_{\bar{x}_1 - \bar{x}_2}$ was also large, and thus 19.7 was not significantly larger than 17. The paired sample test controlled this initial and final variability in weights by looking only at the individual changes in weights. Because of this, it was better able to detect the significance of the weight loss.

Should we treat samples as dependent or independent?

We conclude this section with two examples showing when to treat two samples of equal size as dependent or independent:

1. An agricultural extension service wishes to determine whether a new hybrid seed corn has a greater yield than an old standard variety. If the service asks 10 farmers to record the yield of an acre planted with the new variety and asks another 10 farmers to record the yield of an acre planted with the old variety, the two samples are independent. However, if it asks 10 farmers to plant one acre with each variety and record the results, then the samples are dependent, and the paired difference test is appropriate. In the latter case, differences due to fertilizer, insecticide, rainfall, and so on, are controlled, because each farmer treats his two acres identically. Thus, any differences in yield can be attributed solely to the variety planted.

2. The director of the secretarial pool at a large legal office wants to determine whether typing speed depends on the word-processing software used by a secretary. If she tests seven secretaries using PicosoftWrite and seven using WritePerfect, she should treat her samples as independent. If she tests the same seven secretaries twice (once on each word processor), then the two samples are dependent. In the paired difference test, differences among the secretaries are eliminated as a contributing factor, and the differences in typing speeds can be attributed to the different word processors.

HINTS & ASSUMPTIONS

Often in testing differences between means, it makes sense to take samples that are *not* independent of each other. For example, if you are measuring the effect of a rust inhibitor on the buildup of rust on metal pipe, you would normally sample the rust on the same pipes before and after applying the inhibitor. Doing that controls for the effects of different locations, heat, and moisture. Because the same pipe is involved twice, the samples are not independent. Hint: If we measure the rust on each pipe before and six months after the application, we have a single sample of the grams of rust that have appeared since the application.

Exercises 9.4

Self-Check Exercises

SC 9-5 Sherri Welch is a quality control engineer with the windshield wiper manufacturing division of Emsco, Inc. Emsco is currently considering two new synthetic rubbers for its wiper blades, and Sherri was charged with seeing whether blades made with the two new compounds wear equally well. She equipped 12 cars belonging to other Emsco employees with one blade made of each of the two compounds. On cars 1 to 6, the right blade was made of compound A and the left blade was made of compound B; on cars 7 to 12, compound A was used for the left blade. The cars were driven under normal operating conditions until the blades no longer did a satisfactory job of clearing the windshield of rain. The data below give the usable life (in days) of the blades. At $\alpha = 0.05$, do the two compounds wear equally well?

Car	1	2	3	4	5	6	7	8	9	10	11	12
Left blade	162	323	220	274	165	271	233	156	238	211	241	154
Right blade	183	347	247	269	189	257	224	178	263	199	263	148

SC 9-6 Nine computer-components dealers in major metropolitan areas were asked for their prices on two similar color inkjet printers. The results of this survey are given below. At $\alpha = 0.05$, is it reasonable to assert that, on average, the Apson printer is less expensive than the Okaydata printer?

Dealer	1	2	3	4	5	6	7	8	9
Apson price	$250	319	285	260	305	295	289	309	275
Okaydata price	$270	325	269	275	289	285	295	325	300

Applications

■ **9-14** The data below are a random sample of 9 firms chosen from the "Digest of Earnings Reports" in *The Wall Street Journal* on February 6, 1992:

(a) Find the mean change in earnings per share between 1991 and 1992.

(b) Find the standard deviation of the change and the standard error of the mean.

(c) Were average earnings per share different in 1991 and 1992? Test at $\alpha = 0.02$.

Firm	1	2	3	4	5	6	7	8	9
1991 earnings	1.38	1.26	3.64	3.50	2.47	3.21	1.05	1.98	2.72
1992 earnings	2.48	1.50	4.59	3.06	2.11	2.80	1.59	0.92	0.47

■ **9-15** Jeff Richardson, the receiving clerk for a chemical-products distributor, is faced with the continuing problem of broken glassware, including test-tubes, petri dishes, and flasks. Jeff has determined some additional shipping precautions that can be undertaken to prevent breakage, and he has asked the Purchasing Director to inform the suppliers of the new measures. Data for 8 suppliers are given below in terms of average number of broken items per shipment. Do the data indicate, at $\alpha = 0.05$, that the new measures have lowered the average number of broken items?

Supplier	1	2	3	4	5	6	7	8
Before	16	12	18	7	14	19	6	17
After	14	13	12	6	9	15	8	15

■ **9-16** Additives-R-Us has developed an additive to improve fuel efficiency for trucks that pull very heavy loads. They tested the additive by randomly selecting 18 trucks and dividing them into 9 pairs. In each pair, both trucks hauled the same type of load over the same roadway, but only one truck used fuel with the new additive. Different pairs followed different routes and carried different loads. The resulting fuel efficiencies (in miles per gallon) are given below. Do the data indicate, at $\alpha = 0.01$, that trucks using fuel with the additive achieved significantly better fuel efficiency than trucks using regular fuel?

Pair	1	2	3	4	5	6	7	8	9
Regular	5.7	6.1	5.9	6.2	6.4	5.1	5.9	6.0	5.5
Additive	6.0	6.2	5.8	6.6	6.7	5.3	5.7	6.1	5.9

■ **9-17** Aquarius Health Club has been advertising a rigorous program for body conditioning. The club claims that after 1 month in the program, the average participant should be able to do eight more push-ups in 2 minutes than he or she could do at the start. Does the random sample of 10 program participants given below support the club's claim? Use the 0.025 level of significance.

Participant	1	2	3	4	5	6	7	8	9	10
Before	38	11	34	25	17	38	12	27	32	29
After	45	24	41	39	30	44	30	39	40	41

■ **9-18** Donna Rose is a production supervisor on the disk-drive assembly line at Winchester Technologies. Winchester recently subscribed to an easy listening music service at its factory, hoping that this would relax the workers and lead to greater productivity. Donna is skeptical about this hypothesis and fears the music will be distracting, leading to lower productivity. She sampled weekly production for the same six workers before the music was installed and after it was installed. Her data are given below. At $\alpha = 0.02$, has the average production changed at all?

Employee	1	2	3	4	5	6
Week without music	219	205	226	198	209	216
Week with music	235	186	240	203	221	205

■ **9-19** Modems transmit information across telephone lines from one computer to another. Their speed is rated in baud, the number of bits per second that they can transmit. Because of several technical factors, actual transmission rate varies from file to file. Anne Evans was shopping for a new 28,800 baud modem. In testing two modems to decide which to purchase, she transmitted 7 randomly chosen files with both modems and recorded the following rates (in thousands of baud).

File	1	2	3	4	5	6	7
Haynes Ultima 28.8	9.52	10.17	10.33	10.02	10.72	9.62	9.17
Extel PerFAXtion 28.8	10.92	11.46	11.18	12.21	10.42	11.36	10.47

A review in *PC Reports* said that the magazine's tests had found the Extel PerFAXtion to be significantly faster than the Haynes Ultima. At $\alpha = 0.01$, do Anne's results confirm that conclusion?

Worked-Out Answers to Self-Check Exercises

SC 9-5

Car	1	2	3	4	5	6	7	8	9	10	11	12
Blade A	183	347	247	269	189	257	233	156	238	211	241	154
Blade B	162	323	220	274	165	271	224	178	263	199	263	148
Difference	21	24	27	−5	24	−14	9	−22	−25	12	−22	6

$$\bar{x} = \frac{\Sigma x}{n} = \frac{35}{12} = 2.9167 \text{ days}$$

$$s^2 = \frac{1}{n-1}(\Sigma x^2 - n\bar{x}^2) = \frac{1}{11}(4397 - 12(2.9167)^2) = 390.45, s = \sqrt{s^2}$$

$$= 19.76 \text{ days}$$

$$\hat{\sigma}_{\bar{x}} = s/\sqrt{n} = 19.76/\sqrt{12} = 5.7042 \text{ days}$$

$$H_0: \mu_A = \mu_B \qquad H_1: \mu_A \neq \mu_B \qquad \alpha = 0.05$$

The limits of the acceptance region are $t = \pm 2.201$, or

$$\bar{x} = 0 \pm t\hat{\sigma}_{\bar{x}} = \pm 2.201(5.7042) = \pm 12.55 \text{ days}$$

Because the observed t value $= \dfrac{\bar{x} - \mu_{H_0}}{\hat{\sigma}_{\bar{x}}} = \dfrac{2.9167 - 0}{5.7042} = 0.511 < 2.201$ (or $\bar{x} = 2.9167 < 12.55$), we do not reject H_0. The two compounds are not significantly different with respect to usable life.

SC 9-6

Dealer	1	2	3	4	5	6	7	8	9
Apson price	250	319	285	260	305	295	289	309	275
Okaydata price	270	325	269	275	289	285	295	325	300
Difference	20	6	−16	15	−16	−10	6	16	25

$$\bar{x} = \frac{\Sigma x}{n} = \frac{46}{9} = \$5.1111$$

$$s^2 = \frac{1}{n-1}(\Sigma x^2 - n\bar{x}^2) = \frac{1}{8}(2{,}190 - 9(5.1111)^2) = 244.36,\ s = \sqrt{s^2} = \$15.63$$

$$\hat{\sigma}_{\bar{x}} = s/\sqrt{n} = 15.63/\sqrt{9} = \$5.21$$

H_0: $\mu_O = \mu_A$ $\quad$ H_1: $\mu_O > \mu_A$ $\quad$ $\alpha = 0.05$

The upper limit of the acceptance region is $t = 1.860$, or

$$\bar{x} = 0 + t\hat{\sigma}_{\bar{x}} = 1.860(5.21) = \$9.69$$

Because the observed t value $= \dfrac{\bar{x} - \mu_{H_0}}{\hat{\sigma}_{\bar{x}}} = \dfrac{5.1111 - 0}{5.21} = 0.981 < 1.860$ (or $\bar{x} = \$5.11 < \$9.69$), we do not reject H_0. On average, the Apson inkjet printer is not significantly less expensive than the Okaydata inkjet printer.

9.5 Tests for Differences between Proportions: Large Sample Sizes

Suppose you are interested in finding out whether the Republican party is stronger in New York than in California. Or perhaps you would like to know whether women are as likely as men to purchase sports cars. To reach a conclusion in situations like these, you can take samples from each of the two groups in question (voters in New York and California or women and men) and use the sample proportions to test the difference between the two populations.

The big picture here is very similar to what we did in Section 9.2, when we compared two means using independent samples: We standardize the difference between the two sample proportions and base our tests on the normal distribution. The only major difference will be in the way we find an estimate for the standard error of the difference between the two sample proportions. Let's look at some examples.

Two-Tailed Tests for Differences between Proportions

Consider the case of a pharmaceutical manufacturing company testing two new compounds intended to reduce blood-pressure levels. The compounds are administered to two different sets of laboratory animals. In group one, 71 of 100 animals tested respond to drug 1 with lower blood-pressure levels. In group two, 58 of 90 animals tested respond to drug 2 with lower blood-pressure levels. The company wants to test at the 0.05 level whether there is a difference between the efficacies of these two drugs. How should we proceed with this problem?

$\bar{p}_1 = 0.71$ ← Sample proportion of successes with drug 1

$\bar{q}_1 = 0.29$ ← Sample proportion of failures with drug 1

$n_1 = 100$ ← Sample size for testing drug 1

$\bar{p}_2 = 0.644$ ← Sample proportion of successes with drug 2

$\bar{q}_2 = 0.356$ ← Sample proportion of failures with drug 2

$n_2 = 90$ ← Sample size for testing drug 2

Step 1: State your hypotheses, type of test, and significance level

$H_0\colon p_1 = p_2$ ← Null hypothesis: There is no difference between these two drugs

$H_1\colon p_1 \neq p_2$ ← Alternative hypothesis: There is a difference between them

$\alpha = 0.05$ ← Level of significance for testing this hypothesis

Step 2: Choose the appropriate distribution and find the critical value

Figure 9-8 illustrates this hypothesis test graphically. Because the management of the pharmaceutical company wants to know whether there is a difference between the two compounds, this is a two-tailed test. The significance level of 0.05 corresponds to the colored regions in the figure. Both samples are large enough to justify using the normal distribution to approximate the binomial. From Appendix Table 1, we can determine that the critical value of z for 0.475 of the area under the curve is 1.96.

As in our previous examples, we can begin by calculating the standard deviation of the sampling distribution we are using in our hypothesis test. In this example, the binomial distribution is the correct sampling distribution.

Step 3: Compute the standard error and standardize the sample statistic

We want to find the *standard error of the difference between two proportions;* therefore, we should recall the formula for the *standard error of the proportion:*

$$\sigma_{\bar{p}} = \sqrt{\frac{pq}{n}} \qquad [7\text{-}4]$$

FIGURE 9-8

Two-tailed hypothesis test of the difference between two proportions at the 0.05 level of significance

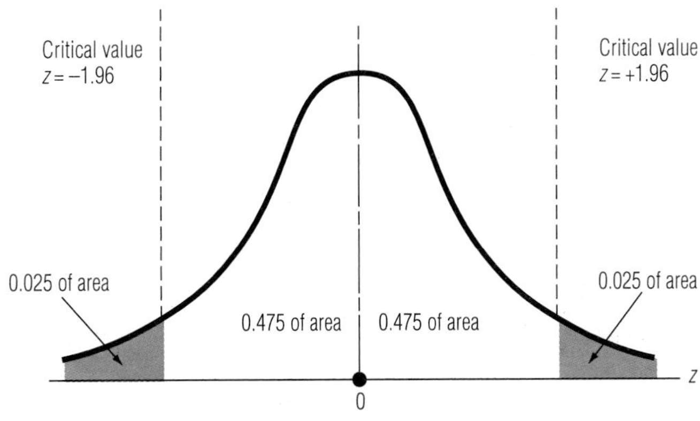

Using this formula and the same form we previously used in Equation 9-1 for the standard error of the difference between two *means,* we get

Standard Error of the Difference between Two Proportions

$$\sigma_{\bar{p}_1 - \bar{p}_2} = \sqrt{\frac{p_1 q_1}{n_1} + \frac{p_2 q_2}{n_2}} \qquad [9\text{-}5]$$

How to estimate this standard error

To test the two compounds, we do not know the population parameters p_1, p_2, q_1, and q_2, and thus we need to estimate them from the sample statistics $\bar{p}_1$, $\bar{p}_2$, $\bar{q}_1$, and $\bar{q}_2$. In this case, we might suppose that the practical formula to use would be

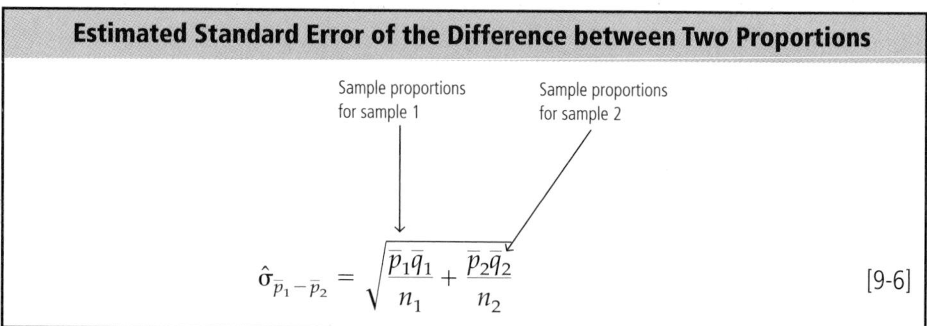

$$\hat{\sigma}_{\bar{p}_1 - \bar{p}_2} = \sqrt{\frac{\bar{p}_1 \bar{q}_1}{n_1} + \frac{\bar{p}_2 \bar{q}_2}{n_2}} \qquad [9\text{-}6]$$

But think about this a bit more. After all, if we hypothesize that there is *no difference* between the two population proportions, then our best estimate of the overall population proportion of successes is probably the *combined proportion of successes* in both samples, that is:

$$\begin{array}{l}\text{Best estimate of the overall}\\ \text{proportion of successes in}\\ \text{the population if the two}\\ \text{proportions are hypothesized}\\ \text{to be equal}\end{array} = \frac{\begin{array}{l}\text{number of successes}\\ \text{in sample 1}\end{array} + \begin{array}{l}\text{number of successes}\\ \text{in sample 2}\end{array}}{\text{total size of both samples}}$$

And in the case of the two compounds, we use this equation with symbols rather than words:

Estimated Overall Proportion of Successes in Two Populations

$$\hat{p} = \frac{n_1\bar{p}_1 + n_2\bar{p}_2}{n_1 + n_2} \qquad [9\text{-}7]$$

$$= \frac{(100)(0.71) + (90)(0.644)}{100 + 90}$$

$$= \frac{71 + 58}{190}$$

$$= 0.6789$$

← Estimate of the overall proportion of successes in the combined populations using combined proportions from both samples ($\hat{q}$ would be $1 - 0.6789 = 0.3211$)

Now we can appropriately modify Equation 9-6 using the values $\hat{p}$ and $\hat{q}$ from Equation 9-7.

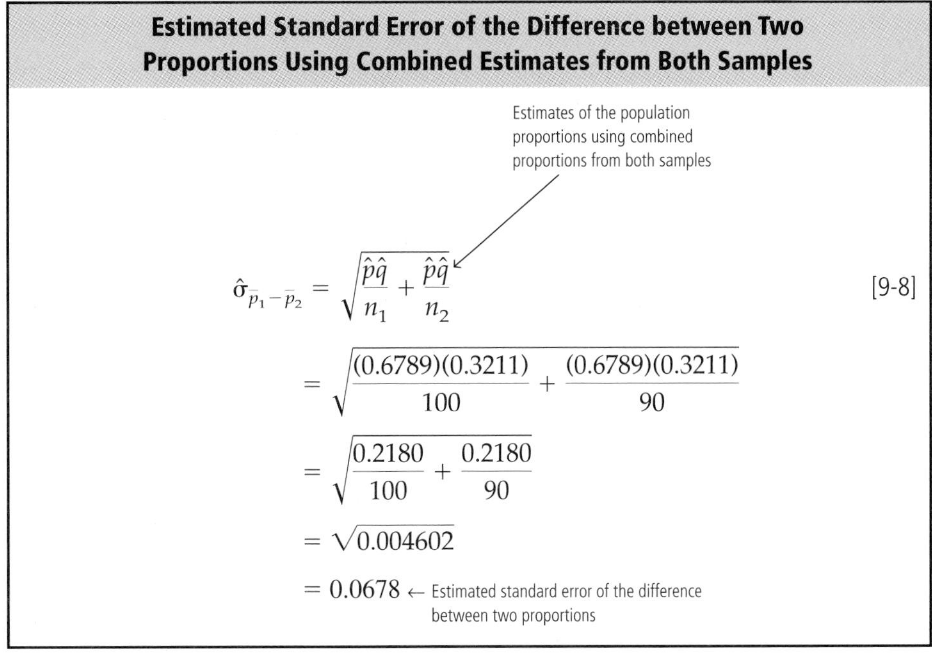

Estimated Standard Error of the Difference between Two Proportions Using Combined Estimates from Both Samples

$$\hat{\sigma}_{\bar{p}_1 - \bar{p}_2} = \sqrt{\frac{\hat{p}\hat{q}}{n_1} + \frac{\hat{p}\hat{q}}{n_2}} \qquad [9\text{-}8]$$

$$= \sqrt{\frac{(0.6789)(0.3211)}{100} + \frac{(0.6789)(0.3211)}{90}}$$

$$= \sqrt{\frac{0.2180}{100} + \frac{0.2180}{90}}$$

$$= \sqrt{0.004602}$$

$$= 0.0678 \leftarrow \text{Estimated standard error of the difference between two proportions}$$

We standardize the difference between the two observed sample proportions, $\bar{p}_1 - \bar{p}_2$, by dividing by the estimated standard error of the difference between two proportions:

$$z = \frac{(\bar{p}_1 - \bar{p}_2) - (p_1 - p_2)_{H_0}}{\hat{\sigma}_{\bar{p}_1 - \bar{p}_2}}$$

$$= \frac{(0.71 - 0.644) - 0}{0.0678}$$

$$= 0.973$$

Step 4: Sketch the distribution and mark the sample value and critical values

Next we plot the standardized value on a sketch of the sampling distribution in Figure 9-9.

FIGURE 9-9

Two-tailed hypothesis test of the difference between two proportions at the 0.05 level of significance, showing the acceptance region and the standardized difference between the sample proportions

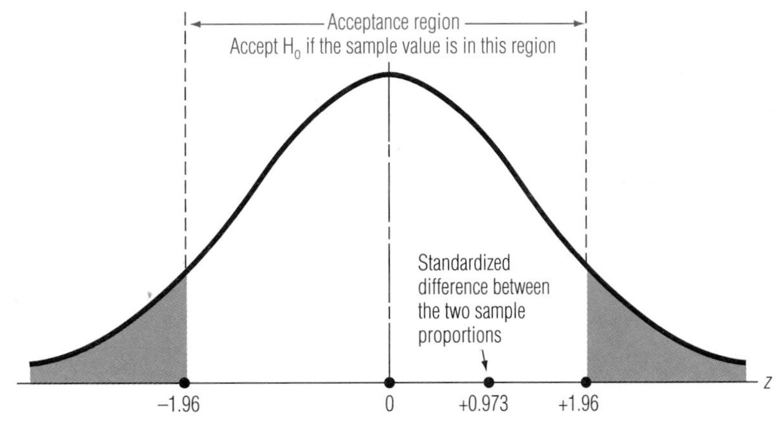

Step 5: Interpret the result

We can see in Figure 9-9 that the standardized difference between the two sample proportions lies within the acceptance region. Thus, we accept the null hypothesis and conclude that these two new compounds produce effects on blood pressure that are *not* significantly different.

One-Tailed Tests for Differences between Proportions

Conceptually, the one-tailed test for the difference between two population proportions is similar to a one-tailed test for the difference between two means. Suppose that for tax purposes, a city government has been using two methods of listing property. The first requires the property owner to appear in person before a tax lister, but the second permits the property owner to mail in a tax form. The city manager thinks the personal-appearance method produces far fewer mistakes than the mail-in method. She authorizes an examination of 50 personal-appearance listings and 75 mail-in listings. Ten percent of the personal-appearance forms contain errors; 13.3 percent of the mail-in forms contain them. The results of her sample can be summarized:

$\bar{p}_1 = 0.10$ ← Proportion of personal-appearance forms with errors

$\bar{q}_1 = 0.90$ ← Proportion of personal-appearance forms without errors

$n_1 = 50$ ← Sample size of personal-appearance forms

$\bar{p}_2 = 0.133$ ← Proportion of mail-in forms with errors

$\bar{q}_2 = 0.867$ ← Proportion of mail-in forms without errors

$n_2 = 75$ ← Sample size of mail-in forms

The city manager wants to test at the 0.15 level of significance the hypothesis that the personal-appearance method produces a lower proportion of errors. What should she do?

Step 1: State your hypotheses, type of test, and significance level

$H_0: p_1 = p_2$ ← Null hypothesis: There is no difference between the two methods

$H_1: p_1 < p_2$ ← Alternative hypothesis: The personal-appearance method has a lower proportion of errors than the mail-in method

$\alpha = 0.15$ ← Level of significance for testing the hypothesis

Step 2: Choose the appropriate distribution and find the critical value

With samples of this size, we can use the standard normal distribution and Appendix Table 1 to determine the critical value of z for 0.35 of the area under the curve $(0.50 - 0.15)$. We can use this value, 1.04, as the boundary of the acceptance region.

Figure 9-10 illustrates this hypothesis test. Because the city manager wishes to test whether the personal-appearance listing is better than the mailed-in listing, the appropriate test is a one-tailed test. Specifically, it is a *left-tailed* test, because to reject the null hypothesis, the test result must fall in the colored portion of the left tail, indicating that *significantly fewer errors* exist in the personal-appearance forms. This colored region in Figure 9-10 corresponds to the 0.15 significance level.

Step 3: Compute the standard error and standardize the sample statistic

To estimate the *standard error of the difference between two proportions,* we first use the combined proportions from both samples to estimate the overall proportion of successes:

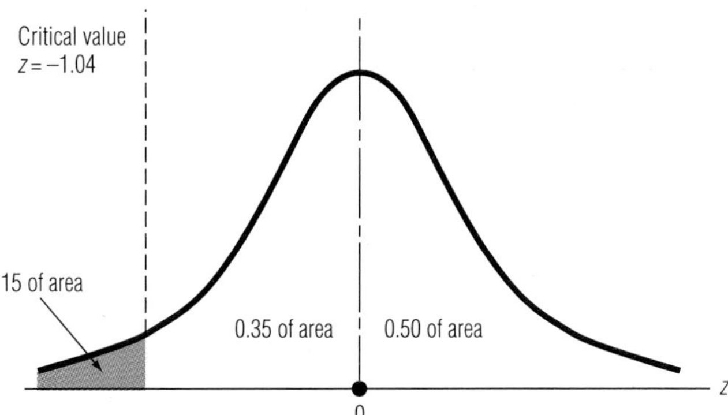

FIGURE 9-10

One-tailed hypothesis test of the difference between two proportions at the 0.15 level of significance

$$\hat{p} = \frac{n_1\bar{p}_1 + n_2\bar{p}_2}{n_1 + n_2} \qquad [9\text{-}7]$$

$$= \frac{(50)(0.10) + (75)(0.133)}{50 + 75}$$

$$= \frac{5 + 10}{125}$$

$$= 0.12 \leftarrow \text{Estimate of the overall proportion of successes in the population using combined proportions from both samples}$$

Now this answer can be used to calculate the estimated standard error of the difference between the two proportions, using Equation 9-8:

$$\hat{\sigma}_{\bar{p}_1 - \bar{p}_2} = \sqrt{\frac{\hat{p}\hat{q}}{n_1} + \frac{\hat{p}\hat{q}}{n_2}} \qquad [9\text{-}8]$$

$$= \sqrt{\frac{(0.12)(0.88)}{50} + \frac{(0.12)(0.88)}{75}}$$

$$= \sqrt{\frac{0.10560}{50} + \frac{0.10560}{75}}$$

$$= \sqrt{0.00352}$$

$$= 0.0593 \leftarrow \text{Estimated standard error of the difference between two proportions using combined estimates}$$

We use the estimated standard error of the difference, $\hat{\sigma}_{\bar{p}_1 - \bar{p}_2}$, to convert the observed difference between the two sample proportions, $\bar{p}_1 - \bar{p}_2$, to a standardized value:

$$z = \frac{(\bar{p}_1 - \bar{p}_2) - (p_1 - p_2)_{H_0}}{\hat{\sigma}_{\bar{p}_1 - \bar{p}_2}}$$

$$= \frac{(0.10 - 0.133) - 0}{0.0593}$$

$$= -0.556$$

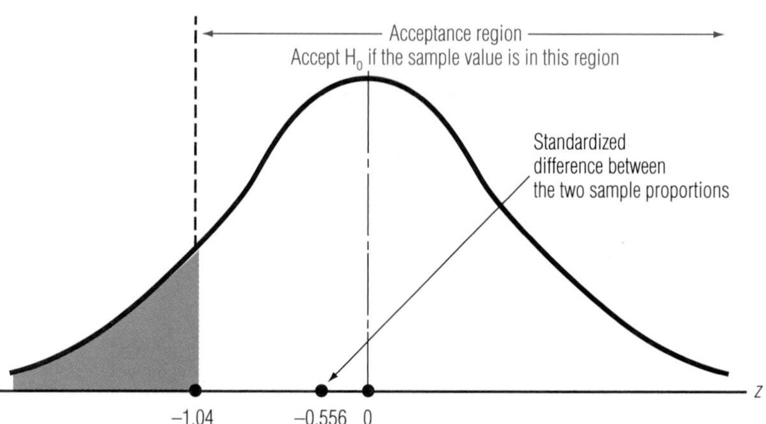

FIGURE 9-11

One-tailed hypothesis test of the difference between two proportions at the 0.15 level of significance, showing the acceptance region and the standardized difference between the sample proportions

Step 4: Sketch the distribution and mark the sample value and critical value

Figure 9-11 shows where this standardized difference lies in comparison to the critical value.

Step 5: Interpret the result

This figure shows us that the standardized difference between the two sample proportions lies well within the acceptance region, and the city manager should accept the null hypothesis that there is no difference between the two methods of tax listing. Therefore, if mailed-in listing is considerably less expensive to the city, the city manager should consider increasing the use of this method.

HINTS & ASSUMPTIONS

The procedure here is almost like the one we used earlier in comparing differences between two means using independent samples. The only difference here is that we first use the combined proportions from both samples to estimate the overall proportion, then we use that answer to estimate the standard error of the difference between the two proportions. Hint: If the test is concerned with whether one proportion is significantly *different* from the other, use a two-tailed test. If the test asks whether one proportion is significantly *higher* or significantly *lower* than the other, then a one-tailed test is appropriate.

Exercises 9.5

Self-Check Exercises

SC 9-7 A large hotel chain is trying to decide whether to convert more of its rooms to nonsmoking rooms. In a random sample of 400 guests last year, 166 had requested nonsmoking rooms. This year, 205 guests in a sample of 380 preferred the nonsmoking rooms. Would you recommend that the hotel chain convert more rooms to nonsmoking? Support your recommendation by testing the appropriate hypotheses at a 0.01 level of significance.

SC 9-8 Two different areas of a large eastern city are being considered as sites for day-care centers. Of 200 households surveyed in one section, the proportion in which the mother worked full-time was 0.52. In another section, 40 percent of the 150 households surveyed had mothers working at full-time jobs. At the 0.04 level of significance, is there a significant difference in the proportions of working mothers in the two areas of the city?

Applications

■ **9-20** On Friday, 11 stocks in a random sample of 40 of the roughly 2,500 stocks traded on the New York Stock Exchange advanced; that is, their price of their shares increased. In a sample of 60 NYSE stocks taken on Thursday, 24 advanced. At $\alpha = 0.10$, can you conclude that a smaller proportion of NYSE stocks advanced on Friday than did on Thursday?

■ **9-21** MacroSwift has recently released a new word-processing product, and they are interested in determining whether people in the 30–39 age group rate the program any differently than members of the 40–49 age group. MacroSwift randomly sampled 175 people in the 30–39 age group who purchased the product and found 87 people who rated the program as excellent, with 52 people who would purchase an upgrade. They also sampled 220 people in the 40–49 age group and found 94 people who gave an excellent rating, with 37 people who plan to purchase an upgrade. Is there any significant difference in the proportions of people in the two age groups who rate the program as excellent at the $\alpha = 0.05$ level? Is the same result true for proportions of people who plan to purchase an upgrade?

■ **9-22** A coal-fired power plant is considering two different systems for pollution abatement. The first system has reduced the emission of pollutants to acceptable levels 68 percent of the time, as determined from 200 air samples. The second, more expensive system has reduced the emission of pollutants to acceptable levels 76 percent of the time, as determined from 250 air samples. If the expensive system is significantly more effective than the inexpensive system in reducing pollutants to acceptable levels, then the management of the power plant will install the expensive system. Which system will be installed if management uses a significance level of 0.02 in making its decision?

■ **9-23** A group of clinical physicians is performing tests on patients to determine the effectiveness of a new antihypertensive drug. Patients with high blood pressure were randomly chosen and then randomly assigned to either the control group (which received a well-established antihypertensive) or the treatment group (which received the new drug). The doctors noted the percentage of patients whose blood pressure was reduced to a normal level within 1 year. At the 0.01 level of significance, test appropriate hypotheses to determine whether the new drug is significantly more effective than the older drug in reducing high blood pressure.

Group	Proportion That Improved	Number of Patients
Treatment	0.45	120
Control	0.36	150

different, doesn't specify direction

■ **9-24** The University Bookstore is facing significant competition from off-campus bookstores, and they are considering targeting a specific class in order to retain student business. The bookstore randomly sampled 150 freshmen and 175 sophomores. They found that 46 percent of the freshmen and 40 percent of the sophomores purchase all of their textbooks at the University Bookstore. At $\alpha = 0.10$, is there a significant difference in the proportions of freshman and sophomores who purchase entirely at the University Bookstore?

■ **9-25** In preparation for contract-renewal negotiations, the United Manufacturing Workers surveyed its members to see whether they preferred a large increase in retirement benefits or a smaller increase in salary. In a group of 1,000 male members who were polled, 743 were in favor of increased retirement benefits. Of 500 female members surveyed, 405 favored the increase in retirement benefits.

(a) Calculate $\hat{p}$.

(b) Compute the standard error of the difference between the two proportions.

(c) Test the hypothesis that equal proportions of men and women are in favor of increased retirement benefits. Use the 0.05 level of significance.

Worked-Out Answers to Self-Check Exercises

SC 9-7 $n_1 = 400 \quad \bar{p}_1 = 0.415 \quad n_2 = 380 \quad \bar{p}_2 = 0.5395$

$H_0: p_1 = p_2 \quad H_1: p_1 < p_2 \quad \alpha = 0.01$

$$\hat{p} = \frac{n_1\bar{p}_1 + n_2\bar{p}_2}{n_1 + n_2} = \frac{400(0.415) + 380(0.5395)}{400 + 380} = 0.4757$$

$$\hat{\sigma}_{\bar{p}_1 - \bar{p}_2} = \sqrt{\hat{p}\hat{q}\left(\frac{1}{n_1} + \frac{1}{n_2}\right)} = \sqrt{0.4757(0.5243)\left(\frac{1}{400} + \frac{1}{380}\right)} = 0.0358$$

The lower limit of the acceptance region is $z = -2.33$, or

$$\bar{p}_1 - \bar{p}_2 = 0 - z\hat{\sigma}_{\bar{p}_1 - \bar{p}_2} = -2.33(0.0358) = -0.0834$$

Because the observed z value $= \dfrac{\bar{p}_1 - \bar{p}_2}{\hat{\sigma}_{\bar{p}_1 - \bar{p}_2}} = \dfrac{0.415 - 0.5395}{0.0358} = -3.48$ < -2.33 (or $\bar{p}_1 - \bar{p}_2 = -0.1245 < -0.0834$), we reject H_0. The hotel chain should convert more rooms to nonsmoking because there was a significant increase in the proportion of guests requesting these rooms over the last year.

SC 9-8 $n_1 = 200 \quad \bar{p}_1 = 0.52 \quad n_2 = 150 \quad \bar{p}_2 = 0.40$

$H_0: p_1 = p_2 \quad H_1: p_1 \neq p_2 \quad \alpha = 0.04$

$$\hat{p} = \frac{n_1\bar{p}_1 + n_2\bar{p}_2}{n_1 + n_2} = \frac{200(0.52) + 150(0.40)}{200 + 150} = 0.4686$$

$$\hat{\sigma}_{\bar{p}_1 - \bar{p}_2} = \sqrt{\hat{p}\hat{q}\left(\frac{1}{n_1} + \frac{1}{n_2}\right)} = \sqrt{0.4686(0.5314)\left(\frac{1}{200} + \frac{1}{150}\right)} = 0.0539$$

The limits of the acceptance region are $z = \pm 2.05$, or

$$\bar{p}_1 - \bar{p}_2 = 0 \pm z\hat{\sigma}_{\bar{p}_1 - \bar{p}_2} = \pm 2.05(0.0539) = \pm 0.1105$$

Because the observed z value $= \dfrac{\bar{p}_1 - \bar{p}_2}{\hat{\sigma}_{\bar{p}_1 - \bar{p}_2}} = \dfrac{0.52 - 0.40}{0.0539} = 2.23 > 2.05$ (or $\bar{p}_1 - \bar{p}_2 = 0.12 > 0.1105$), we reject H_0. The proportions of working mothers in the two areas differ significantly.

9.6 Prob Values: Another Way to Look at Testing Hypotheses

In all the work we've done so far on hypothesis testing, one of the first things we had to do was choose a level of significance, α, for the test. It has been traditional to choose a significance level of $\alpha = 10$ percent, 5 percent, 2 percent, or 1 percent, and almost all our examples have been done at these levels. But why use only these few values?

How do we choose a significance level?

When we discussed Type I and Type II errors on page 409, we saw that the choice of the significance level depended on a trade-off between the costs of each of these two kinds of errors. If the cost of a Type I error (incorrectly rejecting H_0) is relatively high, we want to avoid making this kind of error, so we choose a small value of α. On the other hand, if a Type II error (incorrectly accepting H_0) is relatively more expensive, we are more willing to make a Type I error, and we choose a high value of α. **However, understanding the nature of the trade-off still doesn't tell us how to choose a significance level.**

Deciding before we take a sample

When we test the hypotheses:

$$H_0\colon \mu = \mu_{H_0}$$
$$H_1\colon \mu \neq \mu_{H_0}$$
$$\alpha = 0.05$$

we take a sample, compute $\bar{x}$ and reject H_0 if $\bar{x}$ is so far from μ_{H_0} that the probability of seeing a value of $\bar{x}$ this far (or farther) from μ_{H_0} is less than 0.05. In other words, **before we take the sample,** we specify how unlikely the observed results will have to be in order for us to reject H_0. There is another way to approach this decision about rejecting or accepting H_0 that doesn't require that we specify the significance level before taking the sample. Let's see how it works.

Prob values

Suppose we take our sample, compute $\bar{x}$, and then ask the question, "Supposing H_0 were true, what's the probability of getting a value of $\bar{x}$ this far or farther from μ_{H_0}?" This probability is called a *prob value* or a *p-value*. **Whereas before we asked, "Is the probability of what we've observed less than α?" now we are merely asking, "How unlikely is the result we have observed?" Once the prob value for the test is reported, *then* the decision maker can weigh all the relevant factors and decide whether to accept or reject H_0, without being bound by a prespecified significance level.**

Another advantage

Another benefit of using prob values is that they provide more information. If you know that I rejected H_0 at $\alpha = 0.05$, you know only that $\bar{x}$ was *at least* 1.96 standard errors away from μ_{H_0}. However, a prob value of 0.05 tells you that $\bar{x}$ was *exactly* 1.96 standard errors away from μ_{H_0}. Let's look at an example.

Two-Tailed Prob Values When σ Is Known

A machine is used to cut wheels of Swiss cheese into blocks of specified weight. On the basis of long experience, it has been observed that the weight of the blocks is normally distributed with a standard deviation of 0.3 ounce. The machine is currently set to cut blocks that weigh 12 ounces. A sample of nine blocks is found to have an average weight of 12.25 ounces. Should we conclude that the cutting machine needs to be recalibrated?

Setting up the problem symbolically

Written symbolically, the data in our problem are

$$\mu_{H_0} = 12 \leftarrow \text{Hypothesized value of the population mean}$$

$$\sigma = 0.3 \leftarrow \text{Population standard deviation}$$

$$n = 9 \leftarrow \text{Sample size}$$

$$\bar{x} = 12.25 \leftarrow \text{Sample mean}$$

The hypotheses we wish to test are

$$H_0\text{: } \mu = 12 \leftarrow \text{Null hypothesis: The true population mean weight is 12 ounces}$$

$$H_1\text{: } \mu \neq 12 \leftarrow \text{Alternative hypothesis: The true population mean weight is not 12 ounces}$$

Because this is a two-tailed test, our prob value is the probability of observing a value of $\bar{x}$ at least as far away (on either side) from 12 as 12.25, if H_0 is true. In other words, the prob value is the probability of getting $\bar{x} \geq 12.25$ or $\bar{x} \leq 11.75$ if H_0 is true. To find this probability, we first use Equation 6-1 to calculate the standard error of the mean:

Calculating the standard error of the mean

$$\sigma_{\bar{x}} = \frac{\sigma}{\sqrt{n}} \tag{6-1}$$

$$= \frac{0.3}{\sqrt{9}}$$

$$= \frac{0.3}{3}$$

$$= 0.1 \text{ ounce} \leftarrow \text{Standard error of the mean}$$

Then we use this to convert $\bar{x}$ to a standard z score:

Finding the z score and the prob value

$$z = \frac{\bar{x} - \mu}{\sigma_{\bar{x}}} \tag{6-2}$$

$$= \frac{12.25 - 12}{0.1}$$

$$= \frac{0.25}{0.1}$$

$$= 2.5$$

From Appendix Table 1, we see that the probability that z is greater than 2.5 is $0.5000 - 0.4938 = 0.0062$. Hence, because this is a two-tailed hypothesis test, the prob value is $2(0.0062) = 0.0124$. Our results are illustrated in Figure 9-12. Given this information, our cheese packer can now decide whether to recalibrate the machine (reject H_0) or not (accept H_0).

Relationship between prob values and significance levels

How is this related to what we did before, when we specified a significance level? If a significance level of $\alpha = 0.05$ were adopted, we would reject H_0. You can easily see this by looking at Figure 9-12. At a significance level of $\alpha = 0.05$, we reject H_0 if $\bar{x}$ is so far from μ_{H_0} that less than 0.05 of the area under the curve is left in the two tails. Because our observed value of $\bar{x} = 12.25$ leaves only 0.0124 of the total area in the tails, we would re-

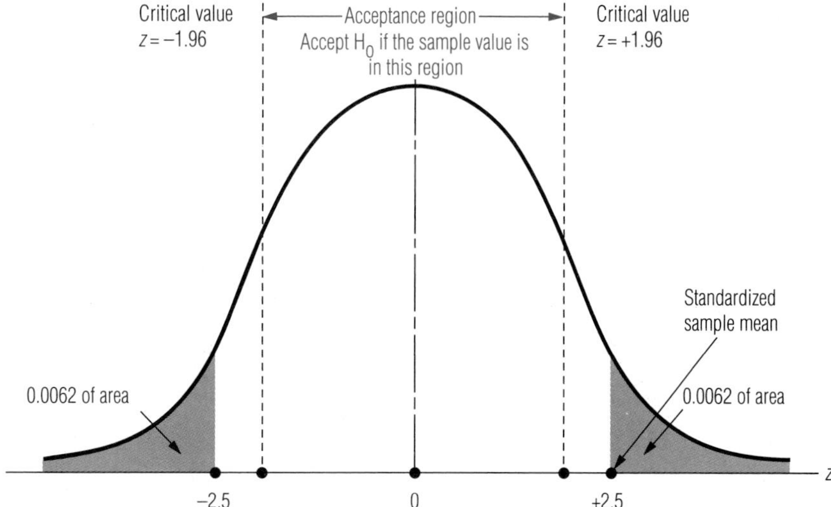

FIGURE 9-12

Two-tailed hypothesis test, showing prob value of 0.0124 (in both tails combined)

ject H_0 at a significance level of $\alpha = 0.05$. (You can also verify this result by noting in Appendix Table 1 that the critical z values for $\alpha = 0.05$ are ± 1.96. Thus, the standardized value of $\bar{x}$ (2.5) is *outside* the acceptance region.)

Similarly, we can see that at a significance level of $\alpha = 0.01$, we would accept H_0, because $\bar{x} = 12.25$ leaves more than 0.01 of the total area in the tails. (In this case, the critical z values for $\alpha = 0.01$ would be ± 2.58, and now the standardized value of $\bar{x}$, 2.5, is *inside* the acceptance region.) In fact, at any level of α above 0.0124, we would reject H_0. **Thus, we see that the prob value is precisely the largest significance level at which we would accept H_0.**

Prob Values under Other Conditions

In our example, we did a two-tailed hypothesis test using the normal distribution. How would we proceed in other circumstances?

One-tailed prob values

1. If σ was known, and we were doing a one-tailed test, we would compute the prob value in exactly the same way except that we would not multiply the probability that we got from Appendix Table 1 by 2, because that table gives one-tailed probabilities directly.

Using the *t* distribution

2. If σ was not known, we would use the t distribution with $n - 1$ degrees of freedom and Appendix Table 2. This table gives two-tailed probabilities, but only a few of them, so we can't get exact prob values from it. For example, for a two-tailed test, if $\mu_{H_0} = 50$, $\bar{x} = 49.2$, $s = 1.4$, and $n = 16$, we find that

$$\hat{\sigma}_{\bar{x}} = \frac{\hat{\sigma}}{\sqrt{n}} \qquad [7\text{-}6]$$

$$= \frac{1.4}{\sqrt{16}}$$

$$= 0.35$$

and that $\bar{x}$ is 2.286 estimated standard errors below μ_{H_0} [(49.2 − 50)/0.35= −2.286]. Looking at the 15 degrees of freedom row in Appendix Table 2, we see that 2.286 is between 2.131 ($\alpha = 0.05$) and 2.602 ($\alpha = 0.02$). Our prob value is therefore something between 0.02 and 0.05, but we can't be more specific.

Prob values in other contexts

Most computer statistics packages report exact prob values, not only for tests about means based on the normal distribution, but for other tests such as chi-square and analysis of variance (which we will discuss in Chapter 11) and tests in the context of linear regression (which we will discuss in Chapters 12 and 13). The discussion we have provided in this section will enable you to understand prob values in those contexts too. Although different statistics and distributions will be involved, the ideas are the same.

HINTS & ASSUMPTIONS

Prob values and computers eliminate having to look up values from a z or t distribution table, and take the drudgery out of hypothesis testing. Warning: The *smaller* the prob value, the greater the significance of the findings. Hint: You can avoid confusion here by remembering that a prob value is the chance that the result you have could have occurred by sampling error, thus, smaller prob values mean smaller chances of sampling error and higher significance.

Exercises 9.6

Self-Check Exercises

SC 9-9 The Coffee Institute has claimed that more than 40 percent of American adults regularly have a cup of coffee with breakfast. A random sample of 450 individuals revealed that 200 of them were regular coffee drinkers at breakfast. What is the prob value for a test of hypotheses seeking to show that the Coffee Institute's claim was correct? (*Hint:* Test H_0: $p = 0.4$, versus H_1: $p > 0.4$.)

SC 9-10 Approximately what is the prob value for the test in Self-Check Exercise 9-3 on page 465?

Applications

■ **9-26** A car retailer thinks that a 40,000-mile claim for tire life by the manufacturer is too high. She carefully records the mileage obtained from a sample of 64 such tires. The mean turns out to be 38,500 miles. The standard deviation of the life of all tires of this type has previously been calculated by the manufacturer to be 7,600 miles. Assuming that the mileage is normally distributed, determine the largest significance level at which we would accept the manufacturer's mileage claim, that is, at which we would not conclude the mileage is significantly less than 40,000 miles.

■ **9-27** The North Carolina Department of Transportation has claimed that at most, 18 percent of passenger cars exceed 70 mph on Interstate 40 between Raleigh and Durham. A random sample of 300 cars found 48 cars exceeding 70 mph. What is the prob value for a test of hypothesis seeking to show the NCDOT's claim is correct?

■ **9-28** Kelly's machine shop uses a machine-controlled metal saw to cut sections of tubing used in pressure-measuring devices. The length of the sections is normally distributed with a standard deviation of 0.06″. Twenty-five pieces have been cut with the machine set to cut sections 5.00″ long. When these pieces were measured, their mean length was found to be 4.97″. Use prob values to determine whether the machine should be recalibrated because the mean length is significantly different from 5.00″.

■ **9-29** SAT Services advertises that 80 percent of the time, its preparatory course will increase an individual's score on the College Board exams by at least 50 points on the combined verbal and quantitative total score. Lisle Johns, SAT's marketing director, wants to see whether this is a reasonable claim. He has reviewed the records of 125 students who took the course and found that 94 of them did, indeed, increase their scores by at least 50 points. Use prob values to determine whether SAT's ads should be changed because the percentage of students whose scores increase by 50 or more points is significantly different from 80 percent.

■ **9-30** What is the prob value for the test in Exercise 9-2?

■ **9-31** What is the prob value for the test in Exercise 9-3?

■ **9-32** Approximately what is the prob value for the test in Exercise 9-8?

■ **9-33** Approximately what is the prob value for the test in Exercise 9-11?

■ **9-34** Approximately what is the prob value for the test in Exercise 9-14?

■ **9-35** Approximately what is the prob value for the test in Exercise 9-15?

■ **9-36** What is the prob value for the test in Exercise 9-22?

■ **9-37** What is the prob value for the test in Exercise 9-25?

Worked-Out Answers to Self-Check Exercises

SC 9-9 $n = 450 \qquad \bar{p} = 200/450 = 0.4444$

H_0: $p = 0.4 \qquad H_1$: $p > 0.4$

The prob value is the probability that $\bar{p} \geq 0.4444$, that is,

$$P\left(z \geq \frac{0.4444 - 0.4}{\sqrt{0.4(0.6)/450}}\right) = P(z \geq 1.92) = 0.5 - 0.4726 = 0.0274$$

SC 9-10 From the solution to exercise SC 9-3 on page 467, we have $t = -2.766$, with $12 + 9 - 2 = 19$ degrees of freedom. From the row in Appendix Table 2 for 19 degrees of freedom, we see that -2.766 is between -2.861 (corresponding to a probability of $.01/2 = .005$ in the lower tail) and -2.539 (corresponding to a probability of $.02/2 = .01$ in the lower tail). Hence the prob value for our test is between .005 and .01.

9.7 Using the Computer to Test Hypotheses

When the final exam for our Fall 1995 statistics course was designed, we expected that the average grade would be about 75 percent (56.25 points out of a maximum possible score of 75). Let's test (at $\alpha = 0.05$) whether our expectation was met.

Setting up the problem symbolically

H_0: $\mu = 56.25$ ← The exam achieved the desired difficulty

H_1: $\mu \neq 56.25$ ← The desired difficulty was not achieved

$\alpha = 0.05$ ← Level of significance for this test

Interpreting the results

In Figure 9-13, we have used Minitab to analyze the data in Appendix 10. The observed t value for this test is -15.45, with an associated (two-tailed) prob value of 0.0000. Because this prob value is less than our significance level of $\alpha = 0.05$, we must reject H_0 and conclude that the test did not achieve the desired level of difficulty. (In fact, the test turned out to be much more difficult than we had intended.)

The university had been receiving many complaints about the caliber of teaching being done by the graduate-student teaching assistants. As a result, we wondered whether the students in sections taught by the graduate TAs really did do worse on the exam than those students in sections taught by the faculty. If we let the TAs' sections be sample 1 and the faculty's sections be sample 2, then the appropriate hypotheses for testing this concern are

Setting up the problem symbolically

$$H_0: \mu_1 = \mu_2 \leftarrow \text{The concern is not supported by the data}$$

$$H_1: \mu_1 < \mu_2 \leftarrow \text{The concern is supported by the data}$$

The Minitab output for doing this test is given in Figure 9-14. Notice that test results are reported assuming that the two population variances are equal. If we can assume that the two variances are equal, then the test reported by Minitab is the test we discussed on pages 471–472, where we found a pooled estimate for σ^2.

Interpreting the results

What should we conclude about whether or not students in sections taught by TAs are at a disadvantage? The reported prob value for this one-tailed test (0.33) is quite large relative

FIGURE 9-13 Using Minitab to test hypotheses about a population mean

```
T-Test of the Mean

Test of mu = 56.250 vs mu not = 56.250

Variable      N       Mean     StDev    SE Mean        T     P-Value
FINAL       199     45.281    10.014      0.710   -15.45      0.0000
```

FIGURE 9-14 Using Minitab to test hypotheses about the difference between two means

```
Two Sample T-Test and Confidence Interval

Twosample T for FINAL
INSTRNUM     N        Mean       StDev    SE Mean
1           89       44.93        9.76        1.0
2          110        45.6        10.2       0.98

95% C.I. for mu 1 - mu 2: ( -3.5,  2.19)

T-Test mu 1 = mu 2 (vs <): T= -0.44  P=0.33  DF=  197

Both use Pooled StDev = 10.0
```

to the typical significance levels we have been using (0.10, 0.05, 0.01, etc.) so we cannot reject H_0. The data do not support the concern expressed in the complaints received by the university.

The earnings data in Appendix 11 contain the 1988 last-quarter earnings for 224 companies, in addition to containing the 1989 last-quarter earnings. Because the U.S. economy had not suffered a recession since 1982, by 1989 many economists were expecting the economy to start slowing down. Let's check (at $\alpha = 0.10$) whether the year-to-year change in last-quarter earnings gave evidence that their expectation had come to pass. In Figure 9-15, we have used Minitab to test this.

Setting up the problem symbolically

$$H_0\colon \mu_{1989} = \mu_{1988} \leftarrow \text{The economy didn't slow down}$$

$$H_1\colon \mu_{1989} < \mu_{1988} \leftarrow \text{The economy did slow down}$$

$$\alpha = 0.10 \leftarrow \text{Level of significance for this test}$$

To perform this paired difference test, we first subtracted the 1988 last-quarter earnings from the 1989 last-quarter earnings and stored the results in a variable named "CHANGE." Looking at CHANGE, our hypotheses become

$$H_0\colon \mu = 0 \quad \leftarrow \text{The economy didn't slow down}$$

$$H_1\colon \mu < 0 \quad \leftarrow \text{The economy did slow down}$$

$$\alpha = 0.10 \leftarrow \text{Level of significance for this test}$$

Interpreting the results

In Figure 9-15, we see that the reported prob value for our one-tailed test is 0.28. Because this prob value is greater than our significance level of $\alpha = 0.10$, we cannot reject H_0. Last-quarter earnings did not decline significantly from year to year, so they don't provide evidence of a slowing economy.

In the test we just did, all 224 companies were used. However, maybe earnings changes for the relatively large companies whose stock is listed on the New York Stock Exchange are different from earnings changes for the smaller companies listed on the American Stock Exchange or traded over-the-counter. If they differ, perhaps one is a better indicator of the direction in which the economy is heading. To check this out, we can divide the 224 companies into two groups (NYSE and OTHER) and do an independent samples test of the difference in the mean values of CHANGE in the two groups. Let's test this at $\alpha = 0.02$.

FIGURE 9-15 Using Minitab to do a paired difference test of means

```
T-Test of the Mean

Test of mu = 0.0000 vs mu < 0.0000

Variable      N      Mean     StDev   SE Mean        T    P-Value
CHANGE      224   -0.0354    0.8967    0.0599    -0.59       0.28
```

FIGURE 9-16 Using Minitab to do an independent-samples test of means

```
Two Sample T-Test and Confidence Interval

Twosample T for CHANGE
NYORNO     N        Mean       StDev    SE Mean
0        149      -0.061       0.645      0.053
1         75        0.02        1.26       0.15

95% C.I. for mu 0 - mu 1: ( -0.327,  0.17)

T-Test mu 0 = mu 1 (vs not =): T= -0.60  P=0.55  DF=  222

Both use Pooled StDev = 0.898
```

Setting up the problem symbolically

$$H_0\text{: } \mu_{NYSE} = \mu_{OTHER} \leftarrow \text{Both mean changes are the same}$$

$$H_1\text{: } \mu_{NYSE} \neq \mu_{OTHER} \leftarrow \text{Both mean changes are not the same}$$

$$\alpha = 0.02 \quad \leftarrow \text{Level of significance for this test}$$

In Figure 9-16, we have used Minitab to perform this test. The EXCHANGE variable was converted from its character values of O, A, and N to the numeric values 0, 0, and 1 in a new variable called NYORNO.

Interpreting the results

In this particular case the prob value of 0.55 for the test of the difference of the NYSE and OTHER mean changes is much larger than our significance level of $\alpha = 0.02$, so we cannot reject H_0. There is not enough evidence to warrant further investigation of using the year-to-year change in last-quarter earnings as evidence of the direction in which the economy was heading.

Statistics at Work

Loveland Computers

Case 9: Two-Sample Tests of Hypotheses When Lee Azko looked over the results of the telephone survey conducted by the marketing department of Loveland Computers, something was troubling. "Hmm, you wouldn't still have the data for the 'Total spent on software' on computer, would you, Margot?" Lee asked the head of the department.

"Hey, I keep *everything*," Margot replied. "It's in a worksheet file on the computer over there. I had the intern camp out in my office last summer. Why do you need to see the data?"

"Well, give me a minute and I'll show you," said Lee, turning on the machine. After a few minutes of muttering over the keyboard, Lee pushed back from the screen. "Thought so! Take a look at that. It looks like there are really two groups of customers here—see how there are two different peaks on this graph?"

"I guess we should have done more than just print out the mean and standard deviation last summer," said Margot disconsolately. "I guess this means the data are no good."

"Not necessarily," said Lee with more optimism. "I'll bet your 'big spenders' are your business customers and the lower peak is the home users. You wouldn't have any way to know which category the response was in, would you?"

"Well, we capture that automatically," Margot said, leaning over and clearing the graph from the screen. "If you look at the first column, you'll see that it's the customer number. All the business customers have a customer number that begins with a *1* and all the home users have a customer number that begins with a *2*."

"Let me copy this file onto a floppy," Lee said, opening the briefcase. "I'll be back this afternoon with the answer."

Study Questions: What graph did Lee plot using the worksheet program? What hypothesis is being tested and what is the appropriate statistical test? Is this a one-tailed or a two-tailed problem?

Computer Database Exercise

HH Industries

Laurel knocked on Hal's half-open door. "Welcome back," she said. "I hear you had a great trip."

Hal looked up and motioned for her to come in and sit down. "Oh, it was great all right. But exhausting! We spent the entire week on our feet!"

Hal, Stan, and John Raymond, the new advertising manager, had just returned the day before from a week-long trade show in Las Vegas. CONEXPO was the largest construction exposition in the world; held only every five years, it drew thousands of exhibitors and participants. Everyone who was anyone in the construction business was there. For the first time, HH Industries had been right in the middle of it all.

"Our booth position was unbelievable," Hal continued. "I don't know what John promised the woman who was arranging everything, but it was worth it!" He winked at Laurel. "We definitely had a prime piece of real estate. Coming off the escalator, you had to walk right by our booth to get to the main part of the exhibition hall. And the displays we had built just before the show were really eye-catching. Not only did we give away all 400 catalogs we took with us, but we have addresses for almost twice that many folks who want to be put on our mailing list."

Laurel grinned. Hal's enthusiasm was infectious. "You conjectured that this show might very well change the future of our business, and it sounds like you may have been right. Stan mentioned that you guys even had to have dinner with clients every evening. I bet you're glad to be back, even if it's only to recuperate."

"It does feel good to have it behind us," Hal agreed. "I just hope our investment actually pays off—all told, we spent almost $15,000 to participate."

Laurel thought for a minute. "The sales figures may take a while to react strongly enough for us to notice. People don't just switch suppliers right away. However, I've got an idea of a simple way by which we could measure a more immediate response. Doesn't Stan keep track of the number of different customers who call us every day?"

Hal nodded and smiled. "The UCC—Unique Customer Count. You know Stan. He keeps track of everything!"

"I thought so. Let me take a look at the UCC data from the last several weeks. Then we'll collect some more data starting Monday. We can compare the pre- and post-CONEXPO figures and determine if we're seeing any difference in the number of people we're talking to. It's a simple technique, but it should give us a feel in the short run. Later we can develop more detailed, in-depth analyses to track sales trends, project a break-even point for our investment, and so on."

"Sounds good to me," Hal said. "Let me know what you come up with."

Laurel collected the following data (which can also be found in the CH09A.xxx files on the data disk):

Pre-CONEXPO UCCs	Post-CONEXPO UCCs
39 22 28 11 33 47 25	41 47 27 27 36 24 28
24 34 28 15 40 27 33	36 46 34 36 44 13 23
27 23 27 18 46 33 17	46 48 48 44 45 26 36
38 38 19 13 30 20 38	21 30 35 36 23 36 34
37 33 17 28 36 23 27	36 48 38 44 35 36 46
34 24 38 35 10 37 23	36 36 24 26 24 23 23
29 32 38 21 43 27 35	51 37 37 17 46 34 28
28 18 39 23 20 30 28	41 30 25 46 33 26 44
17 33 47 28 16 23 37	36 38 28 34 45 46 36

1. Determine whether the pre-CONEXPO and post-CONEXPO call populations have the same mean number of unique customers per day. Test at the 0.05 level of significance.

Hal was understandably enthusiastic about Laurel's findings. "Looks like we were able to reach some new folks," he said at the next staff meeting. John Raymond looked across the table at Laurel. "Is there any way we could tell whether or not it hurt us not having enough catalogs at the show? That is, could we tell if those customers who received a catalog in the mail are ordering less than those that picked up catalogs at our booth?"

Stan looked up. "That would be great," he chimed in. "And since we phoned back here with catalog requests during the show, those that requested catalogs had them as soon as they got home; we could probably even use data from the same time period as this study," he said, indicating the papers in front of him.

Laurel thought for a minute. "That will be somewhat of a challenge," she began. "The population sizes differ by quite a bit, so we'll have to use a proportional approach rather than actual sales figures. Let me see what I can come up with. Stan, I'll need some help from you to pick out the relevant customers from the data for the last few weeks—I'll stop by your office this afternoon."

Laurel started designing the study as soon as she left the staff meeting. She had Stan mark the sales reports for her, indicating customers from each group separately. Then she calculated the percentage of customers placing orders on each day in the study period. (These data are in the CH09B.xxx files on the data disk.)

Picked-Up Catalog

0.019	0.081	0.003	0.052	0.092	0.032	0.021
0.079	0.019	0.014	0.061	0.023	0.007	0.023
0.026	0.017	0.074	0.018	0.072	0.023	0.038
0.022	0.061	0.031	0.025	0.020	0.027	0.029
0.080	0.037	0.021	0.027	0.024	0.057	0.067
0.036	0.091	0.025	0.056	0.046	0.086	0.042
0.028	0.010	0.005	0.056	0.009	0.024	0.061
0.019	0.010	0.021	0.057	0.017	0.017	0.057
0.015	0.054	0.022	0.019	0.031	0.053	0.041

Mailed Catalog

0.016	0.095	0.011	0.002	0.026	0.011	0.055
0.030	0.030	0.051	0.017	0.048	0.050	0.021
0.003	0.046	0.012	0.014	0.072	0.013	0.056
0.052	0.009	0.085	0.024	0.015	0.022	0.045
0.028	0.012	0.013	0.015	0.013	0.027	0.049
0.014	0.061	0.007	0.023	0.023	0.007	0.035
0.019	0.030	0.029	0.042	0.022	0.065	0.033
0.012	0.052	0.019	0.030	0.041	0.014	0.032
0.074	0.023	0.027	0.057	0.056	0.017	0.053

2. Determine whether the daily average proportion of customers placing orders is smaller for customers who had the catalog mailed to them (versus those who picked up catalogs). For what values of alpha will the null hypothesis be accepted?

Stan was pleased about the results so far, but Laurel knew that he wasn't completely satisfied. "I know what you need," she said to him one afternoon after a lengthy discussion. "You need dollars! You're never quite happy until there are dollars involved."

Stan smiled sheepishly. "You know me too well. I have been curious as to how the bottom line has been affected by CONEXPO. To my eye, the sales figures look good, but you and your statistics should be able to convince me that it's not just wishful thinking!"

Stan was definitely from the old school where statistics were for academicians, not businesspeople. He had come a long way in accepting statistical work as both valid and valuable to HH Industries. "Let's pick about 40 SKUs from the inventory and study their sales performance during the same time periods we addressed in the UCC and the catalog studies," she said. "That will give us a pretty good feel for how sales are doing in general."

With Stan's help, Laurel collected the following data for the same 40 SKUs both before and after CONEXPO. (These data are in the CH09C.xxx files on the data disk.)

Pre-CONEXPO Sales Data

1,163	711	394	538	915
850	598	1,619	1,624	486
766	670	469	2,125	860
305	609	1,510	512	782
1,800	818	531	521	1,561
318	1,215	910	1,441	719
360	834	1,195	530	321
266	225	925	1,762	652

Post-CONEXPO Sales Data

1,220	795	316	713	814
932	663	1,801	1,848	538
810	891	471	2,118	888
315	812	1,620	659	950
2,015	930	609	581	1,691
325	1,422	934	1,493	842
500	850	1,300	695	419
358	252	1,287	1,873	775

3. At the 15 percent significance level, determine whether mean sales increased after CONEXPO. Can the effect on sales be attributed entirely to CONEXPO? Explain.

From the Textbook to the Real World

Clinical Trials Use Statistics to Determine the Best Medical Procedures

Medical professionals often joke that one of the most dangerous places to be when you're sick is in a hospital. That's because patients in hospitals sometimes pick up infections from other patients. Research has shown that most of the transmission occurs on the hands of health care workers as they move from one patient to the next, so a group of doctors and nurses at the University of Iowa College of Medicine decided to investigate hand washing in their hospital's three intensive care units (ICUs) over an 8-month period.

Dr. Bradley Doebbling and his colleagues set up a cross-over study to compare two types of cleansers. Each month they switched the type of cleanser available. Both cleansers have some antibacterial activity: One contained the antibiotic chlorhexidine gluconate and the other contained a 60 percent alcohol solution.

The hospital already had procedures in place to watch for infections in ICU patients and to treat them promptly. The researchers also set up random half-hour observation periods to track the number of times the ICU doctors and nurses washed their hands between procedures. Then they compared the number of infections reported under the two hand-washing systems, using the number of patient days under the two regimens (one patient in the hospital for one day counts as a patient day).

	Hand-Washing Agent	
	Chlorhexidine	**Alcohol**
Number of patient days	4,001	3,984
Number of infections	152	202

Demonstrating a Difference between Cleansers The results were that in the months when chlorhexidine was used, the frequency of in-hospital infections was only three-quarters of what it was when the alcohol solution was provided, and statistical analysis of the infection rates of the two groups shows this difference to be significant.

The apparent superior effectiveness of chlorhexidine depends, in part, on professionals' willingness to comply with hand-washing instructions. Overall, the researchers found that staff members washed their hands on only about 40 percent of the opportunities when it might have helped control infection, but they were more likely to wash when the chlorhexidine was available. In one of the three ICUs, the difference in hand-washing compliance was as much as 48 percent compliance with chlorhexidine versus only 30 percent for use of alcohol ($p = 0.002$ by a t test).

The Payoff Is Substantial Studies have estimated the total annual cost of in-hospital infections in the United States to be between \$5 and \$10 billion. Encouraging hospital staff members to thoroughly wash their hands between procedures does seem to make a difference in infection rates, and staff members are more likely to wash when they are provided with a strong antibacterial cleanser.

Source: B. N. Doebbling, G. L. Stanley, C. T. Sheetz, M. A. Pfaller, A. K. Houston, L. Annis, N. Li, and R. P. Wenzel. "Comparative Efficacy of Alternative Hand-Washing Agents in Reducing Nosocomial Infections in Intensive Care Units," *The New England Journal of Medicine*, 327(2), (1992): 88–93.

Chapter Review

Terms Introduced in Chapter 9

Combined Proportion of Successes In comparing two population proportions, the total number of successes in both samples divided by the total size of both samples; used to estimate the proportion of successes common to both populations.

Dependent Samples Samples drawn from two populations in such a way that the elements in one sample are matched or paired with the elements in the other sample, in order to allow a more precise analysis by controlling for extraneous factors.

Paired Difference Test A hypothesis test of the difference between two population means based on the means of two dependent samples.

Paired Samples Another name for dependent samples.

Pooled Estimate of σ^2 A weighted average of s_1^2 and s_2^2 used to estimate the common variance, σ^2, when using small samples to test the difference between two population means.

Prob Value The largest significance level at which we would accept the null hypothesis. It enables us to test hypotheses without first specifying a value for α.

P-value Another name for a prob value.

Two-Sample Tests Hypothesis tests based on samples taken from two populations in order to compare their means or proportions.

Equations Introduced in Chapter 9

■ **9-1**

$$\sigma_{\bar{x}_1 - \bar{x}_2} = \sqrt{\frac{\sigma_1^2}{n_1} + \frac{\sigma_2^2}{n_2}}$$ p. 456

This formula enables us to derive the standard deviation of the distribution of the difference between two sample means, that is, *the standard error of the difference between two means.* To do this, we take the square root of the sum of Population 1's variance divided by its sample size plus Population 2's variance divided by its sample size.

■ **9-2** $$\hat{\sigma}_{\bar{x}_1 - \bar{x}_2} = \sqrt{\frac{\hat{\sigma}_1^2}{n_1} + \frac{\hat{\sigma}_2^2}{n_2}}$$ p. 457

If the two population standard deviations are unknown, we can use this formula to derive the *estimated* standard error of the difference between two means. We can use this equation after we have used the two sample standard deviations and Equation 7–1 to determine the estimated standard deviations of Population 1 and Population 2, ($\hat{\sigma} = s$).

■ **9-3** $$s_p^2 = \frac{(n_1 - 1)s_1^2 + (n_2 - 1)s_2^2}{n_1 + n_2 - 2}$$ p. 463

With this formula, we can get a pooled estimate of σ^2. It uses a weighted average of s_1^2 and s_2^2, where the weights are the numbers of degrees of freedom in each sample. Use of this formula assumes that $\sigma_1^2 = \sigma_2^2$ (that the unknown population variances are equal). We use this formula when testing for the differences between means in situations with small sample sizes (less than 30).

■ **9-4** $$\hat{\sigma}_{\bar{x}_1 - \bar{x}_2} = s_p\sqrt{\frac{1}{n_1} + \frac{1}{n_2}}$$ p. 463

Given the pooled estimate of σ^2 obtained from Equation 9-3, we put this value into Equation 9–2 and simplify the expression. This gives us a formula to estimate the standard error of the difference between sample means when we have small samples (less than 30) but equal population variances.

■ **9-5** $$\sigma_{\bar{p}_1 - \bar{p}_2} = \sqrt{\frac{p_1 q_1}{n_1} + \frac{p_2 q_2}{n_2}}$$ p. 478

This is the formula used to derive the standard error of the difference between two *proportions*. The symbols p_1 and p_2 represent the proportions of successes in Population 1 and Population 2, respectively, and q_1 and q_2 are the proportions of failures in Populations 1 and 2, respectively.

■ **9-6** $$\hat{\sigma}_{\bar{p}_1 - \bar{p}_2} = \sqrt{\frac{\bar{p}_1 \bar{q}_1}{n_1} + \frac{\bar{p}_2 \bar{q}_2}{n_2}}$$ p. 478

If the population parameters p and q are unknown, we can use the sample statistics $\bar{p}$ and $\bar{q}$ and this formula to *estimate* the standard error of the difference between two proportions.

■ **9-7** $$\hat{p} = \frac{n_1\bar{p}_1 + n_2\bar{p}_2}{n_1 + n_2}$$ p. 478

Because the null hypothesis assumes that there is *no difference* between the two population proportions, it would be more appropriate to modify Equation 9-6 and to use the combined proportions from both samples to estimate the overall proportion of successes in the combined populations. Equation 9-7 combines the proportions from both samples. Note that the value of $\hat{q}$ is equal to $1 - \hat{p}$.

■ 9-8 $$\hat{\sigma}_{\bar{p}_1 - \bar{p}_2} = \sqrt{\frac{\hat{p}\hat{q}}{n_1} + \frac{\hat{p}\hat{q}}{n_2}}$$ p. 479

Now we can substitute the results of Equation 9-7, both $\hat{p}$ and $\hat{q}$, into Equation 9-6 and get a more correct version of Equation 9-6. This new equation, 9-8, gives us the *estimated* standard error of the difference between the two proportions using combined estimates from both samples.

● Review and Application Exercises

■ **9-38** Clic Pens has tested two types of point-of-purchase displays for its new erasable pen. A shelf display was placed in a random sample of 40 stores in the test market, and a floor display was placed in 40 other stores in the area. The mean number of pens sold per store in one month with the shelf display was 42, and the sample standard deviation was 8. With the floor display, the mean number of pens sold per store in the same month was 45, and the sample standard deviation was 7. At $\alpha = 0.02$, was there a significant difference between sales with the two types of displays?

■ **9-39** In 1992, a survey of 50 municipal hospitals revealed an average occupancy rate of 73.6 percent, and the sample standard deviation was 18.2 percent. Another survey of 75 municipal hospitals in 1995 found an average occupancy rate of 68.9 percent, and the sample standard deviation was 19.7 percent. At $\alpha = 0.10$, can we conclude that the average occupancy rate changed significantly during the 3 years between surveys?

■ **9-40** General Cereals has just concluded a new advertising campaign for Fruit Crunch, its all-natural breakfast cereal with nuts, grains, and dried fruits. To test the effectiveness of the campaign, brand manager Alan Neebe surveyed 11 customers before the campaign and another 11 customers after the campaign. Given are the customers' reported weekly consumption (in ounces) of Fruit Crunch:

Before	14	5	18	18	30	10	8	26	13	29	24
After	23	14	13	29	33	11	12	25	21	26	34

(a) At $\alpha = 0.05$, can Alan conclude that the campaign has succeeded in increasing demand for Fruit Crunch?

(b) Given Alan's initial survey before the campaign, can you suggest a better sampling procedure for him to follow after the campaign?

■ **9-41** Ben & Jerry's Homemade, Inc., is an unconventional manufacturer of super-premium ice cream known for adventurous flavors such as Chocolate Chip Cookie Dough. A *Wall Street Journal* article reports that part of the company's success is due to its appeal to young adult consumers (who will presumably remain loyal customers throughout their peak ice-cream-eating years). Suppose a market researcher conducts intercept interviews at a local supermarket and asks 200 consecutive purchasers of Ben & Jerry's ice cream and 200 consecutive purchasers of Grand Metropolitan's rival Haagen-Daz super-premium ice cream a single question: "Are you under age 25?" If 7 percent of the Ben & Jerry's enthusiasts say "yes" and only 3 percent of the Haagen-Daz devotees say "yes," is the conclusion in the article confirmed, at the 10 percent level of significance?

Source: Suein L. Hwang, "While Many Competitors See Sales Melt, Ben & Jerry's Scoops Out Solid Market Growth," *The Wall Street Journal* (25 May 1993): B1.

■ **9-42** Students Against Drunk Driving has targeted seat-belt usage as a positive step to reduce accidents and injuries. Before a major campaign at one high school, 44 percent of 150 drivers entering the school parking lot were using their seat belts. After the seat-belt awareness program, the proportion using seat belts had risen to 52 percent in a sample of 200 vehicles. At a 0.04 significance level, can the students conclude that their campaign was effective?

■ **9-43** Allen Distributing Company hypothesizes that a phone call is more effective than a letter in speeding up collection of slow accounts. Two groups of slow accounts were contacted, one by each method, and the length of time between mailing the letter or making the call and the receipt of payment was recorded:

Method Used	Days to Collection						
Letter	10	8	9	11	11	14	10
Phone call	7	4	5	4	8	6	9

(a) At $\alpha = 0.025$, should Allen conclude that slow accounts are collected more quickly with calls than with letters?

(b) Can Allen conclude that slow accounts respond more quickly to calls?

■ **9-44** A buffered aspirin recently lost some of its market share to a new competitor. The competitor advertised that its brand enters the bloodstream faster than the buffered aspirin does and, as a result, it relieves pain sooner. The buffered-aspirin company would like to prove that there is no significant difference between the two products and, hence, that the competitor's claim is false. As a preliminary test, 9 subjects were given buffered aspirin once a day for 3 weeks. For another 3 weeks, the same subjects were given the competitive product. For each medication, the average number of minutes it took to reach each subject's bloodstream was recorded:

Subject	1	2	3	4	5	6	7	8	9
Buffered aspirin	16.5	25.5	23.0	14.5	28.0	10.0	21.5	18.5	15.5
Competitor	12.0	20.5	25.0	16.5	24.0	11.5	17.0	15.0	13.0

At $\alpha = 0.10$, is there any significant difference in the times the two medications take to reach the bloodstream?

■ **9-45** Consider the data at the top of page 500. In the first three months of 1993, sales of luxury cars in the United States declined slightly but the proportion of luxury cars that were imported increased. Is the change in market share for imported versus domestic cars significant, at the 5 percent level?

	Luxury Car Sales, 1992	1st Quarter 1993
Percent domestic	47.5	46.2
Percent imported	52.5	53.8
Total units sold	373,842	372,442

Source: Business Week *(31 May 1993): 40.*

■ **9-46** A chemist developing insect repellents wishes to know whether a newly developed formula gives greater protection from insect bites than that given by the leading product on the market. In an experiment, 14 volunteers each had one arm sprayed with the old product and the other sprayed with the new formula. Then each subject placed his arms into two chambers filled with equal numbers of mosquitoes, gnats, and other biting insects. The numbers of bites received on each arm follow. At $\alpha = 0.01$, should the chemist conclude that the new formula is, indeed, more effective than the current market leader?

Subject	1	2	3	4	5	6	7	8	9	10	11	12	13	14
Old formula	5	2	5	4	3	6	2	4	2	6	5	7	1	3
New formula	3	1	5	1	1	4	4	2	5	2	3	3	1	2

■ **9-47** Long Distance Carrier is trying to see the effect of offering "1 month free" with a monthly fixed fee of $10.95, versus an offer of a low monthly fee—$8.75—with no free month. To test which might be more attractive to consumers, Long Distance runs a brief market test: 12 phone reps make calls using one approach, and 10 use the other. The following number of customers agreed to switch from their present carrier to LDC:

Offer	**Number of Switches**											
1 month free	118	115	122	99	106	125	102	100	92	103	113	129
Low monthly fee	115	126	113	110	135	102	124	137	108	128		

Test at a significance level of 10 percent whether there are significant productivity differences with the two offers.

■ **9-48** Is the perceived level of responsibility for an action related to the severity of its consequences? That question was the basis of a study of responsibility in which the subjects read a description of an accident on an interstate highway. The consequences, in terms of cost and injury, were described as either very minor or serious. A questionnaire was used to rate the degree of responsibility that the subjects believed should be placed on the main figure in the story. Below are the ratings for both the mild-consequences and the severe-consequences groups. High ratings correspond to higher responsibility attributed to the main figure. If a 0.025 significance level was used, did the study conclude that severe consequences lead to a greater attribution of responsibility?

Consequences	**Degree of Responsibility**							
Mild	4	5	3	3	4	1	2	6
Severe	4	5	4	6	7	8	6	5

■ **9-49** In October 1992, a survey of 120 macroeconomists found 87 who believed that the recession had already ended. A survey of 150 purchasing agents found 89 who believed the recession had ended. At $\alpha = 0.10$, should you conclude that the purchasing agents were more pessimistic about the economy than the macroeconomists were?

■ **9-50** Full-length feature films earn huge profits for entertainment giant The Walt Disney Company. Hit movies, such as *Aladdin*, may earn more than $300 million above their production costs. But each year, in addition to these spectacular successes, some modest animated full-length features come to the screen. An analyst obtained a listing of the box office gross (sum of all tickets sold) for the first release of all animated features from 1986 to 1992 and compiled the following data:

Movie	Studio	Box Office Gross ($millions)
An American Tail	Universal	44.9
All Dogs Go to Heaven	MGM/UA	26.2
Ferngully: The Last Rainforest	Twentieth Century Fox	20.9
Fievel Goes West	Universal	20.2
Cool World	Paramount	13.7
Rock-a-Doodle	Twentieth Century Fox	11.6
Bebe's Kids	Paramount	7.5
Care Bears II	Columbia	5.4
Pinocchio & the Emperor of Night	New World	2.7
Care Bears	Cineplex	2.2
Babar: The Movie	New Line	1.4
Oliver and Company	Disney	52.6
Rescuers Down Under	Disney	27.8
The Great Mouse Detective	Disney	24.2
The Rescuers	Disney	21.1
Duck Tales	Disney	18.1

(Note: Excludes Disney "hit" releases earning more than $80 million and excludes Disney re-releases of classic animated features such as Snow White.)

Source: David J. Londoner and William L Kessler, "The Walt Disney Company: Momentum in the Basics," Wertheim Schroeder & Co. research report, New York, February 12, 1993.

At $\alpha = 0.05$, do these data support the conclusion that "even excluding smash hits, Disney's animated films earn more than the competition?"

■ **9-51** The MBA program at Piedmont Business School offers Analytic Skills Workshop (ASW) during the summer to help entering students brush up on their accounting, economics, and mathematics. Program Director Andy Bunch wonders whether ASW has been advantageous to the students enrolled. He has taken random samples of grade-point averages for students enrolled in ASW over the past 5 years and for students who started the MBA program without ASW during the same time span. At $\alpha = 0.02$, have the ASW students gotten significantly higher GPAs? Should Andy advertise that ASW helps student achievement in the MBA program?

	$\bar{x}$	s	n
ASW	3.37	1.13	26
Non-ASW	3.15	1.89	35

■ **9-52** Fifty-eight of 2,000 randomly sampled corporations had their 1995 federal income tax returns audited. In another sample of 2,500 corporations, 61 had their 1994 returns audited. Was the fraction of corporate returns audited in 1995 significantly different from the 1994 fraction? Test the appropriate hypotheses at $\alpha = 0.01$.

■ **9-53** Ellen Singer asserted to one of her colleagues at Triangle Realty that homes in southern Durham County sold for about \$15,000 less than similar homes in Chapel Hill. To test this assertion, her colleague randomly chose 10 recent sales in Chapel Hill and matched them with 10 recent sales in southern Durham County in terms of style, size, age, number of rooms, and size of lot. At $\alpha = 0.05$, do the following data (selling prices in thousands of \$) support Ellen's claim?

Chapel Hill	97.3	108.4	135.7	142.3	151.8	158.5	177.4	183.9	195.2	207.6
Durham County	81.5	92.0	115.8	137.8	150.9	149.2	168.2	173.9	175.9	194.4

■ **9-54** The Dow-Jones Transportation Average is based on the closing prices of the common stocks of 20 airline, rail, and freight companies. On May 24, 1993, the average price of these 20 stocks declined from \$47.156 to \$47.150. Treating these stocks as a random sample of all transportation-related stocks, is the observed decrease significant? Explain.

Stock	Close 5/21/93	Close 5/24/93
Airborne Freight	23.500	23.375
Alaska Airlines	16.750	16.625
American President	50.750	52.000
AMR	71.625	71.875
Burlington Northern	53.875	54.000
Carolina Freightways	13.125	13.000
Conrail	51.375	51.875
Consolidated Freightways	15.375	15.625
CSX	71.125	70.750
Delta Airlines	60.250	60.750
Federal Express	49.750	49.375
Norfolk and Southern	61.875	61.250
Roadway	54.750	55.000
Ryder System	27.250	27.125
Santa Fe Pacific	16.750	17.000
Southwest Airline	40.375	40.500
UAL	138.750	138.750
Union Pacific	63.250	63.000
USAir Group	22.500	22.625
XTRA	40.125	38.500
Average Price	47.156	47.150

Source: The Wall Street Journal *(25 May 1993): C3–C6.*

■ **9-55** TV network executive Terri Black has just received a proposal and a pilot tape for a new show. *Empty Nest No Longer* is a situation comedy about a middle-aged couple whose two college-graduate offspring cannot find jobs and have returned home. Terri wonders whether the show will appeal to twenty-somethings as well as to an older audience. Figuring that people in her office are reasonably representative of their age group in the population as a whole, she asks them to evaluate the pilot tape on a scale from 0 to 100, and gets the following responses.

Age	Responses						
20–29	86	74	73	65	82	78	79
≥ 30	63	72	68	75	73	80	

(a) At a 0.05 significance level, should Terri conclude the show will be equally attractive to the two age groups?

(b) Independent of your answer to (a), do you think Terry should use the results of her office survey to decide how to design an advertising campaign for *Empty Nest No Longer?* Explain.

■ **9-56** A manufacturer of pet foods was wondering whether cat owners and dog owners reacted differently to premium pet foods. They commissioned a consumer survey that yielded the following data.

Pet	Owners Surveyed	Number Using Premium Food
Cat	280	152
Dog	190	81

Is it reasonable to conclude, at $\alpha = 0.02$, that cat owners are more likely than dog owners to feed their pets premium food?

■ **9-57** Robin Wendell has been offered a transfer from Pittsburgh to Boston, but is holding out for more money, "because the cost of living there is so much more." Looking at a grocery receipt and deleting big-ticket items, Robin came up with 36 items under \$2 with a mean of \$0.98, standard deviation \$0.43 in Pittsburgh. The recruiting manager stops by a Boston grocery store, and with the same \$2.00 limit, buys 42 items, with a mean price of \$1.07, standard deviation \$0.38. Is Robin right that the cost of groceries is more in Boston than in Pittsburgh, at a confidence level $\alpha = 0.01$? What could be done to improve the analysis of cost of living in the two cities?

■ **9-58** A group of British physicians replicated a U.S. management survey of medical directors, asking which skills they considered useful and essential for their jobs. Of 100 U.S. surveys mailed, the response rate was 50 percent, and of 59 U.K. surveys mailed, the reported response rate was 45 percent.

(a) How many questionnaires were returned in the U.K. survey?

(b) Did the proportions of responses differ between the two samples?

Source: Trevor Wood, Gabriel Scally and Declan O'Neill, "Management Knowledge and Skills Required by UK and US Medical Directors," *Physician Executive* (August 1995): 26–29.

■ **9-59** A firm is considering offering new-hire MBAs a housing allowance to compensate for differences in the price of housing. One executive points to a table in *The Wall Street Journal* with a survey of typical starter home prices for young executives across the country. The executive notes, "Housing prices are really coming down in California; we should only compensate people who live in the high-priced East Coast and the South."

East and South	Midwest and West
159,125	167,155
206,125	95,000
188,071	197,519
196,750	215,368
143,792	145,767
324,171	154,914
248,157	153,581
199,419	156,690
110,650	178,169
169,586	210,914
174,800	

(a) If the table represents a random sample of house prices in each area, is the mean price significantly different between the two groups of houses?

(b) As the discussion progresses, a colleague points out that the figure of $324,171 in the first group comes from Washington, D.C., and is obviously an outlier. The human resources staff member points to the $95,000 figure from the second group, which is from Eden Prairie, Minnesota, stating, "We don't even have an office in Minnesota." Is the analysis improved by throwing out these outliers and are the conclusions the same?

Source: "Starter Home Prices," *The Wall Street Journal* (29 September 95): B10.

Chapter Concepts Test

Circle the correct answer or fill in the blank. *Answers are in the back of the book.*

T F 1. A paired difference test is appropriate when the two samples being tested are dependent samples.

T F 2. A one-tailed test for the difference between means may be undertaken when the sample sizes are either large or small and the procedures are similar. The only difference is that when the sample sizes are large, we use the normal distribution, whereas the *t* distribution is used when the sample sizes are small.

T F 3. In testing hypotheses about the difference of two means, suppose that the sample sizes are large. If we do not know the actual standard deviations of the two populations, we can use the sample standard deviations as estimates.

T F 4. If we took two independent samples and performed a hypothesis test to see whether their means were significantly different, we would find the results very similar to a paired difference test performed on the same two samples.

T F 5. When doing a two-tailed test for the difference between means, with a null hypothesis of $\mu_1 = \mu_2$, the hypothesized difference between the two population means is zero.

T F 6. Exact prob values can't be determined (from the table) when using the *t* distribution in a hypothesis test.

T F 7. Two-sample tests are used to reach conclusions about the relationships between two populations.

T F 8. When the sample sizes are small, only one-tailed tests of the difference between two population means can be done.

T F 9. When the null hypothesis for testing the difference between two population proportions is H_0: $p_1 = p_2$, you combine the two samples to estimate the common population proportion.

T F 10. Most computer statistics packages do not give prob values for hypothesis tests, so you still have to use tables to decide whether to accept or reject H_0.

T F 11. In testing the difference of two population means, the null hypothesis must be H_0: $\mu_1 = \mu_2$.

T F 12. If the sample sizes are too small to use the normal distribution for a test of the difference of two population proportions, you should use the *t* distribution.

T F 13. If you use prob values, you don't have to specify a value of α before sampling.

T F 14. To compare two population means using small samples, you should always pool the two sample variances.

T F 15. Testing the differences between means with dependent samples becomes a one-sample test once you compute the differences of the paired observations.

T F 16. Although you don't know how to do small-sample tests of two independent means when the two population variances are unequal, most computer statistical packages will perform tests in those circumstances.

T F 17. Paired difference tests of means can be based on either the normal or the *t* distributions, depending on the sample sizes.

T F 18. Prob values can be used for one-sample tests, but not for two-sample tests.

T F 19. To standardize the observed difference of sample means when σ_1 and σ_2 are not known, you always divide by $\sigma_{\bar{x}_1 - \bar{x}_2}$, regardless of the sample sizes.

T F 20. Because most computer statistical packages report two-tailed prob values for tests on means, you must divide the reported prob value by 2 if you are doing a one-tailed test.

T F 21. In testing the difference between two proportions, the divisor used to standardize the difference between the sample proportions is different for one- and two-tailed tests.

A B C D 22. Suppose you are going to test the difference between two sample means, which you have calculated as $\bar{x}_1 = 22$ and $\bar{x}_2 = 27$. You wish to test whether the difference is significant. What value of $\mu_{\bar{x}_1 - \bar{x}_2}$ will you use?

(a) 5.

(b) −5.

(c) 0.

(d) Cannot be determined from information given.

A B C D 23. Why do we sometimes use paired, as opposed to independent, samples?

(a) Taking paired samples always costs less than taking independent samples.

(b) Paired samples allow us to control for extraneous factors.

(c) The sample sizes must be the same for paired samples.

(d) (b) and (c) but not (a).

A B C D 24. A set of two dependent samples of size 15 was taken and a hypothesis test was performed. A *t* value with 14 degrees of freedom was used. If the two sets of samples had been treated as independent, how many degrees of freedom would have been used?

(a) 14.

(b) 28.

(c) 29.

(d) 30.

A B C 25. A farmer has 12 fields of corn in different parts of a certain county. Testing for significantly different yields from year to year, he checks his records for the past 2 years and is able to gather information about production in 11 of the fields for the first year and second year. Should he treat these samples as:

(a) Dependent?

(b) Independent?

(c) Cannot be determined from information given.

A B C D 26. In a test of difference between proportions, two samples are under consideration. In the first, a sample of size 100 shows 20 successes; in the second, a sample of size 50 shows 13 successes. What is the value of $\hat{p}$ for this situation?

(a) $\frac{20 + 13}{150}$.

(b) $\frac{20}{100} + \frac{13}{50}$.

(c) $\frac{33}{150} \times \frac{117}{150}$.

(d) None of these.

A B C D 27. What is the major assumption we made when performing one-tailed tests for differences between means with small samples?

(a) Unknown population variances were equal.

(b) Sampling fractions were quite small.

(c) The samples were chosen using judgmental sampling techniques.

(d) None of these.

A B C D 28. Airline A and Airline B boast successful baggage routing rates of 95 and 98 percent, respectively. From this information we can determine:

(a) Airline A has better baggage service.

(b) Airline B has better baggage service.

(c) The baggage services are equally accurate.

(d) Nothing; we need more information.

A B C D 29. A two-tailed test of a difference between two proportions led to $z = 1.85$ for its standardized difference of sample proportions. For which of the following significance levels would you reject H_0?

(a) $\alpha = 0.05$.

(b) $\alpha = 0.10$.

(c) $\alpha = 0.02$.

(d) (a) and (b), but not (c).

A B C D 30. Let p be the prob value for a given upper-tailed hypothesis test, α be the significance level, t_{CRIT} be the critical value for the test, and t_{OBS} be the standardized test statistic. You will accept H_0 if:

(a) $p > \alpha$.

(b) $p < \alpha$.

(c) $t_{OBS} > t_{CRIT}$.

(d) (b) and (c), but not (a).

A B C D 31. You wish to test whether the mean of population 2 is at least 10 more than the mean of population 1. What value of $(\mu_1 - \mu_2)_{H_0}$ should you use when computing the standardized test statistic?

(a) 0.

(b) 10.

(c) −10.

(d) ±5.

A B C D 32. For which of the following is a test of difference of proportions not appropriate?

(a) Seeing whether the fractions of waste produced by two processes are the same.

(b) Deciding whether the fractions of women in two grades at school are the same.

(c) Testing whether different proportions of people in Boston and Chicago like NBA basketball.

(d) Seeing whether Ford owners have more brand loyalty than Honda owners.

A B C D 33. If sample 1 has 13 elements with $s_1 = 17$ and sample 2 has 9 elements with $s_2 = 22$, then $s_p^2 =$:

(a) 19.

(b) 361.

(c) 367.

(d) 19.5.

A B C D 34. For which of the following is a two-sample test not appropriate?

(a) Seeing whether the proportions of childless couples and couples with children who buy sports cars are different.

(b) Seeing whether the mean beer consumption is higher in Germany than in France.

(c) Testing whether there are more men than women in Alaska.

(d) Deciding whether average attendance at major league baseball games is the same in Los Angeles and San Francisco.

A B C D 35. For an upper-tailed test of the difference of two means based on dependent samples of size 6 and $\alpha = 0.05$, the critical value for the test statistic is:

(a) 2.015.

(b) 1.645.

(c) 1.812.

(d) 1.782.

A B C D E 36. Which of the following tests could be based on the normal distribution?

(a) Difference between independent means.

(b) Difference between dependent means.

(c) Difference between proportions.

(d) All of the above.

(e) (a) and (c), but not (b).

37. A hypothesis test of the difference between two population means based on dependent samples is known as a ______________________ test.

chapter 10

QUALITY AND QUALITY CONTROL

Objectives

- To examine why the concept of quality—making sure that a product or service is consistent, reliable, and free from errors and defects—is important in decision making
- To learn how to use control charts to monitor the output of a process and see whether it is meeting established quality standards
- To recognize patterns that indicate that a process is out-of-control
- To understand how to construct $\bar{x}$, R, and p charts
- To introduce basic concepts of Total Quality Management
- To learn how acceptance sampling is used to monitor the input to a process to ensure that it meets established quality standards

Chapter Contents

The Durham City Executive for TransCarolina Bank has just established an express teller to handle transactions consisting of a single deposit or withdrawal. She hopes ultimately to be able to complete express transactions in an average of less than 60 seconds. For the moment, however, she wants to be sure that the express line works smoothly and consistently. Once the process is in-control, she can devote her attention to reducing its average time to meet her 60-second goal. For the past month, she has randomly sampled six express transactions each business day:

Day	Date	Transaction Times (seconds)						Day	Date	Transaction Times (seconds)					
M	5/03	63	55	56	53	61	64	M	5/17	57	63	56	64	62	59
T	5/04	60	63	60	65	61	66	T	5/18	66	63	65	59	70	61
W	5/05	57	60	61	65	66	62	W	5/19	63	53	69	60	61	58
Th	5/06	58	64	60	61	57	65	Th	5/20	68	67	59	58	65	59
F	5/07	79	68	65	61	74	71	F	5/21	70	62	66	80	71	76
M	5/10	55	66	62	63	56	52	M	5/24	65	59	60	61	62	65
T	5/11	57	61	58	64	55	63	T	5/25	63	69	58	56	66	61
W	5/12	58	51	61	57	66	59	W	5/26	61	56	62	59	57	55
Th	5/13	65	66	62	68	61	67	Th	5/27	65	57	69	62	58	72
F	5/14	73	66	61	70	72	78	F	5/28	70	60	67	79	75	68

Using the techniques discussed in this chapter, the Durham city executive can determine whether the express-teller line is in-control or out-of-control. ■

10.1 Introduction

Responding to global challenge

We often hear that everyone talks about the weather but no one is prepared to do anything about it. Until recently, the same was true about American business and quality. However, as the relative isolation of national economies has been succeeded by the increasing globalization of commerce, American industry has had to respond to challenges from abroad. One of those challenges was a dedication to quality control and the management of quality in production that came to be epitomized by such Japanese products as automobiles and consumer electronics. In response to this challenge, the philosophy and techniques of quality control and management are becoming widespread in American manufacturing. In addition, the rapidly growing circle of applications of *Total Quality Management* (known by the acronym TQM) has expanded from manufacturing industries to service industries such as health care and legal services.

TQM for services as well as for manufacturing

In this chapter, you'll see how simple applications of some of the ideas we've already discussed about estimation and hypothesis testing can be used for quality control and improvement. We'll look at *control charts* and *acceptance sampling,* two commonly used quality control techniques. Along the way, you'll meet some of the pioneers in the field and learn some of the language of quality control.

What Is Quality?

Distinguish between luxury and quality

When you hear a commercial for a "high-quality automobile," do you conjure up images of such luxurious options as leather seats and fancy sound systems? Most of us do connect *luxury* and *quality.* But expensive leather seats don't mean very much if the engine won't start on a cold morning, and the latest noise-reduction technology is hard to appreciate if the tape deck starts chewing up your tapes. These examples show us that it's important to separate the notion of luxury from our discussion of quality.

In fact, some of the cheapest items in everyday life can have very high quality. Consider the paper used in a copying machine. For little more than a penny a page, you can buy smooth white paper, less than one hundredth of an inch thick and of uniform size. You have come to expect such high quality in copier paper that you don't examine individual pages before loading it into a copier. You wouldn't think of measuring the thickness of each page to make sure that it was thin enough not to jam the copier, but thick enough so that you could print on both sides and not have the two images interfere with each other.

Quality means fitness for use

The copy paper example gives us a clue to a working definition of *quality.* Things that are of high quality are those that work in the way we expect them to. As quality expert Joseph M. Juran has put it, *quality implies fitness for use.* In this sense, *quality means conformance to requirements.* Note that this is not quite the same as conformance to specifications. Copy paper that is cut to size for American copy machines won't fit European machines that demand the slightly narrower A4 metric format.

Consistency, reliability, and lack of defects

Note that the idea of "things that work in the way we expect them to" points out that quality is defined by customers as well as by producers. As you shall see, meeting the needs of customers is central to TQM. Working definitions of quality vary in different contexts, especially when we contrast goods and services. But in keeping with our notion of conformance to requirements, most working definitions of quality will include the concepts of *consistency, reliability,* and *lack of errors and defects.*

Variability Is the Enemy of Quality

Mass production makes quality an issue

When a craftsman makes something by hand, there is a continuous process of checking, measuring, and reworking. If you'd watched Michelangelo completing a sculpture, you wouldn't have seen a final "quality control" step before he shipped his artwork to his patron. Indeed, quality control is not an issue when you are producing goods and services that are essentially unique. However, when mass production became common during the nineteenth century, it was soon realized that individual pieces could not be identical—a certain amount of variation is inevitable. But this leads to a problem: With too much variation, parts that are supposed to fit together won't fit! In this sense, you can see why variability is the enemy of quality.

Controlling Variability: Inspection vs. Prevention

How should we deal with variability? Think about a stack of two-by-fours in a lumberyard. Most of them will conform to requirements, but some won't because of twisting and warping as they dried, splitting when the saw hit a knot, or sundry other causes. One approach to mass production says it's cheaper to push material through the process and sort out the defects at the end. This leads our lumberyard to have an inspector examine two-by-fours as they come out of the drying kiln. Defective pieces go to the scrap heap.

Early quality control: Sorting out defective finished goods

In the early days of mass production, sorting out defects became the chief method of quality control. Armies of white-coated inspectors tested goods at the end of a production line and released only some of them to customers. It was widely believed that the cost of a few rejects didn't amount to much because the marginal cost of each unit was small. But by the late 1970s, people were pointing out that the costs of defects were much higher than supposed. The armies of inspectors had to be paid, and if defective products slipped through, there were warranty costs and loss of customers' goodwill.

Zero defects as a goal

They argued that it is simply cheaper to do things right the first time. They preached the concept of *zero defects*. If your electrical power was 99 percent reliable, you'd spend a lot of time resetting your clocks. A major airline with a 99.9 percent safety record would have several crashes each week! If we demand near-perfect performance from power companies and airlines, perhaps we should expect no less from the producers of all our goods and services.

Preventing defects and increasing workers' pride

When poorly made parts are passed down a production line, all subsequent work is wasted when the final product is rejected by quality control inspectors. But it's expensive to keep inspecting components to make sure they conform to requirements. Imagine how much time would be wasted if you had to examine each piece of paper for defects before loading a copier. This leads to the goal of preventing defects at each stage of manufacturing a product or delivering a service. To accomplish this, the people who make things are given the responsibility to check their work before it is passed on, rather than just letting sloppy work slide by to be caught at a final inspection. This also has the benefit of giving workers a greater investment of pride in the work they are doing—in this sense, they are more like craftsmen.

Exercises 10.1

Basic Concepts

- **10-1** Give an example of a very expensive product that has very low quality.
- **10-2** Give an example of a very inexpensive product that has very high quality.
- **10-3** What is a reasonable working definition of quality?
- **10-4** What actually makes quality control an issue of concern to management?
- **10-5** What kinds of costs would you gather to perform an "inspection versus prevention" analysis?
- **10-6** Define *zero defects* as a concept.

10.2 Statistical Process Control

Variability is not inevitable

The key to managing for quality is to believe that excessive variability is not inevitable. When the output of some process is found to be unreliable, not always conforming to requirements, we must carefully examine the process and see how it can be controlled.

In the 1920s, Walter A. Shewhart, a researcher at Bell Labs, created a system for tracking variation and identifying its causes. Shewhart's system of *statistical process control* (or *SPC*) was developed further and championed by his one-time colleague, W. Edwards Deming. For many years, Deming was a prophet without honor in the United States, but when Japan was rebuilding its economy after World War II, Japanese managers incorporated Deming's ideas into their management philosophy. Many American industries, including automobiles and consumer electronics, encountered severe competitive pressures from the Japanese in the late 1970s and 1980s. As a result, the contributions made to quality control by Deming and others were reconsidered by American managers.

Random variation in process output

Let's look at some basic ideas of Shewhart's statistical process control. Consider a production line that makes driveshafts for automobiles. Requirements for well-functioning shafts have been established. We would like to monitor and improve the quality of the shafts we produce. The shafts are made in large quantities on an automatic lathe. If we measured the diameter of each shaft after manufacture, we would expect to see some variability (perhaps a normal distribution) of the measurements around a mean value. These observed random variations in the measurements could result from variations in the hardness of the steel used for the shafts, power surges affecting the lathe, or even errors in making the measurements on the finished shafts.

Nonrandom variation in the output

But imagine what happens as the cutting tool begins to dull. The average diameter will gradually increase unless the lathe is recalibrated. And if the bearings on the lathe wear over time, the cutting edge might move around. Then some shafts would be too large, and some too small. Although the mean diameter might well be the same, the variability in the measurements would increase. It would be important to note such nonrandom (or *systematic*) variation, to identify its source, and to correct the problem.

From this discussion, you can see that there are two kinds of variation that are observed in the output from most processes, in general, and from our automatic lathe, in particular:

- Random variation (sometimes called *common*, or *inherent*, variation)
- Systematic variation (sometimes called *assignable*, or *special cause*, variation)

Managerial responses to inherent and assignable variation

These two kinds of variation call for different managerial responses. Although one of the goals of quality management is *constant improvement* by the reduction of inherent variation, this cannot ordinarily be accomplished without changing the process. And you should not change the process until you are sure that all assignable variation has been identified and brought under control. So the idea is this: **If the process is *out-of-control* because there is still some special cause variation present, identify and correct the cause of that variation. Then, when the process has been brought *in-control,* quality can be improved by redesigning the process to reduce its inherent variability.**

In the next three sections, we shall look at control charts, devices that Shewhart invented for monitoring process outputs to identify when they slip out of control.

HINTS & ASSUMPTIONS

There are a lot of catch phrases associated with quality control programs today: "Put Quality First," "Variation Is the Enemy of Quality," "Make It Right the First Time," and "Zero Defects" are only a few. As you read these phrases in the popular press it may seem like a paradox that *statistical process control,* the topic of this chapter, focuses on *variation.* Hint: Until we can measure a process and find out the sources of the variation (random variation and systematic variation) we aren't able to bring the process into control. Warning: Quality control programs based solely on slogans instead of sound statistical methods don't work.

Exercises 10.2

Basic Concepts

- **10-7** What happened in the 1970s and 1980s to cause American managers to pay more attention to Deming's ideas?
- **10-8** Explain why work produced by a robot might have less random variation than work produced by a human.

■ **10-9** When the manager of a baseball team decides to change pitchers, is he responding to random or assignable variation? Explain.

■ **10-10** What kinds of systematic variation are the managers of supermarkets trying to control when they establish express lanes at some of their cash registers?

10.3 $\bar{x}$ Charts: Control Charts for Process Means

Plot the data to find nonrandom variations

The essence of statistical process control is to identify a parameter that is easy to measure and whose value is important for the quality of the process output (the shaft diameter in our example), plot it in such a way that we can recognize nonrandom variations, and decide when to make adjustments to a process. These plots are known generically as *control charts*. Suppose, for the moment, that we want to produce shafts whose diameters are distributed normally with $\mu = 60$ millimeters and $\sigma = 1$ millimeter. **(An assumption of normality with μ and σ known is unreasonable in most situations, and we will drop it later. However, it facilitates our discussion of the basic ideas of control charts.)**

To monitor the process, we take a random sample of 16 measurements each day and compute their means, $\bar{x}$. From Chapter 6, we know that the sample means have a sampling distribution with

$$\mu_{\bar{x}} = \mu = 60 \qquad [6\text{-}1]$$

$$\begin{aligned}\sigma_{\bar{x}} &= \frac{\sigma}{\sqrt{n}}\\ &= \frac{1}{\sqrt{16}}\\ &= 0.25\end{aligned}$$

$\bar{x}$ charts

For a period of 2 weeks, let's plot the daily sample means against time. This is called an $\bar{x}$ *chart*. In Figure 10-1, we have plotted the results from three hypothetical sets of two weeks' worth of daily sample means. In each of these three $\bar{x}$ charts, we have also included

- A center line (CL), with value $\mu_{\bar{x}} = 60$
- An *upper control limit* (*UCL*) line, with value $\mu_{\bar{x}} + 3\sigma_{\bar{x}} = 60 + 3(0.25) = 60.75$
- A *lower control limit* (*LCL*) line, with value $\mu_{\bar{x}} - 3\sigma_{\bar{x}} = 60 - 3(0.25) = 59.25$

$\pm 3\sigma$ control limits should contain most of the observations

The number 3 in the upper and lower control limits is used by standard convention. Where does it come from? Recall Chebyshev's theorem, which we discussed on page 116. No matter what the underlying distribution, at least 89 percent of all observations fall within ± 3 standard deviations from the mean. And recall that for normal populations (see Appendix Table 1), over 99.7 percent of all observations fall within that interval.

So, if a process is in-control, essentially all observations should fall within the control limits. Conversely, observations that fall outside those limits suggest that the process is out-of-control, and they warrant further investigation to see if some special cause can be found to explain why they fall outside the limits. With this in mind, let's look at Figure 10-1.

FIGURE 10-1

Three $\bar{x}$ charts for the driveshaft production process

(a) Process is in-control

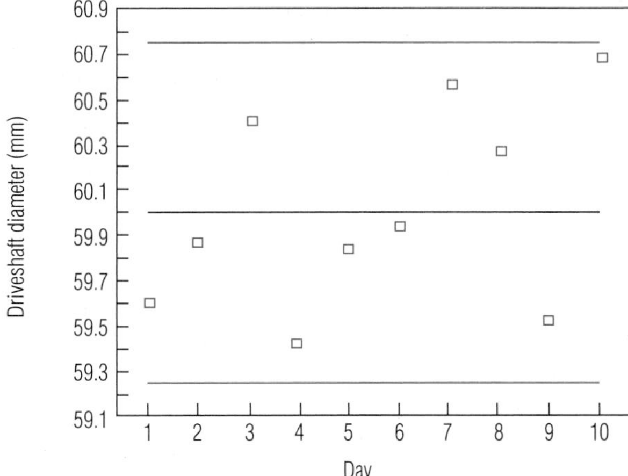

(b) Process is out-of-control: outliers beyond control limits

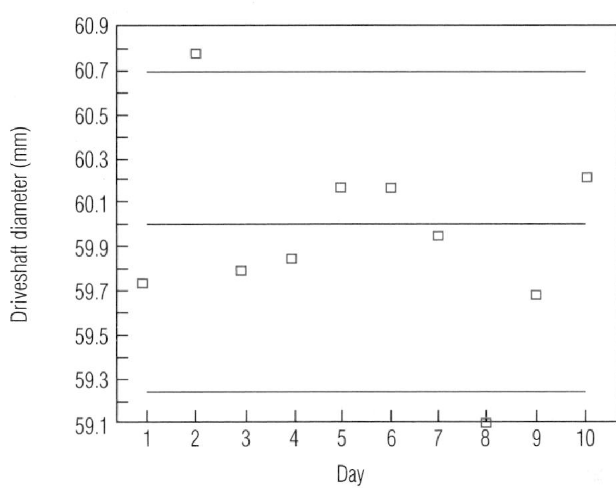

(c) Process is out-of-control: increasing trend in observations

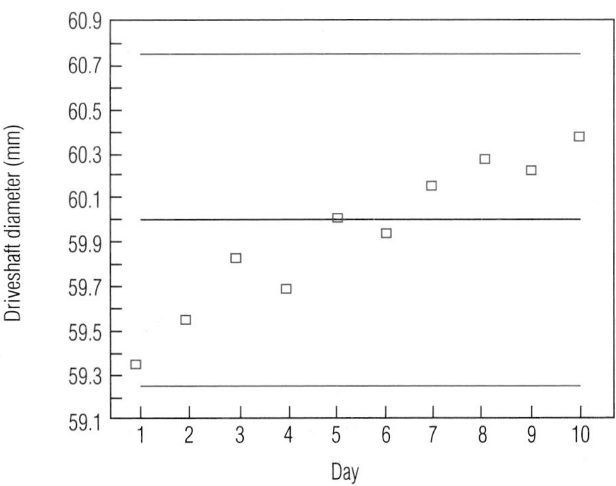

Basic Interpretation of Control Charts

In Figure 10-1(a), all observations fall within the control limits, so the process is in-control. In Figure 10-1(b), the second and eighth observations are *outliers*—they fall outside the control limits. In this instance, the process is out-of-control. The production staff should try to find out whether something out of the ordinary happened on those 2 days. Perhaps the lathe was not recalibrated those mornings, or maybe the regular operator was out sick. An investigation may not turn up anything. After all, even purely random variation will produce outliers 0.3 percent of the time. In such cases, concluding that something has gone awry corresponds to making a Type I error in hypothesis testing. However, because legitimate outliers happen so infrequently, it makes good sense to investigate whenever an outlier is observed.

Outliers should be investigated

What should we conclude about Figure 10-1(c)? Even though all 10 observations fall within the control limits, they exhibit anything but random variation. They show a distinct pattern of increase over time. Whenever you see such lack of randomness, you should assume that something systematic is causing it and seek to determine what that assignable cause is. Even though all the observations fall within the control limits, we still say that the process is out-of-control. In this example, the lathe blade was getting duller each day, and the maintenance department had neglected to sharpen it as scheduled.

Patterns in the data points also indicate out-of-control processes

What sort of patterns should you be looking out for? Among the more commonly noted patterns are

Common out-of-control patterns

- **Individual outliers** (Figure 10-1(b)).
- **Increasing or decreasing trends** (Figure 10-1(c)). These indicate that the process mean may be drifting.
- **Jumps in the level around which the observations vary** (Figure 10-2(a)). These indicate that the process mean may have shifted.
- **Cycles** (Figure 10-2(b)). Such regularly repeating waves above and below the center line could indicate such things as worker fatigue and changeover between work shifts.
- **"Hugging the control limits"** (Figure 10-2(c)). Uniformly large deviations from the mean can indicate that two distinct populations are being observed.
- **"Hugging the center line"** (Figure 10-2(d)). Uniformly small deviations from the mean indicate that variability has been reduced from historic levels; this is generally desirable. If it can be maintained, the control limits should be tightened to make sure that this improved quality continues.

$\bar{x}$ Charts when μ and σ Are Not Known

Now that you understand the basic ideas for interpreting $\bar{x}$ charts, let's see how to construct them when μ and σ aren't known. Recall the express-teller line at TransCarolina Bank, which opened this chapter. Lisa Klein, Durham City Executive for TransCarolina, wants express-teller transactions to be completed in an average of less than 60 seconds. Her sample data for last month are repeated in Table 10-1, which also includes daily sample means and ranges.

As we saw in Chapters 7–9, a common theme in statistics is the use of sample information to estimate unknown parameters. Because Lisa doesn't know the true process mean, μ, she will use the sample mean, $\bar{\bar{x}}$, in its place. But which of the twenty daily $\bar{x}$'s should she use? None of them! Each of them contains information from only six observations, but she has a total of 120

Estimate μ by $\bar{\bar{x}}$

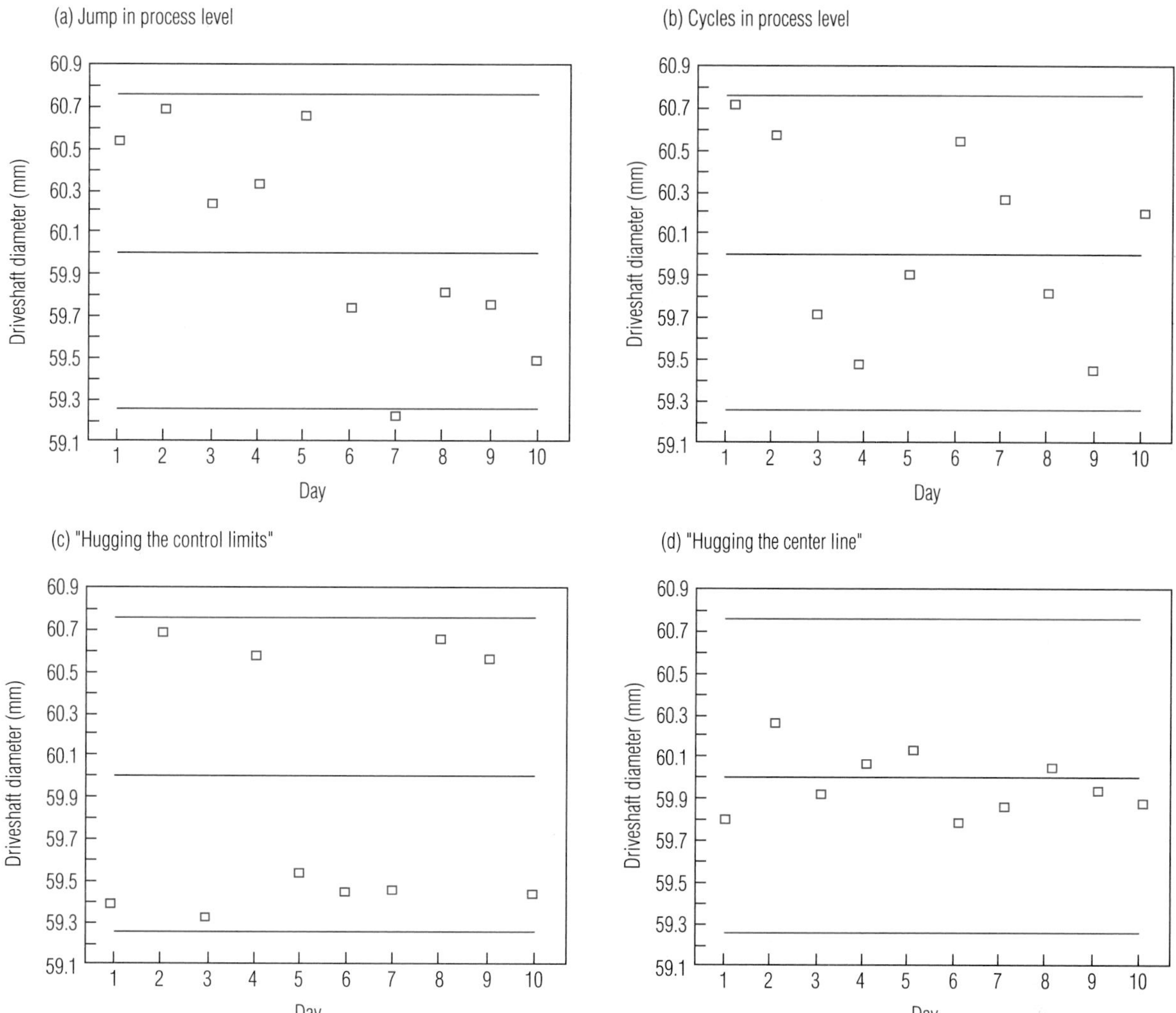

FIGURE 10-2 Nonrandom patterns in control charts

observations available (six observations for each of 20 days). She captures all this information by using $\bar{\bar{x}}$, the *grand mean,* which can be calculated in two equivalent ways:

Grand Mean from Several Samples of the Same Size

$$\bar{\bar{x}} = \frac{\Sigma x}{n \times k} = \frac{\Sigma \bar{x}}{k} \quad [10\text{-}1]$$

where

- $\bar{\bar{x}}$ = grand mean
- Σx = sum of all observations
- $\Sigma \bar{x}$ = sum of the sample means

Table 10-1 Raw Data and Daily Sample Means and Ranges for TransCarolina Bank Express-Teller Line

Day	Date	Transaction Times (seconds)						Mean ($\bar{x}$)	Range (R)
M	5/03	63	55	56	53	61	64	58.7	11
T	5/04	60	63	60	65	61	66	62.5	6
W	5/05	57	60	61	65	66	62	61.8	9
TH	5/06	58	64	60	61	57	65	60.8	8
F	5/07	79	68	65	61	74	71	69.7	18
M	5/10	55	66	62	63	56	52	59.0	14
T	5/11	57	61	58	64	55	63	59.7	9
W	5/12	58	51	61	57	66	59	58.7	15
TH	5/13	65	66	62	68	61	67	64.8	7
F	5/14	73	66	61	70	72	78	70.0	17
M	5/17	57	63	56	64	62	59	60.2	8
T	5/18	66	63	65	59	70	61	64.0	11
W	5/19	63	53	69	60	61	58	60.7	16
TH	5/20	68	67	59	58	65	59	62.7	10
F	5/21	70	62	66	80	71	76	70.8	18
M	5/24	65	59	60	61	62	65	62.0	6
T	5/25	63	69	58	56	66	61	62.2	13
W	5/26	61	56	62	59	57	55	58.3	7
TH	5/27	65	57	69	62	58	72	63.8	15
F	5/28	70	60	67	79	75	68	69.8	19
								$\Sigma\bar{x} = 1{,}260.2$	$\Sigma R = 237$

- n = number of observations in each sample
- k = number of samples taken

In our example, $n = 6$ and $k = 20$, so we find

$$\bar{\bar{x}} = \frac{\Sigma x}{n \times k} = \frac{7{,}561}{6(20)} = 63.0 \quad \text{or} \qquad [10\text{-}1]$$

$$\bar{\bar{x}} = \frac{\Sigma\bar{x}}{k} = \frac{1{,}260.2}{20} = 63.0$$

Once $\bar{\bar{x}}$ has been calculated, its value is used as the center line (CL) in the $\bar{x}$ chart.

How should Lisa estimate σ? In Chapters 7–9, we used s, the sample standard deviation, to estimate σ. However, in control charts, it has become customary to base an estimate of σ on $\bar{R}$, the average of the sample ranges. This custom arose because control charts were often plotted on the factory floor, and it was a lot easier for workers to compute sample ranges (the difference between the highest and lowest observations in the sample) than to compute sample standard deviations using Equation 3-18 (see p. 119). The relationship between σ and $\bar{R}$ is captured in a factor called d_2, which depends on n, the sample size. The values of d_2 are given in Appendix Table 9.

Estimate σ from $\bar{R}$ using d_2

The upper and lower control limits (UCL and LCL) for an $\bar{x}$ chart are computed with the following formulas:

Control Limits for an $\bar{x}$ Chart

$$\text{UCL} = \bar{\bar{x}} + \frac{3\bar{R}}{d_2\sqrt{n}} \quad [10\text{-}2]$$

$$\text{LCL} = \bar{\bar{x}} - \frac{3\bar{R}}{d_2\sqrt{n}}$$

where

- $\bar{\bar{x}}$ = grand mean
- $\bar{R}$ = average of the sample ranges ($= \Sigma R/k$)
- d_2 = control chart factor from Appendix Table 9
- n = number of observations in each sample

To make life simple on the factory floor, these limits are often calculated as $\bar{\bar{x}} \pm A_2\,\bar{R}$, where $A_2 = 3/(d_2\sqrt{n})$. Appendix Table 9 also gives the values of A_2.

Using Equation 10-2, Lisa computes $\bar{R} = \Sigma R/k = 237/20 = 11.85$, looks up d_2 for $n = 6$ in Appendix Table 9 ($d_2 = 2.534$), and then finds the control limits for her $\bar{x}$ chart:

$$\text{UCL} = \bar{\bar{x}} + \frac{3\bar{R}}{d_2\sqrt{n}} = 63.0 + \frac{3(11.85)}{2.534\sqrt{6}} = 63.0 + 5.7 = 68.7 \quad [10\text{-}2]$$

$$\text{LCL} = \bar{\bar{x}} - \frac{3\bar{R}}{d_2\sqrt{n}} = 63.0 - \frac{3(11.85)}{2.534\sqrt{6}} = 63.0 - 5.7 = 57.3$$

Investigating the pattern in the $\bar{x}$ chart

Lisa now plots the CL, UCL, LCL, and the daily values of $\bar{x}$, to get the $\bar{x}$ chart in Figure 10-3. A quick glance at the chart shows her that something is awry: Every Friday, the average service time jumps above the UCL. When she investigates more closely, Lisa discovers that the experienced express-line teller is spending Fridays in a professional development course. On those days, a trainee is manning the express-teller line. Lisa decides to provide more supervision to the trainee to help him improve his processing speed.

Redo the chart, excluding the outliers

Now that she has found out why Fridays are out-of-control, Lisa can see whether the experienced express-line teller is meeting her goal of completing transactions in under 60 seconds on average. To do this, she goes back to the data in Table 10-1, excludes the four Friday outliers, and plots a new control chart from the remaining $k = 16$ daily samples. For that chart, displayed in Figure 10-4, the center line and control limits are given by

$$\bar{\bar{x}} = \frac{\Sigma x}{n \times k} = \frac{5{,}879}{6(16)} = 61.2 \quad [10\text{-}1]$$

$$\text{UCL} = \bar{\bar{x}} + \frac{3\bar{R}}{d_2\sqrt{n}} = 61.2 + \frac{3(10.3)}{2.534\sqrt{6}} = 61.2 + 5.0 = 66.2$$

$$\text{LCL} = \bar{\bar{x}} - \frac{3\bar{R}}{d_2\sqrt{n}} = 61.2 - \frac{3(10.3)}{2.534\sqrt{6}} = 61.2 - 5.0 = 56.2 \quad [10\text{-}2]$$

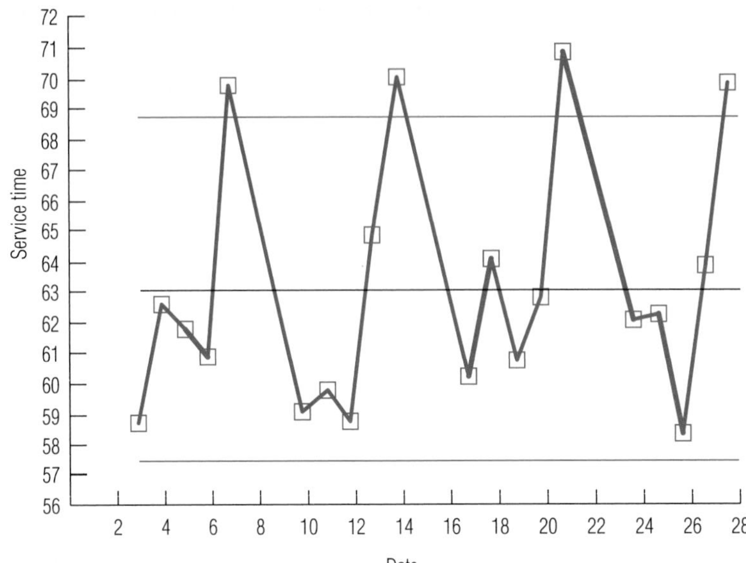

FIGURE 10-3

$\bar{x}$ chart for the express-teller line at the TransCarolina Bank

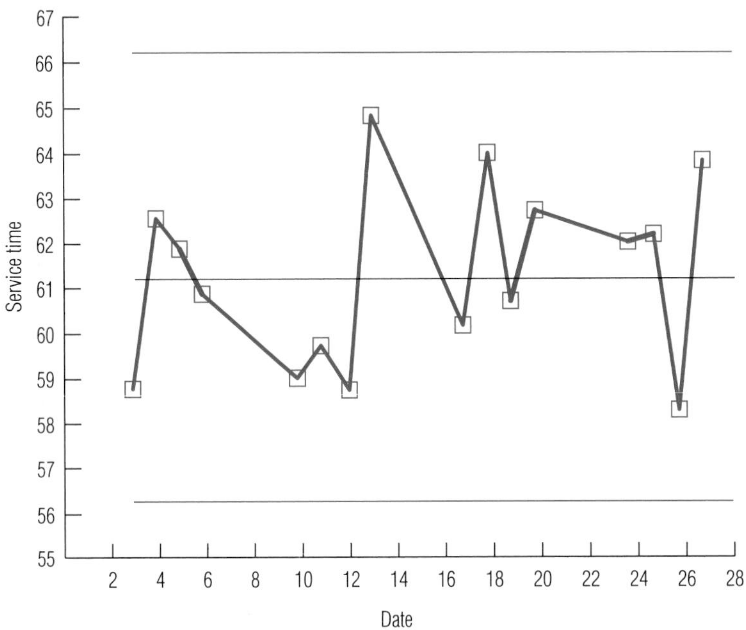

FIGURE 10-4

$\bar{x}$ chart for express-teller line at TransCarolina Bank, with Fridays deleted

Managerial vs. statistical decisions

From Figure 10-4, Lisa sees that the process is in-control. However, with a sample grand mean of 61.2 seconds, even the experienced teller is not yet meeting the under-60-seconds goal. Being in-control does not mean that a process is meeting its goals. In this case, Lisa and the teller will have to work together to analyze the way in which transactions are handled. Perhaps they can redesign procedures to achieve their goal. Or, because the current process is behaving well, they may decide that 61.2 seconds is good enough and not run the risk of spoiling a good system by tinkering with it. This is a managerial decision, not a statistical one. But the statistical analysis has provided Lisa with information she can use in making her managerial decision.

HINTS & ASSUMPTIONS

Recognizing patterns in quality control measurements is the key to fixing an out-of-control situation. When they exist, these patterns focus our attention on something *systematic* that is causing our problem. Hint: The distribution of the variable we measure in quality control does not have to be normal in order for us to use statistical methods to control the process. As we take successive samples, the use of upper and lower control limits is a very practical example of Chebyshev's theorem. You'll remember that Chebyshev assured us back in Chapter 3 that even when the underlying distribution is not normally distributed, we can still make useful statements about the population from information contained in samples. Warning: The statistical quality control methods we will illustrate in this chapter *illuminate* problems. From that point on, it takes focused management and effective communication to *correct* the situation.

Exercises 10.3

Self-Check Exercises

SC 10-1 For each of the following cases, find the CL, UCL, and LCL for an $\bar{x}$ chart based on the given information.

(a) $n = 9, \bar{\bar{x}} = 26.7, \bar{R} = 5.3.$

(b) $n = 17, \bar{\bar{x}} = 138.6, \bar{R} = 15.1.$

(c) $n = 4, \bar{\bar{x}} = 84.2, \bar{R} = 9.6.$

(d) $n = 22, \bar{\bar{x}} = 8.1, \bar{R} = 7.4.$

SC 10-2 Altoona Tire Company sells its ATC-50 tires with a 50,000-mile tread-life warranty. Lorrie Ackerman, a quality control engineer with the company, runs simulated road tests to monitor the life of the output from the ATC-50 production process. From each of the last 12 batches of 1,000 tires, she has tested 5 tires and recorded the following results, with $\bar{x}$ and R measured in thousands of miles:

Batch	1	2	3	4	5	6	7	8	9	10	11	12
$\bar{x}$	50.5	49.7	50.0	50.7	50.7	50.6	49.8	51.1	50.2	50.4	50.6	50.7
R	1.1	1.6	1.8	0.1	0.9	2.1	0.3	0.8	2.3	1.3	2.0	2.1

(a) Use the data above to help Lorrie construct an $\bar{x}$ chart.

(b) Is the production process in-control? Explain.

Basic Concepts

■ **10-11** List four types of patterns that indicate that a process is out-of-control. Give examples where each might arise.

■ **10-12** For each of the following cases, find the CL, UCL, and LCL for an $\bar{x}$ chart based on the given information.

(a) $n = 12, \bar{\bar{x}} = 16.4, \sigma_{\bar{x}} = 1.2.$

(b) $n = 12, \bar{\bar{x}} = 16.4, \bar{R} = 7.6.$

(c) $n = 8, \bar{\bar{x}} = 4.1, \bar{R} = 1.3.$

(d) $n = 15, \bar{\bar{x}} = 141.7, \bar{R} = 18.6.$

Applications

■ **10-13** The Wilson Piston Company manufactures pistons for LawnGuy mowers, and the diameter of each piston must be carefully monitored. Jeff Wilson, the quality control engineer, has sampled 8 pistons from each of the last 15 batches of 500 pistons and has recorded the following results, with $\bar{x}$ and R measured in centimeters:

Batch	1	2	3	4	5	6	7	8	9	10	11	12	13	14	15
$\bar{x}$	15.85	15.95	15.86	15.84	15.91	15.81	15.86	15.84	15.83	15.83	15.72	15.96	15.88	15.84	15.89
R	0.15	0.17	0.18	0.16	0.14	0.21	0.13	0.22	0.19	0.21	0.28	0.12	0.19	0.22	0.24

(a) Use the data above to help Jeff construct an $\bar{x}$ chart.

(b) Is the production process in-control? Explain.

■ **10-14** Dick Burney is director of 911 emergency medical services in Ann Arbor, Michigan. He is concerned about response time, the amount of time that elapses between the receipt of a call at the 911 switchboard and the arrival of a municipal rescue squad crew at the calling location. For the last 3 weeks, he has randomly sampled response times for 9 calls each day to get the following results, with $\bar{x}$ and R measured in minutes:

Day	M	Tu	W	Th	F	Sa	Su
$\bar{x}$	11.6	17.4	14.8	13.8	13.9	22.7	16.6
R	14.1	19.1	22.9	18.0	14.6	23.7	21.0

Day	M	Tu	W	Th	F	Sa	Su
$\bar{x}$	9.5	12.7	17.7	16.3	10.5	22.5	12.6
R	12.6	17.0	12.0	15.1	22.1	24.1	21.3

Day	M	Tu	W	Th	F	Sa	Su
$\bar{x}$	11.4	16.0	11.0	13.3	9.3	21.5	17.9
R	12.1	21.1	13.5	20.3	16.8	20.7	23.2

(a) Construct an $\bar{x}$ chart to help Dick see whether the response-time process is in-control.

(b) What aspect of the chart should disturb him? What action might he take to address this problem?

(c) Excluding the data identified as outlying in part (b), is the process in-control? Explain.

■ **10-15** Track Bicycle Parts manufactures precision ball bearings for wheel hubs, bottom brackets, head sets, and pedals. Seth Adams is responsible for quality control at Track. He has been checking the output of the 5-mm bearings used in front wheel hubs. For each of the last 18 hours, he has sampled 5 bearings, with the following results:

Hour	Bearing Diameters (mm)				
1	5.03	5.06	4.86	4.90	4.95
2	4.97	4.94	5.09	4.78	4.88
3	5.02	4.98	4.94	4.95	4.80
4	4.92	4.93	4.90	4.92	4.96
5	5.01	4.99	4.93	5.06	5.01

(Continued)

Hour	Bearing Diameters (mm)				
6	5.00	4.95	5.10	4.85	4.91
7	4.94	4.91	5.05	5.07	4.88
8	5.00	4.98	5.05	4.96	4.97
9	4.99	5.01	4.93	5.10	4.98
10	5.03	4.96	4.92	5.01	4.93
11	5.02	4.88	5.00	4.98	5.09
12	5.09	5.01	5.13	4.89	5.02
13	4.90	4.93	4.97	4.98	5.12
14	5.04	4.96	5.15	5.04	5.02
15	5.09	4.90	5.04	5.19	5.03
16	5.10	5.01	5.04	5.05	5.02
17	4.97	5.10	5.12	4.92	5.04
18	5.01	4.99	5.06	5.04	5.12

(a) Construct an $\bar{x}$ chart to help Seth determine whether the production of 5-mm bearings is in-control.

(b) Should Seth conclude that the process is in-control? Explain.

■ **10-16** Northern White Metals Corp. uses an extrusion process to produce various kinds of aluminum brackets. Raw aluminum ingots are forced under pressure through steel dies to produce long sections of a desired cross-sectional shape. These sections are then fed through an automatic saw, where they are cut into brackets of the desired length. NWMC operates for three shifts of 4 hours each day, and the saw is recalibrated at the beginning of each shift. This week NWMC is producing #409 brackets with a specified cut length of 4 inches. Silvia Serrano, NWMC's quality specialist, has recorded the lengths of 15 randomly chosen brackets during each half-hour of today's three shifts to get the following data:

Shift 1

Time	0630	0700	0730	0800	0830	0900	0930	1000
$\bar{x}$	4.00	4.02	4.01	4.00	4.03	4.01	4.03	4.00
R	0.09	0.10	0.10	0.11	0.09	0.11	0.11	0.10

Shift 2

Time	1030	1100	1130	1200	1230	1300	1330	1400
$\bar{x}$	4.03	4.06	4.04	4.06	4.04	4.03	4.06	4.05
R	0.12	0.11	0.09	0.10	0.11	0.09	0.10	0.10

Shift 3

Time	1430	1500	1530	1600	1630	1700	1730	1800
$\bar{x}$	4.01	4.01	4.00	4.02	3.99	4.02	4.00	4.00
R	0.10	0.11	0.10	0.09	0.10	0.11	0.09	0.09

(a) Help Silvia construct an $\bar{x}$ chart to monitor the production of the #409 brackets.

(b) What, if anything, can you see in the chart that would cause Silvia some concern? Explain. What should Silvia do to address this concern?

Worked-Out Answers to Self-Check Exercises

SC 10-1 (a) $\bar{\bar{x}} = 26.7$ $\quad \bar{R} = 5.3$ $\quad n = 9$ $\quad d_2 = 2.970$

$\text{CL} = \bar{\bar{x}} = 26.7$

$$UCL = \bar{\bar{x}} + \frac{3\bar{R}}{d_2\sqrt{n}} = 26.7 + \frac{3(5.3)}{2.970\sqrt{9}} = 28.5$$

$$LCL = \bar{\bar{x}} - \frac{3\bar{R}}{d_2\sqrt{n}} = 26.7 - \frac{3(5.3)}{2.970\sqrt{9}} = 24.9$$

(b) $\bar{\bar{x}} = 138.6 \qquad \bar{R} = 15.1 \qquad n = 17 \qquad d_2 = 3.588$

$CL = \bar{\bar{x}} = 138.6$

$$UCL = \bar{\bar{x}} + \frac{3\bar{R}}{d_2\sqrt{n}} = 138.6 + \frac{3(15.1)}{3.588\sqrt{17}} = 141.7$$

$$LCL = \bar{\bar{x}} - \frac{3\bar{R}}{d_2\sqrt{n}} = 138.6 - \frac{3(15.1)}{3.588\sqrt{17}} = 135.5$$

(c) $\bar{\bar{x}} = 84.2 \qquad \bar{R} = 9.6 \qquad n = 4 \qquad d_2 = 2.059$

$CL = \bar{\bar{x}} = 84.2$

$$UCL = \bar{\bar{x}} + \frac{3\bar{R}}{d_2\sqrt{n}} = 84.2 + \frac{3(9.6)}{2.059\sqrt{4}} = 91.2$$

$$LCL = \bar{\bar{x}} - \frac{3\bar{R}}{d_2\sqrt{n}} = 84.2 - \frac{3(9.6)}{2.059\sqrt{4}} = 77.2$$

(d) $\bar{\bar{x}} = 8.1 \qquad \bar{R} = 7.4 \qquad n = 22 \qquad d_2 = 3.819$

$CL = \bar{\bar{x}} = 8.1$

$$UCL = \bar{\bar{x}} + \frac{3\bar{R}}{d_2\sqrt{n}} = 8.1 + \frac{3(7.4)}{3.819\sqrt{22}} = 9.3$$

$$LCL = \bar{\bar{x}} - \frac{3\bar{R}}{d_2\sqrt{n}} = 8.1 - \frac{3(7.4)}{3.819\sqrt{22}} = 6.9$$

SC 10-2 (a) $n = 5 \qquad k = 12 \qquad d_2 = 2.326$

$$\bar{\bar{x}} = \frac{\Sigma\bar{x}}{k} = \frac{605.0}{12} = 50.417 \qquad \bar{R} = \frac{\Sigma R}{k} = \frac{16.4}{12} = 1.367$$

$CL = \bar{\bar{x}} = 50.417$

$$UCL = \bar{\bar{x}} + \frac{3\bar{R}}{d_2\sqrt{n}} = 50.417 + \frac{3(1.367)}{2.326\sqrt{5}} = 51.21$$

$$LCL = \bar{\bar{x}} - \frac{3\bar{R}}{d_2\sqrt{n}} = 50.417 - \frac{3(1.367)}{2.326\sqrt{5}} = 49.63$$

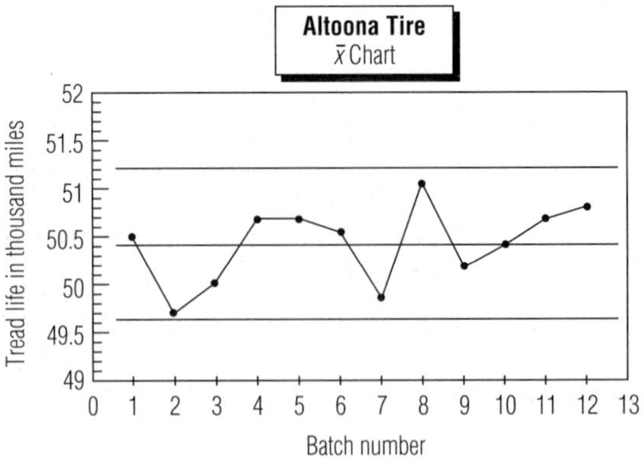

(b) The production process appears to be in-control. However, there are several batches (batches 2, 7 and 8), that approach the control limits.

10.4 *R* Charts: Control Charts for Process Variability

Monitoring variability

Recall our discussion of quality in the first two sections of this chapter. Because quality implies consistency, reliability, and conformance to requirements, variability is the enemy of quality. Stated in a somewhat different way, the way to improve quality is to reduce variability. But before you can decide whether variability is a problem in any instance, you must be able to monitor it.

The control limits in $\bar{x}$ charts place bounds on the amount of variability we are willing to tolerate in our sample means. However, quality concerns are addressed to individual observations (driveshaft diameters, express-teller-line transaction times, and so on). We saw in Chapter 6 that sample means are less variable than individual observations. More precisely, Equation 6-1 tells us that

$$\sigma_{\bar{x}} = \frac{\sigma}{\sqrt{n}} \qquad [6\text{-}1]$$

Center line for *R* charts

To monitor the variability in the individual observations, we use another control chart, known as an *R* chart. In *R* charts, we plot the values of the sample ranges for each of the samples. The center line for *R* charts is placed at $\bar{R}$. To get the control limits, we need to know something about the sampling distribution of *R*. In particular, what is its standard deviation, σ_R? Although the derivation of the result is beyond the scope of this text, it turns out that

Standard Deviation of the Sampling Distribution of *R*

$$\sigma_R = d_3\sigma \qquad [10\text{-}3]$$

where

- σ = population standard deviation
- d_3 = another factor depending on n

Control limits for *R* charts

The values of d_3 are also given in Appendix Table 9. Now we can substitute $\bar{R}/d_2$ for σ as we did in Equation 10-2, to compute the control limits for *R* charts:

Control Limits for an *R* Chart

$$\text{UCL} = \bar{R} + \frac{3d_3\bar{R}}{d_2} = \bar{R}\left(1 + \frac{3d_3}{d_2}\right)$$

$$\text{LCL} = \bar{R} - \frac{3d_3\bar{R}}{d_2} = \bar{R}\left(1 - \frac{3d_3}{d_2}\right) \qquad [10\text{-}4]$$

To make life simple on the factory floor, these limits are often calculated as

$$\text{UCL} = \overline{R}D_4, \text{ where } D_4 = 1 + 3d_3/d_2$$

$$\text{LCL} = \overline{R}D_3, \text{ where } D_3 = 1 - 3d_3/d_2$$

The values of D_3 and D_4 can also be found in Appendix Table 9.

LCL = 0 if $n \leq 6$

There is one slight wrinkle in using Equation 10-4. A sample range is always a nonnegative number (because it is the difference between the largest and smallest observations in the sample). However, when $n \leq 6$, the LCL computed by Equation 10-4 will be negative. In these cases, we set the value of LCL to zero. Accordingly, the entries for D_3 for $n \leq 6$ in Appendix Table 9 are all zeros.

Although she doesn't have any specific goals for the variability in service times on the express-teller line at the Durham office of TransCarolina Bank, Lisa Klein would like to see whether that aspect of the operation is in-control. Returning to the data in Table 10-1, she recalls that $\overline{R} = 11.85$. Using this value in Equation 10-4, she finds the control limits for the $\overline{R}$ chart in Figure 10-5:

$$\text{UCL} = \overline{R}\left(1 + \frac{3d_3}{d_2}\right) = 11.85\left(1 + \frac{3(0.848)}{2.534}\right) = 23.7$$

$$\text{LCL} = \overline{R}\left(1 - \frac{3d_3}{d_2}\right) = 11.85\left(1 - \frac{3(0.848)}{2.534}\right) = 0 \qquad [10\text{-}4]$$

Noticing a pattern in the *R* chart

Although Figure 10-5 seems to indicate that the variability in service times on the express-teller line is in-control, Lisa knows that a teller trainee was at work on Fridays (the 7th, 14th, 21st, and 28th of the month). The effect of this can be seen on the *R* chart, because Fridays have the most variability (the highest sample ranges) during each of the 4 weeks in the sample.

FIGURE 10-5

R chart for express-teller line at TransCarolina Bank

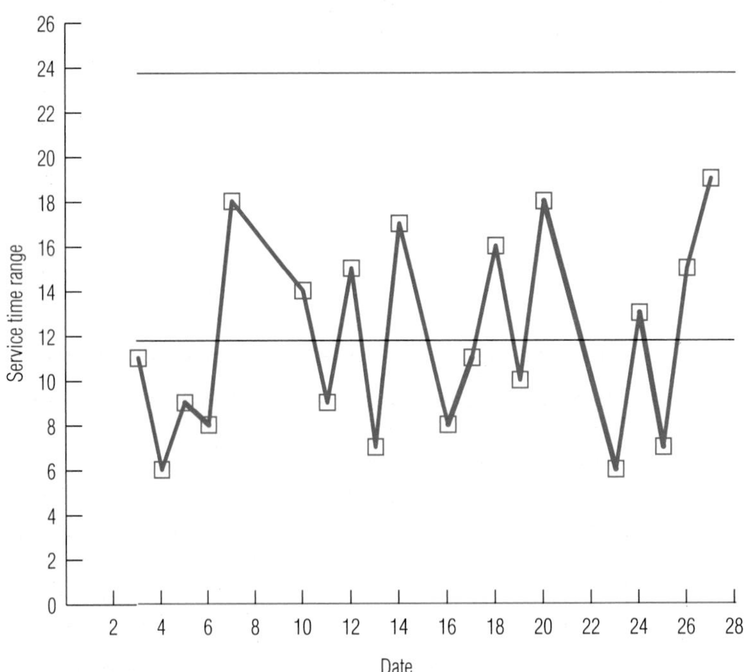

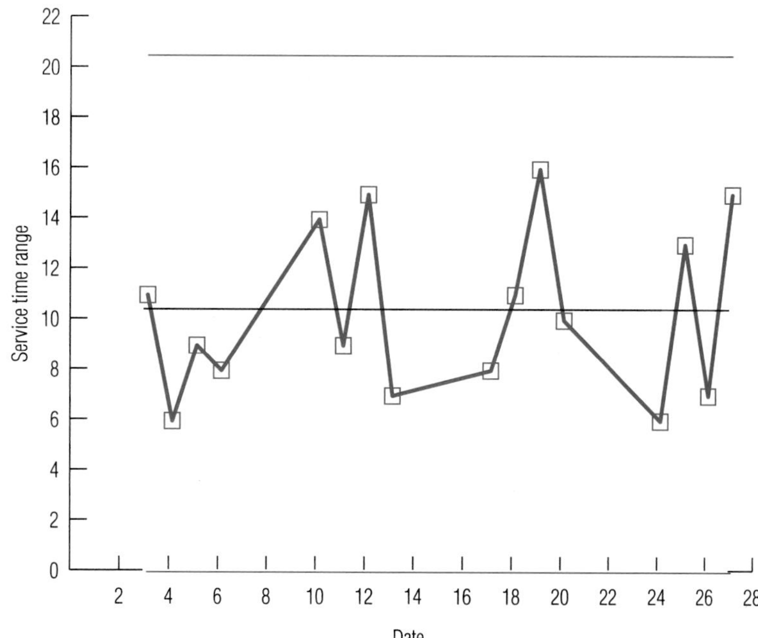

FIGURE 10-6

R chart for express-teller line at TransCarolina Bank, with Fridays excluded

Just as she did when looking at the process mean in Figures 10-3 and 10-4, Lisa now excludes the four Fridays to monitor the variability in service times on the express-teller line when the experienced teller is providing the service. Now $\overline{R} = 10.3$, and the control limits are

$$\text{UCL} = \overline{R}\left(1 + \frac{3d_3}{d_2}\right) = 10.3\left(1 + \frac{3(0.848)}{2.534}\right) = 20.6$$

$$\text{LCL} = \overline{R}\left(1 - \frac{3d_3}{d_2}\right) = 10.3\left(1 - \frac{3(0.848)}{2.534}\right) = 0 \qquad [10\text{-}4]$$

The final *R* chart in Figure 10-6 shows that the experienced teller has service-time variability well in-control. There is nothing evident in the control chart to indicate the presence of any other assignable variation.

HINTS & ASSUMPTIONS

Warning: The range we plot in an *R* chart is only a convenient substitute for the variability of the process we are studying. Its chief advantages are that it is easy to calculate, plot, and understand. But we need to remember from Chapter 3 that the range considers only the highest and lowest values in a distribution and omits all other observations in the data set. Thus, it can ignore the nature of the variation among all of the other observations and is heavily influenced by extreme values. Also, because it measures only two values, the range can change significantly from one sample to the next in a given population.

Exercises 10.4

Self-Check Exercises

SC 10-3 For each of the following cases, find the CL, UCL, and LCL for an R chart based on the given information.

(a) $n = 9, \bar{\bar{x}} = 26.7, \bar{R} = 5.3$.

(b) $n = 17, \bar{\bar{x}} = 138.6, \bar{R} = 15.1$.

(c) $n = 4, \bar{\bar{x}} = 84.2, \bar{R} = 9.6$.

(d) $n = 22, \bar{\bar{x}} = 8.1, \bar{R} = 7.4$.

SC 10-4 Construct an R chart for the data given in Exercise SC 10-2. Is the variability in the tread life of the ATC-50 in control? Explain.

Basic Concepts

■ **10-17** For each of the following cases, find the CL, UCL, and LCL for an R chart based on the given information:

(a) $n = 3, \bar{\bar{x}} = 18.4, \bar{R} = 3.1$.

(b) $n = 19, \bar{\bar{x}} = 16.2, \bar{R} = 6.9$.

(c) $n = 8, \bar{\bar{x}} = 141.7, \bar{R} = 18.2$.

(d) $n = 24, \bar{\bar{x}} = 8.6, \bar{R} = 1.4$.

(e) $\bar{R} = 6.0$, LCL $= 3.0$, find the UCL.

Applications

■ **10-18** Ray Underhall reproduces antique chairs. His apprentices turn spindles for the chair backs on manual lathes. The beads on the spindles are to have average diameters of $^7/_8$ inch at their widest points. Ray monitors the apprentices' work with control charts. Which of the following patterns is he likely to see on the R chart for a new apprentice? Explain.

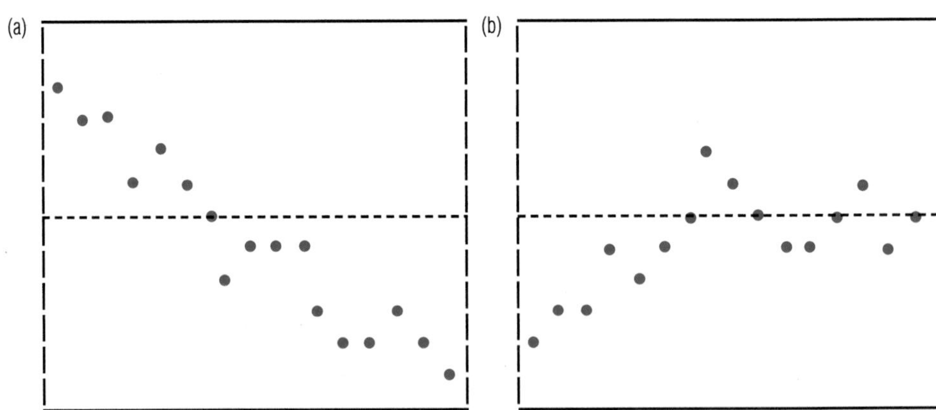

■ **10-19** Construct an R chart for the data given in Exercise 10-13. Is the variability in the piston diameter under control? Explain.

■ **10-20** Consider the emergency medical service data given in Exercise 10-14.

(a) Construct an R chart for these data.

(b) When he looked at the $\bar{x}$ chart for these data, Dick Burney noted that the three Saturdays were outliers. Closer investigation revealed that this happened because the number of calls coming in was higher on Saturdays than on any other day of the week. Does the R chart you constructed in part (a) show any pattern that could be attributed to the same cause? Explain.

(c) Exclude the 3 Saturdays and construct a new R chart. Does this chart exhibit any patterns that Dick should be concerned about? Explain.

■ **10-21** Construct an R chart for the data given in Exercise 10-15. Are there any patterns in this chart that should concern Seth Adams, or does the variability in the process appear to be in-control? Explain.

■ **10-22** Construct an R chart for the data given in Exercise 10-16. Are there any patterns in this chart that should concern Silvia Serrano, or does the variability in the process appear to be in-control? Explain.

Worked-Out Answers to Self-Check Exercises

SC 10-3 (a) $n = 9$ $\quad \bar{R} = 5.3$ $\quad D_4 = 1.816$ $\quad D_3 = 0.184$

$\text{CL} = \bar{R} = 5.3$

$\text{UCL} = \bar{R}D_4 = 5.3(1.816) = 9.62$

$\text{LCL} = \bar{R}D_3 = 5.3(0.184) = 0.98$

(b) $n = 17$ $\quad \bar{R} = 15.1$ $\quad D_4 = 1.622$ $\quad D_3 = 0.378$

$\text{CL} = \bar{R} = 15.1$

$\text{UCL} = \bar{R}D_4 = 15.1(1.622) = 24.49$

$\text{LCL} = \bar{R}D_3 = 15.1(0.378) = 5.71$

(c) $n = 4$ $\quad \bar{R} = 9.6$ $\quad D_4 = 2.282$ $\quad D_3 = 0$

$\text{CL} = \bar{R} = 9.6$

$\text{UCL} = \bar{R}D_4 = 9.6(2.282) = 21.91$

$\text{LCL} = \bar{R}D_3 = 9.6(0) = 0$

(d) $n = 22$ $\quad \bar{R} = 7.4$ $\quad D_4 = 1.566$ $\quad D_3 = 0.434$

$\text{CL} = \bar{R} = 7.4$

$\text{UCL} = \bar{R}D_4 = 7.4(1.566) = 11.59$

$\text{LCL} = \bar{R}D_3 = 7.4(0.434) = 3.21$

SC 10-4 $n = 5$ $\quad D_4 = 2.114$ $\quad D_3 = 0$

$\bar{R} = 1.367$

$\text{CL} = \bar{R} = 1.367$

$$UCL = \overline{R}D_4 = 1.367(2.114) = 2.89$$

$$LCL = \overline{R}D_3 = 1.367(0) = 0$$

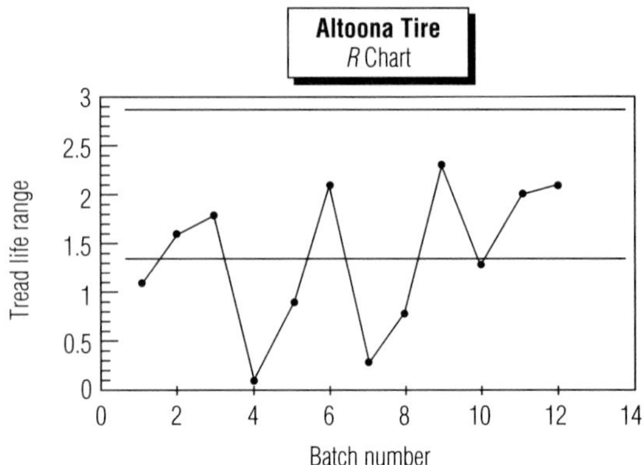

Distinct cycling in the values of R shows that the process is out-of-control.

10.5 *p* Charts: Control Charts for Attributes

Quantitative and *qualitative* variables

$\bar{x}$ charts and R charts are control charts for *quantitative* variables, which take on *numerical* values. Quantitative variables are measured (for example, heights, IQs, or speeds) or counted (for example, numbers of employees, phone calls per hour, or points scored in a basketball game). But not all the variables we encounter are quantitative. Variables such as marital status, heads or tails in a coin toss, or winning or losing a basketball game are *categorical,* or *qualitative.*

Attributes

In the area of statistical process control, a qualitative variable that can take on only two values is called an *attribute.* Recalling, once again, that quality is conformity to requirements, it should not surprise you to learn that the attribute most frequently discussed in SPC is that of conformance or noncomformance of units of output to the process specifications.

A standard to be met

Consider the case of Golden Guernsey Dairies. Harry Galloway is in charge of the milk bottling operations at GGD, an integrated dairy farm and milk packager near Sheboygan, Wisconsin. (Although cartons have long since replaced milk bottles, Harry still refers to the operations as bottling.) There is some variation in the output from GGD's bottling machinery, so Harry monitors the process to be sure that the average half-gallon container is filled with 64.1 ounces of milk. He has long used $\bar{x}$ charts, based on hourly samples of 100 cartons (taken 10 times each day, from 6 A.M. to 3 P.M.), to monitor the bottling operation, and the process is well under control. The Wisconsin State Department of Agriculture recently instituted a new requirement that not only must half-gallon cartons contain at least 64 ounces on average, but in addition, no more than 3 percent of them can contain less than 63.5 ounces.

The relevant data

The attribute that concerns Harry is whether any particular carton contains at least 63.5 ounces or less than that amount. To monitor the output, he has been keeping a record of the proportions of underfilled cartons (the fraction of cartons not conforming to the Department of Agriculture's 63.5-ounce standard) in his hourly samples for the past week. These data are given in Table 10-2.

Table 10-2

Fraction of Underfilled Half-Gallon Cartons in Hourly Samples at Golden Guernsey Dairies

Day	Hour	Fraction Underfilled	Day	Hour	Fraction Underfilled
Sunday	6	0.02	Wednesday	11	0.05
	7	0.01	*cont.*	12	0.05
	8	0.03		1	0.04
	9	0.03		2	0.05
	10	0.04		3	0.04
	11	0.02	Thursday	6	0.01
	12	0.03		7	0.03
	1	0.03		8	0.02
	2	0.03		9	0.02
	3	0.03		10	0.03
Monday	6	0.01		11	0.03
	7	0.01		12	0.03
	8	0.03		1	0.06
	9	0.03		2	0.05
	10	0.03		3	0.05
	11	0.02	Friday	6	0.02
	12	0.02		7	0.02
	1	0.04		8	0.03
	2	0.03		9	0.03
	3	0.05		10	0.02
Tuesday	6	0.02		11	0.03
	7	0.03		12	0.04
	8	0.02		1	0.04
	9	0.02		2	0.05
	10	0.03		3	0.03
	11	0.02	Saturday	6	0.01
	12	0.02		7	0.02
	1	0.03		8	0.03
	2	0.05		9	0.02
	3	0.06		10	0.04
Wednesday	6	0.02		11	0.03
	7	0.03		12	0.04
	8	0.01		1	0.05
	9	0.03		2	0.03
	10	0.03		3	0.04

Testing whether the standard is met

Because the fraction underfilled in the total sample of 7,000 cartons (7 days, 10 samples per day, 100 cartons per sample) is 0.0306, Harry is reasonably confident that GGD is meeting the new requirement. A formal test of the hypothesis H_0: $p = 0.03$, against the alternative H_1: $p > 0.03$, supports his confidence. The standard deviation of the sample proportion is

$$\sigma_{\bar{p}} = \sqrt{\frac{pq}{n}} \qquad [7\text{-}4]$$

$$= \sqrt{\frac{0.03(0.97)}{7{,}000}} = 0.0020$$

Using this value to convert the observed sample fraction (0.0306) to a standard z score,

$$z = \frac{\bar{p} - \mu_{\bar{p}}}{\sigma_{\bar{p}}} = \frac{0.0306 - 0.03}{0.0020} = 0.3$$

It is met!

We find from Appendix Table 1 that the prob value for our test is 0.5000 − 0.1179 = 0.3821. With such a large prob value, Harry can be quite confident in accepting H_0. The fraction of half-gallon cartons being underfilled is not significantly greater than 3 percent; GGD is meeting the Department of Agriculture's new standard.

p charts give more information

However, because he has the overall sample broken down into $k = 70$ hourly samples of size $n = 100$ over the course of the week, there is more information available for Harry to look at. He can plot the hourly sample fractions in a control chart known as a *p chart.* Because

$$\mu_{\bar{p}} = p \quad [7\text{-}3]$$

and

$$\sigma_{\bar{p}} = \sqrt{\frac{pq}{n}} \quad [7\text{-}4]$$

the center line and control limits of p charts are at

Center line and control limits for *p* charts

Center Line for a *p* Chart

$$\text{CL} = \mu_{\bar{p}} = p \quad [10\text{-}5]$$

Control Limits for a *p* Chart

$$\text{UCL} = \mu_{\bar{p}} + 3\sigma_{\bar{p}} = p + 3\sqrt{\frac{pq}{n}} \quad [10\text{-}6]$$

$$\text{LCL} = \mu_{\bar{p}} - 3\sigma_{\bar{p}} = p - 3\sqrt{\frac{pq}{n}}$$

If there is a known or targeted value of p, that value should be used in Equations 10-5 and 10-6. However, if no such value of p is available, then you should estimate p by the overall sample fraction

Estimate of *p*

$$\bar{\bar{p}} = \frac{\Sigma \bar{p}_j}{k} \quad [10\text{-}7]$$

where

- $\bar{p}_j$ = sample fraction in the jth hourly sample
- k = total number of hourly samples

Make sure that LCL ≥ 0 and UCL ≤ 1

Recall the slight wrinkle in using Equation 10-4 for the LCL of an R chart: Ranges cannot be negative; so if Equation 10-4 gave an LCL below 0, we replaced it by 0. In the same way, Equation 10-6 can produce a UCL above 1 or an LCL below 0 for a p chart. Because p is always between 0 and 1, we will replace a negative LCL by 0 and a UCL above 1 by 1.

Because Harry has a target value of $p = 0.03$ (and because he is quite confident that his filling operation is coming close to this target), he uses that value to find the center line and control limits for his p chart:

$$\text{CL} = p = 0.03 \quad [10\text{-}5]$$

$$\text{UCL} = p + 3\sqrt{\frac{pq}{n}} = 0.03 + 3\sqrt{\frac{0.03(0.97)}{100}} = 0.081$$

$$\text{LCL} = p - 3\sqrt{\frac{pq}{n}} = 0.03 - 3\sqrt{\frac{0.03(0.97)}{100}} = -0.021 \quad [10\text{-}6]$$

Harry corrects the LCL to 0 and then plots the p chart in Figure 10-7.

Noting a pattern, finding its cause, and taking action to correct it

All of the observations on the control chart fall within the control limits, but there is a distinct pattern in the chart that repeats every day. The proportion of underfilled cartons tends to start out low in the morning and finish up high in the afternoon. Harry immediately realizes the cause of this pattern. The bottling machinery is cleaned and calibrated each morning and then runs for the entire day. Even though the fraction of underfilled cartons meets the state standard on average, Harry is unhappy with his finding. Fortunately, cleaning and calibrating are quick and easy, so Harry decides to stop the line briefly at 10 A.M. each day to clean and recalibrate the machinery for the second half of the day.

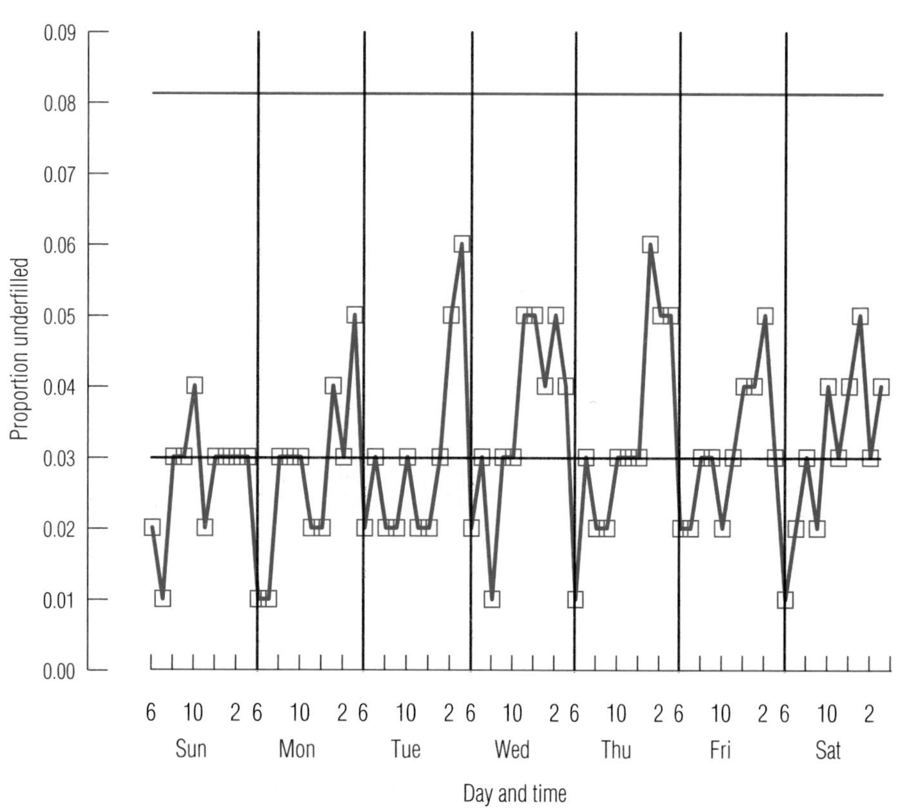

FIGURE 10-7

p chart for bottling machinery at Golden Guernsey Dairies

HINTS & ASSUMPTIONS

Charts of means and ranges help us control quantitative variables that can be measured, such as length of a part, life (in hours) of an engine, or the width of lumber. But many variables take on only two values, such as acceptable part/unacceptable part, fits/doesn't fit, or fast enough/not fast enough. In statistical process control, such a variable is called an *attribute* and we control attributes with p charts. Hint: Think of an attribute in terms of hair color; you are either a redhead or not, you have it or you don't. Warning: If there is a target value for p, you should use it for the center line of the p chart. If no such value is available, then use the overall sample fraction for the center line. Remember that probabilities are between 0 and 1; lower control limits below 0 or upper control limits above 1 are incorrect.

Exercises 10.5

Self-Check Exercises

SC 10-5 For each of the following cases, find the CL, UCL, and LCL for a p chart based on the given information.

(a) $n = 144, \bar{\bar{p}} = 0.10$.

(b) $n = 60, \bar{\bar{p}} = 0.9$.

(c) $n = 125$, 0.36 is the target value for p.

(d) $n = 48$, 0.75 is the target value for p.

SC 10-6 Todd Olmstead is the Meals-on-Wheels dispatcher for the Atlanta metropolitan area. He wants meals delivered to clients within 30 minutes of leaving the kitchens. Meals with longer delivery times tend to be too cold when they arrive. Each of his 10 volunteer drivers is responsible for delivering 15 meals daily. Over the past month, Todd has recorded the percentage of each day's 150 meals that were delivered on-time:

Day	1	2	3	4	5	6	7	8
% on-time	89.33	81.33	95.33	88.67	96.00	86.67	98.00	84.00
Day	9	10	11	12	13	14	15	16
% on-time	90.67	80.67	88.00	86.67	96.67	85.33	78.67	89.33
Day	17	18	19	20	21	22	23	24
% on-time	89.33	78.67	94.00	94.00	99.33	95.33	94.67	92.67
Day	25	26	27	28	29	30		
% on-time	81.33	89.33	99.33	90.67	92.00	88.00		

(a) Help Todd construct a p chart from these data.

(b) How does your chart show that the attribute "fraction of meals delivered on-time" is out-of-control?

(c) What action do you recommend for Todd?

Basic Concepts

■ **10-23** Which of the following qualitative variables are attributes?

(a) Gender of nouns in German.

(b) Gender of nouns in French.

(c) Course grades under a Pass/Fail grading scheme.

(d) Course grades under an A, B, C, D, F grading scheme.

■ **10-24** For each of the following cases, find the CL, UCL, and LCL for a p chart based on the given information.

(a) $n = 30, \bar{\bar{p}} = 0.25$.

(b) $n = 65, \bar{\bar{p}} = 0.15$.

(c) $n = 82, \bar{\bar{p}} = 0.05$.

(d) $n = 97$, 0.42 is the target value for p.

(e) $n = 124$, 0.63 is the target value for p.

Applications

■ **10-25** After finding out his luggage arrived in San Antonio while his destination was Omaha, Will Richardson, a statistician for USA Airlines, decided to do some research. For the last 3 weeks, Will has sampled 200 passengers daily and determined the percentage of luggage delivered to the expected destination with the results given below:

Day	1	2	3	4	5	6	7	8	9	10	11	12	13	14	15	16	17	18	19	20	21
Percent correct	0.89	0.91	0.93	0.95	0.94	0.96	0.92	0.91	0.93	0.90	0.88	0.94	0.97	0.94	0.95	0.92	0.93	0.92	0.91	0.93	0.89

(a) Help Will construct a p chart from these data.

(b) Is the luggage delivery process in-control? Explain.

(c) What recommendations, if any, can you make?

■ **10-26** BioAssist, Inc., manufactures high potency vitamin supplements. C-Assist, a 1,000-mg capsule of vitamin C, is BioAssist's best seller. Sherry Cohen is responsible for monitoring the quality of C-Assist. The capsules are supposed to contain between 999 and 1,001 mg of vitamin C, and BioAssist wants no more than 1.5 percent of them to fail to meet this specification. Every quarter-hour, Sherry samples 500 capsules and records the percentage failing to meet the specification (percent bad). She has gotten the following results for the last 8 hours of production:

Time	**0915**	**0930**	**0945**	**1000**	**1015**	**1030**	**1045**	**1100**	**1115**	**1130**	**1145**
% bad	2.4	1.8	1.6	0.6	1.0	1.4	2.0	2.8	2.4	1.6	1.0
Time	**1200**	**1215**	**1230**	**1245**	**1300**	**1315**	**1330**	**1345**	**1400**	**1415**	**1430**
% bad	0.4	0.6	1.6	2.2	2.6	2.2	1.6	1.0	0.4	1.2	1.6
Time	**1445**	**1500**	**1515**	**1530**	**1545**	**1600**	**1615**	**1630**	**1645**	**1700**	
% bad	2.2	2.8	1.8	1.6	0.8	0.4	1.2	1.4	2.0	2.8	

(a) Consider all 16,000 capsules Sherry has sampled. Can she be sure that the percentage bad is not significantly greater than 1.5 percent? State and test the appropriate hypotheses.

(b) Use the data above to help Sherry construct a p chart.

(c) Is there anything in the p chart about which Sherry should worry? If not, why not? If so, what should she do?

■ **10-27** Andie Duvall is a finance major who has been studying the stock market for her senior honors thesis. On each of the last 100 trading days, she has randomly sampled 100 companies listed on the New York Stock Exchange and recorded the fraction whose share prices increased that day. Andie believes that there is a 50–50 chance that any given stock will increase on any given day. Explain how she can use a p chart based on her 100 days' worth of data to see if her belief is reasonable or not.

■ **10-28** Ross Darrow is a flight operations analyst for Spacious Skies, Unltd. He has been assigned the task of monitoring flights at the company's hub airport in the southeast. Each day, Spacious Skies has 240 takeoffs scheduled from this hub. Ross has been concerned about the fraction of flights with late departures, and four weeks ago he instituted procedures designed to reduce that fraction. Use the data for the last 30 weekdays to construct a p chart to see whether his new procedures have been successful. What further action, if any, should Ross consider?

Weeks 1 & 2

Day	M	T	W	Th	F	M	T	W	Th	F
# late	26	19	26	22	24	19	19	20	18	18

Weeks 3 & 4

Day	M	T	W	Th	F	M	T	W	Th	F
# late	17	9	13	10	12	14	14	13	9	10

Weeks 5 & 6

Day	M	T	W	Th	F	M	T	W	Th	F
# late	12	15	14	15	16	18	17	16	18	17

Worked-Out Answers to Self-Check Exercises

SC 10-5 (a) $\text{CL} = \bar{\bar{p}} = 0.10$

$$\text{UCL} = \bar{\bar{p}} + 3\sqrt{\frac{pq}{n}} = 0.10 + 3\sqrt{\frac{0.10(0.90)}{144}} = 0.175$$

$$\text{LCL} = \bar{\bar{p}} - 3\sqrt{\frac{pq}{n}} = 0.10 - 3\sqrt{\frac{0.10(0.90)}{144}} = 0.025$$

(b) $\text{CL} = \bar{\bar{p}} = 0.9$

$$\text{UCL} = \bar{\bar{p}} + 3\sqrt{\frac{pq}{n}} = 0.9 + 3\sqrt{\frac{0.9(0.1)}{60}} = 1.016\text{, so the UCL} = 1$$

$$\text{LCL} = \bar{\bar{p}} - 3\sqrt{\frac{pq}{n}} = 0.9 - 3\sqrt{\frac{0.9(0.1)}{60}} = 0.784$$

(c) $\text{CL} = p = 0.36$

$$\text{UCL} = p + 3\sqrt{\frac{pq}{n}} = 0.36 + 3\sqrt{\frac{0.36(0.64)}{125}} = 0.489$$

$$\text{LCL} = p - 3\sqrt{\frac{pq}{n}} = 0.36 - 3\sqrt{\frac{0.36(0.64)}{125}} = 0.231$$

(d) $\text{CL} = p = 0.75$

$$\text{UCL} = p + 3\sqrt{\frac{pq}{n}} = 0.75 + 3\sqrt{\frac{0.75(0.25)}{48}} = 0.938$$

$$LCL = p - 3\sqrt{\frac{pq}{n}} = 0.75 - 3\sqrt{\frac{0.75(0.25)}{48}} = 0.563$$

SC 10-6 (a) $n = 150 \qquad \bar{\bar{p}} = \frac{\Sigma \bar{p}}{k} = \frac{26.94}{30} = 0.898$

$$UCL = p + 3\sqrt{\frac{pq}{n}} = 0.898 + 3\sqrt{\frac{0.898(0.102)}{150}} = 0.972$$

$$LCL = p - 3\sqrt{\frac{pq}{n}} = 0.898 - 3\sqrt{\frac{0.898(0.102)}{150}} = 0.824`$$

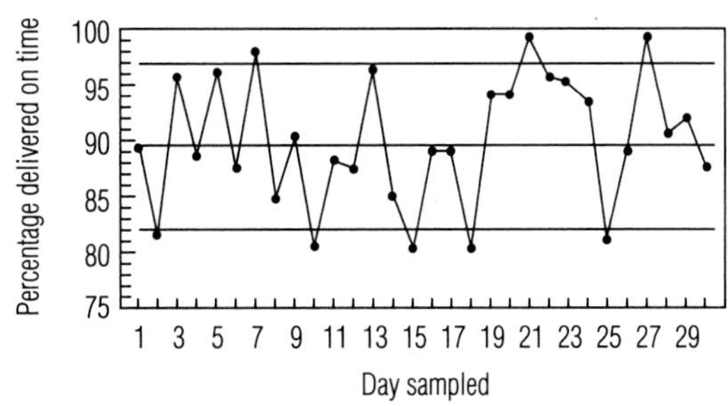

(b) Five of the 30 days sampled had values of "fraction on-time" that were below the lower control limit. (Being above the upper control limit is not worrisome in this context.)

(c) Because the percentage of meals delivered on-time is out-of-control, Todd might investigate the reasons behind the 5 days that are out-of-control. It might be a particular driver, or those days may provide heavier traffic. He might replace or train the volunteer(s) based on his findings.

10.6 Total Quality Management

Some processes are too complicated for control charts

Statistical Process Control is very useful for continuous processes such as oil refineries and mass-production facilities. However, many managers feel that their businesses are altogether too complicated to have their important aspects captured and monitored by control charts. Suppose you were the manager of a regional hub airport and were asked to reduce takeoff delays. Although delays are easy to identify, their causes are harder to pin down. Takeoffs can be delayed by weather, equipment problems, lateness of incoming crews, holiday traffic, and so on. At first glance, you wouldn't know what things to measure in order to control delays.

TQM requires companywide commitment

Total Quality Management (TQM) is a set of approaches that enable the managers of complex systems to match the firm's products to customers' expectations. The airport manager can use TQM to reduce delays so that planes match the schedules that their passengers expect. Because so many factors are involved, and because different workers have responsibility for these factors, successful use of TQM requires commitments at all levels of the firm in order to be successful. In particular, top-level management must provide strong leadership for quality, and workers at all levels must be empowered to identify problems and make changes in the system.

Fishbone Diagrams: Identifying and Grouping Causes

The TQM approach to complex businesses begins with the realization that all errors, defects, and problems have causes, and that there is only a finite number of these. The first step is to identify and discriminate between *things gone right* and *things gone wrong.* In our airport example, some of the planes do leave on time (things gone right). When you look at the late departures (things gone wrong), you can begin to build up a list of causes behind their delays.

Identify what's right and what's wrong

Gather causes into logical groups

Even in complicated systems, causes of problems can be gathered into logical groups. For example, in our airport delays case, some of the late takeoffs are due to problems with the aircraft themselves, others result from baggage handling, and so on. As you collect the various reasons for departure delays into logical groups, it becomes clear that there are cause-and-effect relationships among them. These relationships can be captured pictorially in a *cause-and-effect* diagram such as Figure 10-8. Such cause-and-effect diagrams are sometimes called *Ishikawa diagrams,* after their Japanese developer, Kaoru Ishikawa. But, because of their appearance, these diagrams are most often called *fishbone diagrams.*

The fishbone diagram takes an unstructured list of factors that contribute to delayed takeoffs and organizes that list in two major ways. First, it gathers the factors into logical groups. And then, within the groups, it indicates how the various factors feed into one another in cause-and-effect relationships. Because of this, you can see how the complex system hangs together and recognize that many factors may need to be addressed in order to resolve the problems.

Successful use of TQM involves personnel at all levels

The fishbone diagram also points out why personnel at all levels must be involved if TQM is to be successful. Baggage handlers are much more likely than top management or consultants to be able to identify a complete list of baggage problems that contribute to takeoff delays. In addition, because of their familiarity with details of the baggage-handling operation, they are also very likely to be able to suggest ways to improve that operation.

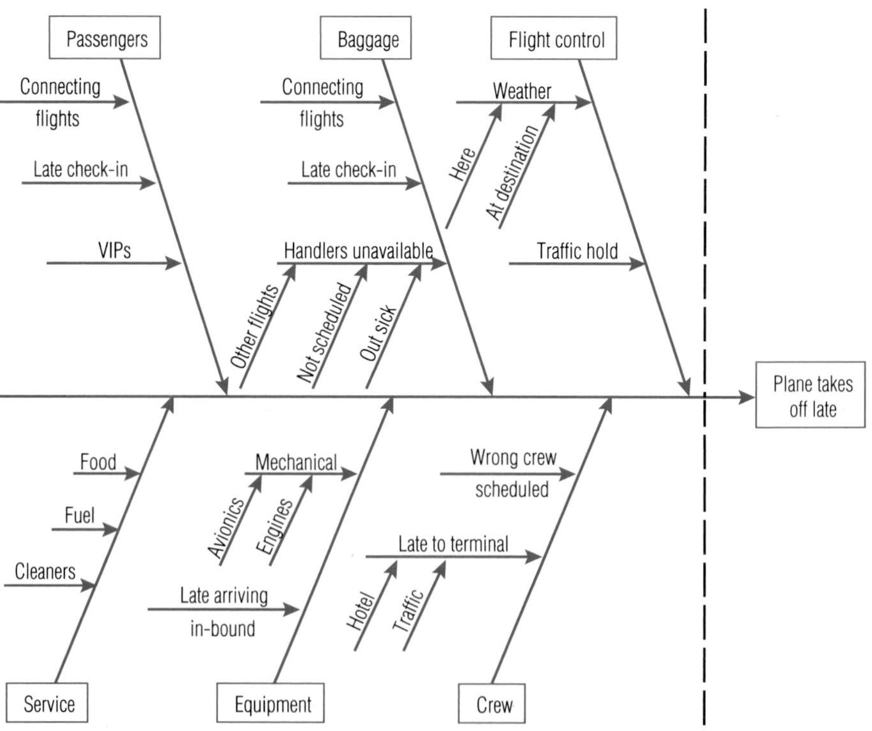

FIGURE 10-8

A fishbone diagram: cause-and-effect reasons for airport takeoff delays

However, unless they are empowered to identify problems and make changes, they are unlikely to be willing to do so.

Slay the Dragons First

In any quality improvement process, as we have seen, there are likely to be a very large number of causes for defects and errors. Looking at all the possible things that can go wrong, even if they are organized into a neat fishbone diagram, can lead even well-motivated people to despair that "this problem is bigger that any of us can handle!" Joseph Juran's important contribution was to insist that TQM companies distinguish between the *vital few* and the *trivial many.* In our airport example, if most of the delays are due to baggage handling, and only one delay a year is attributable to a freak hail storm, it makes good sense to start by looking at ways to improve baggage handling. In TQM parlance, companies must **slay the dragons first** in working to improve the quality of their goods or services.

Concentrate first on common causes

Pareto charts

A *Pareto chart* is a bar graph showing groups of error causes arranged by their frequencies of occurrence. It's constructed by simply counting data from observations of things gone wrong. The results are usually ordered in a sequence from most common to least common, with a residual "other" category at the end. These charts are named after Vilfredo Pareto (1848–1923), an Italian economist who studied the distribution of wealth. Just as Pareto found that most of the wealth in a society is held by relatively few people, Juran noted that in most complex systems, *80 percent of defects and errors can be attributed to 20 percent of the causes.* Looking at the Pareto chart for late departures in Figure 10-9, you can see that about $^2/_3$ of the delays (45 of 68 observations) were caused by baggage-handling and equipment problems. The airport manager should begin system-improvement efforts by concentrating on these two areas.

Continuous Quality Improvement

Once the causes of errors and defects have been identified, resources can be devoted to making changes to improve the quality of the systems' goods or services. This can sometimes involve the institution of SPC methods in the process, but more often it requires reconfiguration of the system or the reallocation of resources within the system. Improved baggage handling could require a fix as simple as hiring more baggage handlers or as complex as installing scanners that

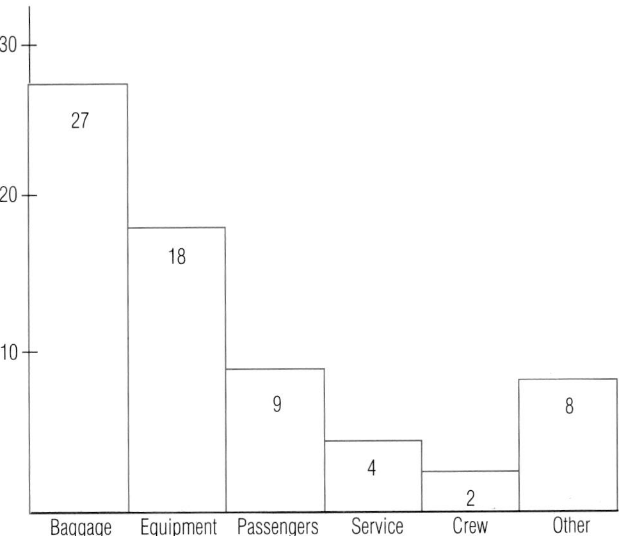

FIGURE 10-9

A Pareto diagram of reasons for airport takeoff delays

read bar-coded destination labels on pieces of luggage to facilitate their automatic routing between connecting flights or to passenger pickup areas when reaching a final destination.

When TQM efforts are successful, it is not uncommon for the leading cause of errors to drop to zero on the Pareto chart. This means that another cause becomes the "dragon," and management attention now will shift to another part of the system. This constant attention to the identification and resolution of problems is known as *Continuous Quality Improvement* (CQI).

HINTS & ASSUMPTIONS

In the typical complex process we study, we find *many* possible causes of failure. Warning: Unless you use an organized, systematic method to look at all of these causes, you run a high risk of missing something that's important. Fishbone diagrams and Pareto charts are very effective ways of focusing and guiding your analysis of quality problems so that everything that affects quality is examined, nothing is overlooked, and the most important things get looked at *first*. A hint learned from many years of quality control experience is that Total Quality Control programs work only when you have strong top management leadership that involves line employees in the responsibility for controlling their own processes.

Exercises 10.6

Self-Check Exercise

SC 10-7 Northway Computers has just begun a TQM program to manage the quality of the personal computers it assembles. A careful analysis of 25,000 computer systems located the following faults:

Component	Number of Faults
CPU	25
Floppy disk drives	106
Hard disk drive	237
I/O ports	36
Keyboard	60
Monitor	42
Power supply	186
RAM memory	30
ROM BIOS	7
Video adapter	47
Other	163

Construct a Pareto chart for Northway. Northway's President, Ted White, is going to set up a series of meetings with his component suppliers. With whom should the first meetings be?

Basic Concepts

■ **10-29** Explain why successful application of TQM requires the participation of employees at all levels of an organization.

■ **10-30** After hearing a lecture on TQM, Joe Smithies said, "Once you've identified and slain the dragon, then you can forget TQM and get on with business as usual." Comment on Joe's understanding of TQM.

Applications

■ **10-31** *The News and Reporter* has a long-standing TQM policy, and it is time to analyze this quarter's complaints and problems. The following problems have been traced by the quality control engineer:

Problem	Department	Number of Occurrences
Omitted advertisement	Classified	18
Incorrect special instructions	Classified	37
Typographical error in a news story	Reporting	14
Advertisement in the wrong section	Classified	16
Incorrectly priced advertisement	Classified	8
Factual error in news story	Reporting	16
Late delivery of all papers	Printing	3
Advertisement placed on incorrect date	Classified	6
Typographical error in commercial advertisement	Advertising	8
Failure to respond to news report	Reporting	16
Editorialized factual story	Reporting	2
Misquoted news story	Reporting	4
Incorrect size of advertisement	Classified	7
Incorrect phone number in advertisement	Classified	9
Incorrect address in advertisement	Classified	3

Construct two Pareto charts for *The News and Reporter.* The first chart should identify which department is in need of most attention and the second chart should identify which area that department should focus on. What's the first order of business for the TQM team?

■ **10-32** Zippy Cola is bottled in several plants around the country. Brand manager Tim Harnett has been keeping track of customer complaints about variability in the drink's flavor. Use the data below to help Tim construct a Pareto chart and decide which plants should first be visited by Zippy Cola's production specialists.

City	Number of Complaints
Atlanta	267
Boston	23
Chicago	37
Houston	175
Milwaukee	19
New Orleans	78
San Francisco	28
Seattle	43

■ **10-33** Construct a fishbone diagram to organize the reasons why you are late to your first class of the day.

Worked-Out Answers to Self-Check Exercise

SC 10-7

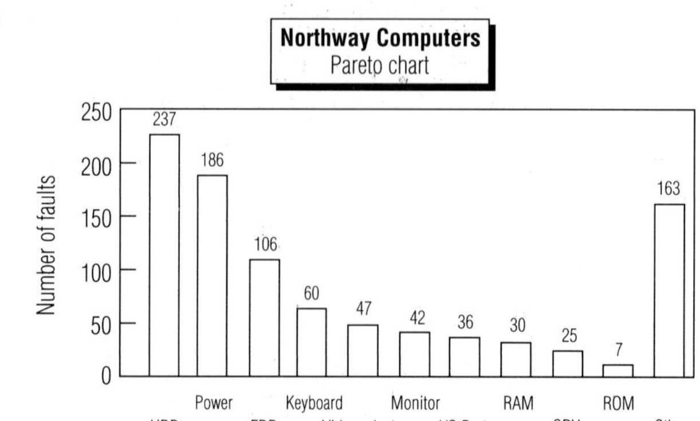

The first meetings should be with the suppliers of the hard disk drives and the power supplies.

10.7 Acceptance Sampling

Testing inputs for conformance to requirements

Adoption of TQM techniques implies a goal that the inputs to each stage of an operation should be defect-free because the operations at the preceding stage are under control. But manufacturers often have to accept raw materials and components from suppliers. To be sure that the results of their own operations are of high quality, they must often test inputs to make sure that they conform to requirements. In most production situations, complete inspection of an entire batch of input is impractical because of time and cost considerations. Instead, a sample of the batch is inspected, and the decision to accept or reject the entire batch is based on the quality of the sample.

You may feel that reliance on sampling to ensure the quality of inputs is just moving the old-time white-coated inspectors from the end of the production line to the beginning. Many experts in quality engineering would agree with you. The whole process of inspection implies that some materials will be rejected and that amounts to a waste of materials and time. However, acceptance sampling can be an effective way to motivate suppliers to improve the quality of their outputs. In fact, it can even be more effective than inspection of the entire batch. Let's look more carefully at this apparently paradoxical assertion.

Acceptance sampling can motivate suppliers to improve quality

Suppose you inspect an entire batch of components sent to you by a supplier. You sort the individual units into two groups, acceptable and unacceptable. Then you send the latter units back to the supplier for replacements. If only 5 percent of the units are rejected, you have imposed a large cost on yourself and a small cost on the supplier. And to boot, you have saved the supplier the cost of being responsible for the quality of its output! On the other hand, suppose you test a small sample from the batch, find 5 percent unsatisfactory units in the sample, and on the basis of the sample send *the entire batch* back for replacement. This imposes a small cost on you and a large cost on the supplier. The supplier may resent the fact that you are sending the acceptable units back along with the unacceptable ones. However, if the supplier values your business, it is ultimately going to take responsibility for ensuring the quality of its output. And if the supplier does not value your business, then you are well served by learning this and seeking another supplier.

The statistical techniques used in *acceptance sampling* will be familiar to you as applications of the sampling and hypothesis-testing ideas we discussed in Chapters 6, 8 and 9.

Much of the original work in acceptance sampling was done in the 1920s and 1930s by Harold F. Dodge and Harry G. Romig, who, like Walter Shewhart, did their research at Bell Labs. They discussed *single-sampling* and *double-sampling* schemes:

Single sampling

In single sampling, two numbers are specified: a sample size, n, and an *acceptance number*, c, the maximum number of allowable pieces with defects. A sample of size n is taken, and the lot is accepted if there are c or fewer defective pieces in the sample, but rejected if the number of defective pieces is greater than c.

Double sampling

Double sampling is more complicated, and depends on four specified numbers, n_1, n_2, c_1, and c_2 ($> c_1$), which are used as follows:
First a sample of size n_1 is taken. Let b_1 (b for *bad*) be the number of defective pieces in this sample:

- If $b_1 \le c_1$, the lot is accepted.
- If $b_1 > c_2$, the lot is rejected.
- If $c_1 < b_1 \le c_2$, an additional n_2 units are sampled.

Let b_2 be the *total number* of defective pieces in the combined sample of $n_1 + n_2$ units:

- If $b_2 \le c_2$, the lot is accepted.
- If $b_2 > c_2$, the lot is rejected.

As you can imagine, the analysis of double-sampling schemes is considerably more complicated than that of single-sampling schemes. Although double-sampling schemes are more powerful and more widely used in practice, we shall restrict our discussion to single sampling. This will enable you to learn the concepts without getting bogged down in the details.

An Example of Acceptance Sampling

Acceptable quality level

Consider a problem faced by Maureen Brennan, the quality control engineer at Northway Computers, a manufacturer of personal computers. Northway is negotiating a contract for batches of 1,000 $3\frac{1}{2}$-inch disk drives with Drives Unlimited. Drives Unlimited has a reputation as a supplier of high-quality drives, but its output is not perfect. It claims that it can produce drives with rates of defects below 1 percent, a level that is acceptable to Maureen Brennan. This 1 percent level is called the *acceptable quality level* (AQL). Loosely speaking, it defines how high a defect level still constitutes a "good" lot.

Now, what happens when Maureen chooses values of n and c for her sampling scheme? For instance, suppose she picks $n = 100$ and $c = 1$. If p is Drives Unlimited's true rate of defects, the probability that any batch will be rejected can be computed using the binomial distribution. This is because Maureen's random sample of 100 taken from a batch of 1,000 drives is also a random sample taken from Drives Unlimited's total output stream. Now, with $n = 100$ and $p = 0.01$,

$$\text{P}(r = 0 \text{ defects}) = \frac{n!}{r!(n-r)!} p^r q^{n-r} \qquad [5\text{-}1]$$

$$= \frac{100!}{0!100!}(0.01)^0(0.99)^{100}$$

$$\text{P}(r = 1 \text{ defect}) = \frac{100!}{1!99!}(0.01)^1(0.99)^{99}$$

Producer's risk: a Type I error

Hence, the probability a batch will be rejected is $1 - 0.3660 - 0.3697 = 0.2643$. This probability is called the *producer's risk.* It is the chance of rejecting a batch even when Drives Unlimited's true rate of defects is only 1 percent. This corresponds to a Type I error in hypothesis testing.

Consumer's risk: a Type II error

Lot tolerance percent defective

The corresponding Type II error leads to *consumer's risk* (a buyer's risk). Suppose that the minimum defect rate Northway would like to reject in a batch of diskette drives is 2 percent. This 2 percent level is called the *lot tolerance percent defective* (LTPD). Loosely speaking, it defines how low a defect level still constitutes a "bad" lot. Suppose that a batch of 1,000 drives with 20 defective units is received by Northway. What is the probability that this batch will be accepted because Maureen's sample of 100 contains no more than one defective unit? This probability is the consumer's risk.

Approximating consumer's risk

Because she is sampling without replacement, the binomial distribution is not the correct distribution for computing this probability. The correct distribution is a relative of the binomial, known as the *hypergeometric distribution.* It is common to use the binomial distribution to approximate consumer's risk. This approximation always *overestimates* the true value of the consumer's risk whenever that risk is less than 0.5. With Maureen's sampling scheme, the approximate binomial probability of accepting a batch of 1,000 units with 20 defective units is computed using Equation 5-1, with $n = 100$ and $p = 0.02$:

$$P(r = 0 \text{ defects}) = \frac{n!}{r!(n-r)!}p^r q^{n-r} \quad [5\text{-}1]$$

$$= \frac{100!}{0!100!}(0.02)^0(0.98)^{100} = 0.1326$$

$$P(r = 1 \text{ defect}) = \frac{100!}{1!99!}(0.02)^1(0.98)^{99} = 0.2707$$

Hence, the approximate probability the batch will be accepted is $0.1326 + 0.2707 = 0.4033$. The exact hypergeometric probability of accepting a batch with 20 defective units is 0.3892, so the approximation is fairly good (the error is only 141/3,892, or about 3.6 percent). In general, the smaller the fraction of the batch that is sampled, the better the job the binomial distribution does to approximate the hypergeometric. This is analogous to the situation we encountered in Chapter 6 (p. 325), where we saw that the finite population multiplier had little effect on the calculation of the standard error of the mean if the sampling fraction was less than 0.05.

Tradeoffs between the two risks

Maureen is unwilling to accept such a high level of risk. She can reduce her risk by lowering c to 0 and rejecting lots in which any defective units show up in her sample of 100. This will reduce her risk to exactly 0.1326 (0.1190 approximate), but it will increase the producer's risk to 0.6340, which Drives Unlimited is unwilling to accept. Is there any way to reduce both the producer's and the consumer's risks? Yes, by increasing the sample size. Suppose she increases her sample size to $n = 250$, and allows 1.2 percent defects in the sample by setting $c = 3$. Then Northway's consumer's risk is now reduced to 0.2225 exact, 0.2622 approximate, and Drives Unlimited's producer's risk is reduced to 0.2419. Of course, this will increase the cost of the inspections that Maureen will have to make. Similar results can be achieved with double sampling without such a drastic increase in total sample size.

Increasing n to decrease both risks

	A	B	C	D	E	F	G	H
1	ACCEPTSA	ACCEPTANCE SAMPLING BY ATTRIBUTES					Alt A View AOQ curve	
2							Alt O View OC curve	
3	INPUT:			OUTPUT:				
4	Lot Size		1000		Producer's risk (Prob. lot with			0.2642
5	Sample size		100		defects = AQL will be rejected)			
6	Acceptance number		1					
7	AQL		1.00%		Consumer's risk (Prob. lot with			0.5578
8	LTPD		1.50%		defects = LTPD will be accepted)			
9	=======	=======	=======	=======	=======	=======	=======	=======
10	# defects		Incoming quality (lot % defective)					
11	in sample	X!	0.0%	1.0%	1.5%	3.0%	4.0%	5.0%
12	0	1	1.0000	0.3679	0.2231	0.0498	0.0183	0.0067
13	1	1	0.0000	0.3679	0.3347	0.1494	0.0733	0.0337
14	2	2	0.0000	0.0000	0.0000	0.0000	0.0000	0.0000
15	3	6	0.0000	0.0000	0.0000	0.0000	0.0000	0.0000
16	4	24	0.0000	0.0000	0.0000	0.0000	0.0000	0.0000
17	5	120	0.0000	0.0000	0.0000	0.0000	0.0000	0.0000
18			------	------	------	------	------	------
19	Prob. accept. lot		1.0000	0.7358	0.5578	0.1991	0.0916	0.0404
20	AOQ		0.00%	0.66%	0.75%	0.54%	0.33%	0.18%

FIGURE 10-10

A spreadsheet to evaluate acceptance-sampling schemes

Acceptance Sampling in Practice: Tables and Computer Programs

The Dodge–Romig tables

As you can see from our example, the relationships between sample size (n), acceptance number (c), and the two types of risk are very complex. Extensive tables exist for helping quality engineers to choose appropriate acceptance sample schemes.*

A spreadsheet template

As an alternative to looking up sampling schemes in tables, there are many computer programs available for evaluating choices of n and c. A particularly easy one to use is a Lotus 1–2–3 spreadsheet template, developed by Everette S. Gardner, Jr.,** and used with his permission. Figure 10-10 shows the application of that spreadsheet to evaluate Maureen Brennan's original ($n = 100$, $c = 1$) sampling scheme.

In cells C4 to C8 (shaded in color), Maureen entered the lot size (1,000), sample size ($n = 100$), acceptance number ($c = 1$), AQL (0.01), and LTPD (0.015). In cells H4 and H7 (shaded in color), the template calculates the producer's risk (0.2642) and the binomial approximation to the consumer's risk (0.5578). (These figures are slightly different from those we calculated earlier because Gardner uses the Poisson approximation to the binomial—see p. 254—in his spreadsheet calculations.)

The OC curve: consumer's risk as a function of input quality

The bottom part of the template calculates various probabilities that give Maureen more information about the behavior of her sampling scheme. Cells C11 to H11 originally contained incoming qualities ranging from 0 to 5 percent, by single percentage points. Because our LTPD was 1.5 percent, we replaced the original 2 percent in cell E11 (shaded in color) by 1.5 percent. The additional information can be seen most easily in two graphs that the template can produce. Maureen can get an *operating characteristic* (OC) graph (Figure 10-11). The height of the OC curve tells her the consumer's risk, the probability that her sampling scheme will *accept* a lot from a production process with an input quality read on the horizontal axis. Subtracting that probability from one gives the producer's risk as the input quality varies. As you would expect, the probability that a lot will be accepted falls as production quality becomes worse.

*For example, see *Sampling Inspection Tables—Single and Double Sampling,* by H. F. Dodge and H. G. Romig, John Wiley, New York, 1959.

***The Spreadsheet Operations Manager,* McGraw-Hill, New York, 1992.

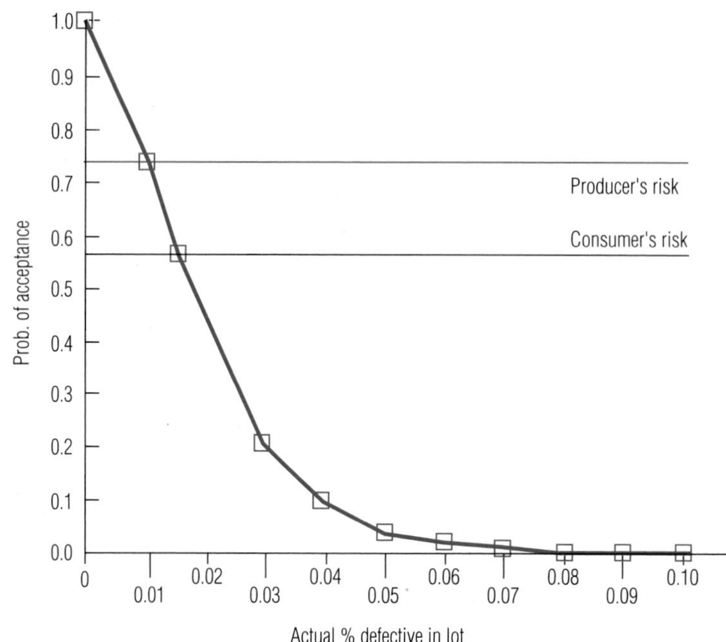

FIGURE 10-11

The operating characteristic (OC) curve for Maureen's acceptance-sampling scheme

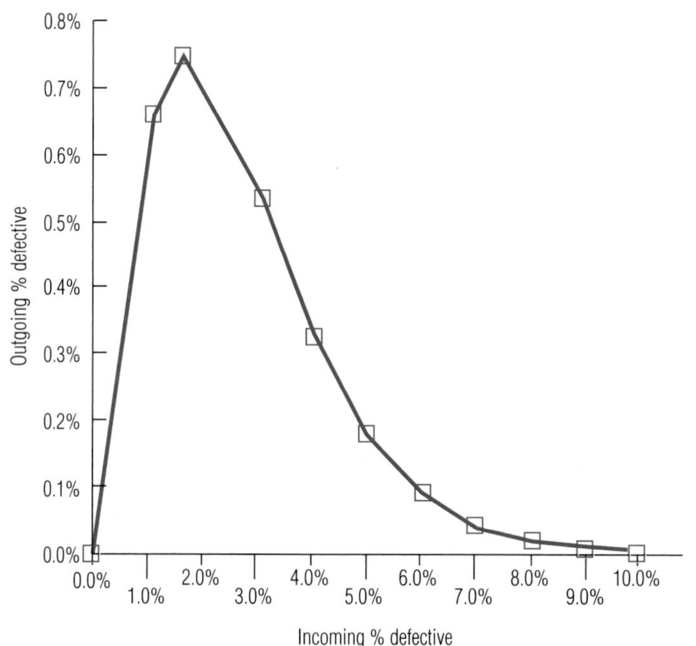

FIGURE 10-12

The average outgoing quality (AOQ) curve for Maureen's acceptance-sampling scheme

The AOQ curve: average outgoing quality as a function of input quality

Maureen can also get an *average outgoing quality* (AOQ) graph (Figure 10-12). The height of the AOQ curve tells her how the long-run average fraction of defective units in lots accepted by her sampling scheme varies as a function of the quality of the drives supplied to Northway by Drives Unlimited. You can see from that graph that the worst long-run average quality would be 0.75 percent, or about 7.5 defective drives per accepted batch of 1,000. Of course, because AOQ is an average, some accepted batches will have more defective drives.

HINTS & ASSUMPTIONS

Warning: Making up or changing your sampling plan as you go generally leads to failure. Carefully planning your sampling plan using sound statistical analysis and then adhering to the plan makes it much less likely that you will be misled by random patterns. Hint: If a municipality tests 200 street lightbulbs from a shipment of 10,000, finds that the first 100 work perfectly, and quits sampling, it can get into serious trouble. Most acceptance situations like this are looking for very low-probability defects, say 1 in 100. Because you know that random events are not uniformly distributed, you should not be swayed by the absence of defects in the first 100 and you should stick with the sampling plan you first designed if you want to benefit from the power of statistical quality control.

Exercises 10.7

Self-Check Exercises

SC 10-8 Compute the producer's risks for the following single-sampling schemes from batches of 2,000 items, with AQL = 0.005.

(a) $n = 150, c = 1$.
(b) $n = 150, c = 2$.
(c) $n = 200, c = 1$.
(d) $n = 200, c = 2$.

SC 10-9 Use the binomial distribution to approximate the consumer's risks in the sampling schemes in Exercise SC 10-8 if LTPD = 0.01.

Basic Concepts

■ **10-34** Why is it impractical to inspect an entire batch of input from a supplier?

■ **10-35** What is the significance of the acceptance number, c, in single sampling?

Applications

■ **10-36** Compute the producer's risks for the following single sampling schemes from batches of 1,500 items, with AQL = 0.02.

(a) $n = 175, c = 3$.
(b) $n = 175, c = 5$.
(c) $n = 250, c = 3$.
(d) $n = 250, c = 5$.

■ **10-37** Use the binomial distribution to approximate the consumer's risks in the sampling schemes in Exercise 10-36 if LTPD = 0.03.

■ **10-38** The graph on page 550 is an OC curve for a single-sampling scheme from batches of 2,500 with $n = 250$ and $c = 2$. Find the producer's risk if the AQL is

(a) 0.005.
(b) 0.010.
(c) 0.015.

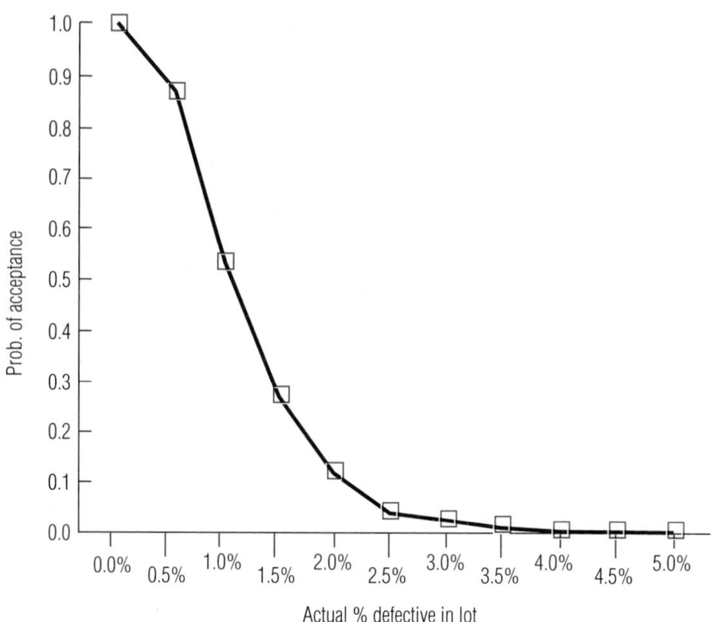

■ **10-39** For the single-sampling scheme in Exercise 10-38, use the OC curve to find the consumer's risk if the LTPD is

(a) 0.010.

(b) 0.015.

(c) 0.020.

Worked-Out Answers to Self-Check Exercises

SC 10-8 AQL = 0.005

(a) $n = 150 \qquad c = 1$

$r = 0$:

$$\frac{n!}{r!(n-r)!}p^r q^{n-r} = \frac{150!}{0!(150)!}(0.005)^0(0.995)^{150} = 0.4715$$

$r = 1$:

$$\frac{n!}{r!(n-r)!}p^r q^{n-r} = \frac{150!}{1!(149)!}(0.005)^1(0.995)^{149} = 0.3554$$

$1 - 0.4715 - 0.3554 = 0.1731$, the producer's risk.

(b) $n = 150 \qquad c = 2$

$r = 2$:

$$\frac{n!}{r!(n-r)!}p^r q^{n-r} = \frac{150!}{2!(148)!}(0.005)^2(0.995)^{148} = 0.1330$$

$1 - 0.4715 - 0.3554 - 0.1330 = 0.0401$ is the producer's risk.

(c) $n = 200 \qquad c = 1$

$r = 0$:

$$\frac{n!}{r!(n-r)!}p^r q^{n-r} = \frac{200!}{0!(200)!}(0.005)^0(0.995)^{200} = 0.3670$$

$r = 1$:

$$\frac{n!}{r!(n-r)!}p^r q^{n-r} = \frac{200!}{1!(199)!}(0.005)^1(0.995)^{199} = 0.3688$$

$1 - 0.3670 - 0.3688 = 0.2642$, the producer's risk.

(d) $n = 200 \qquad c = 2$

$r = 2$:

$$\frac{n!}{r!(n-r)!}p^r q^{n-r} = \frac{200!}{2!(198)!}(0.005)^2(0.995)^{198} = 0.1844$$

$1 - 0.3670 - 0.3688 - 0.1844 = 0.0798$, the producer's risk.

SC 10-9 LTPD = 0.01

(a) $n = 150 \qquad c = 1$

$r = 0$:

$$\frac{n!}{r!(n-r)!}p^r q^{n-r} = \frac{150!}{0!(150)!}(0.01)^0(0.99)^{150} = 0.2215$$

$r = 1$:

$$\frac{n!}{r!(n-r)!}p^r q^{n-r} = \frac{150!}{1!(149)!}(0.01)^1(0.99)^{149} = 0.3355$$

$0.2215 + 0.3355 = 0.557$, the consumer's risk.

(b) $n = 150 \qquad c = 2$

$r = 2$:

$$\frac{n!}{r!(n-r)!}p^r q^{n-r} = \frac{150!}{2!(148)!}(0.01)^2(0.99)^{148} = 0.2525$$

$0.2215 + 0.3355 + 0.2525 = 0.8095$, the consumer's risk.

(c) $n = 200 \qquad c = 1$

$r = 0$:

$$\frac{n!}{r!(n-r)!}p^r q^{n-r} = \frac{200!}{0!(200)!}(0.01)^0(0.99)^{200} = 0.1340$$

$r = 1$:

$$\frac{n!}{r!(n-r)!}p^r q^{n-r} = \frac{200!}{1!(199)!}(0.01)^1(0.99)^{199} = 0.2707$$

$0.1340 + 0.2707 = 0.4047$, the consumer's risk.

(d) $n = 200 \qquad c = 2$

$r = 2$:

$$\frac{n!}{r!(n-r)!}p^r q^{n-r} = \frac{200!}{2!(198)!}(0.01)^2(0.99)^{198} = 0.2720$$

$0.1340 + 0.2707 + 0.2720 = 0.6767$, the consumer's risk.

Statistics at Work

Loveland Computers

Case 10: Quality and Quality Control Walter Azko prided himself on his open-door policy, and any member of the firm was welcome to stop by with ideas. The only difficulty was finding Walter in his office, or indeed, in the country. He still traveled frequently to Pacific Rim countries in search of new suppliers and better prices.

But Walter was in town—and in his office—going over budget projections with Lee when Jeff Cohen from Purchasing and Harry Patel, the firm's financial controller, dropped by. Jeff and Harry were the only two CPAs in the firm so they were often found deep in conversation.

"Boss, we both went to a seminar put on by the State CPA Association," Harry began.

"So we wanted to talk with you about quality initiatives at Loveland Computers," added Jeff. The two were known for finishing each other's sentences.

"I'm not going to pay good money for a bunch of high-priced consultants to come in and preach to us," Walter greeted their enthusiasm with skepticism. "In any case, I've always told you—at this end of the market we compete on price, not on quality. Our customers only care whether a Loveland Computer works and whether we have it in stock when they want to order it. And if it doesn't work, they just have to ship it back to us and we'll send them out a new one."

"Right. And how much is that costing us?" Harry asked.

"You have the figures—the money we write off on computers that we have to scrap is very small compared to our volume. You know that."

"Well, after that seminar, I'm sure that we don't really capture all the costs of a failure," the controller disputed.

"Anyway, we test all the computers overnight at the end of the line before we ship them. What do you want me to do—run them for a week before we ship them out?" Walter remained unconvinced that thinking about quality could change the way Loveland did business.

"Doesn't this relate to customer satisfaction?" Lee interjected. "I read where J. D. Power—the company that reports on what automobile customers think about new models—is going to start rating PCs."

"There's much more to quality than more testing before we ship things. In fact, if we do things right, I'm convinced we'd need *less* testing on the production line," Jeff added. "Let Harry and me buy you lunch and tell you what we learned at the seminar."

Study Questions: What arguments will Jeff and Harry make against Walter's assertion that Loveland competes only on price? What are the total costs of replacing a machine that Harry refers to? How does quality relate to customer satisfaction? Why would Loveland need less end-of-the-line testing if it adopted quality control measures? Does it matter whether Walter Azko ends up with a better understanding of quality by the end of lunch?

Computer Database Exercise

HH Industries

At the next staff meeting, the discussion of Laurel and Gary's O-ring study brought up the general issue of quality control. At Hal's insistence Laurel continued on, talking about processes and statistical control. "What you need to discover," she explained, "is how much variability in a process is due to random variation and how much is due to unique events or individual actions. This will help you determine whether a process is in-control."

She went on. "Let me see if I can give you an intuitive example." She looked around the room. "Peggy," she said, indicating the Accounting and Data Processing manager, "you drive to work from a short distance away. What would you guess is your average one-way commuting time?"

Peggy thought for a moment. "Probably about 25 minutes," she said.

"Okay," Laurel went on, "let's generate some data!" She winked at the group. "Good statisticians always know how to generate data!" Approaching the whiteboard, she drew a table. "Let's say these were the morning commuting times for the last 10 weeks. We want to see if this commuting process is in-control."

Week									
1	2	3	4	5	6	7	8	9	10
18	30	36	23	18	25	40	22	23	33
25	32	25	37	22	28	37	23	28	27
22	20	25	22	32	22	22	30	25	22
27	20	22	20	23	22	28	30	22	21
28	18	22	23	20	23	23	20	26	27

(These data are in the CH10A.xxx files on the data disk.)

Peggy laughed. "Based on the drivers I see, I'd seriously doubt it!"

Laurel chuckled. "I know what you mean." She went on to calculate the average and range of each of the 10 subgroups, the average range, and the process average. She explained how to calculate the upper and lower control limits and sketched the resulting $\bar{x}$ and R control-chart axes.

"Now, when we plot the weekly averages, we can see if the points fall between the limits. Two things will concern us: points falling outside the limits, and unlikely patterns occurring in the data. Both of these could indicate a process out-of-control."

She finished the $\bar{x}$ chart and indicated the first several points. "The fluctuation of the points within the limits results from variation built into the process. In Peggy's case, this would be her choice of route, the other traffic, and so on. These factors could be changed only by changing the system itself. Points outside of the limits, however, each come from a special cause or unique event, something not part of the way the system normally operates."

"Like stopping for gas?" Peggy asked.

"Or having a flat tire?" interjected Stan.

"Or a bad accident along the route?" offered Gary.

"Exactly," said Laurel. "Eliminating these special causes, or simply being able to identify a special cause for each point outside the limits, we can use the control chart as a monitoring tool for this process. Then all we need to do is take samples at regular intervals to make sure that the process doesn't fundamentally change.

"An important point to remember, however, is that 'in-control' doesn't necessarily mean that the process will inherently meet your needs. Imagine continuing this example analysis for the next several years. As the northern part of the country sees population growth, Peggy's commuting time may gradually get longer. Regular patterns like we mentioned earlier will probably appear, and more and more points will start to appear above the upper control limit. This will most likely indicate that the process has fundamentally changed and we need to redo our control chart."

1. Complete the analysis on Laurel's sample data by drawing the $\bar{x}$ and R charts. What can you determine about the process being described?

As they left the meeting over half an hour later, Laurel stopped Hal. "I didn't mean to take over like that," she smiled, "but this quality control stuff can really be valuable for a company like ours—in many areas!"

Hal nodded. "I don't mind at all. It should start people thinking about how it can apply in their individual areas. Just don't blame me if you start getting a bunch of phone calls and requests for help."

As if on cue, Gary walked up. Hal smiled at Laurel. "Told you so," he mocked playfully as he walked away.

"The O-ring supplier we just investigated isn't our only quality concern, as you might guess," Gary began. "We've had reason to question the pumps from Pacific Pumps, the leading supplier of our largest pump. I've kept data for the last several years about pumps we've had to send back. The only problem is, a pump either works or it doesn't—there isn't anything specific we can measure as there was in your example in the staff meeting. Is there anything you can suggest for this situation?"

"Sure," nodded Laurel. "When you have qualitative characteristics rather than quantitative measurements, you can use a *p* chart. It uses the proportion of defective items to create the control chart. Let's see what kind of data you have."

Pumps from Pacific Pumps were ordered in lots of varying size every other month or so. Each pump was individually tested and inspected because these items were large and relatively expensive. The time spent testing the units was well worth it, considering the possible loss of goodwill and extra shipping costs that would be incurred if a customer received a faulty pump. "We expect to reject a pump or two every now and then," Gary had told Laurel. "They're fairly complex pieces of equipment." It was only when rejections had seemed to be more common that a concern had arisen. Laurel had the data from the last 3 years of orders from Pacific Pumps.

	Jan	Mar	May	Jul	Sep	Nov
Number ordered	25	30	10	30	25	10
Number rejected	2	1	0	3	1	0
Number ordered	20	20	25	20	10	35
Number rejected	2	3	0	2	1	4
Number ordered	15	10	30	20	5	15
Number rejected	2	2	4	3	1	2

(These data are in the CH10B.xxx files on the data disk.)

2. Construct a *p* chart for the pump data. What can you conclude about the process being described?

Note: When the individual sample sizes are different, Equation 10-7 must be modified as follows:

$$\bar{\bar{p}} = \frac{\Sigma n_j \bar{p}_j}{\Sigma n_j} \qquad [10\text{-}7a]$$

where

- $\bar{p}_j$ = sample fraction in the *j*th individual sample and
- n_j = size of the *j*th individual sample

In addition, separate control limits are calculated for each individual sample, modifying Equation 10-6 as follows:

$$UCL_j = \mu_{\bar{p}j} + 3\sigma_{\bar{p}_j} = p + 3\sqrt{\frac{pq}{n_j}} \qquad [10\text{-}6a]$$

$$LCL_j = \mu_{\bar{p}j} - 3\sigma_{\bar{p}_j} = p - 3\sqrt{\frac{pq}{n_j}}$$

where UCL_j and LCL_j are the control limits for the *j*th sample.

From the Textbook to the Real World

Statistical Process Control

Improving Billing at a Large Trucking Company Freight companies take responsibility for correctly delivering thousands of dollars' worth of goods in each truck load, so correct paperwork is important. If a trucking company sends an incorrect bill, fixing the problem is time consuming and expensive.

Incorrect documentation can leave a company open to claims for "missing" goods that were never shipped. Even when the correct goods arrive, an incorrect bill of lading (a legal document that lists exactly what the shipper is sending) can disrupt reordering. More importantly, trucking companies get paid by calculating freight charges from bills of lading and then issuing invoices. If the bills of lading aren't correct, then the trucking company may have difficulty in getting paid for the work that's been done.

Getting the Quality Message P*I*E Nationwide became the nation's fourth largest trucking company in 1983 when Ryder Truck Lines and Pacific Intermountain Express merged. Soon after the merger, top executives learned from key customers about the importance of correct paperwork and the costs of correcting errors. With top management leadership, Total Quality Management was adopted and the company's first quality project focused on improving the calculation of freight invoices.

Following the principles of quality expert W. Edwards Deming, P*I*E Nationwide eliminated the auditors and inspectors who used to cross check the documentation. By making the people who calculated invoices responsible for checking their own work, P*I*E reduced the error rate from 10 percent to 0.8 percent in less than one year.

Applying TQM At this point, the billing process was "in-control," with errors occurring at a predictable low rate. But, following the philosophy of *continuous quality improvement*, P*I*E Nationwide sought to further improve the quality of its paperwork. Project staff looked at samples of 20 bills of lading a day for 20 days and found that for 63 percent of loads, shippers made a mistake in completing the bill of lading. When P*I*E Nationwide's employees caught the errors during loading, they corrected them (at an average cost of $1.83 in staff time). But many errors were undetected at that stage.

In a group problem-solving session, a *fishbone diagram* was constructed to suggest possible cause-and-effect relationships for the incorrect bills of lading. Then, using a *Pareto chart* to analyze the most common causes of errors, P*I*E Nationwide was able to institute training programs for drivers and shippers to eliminate the causes of errors.

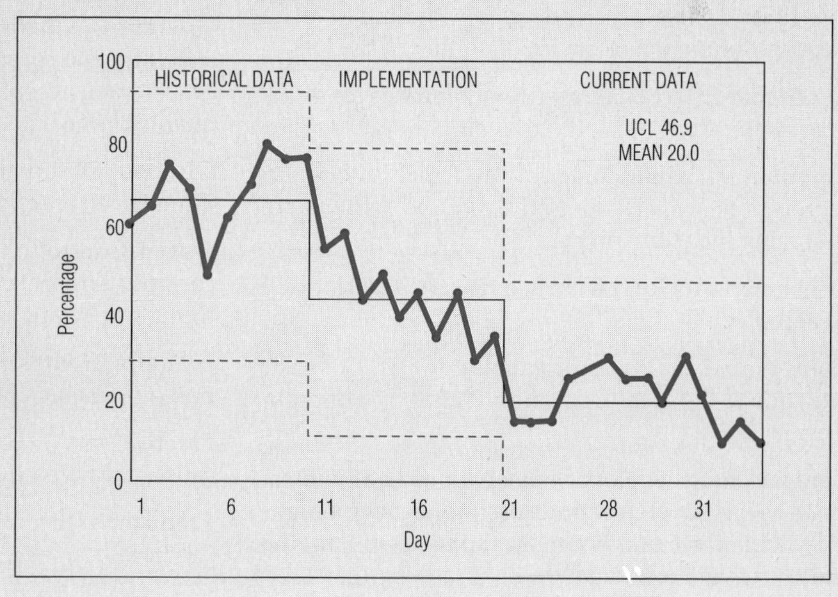

RW10-1

p chart of bill of lading billing defects

The Payoff Training paid off and the proportion of bills of lading with errors dropped from 63 percent to 8 percent (see Figure RW10-1). Although P*I*E Nationwide didn't calculate the system-wide savings from less rework, a study showed an immediate savings of $38,000 at a single terminal.

Many examples of using statistical quality control come from manufacturing, where it's easy to imagine adjusting a machine. But this example shows that in service operations, well-designed training can have the same effect. Collecting data, charting it, and using group problem solving were the techniques that enabled the company to find the causes of errors and then go about correcting them.

Source: Cort Dondero, "SPC Hits the Road," *Quality Progress* 24(1) (January 1991):43–44.

Chapter Review

● Terms Introduced in Chapter 10

Acceptable Quality Level (AQL) The average quality level promised by a producer; the maximum number or percentage of defective pieces in a "good" lot.

Acceptance Number The maximum number of defective pieces with which a lot will still be accepted.

Acceptance Sampling Procedures for deciding whether to accept or reject a batch of input materials based on the quality of a sample taken from that batch.

Assignable Variation Nonrandom, systematic variability in a process. It usually can be corrected without redesigning the entire process.

Attributes Qualitative variables with only two categories.

Average Outgoing Quality (AOQ) Curve A graph showing how the long-run average fraction of defective units in lots accepted by a sampling scheme varies as a function of the input quality of the lots.

Cause-and-Effect Diagram Another name for a *fishbone diagram.*

Common Variation Random variability inherent in a process. It usually cannot be reduced without redesigning the entire process.

Consumer's Risk The chance that a "bad" lot will be accepted.

Continuous Quality Improvement (CQI) Constant attention to the identification and resolution of problems in TQM.

Control Charts A plot of some parameter of interest (such as $\bar{x}$, R, or p) over time, used to identify assignable variations and to make adjustments to the process being monitored.

Control Limits Upper and lower bounds on control charts. For the process to be in-control, all observations must fall within these limits.

Fishbone Diagram A pictorial device for organizing cause-and-effect relationships among the factors causing problems in complex systems.

Hypergeometric Distribution The correct distribution for computing consumer's risk; it is often approximated by the binomial distribution.

Inherent Variation Another name for *common variation.*

Ishikawa Diagram Another name for a *fishbone diagram.*

Lot Tolerance Percent Defective (LTPD) The minimum number or percentage of defective pieces in a "bad" lot.

Operating Characteristic (OC) Curve A graph showing the probability an acceptance-sampling scheme will accept a batch as a function of the input quality of the batch.

Outliers Observations falling outside the control limits on a control chart.

Out-of-Control A process exhibiting outliers on a control chart, or showing nonrandom patterns even though there are no outliers.

***p* Charts** Control charts for monitoring the proportion of items in a batch that meet specifications.

Pareto Chart A bar graph showing groups of error causes arranged by their frequencies of occurrence.

Producer's Risk The chance that a "good" lot will be rejected.

Qualitative Variables Variables whose values are categorical rather than numerical.

Quality Fitness for use or conformance to requirements.

Quantitative Variables Variables with numerical values resulting from measuring or counting.

***R* Charts** Control charts for monitoring process variability.

Special Cause Variation Another name for *assignable variation.*

Statistical Process Control (SPC) Shewhart's system of using control charts to track variation and identify its causes.

Total Quality Management (TQM) A set of approaches that enables the managers of complex systems to match the firm's products to customers' expectations.

$\bar{x}$ Chart Control charts for monitoring process means.

● Equations Introduced in Chapter 10

■ **10-1**

$$\bar{\bar{x}} = \frac{\Sigma x}{n \times k} = \frac{\Sigma \bar{x}}{k}$$ p. 519

To compute the grand mean ($\bar{\bar{x}}$) from several (k) samples of the same size (n), either sum all the original observations (Σx) and divide by the total number of observations ($n \times k$), or else sum the means from each of the samples ($\Sigma \bar{x}$) and divide by the number of samples (k). Then use $\bar{\bar{x}}$ for the center line (CL) of an $\bar{x}$ chart.

■ **10-2**

$$\text{UCL} = \bar{\bar{x}} + \frac{3\bar{R}}{d_2\sqrt{n}}$$ p. 521

$$\text{LCL} = \bar{\bar{x}} - \frac{3\bar{R}}{d_2\sqrt{n}}$$

To compute the control limits for an $\bar{x}$ chart, multiply the average sample range ($\bar{R} = \Sigma R/k$) by 3, and then divide by the product of d_2 (from Appendix Table 9) and $\sqrt{n}$; the result is then added to and subtracted from $\bar{\bar{x}}$. Alternatively, you can compute these limits as $\bar{\bar{x}} \pm A_2\bar{R}$, where A_2 ($= 3/d_2\sqrt{n}$) can also be found in Appendix Table 9.

■ **10-3**

$$\sigma_R = d_3\sigma$$ p. 527

To get the standard deviation of the sampling distribution of R, multiply the population standard deviation, σ, by d_3, another factor that is also given in Appendix Table 9.

■ **10-4**

$$\text{UCL} = \bar{R} + \frac{3d_3\bar{R}}{d_2} = \bar{R}\left(1 + \frac{3d_3}{d_2}\right)$$ p. 527

$$\text{LCL} = \bar{R} - \frac{3d_3\bar{R}}{d_2} = \bar{R}\left(1 - \frac{3d_3}{d_2}\right)$$

To compute the control limits for an R chart, multiply the average sample range ($\bar{R} = \Sigma R/k$) by $1 \pm 3d_3/d_2$. Alternatively, you can compute these limits as

$$\text{UCL} = \overline{R}D_4, \text{ where } D_4 = 1 + 3d_3/d_2$$

$$\text{LCL} = \overline{R}D_3, \text{ where } D_3 = 1 - 3d_3/d_2$$

Values of D_3 and D_4 are also given in Appendix Table 9. Because ranges are always nonnegative, D_3 and the LCL are taken to be 0 when $n \leq 6$.

■ 10-5 $$\text{CL} = \mu_{\overline{p}} = p$$ p. 534

■ 10-6 $$\text{UCL} = \mu_{\overline{p}} + 3\sigma_{\overline{p}} = p + 3\sqrt{\frac{pq}{n}}$$ p. 534

$$\text{LCL} = \mu_{\overline{p}} - 3\,\sigma_{\overline{p}} = p - 3\sqrt{\frac{pq}{n}}$$

If there is a known or targeted value of p, that value should be used in Equations 10-5 and 10-6 to get the center line and control limits for a p chart. However, if no such value of p is available, then you should use the overall sample fraction

■ 10-7 $$\overline{\overline{p}} = \frac{\Sigma \overline{p}_j}{k}$$ p. 534

where

- $\overline{p}_j$ = sample fraction in the jth sample
- k = total number of samples

Review and Application Exercises

■ **10-40** R&H Bloch is a large accounting firm specializing in the preparation of individual federal tax returns. The firm is very conservative in its practices and tries to avoid having more than 2 percent of its clients audited. As part of a summer internship, Jane Bloch has been asked to see whether this goal is being met on a consistent basis. For each week during a 16-week interval centered on April 15 of last year, she has randomly selected 125 returns prepared by the firm. (Those filed after April 15 had paid their estimated taxes due and requested an extension.) Her data follow:

Week Ending	2/25	3/04	3/11	3/18	3/25	4/01	4/08	4/15
# Audited	2	1	2	3	5	4	5	6
Week Ending	4/22	4/29	5/06	5/13	5/20	5/27	6/03	6/10
# Audited	3	1	1	3	2	2	3	2

(a) Are significantly more than 2 percent of R&H Bloch's clients being audited? State and test appropriate hypotheses using all 2,000 clients in Jane's sample.

(b) Notwithstanding your result in part (a), construct a p chart based on Jane's data. Is there anything evident in the chart that Jane should bring to the attention of the partners in the firm? Explain.

■ **10-41** When slaying dragons, should you be concerned with the "trivial many" or the "vital few"? Explain.

■ **10-42** If marital status is coded as "currently married" or "never married," then marital status is an attribute. However, if it is coded as "single," "married," "widowed," or "divorced," then it isn't an attribute. Explain this apparent inconsistency.

■ **10-43** The amount of time a bank teller needs to process a deposit depends on how many items the customer has. Is this inherent or special cause variation? Explain.

■ **10-44** All checks drafted on accounts at Global Bank are returned to the bank's check-processing center. There each check is encoded with optically scannable characters that indicate the amount for which it is drawn. The encoded checks are then scanned so that payment can be made and the accounts on which they have been drawn can be debited. Shih-Hsing Liu has been monitoring the encoding operation, and has counted the number of checks processed in 10 randomly chosen 2-minute periods during each hour of the last two 8-hour shifts. She has recorded the following data:

Shift 1 Time	0700	0800	0900	1000	1100	1200	1300	1400
$\bar{x}$	49.4	49.9	48.8	50.1	49.7	48.1	48.6	48.7
R	4	7	7	4	7	10	7	10
Shift 2 Time	**1500**	**1600**	**1700**	**1800**	**1900**	**2000**	**2100**	**2200**
$\bar{x}$	50.7	51.3	51.1	51.6	50.0	50.5	51.4	50.1
R	6	4	9	9	6	7	4	7

(a) Help Shih-Hsing construct an $\bar{x}$ chart from the data.

(b) Is the process in-control? Does anything in the chart indicate that Shih-Hsing should examine the process more closely? Explain.

■ **10-45** (a) Use Shih-Hsing Liu's data from Exercise 10-44 to construct an R chart.

(b) Does anything in the chart indicate that Shih-Hsing should examine the process more closely? Explain.

■ **10-46** Security Construction uses many subcontractors for the condominium apartments it builds throughout the American sunbelt. Dawn Locklear, Security's customer service representative, has been reviewing the "punch lists" submitted by the purchasers of 500 condos. A punch list is a list of problems noted when the owner moves into the apartment. Security does not receive final payment until the items on the list have been corrected. Dawn has categorized the items on the lists according to the responsible subcontractor. Use her information to construct a Pareto chart to identify which subcontractors require additional supervision.

Subcontractor	Number of Problems
Electrical	257
Flooring	23
Heating/AC	35
Painting	19
Plumbing	22
Roofing	31
Tile	51
Wallboard	303
Windows	16
Other	68

■ **10-47** Compute the producer's risks for the following single-sampling schemes from batches of 2,500 items, with AQL = 0.01.

(a) $n = 200, c = 1$.
(b) $n = 200, c = 2$.
(c) $n = 250, c = 1$.
(d) $n = 250, c = 2$.

■ **10-48** Use the binomial distribution to approximate the consumer's risks in the sampling schemes in Exercise 10-47 if LTPD = 0.015.

■ **10-49** In service operations (as opposed to manufacturing) can the principle *Variation is the enemy of quality* be applied? Aren't all customers different?

■ **10-50** Deshawn Jackson is the quality supervisor for Reliance Storage Media, a manufacturer of diskettes for personal computers. The company has been concerned about the quality of their Reliant economy-grade $3^1/_2$" diskettes, and has completely revamped the production process. Reliant diskettes consist of a cobalt-enhanced iron-oxide coating deposited on a polyethylene terephthalate substrate. The nominal thickness of the coating is 75.0 microns (0.075 mm), but a deviation of ±3.0 microns is acceptable. The diskettes are manufactured in batches of 2,500. In order to evaluate the new production process, Deshawn has sampled two dozen diskettes from each of the last 20 batches and recorded the following data:

Batch	1	2	3	4	5	6	7	8	9	10
$\bar{x}$	75.3	75.0	74.8	75.0	75.3	74.8	74.8	74.9	74.6	74.9
R	3.2	3.3	3.6	3.5	3.8	3.7	3.4	3.3	3.4	3.1
Batch	**11**	**12**	**13**	**14**	**15**	**16**	**17**	**18**	**19**	**20**
$\bar{x}$	75.2	75.1	74.8	74.9	74.9	75.1	75.0	74.9	74.9	75.1
R	3.1	3.0	3.1	2.9	2.8	2.8	2.7	2.9	2.8	2.9

(a) Use the data to construct an $\bar{x}$ chart.
(b) Is the process in-control?
(c) Deshawn looks at the $\bar{x}$ chart and says, "The last 10 batches have means that appear to be less variable than the means of the first 10 batches." Is this observation valid? Explain. Should Deshawn be concerned? Explain.

■ **10-51** Consider the data Deshawn Jackson collected for Exercise 10-50:

(a) Construct an R chart.
(b) Should Deshawn worry about the obvious pattern in the chart? Explain.
(c) Is there any relationship between the pattern in the R chart and the one Deshawn noticed in the $\bar{x}$ chart? (See Exercise 10-50(c).) Is this good news or bad news for Deshawn? Explain.

■ **10-52** Photomatic prints customers' 35 mm film using automated equipment. This high-volume, low-cost approach works for most typical situations, but variation in the input can lead to poor results. For example, if a customer's film has been left in a hot car, it may be printable with special handling, but the results from the automated process are unacceptable. When prints are rejected by customers, Photomatic must reprint by hand—a process that costs more than the price charged—so each "defect" is a loss for the firm. The equipment supplier notes that sophisticated light measuring circuitry should produce acceptable print quality with no more than one defect per thousand. Quality engineer B. J. Nighthorse randomly sampled 2,000 prints from each of the last 20 production runs and recorded the following information:

Run	1	2	3	4	5	6	7	8	9	10
# Defective	3	1	2	4	4	2	2	3	1	0
Run	**11**	**12**	**13**	**14**	**15**	**16**	**17**	**18**	**19**	**20**
# Defective	2	2	1	3	2	2	0	4	2	0

Construct a p chart to see whether the equipment is performing within the manufacturer's specifications and whether the process is in-control.

■ **10-53** Explain how producer's and consumer's risks in acceptance sampling correspond to Type I and Type II errors in hypothesis testing.

■ **10-54** A 14-ounce box of soda crackers will almost never weigh exactly 14 ounces. What sources of common and special cause variation might explain this observation?

■ **10-55** The graph below is an OC curve for a single-sampling scheme from batches of 3,000 with $n = 300$ and $c = 3$. Find the producer's risk if the AQL is:

(a) 0.005.

(b) 0.010.

(c) 0.015.

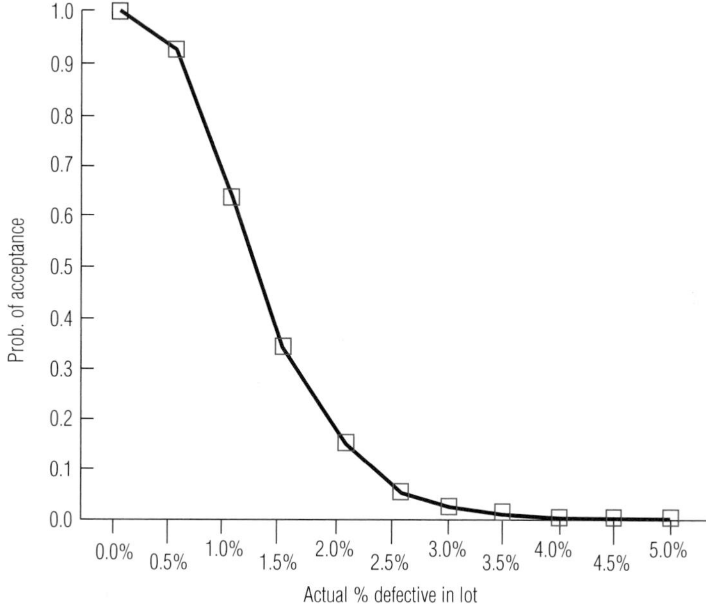

■ **10-56** For the single-sampling scheme in Exercise 10-55, use the OC curve to find the consumer's risk if the LTPD is:

(a) 0.010.

(b) 0.015.

(c) 0.020.

■ **10-57** Connie Rodrigues, the Dean of Students at Midstate College, is wondering about grade inflation at the school. She has randomly selected 200 students from each of the last 20 graduating classes and has looked up their grade-point averages. In addition, for each year's sample she has calculated the percentage of A and B grades for all 200 students as a group. Explain how she can use control charts to analyze whether Midstate has been experiencing grade inflation.

■ **10-58** Explain how acceptance sampling can be more effective in the long run than sampling entire batches of input.

■ **10-59** Education seems to be a difficult field in which to use quality techniques. One possible outcome measure for colleges is the graduation rate (the percentage of students matriculating who graduate on time). Would you recommend using p or R charts to examine graduation rates at a school? Would this be a good measure of quality?

■ **10-60** Few parents would deny that childhood immunizations are important, but studies show that as many as two children out of five reach school age without a complete series of shots. What was once a simple schedule of a few injections for one or two major life-threatening diseases has been expanded to include protection against what were once considered the "normal" diseases of childhood, such as measles. New vaccines—such as one against whooping cough—are being added to the list.

Some vaccinations are effective only if booster shots are given at intervals of several months and may be complicated if a child is ill and misses a planned shot. The age at which recommended vaccinations should be given differs by disease, so more than a dozen visits to the pediatrician's office are required if the full recommended vaccination schedule is to be completed by the time a child registers for school. The situation is complicated for parents with more than one child.

(a) Is checking each child's vaccination status at the time of enrollment to school an example of good quality control?

(b) Draw a fishbone diagram to illustrate causes that lead to an incomplete immunization program.

(c) What would be the next step for a Health Maintenance Organization that was trying to increase compliance with the recommended schedule?

Sources: "Childhood Immunization Schedule," *American Family Physician* (1 June 1995); Jane E. Brody, "Complacent Parents Put Their Children at Risk by Failing to Obtain Recommended Vaccinations," *The New York Times* (11 August 1993):C11.

● Chapter Concepts Test

Circle the correct answer or fill in the blank. *Answers are in the back of the book.*

T F 1. p charts are used to monitor categorical variables with two possible values.

T F 2. Statistical process control was originally developed in Japan and brought to the United States after World War II.

T F 3. Outliers can sometimes be a result of inherent variation.

T F 4. For a given lot size, a single-sampling scheme is completely specified by its sample size and acceptance number.

T F 5. In many complex systems, about 80 percent of the problems can be attributed to about 20 percent of the causes.

T F 6. The grand mean, $\bar{\bar{x}}$, captures more information than the individual sample means.

T F 7. TQM is now being applied in service industries as well as manufacturing industries.

T F 8. Regardless of Equation 10-6, the UCL in a p chart can never be greater than 1.

T F 9. Consumer's risk in acceptance sampling is like a Type II error in hypothesis testing.

T F 10. In control charts, CL denotes either of the two control limits.

T F 11. If you use acceptance sampling, your suppliers won't be motivated to improve the quality of their output.

T F 12. Controlling variability is an essential aspect of maintaining quality.

T F 13. Increasing the sample size enables you to reduce both consumer's and producer's risks.

T F 14. R charts are used to monitor the level of process output.

T F 15. Control charts help us to detect inherent variation.

T F 16. Double sampling requires larger sample sizes than single sampling in order to achieve the same levels of risk.

T F 17. After the causes of outliers have been identified, those points should be discarded and the control chart should be redone.

T F 18. Ishikawa diagrams are also known as fishtail diagrams.

T F 19. The AOQ curve tells you how the output quality of an acceptance-sampling scheme varies as a function of the input quality of the batches being tested.

T F 20. $\bar{x}$ and R charts use the sample standard deviation to measure process variability.

T F 21. The lower control limit on an R chart is always $\bar{R}(1 - 3d_3/d_2)$.

A B C D 22. An OC curve can be used to determine:

(a) Consumer's risk.
(b) Producer's risk.
(c) Both risks.
(d) Neither risk.

A B C D 23. Which of the following diagrams is *not* used in quality control?

(a) $\bar{x}$ chart.
(b) Pareto diagram.
(c) Stem-and-leaf diagram.
(d) AOQ curve.

A B C D 24. *AOQ* stands for:

(a) Approximate outgoing quality.
(b) Average operating quality.
(c) Approximate optimal quality.
(d) Average outgoing quality.

A B C D 25. The UCL for an R chart is:

(a) $\bar{R}D_4$.
(b) $\bar{R}(1 + 3d_3/(d_2\sqrt{n}))$.
(c) $\bar{x} + A_2\bar{R}$.
(d) $\bar{R}D_3$.

A B C D 26. Which of the following terms doesn't belong with the others?

(a) Ishikawa diagram.
(b) Pareto diagram.
(c) Fishbone diagram.
(d) Cause-and-effect diagram.

A B C D 27. Which control-chart patterns indicate that the process is out-of-control?
(a) Decreasing trends.
(b) Cycles.
(c) Hugging the center line
(d) All of the above.

A B C D 28. Who is responsible for the idea that TQM companies should distinguish between the *vital few* and the *trivial many*?
(a) Juran.
(b) Deming.
(c) Pareto.
(d) Shewhart.

A B C D 29. Which of the following charts is used to monitor an attribute?
(a) $\bar{x}$ chart.
(b) A chart.
(c) p chart.
(d) None of the above.

A B C D 30. The correct distribution to use to compute consumer's risk exactly is the:
(a) Normal.
(b) Hypergeometric.
(c) Poisson.
(d) Binomial.

A B C D 31. Which of the following people was *not* directly involved in quality control?
(a) Deming.
(b) Pareto.
(c) Romig.
(d) Ishikawa.

A B C D 32. Which kind of variation can be seen in a control chart?
(a) Inherent variation.
(b) Special cause variation.
(c) Random variation.
(d) All of the above.

A B C D 33. In double sampling, we reject the batch if:
(a) $d_1 > c_2$.
(b) $d_2 > c_2$.
(c) Either (a) or (b).
(d) Neither (a) nor (b).

A B C D 34. Who was primarily responsible for the development of control charts?
(a) Crosby.
(b) Ishikawa.
(c) Dodge.
(d) Shewhart.

A B C D 35. CQI stands for:
(a) Constant quality increments.
(b) Continuous quality improvement.
(c) Continuous quality increases.
(d) Complete quality implementation.

A B C D 36. Which of the following is *not* an aspect of quality?

(a) Luxuriousness.

(b) Fitness for use.

(c) Consistency.

(d) Conformance to requirements.

37. Observations falling beyond the ________________________ are known as outliers.

38. ________________________ diagrams are used to identify and group causes of problems.

39. The probability of rejecting a batch that meets the AQL is called the ________________________risk.

40. ________________________ are used in statistical process control to monitor the output of a product or service and see whether it is meeting standards.

41. ________________________ is used to test the quality of batches of components.

42. In an $\bar{x}$ chart, the center line is determined by $\bar{\bar{x}}$, the ________________________.

43. ________________________ is the enemy of quality.

44. The maximum number of defects allowed before rejecting a batch is called the ________________________.

45. Nonrandom patterns in control charts indicate the presence of ________________________variation.

Flow Chart: Quality and Quality Control

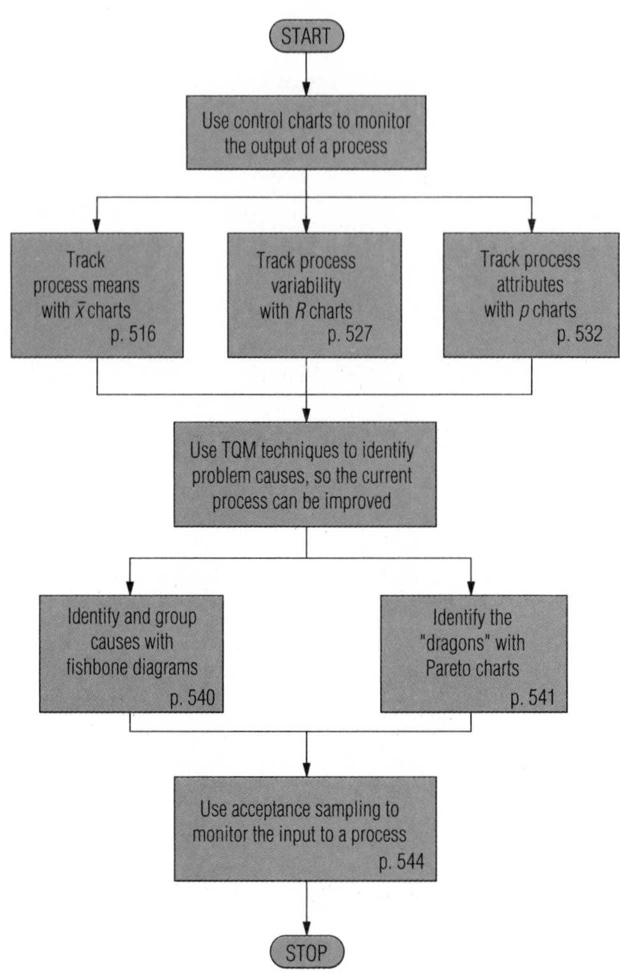

chapter 11

CHI-SQUARE AND ANALYSIS OF VARIANCE

Objectives

- To recognize situations requiring the comparison of more than two means or proportions
- To introduce the chi-square and *F* distributions and learn how to use them in statistical inferences
- To use the chi-square distribution to see whether two classifications of the same data are independent of each other
- To use a chi-square test to check whether a particular collection of data is well described by a specified distribution
- To use the chi-square distribution for confidence intervals and testing hypotheses about a single population variance
- To compare more than two population means using analysis of variance
- To use the *F* distribution to test hypotheses about two population variances

Chapter Contents

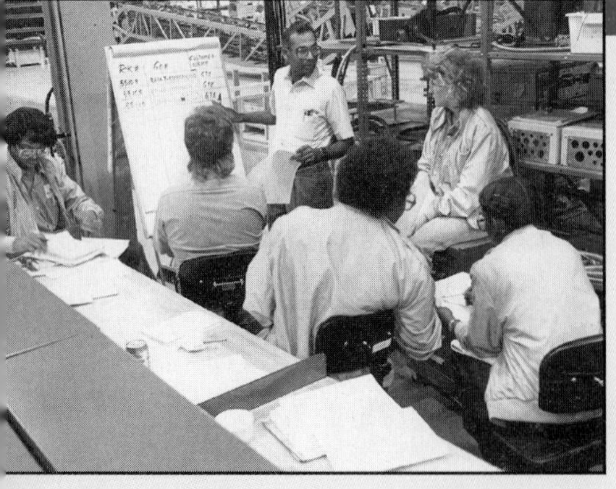

The training director of a company is trying to evaluate three different methods of training new employees. The first method assigns each to an experienced employee for individual help in the factory. The second method puts all new employees in a training room separate from the factory, and the third method uses training films and programmed learning materials. The training director chooses 16 new employees assigned at random to the three training methods and records their daily production after they complete the programs:

Method 1	15	18	19	22	11	
Method 2	22	27	18	21	17	
Method 3	18	24	19	16	22	15

The director wonders whether there are differences in effectiveness among the methods. Using techniques learned in this chapter, we can help answer that question. ■

11.1 Introduction

In Chapters 8 and 9, we learned how to test hypotheses using data from either one or two samples. We used one-sample tests to determine whether a mean or a proportion was significantly different from a hypothesized value. In the two-sample tests, we examined the difference between either two means or two proportions, and we tried to learn whether this difference was significant.

Uses of the chi-square test

Suppose we have proportions from five populations instead of only two. In this case, the methods for comparing proportions described in Chapter 9 do *not* apply; we must use the *chi-square test,* the subject of the first portion of this chapter. Chi-square tests enable us to test whether *more* than two population proportions can be considered equal.

Actually, chi-square tests allow us to do a lot more than just test for the equality of several proportions. If we classify a population into several categories with respect to two attributes (such as age and job performance), we can then use a chi-square test to determine whether the two attributes are independent of each other.

Function of analysis of variance

Managers also encounter situations in which it is useful to test for the equality of more than two population means. Again, we cannot apply the methods introduced in Chapter 9 because they are limited to testing for the equality of only two means. The *analysis of variance,* discussed in the fourth section of this chapter, will enable us to test whether *more* than two population means can be considered equal.

Inferences about population variances

It is clear that we will not always be interested in means and proportions. There are many managerial situations where we will be concerned about the variability in a population. Section 11.5 shows how to use the chi-square distribution to form confidence intervals and test hypotheses about a population variance. In Section 11.6, we show that hypotheses comparing the variances of two populations can be tested using the F distribution.

Exercises 11.1

■ **11-1** Why do we use a chi-square test?

■ **11-2** Why do we use analysis of variance?

■ **11-3** In each of the following situations, state whether a chi-square test, analysis of variance, or inference about population variances should be done.

(a) We want to see whether the variance in spring temperatures is the same on the east and west coasts.

(b) We want to see whether the average speed on Interstate 95 differs depending on the day of the week.

(c) We want to see whether long-term stock performance on Wall Street (classified as good, average, or poor) is independent of the size of the company (classified as small, medium, or large).

(d) Before testing whether $\mu_1 = \mu_2$, we want to test whether the assumption that $\sigma_1^2 = \sigma_2^2$ is reasonable.

■ **11-4** Answer true or false and explain your answers.

(a) After reading this chapter, you should know how to make inferences about two or more population variances.

(b) After reading this chapter, you should know how to make inferences about two or more population means.

(c) After reading this chapter, you should know how to make inferences about two or more population proportions.

■ **11-5** To help remember which distribution or technique is used, complete the following table with either the name of a distribution or the technique involved. The row classification refers to the number of parameters involved in a test, and the column classification refers to the type of parameter involved. Some cells may not have an entry; others may have more than one possible entry.

	Type of Parameter		
Number of Parameters Involved	μ	σ	p
1			
2			
3 or more			

11.2 Chi-Square as a Test of Independence

Sample differences among proportions: Significant or not?

Many times, managers need to know whether the differences they observe among several sample proportions are significant or only due to chance. Suppose the campaign manager for a presidential candidate studies three geographically different regions and finds that 35, 42, and 51 percent, respectively, of the voters surveyed in the three regions recognize the candidate's name. If this difference is significant, the manager may conclude that location will affect the way the candidate should act. But if the difference is not significant (that is, if the manager concludes that the difference is solely due to chance), then he may decide that the place chosen to make a particular policy-making speech will have no effect on its reception. To run the campaign successfully, then, the manager needs to determine whether location and name recognition are dependent or independent.

Contingency Tables

Describing a contingency table

Suppose that in four regions, the National Health Care Company samples its hospital employees' attitudes toward job-performance reviews. Respondents are given a choice between the present method (two reviews a year) and a proposed new method (quarterly reviews). Table 11-1, which illustrates the response to this question from the sample polled, is called a *contingency table.* A table such as this is made up of rows and columns; rows run horizontally, columns vertically. Notice that the four columns in Table 11-1 provide one basis of classification—geographical regions—and that the two rows classify the information another way: preference for review methods. Table 11-1 is called a 2 × 4 contingency table because it consists of two rows and four columns. We describe the dimensions of a contingency table by first stating the number of rows and then the number of columns. The "total" column and the "total" row are not counted as part of the dimensions.

Observed and Expected Frequencies

Setting up the problem symbolically

Suppose we now symbolize the true proportions of the total population of employees who prefer the present plan as

- p_N ← Proportion in Northeast who prefer present plan
- p_S ← Proportion in Southeast who prefer present plan
- p_C ← Proportion in Central region who prefer present plan
- p_W ← Proportion in West Coast region who prefer present plan

Using these symbols, we can state the null and alternative hypotheses as follows:

$$\text{H}_0\text{: } p_N = p_S = p_S = p_W \leftarrow \text{Null hypothesis}$$

$$\text{H}_1\text{: } p_N, p_S, p_C, \text{ and } p_W \text{ are not all equal} \leftarrow \text{Alternative hypothesis}$$

If the null hypothesis is true, we can combine the data from the four samples and then estimate the proportion of the total workforce (the total population) that prefers the present review method:

Table 11-1

Sample Response Concerning Review Schedules for National Health Care Hospital Employees

	Northeast	Southeast	Central	West Coast	Total
Number who prefer present method	68	75	57	79	**279**
Number who prefer new method	32	45	33	31	**141**
Total employees sampled in each region	**100**	**120**	**90**	**110**	**420**

Combined proportion who prefer present method assuming the null hypothesis of no difference is true

$$= \frac{68 + 75 + 57 + 79}{100 + 120 + 90 + 110}$$

$$= \frac{279}{420}$$

$$= 0.6643$$

Determining expected frequencies

Obviously, if the value 0.6643 estimates the population proportion expected to prefer the present compensation method, then 0.3357 (= 1 − 0.6643) is the estimate of the population proportion expected to prefer the proposed new method. Using 0.6643 as the *estimate* of the population proportion who prefer the present review method and 0.3357 as the *estimate* of the population proportion who prefer the new method, we can estimate the number of sampled employees in each region whom we would expect to prefer each of the review methods. The calculations are done in Table 11-2.

Comparing expected and observed frequencies

Table 11-3 combines all the information from Tables 11-1 and 11-2. It illustrates both the actual, or observed, frequency of the employees sampled who prefer each method of job-review and the theoretical, or expected, frequency of sampled employees preferring each method. Remember that the *expected frequencies,* those in color, were estimated from our combined proportion estimate.

Reasoning intuitively about chi-square tests

To test the null hypothesis, $p_N = p_S = p_C = p_W$, we must compare the frequencies that were observed (the black ones in Table 11-3) with the frequencies we would expect if the null hypothesis is true (those in color). If the sets of observed and expected frequencies are

Table 11-2

Proportion of Sampled Employees in Each Region Expected to Prefer the Two Review Methods

	Northeast	Southeast	Central	West Coast
Total number sampled	100	120	90	110
Estimated proportion who prefer present method	×0.6643	×0.6643	×0.6643	×0.6643
Number *expected* to prefer present method	66.43	79.72	59.79	73.07
Total number sampled	100	120	90	110
Estimated proportion who prefer new method	×0.3357	×0.3357	×0.3357	×0.3357
Number *expected* to prefer new method	33.57	40.28	30.21	36.93

Table 11-3

Comparison of Observed and Expected Frequencies of Sampled Employees

	Northeast	Southeast	Central	West Coast
FREQUENCY PREFERRING PRESENT METHOD:				
Observed (actual) frequency	68	75	57	79
Expected (theoretical) frequency	66.43	79.72	59.79	73.07
FREQUENCY PREFERRING NEW METHOD:				
Observed (actual) frequency	32	45	33	31
Expected (theoretical) frequency	33.57	40.28	30.21	36.93

nearly alike, we can reason intuitively that we will accept the null hypothesis. If there is a large difference between these frequencies, we may intuitively reject the null hypothesis and conclude that there are significant differences in the proportions of employees in the four regions preferring the new method.

The Chi-Square Statistic

To go beyond our intuitive feelings about the observed and expected frequencies, we can use the chi-square statistic, which is calculated this way:

Calculating the chi-square statistic

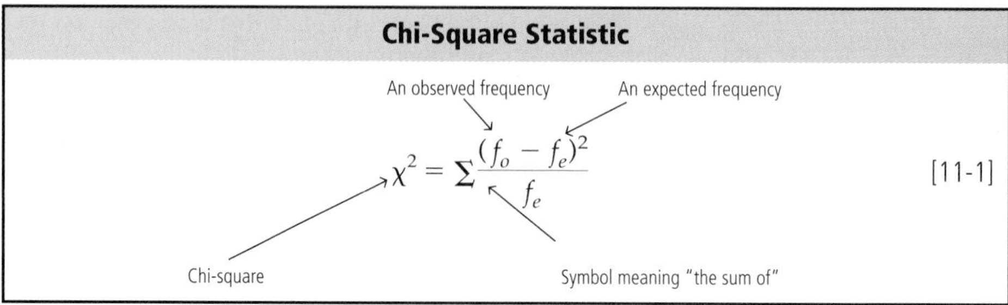

$$\chi^2 = \Sigma \frac{(f_o - f_e)^2}{f_e} \quad [11\text{-}1]$$

This formula says that chi-square, or χ^2, is the sum we will get if we

1. Subtract f_e from f_o for each of the eight values in Table 11-3.
2. Square each of the differences.
3. Divide each squared difference by f_e.
4. Sum all eight of the answers.

Numerically, the calculations are easy to do using a table such as Table 11-4, which shows the steps.

Interpreting the chi-square statistic

The answer of 2.764 is the value for chi-square in our problem comparing preferences for review methods. If this value were as large as, say, 20, it would indicate a substantial difference between our observed values and our expected values. A chi-square of zero, on

Table 11-4 Calculation of χ^2 (Chi-Square) Statistic from Data in Table 11-3

		Step 1	Step 2	Step 3
f_o	f_e	$f_o - f_e$	$(f_o - f_e)^2$	$\frac{(f_o - f_e)^2}{f_e}$
68	66.43	1.57	2.46	0.0370
75	79.72	−4.72	22.28	0.2795
57	59.79	−2.79	7.78	0.1301
79	73.07	5.93	35.16	0.4812
32	33.57	−1.57	2.46	0.0733
45	40.28	4.72	22.28	0.5531
33	30.21	2.79	7.78	0.2575
31	36.93	−5.93	35.16	0.9521
				2.7638

Step 4 $\sum \frac{(f_o - f_e)^2}{f_e} = 2.764 \leftarrow \chi^2$ (chi-square)

the other hand, indicates that the observed frequencies exactly match the expected frequencies. The value of chi-square can never be negative because the differences between the observed and expected frequencies are always *squared*.

The Chi-Square Distribution

Describing a chi-square distribution

If the null hypothesis is true, then the sampling distribution of the chi-square statistic, χ^2, can be closely approximated by a continuous curve known as a *chi-square distribution*. As in the case of the *t* distribution, there is a different chi-square distribution for each different number of degrees of freedom. Figure 11-1 shows the three different chi-square distributions that would correspond to 1, 5, and 10 degrees of freedom. For very small numbers of degrees of freedom, the chi-square distribution is severely skewed to the right. As the number of degrees of freedom increases, the curve rapidly becomes more symmetrical until the number reaches large values, at which point the distribution can be approximated by the normal.

Finding probabilities when using a chi-square distribution

The chi-square distribution is a probability distribution. Therefore, the total area under the curve in each chi-square distribution is 1.0. Like the *t* distribution, so many different chi-square distributions are possible that it is not practical to construct a table that illustrates the areas under the curve for all possible values of the area. Appendix Table 5 illustrates only the areas in the tail most commonly used in significance tests using the chi-square distribution.

Determining Degrees of Freedom

Calculating degrees of freedom

To use the chi-square test, we must calculate the number of degrees of freedom in the contingency table by applying Equation 11-2:

Degrees of Freedom in a Chi-Square Test of Independence

$$\text{Number of degrees of freedom} = (\text{number of rows} - 1)(\text{number of columns} - 1) \quad [11\text{-}2]$$

Let's examine the appropriateness of this equation. Suppose we have a 3×4 contingency table like the one in Figure 11-2. We know the row and column totals that are designated RT_1, RT_2, RT_3, and CT_1, CT_2, CT_3, CT_4. As we discussed in Chapter 7, the number of degrees of freedom is equal to the number of values that we can freely specify.

FIGURE 11-1

Chi-square distributions with 1, 5, and 10 degrees of freedom

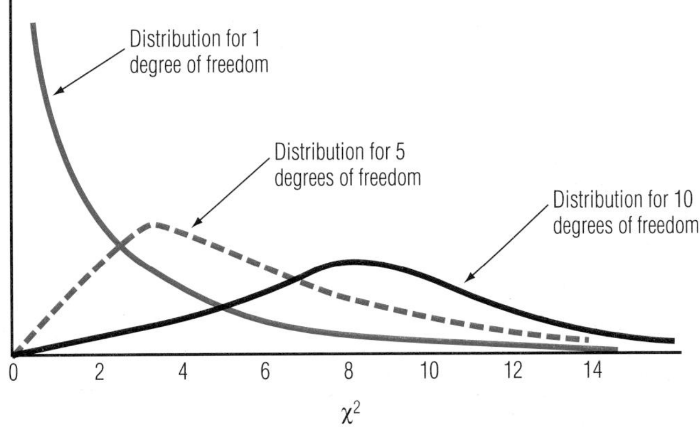

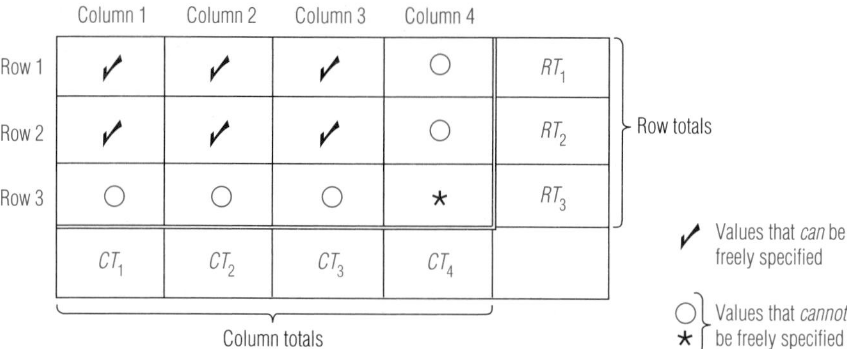

FIGURE 11-2

A 3 × 4 contingency table illustrating determination of the number of degrees of freedom

Look now at the first row of the contingency table in Figure 11-2. Once we specify the first three values in that row (denoted by checks in the figure), the fourth value in that row (denoted by a circle) is already determined; we are not free to specify it because we know the row total.

Likewise, in the second row of the contingency table in Figure 11-2, once we specify the first three values (denoted again by checks), the fourth value is determined and cannot be freely specified. We have denoted this fourth value by a circle.

Turning now to the third row, we see that its first entry is determined *because we already know the first two entries in the first column and the column total;* again, we have denoted this entry with a circle. We can apply this same reasoning to the second and third entries in the third row, both of which have been denoted by circles, too.

Turning finally to the last entry in the third row (denoted by a star), we see that we cannot freely specify its value because we have already determined the first two entries in the fourth column. By counting the number of checks in the contingency table in Figure 11-2, you can see that the number of values we are free to specify is 6 (the number of checks). This is equal to 2 × 3, or (the number of rows − 1) times (the number of columns − 1).

This is exactly what we have in Equation 11-2. Table 11-5 illustrates the row-and-column dimensions of three more contingency tables and indicates the appropriate degrees of freedom in each case.

Using the Chi-Square Test

Stating the problem symbolically

Returning to our example of job-review preferences of National Health Care hospital employees, we use the chi-square test to determine whether attitude about reviews is independent of geographical region. If the company wants to test the null hypothesis at the 0.10 level of significance, our problem can be summarized:

H_0: $p_N = p_S = p_C = p_W$ ← Null hypothesis

H_1: p_N, p_S, p_C, and p_W are not equal ← Alternative hypothesis

$\alpha = 0.10$ ← Level of significance for testing these hypotheses

Table 11-5 Determination of Degrees of Freedom in Three Contingency Tables

Contingency Table	Number of Rows (r)	Number of Columns (c)	r − 1	c − 1	Degrees of Freedom (r − 1)(c − 1)
A	3	4	3 − 1 = 2	4 − 1 = 3	(2)(3) = 6
B	5	7	5 − 1 = 4	7 − 1 = 6	(4)(6) = 24
C	6	9	6 − 1 = 5	9 − 1 = 8	(5)(8) = 40

Calculating degrees of freedom

Because our contingency table for this problem (Table 11-1) has two rows and four columns, the appropriate number of degrees of freedom is

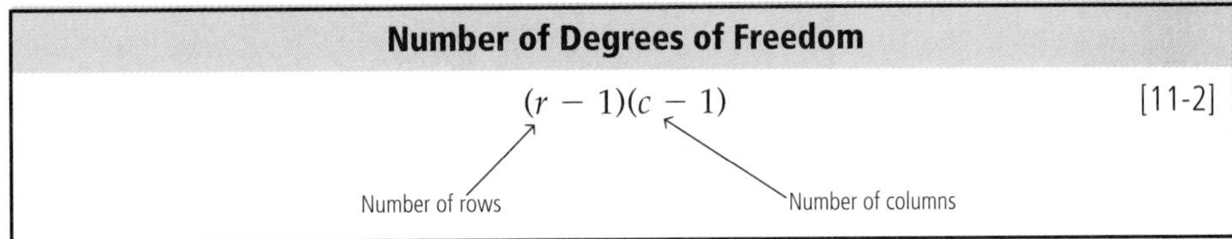

Number of Degrees of Freedom

$$(r - 1)(c - 1) \quad [11\text{-}2]$$

$$= (2 - 1)(4 - 1)$$
$$= (1)(3)$$
$$= 3 \leftarrow \text{Degrees of freedom}$$

Illustrating the hypothesis test

Figure 11-3 illustrates a chi-square distribution with 3 degrees of freedom, showing the significance level in color. In Appendix Table 5, we can look under the 0.10 column and move down to the 3 degrees of freedom row. There we find the value of the chi-square statistic, 6.251. We can interpret this to mean that with 3 degrees of freedom, the region to the right of a chi-square value of 6.251 contains 0.10 of the area under the curve. Thus, the acceptance region for the null hypothesis in Figure 11-3 goes from the left tail of the curve to the chi-square value of 6.251.

Interpreting the results

As we can see from Figure 11-3, the sample chi-square value of 2.764 that we calculated in Table 11-4 falls within the acceptance region. Therefore, we accept the null hypothesis that there is no difference between the attitudes about job interviews in the four geographical regions. In other words, we conclude that attitude about performance reviews is independent of geography.

Contingency Tables with More Than Two Rows

Are hospital stay and insurance coverage independent?

Mr. George McMahon, president of National General Health Insurance Company, is opposed to national health insurance. He argues that it would be too costly to implement, particularly since the existence of such a system would, among other effects, tend to encourage people to spend more time in hospitals. George believes that lengths of stays in hospitals are dependent on the types of health insurance that people have. He asked Donna McClish, his staff statistician, to check the matter. Donna collected data on a random sample of 660 hospital stays and summarized them in Table 11-6.

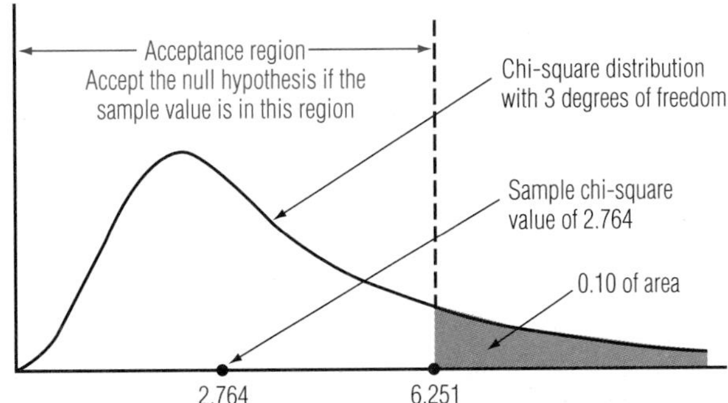

FIGURE 11-3

Chi-square hypothesis test at the 0.10 level of significance, showing acceptance region and sample chi-square value of 2.764

Table 11-6

Hospital-Stay Data Classified by the Type of Insurance Coverage and Length of Stay

		Days in Hospital			
		<5	5–10	>10	**Total**
Fraction of costs	<25%	40	75	65	**180**
covered by	25–50%	30	45	75	**150**
insurance	>50%	40	100	190	**330**
	Total	**110**	**220**	**330**	**660**

Table 11-6 gives observed frequencies in the nine different length-of-stay and type-of-insurance categories (or "cells") into which we have divided the sample. Donna wishes to test the hypotheses:

Stating the hypotheses

H_0: length of stay and type of insurance are independent

H_1: length of stay depends on type of insurance

$\alpha = 0.01 \leftarrow$ Level of significance for testing these hypotheses

Finding expected frequencies

We will use a chi-square test, so we first have to find the expected frequencies for each of the nine cells. Let's demonstrate how to find them by looking at the cell that corresponds to stays of less than 5 days and insurance covering less than 25 percent of costs.

Estimating the proportions in the cells

A total of 180 of the 660 stays in Table 11-6 had insurance covering less than 25 percent of costs. So we can use the figure 180/660 to *estimate* the proportion in the population having insurance covering less than 25 percent of the costs. Similarly, 110/660 *estimates* the proportion of all hospital stays that last fewer than 5 days. If length of stay and type of insurance really are independent, we can use Equation 4-4 to *estimate* the proportion in the first cell (less than 5 days and less than 25 percent coverage).

We let

- A = the event "a stay corresponds to someone whose insurance covers less than 25 percent of the costs"
- B = the event "a stay lasts less than 5 days"

Then,

$$\begin{aligned} \text{P(first cell)} &= \text{P}(A \text{ and } B) \\ &= \text{P}(A) \times \text{P}(B) \\ &= \left(\frac{180}{660}\right)\left(\frac{110}{660}\right) \\ &= 1/22 \end{aligned} \qquad [4\text{-}4]$$

Because 1/22 is the expected *proportion* in the first cell, the expected *frequency* in that cell is

$$(1/22)(660) = 30 \text{ observations}$$

In general, we can calculate the expected frequency for any cell with Equation 11-3:

Calculating the expected frequencies for the cells

Expected Frequency For Any Cell

$$f_e = \frac{RT \times CT}{n} \quad [11\text{-}3]$$

where

- f_e = expected frequency in a given cell
- RT = row total for the row containing that cell
- CT = column total for the column containing that cell
- n = total number of observations

Now we can use Equations 11-3 and 11-1 to compute all of the expected frequencies and the value of the chi-square statistic. The computations are done in Table 11-7.

Figure 11-4 illustrates a chi-square distribution with 4 degrees of freedom (number of rows − 1 = 2) × (number of columns − 1 = 2), showing the 0.01 significance level in color. Appendix Table 5 (in the 0.01 column and the 4 degrees of freedom row) tells Donna that for her problem, the region to the right of a chi-square value of 13.277 contains 0.01 of the area under the curve. Thus, the acceptance region for the null hypothesis in Figure 11-4 goes from the left tail of the curve to the chi-square value of 13.277.

Table 11-7 Calculation of Expected Frequencies and Chi-Square from Data in Table 11-6

Row	Column	f_o	f_e	$= \frac{RT \times CT}{n}$	$f_o - f_e$	$(f_o - f_e)^2$	$\frac{(f_o - f_e)^2}{f_e}$
1	1	40	30	$\frac{180 \times 110}{660}$	10	100	3.333
1	2	75	60	$\frac{180 \times 220}{660}$	15	225	3.750
1	3	65	90	$\frac{180 \times 330}{660}$	−25	625	6.944
2	1	30	25	$\frac{150 \times 110}{660}$	5	25	1.000
2	2	45	50	$\frac{150 \times 220}{660}$	−5	25	0.500
2	3	75	75	$\frac{150 \times 330}{660}$	0	0	0.000
3	1	40	55	$\frac{330 \times 110}{660}$	−15	225	4.091
3	2	100	110	$\frac{330 \times 220}{660}$	−10	100	0.909
3	3	190	165	$\frac{330 \times 330}{660}$	25	625	3.788

$$[11\text{-}1] \quad \sum \frac{(f_o - f_e)^2}{f_e} = 24.315 \leftarrow \chi^2 \text{ (chi-square)}$$

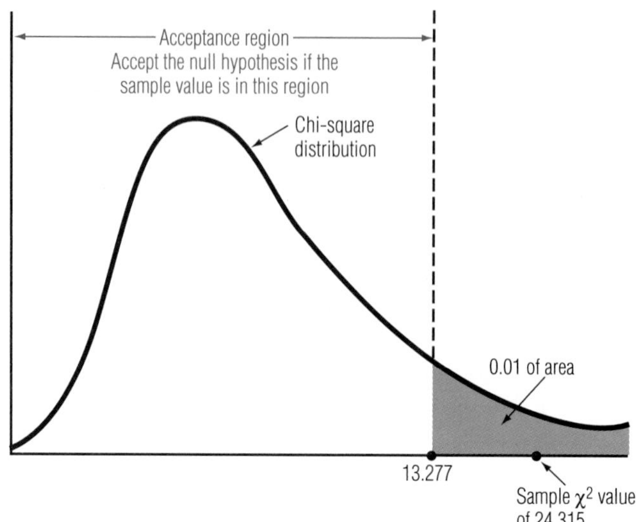

FIGURE 11-4

Chi-square hypothesis test at the 0.01 level of significance, showing acceptance region and sample chi-square value of 24.315

Interpreting the results of the test

As Figure 11-4 shows Donna, the sample chi-square value of 24.315 she calculated in Table 11-7 is not within the acceptance region. Thus, Donna must reject the null hypothesis and inform Mr. McMahan that the evidence supports his belief that length of hospital stay and insurance coverage *are* dependent on each other.

Precautions about Using the Chi-Square Test

Use large sample sizes

To use a chi-square hypothesis test, we must have a sample size large enough to guarantee the similarity between the theoretically correct distribution and our sampling distribution of χ^2, the chi-square statistic. When the expected frequencies are too small, the value of χ^2 will be overestimated and will result in too many rejections of the null hypothesis. **To avoid making incorrect inferences from χ^2 hypothesis tests, follow the general rule that an expected frequency of less than 5 in one cell of a contingency table is too small to use.*** When the table contains more than one cell with an expected frequency of less than 5, we can combine these in order to get an expected frequency of 5 or more. But in doing this, we reduce the number of categories of data and will gain less information from the contingency table.

Use carefully collected data

This rule will enable us to use the chi-square hypothesis test properly, but unfortunately, each test can only reflect (and not improve) the quality of the data we feed into it. So far, we have rejected the null hypothesis if the difference between the observed and expected frequencies—that is, the computed chi-square value—is too large. In the case of the job-review preferences, we would reject the null hypothesis at a 0.10 level of significance if our chi-square value was 6.251 or more. **But if the chi-square value was zero, we should be careful to question whether *absolutely no difference* exists between observed and expected frequencies.** If we have strong feelings that some difference *ought* to exist, we should examine either the way the data were collected or the manner in which measurements were taken, or both, to be certain that existing differences were not obscured or missed in collecting sample data.

Mendel's pea data

In the 1860s, experiments with the characteristics of peas led the monk Gregor Mendel to propose the existence of genes. Mendel's experimental results were astoundingly close

*Statisticians have developed correction factors that, in some cases, allow us to use cells with expected frequencies of less than 5. The derivation and use of these correction factors are beyond the scope of this book.

to those predicted by his theory. A century later, statisticians looked at Mendel's "pea data," performed a chi-square test, and concluded that chi-square was too small; that is, Mendel's reported experimental data were so close to what was expected that they could only conclude that he had fudged the data.

Using the Computer to Do Chi-Square Tests

Using SAS for a chi-square test

Even though the computations necessary to do a chi-square test of independence are relatively simple, for large sets of data they can become rather tedious. Most commonly used computer statistics packages contain routines for doing these tests. In Figure 11-5, we see the output that results when we use the SAS package to analyze the hospital-stay data of Table 11-6. Let's compare the computer output with the analysis we did by hand on pages 575–578.

Comparing computer and hand-computed outputs

In each cell of Figure 11-5, SAS prints out the observed frequency (f_o), the expected frequency (f_e), and the contribution of that cell to the χ^2 statistic $[(f_o - f_e)^2/f_e]$. Then, at the bottom of the table, SAS prints out the sample chi-square value, the number of degrees of freedom, and a prob value. The last of these (the prob value) is the probability of getting an observed chi-square value as large (or larger) than the sample chi-square value if the hypothesis of independence is valid.

Interpreting the results

Recalling our discussion of prob values in Chapter 9, we know that we will reject H_0 if the prob value is less than α, the significance level of the test. In our example, $\alpha = 0.01$ and the prob value reported by SAS is 0.0001, so again we reject H_0 and conclude that length of stay and insurance coverage are not independent.

FIGURE 11-5

Output from SAS from the hospital-stay problem

```
ILLUSTRATING THE USE OF SAS FOR A TEST OF INDEPENDENCE

           DAYS = LENGTH OF STAY
  COVERAGE = % OF COSTS COVERED BY INSURANCE

        TABLE OF DAYS BY COVERAGE

DAYS              COVERAGE

FREQUENCY      |
EXPECTED       |
CELL CHI2      |    UNDER |          |     OVER |
               |      25% | 25 - 50% |      50% |  TOTAL
---------------+----------+----------+----------+
LESS THAN 5    |       40 |       30 |       40 |    110
               |     30.0 |     25.0 |     55.0 |
               |  3.33333 |        1 |  4.09091 |
---------------+----------+----------+----------+
5 TO 10        |       75 |       45 |      100 |    220
               |     60.0 |     50.0 |    110.0 |
               |     3.75 |      0.5 |  .909091 |
---------------+----------+----------+----------+
MORE THAN 10   |       65 |       75 |      190 |    330
               |     90.0 |     75.0 |    165.0 |
               |  6.94444 |        0 |  3.78788 |
---------------+----------+----------+----------+
TOTAL                 180        150        330      660

      STATISTICS FOR TABLE OF DAYS BY COVERAGE

STATISTIC                    DF      VALUE          PROB
---------------------------------------------------------
CHI-SQUARE                    4     24.316        0.0001
```

Using Minitab for a chi-square test

As a second computer-based example of a chi-square test, let's return to the earnings data in Appendix Table 11. We used Minitab to code the year-to-year change in last-quarter earnings in five groups:

Change	Group
$x < -\$0.20$	-2
$-\$0.20 \le x < -\$0.05$	-1
$-\$0.05 \le x < \$0.05$	0
$\$0.05 \le x < \$0.20$	1
$\$0.20 \le x$	2

In addition, the EXCHANGE variable was converted from its character values of O, A, and N to the numeric values 1, 2, and 3 in a new variable called MARKET.

Now, let's test, at $\alpha = 0.01$, whether the year-to-year change in last-quarter earnings depends on where the company's stock is traded.

Stating the hypotheses

H_0: change in earnings and stock exchange are independent

H_1: change in earnings depends on stock exchange

$\alpha = 0.01$ ← Level of significance for testing these hypotheses

Interpreting the results

In Figure 11-6, we have used Minitab to perform this test of independence. In each cell of Figure 11-6, Minitab prints out the observed frequencies (f_o); it also gives the row and column totals. At the bottom of the table, Minitab gives the sample chi-square value and the degrees of freedom. At $\alpha = .01$ with 8 degrees of freedom, the critical chi-square value is 20.090. Therefore we cannot reject H_0. We conclude that change in earnings and stock exchange are independent.

FIGURE 11-6

Using Minitab to do a test of independence

```
Tabulated Statistics

 ROWS: GROUP          COLUMNS: MARKET

                1          2          3        ALL

 -2            24          8         17         49

 -1            14          7         10         31

  0            41         11         11         63

  1            23          6         17         46

  2             9          6         20         35

 ALL          111         38         75        224

CHI-SQUARE =    19.103    WITH D.F. =      8

  CELL CONTENTS --
                   COUNT
```

HINTS & ASSUMPTIONS

Warning: The rows and columns of a chi-square contingency table *must* be mutually exclusive categories that exhaust *all* of the possibilities of the sample. Hint: Think of the cells as little boxes and each member of the sample as a marble. Each marble must be put in a box and there can be no leftover marbles if you want the test to be valid. For example, a survey of voters that has contingency table cells for just Democrats and Republicans ignores the opinions of unaffiliated voters. Hint: The categories "car owner" and "bicycle owner" don't allow for people who own both.

Exercises 11.2

Self-Check Exercises

SC 11-1 A brand manager is concerned that her brand's share may be unevenly distributed throughout the country. In a survey in which the country was divided into four geographic regions, a random sampling of 100 consumers in each region was surveyed, with the following results:

	REGION				
	NE	NW	SE	SW	TOTAL
Purchase the brand	40	55	45	50	190
Do not purchase	60	45	55	50	210
Total	**100**	**100**	**100**	**100**	**400**

Develop a table of observed and expected frequencies for this problem.

SC 11-2 For Exercise SC 11-1:

(a) Calculate the sample χ^2 value.

(b) State the null and alternative hypotheses.

(c) At $\alpha = 0.05$, test whether brand share is the same across the four regions.

Basic Concepts

11-6 Given the following dimensions for contingency tables, how many degrees of freedom will the chi-square statistic for each have?

(a) 5 rows, 4 columns.

(b) 6 rows, 2 columns.

(c) 3 rows, 7 columns.

(d) 4 rows, 4 columns.

Applications

11-7 An advertising firm is trying to determine the demographics for a new product. They have randomly selected 75 people in each of 5 different age groups and introduced the product to them. The results of the survey are given below:

Future Activity	18–29	30–39	Age Group 40–49	50–59	60–69
Purchase frequently	12	18	17	22	32
Seldom purchase	18	25	29	24	30
Never purchase	45	32	29	29	13

Develop a table of observed and expected frequencies for this problem.

11-8 For Exercise 11-7:

(a) Calculate the sample χ^2 value.

(b) State the null and alternative hypotheses.

(c) If the level of significance is 0.01, should the null hypothesis be rejected?

11-9 To see whether silicon chip sales are independent of where the U.S. economy is in the business cycle, data have been collected on the weekly sales of Zippy Chippy, a Silicon Valley firm, and on whether the U.S. economy was rising to a cycle peak, at a cycle peak, falling to a cycle trough, or at a cycle trough. The results are:

	WEEKLY CHIP SALES High	Medium	Low	TOTAL
Economy				
At Peak	20	7	3	30
At Trough	30	40	30	100
Rising	20	8	2	30
Falling	30	5	5	40
Total	**100**	**60**	**40**	**200**

Calculate a table of observed and expected frequencies for this problem.

11-10 For Exercise 11-9:

(a) State the null and alternative hypotheses.

(b) Calculate the sample χ^2 value.

(c) At the 0.10 significance level, what is your conclusion?

11-11 A financial consultant is interested in the differences in capital structure within different firm sizes in a certain industry. The consultant surveys a group of firms with assets of different amounts and divides the firms into three groups. Each firm is classified according to whether its total debt is greater than stockholders' equity or whether its total debt is less than stockholders' equity. The results of the survey are:

	Firm Asset Size (in $ thousands) <500	500–2,000	2,000+	Total
Debt less than equity	7	10	8	**25**
Debt greater than equity	10	18	9	**37**
Total	**17**	**28**	**17**	**62**

Do the three firm sizes have the same capital structure? Use the 0.10 significance level.

11-12 A newspaper publisher, trying to pinpoint his market's characteristics, wondered whether newspaper readership in the community is related to readers' educational achievement. A survey questioned adults in the area on their level of education and their frequency of readership. The results are shown in the following table.

FREQUENCY OF READERSHIP	Professional or postgraduate	College graduate	High school grad	Did not complete high school	TOTAL
	LEVEL OF EDUCATIONAL ACHIEVEMENT				
Never	10	17	11	21	59
Sometimes	12	23	8	5	48
Morning or evening	35	38	16	7	96
Both editions	28	19	6	13	66
Total	**85**	**97**	**41**	**46**	**269**

At the 0.10 significance level, does the frequency of newspaper readership in the community differ according to the readers' level of education?

11-13 An educator has the opinion that the grades high school students make depend on the amount of time they spend listening to music. To test this theory, he has randomly given 400 students a questionnaire. Within the questionnaire are the two questions: "How many hours per week do you listen to music?" "What is the average grade for all your classes?" The data from the survey are in the following table. Using a 5 percent significance level, test whether grades and time spent listening to music are independent or dependent.

HOURS SPENT LISTENING TO MUSIC	A	B	C	D	F	TOTAL
			AVERAGE GRADE			
<5 hrs.	13	10	11	16	5	55
5–10 hrs.	20	27	27	19	2	95
11–20 hrs.	9	27	71	16	32	155
> 20 hrs.	8	11	41	24	11	95
Total	**50**	**75**	**150**	**75**	**50**	**400**

Worked-Out Answers to Self-Check Exercises

SC 11-1

	Region			
	NE	NW	SE	SW
Purchasers				
Observed	40	55	45	50
Expected	47.5	47.5	47.5	47.5
Nonpurchasers				
Observed	60	45	55	50
Expected	52.5	52.5	52.5	52.5

SC 11-2 (a)

f_o	f_e	$f_o - f_e$	$(f_o - f_e)^2$	$\frac{(f_o - f_e)^2}{f_e}$
40	47.5	−7.5	56.25	1.184
55	47.5	7.5	56.25	1.184
45	47.5	−2.5	6.25	0.132
50	47.5	2.5	6.25	0.132
60	52.5	7.5	56.25	1.071
45	52.5	−7.5	56.25	1.071
55	52.5	2.5	6.25	0.119
50	52.5	−2.5	6.25	0.119

$$\chi^2 = \sum \frac{(f_o - f_e)^2}{f_e} = 5.012$$

(b) Two ways, either acceptable:

(1) H_0: Region is independent of purchasing

H_1: Region is related to purchasing (dependent)

(2) H_0: $p_{ne} = p_{nw} = p_{se} = p_{sw}$

H_1: Not all the proportions are equal

(c) With $1 \times 3 = 3$ degrees of freedom and $\alpha = 0.05$, the critical value of χ^2 is 7.815, so don't reject H_0, because $5.012 < 7.815$. Brand share doesn't differ significantly by region.

11.3 Chi-Square as a Test of Goodness of Fit: Testing the Appropriateness of a Distribution

In the preceding section, we used the chi-square test to decide whether to accept a null hypothesis that was a hypothesis of independence between two variables. In our example, these two variables were attitude toward job performance reviews and geographical region.

Function of a goodness-of-fit test

The chi-square test can also be used to decide whether a particular probability distribution, such as the binomial, Poisson, or normal, is the *appropriate* distribution. This is an important ability because as decision makers using statistics, we will need to choose a certain probability distribution to represent the distribution of the data we happen to be considering. We will need the ability to question how far we can go from the assumptions that underlie a particular distribution before we must conclude that this distribution is no longer applicable. **The chi-square test enables us to ask this question and to test whether there is a significant difference between an observed frequency distribution and a theoretical frequency distribution.** In this manner, we can determine the *goodness of fit* of a theoretical distribution (that is, how well it fits the distribution of data that we have actually observed). Thus, we can determine whether we should believe that the observed data constitute a sample drawn from the hypothesized theoretical distribution.

Calculating Observed and Expected Frequencies

Suppose that the Gordon Company requires that college seniors who are seeking positions with it be interviewed by three different executives. This enables the company to obtain a consensus evaluation of each candidate. Each executive gives the candidate either a positive or a negative rating. Table 11-8 contains the interview results of the last 100 candidates.

Table 11-8 Interview Results of 100 Candidates

Possible Positive Ratings from Three Interviews	Number of Candidates Receiving Each of These Ratings
0	18
1	47
2	24
3	11
	100

For staffing purposes, the director of recruitment for this company thinks that the interview process can be approximated by a binomial distribution with $p = 0.40$, that is, with a 40 percent chance of any candidate receiving a positive rating on any one interview. If the director wants to test this hypothesis at the 0.20 level of significance, how should he proceed?

Stating the problem symbolically

H_0: A binomial distribution with $p = 0.40$ is a good description of the interview process ← Null hypothesis

H_1: A binomial distribution with $p = 0.40$ is *not* a good description of the interview process ← Alternative hypothesis

$\alpha = 0.20$ ← Level of significance for testing these hypotheses

Calculating the binomial probabilities

To solve this problem, we must determine whether the discrepancies between the observed frequencies and those we would expect (if the binomial distribution *is* the proper model to use) should be ascribed to chance. We can begin by determining what the binomial probabilities would be for this interview situation. For three interviews, we would find the probability of success in the Binomial Distribution Table (Appendix Table 3) by looking for the column labeled $n = 3$ and $p = 0.40$. The results are summarized in Table 11-9.

Now we can use the theoretical binomial probabilities of the outcomes to compute the expected frequencies. By comparing these expected frequencies with our observed frequencies using the χ^2 test, we can examine the extent of the difference between them. Table 11-10 lists the observed frequencies, the appropriate binomial probabilities from Table 11-9, and the expected frequencies for the sample of 100 interviews.

Table 11-9 Binomial Probabilities for Interview Problem

Possible Positive Ratings from Three Interviews	Binomial Probabilities of These Outcomes
0	0.2160
1	0.4320
2	0.2880
3	0.0640
	1.0000

Table 11-10 Observed Frequencies, Appropriate Binomial Probabilities, and Expected Frequencies for the Interview Problem

Possible Positive Ratings from Three Interviews	Observed Frequency of Candidates Receiving These Ratings	Binomial Probability of Possible Outcomes		Number of Candidates Interviewed		Expected Frequency of Candidates Receiving These Ratings
0	18	0.2160	×	100	=	21.6
1	47	0.4320	×	100	=	43.2
2	24	0.2880	×	100	=	28.8
3	11	0.0640	×	100	=	6.4
	100	**1.0000**				**100.0**

Table 11-11

Calculation of the χ^2 Statistic from the Interview Data Listed in Table 11-10

Observed Frequency (f_o)	Expected Frequency (f_e)	$f_o - f_e$	$(f_o - f_e)^2$	$\frac{(f_o - f_e)^2}{f_e}$
18	21.6	−3.6	12.96	0.6000
47	43.2	3.8	14.44	0.3343
24	28.8	−4.8	23.04	0.8000
11	6.4	4.6	21.16	3.3063
				5.0406

$$\sum\frac{(f_o - f_e)^2}{f_e} = 5.0406 \leftarrow \chi^2$$

Calculating the Chi-Square Statistic

To compute the chi-square statistic for this problem, we can use Equation 11-1:

$$\chi^2 = \sum\frac{(f_o - f_e)^2}{f_e} \qquad [11\text{-}1]$$

and the format we introduced in Table 11-4. This process is illustrated in Table 11-11.

Determining Degrees of Freedom in a Goodness-of-Fit Test

First, count the number of classes

Before we can calculate the appropriate number of degrees of freedom for a chi-square goodness-of-fit test, we must count the number of classes (symbolized k) for which we have compared the observed and expected frequencies. Our interview problem contains four such classes: 0, 1, 2, and 3 positive ratings. Thus, we begin with 4 degrees of freedom. Yet because the four observed frequencies must sum to 100, the total number of observed frequencies we can freely specify is only $k - 1$, or 3. The fourth is determined because the total of the four has to be 100.

Then, subtract degrees of freedom lost from estimating population parameters

To solve a goodness-of-fit problem, we may be forced to impose additional restrictions on the calculation of the degrees of freedom. Suppose we are using the chi-square test as a goodness-of-fit test to determine whether a normal distribution fits a set of observed frequencies. If we have six classes of observed frequencies ($k = 6$), then we would conclude that we have only $k - 1$, or 5 degrees of freedom. If, however, we also have to use the sample mean as an estimate of the population mean, we will have to subtract an additional degree of freedom, which leaves us with only 4. And, third, if we have to use the sample standard deviation to estimate the population standard deviation, we will have to subtract *one more* degree of freedom, leaving us with 3. Our general rule in these cases is, **first employ the (k − 1) rule and then subtract an additional degree of freedom for each population parameter that has to be estimated from the sample data.**

In the interview example, we have four classes of observed frequencies. As a result, $k = 4$, and the appropriate number of degrees of freedom is $k - 1$, or 3. We are not required to estimate any population parameter, so we need not reduce this number further.

Using the Chi-Square Goodness-of-Fit Test

Finding the limit of the acceptance region

In the interview problem, the company desires to test the hypothesis of goodness of fit at the 0.20 level of significance. In Appendix Table 5, then, we must look under the 0.20 column and move down to the row labeled 3 degrees of freedom. There we find that the value

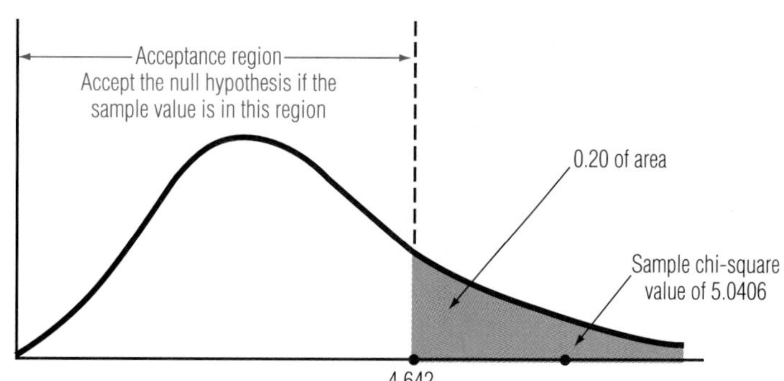

FIGURE 11-7

Goodness-of-fit test at the 0.20 level of significance, showing acceptance region and sample chi-square value of 5.0406

of the chi-square statistic is 4.642. We can interpret this value as follows: With 3 degrees of freedom, the region to the right of a chi-square value of 4.642 contains 0.20 of the area under the curve.

Illustrating the problem

Figure 11-7 illustrates a chi-square distribution with 3 degrees of freedom, showing in color a 0.20 level of significance. Notice that the acceptance region for the null hypothesis (the hypothesis that the sample data came from a binomial distribution with $p = 0.4$) extends from the left tail to the chi-square value of 4.642. Obviously, the sample chi-square value of 5.0406 falls outside this acceptance region. Therefore, we reject the null hypothesis and conclude that the binomial distribution with $p = 0.4$ fails to provide a good description of our observed frequencies.

Interpreting the results

HINTS & ASSUMPTIONS

Lots of folks know that a chi-square test can be used as a test of goodness of fit, and most of them can do the calculations. But fewer of them can explain the logic in using the test for this purpose in common-sense terms. Hint: If we have a distribution that we *think* may be normal, but we're not sure, we use a known normal distribution to generate the *expected values* and then using chi-square methods, we see how much difference there is between these expected values and the values we observed in a sample taken from the distribution we think is normal. If the difference is too large, our distribution isn't normal.

Exercises 11.3

Self-Check Exercises

SC 11-3 At the 0.10 level of significance, can we conclude that the following 400 observations follow a Poisson distribution with $\lambda = 3$?

Number of arrivals per hour	0	1	2	3	4	5 or more
Number of hours	20	57	98	85	78	62

SC 11-4 After years of working at a weighing station for trucks, Jeff Simpson feels that the weight per truck (in thousands of pounds) follows a normal distribution with $\mu = 71$ and $\sigma = 15$. In order to test this assumption, Jeff collected the following data one Monday, recording the weight of each truck that entered his station.

85	57	60	81	89	63	52	65	77	64
89	86	90	60	57	61	95	78	66	92
50	56	95	60	82	55	61	81	61	53
63	75	50	98	63	77	50	62	79	69
76	66	97	67	54	93	70	80	67	73

If Jeff used a chi-square goodness-of-fit test on these data, what would he conclude about the trucks' weight distribution? (Use a 0.10 significance level and be sure to state the hypotheses of interest.) (*Hint:* Use five equally probable intervals.)

Basic Concepts

11-14 Below is an observed frequency distribution. Using a normal distribution with $\mu = 5$ and $\sigma = 1.5$,

(a) Find the probability of falling in each class.

(b) From part (a), compute the expected frequency of each category.

(c) Calculate the chi-square statistic.

(d) At the 0.10 level of significance, does this frequency distribution seem to be well described by the suggested normal distribution?

Observed value of the variable	<2.6	2.6–3.79	3.8–4.99	5–6.19	6.2–7.39	≥7.4
Observed frequency	6	30	41	52	12	9

11-15 At the 0.05 level of significance, can we conclude the following data follow a Poisson distribution with $\lambda = 5$?

Number of calls per minute	0	1	2	3	4	5	6	7 or more
Frequency of occurrences	4	15	42	60	89	94	52	80

Applications

11-16 Louis Armstrong, salesman for the Dillard Paper Company, has five accounts to visit per day. It is suggested that the variable, sales by Mr. Armstrong, may be described by the binomial distribution, with the probability of selling each account being 0.4. Given the following frequency distribution of Armstrong's number of sales per day, can we conclude that the data do in fact follow the suggested distribution? Use the 0.05 significance level.

Number of sales per day	0	1	2	3	4	5
Frequency of the number of sales	10	41	60	20	6	3

11-17 The computer coordinator for the business school believes the amount of time a graduate student spends reading and writing e-mail each weekday is normally distributed with mean $\mu = 14$ and standard deviation $\sigma = 5$. In order to examine this belief, the coordinator collected data one Wednesday, recording the amount of time in minutes each graduate student spent checking e-mail. Using a chi-square goodness-of-fit test on these data, what would you conclude about the distribution of e-mail times? (Use a 0.05 significance level and clearly state your hypotheses.) (*Hint:* Use five equally probable intervals.)

8.2	7.4	9.6	12.8	22.4	6.2	8.7	9.7	12.4	10.6
1.2	18.6	3.3	15.7	18.4	12.4	15.9	19.4	12.8	20.4
12.3	11.3	10.9	18.4	14.3	16.2	6.7	13.9	18.3	19.2
14.3	14.9	16.7	11.3	18.4	18.8	20.4	12.4	18.1	20.1

11-18 In order to plan how much cash to keep on hand in the vault, a bank is interested in seeing whether the average deposit of a customer is normally distributed. A newly hired employee hoping for a raise has collected the following information:

Deposit	\$0–\$999	\$1,000–\$1,999	\$2,000 or more
Observed frequency	20	65	25

(a) Compute the expected frequencies if the data are normally distributed with mean \$1,500 and standard deviation \$600.

(b) Compute the chi-square statistic.

(c) State explicit null and alternative hypotheses.

(d) Test your hypotheses at the 0.10 level and state an explicit conclusion.

11-19 The post office is interested in modeling the mangled-letter problem. It has been suggested that any letter sent to a certain area has a 0.15 chance of being mangled. Because the post office is so big, it can be assumed that two letters' chances of being mangled are independent. A sample of 310 people was selected and two test letters were mailed to each of them. The number of people receiving zero, one, or two mangled letters was 260, 40, and 10, respectively. At the 0.10 level of significance, is it reasonable to conclude that the number of mangled letters received by people follows a binomial distribution with $p = 0.15$?

11-20 A state lottery commission claims that for a new lottery game, there is a 10 percent chance of getting a \$1 prize, a 5 percent chance of \$100, and an 85 percent chance of getting nothing. To test whether this claim is correct, a winner from the last lottery went out and bought 1,000 tickets for the new lottery. He had 87 one-dollar prizes, 48 hundred-dollar prizes, and 865 worthless tickets. At the 0.05 significance level, is the state's claim reasonable?

11-21 Dennis Barry, a hospital administrator, has examined past records from 210 randomly selected 8-hour shifts to determine the frequency with which the hospital treats fractures. The numbers of days in which zero, one, two, three, four, or five or more patients with broken bones were treated were 25, 55, 65, 35, 20, and 10, respectively. At the 0.05 level of significance, can we reasonably believe that the incidence of broken-bone cases follows a Poisson distribution with $\lambda = 2$?

11-22 A large city fire department calculates that for any given precinct, during any given 8-hour shift, there is a 30 percent chance of receiving at least one fire alarm. Here is a random sampling of 60 days:

Number of shifts during which alarms were received	0	1	2	3
Number of days	16	27	11	6

At the 0.05 level of significance, do these fire alarms follow a binomial distribution? (*Hint:* Combine the last two groups so that all expected frequencies are greater than 5.)

11-23 A diligent statistics student wants to see whether it is reasonable to assume that some sales data have been sampled from a normal population before performing a hypothesis test on the mean sales. She collected some sales data, computed $\bar{x} = 78$ and $s = 9$, and tabulated the data as follows:

Sales level	≤ 65	66–70	71–75	76–80	81–85	≥ 86
Number of observations	10	20	40	50	40	40

(a) Is it important for the statistics student to check whether the data are normally distributed? Explain.

(b) State explicit null and alternative hypotheses for checking whether the data are normally distributed.

(c) What is the probability (using a normal distribution with $\mu = 78$ and $\sigma = 9$) that sales will be less than or equal to 65.5, between 65.5 and 70.5, between 70.5 and 75.5, between 75.5 and 80.5, between 80.5 and 85.5, and greater than or equal to 85.5?

(d) At the 0.05 level of significance, does the observed frequency distribution follow a normal distribution?

11-24 A supermarket manager is keeping track of the arrival of customers at checkout counters to see how many cashiers are needed to handle the flow. In a sample of 500 five-minute time periods, there were 22, 74, 115, 95, 94, 80, and 20 periods in which zero, one, two, three, four, five, or six or more customers, respectively, arrived at a checkout counter. Are these data consistent at the 0.05 level of significance with a Poisson distribution with $\lambda = 3$?

11-25 A professional baseball player, Lon Dakestraw, was at bat five times in each of 100 games. Lon claims that he has a probability of 0.4 of getting a hit each time he goes to bat. Test his claim at the 0.05 level by seeing whether the following data are distributed binomially ($p = 0.4$). (*Note:* Combine classes if the expected number of observations is less than 5).

Number of Hits per Game	Number of Games with That Number of Hits
0	12
1	38
2	27
3	17
4	5
5	1

Worked-Out Answers to Self-Check Exercises

SC 11-3 H_0: Poisson with $\lambda = 3$

H_1: Something else

Test at $\alpha = 0.10$, with $6 - 1 = 5$ degrees of freedom.

Arrivals/hour	0	1	2	3	4	5+
Poisson prob.	0.0498	0.1494	0.2240	0.2240	0.1680	0.1848
Observed	20	57	98	85	78	62
Expected	19.92	59.76	89.60	89.60	62.20	73.92
$\frac{(f_o - f_e)^2}{f_e}$	0.000	0.127	0.788	0.236	1.736	1.922

$$\chi^2 = \sum \frac{(f_o - f_e)^2}{f_e} = 4.809$$

With 5 degrees of freedom and $\alpha = 0.10$, the critical value of χ^2 is 9.236, so don't reject H_0, because $4.809 < 9.236$. The data are well described by a Poisson distribution with $\lambda = 3$.

SC 11-4 5 equiprobable intervals; 0.2 probability for each interval, $50 \times 0.2 = 10$ trucks expected per interval.

z	$-\infty$	-0.84	-0.25	0.25	0.84	$+\infty$
$x = 71 + 15z$	$-\infty$	58.40	67.25	74.75	83.60	$+\infty$
Observed	10	16	3	10	11	
Expected	10	10	10	10	10	
$\frac{(f_o - f_e)^2}{f_e}$	0.0	3.6	4.9	0.0	0.1	

$$\chi^2 = 8.6$$

H_0: Truck weights are distributed normally with $\mu = 71$ and $\sigma = 15$

H_1: The weights are distributed differently (either normal with a different μ and/or σ or a nonnormal distribution)

With $5 - 1 = 4$ degrees of freedom and $\alpha = 0.10$, the critical value of χ^2 is 7.779, so reject H_0, because $8.6 > 7.779$. The data are not well described by a normal distribution with $\mu = 71$ and $\sigma = 15$. Jeff is wrong.

11.4 Analysis of Variance

Function of analysis of variance

Earlier in this chapter, we used the chi-square test to examine the differences among more than two sample proportions and to make inferences about whether such samples are drawn from populations each having the same proportion. In this section, we will learn a technique known as ***analysis of variance*** **(often abbreviated ANOVA) that will enable us to test for the significance of the differences among more than two sample means.** Using analysis of variance, we will be able to make inferences about whether our samples are drawn from populations having the same mean.

Situations where we can use ANOVA

Analysis of variance is useful in such situations as comparing the mileage achieved by five different brands of gasoline, testing which of four different training methods produces the fastest learning record, or comparing the first-year earnings of the graduates of half a dozen different business schools. In each of these cases, we would compare the means of *more* than two samples.

Statement of the Problem

In the training director's problem that opened this chapter, she wanted to evaluate three different training methods to determine whether there were any differences in effectiveness.

Calculating the grand mean

After completion of the training period, the company's statistical staff chose 16 new employees assigned at random to the three training methods.* Counting the production output by these 16 trainees, the staff has summarized the data and calculated the mean production of the trainees (see Table 11-12). Now if we wish to determine the *grand mean,* or $\bar{\bar{x}}$ (the mean for the entire group of 16 trainees), we can use one of two methods:

1. $$\bar{\bar{x}} = \frac{15 + 18 + 19 + 22 + 11 + 22 + 27 + 18 + 21 + 17 + 18 + 24 + 19 + 16 + 22 + 15}{16}$$

$$= \frac{304}{16}$$

$$= 19 \leftarrow \text{Grand mean using all data}$$

*Although in real practice, 16 trainees would not constitute an adequate statistical sample, we have limited the number here to be able to demonstrate the basic techniques of analysis of variance and to avoid tedious calculations.

Table 11-12	Method 1	Method 2	Method 3	
Daily Production of 16 New Employees			18	
	15	22	24	
	18	27	19	
	19	18	16	
	22	21	22	
	11	17	15	
	85	**105**	**114**	
	÷5	÷5	÷6	
	$17 = \bar{x}_1$	$21 = \bar{x}_2$	$19 = \bar{x}_3$	← Sample means
	$n_1 = 5$	$n_2 = 5$	$n_3 = 6$	← Sample sizes

2. $\bar{\bar{x}} = (5/16)(17) + (5/16)(21) + (6/16)(19)$

$$= \frac{304}{16}$$

$= 19$ ← Grand mean as a weighted average of the sample means, using the relative sample sizes as the weights

Statement of the Hypotheses

In this case, our reason for using analysis of variance is to decide whether these three samples (a *sample* is the small group of employees trained by any one method) were drawn from populations (a *population* is the total number of employees who could be trained by that method) having the same means. Because we are testing the effectiveness of the three training methods, we must determine whether the three samples, represented by the sample means $\bar{x}_1 = 17$, $\bar{x}_2 = 21$, and $\bar{x}_3 = 19$, could have been drawn from populations having the same mean, μ. A formal statement of the null and alternative hypotheses we wish to test would be

Stating the problem symbolically

H_0: $\mu_1 = \mu_2 = \mu_3$ ← Null hypothesis

H_1: μ_1, μ_2, and μ_3 are *not* all equal ← Alternative hypothesis

Interpreting the results

If we can conclude from our test that the sample means do not differ significantly, we can infer that the choice of training method does not influence the productivity of the employee. On the other hand, if we find differences among the sample means that are too large to attribute to chance sampling error, we can infer that the method used in training *does* influence the productivity of the employee. In that case, we would adjust our training program accordingly.

Analysis of Variance: Basic Concepts

Assumptions made in analysis of variance

In order to use analysis of variance, we must assume that each of the samples is drawn from a normal population and that each of these populations has the same variance, σ^2. However, if the sample sizes are large enough, we do not need the assumption of normality.

In our training-methods problems, our null hypothesis states that the three populations have the same mean. If this hypothesis is true, classifying the data into three columns in Table 11-12 is unnecessary and the entire set of 16 measurements of productivity can be thought of as a sample from one population. This overall population also has a variance of σ^2.

Analysis of variance is based on a comparison of two different estimates of the variance, σ^2, of our overall population. In this case, we can calculate one of these estimates by examining **the variance among the three sample means,** which are 17, 21, and 19. The other estimate of the population variance is determined by **the variation within the three samples** themselves, that is, (15, 18, 19, 22, 11), (22, 27, 18, 21, 17), and (18, 24, 19, 16, 22, 15). Then we compare these two estimates of the population variance. Because both are estimates of σ^2, they should be approximately equal in value *when the null hypothesis is true.* If the null hypothesis is *not* true, these two estimates will differ considerably. The three steps in analysis of variance, then, are

Steps in analysis of variance

1. Determine one estimate of the population variance from the variance *among the sample means.*
2. Determine a second estimate of the population variance from the variance *within the samples.*
3. Compare these two estimates. If they are approximately equal in value, *accept* the null hypothesis.

In the remainder of this section, we shall learn how to calculate these two estimates of the population variance, how to compare these two estimates, and how to perform a hypothesis test and interpret the results. As we learn how to do these computations, however, keep in mind that all are based on the above three steps.

Calculating the Variance among the Sample Means

Finding the first estimate of the population variance

Step 1 in analysis of variance indicates that we must obtain one estimate of the population variance from the variance among the three sample means. In statistical language, this estimate is called the *between-column variance.*

In Chapter 3, we used Equation 3-17 to calculate the sample variance:

Sample variance ⟶ $$s^2 = \frac{\Sigma(x - \bar{x})^2}{n - 1} \qquad [3\text{-}17]$$

First, find the variance among sample means

Now, because we are working with three sample means and a grand mean, let's substitute $\bar{x}$ for x, $\bar{\bar{x}}$ for $\bar{x}$, and k (the number of samples) for n to get a formula for the variance among the sample means:

Variance among the Sample Means

$$s_{\bar{x}}^2 = \frac{\Sigma(\bar{x} - \bar{\bar{x}})^2}{k - 1} \qquad [11\text{-}4]$$

Then, find the population variance using the variance among sample means

Next, we can return for a moment to Chapter 6, where we defined the standard error of the mean as the standard deviation of all possible samples of a given size. The formula to derive the standard error of the mean is Equation 6-1:

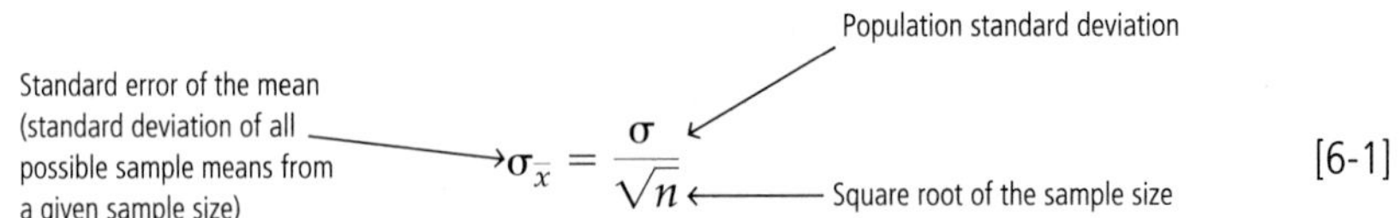

We can simplify this equation by cross-multiplying the terms and then squaring both sides in order to change the population standard deviation, σ, into the population variance, σ^2:

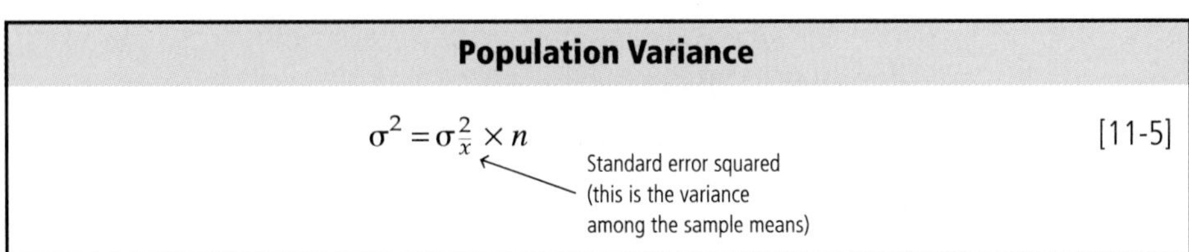

Population Variance
$\sigma^2 = \sigma_{\bar{x}}^2 \times n$
Standard error squared (this is the variance among the sample means)
[11-5]

For our training-method problem, we do not have all the information we need to use this equation to find σ^2. Specifically, we do not know $\sigma_{\bar{x}}^2$. We could, however, calculate the variance among the three sample means, $s_{\bar{x}}^2$, using Equation 11-4. So why not substitute $s_{\bar{x}}^2$ for $\sigma_{\bar{x}}^2$ in Equation 11-5 and calculate an estimate of the population variance? This will give us

$$\hat{\sigma}^2 = s_{\bar{x}}^2 \times n = \frac{\Sigma n(\bar{x} - \bar{\bar{x}})^2}{k - 1}$$

Which sample size to use

There is a slight difficulty in using this equation as it stands. In Equation 6-1, n represents the sample size, but *which* sample size should we use when the different samples have different sizes? We solve this problem with Equation 11-6, where each $(\bar{x}_j - \bar{\bar{x}})^2$ is multiplied by its own appropriate n_j.

Estimate of Between-Column Variance

First estimate of the population variance $\longrightarrow$ $$\hat{\sigma}_b^2 = \frac{\Sigma n_j(\bar{x}_j - \bar{\bar{x}})^2}{k - 1} \qquad [11\text{-}6]$$

where

- $\hat{\sigma}_b^2$ = our first estimate of the population variance based on the variance among the sample means (the *between-column variance*)
- n_j = size of the jth sample
- $\bar{x}_j$ = sample mean of the jth sample
- $\bar{\bar{x}}$ = grand mean
- k = number of samples

Now we can use Equation 11-6 and the data from Table 11-12 to calculate the between-column variance. Table 11-13 shows how to do these calculations.

Table 11-13 Calculation of the Between-Column Variance

n	$\bar{x}$	$\bar{\bar{x}}$	$\bar{x} - \bar{\bar{x}}$	$(\bar{x} - \bar{\bar{x}})^2$	$n(\bar{x} - \bar{\bar{x}})^2$
5	17	19	$17 - 19 = -2$	$(-2)^2 = 4$	$5 \times 4 = 20$
5	21	19	$21 - 19 = 2$	$(2)^2 = 4$	$5 \times 4 = 20$
6	19	19	$19 - 19 = 0$	$(0)^2 = 0$	$6 \times 0 = \underline{0}$
					$\Sigma n_j(\bar{x}_j - \bar{\bar{x}})^2 = 40$

$$\hat{\sigma}_b^2 = \frac{\Sigma n_j(\bar{x}_j - \bar{\bar{x}})^2}{k - 1} = \frac{40}{3 - 1} \quad [11\text{-}6]$$

$$= \frac{40}{2}$$

$$= 20 \text{ Between-column variance}$$

Calculating the Variance within the Samples

Finding the second estimate of the population variance

Step 2 in ANOVA requires a second estimate of the population variance based on the variance within the samples. In statistical terms, this can be called the *within-column variance.* Our employee-training problem has three samples of five or six items each. We can calculate the variance within each of these three samples using Equation 3-17:

$$\text{Sample variance} \longrightarrow s^2 = \frac{\Sigma(x - \bar{x})^2}{n - 1} \quad [3\text{-}17]$$

Because we have assumed that the variances of our three populations are the same, we could use any one of the three sample variances (s_1^2 or s_2^2 or s_3^2) as the second estimate of the population variance. Statistically, we can get a better estimate of the population variance by using a weighted average of all three sample variances. The general formula for this second estimate of σ^2 is

Estimate of Within-Column Variance

$$\text{Second estimate of the population variance} \longrightarrow \hat{\sigma}_w^2 = \Sigma\left(\frac{n_j - 1}{n_T - k}\right)s_j^2 \quad [11\text{-}7]$$

where

- $\hat{\sigma}_w^2$ = our second estimate of the population variance based on the variances within the samples (the *within-column variance*)
- n_j = size of the jth sample
- s_j^2 = sample variance of the jth sample
- k = number of samples
- $n_T = \Sigma n_j$ = total sample size

Using all the information at our disposal

This formula uses all the information we have at our disposal, not just a portion of it. Had there been seven samples instead of three, we would have taken a weighted average of all seven. The weights used in Equation 11-7 will be explained shortly. Table 11-14 illustrates how to calculate this second estimate of the population variance using the variances within all three of our samples.

Table 11-14 Calculation of Variances within the Samples and the Within-Column Variance

Training Method 1 Sample Mean: $\bar{x} = 17$		Training Method 2 Sample Mean: $\bar{x} = 21$		Training Method 3 Sample Mean: $\bar{x} = 19$	
$x - \bar{x}$	$(x - \bar{x})^2$	$x - \bar{x}$	$(x - \bar{x})^2$	$x - \bar{x}$	$(x - \bar{x})^2$
$15 - 17 = -2$	$(-2)^2 = 4$	$22-21 = 1$	$(1)^2 = 1$	$18 - 19 = -1$	$(-1)^2 = 1$
$18 - 17 = 1$	$(1)^2 = 1$	$27-21 = 6$	$(6)^2 = 36$	$24 - 19 = 5$	$(5)^2 = 25$
$19 - 17 = 2$	$(2)^2 = 4$	$18-21 = -3$	$(-3)^2 = 9$	$19 - 19 = 0$	$(0)^2 = 0$
$22 - 17 = 5$	$(5)^2 = 25$	$21-21 = 0$	$(0)^2 = 0$	$16 - 19 = -3$	$(-3)^2 = 9$
$11 - 17 = -6$	$(-6)^2 = \underline{36}$	$17-21 = -4$	$(-4)^2 = \underline{16}$	$22 - 19 = 3$	$(3)^2 = 9$
	$\Sigma(x - \bar{x})^2 = \mathbf{70}$		$\Sigma(x - \bar{x})^2 = \mathbf{62}$	$15 - 19 = -4$	$(-4)^2 = \underline{16}$
					$\Sigma(x - \bar{x})^2 = \mathbf{60}$
	$\frac{\Sigma(x - \bar{x})^2}{n-1} = \frac{70}{5-1} = \frac{70}{4}$		$\frac{\Sigma(x - \bar{x})^2}{n-1} = \frac{62}{5-1} = \frac{62}{4}$		$\frac{\Sigma(x - \bar{x})^2}{n-1} = \frac{60}{6-1} = \frac{60}{5}$
Sample variance $\rightarrow s_1^2 = 17.5$		Sample variance $\rightarrow s_2^2 = 15.5$		Sample variance $\rightarrow s_3^2 = 12.0$	

And:

$$\hat{\sigma}^2 = \sum\left(\frac{n_j - 1}{n_T - k}\right)s_j^2 = (4/13)(17.5) + (4/13)(15.5) + (5/13)(12.0) \qquad [11\text{-}7]$$

$$= \frac{192}{13}$$

$$= 14.769 \leftarrow$$ Second estimate of the population variance based on the variances within the samples (the within-column variance)

The *F* Hypothesis Test: Computing and Interpreting the *F* Statistic

Finding the *F* ratio

Step 3 in ANOVA compares these two estimates of the population variance by computing their ratio, called *F*, as follows:

$$F = \frac{\text{first estimate of the population variance based on the variance among the sample means}}{\text{second estimate of the population variance based on the variances within the samples}} \qquad [11\text{-}8]$$

If we substitute the statistical shorthand for the numerator and denominator of this ratio, Equation 11-8 becomes

F Statistic

$$F = \frac{\text{between–column variance}}{\text{within–column variance}} = \frac{\hat{\sigma}_b^2}{\hat{\sigma}_w^2} \qquad [11\text{-}9]$$

Now we can find the *F ratio* for the training-method problem with which we have been working:

$$F = \frac{\text{between–column variance}}{\text{within–column variance}} = \frac{\hat{\sigma}_b^2}{\hat{\sigma}_w^2} \qquad [11\text{-}9]$$

$$= \frac{20}{14.769}$$

$$= 1.354 \leftarrow F \text{ ratio}$$

Interpreting the F ratio

Having found this F ratio of 1.354, how can we interpret it? First, examine the denominator, which is based on the variance within the samples. The denominator is a good estimator of σ^2 (the population variance) whether the null hypothesis is true or not. What about the numerator? If the null hypothesis that the three methods of training have equal effects is true, then the numerator, or the variation among the sample means of the three methods, is also a good estimate of σ^2 (the population variance). As a result, **the denominator and numerator should be about equal if the null hypothesis is true.** The nearer the F ratio comes to 1, then the more we are inclined to accept the null hypothesis. Conversely, as the F ratio becomes larger, we will be more inclined to reject the null hypothesis and accept the alternative (that a difference does exist in the effects of the three training methods).

Shortly, we shall learn a more formal way of deciding when to accept or reject the null hypothesis. But even now, you should understand the basic logic behind the *F statistic.* **When populations are not the same, the between-column variance (which was derived from the variance among the sample means) tends to be larger than the within-column variance (which was derived from the variances within the samples), and the value of F tends to be large. This leads us to reject the null hypothesis.**

The *F* Distribution

Describing an F distribution

Like other statistics we have studied, if the null hypothesis is true, then the F statistic has a particular sampling distribution. Like the t and chi-square distributions, this F distribution is actually a whole family of distributions, three of which are shown in Figure 11-8. Notice that each is identified by a *pair* of degrees of freedom, unlike the t and chi-square distributions, which have only one value for the number of degrees of freedom. **The first number is the number of degrees of freedom in the numerator of the F ratio; the second is the degrees of freedom in the denominator.**

As we can see in Figure 11-8, the F distribution has a single mode. The specific shape of an F distribution depends on the number of degrees of freedom in both the numerator and the denominator of the F ratio. But, in general, the F distribution is skewed to the right and tends to become more symmetrical as the numbers of degrees of freedom in the numerator and denominator increase.

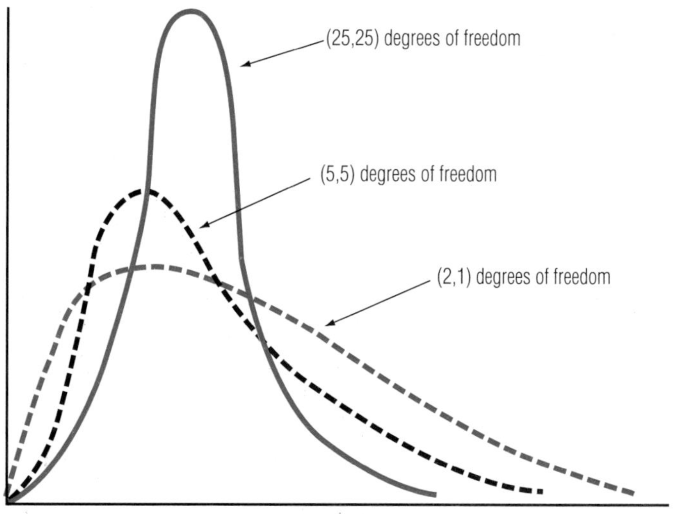

FIGURE 11-8

Three F distributions (first value in parentheses equals number of degrees of freedom in the numerator of the F ratio; second equals number of degrees of freedom in the denominator)

Using the F Distribution: Degrees of Freedom

Calculating degrees of freedom

As we have mentioned, each F distribution has a pair of degrees of freedom, one for the numerator of the F ratio and the other for the denominator. How can we calculate both of these?

Finding the numerator degrees of freedom

First, think about the numerator, the between-column variance. In Table 11-13, we used three values of $\bar{x} - \bar{\bar{x}}$, one for each sample, to calculate $\Sigma n_j(\bar{x}_j - \bar{\bar{x}})^2$. Once we knew two of these $\bar{x} - \bar{\bar{x}}$ values, the third was *automatically determined* and could not be freely specified. Thus, one degree of freedom is lost when we calculate the between-column variance, and the number of degrees of freedom for the numerator of the F ratio is always one fewer than the number of samples. The rule, then, is

Numerator Degrees of Freedom

$$\text{Number of degrees of freedom in the } \textit{numerator} \text{ of the } F \text{ ratio} = (\text{number of samples} - 1) \quad [11\text{-}10]$$

Finding the denominator degrees of freedom

Now, what of the denominator? Look at Table 11-14 for a moment. There we calculated the variances within the samples, and we used all three samples. For the jth sample, we used n_j values of $(x - \bar{x}_j)$ to calculate the $\Sigma(x - \bar{x}_j)^2$ for that sample. Once we knew all but one of these $(x - \bar{x}_j)$ values, the last was *automatically determined* and could not be freely specified. Thus, we lost 1 degree of freedom in the calculations for *each* sample, leaving us with 4, 4, and 5 degrees of freedom in the samples. Because we had three samples, we were left with $4 + 4 + 5 = 13$ degrees of freedom (which could also be calculated as $5 + 5 + 6 - 3 = 13$). We can state the rule like this:

Denominator Degrees of Freedom

$$\text{Number of degrees of freedom in the } \textit{denominator} \text{ of the } F \text{ ratio} = \Sigma(n_j - 1) = n_T - k \quad [11\text{-}11]$$

where

- n_j = size of the jth sample
- k = number of samples
- $n_T = \Sigma n_j$ = total sample size

Now we can see that the weight assigned to s_j^2 in Equation 11-7 on p. 595 was just its fraction of the total number of degrees of freedom in the denominator of the F ratio.

Using the F Table

To do F hypothesis tests, we shall use an F table in which the columns represent the number of degrees of freedom for the numerator and the rows represent the degrees of freedom for the denominator. Separate tables exist for each level of significance.

Suppose we are testing a hypothesis at the 0.01 level of significance, using the F distribution. Our degrees of freedom are 8 for the numerator and 11 for the denominator. In this instance, we would turn to Appendix Table 6(b). In the body of that table, the appropriate value for 8 and 11 degrees of freedom is 4.74. If our calculated sample value of F exceeds this table value of 4.74, we would reject the null hypothesis. If not, we would accept it.

Testing the Hypothesis

Finding the F statistic and the degrees of freedom

We can now test our hypothesis that the three different training methods produce identical results, using the material we have developed to this point. Let's begin by reviewing how we calculated the F ratio:

$$F = \frac{\text{first estimate of the population variance based on the variance among the sample means}}{\text{second estimate of the population variance based on the variances within the samples}} \quad [11\text{-}8]$$

$$= \frac{20}{14.769}$$

$$= 1.354 \leftarrow F \text{ statistic}$$

Next, calculate the number of degrees of freedom in the numerator of the F ratio, using Equation 11-10 as follows:

$$\text{Number of degrees of freedom in the } \textit{numerator} \text{ of the } F \text{ ratio} = (\text{number of samples} - 1) \quad [11\text{-}10]$$

$$= 3 - 1$$

$$= 2 \leftarrow \text{Degrees of freedom in the numerator}$$

And we can calculate the number of degrees of freedom in the denominator of the F ratio by use of Equation 11-11:

$$\text{Number of degrees of freedom in the } \textit{denominator} \text{ of the } F \text{ ratio} = \Sigma(n_j - 1) = n_T - k \quad [11\text{-}11]$$

$$= (5 - 1) + (5 - 1) + (6 - 1)$$

$$= 4 + 4 + 5$$

$$= 13 \leftarrow \text{Degrees of freedom in the denominator}$$

Finding the limit of the acceptance region

Suppose the director of training wants to test at the 0.05 level the hypothesis that there are no differences among the three training methods. We can look in Appendix Table 6(a) for 2 degrees of freedom in the numerator and 13 in the denominator. The value we find there is 3.81. Figure 11-9 shows this hypothesis test graphically. The colored region represents the level of significance. The table value of 3.81 sets the upper limit of the acceptance region. Because the calculated sample value for F of 1.354 lies within the acceptance region, we would accept the null hypothesis and conclude that, according to the sample information we have, there are no significant differences in the effects of the three training methods on employee productivity.

Interpreting the results

Precautions about Using the *F* Test

Use large sample sizes

As we stated earlier, our sample sizes in this problem are too small for us to be able to draw valid inferences about the effectiveness of the various training methods. We chose small samples so that we could explain the logic of analysis of variance without tedious calculations. In actual practice, our methodology would be the same, but our samples would be larger.

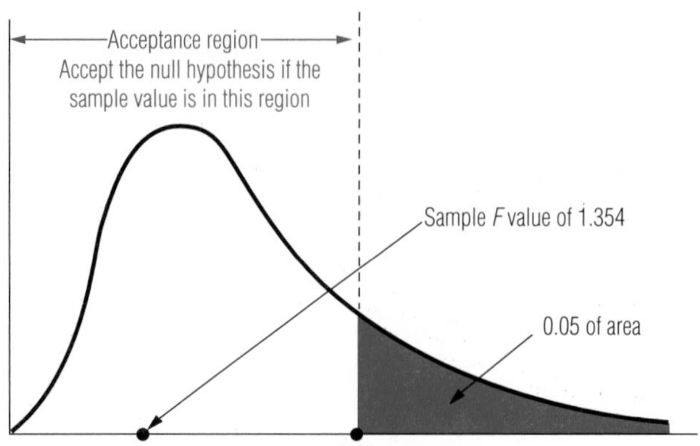

FIGURE 11-9

Hypothesis test at the 0.05 level of significance, using the F distribution and showing the acceptance region and the sample F value

Control all factors but the one being tested

In our example, we have assumed the absence of many factors that might have affected our conclusions. We accepted as given, for example, the fact that all the new employees we sampled had the same demonstrated aptitude for learning, which may or may not be true. We assumed that all the instructors of the three training methods had the same ability to teach and to manage, which may not be true. And we assumed that the company's statistical staff collected the data on productivity during work periods that were similar in terms of time of day, day of the week, time of the year, and so on. To be able to make significant decisions based on analysis of variance, we need to be certain that all these factors are effectively controlled.

A test for one factor only

Finally, notice that we have discussed only *one-way,* or one-factor, analysis of variance. Our problem examined the effect of the type of training method on employee productivity, nothing else. Had we wished to measure the effect of two factors, such as the training program and the age of the employee, we would need the ability to use two-way analysis of variance, a statistical method best saved for more advanced textbooks.

Using the Computer for Analysis of Variance

Using SAS for ANOVA

Once again, let us repeat that we used small sample sizes in our ANOVA example so we could explain the logic of the method without getting bogged down in tedious calculations. For a realistic problem, it would be very convenient to use the ANOVA routines that can be found in all the commonly used statistical packages. So that you can compare one of these with the analysis that we did by hand, Figure 11-10 gives the output when SAS is used to analyze the data in our training-method problem.

Let's look first at the column of SAS's ANOVA table headed "MEAN SQUARE." In the row labeled "MODEL," this column contains the value 20.000, which we recognize as the between-column variance we calculated in Table 11-13. In the row labeled "ERROR," we find the value 14.769, which is the within-column variance we calculated in Table 11-14. Notice also the column headed "DF" (meaning degrees of freedom). It tells us that the MODEL MEAN SQUARE (the between-column variance) has 2 degrees of freedom and the ERROR MEAN SQUARE (the within-column variance) has 13 degrees of freedom.

The last line of the output gives the value of the F statistic, $F = 1.35$, and the prob value 0.2923, which is the probability of getting an F statistic as large or larger than 1.35 if H_0 is true. Because the prob value is larger than our significance level of $\alpha = 0.05$, we conclude that we cannot reject H_0. On the basis of the sample evidence, these three training methods do not appear to have significantly different effects on employee productivity.

Figure 11-11 illustrates the use of Minitab to perform the same test. Minitab provides essentially the same ANOVA table, along with n, $\bar{x}$, and s for the three samples.

```
ILLUSTRATING THE USE OF SAS FOR ANOVA
DOES PRODUCTIVITY DEPEND ON TRAINING METHOD?

ANALYSIS OF VARIANCE PROCEDURE

DEPENDENT VARIABLE:   UNITSUNITS PRODUCED BY TRAINEE

SOURCE              DF     SUM OF SQUARES    MEAN SQUARE

MODEL                2        40.00000000    20.00000000

ERROR               13       192.00000000    14.76923077

CORRECTED TOTAL     15       232.00000000

MODEL F =         1.35                  PR > F = 0.2923
```

FIGURE 11-10

Output from SAS for the employee-training problem

```
One-Way Analysis of Variance

Analysis of Variance
Source      DF        SS        MS        F        p
Factor       2      40.0      20.0     1.35    0.292
Error       13     192.0      14.8
Total       15     232.0

 Level       N      Mean     StDev
METHOD 1     5    17.000     4.183
METHOD 2     5    21.000     3.937
METHOD 3     6    19.000     3.464

Pooled StDev =     3.843
```

FIGURE 11-11

Minitab output for the employee-training problem

Now that we've seen how to interpret the SAS and Minitab output, let's analyze a much more realistic example. Despite the conclusion we reached on pages 489–491 that students in the faculty-taught sections of our statistics course didn't do significantly better on the final exam than students who were taught by teaching assistants, we still received complaints. "I'm in Mr. Jackson's class, and my friends in Professor Rubin's class are learning much more than I am" was typical of what we were hearing. We began to wonder whether perhaps there were *significant differences among the individual sections of the course,* even if the teaching assistants *as a group* were not significantly different from the faculty *as a group.*

We used the Minitab ANOVA procedure to check this out. The formal statement of our hypotheses was

H_0: All six μ's are the same (no difference among sections)

H_1: The six μ's are not the same (sections differ significantly)

Conclusion about student complaints

The output from this analysis is shown in Figure 11-12. The calculated value of the F statistic is 1.75, and the probability of observing such a large value of F if H_0 is true (the prob value for this test) is 0.126. With such a large prob value, we must accept H_0 and conclude that there were no significant differences in the six sections' performances on the final exam.

One-Way Analysis of Variance

Analysis of Variance on FINAL

Source	DF	SS	MS	F	p
SECTION	5	859.4	171.9	1.75	0.126
Error	193	18996.8	98.4		
Total	198	19856.2			

Level	N	Mean	StDev
1	27	45.741	10.679
2	46	44.761	11.900
3	37	49.081	7.365
4	26	44.923	8.064
5	36	44.333	10.373
6	27	42.111	9.435

Pooled StDev = 9.921

FIGURE 11-12

Minitab output for ANOVA of final exam scores

Using ANOVA on the earnings data

Let's use Minitab to do an analysis of variance on the earnings data in Appendix Table 11. Recall that on pages 491–492, we used Minitab to test whether the year-to-year changes in last-quarter earnings for New York Stock Exchange stocks had a different mean than the year-to-year changes in last-quarter earnings for American Stock Exchange and over-the-counter stocks. We grouped the latter two together because at that point we didn't yet know how to compare more than two means. Now let's look at all three groups separately and use analysis of variance to see whether the three means differ significantly.

$$H_0: \mu_{OTC} = \mu_{ASE} = \mu_{NYSE} \text{ (no differences by exchange)}$$

$$H_1: \text{the } \mu\text{'s are not equal (exchanges differ significantly)}$$

Interpreting the results

We used the ONEWAY command in Minitab to perform this analysis of variance. Recall that the MARKET variable is 1 for OTC, 2 for ASE, and 3 for NYSE. The results are given in Figure 11-13. The calculated value of the *F* statistic is 0.88 and the prob value for test-

FIGURE 11-13

Using Minitab for ANOVA of earnings changes

One-Way Analysis of Variance

Analysis of Variance on CHANGE

Source	DF	SS	MS	F	p
MARKET	2	1.421	0.711	0.88	0.415
Error	221	177.906	0.805		
Total	223	179.327			

Level	N	Mean	StDev
1	111	-0.1120	0.5195
2	38	0.0876	0.9121
3	75	0.0156	1.2598

Pooled StDev = 0.8972

ing our hypotheses is 0.415. Because this prob value is larger than all of our customary levels of significance ($\alpha = 0.10, 0.05, 0.01$, and so on), we cannot reject H_0; we conclude that the mean values of year-to-year changes in last-quarter earnings on the three exchanges are not significantly different from each other.

HINTS & ASSUMPTIONS

The focus of analysis of variance is to test whether three or more samples have been drawn from populations having the same mean. Analysis of variance is important in research such as the evaluation of new drugs, where we need to examine the effects of dose, frequency of medication, effects of other drugs, and patient differences in a single study. Analysis of variance compares two estimates of the population variance. One estimate comes from the variance among the sample means, the other from the variance within the samples themselves. If they are approximately equal, the chances are high that the samples came from the same population. Warning: It's vital not to abandon common sense when interpreting results. While it may be true that a study can identify differences in brand preferences for instant coffee that apply to coffee purchases made on weekday mornings, it's hard to say what a coffee company should do with this information.

Exercises 11.4

Self-Check Exercises

SC 11–5 A study compared the effects of four 1-month point-of-purchase promotions on sales. The unit sales for five stores using all four promotions in different months follow.

Free sample	78	87	81	89	85
One-pack gift	94	91	87	90	88
Cents off	73	78	69	83	76
Refund by mail	79	83	78	69	81

(a) Compute the mean unit sales for each promotion and then determine the grand mean.

(b) Estimate the population variance using the between-column variance (Equation 11-6).

(c) Estimate the population variance using the within-column variance computed from the variance within the samples.

(d) Calculate the F ratio. At the 0.01 level of significance, do the promotions produce different effects on sales?

SC 11–6 A research company has designed three different systems to clean up oil spills. The following table contains the results, measured by how much surface area (in square meters) is cleared in 1 hour. The data were found by testing each method in several trials. Are the three systems equally effective? Use the 0.05 level of significance

System A	55	60	63	56	59	55
System B	57	53	64	49	62	
System C	66	52	61	57		

Applications

■ **11-26** A study compared the number of hours of relief provided by five different brands of antacid administered to 25 different people, each with stomach acid considered strong. The results are given below:

Brand	A	B	C	D	E
	4.4	5.8	4.8	2.9	4.6
	4.6	5.2	5.9	2.7	4.3
	4.5	4.9	4.9	2.9	3.8
	4.1	4.7	4.6	3.9	5.2
	3.8	4.6	4.3	4.3	4.4

(a) Compute the mean number of hours of relief for each brand and determine the grand mean.

(b) Estimate the population variance using the between-column variance (Equation 11-6).

(c) Estimate the population variance using the within-column variance computed from the variance within the samples.

(d) Calculate the F ratio. At the 0.05 level of significance, do the brands produce significantly different amounts of relief to people with strong stomach acid?

■ **11-27** Three training methods were compared to see whether they led to greater productivity after training. The following are productivity measures for individuals trained by each method.

Method 1	45	40	50	39	53	44
Method 2	59	43	47	51	39	49
Method 3	41	37	43	40	52	37

At the 0.05 level of significance, do the three training methods lead to different levels of productivity?

■ **11-28** The following data show the number of claims processed per day for a group of four insurance company employees observed for a number of days. Test the hypothesis that the employees' mean claims per day are all the same. Use the 0.05 level of significance.

Employee 1	15	17	14	12		
Employee 2	12	10	13	17		
Employee 3	11	14	13	15	12	
Employee 4	13	12	12	14	10	9

■ **11-29** Given the measurements in the four samples that follow, can we conclude that they come from populations having the same mean value? Use the 0.01 level of significance.

Sample 1	16	21	24	28	29	
Sample 2	29	18	20	19	30	21
Sample 3	14	15	21	19	28	17
Sample 4	21	28	20	22	18	

■ **11-30** The manager of an assembly line in a clock manufacturing plant decided to study how different speeds of the conveyor belt affect the rate of defective units produced in an 8-hour shift. To examine this, he ran the belt at four different speeds for five 8-hour shifts each and measured the number of defective units found at the end of each shift. The results of the study follow:

Defective Units per Shift			
Speed 1	Speed 2	Speed 3	Speed 4
37	27	32	35
35	32	36	27
38	32	33	33
36	34	34	31
34	30	40	29

(a) Calculate the mean number of defective units, $\bar{x}$, for each speed; then determine the grand mean, $\bar{\bar{x}}$.

(b) Using Equation 11-6, estimate the population variance (the between-column variance).

(c) Calculate the variances *within* the samples and estimate the population variance based upon these variances (the within-column variance).

(d) Calculate the F ratio. At the 0.05 level of significance, do the four conveyor-belt speeds produce the same mean rate of defective clocks per shift?

■ **11-31** We are interested in testing for differences in the palatability of three spicy salsas: A, B, and C. For each product, a sample of 25 men was chosen. Each rated the product from -3 (terrible) to $+3$ (excellent). The following SAS output was produced.

```
                 ANALYSIS OF VARIANCE PROCEDURE

DEPENDENT VARIABLE:      SCORE (-3 TO +3)
SOURCE                    DF  SUM OF SQUARES  MEAN SQUARE
MODEL                      2        15.68            7.84
ERROR                     72         94.4      1.31111111
CORRECTED TOTAL           74       110.08
MODEL F =               5.98                 PR > F = 0.004
```

(a) State explicit null and alternative hypotheses.

(b) Test your hypotheses with the SAS output. Use $\alpha = 0.05$.

(c) State an explicit conclusion.

■ **11-32** The supervisor of security at a large department store would like to know whether the store apprehends relatively more shoplifters during the Christmas holiday season than in the weeks before or after the holiday. He gathered data on the number of shoplifters apprehended in the store during the months of November, December, and January over the past 6 years. The information follows:

	Number of Shoplifters					
November	43	37	59	55	38	48
December	54	41	48	35	50	49
January	36	28	34	41	30	32

At the 0.05 level of significance, is the mean number of apprehended shoplifters the same during these 3 months?

■ **11-33** An Introduction to Economics course is offered in 3 sections, each with a different instructor. The final grades from the spring term are presented below. Is there a significant difference in the average grades given by the instructors? State and test appropriate hypotheses at $\alpha = 0.01$.

Section 1	Section 2	Section 3
98.4	97.6	94.5
97.6	99.2	92.3
84.7	82.6	92.4
88.5	81.2	82.3
77.6	64.5	62.6
84.3	82.3	68.6
81.6	68.4	92.7
88.4	75.6	82.3
95.1		91.2
90.4		92.6
89.4		87.4
65.6		
94.5		
99.4		
68.7		
83.4		

■ **11-34** The manufacturer of silicon chips requires so-called clean rooms, where the air is specially filtered to keep the number of dust particles at a minimum. The Outel Corporation wants to make sure that each of its five clean rooms has the same number of dust particles. Five air samples have been taken in each room. The "dust score," on a scale of 1 (low) to 10 (high), was measured. At the 0.05 level of significance, do the rooms have the same average dust score?

	Dust Score (1 to 10)				
Room 1	5	6.5	4	7	6
Room 2	3	6	4	4.5	3
Room 3	1	1.5	3	2.5	4
Room 4	8	9.5	7	6	7.5
Room 5	1	2	3.5	1.5	3

■ **11-35** A lumber company is concerned about how rising interest rates are affecting the new housing starts in the area. To explore this question, the company has gathered data on new housing starts during the past three quarters for five surrounding counties. This information is presented in the following table. At the 0.05 level of significance, are there any differences in the number of new housing starts during the three quarters?

Quarter 1	41	53	54	55	43
Quarter 2	45	51	48	43	39
Quarter 3	34	44	46	45	51

■ **11-36** Genes-and-Jeans, Inc., offers clones of such popular jeans as Generic, DNA, RNA, and Oops. The store wants to see whether there are differences in the number of pairs sold of different brands. The manager has counted the number of pairs sold for each brand on several different days. At the 0.05 significance level, are the sales of the four brands the same?

Pairs of Jeans Sold						
Generic	17	21	13	27	12	
DNA	27	13	29	9		
RNA	13	15	17	23	10	21
Oops	18	25	15	27	12	

■ **11-37** The Government Accounting Office (GAO) is interested in seeing whether similar-sized offices spend similar amounts on personnel and equipment. (Offices spending more are targeted for special auditing.) Monthly expenses for three offices have been examined: one office in the Agriculture Department, one in the State Department, and one in the Interior Department. The data follow. At the 0.01 significance level, are there differences in expenses for the different offices?

Monthly Office Expenses ($ thousands) for Some Past Months						
Agriculture	10	8	11	9	12	
State	15	9	8	10	13	13
Interior	8	16	12			

■ **11-38** In Bigville, a fast-food chain feels it is gaining a bad reputation because it takes too long to serve the customers. Because the chain has four restaurants in this town, it is concerned with whether all four restaurants have the same average service time. One of the owners of the fast-food chain has decided to visit each of the stores and monitor the service time for five randomly selected customers. At his four noontime visits, he records the following service times in minutes:

Restaurant 1	3	4	5.5	3.5	4
Restaurant 2	3	3.5	4.5	4	5.5
Restaurant 3	2	3.5	5	6.5	6
Restaurant 4	3	4	5.5	2.5	3

(a) Using a 0.05 significance level, do all the restaurants have the same mean service time?

(b) Based on his results, should the owner make any policy recommendations to any of the restaurant managers?

Worked-Out Answers to Self-Check Exercises

SC 11-5 (a)

	Free	Gift	Cents	Refund
	78	94	73	79
	87	91	78	83
	81	87	69	78
	89	90	83	69
	85	88	76	81
Σx	**420**	**450**	**379**	**390**
n	5	5	5	5
$\bar{x}$	84	90	75.8	78
Σx^2	35,360	40,530	28,839	30,536
s^2	20	7.5	27.7	29

$$\text{Grand mean} = \bar{\bar{x}} = \frac{420 + 450 + 379 + 390}{20} = 81.95$$

(b)

$$\hat{\sigma}_b^2 = \frac{\Sigma n_j(\bar{x}_j - \bar{\bar{x}})^2}{k - 1} = \frac{5[(84 - 81.95)^2 + (90 - 81.95)^2 + (75.8 - 81.95)^2 + (78 - 81.95)^2]}{4 - 1}$$

$$= \frac{612.15}{3} = 204.05$$

(c) $\hat{\sigma}_w^2 = \Sigma\left(\frac{n_j - 1}{n_T - k}\right)s_j^2 = \frac{4(20 + 7.5 + 27.7 + 29)}{20 - 4} = \frac{336.8}{16} = 21.05$

(d) $F = \frac{204.05}{21.05} = 9.69$

With 3 degrees of freedom in the numerator, 16 degrees of freedom in the denominator, and $\alpha = 0.01$, the critical value of F is 5.29, so reject H_0, because $9.69 > 5.29$. The promotions have significantly different effects on sales.

SC 11-6

	n	$\bar{x}$	s^2
System A	6	58	10.4000
System B	5	57	38.5000
System C	4	59	35.3333

$$\bar{\bar{x}} = \frac{6(58) + 5(57) + 4(59)}{6 + 5 + 4} = 57.9333$$

$$\hat{\sigma}_b^2 = \frac{\Sigma n_j(\bar{x}_j - \bar{\bar{x}})^2}{k - 1}$$

$$= \frac{6(58 - 57.9333)^2 + 5(57 - 57.9333)^2 + 4(59 - 57.9333)^2}{3 - 1}$$

$$= \frac{8.9333}{2} = 4.4667$$

$$\sigma_w^2 = \Sigma\left(\frac{n_j - 1}{n_T - k}\right)s_j^2 = \frac{5(10.4) + 4(38.5) + 3(35.3333)}{15 - 3} = \frac{312}{12} = 26$$

$$F = \frac{\hat{\sigma}_w^2}{\hat{\sigma}_w^2} = \frac{4.4667}{26} = 0.17$$

With 2 degrees of freedom in the numerator, 12 degrees of freedom in the denominator, and $\alpha = 0.05$, the critical value of F is 3.89, so don't reject H_0, because $0.17 < 3.89$. The systems do not have significantly different effectiveness.

11.5 Inferences about a Population Variance

Need to make decisions about variability in a population

In Chapters 7–9, we learned how to form confidence intervals and test hypotheses about one or two population means or proportions. Earlier in this chapter, we used chi-square and F tests to make inferences about more than two means or proportions. But we are not always interested in means and proportions. In many situations, responsible decision makers have to make inferences about the variability in a population. In order to schedule the labor force at harvest time, a peach grower needs to know not only the mean time to maturity of the peaches, but also

Table 11-15

Delivery Time (in Hours) for Letters Going between New York and Chicago

Time x	$\bar{x}$	$x - \bar{x}$	$(x - \bar{x})^2$
50	59	− 9	81
45	59	−14	196
27	59	−32	1,024
66	59	7	49
43	59	−16	256
96	59	37	1,369
45	59	−14	196
90	59	31	961
69	59	10	100
$\Sigma x = \mathbf{531}$			$\Sigma(x - \bar{x})^2 = \mathbf{4{,}232}$

$$\bar{x} = \frac{\Sigma x}{n} = \frac{531}{9} \quad [3\text{–}2]$$

$$= 59 \text{ hours}$$

$$s^2 = \frac{\Sigma(x - \bar{x})^2}{n - 1} = \frac{4{,}232}{8} \quad [3\text{–}17]$$

$$= 529 \text{ hours squared}$$

$$s = \sqrt{s^2} = \sqrt{529} \quad [3\text{–}18]$$

$$= 23 \text{ hours}$$

their variance around that mean. A sociologist investigating the effect of education on earning power wants to know whether the incomes of college graduates are more variable than those of high school graduates. Precision instruments used in laboratory work must be quite accurate on the average but in addition, repeated measurements should show very little variation. In this section, we shall see how to make inferences about a single population variance. The next section looks at problems involving the variances of two populations.

The Distribution of the Sample Variance

In response to a number of complaints about slow mail delivery, the Postmaster General initiates a preliminary investigation. An investigator follows nine letters from New York to Chicago, to estimate the standard deviation in time of delivery. Table 11-15 gives the data and computes $\bar{x}$, s^2, and s. As we saw in Chapter 7, we use s to estimate σ.

Determining the uncertainty attached to estimates of the population standard deviation

We can tell the Postmaster General that the *population* standard deviation, as estimated by the *sample* standard deviation, is approximately 23 hours. But he also wants to know how accurate that estimate is and what uncertainty is associated with it. In other words, he wants a confidence interval, not just a point estimate of σ. In order to find such an interval, we must know the sampling distribution of s. It is traditional to talk about s^2 rather than s, but this will cause us no trouble, because we can always go from s^2 and σ^2 to s and σ by taking square roots; we can go in the other direction by squaring.

Chi-Square Statistic for Inferences about One Variance

$$\chi^2 = \frac{(n - 1)s^2}{\sigma^2} \quad [11\text{-}12]$$

If the population variance is σ^2, then the statistic has a chi-square distribution with $n - 1$ degrees of freedom. This result is exact if the population is normal, but even for samples from nonnormal populations, it is often a good approximation. We can now use the chi-square distribution to form confidence intervals and test hypotheses about σ^2.

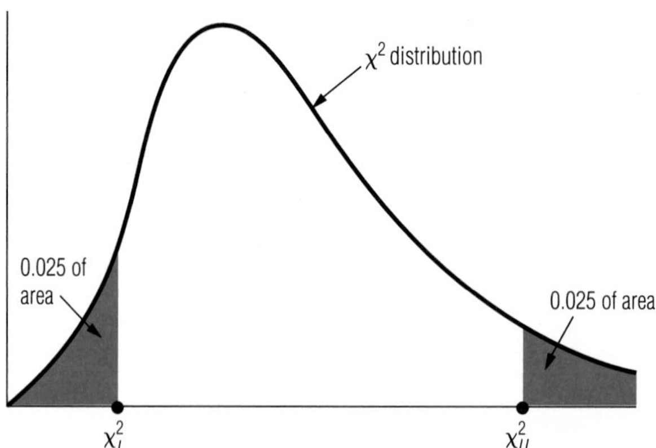

FIGURE 11-14

Constructing a confidence interval for σ^2

Confidence Intervals for the Population Variance

Constructing a confidence interval for a variance

Suppose we want a 95 percent confidence interval for the variance in our mail-delivery problem. Figure 11-14 shows how to begin constructing this interval.

We locate two points on the χ^2 distribution: χ_U^2 cuts off 0.025 of the area in the upper tail of the distribution, and χ_L^2 cuts off 0.025 of the area in the lower tail. (For a 99 percent confidence interval, we would put 0.005 of the area in each tail, and similarly for other confidence levels.) The values of χ_L^2 and χ_U^2 can be found in Appendix Table 5. In our mail problem, with $9 - 1 = 8$ degrees of freedom, $\chi_L^2 = 2.180$ and $\chi_U^2 = 17.535$.

Now Equation 11-12 gives χ^2 in terms of s^2, n, and σ^2. To get a confidence interval for σ^2, we solve Equation 11-12 for σ^2:

Upper and lower limits for the confidence interval

$$\sigma^2 = \frac{(n-1)s^2}{\chi^2} \qquad [11\text{-}13]$$

and then our confidence interval is given by

Confidence Interval for σ^2

$$\sigma_L^2 = \frac{(n-1)s^2}{\chi_U^2} \leftarrow \text{Lower confidence limit}$$

$$\sigma_U^2 = \frac{(n-1)s^2}{\chi_L^2} \leftarrow \text{Upper confidence limit} \qquad [11\text{-}14]$$

Notice that because χ^2 appears in the denominator in Equation 11-13, we can use χ_U^2 to find σ_L^2 and χ_L^2 to find σ_U^2. Continuing with the Postmaster General's problem, we see he can be 95 percent confident that the population variance lies between 241.35 and 1,941.28 hours squared:

$$\sigma_L^2 = \frac{(n-1)s^2}{\chi_U^2} = \frac{8(529)}{17.535} = 241.35$$

$$\sigma_U^2 = \frac{(n-1)s^2}{\chi_L^2} = \frac{8(529)}{2.180} = 1{,}941.28 \qquad [11\text{-}14]$$

So a 95 percent confidence interval for σ would be from $\sqrt{241.35}$ to $\sqrt{1{,}941.28}$ hours, that is, from 15.54 to 44.06 hours.

A Two-Tailed Test of a Variance

Testing hypotheses about a variance: Two-tailed tests

A management professor has given careful thought to the design of examinations. In order for him to be reasonably certain that an exam does a good job of distinguishing the differences in achievement shown by the students, the standard deviation of scores on the examination cannot be too small. On the other hand, if the standard deviation is too large, there will tend to be a lot of very low scores, which is bad for student morale. Past experience has led the professor to believe that a standard deviation of about 13 points on a 100-point exam indicates that the exam does a good job of balancing these two objectives.

The professor just gave an examination to his class of 31 freshmen and sophomores. The mean score was 72.7 and the sample standard deviation was 15.9. Does this exam meet his goodness criterion? We can summarize the data:

$$\sigma_{H_0} = 13 \quad \leftarrow \text{Hypothesized value of the population standard deviation}$$

$$s = 15.9 \leftarrow \text{Sample standard deviation}$$

$$n = 31 \quad \leftarrow \text{Sample size}$$

If the professor uses a significance level of 0.10 in testing his hypothesis, we can symbolically state the problem:

Stating the problem symbolically

$$H_0\colon \sigma = 13 \quad \leftarrow \text{Null hypothesis: The true standard deviation is 13 points}$$

$$H_1\colon \sigma \neq 13 \quad \leftarrow \text{Alternative hypothesis: The true standard deviation is not 13 points}$$

$$\alpha = 0.10 \leftarrow \text{Level of significance for testing these hypotheses}$$

The first thing we do is to use Equation 11-12 to calculate the χ^2 statistic:

Calculating the χ^2 statistic

$$\chi^2 = \frac{(n-1)s^2}{\sigma^2} \qquad [11\text{-}12]$$

$$= \frac{30(15.9)^2}{(13)^2}$$

$$= 44.88$$

This statistic has a χ^2 distribution with $n - 1$ (= 30 in this case) degrees of freedom. We will accept the null hypothesis if χ^2 is neither too big nor too small. From the x^2 distribution table (Appendix Table 5), we can see that the appropriate χ^2 values for 0.05 of the area to lie in each tail of the curve are 18.493 and 43.773. These two limits of the acceptance region and the observed sample statistic ($\chi^2 = 44.88$) are shown in Figure 11-15. We see that the sample value of χ^2 is not in the acceptance region, so the professor should reject the null hypothesis; this exam does not meet his goodness criterion.

Interpreting the results

A One-Tailed Test of a Variance

Testing hypotheses about a variance: One-tailed tests

Precision Analytics manufactures a wide line of precision instruments and has a fine reputation in the field for quality of its instruments. In order to preserve that reputation, it maintains strict quality control on all of its output. It will not release an analytic balance for sale, for example, unless that balance shows a standard deviation

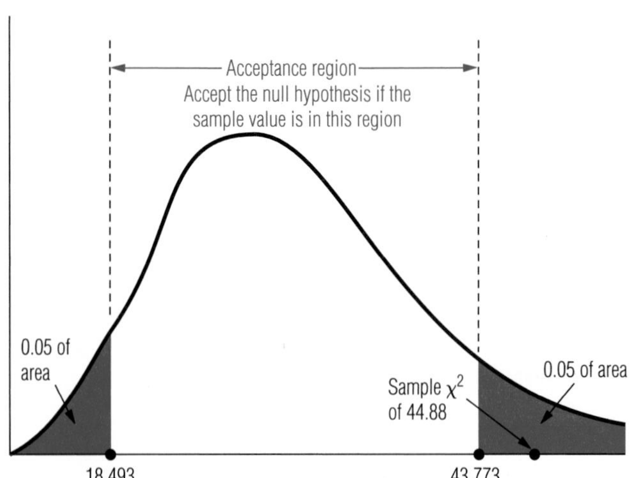

FIGURE 11-15

Two-tailed hypothesis test at the 0.10 level of significance, showing acceptance region and sample χ^2

significantly below one microgram (at $\alpha = 0.01$) when weighing quantities of about 500 grams. A new balance has just been delivered to the quality control division from the production line.

The new balance is tested by using it to weigh the same 500-gram standard weight 30 different times. The sample standard deviation turns out to be 0.73 microgram. Should this balance be sold? We summarize the data:

$$\sigma_{H_0} = 1 \quad \leftarrow \text{Hypothesized value of the population standard deviation}$$

$$s = 0.73 \leftarrow \text{Sample standard deviation}$$

$$n = 30 \quad \leftarrow \text{Sample size}$$

and state the problem:

Stating the problem symbolically

$$H_0\text{: } \sigma = 1 \quad \leftarrow \text{Null hypothesis: The true standard deviation is 1 microgram}$$

$$H_1\text{: } \sigma < 1 \quad \leftarrow \text{Alternative hypothesis: The true standard deviation is less than 1 microgram}$$

$$\alpha = 0.01 \leftarrow \text{Level of significance for testing these hypotheses}$$

Calculating the χ^2 statistic

We begin by using Equation 11-12 to calculate the χ^2 statistic:

$$\chi^2 = \frac{(n-1)s^2}{\sigma^2} \qquad [11\text{-}12]$$

$$= \frac{29(0.73)^2}{(1)^2}$$

$$= 15.45$$

Interpreting the results

We will reject the null hypothesis and release the balance for sale if this statistic is sufficiently small. From Appendix Table 5, we see that with 29 degrees of freedom (30 − 1), the value of χ^2 that leaves an area of 0.01 in the lower tail of the curve is 14.256. The acceptance region and the observed value of χ^2 are shown in Figure 11-16. We see that we cannot reject the null hypothesis. The balance will have to be returned to the production line for adjusting.

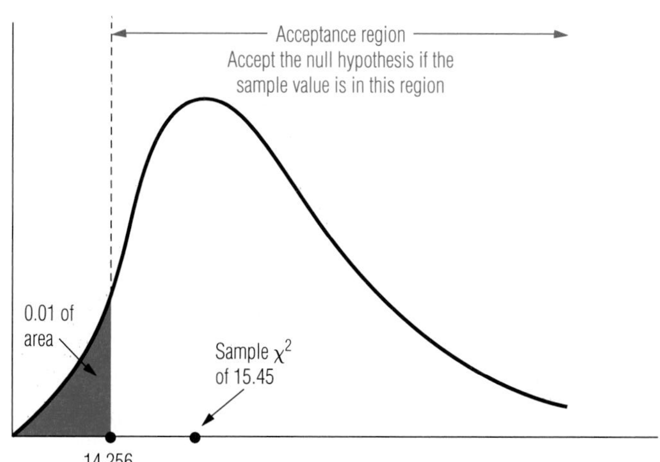

FIGURE 11-16

One-tailed hypothesis test at the 0.01 significance level, showing acceptance region and sample χ^2

HINTS & ASSUMPTIONS

Up to this point, we've seen how to make inferences about one, two, or several *means* or *proportions*. But we're also interested in making inferences about population *variability*. For one population, we do this by using the sample variance and the chi-square distribution. Warning: Chi-square tests can be one-tailed or two-tailed. Hint: If the question to be answered is worded *less than, more than, less than or equal to,* or *greater than or equal to,* use a one-tailed test. If the question concerns *different from,* or *changed from,* use a two-tailed test.

Exercises 11.5

Self-Check Exercises

SC 11-7 Given a sample variance of 127 from a set of nine observations, construct a 95 percent confidence interval for the population variance.

SC 11-8 A production manager feels that the output rate of experienced employees is surely greater than that of new employees, but he does not expect the variability in output rates to differ for the two groups. In previous output studies, it has been shown that the average unit output per hour for new employees at this particular type of work is 20 units per hour with a variance of 56 units squared. For a group of 20 employees with 5 years' experience, the average output for this same type of work is 30 units per hour, with a sample variance of 28 units squared. Does the variability in output appear to differ at the two experience levels? Test the hypotheses at the 0.05 significance level.

Basic Concepts

■ **11-39** A sample of 20 observations from a normal distribution has a mean of 37 and a variance of 12.2. Construct a 90 percent confidence interval for the true population variance.

■ **11-40** The standard deviation of a distribution is hypothesized to be 50. If an observed sample of 30 yields a sample standard deviation of 57, should we reject the null hypothesis that the true standard deviation is 50? Use the 0.05 level of significance.

■ **11-41** Given a sample standard deviation of 6.4 from a sample of 15 observations, construct a 90 percent confidence interval for the population variance.

Applications

■ **11-42** A telescope manufacturer wants its telescopes to have standard deviations in resolution to be significantly below 2 when focusing on objects 500 light-years away. When a new telescope is used to focus on an object 500 light-years away 30 times, the sample standard deviation turns out to be 1.46. Should this telescope be sold?

(a) State explicit null and alternative hypotheses.

(b) Test your hypotheses at the $\alpha = 0.01$ level.

(c) State an explicit conclusion.

■ **11-43** MacroSwift has designed a new operating system that will revolutionize the computing industry. The only problem is, the company expects the average amount of time required to learn the software to be 124 hours. Even though this is a long educational time, the company is truly concerned with the variance of the learning time. Preliminary data indicate the variance is 171 hours squared. Recent testing of 25 people found an average learning time of 123 hours and a sample variance of 196.5 hours squared. Do these data indicate the variability in learning time is different from the previous estimate? Test your hypotheses at the 0.02 significance level.

■ **11-44** A psychologist is aware of studies showing that the variability of attention spans of 5-year-olds can be summarized by $\sigma^2 = 64$ minutes squared. She wonders whether the attention span of 6-year-olds is different. A sample of twenty 6-year-olds gives $s^2 = 28$ minutes squared.

(a) State explicit null and alternative hypotheses.

(b) Test your hypotheses at the $\alpha = 0.05$ level.

(c) State an explicit conclusion.

■ **11-45** In checking its cars for adherence to emissions standards set by the government, an automaker measured emissions of 30 cars. The average number of particles of pollutants emitted was found to be within the required levels, but the sample variance was 50. Find a 90 percent confidence interval for the variance in emission particles for these cars.

■ **11-46** A bank is considering ways to reduce the costs associated with passbook savings accounts. The bank has found that the variance in the number of days between account transactions for passbook accounts is 80 days squared. The bank wants to reduce the variance by discouraging the present use of accounts for short-term storage of cash. Therefore, after implementing a new policy that penalizes the customer with a service charge for withdrawals more than once a month, the bank decides to test for a change in the variance of days between account transactions. From a sample of 25 savings accounts, the bank finds the variance between transactions to be 28 days squared. Is the bank justified in claiming that the new policy reduces the variance of days between transactions? Test the hypotheses at the 0.05 level of significance.

■ **11-47** Sam Bogart, the owner of the Play-It-Again Stereo Company, offers 1-year warranties on all the stereos his company sells. For the 30 stereos that were serviced under the warranty last year, the average cost to fix a stereo was \$75 and sample standard deviation was \$15. Calculate a 95 percent confidence interval for the true standard deviation of the cost of repair. Sam has decided that unless the true standard deviation is less than \$20, he will buy his stereos from a different wholesaler. Help Sam test the appropriate hypotheses, using a significance level of 0.01. Should he switch wholesalers?

Worked-Out Answers to Self-Check Exercises

SC 11-7 For a 95 percent confidence interval with 8 degrees of freedom:

$$\sigma_L^2 = \frac{(n-1)s^2}{\chi_U^2} = \frac{8(127)}{17.535} = 57.941$$

$$\sigma_U^2 = \frac{(n-1)s^2}{\chi_L^2} = \frac{8(127)}{2.180} = 466.055$$

Thus, the confidence interval is (57.941, 466.055).

SC 11-8 For testing H_0: $\sigma^2 = 56$ versus H_1: $\sigma^2 \neq 56$ at $\alpha = 0.05$, the limits of the acceptance region are

$$\chi^2 = 8.907 \quad \text{and} \quad \chi^2 = 32.852$$

The observed $\chi^2 = \frac{(n-1)s^2}{\sigma^2} = \frac{19(28)}{56} = 9.5$, so we don't reject H_0; the variability is not significantly different.

11.6 Inferences about Two Population Variances

Comparing the variances of two populations

In Chapter 9, we saw several situations in which we wanted to compare the means of two different populations. Recall that we did this by looking at the *difference* of the means of two samples drawn from those populations. Here, we want to compare the variances of two populations. However, rather than looking at the *difference* of the two sample variances, it turns out to be more convenient if we look at their *ratio*. The next two examples show how this is done.

A One-Tailed Test of Two Variances

A prominent sociologist at a large midwestern university believes that incomes earned by college graduates show much greater variability than the earnings of those who did not attend college. In order to test this theory, she dispatches two research assistants to Chicago to look at the earnings of these two populations. The first assistant takes a random sample of 21 college graduates and finds that their earnings have a sample standard deviation of s_1 = \$17,000. The second assistant samples 25 nongraduates and obtains a standard deviation in earnings of s_2 = \$7,500. The data of our problem can be summarized as follows:

Data for the problem

$$s_1 = 17{,}000 \leftarrow \text{Standard deviation of first sample}$$

$$n_1 = 21 \quad \leftarrow \text{Size of first sample}$$

$$s_2 = 7{,}500 \quad \leftarrow \text{Standard deviation of second sample}$$

$$n_2 = 25 \quad \leftarrow \text{Size of second sample}$$

Why a one-tailed test is appropriate

Because the sociologist theorizes that the earnings of college graduates are *more* variable than those of people not attending college, a one-tailed test is appropriate. She wishes to verify her theory at the 0.01 level of significance. We can formally state her hypotheses:

Statement of the hypotheses

$$H_0: \sigma_1^2 = \sigma_2^2 \text{ (or } \sigma_1^2/\sigma_2^2 = 1) \quad \leftarrow \text{Null hypothesis: the two variances are the same}$$

$$H_1: \sigma_1^2 > \sigma_2^2 \text{ (or } \sigma_1^2/\sigma_2^2 > 1) \quad \leftarrow \text{Alternative hypothesis: earnings of college graduates have more variance}$$

$$\alpha = 0.01 \leftarrow \text{Level of significance for testing these hypotheses}$$

We know that s_1^2 can be used to estimate σ_1^2, and s_2^2 can be used to estimate σ_2^2. If the alternative hypothesis is true, we would expect that s_1^2 will be greater than s_2^2 (or, equivalently, that s_1^2/s_2^2 will be greater than 1). But how much greater must s_1^2 be in order for us to be able to reject the null hypothesis? To answer this question, we must know the distribution of s_1^2/s_2^2. If we assume that the two populations are reasonably well described by normal distributions, then the ratio

Description of the *F* statistic

_F_ Ratio for Inferences about Two Variances

$$F = \frac{s_1^2}{s_2^2} \quad [11\text{-}15]$$

has an F distribution with $n_1 - 1$ degrees of freedom in the numerator and $n_2 - 1$ degrees of freedom in the denominator.

In the earnings problem, we calculate the sample F statistic:

$$F = \frac{s_1^2}{s_2^2} \quad [11\text{-}15]$$

$$= \frac{(17{,}000)^2}{(7{,}500)^2}$$

$$= \frac{289{,}000{,}000}{56{,}250{,}000}$$

$$= 5.14$$

Interpreting the results

For 20 degrees of freedom $(21 - 1)$ in the numerator and 24 degrees of freedom $(25 - 1)$ in the denominator, Appendix Table 6 tells us that the critical value separating the acceptance and rejection regions is 2.74. Figure 11-17 shows the acceptance region and the

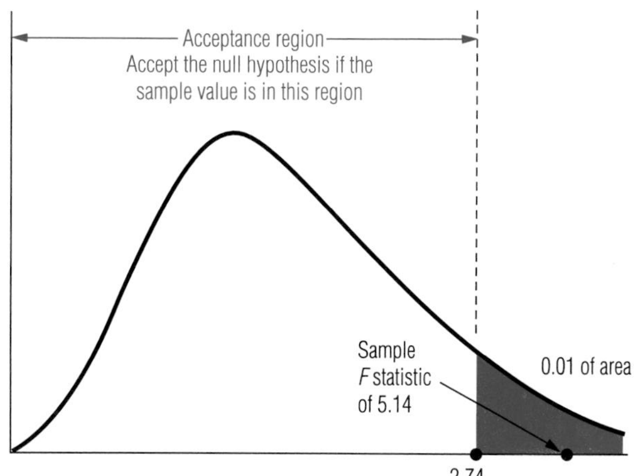

FIGURE 11-17

One-tailed hypothesis test at the 0.01 level of significance, showing the acceptance region and the sample F statistic

observed F statistic of 5.14. Our sociologist rejects the null hypothesis, and the sample data support her theory.

Handling lower-tailed tests in Appendix Table 6

A word of caution about the use of Appendix Table 6 is necessary at this point. You will notice that the table gives values of the F statistic that are appropriate only for *upper-tailed* tests. How can we handle alternative hypotheses of the form $\sigma_1^2 < \sigma_2^2$ (or $\sigma_1^2/\sigma_2^2 < 1$)? This is easily done if we notice that $\sigma_1^2/\sigma_2^2 < 1$ is equivalent to $\sigma_2^2/\sigma_1^2 > 1$. Thus, all we need to do is calculate the ratio s_2^2/s_1^2, which also has an F distribution (but with $n_2 - 1$ numerator degrees of freedom and $n_1 - 1$ denominator degrees of freedom), and then we can use Appendix Table 6. There is another way to say the same thing: **Whenever you are doing a one-tailed test of two variances, number the populations so that the alternative hypothesis has the form**

$$H_1: \sigma_1^2 > \sigma_2^2 \text{ (or } \sigma_1^2/\sigma_2^2 > 1)$$

and then proceed as we did in the earnings example.

A Two-Tailed Test of Two Variances

Finding the critical value in a two-tailed test

The procedure for a two-tailed test of two variances is similar to that for a one-tailed test. The only problem arises in finding the critical value in the lower tail. This is related to the problem about lower-tailed tests discussed in the last paragraph, and we will resolve it in a similar way.

One criterion in evaluating oral anesthetics for use in general dentistry is the variability in the length of time between injection and complete loss of sensation in the patient. (This is called the effect delay time.) A large pharmaceutical firm has just developed two new oral anesthetics, which it will market under the names Oralcaine and Novasthetic. From similarities in the chemical structure of the two compounds, it has been predicted that they should show the same variance in effect delay time. Sample data from tests of the two compounds (which controlled other variables such as age and weight) are given in Table 11-16.

Table 11-16 Effect Delay Times for Two Anesthetics	Anesthetic	Sample Size (n)	Sample Variance (Seconds Squared) (s^2)
	Oralcaine	31	1,296
	Novasthetic	41	784

The company wants to test at a 2 percent significance level whether the two compounds have the same variance in effect delay time. Symbolically, the hypotheses are

Statement of the hypotheses

$$H_0: \sigma_1^2 = \sigma_2^2 \text{ or } (\sigma_1^2/\sigma_2^2 = 1)$$ ← Null hypothesis: the two variances are the same

$$H_1: \sigma_1^2 \neq \sigma_2^2 \text{ (or } \sigma_1^2/\sigma_2^2 \neq 1)$$ ← Alternative hypothesis: the two variances are different

$$\alpha = 0.02$$ ← Significance level of the test

Calculating the *F* statistic

To test these hypotheses, we again use Equation 11-15:

$$F = \frac{s_1^2}{s_2^2} \qquad [11\text{-}15]$$

$$= \frac{1{,}296}{784}$$

$$= 1.65$$

This statistic comes from an F distribution with $n_1 - 1$ degrees of freedom in the numerator (30, in this case) and $n_2 - 1$ degrees of freedom in the denominator (40, in this case). Let us use the notation

Same useful notation for the test

$$F(n, d, \alpha)$$

to denote that value of F with n numerator degrees of freedom, d denominator degrees of freedom, and an area of α in the upper tail. In our problem, the acceptance region extends from $F(30, 40, 0.99)$ to $F(30, 40, 0.01)$, as illustrated in Figure 11-18.

FIGURE 11-18

Two-tailed test of hypotheses at the 0.02 significance level

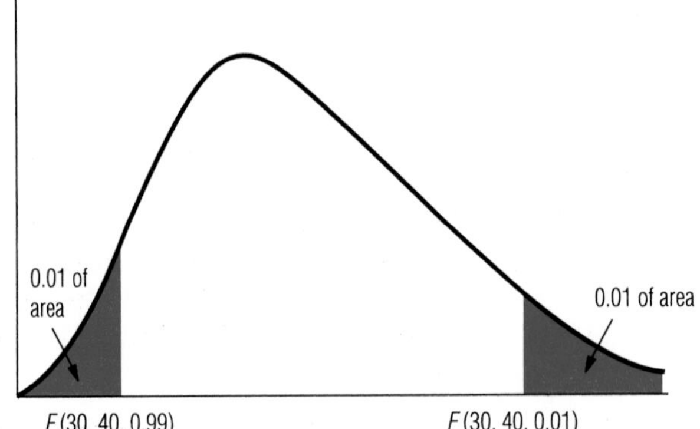

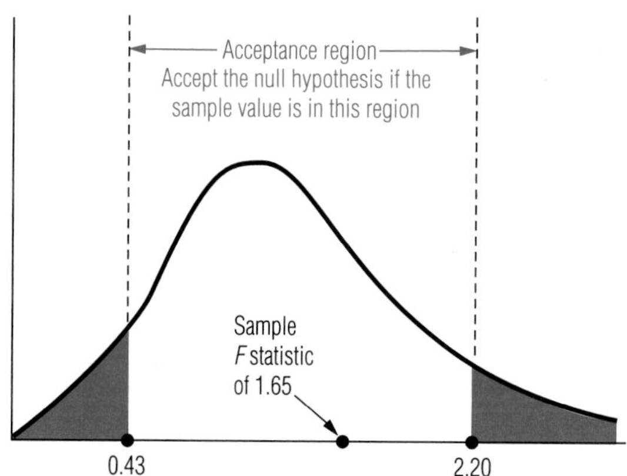

FIGURE 11-19

Two-tailed hypothesis test at the 0.02 level of significance, showing acceptance region and the sample *F* statistic

We can get the value of $F(30, 40, 0.01)$ directly from Appendix Table 6; it is 2.20. However, the value of $F(30, 40, 0.99)$ is not in the table. Now $F(30, 40, 0.99)$ will correspond to a *small* value of s_1^2/s_2^2, and hence to a *large* value of s_2^2/s_1^2, which is just the reciprocal of s_1^2/s_2^2. Given the discussion on page 617 about lower-tailed tests, we might suspect that

Lower-Tail Value of *F* for Two-Tailed Tests

$$F(n, d, \alpha) = \frac{1}{F(d, n, 1 - \alpha)} \qquad [11\text{-}16]$$

and this turns out to be true. We can use this equation to find $F(30, 40, 0.99)$:

$$\begin{aligned} F(30, 40, 0.99) &= \frac{1}{F(40, 30, 0.01)} \\ &= \frac{1}{2.30} \\ &= 0.43 \end{aligned}$$

Interpreting the results

In Figure 11-19 we have illustrated the acceptance region for this hypothesis test and the observed value of *F*. We see there that the null hypothesis is accepted, so we conclude that the observed difference in the sample variances of effect delay times for the two anesthetics is not statistically significant.

HINTS & ASSUMPTIONS

This section has been about using an *F* test to compare the variances of two *populations* by looking at the ratio of the variances from two *samples*. Warning: Appendix Table 6 gives values of *F* that are appropriate for *upper-tailed* tests only. Hint: If you want to do a *lower-tailed* test, be sure to convert it to an upper-tailed test as shown on page 617. And if you want to do a *two-tailed* test, use Equation 11-16 to convert an upper-tailed value from the table into the lower-tailed value needed for your test.

Exercises 11.6

Self-Check Exercises

SC 11-9 A quality control supervisor for an automobile manufacturer is concerned with uniformity in the number of defects in cars coming off the assembly line. If one assembly line has significantly more variability in the number of defects, then changes have to be made. The supervisor has collected the following data:

	Number of Defects	
	Assembly Line A	Assembly Line B
Mean	10	11
Variance	9	25
Sample size	20	16

Does assembly line B have significantly more variability in the number of defects? Test at the 0.05 significance level.

SC 11-10 Techgene, Inc., is concerned about variability in the number of bacteria produced by different cultures. If the cultures have significantly different variability in the number of bacteria produced, then experiments are messed up and some strange things get produced. (The management of the company gets understandably anxious when the scientists produce strange things.) The following data have been collected:

Number of Bacteria (in thousands)

Culture Type A	91	89	83	101	93	98	144	118	108	125	138
Culture Type B	62	76	90	75	88	99	110	140	145	130	110

(a) Compute s_A^2 and s_B^2.

(b) State explicit null and alternative hypotheses and then test at the 0.02 significance level.

Basic Concepts

■ **11-48** For two populations thought to have the same variance, the following information was found. A sample of 16 from population 1 exhibited a sample variance of 3.75, and a sample of 10 from population 2 had a variance of 5.38.

(a) Calculate the F ratio for the test of equality of variances.

(b) Find the critical F value for the upper tail, using the 0.10 significance level.

(c) Find the corresponding F value for the lower tail.

(d) State the conclusion of your test.

■ **11-49** In our study of comparisons between the means of two groups, it was noted that the most common form of the two-group t-test for the difference between two means assumes that the population variances for the two groups are the same. One experimenter, using a control condition and an experimental condition in his study of drug reaction, wished to verify that this assumption held, that is, that the treatment administered affected only the mean, not the variance of the variable under study. From his data, he calculated the variance of the experimental group to be 25.8 and that of the control group to be 20.6. The experimental group had 25 subjects, and the control group had 31. Can he proceed to use the *t*-test, which assumes equal variances for the two groups? Use $\alpha = 0.10$.

■ **11-50** From a sample of 25 observations, the estimate of the standard deviation of the population was found to be 15.0. From another sample of 14 observations, the estimate was found to be 9.7. Can we accept the hypothesis that the two samples come from populations with equal variances, or must we conclude that the variance of the second population is smaller? Use the 0.01 level of significance.

Applications

■ **11-51** Mr. Raj, an investor, has narrowed his search for a mutual fund down to the Oppy fund or the MLPFS fund. Oppy's rate of return is lower, but seems to be more stable than MLPFS's. If Oppy's variability in rate of return is significantly lower than MLPFS's, then he will invest his money there. If there is no significant difference in variability, he'll go with MLPFS. To make a decision, Mr. Raj has taken a sample of 21 monthly rates of return for both firms. For Oppy, the *standard deviation* was 2, and for MLPFS, the standard deviation was 3. Which firm should Mr. Raj invest in? Test at the $\alpha = 0.05$ level.

■ **11-52** An insurance company is interested in the length of hospital-stays for various illnesses. The company has randomly selected 20 patients from hospital A and 25 from hospital B who were treated for the same ailment. The amount of time spent in hospital A had an average of 2.4 days with a standard deviation of 0.6 day. The treatment time in hospital B averaged 2.3 days with a standard deviation of 0.9 day. Do patients at hospital A have significantly less variability in their recovery time? Test at a 0.01 significance level.

■ **11-53** Nation's Broadcasting Company is interested in the number of people who tune in to their hit shows *Buddies* and *Ride to Nowhere;* more importantly, the company is very concerned in the variability in the number of people who watch the shows. Advertisers want consistent viewers in hopes that consistent prolonged advertising will help to sell a product. Data are given below (in millions of viewers) for the past few months.

Number of Viewers (in millions)

Buddies	57.4	62.6	54.6	52.4	60.5	61.8	71.4	67.5	62.6	58.4
Ride to Nowhere	64.5	58.2	39.5	24.7	40.2	41.6	38.4	33.6	34.4	37.8

(a) Compute $s^2_{BUDDIES}$ and s^2_{RIDE}.

(b) State explicit hypotheses to determine whether the variability is the same between the two populations. Test at a 0.10 significance level.

■ **11-54** The HAL Corporation is about to unveil a new, faster personal computer, PAL, to replace its old model, CAL. Although PAL is faster than CAL on average, PAL's processing speed seems more variable. (Processing speed depends on the program being run, the amount of input, and the amount of output.) Two samples of 25 runs, covering the range of jobs expected, were submitted to PAL and CAL (one sample to each). The results were as follows:

	Processing Time (in hundredths of a second)	
	PAL	CAL
Mean	50	75
Standard deviation	20	10

At the 0.05 level of significance, is PAL's processing speed significantly more variable than CAL's?

■ **11-55** Two brand managers were in disagreement over the issue of whether urban homemakers had greater variability in grocery shopping patterns than did rural homemakers. To test their conflicting ideas, they took random samples of 70 homemakers from urban areas and 60 homemakers from rural areas. They found that the variance in days squared between shopping visits for urban homemakers was 14 and the sample variance for the rural homemakers was 3.5. Is the difference between the variances in days between shopping visits significant at the 0.01 level?

■ **11-56** Two competing ice cream stores, Yum-Yum and Goody, both advertise quarter-pound scoops of ice cream. There is some concern about the variability in the serving sizes, so two members of a local consumer group have sampled 25 scoops of Yum-Yum's ice cream and 11 scoops of Goody's. Of course, both members now have stomachaches, so you must help them out. Is there a difference in the variance of ice cream weights between Yum-Yum and Goody? The following data have been collected. Test at the 0.10 level.

	Scoop Weight (in hundredths of a pound)	
	Yum-Yum	Goody
Mean	25	25
Variance	16	10

Worked-Out Answers to Self-Check Exercises

SC 11-9 $H_0: \sigma_B^2 = \sigma_A^2$

$H_1: \sigma_B^2 > \sigma_A^2$

$$\text{Observed } F = \frac{s_B^2}{s_A^2} = \frac{25}{9} = 2.778$$

$$F_{CRIT} = F_{0.05}(15, 19) = 2.23$$

Thus, we reject H_0; assembly line B does have significantly more variability in the number of defects, so some changes have to be made. (Note: We are just checking for uniformity here; the cars could be uniformly bad.)

SC 11–10 (a) $s_A^2 = 423.4 \qquad s_B^2 = 755.818$

(b) $H_0: \sigma_A^2 = \sigma_B^2$

$H_1: \sigma_A^2 \neq \sigma_B^2$

$$\text{Observed } F = \frac{s_B^2}{s_A^2} = \frac{423.4}{755.818} = 0.56$$

$$F_{0.01}(10, 10) = 4.85$$

$$F_{0.99}(10, 10) = \frac{1}{F\,(10, 10, 0.01)} = \frac{1}{4.85} = 0.21$$

Thus, accept H_0; management doesn't have to worry about strange things in the laboratory.

Statistics at Work

Loveland Computers

Case 11: Chi-Square and Anova Tom Hodges had been supervisor of Loveland Computers' technical support team for a little over a year. Like many computer suppliers, Loveland contracted with a nationwide service company to provide 1 year of on-site repair. This guarantee was important in inducing customers to buy computers by phone. But Loveland had found that more than 90 percent of customers' problems could be solved by simply reading the instruction manuals that were packed with each machine, and 95 percent of all problems could be "talked through" if customers were encouraged to call customer service before seeking on-site repair. To save on warranty costs, Loveland had invested heavily in its customer-support center, where as many as 24 staff members would respond to customers' calls.

The customer-support staff were of two types. Most of the staff did not have much background in computers. These first-level support staff had been recruited for their telephone skills and had been trained internally to run through a routine checklist for common problems. When a customer's problem couldn't be corrected with the standard protocol, or when a customer called in with a "difficult" question, the call was transferred to a technician. Some of the technicians were full-time employees, but Hodges had found that plenty of part-time help could be found by recruiting students from the local engineering and computer science graduate programs. To suit their class schedule, most were scheduled to work a late shift, beginning at 4 P.M.

Examples of the kinds of problems that first-level support staff handled included talking customers through loading programs from floppy disks onto the hard drive and helping them check cable connections. The technicians handled problems such as the incompatibility of some "memory-resident" programs, and how to recover "lost" data.

The heads of several departments were meeting together to plan a strategy for improving telephone support. Loveland's support rating had slipped from "excellent" to "good" in a recent poll conducted by a marketing research firm. Walter Azko sent Lee along to "sit in on the meeting and see if you can be of any help."

Margot Derby, head of marketing, began the meeting with an air of finality: "Tom, the problem's obvious. When we call people back who've written complaint letters, they say they can never get through to a technician. They talk with the first-level support staff and then hold forever. It's obvious that it's business customers who are most likely to have a 'difficult' question that's beyond the scope of the first-level staff. You just need to schedule more technicians on the early shift."

Hodges replied, "On the contrary, Margot. It's the home users who need to talk with the technicians, so most of those calls come in on the late shift. They come up with these rocket-scientist questions while they're playing with their machines after work. In any case, the technicians are keeping busy on the late shift—I get a printout of their total time on the phone."

"Yes, but I'll bet that if you look at the average call time, it goes way up in the evening. I think your technicians are just chatting with the customers to fill in time."

"Well, we clearly need to know when the 'difficult' calls typically come in," said Lee, hoping to turn the discussion in a more productive direction. "Because no one ever talks to a technician without talking to a first-level service rep, we can have the first-level support staff assign each question to the easy or difficult category and gather data for each shift. Then, we can test to see if there really are more technical questions on the day shift or the late shift."

"Don't forget that it's my business customers who have more of the difficult questions," said Margot.

"I still think you're wrong on that. And, by the way, I have a gut feeling that the day of the week makes things different," added Tom. "We get a lot of technician-level calls early in the week but not toward the weekend."

Study Questions: In what format should the data be tabulated? Which statistical test might be useful if Lee just focuses on the shift issue (and sets aside the comments about business customers and the day of the week)? And which technique would be most useful for examining the effects of customer type, shift, and day of the week? What might distort the data that Lee asks the customer-support group to collect?

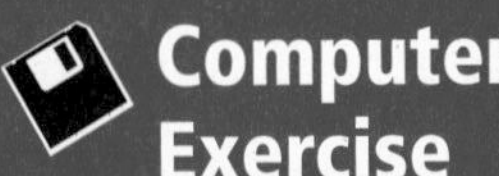

Computer Database Exercise

HH Industries

Stan Hutchings, VP of Sales, stuck his head into Laurel's office one morning a couple of weeks after the sales meeting. "Have you got a minute? I've been meaning to ask you about something."

"Sure," Laurel answered, sliding aside a stack of data. "What can I do for you?"

"For quite some time now, we've been toying with the idea of instituting an 'inside sales' commission program. As it stands now, only our two outside sales reps work on a salary-plus-commission basis. However, the folks who work the phones inside actually account for nearly 75 percent of total sales, and they've been itching for a little incentive in the form of commission. It came up again at the recent sales meeting, and some good ideas were proposed. I have to mention that we tried this kind of program once and it didn't quite work out. The tricky thing is that the calls come in randomly and are answered by the next available sales representative. Some people are just calling for information, some to actually place an order. As it happens, a customer often calls more than once and will probably speak to several reps, resulting in complications in awarding the sale to a single person. The solution that has been proposed is actually quite innovative."

"Each month we have a sales goal, as you know," Stan continued. "The proposed plan involves keeping things as they currently are until we reach 95 percent of our monthly target. Beyond that, a percentage of the sales dollars will be pooled and distributed evenly at the end of the month. Our goal is to encourage a team spirit of sorts, keeping away from the cutthroat competition that commission programs usually foster."

"Sounds great," Laurel agreed, "but how can I help?"

"Well, in the interest of fairness, we need to be sure that sales are actually following a random trend. That is, if I'm assuming correctly, each salesperson's daily average should be about the same over time."

"Ah," said Laurel, "I see what you need. If you can get me some sales data for the different inside sales people, I can do some checking to see what the likelihood is that they actually come from the same distribution."

"Bingo, I thought you might be able to help. I'll get you the data right away. Thanks, Laurel." Stan headed out the door.

Six months of daily sales data for the four full-time inside sales representatives are in the CH11.XXX files on the data disk.

1. Do the sampled data come from populations with the same mean? Test this assumption at the 1 percent significance level.

Stan looked at Laurel's results. "Hmm. Seems like Mike's in a class by himself. Well, he has been here longer than the others and there are certain customers who ask specifically for him. What if we worked up a separate commission program for him and created a pool for the other three? Any validity to that?"

"I'll have to make another run to be sure," Laurel replied, "but I think you've got a better chance that way."

2. Verify Stan's conclusion about Mike by looking at the means and standard deviations by salesperson. Test whether the data for Debbie, Jeff, and Barry seem to indicate populations with the same mean. (Use the 1 percent significance level.)

Later, with a few minutes of free time, Laurel decided to go back and verify her assumptions on the staffing study she had done for Stan (see Chapter 5). She knew the recommendations were based heavily on assuming Poisson arrivals of phone calls.

3. Check the phone call data in the CH05.XXX files on the data disk to see whether they appear to be Poisson-distributed. Use the intervals 0–20, 21–25, 26–30, 31–35, ≥ 36. Test at the 5 percent significance level.

"Darn," muttered Laurel. "I hope I haven't screwed them up too badly with that assumption. If by any chance I'm lucky and the data are actually normally distributed, I can check. At the very least, I've got to let Stan and Hal know." Laurel was never thrilled about admitting mistakes.

4. Check the assumption that the data follow a normal distribution. Test at the 0.05 significance level.
5. If the assumption of normality appears reasonable, reestimate the number of salespeople needed to staff the phones (ignore the information given in question 7 on page 276).

Stan looked at Laurel's data with interest. "I knew something wasn't quite right with our original conclusions, but I couldn't quite put my finger on it. Good thing I kept our six sales people," he winked.

Laurel breathed a sigh of relief.

"However," he went on, "this brings up a new question. These data seem to indicate, and I know from experience, that there are definitely some peak hours. I wonder if we could come up with a more cost-effective solution by using a combination of part-time and full-time sales reps. What do you think?"

"You're probably right," Laurel agreed. "Let me put a few more figures together, and we'll take this back to Hal for his opinion."

6. Calculate the average and standard deviation of the number of calls received during each hour. Assuming that during each hour, the number of calls received is normally distributed, calculate the associated recommended staffing levels in order to be 98 percent certain that a sales rep only has to deal with eight calls an hour. What combination of full-time and part-time reps seems to be appropriate?

From the Textbook to the Real World

Stimulating Response to Mail Surveys

Marketing professionals use statistics to analyze data and determine the effectiveness of various marketing techniques. Marketing research agencies can collect commercial data through labor-intensive telephone or personal interviews. In addition, mail surveys can provide a relatively low-cost alternative for gathering information from widely scattered populations. One major drawback of mail surveys is that their response rates are generally lower than those of face-to-face or telephone interviews; thus, their nonresponse bias is more acute.

In 1987, an experiment was done in London to see whether the response rate to mail surveys could be improved by enclosing a small monetary incentive and/or an informational booklet with the survey. Before 1987, English research agencies usually chose telephone surveys, and only 4 percent of companies in the UK had used monetary incentives with their mail surveys. The experiment was designed to test the following null hypotheses:

H_1:Response to a commercial mail survey is independent of the use of a monetary incentive.

H_2:Response to a commercial mail survey is independent of the use of an informational booklet.

The Experiment The sample consisted of 159 chief executives of building societies. Questionnaires were randomly assigned with either:

1. Monetary incentive/no booklet
2. Monetary incentive/booklet
3. No monetary incentive/booklet
4. No monetary incentive/no booklet

A letter enclosed with the 20-pence coin used as a monetary incentive suggested that it could be used to purchase a cup of coffee to ease the task of completing the questionnaire. The letter enclosed with the booklet indicated that it explained the importance of the survey to the research.

The Results Analysis of variance was used to test the effects of treatments on the response rates. As a check, the chi-square test was also used to test association for the main effects on response rate. The overall response rate to the mailing was 36.5 percent. However, response rates associated with the 20-pence coin were 44.2 percent (versus 29.3 percent with no coin) and for the booklet 33.3 percent (versus 40.0 percent for no booklet). Table RW11-1 presents the ANOVA results. The 14.9 percent increase in the response rate with the coin was significant at $\alpha = 0.05$. The booklet/no booklet difference was not significant. The chi-square test confirmed the ANOVA results.

Table RW 11-1 ANOVA Results for Response Rates

Source of Variation	Sum of Squares	DF	Mean Square	F
Main effects	1.04	2	0.052	2.26
Monetary incentive	0.87	1	0.87	3.76*
Booklet	0.16	1	0.16	0.71

*Denotes significance at 0.05 level.

Practical Significance Practitioners in the UK had voiced skepticism about mail surveys because of nonresponse bias. The experiment indicated that a small monetary incentive could improve response rates to mail surveys without affecting response quality. Expensive booklets had no significant effect on response rate; in fact, response rates were higher without booklets. This evidence suggests that mail surveys are a viable means of obtaining market information and that the time and effort involved in producing a booklet might be better spent more directly on monetary incentives.

Source: David Jobber, Karl Birro, and Stuart Sanderson, "A Factorial Investigation of Methods of Stimulating Response to a Mail Survey," *European Journal of Operational Research* 37 (1988): 158–163.

Chapter Review

● Terms Introduced in Chapter 11

Analysis of Variance (ANOVA) A statistical technique used to test the equality of three or more sample means and thus make inferences as to whether the samples come from populations having the same mean.

Between-Column Variance An estimate of the population variance derived from the variance among the sample means.

Chi-Square Distribution A family of probability distributions, differentiated by their degrees of freedom, used to test a number of different hypotheses about variances, proportions, and distributional goodness of fit.

Contingency Table A table having R rows and C columns. Each row corresponds to a level of one variable, each column to a level of another variable. Entries in the body of the table are the frequencies with which each variable combination occurred.

Expected Frequencies The frequencies we would expect to see in a contingency table or frequency distribution if the null hypothesis is true.

***F* Distribution** A family of distributions differentiated by two parameters (df-numerator, df-denominator), used primarily to test hypotheses regarding variances.

***F* Ratio** A ratio used in the analysis of variance, among other tests, to compare the magnitude of two estimates of the population variance to determine whether the two estimates are approximately equal; in ANOVA, the ratio of between-column variance to within-column variance is used.

Goodness-of-Fit Test A statistical test for determining whether there is a significant difference between an observed frequency distribution and a theoretical probability distribution hypothesized to describe the observed distribution.

Grand Mean The mean for the entire group of subjects from all the samples in the experiment.

Test of Independence A statistical test of proportions of frequencies to determine whether membership in categories of one variable is different as a function of membership in the categories of a second variable.

Within-Column Variance An estimate of the population variance based on the variances within the k samples, using a weighted average of the k sample variances.

● Equations Introduced in Chapter 11

■ **11-1**

$$\chi^2 = \Sigma\frac{(f_o - f_e)^2}{f_e}$$ p. 572

This formula says that the *chi-square statistic* (χ^2) is equal to the sum (Σ) we will get if we

1. Subtract the expected frequencies, f_e, from the observed frequencies, f_o, for each category of our contingency table.
2. Square each of the differences.
3. Divide each squared difference by f_e.
4. Sum all the results of step 3.

■ **11-2** Number of degrees of freedom = (number of rows − 1)(number of columns − 1) p. 575

To calculate number of *degrees of freedom in a chi-square test of independence,* multiply the number of rows (less 1) times the number of columns (less 1).

■ **11-3**

$$f_e = \frac{RT \times CT}{n}$$ p. 577

With this formula, we can calculate the expected frequency for any cell in a contingency table. RT is the row total for the row containing the cell, CT is the column total for the column containing the cell, and n is the total number of observations.

■ **11-4**

$$s_{\bar{x}}^2 = \frac{\Sigma(\bar{x} - \bar{\bar{x}})^2}{k - 1}$$ p. 593

To calculate the *variance among the sample means,* use this formula.

■ **11-5**

$$\sigma^2 = \sigma_{\bar{x}}^2 \times n$$ p. 594

The *population variance* is equal to the product of the square of the standard error of the mean and the sample size.

■ **11-6**

$$\hat{\sigma}_b^2 = \frac{\Sigma n_j(\bar{x}_j - \bar{\bar{x}})^2}{k - 1}$$ p. 594

One estimate of the population variance (the between-column variance) can be obtained by using this equation. We obtain this equation by first substituting $s_{\bar{x}}^2$ for $\sigma_{\bar{x}}^2$ in Equation 11-5, and then by weighting each $(\bar{x}_j - \bar{\bar{x}})^2$ by its own appropriate sample size (n_j).

■ **11-7**

$$\hat{\sigma}_w^2 = \Sigma\left(\frac{n_j - 1}{n_T - k}\right)s_j^2$$ p. 595

A second estimate of the population variance (the within-column variance) can be obtained from this equation. This equation uses a weighted average of all the sample variances. In this formulation, $n_T = \Sigma n_j$, the total sample size.

■ 11-8

$$F = \frac{\text{first estimate of the population variance based on the variance among the sample means}}{\text{second estimate of the popluation variance based on the variances within the samples}}$$

p. 596

This ratio is the way we can compare the two estimates of the population variance, which we calculated in Equations 11-6 and 11-7. In a hypothesis test based on an F distribution, we are more likely to accept the null hypothesis if this *F ratio* or *F statistic* is near to the value of 1. As the F ratio increases, the more likely it is that we will reject the null hypothesis.

■ 11-9

$$F = \frac{\text{between-column variance}}{\text{within-column variance}} = \frac{\hat{\sigma}_b^2}{\hat{\sigma}_w^2}$$

p. 596

This restates Equation 11-8, using statistical shorthand for the numerator and the denominator of the F ratio.

■ 11-10

$$\begin{array}{c}\text{Number of degrees of freedom in}\\ \text{the numerator of the } F \text{ ratio}\end{array} = (\text{number of samples} - 1)$$

p. 598

To do an analysis of variance, we calculate the number of *degrees of freedom in the between-column variance* (the numerator of the F ratio) by subtracting 1 from the number of samples collected.

■ 11-11

$$\begin{array}{c}\text{Number of degrees of freedom in}\\ \text{the denominator of the } F \text{ ratio}\end{array} = \Sigma(n_j - 1) = n_T - k$$

p. 598

We use this equation to calculate the number of degrees of freedom in the denominator of the F ratio. This turns out to be the total sample size, n_T, minus the number of samples, k.

■ 11-12

$$\chi^2 = \frac{(n-1)s^2}{\sigma^2}$$

p. 609

With a population variance of σ^2, the χ^2 statistic given by this equation has a chi-square distribution with $n - 1$ degrees of freedom. This result is exact if the population is normal, but even in samples from nonnormal populations, it is often a good approximation.

■ 11-13

$$\sigma^2 = \frac{(n-1)s^2}{\chi^2}$$

p. 610

To get a confidence interval for σ^2, we solve Equation 11–12 for σ^2.

■ 11-14

$$\sigma_L^2 = \frac{(n-1)s^2}{\chi_U^2} \quad \leftarrow \text{Lower confidence limit}$$

p. 610

$$\sigma_U^2 = \frac{(n-1)s^2}{\chi_L^2} \quad \leftarrow \text{Upper confidence limit}$$

These formulas give the lower and upper confidence limits for a confidence interval for σ^2. (Notice that because χ^2 appears in the denominator, we use χ_U^2 to find σ_L^2 and χ_L^2 to find σ_U^2.)

■ **11-15** $$F = \frac{s_1^2}{s_2^2}$$ p. 616

This ratio has an F distribution with $n_1 - 1$ degrees of freedom in the numerator and $n_2 - 1$ degrees of freedom in the denominator. (This assumes that the two populations are reasonably well described by normal distributions.) It is used to test hypotheses about two population variances.

■ **11-16** $$F(n, d, \alpha) = \frac{1}{F(d, n, 1 - \alpha)}$$ p. 619

Appendix Table 6 gives values of F for upper-tailed tests only, but this equation enables us to find appropriate values of F for lower-tailed and two-tailed tests.

Review and Application Exercises

■ **11-57** The post office is concerned about the variability in the number of days it takes a letter to go from the east coast to the west coast. A sample of letters was mailed from the east coast, and the time taken for the letters to arrive at their address on the west coast was recorded. The following data were collected:

Mailing Time (in days)

2.2	1.7	3.0	2.9	1.9	3.1	4.2	1.5	4.0	2.5

Find a 90 percent confidence interval for the variance in mailing times.

■ **11–58** For the following contingency table, calculate the observed and expected frequencies and the chi-square statistic. State and test the appropriate hypotheses at the 0.05 significance level.

	Attitude Toward Social Legislation		
Occupation	**Favor**	**Neutral**	**Oppose**
Blue-collar	19	16	37
White-collar	15	22	46
Professional	24	11	32

■ **11-59** Marketers know that tastes differ in various regions of the country. In the rental car business, an industry expert has given the opinion that there are strong regional preferences for size of car and quotes the following data in support of that view:

	Region of Country			
Preferred Car Type	**Northeast**	**Southeast**	**Northwest**	**Southwest**
Full-size	105	120	105	70
Intermediate	120	100	130	150
All other	25	30	15	30

(a) State the appropriate null and alternative hypotheses.

(b) Do the data support the expert's opinion at the 0.05 significance level?

(c) What about at the 0.20 significance level?

■ **11-60** What probability distribution is used in each of these types of statistical tests?

(a) Comparing two population proportions.

(b) Value of a single population variance.

(c) Comparing three or more population means.

(d) Comparing two population means from small, dependent samples.

■ **11-61** The Gap is a specialty clothing retailer selling adult casual clothes with a "value" strategy: good quality at a reasonable price. In 1986, the company started a new division, Gap Kids, with separate stores offering similar clothes for the 2–12 age range. After several years of rapid expansion in the United States, the Gap began to open stores in Canada and the United Kingdom. By the third quarter of 1992, the number of stores operating was

	United States	UK	Canada
Gap (adult)	822	20	31
Gap Kids	240	8	14

Source: Company data, reported by Salomon Bros., December 23, 1992.

Test at $\alpha = 0.01$ to see whether the Gap is putting the same emphasis on opening Gap Kids stores in all three countries. Why might this business strategy make sense?

■ **11-62** International inventors and companies know the value of a U.S. patent to protect their ideas, and in recent years, they have received almost half of the patents granted. From the data in the following table, has there been a significant change in the proportion of patents that have originated overseas in the last 10 years? Test at $\alpha = 0.05$.

Patents Awarded	1981	1991
U.S. origin	39,223	51,183
Non-U.S. origin	26,548	45,331

Source: U.S. Patent Office reported by Business Week *(18 January 1993): 79.*

■ **11-63** There are 33 major symphony orchestras in the United States. The numbers of concerts given by each in 1989 are listed and summarized in the following table. It is not immediately clear whether these orchestras can be considered to represent a single population or if there may be several different types (small, medium, and large), distinguished by the number of concerts they give annually. If there are different types of orchestras, a music publishing company might want to develop different marketing programs for dealing with them. For example, the large symphonies could have individual sales representatives assigned to them, but one representative could handle several of the smaller symphonies.

For a first cut at seeing whether the 33 orchestras can be considered a single group, use the information in the table to test at $\alpha = 0.025$ whether the numbers of concerts given in 1989 are well described by a normal distribution with $\mu = 182.3$ (the sample mean) and $\sigma = 57$ (the sample standard deviation).

Numbers of Concerts (raw data)

325	300	267	263	250	230	216	215	200	200	200
200	190	185	185	180	180	180	180	175	175	164
160	160	157	150	135	120	115	105	100	84	70

Frequency Distribution

Class	≤100	101–150	151–200	201–250	251–300	≥301
Frequency	3	5	17	4	3	1

Source: Richard Boyer and David Savageau, Places Rated Almanac *(New York: Prentice Hall Travel, 1989): 226.*

■ **11-64** What probability distribution is used in each of these types of statistical tests?

(a) Comparing the means of two small samples from populations with unknown variances.

(b) Comparing two population variances.

(c) Value of a single population mean based on large samples.

(d) Comparing three or more population proportions.

■ **11-65** Retail stores set prices, but manufacturers have an interest in final retail price as this is part of their promotion strategy. The marketing manager for Brand C ballpoint pens complains that excessive price-cutting by stores results in the perception of Brand C as an "off brand." The sales manager replies that, "Everyone discounts—all the brands—to some extent." During sales calls, they collected data on the final sales price for four brands of pens, including their own, from five different stores. At the 0.05 confidence level, is there significant variation in price between the brands?

Price (in cents)

Brand A	Brand B	Brand C	Brand D
61	52	47	67
55	58	52	63
57	54	49	68
60	55	49	59
62	58	57	65

■ **11-66** An outdoor advertising company must know whether significantly different traffic volumes pass three billboard locations in Newark because the company charges different rates for different traffic volumes. The company measures the volume of traffic at the three locations during randomly selected 5-minute intervals. The table shows the data gathered. At the 0.05 level of significance, are the volumes of traffic passing the three billboards the same?

Volume of Traffic

Billboard 1	30	45	26	44	18	38	42	29	
Billboard 2	29	38	36	21	36	18	17	30	32
Billboard 3	32	44	40	43	24	28	18		

■ **11-67** An investor is interested in seeing whether there are significant differences in the rates of return on stocks, bonds, and mutual funds. He has taken random samples of each type of investment and has recorded the following data.

Rate of Return (percent)

Stocks	2.0	6.0	2.0	2.1	6.2	2.9
Bonds	4.0	3.1	2.2	5.3	5.9	
Mutual funds	3.5	3.1	2.9	6.0		

(a) State null and alternative hypotheses.
(b) Test your hypotheses at the 0.05 significance level.
(c) State an explicit conclusion.

■ **11-68** For the following contingency table:
(a) Construct a table of observed and expected frequencies.
(b) Calculate the chi-square statistic.
(c) State the null and alternative hypotheses.
(d) At a 0.05 level of significance, should the null hypothesis be rejected?

Church Attendance	Income Level Low	Middle	High
Never	27	48	15
Occasional	25	63	14
Regular	22	74	12

■ **11-69** The Overseas Shipholding Group, Inc. (OSG) has three types of vessels: bulk carriers, petroleum products carriers (PPCs), and tankers. Some of these ships are on long-term charters, hauling goods for one supplier over a period of years. Other ships are contracted per voyage. The chief advantage of a long-term charter is locking in revenue, at the cost of forgoing the opportunity to charge a premium price if market forces place ships in high demand. The existence of long-term charters will affect financial analysts' estimates of OSG's future earnings.

Do the following frequency data indicate that the three types of ships are equally likely to be on charter? Test at $\alpha = 0.10$.

	Bulk Carriers	PPCs	Tankers
Charter	7	7	20
No charter	15	10	4

Source: Overseas Shipholding Group, Inc., 1991 Annual Report.

11-70 The Dow-Jones Industrial, Transportation, and Utility Averages are based on the share prices of 30 industrial firms, 20 transportation firms, and 15 utilities listed on the New York Stock Exchange and deemed to be representative of all listed companies in their groups. The following table lists the changes in share prices for these 65 companies on June 21, 1993. At $\alpha = 0.05$, is it reasonable to conclude that the three groups had significantly different average changes in share prices on that day?

Industrial Average

Company	Change	Company	Change
Alcoa	+0.125	Goodyear	−0.125
Allied Signal	+1.625	IBM	−0.125
American Express	−0.375	International Paper	+0.125
AT&T	+0.250	McDonald's	−0.250
Bethlehem Steel	+0.500	Merck	0
Boeing	−0.375	Minnesota Mining & Mfg.	+1.375
Caterpillar	−1.500	JP Morgan	+0.375
Chevron	+1.000	Philip Morris	−0.125
Coca Cola	−0.250	Procter & Gamble	+0.375
Disney	0	Sears	+0.500
DuPont	−0.250	Texaco	+1.000
Eastman Kodak	+0.250	Union Carbide	+0.125
Exxon	−0.125	United Technologies	+0.750
General Electric	+1.000	Westinghouse	0
General Motors	+1.125	Woolworth	+0.250

Transportation Average

Company	Change	Company	Change
Airborne Freight	0	Federal Express	+0.375
Alaska Air	−0.125	Norfolk Southern	+0.250
American President	−0.250	Roadway Services	+0.250
AMR	−0.500	Ryder System	+0.125
Burlington Northern	+0.625	Santa Fe Pacific	+1.000
Carolina Freight	+0.125	Southwest Airlines	−0.625
Consolidated Freightways	−0.125	UAL	−1.500
Conrail	+0.625	Union Pacific	+0.375
CSX	+ 1.125	USAir	0
Delta Air Lines	−0.125	XTRA	0

Utility Average

Company	Change	Company	Change
American Electric Power	+0.375	Niagara Mohawk Power	−0.500
Arkla	+0.125	Pacific Gas & Electric	+0.125
Centerior Energy	−0.125	Panhandle Eastern	+0.625
Commonwealth Edison	+0.625	People's Energy	+0.375
Consolidated Edison	+0.250	Philadelphia Electric	+0.250
Consolidated Natural Gas	+0.250	Public Service	
Detroit Edison	+0.375	Enterprise Group	+0.250
Houston Industries	−0.125	SCEcorp	+0.125

Source: The Wall Street Journal *(22 June 1993): C3.*

■ **11-71** For the following contingency table:

(a) Construct a table of observed and expected frequencies.

(b) Calculate the chi-square statistic.

(c) State the null and alternative hypotheses.

(d) At a 0.01 level of significance, should the null hypothesis be rejected?

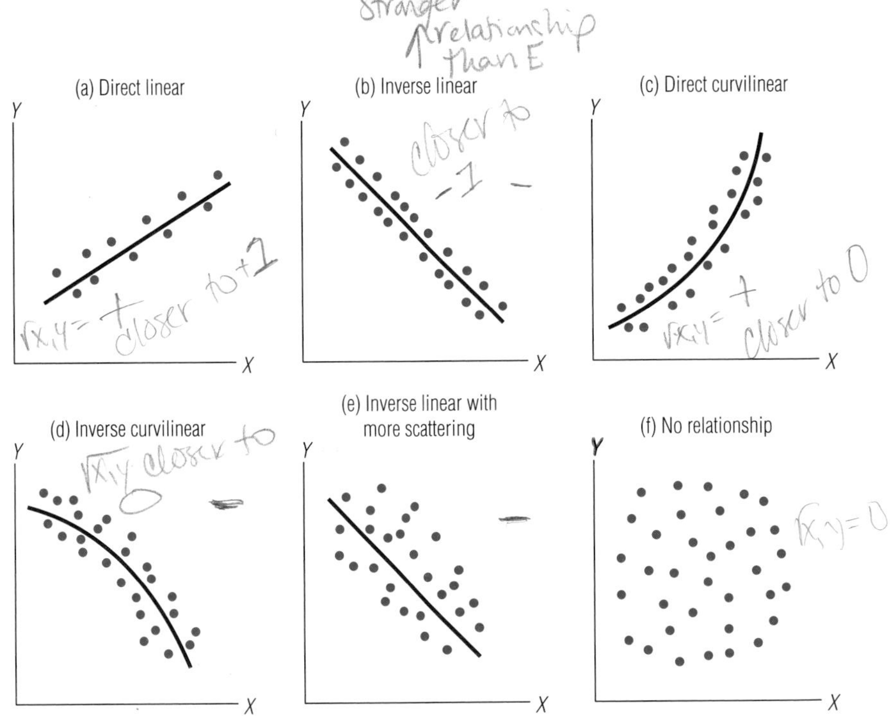

FIGURE 12-5

Possible relationships between X and Y in scatter diagrams

between the two variables; therefore, knowledge of the past concerning one variable does not allow us to predict future occurrences of the other.

Exercises 12.1

Self-Check Exercise

SC 12-1 An instructor is interested in finding out how the number of students absent on a given day is related to the mean temperature that day. A random sample of 10 days was used for the study. The following data indicate the number of students absent (ABS) and the mean temperature (TEMP) for each day.

ABS	8	7	5	4	2	3	5	6	8	9
TEMP	10	20	25	30	40	45	50	55	59	60

(a) State the dependent (Y) variable and the independent (X) variable.
(b) Draw a scatter diagram of these data.
(c) Does the relationship between the variables appear to be linear or curvilinear?
(d) What type of curve could you draw through the data?
(e) What is the logical explanation for the observed relationship?

Basic Concepts

■ **12-1** What is regression analysis?
■ **12-2** In regression analysis, what is an estimating equation?
■ **12-3** What is the purpose of correlation analysis?
■ **12-4** Define direct and inverse relationships.

■ **12-5** To what does the term *causal relationship* refer?

■ **12-6** Explain the difference between linear and curvilinear relationships.

■ **12-7** Explain why and how we construct a scatter diagram.

■ **12-8** What is multiple-regression analysis?

■ **12-9** For each of the following scatter diagrams, indicate whether a relationship exists and, if so, whether it is direct or inverse and linear or curvilinear.

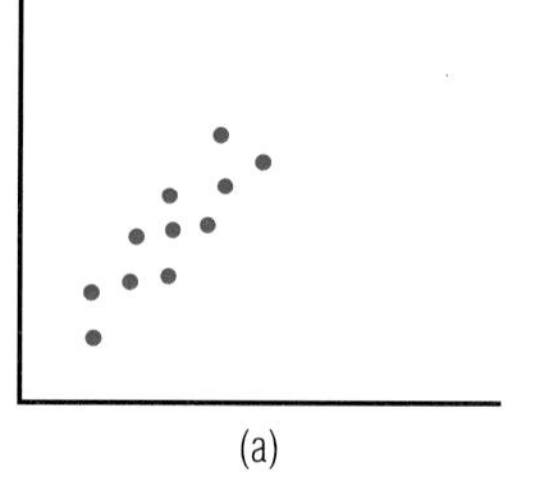

(a)

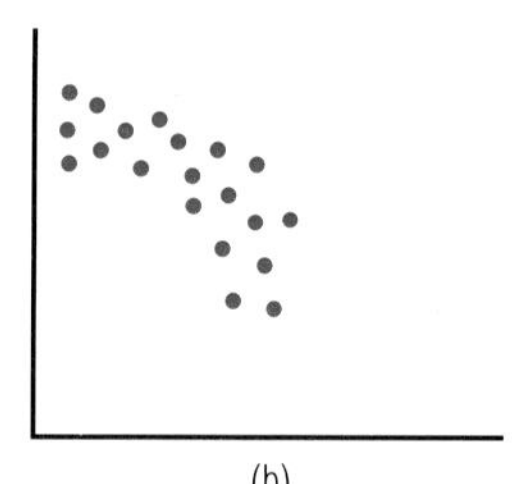

(b)

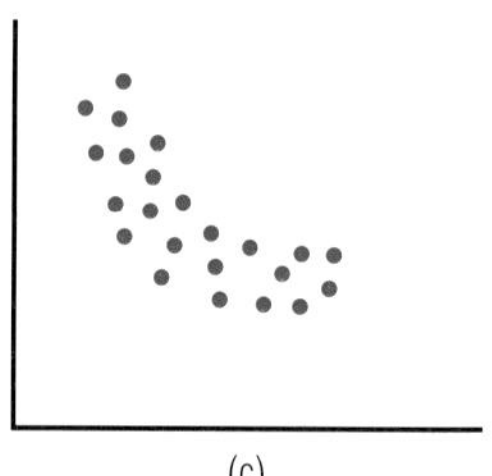

(c)

Applications

■ **12-10** A professor is trying to show his students the importance of quizzes even though 90 percent of the final grade is determined by exams. He believes that the higher the quiz grade, the higher the final grade. A random sample of 15 students in his class was selected with the data given below:

Quiz Average	Final Average
59	65
92	84
72	77
90	80
95	77
87	81
89	80
77	84
76	80
65	69
97	83
42	40
94	78
62	65
91	90

(a) State the dependent (Y) variable and the independent (X) variable.

(b) Draw a scatter diagram of these data.

(c) Does the relationship between the variables appear to be linear or curvilinear?

(d) Does the professor's belief appear to be justified? Explain your reasoning.

■ **12-11** William Hawkins, VP of personnel for International Motors, is working on the relationship between a worker's salary and absentee rate. Hawkins divided the salary range of International into twelve grades or levels (1 being the lowest grade, 12 the highest) and then randomly sampled a group

Basic Concepts

■ **12-13** For the following data

(a) Plot the scatter diagram.

(b) Develop the estimating equation that best describes the data.

(c) Predict Y for $X = 6, 13.4, 20.5$.

X	2.7	4.8	5.6	18.4	19.6	21.5	18.7	14.3
Y	16.66	16.92	22.3	71.8	80.88	81.4	77.46	48.7

X	11.6	10.9	18.4	19.7	12.3	6.8	13.8
Y	50.48	47.82	71.5	81.26	50.1	39.4	52.8

■ **12-14** Using the data given below

(a) Plot the scatter diagram.

(b) Develop the estimating equation that best describes the data.

(c) Predict Y for $X = 5, 6, 7$.

X	16	6	10	5	12	14
Y	−4.4	8.0	2.1	8.7	0.1	−2.9

■ **12-15** Given the following set of data:

(a) Find the best-fitting line.

(b) Compute the standard error of estimate.

(c) Find an approximate prediction interval (with a 95 percent confidence level) for the dependent variable given that X is 44.

X	56	48	42	58	40	39	50
Y	45	38.5	34.5	46.1	33.3	32.1	40.4

Applications

■ **12-16** Sales of major appliances vary with the new housing market: when new home sales are good, so are the sales of dishwashers, washing machines, driers, and refrigerators. A trade association compiled the following historical data (in thousands of units) on major appliance sales and housing starts:

Housing Starts (thousands)	Appliance Sales (thousands)
2.0	5.0
2.5	5.5
3.2	6.0
3.6	7.0
3.3	7.2
4.0	7.7
4.2	8.4
4.6	9.0
4.8	9.7
5.0	10.0

(a) Develop an equation for the relationship between appliance sales (in thousands) and housing starts (in thousands).

(b) Interpret the slope of the regression line.

(c) Compute and interpret the standard error of estimate.

(d) Housing starts next year may be beyond the recorded range; estimates as high as 8.0 million units have been predicted. Compute an approximate 90 percent prediction interval for appliance sales, based on the previous data and the new prediction of housing starts.

■ **12-17** During recent tennis matches, Diane has noticed that her lobs have been less than totally effective because her opponents have been returning more of them. Some of the people she plays are quite tall, so she was wondering whether the height of her opponent could be used to explain the number of lobs not returned during a match. The following data were collected from five recent matches.

Opponent's Height (*H*)	Unreturned Lobs (*L*)
5.0	9
5.5	6
6.0	3
6.5	0
5.0	7

(a) Which variable is the dependent variable?

(b) What is the least-squares estimating equation for these data?

(c) What is your best estimate of the number of unreturned lobs in her match tomorrow with an opponent who is 5.9 feet tall?

■ **12-18** A study by the Atlanta, Georgia, Department of Transportation on the effect of bus-ticket prices on the number of passengers produced the following results:

Ticket price (cents)	25	30	35	40	45	50	55	60
Passengers per 100 miles	800	780	780	660	640	600	620	620

(a) Plot these data.

(b) Develop the estimating equation that best describes these data.

(c) Predict the number of passengers per 100 miles if the ticket price were 50 cents. Use a 95 percent approximate prediction interval.

■ **12-19** William C. Andrews, an organizational behavior consultant for Victory Motorcycles, has designed a test to show the company's supervisors the dangers of oversupervising their workers. A worker from the assembly line is given a series of complicated tasks to perform. During the worker's performance, a supervisor constantly interrupts the worker to assist him or her in completing the tasks. The worker, upon completion of the tasks, is then given a psychological test designed to measure the worker's hostility toward authority (a high score equals low hostility). Eight different workers were assigned the tasks and then interrupted for the purpose of instructional assistance various numbers of times (line *X*). Their corresponding scores on the hostility test are revealed in line *Y*.

X (number of times worker interrupted)	5	10	10	15	15	20	20	25
Y (worker's score on hostility test)	58	41	45	27	26	12	16	3

(a) Plot these data.

(b) Develop the equation that best describes the relationship between the number of times interrupted and the test score.

(c) Predict the expected test score if the worker is interrupted 18 times.

■ **12-20** The editor-in-chief of a major metropolitan newspaper has been trying to convince the paper's owner to improve the working conditions in the pressroom. He is convinced that the noise level when the presses are running creates unhealthy levels of tension and anxiety. He recently had a psychologist conduct a test during which press operators were placed in rooms with varying levels of noise and then given a test to measure mood and anxiety levels. The following table shows the index of their degree of arousal or nervousness and the level of noise to which they were exposed (1.0 is low and 10.0 is high).

Noise level	4	3	1	2	6	7	2	3
Degree of arousal	39	38	16	18	41	45	25	38

(a) Plot these data.

(b) Develop an estimating equation that describes these data.

(c) Predict the degree of arousal we might expect when the noise level is 5.

■ **12-21** A firm administers a test to sales trainees before they go into the field. The management of the firm is interested in determining the relationship between the test scores and the sales made by the trainees at the end of one year in the field. The following data were collected for 10 sales personnel who have been in the field one year.

Salesperson Number	Test Score (T)	Number of Units Sold (S)
1	2.6	95
2	3.7	140
3	2.4	85
4	4.5	180
5	2.6	100
6	5.0	195
7	2.8	115
8	3.0	136
9	4.0	175
10	3.4	150

(a) Find the least-squares regression line that could be used to predict sales from trainee test scores.

(b) How much does the expected number of units sold increase for each 1-point increase in a trainee's test score?

(c) Use the least-squares regression line to predict the number of units that would be sold by a trainee who received an average test score.

■ **12-22** The city council of Bowie, Maryland, has gathered data on the number of minor traffic accidents and the number of youth soccer games that occur in town over a weekend.

X (soccer games)	20	30	10	12	15	25	34
Y (minor accidents)	6	9	4	5	7	8	9

(a) Plot these data.

(b) Develop the estimating equation that best describes these data.

(c) Predict the number of minor traffic accidents that will occur on a weekend during which 33 soccer games take place in Bowie.

(d) Calculate the standard error of estimate.

■ **12-23** In economics, the demand function for a product is often estimated by regressing the quantity sold (Q) on the price (P). The Bamsy Company is trying to estimate the demand function for its new doll "Ma'am," and has collected the following data:

P	20.0	17.5	16.0	14.0	12.5	10.0	8.0	6.5
Q	125	156	183	190	212	238	250	276

(a) Plot these data.
(b) Calculate the least-squares regression line.
(c) Draw the fitted regression line on your plot from part (a).

■ **12-24** A tire manufacturing company is interested in removing pollutants from the exhaust at the factory, and cost is a concern. The company has collected data from other companies concerning the amount of money spent on environmental measures and the resulting amount of dangerous pollutants released (as a percentage of total emissions).

Money Spent ($ thousands)	8.4	10.2	16.5	21.7	9.4	8.3	11.5
Percentage of Dangerous Pollutants	35.9	31.8	24.7	25.2	36.8	35.8	33.4
Money Spent ($ thousands)	18.4	16.7	19.3	28.4	4.7	12.3	
Percentage of Dangerous Pollutants	25.4	31.4	27.4	15.8	31.5	28.9	

(a) Compute the regression equation.
(b) Predict the percentage of dangerous pollutants released when $20,000 is spent on control measures.
(c) Calculate the standard error of estimate.

Worked-Out Answers to Self-Check Exercises

SC 12-2 (a)

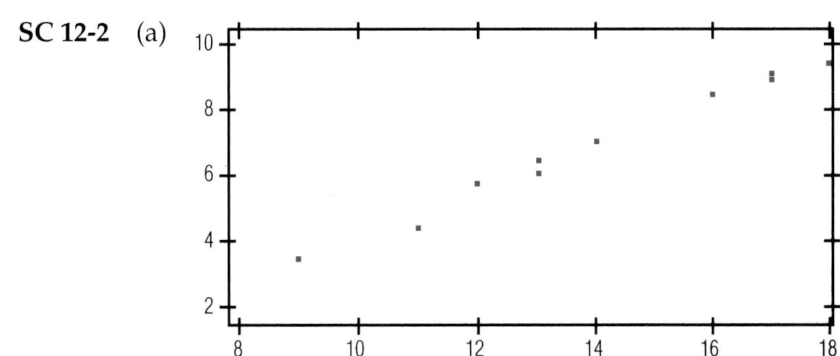

(b)

X	Y	XY	X^2
13	6.2	80.6	169
16	8.6	137.6	256
14	7.2	100.8	196
11	4.5	49.5	121
17	9.0	153.0	289
9	3.5	31.5	81
13	6.5	84.5	169
17	9.3	158.1	289
18	9.5	171.0	324
12	5.7	68.4	144
$\Sigma X = 140$	$\Sigma Y = 70.0$	$\Sigma XY = 1{,}035.0$	$\Sigma X^2 = 2{,}038$

$$\overline{X} = 140/10 = 14 \qquad \overline{Y} = 70.0/10 = 7.0$$

$$b = \frac{\Sigma XY - n\overline{X}\overline{Y}}{\Sigma X^2 - n\overline{X}^2} = \frac{1{,}035.0 - 10(14)(7.0)}{2{,}038 - 10(14)^2} = 0.7051$$

$$a = \overline{Y} - b\overline{X} = 7.0 - (0.7051)(14) = -2.8714$$

Thus, $\hat{Y} = -2.8714 + 0.7051X$. If you used a computer regression package to do your computation, you probably got

$$\hat{Y} = -2.8718 + 0.7051X.$$

This slight difference occurs because most computer packages carry their calculations to more than ten decimal places, but we rounded b to only four places before finding a. For most practical purposes, this slight difference (i.e., $a = -2.8714$ instead of -2.8718) is inconsequential.

(c) $X = 10, \hat{Y} = -2.8714 + 0.7051(10) = 4.1796$

$X = 15, \hat{Y} = -2.8714 + 0.7051(15) = 7.7051$

$X = 20, \hat{Y} = -2.8714 + 0.7051(20) = 11.2306$

SC 12-3 In this problem, Y = overhead and X = units produced.

(a)

X	Y	XY	X^2	Y^2
40	191	7,640	1,600	36,481
42	170	7,140	1,764	28,900
53	272	14,416	2,809	73,984
35	155	5,425	1,225	24,025
56	280	15,680	3,136	78,400
39	173	6,747	1,521	29,929
48	234	11,232	2,304	54,756
30	116	3,480	900	13,456
37	153	5,661	1,369	23,409
40	178	7,120	1,600	31,684
ΣX = **420**	ΣY = **1,922**	ΣXY = **84,541**	ΣX^2 = **18,228**	ΣY^2 = **395,024**

$$\overline{X} = \frac{420}{10} = 42 \qquad \overline{Y} = \frac{1{,}922}{10} = 192.2$$

$$b = \frac{\Sigma XY - n\overline{X}\,\overline{Y}}{\Sigma X^2 - n\overline{X}^2} = \frac{84{,}541 - 10(42)(192.2)}{18{,}228 - 10(42)^2} = 6.4915$$

$$a = \overline{Y} - b\overline{X} = 192.2 - 6.4915(42) = -80.4430$$

Thus, $\hat{Y} = -80.4430 + 6.4915X$ (Computer packages: $\hat{Y} = -80.4428 + 6.4915X$).

(b) $\hat{Y} = -80.4430 + 6.4915(50) = 244.1320$

(c) $$s_e = \sqrt{\frac{\Sigma Y^2 - a\Sigma Y - b\Sigma XY}{n - 2}}$$

$$= \sqrt{\frac{395{,}024 - (-80.4430)(1{,}922) - 6.4915(84{,}541)}{8}} = 10.2320$$

12.3 Correlation Analysis

What correlation analysis does

Correlation analysis is the statistical tool we can use to describe *the degree to which one variable is linearly related to another.* Often, correlation analysis is used in conjunction with regression analysis to measure how well the regression line explains the variation of the dependent variable, Y. Correlation can also be used by itself, however, to measure the degree of association between two variables.

Two measures that describe correlation

Statisticians have developed two measures for describing the correlation between two variables: the *coefficient of determination* and the *coefficient of correlation.* Introducing these two measures of association is the purpose of this section.

The Coefficient of Determination

Developing the sample coefficient of determination

The coefficient of determination is the primary way we can measure the extent, or strength, of the association that exists between two variables, X and Y. Because we have used a sample of points to develop regression lines, we refer to this measure as the *sample coefficient of determination.*

The sample coefficient of determination is developed from the relationship between two kinds of variation: the variation of the Y values in a data set around

1. The fitted regression line
2. Their own mean

The term *variation* in both cases is used in its usual statistical sense to mean "the sum of a group of squared deviations." By using this definition, then, it is reasonable to express the variation of the Y values around the regression line with this equation:

Variation of *Y* Values around the Regression Line

$$\text{Variation of the } Y \text{ values around the regression line} = \Sigma(Y - \hat{Y})^2 \quad [12\text{-}8]$$

The second variation, that of the Y values around their own mean, is determined by

Variation of *Y* Values around Their Own Mean

$$\text{Variation of the } Y \text{ values around their own mean} = \Sigma(Y - \bar{Y})^2 \quad [12\text{-}9]$$

One minus the ratio between these two variations is the sample coefficient of determination, which is symbolized r^2:

Sample Coefficient of Determination

$$r^2 = 1 - \frac{\Sigma(Y - \hat{Y})^2}{\Sigma(Y - \bar{Y})^2} \quad [12\text{-}10]$$

The next two sections will show you that r^2, as defined by Equation 12-10, is a measure of the degree of linear association between X and Y.

Table 12-13 Illustration of Perfect Correlation between Two Variables, X and Y	Data Point	Value of X	Value of Y	
	1st	1	4	
	2nd	2	8	
	3rd	3	12	
	4th	4	16	
	5th	5	20	
	6th	6	24	$\bar{Y} = \frac{144}{8} = 18 \leftarrow$ Mean of the values of Y
	7th	7	28	
	8th	8	32	
			$\Sigma Y =$ **144**	

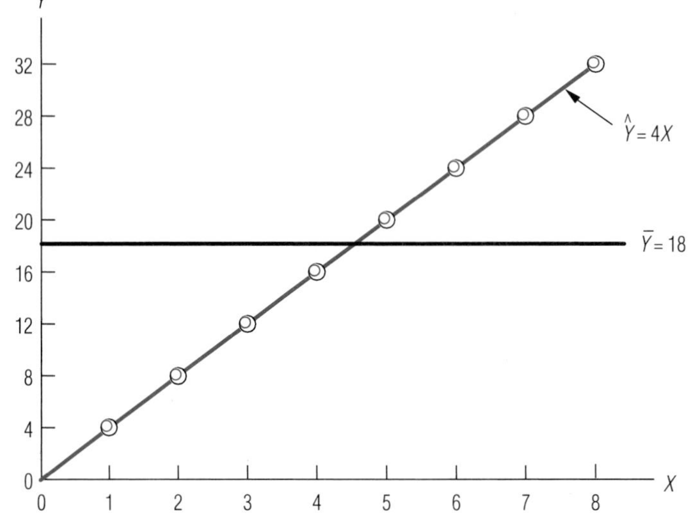

FIGURE 12-13

Perfect correlation between X and Y: Every data point lies on the regression line

An Intuitive Interpretation of r^2

Consider the two extreme ways in which variables X and Y can be related. In Table 12-13, every observed value of Y lies on the estimating line, as can be verified visually by Figure 12-13. This is *perfect correlation.*

Estimating equation appropriate for perfect correlation example

The estimating equation appropriate for these data is easy to determine. Because the regression line passes through the origin, we know that the Y-intercept is zero; because Y increases by 4 every time X increases by 1, the slope must equal 4. Thus, the regression line is

$$\hat{Y} = 4X$$

Determining the sample coefficient of determination for the perfect correlation example

Now, to determine the sample coefficient of determination for the regression line in Figure 12-13, we first calculate the numerator of the fraction in Equation 12-10:

$$\text{Variation of the } Y \text{ values around the regression line} = \Sigma(Y - \hat{Y})^2 \quad [12\text{-}8]$$

$$= \Sigma(0)^2$$

$$= 0$$

Because every Y value is on the regression line, the difference between Y and $\hat{Y}$ is zero in each case

Then we can find the denominator of the fraction:

$$\text{Variation of the } Y \text{ values around their own mean} = \Sigma(Y - \bar{Y})^2 \qquad [12\text{-}9]$$

$$\begin{aligned}
(\ 4 - 18)^2 &= (-14)^2 = 196 \\
(\ 8 - 18)^2 &= (-10)^2 = 100 \\
(12 - 18)^2 &= (-\ 6)^2 = \ \ 36 \\
(16 - 18)^2 &= (-\ 2)^2 = \ \ \ \ 4 \\
(20 - 18)^2 &= (\ \ \ 2)^2 = \ \ \ \ 4 \\
(24 - 18)^2 &= (\ \ \ 6)^2 = \ \ 36 \\
(28 - 18)^2 &= (\ 10)^2 = 100 \\
(32 - 18)^2 &= (\ 14)^2 = \underline{196} \\
& \qquad \qquad \ \ \mathbf{672} \leftarrow \Sigma(Y - \bar{Y})^2
\end{aligned}$$

Interpreting

With these values to substitute into Equation 12-10, we can find that the sample coefficient of determination is equal to $+1$:

$$r^2 = 1 - \frac{\Sigma(Y - \hat{Y})^2}{\Sigma(Y - \bar{Y})^2} \qquad [12\text{-}10]$$

$$= 1 - \frac{0}{672}$$

$$= 1 - 0$$

$$= 1 \leftarrow \text{Sample coefficient of determination when there is perfect correlation}$$

In fact, r^2 is equal to $+1$ whenever the regression line is a perfect estimator.

A second extreme way in which the variables X and Y can be related is that the points could lie at equal distances on both sides of a horizontal regression line, as pictured in Figure 12-14. The data set here consists of eight points, all of which have been recorded in Table 12-14.

Another wa
coefficient o

Explained a

Explained a

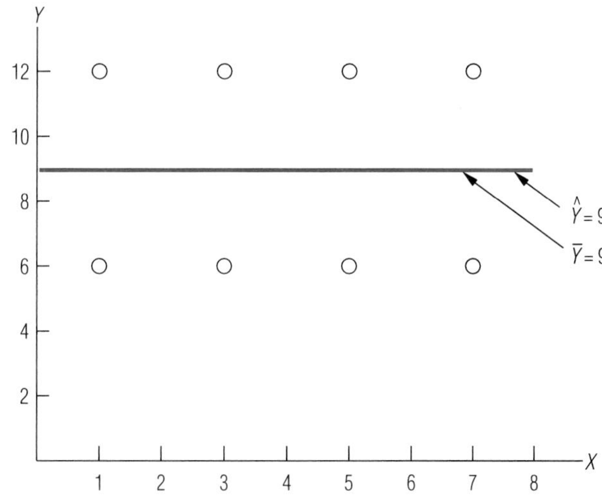

FIGURE 12-14

Zero correlation between X and Y: Same values of Y appear for different values of X

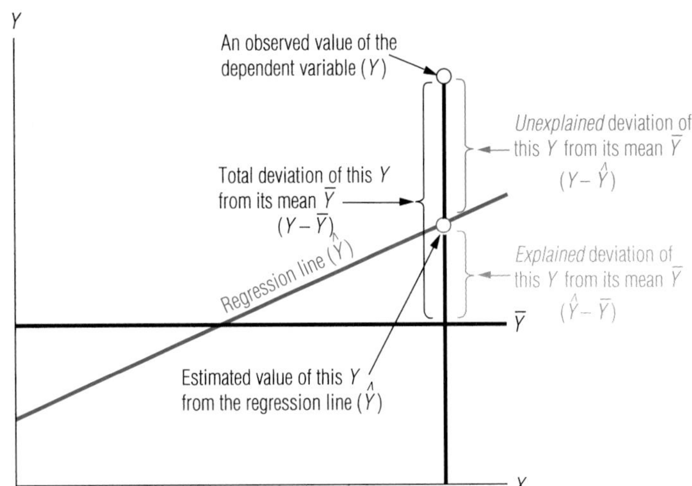

FIGURE 12-15

Total deviation, explained deviation, and unexplained deviation for one observed value of Y

The *unexplained* portion of the total variation (the sum of the squared unexplained deviations) of these points from the regression line would be

$$\Sigma(Y - \hat{Y})^2 \qquad [12\text{-}8]$$

Deter
of de

If we want to express the fraction of the total variation that remains *unexplained,* we would divide the unexplained variation, $\Sigma(Y - \hat{Y})^2$, by the total variation, $\Sigma(Y - \overline{Y})^2$, as follows

$$\frac{\Sigma(Y - \hat{Y})^2}{\Sigma(Y - \overline{Y})^2} \leftarrow \text{Fraction of the total variation that is unexplained}$$

Finally, if we subtract the fraction of the total variation that remains unexplained from 1, we will have the formula for finding that fraction of the total variation of Y that *is* explained by the regression line. That formula is

$$r^2 = 1 - \frac{\Sigma(Y - \hat{Y})^2}{\Sigma(Y - \overline{Y})^2} \qquad [12\text{-}10]$$

the same equation we have previously used to calculate r^2. It is in this sense, then, that r^2 measures how well X explains Y, that is, the degree of association between X and Y.

Short-cut method to calculate r^2

One final word about calculating r^2. To obtain r^2 using Equations 12-8, 12-9, and 12-10 requires a series of tedious calculations. To bypass these calculations, statisticians have developed a short-cut version, using values we would have determined already in the regression analysis. The formula is

Short-Cut Method for Finding Sample Coefficient of Determination

r^2 calculated by short-cut method $\longrightarrow$

$$r^2 = \frac{a\Sigma Y + b\Sigma XY - n\overline{Y}^2}{\Sigma Y^2 - n\overline{Y}^2} \qquad [12\text{-}11]$$

Table 12-15

Calculations of Inputs for Equation 12-11

Year ($n = 6$) (1)	R&D Expense (X) (2)	Annual Profit (Y) (3)	XY (2) × (3)	X^2 $(2)^2$	Y^2 $(3)^2$
1995	5	31	155	25	961
1994	11	40	440	121	1,600
1993	4	30	120	16	900
1992	5	34	170	25	1,156
1991	3	25	75	9	625
1990	2	20	40	4	400
	$\Sigma X = \mathbf{30}$	$\Sigma Y = \mathbf{180}$	$\Sigma XY = \mathbf{1{,}000}$	$\Sigma X^2 = \mathbf{200}$	$\Sigma Y^2 = \mathbf{5{,}642}$

$$\overline{Y} = \frac{180}{6}$$

$$= 30 \leftarrow \text{Mean of the values of the dependent variable}$$

where

- r^2 = sample coefficient of determination
- a = Y-intercept
- b = slope of the best-fitting estimating line
- n = number of data points
- X = values of the independent variable
- Y = values of the dependent variable
- $\overline{Y}$ = mean of the observed values of the dependent variable

Applying the short-cut method

To see why this formula is a short cut, apply it to our earlier regression relating research and development expenditures to profits. In Table 12-15, we have repeated the columns from Table 12-9, adding a Y^2 column. Recall that when we found the values for a and b, the regression line for this problem was

$$\hat{Y} = 20 + 2X$$

Using this line and the information in Table 12-15, we can calculate r^2 as follows:

$$r^2 = \frac{a\Sigma Y + b\Sigma XY - n\overline{Y}^2}{\Sigma Y^2 - n\overline{Y}^2} \quad [12\text{-}11]$$

$$= \frac{(20)(180) + (2)(1{,}000) - (6)(30)^2}{5{,}642 - (6)(30)^2}$$

$$= \frac{3{,}600 + 2{,}000 - 5{,}400}{5{,}642 - 5{,}400}$$

$$= \frac{200}{242}$$

$$= 0.826 \leftarrow \text{Sample coefficient of determination}$$

Interpreting r^2

Thus, we can conclude that the variation in the research and development expenditures (the independent variable X) explains 82.6 percent of the variation in the annual profits (the dependent variable Y).

The Coefficient of Correlation

Sample coefficient of correlation

The coefficient of correlation is the second measure that we can use to describe how well one variable is explained by another. When we are dealing with samples, the *sample coefficient of correlation* is denoted by r and is the square root of the sample coefficient of determination:

Sample Coefficient of Correlation

$$r = \sqrt{r^2} \quad [12\text{-}12]$$

When the slope of the estimating equation is positive, r is the positive square root, but if b is negative, r is the negative square root. Thus, **the sign of r indicates the direction of the relationship between the two variables X and Y.** If an inverse relationship exists—that is, if Y decreases as X increases—then r will fall between 0 and -1. Likewise, if there is a direct relationship (if Y increases as X increases), then r will be a value within the range of 0 to 1. Figure 12-16 illustrates these various characteristics of r.

Interpreting r

The coefficient of correlation is more difficult to interpret than r^2. What does $r = 0.9$ mean? To answer that question, we must remember that $r = 0.9$ is the same as $r^2 = 0.81$. The latter tells us that 81 percent of the variation in Y is explained by the regression line. So we see that r is nothing more than the square root of r^2, and we cannot interpret its meaning directly.

Calculating r for the research and development problem

Now let's find the coefficient of correlation of our problem relating research and development expenditures and annual profits. In the previous section, we found that the sample co-

FIGURE 12-16

Various characteristics of r, the sample coefficient of correlation

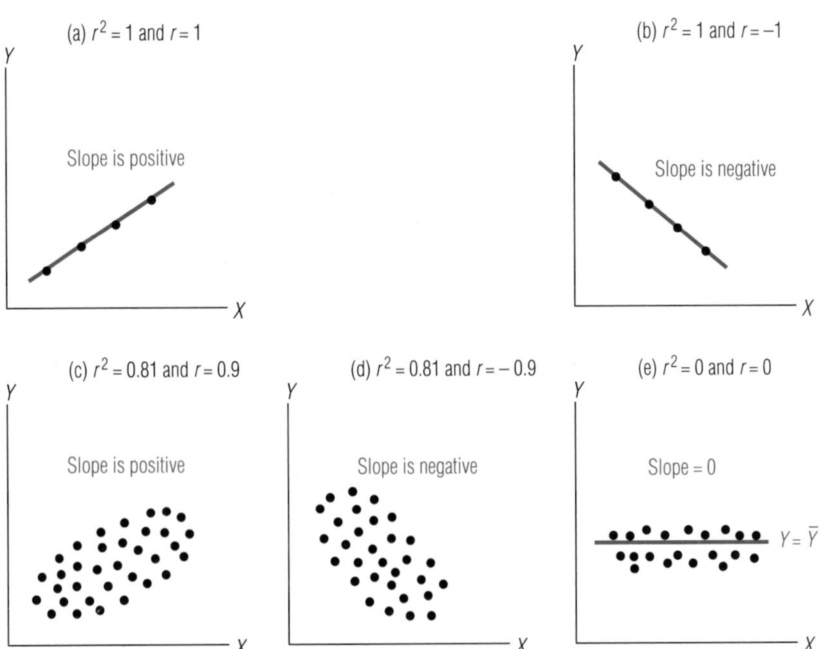

efficient of determination is $r^2 = 0.826$, so we can substitute this value into Equation 12-12 and find that

$$r = \sqrt{r^2} \qquad [12\text{-}12]$$

$$= \sqrt{0.826}$$

$$= 0.909 \leftarrow \text{Sample coefficient of correlation}$$

The relation between the two variables is direct and the slope is positive; therefore, the sign for r is positive.

HINTS & ASSUMPTIONS

Warning: Because you know that the coefficient of determination (r^2) is the square of the coefficient of correlation, r, you should be wary of using all but the highest correlations as the basis for making decisions. Hint: If we find that the amount spent on movies correlates 0.6 with family income, that seems like a fairly strong correlation (0.6 is closer to 1.0 than it is to zero). But when you square 0.6 you see that it accounts for only $0.6 \times 0.6 = 0.36$ or 36 percent of the variation in the amount of money families spend on movies. If you designed your marketing strategy to appeal only to families with high incomes, you'd miss a lot of potential customers. Hint: Instead, try to find what else is influencing family movie decisions.

Exercises 12.3

Self-Check Exercises

SC 12-4 Campus Stores has been selling the *Believe It or Not: Wonders of Statistics Study Guide* for 12 semesters and would like to estimate the relationship between sales and number of sections of elementary statistics taught in each semester. The following data have been collected:

Sales (units)	33	38	24	61	52	45
Number of sections	3	7	6	6	10	12
Sales (units)	65	82	29	63	50	79
Number of sections	12	13	12	13	14	15

(a) Develop the estimating equation that best fits the data.

(b) Calculate the sample coefficient of determination and the sample coefficient of correlation.

SC 12-5 Calculate the sample coefficient of determination and the sample coefficient of correlation for the data in Exercise SC 12-3.

Basic Concepts

■ **12-25** What type of correlation (positive, negative, or zero) should we expect from these variables?

(a) Ability of supervisors and output of their subordinates.

(b) Age at first full-time job and number of years of education.

(c) Weight and blood pressure.

(d) College grade-point average and student's height.

In the following exercises, calculate the sample coefficient of determination and the sample coefficient of correlation for the problems specified.

- **12-26** Calculate the sample coefficient of determination and the sample coefficient of correlation for the data in Exercise 12-17.
- **12-27** Calculate the sample coefficient of determination and the sample coefficient of correlation for the data in Exercise 12-18.
- **12-28** Calculate the sample coefficient of determination and the sample coefficient of correlation for the data in Exercise 12-19.
- **12-29** Calculate the sample coefficient of determination and the sample coefficient of correlation for the data in Exercise 12-20.
- **12-30** Calculate the sample coefficient of determination and the sample coefficient of correlation for the data in Exercise 12-21.

Applications

- **12-31** Bank of Lincoln is interested in reducing the amount of time people spend waiting to see a personal banker. The bank is interested in the relationship between waiting time (Y) in minutes and number of bankers on duty (X). Customers were randomly selected with the data given below:

X	2	3	5	4	2	6	1	3	4	3	3	2	4
Y	12.8	11.3	3.2	6.4	11.6	3.2	8.7	10.5	8.2	11.3	9.4	12.8	8.2

(a) Calculate the regression equation that best fits the data.

(b) Calculate the sample coefficient of determination and the sample coefficient of correlation.

- **12-32** Zippy Cola is studying the effect of its latest advertising campaign. People chosen at random were called and asked how many cans of Zippy Cola they had bought in the past week and how many Zippy Cola advertisements they had either read or seen in the past week.

X (number of ads)	3	7	4	2	0	4	1	2
Y (cans purchased)	11	18	9	4	7	6	3	8

(a) Develop the estimating equation that best fits the data.

(b) Calculate the sample coefficient of determination and the sample coefficient of correlation.

Worked-Out Answers to Self-Check Exercises

SC 12-4 In this problem, Y = sales and X = number of sections.

(a)

X	*Y*	*XY*	X^2	Y^2
3	33	99	9	1,089
7	38	266	49	1,444
6	24	144	36	576
6	61	366	36	3,721
10	52	520	100	2,704
12	45	540	144	2,025
12	65	780	144	4,225
13	82	1,066	169	6,724
12	29	348	144	841
13	63	819	169	3,969
14	50	700	196	2,500
15	79	1,185	225	6,241
$\Sigma X = 123$	$\Sigma Y = 621$	$\Sigma XY = 6{,}833$	$\Sigma X^2 = 1{,}421$	$\Sigma Y^2 = 36{,}059$

$$\overline{X} = 123/12 = 10.25 \qquad \overline{Y} = 621/12 = 51.75$$

$$b = \frac{\Sigma XY - n\overline{X}\overline{Y}}{\Sigma X^2 - n\overline{X}^2} = \frac{6{,}833 - 12(10.25)(51.75)}{1{,}421 - 12(10.25)^2} = 2.9189$$

$$a = \overline{Y} - b\overline{X} = 51.75 - 2.9189(10.25) = 21.8313$$

Thus, $\hat{Y} = 21.8313 + 2.9189X$ (Computer packages: $\hat{Y} = 21.8315 + 2.9189X$).

(b) $$r^2 = \frac{a\Sigma Y + b\Sigma XY - n\overline{Y}^2}{\Sigma Y^2 - n\overline{Y}^2}$$

$$= \frac{21.8313(621) + 2.9189(6{,}833) - 12(51.75)^2}{36{,}059 - 12(51.75)^2} = 0.3481$$

$$r = \sqrt{0.3481} = 0.5900$$

SC 12-5 From the solution to Exercise SC 12-3 on page 676, we have $n = 10$, $\Sigma Y = 1{,}922$, $\overline{Y} = 192.2$, $\Sigma XY = 84{,}541$, $\Sigma Y^2 = 395{,}024$, $a = -80.4430$, and $b = 6.4915$. Hence

$$r^2 = \frac{a\Sigma Y + b\Sigma XY - n\overline{Y}^2}{\Sigma Y^2 - n\overline{Y}^2}$$

$$= \frac{-80.4430(1{,}922) + 6.4915(84{,}541) - 10(192.2)^2}{395{,}024 - 10(192.2)^2}$$

$$= 0.9673$$

$$r = \sqrt{0.9673} = 0.9835$$

12.4 Making Inferences about Population Parameters

Relationship of sample regression line and population regression line

So far, we have used regression and correlation analyses to relate two variables on the basis of sample information. But data from a sample represent only part of the total population. Because of this, we may think of our estimated sample regression line as an estimate of a true but unknown population regression line of the form

Population Regression Line

$$Y = A + BX \qquad [12\text{-}13]$$

Recall our discussion of the Sanitation Department director who tried to use the age of a truck to explain its annual repair expense. That expense will probably consist of two parts:

1. Regular maintenance that does not depend on the age of the truck: tune-ups, oil changes, and lubrication. This expense is captured in the intercept term A in Equation 12-13.

2. Expenses for repairs due to aging: relining brakes, engine and transmission overhauls, and painting. Such expenses tend to increase with the age of the truck, and they are captured in the BX term of the population regression line $Y = A + BX$ in Equation 12-13.

Why data points do not lie exactly on the regression line

Of course, all the brakes of all the trucks will not wear out at the same time, and some of the trucks will run for years without engine overhauls. Because of this, the individual data points will probably not lie exactly on the population regression line. Some will be above it; some will fall below it. So, instead of satisfying

$$Y = A + BX \quad [12\text{-}13]$$

the individual data points will satisfy the formula

Population Regression Line with a Random Disturbance

$$Y = A + BX + e \quad [12\text{-}13a]$$

Random disturbance e and its behavior

where e is a random disturbance from the population regression line. On the average, e equals zero because disturbances above the population regression line are canceled out by disturbances below the line. We can denote the standard deviation of these individual disturbances by σ_e. The standard error of estimate s_e, then, is an estimate of σ_e, the standard deviation of the disturbance.

Let us look more carefully at Equations 12-13 and 12-13a. Equation 12-13a expresses the individual values of Y (in this case, annual repair expense) in terms of the individual values of X (the age of the truck) and the random disturbance (e). Because disturbances above the population regression line are canceled out by those below the line, we know that the expected value of e is zero, and we see that if we had several trucks of the same age, X, we would expect the average annual repair expense on these trucks to be $Y = A + BX$. This shows us that the population regression line (Equation 12-13) gives the mean value of Y associated with each value of X.

Making inferences about B from b

Because our *sample* regression line, $\hat{Y} = a + bX$ (Equation 12-3), estimates the *population* regression line, $Y = A + BX$ (Equation 12-13), we should be able to use it to make inferences about the population regression line. In this section, then, we shall make inferences about the slope B of the "true" regression equation (the one for the entire population) that are based on the slope b of the regression equation estimated from a sample of values.

Slope of the Population Regression Line

Difference between true regression equation and one estimated from sample observations

The regression line is derived from a sample and not from the entire population. As a result, we cannot expect the true regression equation, $Y = A + BX$ (the one for the entire population), to be exactly the same as the equation estimated from the sample observations, or $\hat{Y} = a + bX$. Even so, we can use the value of b, the slope we calculate from a sample, to test hypotheses about the value of B, the slope of the regression line for the entire population.

Testing a hypothesis about B

The procedure for testing a hypothesis about B is similar to procedures discussed in Chapters 8 and 9, on hypothesis testing. To understand this process, return to the problem that related annual expenditures for research and development to profits. On page 663, we pointed out that $b = 2$. The first step is to find some value for B to compare with $b = 2$.

Suppose that over an extended past period of time, the slope of the relationship between X and Y was 2.1. To test whether this is still the case, we could define the hypotheses as

$$H_0: B = 2.1 \leftarrow \text{Null hypothesis}$$

$$H_1: B \neq 2.1 \leftarrow \text{Alternative hypothesis}$$

Standard error of the regression coefficient

In effect, then, we are testing to learn whether current data indicate that B has changed from its historical value of 2.1.

To find the test statistic for B, it is necessary first to find the *standard error of the regression coefficient.* Here, the regression coefficient we are working with is b, so the standard error of this coefficient is denoted s_b. Equation 12-14 presents the mathematical formula for s_b:

Standard Error of *b*

$$s_b = \frac{s_e}{\sqrt{\Sigma X^2 - n\overline{X}^2}} \qquad [12\text{-}14]$$

where

- s_b = standard error of the regression coefficient
- s_e = standard error of estimate
- X = values of the independent variable
- $\overline{X}$ = mean of the values of the independent variable
- n = number of data points

Standardizing the regression coefficient

Once we have calculated s_b, we can use Equation 12-15 to standardize the slope of our fitted regression equation:

Standardized Value of *b*

$$t = \frac{b - B_{H_0}}{s_b} \qquad [12\text{-}15]$$

where

- b = slope of fitted regression
- B_{H_0} = actual slope hypothesized for the population
- s_b = standard error of the regression coefficient

Because the test will be based on the t distribution with $n - 2$ degrees of freedom, we use t to denote the standardized statistic.

A glance at Table 12-15 on page 683 enables us to calculate the values of ΣX^2 and $n\overline{X}^2$. To obtain s_e, we can take the short-cut method, as follows:

Calculating s_e

$$s_e = \sqrt{\frac{\Sigma Y^2 - a\Sigma Y - b\Sigma XY}{n - 2}} \quad [12\text{-}7]$$

$$= \sqrt{\frac{5{,}642 - (20)(180) - (2)(1{,}000)}{6 - 2}}$$

$$= \sqrt{\frac{42}{4}}$$

$$= \sqrt{10.5}$$

$$= 3.24 \leftarrow \text{Standard error of estimate}$$

Now we can determine the standard error of the regression coefficient:

Calculating s_b

$$s_b = \frac{s_e}{\sqrt{\Sigma X^2 - n\overline{X}^2}} \quad [12\text{-}14]$$

$$= \frac{3.24}{\sqrt{200 - (6)(5)^2}}$$

$$= \frac{3.24}{\sqrt{50}}$$

$$= \frac{3.24}{7.07}$$

$$= 0.46 \leftarrow \text{Standard error of the regression coefficient}$$

Standardizing the regression coefficient

Now we use the standard error of the regression coefficient to calculate our standardized test statistic:

$$t = \frac{b - B_{H_0}}{s_b} \quad [12\text{-}15]$$

$$= \frac{2.0 - 2.1}{0.46}$$

$$= -0.217 \leftarrow \text{Standardized regression coefficient}$$

Conducting the hypothesis test

Suppose we have reason to test our hypothesis at the 10 percent level of significance. Because we have six observations in our sample data, we know that we have $n - 2$ or $6 - 2 = 4$ degrees of freedom. We look in Appendix Table 2 under the 10 percent column and come down until we find the 4-degrees-of-freedom row. There we see that the appropriate t value is 2.132. Because we are concerned whether b (the slope of the sample regression line) is significantly *different* from B (the hypothesized slope of the population regression line), this is a two-tailed test, and the critical values are ± 2.132. The standardized regression coefficient is -0.217, which is *inside* the acceptance region for our hypothesis test. Therefore, we accept the null hypothesis that B still equals 2.1. In other words, there is not enough difference between b and 2.1 for us to conclude that B has changed from its historical value. Because of this, we feel that each additional million dollars spent on research and development still increases annual profits by about $2.1 million, as it has in the past.

In addition to hypothesis testing, we can also construct a *confidence interval* for the value of B. In the same way that b is a point estimate of B, such confidence intervals are interval estimates of B. The problem we just completed, and for which we did a hypothesis test, will illustrate the process of constructing a confidence interval. There we found that

$$b = 2.0$$

$$s_b = 0.46$$

$$t = 2.132 \leftarrow \text{10 percent level of significance and 4 degrees of freedom}$$

Confidence interval for B

With this information, we can calculate confidence intervals like this:

$$\begin{aligned} b + t(s_b) &= 2 + (2.132)(0.46) \\ &= 2 + 0.981 \\ &= 2.981 \leftarrow \text{Upper limit} \end{aligned}$$

$$\begin{aligned} b - t(s_b) &= 2 - (2.132)(0.46) \\ &= 2 - 0.981 \\ &= 1.019 \leftarrow \text{Lower limit} \end{aligned}$$

Interpreting the confidence interval

In this situation, then, we are 90 percent confident that the true value of B lies between 1.019 and 2.981; that is, each additional million dollars spent on research and development increases annual profits by some amount between \$1.02 million and \$2.98 million.

HINTS & ASSUMPTIONS

In this section we've been using sample observations to calculate b, the slope of the *sample* regression line, which we then use to test hypotheses about B, the true slope of the *population* regression line. Hint: We use s_e to calculate the standard error of the regression coefficient just as we used the sample standard deviation in Chapter 6 to compute the standard error of the mean. Warning: Whenever you use your computer to develop a regression line, don't forget to ask, "Is this regression coefficient significantly different from zero?" If it's *not*, no matter how much good-looking computer output you have, you haven't demonstrated any significant relationship between the variables, and you need to keep looking for more useful relationships. For example, if you own a tanning salon and you have a hunch that more people come in on cloudy days, you might do a regression of "number of visits" on "hours of sunshine." If you do that and it yields a regression line with a slope that is *not* significant, keeping track of the weather is not going to help your business.

Exercises 12.4

Self-Check Exercises

SC 12-6 In finance, it is of interest to look at the relationship between Y, a stock's average return, and X, the overall market return. The slope coefficient computed by linear regression is called the stock's *beta* by investment analysts. A beta greater than 1 indicates that the stock is relatively sen-

sitive to changes in the market; a beta less than 1 indicates that the stock is relatively insensitive. For the following data, compute the beta and test to see whether it is significantly less than 1. Use $\alpha = 0.05$.

Y (%)	10	12	8	15	9	11	8	10	13	11
X (%)	11	15	3	18	10	12	6	7	18	13

SC 12-7 In a regression problem with a sample size of 17, the slope was found to be 3.73 and the standard error of estimate 28.654. The quantity $(\Sigma X^2 - n\overline{X}^2) = 871.56$.

(a) Find the standard error of the regression slope coefficient.

(b) Construct a 98 percent confidence interval for the population slope.

(c) Interpret the confidence interval of part (b).

Basic Concepts

■ **12-33** In a regression problem with a sample size of 25, the slope was found to be 1.12 and the standard error of estimate 8.516. The quantity $(\Sigma X^2 - n\overline{X}^2) = 327.52$.

(a) Find the standard error of the regression slope coefficient.

(b) Test whether the regression coefficient is different from 0 at a significance level of 0.05.

(c) Construct a 95 percent confidence interval for the population slope.

Applications

■ **12-34** Ned's Beds is considering hiring an advertising firm to stimulate business. Ned's brother Fred has done some research in the bed advertising field, and he has collected the following data concerning the amount of profit (Y) a bed company earns and the amount spent on advertising (X). If Fred computes the regression equation, the slope of the line will indicate the amount of profit increase per dollar spent on advertising. Ned will advertise only if the amount of profit earned from \$1 in advertising exceeds \$1.50. Compute the slope of the regression equation and test whether it is greater than 1.50. At a significance level of 0.05, will Ned advertise?

Amount of Advertising (X), \$ hundreds	3.6	4.8	9.7	12.6	11.5	10.9
Amount of Profit (Y), hundreds	12.13	14.7	22.83	28.4	28.33	27.05
Amount of Advertising (X), \$ hundreds	14.6	18.2	3.7	9.8	12.4	16.9
Amount of Profit (Y), hundreds	33.6	40.8	9.4	24.84	30.17	34.7

■ **12-35** A broker for a local investment firm has been studying the relationship between increases in the price of gold (X) and her customers' requests to liquidate stocks (Y). From a data set based on 15 observations, the sample slope was found to be 2.9. If the standard error of the regression slope coefficient is 0.18, is there reason to believe (at the 0.05 significance level) that the slope has changed from its past value of 3.2?

■ **12-36** For a sample of 25, the slope was found to be 1.685 and the standard error of the regression coefficient was 0.11. Is there reason to believe that the slope has changed from its past value of 1.50? Use the 0.05 significance level.

■ **12-37** Realtors are often interested in seeing how the appraised value of a home varies according to the size of the home. Some data on area (in thousands of square feet) and appraised value (in thousands of dollars) for a sample of 11 homes follow.

Area	1.1	1.5	1.6	1.6	1.4	1.3	1.1	1.7	1.9	1.5	1.3
Value	75	95	110	102	95	87	82	115	122	98	90

(a) Estimate the least-squares regression to predict appraised value from size.

(b) Generally, realtors feel that a home's value goes up by $50,000 (= 50 thousands of dollars) for every additional 1,000 square feet in area. For this sample, does this relationship seem to hold? Use $\alpha = 0.10$.

■ **12-38** In 1969, a government health agency found that in a number of counties, the relationship between smokers and heart-disease fatalities per 100,000 population had a slope of 0.08. A recent study of 18 counties produced a slope of 0.147 and a standard error of the regression slope coefficient of 0.032.

(a) Construct a 90 percent confidence interval estimate of the slope of the true regression line. Does the result from this study indicate that the true slope has changed?

(b) Construct a 99 percent confidence interval estimate of the slope of the true regression line. Does the result from this study indicate that the true slope has changed?

■ **12-39** The local phone company has always assumed that the average number of daily phone calls goes up by 1.5 for each additional person in a household. It has been suggested that people are more talkative than this. A sample of 64 households was taken, and the slope of the regression of Y (average number of daily phone calls) on X (size of household) was computed to be 1.8 with a standard error of the regression slope coefficient of 0.2. Test whether significantly more calls per additional person are being made than the phone company assumes, using $\alpha = 0.05$. State explicit hypotheses and an explicit conclusion.

■ **12-40** College admissions officers are constantly seeking variables with which to predict grade-point averages for applicants. One commonly used variable is high school grade-point average. For one college, past data indicated that the slope was 0.85. A recent small study of 20 students found that the sample slope was 0.70 and the standard error of estimate was 0.60. The quantity $(\Sigma X^2 - n\bar{X}^2)$ was equal to 0.25. At the 0.01 level of significance, should the college conclude that the slope has changed?

Worked-Out Answers to Self-Check Exercises

SC 12-6

X	Y	XY	X^2	Y^2
11	10	110	121	100
15	12	180	225	144
3	8	24	9	64
18	15	270	324	225
10	9	90	100	81
12	11	132	144	121
6	8	48	36	64
7	10	70	49	100
18	13	234	324	169
13	11	143	169	121
$\Sigma X =$ **113**	$\Sigma Y =$ **107**	$\Sigma XY =$ **1,301**	$\Sigma X^2 =$ **1,501**	$\Sigma Y^2 =$ **1,189**

$$\bar{X} = \frac{113}{10} = 11.3 \qquad \bar{Y} = \frac{107}{10} = 10.7$$

$$b = \frac{\Sigma XY - n\bar{X}\bar{Y}}{\Sigma X^2 - n\bar{X}^2} = \frac{1{,}301 - 10(11.3)(10.7)}{1{,}501 - 10(11.3)^2} = 0.4101$$

$$a = \bar{Y} - b\bar{X} = 10.7 - 0.4101(11.3) = 6.0659$$

(Computer packages: 6.0660)

$$s_e = \sqrt{\frac{\Sigma Y^2 - a\Sigma Y - b\Sigma XY}{n - 2}}$$

$$= \sqrt{\frac{1{,}189 - 6.0659(107) - 0.4101(1{,}301)}{8}} = 0.8950$$

(Computer packages: 0.8953)

$$s_b = \frac{s_e}{\sqrt{\Sigma X^2 - n\bar{X}^2}} = \frac{0.8950}{\sqrt{224.1}} = 0.060$$

$$H_0: B = 1 \qquad H_1: B < 1 \qquad \alpha = 0.05$$

The standardized statistic is $t = \dfrac{b - B_{H_0}}{s_b} = \dfrac{0.4101 - 1}{0.06} = -9.83$. Because the critical value of $t(-1.860)$ is greater than -9.83, we reject H_0. Stock is insensitive to changes in the market (the slope is significantly < 1).

SC 12-7 (a) $s_b = \dfrac{s_e}{\sqrt{\Sigma X^2 - n\bar{X}^2}} = \dfrac{28.654}{\sqrt{871.56}} = 0.9706$

(b) The 98 percent confidence interval is

$b \pm t(s_b) = 3.73 \pm 2.602(0.9706) = 3.73 \pm 2.53 = (1.20, 6.26)$.

(c) In repeated sampling, 98 out of 100 intervals constructed as above would contain the true, unknown population slope B. For our single sample, we can say that we are 98 percent confident that our computed interval contains B.

12.5 Using Regression and Correlation Analyses: Limitations, Errors, and Caveats

Misuse of regression and correlation

Regression and correlation analyses are statistical tools that, when properly used, can significantly help people make decisions. Unfortunately, they are often misused. As a result, decision makers often make inaccurate forecasts and less-than-desirable decisions. We'll mention the most common errors made in the use of regression and correlation in the hope that you will avoid them.

Extrapolation beyond the Range of the Observed Data

Specific limited range over which regression equation holds

A common mistake is to assume that the estimating line can be applied over any range of values. Hospital administrators can properly use regression analysis to predict the relationship between costs per bed and occupancy levels at various occupancy levels. Some administrators, however, incorrectly use the same regression equation to predict the costs per bed for occupancy levels that are significantly higher than those that were used to estimate the regression line. Although one relationship holds over the range of sample points, an entirely different relationship may exist for a different range. As a result, these people make decisions on one set of costs and find that the costs change drastically as occupancy increases (owing to things such as overtime costs and capacity constraints). Remember that **an estimating equation is valid only over the same range as the one from which the sample was taken initially.**

Cause and Effect

Regression and correlation analyses do not determine cause and effect

Another mistake we can make when we use regression analysis is to assume that a change in one variable is caused by a change in the other variable. As we discussed earlier, **regression and correlation analyses can in no way determine cause and effect.** If we say that there is a correlation between students' grades in college and their annual earnings 5 years after graduation, we are *not* saying that one causes the other. Rather, both may be caused by other factors, such as sociological background, parental attitudes, quality of teachers, effectiveness of the job-interviewing process, and economic status of parents—to name only a few potential factors.

We have extensively used the example about research and development expenses and annual profits to illustrate various aspects of regression analysis. But it is really highly unlikely that profits in a given year are *caused* by R&D expenditures in that year. Certainly, it would be foolhardy for the VP for R&D to suggest to the chief executive that profits could be immediately increased merely by increasing R&D expenditures. Particularly in high-technology industries, the R&D activity can be used to explain profits, but a better way to do so would be to predict current profits in terms of past research and development expenditures as well as in terms of economic conditions, dollars spent on advertising, and other variables. This can be done by using the multiple-regression techniques, to be discussed in the next chapter.

Using Past Trends to Estimate Future Trends

Conditions change and invalidate the regression equation

We must take care to reappraise the historical data we use to estimate the regression equation. Conditions can change and violate one or more of the assumptions on which our regression analysis depends. Earlier in this chapter, we made the point that we assume that

■ **12-11** $$r^2 = \frac{a\Sigma Y + b\Sigma XY - n\bar{Y}^2}{\Sigma Y^2 - n\bar{Y}^2}$$ p. 682

This is a short-cut equation for calculating r^2.

■ **12-12** $$r = \sqrt{r^2}$$ p. 684

The *sample coefficient of correlation* is denoted by r and is found by taking the square root of the sample coefficient of determination. It is a second measure (in addition to r^2) we can use to describe how well one variable is explained by another. The sign of r is the same as the sign of b; it indicates the direction of the relationship between the two variables X and Y.

■ **12-13** $$Y = A + BX$$ p. 687

Each *population regression line* is of the form in Equation 12-13, where A is the Y-intercept for the population and B is the slope.

■ **12-13a** $$Y = A + BX + e$$ p. 688

Because all the individual points in a population do not lie on the population regression line, the *individual* data points will satisfy Equation 12-13a, where e is a random disturbance from the population regression line. On the average, e equals zero because disturbances above the population regression line are canceled out by disturbances below it.

■ **12-14** $$s_b = \frac{s_e}{\sqrt{\Sigma X^2 - n\bar{X}^2}}$$ p. 689

When we are dealing with a sample, we can use this formula to find the *standard error of the regression coefficient, b.*

■ **12-15** $$t = \frac{b - B_{H_0}}{s_b}$$ p. 689

Once we have calculated s_b using Equation 12-14, we can use this equation to standardize the observed value of the regression coefficient. Then we perform the hypothesis test by comparing this standardized value with the critical value(s) from Appendix Table 2.

● Review and Application Exercises

■ **12-45** A consultant is interested in seeing how accurately a new job-performance index measures what is important for a corporation. One way to check is to look at the relationship between the job-evaluation index and an employee's salary. A sample of eight employees was taken, and information about salary (in thousands of dollars) and job-performance index (1–10; 10 is best) was collected.

Job-performance index (*X*)	9	7	8	4	7	5	5	6
Salary (*Y*)	36	25	33	15	28	19	20	22

(a) Develop an estimating equation that best describes these data.
(b) Calculate the standard error of estimate, s_e, for these data.
(c) Calculate the sample coefficient of determination, r^2, for these data.

■ **12-46** The Stork Foundation wishes to show with statistics that, contrary to popular belief, storks *do* bring babies. Thus, it has collected data on the number of storks and the number of babies (both in thousands) in several large cities in central Europe.

Storks	27	38	13	24	6	19	15
Babies	35	46	19	32	15	31	20

(a) Compute the sample coefficient of determination and the sample correlation coefficient for these data.

(b) Has statistical science disproved popular belief?

■ **12-47** (Fill in the blanks.) Regression and correlation analyses deal with the ____________________ between variables. Regression analysis, through ____________________ equations, enables us to ____________________ an unknown variable from a set of known variables. The unknown variable is called the ____________________ variable; known variables are called ____________________ variables. The correlation between two variables indicates the ____________________ of the linear relationship between them and thus gives an idea of how well the ____________________ in regression describes the relationship between the variables.

■ **12-48** Calculate the sample coefficient of determination and the sample correlation coefficient for Exercise 12-14.

Business Week and *U.S. News & World Report* publish rankings of the top 20 business schools. The *Business Week* overall ranking is based on rankings obtained from students and from firms that recruit MBAs. Along with the rankings, the magazines report information about the cost of getting an MBA degree and the graduates' average starting salaries. Use the data in Table RW12-1 to answer Exercises 12-49 to 12-52.

Table RW12-1

Business School Ranking Surveys

School	1992 Rank *BW*	1992 Rank *USN&WR*	*BW* Ranking by Students	*BW* Ranking by Firms	Cost	Starting Salary
Northwestern	1	4	3	1	37,600	70,200
Chicago	2	6	10	4	38,500	68,600
Harvard	3	2	12	3	37,100	84,960
Wharton	4	3	15	2	37,600	72,200
Michigan	5	7	9	6	37,200	58,110
Dartmouth	6	10	1	12	37,500	74,260
Stanford	7	1	5	7	38,480	82,860
Indiana	8	18	6	8	24,600	49,070
Columbia	9	8	18	5	38,000	66,620
North Carolina	10	16	8	11	17,360	55,500
Virginia	11	11	2	15	28,500	65,280
Duke	12	9	7	14	37,000	59,870
MIT	13	5	14	10	39,000	73,000
Cornell	14	12	4	17	37,000	59,940
NYU	15	17	16	13	36,100	56,730
UCLA	16	14	11	16	22,500	64,540
Carnegie–Mellon	17	15	23	9	37,200	56,980
Berkeley	18	13	13	19	15,400	65,500
Vanderbilt	19	19	19	20	35,000	47,320
Washington	20	20	24	18	33,500	48,200

Source: Adapted from Business Week *(26 October 1992):60, and* U.S. News & World Report *(23 March 1992):66.*

12-49 Plot a scatter diagram of the *USN&WR* ranking vs. the cost of the MBA degree. Do more expensive schools appear to get higher rankings? Calculate the sample coefficient of correlation between these two variables.

12-50 Is there a payoff for spending more on an MBA degree? Plot a scatter diagram of starting salary vs. cost. Fit a regression equation to the data and test appropriate hypotheses about its slope.

12-51 Do graduates from the higher-ranking schools get higher starting salaries? Plot a scatter diagram of starting salary vs. the *Business Week* overall ranking. Fit a regression equation to the data and test appropriate hypotheses about its slope.

12-52 How strongly are the starting salaries related to the rankings? Calculate the sample coefficients of determination between the starting salaries and the three *Business Week* rankings (overall, by students, and by firms). Which of these rankings explains the largest fraction of the variation in starting salaries?

■ 12-53 "Nothing succeeds like success" is an old adage in the advertising business. The president of a multiline auto dealership has observed that sales staff who earn the biggest end-of-year bonus are the ones who are most likely to exceed their quota for sales in the following year (and hence earn another bonus).

Last Year's Bonus ($ thousands)	7.8	6.9	6.7	6.0	6.9	5.2
This Year's Sales Over Quota	64	73	42	49	71	46

Last Year's Bonus ($ thousands)	6.3	8.4	7.2	10.1	10.8	7.7
This Year's Sales Over Quota	32	88	53	84	85	93

(a) Develop the line of best fit to describe these data.
(b) Calculate the standard error of estimate for the relationship.
(c) Develop an approximate 90 percent confidence interval for predicting the sales over quota for a sales staff member who earned a bonus of $9,600 last year.

■ 12-54 For each of the following pairs of plots, state which has a higher value of r, the correlation coefficient, and state the sign of r.

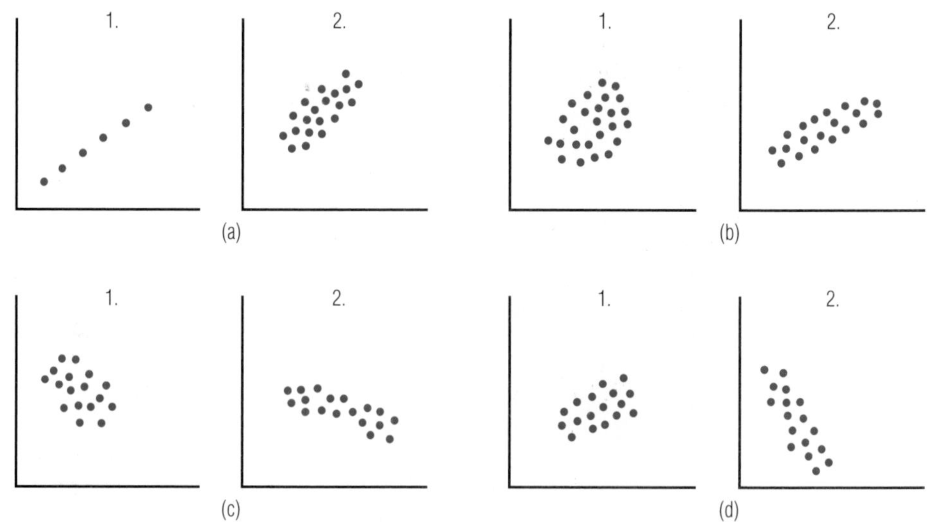

■ **12-55** An operations manager is interested in predicting costs C (in thousands of dollars) based on the amount of raw material input R (in hundreds of pounds) for a jeans manufacturer. If the slope is significantly greater than 0.5 in the following sample data, then there is something wrong with the production process and the assembly-line machinery should be adjusted. At the 0.05 significance level, should the machinery be adjusted? State explicit hypotheses and an explicit conclusion.

C	10	7	5	6	7	6
R	25	20	16	17	19	18

■ **12-56** Calculate the sample coefficient of determination and the sample correlation coefficient for Exercise 12-13.

■ **12-57** We should not extrapolate to predict values outside the range of data used in constructing the regression line. The reason (choose one):

(a) The relationship between the variables may not be the same for different values of the variables.

(b) The independent variable may not have the causal effect on the dependent variable for these values.

(c) The variables' values may change over time.

(d) There may be no common bond to explain the relationship.

Use the data about 50 U.S. metropolitan areas given in Table RW11-2 on p. 636 to answer Exercises 12-58 to 12-60.

12-58 Marketing planners must often estimate geographic demand for a company's product. Demand depends not only on the number of people in a community, but also on the amount of money they have to spend. *Sales & Marketing Management* magazine uses U.S. census data to estimate the "effective buying income" of typical households in U.S. metropolitan areas. EBI is the sum of wages and unearned income, less taxes and fines—in short, a good measure of what economists label "disposable income." The total amount of money available for spending in a community is roughly proportional to the product of EBI and the population.

Compute a new variable TM = (POP × EBI)/1,000. Calculate the sample coefficients of determination between SALES and POP and between SALES and TM. Which of these variables explains more of the variation in SALES?

12-59 Fit a regression equation that uses SINGLE to predict the value of SALES. Find an approximate 90 percent prediction interval for total retail sales in a metropolitan area with 20,000 single-person households. To what extent would this result be useful to a consumer-products company that is developing a new line of single-serving frozen dinners?

12-60 Suppose you wanted to find out whether business is better in communities with more older people. Using median age as a proxy for the number of older people in each metropolitan area, fit a regression equation to explain SALES in terms of AGE. Is the slope of your regression significantly greater than zero? On the basis of this analysis, should you conclude that business *isn't* better in communities with more older people? Explain.

■ **12-61** Economists are often interested in estimating consumption functions. This is done by regressing consumption Y on income X. (For this regression, economists call the slope the *marginal propensity to consume.*) For a sample of 25 families, a slope of 0.87 and a standard error of the regression slope coefficient of 0.035 were computed. For this sample, has the marginal propensity to consume decreased below the standard of 0.94? Use $\alpha = 0.05$. State explicit hypotheses and an explicit conclusion.

■ **12-62** Unlike the coefficient of determination, the coefficient of correlation (choose one)

(a) Indicates whether the slope of the regression line is positive or negative.

(b) Measures the strength of association between the two variables more exactly.

(c) Can never have an absolute value greater than 1.

(d) Measures the percentage of variance explained by the regression line.

■ **12-63** Are good grades in college important for earning a good salary? A business statistics student has taken a random sample of starting salaries and college grade-point averages for some recently graduated friends of his. The data follow:

Starting salary ($ thousands)	36	30	30	24	27	33	21	27
Grade-point average	4.0	3.0	3.5	2.0	3.0	3.5	2.5	2.5

(a) Plot these data.

(b) Develop the estimating equation that best describes these data.

(c) Plot the estimating equation on the scatter plot of part (a).

■ **12-64** A landlord is interested in seeing whether his apartment rents are typical. Thus, he has taken a random sample of 11 rents and apartment sizes of similar apartment complexes. The data follow:

Rent	230	190	450	310	218	185	340	245	125	350	280
Number of bedrooms	2	1	3	2	2	2	2	1	1	2	2

(a) Develop an estimating equation that best describes these data.

(b) Calculate the coefficient of determination.

(c) Predict the rent for a two-bedroom apartment.

■ **12-65** Many small companies buy advertising without considering its effect. "Hamburger wars" (substantial price rivalry with special "value meals") have cut the profits of Ethiopian Burgers of Santa Cruz, California, a small regional chain. The marketing manager is trying to make the case that "you have to spend money to make money." Spending on billboard advertisements, in the manager's opinion, has a direct result on sales. There are records for 7 months:

Monthly expenditure on billboards (× $1,000)	25	16	42	34	10	21	19
Monthly sales revenue (× $100,000)	34	14	48	32	26	29	20

(a) Develop an estimating equation that best describes these data.

(b) Calculate the standard error of estimate for this relationship.

(c) For a month with a billboard expenditure of $28,000, develop an approximate 95 percent confidence interval for the expected monthly sales for that month.

12-66 In 1992, the total U.S. sales of breakfast cereals were estimated to be $3.842 billion. Consider the following information about the 10 best-selling cereals. Find the least-squares equation that uses average retail price to predict market share. Which of the following three generalizations best describes the relationship between these two variables?

(a) Lower price increases sales.

(b) Bigger market share means a higher price can be charged.

(c) Market share doesn't appear to depend on price.

Company	Cereal	Market Share	Volume ($ millions)	Average Retail Price
General Mills	Cheerios	4.58%	175.96	$2.18
Kellogg's	Frosted Flakes	4.08%	156.75	$2.83
General Mills	Honey Nut Cheerios	3.28%	126.02	$2.99
Kellogg's	Rice Krispies	2.99%	114.88	$1.94
Kellogg's	Corn Flakes	2.97%	114.11	$1.47
Kellogg's	Raisin Bran	2.77%	106.42	$2.74
Kellogg's	Frosted Mini-Wheats	2.77%	106.42	$2.91
Kellogg's	Froot Loops	2.33%	89.52	$2.64
General Mills	Lucky Charms	1.85%	71.08	$3.15
General Mills	Total	1.84%	70.69	$2.86

Source: Richard Gibson, "There Is No Way to Sugarcoat This News: Prices of Breakfast Cereals Are Going Up," The Wall Street Journal *(21 January 1993): B1.*

■ **12-67** In an FAA study of airline operations, a survey of 18 companies disclosed that the relationship between the number of pilots employed and the number of planes in service has a slope of 4.3. Previous studies indicated that the slope of this relationship was 4.0. If the standard error of the regression slope coefficient has been calculated to be 0.17, is there reason to believe, at the 0.05 level of significance, that the true slope has changed?

■ **12-68** Dave Proffitt, a second-year MBA student, is doing a study of companies going public for the first time. He is curious to see whether there is a significant relationship between the size of the offering (in millions of dollars) and the price per share.

(a) Given the following data, develop the estimating equation that best fits the data.

Size ($ Millions)	Price($)
108.00	12.00
4.40	4.00
3.50	5.00
3.60	6.00
39.00	13.00
68.40	19.00
7.50	8.50
5.50	5.00
375.00	15.00
12.00	6.00
51.00	12.00
66.00	12.00
10.40	6.50
4.00	3.00

(b) Calculate the sample coefficient of determination. Should Dave use this regression equation for predictive purposes or search elsewhere for additional explanatory variables?

■ **12-69** A manufacturer of cellular phones is testing two different types of batteries to see how long they last in typical use. Provisional data are in the following table:

Hours of Daily Use	Approximate Life (months) Lithium	Approximate Life (months) Alkaline
2.0	3.1	1.3
1.5	4.2	1.6
1.0	5.1	1.8
0.5	6.3	2.2

(a) Develop two linear estimating equations, one to predict product life based on daily use with lithium batteries and one for alkaline batteries.

(b) Find an approximate 90 percent confidence interval for the life (in months) with 1.25 hours of daily use, for each battery type. Can the company make any claims about which battery will provide a longer life based on these numbers?

■ **12-70** A study has been proposed to investigate the relationship between the birthweight of male babies and their adult height. Using the following data, develop the least-squares estimating equation. What percentage of the variation in adult height is explained by this regression line?

Birthweight	Adult Height
5 lb, 8 oz	5′9″
7 lb	6′
6 lb, 4 oz	5′6″
7 lb, 8 oz	5′11″
8 lb, 2 oz	6′1″
6 lb, 12 oz	5′10″

■ **12-71** Many college students transfer in the summer before their junior years. To aid in evaluating the academic potential of these junior transfers, Barbara Hoopes, the Dean of Admissions at Piedmont College, is conducting an analysis that compares students' grade-point averages (GPAs) during their first 2 years of college with their GPAs during their final 2 years, after transferring. Using the following data

Freshman/sophomore GPA	1.7	3.5	2.3	2.6	3.0	2.8	2.4	1.9	2.0	3.1
Junior/senior GPA	2.4	3.7	2.0	2.5	3.2	3.0	2.5	1.8	2.7	3.7

(a) Calculate the least-squares estimating equation Hoopes should use to predict junior/senior GPAs for students transferring to Piedmont College.

(b) Hoopes will not admit junior-transfer applicants unless approximate 90 percent prediction intervals for their junior/senior GPAs fall entirely above 2.0. Will she admit a transfer applicant with a 2.5 freshman/sophomore GPA?

■ **12-72** The salaries of many public officials are less than they could earn from equivalent jobs in the marketplace. *The Wall Street Journal* reported the salaries for 10 states' attorneys general (AGs) and compared them with the typical wage of an entry-level lawyer in the same state. In answering the following questions, assume that the entry-level salaries are a good indicator for the market rate for attorneys in each state.

	Attorney General	Entry-Level Lawyer
Vermont	61,025	26,520
Wyoming	75,000	31,500
Massachusetts	80,000	25,000
Pennsylvania	84,000	33,819
Georgia	90,000	35,880
Washington	92,000	30,000
California	102,000	38,400
Illinois	105,387	27,048
New York	110,000	33,922
Michigan	111,200	35,182

Source: "Paying States' Attorneys General," The Wall Street Journal *(24 July 1995): B8.*

(a) Does the salary offered to the Attorney General vary according to the going rate for attorneys in each state? Test, at $\alpha = 0.05$, whether the slope of the fitted regression is significantly different from 0.

(b) What proportion of the variation in AGs' salaries is accounted for by the going rate for attorneys in the for-profit market?

(c) If an AG wanted to raise the statewide income for lawyers, would lobbying for a pay raise for the AG position help? Why or why not?

■ **12-73** Business travel costs vary considerably among major U.S. cities, as shown in the following table. A corporate controller is attempting to set *per diem* rates that take into account this variation. Should the controller consider both car-rental and hotel costs, or would hotel costs by city provide sufficient information to calculate the rates? (*Hint:* Fit a regression using car-rental costs to explain hotel costs. Then look at r^2).

	Hotel	Car Rental/Day
Atlanta	$121	$54
Boston	199	50
Chicago	159	62
Cleveland	129	52
Dallas	117	44
Denver	92	35
Detroit	102	60
Houston	92	70
Los Angeles	122	51
Miami	111	32
Minneapolis	107	57
New Orleans	116	42
New York	197	60
Orlando	95	36
Phoenix	85	37
Pittsburgh	122	46
St. Louis	115	66
San Francisco	155	52
Seattle	125	45
Washington, D.C.	145	53

Source: "Dow Jones Travel Index," The Wall Street Journal *(4 August 1995): B7.*

● Chapter Concepts Test

Circle the correct answer or fill in the blank. *Answers are in the back of the book.*

T F 1. Regression analysis is used to describe how well an estimating equation describes the relationship being studied.

T F 2. Given that the equation for a line is $Y = 26 - 24X$, we may say that the relationship of Y to X is direct and linear.

T F 3. An r^2 value close to zero indicates a strong correlation between X and Y.

T F 4. Regression and correlation analyses are used to determine cause-and-effect relationships.

T F 5. The sample coefficient of correlation, r, is nothing more than $\sqrt{r^2}$, and we cannot interpret its meaning directly as a percentage of some kind.

T F 6. The standard error of estimate measures the variability of the observed values around the regression equation.

T F 7. The regression line is derived from a sample, not the entire population.

T F 8. We may interpret the sample coefficient of determination as the amount of the variation in Y that is explained by the regression line.

T F 9. Lines drawn on either side of the regression line at ± 1, ± 2, and ± 3 times the value of the standard error of estimate are called confidence lines.

T F 10. The estimating equation is valid over only the same range as that given by the original sample data on which it was developed.

T F 11. In the equation $Y = a + bX$ for dependent variable Y and independent variable X, the Y-intercept is b.

T F 12. If a line is fitted to a set of points by the method of least squares, the individual positive and negative errors from the line sum to zero.

T F 13. If $s_e = 0$ for an estimating equation, it must perfectly estimate the dependent variable at the observed points.

T F 14. Suppose the slope of an estimating equation is positive. Then the value of r must be the positive square root of r^2.

T F 15. If $r = 0.8$, then the regression equation explains 80 percent of the total variation in the dependent variable.

T F 16. The coefficient of correlation is the percentage of the total variation of the dependent variable that is explained by the regression.

T F 17. The standard error of estimate is measured perpendicularly from the regression line rather than on the Y-axis.

T F 18. By squaring individual errors, the least-squares method magnifies all deviations from the estimated regression line.

T F 19. A regression equation may not be valid when extended outside the sample range of the independent variable.

T F 20. An r^2 value measures only the strength of a linear relationship between the two variables X and Y.

T F 21. A small value of r^2 implies that there is not a significant cause-and-effect relationship between X and Y.

A B C D E 22. Suppose that we know the height of a student but do not know her weight. We use an estimating equation to determine an estimate of her weight based on her height. We can therefore surmise that:

(a) Weight is the independent variable.
(b) Height is the dependent variable.
(c) The relationship between weight and height is an inverse one.
(d) None of these.
(e) (b) and (c) but not (a).

A B C D 23. Suppose you are told that there is a direct relationship between the price of artichokes and the amount of rain that fell during the growing season. It can be calculated that:

(a) Prices tend to be high when rainfall is high.
(b) Prices tend to be low when rainfall is high.
(c) A large amount of rain causes prices to rise.
(d) A lack of rain causes prices to rise.

A B C D 24. Suppose it is calculated that a is 4 and b is 2 for a particular estimating line with one independent variable. If the independent variable has a value of 2, what value should be expected for the dependent variable?

(a) 8.
(b) 10.
(c) -1.
(d) 0.

A B C D E 25. Suppose the estimating equation $\hat{Y} = 5 - 2X$ has been calculated for a set of data. Which of the following is true for this situation?

(a) The Y-intercept of the line is 2.
(b) The slope of the line is negative.
(c) The line represents an inverse relationship.
(d) All of these.
(e) (b) and (c) but not (a).

A B C D 26. We know that the standard error is the same at all points on a regression line because we assumed that:

(a) Observed values for Y are normally distributed around each estimated value of $\hat{Y}$.
(b) The variances of the distribution around each possible value of Y are the same.
(c) All available data were taken into account when the regression line was calculated.
(d) None of these.

A B C D 27. The variation of the Y values around the regression line is best expressed as:

(a) $\Sigma(Y + \bar{Y})^2$.
(b) $\Sigma(Y - \bar{Y})^2$.
(c) $\Sigma(Y - \hat{Y})^2$.
(d) $\Sigma(Y + \hat{Y})^2$.

A B C D 28. The value of r^2 for a particular situation is 0.49. What is the coefficient of correlation?

(a) 0.49.
(b) 0.7.
(c) 0.07.
(d) Cannot be determined from the information given.

A B C D 29. The fraction $\Sigma(Y - \hat{Y})^2/\Sigma(Y - \bar{Y})^2$ represents:

(a) The fraction of total variation in Y that is unexplained.
(b) The fraction of total variation in Y that is explained.
(c) The fraction of total variation in Y that was caused by changes in X.
(d) None of these.

A B C D 30. In the equation $Y = A + BX + e$, the e represents:

(a) The X-intercept of the observed data.
(b) The value of Y to which others are compared to determine the best fit.
(c) Random disturbances from the population regression line.
(d) None of these.

A B C D 31. Suppose you wish to compare the hypothesized value of B to a sample value of b that has been calculated. Which of the following *must* be calculated before the others?

(a) s_b.
(b) s_e.
(c) s_p.
(d) Calculations can be made in any order.

A B C D E 32. For the estimating equation to be a perfect estimator of the dependent variable, which of these would have to be true?

(a) The standard error of the estimate is zero.
(b) All the data points are on the regression line.
(c) The coefficient of determination is -1.
(d) (a) and (b) but not (c).
(e) All of these.

A B C D 33. If the dependent variable increases as the independent variable increases in an estimating equation, the coefficient of correlation will be in the range:

(a) 0 to -1.
(b) 0 to -0.05
(c) 0 to -2.
(d) None of these.

A B C D 34. Suppose the fraction of variation in Y that is unexplained by the independent variable X is $\frac{1}{4}$. Then r^2 is:

(a) $\frac{1}{4}$.
(b) $\frac{3}{4}$.
(c) $\frac{15}{16}$.
(d) None of these.

A B C D E 35. The sample coefficient of determination is developed from the variation of the observed Y values around:

(a) The mean of the observed independent variables.
(b) The mean of the observed dependent variables.
(c) The fitted regression line.
(d) (b) and (c) but not (a).
(e) (a), (b), and (c).

A B C D E 36. If $Y = a + bX$, the sample regression line, and $Y = A + BX$, the true unknown population regression equation, are equivalent, then the following must be true:

(a) The estimating equation is a perfect estimator of the dependent variable.
(b) All the data points are on the regression line.
(c) $r^2 = 1$.
(d) All of the above.
(e) None of the above.

37. If the dependent variable in a relationship decreases as the independent variable increases, the relationship is ______________________.

38. An association between two variables that is described by a curved line is a ______________________ one.

39. Every straight line has a ______________________, which represents how much each unit change of the independent variable changes the dependent variable.

40. The extent to which observed values differ from their predicted values on the regression line is measured by the ______________________.

41. ______________________ is a measure of the proportion of variation in the dependent variable that is explained by the regression line.

42. If 75 percent of the variation in the dependent variable is explained by the regression line, then the value of r will be about ______________________.

43. ______________________ is used to measure how well the regression line explains the variation of the dependent variable.

44. The sign of r indicates the ______________________ of the relationship between the two variables X and Y.

45. The method of least squares finds the best-fit line through a set of points, that is, the line that ______________________ the error between the observed points and the estimated points on the line.

Flow Chart: Regression and Correlation

START
To determine the *nature* of the linear relationship between two variables, use linear regression
Organize the data and plot a scatter diagram
Calculate the slope and the Y-intercept of the estimating equation using the least squares method:
$b = \frac{\Sigma XY - n\bar{X}\bar{Y}}{\Sigma X^2 - n\bar{X}^2}$
$a = \bar{Y} - b\bar{X}$
p. 661
Do you want to predict values of the dependent variable, Y ?
Yes
No
For point predictions, use the regression line: $\hat{Y} = a + bX$
Do you want an approximate prediction interval for Y ?
No
Yes

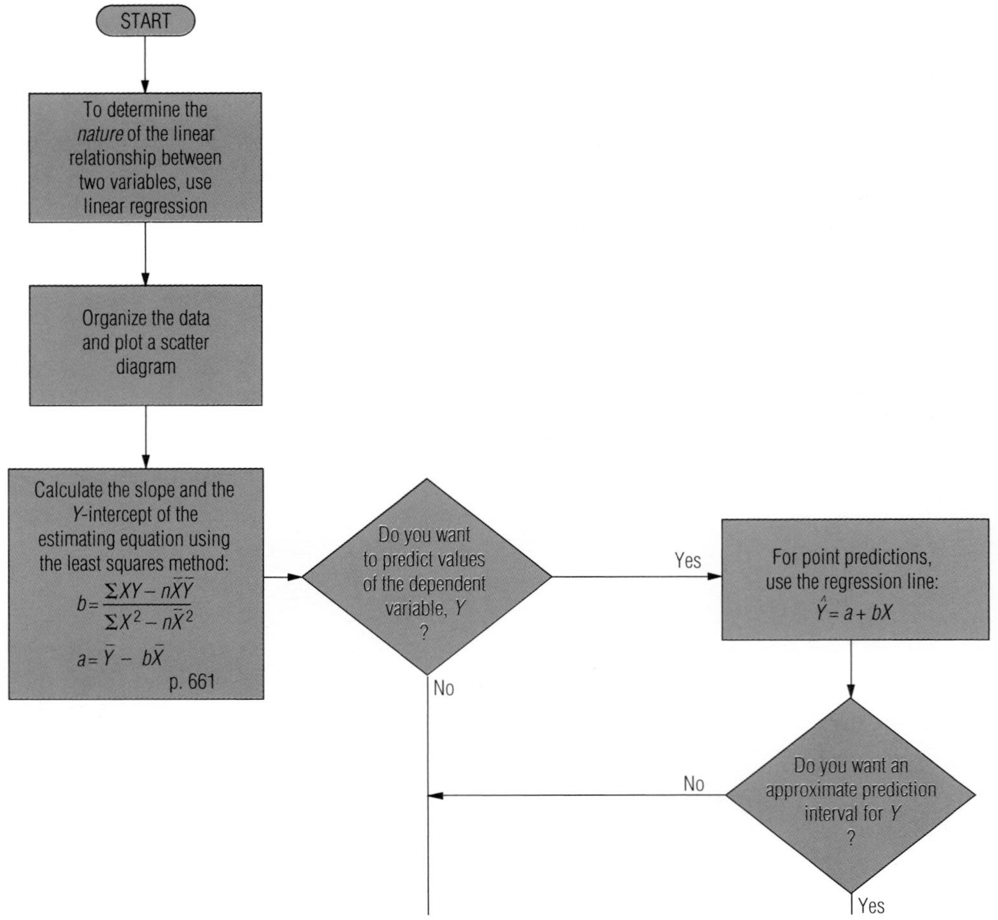

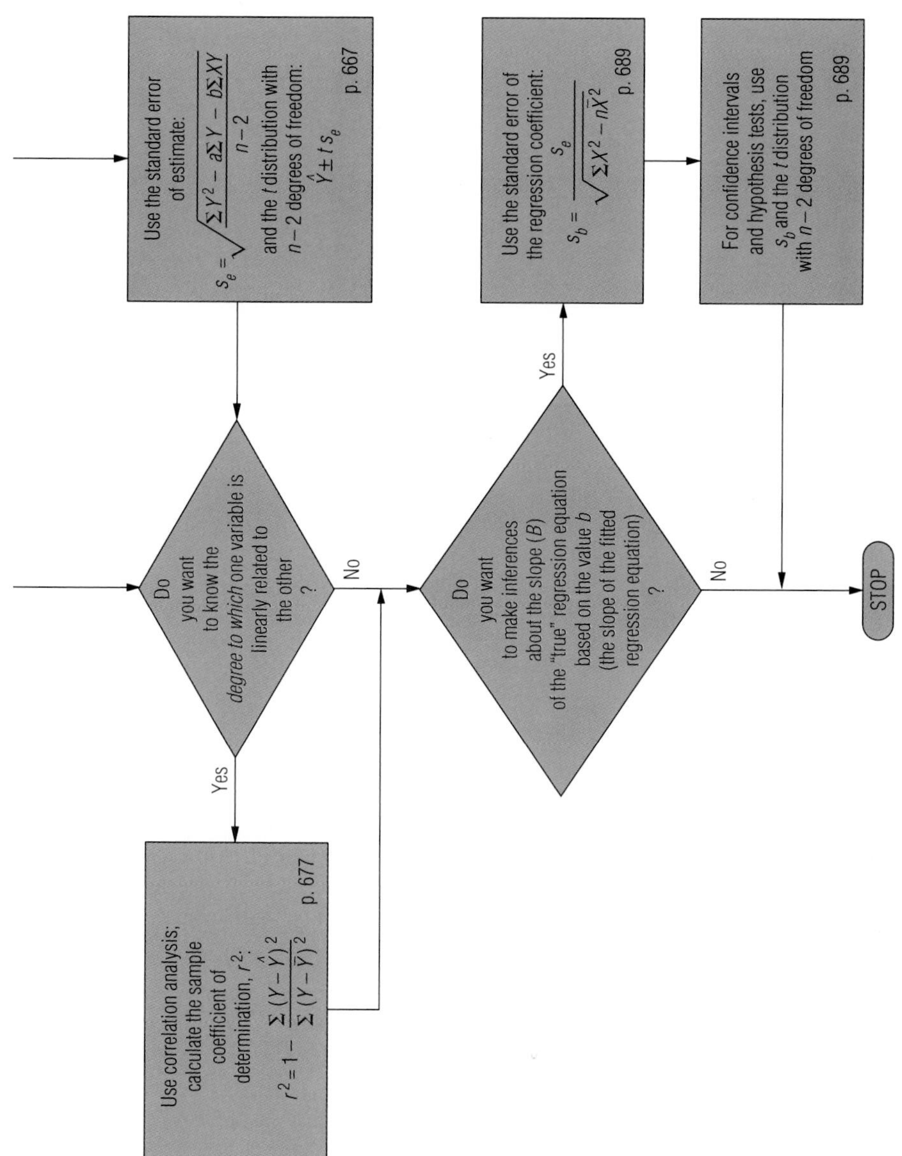

Use the standard error of estimate:
$s_e = \sqrt{\dfrac{\Sigma Y^2 - a\Sigma Y - b\Sigma XY}{n-2}}$
and the t distribution with $n - 2$ degrees of freedom:
$\hat{Y} \pm t s_e$
p. 667
Do you want to know the *degree to which* one variable is linearly related to the other ?
Yes
No
Use correlation analysis; calculate the sample coefficient of determination, r^2:
$r^2 = 1 - \dfrac{\Sigma (Y - \hat{Y})^2}{\Sigma (Y - \bar{Y})^2}$
p. 677
Do you want to make inferences about the slope (B) of the "true" regression equation based on the value b (the slope of the fitted regression equation) ?
Yes
No
Use the standard error of the regression coefficient:
$s_b = \dfrac{s_e}{\sqrt{\Sigma X^2 - n\bar{X}^2}}$
p. 689
For confidence intervals and hypothesis tests, use s_b and the t distribution with $n - 2$ degrees of freedom
p. 689
STOP

chapter 13

MULTIPLE REGRESSION AND MODELING

Objectives

- To extend the regression techniques of the last chapter to handle more than one explanatory variable for a quantity we are trying to predict
- To examine decision-making situations where multiple regression can be used to make predictions
- To interpret the output from computer regression packages
- To test hypotheses about regressions
- To use modeling techniques to incorporate qualitative variables into regression equations
- To learn how to fit curves to data
- To understand the importance of residuals in regression analysis

Chapter Contents

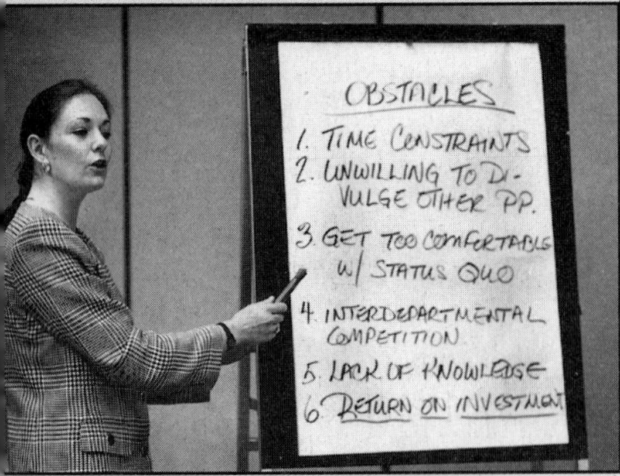

A manufacturer of small office copiers and word-processing machinery pays its salespeople a small base salary plus a commission equal to a fixed percentage of the person's sales. One of the salespeople charges that this salary structure discriminates against women. Current base salaries for the firm's nine salespeople are as follows:

Salesmen		Saleswomen	
Months Employed	Base Salary ($1,000s)	Months Employed	Base Salary ($1,000s)
6	7.5	5	6.2
10	8.6	13	8.7
12	9.1	15	9.4
18	10.3	21	9.8
30	13.0		

The director of personnel sees that base salary depends on length of service, but she does not know how to use the data to learn whether it also depends on gender and whether there is discrimination against women. Methods in this chapter will enable her to find out.

13.1 Multiple Regression and Correlation Analysis

Using more than one independent variable to estimate the dependent variable

As we mentioned in Chapter 12, we can use more than one independent variable to estimate the dependent variable and, in this way, attempt to increase the accuracy of the estimate. This process is called multiple regression and correlation analysis. It is based on the same assumptions and procedures we have encountered using simple regression.

Consider the real-estate agent who wishes to relate the number of houses the firm sells in a month to the amount of her monthly advertising. Certainly, we can find a simple estimating equation that relates these two variables. Could we also improve the accuracy of our equation by including in the estimating process the number of salespeople she employs each month? The answer is probably yes. And now, because we want to use both the number of sales agents and the advertising expenditures to predict monthly house sales, we must use *multiple*, not simple, regression to determine the relationship.

Advantage of multiple regression

The principal advantage of *multiple regression* is that it allows us to use more of the information available to us to estimate the dependent variable. Sometimes the correlation between two variables may be insufficient to determine a reliable estimating equation. Yet, if we add the data from more independent variables, we may be able to determine an estimating equation that describes the relationship with greater accuracy.

Steps in multiple regression and correlation

Multiple regression and correlation analysis involve a three-step process such as the one we used in simple regression. In this process, we

1. Describe the multiple-regression equation.
2. Examine the multiple-regression standard error of estimate.
3. Use multiple-correlation analysis to determine how well the regression equation describes the observed data.

In addition, in multiple regression, we can look at each individual independent variable and test whether it contributes significantly to the way the regression describes the data.

Computer regression packages

In this chapter, we shall see how to find the best-fitting regression equation for a given set of data and how to analyze the equation we get. Although we shall show how to do multiple regression by hand or on a hand-held calculator, it will quickly become obvious to you that you would not want to do even a modest-size real-life problem by hand. Fortunately, there are available many computer packages for doing multiple regressions and other statistical analyses. These packages do the "number crunching" and leave you free to concentrate on analyzing the significance of the resulting estimating equation.

Multiple regression will also enable us to fit curves as well as lines. Using the technique of *dummy variables,* we can even include qualitative factors such as gender in our multiple regression. This technique will enable us to analyze the discrimination problem that opened this chapter. Dummy variables and fitting curves are only two of the many *modeling techniques* that can be used in multiple regression to increase the accuracy of our estimating equations.

Exercises 13.1

Basic Concepts

- **13-1** Why would we use multiple regression instead of simple regression in estimating a dependent variable?
- **13-2** How will dummy variables be used in our study of multiple regression?
- **13-3** To what does the word *multiple* refer in the phrase *multiple regression?*
- **13-4** The owner of a chain of stores would like to predict monthly sales from the size of city in which a store is located. After fitting a simple regression model, she decides that she wants to include the effect of season of the year in the model. Can this be done using the techniques in this chapter?
- **13-5** Describe the three steps in the process of multiple regression and correlation analysis.
- **13-6** Will the procedures used in multiple regression differ greatly from those we used in simple regression? Explain.

13.2 Finding the Multiple-Regression Equation

A problem demonstrating multiple regression

Let's see how we can compute the multiple-regression equation. For convenience, we shall use only two independent variables in the problem we work in this section. Keep in mind, however, that the same sort of technique is, in principle, applicable to any number of independent variables.

The Internal Revenue Service is trying to estimate the monthly amount of unpaid taxes discovered by its auditing division. In the past, the IRS estimated this figure on the basis of the expected number of field-audit labor hours. In recent years, however, field-audit labor hours have become an erratic predictor of the actual unpaid taxes. As a result, the IRS is looking for another factor with which it can improve the estimating equation.

Table 13-1

Data from IRS Auditing Records During the Last 10 Months

Month	X_1 Field-Audit Labor Hours (00s Omitted)	X_2 Computer Hours (00s Omitted)	Y Actual Unpaid Taxes Discovered (millions of dollars)
January	45	16	29
February	42	14	24
March	44	15	27
April	45	13	25
May	43	13	26
June	46	14	28
July	44	16	30
August	45	16	28
September	44	15	28
October	43	15	27

The auditing division does keep a record of the number of hours its computers are used to detect unpaid taxes. Could we combine this information with the data on field-audit labor hours and come up with a more accurate estimating equation for the unpaid taxes discovered each month? Table 13-1 presents these data for the last 10 months.

Appropriate symbols

In simple regression, X is the symbol used for the values of the independent variable. In multiple regression, we have more than one independent variable. So we shall continue to use X, but we shall add a subscript (for example, X_1, X_2) to distinguish between the independent variables we are using.

Defining the variables

In this problem, we will let X_1 represent the number of field-audit labor hours and X_2 represent the number of computer hours. The dependent variable, Y, will be the actual unpaid taxes discovered.

Estimating equation for multiple regression

Recall that in simple regression, the estimating equation $\hat{Y} = a + bX$ describes the relationship between the two variables X and Y. In multiple regression, we must extend that equation, adding one term for each new variable. In symbolic form, Equation 13-1 is the formula we can use when we have two independent variables:

Estimating Equation Describing Relationship among Three Variables

$$\hat{Y} = a + b_1X_1 + b_2X_2 \tag{13-1}$$

where

- $\hat{Y}$ = estimated value corresponding to the dependent variable
- a = Y-intercept
- X_1 and X_2 = values of the two independent variables
- b_1 and b_2 = slopes associated with X_1 and X_2, respectively

Visualizing multiple regression

We can visualize the simple estimating equation as a line on a graph; similarly, we can picture a two-variable multiple regression equation as a plane, such as the one shown in Figure 13-1. Here we have a three-dimensional shape that possesses depth, length, and width. To get an intuitive feel for this three-dimensional shape, visualize the intersection of the axes, Y, X_1, and X_2 as one corner of a room.

Figure 13-1 is a graph of 10 sample points and the plane about which these points seem to cluster. Some points lie above the plane and some fall below it—just as points lie above and below the simple regression line.

Using the least-squares criterion to fit a regression plane

Our problem is to decide which of the possible planes that we could draw will be the best fit. To do this, we shall again use the least-squares criterion and locate the plane that minimizes the sum of the squares of the errors, that is, the distances from the points around the plane to the corresponding points *on* the plane. We use our data and the following three equations (which statisticians call the "normal equations") to determine the values of the numerical constants, a, b_1, and b_2.

Normal Equations

$$\Sigma Y = na + b_1\Sigma X_1 + b_2\Sigma X_2 \quad [13\text{-}2]$$

$$\Sigma X_1Y = a\Sigma X_1 + b_1\Sigma X_1^2 + b_2\Sigma X_1X_2 \quad [13\text{-}3]$$

$$\Sigma X_2Y = a\Sigma X_2 + b_1\Sigma X_1X_2 + b_2\Sigma X_2^2 \quad [13\text{-}4]$$

Solving Equations 13-2, 13-3, and 13-4 for a, b_1, and b_2 will give us the coefficients for the regression plane. Obviously, the best way to compute all the sums in these three equations

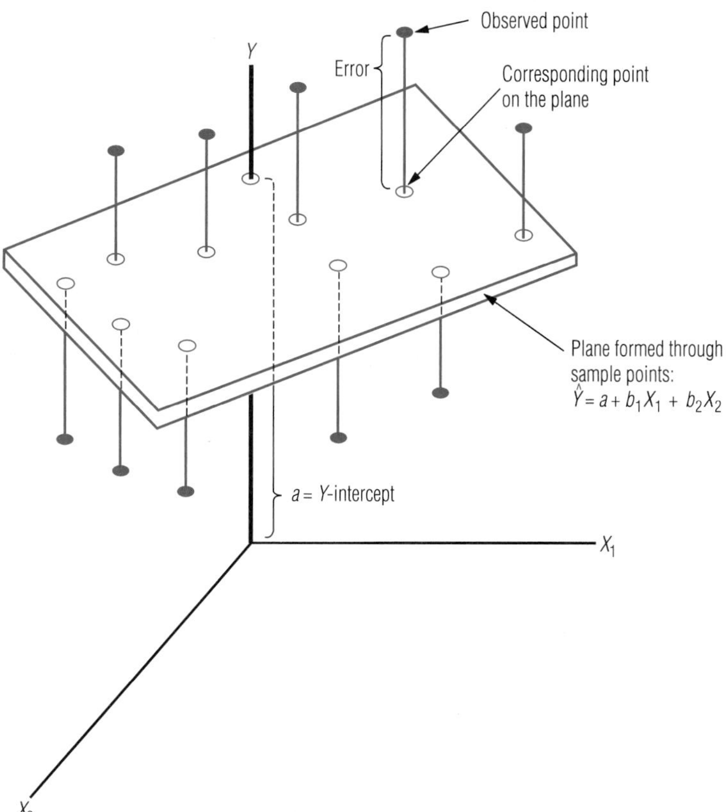

FIGURE 13-1

Multiple regression plane for 10 data points

Table 13-2

Values for Fitting Least-Squares Plane, where $n = 10$

Y (1)	X_1 (2)	X_2 (3)	X_1Y (2) × (1)	X_2Y (3) × (1)	X_1X_2 (2) × (3)	X_1^2 $(2)^2$	X_2^2 $(3)^2$	Y^2 $(1)^2$
29	45	16	1,305	464	720	2,025	256	841
24	42	14	1,008	336	588	1,764	196	576
27	44	15	1,188	405	660	1,936	225	729
25	45	13	1,125	325	585	2,025	169	625
26	43	13	1,118	338	559	1,849	169	676
28	46	14	1,288	392	644	2,116	196	784
30	44	16	1,320	480	704	1,936	256	900
28	45	16	1,260	448	720	2,025	256	784
28	44	15	1,232	420	660	1,936	225	784
27	43	15	1,161	405	645	1,849	225	729
272 ↑ ΣY	**441** ↑ ΣX_1	**147** ↑ ΣX_2	**12,005** ↑ ΣX_1Y	**4,013** ↑ ΣX_2Y	**6,485** ↑ ΣX_1X_2	**19,461** ↑ ΣX_1^2	**2,173** ↑ ΣX_2^2	**7,428** ↑ ΣY^2

$\bar{Y} = 27.2$
$\bar{X}_1 = 44.1$
$\bar{X}_2 = 14.7$

is to use a table to collect and organize the necessary information, just as we did in simple regression. This we have done for the IRS problem in Table 13-2.

Equations 13-2, 13-3, and 13-4 used to solve for a, b_1, and b_2

Now, using the information from Table 13-2 in Equations 13-2, 13-3, and 13-4, we get three equations in the three unknown constants (a, b_1, and b_2):

$$272 = 10a + 441b_1 + 147b_2$$

$$12{,}005 = 441a + 19{,}461b_1 + 6{,}485b_2$$

$$4{,}013 = 147a + 6{,}485b_1 + 2{,}173b_2$$

When we solve these three equations simultaneously, we get

$$a = -13.828$$

$$b_1 = 0.564$$

$$b_2 = 1.099$$

Substituting these three values into the general two-variable regression equation (Equation 13-1), we get an equation that describes the relationship among the number of field-audit labor hours, the number of computer hours, and the unpaid taxes discovered by the auditing division:

$$\hat{Y} = a + b_1X_1 + b_2X_2 \qquad [13\text{-}1]$$

$$= -13.828 + 0.564X_1 + 1.099X_2$$

The auditing division can use this equation monthly to estimate the amount of unpaid taxes it will discover.

Using the multiple-regression equation to estimate

Suppose the IRS wants to increase its discoveries in the coming month. Because trained auditors are scarce, the IRS does not intend to hire additional personnel. The number of field-audit labor hours, then, will remain at October's level of about 4,300 hours. But in order to increase its discoveries of unpaid taxes, the IRS expects to increase the number of computer hours to about 1,600. As a result:

$$X_1 = 43 \leftarrow \text{4,300 hours of field-audit labor}$$

$$X_2 = 16 \leftarrow \text{1,600 hours of computer time}$$

Substituting these values into the auditing division's regression equation, we get

$$\begin{aligned}\hat{Y} &= -13.828 + 0.564X_1 + 1.099X_2 \\ &= -13.828 + (0.564)(43) + (1.099)(16) \\ &= -13.828 + 24.252 + 17.584 \\ &= 28.008 \leftarrow \text{Estimated discoveries of \$28,008,000}\end{aligned}$$

Interpreting our estimate

Therefore, in the November forecast, the audit division can indicate that it expects about $28 million of discoveries for this combination of factors.

a, b_1, and b_2 are the estimated regression coefficients

So far, we have referred to a as the Y-intercept and to b_1 and b_2 as the slopes of the multiple-regression plane. But to be more precise, we should say that these numerical constants are the *estimated regression coefficients*. The constant a is the value of $\hat{Y}$ (in this case, the estimated unpaid taxes) *if* both X_1 and X_2 happen to be zero. The coefficients b_1 and b_2 describe how changes in X_1 and X_2 affect the value of $\hat{Y}$. In our IRS example, we can hold the number of field-audit labor hours, X_1, constant and change the number of computer hours, X_2. When we do, the value of $\hat{Y}$ will increase $1,099,000 for every additional 100 hours of computer time. Likewise, we can hold X_2 constant and find that, for every 100-hour increase in the number of field-audit labor hours, $\hat{Y}$ increases by $564,000.

HINTS & ASSUMPTIONS

Hint: If you have trouble picturing in your mind what multiple regression is actually doing, think back to Chapter 12 and remember that a regression *line* describes the relationship between *two* variables. In multiple regression, the regression *plane* such as the one on page 721 describes the relationship among *three* variables Y, X_1, and X_2. The appropriate regression plane is conceptually the same as the appropriate regression line, that is, the one that minimizes the sum of the squared vertical distances between the data points and the plane in this instance. It may help to remember that each independent variable may account for *some* of the variation in the dependent variable. Multiple regression is just a way to use several independent variables to make a better prediction of the dependent variable.

X_1	X_2	X_3	X_4	Y
21.4	62.9	21.9	−2	22.8
51.7	40.7	42.9	5	93.7
41.8	81.8	69.8	2	64.9
11.8	41.0	90.9	−4	19.2
71.6	22.6	12.9	8	55.8
91.9	61.5	30.9	1	23.1

Applications

■ **13-16** Police stations across the country are interested in predicting the number of arrests they can expect to process each month so as to better schedule office employees. Historically, the average number of arrests (Y) each month is influenced by the number of officers on the police force (X_1), the population of the city in thousands (X_2), and the percentage of unemployed people in the city (X_3). Data for these factors in 15 cities are presented below.

(a) Using whatever computer package is available, determine the best-fitting regression equation for these data.

(b) What percentage of the total variation in the number of arrests (Y) is explained by this equation?

(c) The ChapelBoro police department is trying to predict the number of monthly arrests. ChapelBoro has a population of 75,000, a police force of 82, and an unemployment percentage of 10.5 percent. How many arrests do you predict for each month?

Monthly Average Number of Arrests (Y)	Number of Officers on the Force (X_1)	Size of the City (X_2) in Thousands	Percentage Unemployed (X_3)
390.6	68	81.6	4.3
504.3	94	75.1	3.9
628.4	125	97.3	5.6
745.6	175	123.5	8.7
585.2	113	118.4	11.4
450.3	82	65.4	9.6
327.8	46	61.6	12.4
260.5	32	54.3	18.3
477.5	89	97.4	4.6
389.8	67	82.4	6.7
312.4	47	56.4	8.4
367.5	59	71.3	7.6
374.4	61	67.4	9.8
494.6	87	96.3	11.3
487.5	92	86.4	4.7

■ **13-17** We are trying to predict the annual demand for widgets (DEMAND) using the following independent variables.

PRICE = price of widgets (in $)
INCOME = consumer income (in $)
SUB = price of a substitute commodity (in $)

(*Note:* A substitute commodity is one that can be substituted for another commodity. For example, margarine is a substitute commodity for butter.)

Data have been collected from 1982 to 1996:

Year	Demand	Price ($)	Income ($)	Sub ($)
1982	40	9	400	10
1983	45	8	500	14
1984	50	9	600	12
1985	55	8	700	13
1986	60	7	800	11
1987	70	6	900	15
1988	65	6	1,000	16
1989	65	8	1,100	17
1990	75	5	1,200	22
1991	75	5	1,300	19
1992	80	5	1,400	20
1993	100	3	1,500	23
1994	90	4	1,600	18
1995	95	3	1,700	24
1996	85	4	1,800	21

(a) Using whatever computer package is available, determine the best-fitting regression equation for these data.

(b) Are the signs (+ or −) of the regression coefficients of the independent variables as one would expect? Explain briefly. (*Note:* This is not a statistical question; you just need to think about what the regression coefficients mean.)

(c) State and interpret the coefficient of multiple determination for this problem.

(d) State and interpret the standard error of estimate for this problem.

(e) Using the equation, what would you predict for DEMAND if the price of widgets was $6, consumer income was $1,200, and the price of the substitute commodity was $17?

■ **13-18** Bill Buxton, a statistics professor in a leading business school, has a keen interest in factors affecting students' performance on exams. The midterm exam for the past semester had a wide distribution of grades, but Bill feels certain that several factors explain the distribution: He allowed his students to study from as many different books as they liked, their IQs vary, they are of different ages, and they study varying amounts of time for exams. To develop a predicting formula for exam grades, Bill asked each student to answer, at the end of the exam, questions regarding study time and number of books used. Bill's teaching records already contained the IQs and ages for the students, so he compiled the data for the class and ran a multiple regression with Minitab. The output from Bill's computer run was as follows:

```
Predictor        Coef        Stdev     t-ratio       p
Constant      -49.948        41.55       -1.20   0.268
HOURS         1.06931      0.98163        1.09   0.312
IQ            1.36460      0.37627        3.63   0.008
BOOKS         2.03982      1.50799        1.35   0.218
AGE          -1.79890      0.67332       -2.67   0.319

s = 11.657        R-sq = 76.7%
```

(a) What is the best-fitting regression equation for these data?

(b) What percentage of the variation in grades is explained by this equation?

(c) What grade would you expect for a 21-year-old student with an IQ of 113, who studied 5 hours and used three different books?

■ **13-19** Fourteen Twenty-Two Food Stores, Inc., is planning to expand its convenience store chain. To aid in selecting locations for the new stores, it has collected weekly sales data from each of its 23 stores. To help explain the variability in weekly sales, it has also collected information describing four variables that it believes are related to sales. The data that were collected follow. The variables are defined as follows:

SALES : average weekly sales for each store in thousands of dollars
AUTOS : average weekly auto traffic volume in thousands of cars
ENTRY : ease of entry/exit measured on a scale of 1 to 100
ANNINC : average annual household income for the area in thousands of dollars
DISTANCE : distance in miles from the store to the nearest supermarket

The data were analyzed using Minitab and the output follows:

```
Predictor        Coef       Stdev      t-ratio       p
Constant       175.37       92.62        1.89     0.075
AUTOS          -0.028       0.315       -0.09     0.929
ENTRY           3.775       1.272        2.97     0.008
ANNINC          1.990       4.510        0.44     0.664
DISTANCE       212.41      28.090        7.56     0.000

s = 85.587          R-sq = 95.8%
```

(a) What is the best-fitting regression equation, as given by Minitab?

(b) What is the standard error of estimate for this equation?

(c) What fraction of the variation in sales is explained by this regression?

(d) What sales would you predict for a store located in a neighborhood that had an average annual household income of $20,000, was 2 miles from the nearest supermarket, was on a road with weekly traffic volume of 100,000 autos, and had an ease of entry of 50?

■ **13-20** Rick Blackburn is thinking about selling his house. In order to decide what price to ask, he has collected data for 12 recent closings. He has recorded sales price (in $1,000s), the number of square feet in the house (in 100s of sq ft.), the number of stories, the number of bathrooms, and the age of the house (in years).

Sales Price	Square Feet	Stories	Bathrooms	Age
49.65	8.9	1	1.0	2
67.95	9.5	1	1.0	6
81.15	12.6	2	1.5	11
81.60	12.9	2	1.5	8
91.50	19.0	2	1.0	22
95.25	17.6	1	1.0	17

(Continued)

Sales Price	Square Feet	Stories	Bathrooms	Age
100.35	20.0	2	1.5	12
104.25	20.6	2	1.5	11
112.65	20.5	1	2.0	9
149.70	25.1	2	2.0	8
160.65	22.7	2	2.0	18
232.50	40.8	3	4.0	12

(a) Using whatever computer package is available, determine the best-fitting regression equation for these data.

(b) What is R^2 for this equation? What does this number measure?

(c) If Rick's house has 1,800 square feet (= 18.0 hundreds of square feet), 1 story, 1.5 bathrooms, and is 6 years old, what sale price can Rick expect?

■ **13-21** Allegheny Steel Corporation has been looking into the factors that influence how many millions of tons of steel it is able to sell each year. Management suspects that the following are major factors: the annual national inflation rate, the average price per ton by which imported steel undercuts Allegheny's prices (in dollars), and the number of cars (in millions) that U.S. automakers are planning to produce in that year. Data for 7 years have been collected:

Year	Y Millions of Tons Sold	X_1 Inflation Rate	X_2 Imported Undercut	X_3 Number of Cars
1993	4.2	3.1	3.10	6.2
1992	3.1	3.9	5.00	5.1
1991	4.0	7.5	2.20	5.7
1990	4.7	10.7	4.50	7.1
1989	4.3	15.5	4.35	6.5
1988	3.7	13.0	2.60	6.1
1987	3.5	11.0	3.05	5.9

(a) Using whatever computer package is available, determine the best-fitting regression equation for these data.

(b) What percentage of the total variation in the number of millions of tons of steel sold by Allegheny each year is explained by this equation?

(c) How many tons of steel should Allegheny expect to sell in a year in which the inflation rate is 7.1, American automakers are planning to produce 6.0 million cars, and the average imported price undercut per ton is $3.50?

Worked-Out Answer to Self-Check Exercise

SC 13-3 From the computer output we get the following results:

(a) $\hat{Y} = -1275 + 17.059X_1 + 0.5406X_2 - 0.1743X_3$.

(b) $R^2 = 87.2\%$; 87.2% of the total variation in Y is explained by the model.

(c) $\hat{Y} = -1275 + 17.059(169) + 0.5406(10{,}212) - 0.1743(26{,}925) =$ 2,436 rush returns.

Test of Whether a Variable Is Significant

$$-t_c \leq t_o \leq t_c \qquad [13\text{-}9]$$

where

- t_c = appropriate t value (with $n - k - 1$ degrees of freedom) for the significance level of the test
- $t_o = b_i/s_{b_i}$ = observed (or computed) t value obtained from computer output

If t_o falls between $-t_c$ and t_c, we accept H_0 and conclude X_i is not a significant explanatory variable. Otherwise, we reject H_0 and conclude that X_i is a significant explanatory variable.

Testing the significance of computer hours in the IRS problem

Let's test, at the 0.01 significance level, whether computer hours is a significant explanatory variable for unpaid taxes discovered. From Appendix Table 2, with $n - k - 1 = 10 - 3 - 1 = 6$ degrees of freedom and $\alpha = 0.01$, we see that $t_c = 3.707$. From Figure 13-2, we see that $t_o = 14.00$. Because $t_o > t_c$, we conclude that computer hours *is* a significant explanatory variable. In fact, looking at the computed t values for the other two independent variables (field-audit labor hours $t_o = 7.36$ and rewards to informants, $t_o = 9.59$), we see that each of them is also a significant explanatory variable.

We can also use the column headed "p" to test whether X_i is a significant explanatory variable. In fact, using that information, we don't even need to use Appendix Table 2. The entries in this column are *prob values* for the two-tailed test of the hypotheses:

$$H_0\text{: } B_i = 0$$

$$H_1\text{: } B_i \neq 0$$

Recall from the discussion in Chapter 9 that these prob values are the probabilities that each b_i would be as far (or farther) away from zero than the observed value obtained from our regression, *if* H_0 *is true.* As Figure 13-3 illustrates, we need only compare these prob values with α, the significance level of the test, to determine whether X_i is a significant explanatory variable for Y.

FIGURE 13-3 Using "p" to see whether X_i is a significant explanatory variable

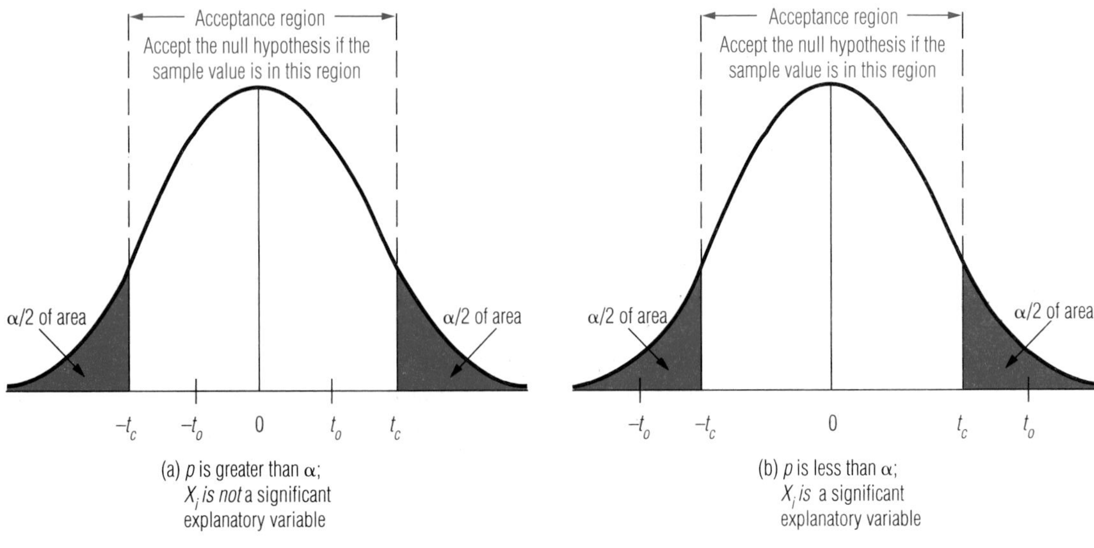

(a) p is greater than α; X_i *is not* a significant explanatory variable

(b) p is less than α; X_i *is* a significant explanatory variable

Testing the significance of an explanatory variable is always a two-tailed test. The independent variable X_i is a significant explanatory variable if b_i is significantly *different* from zero, that is, if t_o is a large positive or a large negative number.

In the IRS example, let's repeat our tests at $\alpha = 0.01$. For each of the three independent variables, p is less than 0.01, so we again conclude that each one is a significant explanatory variable.

Inferences about the Regression as a Whole (Using an F Test)

Suppose you put a piece of graph paper over a dartboard and randomly tossed a bunch of darts at it. After you took out the darts, you would have something that looked very much like a scatter diagram. Suppose you then fit a simple regression line to this set of "observed data points" and calculated r^2. Because the darts were randomly tossed, you would expect to get a low value of r^2 because in this case, X really doesn't explain Y. However, if you did this many times, occasionally you would observe a high value of r^2, just by pure chance.

Significance of the regression as a whole

Given any simple (or multiple) regression, **it's natural to ask whether the value of r^2 (or R^2) really indicates that the independent variables explain Y, or might have happened just by chance.** This question is often phrased, "Is the regression as a whole significant?" In the last section, we looked at how to tell whether an individual X_i was a significant explanatory variable; now we see how to tell whether all the X_i's taken together significantly explain the variability observed in Y. Our hypotheses are

$$H_0: B_1 = B_2 = \cdots = B_k = 0 \leftarrow \text{Null hypothesis: } Y \text{ doesn't depend on the } X_i\text{'s.}$$

$$H_1: \text{at least one } B_i \neq 0 \quad \leftarrow \text{Alternative hypothesis: } Y \text{ depends on at least one of the } X_i\text{'s.}$$

Analyzing the variation in the Y values

When we discussed r^2 in Chapter 12, we looked at the total variation in Y, $\Sigma(Y - \bar{Y})^2$, the part of that variation that is explained by the regression $\Sigma(\hat{Y} - \bar{Y})^2$, and the unexplained part of the variation, $\Sigma\,(Y - \hat{Y})^2$. Figure 13-4 is a duplicate of Figure 12-15. It reviews the relationship between total deviation, explained deviation, and unexplained deviation for a single data point in a simple regression. Although we can't draw a similar picture for a multiple regression, we are doing the same thing conceptually.

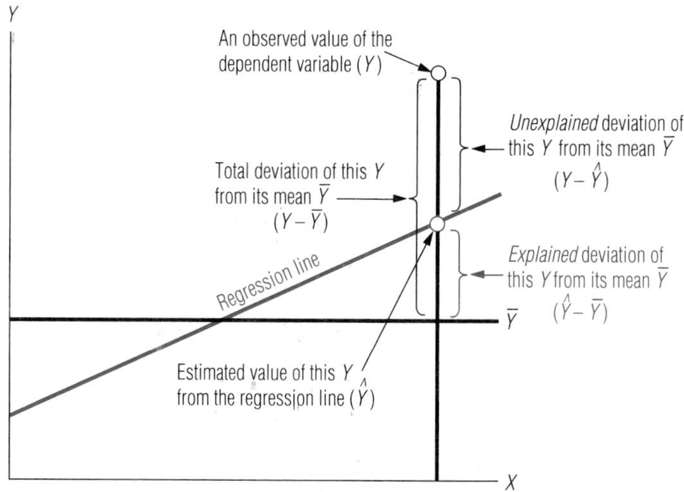

FIGURE 13-4

Total deviation, explained deviation, and unexplained deviation for *one* observed value of Y

dictions, is 3.989, while for the simple regression with the cost of ads as the explanatory variable (output in Figure 13-7), we have $s_e = 3.849$. What we can't do is tell with much precision how sales will change if we increase the number of ads by one. The multiple regression says $b_1 = 0.625$ (that is, each ad increases total pizza sales by about $625), but the standard error of this coefficient is 1.12 (that is, about $1,120).

HINTS & ASSUMPTIONS

Hint: Making inferences about a multiple regression is conceptually just like what we did in Chapter 12 when we made inferences about a regression line, except here we're dealing with two or more independent variables. Warning: Multicollinearity is a problem you have to deal with in multiple regressions, and developing a common-sense understanding of it is necessary. Remember that you can *still* make fairly precise predictions when it's present. But remember that when it's present, you *can't* tell with much precision how much the dependent variable will change if you "jiggle" one of the independent variables. So our aim should be to minimize multicollinearity. Hint: The best multiple regression is one that explains the relationship among the data by accounting for the largest proportion of the variation in the dependent variable, *with the fewest number of independent variables.* Warning: Throwing in too many independent variables just because you have a computer is not a great idea.

Exercises 13.4

Self-Check Exercises

SC 13-4 Edith Pratt is a busy executive in a nationwide trucking company. Edith is late for a meeting because she has been unable to locate the multiple-regression output that an associate produced for her. If the total regression was significant at the 0.05 level, then she wanted to use the computer output as evidence to support some of her ideas at the meeting. The subordinate, however, is sick today and Edith has been unable to locate his work. As a matter of fact, all the information she possesses concerning the multiple regression is a piece of scrap paper with the following on it:

Regression for E. Pratt

SSR	872.4, with df
SSE	, with 17 df
SST	1023.6, with 24 df

Because the scrap paper doesn't even have a complete set of numbers on it, Edith has concluded that it must be useless. You, however, should know better. Should Edith go directly to the meeting or continue looking for the computer output?

SC 13-5 A New England–based commuter airline has taken a survey of its 15 terminals and has obtained the following data for the month of February, where

SALES = total revenue based on number of tickets sold (in thousands of dollars)
PROMOT = amount spent on promoting the airline in the area (in thousands of dollars)
COMP = number of competing airlines at that terminal
FREE = the percentage of passengers who flew free (for various reasons)

Sales ($)	Promot($)	Comp	Free
79.3	2.5	10	3
200.1	5.5	8	6
163.2	6.0	12	9
200.1	7.9	7	16
146.0	5.2	8	15
177.7	7.6	12	9
30.9	2.0	12	8
291.9	9.0	5	10
160.0	4.0	8	4
339.4	9.6	5	16
159.6	5.5	11	7
86.3	3.0	12	6
237.5	6.0	6	10
107.2	5.0	10	4
155.0	3.5	10	4

(a) Use the following Minitab output to determine the best-fitting regression equation for the airline:

```
The regression equation is
SALES = 172 + 25.9 PROMOT - 13.2 COMP - 3.04 FREE

Predictor        Coef        Stdev     t-ratio        p
Constant       172.34        51.38        3.35    0.006
PROMOT         25.950        4.877        5.32    0.000
COMP          -13.238        3.686       -3.59    0.004
FREE           -3.041        2.342       -1.30    0.221
```

(b) Do the passengers who fly free cause sales to decrease significantly? State and test appropriate hypotheses. Use $\alpha = 0.05$.

(c) Does an increase in promotions by \$1,000 change sales by \$28,000, or is the change significantly different from \$28,000? State and test appropriate hypotheses. Use $\alpha = 0.10$.

(d) Give a 90 percent confidence interval for the slope coefficient of COMP.

Applications

■ **13-22** Mark Lowtown publishes the *Mosquito Junction Enquirer* and is having difficulty predicting the amount of newsprint needed each day. He has randomly selected 27 days over the past year and recorded the following information:

POUNDS = pounds of newsprint for that day's newspaper
CLASFIED = number of classified advertisements
DISPLAY = number of display advertisements
FULLPAGE = number of full-page advertisements

Using Minitab to regress POUNDS on the other three variables, Mark got the output that follows.

Predictor	Coef	Stdev	t-ratio	p
Constant	1072.95	872.43	1.23	0.232
CLASFIED	0.251	0.126	1.99	0.060
DISPLAY	1.250	0.884	1.41	0.172
FULLPAGE	250.66	67.92	3.69	0.001

(a) Mark had always felt that each display advertisement used at least 3 pounds of newsprint. Does the regression give him significant reason to doubt this belief at the 5 percent level?

(b) Similarly, Mark had always felt that each classified advertisement used roughly half a pound of newsprint. Does he now have significant reason to doubt this belief at the 5 percent level?

(c) Mark sells full-page advertising space to the local merchants for $30 per page. Should he consider adjusting his rates if newsprint costs him 9¢ per pound? Assume other costs are negligible. State explicit hypotheses and an explicit conclusion. (*Hint:* Holding all else constant, each additional full-page ad uses 250.66 pounds of paper × $0.09 per pound = $22.56 cost. Breakeven is at 333.333 pounds. Why? Thus, if the slope coefficient for FULLPAGE is significantly above 333.333, Mark is not making a profit and his rates should be changed.)

■ **13-23** Refer to Exercise 13-18. At a significance level of 0.10, which variables are significant explanatory variables for exam scores? (There were 12 students in the sample.)

■ **13-24** Refer to Exercise 13-18. The following additional output was provided by Minitab when Bill ran the multiple regression:

Analysis of Variance

SOURCE	DF	SS	MS	F	p
Regression	4	3134.42	783.60		
Error	7	951.25	135.89		
Total	11	4085.67			

(a) What is the observed value of *F*?

(b) At a significance level of 0.05, what is the appropriate critical value of *F* to use in determining whether the regression as a whole is significant?

(c) Based on your answers to (a) and (b), is the regression significant as a whole?

■ **13-25** Refer to Exercise 13-19. At a significance level of 0.01, is DISTANCE a significant explanatory variable for SALES?

■ **13-26** Refer to Exercise 13-19. The following additional output was provided by Minitab when the multiple regression was run:

Analysis of Variance

SOURCE	DF	SS	MS	F	p
Regression	4	2861495	715374	102.39	0.000
Error	18	125761	6896.7		
Total	22	2987256			

At the 0.05 level of significance, is the regression significant as a whole?

■ **13-27** Henry Lander is director of production for the Alecos Corporation of Caracas, Venezuela. Henry has asked you to help him determine a formula for predicting absenteeism in a meatpacking facility. He hypothesizes that percentage absenteeism can be explained by average daily temperature. Data are gathered for several months, you run the simple regression, and you find that temperature explains 66 percent of the variation in absenteeism. But Henry is not convinced that this is a satisfactory predictor. He suggests that daily rainfall may also have something to do with absenteeism. So you gather data, run a regression of absenteeism on rainfall, and get an r^2 of 0.59. "Eureka!" you cry. "I've got it! With one predictor that explains 66 percent and another that explains 59 percent, all I have to do is run a multiple regression using both predictors, and I'll surely have an almost perfect predictor!" To your dismay, however, the multiple regression has an R^2 of only 68 percent, which is just slightly better than the temperature variable alone. How can you account for this apparent discrepancy?

■ **13-28** Juan Armenlegg, manager of Rocky's Diamond and Jewelry Store, is interested in developing a model to estimate consumer demand for his rather expensive merchandise. Because most customers buy diamonds and jewelry on credit, Juan is sure that two factors that must influence consumer demand are the current annual inflation rate and the current prime lending rate at the leading banks in the country. Explain some of the problems that Juan might encounter if he were to set up a regression model based on his two predictor variables.

■ **13-29** A new game show, *Check That Model*, asks contestants to specify the minimum number of parameters they need to determine whether a multiple regression model is significant as a whole at $\alpha = 0.01$. You have won the bidding with 4 parameters. Using the information below, determine whether the regression is significant.

$$R^2 = 0.7452$$
$$SSE = 125.4$$
$$n = 18$$
$$\text{Number of independent variables} = 3$$

■ **13-30** The Scottish Tourist Agency is interested in the number of tourists who enter the country weekly during the high season (Y). Data have been collected and are presented below:

Tourists (Y) = Number of tourists who entered Scotland in a week (in thousands)
Rate (X_1) = Number of Scottish pounds purchased for $1 U.S.
Price (X_2) = Number of Scottish pounds charged for round-trip bus fare from London to Edinburgh
Promot (X_3) = Amount spent on promoting the country (in thousands of Scottish pounds)
Temp (X_4) = Mean temperature during the week in Edinburgh (in degrees Celsius)

Tourists (Y)	Rate (X_1)	Price (X_2)	Promot (X_3)	Temp (X_4)
6.9	0.61	40	8.7	15.4
7.1	0.59	40	8.8	15.6
6.8	0.63	40	8.5	15.4
7.9	0.61	35	8.6	15.3
7.6	0.6	35	9.4	15.8
8.2	0.65	35	9.9	16.2

(Continued)

Tourists (Y)	Rate (X_1)	Price (X_2)	Promot (X_3)	Temp (X_4)
8.0	0.58	35	9.8	16.4
8.4	0.59	35	10.2	16.6
9.7	0.61	30	11.4	17.4
9.8	0.62	30	11.6	17.2
7.2	0.57	40	8.4	17.6
6.7	0.55	40	8.6	16.4

(a) Using whatever computer package is available, determine the best-fitting regression equation for the tourist agency.

(b) Is the currency exchange rate a significant explanatory variable? State and test the appropriate hypotheses at a 0.10 significance level.

(c) Does an increase in promotions by one thousand pounds increase the number of tourists by more than 200? State and test appropriate hypotheses at a 0.05 significance level.

(d) Give a 95 percent confidence interval for the slope coefficient of Temp.

Worked-Out Answers to Self-Check Exercises

SC 13-4 Because SST = SSR + SSE, SSE = SST − SSR = 1,023.6 − 872.4 = 151.2. Because *df* SST = *df* SSR + *df* SSE, *df* SSR = *df* SST − *df* SSE = 24 − 17 = 7.

$$\text{Thus, } F = \frac{\text{SSR}/k}{\text{SSE}/(n-k-1)} = \frac{872.4/7}{151.2/17} = 14.01.$$

$F_{CRIT} = F(7, 17, .05) = 2.61$.
Because $F_{OBS} > F_{CRIT}$, we conclude that the overall regression is significant as a whole; Edith should continue looking for the output so she can use it at the meeting.

SC 13-5 From the computer output, we get the following results:

(a) $\widehat{\text{SALES}} = 172.34 + 25.950\text{PROMOT} - 13.238\text{COMP} - 3.041\text{FREE}$

(b) $H_0\colon B_{FREE} = 0 \qquad H_1\colon B_{FREE} < 0 \qquad \alpha = 0.05$

This is a one-tailed test, and the prob-value on the output is for the two-tailed alternative, $H_1\colon B_{FREE} \neq 0$. So for our test, the prob-value is $0.221/2 = 0.111 > \alpha = 0.05$, so we cannot reject H_0; sales do not decrease significantly as the number of passengers who fly free increases.

(c) $H_0\colon B_{PROMOT} = 28 \qquad H_1\colon B_{PROMOT} \neq 28 \qquad \alpha = 0.10$

The observed t value from the regression results is

$$\frac{(b_{PROMOT} - 28)}{s_{b_{PROMOT}}} = \frac{25.950 - 28}{4.877} = -0.420$$

With 11 degrees of freedom and $\alpha = 0.10$ in both tails combined, the critical t values for the test are ± 1.796, so the observed value is within the acceptance region. We cannot reject H_0; the change in SALES for a one-unit ($1,000) increase in PROMOT is not significantly different from 28, ($28,000).

clearly shows that b
the regression line,
cles tend to be belo
Figure 13-10 giv
From that output, w
variable for base sal
Also, r^2 = 92.6
the variation in bas
before, a table of *re*
nize as the error in t
fitted values and RI

"Squeezing the residuals"

Perhaps the mo residuals. If the re als ought to be ran random patterns, have failed to take what more pictures

Noticing a pattern in the residuals

As we look at th itive. So for the sal low these five data saleswomen, we ha data points. This co

FIGURE 13-10

Minitab regression of base salary on months employed

```
Regressi

The regressi
SALARY = 5.8

Predictor
Constant
MONTHS

s = 0.5494

Analysis of

SOURCE
Regression
Error
Total
```

FIGURE 13-11

Minitab table of residuals

```
ROW  SALARY

 1     7.5
 2     8.6
 3     9.1
 4    10.3
 5    13.0
 6     6.2
 7     8.7
 8     9.4
 9     9.8
```

(d) With 11 degrees of freedom, the t value for a 90 percent confidence interval is 1.796, so that interval is

$$b_{COMP} \pm 1.796 s_{b_{COMP}} = -13.238 \pm 1.796(3.686)$$

$$= -13.238 \pm 6.620 = (-19.858, -6.618)$$

The airline can be 90 percent confident that ticket revenue at an office decreases between approximately \$6,600 and \$19,900 with each additional competing airline.

13.5 Modeling Techniques

Looking at different models

Given a variable we want to explain and a group of potential explanatory variables, there may be several different regression equations we can look at, depending on which explanatory variables we include and how we include them. Each such regression equation is called a *model. Modeling techniques* are the various ways in which we can include the explanatory variables and check the appropriateness of our regression models. There are many different modeling techniques, but we shall look at only two of the most commonly used devices.

Qualitative Data and Dummy Variables

In all the regression examples we have looked at so far, the data have been numerical, or *quantitative.* But, occasionally, we will be faced with a variable that is categorical, or *qualitative.* In our chapter-opening problem, the director of personnel wanted to see whether the base salary of a salesperson depended on the person's gender. Table 13-5 repeats the data of that problem.

Reviewing a previous way to approach the problem

For the moment, ignore the length of employment and use the technique developed in Chapter 9 for testing the difference between means of two populations, to see whether men earn more than women. Test this at $\alpha = 0.01$. If we let the men be population 1 and the women be population 2, we are testing

H_0: $\mu_1 = \mu_2$ ← Null hypothesis: There is no gender discrimination in base salaries

H_1: $\mu_1 > \mu_2$ ← Alternative hypothesis: Women are discriminated against in base salary

$\alpha = 0.01$ ← Level of significance

Table 13-5

Data for Gender-Discrimination Problem

Salesmen		Saleswomen	
Months Employed	Base Salary (\$1,000s)	Months Employed	Base Salary (\$1,000s)
6	7.5	5	6.2
10	8.6	13	8.7
12	9.1	15	9.4
18	10.3	21	9.8
30	13.0		

We sketch t
briefly pages 4

With 7 degre
2.998. Becau

The old approach doesn't detect any discrimination

Our analys
in base salari
the analysis.

"Eyeballing" the data

Before we
points corres

FIGURE 13-9

Scatter diagram of base salaries plotted against months employed

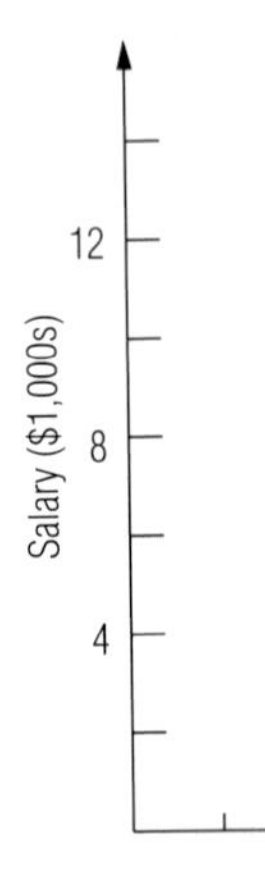

ROW	DAMAGES	FITS1	RESI1
1	0.645	0.1117	0.53333
2	0.750	0.6296	0.12042
3	1.000	1.1475	-0.14750
4	1.300	1.6654	-0.36542
5	1.750	2.1833	-0.43333
6	2.205	2.7013	-0.49625
7	3.500	3.2192	0.28083
8	4.000	3.7371	0.26292
9	4.500	4.2550	0.24500

Of course, you are quite pleased with these results, because R^2 is very high. But the judge is not convinced that you are right. He says, "This is the worst job I've ever seen! I don't care if this line *does* fit the data I gave you, I can tell by looking at the output that it won't work for other data. If you can't do any better, just let me know, and I'll hire a *smart* statistician!"

(a) Why is the judge dissatisfied with the results?

(b) Suggest a better model that will satisfy the judge.

■ **13-39** Jon Grant, supervisor of the Carven Manufacturing Facility, is examining the relationship among an employee's score on an aptitude test, prior work experience, and success on the job. An employee's prior work experience is studied and weighted, yielding a rating between 2 and 12. The measure of on-the-job success is based on a point system involving total output and efficiency, with a maximum possible value of 50. Grant sampled six first-year employees and obtained the following:

X_1 Aptitude Test Score	X_2 Prior Experience	Y Performance Evaluation
74	5	28
87	11	33
69	4	21
93	9	40
81	7	38
97	10	46

(a) Develop the estimating equation best describing these data.

(b) If an employee scored 83 on the aptitude test and had a prior work experience of 7, what performance evaluation would be expected?

■ **13-40** Successful selling is as much an art as a science, but many sales managers believe that personal attributes are important in predicting sales success. Design Alley is a full-service interior design store that sells custom blinds, carpets and wall coverings. The store manager, Dee Dempsey, contracted with a sales-force selection company to conduct pre-hiring tests on four aptitudes. Dee has collected sales growth data for 25 of the salespeople who were hired, along with the scores from the four tests of aptitude: creativity, mechanical ability, abstract thinking, and mathematical calculation. Using a desktop computer, Dee generated the following Minitab output for the best-fitting multiple regression:

```
The regression equation is
GROWTH =   70.1 + 0.422 CREAT + 0.271 MECH + 0.745 ABST = 0.420 MATH

Predictor        Coef          Stdev      t-ratio         p
Constant       70.066          2.130        32.89     0.000
CREAT         0.42160        0.17192         2.45     0.024
MECH          0.27140        0.21840         1.24     0.228
ABST          0.74504        0.28982         2.57     0.018
MATH          0.41955        0.06871         6.11     0.000

s = 2.048         R-sq = 92.6%

Analysis of Variance

SOURCE        DF          SS            MS           F          p
Regression     4     1050.78        262.70       62.64      0.000
Error         20       83.88          4.19
Total         24     1134.66
```

(a) Write the regression equation for sales growth in terms of the four factors tested.

(b) How much of the variation in sales growth is explained by the aptitude tests?

(c) At a significance level of 0.05, which of the aptitude tests are significant explanatory variables for sales growth?

(d) Is the overall model significant as a whole?

(e) Jay is a new applicant with scores on the four tests as follows: CREAT = 12, MECH = 14, ABST = 18, and MATH = 30. What sales growth is predicted by the model for this candidate?

■ **13-41** The Money Bank desires to open new checking accounts for customers who will write at least 30 checks per month. To assist in selecting new customers, the bank has studied the relationship between the number of checks written and the age and annual income of eight of their present customers. AGE was recorded to the nearest year, and annual INCOME was recorded in thousands of dollars. The data follow:

Checks	Age	Income
29	37	16.2
42	34	25.4
9	48	12.4
56	38	25.0
2	43	8.0
10	25	18.3
48	33	24.2
4	45	7.9

(a) Develop an estimating equation to use age and income to predict the number of checks written per month.

(b) How many checks per month would be expected from a 35-year-old with annual income of $22,500?

The proportion of disposable income that consumers spend on different product categories is not the same in all towns—for example, in college towns, sales of pizza are likely to be above average, while the sales of new cars may be below average. Let's investigate how the amount spent on food and drink consumed away from home varies across the 50 metropolitan areas for which we have data in Table RW11-2 on p. 636. In Exercises 13-42 through 13-45, you will construct regressions to try to explain the variability of the EATING variable. (*An important technical note:* Some simple statistical packages have difficulty with large numbers when fitting regressions. If necessary, you can avoid problems by changing the units of the data from thousands of dollars to millions of dollars. For example, for Salem, Oregon, the EATING variable becomes $216.666 million instead of $216,666 thousand.)

13-42 Develop two simple regression models for EATING, using the population and the median effective buying income per household (EBI) as the independent variables. Which independent variable accounts for more of the variation in the observed sales?

13-43 Develop a multiple regression for EATING using both POP and EBI as the explanatory variables. What fraction of the variation in EATING is explained by this model? Is the regression significant as a whole at $\alpha = 0.05$?

13-44 Include SINGLE (the number of single-person households in the area) as a third explanatory variable. How much of the variation in EATING is explained now? Is this a significant improvement over the model developed in Exercise 13-43? (Is SINGLE a significant explanatory variable in this regression?)

13-45 Because POP was no longer significant in the model developed in Exercise 13-44, run a regression using only EBI and SINGLE as explanatory variables. Use this model to find an approximate 90 percent confidence interval for EATING in a metropolitan area with 20,000 single-person households and a median effective buying income of $30,000.

■ **13-46** Dr. Harden Ricci is a veterinarian in Sacramento, California. Recently, he has been trying to develop a predicting equation for the amount of anesthesia (measured in milliliters) to be used in operations. He feels that the amount used will depend on the weight of the animal (in pounds), length of the operation (in hours), and whether the animal is a cat (coded 0) or a dog (coded 1). He used Minitab to run a regression on his data from 13 recent operations, and got these results:

```
The regression equation is
ANESTHES =  90.0 + 99.5 TYPE + 21.5 WEIGHT - 34.5 HOURS

Predictor        Coef         Stdev     t-ratio        p
Constant       90.032        56.842        1.58    0.148
TYPE           99.486        42.374        2.35    0.044
WEIGHT         21.536         2.668        8.07    0.000
HOURS         -34.461        28.607       -1.21    0.259

s = 57.070      R-sq = 95.3%

Analysis of Variance

SOURCE        DF         SS          MS          F        p
Regression     3     590880      196960      60.47    0.000
Error          9      29312      3256.9
Total         12     620192
```

(a) What is the predicting equation for amounts of anesthesia, as given by Minitab?

(b) Give an approximate 95 percent confidence interval for the amount of anesthesia to be used in a 90-minute operation on a 25-pound dog.

(c) At a significance level of 10 percent, is the amount of anesthesia needed significantly different for dogs and cats?

(d) At a significance level of 5 percent, is this regression significant as a whole?

■ **13-47** David Ichikawa is a real estate agent who works with developers who build new houses. Although much of his job concerns marketing the finished houses, he also consults with builders on how much they should pay for each lot. In one residential neighborhood, he has collected the following information on closed sales for buildable lots: Recorded sales PRICE (in $1,000s), SIZE (linear feet of street frontage) and an indicator variable (0 or 1) for whether each lot has a VIEW. From the tax rolls, he can estimate the lot area from the square of an assessment made based on street frontage.

PRICE	SIZE	AREA (= SIZE^2)	VIEW
56.2	175	30625	1
42.5	125	15625	1
67.5	200	40000	1
39.0	115	13225	1
33.3	125	15625	0
29.0	100	10000	0
30.0	108	11664	0
48.0	170	28900	0
44.3	160	25600	0

(a) Using MINITAB, develop the best-fitting regression line for these data.

(b) What fraction of the variation in PRICE is accounted for in this equation?

(c) Find a 90 percent confidence interval for the increase in market value attributable to having a VIEW.

(d) Was it helpful to use AREA (the square of SIZE) in the regression? Explain.

■ **13-48** Camping-R-Us, a newcomer to the outdoor equipment field, plans to market a two-person, three-season tent for weekend campers. To set a fair price, they look at eight comparable tents currently on the market, in terms of weight and square footage. The data follow:

	Weight (oz)	Sq Ft.	Price
Kelty Nautilus	94	37	$225
North Face Salamander	90	36	240
REI Mountain Hut	112	35	225
Sierra Designs Meteor Light	92	40	220
Eureka! Cirrus 3	93	48	167
Sierra Designs Clip 3	98	40	212
Eureka! Timberline Deluxe	114	40	217
Diamond Brand Free Spirit	108	35	200

(a) Calculate the least-squares equation to predict price from weight and square footage.

(b) If Camping-R-Us' tent weighs 100 ounces and has 46 square feet of space, how much should they charge?

■ **13-49** The Carolina Athletic Association is interested in organizing the First Annual Tarheel Triathlon. To attract top competitors, they wish to establish cash incentives for the top finishers by setting times for both men and women overall winners. Because this course has never been run before, the CAA has chosen 10 races of varying lengths that they consider comparable in weather and course conditions.

	Miles			Winning Times (Hr:Min:Sec)	
Triathlon	**Swim**	**Bike**	**Run**	**Men**	**Women**
Bud Light Ironman	2.4	112	26.2	8:09:15	9:00:56
World's Toughest	2.0	100	18.6	8:25:09	9:49:04
Muncie Endurathon	1.2	55.3	13.1	4:05:30	4:40:06
Texas Hill Country	1.5	48	10.0	3:24:24	3:55:02
Leon's Q.E.M.	0.93	24.8	6.2	1:54:32	2:07:10
Sacramento International	0.93	24.8	6.2	1:48:16	2:00:45
Malibu	0.50	18	5.0	1:19:25	1:30:19
Bud Light Endurance	2.4	112	26.2	9:26:30	11:00:29
Wendy's	0.5	20	4.0	1:14:59	1:23:09
Mammoth/Snowcreek	0.6	25	6.2	1:56:07	2:11:49

(a) Determine the regression equations to predict men's and women's winning times, in terms of the length of each individual race segment. (Convert the times to minutes for use in calculations.)

(b) Predict the winning times if the Tarheel Triathlon comprises a 1-mile swim, 50-mile bike ride, and a 12.5-mile run.

(c) If the CAA wants to use the lower limit of an approximate 90 percent confidence interval for the incentive times for men and women, what would these times be?

Table RW13-1 contains financial information about 28 of the largest public companies in North Carolina. The variables in the table are

NAME	Name of the company
PRICE	Closing price of a share of its stock on 4/1/93
DIV	Dividend paid per share in 1992
EPS	1992 earnings per share
ΔSALES	1992 percentage change in total sales
ΔINCOME	1992 percentage change in net income
ΔASSETS	1992 percentage change in assets
OLDPR	Closing price of a share on 12/31/91
NY	1 if the stock traded on the NYSE, 0 otherwise
BANK	1 if the company is a bank or bank holding company, 0 otherwise

Use this information to do Exercises 13-50 through 13-53.

13-50 Use DIV, EPS, ΔSALES, ΔINCOME, ΔASSETS, and OLDPR as explanatory variables in a regression to explain the variation in PRICE. What fraction of the variation is explained by this model?

Table RW13-1 Financial Data for North Carolina Companies

NAME	PRICE	DIV	EPS	ΔSALES	ΔINCOME	ΔASSETS	OLDPR	NY	BANK
Duke Power	39.50	1.76	2.21	3.8	−14.6	3.2	35.00	1	0
First Union	47.50	1.28	3.72	1.4	69.7	11.4	30.00	1	1
Wachovia	36.50	1.00	2.48	−15.7	88.7	0.6	29.00	1	1
Carolina Power & Light	33.00	1.58	2.36	3.0	4.0	2.6	27.00	1	0
Nucor	91.25	0.28	1.83	10.5	22.4	26.1	44.75	1	0
Food Lion	7.00	0.11	0.37	11.8	−13.2	24.9	18.25	0	0
Jefferson-Pilot	55.00	1.30	3.99	2.5	15.7	6.3	37.75	1	0
Unifi	33.88	0.40	1.04	13.4	6.9	64.7	22.38	1	0
Family Dollar Stores	18.50	0.25	1.00	17.1	38.3	19.7	17.25	1	0
BB&T Financial	34.13	0.91	2.75	−3.3	26.4	7.4	22.00	0	1
Lance	23.63	0.92	1.25	2.6	3.8	4.4	21.75	0	0
Cato	30.50	0.08	1.03	24.5	94.7	54.2	14.50	0	0
Piedmont Natural Gas	22.00	0.91	1.40	11.7	71.8	8.7	16.75	1	0
Southern National	21.88	0.50	1.73	6.0	48.0	23.3	13.88	1	1
First Citizens Bancshares	53.00	0.53	5.45	−7.5	77.4	−1.0	27.50	0	1
Ruddick	21.38	0.39	1.30	6.2	14.9	8.8	15.25	1	0
United Dominion Industries	13.13	0.20	0.61	26.7	−12.6	16.4	9.13	1	0
Centura Banks	23.88	0.63	1.66	−6.6	182.3	10.1	12.75	1	1
Guilford Mills	26.13	0.57	1.73	16.3	56.2	9.1	22.25	1	0
CCB Financial	40.50	1.14	3.10	−9.0	18.0	7.1	28.63	0	1
United Carolina Bancshares	22.50	0.66	2.01	−9.6	21.7	7.1	15.88	0	1
Coastal Healthcare Group	21.00	0.00	0.85	30.4	43.0	51.7	27.75	0	0
Public Service of NC	17.25	0.75	1.09	24.4	58.9	8.1	11.88	0	0
Oakwood Homes	20.25	0.06	0.90	42.4	58.0	25.3	10.63	1	0
NC Natural Gas	26.63	0.98	1.79	18.9	38.3	23.0	16.38	1	0
Bank of Granite	30.00	0.38	1.65	−9.7	13.3	7.9	19.63	0	1
PCA International	16.25	0.28	0.89	8.0	5.6	51.4	14.88	0	0
Ingles Markets	6.25	0.22	0.31	2.1	−48.8	2.0	6.13	0	0

Source: Business North Carolina *(May 1993): 34–37.*

13-51 Three of the independent variables used in the model in Exercise 13-50 are insignificant even at α as high as 0.30. Delete these variables and run another regression using only the remaining three. How much less of the variation in PRICE is explained by this model?

13-52 Now add in NY and BANK as explanatory variables. At $\alpha = 0.10$, is there evidence that, other things being equal, being listed on the NYSE has any significant effect on PRICE? At $\alpha = 0.10$, do the share prices of banks and bank holding companies differ significantly from those of other companies in the group?

13-53 Using the model of Exercise 13-51,

(a) Can you conclude, at $\alpha = 0.05$, that increasing dividends leads to significant decreases in share price? State and test appropriate hypotheses.

(b) Other things being equal, does a \$1 increase in earnings per share lead to an increase in share price of significantly more than \$2? State and test appropriate hypotheses at $\alpha = 0.05$.

(c) Find a 98 percent confidence interval for the change in share price on 4/1/93 per \$1 increase in the share price on 12/31/91.

(d) NationsBank had DIV = 1.51, EPS = 4.52, and OLDPR = 40.63. What share price does the model predict on 4/1/93? How does the prediction compare with the true share price of \$54.88 that NationsBank had on that day?

■ **13-54** Peoria, Illinois, is in the process of modifying its tax structure. Twelve cities of comparable size and economic structure were surveyed as to specific taxes and the associated total tax revenue.

(a) Use the following data to determine the least-squares equation relating revenue to the three tax rates.

Tax Rates			Tax Revenue
Property	**Sales**	**Gasoline**	**(\$ thousands)**
1.639%	2.021%	3.300¢/gal	\$28,867.5
1.686	1.972	3.300	28,850.2
1.639	2.041	3.300	29,011.5
1.639	2.363	0.131	28,806.5
1.639	2.200	2.540	28,821.7
1.639	2.201	1.560	28,774.6
1.654	2.363	0.000	28,803.2
2.643	1.000	3.300	28,685.7
2.584	1.091	2.998	28,671.8
2.048	1.752	1.826	28,671.0
2.176	1.648	1.555	28,627.4
1.925	1.991	0.757	28,670.7

(b) Two proposals have been submitted for Peoria. Estimate total tax revenues if the tax rates are

	Property	Sales	Gasoline
Proposal A	2.763%	1.000%	1.0¢/gal
Proposal B	1.639	2.021	3.3

Determine which proposal the city should adopt.

■ **13-55** The National Cranberry Cooperative, an organization formed and owned by growers of cranberries to process and market their berries, is trying to establish a relationship between average price per barrel received in any given year and the total number of barrels sold in the previous year (divided into fresh sales and berries sold for processing).

(a) Calculate the least-squares equation to predict price from these sales figures.

Sales (in thousands of barrels) Fresh	Sales (in thousands of barrels) Process	Following Year's Price	Sales (in thousands of barrels) Fresh	Sales (in thousands of barrels) Process	Following Year's Price
844	256	15.50	320	460	9.79
965	335	17.15	528	860	10.90
470	672	11.71	340	761	15.88

(b) Predict next year's price per barrel if this year's sales are 980 (fresh) and 360 (process).

■ **13-56** Cellular phones were introduced in Europe in 1980, and since then, their growth in popularity has been phenomenal. The number of subscribers in subsequent years is contained in the following table.

1981	3,510	1984	143,300	1987	877,850
1982	34,520	1985	288,420	1988	1,471,200
1983	80,180	1986	507,930	1989	2,342,080

Using the number of years since the introduction of cellular phones as the independent variable (i.e., 1981 = 1, etc.), find the least-squares linear equation relating these two variables. Look at the residuals—do they have a noticeable pattern? Find the least-squares quadratic equation. Which appears to be a better fit?

■ **13-57** While shopping for a new down sleeping bag, Fred Montana is curious about what features of a bag are most important in determining the bag's price. He picks six Gore-Tex sleeping bags and decides to run a linear regression analysis to find out.

	Down Fill (oz)	Total Weight (lb)	Loft (in.)	Temp. Rating (°F)	Price ($)
Swallow	14.0	2.00	5.5	20	255
Snow Bunting	18.0	2.25	6.5	10	285
Puffin	24.0	3.13	6.5	10	329
Widgeon	25.5	3.25	7.5	−10	395
Tern	32.5	3.63	9.0	−30	459
Snow Goose	41.0	4.25	10.0	−40	509

(a) Regress price on ounces of down fill, total weight, loft, and temperature rating. Using the prob values, determine which of these variables are significant at the $\alpha = 0.01$ level.

(b) What about the regression as a whole? Use the ANOVA prob value, again at the $\alpha = 0.01$ level, to determine whether the regression as a whole is significant.

(c) What problem might there be in using all these variables together? Do the answers to parts (a) and (b) seem to indicate this problem might be present?

■ **13-58** Home Depot is a rapidly growing chain of discount home improvement centers. The table gives information from the annual reports, which is typical of the data financial analysts use to predict the company's future revenue.

(a) Develop the multiple regression equation that describes Total Revenue as a function of Number of Stores and Average Store Size. Which factor appears to be more important in determining Revenue growth? As a consultant, would you recommend an expansion strategy that emphasizes broad geographic spread (increasing number of stores) or building a smaller number of very large stores (increasing average store size)?

(b) Develop a column of average revenue per employee. Find the regression line that best describes Average Revenue per Employee as a function of Year (with 1984 coded as 1, 1985 as 2, etc.) and Average Store Size. Are employees more productive in larger stores or is the trend line (the regression factor Year) a more important factor? As an analyst, would you rate the trend to larger stores a successful strategy, or would you judge inflation and other factors to be more important?

Year	Number of Stores	Average Store Size (1,000s of sq ft.)	Total Revenue ($ millions)	Number of Employees
1984	31	77	433	4,000
1985	50	80	701	5,400
1986	60	80	1,001	6,600
1987	75	82	1,454	9,100
1988	96	86	2,000	13,000
1989	118	88	2,758	17,500
1990	145	92	3,815	21,500
1991	174	95	5,136	28,000
1992	214	98	7,148	38,900
1993	264	100	9,239	50,600
1994	340	103	12,477	67,300

Source: Home Depot, Annual Reports, 1993 and 1994.

■ **13-59** Wal-Mart is one of America's largest and most successful companies, with more than 2,400 stores in operation and $82 billion dollars in annual sales. The company was initially able to post handsome returns on shareholders' equity (ROE), but their performance on this benchmark has been falling. Along with rapid growth, the company has expanded beyond its original single-concept store to include more Sam's Clubs, which are very-low-margin, high-turnover operations. The following data show figures for fiscal years ending in January of the date shown, inventory, percentage of all stores that were Sam's Clubs, and ROE:

Year	Inventory ($ billions)	Percentage Sam's Clubs	ROE
1985	1.2	1.5%	36.7%
1986	1.5	2.6	33.3
1987	2.2	4.8	35.2
1988	2.8	7.0	37.1
1989	3.6	7.7	37.1
1990	4.7	8.1	35.8
1991	6.2	8.6	32.6
1992	7.8	10.8	30.0
1993	9.8	12.2	28.5
1994	11.5	17.7	26.6
1995	14.4	17.7	24.9

Source: Wal-Mart Annual Report, 1995.

Develop a multiple-regression equation to predict ROE for Wal-Mart, based on the two variables given. What advice would you give to the firm's management to increase ROE?

Chapter Concepts Test

Circle the correct answer, or fill in the blank. *Answers are in the back of the book.*

T F 1. The principal advantage of multiple regression over simple regression is that it allows us to use more of the information available to estimate the dependent variable.

T F 2. Suppose, in the multiple-regression equation $\hat{Y} = 24.4 + 5.6X_1 + 6.8X_2$, $\hat{Y}$ stands for weight (in pounds) and X_2 stands for age (in years). For each additional year of age, then, it can be expected that weight will increase by 24.4 pounds.

T F 3. Although it is theoretically possible to do multiple-regression calculations by hand, we seldom do so.

T F 4. Suppose you are attempting to form a confidence interval for a value of Y from a multiple-regression equation. If there are 20 elements in the sample and 4 independent variables are used in the regression, you should use 16 degrees of freedom when you get a value from the t table.

T F 5. The standard error of the coefficient b_2 in a multiple regression is denoted s_2.

T F 6. Suppose we wish to test whether the values of Y in a multiple regression really depend on the values of X_1. The null hypothesis for our test will be $B_1 = 0$.

T F 7. To determine whether a regression is significant as a whole, an observed value of F is calculated and compared to a value from a table.

T F 8. If one knows the total sum of squares and regression sum of squares for a multiple regression, the error sum of squares can always be quickly calculated.

T F 9. Certain patterns in the signs of the residuals from a second-degree regression model indicate that we should instead use a straight-line model.

T F 10. Simple regressions of Y on X_1 and Y on X_2 show that X_1 and X_2 are both significant explanatory variables for Y. But a multiple regression of Y on X_1 and X_2 says that neither X_1 nor X_2 is a significant explanatory variable for Y. Clearly, this is a case of multicollinearity.

T F 11. Dummy variables are a technique that can be used to incorporate qualitative data into multiple regressions.

T F 12. When using a dummy variable with values of 0 and 1, it is very important to make sure that the 0's and 1's are used according to standard practice. Reversing the coding will completely destroy the results of the multiple regression.

T F 13. We can form a second-degree regression model by multiplying observed values of an independent variable by 2.

T F 14. Adding additional variables to a multiple regression will always reduce the standard error of estimate.

T F 15. Suppose a multiple regression yielded this equation: $\hat{Y} = 5.6 + 2.8X_1 - 3.9X_2 + 5.6X_3$. If X_1, X_2, and X_3 all had values of zero, then Y could be expected to have a value of 5.6.

T F 16. The analysis of the residuals in a straight-line regression model is done to determine the correct value for s_e.

T F 17. Although it is possible to make inferences about the regression as a whole, it is not possible to make inferences about the estimated regression coefficients.

T F 18. If there is a high level of correlation between explanatory variables, it is usually possible to disentangle the separate contributions of these variables in a regression.

T F 19. The standard error of the population data points is denoted s_e.

T F 20. If a regression includes all relevant explanatory factors, the residuals should be random.

T F 21. A linear relationship between explanatory variables will always produce multicollinearity in the regression model.

A B C D E 22. Suppose that a multiple regression yielded this equation: $\hat{Y} = 51.21 + 6.88X_1 + 7.06X_2 - 3.71X_3$. The value of b_2 for this equation is:

(a) 51.21.

(b) 6.88.

(c) 7.06.

(d) −3.71.

(e) Cannot be determined from information given.

A B C D 23. We have said that the standard error of estimate has $n - k - 1$ degrees of freedom. What does the k stand for in this expression?

(a) Number of elements in the sample.

(b) Number of independent variables in the multiple regression.

(c) Mean of the sample values of the dependent variable.

(d) None of these.

A B C D E 24. Suppose that you have run a multiple regression and have found that the value of b_1 is 1.66. Historical data, however, indicate that the value of B_1 should be 1.34. You wish to test, at a 0.05 level of significance, the null hypothesis that B_1 is still 1.34. Assuming that you have access to any tables you may need, what other information is required for you to perform your test?

(a) Degrees of freedom.

(b) s_{b_1}.

(c) s_e.

(d) (a) and (b) but not (c).

(e) (a) and (c) but not (b).

A B C D 25. Suppose that a toy manufacturer wishes to determine whether his red toys sell better than his blue toys. He gathered data regarding sales levels, color, price, and average age levels for which the toys are intended. He entered these into a computer run. The resulting multiple-regression equation was $\hat{Y} = 70{,}663 - 713X_1 - 59.6X_2 + 66.4X_3$, where $\hat{Y}$ refers to sales levels in units, X_1 refers to color ($0 =$ blue, $1 =$ red), X_2 refers to retail price (in dollars), and X_3 refers to average age level (in years). Which of the following is true if factors of price and age level are held constant?

(a) Red toys should sell 713 more units than blue toys.

(b) Red toys should sell 713 fewer units than blue toys.

(c) Children will always choose a blue toy over a red one.

(d) (b) and (c) but not (a).

Questions 26 through 31 deal with a director of personnel who is trying to determine a predicting equation for longevity in his plant. He has used Minitab to regress months employed for several employees on their education levels (years of schooling), age when hired, score on the company's psychological maturity test, and number of dependents (including the employee). Here are his results:

```
The regression equation is
LONGEV = 82.2 - 1.55 SCHOOL - 1.69 AGE + 0.11 SCORE + 6.88 DEPENDEN

Predictor        Coef        Stdev     t-ratio        p
Constant       82.237       81.738       1.01     0.361
SCHOOL         -1.553        4.362      -0.36     0.736
AGE            -1.685        1.253      -1.35     0.236
SCORE           0.110        0.291       0.38     0.720
DEPENDEN        6.876        7.658       0.89     0.410

s = 13.4        R-sq = 89.1%

Analysis of Variance

SOURCE        DF         SS          MS          F        p
Regression     4    7325.33     1831.33      10.19    0.013
Error          5     898.28      179.66
Total          9    8223.60
```

26. The regression equation for these data is:
    (a) $\hat{Y} = 82.24 - 1.55X_1 - 1.69X_2 + 0.11X_3 + 6.88X_4$.
    (b) $\hat{Y} = 13.40 - 1.55X_1 - 1.69X_2 + 0.11X_3 + 6.88X_4$.
    (c) $\hat{Y} = 81.74 + 4.36X_1 + 1.25X_2 + 0.29X_3 + 7.66X_4$.
    (d) $\hat{Y} = 82.24 - 0.36X_1 - 1.35X_2 + 0.38X_3 + 0.90X_4$.
27. How much of the variation in length of employment is explained by the regression?
    (a) 94 percent.
    (b) 82 percent.
    (c) 89 percent.
    (d) 13 percent.
28. Suppose you wish to test whether years of school is a significant explanatory variable for longevity. The degrees of freedom you would use would be:
    (a) 4.
    (b) 10.
    (c) 6.
    (d) 5.
29. What is the value of s_{b_3}?
    (a) 13.4.
    (b) 0.29.
    (c) 0.38.
    (d) 0.11.
30. How many denominator degrees of freedom would there be for an *F* test to determine whether this regression was significant as a whole?
    (a) 5.
    (b) 4.
    (c) 9.
    (d) 10.

A B C D 31. How many data points did the director enter?

(a) 9.
(b) 10.
(c) 18.
(d) 19.

A B C D 32. In the equation $Y = A + B_1X_1 + B_2X_2$, Y is independent of X_1 if:

(a) $B_2 = 0$.
(b) $B_2 = -1$.
(c) $B_1 = 1$.
(d) None of these.

A B C D E 33. A normal distribution can be used to approximate the t distribution for multiple regression whenever the degrees of freedom (n minus the number of estimated regression coefficients) are:

(a) Less than 40.
(b) More than 10.
(c) Equal to 5.
(d) More than 50.
(e) None of these.

A B C D E 34. Because $r^2 = 1 - \Sigma(Y - \hat{Y})^2/\Sigma(Y - \overline{Y})^2$, r^2 is equivalent to:

(a) 1 − SSR/SST.
(b) 1 − SSE/SST.
(c) 1 − SSE/SSR.
(d) 1 − SST/SSR.
(e) 1 − SST/SSE.

A B C D 35. For the multiple regression $\hat{Y} = a + b_1X_1 + b_2X_2$ used to estimate $Y = A + B_1X_1 + B_2X_2$, the form of a plausible confidence interval for B_1 is:

(a) $B_1 - ts_{b_1}, B_1 + ts_{b_1}$.
(b) $B_1 - ts_e, B_1 + ts_e$.
(c) $b_1 - ts_{b_1}, b_1 + ts_{b_1}$.
(d) $b_1 - ts_e, b_1 + ts_e$.

A B C D 36. Signs of the possible presence of multicollinearity in a multiple regression are:

(a) Significant t values for the coefficients.
(b) Low standard errors for the coefficients.
(c) A sharp increase in a t value for the coefficient of an explanatory variable when another variable is removed from the model.
(d) All of the above.

37. ______________________ are methods for deciding which variables to include in a regression model and the different ways in which they can be included.

38. Mathematical manipulations for converting a variable into a different form so that we can fit regression curves are called ______________________.

39. The ______________________ is a statistic used to test the significance of a regression as a whole.

40. A ______________________ variable takes on the values 0 and 1 to describe qualitative data.

41. A measure of our uncertainty about the exact value of a multiple-regression coefficient is the ______________________ of the coefficient.

42. The coefficient of multiple determination in multiple regression measures the ______________________.

43. The significance of a multiple regression can be tested with the null hypothesis ______________________, which indicates that Y does not depend on the X_i's.

44. The standard error s_e is also called the ______________________.

45. Alternating strings of consecutive ______________________ with like sign in a linear regression model indicate that the data might better fit a curve than a straight line.

chapter 14

NONPARAMETRIC METHODS

Objectives

- To test hypotheses when we cannot make any assumptions about the distribution from which we are sampling
- To know which distribution-free (nonparametric) tests are appropriate for different situations
- To use and interpret each of six standard nonparametric hypothesis tests
- To learn the advantages and disadvantages of nonparametric tests

Chapter Contents

Table 14-2

Evaluation by 40 Students of Two Types of Classes

Panel-member number	1	2	3	4	5	6	7	8	9	10	11	12	13	14	15	16
Score for large lectures (1)	2	1	4	4	3	3	4	2	4	1	3	3	4	4	4	1
Score for small sections (2)	3	2	2	3	4	2	2	1	3	1	2	3	4	4	3	2
Sign of score 1 minus score 2	−	−	+	+	−	+	+	+	+	0	+	0	0	0	+	−

distribution as the appropriate sampling distribution. You may also remember that when np and nq are each at least 5, we can use the normal distribution to approximate the binomial. This is just the case with the results from our panel of college juniors. Thus, we can apply the normal distribution to our test of the two teaching methods.

Setting up the problem symbolically

$$p_{H_0} = 0.5 \leftarrow \text{Hypothesized proportion of the population that prefers large lectures}$$

$$q_{H_0} = 0.5 \leftarrow \text{Hypothesized proportion of the population that prefers small sections } (q_{H_0} = 1 - p_{H_0})$$

$$n = 30 \leftarrow \text{Sample size}$$

$$\bar{p} = 0.633 \leftarrow \text{Proportion of successes in the sample (19/30)}$$

$$\bar{q} = 0.367 \leftarrow \text{Proportion of failures in the sample (11/30)}$$

Testing a Hypothesis of No Difference

Calculating the standard error

Suppose the chancellor's office wants to test the hypothesis that there is no difference between student perception of the two types of classes at the 0.05 level of significance. We shall conduct this test using the methods we introduced in Chapter 8. The first step is to calculate the standard error of the proportion:

$$\sigma_{\bar{p}} = \sqrt{\frac{pq}{n}} \qquad [7\text{-}4]$$

$$= \sqrt{\frac{(0.5)(0.5)}{30}}$$

$$= \sqrt{0.00833}$$

$$= 0.091 \leftarrow \text{Standard error of the proportion}$$

FIGURE 14-1

Two-tailed hypothesis test of a proportion at the 0.05 level of significance

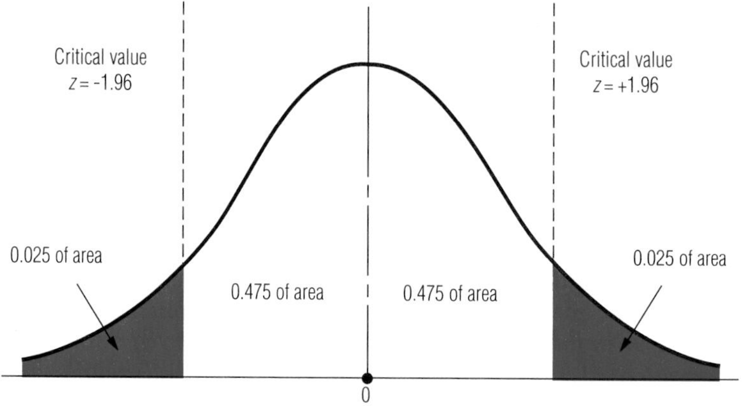

17	18	19	20	21	22	23	24	25	26	27	28	29	30	31	32	33	34	35	36	37	38	39	40
1	2	2	4	4	4	4	3	3	2	3	4	3	4	3	1	4	3	2	2	2	1	3	3
3	2	3	3	1	4	3	3	2	2	1	1	1	3	2	2	4	4	3	3	1	1	4	2
–	0	–	+	+	0	+	0	+	0	+	+	+	+	+	–	0	–	–	–	+	0	–	+

Illustrating the test graphically

Because we want to know whether the true proportion is larger *or* smaller than the hypothesized proportion, this is a two-tailed test. Figure 14-1 illustrates this hypothesis test graphically. The two colored regions represent the 0.05 level of significance.

Next we use Equation 6-2 to *standardize* the sample proportion, $\bar{p}$, by subtracting p_{H_0}, the hypothesized proportion, and dividing by $\sigma_{\bar{p}}$, the standard error of the proportion.

$$z = \frac{\bar{p} - p_{H_0}}{\sigma_{\bar{p}}} \quad [6\text{-}2]$$

$$= \frac{0.633 - 0.5}{0.091}$$

$$= 1.462$$

Interpreting the results

Placing this standardized value, 1.462, on the z scale shows that the sample proportion falls well within the acceptance region as shown in Figure 14-2. Therefore, the chancellor should accept the null hypothesis that students perceive no difference between the two types of classes.

A final word about the sign test

A sign test such as this is quite simple to do and applies to both one-tailed and two-tailed tests. It is usually based on the binomial distribution. Remember, however, that we were able to use the normal approximation to the binomial as our sampling distribution because np and nq were both greater than 5. When these conditions are not met, we must use the binomial instead.

FIGURE 14-2

Two-tailed hypothesis test at the 0.05 level of significance, illustrating the acceptance region and the standardized sample proportion

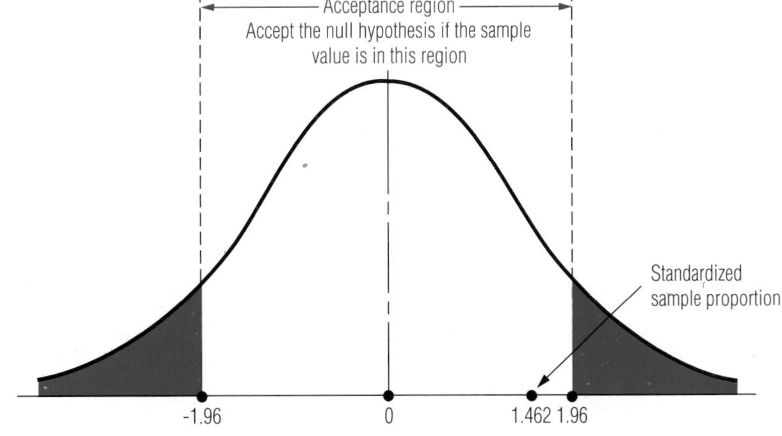

Nonparametric tests are very convenient when the real world presents distribution-free data on which a decision must be taken. Hint: Note that the *sign test* is just another application of the familiar *normal approximation to the binomial,* using + and − instead of "success" and "failure."

Exercises 14.2

Self-Check Exercises

SC 14-1 The following data show employees' rates of defective work before and after a change in the wage incentive plan. Compare the following two sets of data to see whether the change lowered the defective units produced. Use the 0.10 level of significance.

Before	8	7	6	9	7	10	8	6	5	8	10	8
After	6	5	8	6	9	8	10	7	5	6	9	8

SC 14-2 After collecting data on the amount of air pollution in Los Angeles, the Environmental Protection Agency decided to issue strict new rules to govern the amount of hydrocarbons in the air. For the next year, it took monthly measurements of this pollutant and compared them to the preceding year's measurements for corresponding months. Based on the following data, does the EPA have enough evidence to conclude with 95 percent confidence that the new rules were effective in lowering the amount of hydrocarbons in the air? To justify these laws for another year, it must conclude at $\alpha = 0.10$ that they are effective. Will these laws still be in effect next year?

	Last Year*	This Year
Jan.	7.0	5.3
Feb.	6.0	6.1
Mar.	5.4	5.6
April	5.9	5.7
May	3.9	3.7
June	5.7	4.7
July	6.9	6.1
Aug.	7.6	7.2
Sept.	6.3	6.4
Oct.	5.8	5.7
Nov.	5.1	4.9
Dec.	5.9	5.8

*Measured in parts per million.

Applications

■ **14-7** The following data show employees' satisfaction levels (as a percentage) before and after their company was bought by a larger firm. Did the buyout increase employee satisfaction? Use the 0.05 significance level.

Before	98.4	96.6	82.4	96.3	75.4	82.6	81.6	91.4	90.4	92.4
After	82.4	95.4	94.2	97.3	77.5	82.5	81.6	84.5	89.4	90.6

■ **14-8** Use the sign test to see whether there is a difference between the number of days required to collect an account receivable before and after a new collection policy. Use the 0.05 significance level.

Before	33	36	41	32	39	47	34	29	32	34	40	42	33	36	29
After	35	29	38	34	37	47	36	32	30	34	41	38	37	35	28

■ **14-9** A light-aircraft engine repair shop switched the payment method it used from hourly wage to hourly wage plus a bonus computed on the time required to disassemble, repair, and reassemble an engine. The following are data collected for 25 engines before the change and 25 after the change. At a 0.10 significance level, did the new plan increase productivity?

Hours Required		Hours Required	
Before	After	Before	After
29	32	25	34
34	19	42	27
32	22	20	26
19	21	25	25
31	20	33	31
22	24	34	19
28	25	20	22
31	31	21	32
32	18	22	31
44	22	45	30
41	24	43	29
23	26	31	20
34	41		

■ **14-10** Because of the severity of recent winters, there has been talk that the earth is slowly progressing toward another ice age. Some scientists hold different views, however, because the summers have brought extreme temperatures as well. One scientist proposed looking at the mean temperature for each month to see whether it was lower than in the previous year. Another meteorologist at the government weather service argued that perhaps they should look as well at temperatures in the spring and fall months of the last 2 years, so that their conclusions would be based on other than extreme temperatures. In this way, he said, they could detect whether there appeared to be a general warming or cooling trend or just extreme temperatures in the summer and winter months. So 15 dates in the spring and fall were randomly selected, and the temperatures in the last 2 years were noted for a particular location with generally moderate temperatures. Following are the dates and corresponding temperatures for 1994 and 1995.

(a) Is the meteorologist's reasoning as to the method of evaluation sound? Explain.

(b) Using a sign test, determine whether the meteorologist can conclude at $\alpha = 0.05$ that 1995 was cooler than 1994, based on these data.

Date	1994	1995	Date	1994	1995
	Temperature (Fahrenheit)				
Mar. 29	58	57	Oct. 12	54	48
Apr. 4	45	70	May 31	74	79
Apr. 13	56	46	Sept. 28	69	60
May 22	75	67	June 5	80	74
Oct. 1	52	60	June 17	82	79
Mar. 23	49	47	Oct. 5	59	72
Nov. 12	48	45	Nov. 28	50	50
Sept. 30	67	71			

■ **14-11** With the concern over radiation exposure and its relationship to the incidence of cancer, city environmental specialists keep a close eye on the types of industry coming into the area and the degree to which they use radiation in their production. An index of exposure to radioactive contamination has been developed and is being used daily to determine whether the levels are increasing or are higher under certain atmospheric conditions.

Environmentalists claim that radioactive contamination has increased in the last year because of new industry in the city. City administrators, however, claim that new, more stringent regulations on industry in the area have made levels lower than last year, even with new industry using radiation. To test their claim, records for 11 randomly selected days of the year have been checked, and the index of exposure to radioactive contamination has been noted. The following results were obtained:

Index of Radiation Exposure

1994	1.402	1.401	1.400	1.404	1.395	1.402	1.406	1.401	1.404	1.406	1.397
1995	1.440	1.395	1.398	1.404	1.393	1.400	1.401	1.402	1.400	1.403	1.402

Can the administrators conclude at $\alpha = 0.15$ that the levels of radioactive contamination have changed or, more specifically, that they have been reduced?

■ **14-12** As part of the recent interest in population growth and the sizes of families, a population researcher examined a number of hypotheses concerning the family size that various people look upon as ideal. She suspected that variables of race, sex, age, and background might account for some of the different views. In one pilot sample, the researcher tested the hypothesis that women today think of an ideal family as being smaller than the ideal held by their mothers. She asked each of the participants in the pilot study to state the number of children she would choose to have or that she considered ideal. Responses were anonymous, to guard against the possibility that people would feel obligated to give a socially desirable answer. In addition, people of different backgrounds were included in the sample. The following are the responses of the mother–daughter pairs.

Ideal Family Size

Sample Pair	A	B	C	D	E	F	G	H	I	J	K	L	M
Daughter	3	4	2	1	5	4	2	2	3	3	1	4	2
Mother	4	4	4	3	5	3	3	5	3	2	2	3	1

(a) Can the researcher conclude at $\alpha = 0.03$ that the mothers and daughters do not have essentially the same ideal of family size? Use the binomial distribution.

(b) Determine whether the researcher could conclude that the mothers do not have essentially the same family-size preferences as their daughters by using the normal approximation to the binomial.

(c) Assume that for each pair listed, there were 10 more pairs who responded in an identical manner. Calculate the range of the proportion for which the researcher would conclude that there is no difference in the mothers and daughters. Is your conclusion different?

(d) Explain any differences in conclusions obtained in parts (a), (b), and (c).

■ **14-13** A nationwide used-car company has developed a new instructional video to educate salespeople. Twenty employees' average monthly car sales are presented below for time periods both before and after the video's creation. Does the company have enough evidence to conclude with 95 percent confidence that the video was effective in increasing the average number of cars sold? If we just consider the employees with low sales (less than an average of 12 cars per month before the video), did the video increase their selling performance?

Before	18.4	16.9	17.4	11.6	10.5	12.7	22.3	18.5	17.5	16.4
After	18.6	16.8	17.3	15.6	19.5	12.6	22.3	16.5	18.0	16.4
Before	15.9	18.6	23.5	18.7	9.4	16.3	18.5	17.4	11.3	8.4
After	17.4	18.6	23.5	18.9	15.6	15.4	17.6	17.4	16.5	13.4

Worked-Out Answers to Self-Check Exercises

SC 14-1

Before	8	7	6	9	7	10	8	6	5	8	10	8
After	6	5	8	6	9	8	10	7	5	6	9	8
Sign	−	−	+	−	+	−	+	+	0	−	−	0

12 responses: 4(+), 6(−), 2(0).

For $n = 10$, $p = 0.5$, the probability of 6 or more minuses is 0.3770 (Appendix Table 3). Because $0.3770 > 0.10$, we cannot reject H_0. The wage incentive plan did not significantly lower the rates of defective work.

SC 14-2

Before	7.0	6.0	5.4	5.9	3.9	5.7	6.9	7.6	6.3	5.8	5.1	5.9
After	5.3	6.1	5.6	5.7	3.7	4.7	6.1	7.2	6.4	5.7	4.9	5.8
Sign	−	+	+	−	−	−	−	−	+	−	−	−

12 responses: 3(+), 9(−).

For $n = 12$, $p = 0.5$, the probability of 9 or more minuses is 0.0729 (Appendix Table 3). Because $0.10 > 0.0729 > 0.05$, they cannot be 95 percent confident that hydrocarbon levels have been lowered, but they will conclude at $\alpha = 0.10$ that the rules are effective. Hence, they will still be in effect next year.

14.3 Rank Sum Tests: The Mann–Whitney *U* Test and the Kruskal–Wallis Test

In Chapter 11, we showed how to use analysis of variance to test the hypothesis that several population means are equal. We assumed in such tests that the populations were normally distributed with equal variances. Many times these assumptions cannot be met, and in such cases, we can use two nonparametric tests, neither of which depends on the normality assumptions. Both of these tests are called rank sum tests because the test depends on the ranks of the sample observations.

Use based on the number of populations involved

Rank sum tests are a whole family of tests. We shall concentrate on just two members of this family, the Mann–Whitney U test and the Kruskal–Wallis test. We'll use the Mann–Whitney test when only two populations are involved and the Kruskal–Wallis test when more than two populations are involved. Use of these tests will enable us to determine whether independent samples have been drawn from the same population (or from different populations having the same distribution). The use of *ranking* information rather than pluses and minuses is less wasteful of data than the sign test.

Solving a Problem Using the Mann–Whitney *U* Test

Suppose that the board of regents of a large eastern state university wants to test the hypothesis that the mean SAT scores of students at two branches of the state university are equal. The board keeps statistics on all students at all branches of the system. A random sample of 15 students from each branch has produced the data shown in Table 14-3.

Ranking the items to be tested

To apply the Mann–Whitney U test to this problem, we begin by ranking all the scores in order from lowest to highest, indicating beside each the symbol of the branch. Table 14-4 accomplishes this.

Table 14-3

SAT Scores for Students at Two State University Branches

Branch A	1,000	1,100	800	750	1,300	950	1,050	1,250
Branch S	920	1,120	830	1,360	650	725	890	1,600
Branch A	1,400	850	1,150	1,200	1,500	600	775	
Branch S	900	1,140	1,550	550	1,240	925	500	

Table 14-4

SAT Scores Ranked from Lowest to Highest

Rank	Score	Branch	Rank	Score	Branch
1	500	S	16	1,000	A
2	550	S	17	1,050	A
3	600	A	18	1,100	A
4	650	S	19	1,120	S
5	725	S	20	1,140	S
6	750	A	21	1,150	A
7	775	A	22	1,200	A
8	800	A	23	1,240	S
9	830	S	24	1,250	A
10	850	A	25	1,300	A
11	890	S	26	1,360	S
12	900	S	27	1,400	A
13	920	S	28	1,500	A
14	925	S	29	1,550	S
15	950	A	30	1,600	S

Next, let's learn the symbols used to conduct a Mann–Whitney U test in the context of this problem:

Symbols for expressing the problem

n_1 = number of items in sample 1, that is, the number of students at Branch A

n_2 = number of items in sample 2, that is, the number of students at Branch S

R_1 = sum of the ranks of the items in sample 1: the sum from Table 14-5 of the ranks of all the Branch A scores

R_2 = sum of the ranks of the items in sample 2: the sum from Table 14-5 of the ranks of all the Branch S scores

In this case, both n_1 and n_2 are equal to 15, but it is *not* necessary for both samples to be of the same size. Now in Table 14-5, we can reproduce the data from Table 14-3, adding the ranks from Table 14-4. Then we can total the ranks for each branch. As a result, we have all the values we need to solve this problem, because we know that

$$n_1 = 15$$
$$n_2 = 15$$
$$R_1 = 247$$
$$R_2 = 218$$

Calculating the U Statistic

U statistic defined

Using the values for n_1 and n_2 and the rank sums R_1 and R_2, we can determine the *U statistic,* a measure of the difference between the ranked observations of the two samples of SAT scores:

Table 14-5

Raw Data and Rank for SAT Scores

Branch A	Rank	Branch S	Rank
1,000	16	920	13
1,100	18	1,120	19
800	8	830	9
750	6	1,360	26
1,300	25	650	4
950	15	725	5
1,050	17	890	11
1,250	24	1,600	30
1,400	27	900	12
850	10	1,140	20
1,150	21	1,550	29
1,200	22	550	2
1,500	28	1,240	23
600	3	925	14
775	7	500	1
	247 ← Total ranks		218 ← Total ranks

Computing the U statistic

U Statistic

$$U = n_1 n_2 + \frac{n_1(n_1 + 1)}{2} - R_1 \tag{14-1}$$

$$= (15)(15) + \frac{(15)(16)}{2} - 247$$

$$= 225 + 120 - 247$$

$$= 98 \leftarrow U \text{ statistic}$$

If the null hypothesis that the $n_1 + n_2$ observations came from identical populations is true, then this U statistic has a sampling distribution with a mean of

Mean of the Sampling Distribution of U

$$\mu_U = \frac{n_1 n_2}{2} \tag{14-2}$$

$$= \frac{(15)(15)}{2}$$

$$= 112.5 \leftarrow \text{Mean of the } U \text{ statistic}$$

and a standard error of

Standard Error of the U Statistic

$$\sigma_U = \sqrt{\frac{n_1 n_2 (n_1 + n_2 + 1)}{12}} \tag{14-3}$$

$$= \sqrt{\frac{(15)(15)(15 + 15 + 1)}{12}}$$

$$= \sqrt{\frac{6{,}975}{12}}$$

$$= \sqrt{581.25}$$

$$= 24.1 \leftarrow \text{Standard error of the } U \text{ statistic}$$

Testing the Hypotheses

The sampling distribution of the U statistic can be approximated by the normal distribution when both n_1 and n_2 are larger than 10. Because our problem meets this condition, we can use the standard normal probability distribution table to make our test. The board of regents wishes to test at the 0.15 level of significance the hypothesis that these samples were drawn from identical populations.

Stating the hypotheses

H_0: $\mu_1 = \mu_2$ ← Null hypothesis: There is no difference between the two populations, so they have the same mean

H_1: $\mu_1 \neq \mu_2$ ← Alternative hypothesis: There is a difference between the two populations; in particular, they have different means

$\alpha = 0.15$ ← Level of significance for testing these hypotheses

Finding the limits of the acceptance region

The board of regents wants to know whether the mean SAT score for students at either of the two schools is better or worse than the other. Therefore, this is a two-tailed hypothesis test. Figure 14-3 illustrates this test graphically. The two colored areas represent the 0.15 level of significance. Because we are using the normal distribution as our sampling distribution in this test, we can determine from Appendix Table 1 that the critical z value for an area of 0.425 is 1.44.

Next, we use Equation 6-2 to *standardize* the sample U statistic, by subtracting μ_U, its mean, and dividing by σ_U, its standard error.

$$z = \frac{U - \mu_U}{\sigma_U} \quad [6\text{-}2]$$

$$= \frac{98 - 112.5}{24.1}$$

$$= -0.602$$

Figure 14-4 shows the standardized sample value of U and the critical values of z for the test. The board of regents should notice that the sample statistic does lie within the critical values for the test, and conclude that the distributions, and hence the mean SAT scores at the two schools, are the same.

Special Properties of the *U* Test

Another way to compute the *U* statistic

The U statistic has a feature that enables users to save calculating time when the two samples under observation are of unequal size. We just computed the value of U using Equation 14-1:

$$U = n_1n_2 + \frac{n_1(n_1 + 1)}{2} - R_1 \quad [14\text{-}1]$$

FIGURE 14-3

Two-tailed hypothesis test at the 0.15 level of significance

Illustrating the test graphically

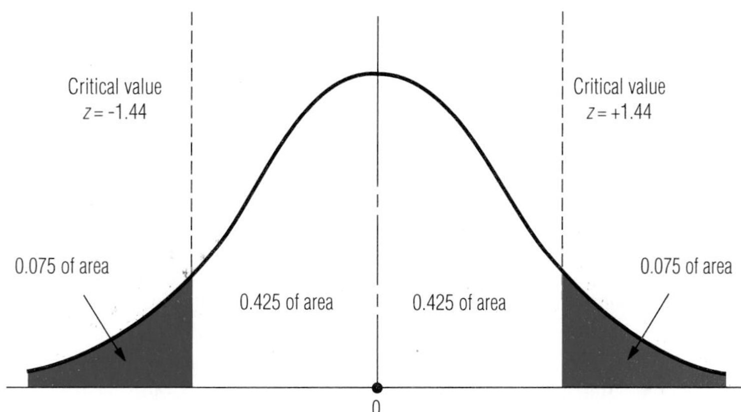

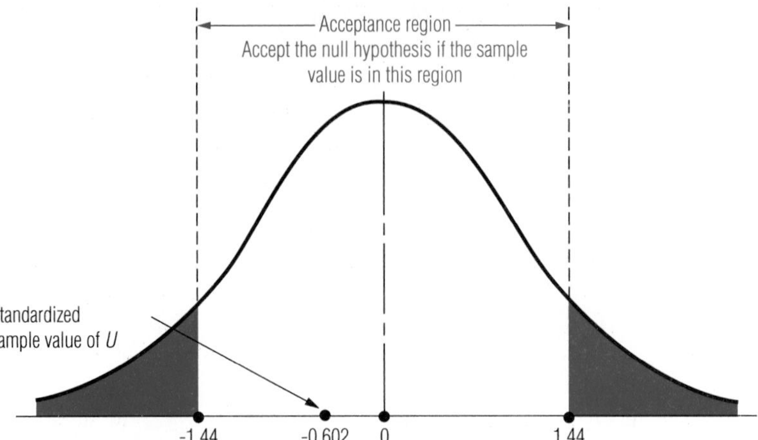

FIGURE 14-4

Two-tailed hypothesis test at the 0.15 level of significance, showing the acceptance region and the standardized sample *U* statistic

But just as easily, we could have computed the U statistic using the R_2 value, like this:

Alternate Formula for the *U* Statistic

$$U = n_1 n_2 + \frac{n_2(n_2 + 1)}{2} - R_2 \qquad [14\text{-}4]$$

The answer would have been 127 (which is just as far *above* the mean of 112.5 as 98 is *below* it). In this problem, we would have spent the same amount of time calculating the value of the U statistic using either Equation 14-1 or Equation 14-4. In other cases, when the number of items is larger in one sample than in the other, choose the equation that will require less work. Regardless of whether you calculate U using Equation 14-1 or 14-4, you will come to the same conclusion. Notice that in this example, the answer 127 falls in the acceptance region just as 98 did.

Handling ties in the data

What about *ties* that may happen when we rank the items for this test? For example, what if the two scores ranked 13 and 14 in Table 14-4 both had the value 920? In this case, we would find the average of their ranks $(13 + 14)/2 = 13.5$, and assign the result to both of them. If there were a three-way tie among the scores ranked 13, 14, and 15, we would average these ranks $(13 + 14 + 15)/3 = 14$, and use that value for all three items.

Solving a Problem Using the Kruskal–Wallis Test

Testing for differences when more than two populations are involved

As we noted earlier in this section, the Kruskal–Wallis test is an extension of the Mann–Whitney test to situations where more than two populations are involved. This test, too, depends on the ranks of the sample observations.

In Table 14-6, we have shown the scores of a sample of 20 student pilots on their Federal Aviation Agency written examination, arranged according to which method was used in their training: video cassette, audio cassette, or classroom training.

The FAA is interested in evaluating the effectiveness of these three training methods. Specifically, it wants to test at the 0.10 level of significance the hypothesis that the mean written examination scores of student pilots trained by each of these three methods are equal. Because we have more than two populations involved, the Kruskal–Wallis test is appropriate in this instance. To apply the Kruskal–Wallis test to this problem, we begin in

Table 14-6

Written Examination Scores for 20 Student Pilots Trained by Three Different Methods

Video cassette	74	88	82	93	55	70			
Audio cassette	78	80	65	57	89				
Classroom	68	83	50	91	84	77	94	81	92

Ranking the items to be tested

Table 14-7 by ranking all the scores in order, from lowest to highest, indicating beside each the symbol of the training method that was used. Ties are handled by averaging ranks, exactly as we did with the Mann–Whitney test.

Next, let's learn the symbols used in a Kruskal–Wallis test:

Symbols used for a Kruskal–Wallis test

n_j = number of items in sample j

R_j = sum of the ranks of all items in sample j

k = number of samples

$n = n_1 + n_2 + \cdots + n_k$, the total number of observations in all samples

Rearranging data to compute sums of ranks

Table 14-8 rearranges the data from Table 14-7 so that we can easily compute the sums of the ranks for each training method. Then we can use Equation 14-5 to compute the K statistic, a measure of the differences among the ranked observations in the three samples.

Computing the K statistic

K Statistic

$$K = \frac{12}{n(n+1)} \sum \frac{R_j^2}{n_j} - 3(n+1) \qquad [14\text{-}5]$$

$$= \frac{12}{20(20+1)}\left[\frac{(61)^2}{6} + \frac{(42)^2}{5} + \frac{(107)^2}{9}\right] - 3(20+1)$$

$$= (0.02857)(620.2 + 352.8 + 1{,}272.1) - 63$$

$$= 1.143$$

Table 14-7

Written Examination Scores Ranked from Lowest to Highest

Rank	Score	Training Method	Rank	Score	Training Method
1	50	C	11	81	C
2	55	VC	12	82	VC
3	57	AC	13	83	C
4	65	AC	14	84	C
5	68	C	15	88	VC
6	70	VC	16	89	AC
7	74	VC	17	91	C
8	77	C	18	92	C
9	78	AC	19	93	VC
10	80	AC	20	94	C

Table 14-8 Data and Rank Arranged by Training Method

Video Cassette	Rank	Audio Cassette	Rank	Classroom	Rank
74	7	78	9	68	5
88	15	80	10	83	13
82	12	65	4	50	1
93	19	57	3	91	17
55	2	89	16	84	14
70	6		42 ← Sum of ranks	77	8
	61 ← Sum of ranks			94	20
				81	11
				92	18
					107 ← Sum of ranks

Testing the Hypotheses

The sampling distribution of the K statistic can be approximated by a chi-square distribution ***when all the sample sizes are at least 5.*** Because our problem meets this condition, we can use the chi-square distribution and Appendix Table 5 for this test. In a Kruskal–Wallis test, the appropriate number of degrees of freedom is $k - 1$, which in this problem is $(3 - 1)$ or 2 because we are dealing with three samples. The hypotheses can be stated as follows:

Stating the hypotheses

H_0: $\mu_1 = \mu_2 = \mu_3$ ← Null hypothesis: There are no differences among the three populations, so they have the same mean

H_1: μ_1, μ_2 and μ_3 are not all equal ← Alternative hypothesis: There are differences among the three populations; in particular, they have different means

$\alpha = 0.10$ ← Level of significance for testing these hypotheses

Figure 14-5 illustrates a chi-square distribution with 2 degrees of freedom. The colored area represents the 0.10 level of significance. Notice that the acceptance region for the null

FIGURE 14-5

Kruskal–Wallis test at the 0.10 level of significance, showing the acceptance region and the sample K statistic

Illustrating the test graphically

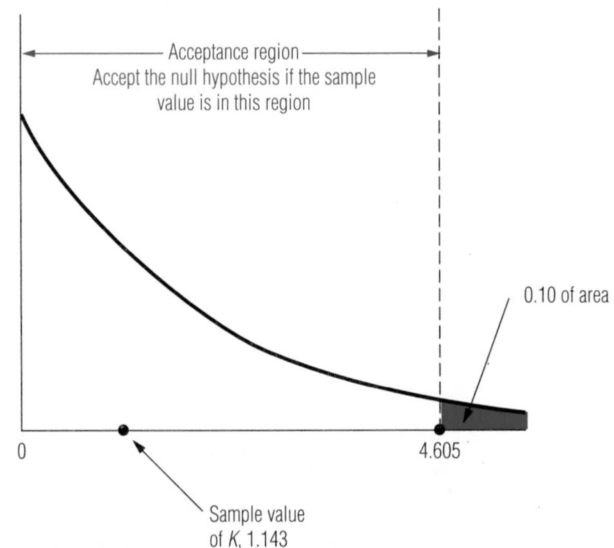

Interpreting the results

hypothesis (that there are no differences among the three populations) extends from zero to a chi-square value of 4.605. Obviously, the sample K value of 1.143 is within this acceptance region; therefore, the FAA should accept the null hypothesis and conclude that there are no differences in the results obtained by using the three training methods.

HINTS & ASSUMPTIONS

Rank sum tests such as the Mann–Whitney and the Kruskal–Wallis tests often produce ties in rankings. Hint: When you encounter ties, remember that each tied value gets an *average* rank. If the 10th and 11th items are tied, each of them gets a rank of 10.5. In the case of ties of more than 2 items, they all still get the average rank (a tie in the 3rd, 4th, 5th, and 6th items means all four of them get a rank of $(3 + 4 + 5 + 6)/4 = 4.5$).

Exercises 14.3

Self-Check Exercises

SC 14-3 Melisa's Boutique has three mall locations. Melisa keeps a daily record for each location of the number of customers who actually make a purchase. A sample of those data follows. Using the Kruskal–Wallis test, can you say at the 0.05 level of significance that her stores have the same number of customers who buy?

Eastowne Mall	99	64	101	85	79	88	97	95	90	100
Craborchard Mall	83	102	125	61	91	96	94	89	93	75
Fairforest Mall	89	98	56	105	87	90	87	101	76	89

SC 14-4 A large hospital hires most of its nurses from the two major universities in the area. Over the last year, they have been giving a test to the newly graduated nurses entering the hospital to determine which school, if either, seems to educate its nurses better. Based on the following scores (out of 100 possible points), help the personnel office of the hospital determine whether the schools differ in quality. Use the Mann–Whitney U test with a 10 percent level of significance.

Test Scores

School A	97	69	73	84	76	92	90	88	84	87	93		
School B	88	99	65	69	97	84	85	89	91	90	87	91	72

Applications

■ **14-14** Test the hypothesis of no difference between the ages of male and female employees of a certain company using the Mann–Whitney U test for the sample data. Use the 0.10 level of significance.

Males	31	25	38	33	42	40	44	26	43	35
Females	44	30	34	47	35	32	35	47	48	34

■ **14-15** The following table shows sample retail prices for three brands of shoes. Use the Kruskal–Wallis test to determine whether there is any difference among the retail prices of the brands throughout the country. Use the 0.01 level of significance.

Brand A	\$89	90	92	81	76	88	85	95	97	86	100
Brand B	\$78	93	81	87	89	71	90	96	82	85	
Brand C	\$80	88	86	85	79	80	84	85	90	92	

■ **14-16** A mail-order gift company has the following sample data on dollar sales, separated according to how the order was paid. Test the hypothesis that there is no difference in the dollar amount of orders paid for by cash, by check, or by credit card. Use the Kruskal–Wallis test with a 0.05 level of significance.

Credit-card orders	78	64	75	45	82	69	60
Check orders	110	70	53	51	61	68	
Cash orders	90	68	70	54	74	65	59

■ **14-17** The following data show annual hours missed due to illness for the 24 men and women at the Northern Packing Company, Inc. At the 0.10 level of significance, is there any difference attributable to gender? Use the Mann–Whitney U test.

Men	31	44	25	30	70	63	54	42	36	22	25	50
Women	38	34	33	47	58	83	18	36	41	37	24	48

■ **14-18** A manufacturer of toys changed the type of plastic molding machines it was using because a new one gave evidence of being more economical. As the Christmas season began, however, productivity seemed somewhat lower than last year. Because production records for the past years were readily available, the production manager decided to compare the monthly output for the 15 months when the old machines were used and the 11 months of production so far this year. Records show these output amounts with the old and new machines.

Monthly Output in Units

Old Machines		**New Machines**	
992	966	965	956
945	889	1,054	900
938	972	912	938
1,027	940	850	
892	873	796	
983	1,016	911	
1,014	897	877	
1,258		902	

Can the company conclude at a significance level of 0.10 that the change in machines has reduced output?

■ **14-19** Hanks' Hot Dogs has four hot dog stands at Memorial Stadium. Hank knows how many hot dogs are sold at each stand during each football game, and he wants to determine whether the four stands are selling the same number. Using the Kruskal–Wallis test, can you say at the 0.10 significance level that the stands have the same number of hot dog sales?

Game	1	2	3	4	5	6	7	8	9
Visitors north	755	698	725	895	886	794	694	827	814
Visitors south	782	724	754	825	815	826	752	784	789
Home north	714	758	684	816	856	884	774	812	734
Home south	776	824	654	779	898	687	716	889	917

■ **14-20** To increase sales during heavy shopping days, a chain of stores selling cheese in shopping malls gives away samples at the stores' entrances. The chain's management defines the heavy shopping days and randomly selects the days for sampling. From a sample of days that were considered heavy shopping days, the following data give one store's sales on days when cheese sampling was done and on days when it was not done.

Sales (in hundreds)

Promotion days	18	21	23	15	19	26	17	18	22	20	18	21	27
Regular days	22	17	15	23	25	20	26	24	16	17	23	21	

Use the Mann–Whitney U test and a 5 percent level of significance to decide whether the storefront sampling produced greater sales.

■ **14-21** A company is interested in knowing whether there is a difference in the output rate for men and women employees in the molding department. Judy Johnson, production manager, was asked to conduct a study in which male and female workers' output was measured for 1 week. Somehow, one of the office clerks misplaced a portion of the data, and Judy was able to locate only the following information from the records of the tests:

$$\sigma_U = 176.4275$$

$$\mu_U = 1{,}624$$

$$R_1 = 3{,}255$$

Judy also remembered that the sample size for men, n_2, had been two units larger than n_1.

Reconstruct a z value for the test and determine whether the weekly output can be assumed, at a 5 percent level of significance, to be the same for both men and women. Indicate also the values for n_1, n_2, and R_2.

■ **14-22** A university that accepts students from both rural and urban high schools is interested in whether the different backgrounds lead to a difference in first-year GPA. Data are presented below for 13 randomly selected first-year students of rural background and 16 students of urban background. Use the Mann–Whitney U test with a 5 percent level of significance.

GPA

Rural	3.19	2.05	2.82	2.16	3.84	4.0	2.91	2.75	3.01	1.98
	2.58	2.76	2.94							
Urban	3.45	3.16	2.84	2.09	2.11	3.08	3.97	3.85	3.72	2.73
	2.81	2.64	1.57	1.87	2.54	2.62				

Stating the hypotheses

H_0: } In a one-sample runs test, a symbolic statement of the hypotheses is not appropriate ← Null hypothesis: The toys are randomly mixed

H_1: } ← Alternative hypothesis: The toys are not randomly mixed

$\alpha = 0.20$ ← Level of significance for testing these hypotheses

Illustrating the test graphically

Because too many *or* too few runs would indicate that the process by which the toys are inserted into the boxes is not random, a two-tailed test is appropriate. Figure 14-6 illustrates this test graphically.

Next we use Equation 6-2 to *standardize* the sample r statistic, 29, by subtracting μ_r, its mean, and dividing by σ_r, its standard error.

$$z = \frac{r - \mu_r}{\sigma_r} \quad [6\text{-}2]$$

$$= \frac{29 - 30.97}{3.84}$$

$$= -0.513$$

Placing the standardized value on the z scale in Figure 14-7 shows that it falls well within the critical values for this test. Therefore, management should accept the null hypothesis and conclude from this test that toys are being inserted in boxes in random order.

FIGURE 14-6

Two-tailed hypothesis test at the 0.20 level of significance

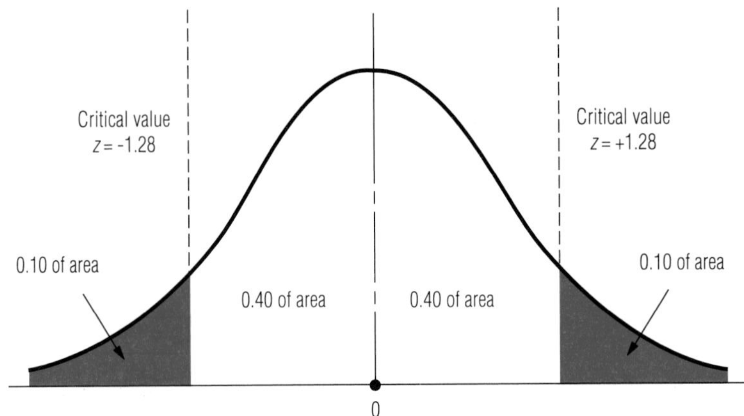

FIGURE 14-7

Two-tailed hypothesis test at the 0.20 level of significance, showing the acceptance region and the standardized observed number of runs

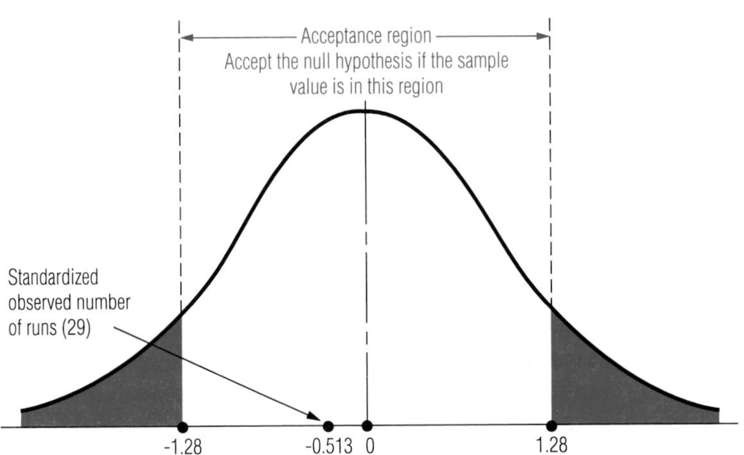

HINTS & ASSUMPTIONS

Runs tests can be used effectively in quality control situations. You will recall from Chapter 10 that variation in quality is either systematic or random, and if it's systematic variation we can correct it. Thus, a runs test can detect the kinds of patterns in output quality that are associated with systematic variation. Hint: Almost all runs tests are two-tailed because the question to be answered is whether there are too many or too few runs. Remember also that runs tests use the r statistic whose distribution can be well described by a normal distribution as long as *either* n_1 *or* n_2 is larger than 20.

Exercises 14.4

Self-Check Exercise

SC 14-5 Professor Ike Newton is interested in determining whether his brightest students (those making the best grades) tend to turn in their tests earlier (because they can recall the material faster) or later (because they take longer to write down all they know) than the others in the class. For a particular physics test, he observes that the students make the following grades in order of turning their tests in:

Order	Grades									
1–10	94	70	85	89	92	98	63	88	74	85
11–20	69	90	57	86	79	72	80	93	66	74
21–30	50	55	47	59	68	63	89	51	90	88

(a) If Professor Newton counts those making a grade of 90 and above as his brightest students, then at a 5 percent level of significance, can he conclude the brightest students turned their tests in randomly?

(b) If 60 and above is passing in Professor Newton's class, then did the students passing versus those not passing turn their tests in randomly? (Also use the 5 percent significance level.)

Basic Concepts

■ **14-24** Test for the randomness of the following sample using the 0.05 significance level:

A, B, A, A, A, B, B, A, B, B, A, A, B, A, B, A, A, B, B, B, B, A, B, B,
A, A, A, B, A, B, A, A, B, B, A, B, B, A, A, A, B, B, A, A, B, A, A, A

Applications

■ **14-25** A sequence of small glass sculptures was inspected for shipping damage. The sequence of acceptable and damaged pieces was as follows:

D, A, A, A, D, D, D, D, D, A, A, D, D, A, A, A, A, D, A, A, D, D, D, D, D

Test for the randomness of the damage to the shipment using the 0.05 significance level.

■ **14-26** The *News and Clarion* kept a record of the gender of people who called the circulation office to complain about delivery problems with the Sunday paper. For a recent Sunday, these data were as follows:

M, F, F, F, M, M, F, M, F, F, F, F, M, M, M, F, M, F, M, F, F, F, F, M, M, M, M, M

Using the 0.05 level of significance, test this sequence for randomness. Is there anything about the nature of this problem that would cause you to believe that such a sequence would not be random?

■ **14-27** Kerwin County Social Services Agency kept this record of the daily number of applicants for marriage counseling in the order in which they appeared at the agency office in 30 working days.

3, 4, 6, 8, 4, 6, 7, 2, 5, 7, 4, 8, 4, 7, 9, 5, 9, 10,
5, 7, 4, 9, 8, 9, 11, 6, 7, 5, 9, 12

Test the randomness of this sequence by seeing whether the values above and below the mean occur in random order. Use the 0.10 level of significance. Can you think of any characteristic of the environment of this problem that would support the statistical finding you reached?

■ **14-28** A restaurant owner has noticed over the years that older couples appear to eat earlier than young couples at his quiet, romantic restaurant. He suspects that perhaps it is because of children having to be left with babysitters and also because the older couples may retire earlier at night. One night, he decided to keep a record of couples' arrivals at the restaurant. He noted whether each couple was over or under 30. His notes are reproduced below. (A = 30 and older; B = younger than 30.)

(5:30 P.M.) A, A, A, A, A, A, B, A, A, A, A, A, A, B, B,
B, A, B, B, B, B, B, A, B, B, B, A, B, B, B, (10 P.M.)

At a 5 percent level of significance, was the restaurant owner correct in his thought that the age of his customers at different dining hours is less than random?

■ **14-29** Kathy Phillips is in charge of production scheduling for a printing company. The company has six large presses, which frequently break down, and one of Kathy's biggest problems is meeting deadlines when there are unexpected breakdowns in presses. She suspects that the older presses break down earlier in the week than the new presses, because all presses are checked and repaired over the weekend. To test her hypothesis, Kathy recorded the number of all the presses as they broke down during the week. Presses numbered 1, 2, and 3 are the older ones.

Number of Press in Order of Breakdown
1, 2, 3, 1, 4, 5, 3, 1, 2, 5, 1, 3, 6, 2, 3, 6, 2, 2, 3, 5, 4,
6, 4, 2, 1, 3, 4, 5, 5, 1, 4, 5, 2, 3, 5, 6, 4, 3, 2, 5, 4, 3

(a) At a 5 percent level of significance, does Kathy have a valid hypothesis that the breakdowns of presses are not random?

(b) Is her hypothesis appropriate for the decision she wishes to make about rescheduling more work earlier in the week on the newer presses?

■ **14-30** Martha Bowen, a department manager working in a large marketing-research firm, is in charge of all the research data analyses done in the firm. Accuracy and thoroughness are her responsibility. The department employs a number of research assistants to do some analyses and uses a computer to do other analyses. Typically, each week Martha randomly chooses completed analyses before they are reported and conducts tests to ensure that they have been done correctly and thoroughly. Martha's assistant, Kim Tadlock, randomly chooses 49 analyses per week from those completed and filed each day, and Martha does the reanalyses. Martha wanted to make certain that the selection process was a random one, so she could provide assurances that the computer analyses and those done by hand were both periodically checked. She arranged to have the research assistants place a special mark on the back of the records, so that they could be identified. Kim was unaware of the mark, so the randomness of the test would not be affected. Kim completed her sample with the following data:

Samples of Data Analyses for 1 Week
(1: by computer, 2: by hand)

1, 1, 1, 1, 1, 1, 1, 1, 1, 2, 1, 1, 1, 1, 1, 1, 1, 1, 1, 2, 1, 1, 1, 1, 1,
1, 1, 1, 1, 2, 1, 1, 1, 1, 1, 1, 1, 1, 1, 2, 1, 1, 1, 1, 1, 1, 1, 1, 1

(a) At a 1 percent significance level, can you conclude that the sample was random?

(b) If the sample were distributed as follows, would the sample be random?

1, 1, 1, 1, 1, 1, 1, 1, 1, 1, 1, 1, 1, 1, 1, 1, 1, 1, 1, 1, 1, 1, 1, 1, 1,
1, 1, 1, 1, 1, 1, 1, 1, 1, 1, 1, 1, 1, 1, 1, 1, 1, 1, 1, 1, 2, 2, 2, 2

(c) Because computer analyses are much faster than those done by hand, and because a number of the analyses can be done by computer, there are about three times as many computer analyses per week as hand analyses. Is there statistical evidence in part (a) to support the belief that somewhere in the sampling process there is something less than randomness occurring? If so, what is the evidence?

(d) Does the conclusion you reached in part (c) lead you to any new conclusions about the one-sample runs test, particularly in reference to your answer in part (a)?

■ **14-31** Bank of America is curious about the grade level of people who use their ATM at the Student Union. Freshmen and sophomores are classified as type A, juniors and seniors as type B. Data are presented below for 45 people who used the ATM during one Friday afternoon. Test this sequence for randomness at the 0.05 significance level.

B B B A A A B A A A A A A B B B B A B A A A A B B A A B B B A B B B A A A A A A A B B B

■ **14-32** The First National Bank of Smithville recorded the gender of the first 40 customers who appeared last Tuesday with this notation:

M, F, M, M, M, M, F, F, M, M, M, F, M, M, M, M, M, F, F, M,
F, M, M, M, F, M, M, M, M, M, M, F, M, M, M, M, M, F, F, M

At the 0.05 level of significance, test the randomness of this sequence. Is there anything in banking or in the nature of this problem that would lead you to accept intuitively what you have found statistically?

Worked-Out Answer to Self-Check Exercise

SC 14-5 (a) Let G denote those at or above 90, and L denote those below 90:

GLLLGGLLLLLGLLLLLGLLLLLLLLLLGL

$n_1 = \#\text{ of } G\text{'s} = 6 \qquad r = 10$

$n_2 = \#\text{ of } L\text{'s} = 24 \qquad \alpha = 0.05$

$$\mu_r = \frac{2n_1n_2}{n_1 + n_2} + 1 = \frac{2(6)(24)}{30} + 1 = 10.6$$

$$\sigma_r = \sqrt{\frac{2n_1n_2(2n_1n_2 - n_1 - n_2)}{(n_1 + n_2)^2(n_1 + n_2 - 1)}} = \sqrt{\frac{2(6)(24)[2(6)(24) - 6 - 24]}{(30)^2(29)}}$$

$$= 1.69$$

The critical values of z are ± 1.96. The standardized value of r is

$$z = \frac{r - \mu_r}{\sigma_r} = \frac{10 - 10.6}{1.69} = -0.355$$

so we accept H_0. The sequence is random.

(b) With P denoting passing (≥ 60) and F denoting failing (< 60), we get

PPPPPPPPPPPPFPPPPPPPPPFFFFPPPPFPP

$n_1 = \#\text{ of } P\text{'s} = 24 \qquad r = 7$

$n_2 = \#\text{ of } F\text{'s} = 6 \qquad \alpha = 0.05$

$$\mu_r = \frac{2(24)(6)}{30} + 1 = 10.6$$

$$\sigma_r = \sqrt{\frac{2(24)(6)[2(24)(6) - 24 - 6]}{(30)^2(29)}} = 1.69$$

The critical values of z are ± 1.96. The standardized value of r is

$$z = \frac{7 - 10.6}{1.69} = -2.13$$

so we reject H_0 because $z < -1.96$. This sequence is not random.

14.5 Rank Correlation

Function of the rank-correlation coefficient

Chapters 12 and 13 introduced us to the notion of correlation and to the correlation coefficient, a measure of the closeness of association between two variables. Often in correlation analysis, information is not available in the form of numerical values such as those we used in the problems of those chapters. But if we can assign rankings to the items in each of the two variables we are studying, a *rank-correlation coefficient* can be calculated. **This is a measure of the correlation that exists between the two sets of ranks, a measure of the degree of association between the variables that we would not have been able to calculate otherwise.**

Another advantage of using rank correlation

A second reason for learning the method of rank correlation is to be able to simplify the process of computing a correlation coefficient from a very large set of data for each of two variables. To prove how tedious this can be, try expanding one of the correlation problems in Chapter 12 by a factor of 10 and performing the necessary calculations. Instead of having to do these calculations, we can compute a measure of association that is based on the *ranks* of the observations, *not the numerical values* of the data. This measure is called the Spearman rank-correlation coefficient, in honor of the statistician who developed it in the early 1900s.

The Coefficient of Rank Correlation

Listing the ranked variables

By working a couple of examples, we can learn how to calculate and interpret this measure of the association between two ranked variables. First, consider Table 14-9, which lists five people and compares the academic rank they achieved in college with the level they have attained in a certain company 10 years after graduation. The value of 5 represents the highest rank in the group; the rank of 1, the lowest.

Calculating the rank-correlation coefficient

Using the information in Table 14-9, we can calculate a coefficient of rank correlation between success in college and company level achieved 10 years later. All we need is Equation 14-8 and a few computations.

Coefficient of Rank Correlation

$$r_s = 1 - \frac{6\Sigma d^2}{n(n^2 - 1)} \qquad [14\text{-}8]$$

where

- r_s = coefficient of rank correlation (notice that the subscript s, from Spearman, distinguishes this r from the one we calculated in Chapter 12)
- n = number of paired observations
- Σ = notation meaning "the sum of"
- d = difference between the ranks for each pair of observations

Table 14-9

Comparison of the Ranks of Five Students

Student	College Rank	Company Rank 10 Years Later
John	4	4
Margaret	3	3
Debbie	1	1
Steve	2	2
Lisa	5	5

The computations are easily done in tabular form, as we show in Table 14-10. Therefore, we have all the information we need to find the rank-correlation coefficient for this problem:

$$r_s = 1 - \frac{6\Sigma d^2}{n(n^2 - 1)} \qquad [14\text{-}8]$$

$$= 1 - \frac{6(0)}{5(25 - 1)}$$

$$= 1 - \frac{0}{120}$$

$$= 1 \leftarrow \text{Rank-correlation coefficient}$$

Explaining values of the rank-correlation coefficient

As we learned in Chapter 12, this correlation coefficient of 1 shows that there is a perfect association or *perfect correlation* between the two variables. This verifies what we saw in Table 14-9, the fact that the college and company ranks for each person were identical.

Computing another rank-correlation coefficient

One more example should make us feel comfortable with the coefficient of rank correlation. Table 14-11 illustrates five more people, but this time the ranks in college and in a company 10 years later seem to be extreme opposites. We can compute the difference between the ranks for each pair of observations, find d^2, and then take the sum of all the d^2s. Substituting these values into Equation 14-8, we find a rank correlation coefficient of -1:

$$r_s = 1 - \frac{6\Sigma d^2}{n(n^2 - 1)} \qquad [14\text{-}8]$$

$$= 1 - \frac{6(40)}{5(25 - 1)}$$

$$= 1 - \frac{240}{120}$$

$$= 1 - 2$$

$$= -1 \leftarrow \text{Rank-correlation coefficient}$$

Interpreting the results

In Chapter 12, we learned that a correlation coefficient of -1 represents *perfect inverse correlation.* And that is just what happened in our case: The people who did the best in college wound up 10 years later in the lowest ranks of an organization. Now let's apply these ideas.

Table 14-10 Generating Information to Compute the Rank-Correlation Coefficient

Student	College Rank (1)	Company Rank (2)	Difference between the Two Ranks (1) − (2)	Difference Squared [(1) − (2)]²
John	4	4	0	0
Margaret	3	3	0	0
Debbie	1	1	0	0
Steve	2	2	0	0
Lisa	5	5	0	0
				$\Sigma d^2 =$ **0** ← Sum of the squared differences

Table 14-11 Generating Data to Compute the Rank-Correlation Coefficient

Student	College Rank (1)	Company Rank (2)	Difference between the Two Ranks (1) − (2)	Difference Squared [(1) − (2)]²
Roy	5	1	4	16
David	1	5	−4	16
Jay	3	3	0	0
Charlotte	2	4	−2	4
Kathy	4	2	2	4
				$\Sigma d^2 =$ **40** ← Sum of the squared differences

Solving a Problem Using Rank Correlation

Rank correlation is a useful technique for looking at the connection between air quality and the evidence of pulmonary-related diseases that we discussed in our chapter-opening problem. Table 14-12 reproduces the data found by the health organization studying the problem. In the same table, we also do some of the calculations needed to find r_s.

Finding the rank-correlation coefficient

Using the data in Table 14-12 and Equation 14-8, we can find the rank-correlation coefficient for this problem:

$$r_s = 1 - \frac{6\Sigma d^2}{n(n^2 - 1)} \qquad [14\text{-}8]$$

$$= 1 - \frac{6(58)}{11(121 - 1)}$$

$$= 1 - \frac{348}{1{,}320}$$

$$= 1 - 0.2636$$

$$= 0.7364 \leftarrow \text{Rank-correlation coefficient}$$

Table 14-12

Ranking of Eleven Cities

City	Air Quality Rank (1)	Pulmonary-Disease Rank (2)	Difference between the Two Ranks (1) − (2)	Difference Squared $[(1) - (2)]^2$
A	4	5	−1	1
B	7	4	3	9
C	9	7	2	4
D	1	3	−2	4
E	2	1	1	1
F	10	11	−1	1
G	3	2	1	1
H	5	10	−5	25
I	6	8	−2	4
J	8	6	2	4
K	11	9	2	4
	Best rank = 11 Worst rank = 1			$\Sigma d^2 = \mathbf{58}$ ← Sum of the squared differences

Interpreting the results

A correlation coefficient of 0.736 suggests a substantial positive association between average air quality and the occurrence of pulmonary disease, at least in the 11 cities sampled; that is, high levels of pollution go with high incidence of pulmonary disease.

How can we test this value of 0.736? We can apply the same methods we used to test hypotheses in Chapter 8 and 9. In performing such tests on r_s, we are trying to avoid the error of concluding that an association exists between two variables if, in fact, no such association exists in the population from which these two samples were drawn, that is, if the *population* rank-correlation coefficient, ρ_s (*rho sub s*), is really equal to zero.

Testing hypotheses about rank correlation

For small values of *n*, (*n* less than or equal to 30), the distribution of r_s is not normal, and unlike other small sample statistics we have encountered, it is not appropriate to use the *t* distribution for testing hypotheses about the rank-correlation coefficient. Instead, we use Appendix Table 7, Spearman's Rank Correlation Values, to determine the acceptance and rejection regions for such hypotheses. In our current problem, suppose that the health organization wants to test, at the 0.05 level of significance, the null hypothesis that there is zero correlation in the ranked data of *all* cities in the world. Our problem then becomes:

Stating the hypotheses

$$H_0: \rho_s = 0$$ ← Null hypothesis: There is no correlation in the ranked data of the population

$$H_1: \rho_s \neq 0$$ ← Alternative hypothesis: There is a correlation in the ranked data of the populations

$$\alpha = 0.05$$ ← Level of significance for testing these hypotheses

A two-tailed test is appropriate, so we look at Appendix Table 7 in the row for $n = 11$ (the number of cities) and the column for a significance level of 0.05. There we find that the critical values for r_s are ± 0.6091, that is, the upper limit of the acceptance region is 0.6091, and the lower limit of the acceptance region is -0.6091.

Figure 14-8 shows the limits of the acceptance region and the rank-correlation coefficient we calculated from the air-quality sample. From this figure, we can see that the rank-correlation coefficient lies outside the acceptance region. Therefore, we would reject the

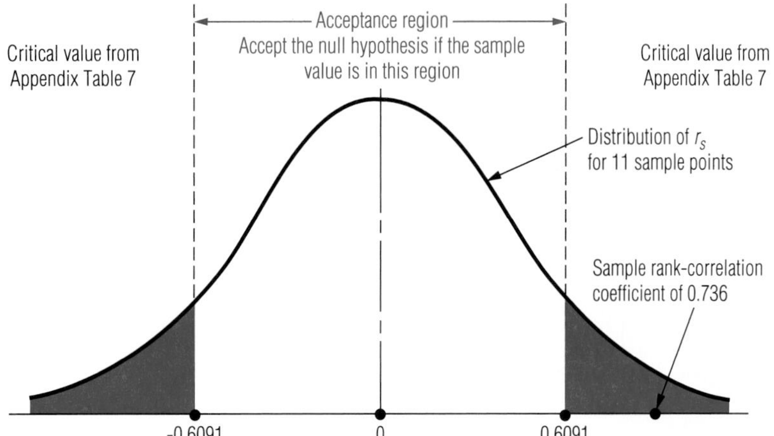

FIGURE 14-8

Two-tailed hypothesis test, using Appendix Table 7 at the 0.05 level of significance, showing the acceptance region and the sample rank-correlation coefficient

null hypothesis of no correlation and conclude that there *is* an association between air-quality levels and the incidence of pulmonary disease in the world's cities.

The appropriate distribution for values of *n* greater than 30

If the sample size is greater than 30, we can no longer use Appendix Table 7. However, when n is greater than 30, the sampling distribution of r_s is approximately normal, with a mean of zero and a standard deviation of $1/\sqrt{n-1}$. Thus, the standard error of r_s is

Standard Error of the Coefficient of Rank Correlation

$$\sigma_{r_s} = \frac{1}{\sqrt{n-1}} \quad [14\text{-}9]$$

and we can use Appendix Table 1 to find the appropriate z values for testing hypotheses about the population rank correlation.

Example with *n* greater than 30

As an example of hypothesis testing of rank-correlation coefficients when n is greater than 30, consider the case of a social scientist who tries to determine whether bright people tend to choose spouses who are also bright. He randomly chooses 32 couples and tests to see whether there is a significant rank correlation in the IQs of the couples. His data and computations are given in Table 14-13.

Using the data in Table 14-13 and Equation 14-8, we can find the rank-correlation coefficient for this problem:

$$r_s = 1 - \frac{6\Sigma d^2}{n(n^2-1)} \quad [14\text{-}8]$$

$$= 1 - \frac{6(1{,}043.5)}{32(1{,}024 - 1)}$$

$$= 1 - \frac{6{,}261}{32{,}736}$$

$$= 1 - 0.1913$$

$$= 0.8087 \leftarrow \text{Rank-correlation coefficient}$$

Table 14-13 Computation of Rank Correlation of Husbands' and Wives' IQs

Couple (1)	Husband's IQ (2)	Wife's IQ (3)	Husband's Rank (4)	Wife's Rank (5)	Difference between Ranks (4) − (5)	Difference Squared $[(4) - (5)]^2$
1	95	95	8	4.5	3.5	12.25
2	103	98	20	8.5	11.5	132.25
3	111	110	26	23	3	9.00
4	92	88	4	2	2	4.00
5	150	106	32	18	14	196.00
6	107	109	24	21.5	2.5	6.25
7	90	96	3	6	−3	9.00
8	108	131	25	32	−7	49.00
9	100	112	17.5	25.5	−8	64.00
10	93	95	5.5	4.5	1	1.00
11	119	112	29	25.5	3.5	12.25
12	115	117	28	30	−2	4.00
13	87	94	1	3	−2	4.00
14	105	109	21	21.5	−0.5	0.25
15	135	114	31	27	4	16.00
16	89	83	2	1	1	1.00
17	99	105	14.5	16.5	−2	4.00
18	106	115	22.5	28	−5.5	30.25
19	126	116	30	29	1	1.00
20	100	107	17.5	19	−1.5	2.25
21	93	111	5.5	24	−18.5	342.25
22	94	98	7	8.5	−1.5	2.25
23	100	105	17.5	16.5	1	1.00
24	96	103	10	15	−5	25.00
25	99	101	14.5	13	1.5	2.25
26	112	123	27	31	−4	16.00
27	106	108	22.5	20	2.5	6.25
28	98	97	12.5	7	5.5	30.25
29	96	100	10	11.5	−1.5	2.25
30	98	99	12.5	10	2.5	6.25
31	100	100	17.5	11.5	6	36.00
32	96	102	10	14	−4	16.00
					Sum of the squared differences → $\Sigma d^2 =$	**1,043.50**

If the social scientist wishes to test his hypothesis at the 0.01 level of significance, his problem can be stated:

H_0: $\rho_s = 0$ ← Null hypothesis: There is no rank correlation in the population; that is, husbands' intelligence and wives' intelligence are randomly mixed

Stating the hypotheses

H_1: $\rho_s > 0$ ← Alternative hypothesis: The population rank correlation is positive; that is, bright people choose bright spouses

$\alpha = 0.01$ ← Level of significance for testing these hypotheses

An upper-tailed test is appropriate. From Appendix Table 1, we find that the critical z value for the 0.01 level of significance is 2.33. Figure 14-9 illustrates this hypothesis test graphically; we show there the colored region in the upper tail of the distribution that corresponds to the 0.01 level of significance.

To compute our test statistic, we first find the standard error of r_s:

$$\sigma_{r_s} = \frac{1}{\sqrt{n-1}} \qquad [14\text{-}9]$$

$$= \frac{1}{\sqrt{32-1}} = 0.1796$$

Now we can use Equation 6-2 to *standardize* the rank correlation coefficient, r_s, by subtracting 0, its hypothesized value, and dividing by σ_{r_s}, its standard error.

$$z = \frac{r_s - 0}{\sigma_{r_s}} \qquad [6\text{-}2]$$

$$= \frac{0.8087}{0.1796}$$

$$= 4.503$$

Interpreting the results

Figure 14-10 shows the limit of the acceptance region and the standardized rank-correlation coefficient we calculated from the IQ data. In Figure 14-10, we can see that the rank-correlation coefficient lies far outside the acceptance region. Therefore, we would reject the null hypothesis of no correlation and conclude that bright people tend to choose bright spouses.

A Special Property of Rank Correlation

Advantage of rank correlation

Rank correlation has a useful advantage over the correlation method we discussed in Chapter 12. Suppose we have cases in which one or several very extreme observations exist in the original data. By the use of numerical values as was done in Chapter 12, the correlation coefficient may not be a good description of the association that exists between two variables. Yet extreme observations in a *rank*-correlation test will never produce a large rank difference.

FIGURE 14-9

Upper-tailed hypothesis test at the 0.01 level of significance

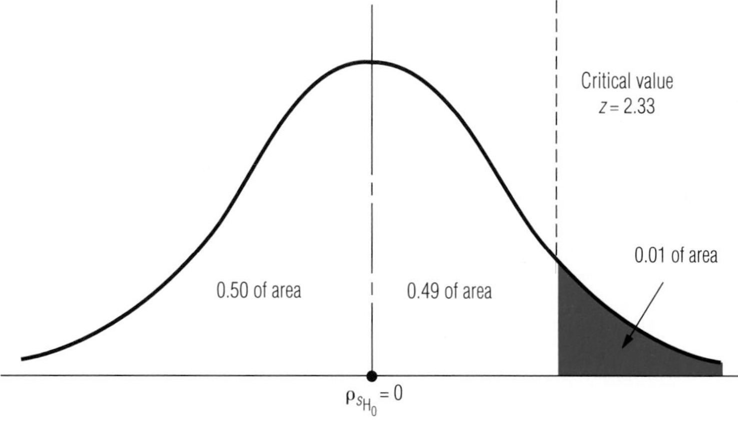

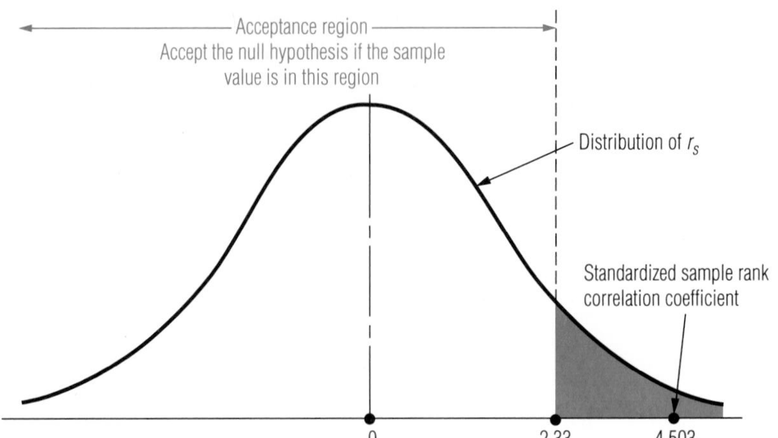

FIGURE 14-10

Upper-tailed hypothesis test at the 0.01 level of significance, showing the acceptance region and the standardized sample rank-correlation coefficient

Consider the following data array of two variables, X and Y:

X	10	13	16	19	25
Y	34	40	45	51	117

Because of the large value of the fifth Y term, we would get two significantly different answers for r using the conventional and the rank-correlation methods. In this case, the rank-correlation method would be less sensitive to the extreme value. We would assign a rank order of 5 to the numerical value of 117 and avoid the unduly large effect on the value of the correlation coefficient.

HINTS & ASSUMPTIONS

When there are extreme values in the original data, rank correlation can produce more useful results than the correlation method explained in Chapter 12 because extreme observations never produce a large difference in *rank*. Hint: Rank correlation is very useful when data are non-normally distributed. Take the case of university fund-raising where you get a few "big hitter" gifts, lots and lots of gifts below $100, and a very broad range in between. Using the correlation techniques of Chapter 12 to investigate the relationship between number of appeal mailings and size of gift with this kind of distribution doesn't make sense because the million-dollar gifts would distort the findings. But using rank correlation in this instance works quite well.

Exercises 14.5

Self-Check Exercise

SC 14-6 The following are ratings of aggressiveness (X) and amount of sales in the last year (Y) for eight salespeople. Is there a significant rank correlation between the two measures? Use the 0.10 significance level.

X	30	17	35	28	42	25	19	29
Y	35	31	43	46	50	32	33	42

Applications

■ **14-33** The following are years of experience (X) and average customer satisfaction (Y) for 10 service providers. Is there a significant rank correlation between the two measures? Use the 0.05 significance level.

X	6.3	5.8	6.1	6.9	3.4	1.8	9.4	4.7	7.2	2.4
Y	5.3	8.6	4.7	4.2	4.9	6.1	5.1	6.3	6.8	5.2

■ **14-34** A plant supervisor ranked a sample of eight workers on the number of hours of overtime worked and length of employment. Is the rank correlation between the two measures significant at the 0.01 level?

Amount of overtime	5.0	8.0	2.0	4.0	3.0	7.0	1.0	6.0
Years employed	1.0	6.0	4.5	2.0	7.0	8.0	4.5	3.0

■ **14-35** Most people believe that managerial experience produces better interpersonal relationships between a manager and her employees. The Quail Corporation has the following data matching years of experience on the part of the manager with the number of grievances filed last year by the employees reporting to that manager. At the 0.05 level of significance, does the rank correlation between these two suggest that experience improves relationships?

Years of experience	7	18	17	4	21	27	20	14	15	10
Number of grievances	5	2	4	4	3	2	4	5	4	6

■ **14-36** The Occupational Safety and Health Administration (OSHA) was conducting a study of the relationship between expenditures for plant safety and the accident rate in the plants. OSHA had confined its studies to the synthetic chemical industry. To adjust for the size differential that existed among some of the plants, OSHA had converted its data into expenditures per production employee. The results follow:

Expenditure by Chemical Companies per Production Employee in Relation to Accidents per Year

Company	A	B	C	D	E	F	G	H	I	J	K
Expenditure	$60	$37	$30	$20	$24	$42	$39	$54	$48	$58	$26
Accidents	2	7	6	9	7	4	8	2	4	3	8

Is there a significant correlation between expenditures and accidents in the chemical-company plants? Use a rank correlation (with 1 representing highest expenditure and accident rate) to support your conclusion. Test at the 1 percent significance level.

■ **14-37** Two business school professors were discussing how difficult it is to predict the success of graduates based on grades alone. One professor thought that the number of years of experience MBAs had before returning for their degrees was probably a better predictor. Using the following data, at the 0.02 level of significance, which rank correlation is a better predictor of career success?

Years experience	4	3	4	3	6	7	1	5	5	2
Grade-point average	3.4	3.2	3.5	3.0	2.9	3.4	2.5	3.9	3.6	3.0
Success rank (10 = top)	4	2	6	5	7	9	1	8	10	3

■ **14-38** The Carolina Lighting Company has two trained interviewers to recruit manager trainees for new sales outlets. Although each of the interviewers has a unique style, both are thought to be good preliminary judges of managerial potential. The personnel manager wondered how closely the interviewers would agree, so she had both of them independently evaluate 14 applicants. They ranked the applicants in terms of their degree of potential contribution to the company. The results follow. Use a rank correlation and a 1 percent significance level to determine whether there is a significant positive correlation between the two interviewers' rankings.

Applicant	1	2	3	4	5	6	7	8	9	10	11	12	13	14
Interviewer 1	1	11	13	2	12	10	3	4	14	5	6	9	7	8
Interviewer 2	4	12	11	2	14	10	1	3	13	8	6	7	9	5

■ **14-39** Nancy McKenzie, supervisor for a lithographic camera assembly process, feels that the longer a group of employees works together, the higher the daily output rate. She gathered the following data during the first 10 days that one group of employees worked together.

Day	1	2	3	4	5	6	7	8	9	10
Output rate	4.0	7.0	5.0	6.0	8.0	2.0	3.0	0.5	9.0	6.0

Can Nancy conclude at a 5 percent significance level that there is no correlation between the number of days worked together and the daily output?

■ **14-40** An electronics firm, which recruits many engineers, wonders whether the cost of extensive recruiting efforts is worth it. If the firm could be confident (using a 1 percent significance level) that the population rank correlation between applicants' résumés scored by the personnel department and interview scores is positive, it would feel justified in discontinuing interviews and relying on résumé scores in hiring. The firm has drawn a sample of 35 engineer applicants in the last 2 years. On the basis of the sample shown, should the firm discontinue interviews and use résumé scores to hire?

Individual	Interview Score	Résumé Score	Individual	Interview Score	Résumé Score
1	81	113	19	81	111
2	88	88	20	84	121
3	55	76	21	82	83
4	83	129	22	90	79
5	78	99	23	63	71
6	93	142	24	78	108
7	65	93	25	73	68
8	87	136	26	79	121
9	95	82	27	72	109
10	76	91	28	95	121
11	60	83	29	81	140
12	85	96	30	87	132
13	93	126	31	93	135
14	66	108	32	85	143
15	90	95	33	91	118
16	69	65	34	94	147
17	87	96	35	94	138
18	68	101			

■ **14-41** The following are salary and age data for the 10 Ph.D. candidates graduating this year from the School of Accounting at Northwest University. At the 0.05 level of significance, does the rank correlation of age and salary suggest that older candidates get higher starting salaries?

Salary	Age
$67,000	29
60,000	25
57,500	30
59,500	35
50,000	27
55,000	31
59,500	32
63,000	38
69,500	28
72,000	34

■ **14-42** Dee Boone operates a repair facility for light-aircraft engines. He is interested in improving his estimates of repair time required and believes that the best predictor is the number of operating hours on the engine since its last major repair. Below are data on ten engines Dee worked on recently. At the 0.10 level of significance, does the rank correlation suggest a strong relationship?

Engine	Hours Since Last Major Repair	Hours Required to Repair
1	1,000	40
2	1,200	54
3	900	41
4	1,450	60
5	2,000	65
6	1,300	50
7	1,650	42
8	1,700	65
9	500	43
10	2,100	66

Worked-Out Answer to Self-Check Exercise

SC 14-6

X(ranks)	6	1	7	4	8	3	2	5
Y(ranks)	4	1	6	7	8	2	3	5
d	2	0	1	−3	0	1	−1	0
d^2	4	0	1	9	0	1	1	0

$\Sigma d^2 = 16 \qquad n = 8 \qquad \alpha = 0.10$

$H_0\colon \rho_s = 0 \qquad H_1\colon \rho_s \neq 0$

$$r_s = 1 - \frac{6\Sigma d^2}{n(n^2 - 1)} = 1 - \frac{6(16)}{8(63)} = 0.8095$$

From Appendix Table 7, the critical values for r_s are ± 0.6190. Because $0.8095 > 0.6190$, we reject H_0. The correlation is significant.

14.6 The Kolmogorov–Smirnov Test

The K–S test and its advantages

The Kolmogorov–Smirnov test, named for statisticians A. N. Kolmogorov and N. V. Smirnov, is a simple nonparametric method for testing whether there is a significant difference between an observed frequency distribution and a theoretical frequency distribution. The K–S test is therefore another measure of the *goodness-of-fit* of a theoretical frequency distribution, as was the chi-square test we studied in Chapter 11. However, the K–S test has several advantages over the χ^2 test: It is a more powerful test, and it is easier to use because it does not require that data be grouped in any way.

A special advantage

The K–S statistic, D_n, is particularly useful for judging how close the observed frequency distribution is to the expected frequency distribution, because the probability distribution of D_n depends on the sample size n but is independent of the expected frequency distribution (D_n is a distribution-free statistic).

A Problem Illustrating the K–S Test

Suppose that the Orange County Telephone Exchange has been keeping track of the number of "senders" (a type of automatic equipment used in telephone exchanges) that were in use at a given instant. Observations were made on 3,754 different occasions. For capital-investment planning purposes, the budget officer of this company thinks that the pattern of usage follows a Poisson distribution with a mean of 8.5. If he wants to test his hypothesis at the 0.01 level of significance, he can use the K–S test.

We would set up our hypotheses like this:

Stating the hypotheses

H_0: A Poisson distribution with $\lambda = 8.5$ is a good description of the pattern of usage ← Null hypothesis

H_1: A Poisson distribution with $\lambda = 8.5$ is not a good description of the pattern of usage ← Alternative hypothesis

$\alpha = 0.01$ ← Level of significance for testing these hypotheses

Computing and comparing expected frequencies

Next, we would list the data that we observed. Table 14-14 lists the observed frequencies and transforms them into observed relative cumulative frequencies.

Now we can use the Poisson formula to compute the expected frequencies.

$$p(x) = \frac{\lambda^x \times e^{-\lambda}}{x!} \qquad [5\text{-}4]$$

By comparing these expected frequencies with our observed frequencies, we can examine the extent of the difference between them: the absolute deviation. Table 14-15 lists the observed relative cumulative frequencies F_o, the expected relative cumulative frequencies F_e, and the absolute deviations for $x = 0$ to 22.

Calculating the K–S Statistic

To compute the K–S statistic for this problem, you simply pick out D_n, the maximum absolute deviation of F_e from F_o.

Computing the K–S statistic

K–S Statistic

$$D_n = \max |F_e - F_o| \quad [14\text{-}10]$$

Computing the critical value

In this problem, $D_n = 0.2582$ at $x = 9$.

A K–S test must always be a one-tailed test. The critical values for D_n have been tabulated and can be found in Appendix Table 8. By looking in the row for $n = 3{,}754$ (the sample size) and the column for a significance level of 0.01, we find that the critical value of D_n must be computed using the formula

$$\frac{1.63}{\sqrt{n}} = \frac{1.63}{\sqrt{3{,}754}} = \frac{1.63}{61.27} = 0.0266$$

Our conclusion

The next step is to compare the calculated value of D_n with the critical value of D_n from the table. If the table value for the chosen significance level is greater than the calculated value of D_n, then we will accept the null hypothesis. Obviously, $0.0266 < 0.2582$, so we reject H_0 and conclude that a Poisson distribution with a mean of 8.5 is *not* a good description of the pattern of sender usage at the Orange County Telephone Exchange.

Table 14-14 Observed and Relative Cumulative Frequencies

Number Busy	Observed Frequency	Observed Cumulative Frequency	Observed Relative Cumulative Frequency
0	0	0	0.0000
1	5	5	0.0013
2	14	19	0.0051
3	24	43	0.0115
4	57	100	0.0266
5	111	211	0.0562
6	197	408	0.1087
7	278	686	0.1827
8	378	1,064	0.2834
9	418	1,482	0.3948
10	461	1,943	0.5176
11	433	2,376	0.6329
12	413	2,789	0.7429
13	358	3,147	0.8383
14	219	3,366	0.8966
15	145	3,511	0.9353
16	109	3,620	0.9643
17	57	3,677	0.9795
18	43	3,720	0.9909
19	16	3,736	0.9952
20	7	3,743	0.9971
21	8	3,751	0.9992
22	3	3,754	1.0000

Table 14–15

Relative Observed Cumulative Frequencies, Expected Relative Cumulative Frequencies, and Absolute Deviations

Number Busy	Observed Frequency	Observed Cumulative Frequency	Observed Relative Cumulative Frequency	Expected Relative Cumulative Frequency	$\|F_e - F_o\|$ Absolute Deviation
0	0	0	0.0000	0.0002	0.0002
1	5	5	0.0013	0.0019	0.0006
2	14	19	0.0051	0.0093	0.0042
3	24	43	0.0115	0.0301	0.0186
4	57	100	0.0266	0.0744	0.0478
5	111	211	0.0562	0.1496	0.0934
6	197	408	0.1087	0.2562	0.1475
7	278	686	0.1827	0.3856	0.2029
8	378	1,064	0.2834	0.5231	0.2397
9	418	1,482	0.3948	0.6530	0.2582
10	461	1,943	0.5176	0.7634	0.2458
11	433	2,376	0.6329	0.8487	0.2158
12	413	2,789	0.7429	0.9091	0.1662
13	358	3,147	0.8383	0.9486	0.1103
14	219	3,366	0.8966	0.9726	0.0760
15	145	3,511	0.9353	0.9862	0.0509
16	109	3,620	0.9643	0.9934	0.0291
17	57	3,677	0.9795	0.9970	0.0175
18	43	3,720	0.9909	0.9987	0.0078
19	16	3,736	0.9952	0.9995	0.0043
20	7	3,743	0.9971	0.9998	0.0027
21	8	3,751	0.9992	0.9999	0.0007
22	3	3,754	1.0000	1.0000	0.0000

HINTS & ASSUMPTIONS

Think of the Kolmogorov–Smirnov test as another *goodness-of-fit* test, just like the chi-square test in Chapter 11, except that this time it's easier to use because we don't have to do all the arithmetic needed to calculate chi-square. The K–S test just finds the relative cumulative distributions for both observed frequencies and expected frequencies and then tests how far apart they are. If the distance is not significant, then the observed distribution is well described by the theoretical distribution. Hint: K–S tests are *always* one-tailed tests because we are always testing whether differences are greater than a specified level.

Exercises 14.6

Self-Check Exercise

SC 14-7 The following is an observed frequency distribution. Using a normal distribution with $\mu = 6.80$ and $\sigma = 1.24$:

(a) Find the probability of falling into each class.

(b) From part (a), compute the expected frequency of each category.

Self-Check Exercise

(continued)

(c) Calculate D_n.

(d) At the 0.15 level of significance, does this distribution seem to be well described by the suggested normal distribution?

Value of the variable	$\leq$4.009	4.010–5.869	5.870–7.729	7.730–9.589	>9.590
Observed frequency	13	158	437	122	20

Basic Concepts

■ **14-43** At the 0.05 level of significance, can we conclude that the following data come from a Poisson distribution with $\lambda = 3$?

Number of arrivals per day	0	1	2	3	4	5	6 or more
Number of days	6	18	30	24	11	2	9

■ **14-44** The following is an observed frequency distribution. Using a normal distribution with $\mu = 98.6$ and $\sigma = 3.78$

(a) Find the probability of falling into each class.

(b) From part (a), compute the expected frequency of each category.

(c) Calculate D_n.

(d) At the 0.10 significance level, does this distribution seem to be well described by the suggested normal distribution?

Value of the variable	<92.0	92.0–95.99	96.0–99.99	100–103.99	$\geq$104
Observed frequency	69	408	842	621	137

■ **14-45** The following is a table of observed frequencies, along with the frequencies to be expected under a normal distribution.

(a) Calculate the K–S statistic.

(b) Can we conclude that these data do in fact come from a normal distribution? Use the 0.10 level of significance.

	Test Score				
	51–60	61–70	71–80	81–90	91–100
Observed frequency	30	100	440	500	130
Expected frequency	40	170	500	390	100

Applications

■ **14-46** Kevin Morgan, national sales manager of an electronics firm, has collected the following salary statistics on his field salesforce earnings. He has both observed frequencies and frequencies expected if the distribution of salaries is normal. At the 0.10 level of significance, can Kevin conclude that the distribution of salesforce earnings is normal?

	Earnings (in thousands)						
	25–30	31–36	37–42	43–48	49–54	55–60	61–66
Observed frequency	9	22	25	30	21	12	6
Expected frequency	6	17	32	35	18	13	4

■ **14-47** Randall Nelson, salesman for the V-Star company, has seven accounts to visit per week. It is thought that the sales by Mr. Nelson may be described by the binomial distribution, with the probability of selling each account being 0.45. Examining the observed frequency distribution of Mr. Nelson's number of sales per week, determine whether the distribution does in fact correspond to the suggested distribution. Use the 0.05 significance level.

Number of sales per week	0	1	2	3	4	5	6	7
Frequency of the number of sales	25	32	61	47	39	21	18	12

■ **14-48** Jackie Denn, an airline food-service administrator, has examined past records from 200 randomly selected cross-country flights to determine the frequency with which low-sodium meals were requested. The number of flights in which 0, 1, 2, 3, or 4 or more low-sodium meals were requested was 25, 45, 67, 43, and 20, respectively. At the 0.05 level of significance, can she reasonably conclude that these requests follow a Poisson distribution with $\lambda = 1$?

Worked-Out Answer to Self-Check Exercise

SC 14-7 (a) The probabilities of falling into the five classes are the indicated areas under the curve below:

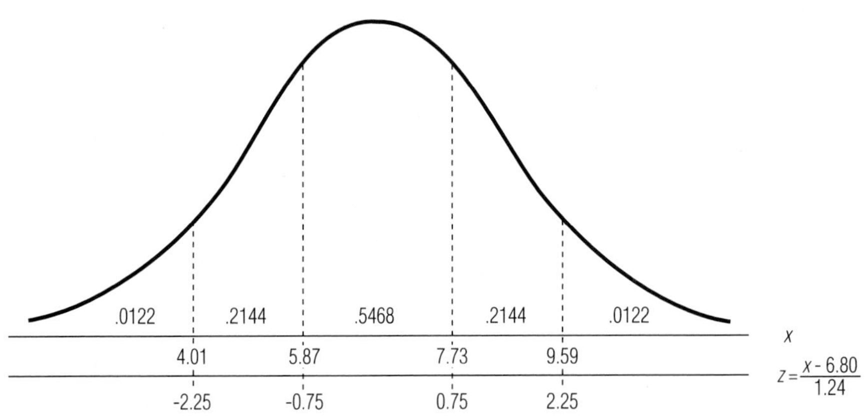

(b) $n = 13 + 158 + 437 + 122 + 20 = 750$. Thus, the expected frequencies are $0.0122(750) = 9.15$, $0.2144(750) = 160.80$, $0.5468(750) = 410.1$, 160.80, and 9.15.

(c)

f_o	cum. f_o	F_o	F_e	$\lvert F_e - F_o \rvert$
13	13	0.0173	0.0122	0.0051
158	171	0.2280	0.2266	0.0014
437	608	0.8107	0.7734	0.0373 ←
122	730	0.9733	0.9878	0.0145
20	750	1.0000	1.0000	0.0000

(d) $D_{table} = \frac{1.14}{\sqrt{n}} = \frac{1.14}{\sqrt{750}} = 0.0416$. $D_n < D_{table}$, so accept H_0.
The data are well described by the suggested normal distribution.

Statistics at Work

Loveland Computers

Case 14: Nonparametric Methods "I forgot to tell you," said Sherrel Wright, the advertising manager, as they headed back to the office, "Margot was looking for you—you better check in with her before you start on this advertising project."

"I need help!" Margot announced in a voice that could be heard in Cheyenne, Wyoming. "I spent a lot of money to get some data, and now that it's here, I don't know what we've got."

"Well I don't either," Lee joked, trying to lighten the mood. "Why don't you tell me what's going on."

"For some of the midrange models—basically PCs with fast chips and a reasonable amount of disk storage—we can make them look three different ways. The old AT style machines are the size of a small suitcase. People liked the big box because it had the image of a big, powerful machine. But in the last year or so, some of the very powerful workstations have been made in a pizza box format with a fairly narrow, flat box. So some companies have been offering the midrange in a low-profile format. It's really just the same innards in a smaller box that doesn't take up as much desk space. Finally, some competitors have offered a tower configuration. That's the old AT style tipped on its edge so it can sit on the floor. That eliminates any need for desk space."

"So which style did Loveland go with?" Lee asked.

"Frankly, we've been all over the place—during different marketing campaigns. Sometimes we've offered two of the three formats, but we've changed back and forth as we've tried to guess what customers want. You'd think that everyone would want the machine on the floor, but it turns out the computer box is a useful place to put the monitor, and people who use a lot of floppies don't want to keep reaching under their desks to use the disk drive."

"Okay. So offer all three styles," Lee smiled at this simple-but-elegant solution.

"That just adds to our costs. If we run three styles, we lose the volume discounts that we can get by going with just one. And then we have to advertise three formats while I'm also launching new high-end products and keeping up with demand for our lowest-price machines. I'd like to be able to recommend the single best format to management."

"Well, I don't have a crystal ball," Lee began.

"I don't expect you to. I hired a market-research firm. They ran focus groups in Boulder, New Jersey, and Oregon. There were eight people in each group, and two groups at each site, so altogether I've got 48 response cards—and several hours of videotaped discussions that I'll save you from watching. As you'd expect, we asked the participants to rank the three formats in terms of the style they'd prefer if they were going to buy a personal computer. Then we asked them, if your first choice weren't available, which of the other two formats would you prefer. Tell me how we're going to make some sense out of this so I can make a recommendation to the product-planning group."

Study Questions: How should Lee organize the data and which statistical tests are appropriate? What should Loveland do if the analysis of data from this small group is inconclusive?

Computer Database Exercise

HH Industries

Still sensitive about what the Poisson assumption had done for the phone-call study, Laurel reflected on the sales commission questions she had recently answered for Stan. The assumption of normal populations with the same standard deviation was critical to the conclusions she had drawn. "Just to be on the safe side," she thought, "I think I'll verify my results with some rank sum analysis."

1. Using the sales data from Chapter 11, test the assumption that these samples come from populations with the same mean. What if Mike is ex-

cluded as before? Test at the 0.05 significance level.

At lunch the following week, Gary and Laurel discussed the results of the hiring-criteria study they had just completed. "As it turns out," Gary said, "that study is even more timely than we initially thought. It appears that Hal's got plans in the works to establish another satellite warehouse—this time in the Midwest region. I guess our business is so solid there that we're advancing on this pretty quickly. This will sure make my staffing job a lot easier."

"By the way," he continued, "remember when we were talking about the UPS study that resulted in our Pennsylvania warehouse? It was shortly after you arrived, and you did a terrific analysis on our success in reaching the targeted geographic area."

"Uh oh," Laurel teased. "I know when praise comes from you, you've got more work for me up your sleeve! Yes, I remember our conversations. What about it?"

"At the time," Gary went on, "you may recall that I made some cryptic comments about what I felt *should have been*, versus what actually *was*, included in the study. At any rate, it's been bugging me and I'd like to know your opinion."

"Go on," Laurel sighed, feigning irritation. "I think I've created a statistical monster!"

Gary laughed. "You sure know how to make a guy feel bad! Seriously, I don't think this will be much trouble—I'm just curious about something. When UPS did that study, it only took into account packages we *shipped*. As it turns out, *receiving* costs are also fairly significant. And, as you could probably guess, here in Florida we pay an extra "penalty" for being at the end of the shipping line. Most of the trucks that deliver to us end up leaving the state empty, unable to find freight that needs delivering back to other areas of the country.

"I'm formulating a proposal that would essentially suggest that our new Midwest site become our *main* warehouse. We would maintain all our administrative functions here in Florida, but from an inventory standpoint, we'd act purely as a satellite. That's a long explanation for a short question: Would it be possible to rank all the states we ship to and receive from, just to see if there's any correlation at all there? That would give me some preliminary information for my proposal."

Laurel realized she had been holding her breath. "Whew," she managed. "That's a much easier question than I had anticipated! The whole study sounds interesting, *and* time-consuming. But in answer to *today's* question—yes, that should be relatively simple. I could probably have it for you by the end of this week. And thanks for the warning. I know you'll be back with more requests for help, and next time they won't be so easy! I'm going to start gathering some data I think might be useful. Be sure and let me know how things are going."

"Somehow I figured I could count on you. Thanks, Laurel," Gary smiled. "Lunch is on me."

2. Using the data in the CH14.xxx files on the data disk, calculate the rank-correlation coefficient between the states HH Industries shipped to and those it received shipments from. At the 0.01 significance level, can we conclude there is a relationship between these two?

From the Textbook to the Real World

Statistics in Medicine

Statistical methods are often used in researching the origin, treatment, and control of various diseases. Because much of the data found in medical research does not conform to the normal distribution, nonparametric methods are particularly useful. Charles H. Kirkpatrick, M.D., and David W. Alling, M.D., Ph.D., applied the Mann–Whitney test in a clever way to assess the results of a randomized clinical trial involving the treatment of chronic oral candidiasis, a disease characterized by recurrent infections of the skin, nails, and mucous membranes. Results of their tests indicated that clotrimazole, which had been used successfully on similar disorders, was a highly effective treatment for chronic oral candidiasis.

The Clinical Trial Twenty patients suffering from persistent oral candidiasis were admitted to the study and assigned by random allocation to treatment with either clotrimazole lozenges or a placebo. Subjects' responses to the treatment were assessed 2 to 7 days after treatment, as shown in Table RW 14-1. This format captures two kinds of outcomes and combines them so that the larger of any two scores connotes the less favorable outcome; these scores define an ordered classification. The results of the clotrimazole and placebo treatments are summarized in Table RW 14-2. All 10 patients on the clotrimazole lozenges appeared to have no symptoms by the fifth day of treatment. This visual observation was confirmed by a Mann–Whitney test, which offered strong statistical support.

Table RW14-1 Scoring System for Outcomes of Treatment for Chronic Oral Candidiasis

Score	Clinical Findings	Laboratory Findings
1	Absent	Negative
2	Improved	Negative
3	Improved	Positive
4	Unimproved	Positive

Table RW14-2 Outcomes After 2 to 7 Days of Treatment in 20 Patients

Treatment Group	Result Score 1	2	3	4	Total Patients
Clotrimazole	6	3	1	0	10
Placebo	1	0	0	9	10

The Bottom Line Successful treatments for diseases are found only through research. In this case, although clotrimazole is known to cause adverse side effects when administered over a prolonged period, preliminary studies using oral clotrimazole on an intermittent schedule have shown clinical benefits. The use of statistical methods enables clinical researchers to quantify results of medical treatments, which lends credibility to their findings.

Source: C. H. Kirkpatrick and D. W. Alling, "Treatment of Chronic Oral Candidiasis with Clotrimazole Troches: A Controlled Clinical Trial," *The New England Journal of Medicine* 299 (1978): 1201–1203.

Chapter Review

● Terms Introduced in Chapter 14

Kolmogorov–Smirnov Test A nonparametric test, which does not require that data be grouped in any way, for determining whether there is a significant difference between an observed frequency distribution and a theoretical frequency distribution.

Kruskal–Wallis Test A nonparametric method for testing whether three or more independent samples have been drawn from populations with the same distribution. It is a nonparametric version of ANOVA, which we studied in Chapter 11.

Mann–Whitney *U* Test A nonparametric method used to determine whether two independent samples have been drawn from populations with the same distribution.

Nonparametric Tests Statistical techniques that do not make restrictive assumptions about the shape of a population distribution when performing a hypothesis test.

One-Sample Runs Test A nonparametric method for determining the randomness with which the items in a sample have been selected.

Rank Correlation A method for doing correlation analysis when the data are not available to use in numerical form, but when information is sufficient to rank the data.

Rank-Correlation Coefficient A measure of the degree of association between two variables that is based on the ranks of observations, not their numerical values.

Rank Sum Tests A family of nonparametric tests that use the order information in a set of data.

Run A sequence of identical occurrences preceded and followed by different occurrences or by none at all.

Sign Test A test for the difference between paired observations where + and − signs are substituted for quantitative values.

Theory of Runs A theory developed to allow us to test samples for the randomness of their order.

● Equations Introduced in Chapter 14

■ **14-1**

$$U = n_1n_2 + \frac{n_1(n_1 + 1)}{2} - R_1$$

p. 804

To apply the Mann–Whitney U test, you need this formula to derive the U statistic, a measure of the difference between the ranked observations of the two variables. R_1 is the sum of the ranks of observations of variable 1; n_1 and n_2 are the numbers of items in samples 1 and 2, respectively. Both samples need not be of the same size.

■ **14-2**

$$\mu_U = \frac{n_1n_2}{2}$$

p. 804

If the null hypothesis of a Mann–Whitney U test is that $n_1 + n_2$ observations came from identical populations, then the U statistic has a sampling distribution with a mean equal to the product of n_1 and n_2 divided by 2.

■ **14-3**

$$\sigma_U = \sqrt{\frac{n_1n_2(n_1 + n_2 + 1)}{12}}$$

p. 804

This formula enables us to derive the *standard error of the U statistic* of a Mann–Whitney U test.

■ **14-4**

$$U = n_1n_2 + \frac{n_2(n_2 + 1)}{2} - R_2$$

p. 806

This formula and Equation 14-1 can be used interchangeably to derive the U statistic in the Mann–Whitney U test. To save time, use this formula if the number of observations in sample 2 is significantly smaller than the number of observations in sample 1.

■ **14-5**

$$K = \frac{12}{n(n + 1)}\sum\frac{R_j^2}{n_j} - 3(n + 1)$$

p. 807

The formula computes the K statistic used in the Kruskal–Wallis test for different means among three or more populations. The appropriate sampling distribution for K is chi-square with $k - 1$ degrees of freedom, when each sample contains at least five observations.

■ **14-6**

$$\mu_r = \frac{2n_1n_2}{n_1 + n_2} + 1$$

p. 815

When doing a one-sample runs test, use this formula to derive the mean of the sampling distribution of the *r statistic*. This *r* statistic is equal to the *number of runs* in the sample being tested.

■ **14-7**

$$\sigma_r = \sqrt{\frac{2n_1n_2(2n_1n_2 - n_1 - n_2)}{(n_1 + n_2)^2(n_1 + n_2 - 1)}}$$

p. 815

This formula enables us to derive the *standard error of the r statistic* in a one-sample runs test.

■ **14-8**

$$r_s = 1 - \frac{6\Sigma d^2}{n(n^2 - 1)}$$

p. 821

The *coefficient of rank correlation*, r_s, is a measure of the closeness of association between two ranked variables.

■ **14-9**

$$\sigma_{r_s} = \frac{1}{\sqrt{n - 1}}$$

p. 825

This formula enables us to calculate the *standard error of* r_s in a hypothesis test on the coefficient of rank correlation.

■ **14-10**

$$D_n = \max |F_e - F_o|$$

p. 833

If we compare this computed value to a critical value of D_n in the K–S table, we can test distributional goodness of fit.

Review and Application Exercises

■ **14-49** A college football coach has a theory that in athletics, success feeds on itself. In other words, he feels that winning a championship one year increases the team's motivation to win it the next year. He expressed his theory to a student of statistics, who asked him for the records of the team's wins and losses over the last several years. The coach gave him a list, specifying whether the team had won (W) or lost (L) the championship that year. The results of this tally are

W, W, W, W, W, W, L, W, W, W, W, W, L, W, W, W, W, L, L, W, W, W, W, W, W

(a) At a 10 percent significance level, is the occurrence of wins and losses a random one?

(b) Does your answer to part (a), combined with a sight inspection of the data, tell you anything about the one-sample runs test?

■ **14-50** A small metropolitan airport recently opened a new runway, creating a new flight path over an upper-income residential area. Complaints of excessive noise had deluged the airport authority to the point that the two major airlines servicing the city had installed special engine baffles on the turbines of the jets to reduce noise and help ease the pressure on the authority. Both airlines wanted to see whether the baffles had helped to reduce the number of complaints that had been brought against the airport. If they had not, the baffles would be removed because they increased fuel consumption. Based on the following random samples of 13 days before the baffles were installed and another 13 days after installation, can it be said at the 0.02 level of significance that installing the baffles had reduced the number of complaints?

Complaints Before and After Baffles Were Installed

Before	27	15	20	24	13	18	30	46	15	29	17	21	18
After	26	23	19	12	25	9	16	12	28	20	16	14	11

■ **14-51** The American Broadcasting System (ABS) has invested a sizable amount of money into a new program for television, *High Times*. *High Times* was ABS's entry into the situation-comedy market and featured the happy-go-lucky life in a college dormitory. Unfortunately, the program had not done as well as expected, and the sponsor was considering canceling. To beef up the ratings, ABS introduced co-ed dormitories into the series. The following are the results of telephone surveys before and after the change in the series. Surveys were conducted in several major metropolitan areas, so the results are a composite from the cities.

(a) Using a U test, can you infer at the 0.10 significance level that the change in the series format helped the ratings?

(b) Do the results of your test say anything about the effect of sex on TV program ratings?

Share of Audience Before and After Change to Co-Ed Dormitories

Before	22	18	19	20	31	22	25	19	22	24	18	16	14	28	23	15	16
After	25	28	18	30	33	25	29	32	19	16	30	33	17	25			

■ **14-52** Overall readiness evaluations for military units are conducted by staff officers, with a maximum score of 100 points. Transport command officers complain that they are rated lower than infantry command officers because most of the staff officers came up through the ranks of the infantry. At the 0.05 level of significance, test the hypothesis of no difference in ratings, based on the readiness evaluations at both units during 10 randomly chosen weeks.

	Evaluation Score									
Infantry command	72	80	86	90	95	92	88	96	91	82
Transport command	80	79	90	82	81	84	78	74	85	71

Table RW 12-1 on p. 703 presented the results of the 1992 *Business Week* and *U.S. News & World Report* rankings of American business schools. Use that information to answer Exercises 14-53 and 14-54.

■ **14-53** Consider the top 10 schools in the overall *Business Week* ranking. Rescaling the student and recruiting-firm rankings for those 10 schools, we get

	Rankings	
School	**by Students**	**by Firms**
Northwestern	2	1
Chicago	7	4

(Continued)

School	Rankings by Students	by Firms
Harvard	8	3
Wharton	9	2
Michigan	6	6
Dartmouth	1	10
Stanford	3	7
Indiana	4	8
Columbia	10	5
North Carolina	5	9

At $\alpha = 0.10$, do the firms' rankings differ from the students' rankings?

■ **14-54** Considering all 20 of the schools, do the rankings by the two magazines differ significantly, at $\alpha = 0.10$?

■ **14-55** The Ways and Means Committee of the U.S. House of Representatives was attempting to evaluate the results of a tax cut given to individuals during the preceding year. The intended purpose had been to stimulate the economy, the theory being that with a tax reduction, the consumer would spend the tax savings. The committee had employed an independent consumer-research group to select a sample of households and maintain records of consumer spending both before and after the legislation was put into effect. A portion of the data from the research group follows:

Schedule of Consumer Spending

Household	Before Legislation	After Legislation	Household	Before Legislation	After Legislation
1	$ 3,578	$ 4,296	17	$11,597	$12,093
2	10,856	9,000	18	9,612	9,675
3	7,450	8,200	19	3,461	3,740
4	9,200	9,200	20	4,500	4,500
5	8,760	8,840	21	8,341	8,500
6	4,500	4,620	22	7,589	7,609
7	15,000	14,500	23	25,750	24,321
8	22,350	22,500	24	14,673	13,500
9	7,346	7,250	25	5,003	6,072
10	10,345	10,673	26	10,940	11,398
11	5,298	5,349	27	8,000	9,007
12	6,950	7,000	28	14,256	14,500
13	34,782	33,892	29	4,322	4,258
14	12,837	14,297	30	6,828	7,204
15	7,926	8,437	31	7,549	7,678
16	5,789	6,006	32	8,129	8,125

At a significance level of 3 percent, determine whether the tax-reduction policy has achieved its desired goals.

■ **14-56** Many entertainment companies have invested in theme parks with tie-ins to hit movies. Attendance depends on many factors, including the weather. Should the weather be considered a random event?

■ **14-57** Two television weather forecasters got into a discussion one day about whether years with heavy rainfall tended to occur in spurts. One of them said he thought that there were patterns of annual rainfall amounts, and that several wet years were often followed by a number of drier-than-average years. The other forecaster was skeptical and said she thought that the amount of rainfall for consecutive years was fairly random. To investigate the question, they decided to look at the annual rainfall for several years back. They found the median amount and classified the rainfall as below (B) or above (A) the median annual rainfall. A summary of their results follows:

A, A, A, B, B, B, A, B, A, A, B, B, A, B, A, B, A, A, B, B, A, A, A, B, A, A,
A, A, A, B, B, B, A, B, B, B, A, B, A, A, A, B, A, A, A, B, A, B, B, A, B, B

If the forecasters test at a 5 percent significance level, will they conclude that the annual rainfall amounts do not occur in patterns?

■ **14-58** Anne J. Montgomery, administrative director of executive education at Southern University, uses two kinds of promotional material to announce seminars: personal letters and brochures. She feels quite strongly that brochures are the more effective method. She has collected data on numbers of people attending each of the last 10 seminars promoted with each method. At the 0.15 level of significance, is her hunch right?

	Number Attending									
Personal letter	35	85	90	92	88	46	78	57	85	67
Brochure	42	74	82	87	45	73	89	75	60	94

■ **14-59** The National Association of Better Advertising for Children (NABAC), a consumer group for improving children's television, was conducting a study on the effect of Saturday morning advertising. Specifically, the group wanted to know whether a significant degree of purchasing was stimulated by advertising directed at children, and if there was a positive correlation between Saturday morning TV advertising time and product sales.

NABAC chose the children's breakfast-cereal market as a sample group. It selected products whose advertising message was aimed entirely at children. The results of the study follow. (The highest-selling cereal has sales rank 1.)

Comparison of TV Advertising Time and Product Sales

Product	Advertising Time in Minutes	Sales Rank
Captain Grumbles	0.50	10
Obnoxious Berries	3.00	1
Fruity Hoops	1.25	9
OO La Granola	2.00	5
Sweet Tweets	3.50	2
Chocolate Chumps	1.00	11
Sugar Spots	4.00	3
County Cavity	2.50	8
Crunchy Munchies	1.75	6
Karamel Kooks	2.25	4
Flakey Flakes	1.50	7

Can the group conclude that there is a *positive* rank correlation between the amount of Saturday morning advertising time and sales volume of breakfast cereals? Test at the 5 percent significance level.

Mutual funds provide an opportunity for small investors to participate in the stock market. Investors can select from more than 3,000 funds, looking for funds that will provide safety for their savings *and* the greatest total return—the dividends earned by the fund plus increases in the prices of the stocks owned by the fund. Successful funds attract more investments, so the amount of money being managed may amount to several billion dollars. Some market observers view large fund size as a disadvantage, because the fund may own so many shares of a particular firm that an attempt to liquidate a position may drive down the price. Table RW14-3 presents information about size and return for the 20 largest funds at the end of September 1992. Use that information to do Exercises 14-60 and 14-61.

14-60 (a) Is there a significant relationship between fund size and the average total return earned over the last 5 years?

(b) Is there a significant relationship between the 1992 total return and the average total return earned over the last 5 years?

14-61 Two large fund managers, Fidelity and Twentieth Century, have multiple entries on the list in Table RW 14-3. Do the performances of the funds offered by these two companies come from a different distribution than the

Table RW14-3

Twenty Largest Mutual Funds, September 1992

Fund	Size ($ billions)	Annualized Total Return (%) 1992	Annualized Total Return (%) 5-yr Avg.
Fidelity Magellan	21.05	9.51	11.24
Investment Co. of America	14.03	11.08	9.50
Washington Mutual	9.48	11.35	8.99
Windsor	8.23	9.53	7.00
Vanguard Index 500	5.77	10.87	8.73
Income Fund of America	5.64	16.33	11.57
Fidelity Puritan	5.62	15.11	9.38
Wellington	5.10	11.44	9.34
AIM Weingarten	4.98	5.77	11.07
Windsor II	4.80	14.71	9.59
Dean Witter Dividend	4.67	11.42	10.03
Janus	4.66	8.55	14.70
Fidelity Equity-Income	4.65	12.45	7.29
American Mutual	4.60	11.59	9.06
Twentieth Century Select	4.47	2.02	6.25
Twentieth Century Growth	4.40	10.84	9.52
Fidelity Growth & Income	4.29	10.51	11.80
Templeton World	4.02	7.00	5.47
Twentieth Century Ultra	4.01	1.24	14.55
Pioneer II	3.97	9.92	4.78

Source: Standard & Poor's/Lipper Mutual Fund Profiles, *6(4), (November 1992).*

performances of the remaining 13 funds? Test this for both the 1992 total returns and the 5-year average total returns.

■ **14-62** *American Motoring Magazine* recently tested two brake-disk materials for stopping effectiveness. Data representing stopping distances for both kinds of materials follow. At the 0.05 level of significance, test the hypothesis that there is no difference in the effectiveness of the materials.

Stopping Distance (feet)

Graphite bonded	110	120	130	110	100	105	110	130	145	125
Sintered bronze	100	110	135	105	105	100	100	115	135	120

■ **14-63** As part of a survey on restaurant quality, a local magazine asked area residents to rank two steak houses. On a scale of 1 to 10, subjects were to rate characteristics such as food quality, atmosphere, service, and price. After data were collected, one of the restaurant owners proposed that various statistical tests be performed. He specifically mentioned that he would like to see a mean and standard deviation for the responses to each question about each restaurant, in order to see which one had scored better. Several of the magazine workers argued against his suggestions, noting that the quality of input data would not justify a detailed statistical analysis. They argued that what was important was the residents' rankings of the two restaurants. Evaluate the arguments presented by the restaurant owner and the magazine employees.

■ **14-64** Senior business students interviewed by the Ohio Insurance Company were asked not to discuss their interviews with others in the school until the recruiter left. The recruiter, however, suspected that the later applicants knew more about what she was looking for. Were her suspicions correct? To find out, rank the interview scores received by subjects given in the table. Then test the significance of the rank correlation coefficient between the scores and interview number. Use the 0.02 significance level.

Interview Number	Score	Interview Number	Score	Interview Number	Score	Interview Number	Score
1	63	6	57	11	77	16	70
2	59	7	76	12	61	17	75
3	50	8	81	13	53	18	90
4	60	9	58	14	74	19	80
5	66	10	65	15	82	20	89

■ **14-65** More than 3 years ago, the Occupational Safety and Health Administration (OSHA) required a number of safety measures to be implemented in the Northbridge Aluminum plant. Now OSHA would like to see whether the changes have resulted in fewer accidents in the plant. It has collected these data:

Accidents at the Northbridge Plant

	Jan.	Feb.	Mar.	Apr.	May	June	July	Aug.	Sept.	Oct.	Nov.	Dec.
1992	5	3	4	2	6	4	3	3	2	4	5	3
1993	4	4	3	3	3	4	0	5	4	2	0	1
1994	3	2	1	1	0	2	4	3	2	1	1	2
1995	2	1	0	0	1	2						

(a) Determine the median number of accidents per month. If the safety measures have been effective, we should find early months falling above the median and later months below the median. Accordingly, there will be a small number of runs above and below the median. Conduct a test at the 0.03 level of significance to see whether the accidents are randomly distributed.

(b) What can you conclude about the effectiveness of the safety measures?

■ **14-66** A large countywide ambulance service calculates that for any given township it serves, during any given 6-hour shift, there is a 35 percent chance of receiving at least one call for assistance. The following is a random sampling of 90 days:

Number of shifts during which calls were received	0	1	2	3	4
Number of days	5	35	30	13	7

At the 0.05 level of significance, do these calls for assistance follow a binomial distribution?

Table RW14-4

Overseas Shipholding Group Fleet Data

Type	Registry	Built	Type	Registry	Built	Type	Registry	Built
Bulk	U.S.	1978	Bulk	Non-U.S.	1973	PPC	Non-U.S.	1981
Bulk	U.S.	1978	Bulk	Non-U.S.	1981	PPC	Non-U.S.	1981
PPC	U.S.	1983	Bulk	Non-U.S.	1983	PPC	Non-U.S.	1982
PPC	U.S.	1982	Bulk	Non-U.S.	1983	Tanker	Non-U.S.	1973
PPC	U.S.	1969	Bulk	Non-U.S.	1989	Tanker	Non-U.S.	1975
PPC	U.S.	1968	Bulk	Non-U.S.	1989	Tanker	Non-U.S.	1974
PPC	U.S.	1968	Bulk	Non-U.S.	1980	Tanker	Non-U.S.	1974
Tanker	U.S.	1974	Bulk	Non-U.S.	1980	Tanker	Non-U.S.	1989
Tanker	U.S.	1973	Bulk	Non-U.S.	1977	Tanker	Non-U.S.	1990
Tanker	U.S.	1977	Bulk	Non-U.S.	1975	Tanker	Non-U.S.	1972
Tanker	U.S.	1977	Bulk	Non-U.S.	1975	Tanker	Non-U.S.	1989
Tanker	U.S.	1978	Bulk	Non-U.S.	1985	Tanker	Non-U.S.	1989
Tanker	U.S.	1977	Bulk	Non-U.S.	1985	Tanker	Non-U.S.	1976
Tanker	U.S.	1971	PPC	Non-U.S.	1986	Tanker	Non-U.S.	1975
Tanker	U.S.	1970	PPC	Non-U.S.	1986	Tanker	Non-U.S.	1975
Bulk	Non-U.S.	1982	PPC	Non-U.S.	1986	Tanker	Non-U.S.	1986
Bulk	Non-U.S.	1982	PPC	Non-U.S.	1987	Tanker	Non-U.S.	1987
Bulk	Non-U.S.	1975	PPC	Non-U.S.	1989	Tanker	Non-U.S.	1980
Bulk	Non-U.S.	1975	PPC	Non-U.S.	1988	Tanker	Non-U.S.	1981
Bulk	Non-U.S.	1990	PPC	Non-U.S.	1989	Tanker	Non-U.S.	1979
Bulk	Non-U.S.	1990	PPC	Non-U.S.	1989			
Bulk	Non-U.S.	1973	PPC	Non-U.S.	1979			

Source: Overseas Shipholding Group, Inc., 1991 Annual Report.

The Overseas Shipholding Group, Inc., has ownership interest in 64 vessels, classified as bulk carriers, petroleum products carriers (PPC), or tankers. The ships' types, registry, and the years in which they were built are given in Table RW14-4. Use this information to do Exercises 14-67 and 14-68.

14-67 Are the U.S. and non-U.S. fleets the same age? That is, can you conclude that the years-built data for the two fleets come from the same distribution?

14-68 Are the age distributions of the three types of carriers significantly different?

■ 14-69 Jim Bailey, owner of Crow's Nest Marina, believes that the number of hours a boat engine has been run in salt water and not the age of the boat is the best predictor of engine failure. His service manager has collected data from his repair records on failed engines. At the 0.05 level of significance, is Jim's hunch right?

Engine	Hours in Salt Water	Age of Engine (years)	Cost of Repair (dollars)
1	300	4	625
2	150	6	350
3	200	3	390
4	250	6	530
5	100	4	200
6	400	5	1,000
7	275	6	550
8	350	6	800
9	325	3	700
10	375	2	600

■ 14-70 SavEnergy, an international activist group concerned about the gross domination of Western areas in energy usage, has claimed that population size and energy consumption are negatively correlated. Their opponents claim no correlation is present. Using the following data, test the hypothesis that no rank correlation exists between population and energy consumption, versus SavEnergy's negative correlation claim. Use the 0.10 level of significance.

	1989 Population (000,000 omitted)	Total Energy Consumption (10^{15} joules)
United States	249	68
Latin America	438	16
Africa	646	11
Europe	499	65
Soviet Union	289	54
India	835	9
China	1,100	24

■ 14-71 Highway crashes killed more than 75,000 occupants of passenger cars during 1993–1996. Using that grim statistic as a starting point, researchers at the Insurance Institute for Highway Safety computed death rates for the 103 largest-selling vehicle series. Vehicles were categorized as station wagons & vans, four-door cars, two-door cars, or sports & specialty cars. Further stratification in each category labeled vehicles as large, midsize, or small. Looking at the rates (deaths per 10,000 registered vehicles) for four-door cars, the figures are as follows:

Large	1.2	1.3	1.4	1.5	1.5	1.5	1.6	1.8		
Midsize	1.1	1.2	1.2	1.2	1.3	1.3	1.3	1.3	1.4	1.4
	1.5	1.6	1.6	1.6	1.7	1.7	1.8	1.9	2.0	2.3
	2.3	2.4	2.5	2.6	2.9					
Small	1.1	1.5	1.6	1.7	1.8	2.0	2.0	2.0	2.3	2.5
	2.6	2.8	3.2	4.1						

Use the Kruskal–Wallis test to test whether the three population means are equal. Test at the 0.05 level of significance.

■ **14-72** The year 1996 was particularly bad for injuries to professional baseball players. From the following data, does a sign test for paired data indicate that American League players suffered significantly more injuries than their National League counterparts? Use a 0.05 level of significance.

Injury Location	AL	NL	Injury Location	AL	NL
Shoulder	46	22	Back	10	7
Neck	3	0	Wrist	10	2
Rib	7	5	Hip	1	1
Elbow	21	19	Hand	6	4
Finger	7	5	Ankle	6	4
Thigh	17	14	Foot	1	4
Groin	7	3	Toe	0	1
Knee	16	18	Other	10	4

■ **14-73** Recent research about the kinds of weather patterns that may be correlated with sunspots, has focused on polar temperature (the average temperature in the stratosphere above the North Pole) during periods when certain equatorial winds are blowing. When these winds are from the west, the polar temperature appears to rise and fall with solar activity. When the winds are easterly, the temperature appears to do the opposite of what the sun is doing. From the data, calculate the coefficients of rank correlation between these variables and test, at the 0.05 level of significance, if the hypothesized relationships hold (i.e., positive correlation for westerly winds, negative correlation for easterly winds).

	Polar Temperature (°F)	
Solar Activity	East Winds	West Winds
230	−85	−76
160	−97	−86
95	−88	−100
75	−85	−110
100	−90	−108
165	−96	−85
155	−91	−70
120	−76	−100
75	−80	−110
65	−86	−112
125	−90	−99
195	−104	−91
190	−95	−93
125	−99	−99
75	−73	−103

■ **14-74** On December 31, 1992, the New Jersey Expressway Authority issued a call to redeem some of its $5,000 bonds. The bonds were part of a $45,000,000 issue of 9,000 bonds, paying an interest rate of 4.85 percent and originally due to mature in 2001. The Authority either had cash on hand or else had found a less expensive source of money, and it called the bonds to reduce its interest expense. The bonds selected for redemption were numbered:

5	8	16	21	183	646	1018	1044	1045	1233
1616	1794	1908	2069	2072	2172	2922	2927	2930	3044
3925	4225	4283	4303	4312	4316	4347	4380	5189	6266
6281	6291	7107	7114	7128	7145	7230	7394	8162	8172
8179	8180								

Source: The Wall Street Journal *(January 7, 1993) p. C20.*

(a) Assuming that the bonds were randomly selected for redemption, how many would you expect to see with numbers between 1 and 1500, 1501 and 3000, . . ., 7501 and 9000?

(b) Use the chi-square goodness-of-fit test discussed in Chapter 11 to see whether it is reasonable to conclude that the called bonds were randomly selected.

(c) Use the Kolmogorov–Smirnov test to see whether random selection of the called bonds is a reasonable hypothesis.

(d) Compare your results in parts (b) and (c).

■ **14-75** "Technical" stock analysts carefully examine trading patterns in stock prices and, at the limit, ignore "fundamental" news about a company's (or an industry's) performance and prospects. One analyst looked at each half hour of trading for the Dow Jones Industrial Average from January 1987 to April 1991 and noted when the average was up (U) or down (D) as compared with the previous half hour. Is the following sequence of up and down half hours of trading during a single week a random pattern?

Monday	DUDDUUUUDUUUUU
Tuesday	UUDDDDUDDDUUDU
Wednesday	UUDUUUUUDDUDUD
Thursday	UDDUUUUUDDUUUD
Friday	UUDUUUUUDDDUUU

Source: Yale Hirsch, The 1993 Stock Trader's Almanac *(Old Tappan, NJ: The Hirsch Organization) 1992, p. 117.*

■ **14-76** Managers in service-operations businesses have to handle peak times, when many customers arrive at once. The manager of the information booth at a suburban mall collected the following data on arrivals per minute between 7:10 and 8:00 on Thursday, the mall's late shopping night:

Number of Arrivals	1	2	3	4	5	6	7	8	9	10	11
Frequency	5	3	2	6	6	2	6	10	4	4	2

Test whether a Poisson distribution with a mean of 6 adequately describes these data. Use the 0.05 level of significance.

■ **14-77** The results of the Carolina Athletic Association's first 10K run showed the following order of male and female finishers:

M M M M M M M M M M M M M W M M M M M M W M M M M
M W M M M M M M M M M W M W M M M M W M M M M W M
M W M M M M M M W M M W M M M W W W W M W M W W M
W M M M W M W W M W W W W M M W M M

Did the women finish randomly throughout? Use the 0.20 level of significance.

■ **14-78** Several groups were given a list of 30 activities and technological advances and were asked to rank them, considering the risk of dying as a consequence of each. The results are in the following table. Calculate the rank correlation coefficient of each group relative to the experts' ranking. Which group seemed to have the most accurate perception of the risks involved?

A = Experts
B = League of Women Voters
C = College Students
D = Civic Club Members

Risk	A	B	C	D
Motor vehicles	1	2	5	3
Smoking	2	4	3	4
Alcoholic beverages	3	6	7	5
Handguns	4	3	2	1
Surgery	5	10	11	9
Motorcycles	6	5	6	2
X-rays	7	22	17	24
Pesticides	8	9	4	15
Electric power (nonnuclear)	9	18	19	19
Swimming	10	19	30	17
Contraceptives	11	20	9	22
General (private) aviation	12	7	15	11
Large construction	13	12	14	13
Food preservatives	14	25	12	28
Bicycles	15	16	24	14
Commercial aviation	16	17	16	18
Police work	17	8	8	7
Fire fighting	18	11	10	6
Railroads	19	24	23	20
Nuclear power	20	1	1	8
Food coloring	21	26	20	30
Home appliances	22	29	27	27
Hunting	23	13	18	10
Prescription antibiotics	24	28	21	26
Vaccinations	25	30	29	29
Spray cans	26	14	13	23
High school & college football	27	23	26	21
Power mowers	28	27	28	25
Mountain climbing	29	15	22	12
Skiing	30	21	25	16

■ **14-79** In testing a new hayfever medication, researchers measured the incidence of adverse side effects of the drug by administering it to a large number of patients and evaluating them against a control group. The percentages of patients reporting 13 types of side effects were recorded. Using a sign test for paired data, can you determine whether, on the whole, either group experienced more adverse side effects? Use the 0.10 significance level.

Side Effect	Drug	Control
A	9.0	18.1
B	6.3	3.8
C	2.9	5.8
D	1.4	1.0
E	0.9	0.6
F	0.9	0.2
G	0.6	0.0
H	4.6	2.7
I	2.3	3.5
J	0.9	0.5
K	0.5	0.5
L	0.0	0.2
M	1.0	1.4

■ **14-80** Commercial banking has experienced substantial consolidation as large regional banks have acquired smaller banks and some mid-sized firms have merged. The following table shows the rank of the top 10 banks (by total assets) in 1995, and the ranking the group members would have had among themselves in 1985. At the 10 percent significance level, is it true that the "big get bigger," or has competition between banks led to significant changes in the rankings?

Bank	1995 Rank	1985 Rank
Citicorp	1	1
BankAmerica	2	2
NationsBank	3	8
Chemical	4	5
J. P. Morgan	5	4
First Union	6	10
Chase Manhattan	7	3
First Chicago	8	7
Bankers Trust	9	6
Banc One	10	9

Source: "Creating New Giants," The Wall Street Journal *(14 July 1995): A4.*

Chapter Concepts Test

Circle the correct answer, or fill in the blank. *Answers are in the back of the book.*

T F 1. One advantage of nonparametric methods is that some of the tests do not require us even to rank the observations.

T F 2. The Mann–Whitney *U* test is one of a family of tests known as rank-difference tests.

T F 3. A sign test for paired data is based on the binomial distribution but can often be approximated by the normal distribution.

T F 4. One disadvantage of nonparametric methods is that they tend to ignore a certain amount of information.

T F 5. In the Mann–Whitney *U* test, two samples, of sizes n_1 and n_2, are taken to determine the *U* statistic. The sampling distribution of the *U* statistic can be approximated by the normal distribution when either n_1 or n_2 is greater than 10.

T F 6. The Mann–Whitney *U* test tends to waste less data than the sign test.

T F 7. Assume that in a rank test, two elements are tied for the tenth rank position. We assign each of them a rank of 10.5 and the next element after these two receives a rank of 11.

T F 8. In contrast to regression analysis, where one may compute a coefficient of correlation, an equivalent measure may be determined in a ranking of two variables in nonparametric testing. This equivalent measure is called a rank-correlation coefficient.

T F 9. In a one-sample runs test, the number of runs is a statistic that has its own sampling distribution.

T F 10. One disadvantage in using the rank-correlation coefficient is that it is very sensitive to extreme observations in the data set.

T F 11. The Kolmogorov–Smirnov test can be used to measure the goodness-of-fit of a theoretical distribution.

T F 12. Nonparametric methods are more efficient than parametric methods.

T F 13. The one-sample runs test enables us to determine whether two independent samples have been drawn from populations with the same distributions.

T F 14. The sequence A, A, B, A, B, contains four runs.

T F 15. A rank correlation coefficient of -1 represents a perfect inverse rank correlation.

T F 16. In a one-sample runs test, the alternative hypothesis is that the sequence of observations is not random.

T F 17. In the Mann–Whitney *U* test, it is not necessary that the two samples be of the same size.

T F 18. The K–S test statistic is simply the minimum absolute deviation between the observed relative cumulative frequencies and the expected relative cumulative frequencies.

T F 19. The rank sum test tests the hypothesis that several population means are equal, provided the populations are normally distributed with equal variances.

T F 20. The Kruskal–Wallis test is a nonparametric version of ANOVA.

T F 21. The sampling distribution of the Kruskal–Wallis *K* statistic can be approximated by a chi-square distribution only if all sample sizes are at least 5.

A B C D 22. In a sign test for paired data, 800 students were asked to give ranks (on a scale of 0 to 10) for their attitudes toward true–false and multiple-choice tests. When signs were calculated for the two sets of paired data, 138 of the 800 paired responses received a value of 0. Does this mean that 138 students:

(a) Did not like either type of test?

(b) Did not answer the survey?

(c) Ranked the types equally?

(d) Thought one of the types was perfect and the other was awful?

A B C D 23. Suppose that, in Question 22, the administration felt that true–false tests were liked three times as well as multiple-choice tests. Assuming that a preference for true–false tests is a "success," what is the null hypothesis for the administration's sign test for paired data?

(a) $p = 0.25$.

(b) $p = 0.75$.

(c) $p \neq 0.25$.

(d) $p \neq 0.75$.

Questions 24 and 25 refer to the following situation. Five former patients are selected at random from Ward A at Trinity Hospital, and four former patients are selected at random from Ward B. The patients stayed the following number of days:

Ward A	13	4	2	10	6
Ward B	10	9	7	8	

A B C D 24. A Mann–Whitney *U* test is to be performed to determine whether there is a significant difference between the lengths of the hospital stays for the two wards. If the lengths of stay are ranked from shortest to longest, what is the ranking for the 13-day stay in Ward A?

(a) 9.

(b) 8.

(c) $9\,{}^{1}/_{2}$.

(d) $7\,{}^{1}/_{2}$.

A B C D 25. If the lengths of stay are ranked from shortest to longest, what is the value of: $(R_1 - R_2)$

(a) $-{}^{1}/_{2}$.

(b) 0.

(c) ${}^{1}/_{2}$.

(d) $2\,{}^{1}/_{2}$.

A B C D 26. What is the maximum number of runs possible in a sequence of length 5 using two symbols?

(a) 6.

(b) 4.

(c) 3.

(d) 5.

A B C D E 27. The sequence of C, D, C, D, C, D, C, D, C, D would probably be rejected by a test of runs as not being truly random because:

(a) The pattern C, D occurs only five times; this is not often enough to guarantee randomness.

(b) The sequence contains too many runs.

(c) The sequence contains too few runs.

(d) The sequence contains only two symbols.

(e) None of these.

A B C D 28. In a Mann–Whitney U test, a particular sampling distribution for U has a mean of 15. One value of U is calculated as $n_1n_2 + n_1(n_1 + 1)/2 - R_1$, which equals 22.5. We immediately conclude that the value of $n_1n_2 + n_2(n_2 + 1)/2 - R_2$ in this situation is:

(a) 10.

(b) 12.5.

(c) 7.5.

(d) Cannot be determined from the information given.

Questions 29 to 31 refer to the following situation: Seven executives (denoted A–G) were ranked from 1 to 7 on a scale of yearly salary level, with 1 being highest. The results were:

A	B	C	D	E	F	G
2	6	4	1	3	5	7

A B C D E 29. Which of the following is correct?

(a) E earned more than four others.

(b) C and F earned the same amount.

(c) C's earnings are less than those of four others.

(d) All of these.

(e) (a) and (c) but not (b).

A B C D 30. Suppose that, as the second part of this study, the seven executives are ranked according to how happy they seem to be, with 1 being the happiest. If salaries and happiness are perfectly correlated, what must be the happiness ranking for businessman A?

(a) 1.

(b) 2.

(c) 3.

(d) 6.

A B C D 31. If, in the happiness ranking of question 30, salaries and happiness were perfectly inversely correlated, what must be the happiness ranking of executive F?

(a) 7.

(b) 2.

(c) 5.

(d) 3.

A B C D E F G 32. When compared to parametric methods, nonparametric methods:

(a) Are less accurate.

(b) Are less efficient.

(c) Are computationally easier.

(d) Require less information.

(e) All of these.

(f) (b), (c), and (d), but not (a).

(g) None of these.

A B C D 33. For a perfect correlation, the coefficient of rank correlation r_s would be:

(a) Equal to 1.

(b) Between 0 and −1.

(c) Equal to 0.

(d) None of these.

A B C D 34. For samples of size greater than 30, the sampling distribution of the rank-correlation coefficient is approximately which distribution?

(a) t.

(b) Binomial.

(c) Chi-square.

(d) Normal.

A B C D 35. In the Kruskal–Wallis test of k samples, the appropriate number of degrees of freedom is:

(a) k.

(b) $k - 1$.

(c) $n_k - 1$.

(d) $n - k$.

A B C D 36. Choose the sample with the largest rank sum if elements are ranked from largest to smallest:

Sample A	1	3	9
Sample B	5	1	8
Sample C	9	4	2

(a) C with rank sum 15.

(b) C with rank sum 20.5.

(c) A with rank sum 16.

(d) B with rank sum 14.5.

37. A sequence of identical occurrences preceded and followed by different occurrences or none at all is a ________________________.

38. A nonparametric method used to determine whether two independent samples have been drawn from populations with the same distribution is the ________________________.

39. A nonparametric technique for determining the randomness with which sampled items have been selected is the ________________________.

40. A ________________________ test tests for the difference between paired observations by substituting +, −, and 0 for quantitative values.

41. A ________________________ coefficient measures the degree of association between two variables and is based on the ranks of the observations.

42. The U statistic has a special property that enables us to save computational time when ________________________.

43. To distinguish it from the coefficient of correlation, the rank coefficient of correlation is denoted ________________.

44. The K–S statistic D_n is a ________________ statistic in that it is independent of the expected frequency distribution.

45. The ________________ test has advantages over the chi-square test for goodness-of-fit because the data need not be grouped in any way.

● Flow Chart: Nonparametric Methods

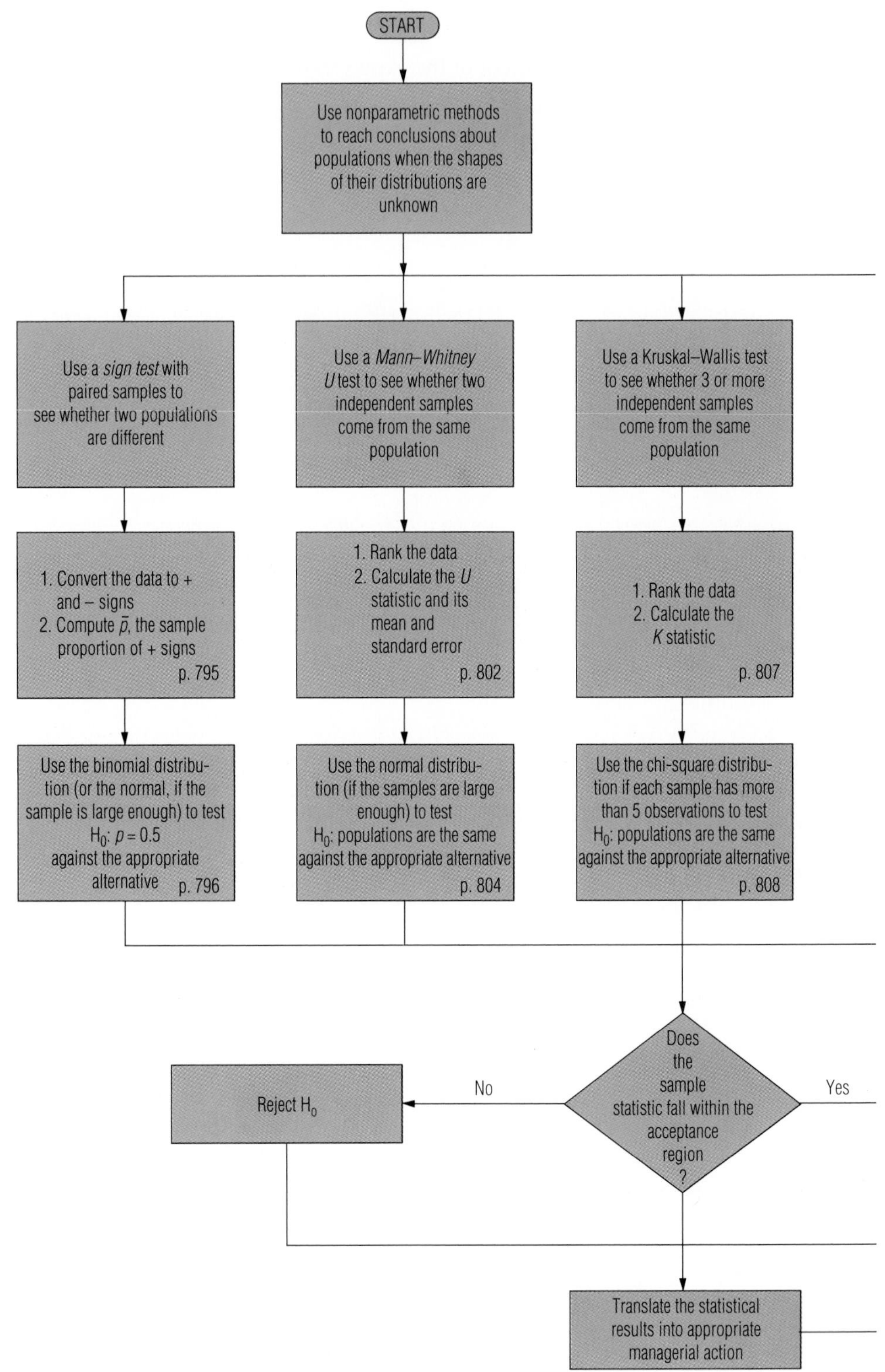

START
Use nonparametric methods to reach conclusions about populations when the shapes of their distributions are unknown
Use a *sign test* with paired samples to see whether two populations are different
Use a *Mann–Whitney U* test to see whether two independent samples come from the same population
Use a Kruskal–Wallis test to see whether 3 or more independent samples come from the same population
1. Convert the data to + and – signs
2. Compute $\bar{p}$, the sample proportion of + signs
p. 795
1. Rank the data
2. Calculate the U statistic and its mean and standard error
p. 802
1. Rank the data
2. Calculate the K statistic
p. 807
Use the binomial distribution (or the normal, if the sample is large enough) to test H_0: $p = 0.5$ against the appropriate alternative
p. 796
Use the normal distribution (if the samples are large enough) to test H_0: populations are the same against the appropriate alternative
p. 804
Use the chi-square distribution if each sample has more than 5 observations to test H_0: populations are the same against the appropriate alternative
p. 808
Does the sample statistic fall within the acceptance region?
No
Yes
Reject H_0
Translate the statistical results into appropriate managerial action

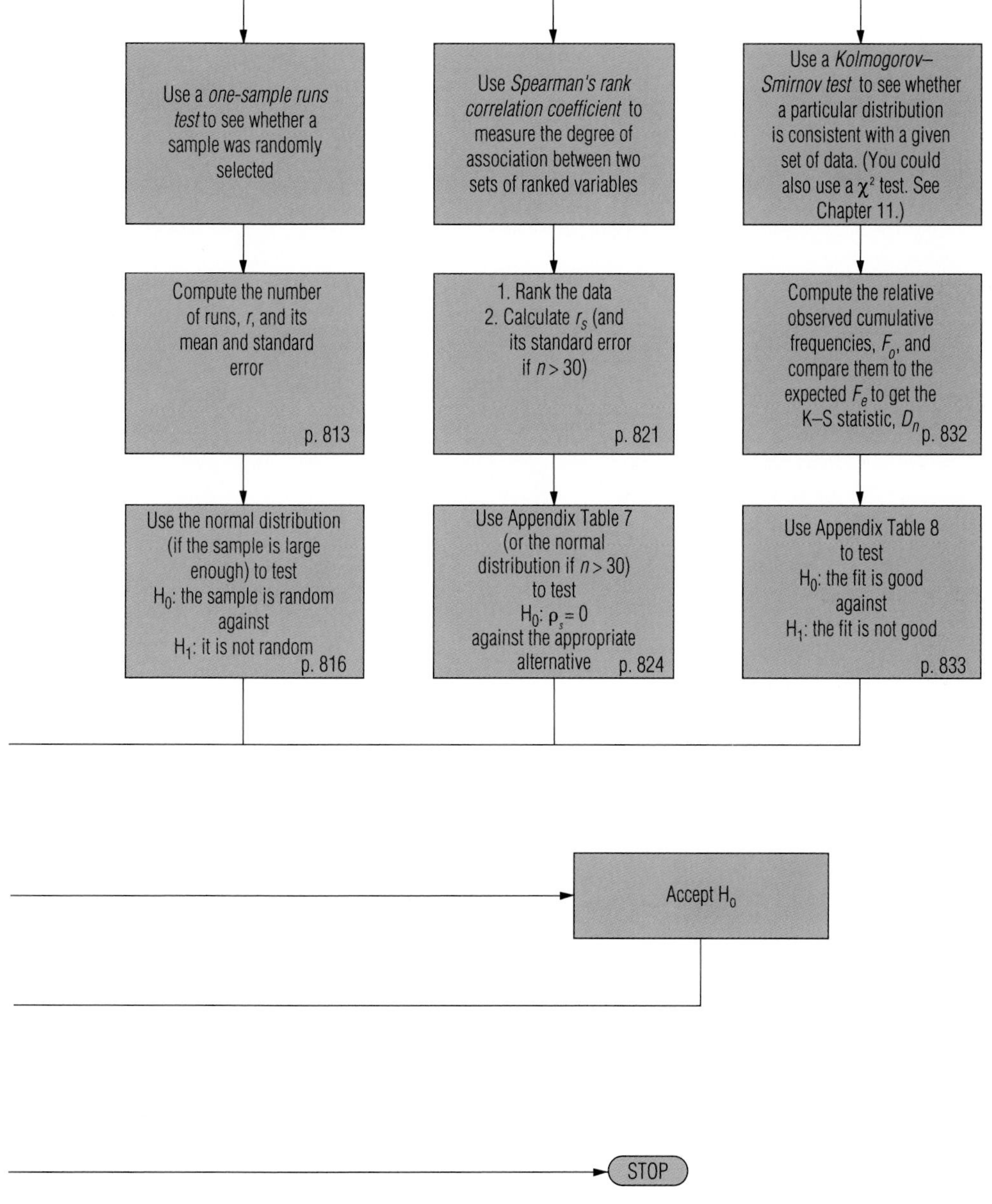

Use a *one-sample runs test* to see whether a sample was randomly selected
Use *Spearman's rank correlation coefficient* to measure the degree of association between two sets of ranked variables
Use a *Kolmogorov–Smirnov test* to see whether a particular distribution is consistent with a given set of data. (You could also use a χ^2 test. See Chapter 11.)
Compute the number of runs, r, and its mean and standard error
p. 813
1. Rank the data
2. Calculate r_s (and its standard error if $n > 30$)
p. 821
Compute the relative observed cumulative frequencies, F_o, and compare them to the expected F_e to get the K–S statistic, D_n
p. 832
Use the normal distribution (if the sample is large enough) to test
H_0: the sample is random
against
H_1: it is not random
p. 816
Use Appendix Table 7 (or the normal distribution if $n > 30$) to test
H_0: $\rho_s = 0$
against the appropriate alternative
p. 824
Use Appendix Table 8 to test
H_0: the fit is good
against
H_1: the fit is not good
p. 833
Accept H_0
STOP

chapter 15

TIME SERIES AND FORECASTING

Objectives

- To learn why forecasting changes that take place over time are an important part of decision making
- To understand the four components of a time series
- To use regression-based techniques to estimate and forecast the trend in a time series
- To learn how to measure the cyclical component of a time series
- To compute seasonal indices and use them to deseasonalize a time series
- To be able to recognize irregular variation in a time series
- To deal simultaneously with all four components of a time series and to use time-series analysis for forecasting

Chapter Contents

The management of a ski resort has these quarterly occupancy data over a 5-year period:

Year	1st Qtr	2nd Qtr	3rd Qtr	4th Qtr
1991	1,861	2,203	2,415	1,908
1992	1,921	2,343	2,514	1,986
1993	1,834	2,154	2,098	1,799
1994	1,837	2,025	2,304	1,965
1995	2,073	2,414	2,339	1,967

To improve service, management must understand the seasonal pattern of demand for rooms. Using methods covered in this chapter, we shall help the hotel discern such a seasonal pattern, if it exists, and use it to forecast demand for rooms. ■

15.1 Introduction

Forecasting, or predicting, is an essential tool in any decision-making process. Its uses vary from determining inventory requirements for a local shoe store to estimating the annual sales of video games. The quality of the forecasts management can make is strongly related to the information that can be extracted and used from past data. *Time-series analysis* is one quantitative method we use to determine patterns in data collected over time. Table 15-1 is an example of time-series data.

Use of time-series analysis

Time-series analysis is used to detect patterns of change in statistical information over regular intervals of time. We *project* these patterns to arrive at an estimate for the future. Thus, time-series analysis helps us cope with uncertainty about the future.

Table 15-1 Time Series for the Number of Ships Loaded at Morehead City, N.C.

Year	1988	1989	1990	1991	1992	1993	1994	1995
Number	98	105	116	119	135	156	177	208

Exercises 15.1

Basic Concepts

- ■ **15-1** Of what value are forecasts in the decision-making process?
- ■ **15-2** For what purpose do we apply time-series analysis to data collected over a period of time?
- ■ **15-3** How can one benefit from determining past patterns?
- ■ **15-4** How would errors in forecasts affect a city government?

15.2 Variations in Time Series

Four kinds of variation in time-series

We use the term *time series* to refer to any group of statistical information accumulated at regular intervals. There are four kinds of change, or variation, involved in time-series analysis:

1. Secular trend
2. Cyclical fluctuation
3. Seasonal variation
4. Irregular variation

Secular trend

With the first type of change, *secular trend,* the value of the variable tends to increase or decrease over a long period of time. The steady increase in the cost of living recorded by the Consumer Price Index is an example of secular trend. From year to individual year, the cost of living varies a great deal, but if we examine a long-term period, we see that the trend is toward a steady increase. Figure 15-1(a) shows a secular trend in an increasing but fluctuating time series.

Cyclical fluctuation

The second type of variation seen in a time series is *cyclical fluctuation.* The most common example of cyclical fluctuation is the business cycle. Over time, there are years when the business cycle hits a peak above the trend line. At other times, business activity is likely to slump, hitting a low point below the trend line. The time between hitting peaks or falling to low points is at least 1 year, and it can be as many as 15 or 20 years. Figure 15-1(b) illustrates a typical pattern of cyclical fluctuation above and below a secular trend line. Note that the cyclical movements do not follow any regular pattern but move in a somewhat unpredictable manner.

Seasonal variation

The third kind of change in time-series data is *seasonal variation.* As we might expect from the name, seasonal variation involves patterns of change within a year that tend to be repeated from year to year. For example, a physician can expect a substantial increase in the number of flu cases every winter and of poison ivy every summer. Because these are regular patterns, they are useful in forecasting the future. In Figure 15-1(c), we see a seasonal variation. Notice how it peaks in the fourth quarter of each year.

Irregular variation

Irregular variation is the fourth type of change in time-series analysis. In many situations, the value of a variable may be completely unpredictable, changing in a random manner. Irregular variations describe such movements. The effects of the Middle East conflict in 1973, the Iranian situation in 1979–1981, the collapse of OPEC in 1986, and the Iraqi situation in 1990 on gasoline prices in the United States are examples of irregular variation. Figure 15-1(d) illustrates irregular variation.

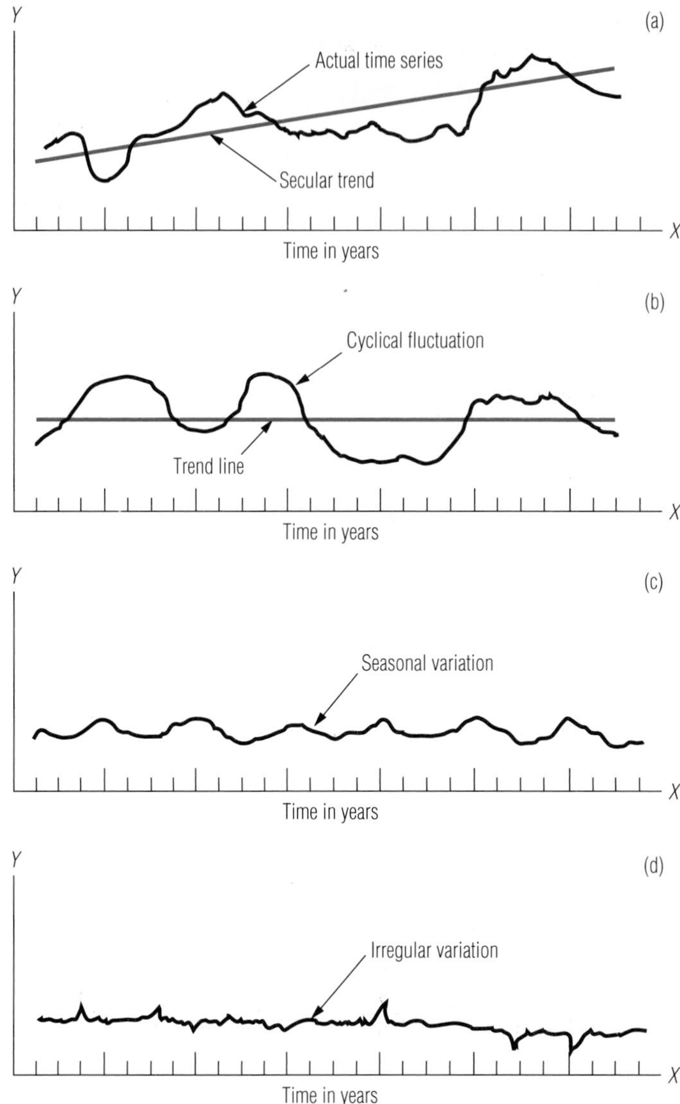

FIGURE 15-1
Time-series variations

Thus far, we have referred to a time series as exhibiting one or another of these four types of variation. In most instances, however, a time series will contain several of these components. Thus, we can describe the overall variation in a single time series in terms of these four different kinds of variation. In the following sections, we will examine the four components and the ways in which we measure each.

Exercises 15.2

Basic Concepts

■ **15-5** Identify the four principal components of a time series and explain the kind of change, over time, to which each applies.

- **15-6** Which of the four components of a time series would we use to describe the effect of Christmas sales on a retail department store?
- **15-7** What is the advantage of decomposing a time series into its four components?
- **15-8** Which of the four components of a time series might the U.S. Department of Agriculture use to describe a 7-year weather pattern?
- **15-9** How would a war be accounted for in a time series?
- **15-10** What component of a time series explains the general growth and decline of the steel industry over the last two centuries?
- **15-11** Using the four kinds of variation, describe the behavior of crude oil prices from 1970 to 1987.

15.3 Trend Analysis

Two methods of fitting a trend line

Of the four components of a time series, secular trend represents the long-term direction of the series. One way to describe the trend component is to fit a line visually to a set of points on a graph. Any given graph, however, is subject to slightly different interpretations by different individuals. We can also fit a trend line by the method of least squares, which we examined in Chapter 12. In our discussion, we will concentrate on the method of least squares because visually fitting a line to a time series is not a completely dependable process.

Reasons for Studying Trends

There are three reasons why it is useful to study secular trends:

Three reasons for studying secular trends

1. **The study of secular trends allows us to describe a historical pattern.** There are many instances when we can use a past trend to evaluate the success of a previous policy. For example, a university may evaluate the effectiveness of a recruiting program by examining its past enrollment trends.
2. **Studying secular trends permits us to project past patterns, or trends, into the future.** Knowledge of the past can tell us a great deal about the future. Examining the growth rate of the world's population, for example, can help us estimate the population for some future time.
3. **In many situations, studying the secular trend of a time series allows us to eliminate the trend component from the series.** This makes it easier for us to study the other three components of the time series. If we want to determine the seasonal variation in ski sales, for example, eliminating the trend component gives us a more accurate idea of the seasonal component.

Trend lines take different forms

Trends can be linear or curvilinear. Before we examine the linear, or straight-line, method of describing trends, we should remember that some relationships do not take that form. The increase of pollutants in the environment follows an upward sloping curve similar to that in Figure 15-2(a). Another common example of a curvilinear relationship is the life cycle of a new business product, illustrated in Figure 15-2(b). When a new product is introduced, its sales volume is low (I). As the product gains recognition and success, unit sales grow at an increasingly rapid rate (II). After the product is firmly established, its unit sales grow at a stable rate (III). Finally, as the product reaches the end of its life cycle, unit sales begin to decrease (IV).

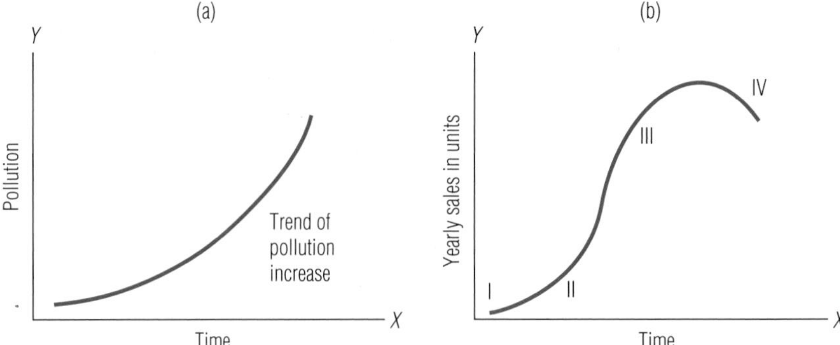

FIGURE 15-2

Curvilinear trend relationships

Fitting the Linear Trend by the Least-Squares Method

Besides trends that can be described by a curved line, there are others that are described by a straight line. These are called linear trends. Before developing the equation for a linear trend, we need to review the general equation for estimating a straight line (Equation 12-3):

Equation for estimating a straight line ⟶ $$\hat{Y} = a + bX \qquad [12\text{-}3]$$

where

- $\hat{Y}$ = estimated value of the dependent variable
- X = independent variable (*time* in trend analysis)
- a = Y-intercept (the value of Y when $X = 0$)
- b = slope of the trend line

Finding the best-fitting trend line

We can describe the general trend of many time series using a straight line. But we are faced with the problem of finding the best-fitting line. As we did in Chapter 12, we can use the least-squares method to calculate the best-fitting line, or equation. There we saw that the best-fitting line was determined by Equations 12-4 and 12-5, which are now renumbered as Equations 15-1 and 15-2.

Slope of the Best-Fitting Regression Line

$$b = \frac{\Sigma XY - n\overline{X}\overline{Y}}{\Sigma X^2 - n\overline{X}^2} \qquad [15\text{-}1]$$

***Y*-Intercept of the Best-Fitting Regression Line**

$$a = \overline{Y} - b\overline{X} \qquad [15\text{-}2]$$

where

- Y = values of the dependent variable
- X = values of the independent variable

- $\bar{Y}$ = mean of the values of the dependent variable
- $\bar{X}$ = mean of the values of the independent variable
- n = number of data points in the time series
- a = Y-intercept
- b = slope

With Equations 15-1 and 15-2, we can establish the best-fitting line to describe time-series data. However, the regularity of time-series data allows us to simplify the calculations in Equations 15-1 and 15-2 through the process we shall now describe.

Translating, or Coding, Time

Coding the time variable to simplify computation

Normally, we measure the independent variable *time* in terms such as *weeks, months,* and *years.* Fortunately, we can convert these traditional measures of time to a form that simplifies the computation. In Chapter 3, we called this process *coding.* To use coding here, we find the mean time and then subtract that value from each of the sample times. Suppose our time series consists of only three points, 1992, 1993, and 1994. If we had to place these numbers in Equations 15-1 and 15-2, we would find the resultant calculations tedious. Instead, we can transform the values 1992, 1993, and 1994 into corresponding values of -1, 0, and 1, where 0 represents the mean (1993), -1 represents the first year ($1992 - 1993 = -1$), and 1 represents the last year ($1994 - 1993 = 1$).

Treating odd and even numbers of elements

We need to consider two cases when we are coding time values. The first is a time series with an *odd number of elements,* as in the previous example. The second is a series with an *even number of elements.* Consider Table 15-2. In part (a), on the left, we have an odd number of years. Thus, the process is the same as the one we just described, using the years 1992, 1993, and 1994. In part (b), on the right, we have an *even* number of elements. In cases like this, when we find the mean and subtract it from each element, the fraction $^1/_2$ becomes part

Table 15-2 Translating, or Coding, Time Values

(a) When there is an *odd* number of elements in the time series

X (1)	$X - \bar{X}$ (2)	Translated, or Coded, Time (3)
1989	1989 − 1992 =	−3
1990	1990 − 1992 =	−2
1991	1991 − 1992 =	−1
1992	1992 − 1992 =	0
1993	1993 − 1992 =	1
1994	1994 − 1992 =	2
1995	1995 − 1992 =	3
$\Sigma X = 13{,}944$		x (the mean year) = 0

$$\bar{X} = \frac{\Sigma X}{n} = \frac{13{,}944}{7} = 1992$$

(b) When there is an *even* number of elements in the time series

X (1)	$X - \bar{X}$ (2)	$(X - \bar{X}) \times 2$ (3)	Translated, or Coded, Time (4)
1990	$1990 - 1992\frac{1}{2} =$	$-2\frac{1}{2} \times 2 =$	−5
1991	$1991 - 1992\frac{1}{2} =$	$-1\frac{1}{2} \times 2 =$	−3
1992	$1992 - 1992\frac{1}{2} =$	$-\frac{1}{2} \times 2 =$	−1
1993	$1993 - 1992\frac{1}{2} =$	$\frac{1}{2} \times 2 =$	1
1994	$1994 - 1992\frac{1}{2} =$	$1\frac{1}{2} \times 2 =$	3
1995	$1995 - 1992\frac{1}{2} =$	$2\frac{1}{2} \times 2 =$	5
$\Sigma X = 11{,}955$			x (the mean year) = 0

$$\bar{X} = \frac{\Sigma X}{n} = \frac{11{,}955}{6} = 1992\frac{1}{2}$$

of the answer. To simplify the coding process and to remove the $^1/_2$, we multiply each time element by 2. We will denote the "coded," or translated, time with a lowercase x.

Why use coding?

We have two reasons for this translation of time. First, it eliminates the need to square numbers as large as 1992, 1993, 1994, and so on. This method also sets the mean year, $\bar{x}$, equal to zero and allows us to simplify Equations 15-1 and 15-2.

Simplifying the calculation of *a* and *b*

Now we can return to our calculations of the slope (Equation 15-1) and the Y-intercept (Equation 15-2) to determine the best-fitting line. Because we are using the coded variable x, we replace X and $\bar{X}$ by x and $\bar{x}$ in Equations 15-1 and 15-2. Then, because the mean of our coded time variable $\bar{x}$ is zero, we can substitute 0 for $\bar{x}$ in Equations 15-1 and 15-2, as follows:

$$b = \frac{\Sigma XY - n\bar{X}\bar{Y}}{\Sigma X^2 - n\bar{X}^2} \quad [15\text{-}1]$$

$$= \frac{\Sigma xY - n\bar{x}\bar{Y}}{\Sigma x^2 - n\bar{x}^2} \leftarrow \begin{cases} x \text{ the coded variable) substituted for } X \\ \text{and } \bar{x} \text{ substituted for } \bar{X} \end{cases}$$

$$= \frac{\Sigma xY - n0\bar{Y}}{\Sigma x^2 - n0^2} \leftarrow \bar{x} \text{ replaced by } 0$$

Slope of the Trend Line for Coded Time Values

$$b = \frac{\Sigma xY}{\Sigma x^2} \quad [15\text{-}3]$$

Equation 15-2 changes as follows:

$$a = \bar{Y} - b\bar{X} \quad [15\text{-}2]$$

$$= \bar{Y} - b\bar{x} \leftarrow \bar{x} \text{ substituted for } \bar{X}$$

$$= \bar{Y} - b0 \leftarrow \bar{x} \text{ replaced by } 0$$

Intercept of the Trend Line for Coded Time Values

$$a = \bar{Y} \quad [15\text{-}4]$$

Equations 15-3 and 15-4 represent a substantial improvement over Equations 15-1 and 15-2.

A Problem Using the Least-Squares Method in a Time Series (Even Number of Elements)

Using the least-squares method

Consider the data in Table 15-1, illustrating the number of ships loaded at Morehead City between 1988 and 1995. In this problem, we want to find the equation that will describe the secular trend of loadings. To calculate the necessary values for Equations 15-3 and 15-4, let us look at Table 15-3.

Table 15-3

Intermediate Calculations for Computing the Trend

X (1)	$Y^{\dagger}$ (2)	$X - \bar{X}$ (3)	x (3) × 2 = (4)	xY (4) × (2)	x^2 $(4)^2$
1988	98	$1988 - 1991\frac{1}{2}^{\ddagger} = -3\frac{1}{2}$	$-3\frac{1}{2} \times 2 = -7$	−686	49
1989	105	$1989 - 1991\frac{1}{2} = -2\frac{1}{2}$	$-2\frac{1}{2} \times 2 = -5$	−525	25
1990	116	$1990 - 1991\frac{1}{2} = -1\frac{1}{2}$	$-1\frac{1}{2} \times 2 = -3$	−348	9
1991	119	$1991 - 1991\frac{1}{2} = -\frac{1}{2}$	$-\frac{1}{2} \times 2 = -1$	−119	1
1992	135	$1992 - 1991\frac{1}{2} = \frac{1}{2}$	$\frac{1}{2} \times 2 = 1$	135	1
1993	156	$1993 - 1991\frac{1}{2} = 1\frac{1}{2}$	$1\frac{1}{2} \times 2 = 3$	468	9
1994	177	$1994 - 1991\frac{1}{2} = 2\frac{1}{2}$	$2\frac{1}{2} \times 2 = 5$	885	25
1995	208	$1995 - 1991\frac{1}{2} = 3\frac{1}{2}$	$3\frac{1}{2} \times 2 = 7$	1,456	49
$\Sigma X = \mathbf{15,932}$	$\Sigma Y = \mathbf{1,114}$			$\Sigma xY = \mathbf{1,266}$	$\Sigma x^2 = \mathbf{168}$

$$\bar{X} = \frac{\Sigma X}{n} = \frac{15,932}{8} = 1,991\tfrac{1}{2}$$

$$\bar{Y} = \frac{\Sigma Y}{n} = \frac{1,114}{8} = 139.25$$

† Y is the number of ships.

‡ $1991\frac{1}{2}$ corresponds to $x = 0$.

Finding the slope and Y-intercept

With these values, we can now substitute into Equations 15-3 and 15-4 to find the slope and the Y-intercept for the line describing the trend in ship loadings:

$$b = \frac{\Sigma xY}{\Sigma x^2} \qquad [15\text{-}3]$$

$$= \frac{1,266}{168}$$

$$= 7.536$$

and

$$a = \bar{Y} \qquad [15\text{-}4]$$

$$= 139.25$$

Thus, the general linear equation describing the secular trend in ship loadings is

$$\hat{Y} = a + bx \qquad [12\text{-}3]$$

$$= 139.25 + 7.536x$$

where

- $\hat{Y}$ = estimated annual number of ships loaded
- x = coded time value representing the number of *half-year* intervals (a minus sign indicates half-year intervals before $1991\frac{1}{2}$; a plus sign indicates half-year intervals after $1991\frac{1}{2}$)

Projecting with the Trend Equation

Once we have developed the trend equation, we can project it to forecast the variable in question. In the problem of finding the secular trend in ship loadings, for instance, we determined that the appropriate secular trend equation was

$$\hat{Y} = 139.25 + 7.536x$$

Using our trend line to predict

Now, suppose we want to estimate ship loadings for 1996. First, we must convert 1996 to the value of the coded time (in half-year intervals).

$$\begin{aligned} x &= 1996 - 1991\tfrac{1}{2} \\ &= 4.5 \text{ years} \\ &= 9 \text{ } \textit{half}\text{-year intervals} \end{aligned}$$

Substituting this value into the equation for the secular trend, we get= 139.25 + 67.82

$$\begin{aligned} \hat{Y} &= 139.25 + 67.82 \\ &= 139.25 + 67.82 \\ &= 207 \text{ ships loaded} \end{aligned}$$

Therefore, we have estimated 207 ships will be loaded in 1996. If the number of elements in our time series had been odd, not even, our procedure would have been the same except that we would have dealt with 1-year intervals, not half-year intervals.

Use of a Second-Degree Trend in a Time Series

Handling time series that are described by curves

So far, we have described the method of fitting a straight line to a time series. But many time series are best described by curves, not straight lines. In these instances, the linear trend model does not adequately describe the change in the variable as time changes. To overcome this problem, we often use a parabolic curve, which is described mathematically by a *second-degree equation.* Such a curve is illustrated in Figure 15-3. The general form for an estimated second-degree equation is

General Form for Fitted Second-Degree Curve

$$\hat{Y} = a + bx + cx^2 \quad [15\text{-}5]$$

where

- $\hat{Y}$ = estimate of the dependent variable
- $a, b,$ and c = numerical constants
- x = coded values of the time variable

Finding the values for *a*, *b*, and *c*

Again we use the least-squares method to determine the second-degree equation to describe the best fit. The derivation of the second-degree equation is beyond the scope of this

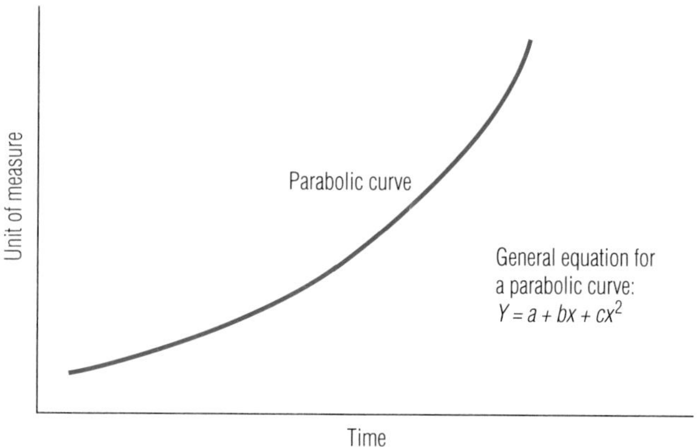

FIGURE 15-3

Form and equation for a parabolic curve

text. However, we can determine the value of the numerical constants (a, b, and c) from the following three equations:

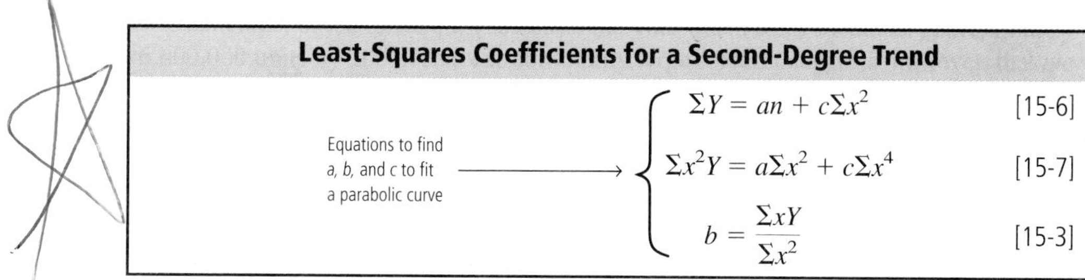

Least-Squares Coefficients for a Second-Degree Trend

Equations to find a, b, and c to fit a parabolic curve

$$\Sigma Y = an + c\Sigma x^2 \qquad [15\text{-}6]$$

$$\Sigma x^2 Y = a\Sigma x^2 + c\Sigma x^4 \qquad [15\text{-}7]$$

$$b = \frac{\Sigma xY}{\Sigma x^2} \qquad [15\text{-}3]$$

When we find the values of a, b, and c by solving Equations 15-6, 15-7, and 15-3 simultaneously, we substitute these values into the second-degree equation, Equation 15-5.

As in describing a linear relationship, we transform the independent variable, time (X), into a coded form (x) to simplify the calculation. We'll now work through a problem in which we fit a parabolic trend to a time series.

A Problem Involving a Parabolic Trend (Odd Number of Elements in the Time Series)

In recent years, the sale of electric quartz watches has increased at a significant rate. Table 15-4 contains sales information that will help us determine the parabolic trend describing watch sales.

Coding the time variable

We organize the necessary calculations in Table 15-5. The first step in this process is to translate the independent variable X into a coded time variable x. Note that the coded variable x is listed in 1-year intervals because there is an odd number of elements in our time series. Thus, it is not necessary to multiply the variable by 2.

Table 15-4

Annual Sales of Electric Quartz Watches

X (year)	1991	1992	1993	1994	1995
Y (unit sales in millions)	13	24	39	65	106

■ **15-19** The State Department of Motor Vehicles is studying the number of traffic fatalities in the state resulting from drunk driving for each of the last 9 years.

Year	1987	1988	1989	1990	1991	1992	1993	1994	1995
Deaths	175	190	185	195	180	200	185	190	205

(a) Find the linear equation that describes the trend in the number of traffic fatalities in the state resulting from drunk driving.

(b) Estimate the number of traffic fatalities resulting from drunk driving that the state can expect in 1996.

Worked-Out Answers to Self-Check Exercises

SC 15-1 (a)

Year	x	Y	xY	x^2
1987	−9	42	−378	81
1988	−7	50	−350	49
1989	−5	61	−305	25
1990	−3	75	−225	9
1991	−1	92	−92	1
1992	1	111	111	1
1993	3	120	360	9
1994	5	127	635	25
1995	7	140	980	49
1996	9	138	1242	81
	0	**956**	**1,978**	**330**

$$a = \bar{Y} = \frac{956}{10} = 95.6 \qquad b = \frac{\Sigma xY}{\Sigma x^2} = \frac{1,978}{330} = 5.9939$$

$\hat{Y} = 95.6 + 5.9939x$ (where $1991.5 = 0$ and x units $= 0.5$ year)

(b) $\hat{Y} = 95.6 + 5.9939(13) = 173.5$ tables

SC 15-2

Year	x	Y	xY	x^2	x^2Y	x^4
1990	−5	50	−250	25	1,250	625
1991	−3	110	−330	9	990	81
1992	−1	350	−350	1	350	1
1993	1	1,020	1,020	1	1,020	1
1994	3	1,950	5,850	9	17,550	81
1995	5	3,710	18,550	25	92,750	625
	0	**7,190**	**24,490**	**70**	**113,910**	**1,414**

(a) $$a = \bar{Y} = \frac{7,190}{6} = 1,198.3333 \qquad b = \frac{\Sigma xY}{\Sigma x^2} = \frac{24,490}{70} = 349.8571$$

$\hat{Y} = 1,198.3333 + 349.8571x$ (where $1992.5 = 0$ and x units $= 0.5$ year)

(b) Equations 15.6 and 15.7 become

$$\Sigma Y = na + c\Sigma x^2 \qquad 7,190 = 6a + 70c$$

$$\Sigma x^2Y = a\Sigma x^2 + c\Sigma x^4 \qquad 113,910 = 70a + 1,414c$$

Solving these simultaneously, we get

$$a = 611.8750, c = 50.2679$$

$$\hat{Y} = 611.8750 + 349.8571x + 50.2679x^2$$

(c) Linear forecast: $\hat{Y} = 1{,}198.3333 + 349.8571(13) = 5{,}746$ PCs

Second-degree equation forecast : $\hat{Y} = 611.8750 + 349.8571(13) + 50.2679(169) = 13{,}655$ PCs

(d) Neither is very good. The linear trend missed the acceleration in the rate of faculty PC acquisition. The second-degree trend assumed the acceleration would continue, ignoring the fact that there are only 8,000 faculty members.

15.4 Cyclical Variation

Cyclical variation defined

Cyclical variation is the component of a time series that tends to oscillate above and below the secular trend line for periods longer than 1 year. The procedure used to identify cyclical variation is the residual method.

Residual Method

When we look at a time series consisting of annual data, only the secular-trend, cyclical, and irregular components are considered. (This is true because seasonal variation makes a complete, regular cycle within each year and thus does not affect one year any more than another.) Because we can describe secular trend using a trend line, we can isolate the remaining cyclical and irregular components from the trend. We will assume that the cyclical component explains most of the variation left unexplained by the trend component. (Many real-life time series do not satisfy this assumption. Methods such as Fourier analysis and spectral analysis can analyze the cyclical component for such time series. However, these are beyond the scope of this book.)

Expressing cyclical variation as a percent of trend

If we use a time series composed of annual data, we can find the fraction of the trend by dividing the actual value (Y) by the corresponding trend value ($\hat{Y}$) for each value in the time series. We then multiply the result of this calculation by 100. This gives us the measure of cyclical variation as a *percent of trend.* We express this process in Equation 15-8:

Percent of Trend

$$\frac{Y}{\hat{Y}} \times 100 \qquad [15\text{-}8]$$

where

- Y = actual time-series value
- $\hat{Y}$ = estimated trend value from the same point in the time series

Table 15-6 Grain Received by Farmers' Cooperative Over 8 Years	X Year	Y Actual Bushels (× 10,000)	$\hat{Y}$ Estimated Bushels (× 10,000)
	1988	7.5	7.6
	1989	7.8	7.8
	1990	8.2	8.0
	1991	8.2	8.2
	1992	8.4	8.4
	1993	8.5	8.6
	1994	8.7	8.8
	1995	9.1	9.0

Now let's apply this procedure.

Measuring variation

A farmers' marketing cooperative wants to measure the variations in its members' wheat harvest over an 8-year period. Table 15-6 shows the volume harvested in each of the 8 years. Column Y contains the values of the linear trend for each time period. The trend line has been generated using the methods illustrated in Section 3 of this chapter. Note that when we graph the actual (Y) and the trend ($\hat{Y}$) values for the 8 years in Figure 15-5, the actual values move above and below the trend line.

Interpreting cyclical variations

Now we can determine the percent of trend for each of the years in the sample (column 4 in Table 15-7). From this column, we can see the variation in actual harvests around the estimated trend (98.7 to 102.5). We can attribute these cyclical variations to factors such as rainfall and temperature. However, because these factors are relatively unpredictable, we cannot forecast any specific patterns of variation using the method of residuals.

Expressing cyclical variations in terms of relative cyclical residual

The *relative cyclical residual* is another measure of cyclical variation. In this method, the *percentage deviation* from the trend is found for each value. Equation 15-9 presents the mathematical formula for determining the relative cyclical residuals. As with percent of trend, this measure is also a percentage.

Relative Cyclical Residual

$$\frac{Y - \hat{Y}}{\hat{Y}} \times 100 \qquad [15\text{-}9]$$

where

- Y = actual time-series value
- $\hat{Y}$ = estimated trend value from the same point in the time series

Table 15-8 shows the calculation of the relative cyclical residual for the farmers' cooperative problem. Note that the easy way to compute the relative cyclical residual (column 5) is to subtract 100 from the percent of trend (column 4).

Comparing the two measures of cyclical variation

These two measures of cyclical variation, percent of trend and relative cyclical residual, are percentages of the trend. For example, in 1993, the *percent of trend* indicated that the actual harvest was 98.8 percent of the expected harvest for that year. For the same year, the *relative cyclical residual* indicated that the actual harvest was 1.2 percent short of the expected harvest (a relative cyclical residual of −1.2).

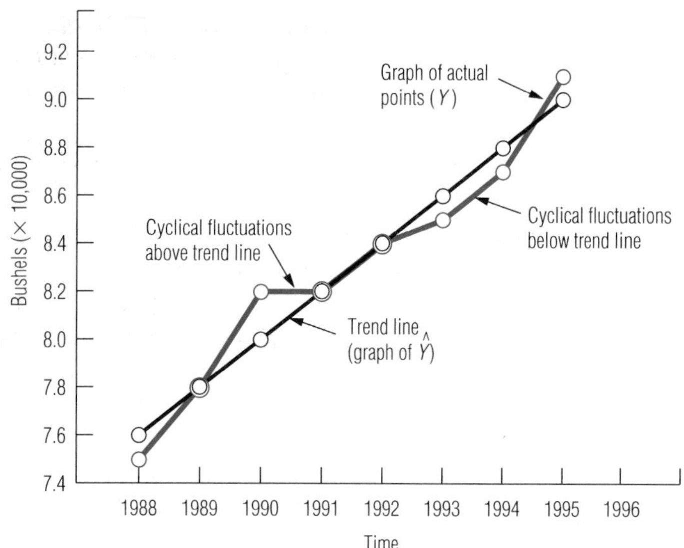

FIGURE 15-5

Cyclical fluctuations around the trend line

Table 15-7

Calculation of Percent of Trend

X Year (1)	Y Actual Bushels (× 10,000) (2)	$\hat{Y}$ Estimated Bushels (× 10,000) (3)	$\frac{Y}{\hat{Y}} \times 100$ Percent of Trend $(4) = \frac{(2)}{(3)} \times 100$
1988	7.5	7.6	98.7
1989	7.8	7.8	100.0
1990	8.2	8.0	102.5
1991	8.2	8.2	100.0
1992	8.4	8.4	100.0
1993	8.5	8.6	98.8
1994	8.7	8.8	98.9
1995	9.1	9.0	101.1

Table 15-8

Calculation of Relative Cyclical Residuals

X Year (1)	Y Actual Bushels (× 10,000) (2)	$\hat{Y}$ Estimated Bushels (× 10,000) (3)	$\frac{Y}{\hat{Y}} \times 100$ Percent of Trend $(4) = \frac{(2)}{(3)} \times 100$	$\frac{Y - \hat{Y}}{\hat{Y}} \times 100$ Relative Cyclical Residual $(5) = (4) - 100$
1988	7.5	7.6	98.7	−1.3
1989	7.8	7.8	100.0	0.0
1990	8.2	8.0	102.5	2.5
1991	8.2	8.2	100.0	0.0
1992	8.4	8.4	100.0	0.0
1993	8.5	8.6	98.8	−1.2
1994	8.7	8.8	98.9	−1.1
1995	9.1	9.0	101.1	1.1

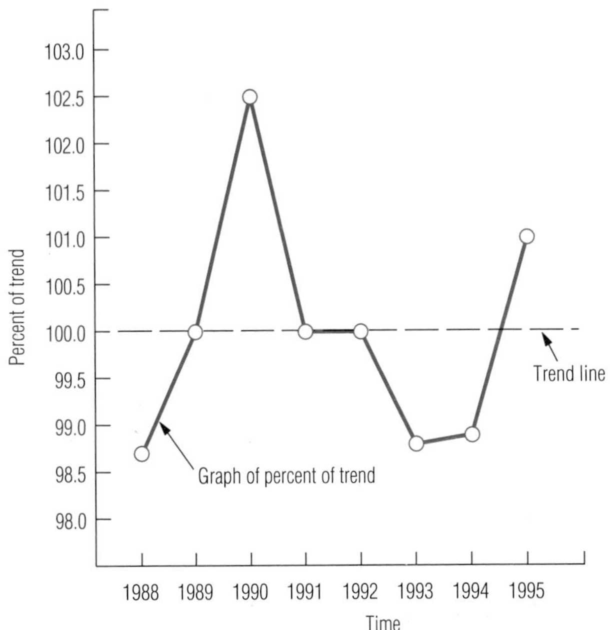

FIGURE 15-6

Graph of percent of trend around the trend line for the data in Table 15-7

Graphing cyclical variation

We often graph cyclical variation as the percent of trend. Figure 15-6 illustrates how this process eliminates the trend line and isolates the cyclical component of the time series. It must be emphasized that the procedures discussed in this section can be used only for describing past cyclical variations and not for predicting future cyclical variations. Predicting cyclical variation requires the use of techniques beyond the scope of this book.

HINTS & ASSUMPTIONS

Remember that *cyclical variation* is the component of a time series that oscillates above and below the trend line for periods *longer* than a year. Warning: *Seasonal variation* makes a complete cycle *within* each year and does not affect one year any more than another. Cyclical variation is measured by two methods. The first method expresses the variation as a percentage *of* the trend, hence its name *percent of trend*. The second method (the *relative cyclical residual*) calculates the variation as a percent deviation *from the trend*.

Exercises 15.4

Self-Check Exercise

SC 15-3 The Western Natural Gas Company has supplied 18, 20, 21, 25, and 26 billion cubic feet of gas, respectively, for the years 1991 to 1995.

(a) Find the linear estimating equation that best describes these data.
(b) Calculate the percent of trend for these data.
(c) Calculate the relative cyclical residual for these data.
(d) In which years does the largest fluctuation from trend occur, and is it the same for both methods?

Applications

■ **15-20** Microprocessing, a computer firm specializing in software engineering, has compiled the following revenue records for the years 1989 to 1995.

Year	1989	1990	1991	1992	1993	1994	1995
Revenue (× $100,000)	1.1	1.5	1.9	2.1	2.4	2.9	3.5

The second-degree equation that best describes the secular trend for these data is

$$\hat{Y} = 2.119 + 0.375x + 0.020x^2, \text{ where } 1992 = 0, \text{ and } x \text{ units} = 1 \text{ year}$$

(a) Calculate the percent of trend for these data.
(b) Calculate the relative cyclical residual for these data.
(c) Plot the percent of trend from part (a).
(d) In which year does the largest fluctuation from trend occur, and is it the same for both methods?

■ **15-21** The BullsEye department store has been expanding market share during the past 7 years, posting the following gross sales in millions of dollars:

Year	1990	1991	1992	1993	1994	1995	1996
Sales	14.8	20.7	24.6	32.9	37.8	47.6	51.7

(a) Find the linear estimating equation that best describes the data.
(b) Calculate the percent of trend for these data.
(c) Calculate the relative cyclical residual for these data.
(d) In which years does the largest fluctuation from trend occur, and is it the same for both methods?

■ **15-22** Joe Honeg, the sales manager responsible for the appliance division of a large consumer-products company, has collected the following data regarding unit sales for his division during the last 5 years:

Year	1991	1992	1993	1994	1995
Units (× 10,000)	32	46	50	66	68

The equation describing the secular trend for appliance sales is

$$\hat{Y} = 52.4 + 9.2x, \text{ where } 1993 = 0, \text{ and } x \text{ units} = 1 \text{ year}$$

(a) Calculate the percent of trend for these data.
(b) Calculate the relative cyclical residual for these data.
(c) Plot the percent of trend from part (a).
(d) In which year does the largest fluctuation from trend occur, and is it the same for both methods?

■ **15-23** Suppose you are the capital budgeting officer of a small corporation whose financing requirements over the last few years have been

Year	1989	1990	1991	1992	1993	1994	1995
Millions of dollars required	2.2	2.1	2.4	2.6	2.7	2.9	2.8

The trend equation that best describes these data is

$$\hat{Y} = 2.53 + 0.13x, \text{ where } 1992 = 0, \text{ and } x \text{ units} = 1 \text{ year}$$

(a) Calculate the percent of trend for these data.
(b) Calculate the relative cyclical residual for these data.
(c) In which year does the largest fluctuation from trend occur, and is it the same for both methods?
(d) As the capital budgeting officer, what would this fluctuation mean for you and the activities you perform?

■ **15-24** Parallel Breakfast Foods has data on the number of boxes of cereal it has sold in each of the last 7 years.

Year	1989	1990	1991	1992	1993	1994	1995
Boxes (× 10,000)	21.0	19.4	22.6	28.2	30.4	24.0	25.0

(a) Find the linear estimating equation that best describes these data.
(b) Calculate the percent of trend for these data.
(c) Calculate the relative cyclical residual for these data.
(d) In which year does the biggest fluctuation from the trend occur under each measure of cyclical variation? Is this year the same for both measures? Explain.

■ **15-25** Wombat Airlines, an Australian company, has gathered data on the number of passengers who have flown on its planes during each of the last 5 years.

Year	1991	1992	1993	1994	1995
Passengers (in tens of thousands)	3.5	4.2	3.9	3.8	3.6

(a) Find the linear estimating equation that best describes these data.
(b) Calculate the percent of trend for these data.
(c) Calculate the relative cyclical residual for these data.
(d) Based on the data and your previous calculations, give a one-sentence summary of the position in which Wombat Airlines finds itself.

Worked-Out Answer to Self-Check Exercise

SC 15-3

Year	x	Y	xY	x^2	$\hat{Y}$	$\frac{Y}{\hat{Y}} \times 100$	$\frac{Y-\hat{Y}}{\hat{Y}} \times 100$
1991	−2	18	−36	4	17.8	101.12	1.12
1992	−1	20	−20	1	19.9	100.50	0.50
1993	0	21	0	0	22.0	95.45	−4.55
1994	1	25	25	1	24.1	103.73	3.73
1995	2	26	52	4	26.2	99.24	−0.76
	0	**110**	**21**	**10**			

(a) $a = \overline{Y} = \frac{110}{5} = 22 \qquad b = \frac{\Sigma xY}{\Sigma x^2} = \frac{21}{10} = 2.1$

$\hat{Y} = 22 + 2.1x$ (where 1993 = 0 and x units = 1 year)

(b) See the next-to-the-last column above for percent of trend.
(c) See the last column above for relative cyclical residual.
(d) Largest fluctuation (by both methods) was in 1993.

15.5 Seasonal Variation

Seasonal variation defined

Besides secular trend and cyclical variation, a time series also includes seasonal variation. *Seasonal variation* is defined as repetitive and predictable movement around the trend line in *one year or less*. In order to detect seasonal variation, time intervals must be measured in small units, such as days, weeks, months, or quarters.

We have three main reasons for studying seasonal variation:

Three reasons for studying seasonal variation

1. **We can establish the pattern of past changes.** This gives us a way to compare two time intervals that would otherwise be too dissimilar. If a flight training school wants to know if a slump in business during December is normal, it can examine the seasonal pattern in previous years and find the information it needs.
2. **It is useful to project past patterns into the future.** In the case of long-range decisions, secular-trend analysis may be adequate. But for short-run decisions, the ability to predict seasonal fluctuations is often essential. Consider a wholesale food chain that wants to maintain a minimum adequate stock of all items. The ability to predict short-range patterns, such as the demand for turkeys at Thanksgiving, candy at Christmas, or peaches in the summer, is useful to the management of the chain.
3. **Once we have established the seasonal pattern that exists, we can eliminate its effects from the time series.** This adjustment allows us to calculate the cyclical variation that takes place each year. When we eliminate the effect of seasonal variation from a time series, we have *deseasonalized* the time series.

Ratio-to-Moving-Average Method

Using the ratio-to-moving-average method of measuring seasonal variation

In order to measure seasonal variation, we typically use the *ratio-to-moving-average method*. This technique provides an *index* that describes the degree of seasonal variation. The index is based on a mean of 100, with the degree of seasonality measured by variations away from the base. For example, if we examine the seasonality of canoe rentals at a summer resort, we might find that the spring-quarter index is 142. The value 142 indicates that 142 percent of the average quarterly rental occur in the spring. If management recorded 2,000 canoe rentals for all of last year, then the average quarterly rental would be 2,000/4 = 500. Because the spring-quarter index is 142, we estimate the number of spring rentals as follows:

Spring-quarter index

$$\text{Average quarterly rental} \longrightarrow 500 \times \frac{142}{100} = 710 \longleftarrow \textit{Seasonalized}\text{ spring-quarter rental}$$

An example of the ratio-to-moving-average method

Our chapter-opening example can illustrate the ratio-to-moving-average method. The resort hotel wanted to establish the seasonal pattern of room demand by its clientele. Hotel management wants to improve customer service and is considering several plans

Table 15-9

Time Series for Hotel Occupancy

Year	Number of Guests per Quarter I	II	III	IV
1991	1,861	2,203	2,415	1,908
1992	1,921	2,343	2,514	1,986
1993	1,834	2,154	2,098	1,799
1994	1,837	2,025	2,304	1,965
1995	2,073	2,414	2,339	1,967

to employ personnel during peak periods to achieve this goal. Table 15-9 contains the quarterly occupancy, that is, the average number of guests during each quarter of the last 5 years.

We will refer to Table 15-9 to demonstrate the six steps required to compute a seasonal index.

Step 1: Calculate the 4-quarter moving total

1. **The first step in computing a seasonal index is to calculate the 4-quarter moving total for the time series.** To do this, we total the values for the quarters during the first year, 1991, in Table 15-9: 1,861 + 2,203 + 2,415 + 1,908 = 8,387. A moving total is associated with the middle data point in the set of values from which it was calculated. Because our first total of 8,387 was calculated from four data points, we place it opposite the midpoint of those quarters, so it falls in column 4 of Table 15-10, between the rows for the 1991-II and 1991-III quarters.

   We find the next moving total by dropping the 1991-I value, 1,861, and adding the 1992-I value, 1,921. By dropping the first value and adding the fifth, we keep four quarters in the total. The four values added now are 2,203 + 2,415 + 1,908 + 1,921 = 8,447. This total is entered in Table 15-10 directly below the first quarterly total of 8,387. We continue the process of "sliding" the 4-quarter total over the time series until we have included the last value in the series. In this example, it is the 1,967 rooms in the fourth quarter of 1995, the last number in column 3 of Table 15-10. The last entry in the moving total column is 8,793. It is between the rows for the 1995-II and 1995-III quarters because it was calculated from the data for the 4 quarters of 1995.

Step 2: Compute the 4-quarter moving average

2. **In the second step, we compute the 4-quarter moving average by dividing each of the 4-quarter totals by 4.** In Table 15-10, we divided the values in column 4 by 4, to arrive at the values for column 5.

Step 3: Center the 4-quarter moving average

3. **In the third step, we center the 4-quarter moving average.** The moving averages in column 5 all fall halfway between the quarters. We would like to have moving averages associated with each quarter. In order to ***center*** our moving averages, we associate with each quarter the average of the two 4-quarter moving averages falling just above and just below it. For the 1991-III quarter, the resulting **4-quarter centered moving average** is 2,104.25, that is, (2,096.75 + 2,111.75)/2. The other entries in column 6 are calculated the same way. Figure 15-7 illustrates how the moving average has smoothed the peaks and troughs of the original time series. The seasonal and irregular components have been smoothed, and the resulting dotted colored line represents the cyclical and trend components of the series.

Table 15-10
Calculating the 4-Quarter Centered Moving Average

Year (1)	Quarter (2)	Occupancy (3)	Step 1: 4-Quarter Moving Total (4)	Step 2: 4-Quarter Moving Average (5) = (4) ÷ 4	Step 3: 4-Quarter Centered Moving Average (6)	Step 4: Percentage of Actual to Moving Average Values (7) = $\frac{(3)}{(6)} \times 100$
1991	I	1,861				
	II	2,203				
			8,387	2,096.75		
	III	2,415			2,104.250	114.8
			8,447	2,111.75		
	IV	1,908			2,129.250	89.6
			8,587	2,146.75		
1992	I	1,921			2,159.125	89.0
			8,686	2,171.50		
	II	2,343			2,181.250	107.4
			8,764	2,191.00		
	III	2,514			2,180.125	115.3
			8,677	2,169.25		
	IV	1,986			2,145.625	92.6
			8,488	2,122.00		
1993	I	1,834			2,070.000	88.6
			8,072	2,018.00		
	II	2,154			1,994.625	108.0
			7,885	1,971.25		
	III	2,098			1,971.625	106.4
			7,888	1,972.00		
	IV	1,799			1,955.875	92.0
			7,759	1,939.75		
1994	I	1,837			1,965.500	93.5
			7,965	1,991.25		
	II	2,025			2,012.000	100.6
			8,131	2,032.75		
	III	2,304			2,062.250	111.7
			8,367	2,091.75		
	IV	1,965			2,140.375	91.8
			8,756	2,189.00		
1995	I	2,073			2,193.375	94.5
			8,791	2,197.75		
	II	2,414			2,198.000	109.8
			8,793	2,198.25		
	III	2,339				
	IV	1,967				

Sometimes step 3 can be skipped

Suppose we were working with the admissions data for a hospital emergency room, and we wanted to compute *daily* indices. In steps 1 and 2, we would compute 7-day moving totals and moving averages, **and the moving averages would already be centered** (because the middle of a 7-day period is the fourth of those 7 days). In this case, step 3 is unnecessary. Whenever the number of periods for which we want indices is odd (7 days in a week, three shifts in a day), we can skip step 3. However, when the number of periods is even (4 quarters, 12 months, 24 hours), then we must use step 3 to center the moving averages we get with step 2.

Step 4: Calculate the percentage of actual value to moving average value

4. **Next, we calculate the percentage of the actual value to the moving-average value for each quarter in the time series having a 4-quarter moving-average entry.** This step allows us to recover the seasonal component for the quarters. We determine this percentage by dividing each of the actual quarter values in column 3 of Table 15-10 by the corresponding 4-quarter centered moving-average values in column 6 and then multiplying the result by 100. For example, we find the percentage for 1991-III as follows:

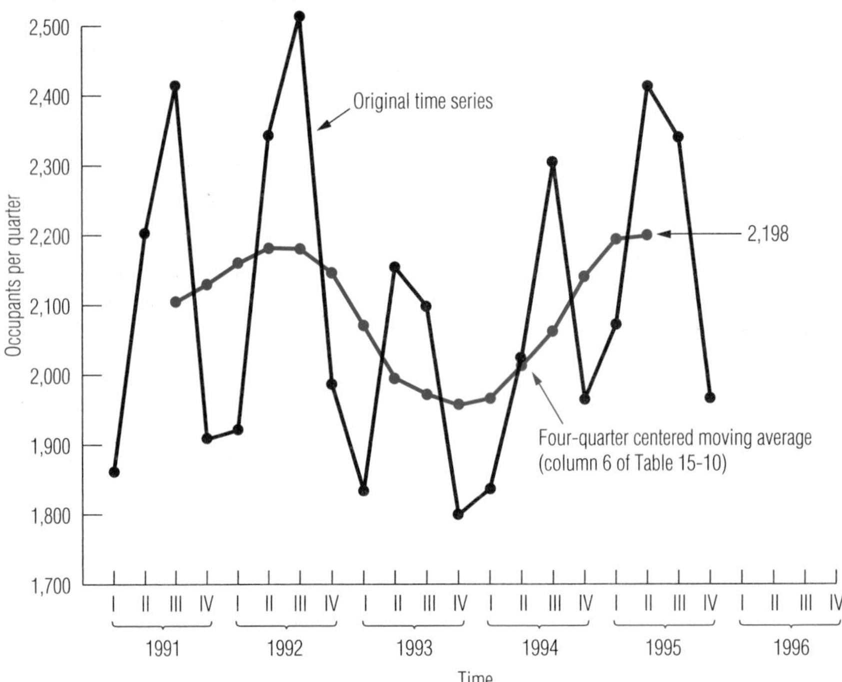

FIGURE 15-7

Using a moving average to smooth the original time series

$$\frac{\text{Actual}}{\text{Moving average}} \times 100 = \frac{2{,}415}{2{,}104.250} \times 100$$
$$= 114.8$$

Step 5: Collect answers from step 4 and calculate the modified mean

5. **To collect all the percentage of actual to moving-average values in column 7 of Table 15-10, arrange them by quarter.** Then calculate the *modified mean* for each quarter. The modified mean is calculated by discarding the highest and lowest values for each quarter and averaging the remaining values. In Table 15-11, we present the fifth step and show the process for finding the modified mean.

Reducing extreme cyclical and irregular variations

The seasonal values we recovered for the quarters in column 7 of Table 15-10 still contain the cyclical and irregular components of variation in the time series. By eliminating the highest and lowest values from each quarter, we *reduce* the extreme cyclical and irregular variations. When we average the remaining values, we further smooth the cyclical and irregular components. Cyclical and irregular variations tend to be removed by this process, so the modified mean is an index of the seasonality component. (Some statisticians prefer to use the median value instead of computing the modified mean to achieve the same outcome.)

Step 6: Adjust the modified mean

6. **The final step, demonstrated in Table 15-12, adjusts the modified mean slightly.** Notice that the four indices in Table 15-11 total 404.1. However, the base for an index is 100. Thus, the four quarterly indices should total 400, and their mean should be 100. To correct for this error, we multiply each of the quarterly indices in Table 15-11 by an adjusting constant. This number is found by dividing the desired sum of the indices (400) by the actual sum (404.1). In this case, the result is 0.9899. Table 15-12 shows that multiplying the indices by the adjusting constant brings the quarterly indices to a total of 400. (Sometimes even after this adjustment, the mean of the seasonal indices

Table 15-11

Demonstration of Step 5 in Computing a Seasonal Index*

Year	Quarter I	Quarter II	Quarter III	Quarter IV
1991	—	—	114.8	~~89.6~~
1992	89.0	107.4	~~115.3~~	~~92.6~~
1993	~~88.6~~	108.0	~~106.4~~	92.0
1994	93.5	~~100.6~~	111.7	91.8
1995	~~94.5~~	~~109.8~~	—	—
	182.5	**215.4**	**226.5**	**183.8**

Modified mean:

$$\text{Quarter I: } \frac{182.5}{2} = 91.25$$

$$\text{Quarter II: } \frac{215.4}{2} = 107.70$$

$$\text{Quarter III: } \frac{226.5}{2} = 113.25$$

$$\text{Quarter IV: } \frac{183.8}{2} = 91.90$$

Total of indices = **404.1**

*Eliminated values are indicated by a colored slash.

Table 15-12

Demonstration of Step 6

Quarter	Unadjusted Indices	×	Adjusting Constant	=	Seasonal Index
I	91.25	×	0.9899	=	90.3
II	107.70	×	0.9899	=	106.6
III	113.25	×	0.9899	=	112.1
IV	91.90	×	0.9899	=	91.0
			Total of seasonal indices	=	**400.0**

$$\text{Mean of seasonal indices} = \frac{400}{4} = 100.0$$

is not exactly 100 because of accumulated rounding errors. In this case, however, it is exactly 100.)

Uses of the Seasonal Index

Deseasonalizing a time series

The ratio-to-moving-average method just explained allows us to identify seasonal variation in a time series. The seasonal indices are used to remove the effects of seasonality from a time series. This is called *deseasonalizing* a time series. Before we can identify either the trend or cyclical components of a time series, we must eliminate seasonal variation. To deseasonalize a time series, we divide each of the actual values in the series by the appropriate seasonal index (expressed as a fraction of 100). To demonstrate, we shall deseasonalize the value of the first four quarters in Table 15-9. In Table 15-13, we show the deseasonalizing process using the values for the seasonal indices from Table 15-12. Once the seasonal

Table 15-13
Demonstration of Deseasonalizing Data

Year (1)	Quarter (2)	Actual Occupancy (3)		$\left(\frac{\text{Seasonal Index}}{100}\right)$ (4)		Deseasonalized Occupancy (5) = (3) ÷ (4)
1991	I	1,861	÷	$\left(\frac{90.3}{100}\right)$	=	2,061
1991	II	2,203	÷	$\left(\frac{106.6}{100}\right)$	=	2,067
1991	III	2,415	÷	$\left(\frac{112.1}{100}\right)$	=	2,154
1991	IV	1,908	÷	$\left(\frac{91.0}{100}\right)$	=	2,097

effect has been eliminated, the deseasonalized values that remain reflect only the trend, cyclical, and irregular components of the time series.

Using seasonality in forecasts

Once we have removed the seasonal variation, we can compute a deseasonalized trend line, which we can then project into the future. Suppose the hotel management in our example estimates from a deseasonalized trend line that the deseasonalized average occupancy for the fourth quarter of the *next* year will be 2,121. When this prediction has been obtained, management must then take the seasonality into account. To do this, it multiplies the deseasonalized predicted average occupancy of 2,121 by the fourth-quarter seasonal index (expressed as a fraction of 100) to obtain a seasonalized estimate of 1,930 rooms for the fourth-quarter average occupancy. Here are the calculations:

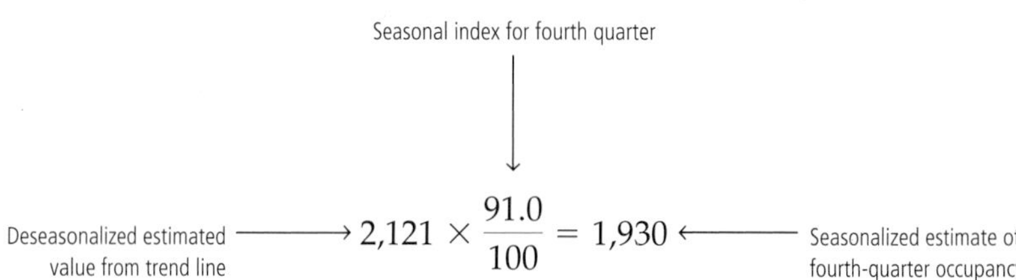

HINTS & ASSUMPTIONS

Using seasonal indices to adjust quarterly and monthly data helps us detect the underlying secular trend. Warning: Most reported figures fail to tell us how much seasonal adjustment was used, and in some management decisions this missing information is valuable. For example, if a state motor vehicle department reports last month's new vehicle registrations were 25,000 at a *seasonally adjusted rate*, how would a distributor of an after-market automobile product such as custom floor mats predict demand for *next month* without knowing the *actual* number of new cars? Often, for internal company planning purposes, it is helpful to know both adjusted and unadjusted figures.

Exercises 15.5

Self-Check Exercise

SC 15-4 Using the following percentages of actual to moving average describing the quarterly amount of cash in circulation at the Village Bank in Carrboro, N.C. over a 4-year period, calculate the seasonal index for each quarter.

	Spring	Summer	Fall	Winter
1992	87	106	86	125
1993	85	110	83	127
1994	84	105	87	128
1995	88	104	88	124

Applications

■ **15-26** The owner of The Pleasure-Glide Boat Company has compiled the following quarterly figures regarding the company's level of accounts receivable over the last 5 years (× \$1,000):

	Spring	Summer	Fall	Winter
1991	102	120	90	78
1992	110	126	95	83
1993	111	128	97	86
1994	115	135	103	91
1995	122	144	110	98

(a) Calculate a 4-quarter centered moving average.

(b) Find the percentage of actual to moving average for each period.

(c) Determine the modified seasonal indices and the seasonal indices.

■ **15-27** Marie Wiggs, personnel director for a pharmaceutical company, recorded these percentage absentee rates for each quarter over a 4-year period:

	Spring	Summer	Fall	Winter
1992	5.6	6.8	6.3	5.2
1993	5.7	6.7	6.4	5.4
1994	5.3	6.6	6.1	5.1
1995	5.4	6.9	6.2	5.3

(a) Construct a 4-quarter centered moving average and plot it on a graph along with the original data.

(b) What can you conclude about absenteeism from part (a)?

■ **15-28** Using the following percentages of actual to moving average describing the seasonal sales of sporting goods over a 5-year period, calculate the seasonal index for each season.

Year	Baseball	Football	Basketball	Hockey
1992	96	128	116	77
1993	92	131	125	69
1994	84	113	117	84
1995	97	118	126	89
1996	91	121	124	81

■ **15-29** A large manufacturer of automobile springs has determined the following percentages of actual to moving average describing the firm's quarterly cash needs for the last 6 years:

	Spring	Summer	Fall	Winter
1990	108	128	94	70
1991	112	132	88	68
1992	109	134	84	73
1993	110	131	90	69
1994	108	135	89	68
1995	106	129	93	72

Calculate the seasonal index for each quarter. Comment on how it compares to the indices you calculated for Exercise 15-26.

■ **15-30** A university's dean of admissions has compiled the following quarterly enrollment figures for the previous 5 years ($\times$ 100):

	Fall	Winter	Spring	Summer
1991	220	203	193	84
1992	235	208	206	76
1993	236	206	209	73
1994	241	215	206	92
1995	239	221	213	115

(a) Calculate a 4-quarter centered moving average.

(b) Find the percentage of actual to moving average for each period.

(c) Determine the modified seasonal indices and the seasonal indices.

■ **15-31** The Ski and Putt Resort, a combination of ski slopes and golf courses, has just recently tabulated its data on the number of customers (in thousands) it has had during each season of the last 5 years. Calculate the seasonal index for each quarter. If 15 people are employed in the summer, what should winter employment be, assuming both sports have equal labor requirements?

	Spring	Summer	Fall	Winter
1991	200	300	125	325
1992	175	250	150	375
1993	225	300	200	450
1994	200	350	225	375
1995	175	300	200	350

■ **15-32** David Curl Builders has collected quarterly data on the number of homes it has started during the last 5 years.

	Spring	Summer	Fall	Winter
1991	8	10	7	5
1992	9	10	7	6
1993	10	11	7	6
1994	10	12	8	7
1995	11	13	9	8

(a) Calculate the seasonal index for each quarter.

(b) If David's working capital needs are related directly to the number of starts, by how much should his working capital need decrease between summer and winter?

Worked-Out Answer to Self-Check Exercise

SC 15-4

Year	Spring	Summer	Fall	Winter
1992	87	106	86	125
1993	85	110	83	127
1994	84	105	87	128
1995	88	104	88	124
Modified sum	172	211	173	252
Modified mean	86	105.5	86.5	126
Seasonal index	85.15	104.46	85.64	124.75

The sum of the modified means was 404, so the adjusting factor was 400/404 = 0.9901. The seasonal indices were obtained by multiplying the modified means by this factor.

15.6 Irregular Variation

Difficulty of dealing with irregular variation

The final component of a time series is irregular variation. After we have eliminated trend, cyclical, and seasonal variations from a time series, we still have an unpredictable factor left. Typically, irregular variation occurs over short intervals and follows a random pattern.

Because of the unpredictability of irregular variation, we do not attempt to explain it mathematically. However, we can often isolate its causes. New York City's financial crisis of 1975, for example, was an irregular factor that severely depressed the municipal bond market. In 1984, the unusually cold temperatures in late December in the southern states were an irregular factor that significantly increased electricity and fuel oil consumption. The Persian Gulf War in 1991 was another irregular factor; it significantly increased airline and ship travel for a number of months as troops and supplies were moved. Not all causes of irregular variation can be identified so easily, however. One factor that allows managers to cope with irregular variation is that over time, these random movements tend to counteract each other.

HINTS & ASSUMPTIONS

Warning: Irregular variation is *very* important but is not explainable mathematically. It's what is "left over" after we eliminate trend, cyclical, and seasonal variation from a time series. In most cases, irregular variation is difficult if not impossible to predict and we never attempt to "fit a line" to account for irregular variation. Hint: Often you will find irregular variation acknowledged with a footnote or a comment on a graph. Examples of this would be "Market closed for Labor Day Holiday" or "Spring break fell in March instead of April last year."

Caution in using the forecast

On the basis of this analysis, the firm estimates that sales for 1996-III will be \$135,000. We must stress, however, that this value is only an estimate and does not take into account the cyclical and irregular components. As we noted earlier, the irregular variation cannot be predicted mathematically. Also, remember that our earlier treatment of cyclical variation was descriptive of past behavior and not predictive of future behavior.

HINTS & ASSUMPTIONS

A *complete* analysis of a time series tries to account for *secular trend, cyclical variation,* and *seasonal variation.* What's left is *irregular variation.* Warning: Even the best analysis of a time series *describes past behavior,* and may not be predictive of future behavior. Hint: The correct way to proceed in analyzing all of the components of a time series is to first deseasonalize the time series, then find the trend line, then calculate the cyclical variation around that trend line, and then identify irregular variation from what is left.

Exercises 15.7

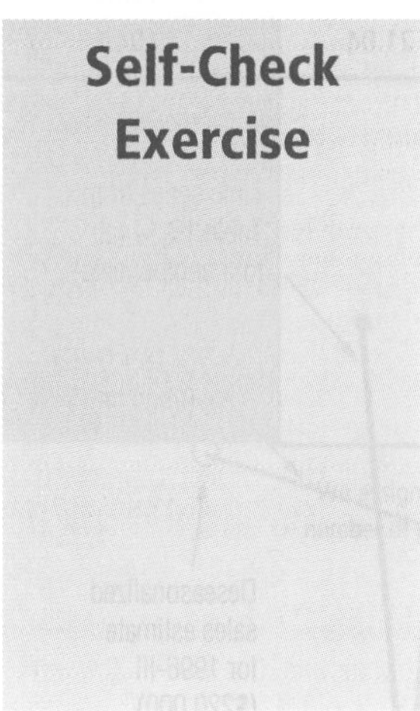

SC 15-5 A state commission designed to monitor energy consumption assembled the following seasonal data regarding natural gas consumption, in millions of cubic feet:

	Winter	Spring	Summer	Fall
1992	293	246	231	282
1993	301	252	227	291
1994	304	259	239	296
1995	306	265	240	300

(a) Determine the seasonal indices and deseasonalize these data (using a 4-quarter centered moving average).

(b) Calculate the least-squares line that best describes these data.

(c) Identify the cyclical variation in these data by the relative cyclical residual method.

(d) Plot the original data, the deseasonalized data, and the trend.

Applications

■ **15-37** An environmental agency has been watching New York air quality over a 5-year period and has assembled the following seasonal data regarding amount of contaminants (in parts per million) in the air:

Year	Winter	Spring	Summer	Fall
1992	452	385	330	385
1993	474	397	356	399
1994	494	409	375	415
1995	506	429	398	437
1996	527	454	421	482

(a) Determine the seasonal indices and deseasonalize these data (using a 4-quarter centered moving average).

(b) Calculate the least-squares line that best describes these data.

(c) Identify the cyclic variation in these data by the relative cyclical residual method.

(d) Plot the original data, the deseasonalized data, and the trend.

■ **15-38** The following data describe the marketing performance of a regional beer producer:

	Sales by Quarter (× $100,000)			
Year	I	II	III	IV
1991	19	24	38	25
1992	21	28	44	23
1993	23	31	41	23
1994	24	35	48	21

(a) Calculate the seasonal indices for these data. (Use a 4-quarter centered moving average.)

(b) Deseasonalize these data using the indices from part (a).

■ **15-39** For Exercise 15-38:

(a) Find the least-squares line that best describes the trend in deseasonalized beer sales.

(b) Identify the cyclical component in this time series by computing the percent of trend.

Worked-Out Answer to Self-Check Exercise

SC 15-5 (a)

Year	Quarter	Actual Gas Usage	4-Quarter Moving Average	Centered Moving Average	Percentage of Actual to Moving Average	Seasonal Index	Deseason-alized Usage
1992	Winter	293				111.66	262.4037
	Spring	246				94.39	260.6208
			263.00				
	Summer	231		264.000	87.50	86.82	266.0677
			265.00				
	Fall	282		265.750	106.11	107.13	263.2316
			266.50				
1993	Winter	301		266.000	113.16	111.66	269.5683
			265.50				
	Spring	252		266.625	94.51	94.39	266.9774
			267.75				
	Summer	227		268.125	84.66	86.82	261.4605
			268.50				
	Fall	291		269.375	108.03	107.13	271.6326
			270.25				
1994	Winter	304		271.750	111.87	111.66	272.2551
			273.25				
	Spring	259		273.875	94.57	94.39	274.3935
			274.50				
	Summer	239		274.750	86.99	86.82	275.2822
			275.00				
	Fall	296		275.750	107.34	107.13	276.2998
			276.50				
1995	Winter	306		276.625	110.62	111.66	274.0462
			276.75				
	Spring	265		277.250	95.58	94.39	280.7501
			277.75				
	Summer	240				86.82	276.4340
	Fall	300				107.13	280.0336

Year	Winter	Spring	Summer	Fall
1992			~~87.50~~	~~106.11~~
1993	~~113.16~~	~~94.51~~	~~84.66~~	~~108.03~~
1994	111.87	94.57	86.99	107.34
1995	~~110.62~~	~~95.58~~		
Modified sum	111.87	94.57	86.99	107.34
Seasonal index	111.66	94.39	86.82	107.13

The sum of the modified means was 400.77, so the adjusting factor was 400/400.77 = 0.99808. The seasonal indices were obtained by multiplying the modified means by this factor.

(b, c)

Year	Quarter	Deseason-alized Usage (Y)	x	xY	x^2	Deseason-alized trend $\hat{Y} = 270.7161 + 0.6301x$	Relative Cyclical Residual $\frac{Y - \hat{Y}}{\hat{Y}} \times 100$
1992	Winter	262.4037	−15	−3936.0555	225	261.2646	0.44
	Spring	260.6208	−13	−3388.0704	169	262.5248	−0.73
	Summer	266.0677	−11	−2926.7447	121	263.7850	0.87
	Fall	263.2316	−9	−2369.0844	81	265.0452	−0.68
1993	Winter	269.5683	−7	−1886.9781	49	266.3054	1.23
	Spring	266.9774	−5	−1334.8870	25	267.5656	−0.22
	Summer	261.4605	−3	−784.3815	9	268.8258	−2.74
	Fall	271.6326	−1	−271.6326	1	270.0860	0.57
1994	Winter	272.2551	1	272.2551	1	271.3462	0.33
	Spring	274.3935	3	823.1805	9	272.6064	0.66
	Summer	275.2822	5	1376.4110	25	273.8666	0.52
	Fall	276.2998	7	1934.0986	49	275.1268	0.43

(Continued)

Year	Quarter	Deseason-alized Usage (Y)	x	xY	x^2	Deseason-alized trend $\hat{Y} = 270.7161 + 0.6301x$	Relative Cyclical Residual $\frac{Y - \hat{Y}}{\hat{Y}} \times 100$
1995	Winter	274.0462	9	2466.4158	81	276.3870	−0.85
	Spring	280.7501	11	3088.2511	121	277.6472	1.12
	Summer	276.4340	13	3593.6420	169	278.9074	−0.89
	Fall	280.0336	15	4200.5040	225	280.1676	−0.05
		4,331.4571	**0**	**856.9239**	**1,360**		

$$a = \bar{Y} = \frac{4{,}331.4571}{16} = 270.7161 \qquad b = \frac{\Sigma xY}{\Sigma x^2} = \frac{856.9239}{1{,}360} = 0.6301$$

$$\hat{Y} = 270.7161 + 0.6301x \text{ (where 1993-IV } {}^1/_2 = 0 \text{ and } x \text{ units} = {}^1/_2 \text{ quarter)}$$

(d)

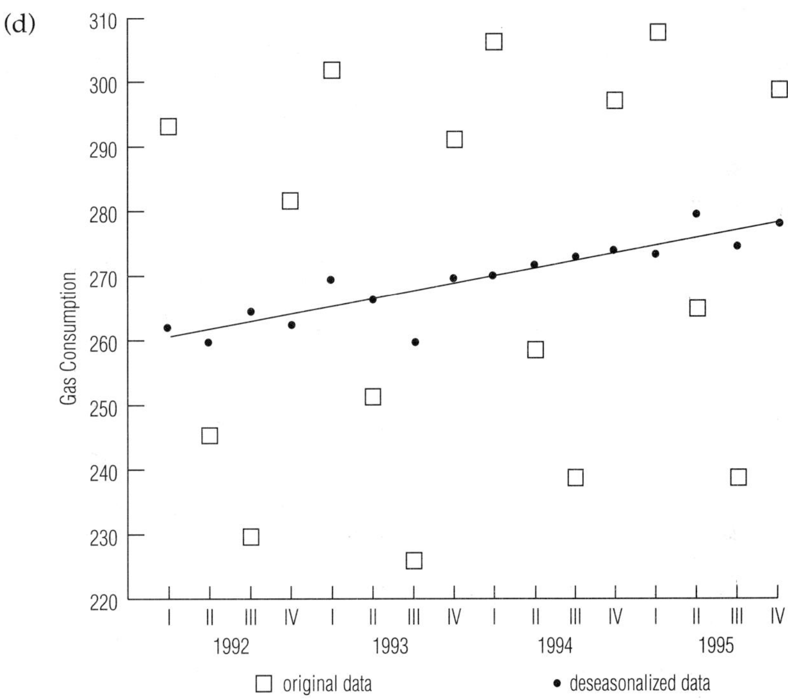

15.8 Time-Series Analysis in Forecasting

In this chapter, we have examined all four components of a time series. We have described the process of projecting past trend and seasonal variation into the future, while taking into consideration the inherent inaccuracies of this analysis. In addition, we noted that although the irregular and cyclical components do affect the future, they are erratic and difficult to use in forecasting.

Recognizing limitations of time-series analysis

We must realize that the mechanical approach of time-series analysis is subject to considerable error and change. It is necessary for management to combine these simple procedures with knowledge of other factors in order to develop workable forecasts. Analysts are constantly revising, updating, and discarding their forecasts. If we wish to cope successfully with the future, we must do the same.

When using the procedures described in this chapter, we should pay particular attention to two problems:

1. In forecasting, we project past trend and seasonal variation into the future. We must ask, "How regular and lasting were the past trends? What are the chances that these patterns are changing?"
2. How accurate are the historical data we use in time series analysis? If a company has changed from a FIFO (first-in, first-out) to a LIFO (last-in, first-out) inventory accounting system in a period during the time under consideration, the data (such as quarterly profits) before and after the change are not comparable and not very useful for forecasting.

HINTS & ASSUMPTIONS

Warning: Smart managers realize that accounting for most of the variation in a time series of *past* data does *not* mean that this same pattern will continue in the future. Hint: These same smart managers combine the predictions available from time series with intuitive answers to broad what-if questions, which are always part of strategic planning. These what-if questions concern the future business environment (sociological, economic, political) and whether it will change significantly from the environment that existed when the time-series data were gathered.

Exercises 15.8

- **15-40** List four errors that can affect forecasting with a time series.
- **15-41** When using a time series to predict the future, what assurances do we need about the historical data on which our forecasts are based?
- **15-42** What problems would you see developing if we used past college enrollments to predict future college enrollments?
- **15-43** How would forecasts using time-series analysis handle things such as
  - (a) Changes in the federal tax laws?
  - (b) Changes in accounting systems?

Statistics at Work

Loveland Computers

Case 15: Time Series Lee Azko was resting on well-earned laurels. The complicated regression analysis for the results of advertising expenditures had given Sherrel Wright new confidence in making the argument for better planning. Even Walter Azko began to accept that some of the firm's success wasn't hit or miss—there really were some rules to this game.

"I never could see the value of running five- or six-page spreads," Uncle Walter said as he rounded the corner of Lee's "office"—a cubicle that was furnished with little except one of the largest and fastest of Loveland's latest personal computers. "Thanks for showing I was right. And you're even making me a believer in that expensive newspaper advertising, too."

"Did Margot say anything about those focus groups?" Lee fished for another compliment.

"We're going to deal with that next week—too early to say. But don't get too comfortable. I have a whole new project for you—go and see Gratia."

Gratia Delaguardia was clearly sharing a joke. The laughter was audible down the corridor—Gratia rated a "real" office, with a door. Lee found Gratia looking at a graph with yet another player on Loveland's team.

"Lee, come on in and meet Roberto Palomar. Bert runs the phone bank—you know, our order department. We were just talking about you."

"Hence the laughter?" Lee was nervous.

"No, no. Take a look at this. Bert's been trying to estimate the number of phone reps we need to have available to take orders. We need to plan for hiring. . . ."

"And to install enough incoming 800 lines," added Roberto, whom everyone called Bert.

"We plotted out the quarterly data," continued Gratia, "and, as an engineer, let me tell you I can recognize a nonlinear trend when I see one." Gratia pointed to a curve that looked like the path of the space shuttle going into orbit. "Of course, we aren't complaining about our growth. It's good to be on a winning team."

"But if we continue this trend," said Bert, sliding a ruler into place on the graph, "within 10 years, we'll have to employ the whole population of Loveland just to staff our phone banks." With that, Gratia and Bert again dissolved with laughter. "Lee, look at these numbers and say it isn't so."

"Well, there's no doubt there's a very strong underlying trend," Lee observed, noting the obvious. "Is there any seasonality—you know, differences from month to month?"

"Good question," Bert replied. "These quarterly totals tend to mask some of the monthly ups and downs. For example, August is always a bust because people are away on vacation. But December is a very heavy month. We're not really in the Christmas gift business, although some home users apparently do ask Santa for a new Loveland Computer. The main effect comes from small businesses that want to book equipment expenditures before the end of the year for tax purposes."

"And I don't suppose the call volume is evenly spaced over the week," Lee ventured.

"Ah, rainy days and Mondays!" Bert answered. "We have a rule of thumb that we do twice as much business on Mondays as on Tuesdays. So we try to avoid training sessions or staff meetings on Mondays. Sometimes the supervisory staff will pitch in—whatever it takes. If we miss a call, a potential customer may buy from one of our competitors.

"But now we're at the point where I really should plan a little better for the number of staff to have available. If I schedule too many people, it's a waste of money and the reps get bored. They'd rather be at home."

"Well I think I can help," Lee offered. "Let me tell you what I'll need."

Study Questions: What data will Lee want to examine? What analysis will be performed? How will Bert make use of the information that Lee develops?

Computer Database Exercise

HH Industries

The following week, Stan approached Laurel about some data for his upcoming quarterly sales meeting. "If you remember those first talks we had about the company's history," he said, "you'll remember my telling you how seals and seal kits, our most extensive product line, are the cornerstone of our sales. In fact, it's the product line Mr. Douglas basically started the business with. As it turns out, it's also the product line that generates our largest gross margin percentage. Is there anything you could do in the way of charts or graphs that would illustrate the behavior of seal sales over the last 10 years or so? I've got either daily or monthly data you could work with."

"What if I deseasonalize the data, to show a more accurate rate of growth?" Laurel suggested. "I could use the monthly sales figures and generate some graphs showing the trends. By calculating a least-squares estimate, I could also give you a rough predictive tool for anticipating seal sales, deseasonalized that is, for the next few years. How does that sound?"

"You lost me on the least-squares part," Stan admitted, "but that sounds exactly like the type of thing I'm looking for. It will be interesting to see how sales look without seasonal trends. Can you have a rough draft of the figures by the first part of next week?"

"You bet," answered Laurel. "I'll bring it all by your office Monday or Tuesday."

1. Do a time-series analysis of seal sales over the last 10 years. (See the sales data in the CH15.xxx files on the data disk.) Deseasonalize sales by month, using the ratio-to-moving-average method. (Use a 12-month centered moving average.) Then find the least-squares linear equation that best describes the deseasonalized data.
2. Use your results to forecast sales for each month of 1994.
3. Look at the residuals associated with the linear regression equation. Is there any pattern that might cause you to be suspicious that a straight line is not the best fit?

From the Textbook to the Real World

Icelandic Fisheries

A model has been developed for the Ministry of Fisheries in Iceland to facilitate decision making in fisheries management. It is used primarily for short-term management of quota systems and long-term investment planning. With this model, predictions can be made about catches of cod and other demersal species several years ahead. Earnings and cost information can also be calculated. Analysts collect data on a number of variables, including the size of the fish stocks in the beginning of the planning period and the size and classification of the fishing fleet. Recent studies indicate that the fishing fleet is far too large, and unless adequate measures can be taken to limit fishing off the Icelandic coast, the backbone of the Icelandic economy may be threatened.

Background Fishing is the dominant industry in Iceland's economy, with fish and fish products representing approximately 70 percent of the country's exports. The demersal species are the most important species of fish in Iceland, and cod accounts for 55 percent of the demersal catch. Until 1976, when Iceland gained full sovereignty over its fishing grounds, foreign vessels accounted for about half of the total catch. Icelandic fishing companies began modernizing their fleets as early as 1970, in anticipation of the removal of foreign competition. As the fleet grew in size and became more efficient, concerns about stock protection arose. Stock-size estimations prepared in 1975 indicated that the cod stock was down to less than half of its average size for the postwar period. Furthermore, the age and structure of the catch was not favorable. Despite the removal of foreign fishing vessels, the total fishing effort hardly decreased due to modern fishing techniques and equipment. By 1983, the cod catch reached an all-time low. Authorities and the fishing industry realized that the fishing fleet, and hence the effort expended, was too large. Expansion of the fleet must be contained. Initially, the fishing period was restricted by enforcing extended Christmas and Easter vacations for fishermen and by setting ceilings on the allowable annual operating time of each trawler. In 1984, general quota systems were introduced.

Fishing Models In 1979, the Ministry of Fisheries established a working group consisting of members from the University of Iceland, the Marine Research Institute, and other groups to develop a model of demersal fisheries. The model would be a decision support tool for long- and short-term management. Short-term planning involves closing areas for fishing, mesh-size regulations, and quota systems. In the long run, fleet size and its composition can be managed through the government's control over banking and the investment in new vessels.

Data on Fisheries Over the last few decades, extensive data on fishing in Iceland have been collected. The government's involvement in transactions between fishermen and the fish-processing industry has made it beneficial for both partners to report catches and other data properly, so the data are found to be very reliable. Although the data are accurate, randomness exists due to the impact of harsh and unstable weather on the fishing grounds. There are four groups of data: landings, stock sizes, fishing power and selectivity, and economic data. From this information, trends can be extrapolated regarding the expected catch for a given fishing unit, the expected profits or losses for the fleet, and other statistics, year by year. The year 1983 is used as a base year by the government committee to compare sustainable yield for different fleet sizes and types. Sustainable yield refers to the equilibrium catch for a given constant effort and standard environmental factors.

Results The main conclusion from the study was that the fleet is too large, and the stock of future fish is being jeopardized by the fishing efforts of so many vessels. Although the problems associated with renewable natural resources involve uncertainty and are often unpredictable, the time-series model used by the Ministry of Fisheries in Iceland provided a tool for determining the nature and severity of the problem. It also allowed policy makers to concentrate on comparisons of different policies through sensitivity analysis, rather than to seek predictions of absolute values. By observing trends in stock size and other variables, politicians can determine the effects of different government policies. In Iceland, decision makers found that early strategies were unsuccessful in decreasing the size of the catch, so quota systems and investment limitations were imposed to preserve the country's fishing industry.

Source: Thorkell Helgason and Snojolfur Olafsson, "An Icelandic Fisheries Model," *European Journal of Operational Research* 33 (1988): 191–199.

Chapter Review

● Terms Introduced in Chapter 15

Coding A method of converting traditional measures of time to a form that simplifies computation (often called *translating*).

Cyclical Fluctuation A type of variation in a time series, in which the value of the variable fluctuates above and below a secular trend line.

Deseasonalization A statistical process used to remove the effects of seasonality from a time series.

Irregular Variation A condition in a time series in which the value of a variable is completely unpredictable.

Modified Mean A statistical method used in time-series analysis. Discards the highest and lowest values when computing a mean.

Ratio-to-Moving-Average Method A statistical method used to measure seasonal variation. Uses an index describing the degree of that variation.

Relative Cyclical Residual A measure of cyclical variation, it uses the percentage deviation from the trend for each value in the series.

Residual Method A method of describing the cyclical component of a time series. It assumes that most of the variation in the series not explained by the secular trend is cyclical variation.

Seasonal Variation Patterns of change in a time series within a year; patterns that tend to be repeated from year to year.

Second-Degree Equation A mathematical form used to describe a parabolic curve that may be used in time-series trend analysis.

Secular Trend A type of variation in a time series, the value of the variable tending to increase or decrease over a long period of time.

Time Series Information accumulated at regular intervals and the statistical methods used to determine patterns in such data.

● Equations Introduced in Chapter 15

■ **15-1** $$b = \frac{\Sigma XY - n\overline{X}\,\overline{Y}}{\Sigma X^2 - n\overline{X}^2}$$ p. 866

This formula, originally introduced in Chapter 12 as Equation 12-4, enables us to calculate the *slope of the best-fitting regression line* for any two-variable set of data points. The symbols $\overline{X}$ and $\overline{Y}$ represent the means of the values of the independent variable and dependent variable respectively; n represents the number of data points with which we are fitting the line.

■ **15-2** $$a = \overline{Y} - b\overline{X}$$ p. 866

We met this formula as Equation 12-5. It enables us to compute the *Y-intercept of the best-fitting regression line* for any two-variable set of data points.

■ **15-3** $$b = \frac{\Sigma xY}{\Sigma x^2}$$ p. 868

When the individual years (X) are changed to coded time values (x) by subtracting the mean ($x = X - \overline{X}$), Equation 15-1 for the slope of the trend line is simplified and becomes Equation 15-3.

■ **15-4** $$a = \overline{Y}$$ p. 868

In a similar fashion, using coded time values also allows us to simplify Equation 15-2 for the intercept of the trend line.

■ **15-5** $$\hat{Y} = a + bx + cx^2$$ p. 870

Sometimes we wish to fit a trend with a parabolic (or second-degree) curve instead of a straight line ($\hat{Y} = a + bx$). The general form for a fitted second-degree curve is obtained by including the second-degree term (cx^2) in the equation for $\hat{Y}$.

■ **15-6** $$\Sigma Y = an + c\Sigma x^2$$ p. 871

■ **15-7** $$\Sigma x^2 Y = a\Sigma x^2 + c\Sigma x^4$$ p. 871

In order to find the least-squares second-degree fitted curve, we must solve Equations 15-6 and 15-7 simultaneously for the values of a and c. The value for b is obtained from Equation 15-3.

■ **15-8** $$\text{Percent of trend} = \frac{Y}{\hat{Y}} \times 100$$ p. 877

We can measure cyclical variation as a *percent of trend* by dividing the actual value (Y) by the trend value ($\hat{Y}$) and then multiplying by 100.

■ **15-9** Relative cyclical residual $= \frac{Y - \hat{Y}}{\hat{Y}} \times 100$ p. 878

Another measure of cyclical variation is the *relative cyclical residual*, obtained by dividing the deviation from the trend $(Y - \hat{Y})$ by the trend value, and multiplying the result by 100. The relative cyclical residual can easily be obtained by subtracting 100 from the percent of trend.

● Review and Application Exercises

■ **15-44** The number of people admitted to Valley Nursing Home per quarter is given in the following table:

	Spring	Summer	Fall	Winter
1992	29	30	41	43
1993	27	34	45	48
1994	33	36	46	51
1995	34	40	47	53

(a) Calculate the seasonal indices for these data (use a 4-quarter centered moving average).

(b) Deseasonalize these data using the indices from part (a).

(c) Find the least-squares line that best describes the trend of the deseasonalized figures.

■ **15-45** Wheeler Airline, a regional carrier, has estimated the number of passengers to be 595,000 (deseasonalized) for the month of December. How many passengers should the company anticipate if the December seasonal index is 128?

■ **15-46** An EPA research group has measured the level of mercury contamination in the ocean at a certain point off the East Coast. The following percentages of mercury were found in the water:

	Jan.	Feb.	Mar.	Apr.	May	June	July	Aug.	Sept.	Oct.	Nov.	Dec.
1993	0.3	0.7	0.8	0.8	0.7	0.7	0.6	0.6	0.4	0.7	0.2	0.5
1994	0.4	0.9	0.7	0.9	0.5	0.8	0.7	0.7	0.4	0.6	0.3	0.4
1995	0.2	0.6	0.6	0.9	0.7	0.7	0.8	0.8	0.5	0.6	0.3	0.5

Construct a 4-month centered moving average, and plot it on a graph along with the original data.

■ **15-47** A production manager for a Canadian paper mill has accumulated the following information describing the millions of pounds processed quarterly:

	Winter	Spring	Summer	Fall
1992	3.1	5.1	5.6	3.6
1993	3.3	5.1	5.8	3.7
1994	3.4	5.3	6.0	3.8
1995	3.7	5.4	6.1	3.9

(a) Calculate the seasonal indices for these data (percentage of actual to centered moving average).

(b) Deseasonalize these data, using the seasonal indices from part (a).

(c) Find the least-squares line that best describes these data.

(d) Estimate the number of pounds that will be processed during the spring of 1996.

■ **15-48** Describe some of the difficulties in using a linear estimating equation to describe these data:

(a) Gasoline mileage achieved by U.S. automobiles.

(b) Fatalities in commercial aviation.

(c) The grain exports of a single country.

(d) The price of gasoline.

15-49 Magna International is a large Canadian manufacturer of automotive components such as molded door panels. Magna's 1992 annual report listed the company's revenues for the previous ten years (in millions of Canadian dollars):

Year	1983	1984	1985	1986	1987	1988	1989	1990	1991	1992
Revenue	302.5	493.6	690.4	1,027.8	1,152.5	1,458.6	1,923.7	1,927.2	2,017.2	2,358.8

(a) Find the least-squares trend line for these data.

(b) Plot the annual data and the trend line on the same graph. Do the variations from the trend appear random or cyclical?

(c) Use a computer-based regression package to find the best-fitting parabolic trend for these data. Is c, the coefficient of x^2, significantly different from zero? Which of the two trend models would you recommend using to forecast Magna's 1993 revenues? Explain.

(d) Forecast Magna's 1993 revenues.

■ **15-50** Comment on the difficulties you would have using a second-degree estimating equation to predict the future behavior of the process that generated these data:

(a) Sales of personal computers in the United States.

(b) Use of video games in the United States.

(c) Premiums for medical malpractice insurance.

(d) The number of MBAs graduated from U.S. universities.

■ **15-51** The following table shows the number of franchisees of Beauty Bar, Inc., operating at the end of each year:

Year	1990	1991	1992	1993	1994	1995
Number of franchisees	596	688	740	812	857	935

(a) Find the linear equation that best describes these data.

(b) Estimate the number of operations manuals (one to a franchisee) that must be printed for 1997.

■ **15-52** An assistant undersecretary in the U.S. Commerce Department has the following data describing the value of grain exported during the last 16 quarters (in billions of dollars):

	I	II	III	IV
1992	1	3	6	4
1993	2	2	7	5
1994	2	4	8	5
1995	1	3	8	6

(a) Determine the seasonal indices and deseasonalize these data (using a 4-quarter centered moving average).

(b) Calculate the least-squares line that best describes these data.

(c) Identify the cyclical variation in these data by the relative cyclical residual method.

(d) Plot the original data, the deseasonalized data, and the trend.

■ **15-53** Richie Bell's College Bicycle Shop has determined from a previous trend analysis that spring sales should be 165 bicycles (deseasonalized). If the spring seasonal index is 143, how many bicycles should the shop sell this spring?

■ **15-54** With the U.S. Interstate Highway program nearly finished, of what use are old data to the manufacturers of heavy earth-moving equipment as they attempt to forecast sales? What new data would you suggest they use in their forecasting?

15-55 Automobile manufacturing is often cited as an example of a cyclical industry (one subject to changes in demand according to an underlying business cycle). Consider automobile production worldwide (in millions of units) and in the former U.S.S.R. (in hundreds of thousands of units) from 1970 through 1990:

Year	World	U.S.S.R.	Year	World	U.S.S.R.
1970	22.5	3.4	1981	27.5	13.2
1971	26.4	5.3	1982	26.6	13.1
1972	27.9	7.3	1983	30.0	13.2
1973	30.0	9.2	1984	30.5	13.3
1974	25.9	11.2	1985	32.3	13.3
1975	25.0	12.0	1986	32.9	13.3
1976	28.8	12.4	1987	33.0	13.3
1977	30.5	12.8	1988	34.3	12.6
1978	31.2	13.1	1989	35.6	12.2
1979	30.8	13.1	1990	35.8	12.6
1980	28.6	13.3			

(a) Find the least-squares trend line for the worldwide data.

(b) Plot the worldwide data and the trend line on the same graph. Do the variations from the trend appear random or cyclical?

(c) Plot the residuals as a percent of trend. Approximately how long is the business cycle shown by these data?

(d) Consider the output of automobiles in the former U.S.S.R. Discuss its similarities and differences with the patterns you found in parts (a), (b), and (c).

■ **15-56** R. B. Fitch Builders has completed these numbers of homes in the 8 years it has been in business:

Year	1988	1989	1990	1991	1992	1993	1994	1995
Completions	12	11	19	17	19	18	20	23

(a) Develop a linear estimating equation to describe the trend of completions.

(b) How many completions should R. B. plan on for 1999?

(c) Along with the answer to part (b), what advice would you give R. B. about using this forecasting technique?

A B C D E 25. Assume that a time series with annual data for the years 1988–1996 is described well by the second-degree equation $\hat{Y} = 5 + 3x + 9x^2$. Based only on this secular trend, what is the forecast value for 1997?

(a) 161.

(b) 245.

(c) 347.

(d) 293.75.

(e) 200.75.

A B C D 26. Suppose that $\hat{Y} = 10 + 3x$ describes well an annual time series for 1987–1993. If the actual value of Y for 1990 is 8, what is the percent of trend for 1990?

(a) 125%.

(b) 112.5%.

(c) 90%.

(d) 80%.

A B C D 27. A time series for the years 1985–1996 had the following relative cyclical residuals, in chronological order: −1%, −2%, 1%, 2%, −1%, −2%, 1%, 2%, −1%, −2%, 1%, 2%. The relative cyclical residual for 1997 should be:

(a) 3%.

(b) −1%.

(c) −2%.

(d) Cannot be determined from information given.

A B C D 28. Assume that you have been given quarterly sales data for a 5-year period. To use the ratio-to-moving-average method of computing a seasonal index, your first step would be:

(a) Compute the 4-quarter moving average.

(b) Discard highest and lowest values for each quarter.

(c) Calculate the 4-quarter moving total.

(d) None of these.

Questions 29 through 31 deal with a seasonal index being computed, using the ratio-to-moving-average method for quarterly data from 1992–1996. The percentages of actual to moving average for the third quarter of each year are 1992, 109.0; 1993, 112.8; 1994, 110.0; 1995, 108.0; 1996, 104.6.

A B C D E 29. What is the *unadjusted* index for the third quarter?

(a) 108.88.

(b) 109.0.

(c) 110.23.

(d) 110.96.

(e) None of these.

A B C D E 30. Assume that the total of the unadjusted indices for the four quarters is 404.04. If the unadjusted index for the first quarter is 97.0, what is the adjusted seasonal index for the first quarter?

(a) 96.03.

(b) 97.98.

(c) 24.01.

(d) 99.00.

(e) Cannot be determined from the information given.

31. The adjusted seasonal index for the fourth quarter is 95.0. If the deseasonalized trend line that was calculated to estimate quarterly sales is $\hat{Y} = 400 + 9x$, what would be the seasonalized sales estimate for the fourth quarter of 1994?
(a) 499.7.
(b) 643.0.
(c)610.85.
(d) 676.8.

32. If a time series has an even number of years, and we use coding, then each coded interval is equal to:
(a) 1 year.
(b) 2 years.
(c) 1 month.
(d) 6 months.
(e) None of these.

33. A method used to deal with cyclical variation when the cyclical component does not explain most of the variation left unexplained by the trend component is:
(a) Spearman analysis.
(b) Specific analysis.
(c) Second-degree analysis.
(d) Relative cyclical residual.
(e) All of these.
(f) None of these.

34. For a given year, if an adjusted seasonal index for some period is greater than 100, then the following must be true:
(a) The adjusted index for some other period is > 100.
(b) The adjusted index for some other period is < 100.
(c) The adjusted index for some other period is $= 100$.
(d) (a) and (b) but not (c).
(e) None of the above.

35. If the percent of trend for a particular year in a time series is greater than 100%, then for this year:
(a) The actual time-series value lies below the trend line and the relative cyclical residual is positive.
(b) The actual time-series value lies below the trend line and the relative cyclical residual is positive.
(c) The actual time-series value lies above the trend line and the relative cyclical residual is negative.
(d) The actual time-series value lies above the trend line and the relative cyclical residual is positive.

36. Which of the following are common reasons for studying both secular trends and seasonal variation:
(a) To allow the elimination of the component from the series.
(b) To describe past patterns.
(c) To project past patterns into the future.
(d) All of the above.
(e) None of the above.

Precision Metal Products manufactures high-quality fabrications for use in the production of machinery for heavy industry. The company's three principal materials are coal, iron ore, and nickel ore. Management has the following data showing prices of these materials in 1975 and 1995 and quantity data for 1988, a year when purchasing patterns were characteristic of the entire 20-year period.

Raw Material	Qty. Used 1988 (000 tons)	Price/Ton 1975	Price/Ton 1995
Coal	158	$7.56	$19.50
Iron ore	12	9.20	21.40
Nickel ore	5	12.30	36.10

Management would like help in constructing some measure of the change in material prices in the 20-year period. Using the methods in this chapter, we can supply it with such a figure to use in its planning. ■

16.1 Defining an Index Number

Why use an index number?

At some time, everyone faces the question of how much something has changed over a period of time. We may want to know how much the price of groceries has increased so we can adjust our budgets accordingly. A factory manager may wish to compare this month's per-unit production cost with that of the past 6 months. Or a medical research team may wish to compare the number of flu cases reported this year with the number reported in previous years. In each of these situations, the degree of change must be determined and defined. Typically, we use *index numbers* to measure such differences.

What is an index number?

An index number measures how much a variable changes over time. We calculate an index number by finding the ratio of the current value to a base value. Then we multiply the resulting number by 100 to express the index as a percentage. This final value is the *percentage relative.* Note that the index number for the base point in time is always 100.

Computing a simple index

The secretary of state of North Carolina has data indicating the number of new businesses incorporated. The data she collects show that 9,300 were started in 1980, 6,500 in 1985, 9,600 in 1990, and 10,100 in 1995. If 1980 is the base year, she can calculate the index numbers reflecting volume changes using the process presented in Table 16-1.

Using these calculations, the secretary of state finds that incorporations in 1985 had an index of 70 relative to 1980. Another way to state this is to say that the number of incorporations in 1985 was 70 percent of the number of incorporations in 1980.

Types of Index Numbers

Price index

There are three principal types of indices: the price index, the quantity index, and the value index. A *price index* is the one most frequently used. It compares levels of prices from one period to another. The familiar *Consumer Price Index* (CPI), tabulated by the Bureau of

Table 16-1

Calculation of Index Numbers (Base Year = 1980)

Year (1)	Number of New Incorporations (000) (2)	Ratio (3) = (2) ÷ 9.3	Index or Percentage Relative (4) = (3) × 100
1980	9.3	$\frac{9.3}{9.3} = 1.00$	1.00 × 100 = 100
1985	6.5	$\frac{6.5}{9.3} = 0.70$	0.70 × 100 = 70
1990	9.6	$\frac{9.6}{9.3} = 1.03$	1.03 × 100 = 103
1995	10.1	$\frac{10.1}{9.3} = 1.09$	1.09 × 100 = 109

Labor Statistics, measures overall price changes of a variety of consumer goods and services and is used to define the cost of living.

Quantity index

A *quantity index* measures how much the number or quantity of a variable changes over time. Our example using incorporations determined a quantity index relating the numbers in 1985, 1990, and 1995 to that in 1980.

Value index

The last type of index, the *value index,* measures changes in total monetary worth. That is, it measures changes in the dollar value of a variable. In effect, the value index combines price and quantity changes to present a more informative index. In our example, we determined only a quantity index. However, we could have included the dollar effect by computing the total incorporated value for the years under consideration. Table 16-2 presents the corresponding value indices for 1985, 1990, and 1995. From this computation, we can say that the *value index* of incorporations in 1995 was 160. Or we can say that the incorporated value of 1995 increased 60 percent relative to the incorporated value of 1980.

Usually, an index measures change in a variable over a period of time, such as in a time series. However, it can also be used to measure differences in a given variable in different locations. This is done by simultaneously collecting data in different locations and then comparing the data. The comparative cost-of-living index, for example, shows that in terms of the cost of goods and services, it is cheaper to live in Austin, Texas, than in New York City.

Composite index numbers

A single index may reflect a composite, or group, of changing variables. The Consumer Price Index measures the general price level for specific goods and services in the economy.

Table 16-2

Computing a Value Index (Base Year = 1980)

Year (1)	Incorporated Value (millions) (2)	Ratio (3) = (2) ÷ 18.4	Index or Percentage Relative (4) = (3) × 100
1980	$18.4	$\frac{18.4}{18.4} = 1.00$	1.00 × 100 = 100
1985	14.6	$\frac{14.6}{18.4} = 0.79$	0.79 × 100 = 79
1990	26.2	$\frac{26.2}{18.4} = 1.42$	1.42 × 100 = 142
1995	29.4	$\frac{29.4}{18.4} = 1.60$	1.60 × 100 = 160

It combines the individual prices of the goods and services to form a composite price index number.

Uses of Index Numbers

Index numbers can be used in several ways. It is most common to use them by themselves, as an end result. Index numbers such as the Consumer Price Index are often cited in news reports as general indicators of the nation's economic condition.

One use of the Consumer Price Index

Management uses index numbers as part of an intermediate computation to understand other information better. In the chapter on time series, seasonal indices were used to modify and improve estimates of the future. The use of the Consumer Price Index to determine the real buying power of money is another example of how index numbers help increase knowledge of other factors. Table 16-3 shows the weekly salary paid to a secretary over a period of years, the corresponding Consumer Price Index values, and computation of the secretary's real salary. The secretary's dollar salary increased substantially, but the actual buying power of her income increased less rapidly. This can be attributed to the simultaneous rise in the cost-of-living index from 100 to 200.

Problems Related to Index Numbers

Several things can distort index numbers. The four most common causes of distortion are:

Limited data

1. Sometimes there is **difficulty in finding suitable data** to compute an index. Suppose the sales manager of Colonial Aircraft is interested in computing an index describing seasonal variation in the sale of the company's small planes. If sales are reported only on an annual basis, he would be unable to determine the seasonal sales pattern.

Incomparability

2. **Incomparability of indices** occurs when attempts are made to compare one index with another after there has been a basic change in what is being measured. If Citizens for Reasonable Transportation compare price indices of automobiles from 1979 to 1989, they find that prices have increased substantially. However, this comparison does not take into consideration technological advances in the quality of automobiles achieved over the time period in consideration.

Inappropriate weighting

3. **Inappropriate weighting of factors** can also distort an index. In developing a composite index, such as the Consumer Price Index, we must consider changes in some variables to be more important than changes in others. The

Table 16-3 Computation of Real Wages

Year (1)	Weekly Salary Paid (2)	Consumer Price Index (3)	$(4) = \frac{(2) \times 100}{(3)}$	Real or Adjusted Salary
1977	\$114.75	100	$114.75 \times \frac{100}{100} =$	\$114.75
1982	145.50	123	$145.50 \times \frac{100}{123} =$	\$118.29
1992	472.98	200	$472.98 \times \frac{100}{200} =$	\$236.49

effect on the economy of a 50-cent-per-gallon increase in the price of gasoline cannot be counterbalanced by a 50-cent decrease in the price of cars. It must be realized that the 50-cent-per-gallon increase in gas cost has a much greater effect on consumers. Thus, greater weight has to be assigned to the increased gas price than to the decrease in the cost of cars.

Use of an improper base

4. Distortion of index numbers also occurs when **selection of an improper base** occurs. Sometimes a firm selects a base that automatically leads to a result that is in its own interest and proves its initial assumption. If Consumers Against Oil Waste wants to portray oil companies in a bad light, it might measure this year's profits with a recession year as its base for oil profits. This would produce an index that shows oil profits have increased substantially. On the other hand, if Consumers for Unlimited Oil Use wishes to show that this year's profits are minimal, it might select a year with high profits for its base year. Using high profit as a base would probably result in an index indicating a small increase, or maybe even a decline, in oil profits this year. Therefore, we must always consider how and why the base period was selected before we accept a claim based on the result of comparing index numbers.

Sources of Index Numbers

Sources of data for index numbers

When managers apply index numbers to everyday problems, they use many sources to obtain the necessary information. The source depends on their information requirements. A firm can use monthly sales reports to determine its seasonal sales pattern. In dealing with broad areas of national economy and the general level of business activity, publications such as the *Federal Reserve Bulletin, Moody's, Monthly Labor Review,* and the *Consumer Price Index* provide a wealth of data. Many federal and state publications are listed in the U.S. Department of Commerce pamphlet *Measuring Markets.* Almost all government agencies distribute data about their activities, from which index numbers can be computed. Many financial newspapers and magazines provide information from which index numbers can be computed. When you read these sources, you will find that many of them use index numbers themselves.

Exercises 16.1

Basic Concepts

- **16-1** What is the index for a base year?
- **16-2** Explain the differences among the three principal types of indices: *price, quantity,* and *value.*
- **16-3** What does the Consumer Price Index measure? Is this based on a single variable or a composite of variables?
- **16-4** What are two basic ways of using index numbers?
- **16-5** What does an index number measure?
- **16-6** How is a percentage relative (index) found?

16.2 Unweighted Aggregates Index

The simplest form of a composite index is an *unweighted aggregates index. Unweighted* means that all the values considered in calculating the index are of equal importance. *Aggregate* means that we add, or sum, all the values. The principal advantage of an unweighted aggregates index is its simplicity.

Computing an unweighted aggregates index

An unweighted aggregates index is calculated by adding all the elements in the composite for the given time period and then dividing this result by the sum of the same elements during the base period. Equation 16-1 presents the mathematical formula for computing an unweighted aggregates quantity index.

Unweighted Aggregates Quantity Index

$$\frac{\Sigma Q_i}{\Sigma Q_0} \times 100 \qquad [16\text{-}1]$$

where

- Q_i = quantity of each element in the composite for the year in which we want the index
- Q_0 = quantity of each element in the composite for the base year

A word of explanation about the use of the subscript i to indicate the year for which we want to compute the index: Suppose we have quantity data for 1990 (the base year), 1991, and 1992, and we want to compute unweighted aggregates quantity indices for 1991 and 1992. If we use the subscripts 0, 1, and 2 to denote 1990, 1991, and 1992, then the index for 1991 is

$$\frac{\Sigma Q_1}{\Sigma Q_0} \times 100$$

and the index for 1992 is

$$\frac{\Sigma Q_2}{\Sigma Q_0} \times 100$$

Both of these are captured by the use of the generic subscript i in the numerator of Equation 16-1. We shall use i in the same fashion *in the formulas* defining all of the index numbers we discuss in this chapter. For sake of brevity, we shall use *current year* to indicate the *year in which we want the index.*

Note that we can substitute *either* prices or values for quantities in Equation 16-1 to find the general equation for a price index or a value index. Because the ratio is multiplied by 100, the resulting index is technically a percentage. However, it is customary to refer only to the value and to omit the percent sign when discussing index numbers.

Computing an unweighted index

The example in Table 16-4 demonstrates how we compute an unweighted index. In this case, we want to measure changes in general price levels on the basis of changes in prices of a few items. The 1990 prices are the base values to which we compare the 1995 prices.

Table 16-4
Computation of an Unweighted Index

Elements in the Composite	Prices 1990 P_0	Prices 1995 P_1
Milk (1 gallon)	$1.92	$3.40
Eggs (1 dozen)	0.81	1.00
Hamburger (1 pound)	1.49	2.00
Gasoline (1 gallon)	1.00	1.17
	$\Sigma P_0 = 5.22$	$\Sigma P_1 = 7.57$

Unweighted aggregates price index

$$= \frac{\Sigma P_i}{\Sigma P_0} \times 100 \quad [16\text{-}1]$$

$$= \frac{7.57}{5.22} \times 100$$

$$= 1.45 \times 100$$

$$= 145$$

Interpreting the index

From these calculations, we determine that the price index describing the change in these items from 1990 to 1995 is 145. If the elements in this composite are representative of the general price level, we can say that prices rose 45 percent from 1990 to 1995. However, we cannot expect a sample of four items to reflect accurate price changes for all goods and services. Thus, this calculation provides us with only a very rough estimate.

Suppose we now add the change in price of hand-held electronic calculators from 1990 to 1995 to our composite (Table 16-5). Again, 1990 is the base period against which we compare the 1995 prices.

Limitations of an unweighted index

Intuitively we know that the previous index of 145 is a more accurate estimate of general price behavior than 92 because more prices rose than fell between 1990 and 1995. Thus, we see **the major disadvantage of an unweighted index. It does not attach greater importance, or weight, to the price change of a high-use item than it does to a low-volume item.** (A family may purchase 50 dozen eggs a year, but it would be unusual for a family to

Table 16-5
Computation of an Unweighted Index

Elements in the Composite	Prices 1990 P_0	Prices 1995 P_1
Milk (1 gallon)	$1.92	$3.40
Eggs (1 dozen)	0.81	1.00
Hamburger (1 pound)	1.49	2.00
Gasoline (1 gallon)	1.00	1.17
Hand-held electronic calculator (1)	15.00	11.00
	$\Sigma P_0 = 20.22$	$\Sigma P_1 = 18.57$

Unweighted aggregates price index

$$= \frac{\Sigma P_i}{\Sigma P_0} \times 100 \quad [16\text{-}1]$$

$$= \frac{18.57}{20.22} \times 100$$

$$= 0.92 \times 100$$

$$= 92$$

own more than one or two calculators.) A substantial price change for slow-moving items can completely distort an index. For this reason, it is not common to use a simple unweighted index in important analyses.

The deficiencies of an unweighted index suggest that we use a weighted index. There are two ways to calculate more sophisticated indices. Each of these will be discussed in detail in the following sections.

HINTS & ASSUMPTIONS

Warning: An unweighted index can be distorted, and lose its value from changes in a few items in the index that do not fairly represent the situation being studied. Hint: Social Security payments have been "indexed" to the Consumer Price Index, which includes average mortgage costs as a measure of housing costs. But most Social Security recipients are not in the market for a new mortgage. With the exception of those who have an adjustable-rate mortgage, their mortgage payments are fixed and thus their costs are not affected by inflation. Warning: The major disadvantage of an unweighted index is that it does *not* attach greater importance to price changes in a high-use item than it does to a low-use item. Hint: Before you decide which index is appropriate, look carefully at the product/service components of that index to see whether their usage has been constant.

Exercises 16.2

Self-Check Exercise

SC 16-1 The VP of sales for Xenon Computer Corporation is examining the commission rate employed for the last 3 years. Below are the commission earnings of the company's top five sales personnel.

	1993	1994	1995
Guy Howell	$48,500	$55,100	$63,800
Skip Ford	41,900	46,200	60,150
Nelson Price	38,750	43,500	46,700
Nina Williams	36,300	45,400	39,900
Ken Johnson	33,850	38,300	50,200

Using 1993 as the base period, express the commission earnings in 1994 and 1995 in terms of an unweighted aggregates index.

Applications

■ **16-7** In an effort to get a measure of economic hardship, the IMF (International Monetary Fund) collected data on the price behavior of five major products imported by a group of less-developed countries. Using 1992 as the base period, express the 1995 prices in terms of an unweighted aggregates index.

Product	A	B	C	D	E
1992 price	$127	$532	$2,290	$60	$221
1995 price	$152	$651	$2,314	$76	$286

■ **16-8** For purposes of bidding on U.S. contracts, the management of a large overseas manufacturing facility are compiling data on wage levels. The following data concern base pay for the different classes of labor in the facility over a 4-year period.

	Wages per Hour			
	1992	1993	1994	1995
Class A	$8.48	$9.32	$10.34	$11.16
Class B	6.90	7.52	8.19	8.76
Class C	4.50	4.99	5.48	5.86
Class D	3.10	3.47	3.85	4.11

Using 1992 as the base period, calculate the unweighted aggregates wage index for 1993, 1994, and 1995.

■ **16-9** A study of college costs has collected data for the amount of tuition a full-time undergraduate paid during the last 4 years at four schools:

	1993	1994	1995	1996
Eastern U.	$3,142	$3,564	$4,109	$4,372
State U.	2,816	3,474	3,682	4,019
Western U.	3,582	3,987	4,406	4,819
Central U.	4,014	4,197	4,384	4,671

Using 1993 as a base period, express tuition charges in 1994, 1995, and 1996 in terms of an unweighted aggregates index.

■ **16-10** Bill Ivey, the administrator of a small rural hospital, has compiled the information shown regarding food purchased for the hospital kitchen. For the commodities listed, the corresponding price indicates the average price for that year. Using 1994 as the base period, express the prices in 1993 and 1995 in terms of an unweighted aggregates index.

Commodity	1993	1994	1995
Dairy products	$2.34	$2.38	$2.60
Meat products	3.19	3.41	3.36
Vegetable products	0.85	0.89	0.94
Fruit products	1.11	1.19	1.18

■ **16-11** A chemical processing plant used five materials in the manufacture of an industrial cleaning agent. The following data indicate the final inventory levels for these materials for the years 1993 and 1995.

Material	A	B	C	D	E
Inventory (tons) 1993	86	395	1,308	430	113
Inventory (tons) 1995	95	380	1,466	469	108

Using 1993 as the base period, express the 1995 inventory levels in terms of an unweighted aggregates index.

■ **16-12** John Dykstra, a management trainee in a bank, has collected information on the bank's transactions for the years 1994 and 1995:

	Withdrawals		Deposits	
	Savings	Checking	Savings	Checking
Number of transactions 1994	169,000	21,843,000	293,000	2,684,000
Number of transactions 1995	158,000	23,241,000	303,000	3,361,000

Using 1994 as the base period, express the number of banking transactions in 1995 in terms of an unweighted aggregates index.

■ **16-13** The Bookster Publishing Company began its business of publishing college textbooks in 1993. It is interested in determining how its sales have changed compared to its first year. A summary of the company's records shows how many new books it published in each year in the following areas:

	1993	1994	1995
Biology	48	53	50
Mathematics	32	37	35
History	19	15	22
English	16	20	21
Sociology	24	18	26
Physics	10	26	32
Chemistry	27	26	30
Philosophy	11	8	15

Using 1993 as the base year, calculate the unweighted aggregates quantity index for 1994 and 1995. Interpret the results for the publishing company.

Worked-Out Answer to Self-Check Exercise

SC 16-1

	1993 Q_0	1994 Q_1	1995 Q_2
Howell	48,500	55,100	63,800
Ford	41,900	46,200	60,150
Price	38,750	43,500	46,700
Williams	36,300	45,400	39,900
Johnson	33,850	38,300	50,200
	199,300	**228,500**	**260,750**
	19,930,000	22,850,000	26,075,000
Index $= \dfrac{\Sigma Q_i}{\Sigma Q_0} \times 100$:	99,300	199,300	199,300
	= 100.0	= 114.7	= 130.8

16.3 Weighted Aggregates Index

Advantages of weighting in an index

As we have said, often we have to attach greater importance to changes in some variables than to others when we compute an index. This weighting allows us to include more information than just the change in price over time. It also lets us improve the accuracy of the general price level estimate based on our sample. The problem is to decide how much weight to attach to each of the variables in the sample.

Computing a weighted aggregates index

The general formula for computing a weighted aggregates price index is

Weighted Aggregates Price Index

$$\frac{\Sigma P_i Q}{\Sigma P_0 Q} \times 100 \qquad [16\text{-}2]$$

where

- P_i = price of each element in the composite in the current year
- P_0 = price of each element in the composite in the base year
- Q = quantity weighting factor chosen

Consider the sample in Table 16-6. Each of the elements in the composite is taken from Table 16-5 and is weighted according to the volume of sales. The process of weighted aggregates confirms our earlier intuitive impression from page 927 that the general price level had risen (index = 129).

Typically, management uses the quantity of an item consumed as the measure of its importance in computing a weighted aggregates index. This leads to an important question in applying the process: Which quantities are used?

Three ways to weight an index

In general, there are three ways to weight an index. The first involves using quantities consumed during the base period in computing each index number. This is called the *Laspeyres method,* after the statistician who developed it. The second uses quantities consumed during the period in question for each index. This is the *Paasche method,* in honor of the person who devised it. The third way is called the *fixed-weight aggregates method.* With this method, one period is chosen, and its quantities are used to find *all* indices. (Note that if the chosen period is the base period, the fixed-weight aggregates method is the same as the Laspeyres method.)

Table 16-6

Computation of a Weighted Aggregates Index

Elements in the Composite	Q Volume (billions) (1)	P_0 1990 Prices (2)	P_1 1995 Prices (3)	P_0Q Weighted Sales (4) = (2) × (1)	P_1Q Weighted Sales (5) = (3) × (1)
Milk	20.000 (gal)	$ 1.92	$ 3.40	1.92 × 20.000 = 38.40	3.40 × 20.000 = 68.00
Eggs	3.500 (doz)	0.81	1.00	0.81 × 3.500 = 2.84	1.00 × 3.500 = 3.50
Hamburger	11.000 (lb)	1.49	2.00	1.49 × 11.000 = 16.39	2.00 × 11.000 = 22.00
Gasoline	154.000 (gal)	1.00	1.17	1.00 × 154.000 = 154.00	1.17 × 154.000 = 180.18
Calculators	0.002 (units)	15.00	11.00	15.00 × 0.002 = 0.03	11.00 × 0.002 = 0.02
				ΣP_0Q = 211.66	ΣP_1Q = 273.70

$$\text{Weighted aggregates index} = \frac{\Sigma P_i Q}{\Sigma P_0 Q} \times 100 \qquad [16\text{-}2]$$

$$= \frac{273.70}{211.66} \times 100$$

$$= 1.29 \times 100$$

$$= 129$$

Laspeyres Method

The Laspeyres method

The Laspeyres method, which uses quantities consumed during the base period, is the method most commonly used because it requires quantity measures for only one period. Because each index number depends on the same base price and quantity, management can compare the index of one period directly with the index of another. Suppose a steel manufacturer's price index is 103 in 1992 and 125 in 1995, using 1990 base prices and quantities. The company concludes that the general price level has increased 22 percent from 1992 to 1995. To calculate the Laspeyres index, the company first multiplies the current-period price by the base-period quantity for each element in the composite, and then it sums each of the resulting values. Next it multiplies the base-period price by the base-period quantity for each element, and again it sums the resulting values. By dividing the first sum by the second and multiplying the result by 100, management can convert this value to a percentage relative. Equation 16-3 presents the formula used to determine the Laspeyres index.

Computing a Laspeyres index

Laspeyres Price Index

$$\frac{\Sigma P_i Q_0}{\Sigma P_0 Q_0} \times 100 \qquad [16\text{-}3]$$

where

- P_i = prices in the current year
- P_0 = prices in the base year
- Q_0 = quantities sold in the base year

Example using the Laspeyres method

Let's work an example to demonstrate how the Laspeyres method is used. Suppose we want to determine changes in price level between 1991 and 1995. Table 16-7 contains the pertinent data for 1991 and 1995.

Table 16-7

Calculation of a Laspeyres Index

Elements in the Composite (1)	P_0 Base Price 1991 (2)	P_1 Current Price 1995 (3)	Q_0 Average Quantity Consumed in 1991 by a Family (4)	P_0Q_0 (5) = (2) × (4)	P_1Q_0 (6) = (3) × (4)
Bread (1 loaf)	$0.91	$1.19	200 loaves	$182	$238
Potatoes (1 lb)	0.79	0.99	300 lb	237	297
Chicken (3-lb fryer)	3.92	4.50	100 chickens	392	450
				$\Sigma P_0Q_0 = 811$	$\Sigma P_1Q_0 = 985$

$$\text{Laspeyres price index} = \frac{\Sigma P_i Q_0}{\Sigma P_0 Q_0} \times 100 \qquad [16\text{-}3]$$

$$= \frac{985}{811} \times 100$$

$$= 1.21 \times 100$$

$$= 121$$

Drawing conclusions from the calculated index

If we have selected a representative sample of goods, we can conclude that the general price index for 1995 is 121 based on the 1991 index of 100. Alternatively, we can say that prices have increased by 21 percent. Notice that we have used the average quantity consumed in 1991 rather than the total quantity consumed. Actually, it does not matter which is used, as long as we apply the same quantity measure throughout the problem. Typically, we select the quantity measure that is easiest to find.

Advantages of the Laspeyres method

One advantage of the Laspeyres method is the comparability of one index with another. If we had the 1992 prices for the previous example, we would be able to find a value for the 1992 general price index. This index could be compared directly with the 1995 index. Using the same base-period quantity allows us to make a direct comparison.

Another advantage is that many commonly used quantity measures are not tabulated every year. A firm might be interested in some variable whose quantity measure is computed once every 10 years. The Laspeyres method uses only one quantity measure, that of the base year, so the firm does not need yearly tabulations to measure quantities consumed.

Disadvantage of the Laspeyres method

The primary disadvantage of the Laspeyres method is that it does not take into consideration changes in consumption patterns. Items purchased in large quantities just a few years ago may be relatively unimportant today. Suppose the base quantity of an item differs greatly from the quantity for the period in question. Then the change in that item's price indicates very little about the change in the general price level.

Paasche Method

Difference between Paasche and Laspeyres methods

The second way to compute a weighted aggregates price index is the Paasche method. Finding a Paasche index is similar to finding a Laspeyres index. The difference is that the weights used in the Paasche method are the quantity measures for the *current* period rather than for the *base* period.

Computing a Paasche index

The Paasche index is calculated by multiplying the current-period price by the current-period quantity for each item in the composite and summing these products. Then the base-period price is multiplied by the current-period quantity for each item, and the results are summed. The first sum is divided by the second sum, and the resulting value is multiplied by 100 to convert the value into a percentage relative. Equation 16-4 defines the method for calculating a Paasche index.

Paasche Price Index

$$\frac{\Sigma P_i Q_i}{\Sigma P_0 Q_i} \times 100 \qquad [16\text{-}4]$$

where

- P_i = current-period prices
- P_0 = base-period prices
- Q_i = current-period quantities

With this equation, we can rework the problem in Table 16-7. Notice that we have discarded the quantities consumed in 1991. They have been replaced by the quantities consumed in 1995. Table 16-8 presents the information necessary for this modified problem.

Table 16-8

Calculation of a Paasche Index

Elements in the Composite (1)	P_1 Current Price 1995 (2)	P_0 Base Price 1995 (3)	Q_1 Average Quantity Consumed in 1995 by a Family (4)	P_1Q_1 (5) = (2) × (4)	P_0Q_1 (6) = (3) × (4)
Bread (1 loaf)	$1.19	$0.91	200 loaves	$ 238	$ 182
Potatoes (1 lb)	0.99	0.79	100 lb	99	79
Chicken (3-lb fryer)	4.50	3.92	300 chickens	1,350	1,176
				$\Sigma P_1Q_1 = 1{,}687$	$\Sigma P_0Q_1 = 1{,}437$

$$\text{Paasche price index} = \frac{\Sigma P_iQ_i}{\Sigma P_0Q_i} \times 100 \qquad [16\text{-}4]$$

$$= \frac{1{,}687}{1{,}437} \times 100$$

$$= 1.17 \times 100$$

$$= 117$$

Interpreting the difference between the two methods

In this analysis, we find that the price index for 1995 is 117. As you see from Table 16-7, the price index calculated by the Laspeyres method is 121. The difference between these indices reflects the change in consumption patterns of the three variables in the composite.

Advantage of the Paasche method

The Paasche method is particularly helpful because it combines the effects of changes in price and consumption patterns. Thus, it is a better indicator of general changes in the economy than the Laspeyres method. In our examples, the Paasche index shows a trend toward less-expensive goods and services because it indicates a price level increase of 17 percent instead of the 21 percent increase calculated using the Laspeyres method.

Disadvantages of the Paasche method

One of the principal disadvantages of the Paasche method is the need to tabulate quantity measures for each period examined. Often, quantity information for each period is either expensive to gather or unavailable. It would be hard, for example, to find reliable sources of data to determine quantity measures of 100 food products consumed in different countries for each of several years.

Each value for a Paasche price index is the result of both price and quantity changes from the base period. **Because the quantity measures used for one index period are usually different from the quantity measures for another index period, it is impossible to attribute the difference between the two indices to price changes only.** Thus, it is difficult to compare indices from different periods as calculated by the Paasche method.

Fixed-Weight Aggregates Method

Fixed-weight aggregates index

The third technique used to assign weights to elements in a composite is the fixed-weight aggregates method. It is similar to both the Laspeyres and Paasche methods. However, instead of using base-period or current-period weights (quantities), it uses weights from a representative period. The representative weights are referred to as fixed weights. The fixed weights and the base prices do not have to come from the same period.

Computing a fixed-weight aggregates index

We calculate a fixed-weight aggregates price index by multiplying the current-period prices by the fixed weights and summing the results. Then we multiply the base-period prices by the fixed weights and sum them. Finally, we divide the first sum by the second and multiply by 100 to convert the ratio to a percentage relative. The formula used to calculate a fixed-weight aggregates price index is presented in Equation 16-5.

Fixed-Weight Aggregates Price Index	
$$\frac{\Sigma P_i Q_2}{\Sigma P_0 Q_2} \times 100$$	[16-5]

where

- P_i = current-period prices
- P_0 = base-period prices
- Q_2 = fixed weights

Example of a fixed-weight aggregates index

We can demonstrate the process used to calculate a fixed-weight aggregates price index by solving our chapter-opening example. Recall that management wants to determine the price-level changes of raw materials consumed by the company between 1975 and 1995. It has accumulated the information in Table 16-9. From examination of past purchasing records, management has decided that the quantities purchased in 1988 were characteristic of the purchasing patterns during the 20-year period. The 1975 price level is the base price in this analysis. Calculation of the fixed-weight aggregates index is shown in Table 16-9. The company management concludes from this analysis that the general price level has increased 157 percent over the 20-year period.

Advantage of a fixed-weight aggregates index

The primary advantage of a fixed-weight aggregates price index is the flexibility in selecting the base price and the fixed weight (quantity). In many cases, the period that a company wishes to use as the base-price level may have an uncharacteristic consumption level. Therefore, by being able to select a different period for the fixed weight, the company can improve the accuracy of the index. This index also allows a company to change the price base without changing the fixed weight. This is useful because quantity measures are often expensive or impossible to obtain for certain periods.

Table 16-9 Computation of a Fixed-Weight Aggregates Index

Raw Materials (1)	Q_2 Quantity Consumed 1988 (thousands of tons) (2)	P_0 Average Price 1975 ($ per ton) (3)	P_1 Average Price 1995 ($ per ton) (4)	P_0Q_2 Weighted Aggregate 1975 (5) = (3) × (2)	P_1Q_2 Weighted Aggregate 1995 (6) = (4) × (2)
Coal	158	$ 7.56	$19.50	$ 1,194.48	$3,081.00
Iron ore	12	9.20	21.40	110.40	256.80
Nickel ore	5	12.30	36.10	61.50	180.50
				ΣP_0Q_2 = **1,366.38**	ΣP_1Q_2 = **3,518.30**

$$\text{Fixed-weight aggregates price index} = \frac{\Sigma P_i Q_2}{\Sigma P_0 Q_2} \times 100 \qquad [16\text{-}5]$$

$$= \frac{3{,}518.30}{1{,}366.38} \times 100$$

$$= 2.57 \times 100$$

$$= 257$$

HINTS & ASSUMPTIONS

The three methods covered in this section all produce a *weighted aggregates index* by using the *quantities consumed* as a basis for the weighting. Hint: The only real difference among them is the *period* each uses to select these quantities. The *Laspeyres* method uses quantities from the base period. The *Paasche* method uses quantities from the period in question. The *fixed-weight aggregates* method uses quantities from a chosen period. Hint: If the chosen period in the *fixed-weight aggregates* method is the base period, this method becomes the *Laspeyres* method. Warning: Choosing the period to use for weighting requires careful observation and common sense. The decision maker is looking for a period that has *characteristic consumption*, which means a period that most nearly reflects the reality of the situation. There is no mathematical formula that will give you the right answer to this.

Exercises 16.3

Self-Check Exercises

SC 16-2 Bill Simpson, owner of a California vineyard, has collected the following information describing the prices and quantities of harvested crops for the years 1992–1995.

	Price (per ton)				Quantity Harvested (tons)			
Type of Grape	1992	1993	1994	1995	1992	1993	1994	1995
Ruby Cabernet	$108	$109	$113	$111	1,280	1,150	1,330	1,360
Barbera	93	96	96	101	830	860	850	890
Chenin Blanc	97	99	106	107	1,640	1,760	1,630	1,660

Construct a Laspeyres index for each of these 4 years using 1992 as the base period.

SC 16-3 Use the data from Exercise SC 16-2 to calculate a fixed-weight index for each year using 1992 prices as the base and the 1995 quantities as the fixed weight.

SC 16-4 Use the data from Exercise SC 16-2 to calculate a Paasche index for each year using 1993 as the base period.

Applications

■ **16-14** Eastern Digital has developed a substantial market share in the PC computer industry. The prices and number of units sold for their top four computer products from 1993 to 1996 were:

	Selling Price ($)				Number Sold (thousands)			
Model	1993	1994	1995	1996	1993	1994	1995	1996
ED 107	1,894	1,906	1,938	1,957	84.6	86.9	98.4	107.5
ED Electra	2,506	2,560	2,609	2,680	38.4	42.5	55.6	67.5
ED Optima	1,403	1,440	1,462	1,499	87.4	99.4	109.7	134.6
ED 821	1,639	1,650	1,674	1,694	75.8	78.9	82.4	86.4

Construct a Laspeyres index for each of these 4 years using 1993 as the base period.

■ **16-15** Use the data from Exercise 16-14 to calculate a fixed-weight index for each year using 1993 prices as the base and the 1996 quantities as the fixed weights.

■ **16-16** Use the data from Exercise 16-14 to calculate a Paasche index for each year using 1994 as the base period.

■ **16-17** Julie Pristash, the marketing manager of Mod-Stereo, a manufacturer of blank cassette tapes, has compiled the following information regarding unit sales for 1993–1995. Using the average quantities sold from 1993 to 1995 as the fixed weights, calculate the fixed-weight index for each of the years 1993 to 1995 based on 1993.

Length of Tape (minutes)	Retail Price 1993	1994	1995	Average Quantity (× 100,000) 1993–1995
30	$2.20	$2.60	$2.85	32
60	2.60	2.90	3.15	119
90	3.10	3.20	3.25	75
120	3.30	3.35	3.40	16

■ **16-18** Gray P. Saeurs owns the corner fruitstand in a small town. After hearing many complaints that his prices constantly change during the summer, he has decided to see whether this is true. Based on the following data, help Mr. Saeurs calculate the appropriate weighted aggregate price indices for each month. Use June as the base period. Is your result a Laspeyres index or a Paasche index?

Fruit	Price per Pound June	July	Aug.	No. of Pounds Sold June
Apples	$0.59	$0.64	$0.69	150
Oranges	0.75	0.65	0.70	200
Peaches	0.87	0.90	0.85	125
Watermelons	1.00	1.10	0.95	350
Cantaloupes	0.95	0.89	0.90	150

■ **16-19** Charles Widget is in charge of keeping in stock certain items that his company needs in repairing its machines. Since he started this job 3 years ago, he has been observing the changes in the prices for the items he keeps in stock. He arranged the data in the following table in order to calculate a fixed-weight aggregates price index. Perform the calculations Mr. Widget would do using 1993 as the base year.

Item	Price per Item 1993	1994	1995	Average No. Used During 3-Year Period
W-gadget	$1.25	$1.50	$2.00	900
X-gadget	6.50	7.00	6.25	50
Y-gadget	5.25	5.90	6.40	175
Z-gadget	0.50	0.80	1.00	200

Worked-Out Answers to Self-Check Exercises

SC 16-2

Type of Grape	1992 Q_0	1992 P_0	1993 P_1	1994 P_2	1995 P_3
Ruby Cabernet	1,280	108	109	113	111
Barbera	830	93	96	96	101
Chenin Blanc	1,640	97	99	106	107

1992 P_0Q_0	1993 P_1Q_0	1994 P_2Q_0	1995 P_3Q_0
138,240	139,520	144,640	142,080
77,190	79,680	79,680	83,830
159,080	162,360	173,840	175,480
374,510	**381,560**	**398,160**	**401,390**

$$\text{Laspeyres Index} = \frac{\Sigma P_iQ_0}{\Sigma P_0Q_0} \times 100: \quad \frac{37{,}451{,}000}{374{,}510} = 100.0 \quad \frac{38{,}156{,}000}{374{,}510} = 101.9 \quad \frac{39{,}816{,}000}{374{,}510} = 106.3 \quad \frac{40{,}139{,}000}{374{,}510} = 107.2$$

SC 16-3

Type of Grape	1995 Q_3	1992 P_0	1993 P_1	1994 P_2	1995 P_3
Ruby Cabernet	1,360	108	109	113	111
Barbera	890	93	96	96	101
Chenin Blanc	1,660	97	99	106	107

1992 P_0Q_3	1993 P_1Q_3	1994 P_2Q_3	1995 P_3Q_3
146,880	148,240	153,680	150,960
82,770	85,440	85,440	89,890
161,020	164,340	175,960	177,620
390,670	**398,020**	**415,080**	**418,470**

$$\text{Fixed-Weight Index} = \frac{\Sigma P_iQ_3}{\Sigma P_0Q_3} \times 100: \quad \frac{39{,}067{,}000}{390{,}670} = 100.0 \quad \frac{39{,}802{,}000}{390{,}670} = 101.9 \quad \frac{41{,}508{,}000}{390{,}670} = 106.2 \quad \frac{41{,}847{,}000}{390{,}670} = 107.1$$

SC 16-4

Type of Grape	1992 P_1	1993 P_0	1994 P_2	1995 P_3	1992 Q_1	1993 Q_0	1994 Q_2	1995 Q_3
Ruby Cabernet	108	109	113	111	1,280	1,150	1,330	1,360
Barbera	93	96	96	101	830	860	850	890
Chenin Blanc	97	99	106	107	1,640	1,760	1,630	1,660

1992		1994		1995	
P_1Q_1	P_0Q_1	P_2Q_2	P_0Q_2	P_3Q_3	P_0Q_3
138,240	139,520	150,290	144,970	150,960	148,240
77,190	79,680	81,600	81,600	89,890	85,440
159,080	162,360	172,780	161,370	177,620	164,340
374,510	**381,560**	**404,670**	**387,940**	**418,470**	**398,020**

$$\text{Paasche Index} = \frac{\Sigma P_iQ_i}{\Sigma P_0Q_i} \times 100: \quad \frac{37{,}451{,}000}{381{,}560} = 98.2 \qquad \frac{40{,}467{,}000}{387{,}940} = 104.3 \qquad \frac{41{,}847{,}000}{398{,}020} = 105.1$$

16.4 Average of Relatives Methods

Unweighted Average of Relatives Method

As an alternative to the aggregates methods, we can use the average of relatives method to construct an index. Once again, we will use a price index to introduce the process.

Actually, we used a form of the average of relatives method in calculating the simple index in Table 16-1 on page 923. In that one-product example, we calculated the percentage relative by dividing the number of incorporations in the current year, Q_1, by the number in the base year, Q_0, and multiplying the result by 100.

Computing an unweighted average of relatives index

With more than one product (or activity), we first find the ratio of the current price to the base price for each product and multiply each ratio by 100. We then add the resulting percentage relatives and divide by the number of products. (Notice that the aggregates methods discussed in Section 16-3 differ from this method. They sum all the prices *before* finding the ratio.) Equation 16-6 presents the general form for the *unweighted average of relatives* method.

Unweighted Average of Relatives Price Index

$$\frac{\Sigma\left(\frac{P_i}{P_0} \times 100\right)}{n} \qquad [16\text{-}6]$$

where

- P_i = current-period prices
- P_0 = base-period prices
- n = number of elements (or products) in the composite

Comparing the unweighted aggregates index and the unweighted average of relatives index

In Table 16-10, we rework the problem in Table 16-4 on page 927 using the unweighted average of relatives method rather than the unweighted aggregates method.

Based on this analysis, the general price-level index for 1995 is 138. In Table 16-4, the unweighted aggregates index for the same problem is 145. Obviously, there is a difference between these two indices. With the unweighted average of relatives method, we compute

Table 16–10

Computation of an Unweighted Average of Relatives Index

Product (1)	P_0 1990 Prices (2)	P_1 1995 Prices (3)	Ratio × 100 (4) = $\frac{(3)}{(2)} \times 100$
Milk (1 gal)	\$1.92	\$3.40	$\frac{3.40}{1.92} \times 100 = 1.77 \times 100 = 177$
Eggs (1 doz)	0.81	1.00	$\frac{1.00}{0.81} \times 100 = 1.23 \times 100 = 123$
Hamburger (1 lb)	1.49	2.00	$\frac{2.00}{1.49} \times 100 = 1.34 \times 100 = 134$
Gasoline (1 gal)	1.00	1.17	$\frac{1.17}{1.00} \times 100 = 1.17 \times 100 = 117$
			$\sum\left(\frac{P_1}{P_0} \times 100\right) = 551$

$$\text{Unweighted average of relatives index} = \frac{\sum\left(\frac{P_i}{P_0} \times 100\right)}{n} \qquad [16\text{-}6]$$

$$= \frac{551}{4}$$

$$= 138$$

the average of the ratios of the prices for each product. With the unweighted aggregates method, we compute the ratio of the sums of the prices of each product. Notice that this is not the same as assigning some items more weight than others. Rather, the average of relatives method converts each element to a relative scale where each element is represented as a *percentage* rather than an *amount.* Because of this, each of the elements in the composite is measured against a base of 100.

Weighted Average of Relatives Method

Most problems management has to deal with require weighting by *importance.* Thus, it is more common to use the *weighted average of relatives method* than the unweighted method. When we computed a weighted aggregates price index in Section 16-3, we used the quantity consumed to weight the elements in the composite. To assign weights using the weighted average of relatives, we use the value of each element in the composite. (The value is the total dollar volume obtained by multiplying price by quantity.)

Different ways to determine weights

With the weighted average of relatives method, there are several ways to determine weighted value. As in the Laspeyres method, we can use the base value found by multiplying the base quantity by the base price. Using the base value will produce exactly the same result as calculating the index using the Laspeyres method. Because the result is the same, the decision to use the Laspeyres method or the weighted average of relatives method often depends on the availability of data. If value data are more readily available, the weighted average of relatives method is used. We use the Laspeyres method when quantity data are more readily obtained.

Computing a weighted average of relatives index

Equation 16-7 is used to compute a weighted average of relatives price index. This is a general equation into which we can substitute values from the base period, the current period, or any fixed period.

Weighted Average of Relatives Price Index

$$\frac{\sum\left[\left(\frac{P_i}{P_0} \times 100\right)(P_nQ_n)\right]}{\Sigma P_nQ_n} \quad [16\text{-}7]$$

where

- P_nQ_n = value
- P_0 = prices in the base period
- P_i = prices in the current period
- P_n and Q_n = quantities and prices that determine values we use for weights. In particular, $n = 0$ for the base period, $n = i$ for the current period, and $n = 2$ for a fixed period that is not a base or current period.

If we wish to compute a weighted average of relatives index using base values, P_0Q_0, the equation would be

Weighted Average of Relatives Price Index with Base Year Values as Weights

$$\frac{\sum\left[\left(\frac{P_i}{P_0} \times 100\right)(P_0Q_0)\right]}{\Sigma P_0Q_0} \quad [16\text{-}8]$$

Relation of weighted average of relatives to the Laspeyres method

Equation 16-8 is equivalent to the Laspeyres method for any given problem.

In addition to the specific cases of the general form of the weighted average of relatives method, we can use values determined by multiplying the price from one period by the quantity from a different period. Usually, however, we find Equations 16-7 and 16-8 adequate.

Example of a weighted average of relatives index

Here is an example. The information in Table 16-11 comes from Table 16-7 on page 933. We have base quantities and base prices, so we will use Equation 16-8. The price index of 122 differs slightly from the 121 calculated in Table 16-7 using the Laspeyres method, but only because of intermediate rounding.

Using base values, fixed values, or current values

As was the case for weighted aggregates, when we use base values, P_0Q_0, or fixed values, P_2Q_2, for weighted averages, we can readily compare the price level of one period with that of another. However, when we use current values, P_1Q_1, in computing a weighted average of relatives price index, we *cannot* directly compare values from different periods because both the prices and the quantities may have changed. Thus, we usually use either base values or fixed values when computing a weighted average of relatives index.

Hint: The *average of relatives* methods described in this section differ from those in the last section because they use the *total dollar volume consumed* as a basis for the weighting instead of just the quantities consumed. That's why each of them involves a price × quantity calculation. These kinds of indices are used by gasoline refineries and coffee blenders that must use different amounts of raw materials to produce a blended product that is pretty much the same month after month.

Table 16–11 Computing a Weighted Average of Relatives Index

Elements in the Composite (1)	Prices 1991 P_0 (2)	Prices 1995 P_1 (3)	Quantity 1991 Q_0 (4)	Percentage Price Relative $\frac{P_1}{P_0} \times 100$ (5) = $\frac{(3)}{(2)} \times 100$	Base Value P_0Q_0 (6) = (2) × (4)	Weighted Percentage Relative (7) = (5) × (6)
Bread (1 loaf)	\$0.91	\$1.19	200 loaves	$\frac{1.19}{0.91} \times 100 = 131$	182	23,842
Potatoes (1 lb)	0.79	0.99	300 lb	$\frac{0.99}{0.79} \times 100 = 125$	237	29,625
Chicken (3-lb fryer)	3.92	4.50	100 fryers	$\frac{4.50}{3.92} \times 100 = 115$	392	45,080
					$\Sigma P_0Q_0 = 811$	

$$\Sigma\left[\left(\frac{P_1}{P_0} \times 100\right)(P_0Q_0)\right] = 98,547$$

$$\text{Weighted average of relatives index} = \frac{\Sigma\left[\left(\frac{P_i}{P_0} \times 100\right)(P_0Q_0)\right]}{\Sigma P_0Q_0} \quad [16\text{-}8]$$

$$= \frac{98,547}{811}$$

$$= 122$$

Exercises 16.4

Self-Check Exercise

SC 16-5 As a part of the evaluation of a possible acquisition, a New York City conglomerate has collected this sales information:

Product	Average Annual Price 1993	Average Annual Price 1995	Total Dollar Value (Thousands) 1993
Calculators	\$ 27	\$ 20	\$ 150
Radios	30	42	900
Portable TVs	157	145	1,370

(a) Calculate the unweighted average of relatives price index using 1993 as the base period.

(b) Calculate the weighted average of relatives price index using the dollar value for each product in 1993 as the appropriate set of weights and 1995 as the base year.

Applications

■ **16-20** F. C. Linley, owner of the San Mateo Seals, collected information regarding the ticket prices and volume for his franchise over the last 4 years.

	Average Annual Price				Tickets Sold (× 10,000)			
	1992	1993	1994	1995	1992	1993	1994	1995
Box seats	$6.50	$7.25	$7.50	$8.10	26	27	31	28
General admission	3.50	3.85	4.30	4.35	71	80	89	90

Calculate a weighted average of relatives price index for each of the years 1992 through 1995 using 1993 as the base year and for weighting.

■ **16-21** The following table contains information from the raw-material purchase records of a tire manufacturer for the years 1993–1995.

Material	Average Annual Purchase Price/Ton 1993	1994	1995	Value of Purchase (thousands) 1995
Butadiene	$ 17	$ 15	$ 11	$ 50
Styrene	85	89	95	210
Rayon cord	348	358	331	1,640
Carbon black	62	58	67	630
Sodium pyrophosphate	49	56	67	90

Calculate a weighted average of relatives price index for each of those 3 years using 1995 for weighting and for the base year.

■ **16-22** A Tennessee public interest group has surveyed the labor cost of automobile repairs in three major Tennessee cities (Knoxville, Memphis, and Nashville). With the following information, construct an unweighted average of relatives price index using the 1991 prices as a base.

Type of Repair	1991	1993	1995
Replacement of water pump	$ 35	$ 37	$ 41
Regrinding of engine valves (6 cyl.)	189	205	216
Wheel balancing	26	29	30
Tune-up (minor)	16	16	18

■ **16-23** Garret Cage, the president of a local bank, is interested in the average levels of total savings and checking accounts for each of the last 3 years. He sampled days from each of these years; using the levels on those days, he determined the following yearly averages:

	1993	1994	1995
Savings accounts	$1,845,000	$2,320,000	$2,089,000
Checking accounts	385,000	447,000	491,000

Calculate an unweighted average of relatives index for each year using 1993 as the base period.

■ **16-24** InfoTech has researched the unit price and total value of memory chips imported into the United States in 1994 and 1996.

Product	Price 1994	1996	Total Dollar Value (Thousands) 1994
1-megabyte chips	$ 42	$ 65	957
4-megabyte chips	$180	$247	487
16-megabyte chips	$447	$612	349

(a) Calculate the unweighted average of relatives price index for 1996 using 1994 as the base period.

(b) Calculate the weighted average of relatives price index for 1996 using the dollar value for each product in 1994 as the appropriate set of weights and 1994 as the base year.

■ **16-25** A survey of transatlantic passenger rates for roundtrip flights from New York to various European cities produced these results:

	Average Annual Passenger Rates					Passengers (× 1,000)
Destination	**1991**	**1992**	**1993**	**1994**	**1995**	**1995**
Paris	$690	$714	$732	$777	$783	2,835
London	648	654	675	696	744	5,175
Munich	702	723	753	768	798	2,505
Rome	840	867	903	939	975	2,145

Calculate the weighted average of relatives index for each of the years 1991 through 1994 using 1995 as the base year and for weighting.

■ **16-26** In a study of group health insurance policies commissioned by the Rhode Island Medical Care Association, the following sample of average individual rates was collected. Using 1994 as the base period, calculate an unweighted average of relatives price index for each year.

Insurance Group	1992	1993	1994	1995
Physicians	$54	$65	$86	$103
Students	39	41	55	76
Government employees	48	61	76	93
Teachers	46	58	75	96

■ **16-27** A new motel chain hopes to place its first motel in Boomingville, but before it makes a commitment to start construction, it wants to check the room prices charged nightly by the other motels and hotels. After sending an employee to investigate the prices, the motel chain received data in the following form:

	Price per Room per Night			No. Rooms Rented
Hotel	**1993**	**1994**	**1995**	**1993**
Happy Hotel	$35	$37	$42	1,250
Room Service Rooms	25	26	28	950
Executive Motel	45	45	51	1,000
Country Inn	37	38	44	600
Family Fun Motel	26	30	31	2,075

Help the company determine the relative prices using 1993 as the base year and using an unweighted average of relatives index.

■ **16-28** The Quick-Stop Gas Station has been selling road maps to its customers for the past 3 years. The maps that are sold are of the nearest city, the county the gas station is in, the state it is in, and the entire United States. From the following table, calculate the weighted average of relatives price indices for 1994 and 1995 using 1993 as the base year.

Maps	1993	1994	1995	Quantity Sold 1993
City	$0.75	$0.90	$1.10	1,000
County	0.75	0.90	1.00	400
State	1.00	1.50	1.50	1,000
United States	2.50	2.75	2.75	220

Worked-Out Answer to Self-Check Exercise

SC 16-5

Product	1993 P_0	1995 P_1	$\frac{P_1}{P_0}$	P_0Q_0	$\left(\frac{P_1}{P_0}\right)(P_0Q_0)$
Calculators	$ 27	$ 20	0.7407	150	111.11
Radios	30	42	1.4000	900	1,260.00
TVs	157	145	0.9236	1,370	1,265.33
			3.0643	**2,420**	**2,636.44**

$$\text{(a)}\quad \text{Index} = \frac{\sum\left(\frac{P_i}{P_0} \times 100\right)}{n} = \frac{306.43}{3} = 102.1$$

$$\text{(b)}\quad \text{Index} = \frac{\sum\left(\frac{P_i}{P_0} \times 100\right)(P_0Q_0)}{\sum P_0Q_0} = \frac{263{,}644}{2{,}420} = 108.9$$

16.5 Quantity and Value Indices

Quantity Indices

Using a quantity index

Our discussion of index numbers up to now has concentrated on price indices so that it would be easier to understand the general concepts. However, we can also use index numbers to describe quantity and value changes. Of these two, we use quantity indices more often. The Federal Reserve Board calculates quarterly indices in its monthly publication *The Index of Industrial Production* (IIP). The IIP measures the quantity of production in the areas of manufacturing, mining, and utilities. It is computed using a weighted average of relatives quantity index in which the fixed weights (prices) and the base quantities are measured from 1977.

Advantages of a quantity index

In times of inflation, a quantity index provides a more reliable measure of actual output of raw materials and finished goods than a corresponding value index does. Similarly, agricultural production is best measured using a quantity index because it eliminates misleading effects due to fluctuating prices. We often use a quantity index to measure commodities that are subject to considerable price variation.

Any of the methods discussed in previous sections of this chapter to determine price indices can be used to calculate quantity indices. When we computed price indices, we used quantities or values as weights. Now that we want to compute quantity indices, we use prices or values as weights. Let's consider the construction of a weighted average of relatives quantity index.

Computing a weighted average of relatives quantity index

The general process for computing a weighted average of relatives quantity index is the same as that used to compute a price index. Equation 16-9 describes the formula for this type of quantity index. In this equation, value is determined by multiplying quantity by price. The value associated with each quantity is used to weight the elements in the composite.

Weighted Average of Relatives Quantity Index

$$\frac{\Sigma\left[\left(\frac{Q_i}{Q_0} \times 100\right)(Q_nP_n)\right]}{\Sigma Q_nP_n} \qquad [16\text{-}9]$$

where

- Q_i = quantities for the current period
- Q_0 = quantities for the base period
- P_n and Q_n = quantities and prices that determine values we use for weights. In particular, $n = 0$ for the base period, $n = 1$ for the current period, and $n = 2$ for a fixed period that is not a base or current period.

Consider the problem in Table 16-12. We use Equation 16-9 to compute a weighted average of relatives quantity index. The value Q_nP_n is determined from the base period and is therefore symbolized Q_0P_0.

Table 16-12 Computation of a Weighted Average of Relatives Quantity Index

Elements in the Composite (1)	Quantities (billions of bushels) 1991 Q_0 (2)	1995 Q_1 (3)	Price (per bushel) 1991 P_0 (4)	$\frac{Q_1}{Q_0} \times 100$ Percentage Relatives (5) = $\frac{(3)}{(2)} \times 100$	Base Value Q_0P_0 (6) = (2) × (4)	$\frac{Q_1}{Q_0} \times 100 \times Q_0P_0$ Weighted Relatives (7) = (5) × (6)
Wheat	29	24	\$3.80	$\frac{24.0}{29.0} \times 100 = 83$	29 × 3.80 = 110.20	9,146.60
Corn	3	2.5	2.91	$\frac{2.5}{3} \times 100 = 83$	3 × 2.91 = 8.73	724.59
Soybeans	12	14	6.50	$\frac{14.0}{12.0} \times 100 = 117$	12 × 6.50 = 78.00	9,126.00
					ΣQ_0P_0 = **196.93**	

$$\Sigma\left[\left(\frac{Q_1}{Q_0} \times 100\right)(Q_0P_0)\right] = \mathbf{18{,}997.19}$$

$$\text{Weighted average of relatives quantity index} = \frac{\Sigma\left[\left(\frac{Q_i}{Q_0} \times 100\right)(Q_0P_0)\right]}{\Sigma Q_0P_0} \qquad [16\text{-}9]$$

$$= \frac{18{,}997.19}{196.93}$$

$$= 96$$

Value Indices

A disadvantage of a value index

A value index measures general changes in the total value of some variable. Because value is determined both by price and quantity, a value index actually measures the combined effects of price and quantity changes. The principal disadvantage of a value index is that it does not distinguish between the effects of these two components.

Advantages of a value index

Nevertheless, a value index is useful in measuring overall changes. Medical insurance companies, for example, often cite the sharp increase in the *value* of payments awarded in medical malpractice suits as the primary reason for discontinuing malpractice insurance. In this situation, value involves both a greater number of payments and larger cash amounts awarded.

HINTS & ASSUMPTIONS

A quantity index is often used in production decisions because it avoids the effects of inflation and price fluctuations due to market dynamics. Hint: Think about your pizza delivery service, whose total dollar revenue may decrease during periods of high use of discount coupons. Because the company expects the *quantity* of pizzas to increase as a result of discounting, a quantity index is more useful in making decisions about reordering cheese, toppings, and dough and scheduling delivery people.

Exercises 16.5

Self-Check Exercise

SC 16-6 William Olsen, owner of a real estate office, has collected the following sales information for each of the firm's sales personnel:

	Value of Sales ($\times$ \$1,000)			
Salesperson	**1992**	**1993**	**1994**	**1995**
Thompson	490	560	530	590
Alfred	630	590	540	680
Jackson	760	790	810	840
Blockard	230	250	240	360

Calculate an unweighted average of relatives value index for each year using 1992 as the base period.

Basic Concepts

- **16-29** Explain the principal disadvantage in using value indices.
- **16-30** What is the major difference between a weighted aggregates index and a weighted average of relatives index?

Applications

■ **16-31** The financial VP of the American division of Banshee Camera Company is examining the company's cash and credit sales over the last 5 years.

	Value of Sales (× $100,000)				
	1991	**1992**	**1993**	**1994**	**1995**
Credit	5.66	6.32	6.53	6.98	7.62
Cash	2.18	2.51	2.48	2.41	2.33

Calculate an unweighted average of relatives value index for each year using 1991 as the base period.

■ **16-32** A Georgia firm manufacturing heavy equipment has collected the following production information about the company's principal products. Calculate a weighted aggregates quantity index using the quantities and prices from 1995 as the bases and the weights.

	Quantities Produced			Cost of Production/Unit (thousands)
Product	**1993**	**1994**	**1995**	**1995**
River barges	92	118	85	$ 33
Railroad gondola cars	456	475	480	56
Off-the-road trucks	52	56	59	116

■ **16-33** Arkansas Electronics has marketed three basic types of calculators: for the business sector, the scientific sector, and a simple model capable of basic computational functions. The following information describes unit sales for the past 3 years:

	Number Sold (× 100,000)			Price
Model	**1993**	**1994**	**1995**	**1995**
Business	11.85	13.32	15.75	$34.00
Scientific	10.32	11.09	10.18	69.00
Basic	7.12	7.48	7.89	13.00

Calculate the weighted average of relatives quantity indices using the prices and quantities from 1995 to compute the value weights with 1993 as the base year.

■ **16-34** In preparation for an appropriations hearing, the police commissioner of a Maryland town has collected the following information:

Type of Crime	1992	1993	1994	1995
Assault and rape	110	128	134	129
Murder	30	45	40	48
Robbery	610	720	770	830
Larceny	2,450	2,630	2,910	2,890

Calculate the unweighted average of relatives quantity index for each of these years using 1995 as the base period.

■ **16-35** Recycled Sounds has collected the following sales information for five different styles of music. Data are presented in hundreds of compact discs sold per year.

Type	1991	1992	1993	1994	1995	1996
			Number of Sales			
Soft rock	642.4	721.5	842.6	895.3	905.6	951.2
Hard rock	325.8	347.8	398.5	406.3	418.7	426.4
Classical	118.3	123.6	174.3	176.2	174.9	185.3
Jazz	125.6	122.4	137.8	149.6	172.9	205.4
Alternative	208.7	252.7	405.9	608.9	942.7	987.4

Calculate an unweighted average of relatives quantity index for each year using 1991 as the base year.

■ **16-36** After encouraging a chemical company to make its employees handle certain dangerous chemicals with protective gloves, the Public Health Agency is now interested in seeing whether this ruling has had its effect in curbing the number of cancer deaths in that area. Before this rule went into effect, cancer was widespread not only among the workers at the company, but also among their families, close friends, and neighbors. The following data show what these numbers were in 1973 before the ruling and what they were after the ruling in 1993.

Age Group	No. in Population for 1973	Deaths in 1973	Deaths in 1993
<4 yr	5,000	400	125
4–15 yr	4,000	295	200
16–35 yr	24,000	1,230	1,000
36–60 yr	19,000	700	450
>60 yr	7,000	1,100	935

Use a weighted aggregates index of the number of deaths using the 1973 population size as the weights to help the Public Health Agency understand what has happened to the cancer rate.

■ **16-37** A veterinarian has noticed she has treated a large number of pets this past winter. She wonders whether this number was spread across the 3 winter months evenly or whether she treated more pets in any certain month. Using December as the base period, calculate the weighted average of relatives quantity indices for January and February.

	Number Treated			Price per Visit:
	Dec.	Jan.	Feb.	Average for 3 Months
Cats	100	200	95	$ 55
Dogs	125	75	200	65
Parrots	15	20	15	85
Snakes	10	5	5	100

Worked-Out Answer to Self-Check Exercise

SC 16-6

Salesperson	1992 V_0	1993 V_1	1994 V_2	1995 V_3	1992 V_0/V_0	1993 V_1/V_0	1994 V_2/V_0	1995 V_3/V_0
Thompson	490	560	530	590	1.000	1.143	1.082	1.204
Alfred	630	590	540	680	1.000	0.937	0.857	1.079
Jackson	760	790	810	840	1.000	1.039	1.066	1.105
Blockard	230	250	240	360	1.000	1.087	1.043	1.565
					4.000	**4.206**	**4.048**	**4.953**

$$\text{Index} = \frac{\sum\left(\frac{V_i}{V_0} \times 100\right)}{4}: \quad \frac{400.0}{4} \quad \frac{420.6}{4} \quad \frac{404.8}{4} \quad \frac{495.3}{4}$$

$$100.0 \quad 105.2 \quad 101.2 \quad 123.8$$

16.6 Issues in Constructing and Using Index Numbers

Imperfections in index numbers

In this chapter, we have used examples with small samples and short time spans. Actually, index numbers are computed for composites with many elements, and they cover long periods of time. This produces relatively accurate measures of changes. However, even the best index numbers are imperfect.

Problems in Construction

Although there are many problems in constructing index numbers, there are three principal areas of difficulty:

Which items should be included in a composite?

1. **Selecting an item to be included in a composite.** Almost all indices are constructed to answer a particular question. Thus, the items included in the composite depend on the question. The Consumer Price Index asks, "How much has the price of a certain group of items purchased by moderate-income urban Americans changed from one period to another?" From this question, we know that only the items that reflect the purchases of moderate-income urban families should be included in the composite. We must realize that the Consumer Price Index will less accurately reflect price changes of goods purchased by low- or high-income rural families than by moderate-income urban families.

Need for selection of appropriate weights

2. **Selecting the appropriate weights.** In the previous sections of this chapter, we emphasized that the weights selected should represent the relative importance of the various elements. Unfortunately, what is appropriate in one period may become inappropriate in a short period of time. This must be kept in mind when comparing values of indices computed at different times.

What is a normal base period?

3. **Selecting the base period.** Typically, the base period selected should be a normal period, preferably a fairly recent period. "Normal" means that the pe-

riod should not be at either the peak or the trough of a fluctuation. One technique to avoid using an irregular period is to average the values of several consecutive periods to determine a normal value. The U.S. Bureau of Labor Statistics uses the average of 1982, 1983, and 1984 consumption patterns to compute the Consumer Price Index. Management often tries to select a base period that coincides with the base period for one or more of the major indices, such as the Index of Industrial Production. Use of a common base allows management to relate its index to the major indices.

Caveats in Interpreting an Index

In addition to these problems in constructing indices, there are several common errors made in interpreting indices:

Problems with generalizing from an index

1. **Generalization from a specific index.** One of the most common misinterpretations of an index is generalization of the results. The Consumer Price Index measures how prices of a particular combination of goods purchased by moderate-income urban Americans have changed. Despite its specific definition, the Consumer Price Index is often described as reflecting the cost of living for all Americans. Although it is related to the cost of living to some degree, to say that it measures the change in the cost of living is not correct.

Additional knowledge needed

2. **Lack of general knowledge regarding published indices.** Part of the problem leading to the first error is lack of knowledge of what the various published indices measure. All the well-known indices are accompanied by detailed statements concerning measurement. Management should become familiar with exactly what each index measures.

Time affects an index

3. **Effect of time span on an index.** Factors related to an index tend to change with time. In particular, the appropriate weights tend to change. Thus, unless the weights are changed accordingly, the index becomes less reliable.

Lack of measurement of quality

4. **Quality changes.** One common criticism of index numbers is that they do not reflect changes in the quality of the items they measure. If the quality has indeed changed, then the index either understates or overstates the price-level changes. For example, if we construct an index number to describe price changes in pocket calculators over the last decade, the resulting index would understate the actual change that is due to rapid technological improvements in calculators.

Exercises 16.6

Basic Concepts

■ **16-38** What is the effect of time on the weighting of a composite index?

■ **16-39** List several preferences for the choice of base period.

■ **16-40** Describe a technique used to avoid the use of an irregular period for a base.

■ **16-41** Is it correct to say that the Consumer Price Index measures the cost of living?

■ **16-42** What problems exist with index numbers if the quality of an item changes?

Statistics at Work

Loveland Computers

Case 16: Index Numbers "Lee, help me figure out these shipping charges." Walter Azko was looking at a contract about half an inch thick. "The way we do our buying, the manufacturers are responsible for delivering an order to the airport and then an international shipping agent arranges for all the paperwork and loading. Sometimes it feels as if I'm paying the agents more for shipping the goods than I pay the manufacturer for making them. This contract right here is a good example. They want more than 10 percent more than I paid them for a similar shipment last quarter. When I called them, they gave some excuse about the cost of living going up."

"But not by 10 percent," Lee interjected.

"No, and the price of jet fuel went down, so the air-freight bill should be less."

"Well, at least you don't have to worry about exchange rates," Lee said, glancing over the contract. "This says you're to make payment in U.S. dollars."

"That's true—we do send them a check in dollars and they clear it through the local branch of an American bank. Even though the dollar isn't quite the universal currency it once was, people still think it's less risky than many other currencies. But once the agent has cashed the check, they still have to exchange dollars for local currency. They can't pay their warehouse workers in dollars. So, even though the price is stated in dollars, I can tell that I get a better deal when the dollar is 'strong' against other currencies."

"The cost of living is one factor, the cost of aviation fuel is another, and the exchange rate is the third. Does that cover everything?"

"I suppose so," Walter replied. "But with three things going up and down, it's hard to bargain with the agent and tell him I think they're too high."

"I think I have a way I can help," Lee offered cheerfully. "Can I take the afternoon to go down to Denver and talk with the international department of our bank?"

Study Questions: What solution is Lee going to propose as a way to evaluate the proposed price for the shipping agent's contract? What information will Lee be looking for in the bank's international department?

Computer Database Exercise

HH Industries

Laurel knocked on Hal's door. "You wanted to see me?" she asked.

"Yes, please come in Laurel, and close the door behind you," Hal said, looking up from the stack of papers on his desk. "Thanks for coming by. I've got some decision making to do that, unfortunately, won't be a lot of fun, and I could use your help."

"Sure," Laurel nodded. "I'll be glad to do what I can." Hal looked unusually troubled, and Laurel wondered what was up.

"It's about our employee benefits," Hal began. "I don't know if you're aware of how health insurance costs have skyrocketed in recent years, but it's getting incredibly expensive for us to carry policies for our employees. Several small business owners I know have stopped providing health insurance altogether, but I just can't do that. I've always tried to do the best by my employees, but I need help with some justification for my next move, which may seem rather drastic to the people on my staff. I think if I have some information about previous trends and how the current situation fits in, it will be easier to convince them of its necessity."

"Let me give you some background," he continued. "Until a few years ago, we could expect a 10–12 percent yearly increase in insurance costs. More recently, however, the increase has been closer to 20 percent per year, and our agent is predicting as high as 30 percent increases in the near future. The company policy has always been to pay at least 75 percent of the premium, with the rest being covered by paycheck deductions. Family coverage costs us 2.5 times that for individuals, so that's what is reflected in the deductions the employees see. For a long time, we managed to get by without increasing the rates to employees, but it became necessary to implement yearly increases several years ago. In my efforts to give employees the best deal possible, I'm afraid the deductions haven't kept pace with what is required. I don't mind the company bearing a *little* more of the cost, but we can't survive that much longer at this rate. What I need from you is an idea of what's reasonable, based on past history. What do you think?"

"I'll see what I can do," answered Laurel. "I think I can generate some index numbers that capture past trends, and come up with some recommendations for you."

"Great," smiled Hal, "here are some historical figures. You know, I hate being caught between being a nice guy and running a business!"

1. Compute a weighted aggregates price index of employee contribution to health insurance using the number of "individual" and "family" employees covered each year from 1973 to 1993 as given in the CH16.xxx files on the data disk. Use 1973 as the base year. Compare this to an index of the total company insurance cost per year.
2. The anticipated insurance policy cost for 1994 is $270,000, and there are 20 "individual" and 45 "family" employees to be insured. If Hal doesn't mind the total-cost-index to employee-contribution-index ratio running as high as 1.2, what must be the individual and family deductions for 1994?

From the Textbook to the Real World

Index of Leading Economic Indicators

For businesses suffering through cycles of economic prosperity and depression, the composite index of leading economic indicators provides a means of attaining advance information about the future direction of the economy. Although not infallible, this index number provides a tool economists have used for more than 50 years to divine future trends. The system of leading, coincident, and lagging indicators was originally developed by Arthur F. Burns, Wesley C. Mitchell, and their colleagues at the National Bureau of Economic Research (NBER) during the Great Depression. It is currently maintained by the U.S. Department of Commerce and updated on a monthly basis.

Composition and History The index is a weighted average consisting of eleven components (Table RW 16-1), each of which has historically moved ahead of periods of general business expansion and decline. The data are combined into an index that measures the change from the base year (1982) value of 100. The index tends to foreshadow movements in the general economy and was first used to determine when the United States would come out of the Depression of the 1930s. From 1923 to 1969, the NBER predicted

Table RW16-1 Components of the Leading Indicator Index

- Average weekly hours of production or nonsupervisory workers, manufacturing.
- Average weekly initial claims for unemployment insurance, state programs.
- Manufacturers' new orders in 1982 dollars, consumer goods and materials industries.
- Index of stock prices, 500 common stocks.
- Contracts and orders for plant and equipment in 1982 dollars.
- Index of new private housing units authorized by local building permits.
- Vendor performance, slower deliveries diffusion index.
- Index of consumer expectations.
- Change in manufacturers' unfilled orders in 1982 dollars, durable goods industries.
- Change in sensitive material prices.
- Money supply M2 in 1982 dollars.

seven major economic contractions. Analysis of the leading indicators during this period shows that on average, 75 percent of the indicators turned down before the peak of the economic cycle. Periodically, the index is tested and recalibrated to ensure its continued accuracy. For example, in 1975 it was modified to reflect the influence of rampant price inflation, which had begun to distort its forecasts.

Benefit and Limitations The importance of the index of leading economic indicators is demonstrated in its use as the government's chief economic forecasting tool. Although it sometimes signals turning points that never materialize, it has generally been successful in signaling those that *have* occurred. A rule of thumb among economists is that 3 successive months of decline in the index are a sign of an impending recession. The index may sometimes be misleading in that indicators may exhibit random fluctuations due to events such as strikes or severe weather. Reporting lags create another deficiency in the index. Regardless of the frequency of reporting, data are reported with lags and are subject to revision weeks, months, or years later. The index is only one tool that provides information that is more qualitative than quantitative. An analysis of underlying economic factors using the index of leading economic indicators in conjunction with other forecasting devices benefits businesses by providing a broad picture of economic activity that can be translated into effective data for policy and strategic decisions.

Chapter Review

● Terms Introduced in Chapter 16

Consumer Price Index The U.S. government prepares this index, which measures changes in the prices of a representative set of consumer items.

Fixed-Weight Aggregates Method To weight an aggregates index, this method uses as weights quantities consumed during some representative period.

Index of Industrial Production Prepared monthly by the Federal Reserve Board, the IIP measures the quantity of production in the areas of manufacturing, mining, and utilities.

Index Number A ratio that measures how much a variable changes over time.

Laspeyres Method To weight an aggregates index, this method uses as weights the quantities consumed during the base period.

Paasche Method In weighting an aggregates index, the Paasche method uses as weights the quantities consumed during the current period.

Percentage Relative Ratio of a current value to a base value with the result multiplied by 100.

Price Index Compares levels of prices from one period to another.

Quantity Index A measure of how much the number or quantity of a variable changes over time.

Unweighted Aggregates Index Uses all the values considered and assigns equal importance to each of these values.

Unweighted Average of Relatives Method To construct an index number, this method finds the ratio of the current price to the base price for each product, adds the resulting percentage relatives, and then divides by the number of products.

Weighted Aggregates Index Using all the values considered, this index assigns weights to these values.

Weighted Average of Relatives Method To construct an index number, this method weights by importance the value of each element in the composite.

● Equations Introduced in Chapter 16

■ **16-1** Unweighted aggregates quantity index $= \frac{\Sigma Q_i}{\Sigma Q_0} \times 100$ p. 926

To compute an unweighted aggregates index, divide the sum of the current-year quantities of the elements in the index by the sum of the base-year quantities and multiply the result by 100.

■ **16-2** Weighted aggregates price index $= \frac{\Sigma P_i Q}{\Sigma P_0 Q} \times 100$ p. 931

For a weighted aggregates price index using quantities as weights, obtain the weighted sum of the current-year prices by multiplying each price in the index by its associated quantity and summing the results. Then divide this weighted sum by the weighted sum of the base-year prices and multiply the result by 100.

■ **16-3** Laspeyres index $= \frac{\Sigma P_i Q_0}{\Sigma P_0 Q_0} \times 100$ p. 932

The Laspeyres price index is a weighted aggregates price index using the base-year quantities as weights.

■ **16-4** Paasche index $= \frac{\Sigma P_i Q_i}{\Sigma P_0 Q_i} \times 100$ p. 933

To get the Paasche price index, we compute a weighted aggregates price index using the current-year quantities for weights.

■ **16-5** Fixed-weight aggregates price index $= \frac{\Sigma P_i Q_2}{\Sigma P_0 Q_2} \times 100$ p. 935

The fixed-weight aggregates price index is a weighted aggregates price index whose weights are the quantities from a representative year, not necessarily either the base year or the current year.

■ **16-6** Unweighted average of relatives price index $= \frac{\Sigma\left(\frac{P_i}{P_0} \times 100\right)}{n}$ p. 939

We compute an unweighted average of relatives price index by multiplying the ratios of current prices to base prices by 100, summing the results, and then dividing by the number of elements used in the index.

■ **16-7** Weighted average of relatives price index $= \frac{\Sigma\left[\left(\frac{P_i}{P_0} \times 100\right)(P_n Q_n)\right]}{\Sigma P_n Q_n}$ p. 941

With this index, we weight the relative prices by the values for a fixed reference period and divide the weighted sum of relative prices by the sum of the weights. If we use the base year values as weights, we get

■ **16-8** $$\frac{\Sigma\left[\left(\frac{P_i}{P_0} \times 100\right)(P_0 Q_0)\right]}{\Sigma P_0 Q_0}$$ p. 941

which is the same as the Laspeyres price index.

■ **16-9** Weighted average of relatives quantity index $$= \frac{\Sigma\left[\left(\frac{Q_i}{Q_0} \times 100\right)(Q_n P_n)\right]}{\Sigma Q_n P_n}$$ p. 946

In this quantity index, we weight the relative quantities by the values for a fixed reference period and divide the weighted sum by the sum of the weights.

● Review and Application Exercises

■ **16-43** Kamischika Motorcycles began producing three models of mopeds in 1993. For the 3 years 1993 through 1995, sales were as follows:

	Average Annual Price			Units Sold (× 10,000)		
Model	**1993**	**1994**	**1995**	**1993**	**1994**	**1995**
I	$139	$155	$149	3.7	4.1	7.6
II	169	189	189	2.3	4.6	8.1
III	199	205	219	1.6	2.1	3.4

(a) Calculate the weighted average of relatives price indices using the prices and quantities from 1995 as the bases and weights.

(b) Calculate the weighted average of relatives price indices using the total dollar values for each year as the weights and 1995 as the base year.

■ **16-44** These data indicate the value (in millions of dollars) of the principal products exported by a developing country. Determine unweighted aggregate value indices for 1993 and 1995 based on 1991.

Commodity	1991	1993	1995
Coffee	$834	$1,436	$1,321
Sugar	96	118	122
Copper	241	258	269
Zinc	142	125	106

■ **16-45** In a survey of U.S. coal production for 4 years, the following information was collected. Using the value of the 1992 production for weighting and 1992 as the base year, calculate the weighted average of relatives quantity index for each of the 4 years.

Type of Coal	Production (millions of tons)				Value ($ millions)
	1989	1990	1991	1992	1992
Anthracite	7.4	6.8	7.1	7.2	90
Bituminous	595	580	601	625	5,050

■ **16-46** A survey by the National Dairy Products Association produced the following information. Construct a Laspeyres index with 1991 as the base period.

Product	Average Price per Unit		Total Quantity (billions)
	1991	1995	1991
Cheese (lb)	$1.45	$1.49	2.6
Milk (gal)	1.60	1.61	47.6
Butter (lb)	0.70	0.80	3.1

■ **16-47** Robert Barry, Ltd., a garment consulting firm, has examined the pricing trends of clothing items for a client. This table contains the results of the survey (shown in unit prices):

Products	1992	1993	1994	1995
Jeans	$13.00	$13.00	$15.00	$15.00
Jackets	19.00	19.50	22.00	24.00
Shirts	12.00	11.00	12.00	13.00

Calculate an unweighted average of relatives index for each year using 1992 as the base period.

■ **16-48** What problem would exist in comparing price indices describing computer sales over the past few decades?

■ **16-49** The VP of sales for the National Hospital Supply Company conducted a survey of travel expenses incurred by selected salespeople. Of particular interest were the following data regarding expenditures for taxis and the price paid per mile.

Salespeople	Expenditures on Taxis			Average Price/Mile
	1991	1992	1993	1991
A	$704	$ 985	$1,391	0.52
B	635	875	1,306	0.55
C	752	1,023	1,523	0.59
D	503	696	1,106	0.56
E	593	781	1,215	0.55

Calculate an unweighted average of relatives index for each year using 1993 as the base period.

■ **16-50** This information describes the unit sales of a bicycle shop for 3 years:

Model	Number Sold			Price
	1993	1994	1995	1993
Sport	45	48	56	$ 89
Touring	64	67	71	104
Cross-country	28	35	27	138
Sprint	21	16	28	245

Calculate the weighted average of relatives quantity indices using the prices and quantities from 1993 to compute the value weights, with 1993 as the base year.

■ **16-51** The Dow Jones Industrial Average (DJIA) is an index number used by many people as a proxy for describing the overall strength of prices on the New York Stock Exchange. It is based on the sum of the prices of single shares of the common stock of 30 large companies traded on the exchange. This sum is then adjusted to account for splits and changes in the companies whose shares make up the index.

(a) Two of the stocks in the index are Coca Cola, which was trading around $44 per share in late July 1993, and Westinghouse, which was then trading around $17 per share. What information does the DJIA ignore by simply adding single-share prices? Does a 10-percent rise in the price of Westinghouse stock have the same effect as a 10-percent rise in the share price of Coca Cola?

(b) The total annual return of U.S. common stocks has been about 11 percent, as an average, over long time periods. But stockbrokers sometimes choose low points in the market (selected with hindsight) to express gains over time. At the end of 1992, the DJIA stood at 3301. Calculate an index number for how well stocks have done recently, based on the bottom of the market after the October 1987 crash, when the DJIA stood at 1739. Compare this with an index number based on the August 1987 high point of the market, when the DJIA was 2722.

■ **16-52** Pem Jenkins runs a lumberyard and has the following information on costs for 3 years:

Costs	1991	1993	1995
Wages	$24,378	$36,421	$37,613
Lumber	1,816	2,019	2,136
Utilities	638	681	701

Construct an unweighted aggregates index for production costs in 1991 and 1995 using 1993 as the base year.

■ **16-53** An Ohio consumer protection agency has surveyed the price changes of a meatpacking company. The following table contains the average annual per-pound prices for a sample of the firm's products. Construct an unweighted average of relatives price index using the prices from 1993 as the base period.

Products	1993	1994	1995
Sirloin	$1.69	$1.81	$1.85
Chuck	0.91	1.15	1.24
Bologna	1.45	1.58	1.53
Hot dogs	0.99	1.03	1.01
Rib eyes	2.39	2.61	2.56

■ **16-54** Why must one exercise caution in selecting a base period?

■ **16-55** Tameka Robinson, a purchasing agent, has compiled the following price information. Using 1992 as the base period, calculate the unweighted aggregates price index for 1993, 1994, and 1995.

Material	1992	1993	1994	1995
Aluminum	$0.96	$0.99	$1.03	$1.06
Steel	1.48	1.54	1.55	1.59
Brass tubing	0.21	0.25	0.26	0.31
Copper wire	0.06	0.08	0.07	0.09

■ **16-56** A USDA survey of grain production for selected areas in the United States yielded this information:

	Quantities Produced (millions of bushels)					Price per Bushel
Product	**1991**	**1992**	**1993**	**1994**	**1995**	**1991**
Wheat	610	620	640	630	650	$ 4.40
Corn	390	390	410	440	440	3.60
Oats	100	90	120	130	150	1.20
Rye	10	20	10	10	20	24.00
Barley	160	150	120	190	180	2.10
Soybeans	130	140	160	120	130	5.60

Using the prices from 1991 for weights, calculate the weighted aggregates quantity indices for each year.

■ **16-57** John Pringle, an international mineral trader, has collected the following information on prices and quantities of minerals exported by an African country for the years 1994 and 1995. Calculate a Paasche index for 1995 using 1994 as the base period.

	Quantity (million tons)	Price (per lb)	
Mineral	**1995**	**1994**	**1995**
Copper	38.1	$0.59	$0.63
Lead	53.5	0.17	0.16
Zinc	86.4	0.21	0.23

■ **16-58** A European automobile manufacturer has compiled the following information on car sales of one U.S. manufacturer:

	Average Annual Price (hundreds)			Units Sold (× 1,000)		
Size	**1991**	**1993**	**1995**	**1991**	**1993**	**1995**
Subcompact	$62	$68	$ 70	32	65	86
Compact	76	78	80	45	68	73
Sedan	90	98	106	462	325	386

(a) Calculate the weighted average of relatives price indices using the prices and quantities from 1993 as the bases and weights.

(b) Calculate the weighted average of relatives price indices using the total dollar values for each year as the weights and 1993 as the base year.

■ **16-59** Sylvia Jensen, cost analyst for a major appliance firm, has compiled price data for four of the company's products. The figures (given in unit prices) for 1993 through 1996 are shown in the table.

Town	1992	Average Selling Price per Bus 1994	1996	Number of Buses Sold 1994
Greenville	$21,206	$24,210	$26,235	17
Hampton	17,129	19,722	22,109	14
Middletown	25,723	28,657	32,481	21

Construct a Laspeyres index using 1994 as the base period.

■ **16-68** A local fast-food restaurant wants to examine how sales are changing for each of its four most popular menu items. The data for the years 1993 through 1996 follow.

Menu Item	Unit Price 1993	1994	1995	1996	Quantity Sold (millions) 1993	1994	1995	1996
Hamburger	$0.58	$0.62	$0.69	$0.79	2.1	2.5	2.0	1.8
Chicken sandwich	1.89	2.09	2.18	2.25	1.5	1.2	1.8	2.1
French fries	0.84	0.89	0.99	0.99	2.9	2.7	2.3	2.4
Onion rings	0.91	0.99	1.14	1.19	3.1	2.4	2.0	1.6

Calculate a fixed-weight aggregates index for each year using 1993 prices as the base and the 1996 quantities as the fixed weights.

■ **16-69** Use the data from Exercise 16-68 to calculate a Paasche index for each year using 1995 as the base period.

■ **16-70** To compare the quality of undergraduate colleges, *U.S. News & World Report* constructs an index number, based on weighted scores for factors such as the test scores and high school class rank of admitted students and graduation rates reported by each school. But some schools submit incomplete or misleading data by excluding some students admitted under preference programs from the averages they report.

For the 1995 *College Guide,* the magazine staff decided not to include data for test scores they believed to be incomplete, but instead doubled the weight of class standing. Schools that refused to fill out a form were assigned the lowest number of points possible for each factor.

Missing or incomplete data is a common problem for managers. Discuss the pros and cons of the two approaches (doubling another factor and assigning low scores to some schools). What other procedures might have been used?

Source: G. Putka, "U.S. News Addresses Flaws in College Guide," The Wall Street Journal *(7 Sept 1995): B1.*

16-71 The following table gives the number of automobiles produced in the first half of 1994 and 1995 by all companies operating plants in the United States. Note that BMW did not operate in 1994 and that Nummi is a Toyota/GM joint venture that produces the Toyota Corolla and the Chevrolet Prizm on the same production line.

Company	1995, 6 months	1994, 6 months
GM	1,351,471	1,518,162
Ford	819,088	864,029
Chrysler	316,821	290,899
BMW	4,866	—

(Continued)

Company	1995, 6 months	1994, 6 months
Honda	286,122	250,641
Nissan	184,284	174,804
Nummi	119,572	114,589
Toyota	199,840	140,090
Mazda	85,345	125,923
Mitsubishi	114,752	75,352
Subaru–Isuzu	39,579	14,098
Industry Total	**3,521,740**	**3,568,587**

(a) Construct an index for each firm's production for the first six months of 1995 based on the first six months of 1994.

(b) Construct an industrywide index for 1995 production using 1994 as the base. How does this index compare with a simple average of the individual firms' 1995 indices and with a weighted average of relatives index constructed by weighting each element by the 1994 production of that firm?

Source: "U.S. Auto Makers Trimming Overtime, Idling Certain Plants," The Wall Street Journal *(21 July 1995): A4.*

● Chapter Concepts Test

Circle the correct answer, or fill in the blank. *Answers are in the back of the book.*

T F 1. The index number for a base year is always zero.
T F 2. Index numbers can measure differences in a given variable in several locations.
T F 3. The simplest form of a composite index is an unweighted aggregates index.
T F 4. A disadvantage of Laspeyres indices is that they are not comparable to one another.
T F 5. If the fixed-weight aggregates method is used, with the chosen value period being the base period, this is the same as the Paasche method.
T F 6. The average of relatives method sums percentages, not amounts.
T F 7. A substantial price change for a slow-moving item can completely distort an unweighted index.
T F 8. In times of inflation, a quantity index provides a better measure of actual output than a corresponding value index.
T F 9. A value index measures the combined effects of price and quantity changes.
T F 10. When using the weighted average of relatives price index, indices from different periods are always comparable.
T F 11. The Laspeyres method is most commonly used because it requires quantity measures for only one period.
T F 12. An index number is always found by taking the ratio of a current value to a base value and multiplying by 100.
T F 13. Selection of an improper base does not distort index numbers.
T F 14. Although often used as measurements in and of themselves, index numbers can also be used as parts of intermediate computations.
T F 15. Whenever we use the symbol P_i in one of our index formulas, we are referring to the price in the base year.
T F 16. With the aggregates or average of relatives index, it is more common to weight the elements making up the index.

T F 17. An unweighted aggregates index does not allow for changes in price.

T F 18. The CPI and the IIP are both examples of value indices.

T F 19. The weighted average of relatives method divides the weighted sum by the sum of the weights.

T F 20. Index numbers are inherently confusing and thus are seldom used in the real world.

T F 21. The CPI measure is based on a single variable.

A B C D E 22. If an index number calculation over 8 years with a base value of 100 gave an index for 1993 of 110, what would be the percentage relative for 1993?

(a) 110.

(b) 90.9.

(c) 13.75.

(d) 880.

(e) Cannot be determined from the information given.

A B C D 23. To measure changes in total monetary worth, one should calculate:

(a) A price index.

(b) A quantity index.

(c) A value index.

(d) None of these.

A B C D E 24. Suppose a composite price index for 1 gallon of milk, 2 loaves of bread, and 1 pound of hamburger was 110 in 1995 and 119 in 1996. If both indices were computed from a 1994 base of 100, how much did the general price level rise from 1995 to 1996?

(a) 9%.

(b) 8.18%.

(c) 19%.

(d) 7.56%.

(e) Cannot be determined from the information given.

A B C D E 25. Which of the following describes an advantage of using the Laspeyres method?

(a) Many commonly used quantity measures are not tabulated for every period.

(b) Changes in consumption patterns are taken into account.

(c) One index can be easily compared with another.

(d) All of these.

(e) (a) and (c) but not (b).

A B C D E 26. What can be concluded if the weighted aggregates price index for a set of prices was calculated as 106 using the Laspeyres method and 112 using the Paasche method?

(a) The Paasche index is incorrect.

(b) There is a trend toward less expensive goods.

(c) There is a trend toward more expensive goods.

(d) The difference can be attributed to a poor estimation of consumer attitudes.

(e) (a) and (d) only.

A B C D E 27. When computing a weighted average of relatives index, we would be best able to compare indices from various periods if:

(a) Base values were used as P_nQ_n.

(b) Current values were used as P_nQ_n.

(c) Fixed values were used as P_nQ_n.
(d) Either base or fixed values were used as P_nQ_n.
(e) Either current values or fixed values were used as P_nQ_n.

A B C D 28. Commodities subject to considerable price variations could best be measured by a:
(a) Price index.
(b) Quantity index.
(c) Value index.
(d) None of these.

A B C D 29. A base period can be described as a "normal" period if:
(a) It is at neither the peak nor the trough of a fluctuation.
(b) It is the most recent period for which we have data.
(c) There was no inflation or deflation of prices during the period.
(d) It is the average of several consecutive periods.

A B C D 30. The weights used in a quantity index are:
(a) Percentages of total quantity.
(b) Prices.
(c) Average of quantities.
(d) None of these.

A B C D 31. In an unweighted average of relatives index, $(P_i/P_0) \times 100$ is calculated for each product in the composite. What is then done with these values to finish the calculation?
(a) The values are multiplied together.
(b) The largest value is found.
(c) The values are averaged.
(d) The average difference from the median of the values is found and then squared.

A B C D E 32. To measure how much the cost of some variable changes over time, you would use:
(a) A value index.
(b) An inflation index.
(c) A quantity index.
(d) All of these.
(e) None of these.

A B C D 33. It is possible to change the base year without changing the quantities used for weights when using:
(a) The Paasche method.
(b) The Laspeyres method.
(c) The weighted aggregates method.
(d) None of these.

A B C D 34. When the base year values are used as weights, the weighted average of relatives price index is the same as:
(a) The Paasche index.
(b) The Laspeyres index.
(c) The unweighted average of relatives price index.
(d) None of the above.

A B C D E 35. A primary difference between average of relatives and aggregates methods is that:

(a) Aggregates methods sum all prices before finding the ratio.
(b) Average of relatives methods sum all prices before finding the ratio.
(c) Aggregates methods are useful only for price indices.
(d) (a) and (c) but not (b).
(e) None of the above.

A B C D 36. Comparing price indices of military airplanes from 1976 to 1996:

(a) Would clearly prove how defense spending has skyrocketed in the last 20 years.
(b) Would best be accomplished using the Paasche method.
(c) Should use the average of 1974 and 1975 for the base period.
(d) Would make little sense, given the significant technological differences in the items being compared.

A B C D E 37. If the organizers of the 1995 Ironman Triathlon wished to evaluate the winning times each year, relative to the winning time in 1980 (the first year of the competition), they might use:

(a) An unweighted aggregates index, with 1980 as the base.
(b) A weighted aggregates index with 1980 as the base using the number of competitors each year as the weights.
(c) The Paasche method.
(d) Any of the above.
(e) (a) or (b) but not (c).

38. If all the values considered in calculating an index are of equal importance, the index is ______________________.

39. The weighted index method in which quantities consumed during the base period are used as weights is the ______________________ method.

40. If we sum all the values used in calculating an index, the resulting index is called ______________________.

41. Using weights from some representative period (which need not necessarily be the base period or the current period) to compute a weighted aggregates price index is the ______________________ aggregates method.

42. The ______________________ method uses quantities consumed in the current period in question when computing a weighted index.

43. We must realize that the mechanical approach of index numbers is subject to considerable ______________________ and ______________________.

44. The three principal types of indices are the ______________________ index, the ______________________ index and the ______________________ index.

45. The ______________________ is calculated by taking a ratio of the current value to a base value and multiplying by 100.

Flow Chart: Index Numbers

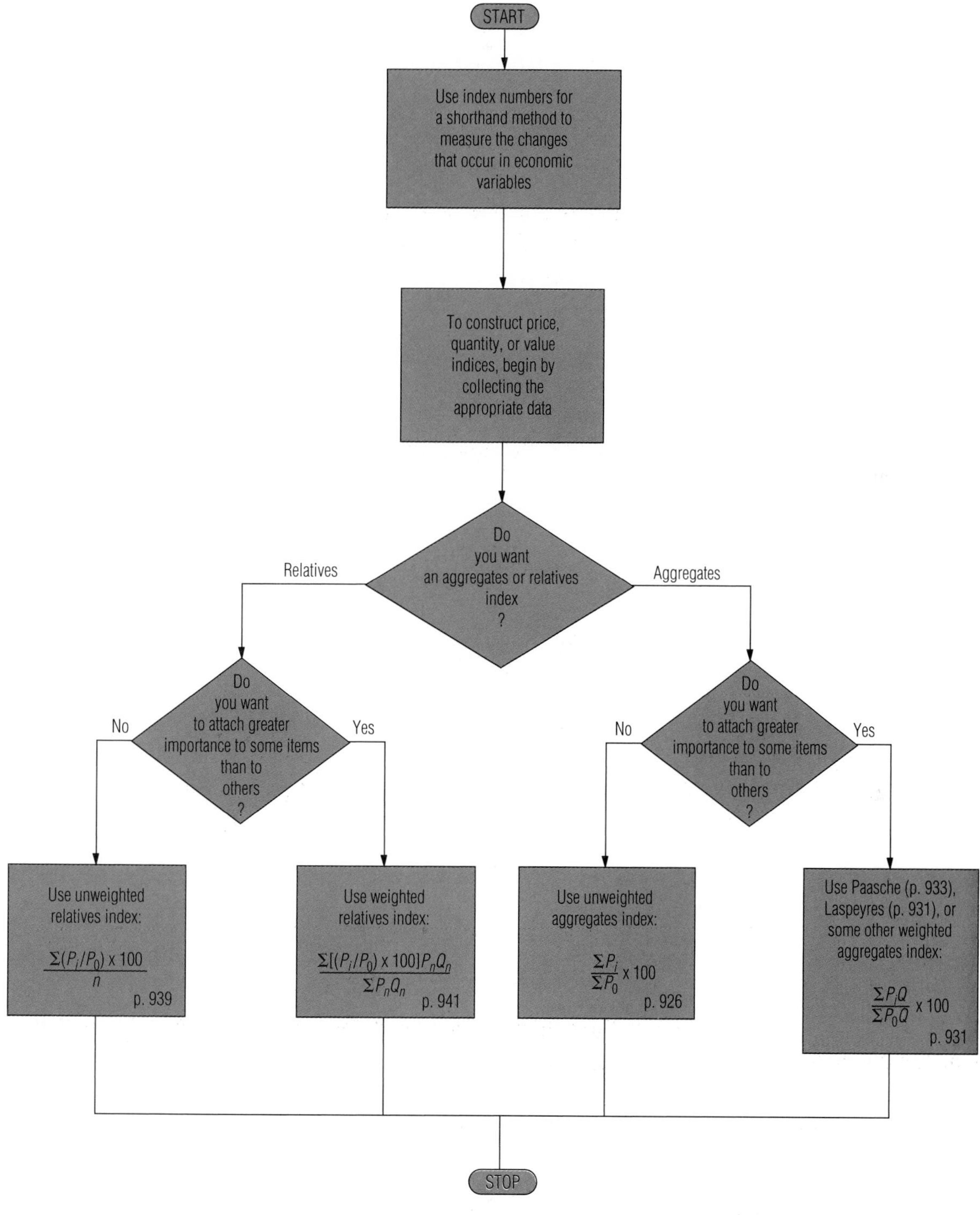

START
Use index numbers for a shorthand method to measure the changes that occur in economic variables
To construct price, quantity, or value indices, begin by collecting the appropriate data
Do you want an aggregates or relatives index ?
Relatives
Aggregates
Do you want to attach greater importance to some items than to others ?
No
Yes
Do you want to attach greater importance to some items than to others ?
No
Yes
Use unweighted relatives index:
$\frac{\Sigma(P_i/P_0) \times 100}{n}$
p. 939
Use weighted relatives index:
$\frac{\Sigma[(P_i/P_0) \times 100]P_nQ_n}{\Sigma P_nQ_n}$
p. 941
Use unweighted aggregates index:
$\frac{\Sigma P_i}{\Sigma P_0} \times 100$
p. 926
Use Paasche (p. 933), Laspeyres (p. 931), or some other weighted aggregates index:
$\frac{\Sigma P_iQ}{\Sigma P_0Q} \times 100$
p. 931
STOP

chapter 17

DECISION THEORY

Objectives

- To learn methods for making decisions under uncertainty
- To use expected value and utility as decision criteria
- To understand why additional information is useful and to calculate its value
- To help decision makers supply needed probability values even when they do not understand probability theory
- To learn how to use decision trees to structure and analyze complex decision-making problems

Chapter Contents

Acme Fruit and Produce Wholesalers buys tomatoes, then sells them to retailers. Acme currently pays \$20 a box. Tomatoes sold on the same day bring \$32 a box. Extremely perishable, tomatoes not sold on the first day are worth only \$2 a box. Acme has calculated that the mean past daily sales is 60 boxes and that the standard deviation of past daily sales is 10 boxes. Using the techniques introduced in this chapter, we can tell Acme how many boxes to order each day to maximize profits. ■

In Section 5-3 (beginning on page 232), we introduced you to the idea of using expected value in decision making. There we worked through a simple problem involving the purchase of strawberries for resale. That kind of problem is part of a set of problems that can be solved using the techniques developed in this chapter.

What is decision theory?

In the last 35 years, managers have used newly developed statistical techniques to solve problems for which information was incomplete, uncertain, or in some cases almost completely lacking. This new area of statistics has a variety of names: *statistical decision theory, Bayesian decision theory* (after the Reverend Thomas Bayes, whom we introduced in Chapter 4), or simply *decision theory.* These names are used interchangeably.

When we did hypothesis testing, we had to decide whether to accept or to reject the stated hypothesis. In decision theory, we must decide among alternatives by taking into account the *monetary* repercussions of our actions. A manager who must select from among a number of available investments should consider the profit or loss that might result from each alternative. Applying decision theory involves selecting an alternative and having a reasonable idea of the economic consequences of choosing that action.

17.1 The Decision Environment

Decision theory can be applied to problems whether the time span is 5 years or 1 day, whether they involve financial management or a plant assembly line, and whether they are in the public or private sector. Regardless of the environment, most of these problems have common characteristics. As a result, decision makers approach their solutions in fairly consistent ways. The elements common to most decision-theory problems are these:

Elements common to decision-theory problems

1. **An objective the decision maker is trying to reach.** If the objective is to minimize downtime of expensive machinery, the manager may try to find the optimal number of spare motors to be kept on hand for quick repairs. Success in finding that number can be measured by counting downtime each month.
2. **Several courses of action.** The decision should involve a choice among alternatives (called *acts*). In our example involving spare motors, the various acts open to the decision maker include stocking one, two, three, four, or five spare motors or choosing not to stock any spare motors.
3. **A calculable measure of the benefit or worth of the various alternatives.** In general, these costs can be negative or positive and are called *payoffs*. Cost accountants should be able to determine the cost of lost production time resulting from a motor burnout both when a spare is on hand and when one is not available. But sometimes the payoffs involve consequences that are more

than solely financial. Imagine trying to decide the optimal number of spare generators a hospital might require in the event of a power failure. Not having enough could cost lives as well as money.

4. **Events beyond the control of the decision maker.** These uncontrollable occurrences are often called *outcomes* or *states of nature*, and their existence creates difficulties as well as interest in decision making under uncertainty. Such events could be the number of motors in our expensive production machinery that will burn out in a given month. Preventive maintenance will reduce motor burnouts, but they will still happen.
5. **Uncertainty concerning which outcome or state of nature will actually happen.** In our example, we are uncertain about how many motors will burn out. This uncertainty is generally handled by the use of probabilities assigned to the various events that might take place, say, a 0.1 chance of losing five motors a month.

Exercises 17.1

Applications

■ **17-1** Wholesale Lamps has been in contact with Leerie's, a local retail lamp shop, about supplying it with a special chrome tree lamp, which the shop wants to use as a drawing card in an upcoming sale. Wholesale Lamps must order the lamps in 2 days to deliver them by the sale date. Wholesale's cost is $49 for the lamps; it will sell them to Leerie's for $54. Wholesale is uncertain about the number Leerie's desires but guesses that it will be between 15 and 20. One of the managers has assigned probabilities to the various numbers that Leerie's might order. The manager of Wholesale Lamps does not foresee a market for the lamps it does not sell to Leerie's. Leerie's is expected to submit the order tomorrow. Should the manager of Wholesale Lamps use decision theory to order the lamps for Leerie's?

■ **17-2** Adventures, Inc., is a source of capital for entrepreneurs starting new firms in the field of genetic engineering. Lisa Levin, a partner in Adventures, has been examining several business proposals that have recently been made to her. Each proposal describes a new venture, outlines its potential market, and solicits investment by Adventures. Lisa has just finished reading the chapter on decision theory in her father's statistics text. She thinks decision theory provides a methodology that can help her decide which ventures to support and at what level. Is Lisa correct? If so, what information does she need in order to apply decision theory to her problem? If not, why not?

■ **17-3** The 8th Avenue Book Store relied on Grambler News Service to supply it with several well-known magazines. Each week, Grambler would deliver a predetermined number of *Today's Romances*, among others, and pick up any unsold copies of the previous week's magazines. The number of copies that the bookstore would sell was never known for sure, but the manager did have past sales data. Grambler charged its bookstands $1.60 for magazines that sold for $2.95. Management of the bookstore wanted to get maximum profitability from the sale of its magazines and was considering the optimal number of *Today's Romances* to order. Should the manager of the bookstore use decision theory to decide the number of magazines to stock?

17.2 Expected Profit under Uncertainty: Assigning Probability Values

Buying decision under conditions of uncertainty

Buying and selling strawberries, as in our example in Chapter 5, is only one case in which decisions have to be made under uncertainty. Another involves a newspaper dealer who buys newspapers for 30¢ each and sells them for 50¢ each. Any papers not sold by the end of the day are completely worthless to him. The dealer's problem is to determine the optimal number he should order each day. On days when he stocks more than he sells, his profits are reduced by the cost of the unsold papers. On days when buyers request more copies than he has in stock, he loses sales and makes smaller profits than he could have.

The dealer has kept a record of his sales for the past 100 days (Table 17-1). This information is a distribution of the dealer's past sales. Because sales volume can take on only a limited number of values, the distribution is discrete. We will assume, for purposes of discussion, that the dealer will sell only the numbers of papers listed—not, say, 412, 525, or 637. Furthermore, the dealer has no reason to believe that sales volume will take on any other value in the future.

Computing probabilities of sales levels

This information tells the dealer something about the historical pattern of his sales. Although it does not tell him what quantity the buyers will request tomorrow, it does tell him that there are 45 chances in 100 that the quantity will be 500 papers. Therefore, a probability of 0.45 is assigned to the sales figure of 500 papers. The probability column in Table 17-1 shows the relationship between the total observations of sales (100 days) and the number of times each possible value of daily sales appeared in the 100 observations. The probability of each sales level occurring is thus derived by dividing the total number of times each value has appeared in the 100 observations by the total number of observations, that is, 15/100, 20/100, 45/100, 15/100, and 5/100.

Maximizing Profits Instead of Minimizing Losses

Back in Section 5-3, when we first introduced you to using expected value in decision making, we used an approach that minimized losses and led us to an optimal stocking pattern for our strawberry dealer. It is just as easy to find the optimal stocking pattern by *maximizing profits,* and that's just what we'll do at this point.

A Chapter 5 problem worked another way

Recall that our fruit and vegetable wholesaler in Chapter 5 bought strawberries at $20 a case and resold them at $50 a case. There we assumed that the product had no value if not sold on the first day (a restriction we shall soon lift). If buyers call for more cases tomor-

Table 17-1

Distribution of Newspaper Sales

Daily Sales	Number of Days Sold	Probability of Each Number Being Sold
300	15	0.15
400	20	0.20
500	45	0.45
600	15	0.15
700	5	0.05
	100	**1.00**

row than the wholesaler has in stock, profits suffer by $30 (selling price minus cost) for each case he cannot sell. On the other hand, costs also result from stocking *too many* units on a given day. If the wholesaler has 13 cases in stock but sells only 10, he makes a profit of $300, or $30 a case on 10 cases. But this profit must be reduced by $60, the cost of the three cases not sold and of no value.

A 100-day observation of past sales gives the information shown in Table 17-2. The probability values there are obtained just as they were in Table 5-6.

Notice that there are only four discrete values for sales volume, and as far as we know, there is no discernible pattern in the sequence in which these four values occur. We assume that the retailer has no reason to believe sales volume will behave differently in the future.

Calculating Conditional Profits

To illustrate this retailer's problem, we can construct a table showing the results in dollars of all possible combinations of purchases and sales. The only values for purchases and for sales that have meaning to us are 10, 11, 12, and 13 cases, because the retailer has no reason to consider buying fewer than 10 or more than 13 cases.

Conditional profit table

Table 17-3, called a *conditional profit table,* shows the profit resulting from any possible combination of supply and demand. The profits could be either positive or negative (although they are all positive in this example) and are conditional in that a certain profit results from taking a specific stocking action (ordering 10, 11, 12, or 13 cases) and selling a specific number of cases (10, 11, 12, or 13 cases).

Explaining elements in the conditional profit table

Table 17-3 reflects the losses that occur when stock remains unsold at the end of a day. Notice, too, that the retailer forgoes potential additional profit when customers demand more cases than he has stocked.

Observe that the stocking of 10 cases each day will always result in a profit of $300. Even on days when buyers want 13 cases, the retailer can sell only 10. When the retailer stocks 11 cases, his profit will be $330 on days when buyers request 11, 12, or 13 cases. But on days when he has 11 cases in stock and buyers buy only 10 cases, profit drops to $280. The $300 profit on the 10 cases sold must be reduced by $20, the cost of the unsold case. A stock of 12 cases will increase daily profits to $360, but only on days when buyers want 12 or 13 cases. Should buyers want only 10 cases, profit is reduced to $260; the $300 profit

Table 17-2

Cases Sold During 100 Days

Daily Sales	Number of Days Sold	Probability of Each Number Being Sold
10	15	0.15
11	20	0.20
12	40	0.40
13	25	0.25
	100	**1.00**

Table 17-3

Conditional Profit Table

Possible Demand (sales) in Cases	Possible Stock Action			
	10 Cases	11 Cases	12 Cases	13 Cases
10	$300	$280	$260	$240
11	300	330	310	290
12	300	330	360	340
13	300	330	360	390

on the sale of 10 cases is reduced by $40, the cost of two unsold cases. Stocking 13 cases will result in a profit of $390 (a $30 profit on each case sold, with no unsold cases) when there is a market for 13 cases. When buyers purchase fewer than 13 cases, such a stock action results in profits of less than $390. For example, with a stock of 13 cases and sale of only 11 cases, the profit is $290; the profit on 11 cases, $330, is reduced by the cost of two unsold cases ($40).

Function of the conditional profit table

Such a conditional profit table does *not* show the retailer how many cases he *should* stock each day in order to maximize profits. It reveals the outcome only if a specific number of cases is stocked and a specific number of cases is sold. Under conditions of uncertainty, the retailer does not know in advance the size of any day's market. However, he must still decide which number of cases, stocked consistently, will maximize profits over a long period of time.

Calculating Expected Profits

The next step in determining the best number of cases to stock is assigning probabilities to the possible outcomes or profits. We saw in Table 17-2 that the probabilities of the possible values for the retailer's sales are as follows:

Cases	10	11	12	13
Probability	0.15	0.20	0.40	0.25

Using these probabilities and the information contained in Table 17-3, we can now compute the expected profit of each possible stock action.

Computing expected profit

We stated in Chapter 5 that **we can compute the expected value of a random variable by weighting each possible value the variable can take by the probability of its taking on that value**. Using this procedure, we can compute the expected daily profit from stocking 10 cases each day. See Table 17-4. The figures in column 4 of Table 17-4 are obtained by weighting the conditional profit of each possible sales volume (column 2) by the probability of that conditional profit occurring (column 3). The sum in the last column is the expected daily profit resulting from stocking 10 cases each day. It is not surprising that this expected profit is $300 because we saw in Table 17-3 that stocking 10 cases each day would always result in a daily profit of $300, regardless of whether buyers wanted 10, 11, 12, or 13 cases.

For 10 units

For 11 units

The same computation for a daily stock of 11 units can be made, as we have done in Table 17-5. This tells us that if the retailer stocks 11 cases each day, his expected daily profit over time will be $322.50. Eighty-five percent of the time the daily profit will be $330; on these days, buyers ask for 11, 12, or 13 cases. However, column 3 tells us that 15 percent of the time the market will take only 10 cases, resulting in a profit of only $280. It is this fact that reduces the daily expected profit to $322.50.

For 12 and 13 units

For 12 and 13 units, the expected daily profit is computed as shown in Tables 17-6 and 17-7, respectively.

Table 17-4

Expected Profit from Stocking 10 Cases

Market Size in Cases (1)	Conditional Profit (2)		Probability of Market Size (3)		Expected Profit (4)
10	$300	×	0.15	=	$ 45.00
11	300	×	0.20	=	60.00
12	300	×	0.40	=	120.00
13	300	×	0.25	=	75.00
			1.00		**$300.00**

Table 17-5

Expected Profit from Stocking 11 Cases

Market Size in Cases	Conditional Profit		Probability of Market Size		Expected Profit
10	$280	×	0.15	=	$ 42.00
11	330	×	0.20	=	66.00
12	330	×	0.40	=	132.00
13	330	×	0.25	=	82.50
			1.00		**$322.50**

Table 17-6

Expected Profit from Stocking 12 Cases

Market Size in Cases	Conditional Profit		Probability of Market Size		Expected Profit	
10	$260	×	0.15	=	$ 39.00	
11	310	×	0.20	=	62.00	
12	360	×	0.40	=	144.00	
13	360	×	0.25	=	90.00	
			1.00		**$335.00**	← Optimal stock action

Table 17-7

Expected Profit from Stocking 13 Cases

Market Size in Cases	Conditional Profit		Probability of Market Size		Expected Profit
10	$240	×	0.15	=	$ 36.00
11	290	×	0.20	=	58.00
12	340	×	0.40	=	136.00
13	390	×	0.25	=	97.50
			1.00		**$327.50**

We have now computed the expected profit of each of the four stock actions open to the retailer. These expected profits are

- If 10 cases are stocked each day, the expected daily profit is $300.00.
- If 11 cases are stocked each day, the expected daily profit is $322.50.
- If 12 cases are stocked each day, the expected daily profit is $335.00.
- If 13 cases are stocked each day, the expected daily profit is $327.50.

Optimal solution

The *optimal stock action* is the one that results in the greatest expected profit—the largest daily average profits and thus the maximum total profits over a period of time. In this illustration, the proper number to stock each day is 12 cases, because that quantity will give the highest possible average daily profits under the conditions given.

What the solution means

We have *not* reduced uncertainty in the problem facing the retailer. Rather, we have used his past experience to determine the best stock action open to him. He still does not know how many cases will be requested on any given day. There is no guarantee that he will make a profit of $335.00 tomorrow. However, if he stocks 12 cases each day under the conditions given, he will have *average* profits of $335.00 per day. This is the *best* he can do, because the choice of any one of the other three possible stock actions will result in a lower expected daily profit.

Expected Profit with Perfect Information

Definition of perfect information

Now suppose that the retailer in our illustration could remove all uncertainty from his problem by obtaining complete and accurate information about the future, referred to as *perfect* information. This does not mean that sales would not vary from 10 to 13 cases per day. Sales would still be 10 cases per day 15 percent of the time, 11 cases 20 percent of the time, 12 cases 40 percent of the time, and 13 cases 25 percent of the time. However, with perfect information, the retailer would know in advance how many cases were going to be called for each day.

Use of perfect information

Under these circumstances, the retailer would stock today the exact number of cases buyers will want tomorrow. For sales of 10 cases, the retailer would stock 10 cases and realize a profit of $300. When sales were going to be 11 cases, he would stock exactly 11 cases, thus realizing a profit of $330.00.

Table 17-8 shows the conditional profit values that are applicable to the retailer's problem if he has perfect information. Knowing the size of the market in advance for a particular day, the retailer chooses the stock action that will maximize his profits. This means he buys and stocks quantities that avoid *all* losses from obsolete stock as well as *all* losses that reflect lost profits on unfilled requests for strawberries.

Expected profit with perfect information

We can now compute the expected profit with perfect information. This is shown in Table 17-9. The procedure is the same as that already used, but you will notice that the conditional profit figures in column 2 of Table 17-9 are the maximum profits possible for each sales volume. When buyers buy 12 cases, for example, the retailer will always make a profit of $360 with perfect information because he will have stocked exactly 12 cases. With perfect information, then, our retailer could count on making an average profit of $352.50 a day. This is a significant figure because it is the *maximum expected profit* possible.

Expected Value of Perfect Information

Value of perfect information

Assuming that a retailer could obtain a perfect predictor about the future, what would be its value to him? He must compare the cost of that information with the additional profit he would realize as a result of having the information.

Table 17-8

Conditional Profit Table with Perfect Information

Possible Sales in Cases	Possible Stock Action: 10 Cases	11 Cases	12 Cases	13 Cases
10	$300	—	—	—
11	—	$330	—	—
12	—	—	$360	—
13	—	—	—	$390

Table 17-9

Expected Profit with Perfect Information

Market Size in Cases	Conditional Profit with Perfect Information		Probability of Market Size		Expected Profit with Perfect Information
10	$300	×	0.15	=	$ 45.00
11	330	×	0.20	=	66.00
12	360	×	0.40	=	144.00
13	390	×	0.25	=	97.50
			1.00		**$352.50**

Why do we need the value of perfect information?

The retailer in our example can earn average daily profits of $352.50 if he has perfect information about the future (see Table 17-9). His best expected daily profit without the predictor is only $335.00 (see Tables 17-4 to 17-7). The difference of $17.50 is the maximum amount the retailer would be willing to pay, per day, for a perfect predictor, because that is the maximum amount by which he can increase his expected daily profit. The difference is the *expected value of perfect information* and is referred to as EVPI. There is no sense in paying more than $17.50 for the predictor; to do so would cost more than the knowledge is worth.

Calculating the value of additional information in the decision-making process is a serious problem for managers. In our illustration, we found that our retailer would pay $17.50 a day for a perfect predictor. Only infrequently, however, can we secure a perfect predictor. In most decision-making situations, managers are really attempting to evaluate the worth of information that will enable them to make better, rather than perfect, decisions.

HINTS & ASSUMPTIONS

Warning: All of the examples used in this section have involved discrete distributions; that is, we've allowed the random variable to take on only a few values. This is not reflective of most real-world situations, but makes it easy for us to do the calculations necessary to introduce this idea. With discrete outcomes, the expected profit is *not* necessarily one of the outcomes. Hint: A 50 percent chance of making a $10 profit coupled with a 50 percent chance of making no profit gives an expected profit of $5. But with a discrete distribution the outcome will be *either* $10 or zero! Some real-world situations also turn out like this. A parcel of undeveloped land can be worth either $5 million or $250,000, depending on where a new airport is finally located. The land may also be sold for $500,000 to a speculator who hopes for the final $5 million sale.

Exercises 17.2

Self-Check Exercise

SC 17-1 The Writer's Workbench operates a chain of word-processing franchises in college towns. For an hourly fee of $8.00, Writer's Workbench provides access to a personal computer, word-processing software, and a printer to students who need to prepare papers for their classes. Paper is provided at no additional cost. The firm estimates that its hourly variable cost per machine (principally due to paper, ribbons, electricity, and wear and tear on the computers and printers) is about 85¢. Deborah Rubin is considering opening a Writer's Workbench franchise in Ames, Iowa. A preliminary market survey has resulted in the following probability distribution of the number of machines demanded per hour during the hours she plans to operate:

Number of machines	22	23	24	25	26	27
Probability	0.12	0.16	0.22	0.27	0.18	0.05

If she wishes to maximize her profit contribution, how many machines should Deborah plan to have? What is the hourly expected value of perfect information in this situation? Even if Deborah could obtain a perfectly accurate forecast of the demand for each and every hour, why wouldn't she be willing to pay up to the EVPI for that information in this situation?

Applications

■ **17-4** Center City Motor Sales has recently incorporated. Its chief asset is a franchise to sell automobiles of a major American manufacturer. CCMS's general manager is planning the staffing of the dealership's garage facilities. From information provided by the manufacturer and from other nearby dealerships, he has estimated the number of annual mechanic hours that the garage will be likely to need.

Hours	10,000	12,000	14,000	16,000
Probability	0.2	0.3	0.4	0.1

The manager plans to pay each mechanic $9.00 per hour and to charge customers $16.00. Mechanics will work a 40-hour week and get an annual 2-week vacation.

(a) Determine how many mechanics Center City should hire.

(b) How much should Center City pay to get perfect information about the number of mechanics it needs?

■ **17-5** Airport Rent-A-Car is a locally operated business in competition with several major firms. ARC is planning a new deal for customers who want to rent a car for only one day and return it to the airport. For $24.95, the company will rent a small economy car to a customer, whose only other expense is to fill the car with gas at the day's end. ARC is planning to buy a number of small cars from the manufacturer at a reduced price of $6,750. The big question is how many to buy. Company executives have decided on the following estimated probability distribution of the number of cars rented per day:

Number of cars rented	10	11	12	13	14	15
Probability	0.18	0.19	0.21	0.15	0.14	0.13

The company intends to offer the plan 6 days a week (312 days per year) and anticipates that its variable cost per car per day will be $2.25. After using the cars for 1 year, ARC expects to sell them and recapture 45 percent of the original cost. Ignoring the time value of money and any noncash expenses, determine the optimal number of cars for ARC to buy.

■ **17-6** For several years, the Madison Rhodes Department Store had featured personalized pencils as a Christmas special. Madison Rhodes purchased the pencils from its supplier, who provided the embossing machine. The personalizing was done on the department store premises. Despite the success of the pencil sales, Madison Rhodes had received comments that the quality of the lead in the pencils was poor, and the store had found a different supplier. The new supplier, however, would be unable to begin servicing the department store until after the first of January. Madison Rhodes was forced to purchase its pencils one final time from its original supplier to meet Christmas demand. It was important, therefore, that pencils not be overstocked, and yet the manager was adamant about not losing too many customers because of stockouts. The pencils came packed 15 to the box,

72 boxes to the case. Madison Rhodes paid \$60 per case and sold the pencils for \$1.50 per box. Labor costs are 37.5¢ per box sold. Based on previous years' sales, management constructed the following schedule:

Expected sales (cases)	15	16	17	18	19	20
Probability	0.05	0.20	0.30	0.25	0.10	0.10

(a) How many cases should Madison Rhodes order?

(b) What's the expected profit?

■ **17-7** Emily Scott, head of a small business consulting firm, must decide how many M.B.A.s to hire as full-time consultants for the next year. (Emily has decided that she will not bother with any part-time employees.) Emily knows from experience that the probability distribution on the number of consulting jobs her firm will get each year is as follows:

Consulting jobs	24	27	30	33
Probability	0.3	0.2	0.4	0.1

Emily also knows that each M.B.A. hired will be able to handle exactly three consulting jobs per year. The salary of each M.B.A. is \$60,000. Each consulting job is worth \$30,000 to Emily's firm. Each consulting job that the firm is awarded but cannot complete costs the firm \$10,000 in future business lost.

(a) How many M.B.A.s should Emily hire?

(b) What is the expected value of perfect information to Emily?

■ **17-8** As a fund-raiser for a student organization, some students have decided to sell individual pizzas outside the Union on Friday. Each pizza will sell for \$1.75 and costs the organization \$.77. Historical sales indicated that between 55 and 60 dozen pizzas will be sold with the probability distribution given below:

Dozens of pizzas	55	56	57	58	59	60
Probability	0.15	0.20	0.10	0.35	0.15	0.05

To maximize the profit contribution, how many pizzas should be ordered? Assume pizzas must be ordered by the dozen. What is the expected value of perfect information in this problem? What is the maximum amount the organization would be willing to pay for perfect information?

■ **17-9** Manfred Baum, merchandise manager for the Grant Shoe Company, is planning production decisions for the coming year's summer line of shoes. His chief concern is estimating the sales of a new design of fashion sandals. These sandals have posed problems in the past for two reasons: (1) the limited selling season does not provide enough time for the company to produce a second run of a popular item, and (2) the styles change dramatically from year to year, and unsold sandals become worthless. Manfred has discussed the newest design with salespeople and has formulated the following estimates of how the item will sell:

Pairs (thousands)	45	50	55	60	65
Probability	0.25	0.30	0.20	0.15	0.10

Information from the production department reveals that the sandal will cost \$15.25 per pair to manufacture, and marketing has informed Manfred that the wholesale price will be \$31.35 a pair. Using the expected-value decision criterion, calculate the number of pairs that Manfred should recommend that the company produce.

Worked-Out Answer to Self-Check Exercise

SC 17-1 The payoff table below gives both conditional and expected profits.

Machines needed		22	23	24	25	26	27	**Expected**
Probability		0.12	0.16	0.22	0.27	0.18	0.05	**Profit**
	22	157.30	157.30	157.30	157.30	157.30	157.30	157.30
	23	156.45	164.45	164.45	164.45	164.45	164.45	163.49
Machines	24	155.60	163.60	171.60	171.60	171.60	171.60	168.40
supplied	25	154.75	162.75	170.75	178.75	178.75	178.75	171.55
	26	153.90	161.90	169.90	177.90	185.90	185.90	172.54 ←
	27	153.05	161.05	169.05	177.05	185.05	193.25	172.09

She should have 26 machines.

$$\text{EVPI} = 157.30(0.12) + 164.45(0.16) + 171.60(0.22) + 178.75(0.27) + 185.90(0.18) + 193.25(0.05) - 172.54 = \$1.787$$

Because she cannot every hour adjust the number of machines she will have available, an hour-by-hour forecast of demand is of little value to her in this situation.

17.3 Using Continuous Distributions: Marginal Analysis

Limitations of the tabular approach

In many inventory problems, the number of computations required makes the use of conditional-profit and expected-profit tables difficult. Our previous illustration contained only four possible stock actions and four possible sales levels, resulting in a conditional-profit table containing 16 possibilities for conditional profits. If we had 300 possible values for sales volume and an equal number of calculations for determining conditional and expected profit, we would have to do a great many computations. The marginal approach avoids this problem.

Marginal analysis is based on the fact that when an additional unit of an item is bought, two fates are possible: the unit will be sold or it will not be sold. The sum of the probabilities of these two events must be 1. (For example, if the probability of selling the additional unit is 0.6, then the probability of not selling it must be 0.4.)

Derivation of marginal profit

If we let p represent the probability of selling one additional unit, then $1 - p$ must be the probability of not selling it. If the additional unit is sold, we shall realize an increase in our conditional profits as a result of the profit from the additional unit. We refer to this as *marginal profit,* or *MP.* In our previous illustration about the retailer, the marginal profit resulting from the sale of an additional unit is \$30, the selling price (\$50) minus the cost (\$20).

Table 17-10 illustrates this point. If we stock 10 units each day and daily demand is for 10 or more units, our conditional profit is \$300 per day. Now we decide to stock 11 units each day. If the eleventh unit is sold (and this is the case when demand is for 11, 12, or 13 units), our conditional profit is increased to \$330 per day. Notice that the increase in conditional profit does not follow merely from *stocking* the eleventh unit. Under the conditions assumed in the problem, this increase in profit will result only when demand is for 11 or more units. This will be the case 85 percent of the time.

Marginal loss

We must also consider how profits would be affected by stocking an additional unit and not selling it. This reduces our conditional profit. The amount of the reduction is referred to as the *marginal loss (ML)* resulting from the stocking of an item that is not sold. In our previous example, the marginal loss was \$20 per unit, the cost of the item.

Table 17-10

Conditional Profit Table

Possible Demand (sales) in Cases	Probability of Market Size	Possible Stock Actions			
		10 Cases	11 Cases	12 Cases	13 Cases
10	0.15	$300	$280	$260	$240
11	0.20	300	330	310	290
12	0.40	300	330	360	340
13	0.25	300	330	360	390

Table 17-10 also illustrates marginal loss. Once more we decide to stock 11 units. If the eleventh unit (the marginal unit) is not sold, the conditional profit is $280. The $300 conditional profit when 10 units were stocked and 10 were sold is reduced by $20, the cost of the unsold unit.

Derivation of stocking rule

Additional units should be stocked as long as the expected marginal profit from stocking each of them is greater than the expected marginal loss from stocking each. **The size of each day's order should be increased up to the point where the expected marginal profit from stocking one more unit if it sells is just equal to the expected marginal loss from stocking that unit if it remains unsold.**

In our illustration, the probability distribution of demand is

Market Size	Probability of Market Size
10	0.15
11	0.20
12	0.40
13	0.25
	1.00

This distribution tells us that as we increase our stock, the probability of selling one additional unit (this is p) decreases. If we increase our stock from 10 to 11 units, the probability of selling all eleven is 0.85. This is the probability that demand will be for 11 units or more. Here is the computation:

Probability that demand will be for 11	0.20
Probability that demand will be for 12	0.40
Probability that demand will be for 13	0.25
Probability that demand will be for 11 or more units	**0.85**

If we add a twelfth unit, the probability of selling all 12 units is reduced to 0.65 (the sum of the probabilities of demand for 12 or 13 units). Finally, the addition of a thirteenth unit carries with it only a 0.25 probability of our selling all 13 units, because demand will be for 13 units only 25 percent of the time.

Deriving the Minimum Probability Equation

Expected marginal profit and *loss* defined

The *expected marginal profit* from stocking and selling an additional unit is the marginal profit of the unit multiplied by the probability that the unit will be sold; this is $p(MP)$. The *expected marginal loss* from stocking and not selling an additional unit is the marginal loss incurred if the unit is unsold multiplied by the probability that the unit will not be sold; this is $(1 - p)(ML)$. We can generalize that the retailer in this situation would stock up to the point at which

$$p(MP) = (1 - p)(ML) \qquad [17\text{-}1]$$

This equation describes the point at which the expected marginal profit from stocking and selling an additional unit, $p(MP)$, is equal to the expected marginal loss from stocking and not selling the unit, $(1 - p)(ML)$. As long as $p(MP)$ is larger than $(1 - p)(ML)$, additional units should be stocked, because the expected profit from such a decision is greater than the expected loss.

Optimal inventory stock action

In any given inventory problem, there will be only *one* value of p for which the maximizing equation will be true. We must determine that value in order to know the optimal stock action to take. We can do this by taking our maximizing equation and solving it for p in the following manner:

$$p(MP) = (1 - p)(ML) \qquad [17\text{-}1]$$

Multiplying the two terms on the right side of the equation, we get

$$p(MP) = ML - p(ML)$$

Collecting terms containing p, we have

$$p(MP) + p(ML) = ML$$

or

$$p(MP + ML) = ML$$

Dividing both sides of the equation by $MP + ML$ gives

Minimum-probability equation

Minimum Probability Required to Stock Another Unit

$$p^* = \frac{ML}{MP + ML} \qquad [17\text{-}2]$$

The symbol p^* represents the minimum required probability of selling at least one additional unit to justify the stocking of that additional unit. The retailer should stock additional units as long as the probability of selling at least an additional unit is greater than p^*.

We can now compute p^* for our illustration. The marginal profit per unit is \$30 (the selling price minus the cost); the marginal loss per unit is \$20 (the cost of each unit); thus

$$p^* = \frac{ML}{MP + ML} = \frac{\$20}{\$30 + \$20} = \frac{\$20}{\$50} = 0.40 \qquad [17\text{-}2]$$

This value of 0.40 for p^* means that in order to make the stocking of an additional unit justifiable, we must have at least a 0.40 *cumulative* probability of selling that unit or more. In order to determine the probability of selling each additional unit we consider stocking, we must compute a series of cumulative probabilities, as we have done in Table 17-11.

Calculation of cumulative probabilities

The cumulative probabilities in the right-hand column of Table 17-11 represent the probabilities that sales will reach or exceed each of the four sales levels. For example, the 1.00 that appears beside the 10-unit sales level means that we are 100 percent certain of selling 10 or more units. This must be true because our problem assumes that one of the four sales levels will *always* occur.

Table 17-11 Cumulative Probabilities of Sales

Sales Units	Probability of This Sales Level	Cumulative Probability That Sales Will Be at This Level or Greater
10	0.15	1.00
11	0.20	0.85
12	0.40	0.65
13	0.25	0.25

The 0.85 probability value beside the 11-unit sales figure means that we are only 85 percent sure of selling 11 or more units. This can be calculated in two ways. First, we could add the chances of selling 11, 12, or 13 units:

11 units	0.20
12 units	0.40
13 units	+0.25
	0.85 = probability of selling 11 or more

Or we could reason that sales of 11 or more units include all possible outcomes except sales of 10 units, which has a probability of 0.15.

All possible outcomes	1.00
Probability of selling 10	−0.15
	0.85 = probability of selling 11 or more

The cumulative probability value of 0.65 assigned to sales of 12 units or more can be established in similar fashion. Sales of 12 or more must mean sales of 12 or 13 units.

Probability of selling 12	0.40
Probability of selling 13	+0.25
	0.65 = probability of selling 12 or more

And, of course, the cumulative probability of selling 13 units is still 0.25, because we have assumed that sales will never exceed 13.

As we mentioned previously, the value of p decreases as the level of stock increases. This causes the expected marginal profit to decrease and the expected marginal loss to increase until, at some point, stocking an additional unit would not be profitable.

Stocking rule

We have said that additional units should be stocked as long as the probability of selling at least an additional unit is greater than p^*. We can now apply this rule to our probability distribution of sales and determine how many units should be stocked.

In this case, the probability of selling 11 or more units is 0.85, a figure clearly greater than our p^* of 0.40; thus, we should stock an eleventh unit. The expected marginal profit from stocking this unit is greater than the expected marginal loss from stocking it. We can verify this as follows:

$$p(MP) = 0.85(\$30) = \$25.50 \text{ expected marginal profit}$$
$$(1 - p)(ML) = 0.15(\$20) = \$3.00 \text{ expected marginal loss}$$

A twelfth unit should be stocked because the probability of selling 12 or more units (0.65) is greater than the required p^* of 0.40. Such action will result in the following expected marginal profit and expected marginal loss:

$$p(MP) = 0.65(\$30) = \$19.50 \text{ expected marginal profit}$$

$$(1 - p)(ML) = 0.35(\$20) = \$7.00 \text{ expected marginal loss}$$

Optimal stocking level for this problem

Twelve is the *optimal* number of units to stock, because the addition of a thirteenth unit carried with it only a 0.25 probability that it will be sold, and that is less than our required p^* of 0.40. The following figures reveal why the thirteenth unit should not be stocked:

$$p(MP) = 0.25(\$30) = \$7.50 \text{ expected marginal profit}$$

$$(1 - p)(ML) = 0.75(\$20) = \$15.00 \text{ expected marginal loss}$$

If we stock a thirteenth unit, we add more to expected loss than we add to expected profit.

Notice that the use of marginal analysis leads us to the same conclusion that we reached with the use of conditional profit and expected profit tables. Both methods of analysis suggest that the retailer should stock 12 units each period.

Adjusting the optimal stocking level

Our strategy, to stock 12 cases every day, assumes that daily sales is a random variable. In actual practice, however, daily sales often take on recognizable patterns depending on the particular day of the week. In retail sales, Saturday is generally recognized as being a higher-volume day than, say, Tuesday. Similarly, Monday retail sales are typically less than those on Friday. In situations with recognizable patterns in daily sales, we can apply the techniques we have learned by computing an optimal stocking level for *each* day of the week. For Saturday, we would use as our input data past sales experience for Saturdays only. Each of the other 6 days could be treated in the same fashion. Essentially, this approach represents nothing more than recognition of, and reaction to, discernible patterns in what may at first appear to be a completely random environment.

Using the Standard Normal Probability Distribution

We first learned the concept of the standard normal probability distribution in Chapter 5. We can now use this idea to help us solve a decision-theory problem using a continuous distribution.

Solving a problem using marginal analysis

Assume that a manager sells an article having normally distributed sales with a mean of 50 units daily and a standard deviation in daily sales of 15 units. The manager purchases this article for \$4 per unit and sells it for \$9 per unit. If the article is not sold on the selling day, it is worth nothing. Using the marginal method of calculating optimal inventory purchase levels, we can calculate our required p^*:

$$p^* = \frac{ML}{MP + ML} \quad [17\text{-}2]$$

$$= \frac{\$4}{\$5 + \$4} = 0.44$$

This means that the manager must be 0.44 sure of selling at least an additional unit before it would pay to stock that unit. Let us reproduce the curve of past sales and determine how to incorporate the marginal method with continuous distributions of past daily sales.

Using the standard normal probability distribution in marginal analysis

Now refer to Figure 17-1. If we erect a vertical line b at 50 units, the area under the curve to the right of this line is one-half the total area. This tells us that the probability of selling 50 or more units is 0.5. *The area to the right of any such vertical line represents the probability of selling that quantity or more.* As the area to the right of any vertical line decreases, so does the probability that we will sell that quantity or more.

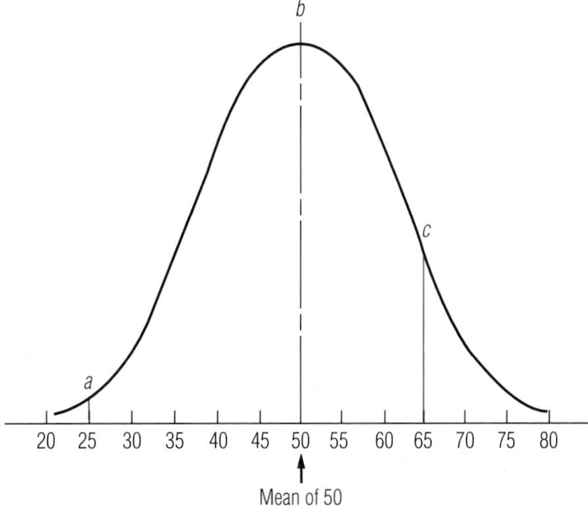

FIGURE 17-1

Normal distribution of past daily sales

Suppose the manager considers stocking 25 units, line *a*. Most of the entire area under the curve lies to the right of the vertical line drawn at 25; thus, the probability is great that the manager will sell 25 units or more. If he considers stocking 50 units (the mean), one-half the entire area under the curve lies to the right of vertical line *b;* thus, he is 0.5 sure of selling the 50 units or more. Now, say he considers stocking 65 units. Only a small portion of the entire area under the curve lies to the right of line *c;* thus, the probability of selling 65 or more units is quite small.

Figure 17-2 illustrates the 0.44 probability that must exist before it pays our manager to stock another unit. He will stock additional units until he reaches point *Q*. If he stocks a larger quantity, the shaded area under the curve drops below 0.44 and the probability of selling another unit or more falls below the required 0.44. How can we locate point *Q?* As we saw in Chapter 5, we can use Appendix Table 1 to determine how many standard deviations it takes to include any portion of the area under the curve measuring from the mean to any point such as *Q*. In this particular case, because we know that the shaded area must be 0.44 of the total area, the area from the mean to point *Q* must be 0.06 (the total area from the mean to the right tail is 0.50). Looking in the body of the table, we find that 0.06 of the area under the curve is located between the mean and a point 0.15 standard deviation to the right of the mean. Thus we know that point *Q* is 0.15 standard deviation to the right of the mean (50).

Optimal solution for this problem

We have been given the information that 1 standard deviation for this distribution is 15 units; so 0.15 times this would be 2.25 units. Because point *Q* is 2.25 units to the right of the mean (50), it must be at about 52 units. This is the optimal order for the manager to place: 52 units per day.

FIGURE 17-2

Normal probability distribution, with 0.44 of the area under the curve shaded

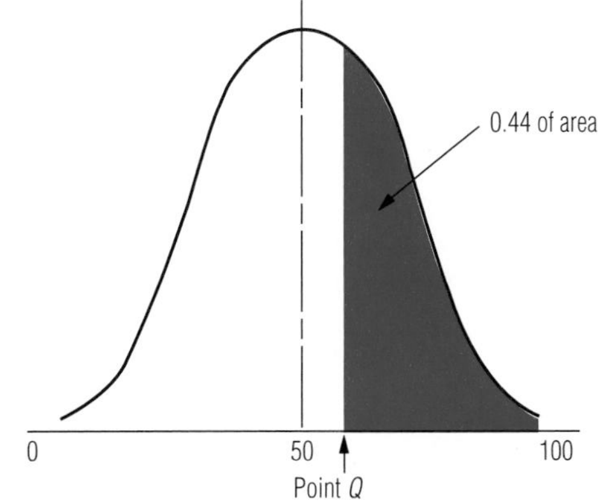

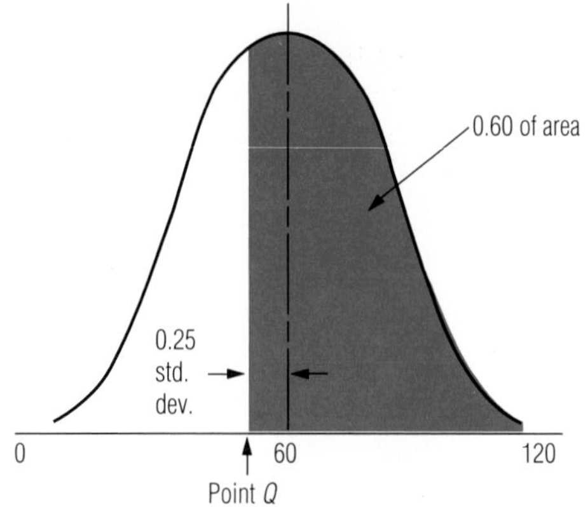

FIGURE 17-3

Normal probability distribution, with 0.60 of the area under the curve shaded

Chapter-opening problem

Now that we have been through one problem using a continuous probability distribution, we can work our chapter-opening problem involving these data for a normally distributed daily sales record:

Mean of past daily sales	60 boxes
Standard deviation of past daily sales distribution	10 boxes
Cost per box	\$20
Selling price per box	\$32
Value if not sold on first day	\$ 2

As we did in the previous problem, we first calculate the p^* that is required to justify the stocking of an additional box. In this instance,

Minimum required probability

$$p^* = \frac{ML}{MP + ML} \qquad [17\text{-}2]$$

$$= \frac{\$20 - \$2}{\$12 + (\$20 - \$2)}$$

Notice that a salvage value of \$2 is deducted from the cost of \$20 to obtain the *ML*

$$= \frac{\$18}{\$12 + \$18}$$

$$= \frac{\$18}{\$30} = 0.60$$

We can now illustrate the probability on a normal curve by marking off 0.60 of the area under the curve, starting from the right-hand end of the curve, as in Figure 17-3.

The manager wants to increase his order size until it reaches point Q. Now point Q lies to the *left* of the mean, whereas in the preceding problem it lay to the *right.* How can we locate point Q? Because 0.50 of the area under the curve is located between the mean and the right-hand tail, 0.10 of the shaded area must be to the left of the mean, $(0.60 - 0.50 = 0.10)$. In the body of Appendix Table 1, the nearest value to 0.10 is 0.0987, so we want to find a point Q with 0.0987 of the area under the curve contained between the mean and point Q. The table indicates point Q is 0.25 standard deviation from the mean. We now solve for point Q as follows:

Optimal solution for chapter-opening problem

$$0.25 \times \text{standard deviation} = 0.25 \times 10 \text{ boxes} = 2.5 \text{ boxes}$$

$$\text{Point } Q = \text{mean less } 2.5 \text{ boxes}$$

$$= 60 - 2.5 \text{ boxes} = 57.5 \text{ or } 57 \text{ boxes}$$

HINTS & ASSUMPTIONS

Warning: Use of the maximum *expected profit* calculated from a single sales distribution as your decision rule assumes that the sales distribution you are dealing with represents *all* of the information you have about demand. If you have information that sales on Saturday, for example, are better represented by a different distribution, then you must treat Saturday as a separate decision and calculate a stocking level for Saturday that will probably be different from that for the other 6 days. Hint: This is how good managers make decisions anyhow. Instead of accepting that every day of the week has identical market characteristics, it's long been known that strong, discernable daily differences exist. These daily differences are themselves quite different in certain countries. Hint: Whereas Saturday is a prime shopping day in the United States, Saturday sales would be near zero in Israel because it is their sabbath.

Exercises 17.3

Self-Check Exercise

SC 17-2 Floyd Guild operates a newsstand near the 53rd Street station of the IC South Shore and Suburban line. The *City Herald* is the most popular of the newspapers that Floyd stocks. Over many years, he has observed that daily demand for the *Herald* is well described by a normal distribution with mean $\mu = 165$ and standard deviation $\sigma = 40$. Copies of the *Herald* sell for 30¢, but the publisher charges Floyd only 20¢ for each copy he orders. If any *Herald*s are left over at the end of the evening commuting hours, Floyd sells them to Jesselman's Fish Market down the street for a dime each. If Floyd wishes to maximize his expected daily profit, how many copies of the *Herald* should he order?

Applications

■ **17-10** Highway construction in North Dakota is concentrated in the months from May through September. To provide some protection to the crews at work on the highways, the Department of Transportation (DOT) requires that large, orange MEN WORKING signs be placed in advance of any construction. Because of vandalism, wear and tear, and theft, the DOT purchases new signs each year. Although the signs are made under the auspices of the Department of Correction, the DOT is charged a price equivalent to one it would pay were it to buy the signs from an outside source. The interdepartmental charge for the signs is $21 if more than 35 of the same kind are ordered. Otherwise, the cost per sign is $29. Because of budget pressures, the DOT attempts to minimize its costs both by not buying too many signs and by attempting to buy in sufficiently large quantity to get the $21 price. In recent years, the department has averaged purchases of 78 signs per year, with a standard deviation of 15. Determine the number of signs the DOT should purchase.

■ **17-11** The town of Green Lake, Wisconsin, is preparing for the celebration of the seventy-ninth Annual Milk and Dairy Day. As a fund-raising device, the city council once again plans to sell souvenir T-shirts. The T-shirts, printed

(a) $^{8}/_{16}$.

(b) $^{3}/_{8}$.

(c) $^{5}/_{8}$.

(d) $^{5}/_{16}$.

A B C D 27. A certain product sells for $25 and is purchased by the retailer for $17. If it is not sold within 2 weeks, the retailer will recoup only $8 of his original $17 investment because of spoilage. The value of *MP* for this situation is:

(a) $9.

(b) $17.

(c) $8.

(d) $25.

A B C D E 28. Assume that for a particular stocking operation, $ML = \$10$ and $MP = \$30$. Then, $p^* = 0.25$. For which of the following situations would you stock the unit in question?

(a) The fifth unit when P(requests for 5 or more units) = 0.50.

(b) The third unit when P(requests for fewer than 3 units) = 0.10 and P(requests for exactly 3 units) = 0.09.

(c) The ninth unit when P(requests for more than 9 units) = 0.16 and P(requests for exactly 9 units) = 0.05.

(d) All of these.

(e) (a) and (b) but not (c).

A B C D 29. A manager is deciding whether to buy a new building or to rent it. If he buys, the cost for the next year will be $5,500, which will include mortgage interest, insurance, and other usual expenses. If he rents, the comparable expense for the next year will be either $6,000, $5,300, or $4,200, depending on market fluctuations. The manager wishes to make his choice based on expected monetary values for the next year. The decision tree for this situation would have:

(a) One decision point and no chance events.

(b) One chance event and one decision point.

(c) Two decision points and three chance events.

(d) One decision point and three chance events.

A B C D E 30. For a particular decision, the total benefit of a new plant is $18,200,000. If the expected net benefit of this plant is $11,500,000, what is the cost of the plant?

(a) $6,700,000.

(b) $8,400,000.

(c) $29,700,000.

(d) $11,500,000.

(e) Cannot be determined from the information given.

A B C D E 31. Assume that three businesswomen are questioned regarding their utilities in risk situations. It is found that Laura is averse to risk, Lisa plays long shots, and Leslie is so well-off financially that the amounts of money in question are negligible when compared to her wealth. For the situations in question, utility could be used as the decision criterion for:

(a) Laura.

(b) Lisa.

(c) Leslie.
(d) All three.
(e) (a) and (b) but not (c).

A B C D 32. A person who is attempting to maximize his expected utility would use the expected value criterion if:
(a) He is risk-averse.
(b) He is a risk seeker.
(c) He has a nonlinear utility curve.
(d) None of these.

A B C D E 33. When a problem has a large number of possible actions, we would normally use a:
(a) Conditional table.
(b) Marginal table.
(c) Utility table.
(d) Marginal analysis.
(e) None of these.

A B C D E 34. Decision theory deals with:
(a) Making decisions under conditions of uncertainty.
(b) Quantity-oriented decision, ignoring financial repercussions.
(c) The worth of additional information to the decision maker.
(d) (a) and (b) but not (c).
(e) (a) and (c) but not (b).

A B C D E 35. Once a decision tree is "solved," the analyst should:
(a) Immediately go out and make the decision.
(b) Specify underlying assumptions to point out, among other things, the limits under which the decision tree is valid.
(c) Perform sensitivity analysis to determine how the solution reacts to changes in the inputs.
(d) (b) and (c) but not (a).
(e) All of the above.

A B C D 36. An item costs the retailer \$3.25 and can be sold for \$5.75. If unsold, the item can be sold for a salvage value of \$1.50. Which of the following statements are true?
(a) $ML = \$4.25$.
(b) $p^* = (\$3.25 - \$1.50)/(\$5.75 - \$1.50)$.
(c) In order to justify the stocking of an additional item, the cumulative probability of selling that unit or more must be 50%.
(d) None of the above.

37. Events beyond the control of the decision maker are called
_________________________ or _________________________ of nature.

38. The maximum amount that a retailer will be willing to pay for a perfect predictor is called the _________________________ .

39. There are two types of losses in a stocking operation:
_________________________ losses and _________________________ losses.

40. The pleasure or displeasure one receives from certain outcomes is known as one's _________________________ .

41. The act of calculating expected benefits for each circle and square of a decision tree is called ________________________ .

42. If a profit increases a person's utility by much more than a loss of the same size would decrease her utility, that person will often act when the expected value is ________________________ .

43. The loss incurred from stocking an item that is not subsequently sold is called ________________________ .

44. Observing how optimal decisions and profits change when payoffs or probabilities vary is called ________________________ .

45. Time sequencing in a decision tree occurs from ________________________ to ________________________; rollback is accomplished from ________________________ to ________________________ .

Appendix Tables

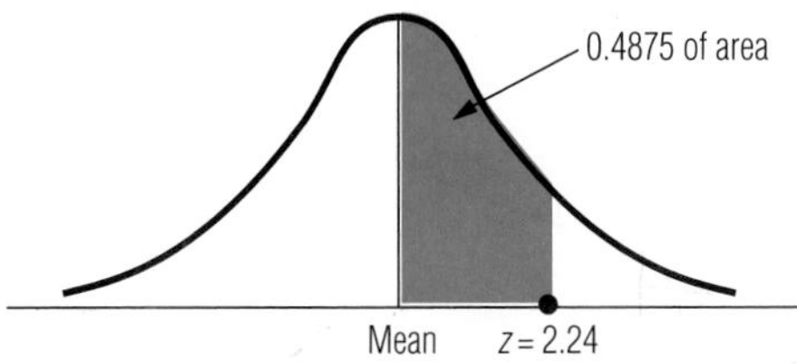

Appendix Table 1

Areas under the Standard Normal Probability Distribution between the Mean and Positive Values of z

Example: To find the area under the curve between the mean and a point 2.24 standard deviations to the right of the mean, look up the value opposite 2.2 and under 0.04 in the table; 0.4875 of the area under the curve lies between the mean and a **z** value of 2.24.

z	0.00	0.01	0.02	0.03	0.04	0.05	0.06	0.07	0.08	0.09
0.0	0.0000	0.0040	0.0080	0.0120	0.0160	0.0199	0.0239	0.0279	0.0319	0.0359
0.1	0.0398	0.0438	0.0478	0.0517	0.0557	0.0596	0.0636	0.0675	0.0714	0.0753
0.2	0.0793	0.0832	0.0871	0.0910	0.0948	0.0987	0.1026	0.1064	0.1103	0.1141
0.3	0.1179	0.1217	0.1255	0.1293	0.1331	0.1368	0.1406	0.1443	0.1480	0.1517
0.4	0.1554	0.1591	0.1628	0.1664	0.1700	0.1736	0.1772	0.1808	0.1844	0.1879
0.5	0.1915	0.1950	0.1985	0.2019	0.2054	0.2088	0.2123	0.2157	0.2190	0.2224
0.6	0.2257	0.2291	0.2324	0.2357	0.2389	0.2422	0.2454	0.2486	0.2517	0.2549
0.7	0.2580	0.2611	0.2642	0.2673	0.2704	0.2734	0.2764	0.2794	0.2823	0.2852
0.8	0.2881	0.2910	0.2939	0.2967	0.2995	0.3023	0.3051	0.3078	0.3106	0.3133
0.9	0.3159	0.3186	0.3212	0.3238	0.3264	0.3289	0.3315	0.3340	0.3365	0.3389
1.0	0.3413	0.3438	0.3461	0.3485	0.3508	0.3531	0.3554	0.3577	0.3599	0.3621
1.1	0.3643	0.3665	0.3686	0.3708	0.3729	0.3749	0.3770	0.3790	0.3810	0.3830
1.2	0.3849	0.3869	0.3888	0.3907	0.3925	0.3944	0.3962	0.3980	0.3997	0.4015
1.3	0.4032	0.4049	0.4066	0.4082	0.4099	0.4115	0.4131	0.4147	0.4162	0.4177
1.4	0.4192	0.4207	0.4222	0.4236	0.4251	0.4265	0.4279	0.4292	0.4306	0.4319
1.5	0.4332	0.4345	0.4357	0.4370	0.4382	0.4394	0.4406	0.4418	0.4429	0.4441
1.6	0.4452	0.4463	0.4474	0.4484	0.4495	0.4505	0.4515	0.4525	0.4535	0.4545
1.7	0.4554	0.4564	0.4573	0.4582	0.4591	0.4599	0.4608	0.4616	0.4625	0.4633
1.8	0.4641	0.4649	0.4656	0.4664	0.4671	0.4678	0.4686	0.4693	0.4699	0.4706
1.9	0.4713	0.4719	0.4726	0.4732	0.4738	0.4744	0.4750	0.4756	0.4761	0.4767
2.0	0.4772	0.4778	0.4783	0.4788	0.4793	0.4798	0.4803	0.4808	0.4812	0.4817
2.1	0.4821	0.4826	0.4830	0.4834	0.4838	0.4842	0.4846	0.4850	0.4854	0.4857
2.2	0.4861	0.4864	0.4868	0.4871	0.4875	0.4878	0.4881	0.4884	0.4887	0.4890
2.3	0.4893	0.4896	0.4898	0.4901	0.4904	0.4906	0.4909	0.4911	0.4913	0.4916
2.4	0.4918	0.4920	0.4922	0.4925	0.4927	0.4929	0.4931	0.4932	0.4934	0.4936
2.5	0.4938	0.4940	0.4941	0.4943	0.4945	0.4946	0.4948	0.4949	0.4951	0.4952
2.6	0.4953	0.4955	0.4956	0.4957	0.4959	0.4960	0.4961	0.4962	0.4963	0.4964
2.7	0.4965	0.4966	0.4967	0.4968	0.4969	0.4970	0.4971	0.4972	0.4973	0.4974
2.8	0.4974	0.4975	0.4976	0.4977	0.4977	0.4978	0.4979	0.4979	0.4980	0.4981
2.9	0.4981	0.4982	0.4982	0.4983	0.4984	0.4984	0.4985	0.4985	0.4986	0.4986
3.0	0.4987	0.4987	0.4987	0.4988	0.4988	0.4989	0.4989	0.4989	0.4990	0.4990

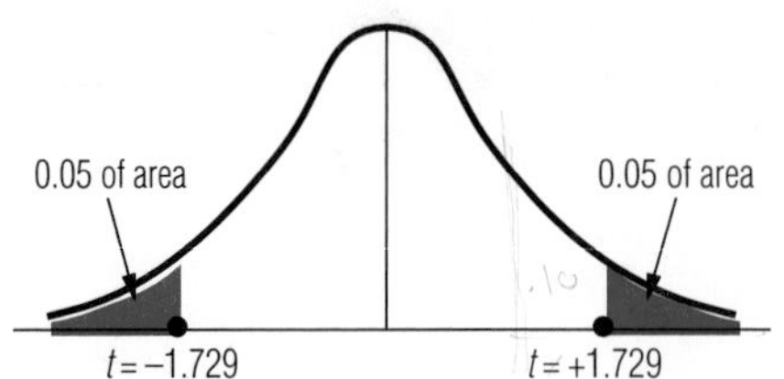

Appendix Table 2

Areas in Both Tails Combined for Student's *t* Distribution

Example: To find the value of *t* that corresponds to an area of 0.10 in both tails of the distribution combined, when there are 19 degrees of freedom, look under the 0.10 column, and proceed down to the 19 degrees of freedom row; the appropriate *t* value there is 1.729.

Degrees of Freedom	Area in Both Tails Combined			
	0.10	**0.05**	**0.02**	**0.01**
1	6.314	12.706	31.821	63.657
2	2.920	4.303	6.965	9.925
3	2.353	3.182	4.541	5.841
4	2.132	2.776	3.747	4.604
5	2.015	2.571	3.365	4.032
6	1.943	2.447	3.143	3.707
7	1.895	2.365	2.998	3.499
8	1.860	2.306	2.896	3.355
9	1.833	2.262	2.821	3.250
10	1.812	2.228	2.764	3.169
11	1.796	2.201	2.718	3.106
12	1.782	2.179	2.681	3.055
13	1.771	2.160	2.650	3.012
14	1.761	2.145	2.624	2.977
15	1.753	2.131	2.602	2.947
16	1.746	2.120	2.583	2.921
17	1.740	2.110	2.567	2.898
18	1.734	2.101	2.552	2.878
19	1.729	2.093	2.539	2.861
20	1.725	2.086	2.528	2.845
21	1.721	2.080	2.518	2.831
22	1.717	2.074	2.508	2.819
23	1.714	2.069	2.500	2.807
24	1.711	2.064	2.492	2.797
25	1.708	2.060	2.485	2.787
26	1.706	2.056	2.479	2.779
27	1.703	2.052	2.473	2.771
28	1.701	2.048	2.467	2.763
29	1.699	2.045	2.462	2.756
30	1.697	2.042	2.457	2.750
40	1.684	2.021	2.423	2.704
60	1.671	2.000	2.390	2.660
120	1.658	1.980	2.358	2.617
Normal Distribution	1.645	1.960	2.326	2.576

Appendix Table 3

Binomial Probabilities

For a given combination of ***n*** and ***p***, entry indicates the probability of obtaining a specified value of ***r***. To locate entry: **when *p* ≤ 0.50,** read ***p*** across the top and both ***n*** and ***r*** down the left margin; **when *p* ≥ 0.50,** read ***p*** across the bottom and both ***n*** and ***r*** up the right margin.

		p																			
n	***r***	**0.01**	**0.02**	**0.03**	**0.04**	**0.05**	**0.06**	**0.07**	**0.08**	**0.09**	**0.10**	**0.11**	**0.12**	**0.13**	**0.14**	**0.15**	**0.16**	**0.17**	**0.18**	***r***	***n***
2	0	0.9801	0.9604	0.9409	0.9216	0.9025	0.8836	0.8649	0.8464	0.8281	0.8100	0.7921	0.7744	0.7569	0.7396	0.7225	0.7056	0.6889	0.6724	2	
	1	0.0198	0.0392	0.0582	0.0768	0.0950	0.1128	0.1302	0.1472	0.1638	0.1800	0.1958	0.2112	0.2262	0.2408	0.2550	0.2688	0.2822	0.2952	1	
	2	0.0001	0.0004	0.0009	0.0016	0.0025	0.0036	0.0049	0.0064	0.0081	0.0100	0.0121	0.0144	0.0169	0.0196	0.0225	0.0256	0.0289	0.0324	0	2
3	0	0.9703	0.9412	0.9127	0.8847	0.8574	0.8306	0.8044	0.7787	0.7536	0.7290	0.7050	0.6815	0.6585	0.6361	0.6141	0.5927	0.5718	0.5514	3	
	1	0.0294	0.0576	0.0847	0.1106	0.1354	0.1590	0.1816	0.2031	0.2236	0.2430	0.2614	0.2788	0.2952	0.3106	0.3251	0.3387	0.3513	0.3631	2	
	2	0.0003	0.0012	0.0026	0.0046	0.0071	0.0102	0.0137	0.0177	0.0221	0.0270	0.0323	0.0380	0.0441	0.0506	0.0574	0.0645	0.0720	0.0797	1	
	3	0.0000	0.0000	0.0000	0.0001	0.0001	0.0002	0.0003	0.0005	0.0007	0.0010	0.0013	0.0017	0.0022	0.0027	0.0034	0.0041	0.0049	0.0058	0	3
4	0	0.9606	0.9224	0.8853	0.8493	0.8145	0.7807	0.7481	0.7164	0.6857	0.6561	0.6274	0.5997	0.5729	0.5470	0.5220	0.4979	0.4746	0.4521	4	
	1	0.0388	0.0753	0.1095	0.1416	0.1715	0.1993	0.2252	0.2492	0.2713	0.2916	0.3102	0.3271	0.3424	0.3562	0.3685	0.3793	0.3888	0.3970	3	
	2	0.0006	0.0023	0.0051	0.0088	0.0135	0.0191	0.0254	0.0325	0.0402	0.0486	0.0575	0.0669	0.0767	0.0870	0.0975	0.1084	0.1195	0.1307	2	
	3	0.0000	0.0000	0.0001	0.0002	0.0005	0.0008	0.0013	0.0019	0.0027	0.0036	0.0047	0.0061	0.0076	0.0094	0.0115	0.0138	0.0163	0.0191	1	
	4	—	—	0.0000	0.0000	0.0000	0.0000	0.0000	0.0000	0.0001	0.0001	0.0001	0.0002	0.0003	0.0004	0.0005	0.0007	0.0008	0.0010	0	4
5	0	0.9510	0.9039	0.8587	0.8154	0.7738	0.7339	0.6957	0.6591	0.6240	0.5905	0.5584	0.5277	0.4984	0.4704	0.4437	0.4182	0.3939	0.3707	5	
	1	0.0480	0.0922	0.1328	0.1699	0.2036	0.2342	0.2618	0.2866	0.3086	0.3280	0.3451	0.3598	0.3724	0.3829	0.3915	0.3983	0.4034	0.4069	4	
	2	0.0010	0.0038	0.0082	0.0142	0.0214	0.0299	0.0394	0.0498	0.0610	0.0729	0.0853	0.0981	0.1113	0.1247	0.1382	0.1517	0.1652	0.1786	3	
	3	0.0000	0.0001	0.0003	0.0006	0.0011	0.0019	0.0030	0.0043	0.0060	0.0081	0.0105	0.0134	0.0166	0.0203	0.0244	0.0289	0.0338	0.0392	2	
	4	—	0.0000	0.0000	0.0000	0.0000	0.0001	0.0001	0.0002	0.0003	0.0004	0.0007	0.0009	0.0012	0.0017	0.0022	0.0028	0.0035	0.0043	1	
	5	—	—	—	—	—	0.0000	0.0000	0.0000	0.0000	0.0000	0.0000	0.0000	0.0000	0.0001	0.0001	0.0001	0.0001	0.0002	0	5
6	0	0.9415	0.8858	0.8330	0.7828	0.7351	0.6899	0.6470	0.6064	0.5679	0.5314	0.4970	0.4644	0.4336	0.4046	0.3771	0.3513	0.3269	0.3040	6	
	1	0.0571	0.1085	0.1546	0.1957	0.2321	0.2642	0.2922	0.3164	0.3370	0.3543	0.3685	0.3800	0.3888	0.3952	0.3993	0.4015	0.4018	0.4004	5	
	2	0.0014	0.0055	0.0120	0.0204	0.0305	0.0422	0.0550	0.0688	0.0833	0.0984	0.1139	0.1295	0.1452	0.1608	0.1762	0.1912	0.2057	0.2197	4	
	3	0.0000	0.0002	0.0005	0.0011	0.0021	0.0036	0.0055	0.0080	0.0110	0.0146	0.0188	0.0236	0.0289	0.0349	0.0415	0.0486	0.0562	0.0643	3	
	4	—	0.0000	0.0000	0.0000	0.0001	0.0002	0.0003	0.0005	0.0008	0.0012	0.0017	0.0024	0.0032	0.0043	0.0055	0.0069	0.0086	0.0106	2	
	5	—	—	—	—	0.0000	0.0000	0.0000	0.0000	0.0000	0.0001	0.0001	0.0001	0.0002	0.0003	0.0004	0.0005	0.0007	0.0009	1	
	6	—	—	—	—	—	—	—	—	—	0.0000	0.0000	0.0000	0.0000	0.0000	0.0000	0.0000	0.0000	0.0000	0	6
7	0	0.9321	0.8681	0.8080	0.7514	0.6983	0.6485	0.6017	0.5578	0.5168	0.4783	0.4423	0.4087	0.3773	0.3479	0.3206	0.2951	0.2714	0.2493	7	
	1	0.0659	0.1240	0.1749	0.2192	0.2573	0.2897	0.3170	0.3396	0.3578	0.3720	0.3827	0.3901	0.3946	0.3965	0.3960	0.3935	0.3891	0.3830	6	
	2	0.0020	0.0076	0.0162	0.0274	0.0406	0.0555	0.0716	0.0886	0.1061	0.1240	0.1419	0.1596	0.1769	0.1936	0.2097	0.2248	0.2391	0.2523	5	
	3	0.0000	0.0003	0.0008	0.0019	0.0036	0.0059	0.0090	0.0128	0.0175	0.0230	0.0292	0.0363	0.0441	0.0525	0.0617	0.0714	0.0816	0.0923	4	
	4	—	0.0000	0.0000	0.0001	0.0002	0.0004	0.0007	0.0011	0.0017	0.0026	0.0036	0.0049	0.0066	0.0086	0.0109	0.0136	0.0167	0.0203	3	
	5	—	—	—	0.0000	0.0000	0.0000	0.0000	0.0001	0.0001	0.0002	0.0003	0.0004	0.0006	0.0008	0.0012	0.0016	0.0021	0.0027	2	
	6	—	—	—	—	—	—	—	0.0000	0.0000	0.0000	0.0000	0.0000	0.0000	0.0000	0.0001	0.0001	0.0001	0.0002	1	
	7	—	—	—	—	—	—	—	—	—	—	—	—	—	—	0.0000	0.0000	0.0000	0.0000	0	7
n	***r***	**0.99**	**0.98**	**0.97**	**0.96**	**0.95**	**0.94**	**0.93**	**0.92**	**0.91**	**0.90**	**0.89**	**0.88**	**0.87**	**0.86**	**0.85**	**0.84**	**0.83**	**0.82**	***r***	***n***
		p																			

P(x=r/n,p)

n	r	0.01	0.02	0.03	0.04	0.05	0.06	0.07	0.08	0.09	0.10	0.11	0.12	0.13	0.14	0.15	0.16	0.17	0.18	r	n
8	0	0.9227	0.8508	0.7837	0.7214	0.6634	0.6096	0.5596	0.5132	0.4703	0.4305	0.3937	0.3596	0.3282	0.2992	0.2725	0.2479	0.2252	0.2044	8	
	1	0.0746	0.1389	0.1939	0.2405	0.2793	0.3113	0.3370	0.3570	0.3721	0.3826	0.3892	0.3923	0.3923	0.3897	0.3847	0.3777	0.3691	0.3590	7	
	2	0.0026	0.0099	0.0210	0.0351	0.0515	0.0695	0.0888	0.1087	0.1288	0.1488	0.1684	0.1872	0.2052	0.2220	0.2376	0.2518	0.2646	0.2758	6	
	3	0.0001	0.0004	0.0013	0.0029	0.0054	0.0089	0.0134	0.0189	0.0255	0.0331	0.0416	0.0511	0.0613	0.0723	0.0839	0.0959	0.1084	0.1211	5	
	4	0.0000	0.0000	0.0001	0.0002	0.0004	0.0007	0.0013	0.0021	0.0031	0.0046	0.0064	0.0087	0.0115	0.0147	0.0185	0.0228	0.0277	0.0332	4	
	5	—	—	0.0000	0.0000	0.0000	0.0000	0.0001	0.0001	0.0002	0.0004	0.0006	0.0009	0.0014	0.0019	0.0026	0.0035	0.0045	0.0058	3	
	6	—	—	—	—	—	—	0.0000	0.0000	0.0000	0.0000	0.0000	0.0001	0.0001	0.0002	0.0002	0.0003	0.0005	0.0006	2	
	7	—	—	—	—	—	—	—	—	—	—	—	0.0000	0.0000	0.0000	0.0000	0.0000	0.0000	0.0000	1	
	8	—	—	—	—	—	—	—	—	—	—	—	—	—	—	—	—	—	—	0	8
9	0	0.9135	0.8337	0.7602	0.6925	0.6302	0.5730	0.5204	0.4722	0.4279	0.3874	0.3504	0.3165	0.2855	0.2573	0.2316	0.2082	0.1869	0.1676	9	
	1	0.0830	0.1531	0.2116	0.2597	0.2985	0.3292	0.3525	0.3695	0.3809	0.3874	0.3897	0.3884	0.3840	0.3770	0.3679	0.3569	0.3446	0.3312	8	
	2	0.0034	0.0125	0.0262	0.0433	0.0629	0.0840	0.1061	0.1285	0.1507	0.1722	0.1927	0.2119	0.2295	0.2455	0.2597	0.2720	0.2823	0.2908	7	
	3	0.0001	0.0006	0.0019	0.0042	0.0077	0.0125	0.0186	0.0261	0.0348	0.0446	0.0556	0.0674	0.0800	0.0933	0.1069	0.1209	0.1349	0.1489	6	
	4	0.0000	0.0000	0.0001	0.0003	0.0006	0.0012	0.0021	0.0034	0.0052	0.0074	0.0103	0.0138	0.0179	0.0228	0.0283	0.0345	0.0415	0.0490	5	
	5	—	—	0.0000	0.0000	0.0000	0.0001	0.0002	0.0003	0.0005	0.0008	0.0013	0.0019	0.0027	0.0037	0.0050	0.0066	0.0085	0.0108	4	
	6	—	—	—	—	—	0.0000	0.0000	0.0000	0.0000	0.0001	0.0001	0.0002	0.0003	0.0004	0.0006	0.0008	0.0012	0.0016	3	
	7	—	—	—	—	—	—	—	—	—	0.0000	0.0000	0.0000	0.0000	0.0000	0.0000	0.0001	0.0001	0.0001	2	
	8	—	—	—	—	—	—	—	—	—	—	—	—	—	—	—	0.0000	0.0000	0.0000	1	
	9	—	—	—	—	—	—	—	—	—	—	—	—	—	—	—	—	—	—	0	9
10	0	0.9044	0.8171	0.7374	0.6648	0.5987	0.5386	0.4840	0.4344	0.3894	0.3487	0.3118	0.2785	0.2484	0.2213	0.1969	0.1749	0.1552	0.1374	10	
	1	0.0914	0.1667	0.2281	0.2770	0.3151	0.3438	0.3643	0.3777	0.3851	0.3874	0.3854	0.3798	0.3712	0.3603	0.3474	0.3331	0.3178	0.3017	9	
	2	0.0042	0.0153	0.0317	0.0519	0.0746	0.0988	0.1234	0.1478	0.1714	0.1937	0.2143	0.2330	0.2496	0.2639	0.2759	0.2856	0.2929	0.2980	8	
	3	0.0001	0.0008	0.0026	0.0058	0.0105	0.0168	0.0248	0.0343	0.0452	0.0574	0.0706	0.0847	0.0995	0.1146	0.1298	0.1450	0.1600	0.1745	7	
	4	0.0000	0.0000	0.0001	0.0004	0.0010	0.0019	0.0033	0.0052	0.0078	0.0112	0.0153	0.0202	0.0260	0.0326	0.0401	0.0483	0.0573	0.0670	6	
	5	—	—	0.0000	0.0000	0.0001	0.0001	0.0003	0.0005	0.0009	0.0015	0.0023	0.0033	0.0047	0.0064	0.0085	0.0111	0.0141	0.0177	5	
	6	—	—	—	—	0.0000	0.0000	0.0000	0.0000	0.0001	0.0001	0.0002	0.0004	0.0006	0.0009	0.0012	1.0018	0.0024	0.0032	4	
	7	—	—	—	—	—	—	—	—	0.0000	0.0000	0.0000	0.0000	0.0000	0.0001	0.0001	0.0002	0.0003	0.0004	3	
	8	—	—	—	—	—	—	—	—	—	—	—	—	—	0.0000	0.0000	0.0000	0.0000	0.0000	2	
	9	—	—	—	—	—	—	—	—	—	—	—	—	—	—	—	—	—	—	1	
	10	—	—	—	—	—	—	—	—	—	—	—	—	—	—	—	—	—	—	0	10
n	r	0.99	0.98	0.97	0.96	0.95	0.94	0.93	0.92	0.91	0.90	0.89	0.88	0.87	0.86	0.85	0.84	0.83	0.82	r	n

p (upper header row spans the 0.01–0.18 columns; lower row spans the 0.99–0.82 columns)

n	r	0.01	0.02	0.03	0.04	0.05	0.06	0.07	0.08	0.09	0.10	0.11	0.12	0.13	0.14	0.15	0.16	0.17	0.18	r	n
		p																			
12	0	0.8864	0.7847	0.6938	0.6127	0.5404	0.4759	0.4186	0.3677	0.3225	0.2824	0.2470	0.2157	0.1880	0.1637	0.1422	0.1234	0.1069	0.0924	12	
	1	0.1074	0.1922	0.2575	0.3064	0.3413	0.3645	0.3781	0.3837	0.3827	0.3766	0.3663	0.3529	0.3372	0.3197	0.3012	0.2821	0.2627	0.2434	11	
	2	0.0060	0.0216	0.0438	0.0702	0.0988	0.1280	0.1565	0.1835	0.2082	0.2301	0.2490	0.2647	0.2771	0.2863	0.2924	0.2955	0.2960	0.2939	10	
	3	0.0002	0.0015	0.0045	0.0098	0.0173	0.0272	0.0393	0.0532	0.0686	0.0852	0.1026	0.1203	0.1380	0.1553	0.1720	0.1876	0.2021	0.2151	9	
	4	0.0000	0.0001	0.0003	0.0009	0.0021	0.0039	0.0067	0.0104	0.0153	0.0213	0.0285	0.0369	0.0464	0.0569	0.0683	0.0804	0.0931	0.1062	8	
	5	—	0.0000	0.0000	0.0001	0.0002	0.0004	0.0008	0.0014	0.0024	0.0038	0.0056	0.0081	0.0111	0.0148	0.0193	0.0245	0.0305	0.0373	7	
	6	—	—	—	0.0000	0.0000	0.0000	0.0001	0.0001	0.0003	0.0005	0.0008	0.0013	0.0019	0.0028	0.0040	0.0054	0.0073	0.0096	6	
	7	—	—	—	—	—	—	0.0000	0.0000	0.0000	0.0000	0.0001	0.0001	0.0002	0.0004	0.0006	0.0009	0.0013	0.0018	5	
	8	—	—	—	—	—	—	—	—	—	—	0.0000	0.0000	0.0000	0.0000	0.0001	0.0001	0.0002	0.0002	4	
	9	—	—	—	—	—	—	—	—	—	—	—	—	—	—	0.0000	0.0000	0.0000	0.0000	3	
	10	—	—	—	—	—	—	—	—	—	—	—	—	—	—	—	—	—	—	2	
	11	—	—	—	—	—	—	—	—	—	—	—	—	—	—	—	—	—	—	1	
	12	—	—	—	—	—	—	—	—	—	—	—	—	—	—	—	—	—	—	0	12
15	0	0.8601	0.7386	0.6333	0.5421	0.4633	0.3953	0.3367	0.2863	0.2430	0.2059	0.1741	0.1470	0.1238	0.1041	0.0874	0.0731	0.0611	0.0510	15	
	1	0.1303	0.2261	0.2938	0.3388	0.3658	0.3785	0.3801	0.3734	0.3605	0.3432	0.3228	0.3006	0.2775	0.2542	0.2312	0.2090	0.1878	0.1678	14	
	2	0.0092	0.0323	0.0636	0.0988	0.1348	0.1691	0.2003	0.2273	0.2496	0.2669	0.2793	0.2870	0.2903	0.2897	0.2856	0.2787	0.2692	0.2578	13	
	3	0.0004	0.0029	0.0085	0.0178	0.0307	0.0468	0.0653	0.0857	0.1070	0.1285	0.1496	0.1696	0.1880	0.2044	0.2184	0.2300	0.2389	0.2452	12	
	4	0.0000	0.0002	0.0008	0.0022	0.0049	0.0090	0.0148	0.0223	0.0317	0.0428	0.0555	0.0694	0.0843	0.0998	0.1156	0.1314	0.1468	0.1615	11	
	5	—	0.0000	0.0001	0.0002	0.0006	0.0013	0.0024	0.0043	0.0069	0.0105	0.0151	0.0208	0.0277	0.0357	0.0449	0.0551	0.0662	0.0780	10	
	6	—	—	0.0000	0.0000	0.0000	0.0001	0.0003	0.0006	0.0011	0.0019	0.0031	0.0047	0.0069	0.0097	0.0132	0.0175	0.0226	0.0285	9	
	7	—	—	—	—	—	0.0000	0.0000	0.0001	0.0001	0.0003	0.0005	0.0008	0.0013	0.0020	0.0030	0.0043	0.0059	0.0081	8	
	8	—	—	—	—	—	—	—	0.0000	0.0000	0.0000	0.0001	0.0001	0.0002	0.0003	0.0005	0.0008	0.0012	0.0018	7	
	9	—	—	—	—	—	—	—	—	—	—	0.0000	0.0000	0.0000	0.0000	0.0001	0.0001	0.0002	0.0003	6	
	10	—	—	—	—	—	—	—	—	—	—	—	—	—	—	0.0000	0.0000	0.0000	0.0000	5	
	11	—	—	—	—	—	—	—	—	—	—	—	—	—	—	—	—	—	—	4	
	12	—	—	—	—	—	—	—	—	—	—	—	—	—	—	—	—	—	—	3	
	13	—	—	—	—	—	—	—	—	—	—	—	—	—	—	—	—	—	—	2	
	14	—	—	—	—	—	—	—	—	—	—	—	—	—	—	—	—	—	—	1	
	15	—	—	—	—	—	—	—	—	—	—	—	—	—	—	—	—	—	—	0	15
20	0	0.8179	0.6676	0.5438	0.4420	0.3585	0.2901	0.2342	0.1887	0.1516	0.1216	0.0972	0.0776	0.0617	0.0490	0.0388	0.0306	0.0241	0.0189	20	
	1	0.1652	0.2725	0.3364	0.3683	0.3774	0.3703	0.3526	0.3282	0.3000	0.2702	0.2403	0.2115	0.1844	0.1595	0.1368	0.1165	0.0986	0.0829	19	
	2	0.0159	0.0528	0.0988	0.1458	0.1887	0.2246	0.2521	0.2711	0.2818	0.2852	0.2822	0.2740	0.2618	0.2466	0.2293	0.2109	0.1919	0.1730	18	
	3	0.0010	0.0065	0.0183	0.0364	0.0596	0.0860	0.1139	0.1414	0.1672	0.1901	0.2093	0.2242	0.2347	0.2409	0.2428	0.2410	0.2358	0.2278	17	
	4	0.0000	0.0006	0.0024	0.0065	0.0133	0.0233	0.0364	0.0523	0.0703	0.0898	0.1099	0.1299	0.1491	0.1666	0.1821	0.1951	0.2053	0.2125	16	
	5	—	0.0000	0.0002	0.0009	0.0022	0.0048	0.0088	0.0145	0.0222	0.0319	0.0435	0.0567	0.0713	0.0868	0.1028	0.1189	0.1345	0.1493	15	
	6	—	—	0.0000	0.0001	0.0003	0.0008	0.0017	0.0032	0.0055	0.0089	0.0134	0.0193	0.0266	0.0353	0.0454	0.0566	0.0689	0.0819	14	
	7	—	—	—	0.0000	0.0000	0.0001	0.0002	0.0005	0.0011	0.0020	0.0033	0.0053	0.0080	0.0115	0.0160	0.0216	0.0282	0.0360	13	
	8	—	—	—	—	—	0.0000	0.0000	0.0001	0.0002	0.0004	0.0007	0.0012	0.0019	0.0030	0.0046	0.0067	0.0094	0.0128	12	
	9	—	—	—	—	—	—	—	0.0000	0.0000	0.0001	0.0001	0.0002	0.0004	0.0007	0.0011	0.0017	0.0026	0.0038	11	
	10	—	—	—	—	—	—	—	—	—	0.0000	0.0000	0.0000	0.0001	0.0001	0.0002	0.0004	0.0006	0.0009	10	
	11	—	—	—	—	—	—	—	—	—	—	—	—	0.0000	0.0000	0.0000	0.0001	0.0001	0.0002	9	
	12	—	—	—	—	—	—	—	—	—	—	—	—	—	—	—	0.0000	0.0000	0.0000	8	
	13	—	—	—	—	—	—	—	—	—	—	—	—	—	—	—	—	—	—	7	
	14	—	—	—	—	—	—	—	—	—	—	—	—	—	—	—	—	—	—	6	
	15	—	—	—	—	—	—	—	—	—	—	—	—	—	—	—	—	—	—	5	
	16	—	—	—	—	—	—	—	—	—	—	—	—	—	—	—	—	—	—	4	
	17	—	—	—	—	—	—	—	—	—	—	—	—	—	—	—	—	—	—	3	
	18	—	—	—	—	—	—	—	—	—	—	—	—	—	—	—	—	—	—	2	
	19	—	—	—	—	—	—	—	—	—	—	—	—	—	—	—	—	—	—	1	
	20	—	—	—	—	—	—	—	—	—	—	—	—	—	—	—	—	—	—	0	20
n	**r**	**0.99**	**0.98**	**0.97**	**0.96**	**0.95**	**0.94**	**0.93**	**0.92**	**0.91**	**0.90**	**0.89**	**0.88**	**0.87**	**0.86**	**0.85**	**0.84**	**0.83**	**0.82**	**r**	**n**
		p																			

n	r	0.19	0.20	0.21	0.22	0.23	0.24	0.25	0.26	0.27	0.28	0.29	0.30	0.31	0.32	0.33	0.34	0.35	0.36	r	n
2	0	0.6561	0.6400	0.6241	0.6084	0.5929	0.5776	0.5625	0.5476	0.5329	0.5184	0.5041	0.4900	0.4761	0.4624	0.4489	0.4356	0.4225	0.4096	2	
	1	0.3078	0.3200	0.3318	0.3432	0.3542	0.3648	0.3750	0.3848	0.3942	0.4032	0.4118	0.4200	0.4278	0.4352	0.4422	0.4488	0.4550	0.4608	1	
	2	0.0361	0.0400	0.0441	0.0484	0.0529	0.0576	0.0625	0.0676	0.0729	0.0784	0.0841	0.0900	0.0961	0.1024	0.1089	0.1156	0.1225	0.1296	0	2
3	0	0.5314	0.5120	0.4930	0.4746	0.4565	0.4390	0.4219	0.4052	0.3890	0.3732	0.3579	0.3430	0.3285	0.3144	0.3008	0.2875	0.2746	0.2621	3	
	1	0.3740	0.3840	0.3932	0.4015	0.4091	0.4159	0.4219	0.4271	0.4316	0.4355	0.4386	0.4410	0.4428	0.4439	0.4444	0.4443	0.4436	0.4424	2	
	2	0.0877	0.0960	0.1045	0.1133	0.1222	0.1313	0.1406	0.1501	0.1597	0.1693	0.1791	0.1890	0.1989	0.2089	0.2189	0.2289	0.2389	0.2488	1	
	3	0.0069	0.0080	0.0093	0.0106	0.0122	0.0138	0.0156	0.0176	0.0197	0.0220	0.0244	0.0270	0.0298	0.0328	0.0359	0.0393	0.0429	0.0467	0	3
4	0	0.4305	0.4096	0.3895	0.3702	0.3515	0.3336	0.3164	0.2999	0.2840	0.2687	0.2541	0.2401	0.2267	0.2138	0.2015	0.1897	0.1785	0.1678	4	
	1	0.4039	0.4096	0.4142	0.4176	0.4200	0.4214	0.4219	0.4214	0.4201	0.4180	0.4152	0.4116	0.4074	0.4025	0.3970	0.3910	0.3845	0.3775	3	
	2	0.1421	0.1536	0.1651	0.1767	0.1882	0.1996	0.2109	0.2221	0.2331	0.2439	0.2544	0.2646	0.2745	0.2841	0.2933	0.3021	0.3105	0.3185	2	
	3	0.0222	0.0256	0.0293	0.0332	0.0375	0.0420	0.0469	0.0520	0.0575	0.0632	0.0693	0.0756	0.0822	0.0891	0.0963	0.1038	0.1115	0.1194	1	
	4	0.0013	0.0016	0.0019	0.0023	0.0028	0.0033	0.0039	0.0046	0.0053	0.0061	0.0071	0.0081	0.0092	0.0105	0.0119	0.0134	0.0150	0.0168	0	4
5	0	0.3487	0.3277	0.3077	0.2887	0.2707	0.2536	0.2373	0.2219	0.2073	0.1935	0.1804	0.1681	0.1564	0.1454	0.1350	0.1252	0.1160	0.1074	5	
	1	0.4089	0.4096	0.4090	0.4072	0.4043	0.4003	0.3955	0.3898	0.3834	0.3762	0.3685	0.3601	0.3513	0.3421	0.3325	0.3226	0.3124	0.3020	4	
	2	0.1919	0.2048	0.2174	0.2297	0.2415	0.2529	0.2637	0.2739	0.2836	0.2926	0.3010	0.3087	0.3157	0.3220	0.3275	0.3323	0.3364	0.3397	3	
	3	0.0450	0.0512	0.0578	0.0648	0.0721	0.0798	0.0879	0.0962	0.1049	0.1138	0.1229	0.1323	0.1418	0.1515	0.1613	0.1712	0.1811	0.1911	2	
	4	0.0053	0.0064	0.0077	0.0091	0.0108	0.0126	0.0146	0.0169	0.0194	0.0221	0.0251	0.0283	0.0319	0.0357	0.0397	0.0441	0.0488	0.0537	1	
	5	0.0002	0.0003	0.0004	0.0005	0.0006	0.0008	0.0010	0.0012	0.0014	0.0017	0.0021	0.0024	0.0029	0.0034	0.0039	0.0045	0.0053	0.0060	0	5
6	0	0.2824	0.2621	0.2431	0.2252	0.2084	0.1927	0.1780	0.1642	0.1513	0.1393	0.1281	0.1176	0.1079	0.0989	0.0905	0.0827	0.0754	0.0687	6	
	1	0.3975	0.3932	0.3877	0.3811	0.3735	0.3651	0.3560	0.3462	0.3358	0.3251	0.3139	0.3025	0.2909	0.2792	0.2673	0.2555	0.2437	0.2319	5	
	2	0.2331	0.2458	0.2577	0.2687	0.2789	0.2882	0.2966	0.3041	0.3105	0.3160	0.3206	0.3241	0.3267	0.3284	0.3292	0.3290	0.3280	0.3261	4	
	3	0.0729	0.0819	0.0913	0.1011	0.1111	0.1214	0.1318	0.1424	0.1531	0.1639	0.1746	0.1852	0.1957	0.2061	0.2162	0.2260	0.2355	0.2446	3	
	4	0.0128	0.0154	0.0182	0.0214	0.0249	0.0287	0.0330	0.0375	0.0425	0.0478	0.0535	0.0595	0.0660	0.0727	0.0799	0.0873	0.0951	0.1032	2	
	5	0.0012	0.0015	0.0019	0.0024	0.0030	0.0036	0.0044	0.0053	0.0063	0.0074	0.0087	0.0102	0.0119	0.0137	0.0157	0.0180	0.0205	0.0232	1	
	6	0.0000	0.0001	0.0001	0.0001	0.0001	0.0002	0.0002	0.0003	0.0004	0.0005	0.0006	0.0007	0.0009	0.0011	0.0013	0.0015	0.0018	0.0022	0	6
7	0	0.2288	0.2097	0.1920	0.1757	0.1605	0.1465	0.1335	0.1215	0.1105	0.1003	0.0910	0.0824	0.0745	0.0672	0.0606	0.0546	0.0490	0.0440	7	
	1	0.3756	0.3670	0.3573	0.3468	0.3356	0.3237	0.3115	0.2989	0.2860	0.2731	0.2600	0.2471	0.2342	0.2215	0.2090	0.1967	0.1848	0.1732	6	
	2	0.2643	0.2753	0.2850	0.2935	0.3007	0.3067	0.3115	0.3150	0.3174	0.3186	0.3186	0.3177	0.3156	0.3127	0.3088	0.3040	0.2985	0.2922	5	
	3	0.1033	0.1147	0.1263	0.1379	0.1497	0.1614	0.1730	0.1845	0.1956	0.2065	0.2169	0.2269	0.2363	0.2452	0.2535	0.2610	0.2679	0.2740	4	
	4	0.0242	0.0287	0.0336	0.0389	0.0447	0.0510	0.0577	0.0648	0.0724	0.0803	0.0886	0.0972	0.1062	0.1154	0.1248	0.1345	0.1442	0.1541	3	
	5	0.0034	0.0043	0.0054	0.0066	0.0080	0.0097	0.0115	0.0137	0.0161	0.0187	0.0217	0.0250	0.0286	0.0326	0.0369	0.0416	0.0466	0.0520	2	
	6	0.0003	0.0004	0.0005	0.0006	0.0008	0.0010	0.0013	0.0016	0.0020	0.0024	0.0030	0.0036	0.0043	0.0051	0.0061	0.0071	0.0084	0.0098	1	
	7	0.0000	0.0000	0.0000	0.0000	0.0000	0.0000	0.0001	0.0001	0.0001	0.0001	0.0002	0.0002	0.0003	0.0003	0.0004	0.0005	0.0006	0.0008	0	7
n	r	0.81	0.80	0.79	0.78	0.77	0.76	0.75	0.74	0.73	0.72	0.71	0.70	0.69	0.68	0.67	0.66	0.65	0.64	r	n

p (column headings across the top and bottom)

n	r	0.19	0.20	0.21	0.22	0.23	0.24	0.25	0.26	0.27	0.28	0.29	0.30	0.31	0.32	0.33	0.34	0.35	0.36	r	n
8	0	0.1853	0.1678	0.1517	0.1370	0.1236	0.1113	0.1001	0.0899	0.0806	0.0722	0.0646	0.0576	0.0514	0.0457	0.0406	0.0360	0.0319	0.0281	8	
	1	0.3477	0.3355	0.3226	0.3092	0.2953	0.2812	0.2670	0.2527	0.2386	0.2247	0.2110	0.1977	0.1847	0.1721	0.1600	0.1484	0.1373	0.1267	7	
	2	0.2855	0.2936	0.3002	0.3052	0.3087	0.3108	0.3115	0.3108	0.3089	0.3058	0.3017	0.2965	0.2904	0.2835	0.2758	0.2675	0.2587	0.2494	6	
	3	0.1339	0.1468	0.1596	0.1722	0.1844	0.1963	0.2076	0.2184	0.2285	0.2379	0.2464	0.2541	0.2609	0.2668	0.2717	0.2756	0.2786	0.2805	5	
	4	0.0393	0.0459	0.0530	0.0607	0.0689	0.0775	0.0865	0.0959	0.1056	0.1156	0.1258	0.1361	0.1465	0.1569	0.1673	0.1775	0.1875	0.1973	4	
	5	0.0074	0.0092	0.0113	0.0137	0.0165	0.0196	0.0231	0.0270	0.0313	0.0360	0.0411	0.0467	0.0527	0.0591	0.0659	0.0732	0.0808	0.0888	3	
	6	0.0009	0.0011	0.0015	0.0019	0.0025	0.0031	0.0038	0.0047	0.0058	0.0070	0.0084	0.0100	0.0118	0.0139	0.0162	0.0188	0.0217	0.0250	2	
	7	0.0001	0.0001	0.0001	0.0002	0.0002	0.0003	0.0004	0.0005	0.0006	0.0008	0.0010	0.0012	0.0015	0.0019	0.0023	0.0028	0.0033	0.0040	1	
	8	0.0000	0.0000	0.0000	0.0000	0.0000	0.0000	0.0000	0.0000	0.0000	0.0000	0.0001	0.0001	0.0001	0.0001	0.0001	0.0002	0.0002	0.0003	0	8
9	0	0.1501	0.1342	0.1199	0.1069	0.0952	0.0846	0.0751	0.0665	0.0589	0.0520	0.0458	0.0404	0.0355	0.0311	0.0272	0.0238	0.0207	0.0180	9	
	1	0.3169	0.3020	0.2867	0.2713	0.2558	0.2404	0.2253	0.2104	0.1960	0.1820	0.1685	0.1556	0.1433	0.1317	0.1206	0.1102	0.1004	0.0912	8	
	2	0.2973	0.3020	0.3049	0.3061	0.3056	0.3037	0.3003	0.2957	0.2899	0.2831	0.2754	0.2668	0.2576	0.2478	0.2376	0.2270	0.2162	0.2052	7	
	3	0.1627	0.1762	0.1891	0.2014	0.2130	0.2238	0.2336	0.2424	0.2502	0.2569	0.2624	0.2668	0.2701	0.2721	0.2731	0.2729	0.2716	0.2693	6	
	4	0.0573	0.0661	0.0754	0.0852	0.0954	0.1060	0.1168	0.1278	0.1388	0.1499	0.1608	0.1715	0.1820	0.1921	0.2017	0.2109	0.2194	0.2272	5	
	5	0.0134	0.0165	0.0200	0.0240	0.0285	0.0335	0.0389	0.0449	0.0513	0.0583	0.0657	0.0735	0.0818	0.0904	0.0994	0.1086	0.1181	0.1278	4	
	6	0.0021	0.0028	0.0036	0.0045	0.0057	0.0070	0.0087	0.0105	0.0127	0.0151	0.0179	0.0210	0.0245	0.0284	0.0326	0.0373	0.0424	0.0479	3	
	7	0.0002	0.0003	0.0004	0.0005	0.0007	0.0010	0.0012	0.0016	0.0020	0.0025	0.0031	0.0039	0.0047	0.0057	0.0069	0.0082	0.0098	0.0116	2	
	8	0.0000	0.0000	0.0000	0.0000	0.0001	0.0001	0.0001	0.0001	0.0002	0.0002	0.0003	0.0004	0.0005	0.0007	0.0008	0.0011	0.0013	0.0016	1	
	9	—	—	—	—	0.0000	0.0000	0.0000	0.0000	0.0000	0.0000	0.0000	0.0000	0.0000	0.0000	0.0000	0.0001	0.0001	0.0001	0	9
10	0	0.1216	0.1074	0.0947	0.0834	0.0733	0.0643	0.0563	0.0492	0.0430	0.0374	0.0326	0.0282	0.0245	0.0211	0.0182	0.0157	0.0135	0.0115	10	
	1	0.2852	0.2684	0.2517	0.2351	0.2188	0.2030	0.1877	0.1730	0.1590	0.1456	0.1330	0.1211	0.1099	0.0995	0.0898	0.0808	0.0725	0.0649	9	
	2	0.3010	0.3020	0.3011	0.2984	0.2942	0.2885	0.2816	0.2735	0.2646	0.2548	0.2444	0.2335	0.2222	0.2107	0.1990	0.1873	0.1757	0.1642	8	
	3	0.1883	0.2013	0.2134	0.2244	0.2343	0.2429	0.2503	0.2563	0.2609	0.2642	0.2662	0.2668	0.2662	0.2644	0.2614	0.2573	0.2522	0.2462	7	
	4	0.0773	0.0881	0.0993	0.1108	0.1225	0.1343	0.1460	0.1576	0.1689	0.1798	0.1903	0.2001	0.2093	0.2177	0.2253	0.2320	0.2377	0.2424	6	
	5	0.0218	0.0264	0.0317	0.0375	0.0439	0.0509	0.0584	0.0664	0.0750	0.0839	0.0933	0.1029	0.1128	0.1229	0.1332	0.1434	0.1536	0.1636	5	
	6	0.0043	0.0055	0.0070	0.0088	0.0109	0.0134	0.0162	0.0195	0.0231	0.0272	0.0317	0.0368	0.0422	0.0482	0.0547	0.0616	0.0689	0.0767	4	
	7	0.0006	0.0008	0.0011	0.0014	0.0019	0.0024	0.0031	0.0039	0.0049	0.0060	0.0074	0.0090	0.0108	0.0130	0.0154	0.0181	0.0212	0.0247	3	
	8	0.0001	0.0001	0.0001	0.0002	0.0002	0.0003	0.0004	0.0005	0.0007	0.0009	0.0011	0.0014	0.0018	0.0023	0.0028	0.0035	0.0043	0.0052	2	
	9	0.0000	0.0000	0.0000	0.0000	0.0000	0.0000	0.0000	0.0000	0.0001	0.0001	0.0001	0.0001	0.0002	0.0002	0.0003	0.0004	0.0005	0.0006	1	
	10	—	—	—	—	—	—	—	—	0.0000	0.0000	0.0000	0.0000	0.0000	0.0000	0.0000	0.0000	0.0000	0.0000	0	10
12	0	0.0798	0.0687	0.0591	0.0507	0.0434	0.0371	0.0317	0.0270	0.0229	0.0194	0.0164	0.0138	0.0116	0.0098	0.0082	0.0068	0.0057	0.0047	12	
	1	0.2245	0.2062	0.1885	0.1717	0.1557	0.1407	0.1267	0.1137	0.1016	0.0906	0.0804	0.0712	0.0628	0.0552	0.0484	0.0422	0.0368	0.0319	11	
	2	0.2897	0.2835	0.2756	0.2663	0.2558	0.2444	0.2323	0.2197	0.2068	0.1937	0.1807	0.1678	0.1552	0.1429	0.1310	0.1197	0.1088	0.0986	10	
	3	0.2265	0.2362	0.2442	0.2503	0.2547	0.2573	0.2581	0.2573	0.2549	0.2511	0.2460	0.2397	0.2324	0.2241	0.2151	0.2055	0.1954	0.1849	9	
	4	0.1195	0.1329	0.1460	0.1589	0.1712	0.1828	0.1936	0.2034	0.2122	0.2197	0.2261	0.2311	0.2349	0.2373	0.2384	0.2382	0.2367	0.2340	8	
	5	0.0449	0.0532	0.0621	0.0717	0.0818	0.0924	0.1032	0.1143	0.1255	0.1367	0.1477	0.1585	0.1688	0.1787	0.1879	0.1963	0.2039	0.2106	7	
	6	0.0123	0.0155	0.0193	0.0236	0.0285	0.0340	0.0401	0.0469	0.0542	0.0620	0.0704	0.0792	0.0885	0.0981	0.1079	0.1180	0.1281	0.1382	6	
	7	0.0025	0.0033	0.0044	0.0057	0.0073	0.0092	0.0115	0.0141	0.0172	0.0207	0.0246	0.0291	0.0341	0.0396	0.0456	0.0521	0.0591	0.0666	5	
	8	0.0004	0.0005	0.0007	0.0010	0.0014	0.0018	0.0024	0.0031	0.0040	0.0050	0.0063	0.0078	0.0096	0.0116	0.0140	0.0168	0.0199	0.0234	4	
	9	0.0000	0.0001	0.0001	0.0001	0.0002	0.0003	0.0004	0.0005	0.0007	0.0009	0.0011	0.0015	0.0019	0.0024	0.0031	0.0038	0.0048	0.0059	3	
	10	—	0.0000	0.0000	0.0000	0.0000	0.0000	0.0000	0.0001	0.0001	0.0001	0.0001	0.0002	0.0003	0.0003	0.0005	0.0006	0.0008	0.0010	2	
	11	—	—	—	—	—	—	—	0.0000	0.0000	0.0000	0.0000	0.0000	0.0000	0.0000	0.0000	0.0001	0.0001	0.0001	1	
	12	—	—	—	—	—	—	—	—	—	—	—	—	—	—	—	0.0000	0.0000	0.0000	0	12
n	r	0.81	0.80	0.79	0.78	0.77	0.76	0.75	0.74	0.73	0.72	0.71	0.70	0.69	0.68	0.67	0.66	0.65	0.64	r	n

(Column headings across the top and bottom: *p*)

n	r	0.19	0.20	0.21	0.22	0.23	0.24	0.25	0.26	0.27	0.28	0.29	0.30	0.31	0.32	0.33	0.34	0.35	0.36	r	n
15	0	0.0424	0.0352	0.0291	0.0241	0.0198	0.0163	0.0134	0.0109	0.0089	0.0072	0.0059	0.0047	0.0038	0.0031	0.0025	0.0020	0.0016	0.0012	15	
	1	0.1492	0.1319	0.1162	0.1018	0.0889	0.0772	0.0668	0.0576	0.0494	0.0423	0.0360	0.0305	0.0258	0.0217	0.0182	0.0152	0.0126	0.0104	14	
	2	0.2449	0.2309	0.2162	0.2010	0.1858	0.1707	0.1559	0.1416	0.1280	0.1150	0.1029	0.0916	0.0811	0.0715	0.0627	0.0547	0.0476	0.0411	13	
	3	0.2489	0.2501	0.2490	0.2457	0.2405	0.2336	0.2252	0.2156	0.2051	0.1939	0.1821	0.1700	0.1579	0.1457	0.1338	0.1222	0.1110	0.1002	12	
	4	0.1752	0.1876	0.1986	0.2079	0.2155	0.2213	0.2252	0.2273	0.2276	0.2262	0.2231	0.2186	0.2128	0.2057	0.1977	0.1888	0.1792	0.1692	11	
	5	0.0904	0.1032	0.1161	0.1290	0.1416	0.1537	0.1651	0.1757	0.1852	0.1935	0.2005	0.2061	0.2103	0.2130	0.2142	0.2140	0.2123	0.2093	10	
	6	0.0353	0.0430	0.0514	0.0606	0.0705	0.0809	0.0917	0.1029	0.1142	0.1254	0.1365	0.1472	0.1575	0.1671	0.1759	0.1837	0.1906	0.1963	9	
	7	0.0107	0.0138	0.0176	0.0220	0.0271	0.0329	0.0393	0.0465	0.0543	0.0627	0.0717	0.0811	0.0910	0.1011	0.1114	0.1217	0.1319	0.1419	8	
	8	0.0025	0.0035	0.0047	0.0062	0.0081	0.0104	0.0131	0.0163	0.0201	0.0244	0.0293	0.0348	0.0409	0.0476	0.0549	0.0627	0.0710	0.0798	7	
	9	0.0005	0.0007	0.0010	0.0014	0.0019	0.0025	0.0034	0.0045	0.0058	0.0074	0.0093	0.0116	0.0143	0.0174	0.0210	0.0251	0.0298	0.0349	6	
	10	0.0001	0.0001	0.0002	0.0002	0.0003	0.0005	0.0007	0.0009	0.0013	0.0017	0.0023	0.0030	0.0038	0.0049	0.0062	0.0078	0.0096	0.0118	5	
	11	0.0000	0.0000	0.0000	0.0000	0.0000	0.0001	0.0001	0.0002	0.0002	0.0003	0.0004	0.0006	0.0008	0.0011	0.0014	0.0018	0.0024	0.0030	4	
	12	—	—	—	—	—	0.0000	0.0000	0.0000	0.0000	0.0000	0.0001	0.0001	0.0001	0.0002	0.0002	0.0003	0.0004	0.0006	3	
	13	—	—	—	—	—	—	—	—	—	—	0.0000	0.0000	0.0000	0.0000	0.0000	0.0000	0.0001	0.0001	2	
	14	—	—	—	—	—	—	—	—	—	—	—	—	—	—	—	—	0.0000	0.0000	1	
	15	—	—	—	—	—	—	—	—	—	—	—	—	—	—	—	—	—	—	0	15
20	0	0.0148	0.0115	0.0090	0.0069	0.0054	0.0041	0.0032	0.0024	0.0018	0.0014	0.0011	0.0008	0.0006	0.0004	0.0003	0.0002	0.0002	0.0001	20	
	1	0.0693	0.0576	0.0477	0.0392	0.0321	0.0261	0.0211	0.0170	0.0137	0.0109	0.0087	0.0068	0.0054	0.0042	0.0033	0.0025	0.0020	0.0015	19	
	2	0.1545	0.1369	0.1204	0.1050	0.0910	0.0783	0.0669	0.0569	0.0480	0.0403	0.0336	0.0278	0.0229	0.0188	0.0153	0.0124	0.0110	0.0080	18	
	3	0.2175	0.2054	0.1920	0.1777	0.1631	0.1484	0.1339	0.1199	0.1065	0.0940	0.0823	0.0716	0.0619	0.0531	0.0453	0.0383	0.0323	0.0270	17	
	4	0.2168	0.2182	0.2169	0.2131	0.2070	0.1991	0.1897	0.1790	0.1675	0.1553	0.1429	0.1304	0.1181	0.1062	0.0947	0.0839	0.0738	0.0645	16	
	5	0.1627	0.1746	0.1845	0.1923	0.1979	0.2012	0.2023	0.2013	0.1982	0.1933	0.1868	0.1789	0.1698	0.1599	0.1493	0.1384	0.1272	0.1161	15	
	6	0.0954	0.1091	0.1226	0.1356	0.1478	0.1589	0.1686	0.1768	0.1833	0.1879	0.1907	0.1916	0.1907	0.1881	0.1839	0.1782	0.1712	0.1632	14	
	7	0.0448	0.0545	0.0652	0.0765	0.0883	0.1003	0.1124	0.1242	0.1356	0.1462	0.1558	0.1643	0.1714	0.1770	0.1811	0.1836	0.1844	0.1836	13	
	8	0.0171	0.0222	0.0282	0.0351	0.0429	0.0515	0.0609	0.0709	0.0815	0.0924	0.1034	0.1144	0.1251	0.1354	0.1450	0.1537	0.1614	0.1678	12	
	9	0.0053	0.0074	0.0100	0.0132	0.0171	0.0217	0.0271	0.0332	0.0402	0.0479	0.0563	0.0654	0.0750	0.0849	0.0952	0.1056	0.1158	0.1259	11	
	10	0.0014	0.0020	0.0029	0.0041	0.0056	0.0075	0.0099	0.0128	0.0163	0.0205	0.0253	0.0308	0.0370	0.0440	0.0516	0.0598	0.0686	0.0779	10	
	11	0.0003	0.0005	0.0007	0.0010	0.0015	0.0022	0.0030	0.0041	0.0055	0.0072	0.0094	0.0120	0.0151	0.0188	0.0231	0.0280	0.0336	0.0398	9	
	12	0.0001	0.0001	0.0001	0.0002	0.0003	0.0005	0.0008	0.0011	0.0015	0.0021	0.0029	0.0039	0.0051	0.0066	0.0085	0.0108	0.0136	0.0168	8	
	13	0.0000	0.0000	0.0000	0.0000	0.0001	0.0001	0.0002	0.0002	0.0003	0.0005	0.0007	0.0010	0.0014	0.0019	0.0026	0.0034	0.0045	0.0058	7	
	14	—	—	—	—	0.0000	0.0000	0.0000	0.0000	0.0001	0.0001	0.0001	0.0002	0.0003	0.0005	0.0006	0.0009	0.0012	0.0016	6	
	15	—	—	—	—	—	—	—	—	0.0000	0.0000	0.0000	0.0000	0.0001	0.0001	0.0001	0.0002	0.0003	0.0004	5	
	16	—	—	—	—	—	—	—	—	—	—	—	—	0.0000	0.0000	0.0000	0.0000	0.0000	0.0001	4	
	17	—	—	—	—	—	—	—	—	—	—	—	—	—	—	—	—	—	0.0000	3	
	18	—	—	—	—	—	—	—	—	—	—	—	—	—	—	—	—	—	—	2	
	19	—	—	—	—	—	—	—	—	—	—	—	—	—	—	—	—	—	—	1	
	20	—	—	—	—	—	—	—	—	—	—	—	—	—	—	—	—	—	—	0	20
n	**r**	**0.81**	**0.80**	**0.79**	**0.78**	**0.77**	**0.76**	**0.75**	**0.74**	**0.73**	**0.72**	**0.71**	**0.70**	**0.69**	**0.68**	**0.67**	**0.66**	**0.65**	**0.64**	**r**	**n**
										p											

n	r	0.37	0.38	0.39	0.40	0.41	0.42	0.43	0.44	0.45	0.46	0.47	0.48	0.49	0.50	r	n
2	0	0.3969	0.3844	0.3721	0.3600	0.3481	0.3364	0.3249	0.3136	0.3025	0.2916	0.2809	0.2704	0.2601	0.2500	2	
	1	0.4662	0.4712	0.4758	0.4800	0.4838	0.4872	0.4902	0.4928	0.4950	0.4968	0.4982	0.4992	0.4998	0.5000	1	
	2	0.1369	0.1444	0.1521	0.1600	0.1681	0.1764	0.1849	0.1936	0.2025	0.2116	0.2209	0.2304	0.2401	0.2500	0	2
3	0	0.2500	0.2383	0.2270	0.2160	0.2054	0.1951	0.1852	0.1756	0.1664	0.1575	0.1489	0.1406	0.1327	0.1250	3	
	1	0.4406	0.4382	0.4354	0.4320	0.4282	0.4239	0.4191	0.4140	0.4084	0.4024	0.3961	0.3894	0.3823	0.3750	2	
	2	0.2587	0.2686	0.2783	0.2880	0.2975	0.3069	0.3162	0.3252	0.3341	0.3428	0.3512	0.3594	0.3674	0.3750	1	
	3	0.0507	0.0549	0.0593	0.0640	0.0689	0.0741	0.0795	0.0852	0.0911	0.0973	0.1038	0.1106	0.1176	0.1250	0	3
4	0	0.1575	0.1478	0.1385	0.1296	0.1212	0.1132	0.1056	0.0983	0.0915	0.0850	0.0789	0.0731	0.0677	0.0625	4	
	1	0.3701	0.3623	0.3541	0.3456	0.3368	0.3278	0.3185	0.3091	0.2995	0.2897	0.2799	0.2700	0.2600	0.2500	3	
	2	0.3260	0.3330	0.3396	0.3456	0.3511	0.3560	0.3604	0.3643	0.3675	0.3702	0.3723	0.3738	0.3747	0.3750	2	
	3	0.1276	0.1361	0.1447	0.1536	0.1627	0.1719	0.1813	0.1908	0.2005	0.2102	0.2201	0.2300	0.2400	0.2500	1	
	4	0.0187	0.0209	0.0231	0.0256	0.0283	0.0311	0.0342	0.0375	0.0410	0.0448	0.0488	0.0531	0.0576	0.0625	0	4
5	0	0.0992	0.0916	0.0845	0.0778	0.0715	0.0656	0.0602	0.0551	0.0503	0.0459	0.0418	0.0380	0.0345	0.0312	5	
	1	0.2914	0.2808	0.2700	0.2592	0.2484	0.2376	0.2270	0.2164	0.2059	0.1956	0.1854	0.1755	0.1657	0.1562	4	
	2	0.3423	0.3441	0.3452	0.3456	0.3452	0.3442	0.3424	0.3400	0.3369	0.3332	0.3289	0.3240	0.3185	0.3125	3	
	3	0.2010	0.2109	0.2207	0.2304	0.2399	0.2492	0.2583	0.2671	0.2757	0.2838	0.2916	0.2990	0.3060	0.3125	2	
	4	0.0590	0.0646	0.0706	0.0768	0.0834	0.0902	0.0974	0.1049	0.1128	0.1209	0.1293	0.1380	0.1470	0.1562	1	
	5	0.0069	0.0079	0.0090	0.0102	0.0116	0.0131	0.0147	0.0165	0.0185	0.0206	0.0229	0.0255	0.0282	0.0312	0	5
6	0	0.0625	0.0568	0.0515	0.0467	0.0422	0.0381	0.0343	0.0308	0.0277	0.0248	0.0222	0.0198	0.0176	0.0156	6	
	1	0.2203	0.2089	0.1976	0.1866	0.1759	0.1654	0.1552	0.1454	0.1359	0.1267	0.1179	0.1095	0.1014	0.0937	5	
	2	0.3235	0.3201	0.3159	0.3110	0.3055	0.2994	0.2928	0.2856	0.2780	0.2699	0.2615	0.2527	0.2436	0.2344	4	
	3	0.2533	0.2616	0.2693	0.2765	0.2831	0.2891	0.2945	0.2992	0.3032	0.3065	0.3091	0.3110	0.3121	0.3125	3	
	4	0.1116	0.1202	0.1291	0.1382	0.1475	0.1570	0.1666	0.1763	0.1861	0.1958	0.2056	0.2153	0.2249	0.2344	2	
	5	0.0262	0.0295	0.0330	0.0369	0.0410	0.0455	0.0503	0.0554	0.0609	0.0667	0.0729	0.0795	0.0864	0.0937	1	
	6	0.0026	0.0030	0.0035	0.0041	0.0048	0.0055	0.0063	0.0073	0.0083	0.0095	0.0108	0.0122	0.0138	0.0156	0	6
7	0	0.0394	0.0352	0.0314	0.0280	0.0249	0.0221	0.0195	0.0173	0.0152	0.0134	0.0117	0.0103	0.0090	0.0078	7	
	1	0.1619	0.1511	0.1407	0.1306	0.1211	0.1119	0.1032	0.0950	0.0872	0.0798	0.0729	0.0664	0.0604	0.0547	6	
	2	0.2853	0.2778	0.2698	0.2613	0.2524	0.2431	0.2336	0.2239	0.2140	0.2040	0.1940	0.1840	0.1740	0.1641	5	
	3	0.2793	0.2838	0.2875	0.2903	0.2923	0.2934	0.2937	0.2932	0.2918	0.2897	0.2867	0.2830	0.2786	0.2734	4	
	4	0.1640	0.1739	0.1838	0.1935	0.2031	0.2125	0.2216	0.2304	0.2388	0.2468	0.2543	0.2612	0.2676	0.2734	3	
	5	0.0578	0.0640	0.0705	0.0774	0.0847	0.0923	0.1003	0.1086	0.1172	0.1261	0.1353	0.1447	0.1543	0.1641	2	
	6	0.0113	0.0131	0.0150	0.0172	0.0196	0.0223	0.0252	0.0284	0.0320	0.0358	0.0400	0.0445	0.0494	0.0547	1	
	7	0.0009	0.0011	0.0014	0.0016	0.0019	0.0023	0.0027	0.0032	0.0037	0.0044	0.0051	0.0059	0.0068	0.0078	0	7
n	r	0.63	0.62	0.61	0.60	0.59	0.58	0.57	0.56	0.55	0.54	0.53	0.52	0.51	0.50	r	n

The column headings are values of *p* (top row of headings, and bottom row of headings).

n	r	0.37	0.38	0.39	0.40	0.41	0.42	0.43	0.44	0.45	0.46	0.47	0.48	0.49	0.50	r	n
8	0	0.0248	0.0218	0.0192	0.0168	0.0147	0.0128	0.0111	0.0097	0.0084	0.0072	0.0062	0.0053	0.0046	0.0039	8	
	1	0.1166	0.1071	0.0981	0.0896	0.0816	0.0742	0.0672	0.0608	0.0548	0.0493	0.0442	0.0395	0.0352	0.0312	7	
	2	0.2397	0.2297	0.2194	0.2090	0.1985	0.1880	0.1776	0.1672	0.1569	0.1469	0.1371	0.1275	0.1183	0.1094	6	
	3	0.2815	0.2815	0.2806	0.2787	0.2759	0.2723	0.2679	0.2627	0.2568	0.2503	0.2431	0.2355	0.2273	0.2187	5	
	4	0.2067	0.2157	0.2242	0.2322	0.2397	0.2465	0.2526	0.2580	0.2627	0.2665	0.2695	0.2717	0.2730	0.2734	4	
	5	0.0971	0.1058	0.1147	0.1239	0.1332	0.1428	0.1525	0.1622	0.1719	0.1816	0.1912	0.2006	0.2098	0.2187	3	
	6	0.0285	0.0324	0.0367	0.0413	0.0463	0.0517	0.0575	0.0637	0.0703	0.0774	0.0848	0.0926	0.1008	0.1094	2	
	7	0.0048	0.0057	0.0067	0.0079	0.0092	0.0107	0.0124	0.0143	0.0164	0.0188	0.0215	0.0244	0.0277	0.0312	1	
	8	0.0004	0.0004	0.0005	0.0007	0.0008	0.0010	0.0012	0.0014	0.0017	0.0020	0.0024	0.0028	0.0033	0.0039	0	8
9	0	0.0156	0.0135	0.0117	0.0101	0.0087	0.0074	0.0064	0.0054	0.0046	0.0039	0.0033	0.0028	0.0023	0.0020	9	
	1	0.0826	0.0747	0.0673	0.0605	0.0542	0.0484	0.0431	0.0383	0.0339	0.0299	0.0263	0.0231	0.0202	0.0176	8	
	2	0.1941	0.1831	0.1721	0.1612	0.1506	0.1402	0.1301	0.1204	0.1110	0.1020	0.0934	0.0853	0.0776	0.0703	7	
	3	0.2660	0.2618	0.2567	0.2508	0.2442	0.2369	0.2291	0.2207	0.2119	0.2027	0.1933	0.1837	0.1739	0.1641	6	
	4	0.2344	0.2407	0.2462	0.2508	0.2545	0.2573	0.2592	0.2601	0.2600	0.2590	0.2571	0.2543	0.2506	0.2461	5	
	5	0.1376	0.1475	0.1574	0.1672	0.1769	0.1863	0.1955	0.2044	0.2128	0.2207	0.2280	0.2347	0.2408	0.2461	4	
	6	0.0539	0.0603	0.0671	0.0743	0.0819	0.0900	0.0983	0.1070	0.1160	0.1253	0.1348	0.1445	0.1542	0.1641	3	
	7	0.0136	0.0158	0.0184	0.0212	0.0244	0.0279	0.0318	0.0360	0.0407	0.0458	0.0512	0.0571	0.0635	0.0703	2	
	8	0.0020	0.0024	0.0029	0.0035	0.0042	0.0051	0.0060	0.0071	0.0083	0.0097	0.0114	0.0132	0.0153	0.0176	1	
	9	0.0001	0.0002	0.0002	0.0003	0.0003	0.0004	0.0005	0.0006	0.0008	0.0009	0.0011	0.0014	0.0016	0.0020	0	9
10	0	0.0098	0.0084	0.0071	0.0060	0.0051	0.0043	0.0036	0.0030	0.0025	0.0021	0.0017	0.0014	0.0012	0.0010	10	
	1	0.0578	0.0514	0.0456	0.0403	0.0355	0.0312	0.0273	0.0238	0.0207	0.0180	0.0155	0.0133	0.0114	0.0098	9	
	2	0.1529	0.1419	0.1312	0.1209	0.1111	0.1017	0.0927	0.0843	0.0763	0.0688	0.0619	0.0554	0.0494	0.0439	8	
	3	0.2394	0.2319	0.2237	0.2150	0.2058	0.1963	0.1865	0.1765	0.1665	0.1564	0.1464	0.1364	0.1267	0.1172	7	
	4	0.2461	0.2487	0.2503	0.2508	0.2503	0.2488	0.2462	0.2427	0.2384	0.2331	0.2271	0.2204	0.2130	0.2051	6	
	5	0.1734	0.1829	0.1920	0.2007	0.2087	0.2162	0.2229	0.2289	0.2340	0.2383	0.2417	0.2441	0.2456	0.2461	5	
	6	0.0849	0.0934	0.1023	0.1115	0.1209	0.1304	0.1401	0.1499	0.1596	0.1692	0.1786	0.1878	0.1966	0.2051	4	
	7	0.0285	0.0327	0.0374	0.0425	0.0480	0.0540	0.0604	0.0673	0.0746	0.0824	0.0905	0.0991	0.1080	0.1172	3	
	8	0.0063	0.0075	0.0090	0.0106	0.0125	0.0147	0.0171	0.0198	0.0229	0.0263	0.0301	0.0343	0.0389	0.0439	2	
	9	0.0008	0.0010	0.0013	0.0016	0.0019	0.0024	0.0029	0.0035	0.0042	0.0050	0.0059	0.0070	0.0083	0.0098	1	
	10	0.0000	0.0001	0.0001	0.0001	0.0001	0.0002	0.0002	0.0003	0.0003	0.0004	0.0005	0.0006	0.0008	0.0010	0	10
n	r	0.63	0.62	0.61	0.60	0.59	0.58	0.57	0.56	0.55	0.54	0.53	0.52	0.51	0.50	r	n

(Top and bottom column headers are labelled *p*.)

n	r	p														r	n
		0.37	**0.38**	**0.39**	**0.40**	**0.41**	**0.42**	**0.43**	**0.44**	**0.45**	**0.46**	**0.47**	**0.48**	**0.49**	**0.50**		
12	0	0.0039	0.0032	0.0027	0.0022	0.0018	0.0014	0.0012	0.0010	0.0008	0.0006	0.0005	0.0004	0.0003	0.0002	12	
	1	0.0276	0.0237	0.0204	0.0174	0.0148	0.0126	0.0106	0.0090	0.0075	0.0063	0.0052	0.0043	0.0036	0.0029	11	
	2	0.0890	0.0800	0.0716	0.0639	0.0567	0.0502	0.0442	0.0388	0.0339	0.0294	0.0255	0.0220	0.0189	0.0161	10	
	3	0.1742	0.1634	0.1526	0.1419	0.1314	0.1211	0.1111	0.1015	0.0923	0.0836	0.0754	0.0676	0.0604	0.0537	9	
	4	0.2302	0.2254	0.2195	0.2128	0.2054	0.1973	0.1886	0.1794	0.1700	0.1602	0.1504	0.1405	0.1306	0.1208	8	
	5	0.2163	0.2210	0.2246	0.2270	0.2284	0.2285	0.2276	0.2256	0.2225	0.2184	0.2134	0.2075	0.2008	0.1934	7	
	6	0.1482	0.1580	0.1675	0.1766	0.1851	0.1931	0.2003	0.2068	0.2124	0.2171	0.2208	0.2234	0.2250	0.2256	6	
	7	0.0746	0.0830	0.0918	0.1009	0.1103	0.1198	0.1295	0.1393	0.1489	0.1585	0.1678	0.1768	0.1853	0.1934	5	
	8	0.0274	0.0318	0.0367	0.0420	0.0479	0.0542	0.0611	0.0684	0.0762	0.0844	0.0930	0.1020	0.1113	0.1208	4	
	9	0.0071	0.0087	0.0104	0.0125	0.0148	0.0175	0.0205	0.0239	0.0277	0.0319	0.0367	0.0418	0.0475	0.0537	3	
	10	0.0013	0.0016	0.0020	0.0025	0.0031	0.0038	0.0046	0.0056	0.0068	0.0082	0.0098	0.0116	0.0137	0.0161	2	
	11	0.0001	0.0002	0.0002	0.0003	0.0004	0.0005	0.0006	0.0008	0.0010	0.0013	0.0016	0.0019	0.0024	0.0029	1	
	12	0.0000	0.0000	0.0000	0.0000	0.0000	0.0000	0.0000	0.0001	0.0001	0.0001	0.0001	0.0001	0.0002	0.0002	0	12
15	0	0.0010	0.0008	0.0006	0.0005	0.0004	0.0003	0.0002	0.0002	0.0001	0.0001	0.0001	0.0001	0.0000	0.0000	15	
	1	0.0086	0.0071	0.0058	0.0047	0.0038	0.0031	0.0025	0.0020	0.0016	0.0012	0.0010	0.0008	0.0006	0.0005	14	
	2	0.0354	0.0303	0.0259	0.0219	0.0185	0.0156	0.0130	0.0108	0.0090	0.0074	0.0060	0.0049	0.0040	0.0032	13	
	3	0.0901	0.0805	0.0716	0.0634	0.0558	0.0489	0.0426	0.0369	0.0318	0.0272	0.0232	0.0197	0.0166	0.0139	12	
	4	0.1587	0.1481	0.1374	0.1268	0.1163	0.1061	0.0963	0.0869	0.0780	0.0696	0.0617	0.0545	0.0478	0.0417	11	
	5	0.2051	0.1997	0.1933	0.1859	0.1778	0.1691	0.1598	0.1502	0.1404	0.1304	0.1204	0.1106	0.1010	0.0916	10	
	6	0.2008	0.2040	0.2059	0.2066	0.2060	0.2041	0.2010	0.1967	0.1914	0.1851	0.1780	0.1702	0.1617	0.1527	9	
	7	0.1516	0.1608	0.1693	0.1771	0.1840	0.1900	0.1949	0.1987	0.2013	0.2028	0.2030	0.2020	0.1997	0.1964	8	
	8	0.0890	0.0985	0.1082	0.1181	0.1279	0.1376	0.1470	0.1561	0.1647	0.1727	0.1800	0.1864	0.1919	0.1964	7	
	9	0.0407	0.0470	0.0538	0.0612	0.0691	0.0775	0.0863	0.0954	0.1048	0.1144	0.1241	0.1338	0.1434	0.1527	6	
	10	0.0143	0.0173	0.0206	0.0245	0.0288	0.0337	0.0390	0.0450	0.0515	0.0585	0.0661	0.0741	0.0827	0.0916	5	
	11	0.0038	0.0048	0.0060	0.0074	0.0091	0.0111	0.0134	0.0161	0.0191	0.0226	0.0266	0.0311	0.0361	0.0417	4	
	12	0.0007	0.0010	0.0013	0.0016	0.0021	0.0027	0.0034	0.0042	0.0052	0.0064	0.0079	0.0096	0.0116	0.0139	3	
	13	0.0001	0.0001	0.0002	0.0003	0.0003	0.0004	0.0006	0.0008	0.0010	0.0013	0.0016	0.0020	0.0026	0.0032	2	
	14	0.0000	0.0000	0.0000	0.0000	0.0000	0.0000	0.0001	0.0001	0.0001	0.0002	0.0002	0.0003	0.0004	0.0005	1	
	15	—	—	—	—	—	—	0.0000	0.0000	0.0000	0.0000	0.0000	0.0000	0.0000	0.0000	0	15
20	0	0.0001	0.0001	0.0001	0.0000	0.0000	0.0000	0.0000	0.0000	0.0000	0.0000	0.0000	—	—	—	20	
	1	0.0011	0.0009	0.0007	0.0005	0.0004	0.0003	0.0002	0.0001	0.0001	0.0001	0.0001	0.0000	0.0000	0.0000	19	
	2	0.0064	0.0050	0.0040	0.0031	0.0024	0.0018	0.0014	0.0011	0.0008	0.0006	0.0005	0.0003	0.0002	0.0002	18	
	3	0.0224	0.0185	0.0152	0.0123	0.0100	0.0080	0.0064	0.0051	0.0040	0.0031	0.0024	0.0019	0.0014	0.0011	17	
	4	0.0559	0.0482	0.0412	0.0350	0.0295	0.0247	0.0206	0.0170	0.0139	0.0113	0.0092	0.0074	0.0059	0.0046	16	
	5	0.1051	0.0945	0.0843	0.0746	0.0656	0.0573	0.0496	0.0427	0.0365	0.0309	0.0260	0.0217	0.0180	0.0148	15	
	6	0.1543	0.1447	0.1347	0.1244	0.1140	0.1037	0.0936	0.0839	0.0746	0.0658	0.0577	0.0501	0.0432	0.0370	14	
	7	0.1812	0.1774	0.1722	0.1659	0.1585	0.1502	0.1413	0.1318	0.1221	0.1122	0.1023	0.0925	0.0830	0.0739	13	
	8	0.1730	0.1767	0.1790	0.1797	0.1790	0.1768	0.1732	0.1683	0.1623	0.1553	0.1474	0.1388	0.1296	0.1201	12	
	9	0.1354	0.1444	0.1526	0.1597	0.1658	0.1707	0.1742	0.1763	0.1771	0.1763	0.1742	0.1708	0.1661	0.1602	11	
	10	0.0875	0.0974	0.1073	0.1171	0.1268	0.1359	0.1446	0.1524	0.1593	0.1652	0.1700	0.1734	0.1755	0.1762	10	
	11	0.0467	0.0542	0.0624	0.0710	0.0801	0.0895	0.0991	0.1089	0.1185	0.1280	0.1370	0.1455	0.1533	0.1602	9	
	12	0.0206	0.0249	0.0299	0.0355	0.0417	0.0486	0.0561	0.0642	0.0727	0.0818	0.0911	0.1007	0.1105	0.1201	8	
	13	0.0074	0.0094	0.0118	0.0146	0.0178	0.0217	0.0260	0.0310	0.0366	0.0429	0.0497	0.0572	0.0653	0.0739	7	
	14	0.0022	0.0029	0.0038	0.0049	0.0062	0.0078	0.0098	0.0122	0.0150	0.0183	0.0221	0.0264	0.0314	0.0370	6	
	15	0.0005	0.0007	0.0010	0.0013	0.0017	0.0023	0.0030	0.0038	0.0049	0.0062	0.0078	0.0098	0.0121	0.0148	5	
	16	0.0001	0.0001	0.0002	0.0003	0.0004	0.0005	0.0007	0.0009	0.0013	0.0017	0.0022	0.0028	0.0036	0.0046	4	
	17	0.0000	0.0000	0.0000	0.0000	0.0001	0.0001	0.0001	0.0002	0.0002	0.0003	0.0005	0.0006	0.0008	0.0011	3	
	18	—	—	—	—	0.0000	0.0000	0.0000	0.0000	0.0000	0.0000	0.0001	0.0001	0.0001	0.0002	2	
	19	—	—	—	—	—	—	—	—	—	—	0.0000	0.0000	0.0000	0.0000	1	
	20	—	—	—	—	—	—	—	—	—	—	—	—	—	—	0	20
n	r	**0.63**	**0.62**	**0.61**	**0.60**	**0.59**	**0.58**	**0.57**	**0.56**	**0.55**	**0.54**	**0.53**	**0.52**	**0.51**	**0.50**	r	n
		p															

Appendix Table 4(a)

Values of $e^{-\lambda}$ for Computing Poisson Probabilities

λ	$e^{-\lambda}$	λ	$e^{-\lambda}$	λ	$e^{-\lambda}$	λ	$e^{-\lambda}$
0.1	0.90484	2.6	0.07427	5.1	0.00610	7.6	0.00050
0.2	0.81873	2.7	0.06721	5.2	0.00552	7.7	0.00045
0.3	0.74082	2.8	0.06081	5.3	0.00499	7.8	0.00041
0.4	0.67032	2.9	0.05502	5.4	0.00452	7.9	0.00037
0.5	0.60653	3.0	0.04979	5.5	0.00409	8.0	0.00034
0.6	0.54881	3.1	0.04505	5.6	0.00370	8.1	0.00030
0.7	0.49659	3.2	0.04076	5.7	0.00335	8.2	0.00027
0.8	0.44933	3.3	0.03688	5.8	0.00303	8.3	0.00025
0.9	0.40657	3.4	0.03337	5.9	0.00274	8.4	0.00022
1.0	0.36788	3.5	0.03020	6.0	0.00248	8.5	0.00020
1.1	0.33287	3.6	0.02732	6.1	0.00224	8.6	0.00018
1.2	0.30119	3.7	0.02472	6.2	0.00203	8.7	0.00017
1.3	0.27253	3.8	0.02237	6.3	0.00184	8.8	0.00015
1.4	0.24660	3.9	0.02024	6.4	0.00166	8.9	0.00014
1.5	0.22313	4.0	0.01832	6.5	0.00150	9.0	0.00012
1.6	0.20190	4.1	0.01657	6.6	0.00136	9.1	0.00011
1.7	0.18268	4.2	0.01500	6.7	0.00123	9.2	0.00010
1.8	0.16530	4.3	0.01357	6.8	0.00111	9.3	0.00009
1.9	0.14957	4.4	0.01228	6.9	0.00101	9.4	0.00008
2.0	0.13534	4.5	0.01111	7.0	0.00091	9.5	0.00007
2.1	0.12246	4.6	0.01005	7.1	0.00083	9.6	0.00007
2.2	0.11080	4.7	0.00910	7.2	0.00075	9.7	0.00006
2.3	0.10026	4.8	0.00823	7.3	0.00068	9.8	0.00006
2.4	0.09072	4.9	0.00745	7.4	0.00061	9.9	0.00005
2.5	0.08208	5.0	0.00674	7.5	0.00055	10.0	0.00005

Appendix Table 4(b)

Direct Values for Determining Poisson Probabilities

For a given value of λ, entry indicates the probability of obtaining a specified value of *X*.

X	λ = 0.1	0.2	0.3	0.4	0.5	0.6	0.7	0.8	0.9	1.0
0	0.9048	0.8187	0.7408	0.6703	0.6065	0.5488	0.4966	0.4493	0.4066	0.3679
1	0.0905	0.1637	0.2222	0.2681	0.3033	0.3293	0.3476	0.3595	0.3659	0.3679
2	0.0045	0.0164	0.0333	0.0536	0.0758	0.0988	0.1217	0.1438	0.1647	0.1839
3	0.0002	0.0011	0.0033	0.0072	0.0126	0.0198	0.0284	0.0383	0.0494	0.0613
4	0.0000	0.0001	0.0003	0.0007	0.0016	0.0030	0.0050	0.0077	0.0111	0.0153
5	0.0000	0.0000	0.0000	0.0001	0.0002	0.0004	0.0007	0.0012	0.0020	0.0031
6	0.0000	0.0000	0.0000	0.0000	0.0000	0.0000	0.0001	0.0002	0.0003	0.0005
7	0.0000	0.0000	0.0000	0.0000	0.0000	0.0000	0.0000	0.0000	0.0000	0.0001

X	λ = 1.1	1.2	1.3	1.4	1.5	1.6	1.7	1.8	1.9	2.0
0	0.3329	0.3012	0.2725	0.2466	0.2231	0.2019	0.1827	0.1653	0.1496	0.1353
1	0.3662	0.3614	0.3543	0.3452	0.3347	0.3230	0.3106	0.2975	0.2842	0.2707
2	0.2014	0.2169	0.2303	0.2417	0.2510	0.2584	0.2640	0.2678	0.2700	0.2707
3	0.0738	0.0867	0.0998	0.1128	0.1255	0.1378	0.1496	0.1607	0.1710	0.1804
4	0.0203	0.0260	0.0324	0.0395	0.0471	0.0551	0.0636	0.0723	0.0812	0.0902
5	0.0045	0.0062	0.0084	0.0111	0.0141	0.0176	0.0216	0.0260	0.0309	0.0361
6	0.0008	0.0012	0.0018	0.0026	0.0035	0.0047	0.0061	0.0078	0.0098	0.0120
7	0.0001	0.0002	0.0003	0.0005	0.0008	0.0011	0.0015	0.0020	0.0027	0.0034
8	0.0000	0.0000	0.0001	0.0001	0.0001	0.0002	0.0003	0.0005	0.0006	0.0009
9	0.0000	0.0000	0.0000	0.0000	0.0000	0.0000	0.0001	0.0001	0.0001	0.0002

X	λ = 2.1	2.2	2.3	2.4	2.5	2.6	2.7	2.8	2.9	3.0
0	0.1225	0.1108	0.1003	0.0907	0.0821	0.0743	0.0672	0.0608	0.0550	0.0498
1	0.2572	0.2438	0.2306	0.2177	0.2052	0.1931	0.1815	0.1703	0.1596	0.1494
2	0.2700	0.2681	0.2652	0.2613	0.2565	0.2510	0.2450	0.2384	0.2314	0.2240
3	0.1890	0.1966	0.2033	0.2090	0.2138	0.2176	0.2205	0.2225	0.2237	0.2240
4	0.0992	0.1082	0.1169	0.1254	0.1336	0.1414	0.1488	0.1557	0.1622	0.1680
5	0.0417	0.0476	0.0538	0.0602	0.0668	0.0735	0.0804	0.0872	0.0940	0.1008
6	0.0146	0.0174	0.0206	0.0241	0.0278	0.0319	0.0362	0.0407	0.0455	0.0504
7	0.0044	0.0055	0.0068	0.0083	0.0099	0.0118	0.0139	0.0163	0.0188	0.0216
8	0.0011	0.0015	0.0019	0.0025	0.0031	0.0038	0.0047	0.0057	0.0068	0.0081
9	0.0003	0.0004	0.0005	0.0007	0.0009	0.0011	0.0014	0.0018	0.0022	0.0027
10	0.0001	0.0001	0.0001	0.0002	0.0002	0.0003	0.0004	0.0005	0.0006	0.0008
11	0.0000	0.0000	0.0000	0.0000	0.0000	0.0001	0.0001	0.0001	0.0002	0.0002
12	0.0000	0.0000	0.0000	0.0000	0.0000	0.0000	0.0000	0.0000	0.0000	0.0001

	λ									
x	**3.1**	**3.2**	**3.3**	**3.4**	**3.5**	**3.6**	**3.7**	**3.8**	**3.9**	**4.0**
0	0.0450	0.0408	0.0369	0.0334	0.0302	0.0273	0.0247	0.0224	0.0202	0.0183
1	0.1397	0.1304	0.1217	0.1135	0.1057	0.0984	0.0915	0.0850	0.0789	0.0733
2	0.2165	0.2087	0.2008	0.1929	0.1850	0.1771	0.1692	0.1615	0.1539	0.1465
3	0.2237	0.2226	0.2209	0.2186	0.2158	0.2125	0.2087	0.2046	0.2001	0.1954
4	0.1734	0.1781	0.1823	0.1858	0.1888	0.1912	0.1931	0.1944	0.1951	0.1954
5	0.1075	0.1140	0.1203	0.1264	0.1322	0.1377	0.1429	0.1477	0.1522	0.1563
6	0.0555	0.0608	0.0662	0.0716	0.0771	0.0826	0.0881	0.0936	0.0989	0.1042
7	0.0246	0.0278	0.0312	0.0348	0.0385	0.0425	0.0466	0.0508	0.0551	0.0595
8	0.0095	0.0111	0.0129	0.0148	0.0169	0.0191	0.0215	0.0241	0.0269	0.0298
9	0.0033	0.0040	0.0047	0.0056	0.0066	0.0076	0.0089	0.0102	0.0116	0.0132
10	0.0010	0.0013	0.0016	0.0019	0.0023	0.0028	0.0033	0.0039	0.0045	0.0053
11	0.0003	0.0004	0.0005	0.0006	0.0007	0.0009	0.0011	0.0013	0.0016	0.0019
12	0.0001	0.0001	0.0001	0.0002	0.0002	0.0003	0.0003	0.0004	0.0005	0.0006
13	0.0000	0.0000	0.0000	0.0000	0.0001	0.0001	0.0001	0.0001	0.0002	0.0002
14	0.0000	0.0000	0.0000	0.0000	0.0000	0.0000	0.0000	0.0000	0.0000	0.0001

	λ									
x	**4.1**	**4.2**	**4.3**	**4.4**	**4.5**	**4.6**	**4.7**	**4.8**	**4.9**	**5.0**
0	0.0166	0.0150	0.0136	0.0123	0.0111	0.0101	0.0091	0.0082	0.0074	0.0067
1	0.0679	0.0630	0.0583	0.0540	0.0500	0.0462	0.0427	0.0395	0.0365	0.0337
2	0.1393	0.1323	0.1254	0.1188	0.1125	0.1063	0.1005	0.0948	0.0894	0.0842
3	0.1904	0.1852	0.1798	0.1743	0.1687	0.1631	0.1574	0.1517	0.1460	0.1404
4	0.1951	0.1944	0.1933	0.1917	0.1898	0.1875	0.1849	0.1820	0.1789	0.1755
5	0.1600	0.1633	0.1662	0.1687	0.1708	0.1725	0.1738	0.1747	0.1753	0.1755
6	0.1093	0.1143	0.1191	0.1237	0.1281	0.1323	0.1362	0.1398	0.1432	0.1462
7	0.0640	0.0686	0.0732	0.0778	0.0824	0.0869	0.0914	0.0959	0.1022	0.1044
8	0.0328	0.0360	0.0393	0.0428	0.0463	0.0500	0.0537	0.0575	0.0614	0.0653
9	0.0150	0.0168	0.0188	0.0209	0.0232	0.0255	0.0280	0.0307	0.0334	0.0363
10	0.0061	0.0071	0.0081	0.0092	0.0104	0.0118	0.0132	0.0147	0.0164	0.0181
11	0.0023	0.0027	0.0032	0.0037	0.0043	0.0049	0.0056	0.0064	0.0073	0.0082
12	0.0008	0.0009	0.0011	0.0014	0.0016	0.0019	0.0022	0.0026	0.0030	0.0034
13	0.0002	0.0003	0.0004	0.0005	0.0006	0.0007	0.0008	0.0009	0.0011	0.0013
14	0.0001	0.0001	0.0001	0.0001	0.0002	0.0002	0.0003	0.0003	0.0004	0.0005
15	0.0000	0.0000	0.0000	0.0000	0.0001	0.0001	0.0001	0.0001	0.0001	0.0002

	λ									
x	**5.1**	**5.2**	**5.3**	**5.4**	**5.5**	**5.6**	**5.7**	**5.8**	**5.9**	**6.0**
0	0.0061	0.0055	0.0050	0.0045	0.0041	0.0037	0.0033	0.0030	0.0027	0.0025
1	0.0311	0.0287	0.0265	0.0244	0.0225	0.0207	0.0191	0.0176	0.0162	0.0149
2	0.0793	0.0746	0.0701	0.0659	0.0618	0.0580	0.0544	0.0509	0.0477	0.0446
3	0.1348	0.1293	0.1239	0.1185	0.1133	0.1082	0.1033	0.0985	0.0938	0.0892
4	0.1719	0.1681	0.1641	0.1600	0.1558	0.1515	0.1472	0.1428	0.1383	0.1339
5	0.1753	0.1748	0.1740	0.1728	0.1714	0.1697	0.1678	0.1656	0.1632	0.1606
6	0.1490	0.1515	0.1537	0.1555	0.1571	0.1584	0.1594	0.1601	0.1605	0.1606
7	0.1086	0.1125	0.1163	0.1200	0.1234	0.1267	0.1298	0.1326	0.1353	0.1377
8	0.0692	0.0731	0.0771	0.0810	0.0849	0.0887	0.0925	0.0962	0.0998	0.1033
9	0.0392	0.0423	0.0454	0.0486	0.0519	0.0552	0.0586	0.0620	0.0654	0.0688
10	0.0200	0.0220	0.0241	0.0262	0.0285	0.0309	0.0334	0.0359	0.0386	0.0413
11	0.0093	0.0104	0.0116	0.0129	0.0143	0.0157	0.0173	0.0190	0.0207	0.0225
12	0.0039	0.0045	0.0051	0.0058	0.0065	0.0073	0.0082	0.0092	0.0102	0.0113
13	0.0015	0.0018	0.0021	0.0024	0.0028	0.0032	0.0036	0.0041	0.0046	0.0052
14	0.0006	0.0007	0.0008	0.0009	0.0011	0.0013	0.0015	0.0017	0.0019	0.0022
15	0.0002	0.0002	0.0003	0.0003	0.0004	0.0005	0.0006	0.0007	0.0008	0.0009
16	0.0001	0.0001	0.0001	0.0001	0.0001	0.0002	0.0002	0.0002	0.0003	0.0003
17	0.0000	0.0000	0.0000	0.0000	0.0000	0.0000	0.0001	0.0001	0.0001	0.0001

	λ									
x	**6.1**	**6.2**	**6.3**	**6.4**	**6.5**	**6.6**	**6.7**	**6.8**	**6.9**	**7.0**
0	0.0022	0.0020	0.0018	0.0017	0.0015	0.0014	0.0012	0.0011	0.0010	0.0009
1	0.0137	0.0126	0.0116	0.0106	0.0098	0.0090	0.0082	0.0076	0.0070	0.0064
2	0.0417	0.0390	0.0364	0.0340	0.0318	0.0296	0.0276	0.0258	0.0240	0.0223
3	0.0848	0.0806	0.0765	0.0726	0.0688	0.0652	0.0617	0.0584	0.0552	0.0521
4	0.1294	0.1249	0.1205	0.1162	0.1118	0.1076	0.1034	0.0992	0.0952	0.0912
5	0.1579	0.1549	0.1519	0.1487	0.1454	0.1420	0.1385	0.1349	0.1314	0.1277
6	0.1605	0.1601	0.1595	0.1586	0.1575	0.1562	0.1546	0.1529	0.1511	0.1490
7	0.1399	0.1418	0.1435	0.1450	0.1462	0.1472	0.1480	0.1486	0.1489	0.1490
8	0.1066	0.1099	0.1130	0.1160	0.1188	0.1215	0.1240	0.1263	0.1284	0.1304
9	0.0723	0.0757	0.0791	0.0825	0.0858	0.0891	0.0923	0.0954	0.0985	0.1014
10	0.0441	0.0469	0.0498	0.0528	0.0558	0.0588	0.0618	0.0649	0.0679	0.0710
11	0.0245	0.0265	0.0285	0.0307	0.0330	0.0353	0.0377	0.0401	0.0426	0.0452
12	0.0124	0.0137	0.0150	0.0164	0.0179	0.0194	0.0210	0.0227	0.0245	0.0264
13	0.0058	0.0065	0.0073	0.0081	0.0089	0.0098	0.0108	0.0119	0.0130	0.0142
14	0.0025	0.0029	0.0033	0.0037	0.0041	0.0046	0.0052	0.0058	0.0064	0.0071
15	0.0010	0.0012	0.0014	0.0016	0.0018	0.0020	0.0023	0.0026	0.0029	0.0033
16	0.0004	0.0005	0.0005	0.0006	0.0007	0.0008	0.0010	0.0011	0.0013	0.0014
17	0.0001	0.0002	0.0002	0.0002	0.0003	0.0003	0.0004	0.0004	0.0005	0.0006
18	0.0000	0.0001	0.0001	0.0001	0.0001	0.0001	0.0001	0.0002	0.0002	0.0002
19	0.0000	0.0000	0.0000	0.0000	0.0000	0.0000	0.0000	0.0001	0.0001	0.0001

	λ									
x	**7.1**	**7.2**	**7.3**	**7.4**	**7.5**	**7.6**	**7.7**	**7.8**	**7.9**	**8.0**
0	0.0008	0.0007	0.0007	0.0006	0.0006	0.0005	0.0005	0.0004	0.0004	0.0003
1	0.0059	0.0054	0.0049	0.0045	0.0041	0.0038	0.0035	0.0032	0.0029	0.0027
2	0.0208	0.0194	0.0180	0.0167	0.0156	0.0145	0.0134	0.0125	0.0116	0.0107
3	0.0492	0.0464	0.0438	0.0413	0.0389	0.0366	0.0345	0.0324	0.0305	0.0286
4	0.0874	0.0836	0.0799	0.0764	0.0729	0.0696	0.0663	0.0632	0.0602	0.0573
5	0.1241	0.1204	0.1167	0.1130	0.1094	0.1057	0.1021	0.0986	0.0951	0.0916
6	0.1468	0.1445	0.1420	0.1394	0.1367	0.1339	0.1311	0.1282	0.1252	0.1221
7	0.1489	0.1486	0.1481	0.1474	0.1465	0.1454	0.1442	0.1428	0.1413	0.1396
8	0.1321	0.1337	0.1351	0.1363	0.1373	0.1382	0.1388	0.1392	0.1395	0.1396
9	0.1042	0.1070	0.1096	0.1121	0.1144	0.1167	0.1187	0.1207	0.1224	0.1241
10	0.0740	0.0770	0.0800	0.0829	0.0858	0.0887	0.0914	0.0941	0.0967	0.0993
11	0.0478	0.0504	0.0531	0.0558	0.0585	0.0613	0.0640	0.0667	0.0695	0.0722
12	0.0283	0.0303	0.0323	0.0344	0.0366	0.0388	0.0411	0.0434	0.0457	0.0481
13	0.0154	0.0168	0.0181	0.0196	0.0211	0.0227	0.0243	0.0260	0.0278	0.0296
14	0.0078	0.0086	0.0095	0.0104	0.0113	0.0123	0.0134	0.0145	0.0157	0.0169
15	0.0037	0.0041	0.0046	0.0051	0.0057	0.0062	0.0069	0.0075	0.0083	0.0090
16	0.0016	0.0019	0.0021	0.0024	0.0026	0.0030	0.0033	0.0037	0.0041	0.0045
17	0.0007	0.0008	0.0009	0.0010	0.0012	0.0013	0.0015	0.0017	0.0019	0.0021
18	0.0003	0.0003	0.0004	0.0004	0.0005	0.0006	0.0006	0.0007	0.0008	0.0009
19	0.0001	0.0001	0.0001	0.0002	0.0002	0.0002	0.0003	0.0003	0.0003	0.0004
20	0.0000	0.0000	0.0001	0.0001	0.0001	0.0001	0.0001	0.0001	0.0001	0.0002
21	0.0000	0.0000	0.0000	0.0000	0.0000	0.0000	0.0000	0.0000	0.0001	0.0001

x	λ = 8.1	8.2	8.3	8.4	8.5	8.6	8.7	8.8	8.9	9.0
0	0.0003	0.0003	0.0002	0.0002	0.0002	0.0002	0.0002	0.0002	0.0001	0.0001
1	0.0025	0.0023	0.0021	0.0019	0.0017	0.0016	0.0014	0.0013	0.0012	0.0011
2	0.0100	0.0092	0.0086	0.0079	0.0074	0.0068	0.0063	0.0058	0.0054	0.0050
3	0.0269	0.0252	0.0237	0.0222	0.0208	0.0195	0.0183	0.0171	0.0160	0.0150
4	0.0544	0.0517	0.0491	0.0466	0.0443	0.0420	0.0398	0.0377	0.0357	0.0337
5	0.0882	0.0849	0.0816	0.0784	0.0752	0.0722	0.0692	0.0663	0.0635	0.0607
6	0.1191	0.1160	0.1128	0.1097	0.1066	0.1034	0.1003	0.0972	0.0941	0.0911
7	0.1378	0.1358	0.1338	0.1317	0.1294	0.1271	0.1247	0.1222	0.1197	0.1171
8	0.1395	0.1392	0.1388	0.1382	0.1375	0.1366	0.1356	0.1344	0.1332	0.1318
9	0.1256	0.1269	0.1280	0.1290	0.1299	0.1306	0.1311	0.1315	0.1317	0.1318
10	0.1017	0.1040	0.1063	0.1084	0.1104	0.1123	0.1140	0.1157	0.1172	0.1186
11	0.0749	0.0776	0.0802	0.0828	0.0853	0.0878	0.0902	0.0925	0.0948	0.0970
12	0.0505	0.0530	0.0555	0.0579	0.0604	0.0629	0.0654	0.0679	0.0703	0.0728
13	0.0315	0.0334	0.0354	0.0374	0.0395	0.0416	0.0438	0.0459	0.0481	0.0504
14	0.0182	0.0196	0.0210	0.0225	0.0240	0.0256	0.0272	0.0289	0.0306	0.0324
15	0.0098	0.0107	0.0116	0.0126	0.0136	0.0147	0.0158	0.0169	0.0182	0.0194
16	0.0050	0.0055	0.0060	0.0066	0.0072	0.0079	0.0086	0.0093	0.0101	0.0109
17	0.0024	0.0026	0.0029	0.0033	0.0036	0.0040	0.0044	0.0048	0.0053	0.0058
18	0.0011	0.0012	0.0014	0.0015	0.0017	0.0019	0.0021	0.0024	0.0026	0.0029
19	0.0005	0.0005	0.0006	0.0007	0.0008	0.0009	0.0010	0.0011	0.0012	0.0014
20	0.0002	0.0002	0.0002	0.0003	0.0003	0.0004	0.0004	0.0005	0.0005	0.0006
21	0.0001	0.0001	0.0001	0.0001	0.0001	0.0002	0.0002	0.0002	0.0002	0.0003
22	0.0000	0.0000	0.0000	0.0000	0.0001	0.0001	0.0001	0.0001	0.0001	0.0001

x	λ = 9.1	9.2	9.3	9.4	9.5	9.6	9.7	9.8	9.9	10
0	0.0001	0.0001	0.0001	0.0001	0.0001	0.0001	0.0001	0.0001	0.0001	0.0000
1	0.0010	0.0009	0.0009	0.0008	0.0007	0.0007	0.0006	0.0005	0.0005	0.0005
2	0.0046	0.0043	0.0040	0.0037	0.0034	0.0031	0.0029	0.0027	0.0025	0.0023
3	0.0140	0.0131	0.0123	0.0115	0.0107	0.0100	0.0093	0.0087	0.0081	0.0076
4	0.0319	0.0302	0.0285	0.0269	0.0254	0.0240	0.0226	0.0213	0.0201	0.0189
5	0.0581	0.0555	0.0530	0.0506	0.0483	0.0460	0.0439	0.0418	0.0398	0.0378
6	0.0881	0.0851	0.0822	0.0793	0.0764	0.0736	0.0709	0.0682	0.0656	0.0631
7	0.1145	0.1118	0.1091	0.1064	0.1037	0.1010	0.0982	0.0955	0.0928	0.0901
8	0.1302	0.1286	0.1269	0.1251	0.1232	0.1212	0.1191	0.1170	0.1148	0.1126
9	0.1317	0.1315	0.1311	0.1306	0.1300	0.1293	0.1284	0.1274	0.1263	0.1251
10	0.1198	0.1210	0.1219	0.1228	0.1235	0.1241	0.1245	0.1249	0.1250	0.1251
11	0.0991	0.1012	0.1031	0.1049	0.1067	0.1083	0.1098	0.1112	0.1125	0.1137
12	0.0752	0.0776	0.0799	0.0822	0.0844	0.0866	0.0888	0.0908	0.0928	0.0948
13	0.0526	0.0549	0.0572	0.0594	0.0617	0.0640	0.0662	0.0685	0.0707	0.0729
14	0.0342	0.0361	0.0380	0.0399	0.0419	0.0439	0.0459	0.0479	0.0500	0.0521
15	0.0208	0.0221	0.0235	0.0250	0.0265	0.0281	0.0297	0.0313	0.0330	0.0347
16	0.0118	0.0127	0.0137	0.0147	0.0157	0.0168	0.0180	0.0192	0.0204	0.0217
17	0.0063	0.0069	0.0075	0.0081	0.0088	0.0095	0.0103	0.0111	0.0119	0.0128
18	0.0032	0.0035	0.0039	0.0042	0.0046	0.0051	0.0055	0.0060	0.0065	0.0071
19	0.0015	0.0017	0.0019	0.0021	0.0023	0.0026	0.0028	0.0031	0.0034	0.0037
20	0.0007	0.0008	0.0009	0.0010	0.0011	0.0012	0.0014	0.0015	0.0017	0.0019
21	0.0003	0.0003	0.0004	0.0004	0.0005	0.0006	0.0006	0.0007	0.0008	0.0009
22	0.0001	0.0001	0.0002	0.0002	0.0002	0.0002	0.0003	0.0003	0.0004	0.0004
23	0.0000	0.0001	0.0001	0.0001	0.0001	0.0001	0.0001	0.0001	0.0002	0.0002
24	0.0000	0.0000	0.0000	0.0000	0.0000	0.0000	0.0000	0.0001	0.0001	0.0001

x	λ = 11	12	13	14	15	16	17	18	19	20
0	0.0000	0.0000	0.0000	0.0000	0.0000	0.0000	0.0000	0.0000	0.0000	0.0000
1	0.0002	0.0001	0.0000	0.0000	0.0000	0.0000	0.0000	0.0000	0.0000	0.0000
2	0.0010	0.0004	0.0002	0.0001	0.0000	0.0000	0.0000	0.0000	0.0000	0.0000
3	0.0037	0.0018	0.0008	0.0004	0.0002	0.0001	0.0000	0.0000	0.0000	0.0000
4	0.0102	0.0053	0.0027	0.0013	0.0006	0.0003	0.0001	0.0001	0.0000	0.0000
5	0.0224	0.0127	0.0070	0.0037	0.0019	0.0010	0.0005	0.0002	0.0001	0.0001
6	0.0411	0.0255	0.0152	0.0087	0.0048	0.0026	0.0014	0.0007	0.0004	0.0002
7	0.0646	0.0437	0.0281	0.0174	0.0104	0.0060	0.0034	0.0018	0.0010	0.0005
8	0.0888	0.0655	0.0457	0.0304	0.0194	0.0120	0.0072	0.0042	0.0024	0.0013
9	0.1085	0.0874	0.0661	0.0473	0.0324	0.0213	0.0135	0.0083	0.0050	0.0029
10	0.1194	0.1048	0.0859	0.0663	0.0486	0.0341	0.0230	0.0150	0.0095	0.0058
11	0.1194	0.1144	0.1015	0.0844	0.0663	0.0496	0.0355	0.0245	0.0164	0.0106
12	0.1094	0.1144	0.1099	0.0984	0.0829	0.0661	0.0504	0.0368	0.0259	0.0176
13	0.0926	0.1056	0.1099	0.1060	0.0956	0.0814	0.0658	0.0509	0.0378	0.0271
14	0.0728	0.0905	0.1021	0.1060	0.1024	0.0930	0.0800	0.0655	0.0514	0.0387
15	0.0534	0.0724	0.0885	0.0989	0.1024	0.0992	0.0906	0.0786	0.0650	0.0516
16	0.0367	0.0543	0.0719	0.0866	0.0960	0.0992	0.0963	0.0884	0.0772	0.0646
17	0.0237	0.0383	0.0550	0.0713	0.0847	0.0934	0.0963	0.0936	0.0863	0.0760
18	0.0145	0.0256	0.0397	0.0554	0.0706	0.0830	0.0909	0.0936	0.0911	0.0844
19	0.0084	0.0161	0.0272	0.0409	0.0557	0.0699	0.0814	0.0887	0.0911	0.0888
20	0.0046	0.0097	0.0177	0.0286	0.0418	0.0559	0.0692	0.0798	0.0866	0.0888
21	0.0024	0.0055	0.0109	0.0191	0.0299	0.0426	0.0560	0.0684	0.0783	0.0846
22	0.0012	0.0030	0.0065	0.0121	0.0204	0.0310	0.0433	0.0560	0.0676	0.0769
23	0.0006	0.0016	0.0037	0.0074	0.0133	0.0216	0.0320	0.0438	0.0559	0.0669
24	0.0003	0.0008	0.0020	0.0043	0.0083	0.0144	0.0226	0.0328	0.0442	0.0557
25	0.0001	0.0004	0.0010	0.0024	0.0050	0.0092	0.0154	0.0237	0.0336	0.0446
26	0.0000	0.0002	0.0005	0.0013	0.0029	0.0057	0.0101	0.0164	0.0246	0.0343
27	0.0000	0.0001	0.0002	0.0007	0.0016	0.0034	0.0063	0.0109	0.0173	0.0254
28	0.0000	0.0000	0.0001	0.0003	0.0009	0.0019	0.0038	0.0070	0.0117	0.0181
29	0.0000	0.0000	0.0001	0.0002	0.0004	0.0011	0.0023	0.0044	0.0077	0.0125
30	0.0000	0.0000	0.0000	0.0001	0.0002	0.0006	0.0013	0.0026	0.0049	0.0083
31	0.0000	0.0000	0.0000	0.0000	0.0001	0.0003	0.0007	0.0015	0.0030	0.0054
32	0.0000	0.0000	0.0000	0.0000	0.0001	0.0001	0.0004	0.0009	0.0018	0.0034
33	0.0000	0.0000	0.0000	0.0000	0.0000	0.0001	0.0002	0.0005	0.0010	0.0020
34	0.0000	0.0000	0.0000	0.0000	0.0000	0.0000	0.0001	0.0002	0.0006	0.0012
35	0.0000	0.0000	0.0000	0.0000	0.0000	0.0000	0.0000	0.0001	0.0003	0.0007
36	0.0000	0.0000	0.0000	0.0000	0.0000	0.0000	0.0000	0.0001	0.0002	0.0004
37	0.0000	0.0000	0.0000	0.0000	0.0000	0.0000	0.0000	0.0000	0.0001	0.0002
38	0.0000	0.0000	0.0000	0.0000	0.0000	0.0000	0.0000	0.0000	0.0000	0.0001
39	0.0000	0.0000	0.0000	0.0000	0.0000	0.0000	0.0000	0.0000	0.0000	0.0001

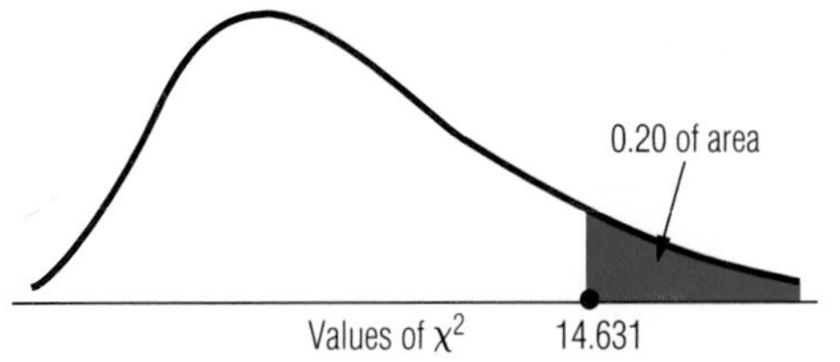

Appendix Table 5

Area in the Right Tail of a Chi-square (χ^2) Distribution

Example:
In a chi-square distribution with 11 degrees of freedom, to find the chi-square value for 0.20 of the area under the curve (the colored area in the right tail) look under the 0.20 column in the table and the 11 degrees of freedom row; the appropriate chi-square value is 14.631.

Degrees of Freedom	Area in Right Tail 0.99	0.975	0.95	0.90	0.800
1	0.00016	0.00098	0.00398	0.0158	0.0642
2	0.0201	0.0506	0.103	0.211	0.446
3	0.115	0.216	0.352	0.584	1.005
4	0.297	0.484	0.711	1.064	1.649
5	0.554	0.831	1.145	1.610	2.343
6	0.872	1.237	1.635	2.204	3.070
7	1.239	1.690	2.167	2.833	3.822
8	1.646	2.180	2.733	3.490	4.594
9	2.088	2.700	3.325	4.168	5.380
10	2.558	3.247	3.940	4.865	6.179
11	3.053	3.816	4.575	5.578	6.989
12	3.571	4.404	5.226	6.304	7.807
13	4.107	5.009	5.892	7.042	8.634
14	4.660	5.629	6.571	7.790	9.467
15	5.229	6.262	7.261	8.547	10.307
16	5.812	6.908	7.962	9.312	11.152
17	6.408	7.564	8.672	10.085	12.002
18	7.015	8.231	9.390	10.865	12.857
19	7.633	8.907	10.117	11.651	13.716
20	8.260	9.591	10.851	12.443	14.578
21	8.897	10.283	11.591	13.240	15.445
22	9.542	10.982	12.338	14.041	16.314
23	10.196	11.689	13.091	14.848	17.187
24	10.856	12.401	13.848	15.658	18.062
25	11.524	13.120	14.611	16.473	18.940
26	12.198	13.844	15.379	17.292	19.820
27	12.879	14.573	16.151	18.114	20.703
28	13.565	15.308	16.928	18.939	21.588
29	14.256	16.047	17.708	19.768	22.475
30	14.953	16.791	18.493	20.599	23.364

Note: If v, the number of degrees of freedom, is greater than 30, we can approximate χ^2_α, the chi-square value leaving α of the area in the right tail, by

$$\chi^2_\alpha = v\left(1 - \frac{2}{9v} + z_\alpha\sqrt{\frac{2}{9v}}\right)^3$$

where z_α is the standard normal value (from Appendix Table 1) that leaves α of the area in the right tail.

		Area in Right Tail			Degrees of
0.20	0.10	0.05	0.025	0.01	Freedom
1.642	2.706	3.841	5.024	6.635	1
3.219	4.605	5.991	7.378	9.210	2
4.642	6.251	7.815	9.348	11.345	3
5.989	7.779	9.488	11.143	13.277	4
7.289	9.236	11.070	12.833	15.086	5
8.558	10.645	12.592	14.449	16.812	6
9.803	12.017	14.067	16.013	18.475	7
11.030	13.362	15.507	17.535	20.090	8
12.242	14.684	16.919	19.023	21.666	9
13.442	15.987	18.307	20.483	23.209	10
14.631	17.275	19.675	21.920	24.725	11
15.812	18.549	21.026	23.337	26.217	12
16.985	19.812	22.362	24.736	27.688	13
18.151	21.064	23.685	26.119	29.141	14
19.311	22.307	24.996	27.488	30.578	15
20.465	23.542	26.296	28.845	32.000	16
21.615	24.769	27.587	30.191	33.409	17
22.760	25.989	28.869	31.526	34.805	18
23.900	27.204	30.144	32.852	36.191	19
25.038	28.412	31.410	34.170	37.566	20
26.171	29.615	32.671	35.479	38.932	21
27.301	30.813	33.924	36.781	40.289	22
28.429	32.007	35.172	38.076	41.638	23
29.553	33.196	36.415	39.364	42.980	24
30.675	34.382	37.652	40.647	44.314	25
31.795	35.563	38.885	41.923	45.642	26
32.912	36.741	40.113	43.194	46.963	27
34.027	37.916	41.337	44.461	48.278	28
35.139	39.087	42.557	45.722	49.588	29
36.250	40.256	43.773	46.979	50.892	30

0.05 of area

3.94

Appendix Table 6(a)

Values of *F* for *F* Distributions with 0.05 of the Area in the Right Tail

Example: In an ***F*** distribution with 15 degrees of freedom for the numerator and 6 degrees of freedom for the denominator, to find the ***F*** value for 0.05 of the area under the curve look under the 15 degrees of freedom column and across the 6 degrees of freedom row; the appropriate ***F*** value is 3.94.

Degrees of Freedom for Denominator	Degrees of Freedom for Numerator																		
	1	**2**	**3**	**4**	**5**	**6**	**7**	**8**	**9**	**10**	**12**	**15**	**20**	**24**	**30**	**40**	**60**	**120**	∞
1	161	200	216	225	230	234	237	239	241	242	244	246	248	249	250	251	252	253	254
2	18.5	19.0	19.2	19.2	19.3	19.3	19.4	19.4	19.4	19.4	19.4	19.4	19.4	19.5	19.5	19.5	19.5	19.5	19.5
3	10.1	9.55	9.28	9.12	9.01	8.94	8.89	8.85	8.81	8.79	8.74	8.70	8.66	8.64	8.62	8.59	8.57	8.55	8.53
4	7.71	6.94	6.59	6.39	6.26	6.16	6.09	6.04	6.00	5.96	5.91	5.86	5.80	5.77	5.75	5.72	5.69	5.66	5.63
5	6.61	5.79	5.41	5.19	5.05	4.95	4.88	4.82	4.77	4.74	4.68	4.62	4.56	4.53	4.50	4.46	4.43	4.40	4.37
6	5.99	5.14	4.76	4.53	4.39	4.28	4.21	4.15	4.10	4.06	4.00	3.94	3.87	3.84	3.81	3.77	3.74	3.70	3.67
7	5.59	4.74	4.35	4.12	3.97	3.87	3.79	3.73	3.68	3.64	3.57	3.51	3.44	3.41	3.38	3.34	3.30	3.27	3.23
8	5.32	4.46	4.07	3.84	3.69	3.58	3.50	3.44	3.39	3.35	3.28	3.22	3.15	3.12	3.08	3.04	3.01	2.97	2.93
9	5.12	4.26	3.86	3.63	3.48	3.37	3.29	3.23	3.18	3.14	3.07	3.01	2.94	2.90	2.86	2.83	2.79	2.75	2.71
10	4.96	4.10	3.71	3.48	3.33	3.22	3.14	3.07	3.02	2.98	2.91	2.85	2.77	2.74	2.70	2.66	2.62	2.58	2.54
11	4.84	3.98	3.59	3.36	3.20	3.09	3.01	2.95	2.90	2.85	2.79	2.72	2.65	2.61	2.57	2.53	2.49	2.45	2.40
12	4.75	3.89	3.49	3.26	3.11	3.00	2.91	2.85	2.80	2.75	2.69	2.62	2.54	2.51	2.47	2.43	2.38	2.34	2.30
13	4.67	3.81	3.41	3.18	3.03	2.92	2.83	2.77	2.71	2.67	2.60	2.53	2.46	2.42	2.38	2.34	2.30	2.25	2.21
14	4.60	3.74	3.34	3.11	2.96	2.85	2.76	2.70	2.65	2.60	2.53	2.46	2.39	2.35	2.31	2.27	2.22	2.18	2.13
15	4.54	3.68	3.29	3.06	2.90	2.79	2.71	2.64	2.59	2.54	2.48	2.40	2.33	2.29	2.25	2.20	2.16	2.11	2.07
16	4.49	3.63	3.24	3.01	2.85	2.74	2.66	2.59	2.54	2.49	2.42	2.35	2.28	2.24	2.19	2.15	2.11	2.06	2.01
17	4.45	3.59	3.20	2.96	2.81	2.70	2.61	2.55	2.49	2.45	2.38	2.31	2.23	2.19	2.15	2.10	2.06	2.01	1.96
18	4.41	3.55	3.16	2.93	2.77	2.66	2.58	2.51	2.46	2.41	2.34	2.27	2.19	2.15	2.11	2.06	2.02	1.97	1.92
19	4.38	3.52	3.13	2.90	2.74	2.63	2.54	2.48	2.42	2.38	2.31	2.23	2.16	2.11	2.07	2.03	1.98	1.93	1.88
20	4.35	3.49	3.10	2.87	2.71	2.60	2.51	2.45	2.39	2.35	2.28	2.20	2.12	2.08	2.04	1.99	1.95	1.90	1.84
21	4.32	3.47	3.07	2.84	2.68	2.57	2.49	2.42	2.37	2.32	2.25	2.18	2.10	2.05	2.01	1.96	1.92	1.87	1.81
22	4.30	3.44	3.05	2.82	2.66	2.55	2.46	2.40	2.34	2.30	2.23	2.15	2.07	2.03	1.98	1.94	1.89	1.84	1.78
23	4.28	3.42	3.03	2.80	2.64	2.53	2.44	2.37	2.32	2.27	2.20	2.13	2.05	2.01	1.96	1.91	1.86	1.81	1.76
24	4.26	3.40	3.01	2.78	2.62	2.51	2.42	2.36	2.30	2.25	2.18	2.11	2.03	1.98	1.94	1.89	1.84	1.79	1.73
25	4.24	3.39	2.99	2.76	2.60	2.49	2.40	2.34	2.28	2.24	2.16	2.09	2.01	1.96	1.92	1.87	1.82	1.77	1.71
30	4.17	3.32	2.92	2.69	2.53	2.42	2.33	2.27	2.21	2.16	2.09	2.01	1.93	1.89	1.84	1.79	1.74	1.68	1.62
40	4.08	3.23	2.84	2.61	2.45	2.34	2.25	2.18	2.12	2.08	2.00	1.92	1.84	1.79	1.74	1.69	1.64	1.58	1.51
60	4.00	3.15	2.76	2.53	2.37	2.25	2.17	2.10	2.04	1.99	1.92	1.84	1.75	1.70	1.65	1.59	1.53	1.47	1.39
120	3.92	3.07	2.68	2.45	2.29	2.18	2.09	2.02	1.96	1.91	1.83	1.75	1.66	1.61	1.55	1.50	1.43	1.35	1.25
∞	3.84	3.00	2.60	2.37	2.21	2.10	2.01	1.94	1.88	1.83	1.75	1.67	1.57	1.52	1.46	1.39	1.32	1.22	1.00

0.01 of area

10.5

Appendix Table 6(b)

Values of *F* for *F* Distributions with 0.01 of the Area in the Right Tail

Example: In an *F* distribution with 7 degrees of freedom for the numerator and 5 degrees of freedom for the denominator, to find the *F* value for 0.01 of the area under the curve look under the 7 degrees of freedom column and across the 5 degrees of freedom row; the appropriate *F* value is 10.5.

Degrees of Freedom for Numerator (columns); **Degrees of Freedom for Denominator** (rows)

	1	2	3	4	5	6	7	8	9	10	12	15	20	24	30	40	60	120	∞
1	4,052	5,000	5,403	5,625	5,764	5,859	5,928	5,982	6,023	6,056	6,106	6,157	6,209	6,235	6,261	6,287	6,313	6,339	6,366
2	98.5	99.0	99.2	99.2	99.3	99.3	99.4	99.4	99.4	99.4	99.4	99.4	99.4	99.5	99.5	99.5	99.5	99.5	99.5
3	34.1	30.8	29.5	28.7	28.2	27.9	27.7	27.5	27.3	27.2	27.1	26.9	26.7	26.6	26.5	26.4	26.3	26.2	26.1
4	21.2	18.0	16.7	16.0	15.5	15.2	15.0	14.8	14.7	14.5	14.4	14.2	14.0	13.9	13.8	13.7	13.7	13.6	13.5
5	16.3	13.3	12.1	11.4	11.0	10.7	10.5	10.3	10.2	10.1	9.89	9.72	9.55	9.47	9.38	9.29	9.20	9.11	9.02
6	13.7	10.9	9.78	9.15	8.75	8.47	8.26	8.10	7.98	7.87	7.72	7.56	7.40	7.31	7.23	7.14	7.06	6.97	6.88
7	12.2	9.55	8.45	7.85	7.46	7.19	6.99	6.84	6.72	6.62	6.47	6.31	6.16	6.07	5.99	5.91	5.82	5.74	5.65
8	11.3	8.65	7.59	7.01	6.63	6.37	6.18	6.03	5.91	5.81	5.67	5.52	5.36	5.28	5.20	5.12	5.03	4.95	4.86
9	10.6	8.02	6.99	6.42	6.06	5.80	5.61	5.47	5.35	5.26	5.11	4.96	4.81	4.73	4.65	4.57	4.48	4.40	4.31
10	10.0	7.56	6.55	5.99	5.64	5.39	5.20	5.06	4.94	4.85	4.71	4.56	4.41	4.33	4.25	4.17	4.08	4.00	3.91
11	9.65	7.21	6.22	5.67	5.32	5.07	4.89	4.74	4.63	4.54	4.40	4.25	4.10	4.02	3.94	3.86	3.78	3.69	3.60
12	9.33	6.93	5.95	5.41	5.06	4.82	4.64	4.50	4.39	4.30	4.16	4.01	3.86	3.78	3.70	3.62	3.54	3.45	3.36
13	9.07	6.70	5.74	5.21	4.86	4.62	4.44	4.30	4.19	4.10	3.96	3.82	3.66	3.59	3.51	3.43	3.34	3.25	3.17
14	8.86	6.51	5.56	5.04	4.70	4.46	4.28	4.14	4.03	3.94	3.80	3.66	3.51	3.43	3.35	3.27	3.18	3.09	3.00
15	8.68	6.36	5.42	4.89	4.56	4.32	4.14	4.00	3.89	3.80	3.67	3.52	3.37	3.29	3.21	3.13	3.05	2.96	2.87
16	8.53	6.23	5.29	4.77	4.44	4.20	4.03	3.89	3.78	3.69	3.55	3.41	3.26	3.18	3.10	3.02	2.93	2.84	2.75
17	8.40	6.11	5.19	4.67	4.34	4.10	3.93	3.79	3.68	3.59	3.46	3.31	3.16	3.08	3.00	2.92	2.83	2.75	2.65
18	8.29	6.01	5.09	4.58	4.25	4.01	3.84	3.71	3.60	3.51	3.37	3.23	3.08	3.00	2.92	2.84	2.75	2.66	2.57
19	8.19	5.93	5.01	4.50	4.17	3.94	3.77	3.63	3.52	3.43	3.30	3.15	3.00	2.92	2.84	2.76	2.67	2.58	2.49
20	8.10	5.85	4.94	4.43	4.10	3.87	3.70	3.56	3.46	3.37	3.23	3.09	2.94	2.86	2.78	2.69	2.61	2.52	2.42
21	8.02	5.78	4.87	4.37	4.04	3.81	3.64	3.51	3.40	3.31	3.17	3.03	2.88	2.80	2.72	2.64	2.55	2.46	2.36
22	7.95	5.72	4.82	4.31	3.99	3.76	3.59	3.45	3.35	3.26	3.12	2.98	2.83	2.75	2.67	2.58	2.50	2.40	2.31
23	7.88	5.66	4.76	4.26	3.94	3.71	3.54	3.41	3.30	3.21	3.07	2.93	2.78	2.70	2.62	2.54	2.45	2.35	2.26
24	7.82	5.61	4.72	4.22	3.90	3.67	3.50	3.36	3.26	3.17	3.03	2.89	2.74	2.66	2.58	2.49	2.40	2.31	2.21
25	7.77	5.57	4.68	4.18	3.86	3.63	3.46	3.32	3.22	3.13	2.99	2.85	2.70	2.62	2.53	2.45	2.36	2.27	2.17
30	7.56	5.39	4.51	4.02	3.70	3.47	3.30	3.17	3.07	2.98	2.84	2.70	2.55	2.47	2.39	2.30	2.21	2.11	2.01
40	7.31	5.18	4.31	3.83	3.51	3.29	3.12	2.99	2.89	2.80	2.66	2.52	2.37	2.29	2.20	2.11	2.02	1.92	1.80
60	7.08	4.98	4.13	3.65	3.34	3.12	2.95	2.82	2.72	2.63	2.50	2.35	2.20	2.12	2.03	1.94	1.84	1.73	1.60
120	6.85	4.79	3.95	3.48	3.17	2.96	2.79	2.66	2.56	2.47	2.34	2.19	2.03	1.95	1.86	1.76	1.66	1.53	1.38
∞	6.63	4.61	3.78	3.32	3.02	2.80	2.64	2.51	2.41	2.32	2.18	2.04	1.88	1.79	1.70	1.59	1.47	1.32	1.00

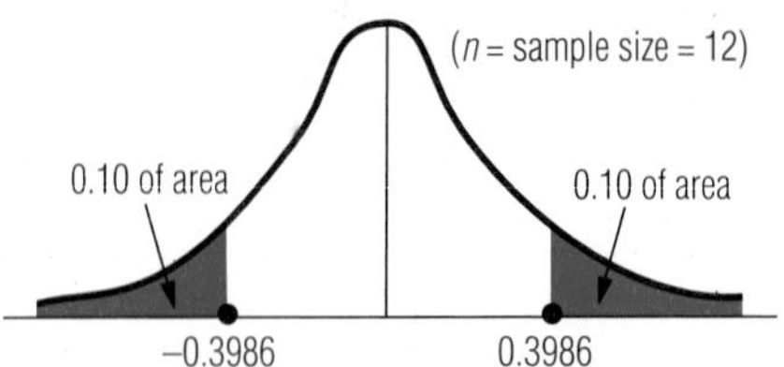

Appendix Table 7

Values for Spearman's Rank Correlation (r_s) for Combined Areas in Both Tails

Example:
For a two-tailed test of significance at the 0.20 level, with n = 12, the appropriate value for r_s can be found by looking under the 0.20 column and across the 12 row; the appropriate r_s value is 0.3986.

n	**0.20**	**0.10**	**0.05**	**0.02**	**0.01**	**0.002**
4	0.8000	0.8000				
5	0.7000	0.8000	0.9000	0.9000		
6	0.6000	0.7714	0.8286	0.8857	0.9429	
7	0.5357	0.6786	0.7450	0.8571	0.8929	0.9643
8	0.5000	0.6190	0.7143	0.8095	0.8571	0.9286
9	0.4667	0.5833	0.6833	0.7667	0.8167	0.9000
10	0.4424	0.5515	0.6364	0.7333	0.7818	0.8667
11	0.4182	0.5273	0.6091	0.7000	0.7455	0.8364
12	0.3986	0.4965	0.5804	0.6713	0.7273	0.8182
13	0.3791	0.4780	0.5549	0.6429	0.6978	0.7912
14	0.3626	0.4593	0.5341	0.6220	0.6747	0.7670
15	0.3500	0.4429	0.5179	0.6000	0.6536	0.7464
16	0.3382	0.4265	0.5000	0.5824	0.6324	0.7265
17	0.3260	0.4118	0.4853	0.5637	0.6152	0.7083
18	0.3148	0.3994	0.4716	0.5480	0.5975	0.6904
19	0.3070	0.3895	0.4579	0.5333	0.5825	0.6737
20	0.2977	0.3789	0.4451	0.5203	0.5684	0.6586
21	0.2909	0.3688	0.4351	0.5078	0.5545	0.6455
22	0.2829	0.3597	0.4241	0.4963	0.5426	0.6318
23	0.2767	0.3518	0.4150	0.4852	0.5306	0.6186
24	0.2704	0.3435	0.4061	0.4748	0.5200	0.6070
25	0.2646	0.3362	0.3977	0.4654	0.5100	0.5962
26	0.2588	0.3299	0.3894	0.4564	0.5002	0.5856
27	0.2540	0.3236	0.3822	0.4481	0.4915	0.5757
28	0.2490	0.3175	0.3749	0.4401	0.4828	0.5660
29	0.2443	0.3113	0.3685	0.4320	0.4744	0.5567
30	0.2400	0.3059	0.3620	0.4251	0.4665	0.5479

Appendix Table 8 Critical Values of *D* in the Kolmogorov-Smirnov Goodness-of-Fit Test

Sample Size (n)	Level of Significance for D = Maximum $\lvert F_e - F_o \rvert$				
	0.20	0.15	0.10	0.05	0.01
1	0.900	0.925	0.950	0.975	0.995
2	0.684	0.726	0.776	0.842	0.929
3	0.565	0.597	0.642	0.708	0.828
4	0.494	0.525	0.564	0.624	0.733
5	0.446	0.474	0.510	0.565	0.669
6	0.410	0.436	0.470	0.521	0.618
7	0.381	0.405	0.438	0.486	0.577
8	0.358	0.381	0.411	0.457	0.543
9	0.339	0.360	0.388	0.432	0.514
10	0.322	0.342	0.368	0.410	0.490
11	0.307	0.326	0.352	0.391	0.468
12	0.295	0.313	0.338	0.375	0.450
13	0.284	0.302	0.325	0.361	0.433
14	0.274	0.292	0.314	0.349	0.418
15	0.266	0.283	0.304	0.338	0.404
16	0.258	0.274	0.295	0.328	0.392
17	0.250	0.266	0.286	0.318	0.381
18	0.244	0.259	0.278	0.309	0.371
19	0.237	0.252	0.272	0.301	0.363
20	0.231	0.246	0.264	0.294	0.356
25	0.21	0.22	0.24	0.27	0.32
30	0.19	0.20	0.22	0.24	0.29
35	0.18	0.19	0.21	0.23	0.27
Over 35	$\frac{1.07}{\sqrt{n}}$	$\frac{1.14}{\sqrt{n}}$	$\frac{1.22}{\sqrt{n}}$	$\frac{1.36}{\sqrt{n}}$	$\frac{1.63}{\sqrt{n}}$

Note: The values of D given in the table are critical values associated with selected values of n. Any value of D that is greater than or equal to the tabulated value is significant at the indicated level of significance.

Appendix Table 9 Control Chart Factors

Sample Size, n	Factors for $\bar{x}$ Charts		Factors for R Charts		
	$d_2 = \frac{R}{\sigma}$	$A_2 = \frac{3}{d_2\sqrt{n}}$	$d_3 = \frac{\sigma_R}{\sigma}$	$D_3 = 1 - \frac{3d_3}{d_2}$	$D_4 = 1 + \frac{3d_3}{d_2}$
2	1.128	1.881	0.853	0	3.269
3	1.693	1.023	0.888	0	2.574
4	2.059	0.729	0.880	0	2.282
5	2.326	0.577	0.864	0	2.114
6	2.534	0.483	0.848	0	2.004
7	2.704	0.419	0.833	0.076	1.924
8	2.847	0.373	0.820	0.136	1.864
9	2.970	0.337	0.808	0.184	1.816
10	3.078	0.308	0.797	0.223	1.777
11	3.173	0.285	0.787	0.256	1.744
12	3.258	0.266	0.779	0.283	1.717
13	3.336	0.249	0.770	0.308	1.692
14	3.407	0.235	0.763	0.328	1.672
15	3.472	0.223	0.756	0.347	1.653
16	3.532	0.212	0.750	0.363	1.637
17	3.588	0.203	0.744	0.378	1.622
18	3.640	0.194	0.739	0.391	1.609
19	3.689	0.187	0.734	0.403	1.597
20	3.735	0.180	0.729	0.414	1.586
21	3.778	0.173	0.724	0.425	1.575
22	3.819	0.167	0.720	0.434	1.566
23	3.858	0.162	0.716	0.443	1.557
24	3.895	0.157	0.712	0.452	1.548
25	3.931	0.153	0.708	0.460	1.540

Note: If $1 - 3d_3/d_2 < 0$, then $D_3 = 0$.

Appendix Table 10

Student Records for Computer Examples

The records for the 199 students who used this text in our course in the fall semester of 1995 are included on the data disk that accompanies the text. Each observation contains the following nine variables:

STUDENT	— the student's position on the roster
SECTION	— which of the six sections of the class the student was enrolled in
INSTRUCT	— the type of instructor (TA or PROF)
EXAM1	— score on first midterm (75 points possible)
EXAM2	— score on second midterm (75 points possible)
HWK	— score on homework (137 points possible)
FINAL	— score on final exam (75 points possible)
TOTAL	— raw score, computed as

20 *(EXAM1 + EXAM2 + 2*FINAL)/75 + 20 *HWK/137

GRADE—letter grade in class determined by

TOTAL	GRADE
0–49	F
50–59	D
60–63	C–
64–69	C
70–73	C+
74–75	B–
76–78	B
79–80	B+
81–85	A–
86–100	A

Appendix Table 11

Company Earnings Data for Computer Examples

The earnings data for 224 companies whose 1989 last-quarter earnings were published in *The Wall Street Journal* during the week of February 12, 1990 are included on the data disk that accompanies the text. Each observation contains the following seven variables:

COMPANY	— the name of the company
EXCHANGE	— the exchange where the stock is traded (N for New York Stock Exchange, A for American Stock Exchange, O for over-the-counter)
LQ89	— 1989 last-quarter earnings
LQ88	— 1988 last-quarter earnings
CHANGE	— the change in last-quarter earnings (LQ89–LQ88)
GRPLQ89	— grouped 1989 last-quarter earnings; each earnings value is rounded to the nearest 25¢
GRPLQ88	— grouped 1988 last-quarter earnings; each earnings value is rounded to the nearest 25¢

Answers to Chapter Concepts Tests

Chapter 2

1. T	16. F	31. c
2. T	17. T	32. e
3. F	18. F	33. e
4. F	19. T	34. e
5. T	20. F	35. e
6. T	21. F	36. b
7. T	22. d	37. incomplete, biased
8. T	23. b	38. representative
9. F	24. a	39. data array, frequency distribution
10. F	25. c	40. population, sample
11. F	26. c	41. frequency
12. F	27. a	42. discrete, continuous
13. T	28. d	43. fractions, percentages
14. T	29. b	44. ogive
15. F	30. e	45. data point

Chapter 3

1. F	19. T	37. b	55. f
2. T	20. F	38. a	56. e
3. F	21. T	39. b	57. symmetrical, skewed
4. F	22. T	40. c	58. sample, population
5. F	23. F	41. d	59. coding
6. T	24. T	42. b	60. geometric, arithmetic
7. T	25. F	43. c	61. bimodal
8. F	26. T	44. e	62. dispersion
9. T	27. F	45. f	63. fractile
10. F	28. T	46. e	64. interquartile
11. T	29. T	47. c	65. variance, standard deviation
12. F	30. F	48. c	
13. T	31. T	49. a	66. coefficient of variation
14. F	32. T	50. a	67. standard score
15. F	33. F	51. c	68. percentiles
16. F	34. F	52. d	69. d
17. F	35. c	53. d	70. b
18. T	36. d	54. e	

Chapter 4

1. F	16. F	31. d
2. F	17. T	32. c
3. T	18. F	33. c
4. T	19. F	34. e
5. T	20. T	35. e
6. F	21. F	36. d
7. F	22. b	37. event, experiment
8. T	23. d	38. sample space
9. T	24. c	39. Venn diagram
10. T	25. b	40. mutually exclusive
11. F	26. c	41. conditional
12. F	27. b	42. subjective approach
13. F	28. e	43. Bayes'
14. T	29. a	44. collectively exhaustive
15. T	30. d	45. classical, relative frequency, subjective

Chapter 5

1. F	16. F	31. c
2. F	17. F	32. e
3. T	18. F	33. a
4. F	19. F	34. c
5. T	20. T	35. d
6. T	21. T	36. f
7. F	22. e	37. expected value
8. F	23. d	38. binomial, Bernoulli
9. F	24. d	39. continuity
10. T	25. e	40. np, $\sqrt{npq}$
11. T	26. b	41. λ (lambda)
12. F	27. a	42. probability distribution
13. T	28. d	43. mean, standard deviation
14. F	29. d	44. random
15. F	30. c	45. discrete, continuous

Chapter 6

1. T 16. T 31. d
2. F 17. T 32. e
3. F 18. T 33. d
4. F 19. T 34. d
5. T 20. F 35. d
6. T 21. T 36. b
7. T 22. d 37. sample
8. F 23. b 38. sampling fraction
9. T 24. e 39. statistical inference
10. F 25. e 40. theoretical sampling distribution
11. T 26. d 41. stratified
12. F 27. b 42. systematic
13. T 28. a 43. Precision
14. F 29. c 44. clusters
15. F 30. b 45. sample proportions

Chapter 7

1. F 16. F 31. d
2. F 17. T 32. e
3. T 18. F 33. d
4. T 19. T 34. e
5. F 20. F 35. d
6. F 21. T 36. b
7. T 22. F 37. d
8. T 23. e 38. point
9. T 24. b 39. interval
10. T 25. a 40. degrees of freedom
11. T 26. c 41. Student's *t*-distribution
12. F 27. e 42. confidence
13. T 28. d 43. distance, mean
14. T 29. a 44. binomial
15. F 30. a 45. $p = 0.5$

Chapter 8

1. F 16. F 31. b
2. T 17. F 32. d
3. F 18. T 33. a
4. T 19. F 34. b
5. T 20. T 35. a
6. F 21. F 36. f
7. T 22. b 37. scales
8. T 23. c 38. normally, unknown
9. T 24. e 39. 1
10. F 25. d 40. reject, null, false
11. F 26. b 41. hypothesis
12. F 27. a 42. II, β (beta)
13. F 28. c 43. null, alternative
14. F 29. c 44. tailed
15. T 30. b 45. upper-tailed (or right-tailed)

Chapter 9

1. T 16. T 31. c
2. F 17. T 32. a
3. T 18. F 33. c
4. F 19. T 34. c
5. T 20. T 35. a
6. T 21. F 36. d
7. T 22. c 37. paired sample (paired difference)
8. F 23. b 38. prob values
9. T 24. b 39. pooled
10. F 25. c 40. difference, sample means
11. F 26. a 41. extraneous factors
12. F 27. a 42. largest, accept
13. T 28. d 43. critical
14. F 29. b 44. statistics, prob
15. T 30. d 45. binomial, normal

Chapter 10

1. T 16. F 31. b
2. F 17. T 32. d
3. T 18. F 33. c
4. T 19. T 34. d
5. T 20. F 35. b
6. T 21. F 36. a
7. T 22. c 37. control limits
8. T 23. c 38. fishbone (Ishikawa, cause-and-effect)
9. T 24. d 39. producer's
10. F 25. a 40. control charts
11. F 26. b 41. acceptance sampling
12. T 27. d 42. grand mean
13. T 28. a 43. variability
14. F 29. c 44. acceptance number
15. F 30. b 45. systematic (assignable, special cause)

Chapter 11

1. T 16. T 31. c
2. T 17. F 32. a
3. F 18. T 33. a
4. T 19. T 34. e
5. T 20. F 35. c
6. F 21. T 36. e
7. T 22. b 37. f
8. T 23. a 38. grand
9. T 24. d 39. analysis of variance (ANOVA)
10. F 25. e 40. independence
11. T 26. c 41. *F*
12. F 27. b 42. goodness-of-fit
13. T 28. d 43. within-column variance, between-column variance, *F*
14. F 29. c 44. lower, 100(1 − α)
15. F 30. e 45. number of samples, total sample size

Chapter 12

1. F 16. F 31. b
2. F 17. F 32. d
3. F 18. F 33. d
4. F 19. T 34. b
5. T 20. T 35. d
6. T 21. F 36. e
7. T 22. d 37. inverse
8. T 23. a 38. curvilinear
9. F 24. a 39. slope
10. T 25. e 40. standard error of estimate
11. F 26. b 41. r^2, the coefficient of determination
12. T 27. c 42. ±0.866
13. T 28. d 43. Correlation analysis
14. T 29. a 44. direction (direct or inverse)
15. F 30. c 45. minimizes

Chapter 13

1. T 16. F 31. b
2. F 17. F 32. d
3. T 18. F 33. e (or perhaps d)
4. F 19. F 34. b
5. F 20. T 35. c
6. T 21. T 36. c
7. T 22. c 37. modeling techniques
8. T 23. b 38. transformations
9. F 24. d 39. (computed) *F*-ratio
10. T 25. b 40. dummy
11. T 26. a 41. standard error
12. F 27. c 42. fraction of the variation in *Y* explained by the regression
13. F 28. d
14. F 29. b 43. $B_1 = B_2 = \cdots = B_k = 0$
15. T 30. a 44. root-mean-square error

45. residuals

Chapter 14

1. T 16. T 31. d
2. F 17. T 32. f
3. T 18. F 33. d
4. T 19. F 34. d
5. F 20. T 35. b
6. T 21. T 36. c
7. F 22. c 37. run
8. T 23. b 38. Mann–Whitney *U* test
9. T 24. a 39. one-sample runs test
10. F 25. b 40. sign
11. T 26. d 41. rank correlation
12. F 27. b 42. the sample sizes are unequal
13. F 28. c 43. r_s
14. T 29. a 44. distribution-free
15. T 30. b 45. Kolmogorov–Smirnov

Chapter 15

1. T 16. F 31. c
2. T 17. T 32. d
3. F 18. T 33. f
4. F 19. F 34. b
5. F 20. F 35. d
6. F 21. T 36. d
7. T 22. e 37. percent of trend
8. F 23. c 38. seasonal
9. F 24. a 39. irregular
10. F 25. b 40. cyclical
11. T 26. d 41. deseasonalizing
12. T 27. d 42. four-quarter moving total
13. T 28. c 43. secular trend
14. F 29. b 44. modified mean
15. T 30. a 45. forecast

Chapter 16

1. F
2. T
3. T
4. F
5. F
6. T
7. T
8. T
9. T
10. F
11. T
12. T
13. F
14. T
15. F
16. T
17. F
18. F
19. T
20. F
21. F
22. a
23. c
24. e
25. e
26. c
27. d
28. b
29. a
30. b
31. c
32. e
33. d
34. b
35. a
36. d
37. a
38. unweighted
39. Laspeyres
40. aggregate
41. fixed weight
42. Paasche
43. error, change
44. price, quantity, value
45. percentage relative (or index number)

Chapter 17

1. F
2. T
3. F
4. F
5. T
6. T
7. F
8. T
9. T
10. F
11. F
12. T
13. T
14. T
15. F
16. T
17. F
18. T
19. F
20. T
21. F
22. e
23. a
24. b
25. c
26. d
27. c
28. e
29. b
30. a
31. d
32. d
33. d
34. e
35. d
36. b
37. outcomes, states
38. expected value of perfect information, or EVPI
39. opportunity, obsolescence
40. utility
41. rollback
42. negative
43. obsolescence (or marginal)
44. sensitivity analysis
45. left, right; right, left

Answers to Selected Even-Numbered Exercises

Chapter 2

- **2-2** Because the Department of Commerce keeps statistics on all the cars sold in the United States, this conclusion is drawn from a *population.*
- **2-4** On the basis of German history since the end of World War II, and given the bias produced by his own strong belief in the validity of communism, Ulbricht was unable to foresee the possibility of the changes that resulted from Gorbachev's hands-off policy toward the eastern European satellite nations.
- **2-6** No conclusions follow easily from the data in their current form. Some rearrangement, such as listing in ascending order or finding the most frequent pair, might help in drawing conclusions.
- **2-8** No. In this case, the raw data would be a list of sample units indicating which were defective. The quality control section has already done some analysis in calculating the averages contained in the report.
- **2-10** In addition to the 7 stores with under 475 service actions that are not breaking even, another 6 stores fall on the "store watch list."
- **2-12**

5 Intervals

Class	Frequency	Relative Frequency
15–25	3	0.0667
26–36	4	0.0889
37–47	12	0.2667
48–58	18	0.4000
59–69	8	0.1778
	45	1.0000

11 Intervals

Class	Frequency	Relative Frequency
15–19	3	0.0667
20–24	0	0.0000
25–29	2	0.0444
30–34	2	0.0444
35–39	5	0.1111
40–44	3	0.0667
45–49	11	0.2444
50–54	3	0.0667
55–59	8	0.1778
60–64	5	0.1111
65–69	3	0.0667
	45	1.0000

(a) No: we can see from either distribution that more than 10 percent of the motorists drive at 55 mph or more. (5 intervals → over 17.78 percent; 11 intervals → 35.56 percent)

(b) Either can be used; the 11-interval distribution gives a more precise answer.

(c) The 5-interval distribution shows that 66.67 percent of the motorists drive between 37 and 58 mph, inclusive.

2-14 Sorting by either variable shows that hours watching television decreases as number of channels purchased increases.

2-16 (a)

Spread	SAT Differential	Spread	SAT Differential
1.3	140	0.1	−20
0.8	150	0.0	10
0.6	60	−0.1	−10
0.4	60	−0.2	20
0.3	60	−0.2	0
0.3	50	−0.5	−30
0.2	0	−0.5	−90
0.1	20	−0.6	−120
0.1	−10	−0.7	−100
0.1	−10	−1.1	−120

(b) 0.1.

(c) −10.

(d) High (low) spreads and high (low) SAT differentials tend to go together, so the SAT differential appears to be a good indicator of spread.

2-18

Pressure (lb/sq in.)	Relative Frequency
2,490.0–2,493.9	0.150
2,494.0–2,497.9	0.175
2,498.0–2,501.9	0.325
2,502.0–2,505.9	0.225
2,506.0–2,509.9	0.125
	1.000

The greatest number of samples (32.5%) fell in class 2,498.0–2,501.9 lb/sq in.

2-20 (a) Before:

Boxes Bought	Frequency	Relative Frequency
1– 2	5	0.25
3– 4	6	0.30
5– 6	7	0.35
7– 8	2	0.10
9–10	0	0.00
	20	**1.00**

(b) After:

Boxes Bought	Frequency	Relative Frequency
1– 2	2	0.10
3– 4	4	0.20
5– 6	6	0.30
7– 8	6	0.30
9–10	2	0.10
	20	**1.00**

(c) In order to be able to compare the two distributions.

(d)

"Change" Class	Frequency	Relative Frequency
−5 to −4	1	0.05
−3 to −2	0	0.00
−1 to 0	5	0.25
1 to 2	8	0.40
3 to 4	5	0.25
5 to 6	1	0.05
	20	**1.00**

(e) Sales appear to have increased, but the apparent increase could be due to other factors we don't know about, so we can't say for sure that the new slogan has helped.

■ **2-22**

Age	<25	25–34	35–44	45–54	≥55
Frequency	6	9	7	3	5
Relative frequency	0.200	0.300	0.233	0.100	0.167

(a) Most purchasers are under 45.

(b) About 75% of the purchasers are under 45.

■ **2-24** (a) No, not enough classes in relevant ranges.

(b) Five classes with midpoints at 25, 27, 29, 31, and 33.

■ **2-26** Closed: single, married, divorced, separated, widowed.
Open: single, married, other.

■ **2-28** The classes are <85, 85–114, 115–144, and ≥145 dB. Because the group wants to highlight the noisy flights, this distribution is not adequate because the 115–144 class includes noise levels on both sides of the 140 dB limit.

■ **2-30** (a)

Days	Frequency
22–24	3
25–27	3
28–30	6
31–33	12
34–36	8
37–39	6
40–42	5
43–45	4
46–48	2
49–51	1
	50

(b)

Days	Frequency
22–27	6
28–33	18
34–39	14
40–45	9
46–51	3
	50

(c) Yes, he wants to know the relative proportions at each level.

■ **2-32** (a) Discrete and closed.

(b) Discrete and closed.

(c) Flavor is qualitative, amount is quantitative.

(d) Collect data on how often stores run out of each flavor and how much of each is left over.

■ **2-34**

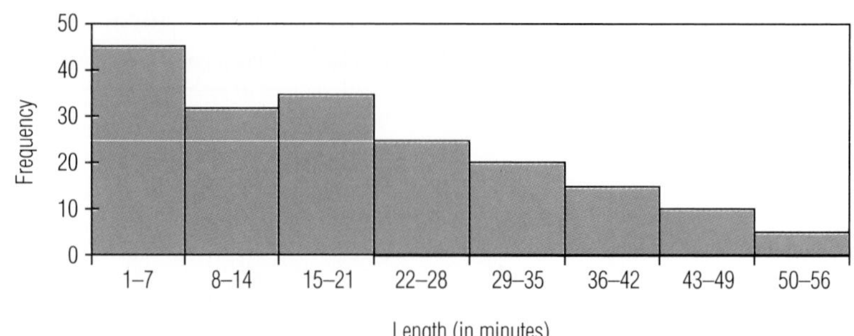

(a) The heights of the bars decrease from left to right: as the length of the call increases, the number of calls decreases.

(b) Whenever a phone becomes free, let the next longest call be made from it.

(c) Yes.

■ **2-36**

Class	Frequency	Cumulative Relative Frequency
2,000–3,999	3	0.15
4,000–5,999	7	0.50
6,000–7,999	7	0.85
8,000–9,999	3	1.00

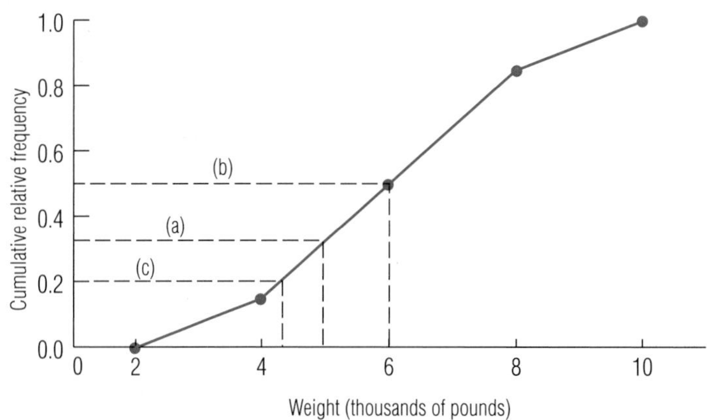

(a) About 65% break even, that is, catch 5,000 pounds or more.

(b) Approximately 6,000 pounds.

(c) Approximately 4,300 pounds.

■ **2-38** (a)

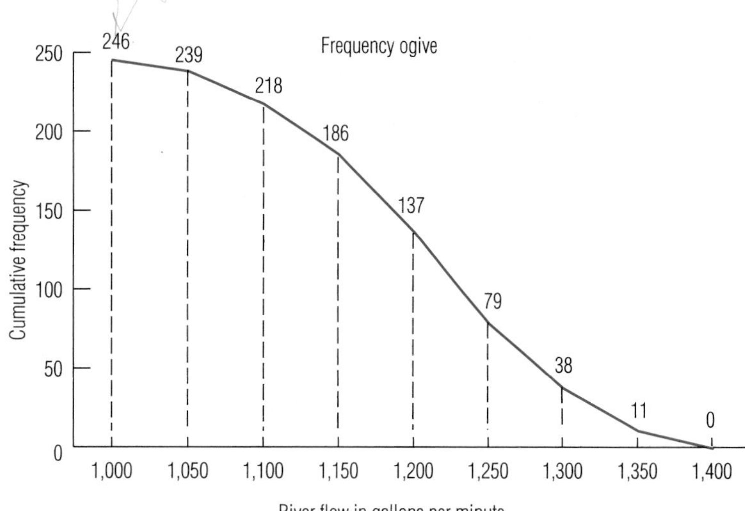

River flow more than	1,000	1,050	1,100	1,150	1,200	1,250	1,300	1,350	1,400
Cumulative frequency	246	239	218	186	137	79	38	11	0

(b)

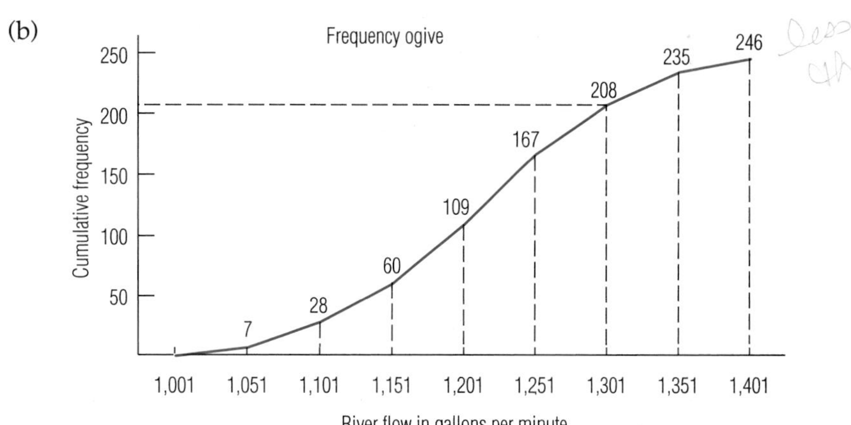

River flow less than	1,001	1,051	1,101	1,151	1,201	1,251	1,301	1,351	1,401
Cumulative frequency	0	7	28	60	109	167	208	235	246

(c) About 85%.

■ **2-40** (b)

Minutes	**Frequency**	**Cumulative Frequency**
19.0–19.7	4	4
19.8–20.5	4	8
20.6–21.3	10	18
21.4–22.1	5	23
22.2–22.9	7	30
23.0–23.7	5	35
23.8–24.5	11	46
24.6–25.3	4	50

(c)

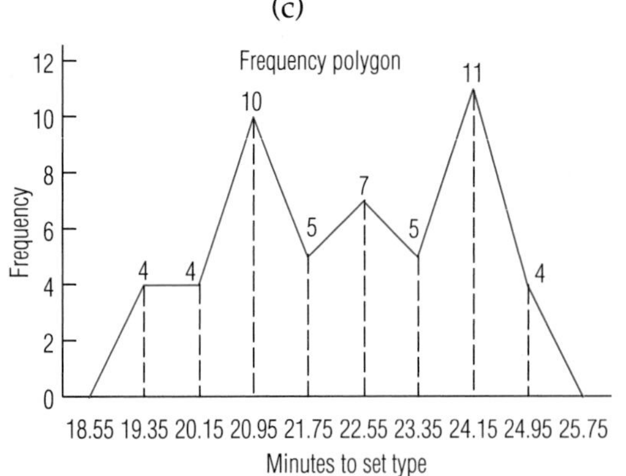

(d)

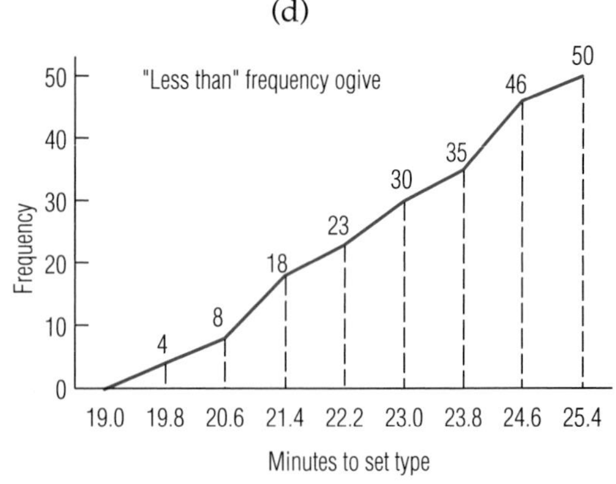

(e) About 78% of the time.

2-42

Earnings	Frequency	Cumulative Frequency
≤$ 5,000	5	0.038
$ 5,001– 10,000	9	0.108
10,001– 15,000	11	0.192
15,001– 20,000	33	0.446
20,001–30,000	37	0.731
30,001–40,000	19	0.877
40,001–50,000	9	0.946
≥50,001	7	1.000
	Total 130	

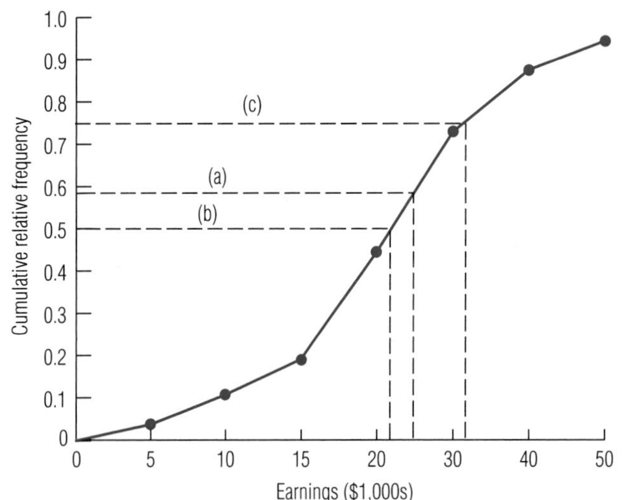

(a) About 42%. (b) About $22,000. (c) About $31,000.

2-44 By grouping those of the same educational level together, we can see group differences associated with educational level more clearly:

Educational Level	Salary Range
Did not finish high school	$14,400– 17,600
High school graduates	17,000– 30,400
One or two years of college	14,400– 22,400
College graduates	19,600– 34,400
Master's degrees	23,200– 36,200
Ph.D. degrees	29,000– 64,000
Doctors and lawyers	52,000–100,000

■ **2-46** (a)

1.9	1.8	1.7	1.6	1.5	1.5	1.5	1.5	1.2	0.9
0.9	0.9	0.9	0.8	0.7	0.7	0.5	0.4	0.4	0.3

(b)

Growth (inches)	Frequency	Relative Frequency	Cumulative Relative Frequency
0.000–0.249	0	0.00	0.00
0.250–0.499	3	0.15	0.15
0.500–0.749	3	0.15	0.30
0.750–0.999	5	0.25	0.55
1.000–1.249	1	0.05	0.60
1.250–1.499	0	0.00	0.60
1.500–1.749	6	0.30	0.90
1.750–1.999	2	0.10	1.00

(c) The data are distinctly bimodal, with modal classes 0.750–0.999 and 1.500–1.749.

(d)

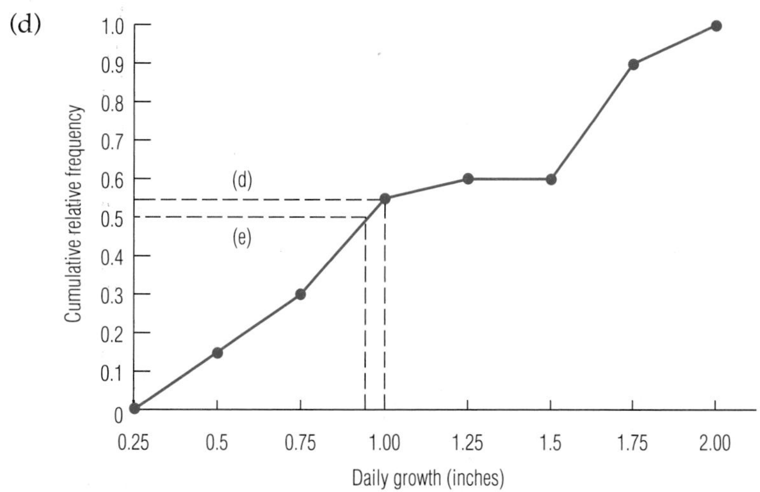

About 45% grew more than 1.0 inch per week.

(e) About 0.95 inch.

■ **2-48** The five classes used are 9,700–9,899 units, 9,900–10,099 units, . . . , 10,500–10,699 units, with cumulative relative frequencies 0.200, 0.733, 0.867, 0.867, and 1.000.

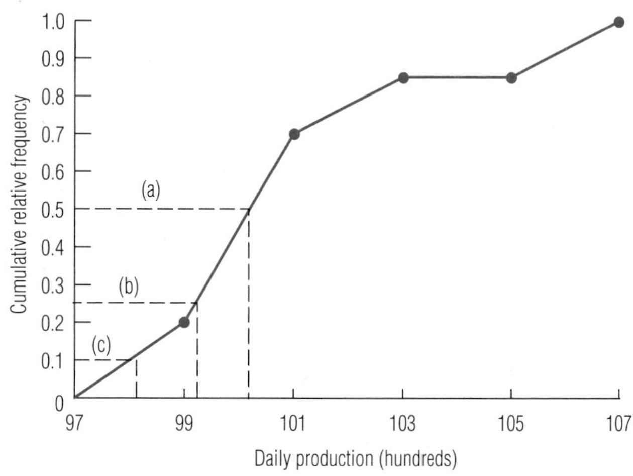

(a) About 50% (seven or eight items) exceeded the breakeven point.

(b) About 9,900 units.

(c) About 9,800 units.

■ **2-50** It tells you what fraction of the observations fit in each class, making it easier to compare samples or populations of different sizes.

■ **2-52** 2,000/(2,000 + 8,000) = 0.2; 0.2(250) = 50 women.

■ **2-54**

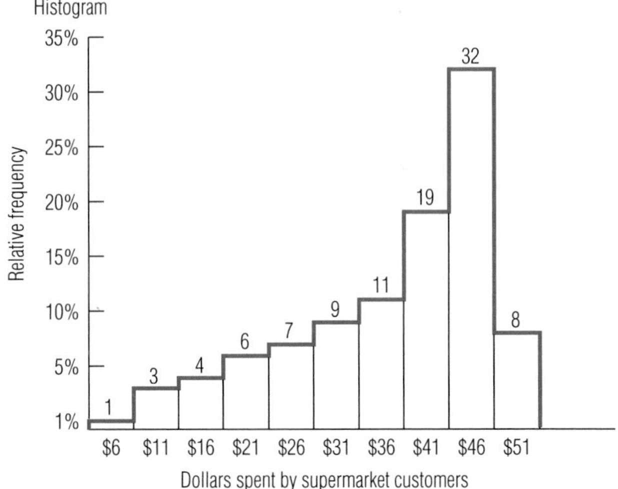

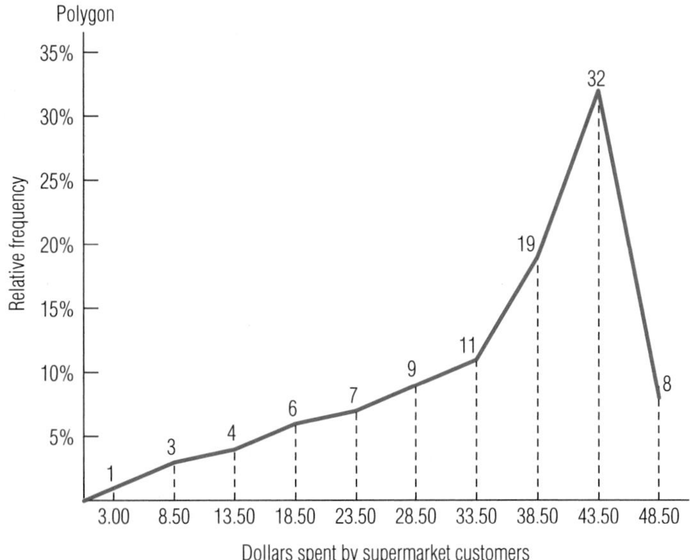

■ **2-56** About 75%.

■ **2-58** Because Ivy League schools tend to have more male undergraduates, the sample is not representative.

2-60 (a)

Journal	Frequency	Relative Frequency
1	1	0.0417
2	2	0.0833
3	2	0.0833
4	0	0.0000
5	2	0.0833
6	2	0.0833
7	3	0.1250
8	1	0.0417

Journal	Frequency	Relative Frequency
9	2	0.0833
10	1	0.0417
11	2	0.0833
12	2	0.0833
13	0	0.0000
14	2	0.0833
15	2	0.0833

(b)

Branch	Frequency	Relative Frequency
North	11	0.4583
West	8	0.3333
South	5	0.2083

(c)

Number of Publications	Frequency	Relative Frequency
1– 3	6	0.2500
4– 6	5	0.2083
7– 9	4	0.1667
10–12	4	0.1667
13–15	2	0.0833
16–18	2	0.0833
19–21	1	0.0417

(d) Faculty use of journals is widespread, but the North branch accounts for most of the publications. Well over half of the faculty publish 9 or fewer articles.

2-62 (1,2) Quantitative, discrete, open-ended. (3) Qualitative, discrete, closed. (4,5) Qualitative, discrete, open-ended (would probably include an "other" class).

2-64 Group I: None, 3; Mild, 7; Moderate, 5; Severe, 3.
Group II: None, 1; Mild, 4; Moderate, 8; Severe, 5.
This way it's much easier to compare the two groups.

2-66

Specialty	Frequency	Relative Frequency
Accounting	17	0.140
Marketing	41	0.339
Statistics	40	0.331
Finance	22	0.182
No publications	1	0.008

2-68 (a,b)

Percentage Won	Frequency	Relative Frequency	Cumulative Relative Frequency
0.000–0.199	2	0.0714	0.0714
0.200–0.399	8	0.2857	0.3571
0.400–0.599	7	0.2500	0.6071
0.600–0.799	10	0.3571	0.9643
0.800–0.999	1	0.0357	1.0000

(c)

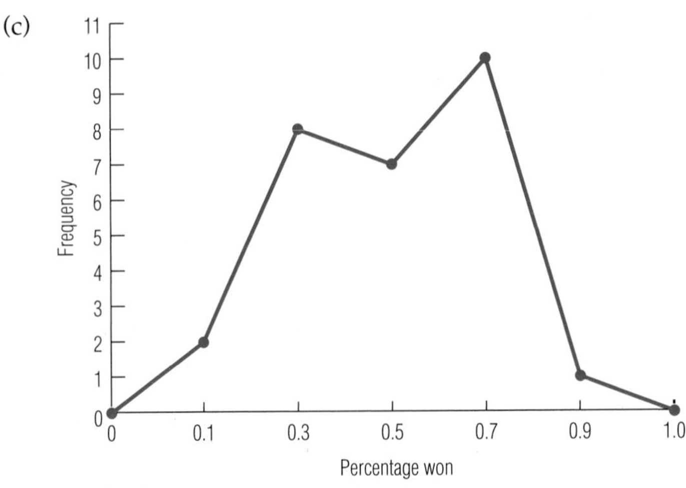

(d) See part (a) for the cumulative relative frequencies.

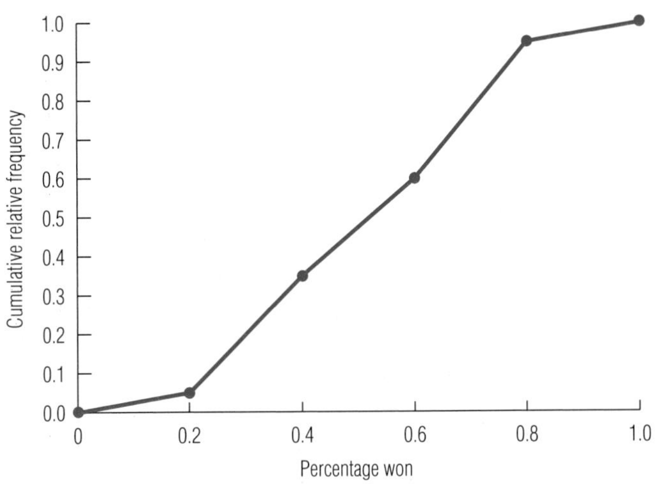

(e) The one team in the 0.800–0.999 class gets a playoff berth, as do 5 of the 10 teams in the 0.600–0.799 class.

■ **2-70** (b) 16 above the limit, 18 below, 1 exactly at.

(c)

Class (minutes)	60–69	70–79	80–89	90–99	100–109	110–119	120–129	130–139
Frequency	2	2	3	6	6	11	4	1
Relative frequency	0.057	0.057	0.086	0.171	0.171	0.314	0.114	0.029

(d) If 108 minutes is typical, then about half should be above 108 and half below. The data support this. Because we don't know how much downtime per shift is viewed as excessive, we cannot tell whether Cline should be concerned.

■ **2-72** (b) 92%; 4%.

(c) 64%; stop ordering from the new supplier.

2-74 (b)

1. Class (sales)	1	2	3	4	5	6	7	8	[illegible]
Frequency	10	3	4	1	4	2	2	1	[illegible]
Relative frequency	0.357	0.107	0.143	0.036	0.143	0.071	0.071	0.036	0.0[illegible]

2. Class (sales)	1–3	4–6	7–9
Frequency	17	7	4
Relative frequency	0.607	0.250	0.143

Both distributions are skewed: many countries have relatively few sales, and then the distribution tails off to the right.

2-76 (a) 4,600–5,199, 5,200–5,799, 5,800–6,399, 6,400–6,999, 7,000–7,599, and 7,600–8,199.

(b) 0.00–1.39, 1.40–2.79, 2.80–4.19, 4.20–5.59, 5.60–6.99, and 7.00–8.39.

2-78 (a) 13.1%. (b) 47.5%.

2-80 A histogram will further highlight the pattern of low numbers of customers from 11 P.M. to 6 A.M., then increasing fairly steadily until 11 A.M. or noon, remaining reasonably steady until 5 P.M., and then decreasing fairly steadily until 11 P.M. One limitation: national data may not apply to Utah. For example, if there were many factories close by, the number of customers at Fresh Foods might reflect changes in work shifts at those factories.

Chapter 3

3-2

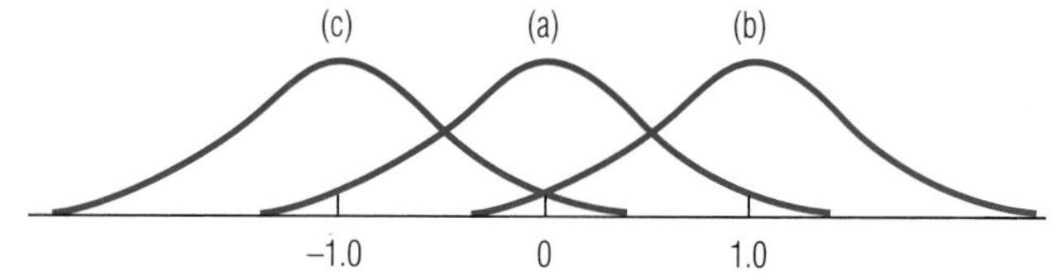

3-4 (a) B. (b) A. (c) A. (d) B. (e) B. (f) A. (g) Neither.

3-6 $\bar{x} = 9.091$; they don't qualify.

3-8 (a)

Age	40–49	50–59	60–69	70–79	80–89
Frequency	4	4	3	2	7

(b) 67. (c) 66.75.

(d) As expected, they are close, but not exactly the same.

3-10 For the first six months, the average is $272.33 < 300$, so the owner will not build the new store.

3-12 $\bar{x} = 23.295$ seconds: the manager should be concerned.

3-14 (a) Q1: 20, Q2: 10, Q3: 30, Q4: 25 (all values in thousands of dollars).

(b) Y1: 13.75, Y2: 15, Y3: 35.

(c) All three averages mentioned are equal to 21.25.

3-16 88.55, 87.75, 89.55, 86.65, 88.50.

3-18 2.021 times.

3-20 $0.1162 per ounce.

3-22 7.58% per year.

3-24 8.98% per year; 22,819 units.

3-26 7.24% per week.

3-28 4.66% per year; $75.66.

3-30 (a) 722.5 miles. (b) 709.1 miles. (c) Both equally good.
3-32 (a) The 192nd item. (b) 70–79.5 (c) 0.1190 (d) 71.190
(e) 71.1905; (d) and (e) differ slightly because of rounding.
3-34 Median = 31 minutes; speeds are not excessive.
3-36 $877.54.
3-38 (a) 2 books (b) 2.3 books
(c) Since the distribution is skewed, the mode is better.
3-40 (a) Brunette. (b) A. (c) Wednesday and Saturday.
3-42 $928.57.
3-44 (a) $1,000–1,499. (b) $1,240. (c) Approximately 628.
3-46 C
3-48 A, because it has less variability.
3-50 There are many ways that the concept may be involved. Certainly, the FTC would examine the price variability for the industry and compare the result to that of the suspect companies. The agency might examine price distributions for similar products, for the same products in a city, or for the same products in different cities. If the variability was significantly different in any of these cases, this result might constitute evidence of a conspiracy to set prices at the same levels.
3-52 29.
3-54 94 degrees.
3-56 Range: 1.10 minutes; interquartile range: 0.32 minute.
3-58 Range = 496.3 megabytes; interquartile range = 376.5 megabytes.
3-60 (a) 410. (b) 236.5, 104, 467. (c) 276.
3-62 The standard deviation of 3.1 boats represents an unacceptable level of variability.
3-64 With a standard deviation of 242.3 checks per day, he should worry.
3-66 (a) $\bar{x} = 7.715$ days, $s = 4.69$ days.
(b) at least 150 expected, something between 182 and 191 observed.
(c) 190 expected.
3-68 5 weeks; 1 week.
3-70

Product	1	2	3
Standard score	−1.25	−1.67	2.22

Product 3 is farthest from average.
3-72 $390,000 ± $20,000.
3-74

Team	Bullets	Trailblazers
CV	8.04%	6.15%

The Bullets' weights have the greater coefficient of variance (CV).
3-76

Program	Regular	Evening
CV	10.02%	9.46%

There isn't much difference between the two groups.
3-78

Company	1	2
CV	18.93%	12.70%

Company 1 pursued the riskier strategy.

■ **3-80**

Employee	John	Jeff	Mary	Tammy
CV	5.67%	1.69%	13.51%	7.61%

Jeff is the best employee.

■ **3-82**

Configuration	1	II	III
CV	13.79%	29.41%	10.13%

Configuration III has least relative variation.

■ **3-84** The statement is incorrect because it completely ignores the variability in yards gained per carry.

■ **3-86** Officer salaries: A, aircraft maintenance: C, food purchases: B.

■ **3-88** The company may be hiring less experienced sales reps while its established sales reps are increasing their sales levels. Another possibility is that it is simultaneously hiring inexperienced and highly experienced sales reps.

■ **3-90** The later period has both a higher mean and more variability.

■ **3-92** (a) 90.8889. (b) 79. (c) No mode for ungrouped data.
(d) Median. (e) 64.0736.

■ **3-94** $CV_1 = 5.0\%$, $CV_2 = 5.3\%$, #2 is less accurate.

■ **3-96** (a) Neither.
(b) The weekend (Friday and Saturday) and weekday (Sunday through Thursday) populations are distinctly different, so the data should not be treated as a single population.

■ **3-98** 9.9, 11.2, 12.7, 13.6, 14.5, 15.3, 16.6, 17.7, 18.6, 19.6; 17.8.

■ **3-100** (a) Standard deviation. (b) Range.
(c) Since the data are fairly evenly spread, the range is a reasonable measure of the variability.

■ **3-102** (a) 10 days. (b) 7.5 days.

■ **3-104** The weekly news magazines would probably have the highest average readerships, the medical journals the smallest average readerships, with the monthly magazines somewhere in the middle.

Monthly magazines and medical journals with many low-circulation items and few high-circulation items are likely to be skewed to the right. There are only a few weekly news magazines, so it's difficult to assess the skewness of this distribution.

■ **3-106** (a) 5.51 mpg. (b) 5.5325 mpg.
(c)

Class (mpg)	4.77–5.03	5.04–5.30	5.31–5.57	5.58–5.84	5.85–6.11
Frequency	4	4	0	1	7

The modal class is 5.85–6.11 mpg.

(d) It depends. If she is ordering fuel for only one car, she should be cautious and use the modal value. If she is ordering fuel for several cars running in the same race, the mean or median is probably OK.

■ **3-108** (a) Mean = 35.4 bulbs, median = 35 bulbs.
(b) Skewed right.

■ **3-110** (a) Median = 4.32 mm; modal class = 4.01–4.50 mm.
(b) 3.5mm screen.

■ **3-112** Mean = \$4.12, median = \$4.61.
The median is better, since the mean is distorted by the observation for Southwest (\$0.14), which is clearly an outlier.

Chapter 4

- **4-2** Extensive tests with animals indicated (with other factors held as constant as possible) that subjects that consumed saccharin were more likely to develop cancer than those not exposed to saccharin. Extrapolating these results to humans, it was concluded that saccharin consumption produces an increased risk of cancer.
- **4-4** This decision involves estimates of consumer preference, brand loyalty, competitor response, and numerous other factors, all involving uncertainty. Hence the estimates are based on probabilities.
- **4-6** (a) (B,S) (B,B) (S,S) (S,B). (b) (B,B,B) (B,B,S) (B,S,S) (B,S,B) (S,B,B) (S,B,S) (S,S,B) (S,S,S).
- **4-8** 0; 1/54; 6/54; 6/54; 5/54; 3/54; 1/54.
- **4-10** (a) They are collectively exhaustive, but not mutually exclusive.
  (b) There are 17 possible subsets of the set of target segments that can be covered within the $800,000 budget:

M	Bu	W	P	Bl	M,W	M,P
M,Bl	M,W,P	M,P,Bl	Bu,W	Bu,P	Bu,Bl	W,P
W,Bl	W,P,Bl	P,Bl				

  (c) The only subsets for which the entire budget is spent are

  Bu,W Bu,Bl M,W,P M,P,Bl
- **4-12** (a) 6/26. (b) 5/26. (c) 1/2. (d) 1/4.
- **4-14**

Interval	0.00–0.24	0.25–0.49	0.50–0.74	0.75–0.99	1.00
Probability	0.00	0.20	0.50	0.25	0.05

- **4-16** (a) Subjective. (b) Relative frequency or subjective. (c) Classical. (d) Relative frequency. (e) Classical. (f) Relative frequency or subjective.
- **4-18** P(*A*) = 21/100; P(*B*) = 29/100; P(C) = 38/100; P(*A* or *B*) = 45/100; P(*A* or C) = 50/100 P(*B* but not (*A* or C)) = 20/100
- **4-20** (a) When *A* and *B* are mutually exclusive, P(*A* and *B*) = 0
  (b) P(*A* or *B* or C) = P(*A*) + P(*B*) + P(C) − P(*A* and *B*) − P(*A* and C) − P(*B* and C) + P(*A* and *B* and C)
  (c) P(*A* or *B* or C) = P(*A*) + P(*B*) + P(C) − P(*A* and C) − P(*B* and C)
  (d) P(*A* or *B* or C) = P(*A*) + P(*B*) + P(C) − P(*B* and C)
  (e) P(*A* or *B* or C) = P(*A*) + P(*B*) + P(C)
- **4-22** (a) 0.0625.
  (b) Lower (86.25 percent).
- **4-24** (a) 1/2. (b) 1/2.
- **4-26** (a) 6/32. (b) 6/32. (c) 1/32.
- **4-28** (a) 0.02.
  (b) 0.07.
  (c) 0.0014.
- **4-30** (a) 0.5576.
  (b) 0.1224.
- **4-32** (a) 0.481545. (b) 0.015795. (c) 0.0136. (d) 0.000585.
  (e) 0.013.
- **4-34** 3/7; 2/3; 5/63; 10/21.
- **4-36** 0.356.

■ **4-38** (a) 0.646. (b) 0.4845.
■ **4-40** 0.5525
■ **4-42** (a) 0.585. (b) 0.78.
■ **4-44** (a) 0.739. (b) 0.169. (c) 0.092.
■ **4-46** P(storm) = 0.61; P(moist | storm) = 0.4426
■ **4-48** (a) 0.336. (b) 0.5.
■ **4-50** (a) 0.3810. (b) 0.5.
■ **4-52** The difference in life insurance premiums agrees with our common-sense belief that the risk of dying in any given year increases as we get older. Higher automobile insurance rates for younger drivers suggest that they have a higher probability of being involved in accidents.
■ **4-54** They have used data on the past rate of failure for restaurants to predict the current rate.
■ **4-56** (a) 1/5. (b) 2/5. (c) 3/5. (d) classical.
■ **4-58** (a) No: There are no vice-presidential nominations during the midterm elections.
(b) No: He could be renominated and reelected. However, winning and losing the nomination are clearly mutually exclusive.
(c) No: He could be renominated but lose the election.
■ **4-60** Only (c).
■ **4-62** (a) 2/6 = 0.3333. (b) Relative frequency.
(c) Inaccurate: small number of observations; sampled plants similar, but not the same.
■ **4-64** (a) 0.75.
(b) The given information is not sufficient to answer the question.
■ **4-66** (a) P(collision) = 0.0295 > 0.025; diversion required.
(b) P(collision | flight 100 five minutes late) = 0.02 < 0.025; diversion not required.
(c) P(collision | flight 200 five minutes early) = 0.03 > 0.025; diversion required.
■ **4-68** (a) 120/300 = 0.4. (b) 21/300 = 0.07.
■ **4-70** (a) 0.5746. (b) 0.2388. (c) 0.1866.
■ **4-72**

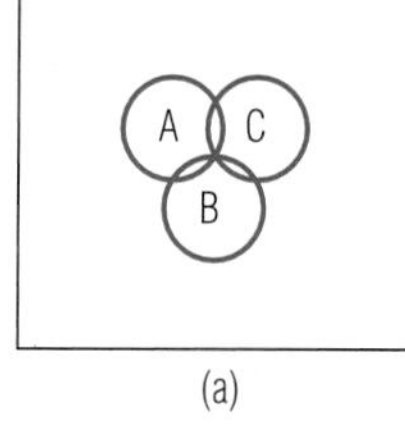

(a)

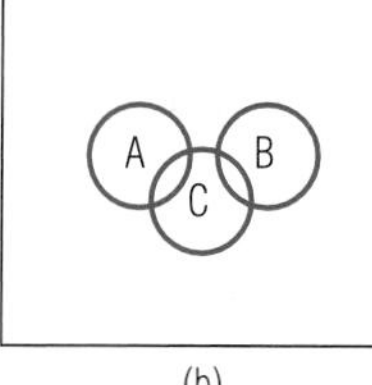

(b)

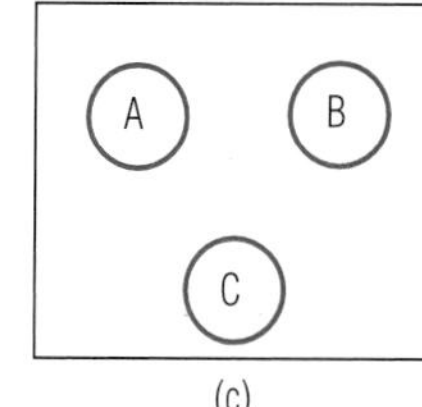

(c)

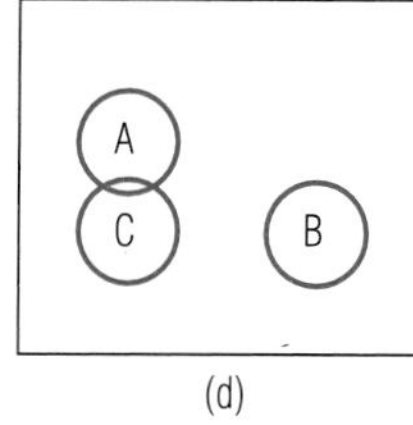

(d)

■ **4-74** (a) 0.005. (b) 0.003. (c) 0.175.
■ **4-76** (a) 3/15, 2/15. (b) 10/45. (c) 15/30.
■ **4-78** (a) 0.0565, 0.1135. (b) 1. (c) 0.2599.
(d) 0.17, not enough information.
■ **4-80** (a) 0.0667. (b) 0.2000. (c) 0.0667.
■ **4-82** (a) 0.0011, 0.0120. (b) 0.0093.
■ **4-84** 0.96.
■ **4-86** (a) Once in every 4,167 flights. (b) 6/50,000. (c) $(6/50{,}000)^2$.

Chapter 5

5-2

Total	2	3	4	5	6	7	8	9	10	11	12
Probability	1/36	2/36	3/36	4/36	5/36	6/36	5/36	4/36	3/36	2/36	1/36

5-4

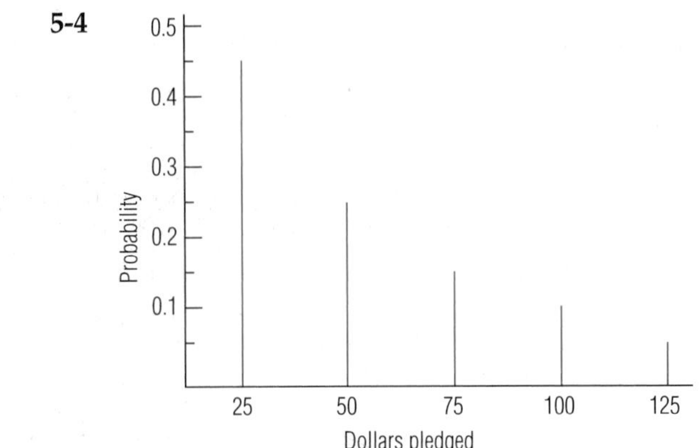

5-6

Number sold	2,500	5,000	5,500
Probability	0.2	0.7	0.1

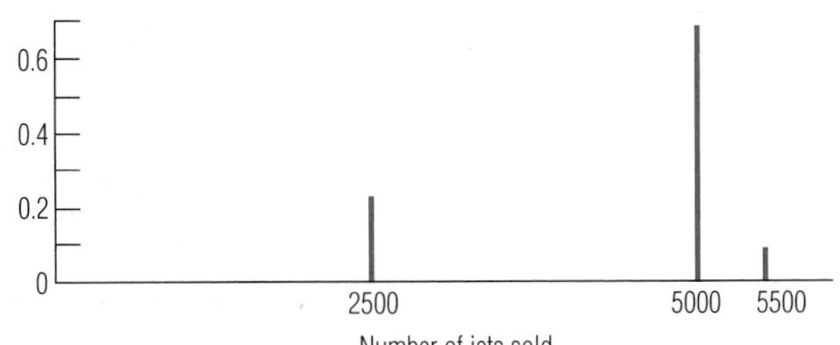

5-8 (a)

Outcome	8,000	9,000	10,000	11,000	12,000	13,000
Probability	0.05	0.15	0.25	0.30	0.20	0.05

(b) \$10,600.

5-10 The expected value of the maintenance cost is \$77, so Jim should not spend \$100 for the insurance.

5-12 13.29 months.

5-14 For the truck and air divisions, respectively, the expected numbers of lost letters per month are 3.083 and 3.167, so he should investigate the air division.

5-16 16 cars.

5-18 (a) 0.0043. (b) 0.1480. (c) 1. (d) 0.0333.

5-20 (a) $\mu = 3$, $\sigma = 1.549$. (b) $\mu = 3.36, \sigma = 1.396$.
(c) $\mu = 4.32$, $\sigma = 2.015$. (d) $\mu = 14.21, \sigma = 2.692$.
(e) $\mu = 134.82$, $\sigma = 10.320$.

5-22 (a) 0.0009. (b) 0.8171.

5-24 (a) Claim 1 implies that $p = 0.40$, claim 2 that $p = 0.467$; so they are not consistent.
(b) No, since they claim that $p = 0.40$.

5-26 (a) 0.9953. (b) 0.7031. (c) 0.0047. (d) 0.5155.

5-28 (a) 0.0183. (b) 0.1465. (c) 0.1954. (d) 0.3711.

■ **5-30** (a) 0.1424 (b) 0.9841 (c) 0.1605 (d) 0.2696

■ **5-32** Yes, the probability of resting at least 12 minutes is 0.5859.

■ **5-34** (a) 0.323323. (b) 0.135335.

■ **5-36** (a) 0.00674. (b) 0.01813. (c) 0.00016.

■ **5-38** (a) 0.7422. (b) 0.9484. (c) 0.0016. (d) 0.4658.

■ **5-40** (a) 0.2712. (b) 0.2946. (c) 0.8749. (d) 0.1492. (e) 0.5496.

■ **5-42** 0.4870.

■ **5-44** $P(3.9 < x < 4.1) = 0.7745$; the standards are not satisfied.

■ **5-46** (a) 0.2537. (b) 0.1210. (c) 0.1489.

■ **5-48** (a) 0.1056

(b) Yes: the $200 cost is less than the $528 expected loss to future business.

■ **5-50** (a) 0.3372. (b) 0.1587. (c) 0.68. (d) 0.32.

■ **5-52** (a) Normal. (b) Poisson. (c) Binomial. (d) Normal.

■ **5-54** A random variable is discrete if it can assume only a limited number of values, and continuous if it can assume all values in a given range. The different types of random variables have different probability functions (also called discrete and continuous) associated with them.

■ **5-56** (a) 0.0413. (b) 0.1606.

■ **5-58** 11 interns.

■ **5-60** (a) Normal. (b) Binomial. (c) Poisson. (d) Normal.

■ **5-62** 0.01832; 0.00529.

■ **5-64** (a) 0.2252. (b) 0.0131. (c) 0.2361. (d) 0.1484.

■ **5-66** (a) 0.9943. (b) 0.0208. (c) 0.7346.

■ **5-68** (a)

Number of copies	7,700	8,500	10,000	11,000	15,000
Probability	0.10	0.25	0.45	0.10	0.10

(b) 15,000 pamphlets.

■ **5-70** (a) $1,324 (b) $1,248

■ **5-72** (a) Yes: knowing that the average number of customers varies from day to day enables the manager to know how convenient the ATM maintenance will be, on average.

(b) Yes: only the Friday data are relevant if the maintenance is rescheduled for Friday.

■ **5-74** (a) $P(x > 20{,}000) = P(z > 1.58) = 0.5 - 0.4429 = 0.0571$.

(b) $P(x < 10{,}000) = P(z < -2.42) = 0.5 - 0.4922 = 0.0078$.

(c) $P(14{,}000 < x < 17{,}500) = P(-0.82 < z < 0.58) = 0.2939 + 0.2190 = 0.5129$.

■ **5-76** (a) $P(x \geq 28) = P(z \geq 0.53) = 0.5 - 0.2019 = 0.2981$.

(b) $P(x < 12) = P(z < -1.60) = 0.5 - 0.4452 = 0.0548$.

■ **5-78** (a) $\mu = \$77{,}685$, $\sigma = \$13{,}751$

(b.1) 0.0526 (b.2) 0.0985 (b.3) 0.4755

(c) 2.74

(d.1) 0.2415 (d.2) 0.4638 (d.3) 0.2947

■ **5-80** (a) 0.9984 (exact answer is 0.9943, 0.4 percent error).

(b) 0.0146 (exact answer is 0.0208, 30 percent error).

(c) 0.7123 (exact answer is 0.7346, 3 percent error).

■ **5-82** 25,000 roses.
■ **5-84** The probabilities of 0, 1, 2, 3, or 4 towers going dark are 0.62742, 0.31019, 0.05751, 0.00474, and 0.00015, respectively.
■ **5-86** (a) $\mu = 1{,}168$, $\sigma = 15.28$. (b) $\mu = 1{,}021.79$, $\sigma = 15.33$.
■ **5-88** 0.0197; the 40% estimate appears to be overly optimistic.
■ **5-90** (a) 10/39 or 0.2564. (a.1) 0.0049. (a.2) 0.5189. (a.3) 0.1796.
(b) $\bar{x} = 10.967$, $s = 20.904$.
(c.1) 0.2514. (c.2) 0.3859. (c.3) 0.4678.

Chapter 6

■ **6-2** Not necessarily. If there is little information available about the population of interest, the best judgment of the individual conducting the study could suggest that probability sampling be used.
■ **6-4** Probability samples involve more statistical analysis and planning at the beginning of a study and usually take more time and money than judgment samples.
■ **6-6** From what we've been told in the problem, Jean's position is apparently quite defensible. Perhaps what makes statistical sampling unique is that it permits statistical inference to be made about a population and its parameters. This is apparently what Jean has done. There are no hard and fast rules as to the size of the sample that must be drawn before inferences can be made. Specifically, there is nothing magic about the 50 percent mark. Common sense would seem to point out that gathering data from 50 percent of some populations might tend to be just as difficult as gathering data from the entire population—for instance, the population of the United States or the world. The defense for Jean's position lies in empirical evidence and some explanation and reasoning with management, educating it about the abilities of statistical inference.
■ **6-8** (b), because there is greater between-group and lesser within-group variance.
■ **6-10** Assuming a nonleap year: 1/6, 1/24, 2/11, 3/1, 3/19, 4/6, 4/24, 5/12, 5/30, 6/17, 7/5, 7/23, 8/10, 8/28, 9/15, 10/3, 10/21, 11/8, 11/26, 12/14.
■ **6-12** The probability of each is 0.10; you would expect to see each one 11.5 times; sixteen 4's, thirteen 7's, and ten 2's; random variation and small sample size.
■ **6-14** No. If both parents work, no one will be at home between noon and 5:00, and some of the heaviest users of day care will be excluded from the survey.
■ **6-16** Every seventh is better, because every fifth examines the same positions in each batch.
■ **6-18** Stratified sampling would work in this case, because there appear to be three homogeneous groups.
■ **6-20** Sampling error.
■ **6-22** In general, overestimating the mean is neither better nor worse than underestimating. In this case, the underestimate (30¢) is closer to the true mean (31.4¢) than is the overestimate (35¢).
■ **6-24** Average weekly sales have decreased from 3,538 cartons to 3,462 cartons.
■ **6-26** It is a sample from the sampling distribution of the mean of samples of size 30 drawn from the population.
■ **6-28** (a) 0.9312. (b) 0.9312. (c) 0.9962.
■ **6-30** At least 355.

■ **6-32** (a) $P(z \geq 0.71) = 0.5000 - 0.2611 = 0.2389$.
(b) $P(z \geq 1.01) = 0.5000 - 0.3438 = 0.1562$.
It has decreased by 0.0827.

■ **6-34** (a) $P(z \geq 0.08) = 0.5000 - 0.0319 = 0.4681$.
(b) $P(z \leq -0.21) = 0.5000 - 0.0832 = 0.4168$.

■ **6-36** $P(z < 1.08) = 0.5000 + 0.3599 = 0.8599 > 0.80$.
The overhaul will not be ordered.

■ **6-38** (a) 120 bu. (b) 1.549 bu.
(c) $P(z > 2.45) = 0.5000 - 0.4929 = 0.0071$.
(d) $P(-1.94 < z < 1.29) = 0.4738 + 0.4015 = 0.8753$.

■ **6-40** (a) 0.572 (b) 0.9599 (c) 0.750

■ **6-42** (a) 0.4725. (b) 0.3504. (c) 0.1879.

■ **6-44** $P(z \geq 0.71) = 0.5000 - 0.2611 = 0.2389$.

■ **6-46** $P(-1.78 < z < 1.64) = 0.4625 + 0.4495 = 0.9120$.

■ **6-48** $P(-1.15 \leq z \leq 1.15) = 0.3749 + 0.3749 = 0.7498$.

■ **6-50** Judgmental, because a pair of skates is inspected only if its size is sufficiently close to Crash's skate size.

■ **6-52** Yes.

■ **6-54** At least 128 customers.

■ **6-56** Although there are apparently no constraints due to time, cost, destructive sampling, or accessibility, sampling can still be appropriate. It will get essentially the same information with less effort, and the clerks will be reassigned earlier.

■ **6-58** No. A sampling distribution of $\bar{x}$ is a frequency distribution of the means of all possible samples. It is not a graph of the individual observations in samples.

■ **6-60** (a) $\mu = \$11.108, \sigma = \$2.320$. (b) $\bar{x} = \$12.152$.
(c) $\mu_{\bar{x}} = \$11.108, \sigma_{\bar{x}} = \$0.773$.
(d) No: sample small, population not even approximately normal (skewed right, mode too frequent).
(e) $P(-0.79 \leq z \leq 0.77) = 0.2852 + 0.2794 = 0.5646$.

■ **6-62** $P(z < 2.76) = 0.5000 + 0.4971 = 0.9971$.

■ **6-64** At least 25 alarms.

■ **6-66** (a) Enumeration. (b) Finite population.

Chapter 7

■ **7-2** Measuring an entire population may not be feasible because of time and cost considerations. A sample yields only an estimate and is subject to sampling errors.

■ **7-4** An estimator is a sample statistic used to estimate a population parameter. An estimate is a specific numerical value for an estimator resulting from the particular sample observed.

■ **7-6** It assures us that the estimator becomes more reliable with larger samples.

■ **7-8** $\bar{x} = 296.583$ people, $s = 40.751$ people

■ **7-10** 0.46.

■ **7-12** (a) 0.181. (b) (6.019, 6.381).

■ **7-14** (a) 0.0390 pounds. (b) (14.122, 14.278) pounds.

■ **7-16** 7 ± 0.208 cars.

■ **7-18** (a) 29.8 ± 1.786 students.

(b) No, we cannot be 95.5% certain that the average class size in Forsight County is less than that in Hindsight County.

■ **7-20** The range of an estimate between and including the upper and lower confidence limits.

■ **7-22** (a) High confidence levels produce wide intervals, so we sacrifice precision to gain confidence.

(b) Narrow intervals result from low confidence levels, so we sacrifice confidence to gain precision.

■ **7-24** No, it is based on the expected results if the sampling process is repeated many times.

■ **7-26** (a) 25 ± 4.9 minutes. (b) 15 ± 3.267 minutes.

(c) 38 ± 1.96 minutes. (d) 20 ± 9.8 minutes.

(e) These are prediction intervals for the next observation rather than confidence intervals for the population mean based on a sample that has already been taken.

■ **7-28** (a) 112.4 ± 1.697. (b) 112.4 ± 2.234.

■ **7-30** (a) 0.184 typos per page. (b) (4.00, 4.60) typos per page.

■ **7-32** 24.3 ± 0.935 minutes.

■ **7-34** $250,000 ± $2,380.

■ **7-36** (a) 0.0520 (b) 0.1818 ± 0.0855

■ **7-38** (a) 0.0238. (b) 0.87 ± 0.0555.

■ **7-40** (a) 0.6 ± 0.076. (b) 1,800 ± 228 accounts.

■ **7-42** 0.6 ± 0.1497.

■ **7-44** (a) 1.761. (b) 2.571. (c) 2.878. (d) 2.492. (e) 3.250.

(f) 1.684.

■ **7-46** (55.65, 68.35).

■ **7-48** (68.58, 75.42).

■ **7-50** 31 ± 5.58 accidents.

■ **7-52** $n \geq 1413$.

■ **7-54** $n \geq 385$; $n \geq 289$; $n \geq 289$.

■ **7-56** $n \geq 23$ bags.

■ **7-58** $n \geq 60$ days.

■ **7-60** An interval estimate gives an indication of possible error through the extent of its range and its associated confidence level. A point estimate is only a single number, and thus one needs additional information to determine its reliability.

■ **7-62** $n \geq 9{,}604$ grades.

■ **7-64** (a) 0.3 mph. (b) 0.0397 mph. (c) 23.2 ± 0.0778 mph.

■ **7-66** It is unbiased, consistent, efficient, and sufficient.

■ **7-68** (a) 78.88%. (b) 98.36%. (c) 90.70%.

■ **7-70** $n \geq 543$ stocks (using $p = 0.5$; $p = 0.85$ gives $n \geq 277$).

■ **7-72** Yes. The entire interval (0.5314, 0.8760) is above 0.50, so they can be more than 95% confident of breaking even at least half the time.

■ **7-74** (a) 3.56%. (b) $n \geq 338$.

■ **7-76** 2.88% ± 1.59%; because $n < 30$, normality must be assumed.

■ **7-78** (a) 0.0195 apple. (b) 3.2 ± 0.0195 apples.

■ **7-80** (a) $\bar{x}$ = $425.39, s = $107.10. (b) $425.39 ± $14.84.

7-82 (a) 0.0990 mg/li. (b) 5.2 ± 0.0990 mg/li.

7-84 0.3333 ± 0.0843.

7-86 (a) 0.0440 mph. (b) 66.3 ± 0.0880 mph.
(c) Yes, since the entire interval lies below 67 mph.

7-88 $n \geq 11$ acres.

Chapter 8

For the solutions of exercises that require testing specific hypotheses, we give the observed value of the test statistic, the appropriate limit(s) of the acceptance region (denoted by subscripts L or U), and the conclusion.

8-2 Theoretically, one could toss a coin a large number of times to see if the proportion of heads was very different from 0.5. Similarly, by recording the outcomes of many dice rolls, one could see if the proportion of any side was very different from 1/6. A large number of trials would be needed for each of these examples.

8-4 Assume a hypothesis about a population, collect sample data, calculate a sample statistic, then use the sample statistic to evaluate the hypothesis.

8-6 We mean that we would not have reasonably expected to find that particular sample if in fact the hypothesis had been true.

8-8 0.0802.

8-10 $\bar{x} = 26{,}100$, $\bar{x}_L = 27{,}000$, $\bar{x}_U = 30{,}000$, so Ned should not purchase the Stalwarts. If σ has increased, the conclusion might not be valid.

8-12 $\bar{x} = 2.2$, $\bar{x}_L = 2.423$, $\bar{x}_U = 2.577$, so the claim is unreasonable.

8-14 A null hypothesis represents the hypothesis you are trying to reject; the alternative hypothesis represents all other possibilities.

8-16 Type I: rejecting a null hypothesis when in fact it is true.
Type II: accepting a null hypothesis when in fact it is false.

8-18 The significance level of a test is the probability of a Type I error.

8-20 (a) t with 34df (normal). (b) Normal. (c) Normal.
(d) t with 28 df. (e) t with 23 df.

8-22 A one-tailed test would be used when we are testing whether the population mean is higher (upper-tailed test) or lower (lower-tailed test) than some hypothesized value. We use a two-tailed test to determine whether the population mean is different (in either direction) from the hypothesized value.

8-24 H_0: $\mu = 3124$, H_1: $\mu < 3124$.

8-26 $z = -1.74$ ($\bar{x} = \$42.95$), $z_L = -2.05$ ($\bar{x}_L = \$42.59$), so don't reject H_0. Atlas should not believe the price has decreased.

8-28 $z = -1.46$ ($\bar{x} = 954$ hours), $z_{CRIT} = \pm 1.96$ ($\bar{x}_L = 951.94$, $\bar{x}_U = 968.06$), so do not reject H_0. The new bulb is meeting specifications.

8-30 $z = 1.48$ ($\bar{x} = \$151$), $z_U = 1.28$($\bar{x}_U = \$150$), so reject H_0. Their commissions are significantly higher.

8-32 $z = -9.30$ ($\bar{x} = 0.33$ percent), $z_L = -2.33$ ($\bar{x}_L = 0.51$ percent), so reject H_0. The growth rate has decreased significantly.

8-34 0.0505, 0.1271, 0.2611.

8-36 0.0202, 0.0606, 0.1469.

8-38 $z = -1.15$ ($\bar{p} = 0.1412$), $z_L = -1.75$ ($\bar{p}_L = 0.1155$), so don't reject H_0. There is not evidence that West Coast distribution is significantly worse.

8-40 (a) $z = -2.12$ ($\bar{p} = 0.0944$), $z_L = -1.64$ ($\bar{p}_L = 0.1072$), so reject H_0. Yes, they should conclude that transmission is reduced.

(b) $z_L = -2.05$ ($\bar{p}_L = 0.0963$), so the conclusion is unchanged.

(c) Not necessarily: Among other reasons, we have been given no information about potential adverse side effects of the spray.

- **8-42** $z = -3.82$ ($\bar{p} = 0.3167$), $z_L = -1.64$ ($\bar{p}_L = 0.3357$), so reject H_0. The proportion of skeptical people has decreased significantly.
- **8-44** $t = -1.662$ ($\bar{x} = 94.3$), $t_L = -2.015$ ($\bar{x}_L = 93.09$), so do not reject H_0.
- **8-46** $t = -3.181$ ($\bar{x} = 780{,}000$), $t_L = -1.796$ ($\bar{x}_L = 799{,}595$), so reject H_0.
- **8-48** $t = -2.179$ ($\bar{x} = 7.2$), $t_L = -2.33$ ($\bar{x}_L = 7.14$), so do not reject H_0. The new terminals are not easier to learn to operate.
- **8-50** $t = 3.771$ ($\bar{x} = 12.4$), $t_{CRIT} = \pm 2.898$ ($\bar{x}_L = 8.16$, $\bar{x}_U = 11.84$), so reject H_0. The claim does not appear to be valid.
- **8-52** (a) H_1: $p_{NY} \neq p_N$. (b) H_1: $\mu_A > \mu_B$. (c) H_1: $\mu \neq 8$. (d) H_1: $\mu < 34$.
- **8-54** No, because each is equally distant from the hypothesized mean and hence equally likely to lead to acceptance in a two-tailed test.
- **8-56** (a) 0.4641. (b) 0.8643. (c) 0.9890.
- **8-58** $z = -1.23$ ($\bar{p} = 0.00225$), $z_L = -1.28$ ($\bar{p}_L = 0.00222$), so do not reject H_0. The new procedures have not achieved their goal.
- **8-60** $z = -0.77$ ($\bar{p} = 0.4$), $z_L = -2.33$ ($\bar{p}_L = 0.1992$), so do not reject H_0. The proportion of funds selling at a discount is not significantly less than the proportion selling at a premium.
- **8-62** (a) ± 1.44. (b) ± 2.33.
- **8-64** $z = -2.83$ ($\bar{x} = 31.7$), $z_L = -2.05$ ($\bar{x}_L = 31.78$), so reject H_0. The bottles are being underfilled.
- **8-66** $z = 2.07$ ($\bar{p} = 0.19$), $z_U = 1.64$ ($\bar{p}_U = 0.1816$), so reject H_0. They should open the store.
- **8-68** $z = 1.97$ ($\bar{p} = 0.7760$), $z_U = 2.05$ ($\bar{p}_U = 0.7782$), so do not reject H_0. The survey does not support the editor's belief.
- **8-70** $t = 2.228$ ($\bar{x} = 87.61$), $t_U = 2.110$ ($\bar{x}_U = 87.07$), so reject H_0. However, if Drive-a-Lemon does not have the same nationwide presence as the major national chains, then a comparison of their average rates to the national average of the large chains can lead to a misleading conclusion.
- **8-72** $z = 0.89$ ($\bar{p} = 0.6$), $z_{CRIT} = \pm 1.64$ ($\bar{p}_L = 0.3166$, $\bar{p}_U = 0.6834$), so do not reject H_0. The proportion is not significantly different from 0.5.
- **8-74** (a) 0.7123. (b) 0.3783. (c) 0.1190.
- **8-76** (a) 0.1271. (b) 0.5199. (c) 0.8925.
- **8-78** (a) 0.8340. (b) 0.5398. (c) 0.2206.
- **8-80** $z = -2.36$ ($\bar{p} = 0.43$), $z_L = -2.33$ ($\bar{p}_L = 0.4306$), so reject H_0. The company failed to reach its goal.

Chapter 9

- **9-2** $z = -2.41$ ($\bar{x}_S - \bar{x}_A = -8$ chips per hour), $z_L = -2.05$ ($(\bar{x}_S - \bar{x}_A)_L = -6.81$ chips per hour), so reject H_0. Block should upgrade.
- **9-4** $z = 6.92$ ($\bar{x}_1 - \bar{x}_2 = 1.13$ percent), $z_U = 1.64$ ($(\bar{x}_1 - \bar{x}_2)_U = 0.27$ percent), so reject H_0.
- **9-6** $z = 2.69$ ($\bar{x}_M - \bar{x}_W = \$2.96$), $z_U = 2.33$ ($(\bar{x}_M - \bar{x}_W)_U = \$2.83$), so reject H_0. The male operators earn significantly more than \$2.00 above what the female operators earn.

■ **9-8** $t = -1.544$ ($\bar{x}_O - \bar{x}_N = -\$18$), $t_L = -1.708$ ($(\bar{x}_O - \bar{x}_N)_L = -\$19.91$), so do not reject H_0. Average daily sales have not increased significantly.

■ **9-10** $t = -0.246$ ($\bar{x}_1 - \bar{x}_2 = -\$75$), $t_L = -1.771$ ($(\bar{x}_1 - \bar{x}_2)_L = -\$539$), so do not reject H_0. The pear-shaped stones are not significantly more expensive.

■ **9-12** $t = -2.162$ ($\bar{x}_M - \bar{x}_E = -\$395$), $t_L = -2.467$ ($(\bar{x}_M - \bar{x}_E)_L = -\$451$), so do not reject H_0. The data do not support the commissioner's speculation.

■ **9-14** (a) $\bar{x} = -0.1878$. (b) $s = 3.8586$, $\hat{\sigma}_{\bar{x}} = 0.3500$.
(c) $t = -0.537$ ($\bar{x} = -0.1878$), $t_{CRIT} = \pm 2.896$ ($\bar{x}_{CRIT} = \pm 1.01$), so do not reject H_0. They were not significantly different.

■ **9-16** $t = 2.358$ ($\bar{x} = 0.1667$ mpg), $t_U = 2.896$ ($\bar{x}_U = 0.2047$ mpg), so do not reject H_0. The additive does not yield significantly better fuel efficiency.

■ **9-18** $t = 0.478$ ($\bar{x} = 2.83$), $t_{CRIT} = \pm 3.365$ ($\bar{x}_{CRIT} = \pm 19.95$), so do not reject H_0. The music has no significant effect.

■ **9-20** $z = -1.283$ ($\bar{p}_1 - \bar{p}_2 = -0.125$), $z_L = -1.28$ ($(\bar{p}_1 - \bar{p}_2)_L = -0.1247$), so reject H_0. A smaller proportion advanced on Friday.

■ **9-22** $z = -1.89$ ($\bar{p}_1 - \bar{p}_2 = -0.08$), $z_L = -2.05$ ($(\bar{p}_1 - \bar{p}_2)_L = -0.0869$), so do not reject H_0. Install the less expensive system.

■ **9-24** $z = 1.09$ ($\bar{p}_F - \bar{p}_S = 0.06$), $z_{CRIT} = \pm 1.64$ ($(\bar{p}_F - \bar{p}_S)_{CRIT} = \pm 0.0904$), so do not reject H_0. The proportions of freshmen and sophomores buying all their books at the University Bookstore are not significantly different.

■ **9-26** Prob value = 0.0571.

■ **9-28** Prob value = 0.0124, so recalibrate if $\alpha > 0.0124$.

■ **9-30** 0.0080.

■ **9-32** More than 0.05.

■ **9-34** More than 0.10.

■ **9-36** 0.0294.

■ **9-38** $z = -1.78$ ($\bar{x}_S - \bar{x}_F = -3$), $z_{CRIT} = \pm 2.33$ ($(\bar{x}_S - \bar{x}_F)_{CRIT} = \pm 3.92$), so do not reject H_0. The displays don't result in significantly different sales levels.

■ **9-40** (a) $t = 1.154$ ($\bar{x}_A - \bar{x}_B = 4.18$), $t_U = 1.725$ ($(\bar{x}_A - \bar{x}_B)_U = 6.25$), so do not reject H_0. The demand has not increased significantly.
(b) Reinterview the same 11 customers who were interviewed before the campaign.

■ **9-42** $z = 1.48$ ($\bar{p}_A - \bar{p}_B = 0.08$), $z_U = 1.75$ ($(\bar{p}_A - \bar{p}_B)_U = 0.0945$), so do not reject H_0. The campaign was not significantly effective.

■ **9-44** $t = 2.053$ ($\bar{x} = -2.0556$), $t_{CRIT} = \pm 1.860$ ($\bar{x}_{CRIT} = \pm 1.8628$), so reject H_0. There is a significant difference.

■ **9-46** $t = -2.386$ ($\bar{x} = -1.29$), $t_L = -2.650$ ($\bar{x}_L = -1.43$), so do not reject H_0. The new formula is not significantly more effective.

■ **9-48** $t = -2.817$ ($\bar{x}_M - \bar{x}_S = -2.125$), $t_L = -2.145$ ($(\bar{x}_M - \bar{x}_S)_L = -1.618$), so reject H_0. Severe consequences lead to significantly greater attribution of responsibility.

■ **9-50** $t = 2.014$ ($\bar{x}_D - \bar{x}_C = 14.51$), $t_U = 1.761$ ($(\bar{x}_D - \bar{x}_C)_U = 12.69$), so reject H_0. Disney's films earn significantly more than the competitors' films earn.

■ **9-52** $z = 0.96$ ($\bar{p}_{95} - \bar{p}_{94} = 0.0046$), $z_{CRIT} = \pm 2.575$ ($(\bar{p}_{95} - \bar{p}_{94})_{CRIT} = \pm 0.0124$), so do not reject H_0. The fraction of returns audited did not change significantly.

■ **9-54** $t = -0.051$, which is very close to 0. The observed decrease in price is not significant.

■ **9-56** $z = 2.48$ ($\bar{p}_C - \bar{p}_D = 0.1166$), $z_U = 2.05$ ($(\bar{p}_C - \bar{p}_D)_U = 0.0964$), so reject H_0. Cat owners are more likely to feed their pets premium foods.

9-58 (a) 26/59 = 0.4407, but 27/59 = 0.4576, so the 45 percent reported response rate suggests that a rounding error was made.

(b) Even with the greatest difference in response rates (taking 26 as the number of U.K. responses), $z = 0.72$, so the response rates are not significantly different.

Chapter 10

10-2 There are many examples of inexpensive, high-quality products: pennies, toothpicks, paper for copy machines, straight pins, and so on.

10-4 Because good managers want to keep their customers satisfied, quality control is an important management concern.

10-6 The concept of zero defects says things should be done right the first time, so that production processes have near-perfect performances.

10-8 The robot can be more precisely controlled and adjusted.

10-10 Limiting the number on an express line reduces the variability in how long it takes to check out the customers on the line. It also tends to reduce the total amount of time that customers with small orders have to spend in the checkout lines.

10-12 (a) CL = 16.4, UCL = 20.0, LCL = 12.8.

(b) CL = 16.4, UCL = 18.42, LCL = 14.38.

(c) CL = 4.1, UCL = 4.58, LCL = 3.62.

(d) CL = 141.7, UCL = 145.85, LCL = 137.55.

10-14 (a) CL = 14.90, UCL = 21.08, LCL = 8.72.

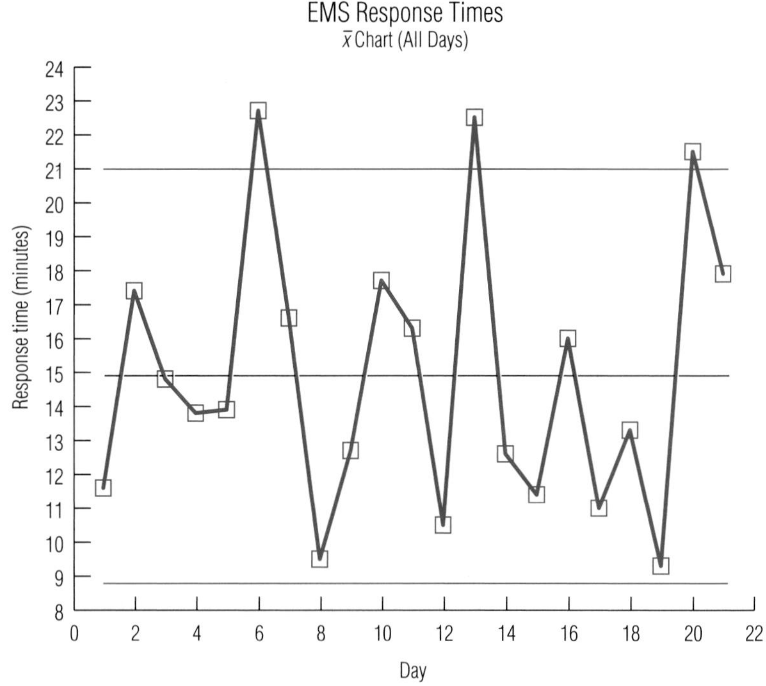

(b) All three Saturdays are outliers on the high side. Dick should investigate whether there are any special circumstances that tend to repeat on Saturdays. For example, there might be more calls coming in on Saturdays, which burden the capabilities of the rescue squads. If this is the case, Dick can consider increasing the number of squads on call on Saturdays.

(c) CL = 13.68, UCL = 19.61, LCL = 7.75.

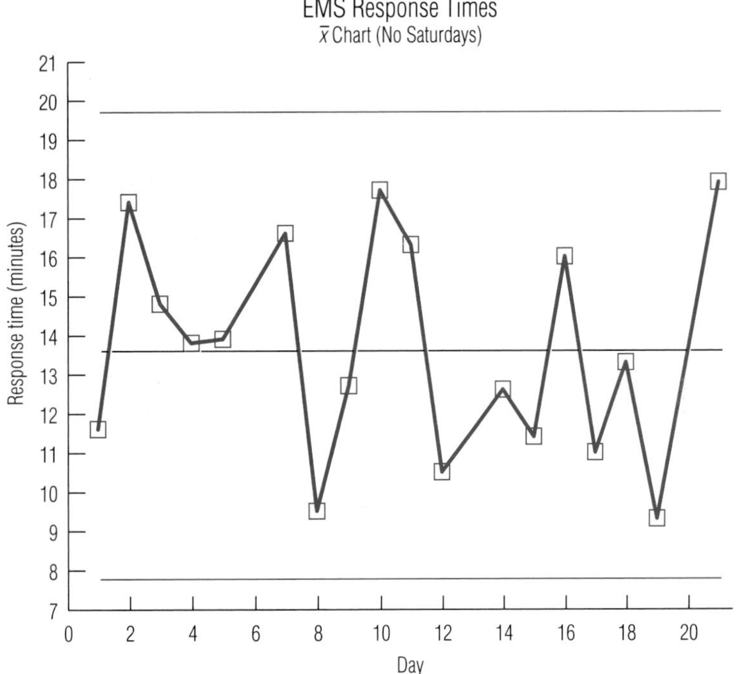

With Saturdays excluded, the process is in-control.

■ **10-16** (a) CL = 4.022, UCL = 4.045, LCL = 4.000.

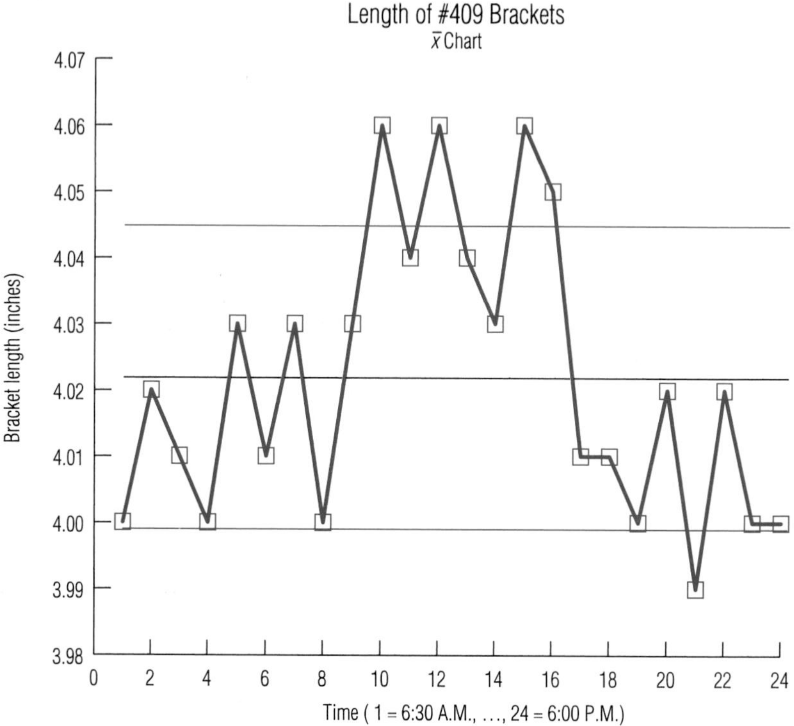

(b) The three shifts seem to be at different levels, with the bracket lengths in the second shift higher than in the first and third shifts. Silvia should check out the procedures for recalibrating the saw at the beginning of each shift.

■ **10-18** We would expect the spindles produced by a new apprentice to show a relatively large variability in diameters initially, with this variability decreasing as the apprentice became more experienced. Pattern (a) conforms to this expectation.

■ **10-20** (a) CL = 18.35, UCL = 33.32, LCL = 3.38.

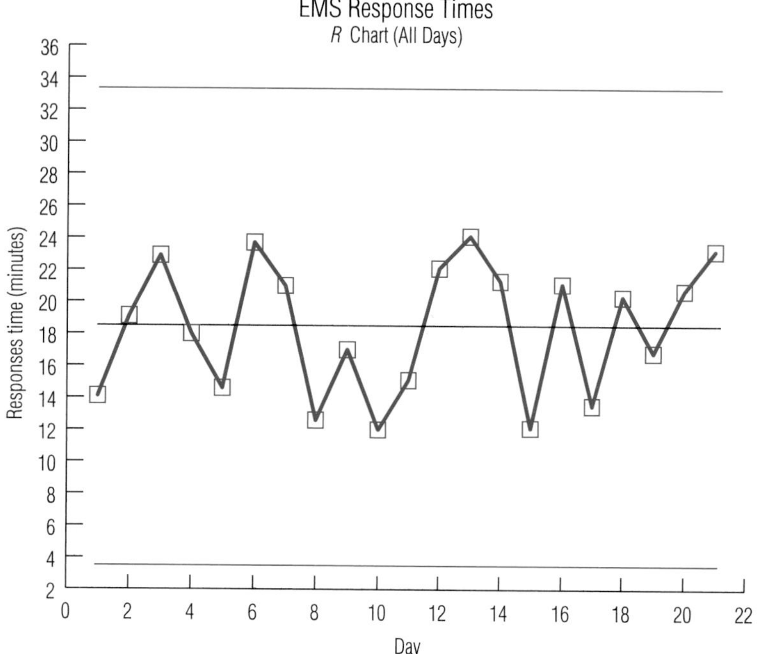

(b) The Saturdays are no longer outliers, but they do tend to have higher variability than the other days. This could well arise because of the greater number of calls coming in on Saturdays.

(c) CL = 17.60, UCL = 31.96, LCL = 3.24.

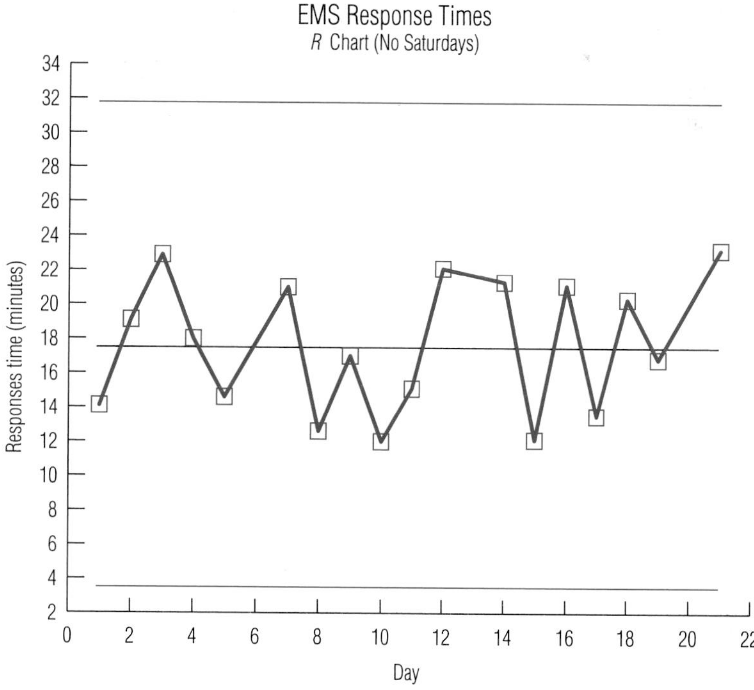

■ **10-22** CL = 0.101, UCL = 0.167, LCL = 0.035.

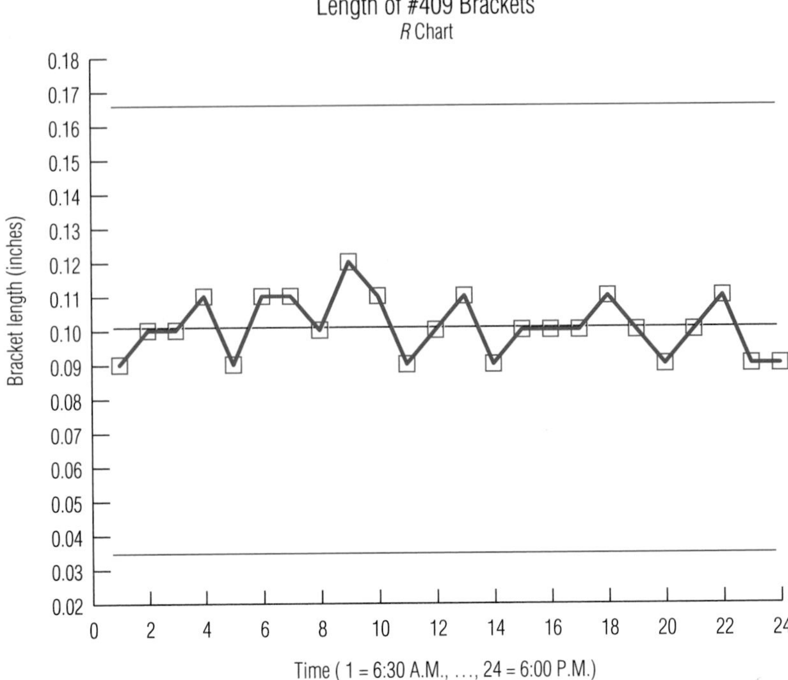

The variability in the process appears to be well in-control.

■ **10-24** (a) CL = 0.25, UCL = 0.487, LCL = 0.013
(b) CL = 0.15, UCL = 0.283, LCL = 0.017
(c) CL = 0.05, UCL = 0.122, LCL = 0
(d) CL = 0.42, UCL = 0.570, LCL = 0.270
(e) CL = 0.63, UCL = 0.760, LCL = 0.500

■ **10-26** (a) H_0: $p = 0.015$, H_1: $p > 0.015$
$\bar{\bar{p}} = 0.01594$, $z = 0.98$, prob value = 0.1635, so accept H_0. She can be reasonably sure that the proportion of bad capsules is not significantly greater than 1.5 percent.

(b) CL = 0.015, UCL = 0.0313, LCL = 0.

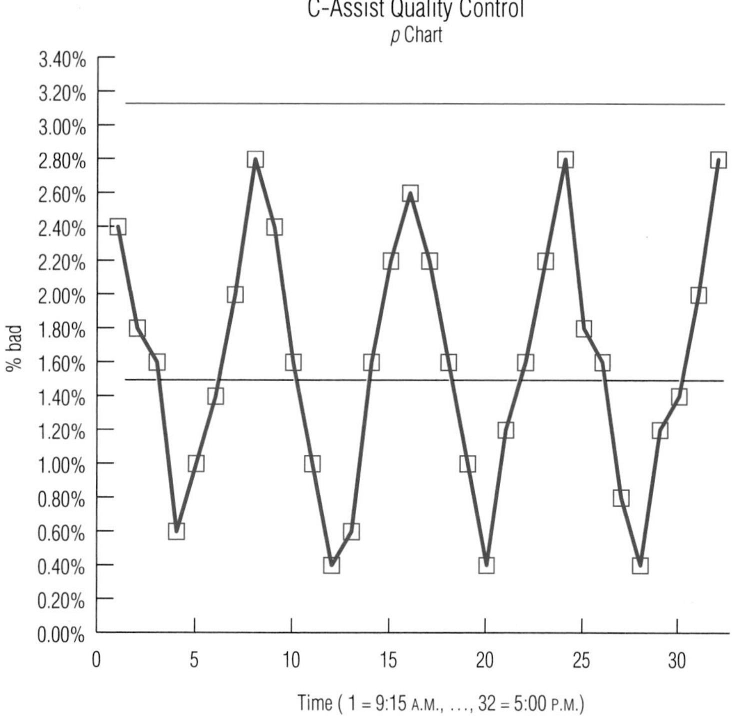

(c) The p chart shows a distinct 2-hour cycle in the percentage of nonconforming capsules.

■ **10-28** CL = 0.0681, UCL = 0.1169, LCL = 0.0193.

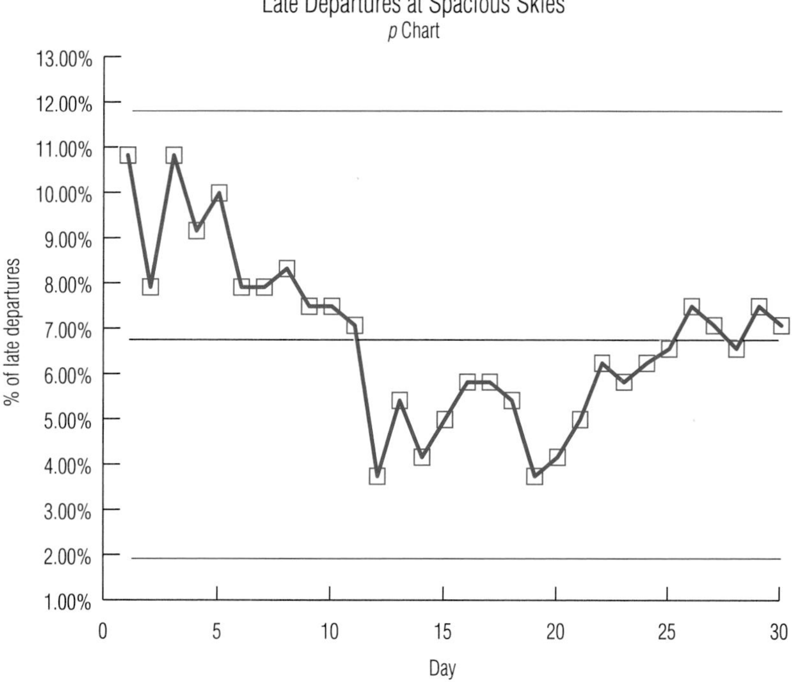

Four weeks ago, the fraction of late departures dropped dramatically, presumably in response to Ross's new procedures. However, in the past two weeks, that fraction has again started drifting upward. If the new procedures aren't being used, he should insist that they be used. If they are being used, he needs to find out why they aren't working.

■ **10-30** The focus must be on *continuous* quality improvement.

■ **10-32** Atlanta and Houston.

■ **10-34** Total inspection is frequently impractical because of the time and cost involved.

■ **10-36** (a) 0.4645. (b) 0.1404. (c) 0.7378. (d) 0.3840.

■ **10-38** (a) 0.13. (b) 0.46. (c) 0.72.

■ **10-40** (a) H_0: $p = 0.02$. H_1: $p > 0.02$.
$\bar{\bar{p}} = 0.0225$, $z = 0.80$, prob value = 0.2119, so accept H_0. She can be reasonably sure that the proportion of audited clients is not significantly greater than 2 percent.
(b) CL = 0.02, UCL = 0.0576, LCL = 0.

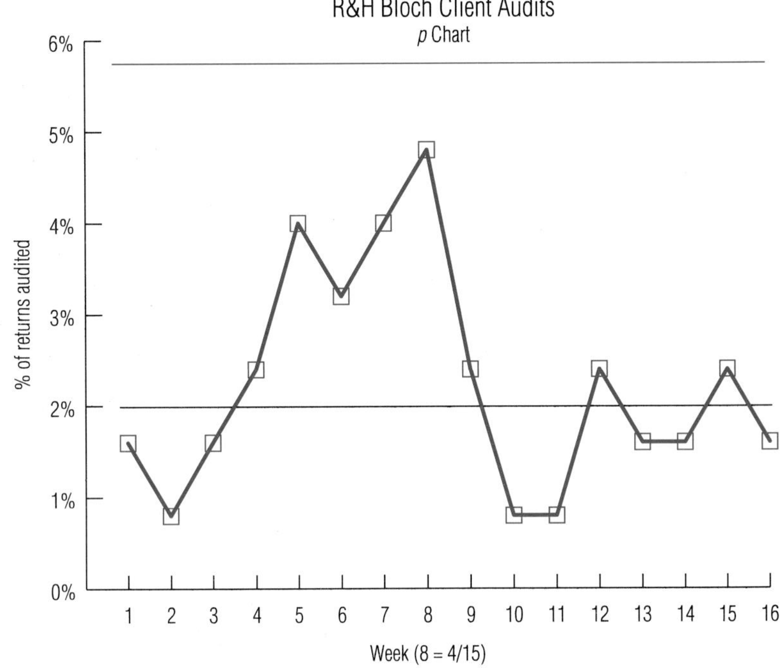

The percent audited has taken a jump upwards in the four weeks before April 15. This may indicate something about the clients who wait until the last minute or something about how the IRS chooses which returns to audit. In either case, the partners should be aware of this phenomenon.

■ **10-42** Attributes are categorical variables with only two possible categories.

■ **10-44** (a) CL = 50.00, UCL = 52.08, LCL = 47.92.

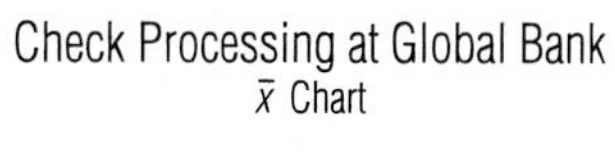

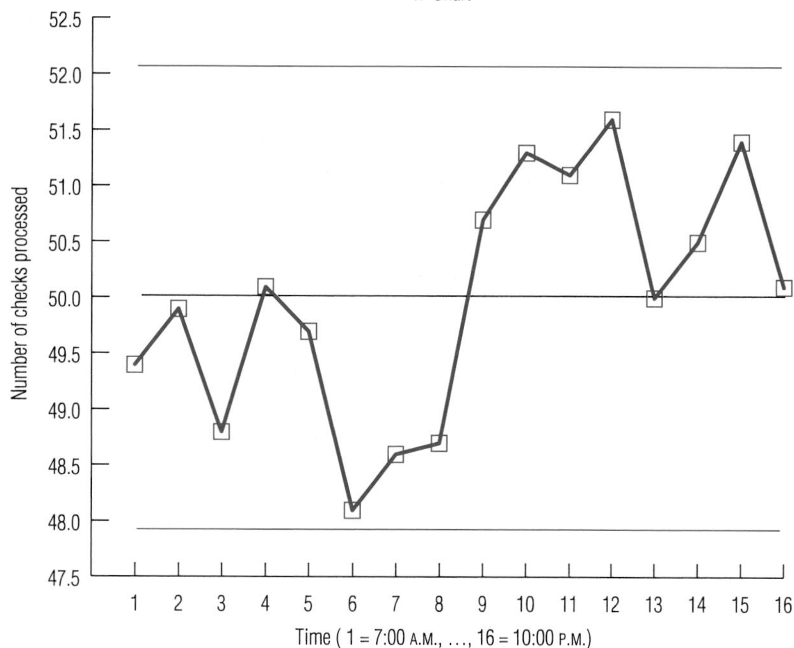

(b) The output during the second shift is at a higher level. Shih-Hsing should try to learn why productivity is higher on that shift.

■ **10-46** The wallboard and electrical subcontractors need additional supervision.

■ **10-48** (a) 0.1969. (b) 0.4215. (c) 0.1099. (d) 0.2749.

■ **10-50** (a) CL = 74.965, UCL = 75.462, LCL = 74.468.

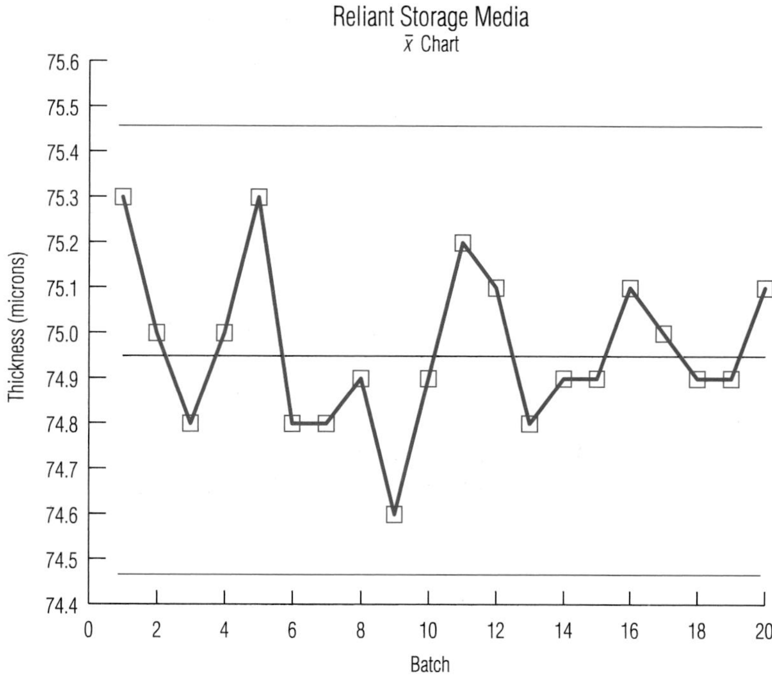

(b) Yes. There are no outliers or other out-of-control patterns.

(c) Yes. The last 10 observations do cluster closer to the center line than the first 10 do. Deshawn should be happy to see this because it indicates that the inherent variability of the process has decreased. To the extent that this is true, he might want to use the last 10 observations to recompute the $\bar{x}$ chart. The new chart will have narrower control limits.

■ **10-52** $\bar{\bar{p}} = 0.001$, so the goal is being met. CL = 0.001, UCL = 0.0031, LCL = 0.

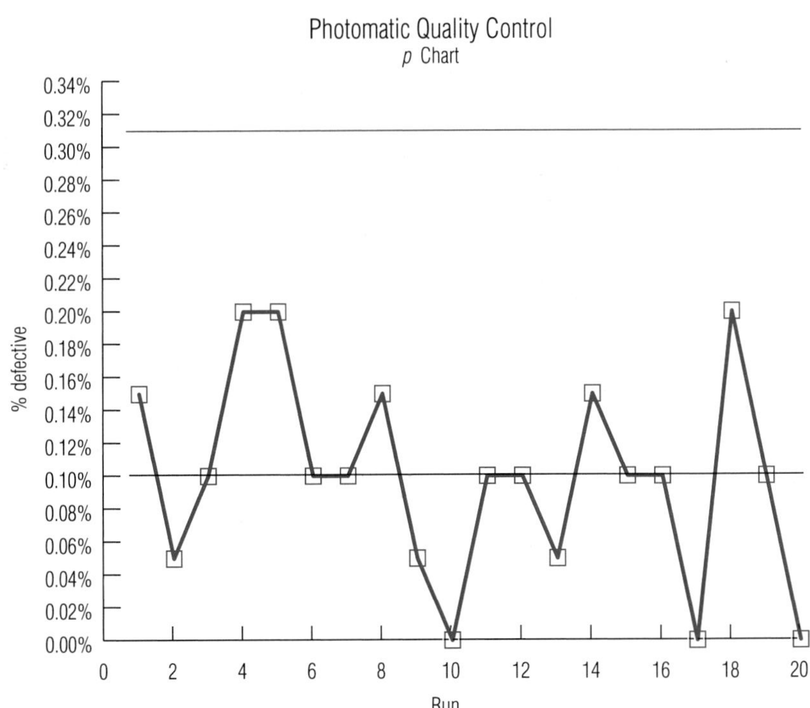

The chart shows that the process is in-control.

■ **10-54** Common variation: density of flour, variability in measuring ingredients, variability in amount of dough per cracker.

Special cause: improper calibration of measuring machinery, drifting temperature in ovens, miscounting by packaging machinery.

■ **10-56** (a) 0.64. (b) 0.34. (c) 0.15.

■ **10-58** By forcing the supplier to take responsibility for the quality of its output.

■ **10-60** (a) No. This is a good example of *inspection* instead of *prevention.*

(b) Major bones could collect causes by parent (failure to make appointment, failure to keep appointment, etc.), by child (illness at time of appointment, allergic reactions, etc.), and by health care professionals (shortage of vaccine, errors in record keeping, etc.).

(c) Collecting data from a sample of missed immunizations would enable the HMO to construct a Pareto diagram to help identify the principal causes of the problem.

Chapter 11

- **11-2** To determine whether three or more population means can be considered equal.
- **11-4** (a) False; you can do inferences on only one or two variances.
  (b) True; use analysis of variance.
  (c) True; use a chi-square test.
- **11-6** (a) 12. (b) 5. (c) 12. (d) 9.
- **11-8** (a) $\chi^2 = 32.2724$.
  (b) H_0: Age group and purchasing plans are independent.
  H_1: Age group and purchasing plans are dependent.
  (c) $\chi^2_U = 20.090$, so we reject H_0; there is a relationship between age group and purchasing plans.
- **11-10** (a) H_0: sales and economy are independent.
  H_1: sales and economy are dependent.
  (b) $\chi^2 = 34.597$.
  (c) $\chi^2_U = 10.645$, so we reject H_0.
- **11-12** $\chi^2 = 32.855$, $\chi^2_U = 14.684$, so we reject H_0. Different levels of education do correspond to different frequencies of readership.
- **11-14** (a) 0.0548, 0.1571, 0.2881, 0.2881, 0.1571, 0.0548
  (b) 8.220, 23.565, 43.215, 43.215, 23.565, 8.220
  (c) $\chi^2 = 10.007$
  (d) $\chi^2_U = 9.236$, so we reject H_0. The data are not well described by a normal distribution with $\mu = 5$ and $\sigma = 1.5$.
- **11-16** $\chi^2 = 8.964$, $\chi^2_U = 9.488$, so we do not reject H_0. The data are well described by the binomial distribution with $n = 5$ and $p = 0.4$.
- **11-18** (a)

Deposit	\$0–999	\$1,000–1,999	\$2,000+
f_e	22.36	65.27	22.36

  (b) $\chi^2 = 0.562$.
  (c) H_0: Deposits normally distributed with $\mu = \$1,500$, $\sigma = \$600$.
  H_1: They are not so distributed.
  (d) $\chi^2_U = 4.605$, so we do not reject H_0. The data are well described by the normal distribution with $\mu = \$1,500$ and $\sigma = \$600$.
- **11-20** $\chi^2 = 2.035$, $\chi^2_U = 5.991$, so we do not reject H_0. The state's claim is reasonable.
- **11-22** $\chi^2 = 2.289$, $\chi^2_U = 5.991$, so we do not reject H_0. The number of alarms is well described by a binomial distribution with $n = 3$ and $p = 0.3$.
- **11-24** $\chi^2 = 33.103$, $\chi^2_U = 12.592$, so we reject H_0. The number of customer arrivals is not well described by a Poisson distribution with $\lambda = 3$.
- **11-26** (a) Brands A-E have means 4.28, 5.04, 4.90, 3.34, and 4.46. The grand mean is 4.404.
  (b) 2.2514
  (c) 0.2942
  (d) $F = 7.65$, $F_U = 2.87$, so we reject H_0. The brands produce significantly different amounts of relief.
- **11-28** $F = 1.47$, $F_U = 3.29$, so we do not reject H_0. The employees' productivities are not significantly different.

■ **11-30** (a) $\bar{x}_j = 36, 31, 35, 31; \bar{\bar{x}} = 33.25$.

(b) 34.5833.

(c) 7.375.

(d) $F = 4.69$, $F_U = 3.24$, so we reject H_0. The different speeds lead to significantly different numbers of defective clocks.

■ **11-32** $F = 6.67$, $F_U = 3.68$, so we reject H_0. The average numbers of apprehended shoplifters differ significantly during these months.

■ **11-34** $F = 18.17$, $F_U = 2.87$, so we reject H_0. The rooms have significantly different average dust scores.

■ **11-36** $F = 0.23$, $F_U = 3.24$, so we do not reject H_0. The sales of the four brands are not significantly different.

■ **11-38** (a) $F = 0.51$, $F_U = 3.24$, so we do not reject H_0. The mean service times are not significantly different.

(b) Because no restaurant is significantly worse than the others, any recommendations would have to be made to all of the managers.

■ **11-40** $\chi^2 = 37.688$, $\chi_U^2 = 45.722$, so we do not reject H_0.

■ **11-42** (a) $H_0 : \sigma = 2$ (or $\sigma^2 = 4$), $H_1 : \sigma < 2$ (or $\sigma^2 < 4$)

(b) $\chi^2 = 15.4541$, $\chi_L^2 = 14.256$, so we do not reject H_0.

(c) The telescope should not be sold.

■ **11-44** (a) H_0: $\sigma^2 = 64$, H_1: $\sigma^2 \neq 64$.

(b) $\chi^2 = 8.31$, $\chi_L^2 = 8.907$, $\chi_U^2 = 32.852$, so we reject H_0.

(c) Six-year-olds' attention spans have significantly different variabilities than five-year-olds' attention spans.

■ **11-46** $\chi^2 = 8.4$, $\chi_L^2 = 13.848$, so we reject H_0. The variance has been reduced significantly.

■ **11-48** (a) $F = 0.70$ (b) $F_U = 3.01$ (c) $F_L = 0.39$

(d) Do not reject H_0. The two variances are not significantly different.

■ **11-50** $F = 2.39$, $F_U = 3.59$, so we do not reject H_0. The second variance is not significantly smaller.

■ **11-52** $F = 2.25$, $F_U = 2.92$, so we do not reject H_0. Patients at hospital A do not have significantly less variability in their recovery times.

■ **11-54** $F = 4$, $F_U = 1.98$, so we reject H_0. PAL's processing speed is significantly more variable.

■ **11-56** $F = 1.6$, $F_L = 1/2.25 = 0.44$, $F_U = 2.74$, so we do not reject H_0. The variances are not significantly different.

■ **11-58** H_0: occupation and attitude are independent.
H_1: occupation and attitude are dependent.
$\chi^2 = 6.607$, $\chi_U^2 = 9.488$, so we do not reject H_0.

■ **11-60** (a) Normal. (b) Chi-square. (c) F (ANOVA).

(d) t.

■ **11-62** $\chi^2 = 691.396$, $\chi_U^2 = 3.841$, so we reject H_0. The proportion of patents originating overseas has changed significantly over the past ten years.

■ **11-64** (a) t-test (t-distribution). (b) F-distribution. (c) Normal.

(d) χ^2.

■ **11-66** $F = 0.82$, $F_U = 3.47$, so we do not reject H_0. The three traffic volumes are not significantly different.

- **11-68** $\chi^2 = 4.792$, $\chi^2_U = 9.488$, so we do not reject H_0. Church attendance seems to be unrelated to income level.
- **11-70** $F = 0.52$, $F_U = 3.15$, so we do not reject H_0. The price changes in the three groups are not significantly different.
- **11-72** (a) x = number of correct guesses.
  H_0: x is distributed binomially, with $n = 10$ and $p = 0.5$.
  H_1: x has some other distribution.
  (b) $\chi^2 = 396.147$ (last two categories combined because $f_e < 5$ for 9-10 correct), $\chi^2_U = 4.605$, so we reject H_0. His probability of guessing the correct card is not 0.5.
  (c) $\chi^2 = 0.2628$ (last three categories, $\chi^2_U = 2.706$, so we do not reject H_0. He has no psychic power.)
- **11-74** H_0: Jim's errors are $N(\mu = 0, \sigma^2 = 16)$.
  H_1: Jim's errors follow another distribution.
  $\chi^2 = 1.228$, $\chi^2_U = 7.815$, so we do not reject H_0. His errors are $N(0,16)$.
- **11-76** $F = 3.80$, $F_U = 3.35$, so we reject H_0. The mean average ages in the three regions are significantly different.
- **11-78** Estimate μ by $\bar{x} = 1{,}764{,}857.8$ and σ by $s = 409{,}322.2$, losing 2 degrees of freedom as a result. Divide the range of retail sales into five equally likely intervals, with boundaries $-\infty$, 1,421,027.2; 1,662,527.3; 1,867,188.4; 2,108,688.4; and $+\infty$. The observed frequencies are 9, 11, 12, 10, and 8. All expected frequencies are 10. Then $\chi^2 = 1.0$. No α is given, but the prob value for this test is greater than 0.20 (from Appendix Table 5, $\chi^2_{.20,2} = 3.219$), so we do not reject H_0. The retail sales data are well-described by a normal distribution.
- **11-80** $F = 18.96$, $F_U = 3.34$, so we reject H_0. The drugs have significantly different effects on driving skills.
- **11-82** $F = 7.72$, $F_U = 7.21$, so we reject H_0. The three types have significantly different fuel costs.
- **11-84** $F = 1.09$, with a prob-value of $0.4171 > 0.10 = \alpha$, so we do not reject H_0. Batting skills are not significantly more variable in the American League.

Chapter 12

Note: Regression results are given from analysis with SAS. Hand calculations will differ slightly because of rounding errors.

- **12-2** An estimating equation is the formula describing the relationship between a dependent variable and one or more independent variables.
- **12-4** In a *direct relationship,* the dependent variable increases as the independent variable increases; in an *inverse relationship,* the dependent variable decreases as the independent variable increases.
- **12-6** In a *linear* relationship, the dependent variable changes a constant amount for equal incremental changes in the independent variable(s); in a *curvilinear* relationship, the dependent variable does not change at a constant rate with equal incremental changes in the independent variable(s).
- **12-8** Multiple regression is a process that determines the relationship between a dependent variable and more than one independent variable.
- **12-10** (a) Final Average (FA) is the dependent variable and Quiz Average (QA) is the independent variable.

(b)

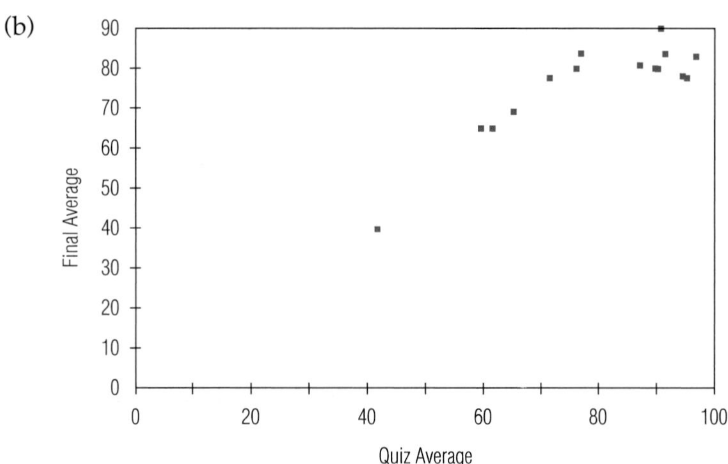

(c) Curvilinear

(d) For the most part FA does increase as QA increases. However, for very high quiz averages, it appears that final averages actually start to decrease.

■ **12-12** A scatter diagram suggests a direct, linear relationship. Clearly, use of facial tissues does not cause colds.

■ **12-14** (a)

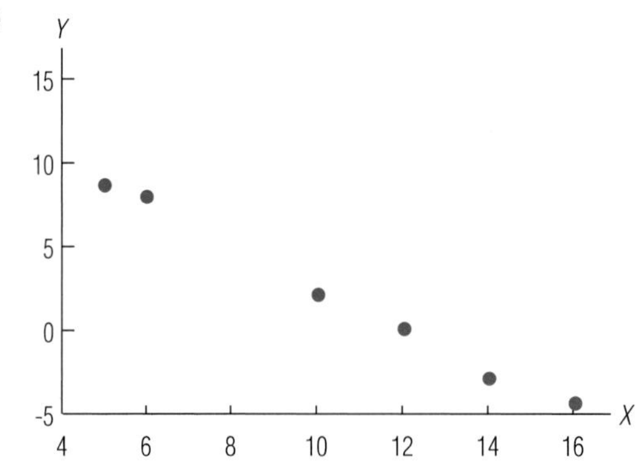

(b) $\hat{Y} = 15.0281 - 1.2471X$.

(c) 8.7926, 7.5455, 6.2984.

■ **12-16** (a) $\widehat{\text{APPLIANCE}} = 1.1681 + 1.7156 \cdot \text{HOUSING}$

(b) When housing starts increase by 1000 units, appliance sales increase by 1715.6 units.

(c) $s_e = 0.3737$. The standard deviation of the data points around the regression line is about 374 units.

(d) 14.89 ± 0.69 thousand units.

■ **12-18** (a)

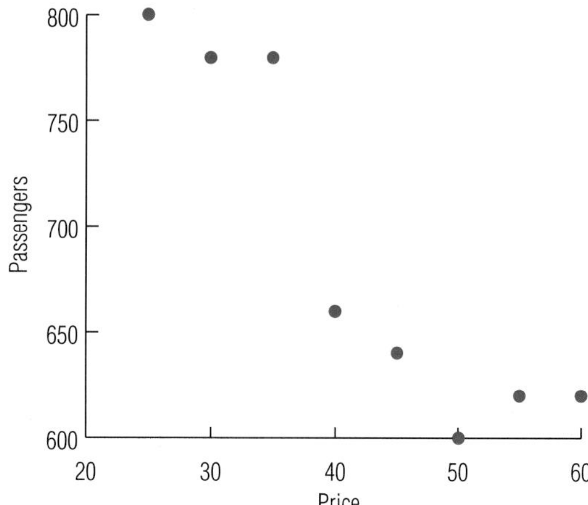

(b) $\widehat{\text{PASSENGERS}} = 952.6190 - 6.2381 \cdot \text{PRICE}.$

(c) 640.7140 ± 93.1279 passengers.

■ **12-20** (a)

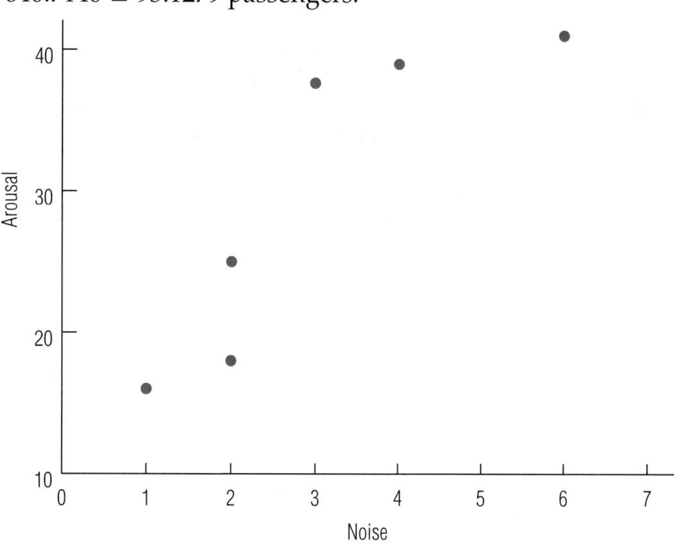

(b) $\widehat{\text{AROUSAL}} = 16.5167 + 4.5667 \cdot \text{NOISE}$

(c) 39.35

■ **12-22** (a)

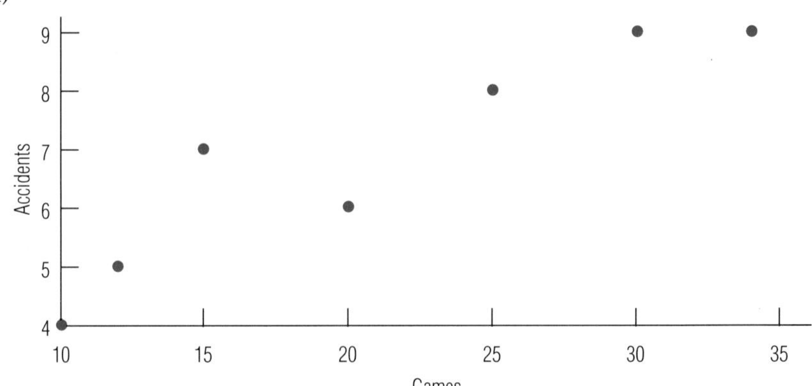

(b) $\widehat{\text{ACCIDENTS}} = 2.7317 + 0.1978 \cdot \text{GAMES}$.

(c) 9.3 accidents.

(d) 0.7882 accident.

■ **12-24** (a) $\widehat{\text{POLLUTANTS}} = 40.7179 - 0.7822 \cdot \text{MONEY}$

(b) 25.0739 percent dangerous pollutants

(c) 2.9188

■ **12-26** $r^2 = 0.9530$; $r = -0.9762$.

■ **12-28** $r^2 = 0.9858$; $r = -0.9929$.

■ **12-30** $r^2 = 0.9269$; $r = 0.9628$.

■ **12-32** (a) $\text{PURCHASES} = 3.3308 + 1.7110 \cdot \text{ADS}$.

(b) $r^2 = 0.6189$, $r = 0.7867$.

■ **12-34** $\hat{Y} = 4.6472 + 1.9517X$, $s_b = 0.0952$, $t = 4.745$, $t_U = 1.812$ ($b_U = 1.6725$), so we reject H_0. Ned should advertise.

■ **12-36** $t = 1.682$ ($b = 1.685$), $t_{CRIT} = \pm 2.069$ ($b_L = 1.27$, $b_U = 1.73$), so we do not reject H_0. The slope has not changed significantly from its past value.

■ **12-38** (a) $b_L = 0.091$ and $b_U = 0.203$, so at $\alpha = 0.10$, we reject H_0 and conclude that the slope has changed since 1969.

(b) $b_L = 0.054$ and $b_U = 0.241$, so at $\alpha = 0.01$, the slope hasn't changed significantly.

■ **12-40** $t = -0.125$ ($b = 0.70$), $t_{CRIT} = \pm 2.878$ ($b_L = -2.6$ and $b_U = 4.3$), so we do not reject H_0. The slope has not changed significantly.

■ **12-42** The coefficient of determination is the fraction of the variation in Y that is explained by X. Its square root, the coefficient of correlation, indicates whether the relationship is direct or inverse.

■ **12-44** Correlation only measures the strength of the relationship between the values of two variables. In no way does it address the cause of that relationship.

■ **12-46** (a) $r^2 = 0.9581$, $r = 0.9788$.

(b) No, the high correlation is spurious. It simply reflects the fact that both the number of storks and the number of births tend to rise when the population increases. Higher population means more people to have children and more roofs for storks to nest on.

■ **12-48** $r^2 = 0.9938$, $r = -0.9969$.

■ **12-50**

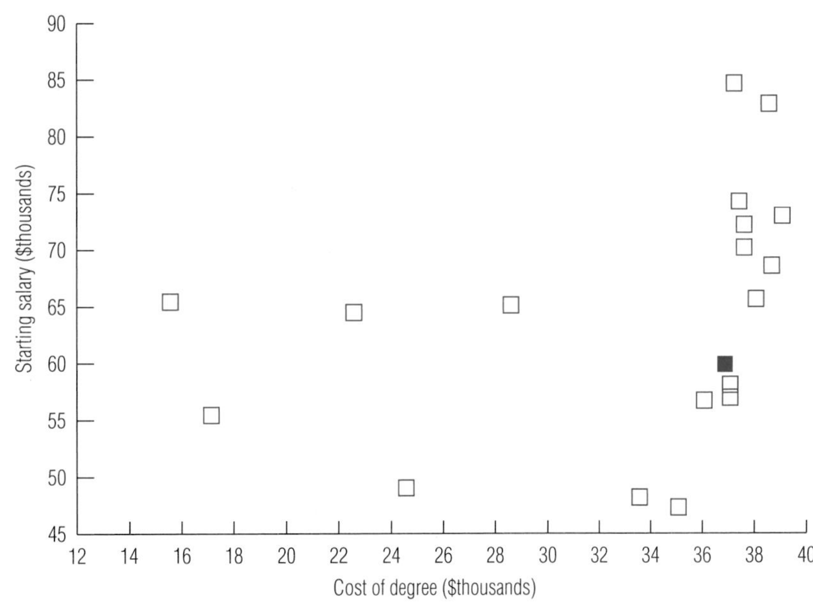

Note: The solid box represents both Duke and Cornell.

$\widehat{\text{SALARY}} = 49.0945 + 0.4478 \cdot \text{COST}$ (both variables in thousands of dollars).
H_0: $B = 0$. H_1: $B > 0$. $t = 1.401$.
With 18 *df*, the prob value for the test is greater than 5%, so we would probably accept H_0. Starting salaries do not increase significantly with the cost of the degree, so it doesn't appear to be worthwhile to spend more on the degree.

■ **12-52** Overall: 0.3527, student: 0.1270, firm: 0.2822.
The overall ranking explains the largest fraction of the variation in starting salaries.

■ **12-54** (a) 1, +. (b) 2, +. (c) 2, −. (d) 2, −.

■ **12-56** $r^2 = 0.9613$, $r = 0.9805$.

■ **12-58** For SALES and POP, $r^2 = 0.1536$; for SALES and TM, $r^2 = 0.2874$. TM explains more of the variation in SALES.

■ **12-60** $\widehat{\text{SALES}} = 1304.37 + 14.05 \cdot \text{AGE}$ (SALES in millions of dollars).
H_0:$B = 0$. H_1: $B > 0$. $t = 0.846$.
With 48 *df*, the prob value for the test is greater than 10%, so we would probably accept H_0. Although this appears to indicate that business isn't better in communities with more older people, it would be erroneous to draw such a conclusion. As we saw in Exercise 12-58, POP explains 15% of the variation in SALES, and a simple regression of SALES on AGE ignores this factor. In order to legitimately draw the suggested conclusion, you should first do a multiple regression analysis.

■ **12-62** (a)

■ **12-64** (a) $\widehat{\text{RENT}} = 55.0018 + 115.8991 \cdot \text{BEDROOMS}$. (b) 0.5762.
(c) \$286.80.

■ **12-66** $\widehat{\text{SHARE}} = 4.2906 - 0.5230 \cdot \text{PRICE}$.
$t = -0.950$, so generalization (c) best describes the relationship.

■ **12-68** (a) $\widehat{\text{PRICE}} = 7.5294 + 0.0285 \cdot \text{SIZE}$.

(b) $r^2 = 0.3412$; Dave should search elsewhere.

■ **12-70** $\widehat{\text{HEIGHT}} = 56.4667 + 0.1249 \cdot \text{WEIGHT}$.

$r^2 = 0.5524$; 55 percent of the variation is explained.

■ **12-72** (a) $\widehat{\text{AGSAL}} = 32.8229 + 1.8356 \cdot \text{ENTRYSAL}$, $t = 1.635$, $t_{CRIT} = \pm 2.306$ ($b_{CRIT} = \pm 2.5885$), so we do not reject H_0. Attorney-General salaries are not significantly related to Entry-level salaries.

(b) $r^2 = 0.2505$, so 25.05 percent of the variation in AG salaries is explained by the going rate.

(c) No. Even if the correlation were strong, correlation does not imply causation.

Chapter 13

■ **13-2** To include qualitative factors in our regressions.

■ **13-4** Yes. Season is a qualitative factor that can be modeled with *dummy variables*.

■ **13-6** No. Multiple regression is based on the same assumptions and procedures as simple regression.

■ **13-8** (a) $\hat{Y} = 2.5915 + 0.8897X_1 + 0.0592X_2$.

(b) 28.10.

■ **13-10** (a) $\hat{Y} = 219.2306 + 6.3815X_1 - 1.6708X_2$.

(b) 43.33 units.

■ **13-12** (a) $\hat{Y} = -4243.1682 + 2.1315X_1 + 0.2135X_2$.

(b) \$9,188.

■ **13-14** (a) $\hat{Y} = 34.8079 + 5.2618X_1 - 8.0187X_2 + 6.8084X_3$.

(b) 4.0688. (c) 0.9834. (d) 66.37.

■ **13-16** (a) $\hat{Y} = 142.4363 + 3.2741X_1 + 0.5269X_2 - 0.3203X_3$.

(b) 98.54%. (c) 447.1 arrests.

■ **13-18** (a) $\widehat{\text{GRADE}} = -49.95 + 1.07 \cdot \text{HOURS} + 1.36 \cdot \text{IQ} + 2.04 \cdot \text{BOOKS} - 1.80 \cdot \text{AGE}$.

(b) 76.7%. (c) About 77.

■ **13-20** (a) $\widehat{\text{PRICE}} = -1.381 + 2.852 \cdot \text{SQFT} - 3.713 \cdot \text{STORIES} + 30.285 \cdot \text{BATHS} + 1.172 \cdot \text{AGE}$.

(b) $R^2 = 0.952$, 95.2 percent of the variation in sales price is explained by the four explanatory variables.

(c) \$98,700.

■ **13-22** (a) H_1: $B_2 < 3$, $t = -1.980$ ($b_2 = 1.25$), $t_L = -1.714$ ($(b_2)_L = 1.485$), so we reject H_0. The regression does not support Mark's belief.

(b) H_1: $B_1 \neq 0.5$, $t = -1.976$ ($b_1 = 0.251$), $t_{CRIT} = \pm 2.069$ ($(b_1)_L = 0.24$, $(b_1)_U = 0.76$), so we do not reject H_0. This belief is supported by the regression.

(c) H_1: $B_3 > 333.333$. Because $b_3 = 250.66$, which is less than 333.333, we do not reject H_0. Mark's rates are OK.

■ **13-24** (a) $F = 5.77$. (b) $F_U = 4.12$. (c) Yes, because we reject H_0.

■ **13-26** Yes, because the analysis of variance prob value (0.000) is less than α (0.05). It is significant as a whole.

■ **13-28** Multicollinearity is present because the prime rate at banks is dependent on the Federal Reserve discount rate, which, for the most part, moves directly with the inflation rate.

■ **13-30** (a) $\hat{Y} = 5.9188 + 3.5470X_1 - 0.1709X_2 + 0.2426X_3 + 0.2273X_4$.

(b) No, because the prob value (0.2809) is greater than α (0.10).

(c) H_1: $B_3 > 0.2$, $t = 0.262$ ($b_3 = 0.2426$), $t_U = 1.895$ ($(b_3)_U = 0.5085$), so we do not reject H_0. Increasing promotions by 1000 pounds does not increase the number of tourists by more than 200.

(d) (−0.0539, 0.5086).

■ **13-32** (a) $\widehat{\text{REVENUE}} = a + b_1 \cdot \text{FLOW} + b_2 \cdot \text{FLOW}^2$.

(b) Let CITY be 0 for the first city, 1 for the second.
$\widehat{\text{REVENUE}} = a + b_1 \cdot \text{FLOW} + b_2 \cdot \text{FLOW}^2 + b_3 \cdot \text{CITY}$.

■ **13-34** (a) $t = 0.860$ ($b_1 = 2.79$), $t_{CRIT} = \pm 2.110$ ($(b_1)_{CRIT} = \pm 6.85$), so do not reject H_0. X_1 is not a significant explanatory variable.

(b) $t = -2.562$ ($b_2 = -3.92$), $t_{CRIT} = \pm 2.110$ ($(b_2)_{CRIT} = \pm 3.23$), so reject H_0. X_2 is a significant explanatory variable.

■ **13-36** (a) $\widehat{\text{DEMAND}} = -0.9705 + 4.4146 \text{ TIME}$.

(b) $\widehat{\text{DEMAND}} = 3.4101 + 2.8686 \text{ TIME} + 0.0966 \text{ TIME}^2$. This model is better: the residuals are now random, and R^2 has increased from 0.9886 to 0.9956.

■ **13-38** (a) He has spotted the obvious pattern in the residuals.

(b) Include the square of the number of days in court as an additional explanatory variable.

■ **13-40** (a) $\widehat{\text{GROWTH}} = 70.066 + 0.422 \cdot \text{CREAT} + 0.271 \cdot \text{MECH} + 0.745 \cdot \text{ABST} + 0.420 \cdot \text{MATH}$.

(b) 92.6%. (c) CREAT, ABST, and MATH.

(d) Yes, since the analysis of variance prob value = 0.000.

(e) 104.93.

■ **13-42** $\widehat{\text{EATING}} = 56{,}177.927 + 506.352\text{POP}$, $r^2 = 0.0775$;
$\widehat{\text{EATING}} = 22{,}170.308 + 5.029\text{EBI}$, $r^2 = 0.2583$.

■ **13-44** EATING = −104,304.617 + 142.356POP + 4.745EBI + 4759.177SINGLE. 44.19% of the variation in EATING is explained by this model. Yes, since the prob value for b_{SINGLE} (0.002) is smaller than our usual significance levels.

■ **13-46** (a) $\widehat{\text{ANESTHES}} = 90.032 + 99.486 \cdot \text{TYPE} + 21.536 \cdot \text{WEIGHT} - 34.461 \cdot \text{HOURS}$.

(b) (547,805) milliliters.

(c) H_1:$B_1 \neq 0$. Because the (two-tailed) prob value (0.044) is less than α (0.10), we reject H_0. The amounts of anesthesia needed for dogs and cats are significantly different.

(d) Yes, because the analysis of variance prob value (0.000) is less than α (0.05).

■ **13-48** (a) $\widehat{\text{PRICE}} = 444.7183 - 0.6124 \cdot \text{WEIGHT} - 4.3769 \cdot \text{SQFT}$.

(b) \$182.

■ **13-50** $\widehat{\text{PRICE}} = -5.789 - 7.713\text{DIV} + 3.823\text{EPS} + 0.035\Delta\text{SALES} + 0.040\Delta\text{INCOME} - 0.018\Delta\text{ASSETS} + 1.533\text{OLDPR}$.
$R^2 = 0.8043$.

■ **13-52** $\widehat{\text{PRICE}} = -5.937 - 9.926\text{DIV} + 4.584\text{EPS} + 1.447\text{OLDPR} + 5.168\text{NY} + 1.277\text{BANK}.$

H_0: $B_{NY} = 0$. H_1: $B_{NY} \neq 0$. prob value $= 0.137 > \alpha = 0.10$, so we do not reject H_0;

NYSE listing has no significant effect on share price.

H_0: $B_{BANK} = 0$. H_1: $B_{BANK} \neq 0$. prob value $= 0.772 > \alpha = 0.10$, so we do not reject H_0; share prices of banks and bank holding companies do not differ significantly from those of other companies in the group.

■ **13-54** (a) $\widehat{\text{REVENUE}} = 28{,}725.416 - 139.760 \cdot \text{PROPERTY} + 105.176 \cdot \text{SALES} + 56.065 \cdot \text{GASOLINE}.$

(b) A: 28,500.50, B: 28,893.92; they should adopt proposal B.

■ **13-56** $\widehat{\text{PHONES}} = -6.6325 + 2.6040 \cdot \text{YEARS}$ (in 100,000s of units), $r^2 = 0.7951$. The residuals show that curvature is present.

$\widehat{\text{PHONES}} = 3.6280 - 2.9926 \cdot \text{YEARS} + 0.5597\,(\text{YEARS})^2$, $r^2 = 0.9836$. The quadratic equation is a better fit.

■ **13-58** (a) $\widehat{\text{REVENUE}} = 8085.6084 + 51.4201\ \text{STORES} - 125.7441\ \text{SIZE}$. The number of stores is more important in determining revenue growth. In fact, larger stores seem to be leading to a decline in revenues. This regression might lead a consultant to emphasize geographic spread.

(b) With sales, per employee measured in $1000s,

$\widehat{\text{SALES/EMPLOYEE}} = +497.08 + 20.8462\ \text{YEAR} - 5.1665\ \text{SIZE}$

Because the coefficient of SIZE is negative, employees are not more productive in larger stores. The positive coefficient of YEARS shows that employee productivity is increasing over time.

Chapter 14

■ **14-2** (b).

■ **14-4** They do not use all the information in the data because they usually rely on ranks or counts.

■ **14-6** Yes. If the data were examined by graphing the number of preferences against the combination number, it could be seen that there is a very distinct bimodal distribution. In this instance, the choice of two packages might well be the better alternative.

■ **14-8** P($\leq$6 or $\geq$7 +'s) = 1, so we do not reject H_0. There has not been a significant change in collection time.

■ **14-10** (a) No. Even if 1995 is significantly cooler than 1994, that alone is not strong evidence of a *long-run trend* toward cooler weather.

(b) P(9 or more +'s) = 0.2120, so we do not reject H_0. 1995 was not significantly cooler than 1994.

■ **14-12** (a) P(6 or more +'s) = 0.3770, so we do not reject H_0. Mothers' ideal family sizes are not significantly greater than daughters'.

(b) $\bar{p} = 0.6$, $\bar{p}_U = 0.798$, so again we do not reject H_0.

(c) Now $\bar{p}_U = 0.590$, so we reject H_0. Ideal family size has decreased significantly.

(d) With larger n, $\sigma_{\bar{p}}$ decreases, so the width of the acceptance region gets smaller. Thus, with the larger sample we could be confident that 0.6 was significantly greater than 0.5, whereas with the smaller sample we could not draw that conclusion.

■ **14-14** $U = 61.5$, $U_L = 28.30$, $U_U = 71.70$, so we do not reject H_0. The mean ages are not significantly different.

■ **14-16** $K = 0.341$, $\chi^2_U = 5.991$, so we do not reject H_0. The average amounts paid by the three methods are not significantly different.

■ **14-18** $U = 115.5$, $U_U = 107.2$, so we reject H_0. The output has been significantly reduced.

■ **14-20** $U = 73$, $U_U = 108.1$, so we do not reject H_0. The promotion has not increased sales significantly. (In fact, sales haven't increased at all!)

■ **14-22** $U = 98$, $U_L = 59.31$, $U_U = 148.69$, so we do not reject H_0. The two backgrounds do not lead to significantly different first-year GPAs.

■ **14-24** $n_1 = 26$, $n_2 = 22$, $r = 27$, $r_L = 18.2$, $r_U = 31.5$, so we do not reject H_0. The sequence appears to be random.

■ **14-26** $n_1 = 14$, $n_2 = 14$, $r = 13$, $r_L = 9.9$, $r_U = 20.1$, so we do not reject H_0. The sequence appears to be random, as we would have expected.

■ **14-28** $n_1 = 15$, $n_2 = 16$, $r = 10$, $r_L = 12.0$, so we reject H_0. The sequence is not random, as the owner suspected.

■ **14-30** (a) $n_1 = 45$, $n_2 = 4$, $r = 9$, $r_L = 5.80$, $r_U = 10.90$, so we do not reject H_0. The sample appears to be random.

(b) With the same acceptance region, r is now 2, so we reject H_0. The sample is not random (which was obvious by inspection).

(c) The sample proportion of computer analyses should be about 0.75. P(45 or more computer analyses out of 49 $| p = 0.75) = 0.0033$, so there are many more computer analyses in the sample than we could reasonably expect to see. Even odder is the particular sequence that was reported: nine 1's, one 2, etc.

(d) The test looks only at the number of runs in the sample, not at other patterns in the data. In addition, it does not check to see whether the sample proportion is reasonable.

■ **14-32** $n_1 = 29$, $n_2 = 11$, $r = 17$, $r_L = 12.1$, $r_U = 21.8$, so we do not reject H_0. The sample appears to be random, as we would have expected.

■ **14-34** $r_s = 0.185$, the critical values are ± 0.8571, so we do not reject H_0. The rank correlation is not significant.

■ **14-36** $r_s = -0.86$, the critical values are ± 0.7455, so we reject H_0. The rank correlation is significant.

■ **14-38** $r_s = 0.89$, the upper-tail critical value is 0.6220, so we reject H_0. The rank correlation is significantly positive.

■ **14-40** $r_s = 0.498$, the upper-tail critical value is 0.400, so we reject H_0. The rank correlation is significantly positive, so the interviews should no longer be used.

■ **14-42** $r_s = 0.791$, the critical values are ± 0.5515, so we reject H_0. The rank correlation is significant.

■ **14-44** (a) 0.0401, 0.2050, 0.3992, 0.2793, 0.0764.

(b) 83.29, 425.79, 829.14, 580.11, 158.68.

(c) $D_n = 0.0154$.

(d) The upper-tail critical value is 0.0268, so we do not reject H_0. The data are well described by the suggested normal distribution.

■ **14-46** $D_n = 0.064$, the upper-tail critical value is 0.1091, so we do not reject H_0. The data are well-described by the suggested distribution.

■ **14-48** $D_n = 0.3858$, the upper-tail critical value is 0.0962, so we reject H_0. The data are not well-described by a Poisson distribution with $\lambda = 1$.

- **14-50** $U = 113.5$, $U_U = 124.47$, so we do not reject H_0. The number of complaints has not been significantly reduced.
- **14-52** $U = 79.5$, $U_U = 71.7$, so we reject H_0. Ratings are significantly lower in the transport command.
- **14-54** $\bar{p} = 0.3529$, $\bar{p}_L = 0.3005$, $\bar{p}_U = 0.6995$, so we do not reject H_0. The two rankings are not significantly different.
- **14-56** Although historical data enable us to know what sort of weather to expect at any season of the year, the weather conditions that actually occur on any given day are quite random.
- **14-58** $U = 53 > U_U = 50$. Because a lower-tail test is appropriate, we do not reject H_0. The data do not support her hunch.
- **14-60** (a) $r_s = 0.0902$, the prob value is > 0.20, so we do not reject H_0. There is not a significant relationship between fund size and the annualized 5-year total return.

  (b) $r_s = -0.0241$, so again we accept H_0. There is not a significant relationship between the 1992 total return and the annualized 5-year total return.
- **14-62** $U = 63.5$, $U_L = 24.07$, $U_U = 75.93$, so we do not reject H_0. The mean stopping distances are not significantly different.
- **14-64** $r_s = 0.6346$ the critical values are ± 0.5203, so we reject H_0. The rank correlation is significant, which supports her suspicion.
- **14-66** $D_n = 0.1229$, the upper-tail critical value is 0.1434, so we do not reject H_0. The data are well-described by a binomial distribution with $n = 4$ and $p = 0.35$.
- **14-68** $K = 4.243$, the prob value is > 0.10, so we do not reject H_0. The average ages of the three types of vessels are not significantly different.
- **14-70** $r_s = -0.6429$, the lower-tail critical value is -0.5357, so we reject H_0. The data support the claim.
- **14-72** P(12 or more −'s) = 0.0176, so we reject H_0. American League players do suffer more injuries.
- **14-74** (a) 7 in each group.

  (b) $\chi^2 = 9.4285$, the prob value is > 0.10, so we do not reject H_0. The called bonds appear to have been selected randomly.

  (c) $D_n = 0.1667$, the prob value is > 0.15, so we do not reject H_0. The called bonds appear to have been selected randomly.
- **14-76** $D_n = 0.1440$, the upper-tail critical value is 0.1923, so we do not reject H_0. The data are well described by a Poisson distribution with $\lambda = 6$.
- **14-78** The rank correlations are 0.5933, 0.6374, and 0.5359 for the three groups. The college students have the most accurate perception. However, we do not know how to test whether the observed differences are significant.
- **14-80** $r_s = 0.5758$, $(r_s)_{CRIT} = 0.5515$, so we reject H_0. As measured by their correlation, the rankings have not changed significantly.

Chapter 15

- **15-2** To determine what patterns exist within the data over the period being examined.
- **15-4** Demands for services such as water and sewer would perhaps not be met. Adjustment of the tax rate to provide for municipal services might lag be-

hind the actual demand for those services. Extra resources would probably be needed to allow a smooth municipal operation in a situation in which forecasting is poor.

■ **15-6** Seasonal variation.

■ **15-8** Cyclical fluctuation.

■ **15-10** Secular trend.

■ **15-12** (a) $\hat{Y} = 36.6091 + 8.1155x$.
(b) 85.3, 93.4, and 101.5 homes per month.

■ **15-14** (a) $\hat{Y} = 466.8125 + 61.7744x$.
(b) $\hat{Y} = 455.0719 + 61.7744x + 0.5591x^2$.
(c) Linear forecast 1.1463 million mice; quadratic forecast 1.2022 million mice.
(d) Neither model will be valid.

■ **15-16** (a) $\hat{Y} = 18.6667 + 2.0500x$, where $x = 0$ in 1982.
(b) $\hat{Y} = 17.3647 + 2.0500x + 0.0126x^2$.
(c) Political resistance to increased rates makes it unlikely that the quadratic trend would continue to be a good predictor. In fact, the second-degree term is not significant.

■ **15-18** (a) Because the rate of increase in the pollution rating is itself increasing, a second-degree trend would fit the data better than a linear trend.
(b) However, as the air gets more polluted and citizens get more concerned, actions will be taken to control pollution, so the predictions of the second-degree trend will in all likelihood be too dire.
(c) Because public or political action is likely to reduce pollution, neither estimating equation will continue to be accurate.

■ **15-20** (a) 93.70, 103.52, 107.71, 99.10, 95.47, 98.34, 102.22.
(b) −6.30, 3.52, 7.71, −0.90, −4.53, −1.66, 2.22.
(d) Largest fluctuation (by both methods) was in 1991.

■ **15-22** (a) 94.12, 106.48, 95.42, 107.14, 96.05.
(b) −5.88, 6.48, −4.58, 7.14, −3.95.
(d) Largest fluctuation (by both methods) was in 1994.

■ **15-24** (a) $\hat{Y} = 24.3714 + 1.0357x$.
(b) 98.76, 87.00, 96.85, 115.71, 119.65, 90.76, 90.98.
(c) −1.24, −13.00, −3.15, 15.71, 19.65, −9.24, −9.02.
(d) Largest fluctuation (by both methods) was in 1993.

■ **15-26** (a) 98.5, 100.25, 101.625, 102.875, 103.625, 104, 104.5, 105.125, 106, 107.375, 109, 110.375, 111.875, 113.875, 115.875, 117.625.
(b) 91.37, 77.81, 108.24, 122.48, 91.68, 79.81, 106.22, 121.76, 91.51, 80.09, 105.50, 122.31, 92.07, 79.91, 105.29, 122.42.
(c) Modified indices: 105.86, 122.36, 91.59, 79.86.
Seasonal indices: 105.95, 122.46, 91.67, 79.93.

■ **15-28** 89.0; 117.1; 116.7; 77.2.

■ **15-30** (a) 176.875, 179.375, 181.625, 182.25, 181.375, 181.25, 181.375, 181.375, 181.625, 183.375, 184.125, 186.125, 188.25, 188.75, 190.375, 194.125.
(b) 109.117, 46.829, 129.387, 114.129, 113.577, 41.931, 130.117, 113.577, 115.072, 39.809, 130.889, 115.514, 109.429, 48.742, 125.542, 113.844.
(c) Modified indices: 129.752, 113.987, 111.503, 44.380.
Seasonal indices: 129.875, 114.095, 111.609, 44.422.

■ **15-32** (a) 114.50, 129.02, 85.81, 70.67. (b) 45.23 percent.

■ **15-34** (c) and (d).

■ **15-36** They even themselves out over time and they are often minor in magnitude.

■ **15-38** (a) 75.886, 105.081, 142.050, 76.984.

(b) 25.038, 22.840, 26.751, 32.474, 27.673, 26.646, 30.975, 29.876, 30.309, 29.501, 28.863, 29.876, 31.626, 33.308, 33.791, 27.278.

■ **15-40** A large irregular component, a change in the weather that produces a larger or smaller than expected seasonal index, a change in technology that affects the secular trend, and an economic change that alters the time scale of the cyclical component.

■ **15-42** The decline in birth rates that has occurred will no doubt affect future college enrollments; we need to be especially careful about the behavior in birth rates 17 or 18 years in the past when estimating college enrollments.

■ **15-44** (a) 78.51, 88.88, 113.51, 119.09.

(b) 36.938, 33.753, 36.120, 36.107, 34.391, 38.254, 39.644, 40.306, 42.033, 40.504, 40.525, 42.825, 43.307, 45.005, 41.406, 44.504.

(c) $\hat{Y} = 39.7263 + 0.3310x$.

■ **15-46** 0.7000, 0.7500, 0.7250, 0.6750, 0.6125, 0.5750, 0.5250, 0.4625, 0.4500, 0.4750, 0.5625, 0.6750, 0.7375, 0.7375, 0.7250, 0.7000, 0.6625, 0.6250, 0.5500, 0.4625, 0.4000, 0.3750, 0.4125, 0.5125, 0.6375, 0.7125, 0.7500, 0.7625, 0.7250, 0.6875, 0.6125, 0.5125.

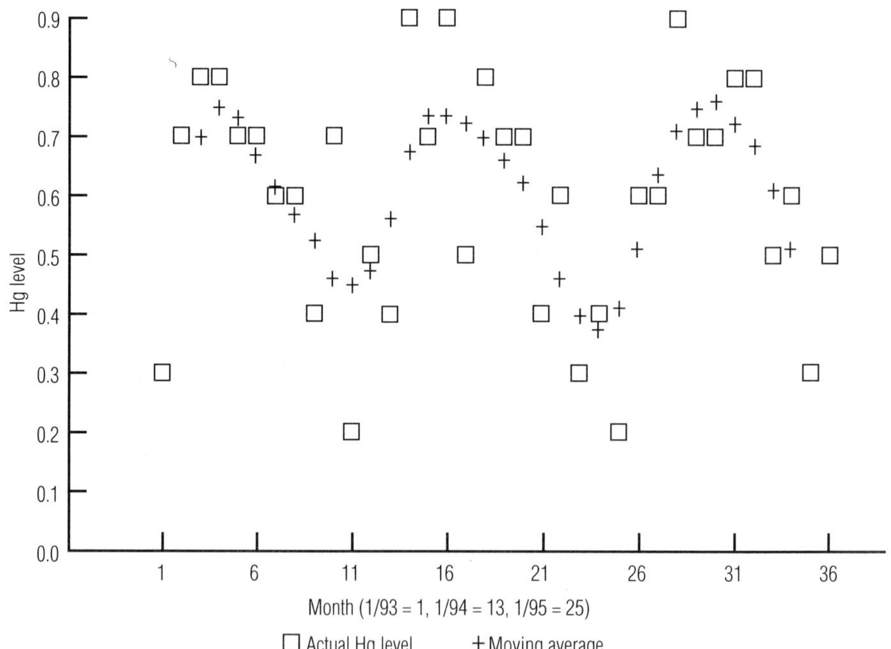

■ **15-48** (a) Gasoline mileage is affected by such things as government responses to the 1973 oil embargo and the resultant mandated fleet-mileage standards.

(b) This series is almost entirely irregular variation because commercial aviation fatalities occur in random batches as the result of unpredictable airplane crashes.

(c) Although total world demand has a long-run increasing trend, there are so many grain growers that each one's exports do not grow smoothly over time but depend instead on political and economic conditions in both importing and exporting nations.

(d) In addition to seasonalities resulting from higher usage in the summer months, gasoline prices are also greatly affected by unpredictable geopolitical events.

■ **15-50** (a) Although sales of PCs have been growing at increasing rates, this growth cannot be sustained as even larger fractions of the population eventually come to own PCs. Because of this, a second-degree predicting equation will soon tend to overestimate the sales of PCs.

(b) Here, too, a forecast based on a second-degree predicting equation will tend to be an overestimate, because of the saturation phenomenon mentioned in part (a), and also because kids will tend to play with them less as the novelty of the games wears off.

(c) As more states act to place caps on damage awards for malpractice, the amounts paid for such claims will cease their rapid growth. As the insurance companies' liabilities stop growing so rapidly, so will the premiums they charge. Once again, second-degree forecasts will tend to be overestimates as a result.

(d) Here is another instance of a growth rate that cannot be sustained, which will lead to overestimates from a second-degree predicting equation.

■ **15-52** (a) Indices: 43.343, 68.730, 173.375, 114.551.
Deseasonalized data: 2.307, 4.365, 3.461, 3.492, 4.614, 2.910, 4.037, 4.365, 4.614, 5.820, 4.614, 4.365, 2.307, 4.365, 4.614, 5.238.

(b) $\hat{Y} = 4.0930 + 0.0433x$.

(c) $-33.014, 23.654, -4.313, -5.698, 21.741, -24.942, 1.867, 7.778, 11.557, 37.817, 7.053, -0.705, -48.539, -4.465, -0.902, 10.436$.

(d)

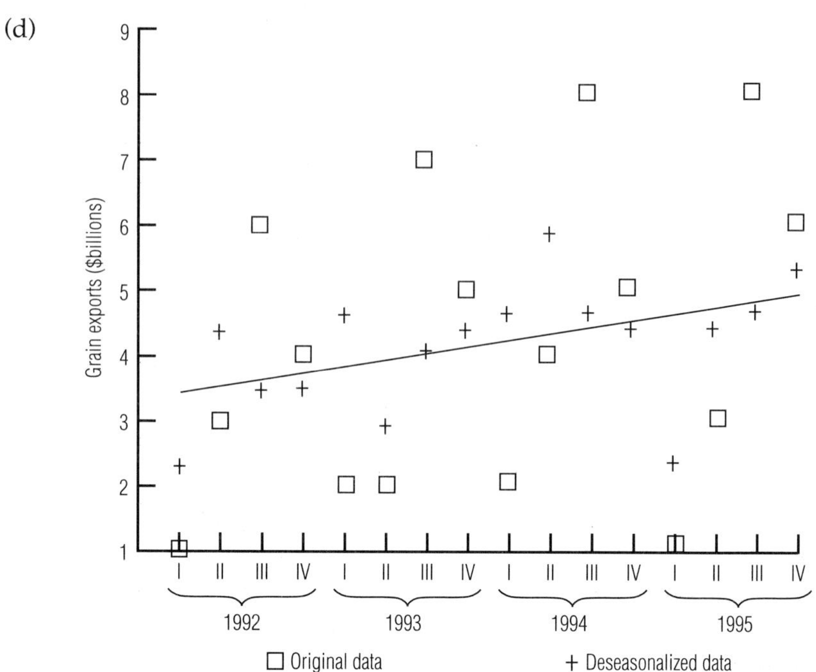

15-54 Because such a major source of demand for heavy earth-moving equipment is going to be lost, historic trends in sales of such equipment will be poor predictors of future sales. The manufacturers would be better advised to abandon a time-series forecasting model for an econometric model that includes such explanatory variables as the number of miles of roads currently under construction and scheduled for the next few years and the age of the current stocks of earth-moving equipment.

15-56 (a) $\hat{Y} = 17.3750 + 0.7202x$.

(b) About 28 completions.

(c) He should be very careful about predicting so far in advance, because of the many things that can change in the home-building business in the meantime.

15-58 (a) $\widehat{\text{UNEMPLOYMENT}} = 8.175 - 0.0379x$.

(b) 82.1, 81.6, 83.5, 93.5, 101.3, 108.0, 116.1, 125.5, 123.1, 120.5, 113.1, 103.0, 95.2, 93.6, 95.7, 98.0, 96.3, 92.0, 90.3, 87.2.

(c)

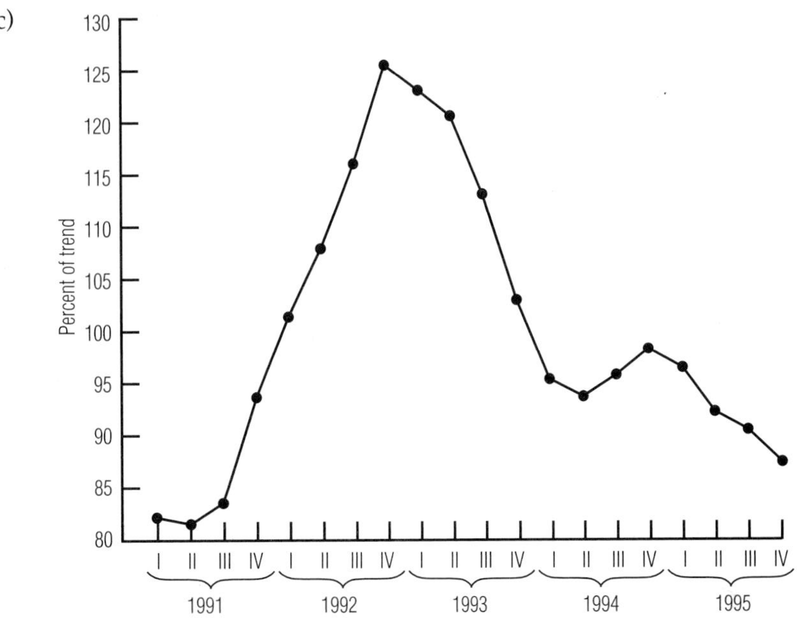

■ **15-60** (a) $\widehat{\text{SALES}} = 60 + 0.25x$.
(b) 61.
(c) No, a second-degree curve would have been better.

■ **15-62** (a) 652.3, 397.85, 689.30, 598.00, 704.00, 408.80, 678.00, 577.20.
(b) Summer, spring.
(c) About 654,000 riders.

■ **15-64** 78.8914, 72.3445, 70.9335, 89.4580, 121.4460, 138.2389, 128.6877.

■ **15-66** (a) 1993. (b) 1995.

Chapter 16

■ **16-2** Price and quantity indices describe the change (usually over time) in a single variable, price and quantity (or number), respectively. Value indices describe the change in the product of price and quantity.

■ **16-4** An index may be used by itself or as part of an intermediate computation, the better to understand some other information.

■ **16-6** Percentage relative = (current value/base value) × 100.

■ **16-8** 110.1, 121.2, 130.1.

■ **16-10** 95.2, 102.7.

■ **16-12** 108.3.

■ **16-14** 100.0, 101.4, 103.1, 104.9.

■ **16-16** 98.6, 100.0, 101.6, 103.5.

■ **16-18** July: 102.1; August: 97.3; these are Laspeyres indices.

■ **16-20** 90.4, 100.0, 108.5, 112.5.

■ **16-22** 100.0, 106.4, 114.8.

■ **16-24** (a) 143.0. (b) 146.5.

■ **16-26** 64.5, 76.9, 100.0, 127.1.

■ **16-28** 129.4, 138.7.

16-30 The weighted aggregates index uses *quantities* for weights; the weighted average of relatives index uses *values*.

16-32 94.7, 101.3, 100.0.

16-34 76.5, 92.7, 95.2, 100.0.

16-36 75.5.

16-38 Appropriate weighting for one period may become inappropriate in a short time. Unless the weights are changed, the index becomes less informative.

16-40 The values from several adjoining periods are averaged.

16-42 By not reflecting the change in quality, the index may not accurately reflect the change in price level.

16-44 147.5, 138.5.

16-46 101.1.

16-48 The problem of incomparability of indices would be present because computer technology has changed so significantly over the past few decades.

16-50 100.0, 101.6, 116.7.

16-52 68.6, 103.4.

16-54 Depending on what is being measured, the choice of base periods can significantly distort the importance of a particular value.

16-56 100.0, 105.6, 105.7, 105.6, 112.7.

16-58 (a) 92.5, 100.0, 106.9.

(b) 92.2, 100.0, 106.9.

16-60 100.0, 108.0, 114.0.

16-62 \$342.99.

16-64 63.2, 72.9, 102.0, 100.0.

16-66 122.9.

16-68 100.0, 108.7, 118.1, 122.9.

16-70 Doubling a factor weight gives that factor extra impact in lieu of the missing factor; assigning low scores to a missing factor calls into question the entire rating process. Alternative responses to missing data include leaving out schools with missing information, or assigning average values to the missing factors. However, these alternatives still produce some distortions in the ratings.

Chapter 17

17-2 Lisa is correct only if she can obtain all of the following information: her objective (presumably Adventures, Inc.'s profit), the available courses of action (which investments to make), the payoffs from these actions, and the probabilities of the various payoffs being realized. The last two of these will be, in all likelihood, difficult to obtain.

17-4 (a) Six mechanics.

(b) EVPI = \$11,712 (assuming the mechanics get paid vacations).

17-6 (a) 17 cases. (b) \$332.70.

17-8 58 dozen, EVPI = \$24.948.

17-10 $p^* = 0.7241$, so order 69 signs.

■ **17-12** (a) $p^* = 0.4467$, so order 378 hot dogs.

(b) $p^* = 0.1700$, so order 394 hot dogs.

■ **17-14** $p^* = 0.6279$, so order 90 chickens.

■ **17-16** (a) $301,760.

(b)

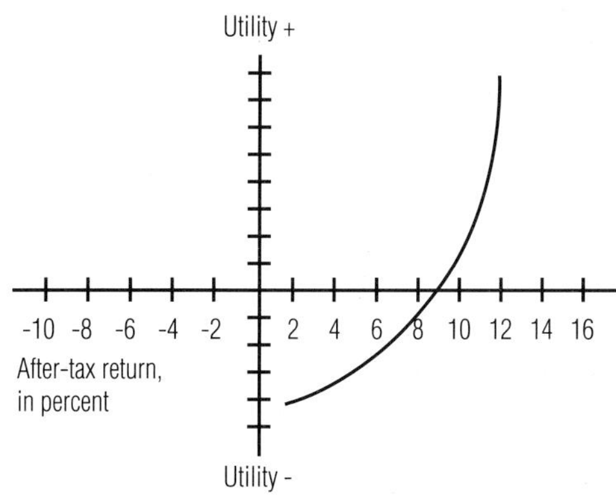

■ **17-18**

Alternative	2-month option	4-month option	No purchase
Expected utility	0.685	0.870	0.700

She should purchase the 4-month option.

■ **17-20** P(lasting ≥ 6 months) = 0.9927, so he should hire.

■ **17-22** P(lasting ≥ 116,224 miles) = 0.5987.

■ **17-24** $P_A = 0.9394$, $P_B = 0.9162$, so buy the stock.

■ **17-26** (a) Payoffs on "operate by self, with snowmaker" branches become 95, 43, −9, with an expected value of 43. She should let the hotel operate the resort.

(b) Now the payoffs and EV become 96, 48, 0, and 48. She should operate by herself, using the snowmaking equipment.

(c) She is indifferent at a 26% increase in operating cost; her profit from either alternative is $45,000 at this point.

■ **17-28** (a)

Option	Bus	Walk	Bike	Car
Expected lateness	15.50	16.00	14.00	15.25

He should ride his bike.

(b)

Option	Bus	Walk	Bike	Car
Expected utility	82.50	82.00	86.00	83.25

He should still ride his bike.

■ **17-30** (a) P(demand ≥ 2213) = 0.8686.

(b) P(demand ≥ 3263) ≤ 0.5, so they should buy the modules.

■ **17-32** (a) $p^* = 0.545$, so order 44 tails.

(b) EVPI = $21.88, the expected increase in profit if the requirement of advance orders doesn't change the demand distribution.

■ **17-34** $p^* = 0.608$, so order 35 bags.

17-36 (a) The three numbers at some of the nodes are the expected costs for parts b, d.i, and d.ii.

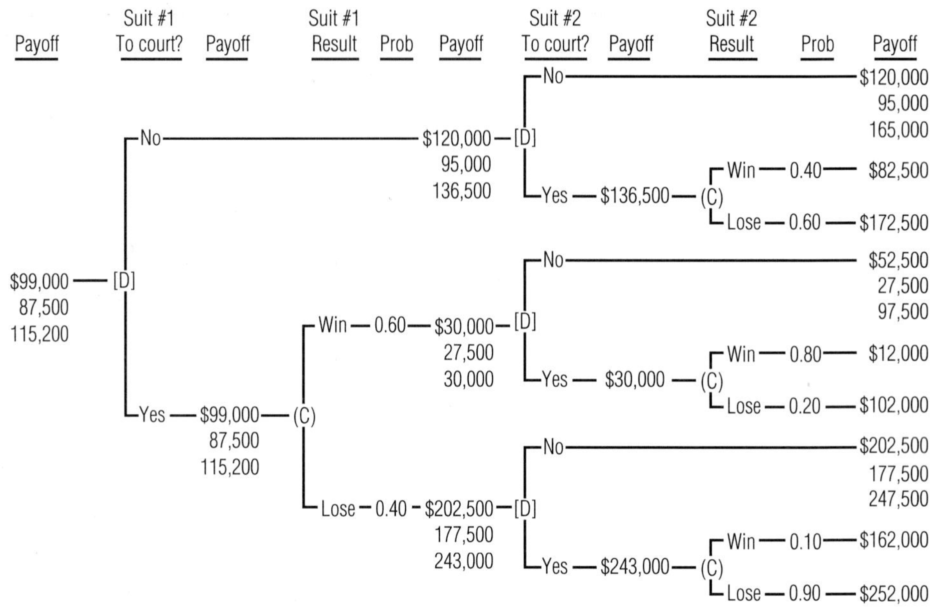

(b) Try #1. If he wins, he should try #2; otherwise, he should settle #2.

(c) $99,000 − $66,000 = $33,000.

(d) (i) Try #1. Settle #2 regardless of the trial #1 outcome.
(ii) Try #1. Try #2 regardless of the trial #1 outcome.

17-38 $p^* = 0.065$, so stock 25 suits.

17-40

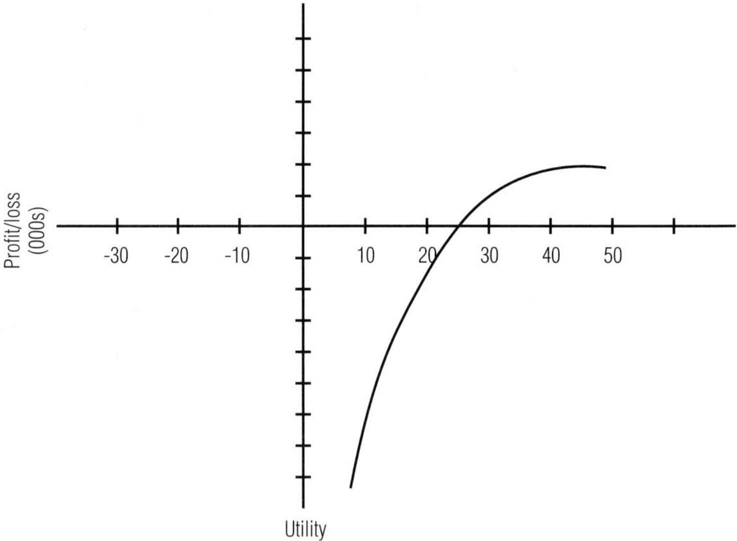

■ **17-42**

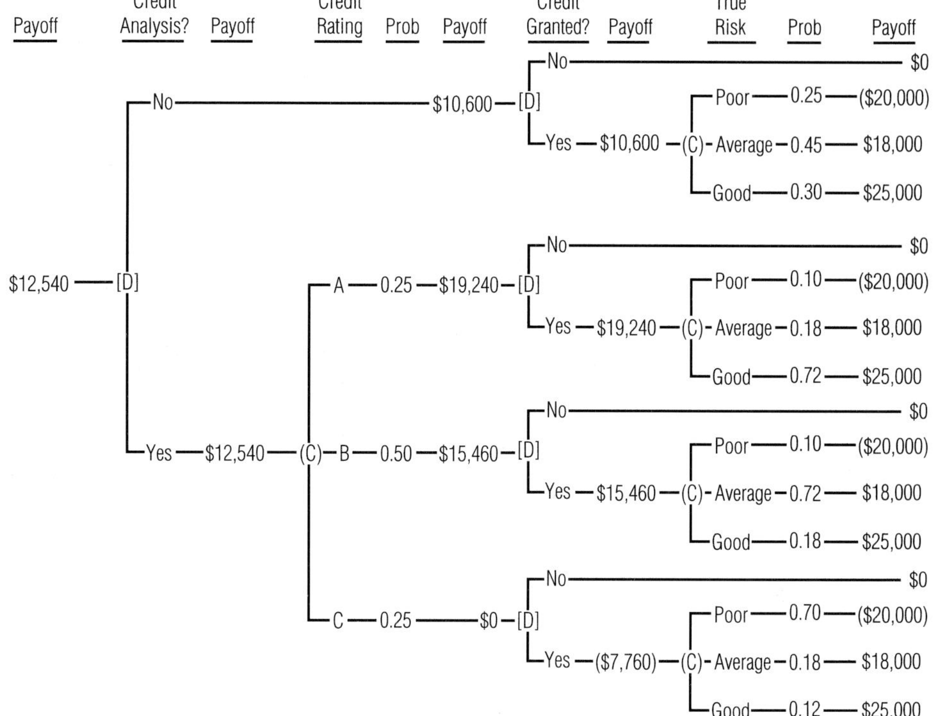

(a) Yes; because $12,540 − $10,600 > $750, they should purchase the credit rating.

(b) If the rating is A or B, grant credit.

(c) $12,540 − $10,600 = $1,940.

(d) $5,000.

■ **17-44** (a) Enduro would accept.

(b)

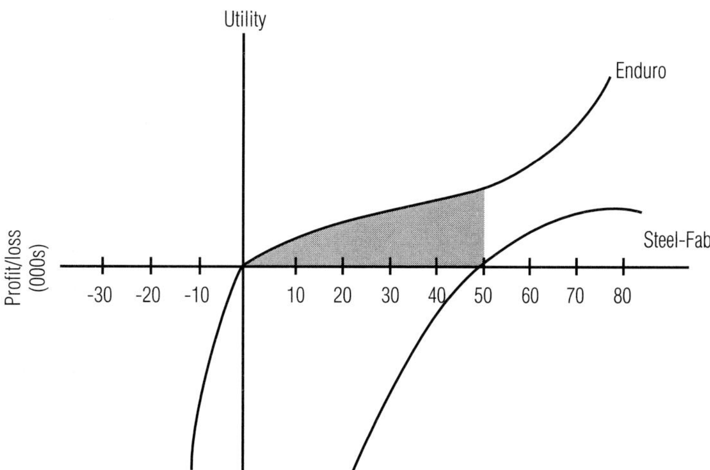

(c) Both would. Steel-Fab would bid up to $611,111.

- **17-46** (a) Use 35 games. (b) EVPI = \$885.
- **17-48** 800.
- **17-50** (a) 75-bed. (b) \$87,100. (c) EVPI = \$29,100.
- **17-52** 16.
- **17-54** (a) \$3402. (b. i) \$3625. (b. ii) \$3937.50. (c) Buy LEAPs.

Bibliography

Data Analysis and Presentation

CLEVELAND, W. S., *The Elements of Graphing Data,* rev. ed., Murray Hill, NJ, AT&T Bell Laboratories, 1994.

EVERITT, B. S., AND G. DUNN. *Advanced Methods of Data Exploration and Modelling,* London, Heinemann Education Books, Ltd., 1983.

TUFTE, E. R., *The Visual Display of Quantitative Information,* Chelshire, CT, Graphics Press, 1983.

TUKEY, J. W., *Understanding Robust and Exploratory Data Analysis,* New York, John Wiley & Sons, 1983.

History of Statistics

STIGLER, S. M., *The History of Statistics: The Measurement of Uncertainty before 1900,* Cambridge, MA, Belknap Press, 1986.

Introductory Statistics

BERENSON, M. L., AND D. M. LEVINE, *Basic Business Statistics: Concepts and Applications,* 6th ed., Englewood Cliffs, NJ, Prentice Hall, 1996.

FREUND, J. E., F. J. WILLIAMS, AND B. M. PERLES, *Elementary Business Statistics,* 6th ed., Englewood Cliffs, NJ, Prentice Hall, 1993.

MCCLAVE, J. T., AND P. G. BENSON, *Statistics for Business and Economics,* 6th ed., Englewood Cliffs, NJ, Prentice Hall, 1994.

Nonparametric Statistics

CONOVER, W. J., *Practical Nonparametric Statistics,* 2d ed., New York, John Wiley & Sons, 1980.

GIBBONS, J. D., AND S. CHAKRABORTI, *Nonparametric Statistical Inference,* 3d ed., New York, Marcel Dekker, 1992.

Probability

HOGG, R. V., AND E. A. TANIS, *Probability and Statistical Inference,* 5th ed., Englewood Cliffs, NJ, Prentice Hall, 1997.

ROWNTREE, D., *Probability,* New York, Charles Scribner's Sons, 1984.

Quality and Quality Control

DEMING, W. E., *Out of the Crisis,* Cambridge, MA, MIT Center for Advanced Engineering Study, 1986.

GITLOW, H., S. GITLOW, A. OPPENHEIM, AND R. OPPENHEIM, 2d ed., *Quality Management: Tools and Methods for Improvement,* Homewood, IL, Richard D. Irwin, Inc., 1995.

GRANT, E. L., AND R. S. LEAVENWORTH, *Stastistical Quality Control,* 7th ed., New York, McGraw-Hill Book Co., 1996.

ISHIKAWA, K., *Guide to Quality Control,* 2d ed., White Plains, NY, Kraus International Publications, 1986.

Regression and Analysis of Variance

BERRY, W. D., *Multiple Regression in Practice*, Beverly Hills, Sage Publications, 1985.
KLEINBAUM, D. G., L. L. KUPPER, AND K. E. MULLER, *Applied Regression Analysis and Other Multivariable Methods*, 2d ed., Boston, PWS-Kent Publishing Co., 1988.
MENDENHALL, W. AND T. SINCICH, *A Second Course in Statistics: Regression Analysis*, 5th ed., Englewood Cliffs, NJ, Prentice Hall, 1996.
NETER, J., W. WASSERMAN, AND M. H. KUTNER, *Applied Linear Statistical Models*, 2d ed., Homewood, IL, Richard D. Irwin, Inc., 1985.

Sampling

GUY, D. M., D. R. CARMICHAEL, AND O. R. WHITTINGTON, *Audit Sampling: An Introduction*, 3rd ed., New York, John Wiley & Sons, 1994.
SCHAEFER, R. L., W. MENDENHALL, AND L. OTT, *Elementary Survey Sampling*, Boston, 5th ed., Duxbury Press, 1996.

Special Topics in Statistics

HUFF, D., *How to Lie with Statistics*, New York, W. W. Norton & Co., 1954.
JAFFE, A. J., *Misused Statistics: Straight Talk for Twisted Numbers*, New York, Marcel Dekker, 1987.
MADANSKY, A., *Prescriptions for Working Statisticians*, New York, Springer-Verlag, 1988.

Statistical Decision Theory

COOK, T. M., AND R. A. RUSSELL, *Introduction to Management Science*, 5th ed., Englewood Cliffs, NJ, Prentice Hall, 1993.
HILLIER, F. S., AND G. J. LIEBERMAN, *Introduction to Operations Research*, 6th ed., New York, McGraw-Hill Book Co., 1995.
LEVIN, R. I., D. S. RUBIN, J. P. STINSON, AND E. S. GARDNER, JR., *Quantitative Approaches to Management*, 8th ed., New York, McGraw-Hill Book Co., 1992.

Statistical Software

MINITAB, INC., *MINITAB User's Guide: Release 10 Xtra*, State College, PA, 1995.
SAS INSTITUTE, INC., *SAS Introductory Guide for Personal Computers*, Release 6.03 ed., Cary, NC, 1988.

Time Series

BOWERMAN, B. L. AND R. T. O'CONNELL, *Forecasting and Time Series: An Applied Approach*, 3d ed., Boston, Duxbury Press, 1993.
FARNUM, N. R., AND L. W. STANTON, *Quantitative Forecasting Methods*, Boston, PWS-Kent Publishing Co., 1989.
MILLS, T. C., *Time Series Techniques for Economists*, Cambridge, Cambridge University Press, 1990.

Index

License Agreement and Limited Warranty

READ THE FOLLOWING TERMS AND CONDITIONS CAREFULLY BEFORE OPENING THIS DATA DISK PACKAGE. THIS IS AN AGREEMENT BETWEEN YOU AND PRENTICE-HALL, INC. (THE "COMPANY"). BY OPENING THIS SEALED PACKAGE, YOU ARE AGREEING TO BE BOUND BY THESE TERMS AND CONDITIONS. IF YOU DO NOT AGREE WITH THESE TERMS AND CONDITIONS, DO NOT OPEN THE DISK PACKAGE. PROMPTLY RETURN THE DISK PACKAGE TO THE COMPANY.

1. GRANT OF LICENSE: In consideration of your purchase of textbooks and/or other materials published by the Company, and your agreement to abide by the terms and conditions of this Agreement, the Company grants to you a nonexclusive right to use and display the copy of the enclosed data disk (hereinafter "the SOFTWARE"). The Company reserves all rights not expressly granted to you under this Agreement. This license is not a sale of the original SOFTWARE or any copy to you.
2. USE RESTRICTIONS: You may not sell or license copies of the SOFTWARE or the Documentation to others or transfer or distribute it, except to instructors and students in your school who are users of the Company textbook that accompanies this SOFTWARE.
3. LIMITED WARRANTY AND DISCLAIMER OF WARRANTY: The Company makes no warranties about the SOFTWARE, which is provided "AS-IS." IF THE DISK IS DEFECTIVE IN MATERIALS OR WORKMANSHIP, YOUR ONLY REMEDY IS TO RETURN IT TO THE COMPANY, WHICH SHALL REPLACE IT UNLESS THE COMPANY DETERMINES IN GOOD FAITH THAT THE DISK HAS BEEN MISUSED OR IMPROPERLY INSTALLED, REPAIRED, ALTERED OR DAMAGED. THE COMPANY DISCLAIMS ALL WARRANTIES, EXPRESS OR IMPLIED, INCLUDING WITHOUT LIMITATION, THE IMPLIED WARRANTIES OF MERCHANTABILITY AND FITNESS FOR A PARTICULAR PURPOSE. THE COMPANY DOES NOT WARRANT, GUARANTEE OR MAKE ANY REPRESENTATION REGARDING THE USE OR THE RESULTS OF THE USE OF THE SOFTWARE. IN NO EVENT, SHALL THE COMPANY OR ITS EMPLOYEES, AGENTS, SUPPLIERS OR CONTRACTORS BE LIABLE FOR ANY INCIDENTAL, INDIRECT, SPECIAL OR CONSEQUENTIAL DAMAGES ARISING OUT OF OR IN CONNECTION WITH THE LICENSE GRANTED UNDER THIS AGREEMENT INCLUDING, WITHOUT LIMITATION, LOSS OF USE, LOSS OF DATA, LOSS OF INCOME OR PROFIT, OR OTHER LOSSES SUSTAINED AS A RESULT OF INJURY TO ANY PERSON, OR LOSS OF OR DAMAGE TO PROPERTY, OR CLAIMS OF THIRD PARTIES, EVEN IF THE COMPANY OR AN AUTHORIZED REPRESENTATIVE OF THE COMPANY HAS BEEN ADVISED OF THE POSSIBILITY OF SUCH DAMAGES.

SOME JURISDICTIONS DO NOT ALLOW THE LIMITATION OF IMPLIED WARRANTIES OR LIABILITY FOR INCIDENTAL, INDIRECT, SPECIAL OR CONSEQUENTIAL DAMAGES, SO THE ABOVE LIMITATIONS MAY NOT ALWAYS APPLY. THE WARRANTIES IN THIS AGREEMENT GIVE YOU SPECIFIC LEGAL RIGHTS AND YOU MAY ALSO HAVE OTHER RIGHTS WHICH VARY IN ACCORDANCE WITH LOCAL LAW.